Yarnton: Iron Age and Romano-British Settlement and Landscape

Results of Excavations 1990–98

by Gill Hey, Paul Booth and Jane Timby

with major contributions by
Alex Bayliss, Christopher Bell, Angela Boyle, Neil Linford, Jacqui Mulville, Mark Robinson and Dan Stansbie

with contributions by
Leigh Allen, Kathy Ayres, Alistair Barclay, R. Berstan, Edward Biddulph, Philippa Bradley, Chris Bronk Ramsey, Gordon Cook, M.S. Copley, Caroline Dennis, Roger Doonan, Caroline Dyer, S.N. Dudd, Emily Edwards, R.P. Evershed, Roger Featherstone, Vanessa Fell, Brian Gilmour, James Greig, Chris Hayden, Martin Henig, Grace Jones, Paul Linford, Gerry McCormac, Elaine Morris, Peter Northover, Ruth Pelling, Julie Rees-Jones, Fiona Roe, Chris Salter, Alex Smith, Pippa Smith, Chris Stevens, Maisie Taylor and Jonathan Wallis

Illustrations by
Amy Hemingway, Hannah Kennedy, Rosalyn Lorimer, Sarah Lucas and Magdalena Wachnik

Thames Valley Landscapes Monograph 35

2011

The publication of this volume has been generously funded by English Heritage

Published for Oxford Archaeology by Oxford University School of Archaeology as part of the Thames Valley Landscapes Monograph series

Designed by Oxford Archaeology Graphics Office

Edited by Chris Hayden and Paul Booth

This book is part of a series about the Thames Valley Landscapes, which can be bought from all good bookshops and internet bookshops. For more information visit http://thehumanjourney.net/

Front cover: artist's reconstruction of Iron Age roundhouses by Peter Lorimer. Design by Peter Lorimer.

ISBN 978-1-905905-21-8

Typeset by Production Line, Oxford
Printed in Great Britain at the Information Press, Eynsham, Oxford

Contents

Chapter 4 The wider view

PART THREE: THE SITES

Chapter 5 The early Iron Age *by Christopher Bell and Dan Stansbie*

Chapter 6 The middle Iron Age *by Christopher Bell and Dan Stansbie*

Chapter 7 The late Iron Age and early Roman transition *by Dan Stansbie*

Chapter 8 The early Roman period *by Dan Stansbie with a contribution by Paul Booth*

Chapter 9 The late Roman period *by Dan Stansbie*

List of Figures

List of Tables

Summary

This is the second in a series of three volumes reporting on a wide-ranging programme of fieldwork undertaken by Oxford Archaeology, mainly between 1989 and 1998, in and around the ARC (now Hanson) gravel extraction pit lying between Yarnton and Cassington, Oxfordshire. This landscape, stretching from the floodplain to the Second Gravel Terrace of the Thames valley, has witnessed human activity from the Neolithic to the present day, although earlier prehistoric occupation concentrated on the floodplain, to be the subject of a separate volume on Neolithic and Bronze Age settlement and landscape (Hey *et al.* forthcoming).

At the end of the Bronze Age/beginning of the Iron Age the floodplain at Yarnton appears to have been abandoned for settlement, although small middle Iron Age occupation sites are known on the Cassington floodplain in the south-west of the study area. Small and permanently-occupied settlements were established on the edge of the Second Gravel Terrace overlooking the low-lying ground at this time, to the west at Worton, and at Yarnton. The latter site, with two adjacent components (known as Yarnton and Cresswell Field), was occupied throughout the Iron Age and Roman periods, and it is the excavation of these sites and examination of their surrounding landscape which form the subject of this volume. Evidence for Saxon and medieval settlement has already been published (Hey 2004).

The Yarnton and Cresswell Field terrace site may have been the home of only two or three families, the focus of use gradually shifting to the east through the Iron Age and Roman periods. Post-built buildings of round, D-shaped and four-post plan were all present in the Iron Age, and houses were increasingly surrounded by gullies from the middle Iron Age. These structures included a possible early Iron Age shrine and a middle Iron Age D-shaped smithy. Buildings were accompanied by extensive spreads of pits, of which about 1000 were identified. Associated with the middle Iron Age settlement was a small cemetery of some 35 crouched inhumation burials, rare for this period, which radiocarbon dating suggests were interred over a relatively short period during the third century BC. Further burials were made in the Roman period. The late Iron Age and Roman settlement at Yarnton was marked by repeatedly redefined ditched enclosures. Some of these may have been small paddocks suggesting intensive stock management, but domestic activity was widespread, although structural evidence was typically sparse. Ancillary structures included corn-drying ovens and two pottery kilns of late 1st century AD date.

The wider landscape context of these settlements was investigated by fieldwalking, geophysical survey and trench evaluation, revealing manuring scatters, field boundaries, ploughsoils and trackways. Former river channels on the floodplain were valuable sources of pollen and waterlogged macrobotanical and invertebrate remains important for reconstructing the landscape and changes in agricultural practice over time

The floodplain was mainly used for grazing and parts of it were accessed by causeways built across palaeochannels in the middle Iron Age. Intensification of agriculture in the Roman period involved use of parts of the floodplain for arable, despite changing environmental conditions which eventually led to abandonment of these fields because of flooding, probably causing them to be relocated on higher ground. One of the middle Iron Age causeways was particularly carefully constructed, overlying a foundation deposit of a middle Bronze Age side-looped spearhead and other Bronze Age metal objects and incorporating unusual deposits of animal bone. Other special deposits, mainly of animal bone but including an iron adze head, were found in Iron Age pits on the settlement site.

The later prehistoric and Romano-British community appears to have been small and self-sufficient and shows little in the way of exotic material culture. Substantial pottery assemblages included several important late Bronze Age/early Iron Age groups, but most of the pottery was derived from fairly local sources throughout the life of the site. The few particularly noteworthy individual objects of Roman date included a fine Aesica-type brooch and a fragment of a late Roman belt buckle. Occupation clearly continued at least to the end of the 4th century AD, and landscape evidence suggests continuity of use of the area through the 5th century, with Anglo-Saxon settlement evidence apparent by the end of that century. The interest of the settlement lies in the manner in which it was used for occupation, apparently continuously from the later Bronze Age through to the end of the Roman period and beyond, with a gradual shift of focus over time, accompanied by evidence of changing land use and landscape.

Résumé

Il s'agit du second volume d'une série de trois sur le programme de travaux de terrains de grande envergure entrepris par Oxford Archaeology, principalement entre 1989 et 1998, au sein et autour de la fosse d'exploitation gravière d'ARC (aujourd'hui Hanson) située entre Yarnton et Cassington, Oxfordshire. Ce paysage, qui s'étend de la plaine inondable à la Seconde Terrasse gravière de la Vallée de la Tamise, a été le témoin de l'activité humaine du néolithique à nos jours, bien qu'une occupation préhistorique préalable se concentrait dans la plaine inondable. Cette occupation sera l'objet d'un volume distinct sur l'habitat et le paysage au Néolithique et à l'Age du Bronze (Hey, et al, à venir).

A l'Age du Bronze final/début de l'Age du Fer, la plaine inondable à Yarnton semble avoir été abandonnée pour laisser place à un habitat, bien que des sites d'occupation du milieu de l'Age du Fer soient connus dans la plaine inondable de Cassington au sud ouest de l'aire d'étude. De petits habitats occupés de manière permanente étaient établis au bord de la Seconde Terrasse gravière surplombant les basses terres à ce moment-là, à l'ouest de Worton et à Yarnton. Ce dernier site, avec deux éléments adjacents (surnommés Yarnton et Cresswell Field) fut occupé tout au long de l'Age du Fer et à la période romaine. C'est la fouille de ces sites et l'examen de leur paysage environnant qui font l'objet de ce volume. Les éléments de preuve relatifs aux habitats saxons et médiévaux ont déjà été publiés (Hey 2004).

La terrasse de Yarnton et de Cresswell Field a peut-être abrité deux ou trois familles, le foyer d'utilisation s'étant graduellement déplacé vers l'est tout au long de l'Age du Fer et de l'époque romaine. Les structures construits sur poteaux, de forme ronde, en D ou en plan sur quatre poteaux existaient tous à l'Age du Fer et les habitations étaient de plus en plus entourées de ravines à partir du milieu de l'Age du Fer. Ces structures incluaient une possible structure rituelle du début de l'Age du Fer et une forge de forme en D du milieu de l'Age du Fer. Les bâtiments étaient entourés de grandes étendues de fosses, dont 1000 ont été identifiées. A l'habitat du milieu de l'Age du Fer, on a pu associer un petit cimetière de 35 sépultures en position accroupie, rares pour cette période, et dont la datation au radiocarbone suggère des inhumations sur une période relativement courte durant le troisième siècle av. J.-C. D'autres sépultures ont été déposées à la période romaine. L'habitat de la fin de l'Age du Fer et Romano-britannique à Yarnton a été marqué par des enclos fossoyés constamment redéfinis. Certains d'entre eux ont peut-être constitué de petits enclos suggérant la gestion intensive de bétail, mais l'activité domestique était répandue, bien que les indices structuraux recueillis soient typiquement épars. Les structures auxiliaires contenaient des fours domestiques et deux fours de potier datés de la fin du Ier siècle ap. J.-C.

Le contexte paysager plus vaste de ces habitats a été examiné grâce à la prospection pédestre, la prospection géophysique et le diagnostic, qui ont révélé les limites de champs, des sols en labour, des débris de fumure, et des sentiers. D'anciens chenaux de rivières dans la plaine inondable ont constitué des sources riches de pollen et de restes macrobotaniques imprégnés d'eau et des restes invertébrés, importants pour la reconstruction du paysage et des changements liés à la pratique agricole à travers le temps.

La plaine inondable servait principalement au pâturage et certaines parties étaient accédées par des chaussées construites au-dessus des paléochenaux au milieu de l'Age du Fer. L'intensification de l'agriculture à la période romaine a engendré l'utilisation de certaines parties de la plaine inondable pour cultiver la terre malgré le changement des conditions environnementales. Celles-ci ont finalement entraîner l'abandon de ces champs à cause des inondations, aboutissant probablement à la re-localisation de ces champs sur des terres surélevées. Une des chaussées de l'Age du Fer était particulièrement bien construite et contenait un fer de lance de l'Age du Bronze et était associé à des dépôts inhabituels d'ossements animaux. D'autres dépôts peu ordinaires, principalement d'ossements animaux mais incluant une tête d'herminette en fer et des restes humains, ont été trouvés dans les fosses de l'Age du Fer sur le site de l'habitat.

La communauté préhistorique tardive et Romano-britannique semble avoir été petite et autonome et présente peu de matériel de culture exotique. Des ensembles importants de céramique incluaient plusieurs groupes importants de l'Age du Bronze final/début de l'Age de Fer, mais la plupart de la céramique provenait de sources locales tout au long de l'existence du site. Les quelques objets particulièrement notables de l'époque romaine incluent une broche fine de type Aesica et un fragment d'une boucle de ceinture de la fin de l'époque romaine. Il est clair que l'occupation a perduré au moins jusqu'à la fin du IVe siècle ap. J.-C., et les témoins paysagers suggèrent l'utilisation de l'aire en continu durant le Ve siècle ap. J.-C., avec la preuve d'un habitat anglo-saxon apparent dès la fin de ce siècle. L'intérêt de cet habitat réside dans la manière dont il était utilisé durant son occupation, apparemment continuellement de l'Age du Bronze final à la fin de la période romaine, avec un déplacement graduel du foyer sur le temps, accompagné d'indices de changement de l'utilisation de la terre et du paysage.

Zusammenfassung

Dies ist der zweite Band einer dreiteiligen Serie, welche sich mit der umfassenden Feldarbeit beschäftigt, die zwischen den Jahren 1989 und 1998 in und um die ARC (heute Hanson) Kiesgruben zwischen Yarnton und Cassington (Oxfordshire) von Oxford Archaeology durchgeführt wurde. Das Areal, erstreckt sich vom Überschwemmungsgebiet bis hin zur zweiten Kiesterrasse der Themse und hat in seiner Geschichte menschliche Aktivität vom Neolithikum bis zum heutigen Tag gesehen, wobei sich die Besiedlung in der frühen Vorgeschichte auf das Überschwemmungsgebiet konzentrierte und in einem eigenständigen Band, Neolithikum und Bronzezeit – Siedlungen und Landschaft, behandelt wird (Hey et al. in Kürze erscheinend).

Gegen Ende der Bronze- / Anfang der Eisenzeit scheint das Überschwemmungsgebiet bei Yarnton nicht besiedelt gewesen zu sein, obwohl kleine mitteleisenzeitliche Ansiedlungen im Überschwemmungsgebiet bei Cassington, im Südwesten des Untersuchungsgebiets, bekannt sind. Während dieser Zeit wurden kleine, permanent bewohnte Siedlungen am Rande der zweiten Kiesterrasse, mit Blick über die tiefer liegenden Gebiete, in Yarnton als auch im Westen bei Worton, gegründet. Die zuerst genannte Siedlung, bestehend aus zwei nebeneinanderliegenden Einheiten (Yarnton und Cresswell Field), war in der Eisen- und Römerzeit durchgehend besiedelt, und es sind diese Stätten und ihre angrenzende Umgebung, welche im vorliegenden Band behandelt werden. Nachweise sächsischer und mittelalterlicher Siedlungen wurden bereits publiziert (Hey 2004).

Die Stätten auf der Yarnton und Cresswell Field Terrasse waren scheinbar die Heimat von nur zwei oder drei Familien. Der Nutzungsschwerpunkt verschiebt sich während der Eisen- und Römerzeit stufenweise Richtung Osten. Runde, D-förmige und vierpfostige Pfostengebäude wurden vorgefunden. Die Häuser wurden vermehrt von mitteleisenzeitlichen Abwasserrinnen umfasst. Die besprochenen Gebäude beinhalteten unter anderem einen möglichen früheisenzeitlichen Schrein und eine mitteleisenzeitliche Schmiede und wurden von einer umfangreichen Anzahl Gruben umgeben, von denen ungefähr 1000 nachgewiesen wurden. Außerdem wird ein kleines Gräberfeld mit 35 Hockerbestattungen der mitteleisenzeitlichen Siedlung zugeordnet, dies ist selten für diesen Zeitabschnitt und Radiokarbondaten legen nahe, dass die Beisetzungen in einer kurzen Zeitspanne während des dritten Jahrhunderts vor Christus stattfanden. Weitere Bestattungen wurden in römischer Zeit hinzugefügt. Die späteisenzeitliche und römische Siedlung bei Yarnton ist durch sich wiederholende, nachdefinierte und umgrabene Einschließungen gekennzeichnet. Einige davon könnten kleine Weiden gewesen sein, was auf intensive Viehhaltung hinweisen würde. Viehwirtschaft war weit verbreitet, doch Nachweise von Gebäuden für diesen Zweck sind sehr selten. Weitere Gebäude beinhalteten Öfen zum Korn trocknen und zwei Topferöfen die in das späte erste Jahrhunderts nach Christus datiert wurden.

Der Zusammenhang zwischen der Siedlungen und der weiteren Umgebung wurde mittels Feldbegehungen, geophysichen Untersuchungen, Sondagen, der Analyse von Feldbegrenzungen und gepflügten Böden, Düngerstreubereichen und historischen Verkehrswegen untersucht. Ehemalige Flussbetten im Uferbereich waren wichtige Quellen für Pollenentnahmen, makrobotanischen und invertebraten Proben, sowie unabdinglich für die Rekonstruktion der Landschaft und zum Aufzeigen der Veränderungen der landwirtschaftlicher Methoden im Laufe der Zeit.

Das Überschwemmungsgebiet wurde hauptsächlich als Weidefläche genutzt, Teile davon wurden durch erhöht angelegte Wege (engl. „Causeways") zugänglich gemacht, die in der mittleren Eisenzeit über ehemalige und mit der Zeit verfüllte Flussbetten angelegt wurden. Eine Intensivierung der Landwirtschaft in römischer Zeit bedeutete die ackerbauliche Nutzung von Teilen der Überschwemmungsgebiete trotz sich ändernder Umweltbedingungen. Diese führten schließlich aufgrund von Überflutungen zur Aufgabe der Äcker und wahrscheinlich ebenso zu einer Umsiedlung derselben auf höherliegende Anbauflächen. Einer der mitteleisenzeitlichen Causeways war besonders sorgfältig angelegt. In dessen Unterbau wurde ein Depot mit einer mittelbronzezeitlichen geflügelten Lanzenspitze, weiteren bronzezeitliche Metallobjekten sowie einer ungewöhnlichen Ansammlung von Tierknochen gefunden. In eisenzeitlichen Gruben innerhalb der Siedlung wurden weitere Depots ausgemacht, hauptsächlich mit Tierknochen doch auch ein eisernes Beil und menschliche Überreste kamen zutage.

Die spätprähistorische und romano-britische Gesellschaft scheint klein und autark gewesen zu sein und kam allem Anschein nach nicht oft mit exotischen Kulturgütern in Kontakt. Eine erhebliche Ansammlung an Keramik, darunter auch einige bedeutende bronzezeitliche/ früheisenzeitliche Funde, kamen zum Vorschein. Der Großteil der Keramik kam jedoch während der gesamten Lebensdauer der Siedlung aus lokalen Quellen. Die wenigen nennenswerten Objekte aus römischer Zeit beinhalten eine Brosche vom Typ Aesica und

Fragmente einer spätrömischen Gürtelschnalle. Die Besatzungszeit dauerte mindestens bis zum Ende des 4. Jahrhunderts n. Chr. und Hinweise in der Landschaft deuten darauf hin, dass das Gebiet noch durch das 5. Jahrhundert hindurch genutzt wurde. Angelsächsische Siedlungen sind gegen Ende des 5. Jahrhunderts nachweisbar. Die Siedlung findet Bedeutung durch die Tatsache, dass sie durchgehend, von der späten Bronzezeit bis zum Ende der römischen Besatzung und darüber hinaus bewohnt wurde und sich dabei schrittweise verschob, sowie nachgewiesen zu sein scheint, dass sich in der Zeit die Landnutzung und die Landschaft selbst veränderte.

Acknowledgements

The Yarnton-Cassington project investigations were a considerable undertaking, with over nine years of fieldwork which involved the majority of the (then) Oxford Archaeological Unit field staff. Some of this work was undertaken in miserable conditions, through snow, blizzards, gales and winter flooding on the floodplain and, although they are too numerous to mention individually, a huge debt of gratitude is owed to the hard work, diligence and perseverance of the field staff. Some people worked on the project for extended periods of time and/or supervised work in the Iron Age and Roman excavation areas and deserve special thanks: Christopher Bell, Helen Glass, Granville Laws, Jeff Muir, Rachel Morse, Mark Roberts and Jeff Tann.

English Heritage provided the bulk of the funds for this project, which would otherwise not have taken place. Tony Fleming, Steve Trow, Roger Thomas, Rob Perrin and Chris Welch were English Heritage Inspectors of Ancient Monuments during the life of the project, and Jon Humble and Helen Keeley were Project Monitors. We are grateful for their advice and support, and that of the English Heritage contract specialists, particularly in the field of environmental work, geophysical survey and dating. In addition to his own work on macro-botanical remains and invertebrates, Mark Robinson has co-ordinated the environmental aspects of the project and his considerable experience and expertise has proved invaluable in the interpretation of both the site evidence and that of the wider landscape. We are also grateful to him for commenting on parts of the report to which he did not contribute directly and to James Greig for commenting upon the landscape sections of the overview.

ARC (now Hanson) provided machinery for stripping the very large areas opened, and for other investigative purposes. They provided other practical support and were very co-operative about access and time available on site. Bob Turner, the pit manager (now retired), deserves special mention for his help and constant good humour, but also Peter Lawless, Phillip Duncan and Julia Edwards who were then in the ARC area office. We would like to thank the landowners, Worton Farms Ltd, especially Mr Guy Pharoan, who have shown great interest in the project and allowed us access to land whilst still under cultivation. We are also very grateful to all the farmers and landowners who allowed access to fields for fieldwalking and evaluation, particularly Malcolm Hastings of Begbroke Hall Farm and Mr Franks of Yarnton Manor.

Several archives have been consulted during site analysis and the preparation of this report and we are grateful to the Oxfordshire County Historic Environment Record, the staff of the Ashmolean Museum, RCHME (now English Heritage) especially Bob Bewley, the Cambridge University Collection of Air Photographs and the Oxford County Record Office.

All the specialists are thanked for their various contributions. The work of James Greig, Mark Robinson, Jacqui Mulville and Kathy Ayres was funded by the Ancient Monuments Laboratory of English Heritage. Jacqui Mulville and Kathy Ayres would like to thank Pippa Smith who identified the animal bone from the Yarnton site and also provided preliminary tables and discussion, which have been incorporated into the report published here. Kate Clark examined the pathological material, Dale Serjeantson assisted with bird bone identification and finally Simon Davies offered helpful comments. James Greig would like to thank Petra Dark (Day) and James Wells for commenting helpfully upon the text. Mark Robinson's work was undertaken in the Environmental Archaeology Laboratory of the Oxford University Museum of Natural History. The samples were processed and sorted by Ruth Pelling. Conservation was undertaken by Vanessa Fell, Margaret Brooks and Glynis Edwards.

Julie Rees-Jones took samples from palaeochannels on the Yarnton floodplain as part of her doctoral thesis to develop optically-stimulated luminescence (OSL) dating of sediments, at the Oxford University Research Laboratory (Rees-Jones 1995; Chapter 13). The charred plant remains from the Yarnton excavation site were analysed by Chris Stevens as part of a CASE studentship undertaken at the McDonald Institute for Archaeological Research, Cambridge University (Stevens 1996; Chapter 19).

The report was edited by Chris Hayden and Paul Booth. The illustrations were drawn by Amy Hemingway and Hannah Kennedy and objects were photographed by Magdalena Wachnik. Further support for the later stages of the post-excavation project from Alex Smith and Leigh Allen is gratefully acknowledged. Translations of the summary were provided by Nathalie Haudecoeur-Wilks and Markus Dylewski.

Chapter 1 Introduction

by Gill Hey and Jane Timby with Mark Robinson

INTRODUCTION

Since 1989, archaeological investigations have revealed a remarkable landscape near the confluence of the rivers Thames and Evenlode around Yarnton, Oxfordshire, with features dating from the Neolithic to the later Saxon period. The following report is the second in a series of three reports discussing the archaeology of the Yarnton-Cassington area, a landscape study spanning a decade of fieldwork by the Oxford Archaeological Unit (now Oxford Archaeology – OA) largely funded by English Heritage. This report, (Volume 2), is specifically concerned with the Iron Age and Romano-British occupation and acts as a companion volume to the report on the Saxon and medieval settlement (Hey 2004) and that on the Neolithic and Bronze Age activity which will follow (Hey *et al.* forthcoming).

STRUCTURE OF THE VOLUME

There are five main Yarnton fieldwork projects of which two are of prime importance to this volume: Yarnton (Yarnton Worton Rectory Farm, site code YWRF) and Yarnton Cresswell Field (site code YCF). Other evidence for activity pertinent to the Iron Age and Romano-British occupation also comes from the Yarnton Floodplain projects (YFP and YFPB) and the Yarnton-Cassington evaluation (YCE). Further smaller-scale evaluation work relevant to the project was carried out as part of the proposed A40 Witney to Cassington Road Dualling Scheme, and small trenches and a watching brief area excavated to the north of the Yarnton site for a recycling plant in 1996-7 (YRP). The Yarnton (ie YWRF) and Cresswell Field sites were part of a continuous belt of settlement before medieval field division and 19th-century railway construction. For this reason the evidence from the two sites has been considered together on a period by period basis, as far as is practical given that both the excavations and the post-excavation work were carried out at separate times.

The Yarnton study is specifically a landscape project where the aim has been not only to understand individual settlements but also their broader environment, changing land-use patterns associated with them and their relationship with neighbouring settlements. In order to optimise the wide range of information available, it was decided not to treat the excavations on a site by site basis, but to split the volumes chronologically. The weakness of this approach is that the transitions between traditionally-defined periods cannot be as fully explored as may be desirable. Being the middle volume in the sequence, this report suffers at its beginning and end in this respect, in that both the later Bronze Age/early Iron Age and late Roman to Saxon transitions are times of change. To try and minimise this acknowledged deficiency, a summary of the late Bronze Age and Saxon evidence is given to allow the wider picture to be appreciated.

Following this introduction (Part 1), an overview of the evidence is presented using the results from the excavations and the specialist reports to discuss Iron Age and Roman landscape and settlement at Yarnton (Part 2, Chapters 2-4). Chapter 2 discusses the environmental evidence and changes in the landscape and settlement through time. Chapter 3 examines society at Yarnton, considering the physical evidence in terms of the buildings, settlement organisation and domestic activities, whilst Chapter 4 places Yarnton into a wider context from the perspective of inter-regional contacts, status and social organisation and continuity and change. In Part 3 (Chapters 5-12), Chapters 5 to 9 describe the archaeological evidence from the early Iron Age to the later Roman period for the Yarnton/Cresswell Field site. Chapter 10 presents the Iron Age and Roman evidence gleaned from the evaluation work at the adjacent settlement of Worton, whilst Chapter 11 looks at the evidence in the wider surrounding landscape including the floodplain. Chapter 12 describes the results of the geophysical survey work. The final section of the report (Part 4, Chapters 13-19) present the absolute dating, the pottery and other artefactual material, the human remains and the ecofactual evidence.

It should be noted that the report was completed in first draft by early 2005 and that most of the specialist work contained within it was undertaken in the period up to 2003. For the most part it has only been possible to carry out very limited updating of text and references since that time, although Chapters 16 and 17 (human remains and animal bone) have been revised more extensively, by Angela Boyle and Jacqui Mulville respectively. In addition, the fact that the two main sites reported here were examined at different times means that close integration of the work of specialists on their respective assemblages was not always possible.

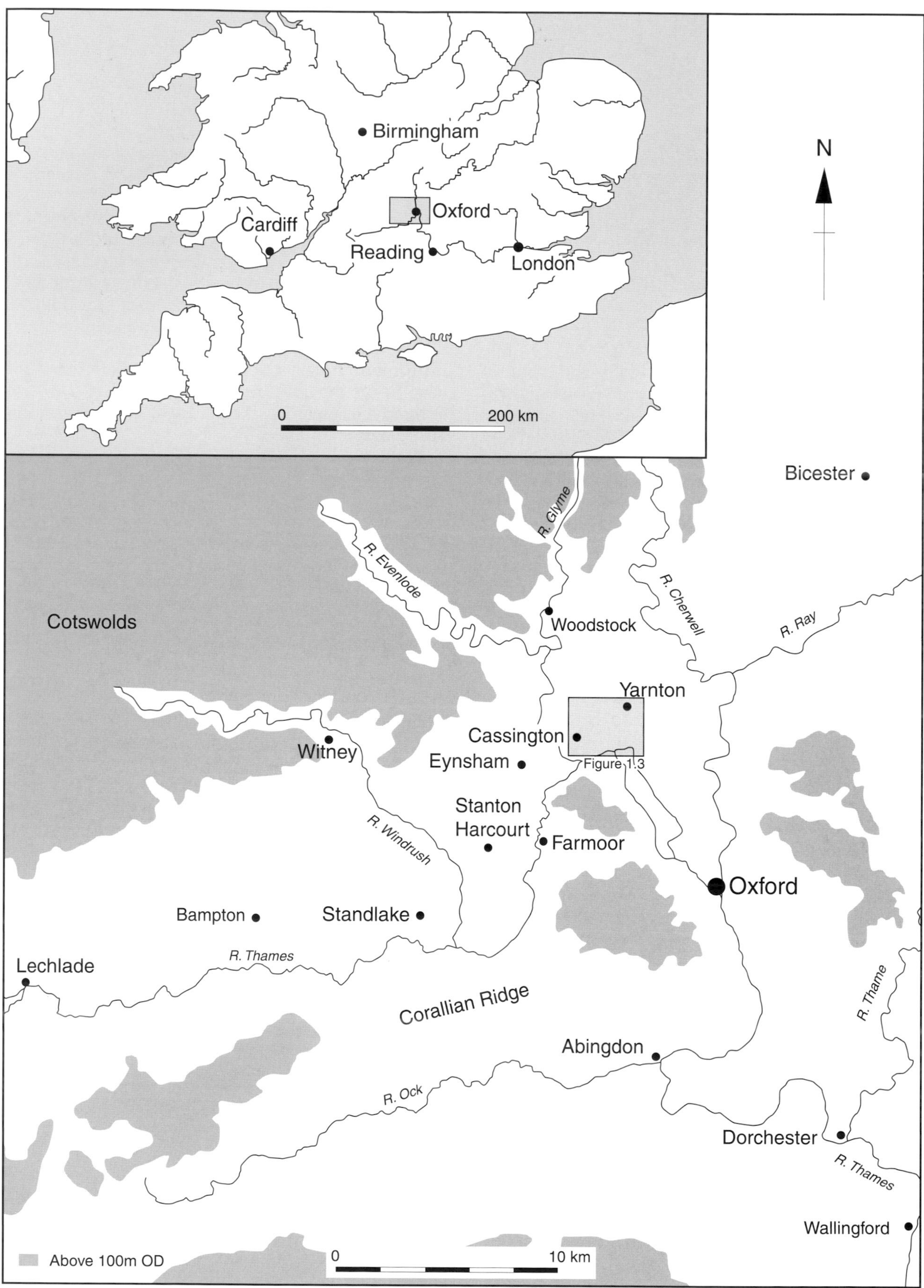

Fig. 1.1 Location of Yarnton-Cassington study area

SITE LOCATION, GEOLOGY AND TOPOGRAPHY

The Yarnton-Cassington study area lies in the Upper Thames Valley, 8 km (5 miles) north-west of Oxford (NGR SP 4711) (Figs 1.1 and 1.2). It is situated north of the River Thames on an area of Second (Summertown-Radley) Gravel Terrace and floodplain between the modern villages of Yarnton to the east and Cassington to the west. It is located 1 km east of the Thames/Evenlode confluence and immediately west of a sharp bend in the Thames where it turns to flow south-east to Oxford (Fig. 1.1). The River Thames forms the southern parish boundary of Yarnton and a tributary stream, known as the Rowel Brook in the south, formed the eastern boundary until 1788-89 when the Oxford canal took much of the stream bed (Day 1990). The modern terrain is relatively flat with the areas investigated mainly lying just below 60 m OD (200 ft). The ground rises more steeply to the NNW to a high point of 96 m OD about 1 km from the Yarnton site and west of the modern village of Yarnton.

The focus of the archaeological work has been the site of the ARC (now Hanson) Cassington gravel extraction pit which covers an area of some 140 ha on Second Gravel Terrace and Thames floodplain, with some Oxford clay, in the parishes of Yarnton and Cassington (Fig. 1.3). The pit lies to the north of the A40 Oxford to Cheltenham road and is bounded on the east and north-east by the Oxford to Worcester railway line. Its western boundary is dictated by a 350 m exclusion zone around Cassington village. A branch line from the Oxford to Worcester railway running south-westwards to Witney and Fairford originally crossed the area and this has been used as a haul road by the gravel company.

The modern, fairly flat, landscape (Fig. 1.2) masks a much more varied past topography. In the prehistoric period stream channels crossed the floodplain, creating islands in the gravel, and palaeosols developed on low-lying ground over early channel silts. Terrace edges would have been more pronounced. Alluvium and colluvium, mostly of Roman and medieval date and created through tree clearance and subsequent intensification of agriculture, have blanketed these features, sealing archaeological remains.

The two main excavation sites presented in this report, Cresswell Field (YCF) to the west and Yarnton Worton Rectory Farm (YWRF, hereafter referred to as the Yarnton site) to the east, lay in the northern zone of the gravel pit on the edge of the Second Gravel Terrace, divided by an old stream course (palaeochannel) forming the western

Fig. 1.2 Air photograph of the Yarnton-Cassington study area from the east. The village of Yarnton lies in the right foreground, Cassington is centred in the middle distance and Eynsham is at the top left. Copyright OA

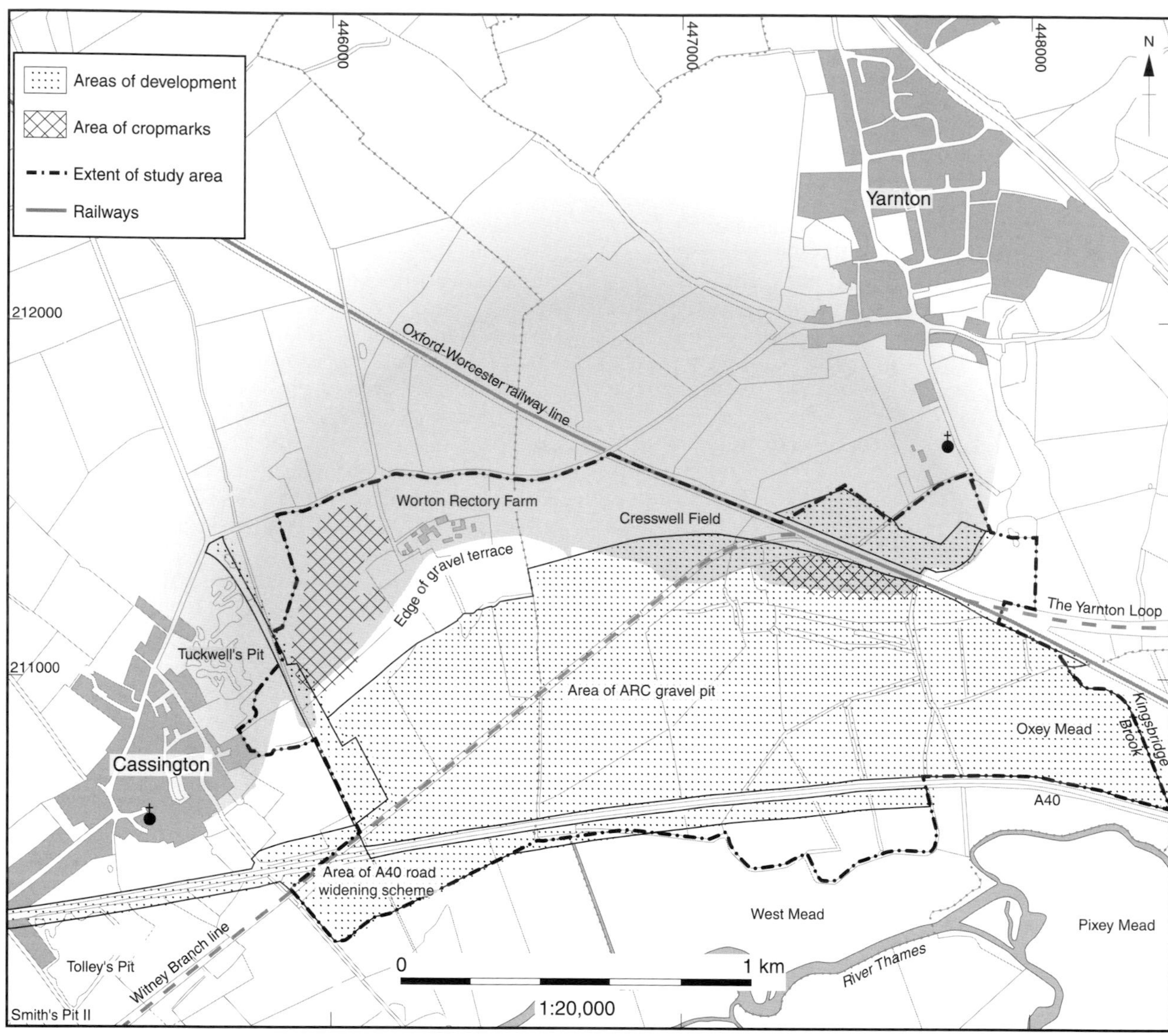

Fig. 1.3 Modern development and the edge of the gravel terrace in the study area

boundary of the Yarnton site (Fig. 1.4). The western edge of the Cresswell Field Iron Age settlement sloped down to the edge of another palaeochannel. The Roman settlement at Yarnton extended below the edge of the gravel terrace, where it was overlain by medieval colluvium.

Geology

The study area at Yarnton-Cassington extends from the Second Gravel Terrace onto the alluvial deposits of the floodplain (Fig. 1.4). At present the floodplain carries poorly drained alluvial clays, the Thames series (Jarvis 1973, 112-3), but prior to alluviation only a thin, non-calcareous ungleyed brown earth of sandy loam to silty clay covered the gravel over much of the floodplain. Major alluviation did not occur until the Roman period (Robinson and Lambrick 1984; see also Chapter 2 below).

The gravels of the Upper Thames Valley are the result of the deposition of largely calcareous material, derived from the northern limestone outcrops washed down by post-glacial rivers. The present fragmented distribution of these deposits is due to changes in the course of the Thames, combined with successive lowering of its bed, leaving the gravel isolated in terraced form (Leech 1977, 2). The Second Terrace lies at around 8.5 m above the present river level. Underlying and extending beyond the gravels to the north-west, the solid geology comprises the Oxford Clay and Kellaways Beds of the Upper Jurassic series (Institute of Geological Sciences 1972).

BACKGROUND TO THE PROJECT

The project is set against the background of a national shift in the focus of gravel extraction from higher gravel terraces onto floodplains. ARC Ltd (now Hanson) obtained planning permission to extract gravel from an area of 140 ha at Cassington and Yarnton prior to the introduction of Planning Policy Guidance 16 in 1990, and thus with no

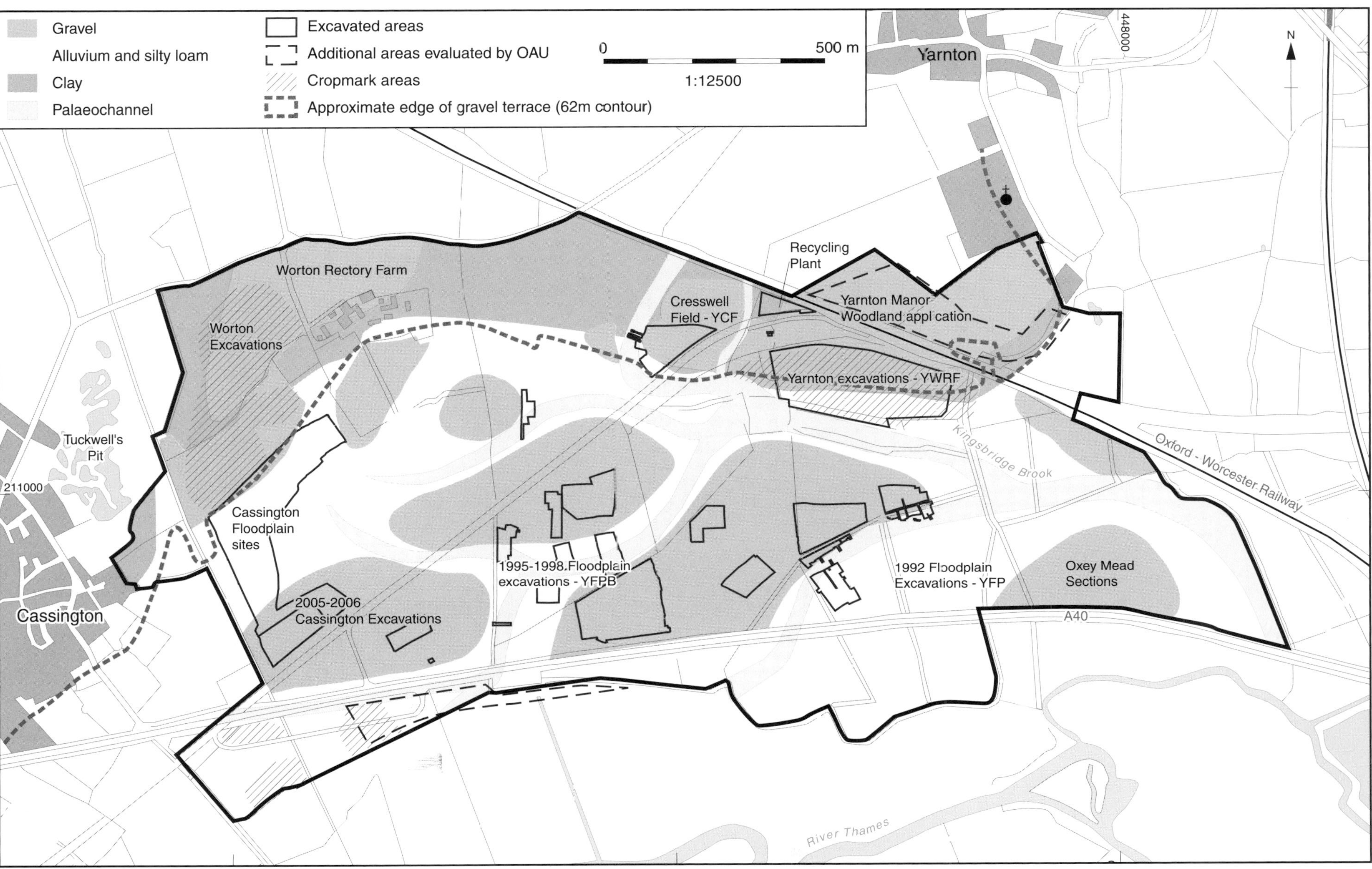

Fig. 1.4 Drift geology and areas of fieldwork in the study area

archaeological conditions imposed. This clearly posed a considerable and imminent threat to the archaeological resource, although road construction, plough damage and the effects of dewatering upon waterlogged deposits (consequent upon gravel extraction) also constituted threats of longer term damage to archaeological remains. Previous salvage finds from the general area, combined with aerial photography, suggested that this was an area of high archaeological potential for the Iron Age and Romano-British periods.

As one of the first gravel pits in the region to have operated on the floodplain, the ARC Cassington pit presented the first opportunity to investigate floodplain archaeology on any scale. The problems of detecting sites beneath alluviated landscapes have been known for some time but the complex interrelationship between the location of early features, subsequent land use, alluviation and colluviation was not then appreciated. The present project enabled these factors to be more fully realised (Hey 1998).

In the early 1960s Professor St Joseph took a series of aerial photographs of the area before the axing of the Oxford to Fairford branch line by Dr Beeching. Figure 1.5, taken in 1962, shows a

Fig. 1.5 Yarnton cropmarks as photographed from the south-west by St Joseph. Cambridge University Collection of Air Photographs (AFU-65)

cropmark site in one of the fields belonging to Worton Rectory Farm and scheduled for gravel extraction (University of Cambridge Committee for Aerial Photography, AFU 65). The discovery of this photograph immediately before quarrying was due to start prompted emergency action and the initiation of archaeological work in 1989.

The subsequent excavations, largely funded by English Heritage, were to extend over a 10 year period, while fieldwork on the Cassington floodplain was not completed until 2006. The project has comprised a combination of large-scale landscape survey with site-specific investigation permitting the examination of landscape in greater depth whilst still recovering an overview of its development.

Sequence of investigations (Fig. 1.6)

In September 1989, OAU (now OA) funded a rapid evaluation of the western two hectares of the Worton Rectory Farm field with cropmarks (Fig 1.6). This field, in common with all the land in the extraction area, had been ploughed in recent years. Nine trenches, representing 3% of the available area, were excavated to coincide with cropmarks identified by Professor St Joseph in 1962, and to assess parts of the site apparently buried beneath colluvium below the edge of the gravel terrace. A high density of features, largely of Iron Age and Roman date, was revealed, a sample of which was excavated by hand. The results were sufficiently important to persuade English Heritage to fund the rescue excavation of one hectare of the most densely-occupied area (Figs 1.7 and 1.8), comprising the western part of the Yarnton site, in Spring 1990. This excavation revealed further Iron Age and Roman occupation with, in addition, evidence of Saxon settlement. Subsequent topsoil stripping by machine of a one hectare area to the east by ARC in May 1990 revealed more Iron Age, Roman and Saxon features which could only be cursorily examined, given limited time and resources. Within this salvage area were at least two Roman pottery kilns and a number of burials.

In Autumn 1990, the eastern side of the field was stripped of topsoil and a grant from English Heritage allowed a further 2.5 ha to be examined, largely to investigate the Saxon settlement (Fig. 1.7, Site 23; for the full extent of this area see Hey 2004, 9, fig. 1.4), although the cropmarks (Fig. 1.5) suggested that a late Roman enclosure was also present. The remains of a middle Saxon settlement, overlain by late Saxon features, were uncovered (Hey 2004).

Overall, therefore, the Yarnton site comprised area excavation and observation of *c* 5 ha on the second gravel terrace along with some wider survey work. Occupation features at Yarnton dated from the late Bronze Age/early Iron Age period, continuing through the Iron Age into the Roman period with some evidence of settlement shift from west to east. It is unclear if there was a break in the occupation sequence at the end of the Roman period, but there was certainly settlement from the late 5th or early 6th century AD (Hey 2004). The later prehistoric activity was mainly domestic in character with a series of structures and enclosures with accompanying pits, but also included several burials and, most notably, a designated middle Iron Age burial ground. The Roman evidence combined domestic and agricultural elements, with field ditches and trackways and a small number of burials.

A programme of fieldwalking was undertaken in arable fields in the autumn of 1990 covering 182 ha within the extraction area and beyond it, to provide landscape evidence associated with the settlement site such as, for example, Roman manuring scatters. The exercise recorded a dense scatter of early and middle Iron Age pottery in the east of Cresswell Field and immediately west of the Yarnton excavation site, with only a small number of later Iron Age and Roman sherds and a single sherd of Saxon pottery (Hey 1991c).

In 1990, 24 evaluation trenches were excavated in the east of Cresswell Field (YCE), representing 1.5% of the 8 ha area which would be affected by gravel extraction. Two supplementary trenches were also excavated in the field to the south. The evaluation was designed to examine the finds scatter and area of cropmarks visible in the field in the summer of 1990 and establish the western limit of the Iron Age settlement excavated at Yarnton. The recorded field names of 'chissels' and 'black patch' were indicative of occupation of some nature in this area (Hey 2004, 33).

Archaeological features, predominantly of later Bronze Age and early-middle Iron Age date, were identified in 22 of the trenches. No late Iron Age contexts were excavated and Roman features were sparse. The examination of the alluvial sequence within the dry river bed to the west indicated that the channel had been dry throughout the life of the settlement. In the field to the south the two trenches showed some Iron Age features and significant Roman remains which were mostly late in date. A series of ditches running parallel to the edge of the terrace were found at the south end of the trenches, north of which lay pits, postholes and gullies.

An evaluation was carried out on Yarnton Floodplain (YFP) in autumn 1991, followed by an excavation of 3.5 ha of the floodplain in 1992-3 revealing domestic occupation, ceremonial monuments and burial sites dating from the early Neolithic to the end of the Bronze Age. A small number of later features were also encountered, dating to the later Bronze Age, Iron Age and Roman periods. Amongst these were a later prehistoric causeway, Romano-British field boundaries and various other surface deposits within the palaeochannels (Fig. 2.2).

In the early 1990s, a proposal to turn the A40 from Witney to Oxford into a dual carriageway prompted archaeological evaluation of this route, funded by English Heritage. As part of this work, a

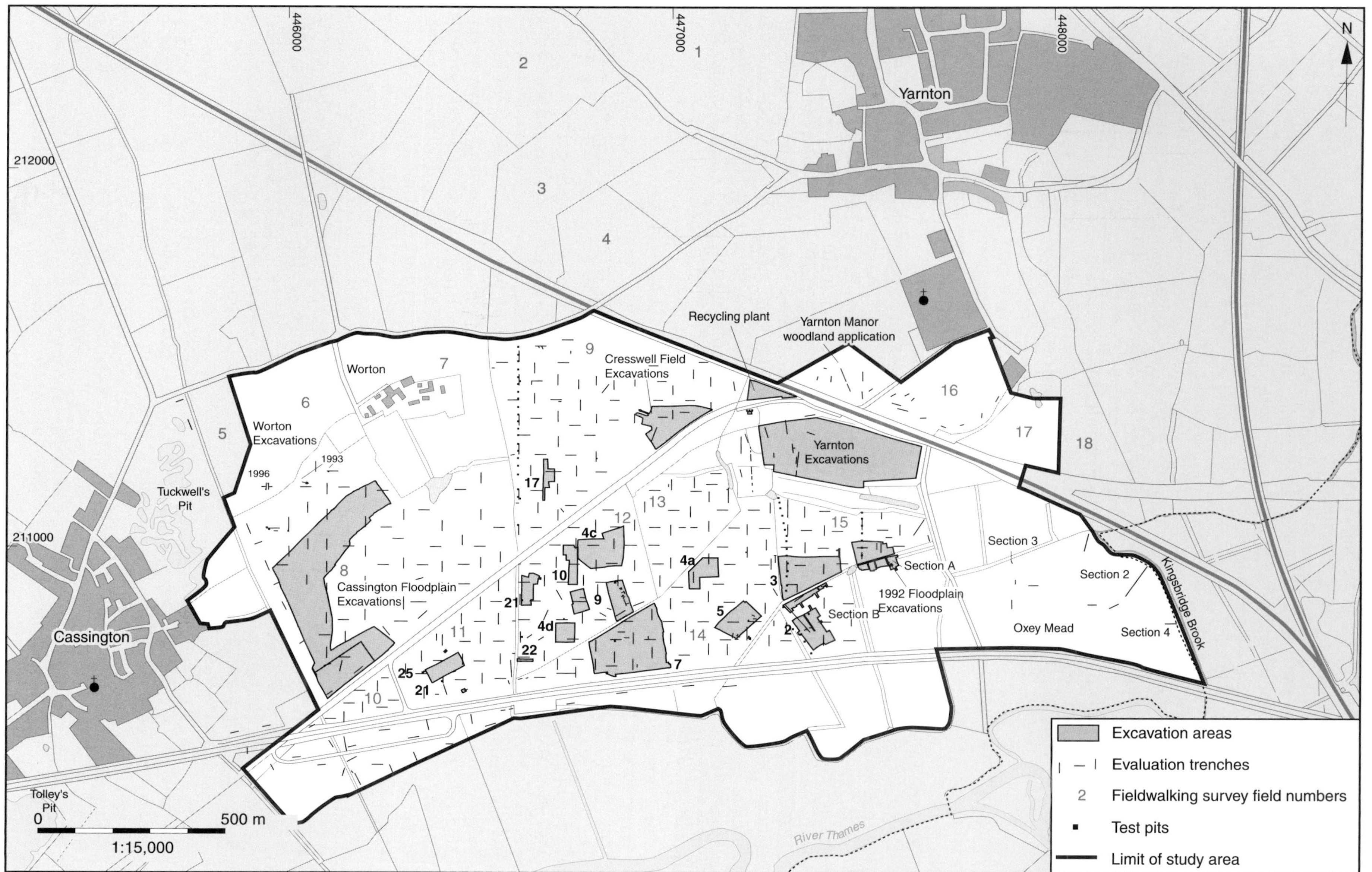

Fig. 1.6 Yarnton-Cassington project fieldwork locations

Fig. 1.7 Yarnton and Cresswell Field excavations: all periods

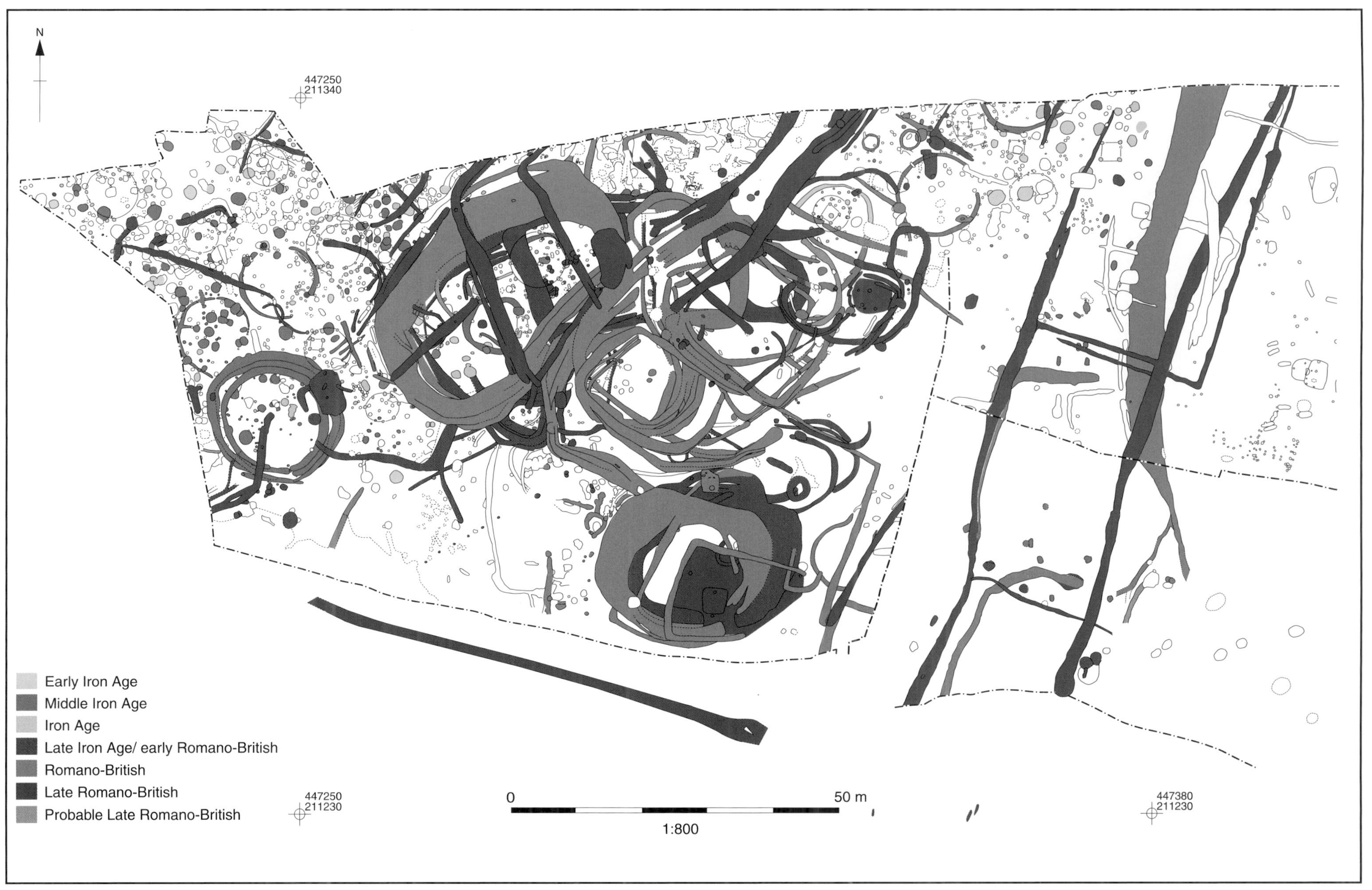

Fig. 1.8 Yarnton site: plan of later prehistoric and Roman phases

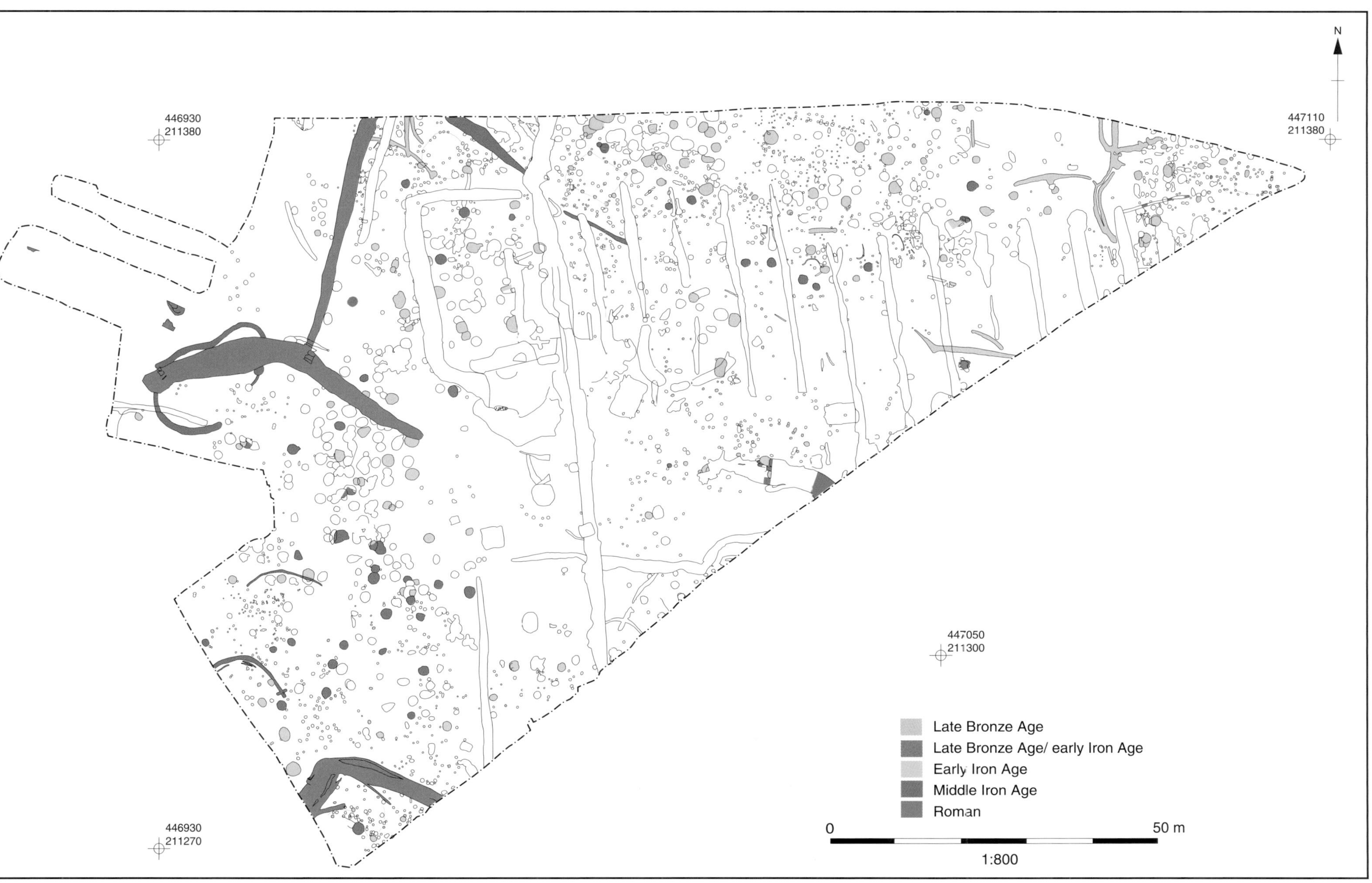

Fig. 1.9 Cresswell Field site: plan of later prehistoric and Roman phases

new access road was planned for Cassington along the west edge of the study area from a roundabout junction on the south-west corner (Fig. 1.3). The archaeological investigation was undertaken by OAU in 1991 and 1992 (Hey 1993a) although the scheme has never been adopted.

In 1993 English Heritage funded OA to undertake a machine-trenched evaluation to assess the archaeological resource of all parts of the study area not previously investigated (Hey 1994a). Some 340 trenches, mostly 30 m by 2 m, and 51 test-pits were excavated within an area of 70 ha covering the ARC/Hanson pit, floodplain and gravel terrace (Fig. 1.6). For the purposes of fully understanding the settlement and landscape context of the sites within the gravel pit, the study area was redefined to include the adjacent site at Worton which lies just beyond the limit of extraction to the north-west, and the land around both the Yarnton and the Worton settlements. The trenches were targeted to examine cropmarks at Worton (Fig. 1.11), first recorded by Major Allen in the 1930s and clearly visible in the summer of 1990 to the west of the modern hamlet (see Chapter 10, Figs 10.1 and 10.2, see also Fig. 11.1).

The research design (Hey 1994a) that was adopted following this work entailed large-scale excavation (a further 10.5 ha) and observation work (5 ha) on the floodplain, and the excavation of a substantial site on the gravel terrace (Cresswell Field). More systematic collection of environmental evidence over the area, and methodological studies, particularly of the use of geophysical survey in alluviated areas, were also undertaken.

Excavations at Yarnton Cresswell Field took place in the Spring of 1995. An area of approximately 1 ha was investigated revealing a dense scatter of features representing occupation activity mainly from the late Bronze Age through to the middle Iron Age (Figs 1.7 and 1.9). Earlier prehistoric and Saxon occupation evidence was also found, and also a little evidence of Romano-British activity (Fig. 1.9). The later Bronze Age and Iron Age features were mostly domestic in nature and consisted of pits, small posthole structures, house gullies and a few small enclosures. There were, however, a few features and deposits of a more ritual nature. These consisted of deliberately placed deposits in some of the pits, including a human skull, whole and partial animal burials and a deposit of smashed, decorated pots. The lowest fills of the adjacent channel were probably contemporary with the Iron Age settlement. The early Iron Age was the main period represented on the site, with a smaller number of middle Iron Age features. There was no obvious late Iron Age occupation and the only possible Romano-British features were a ditched enclosure and two probable field ditches. This confirmed that Cresswell Field formed the earliest part of the Iron Age settlement which gradually shifted eastwards along the terrace, the main focus of the middle and late Iron Age and Romano-British settlement lying within Yarnton.

Work related to a proposed recycling plant was undertaken in 1996 and 1997 (YRP). A small area just north-west of the north-west corner of the Yarnton site was examined in 1996, revealing the corner of a ditched enclosure and numerous postholes. In 1997 a larger, triangular area of *c* 3500 sq m, lying north of the former Oxford-Fairford railway line, just east of Cresswell Field and some 60 m north of the west end of the Yarnton site, was examined (Fig. 1.7). This revealed a limited number of linear features, all on a broad north-south alignment. Their character suggests a Roman or later date, but while occasional burnt stone and animal bone fragments were noted, no dating material was recovered.

The fifth major component of the Yarnton project was the Yarnton Floodplain Project B (YFPB), carried out in 1995-8 and designed to investigate selected Neolithic and Bronze Age domestic and funerary sites on the floodplain. During the course of these excavations, the extent of Roman land use on the floodplain became apparent, with droveways, field ditches and Roman ploughsoils revealed. Examination of the palaeochannels enabled further environmental sampling which illuminated landscape and land-use change throughout the 1st millennia BC and AD, and a number of structures were revealed which date to these periods, including a spectacular limestone causeway (Chapter 11).

A final piece of fieldwork consisted of an excavation and watching brief carried out for Hanson Aggregates Ltd in 2005 and 2006 in the Cassington Pit Western Extension, covering 11.8 ha at the western edge of the Yarnton project area. Scattered finds and features indicated activity of Mesolithic to middle Bronze Age date, but the most extensive remains belonged to a late Bronze Age settlement. Later finds included an isolated middle Iron Age pit and late Iron Age/Romano-British field boundaries. The results of this work will be published with the other evidence for the Neolithic and Bronze Age elements of the project (Hayden *et al.* forthcoming). In that context and below the site is referred to as Cassington floodplain.

PREVIOUS WORK ON THE SITE AND IN THE LOCALITY

Introduction

The Thames/Evenlode confluence is rich in archaeological remains of all periods, with important sites from the Neolithic to the Saxon period found within a small area. Most notable for the Iron Age period is the large late Iron Age enclosure at Cassington Mill (Benson and Miles 1974, 52-3; Case 1982a). It has been recognised for a long time that cropmarks are commonly found on lowland gravels, and the Upper Thames Valley was one of the prime targets for early pioneers in aerial photography such as Major Allen in the 1930s and Derrick Riley in the

Fig. 1.10 Previous discoveries in the locality

1940s, and subsequently for Professor St Joseph in the 1960s-1970s. It has been increasingly obvious from fieldwork that the visible cropmarks are only part of the story and that further extensive areas of settlement exist, masked by deposits of alluvium. Unfortunately, over the last two centuries many sites have been lost through gravel extraction, road and railway construction and house building with only limited recording having taken place (Benson and Miles 1974).

Yarnton study area

There have been varied and intermittent discoveries in the Yarnton study area (as shown on Figure 1.10) in the last two centuries, largely arising from major groundworks such as those for gravel extraction, road and railway construction and house building. In the early 1850s the construction of the Oxford to Worcester railway and a branch line to Witney and Fairford cut through the pit area (Day 1990, 471-2).

One of the first discoveries was made in 1854 in a field of Manor Farm, called the Park (between Yarnton church and station) in which lay a ballast pit (Fig 1.10, no. 1). The Park lies north of the ARC/Hanson gravel pit and thus outside the archaeologically investigated area. A considerable quantity of urns and human remains was noted (Dawkins 1862, 145). Unfortunately most of the finds were disposed of and only one Iron Age pot

Fig. 1.11 Worton cropmarks from the north. Cambridge University Collection of Air Photographs (AY-94).

was salvaged, now in the Ashmolean Museum (Bradford 1942a, fig. 12, no. 36). This would appear to be of middle Iron Age date. Boyd Dawkins, later Professor of Natural History at Oxford, visited the area in May 1861 and discovered further remains in the railway cutting of the Witney railway close to its junction with the main Oxford-Worcester line, about a quarter of a mile west of the earlier discoveries (ibid.; Fig. 1.10, no. 2). He observed a black horizon containing pot and bones and a skeleton buried in a crouched position sliced by the railway cutting. In November of that year, he observed an extended inhumation considered to be of Anglo-Saxon date. Sherds were also collected in 1861 on the south-east and north-west sides of the cutting on the Witney line, 0.4 km west of Yarnton station, from storage pits. The sherds are decorated and probably date to the early Iron Age (ibid.; Fig. 1.10, no. 3).

In 1875-6 the old quarry of 1854 was extended to provide ballast for further railway works, and Professor George Rolleston excavated two probable ring ditches and a number of contracted burials, near one of which was found a decorated sherd, probably of Anglo-Saxon date. Other finds included a copper neckring or diadem, a bronze implement, pottery and a net sinker (Rolleston 1884). It is unclear from the descriptions which of the burials might have been Saxon and which were prehistoric.

Flights by Major Allen in the 1930s (Allen Collection, Ashmolean Museum), by Cambridge and more recently by the RCHME revealed various cropmarks north-west of Worton Rectory Farm (Figs 1.10, no. 8 and 1.11, see also Figs 10.2 and 11.1). These included probable Iron Age occupation features and Romano-British enclosures. A small rectangular enclosure with an entrance to the north (Oxfordshire HER PRN 1382), was also photographed by Allen just north of the A40 in the south of the pit area. Faint traces of other possible features are visible to the north in other photographs (eg NMR SP 4610/1 and SP 4610/2).

The site on the Yarnton gravel terrace was discovered by Professor St Joseph in 1962 (University of Cambridge Committee for Aerial Photography, AFU 65-7) (Fig. 1.5). An earlier flight had led him to believe that there was a villa south of Yarnton (St Joseph 1961, 134), but the published grid reference (SP 473 111), is so close to the south-western corner of the excavated Yarnton site as to suggest that features within that area, seen more clearly in 1962, were originally mistaken for part of a small villa.

Other adjacent sites

Cassington

During the construction of the Oxford northern by-pass between Eynsham and Wolvercote in 1931, a number of new discoveries were made in the area around Cassington village, which were drawn to the attention of E T Leeds (Leeds 1935). Three distinct Iron Age/Romano-British settlements were examined north of the A40: Cassington North-West, the most substantial, in Smith's and Partridge's No. 1 pits (Fig. 1.10, no. 4); Cassington West at the south-west end of the modern village (Fig. 1.10, no. 5), and Cassington East in Tuckwell's pit (Fig. 1.10, no. 6). The western site revealed circular pits and a short length of ditch associated with Iron Age pottery. Some of the features are described as smelting pits. In addition Romano-British pits, ditches and burials were noted (Leeds 1935; Anon 1937, 201). As no pits were observed south of the road it was concluded that the site probably extended to the north. A small excavation was carried out by the Oxford University Archaeological Society in the summer of 1932 on land belonging to Manor Farm, exposing further pits and associated features. Finds included pottery, animal bone, burnt stone, part of a triangular loomweight and a quernstone.

The eastern site fell within Tuckwell's Pit which lies adjacent to the modern hamlet of Worton (Fig. 1.10, no. 6). Further pits were found, again with associated animal bone, pottery and burnt stone. Of particular note amongst the pottery was a globular bowl decorated with triple line swags with horizontal lines above and below in the 'Frilford style' (Leeds 1935, pl. V, no. 2). The base had been perforated.

South of the A40, a large enclosure was discovered from they air by Major Allen in 1933 at Cassington Mill (SP 451 101) adjacent to the River Evenlode (PRN 1265) (Fig. 1.10, no. 7). A broad defensive ditch could be traced around the western, northern and eastern sides enclosing an area of some 5 ha. The enclosure is now largely destroyed as a result of large scale extraction in Smith's Pit 2. Many small-scale excavations and sections were made in advance of extraction between 1930 and 1952, summarised by Case (1982a). The enclosure lies within a complex of archaeological features dating from the earlier prehistoric through to the Saxon period.

The enclosure, sometimes referred to as the Big Enclosure, was roughly circular in shape and over 300 m in diameter, situated above a dramatic drop to the confluence of the Evenlode and the Thames. It was surrounded by a ditch and rampart, the former having produced late Iron Age pottery, with early Roman pottery from higher levels. Harding (1972, 56) classified Cassington as a valley fort initially built in the later years of the 1st century BC. The ditches were recut in the second quarter of the 1st century AD and then shortly afterwards the defences were apparently levelled (Case 1982a, 136). Two skeletons were found in the main enclosure ditch: an adult female and child in the primary filling in crouched position. A crouched female burial of unknown date was also found on the edge of the enclosure ditch (at SP 4481 1001) in 1976 (Chambers 1977).

Roman pottery of 2nd- to 3rd-century date attests continued occupation in the locality, albeit on a much reduced scale. Increased quantities of material dating to the later Roman period suggest more intensive occupation in the 3rd and 4th centuries. Three late Roman inhumation burials were reported from within the south end of the enclosure (Case 1982a, fig. 66). A large late Roman cemetery of over 110 graves was excavated immediately to the north near the junction of the A40 with the Cassington-Eynsham road. Of the 110 graves excavated, 15 were decapitated and three were cremations, but no coffins or grave goods were found (Anon 1936, 201; 1938, 165; for a plan see Harding 1972, plate 27). Other Roman features inside the enclosure included pits and ditches, a large sub-rectangular enclosure, pottery kilns and numerous scatters of pottery and other stray finds. One pottery kiln is datable to the second half of the 1st century AD, and two to the late 2nd century AD. The kilns produced utilitarian vessels such as jars, with no evidence of any fine ware production (Young 1982). Quarrying of the north-eastern area revealed a settlement of round houses dating to the 1st and 2nd centuries AD and following the line of the ditch.

Purwell Farm

Other Iron Age settlements in the immediate environs of Yarnton include Purwell Farm in the northern part of Cassington parish (SP 443 117/9) (Fig. 1.10, no. 10). The site, located on a hill of Oxford Clay capped by gravel, when excavated by Dawson (1961-2) revealed a number of storage pits and gullies containing early Iron Age pottery. Part of a Saxon settlement and associated burial ground have also been investigated at this site (Arthur and Jope 1962-3, 2).

Bladon Castle

The Bladon Castle hillfort lies 1.5 km north-west of the Yarnton Iron Age site upon a small hill rising some 35 m above the surrounding area. Today it is covered in trees, but a single bank and ditch can be discerned on its north-east side and a double bank around its south and west perimeter (Ainslie 1988). A drainage ditch, dug across the north-east rampart by the Blenheim Estate, was cleaned and examined by Tim Allen of Oxford Archaeology and the Oxford University Archaeological Society in 1987. This showed that the rampart was mainly of clay with dump lines of sand, faced front and rear by thin stone walls. Two successive pebbled surfaces abutted it (ibid.). Dating was inconclusive, but the rampart had been burnt, like that at Burroway Brook (Lambrick 2009, 356) and this may suggest a similar early Iron Age date for this event (Allen 2000, 17).

Sandy Lane, Yarnton and Begbroke

Further evidence of Iron Age and Roman occupation has been noted at Sandy Lane gravel pit in the north of Yarnton parish about 1.6 km north of Yarnton village close to the railway junction. Here a large number of Iron Age sherds were salvaged from pits exposed in gravel extraction in the 1920s (Fig. 1.10, no. 11). Iron Age and Roman ditches and pits have also been observed in the area, containing pottery and a Roman bronze brooch of 1st-century type (Anon 1936, 201). Further Roman pottery was found just to the north on fields of the Weed Research Station at Begbroke (Fig. 1.10, no. 12). Aerial photographs have revealed indeterminate cropmarks in this area (Sturdy and Case 1963), while a possible hut site with associated hearths and storage pits was found at Begbroke Hill Farm (SP 483 137) (Fig. 1.10, no. 13). The evidence from this site suggested that stock rearing, particularly of sheep, was important. A loomweight, quern and net sinker were also found.

Port Meadow

In Port Meadow, just to the south-east of Yarnton, a complex of cropmarks was photographed by Major Allen in 1933 and subsequently surveyed on the ground (Atkinson 1942; see also Lambrick and McDonald 1985). These comprise some 19 sites of several periods spread over the floodplain, including ring ditches and rectangular and circular enclosures. Finds from site 5/6, described as 'ring ditches with a diameter of *c* 60 ft' (18 m), produced what was described as late Bronze Age and Iron Age pottery (Atkinson 1942, 32-3); at least some of the illustrated examples (ibid., 33, fig. 6, nos 3-4) are likely to be middle Iron Age in date.

Wytham

On the opposite side of the river Thames, on Wytham Hill *c* 5 km south of the Yarnton site (Fig. 2.1), a possible ditch terminal of defensive proportions has been found and a possible rampart observed in Wytham Wood (Allen 2000, 17). This fragmentary evidence may represent the remains of a hillfort, but the features have not been dated.

PROJECT OBJECTIVES AND METHODS

Objectives

The original research design for the project (Hey and Miles 1989) recognised the rich archaeological resource of the Evenlode confluence and stressed the importance of understanding changing settlement patterns from the Neolithic to the Saxon period. A review undertaken in 1994 (Hey 1994b), in the light of fieldwork already completed at Yarnton and on parts of the floodplain, but prior to further work in the latter area and the excavation of Cresswell Field, set the ongoing project in its national research framework. This review identified a series of major questions to be addressed by further work both in the field and subsequently, informing the approach adopted to post-excavation analysis. With regard to the later prehistoric and Roman periods the principal questions were:

What is the character of the late Bronze Age/early Iron Age transition and why and how did the landscape become permanently settled and bounded and the emphasis change from the monument-dominated landscape of earlier periods?

How did land-use strategies change through the Iron Age, Roman and early Saxon periods, particularly in relation to changing hydrological conditions on the floodplain?

What are the processes which characterise changes in settlement from the mid to the late Iron Age and how do small rural communities become Romanised?

What is the nature of the transition from the late Roman to early Saxon settlement?

How can well-preserved but fragile landscapes (especially those on the floodplain) be effectively evaluated and how can scattered but important remains be adequately and cost-effectively investigated?

One research aim specific to the palaeoenvironmental investigations of the Iron Age to Roman periods of the project, in addition to determining more generally the environmental setting of the site and the biological aspects of its economy was:

To refine further the palaeohydrological and alluvial sequences which have been constructed for the Upper Thames Basin (Robinson and Lambrick 1984; Robinson 1992b).

Methods

Evidence for Iron Age and Roman settlement and landscape is drawn from four main sources: area excavation, evaluation trenching, field survey and environmental sampling within old river channels which once crossed the floodplain area. In all cases priority has been given to extensive rather than intensive detailed investigation to maximise the understanding of overall patterns.

Excavation

The Iron Age and Roman sites at Yarnton (YWRF) and Cresswell Field (YCF) were investigated in open-area excavation. The Yarnton excavation area totalled some 4.5 ha in size whilst Cresswell Field formed a rough triangle of approximately 1 ha. The locations were partly dictated by the permitted limit of gravel extraction, though the excavation at Cresswell Field did extend 20 m north of that in order to encompass an area where the evaluation suggested denser feature distribution. It was also partly determined by the results of the geophysical survey (see Linford, Chapter 12). As time and money were limited, a decision was taken to expose as large an area as possible and sample the exposed features, rather than excavating a smaller area in detail. A three-phase approach was adopted to the excavations with periods of review built in:

1. Mechanical stripping of ploughsoil under archaeological supervision, cleaning and planning the site, was followed by initial sampling of a range of features to provide an interpretable site plan and a rudimentary understanding of basic phasing, the extent of settlement, the degree of planning in settlement layout and the range of structural elements.
2. Excavation priorities were then established for investigating stratigraphic and spatial relationships. Consideration was given to excavating a representative sample of features and also a spatial spread of deposits to allow finds-distribution patterns to be assessed. Sampling provided a more detailed structural sequence for the site, some understanding of date, intensity of occupation, economy and organisation within the settlement.
3. A programme of more detailed work on selected structural features and feature groups was devised to create an understanding of life on the site, involving more work on physical relationships of features and targeting features for finds recovery to provide sizeable assemblages which could be more confidently dated.

The extent of excavation in each fieldwork season varied according to time available and research priorities. The density of features across the site made it impractical to excavate all the discrete features and a sampling strategy was employed. Where they existed, the junctions between intercutting features were excavated to establish the stratigraphic sequence. Additional cross-sections were excavated through linear features to establish their character and date.

Pits were examined by stratified random sampling (Orton 2000). The site was divided up into areas of 30 by 20 m and initially 20% of the pits within each area were excavated. Pits were selected on the basis of sampling a range of types and sizes within each area. At Cresswell Field, once 20% of the pits had been excavated this sample was increased by 10% and subsequently by another 10% across the site. At Cresswell Field 186 pits were sectioned, comprising approximately 40% of the total. At Yarnton some 379 pits (25%) were excavated. Any pits particularly prolific in terms of pottery or other significant deposits were excavated in plan.

A similar strategy to that used for the pits was applied to the postholes to obtain an initial 20% sample. Concentrations of postholes were then examined more closely to elucidate spatial patterns, for example of structures, and where these were identified further features were sampled. At Cresswell Field some 169 postholes dating to the

Iron Age and Roman periods were excavated and at Yarnton 520 such postholes were excavated. In addition, some 547 contexts were allocated to sections dug through ditches and a further 249 to gullies at Yarnton and at Cresswell Field. In total 150 ditch and gully sections were investigated. All contexts were given a unique number (see below for site recording procedures). Contexts from both sites were subsequently assigned to context groups, usually structures or enclosures, during the post-excavation analysis. At Yarnton, a total of 1971 individual contexts were recorded which have been ordered into 31 context groups. At Cresswell Field a total of 1775 individual contexts were recorded which have been ordered into 39 different context groups. Unexcavated features were not given context numbers. Soil samples were taken from deposits across a range of dates and feature types. Metal detectors were used on site during machine stripping and to monitor finds retrieval during hand excavation. After excavation had been completed, a short watching brief and selective salvage operation was carried out during the removal of the top of the gravel by ARC/Hanson.

Regular site visits by Mark Robinson of the Oxford University Museum allowed an appropriate environmental sampling strategy to be devised and general palaeoenvironmental observations to be made about the context of these samples. Usually the only surviving botanical remains were of charred plants. Care was taken to develop a strategy which sampled deposits from the range of features and chronological periods represented, as well as targeting those deposits which were particularly charcoal-rich. Postholes of structures were not very productive in terms of quantities of material, but their sampling was seen to be important in order to provide material contemporary with the use of the structure (Reynolds 1995). In particular, the retrieval of samples suitable for radiocarbon dating was vital in the absence of other diagnostic finds.

The two sites lay in fields which had been cultivated since the medieval period; all had experienced truncation and no floor or ground surfaces survived. The sites were covered by modern ploughsoil *c* 0.25 m deep, which in some places overlay medieval ploughsoil, for example to the east of the Yarnton site. On the higher part of these sites, medieval furrows had cut down into the underlying natural soils leaving distinctive linear grooves (Hey 2004, 206-213). Medieval colluvium was also present on the slopes below the terrace edge to the south and in the western part of the Cresswell Field site. These ploughsoils directly overlay natural gravel or an undisturbed reddish-brown silt deposited as glacial outwash in the Devensian. It was extremely difficult to distinguish archaeological soils from glacial silt and also early ploughsoil/ploughwash. The disturbed upper fills of features, especially those with distinctive charcoal-rich fills, became visible before all the ploughsoil had been removed, as ploughing had not been sufficiently thorough to fully mix the soil. Even where colluviation was not present smaller features were not readily seen.

After the main excavation had been completed at Yarnton a further area to the east was mechanically stripped and any recognisable archaeological features were noted as part of a salvage operation.

Evaluation trenching

Evaluation trenching was employed to illuminate the character of Iron Age and Roman settlement in the study area in two ways:

1. Trenching on a grid to expose 2% of the area threatened by gravel extraction, road building and other development schemes was undertaken to reveal the extent of settlement of different periods, and assess its character and state of preservation (Fig. 1.3). In this exercise negative evidence was as important as recovery of features for an assessment of the limits of settlement for particular periods. Over the course of the project, 393 evaluation trenches, usually 30 m x 2 m in size, were excavated in the threatened areas. Trenches were usually placed on the Ordnance Survey grid in the first instance, but additional trenches of varying shapes and sizes were then excavated to answer particular questions raised during the evaluation process (Fig. 1.6).
2. To investigate sites in the study area not under threat, for example at Worton (Hey 2004, 15).

Where features were revealed in evaluation trenches, 50% of each context was usually excavated, and recording methods were those employed on the main excavation areas. Samples were also taken for charred plant remains and waterlogged material where these were present, in order to gain an understanding of the wider environment.

In addition to the evaluation trenches, test pits were dug in three transects across the study area in order to provide information on ploughsoils, buried soils and colluvium, and the extent of finds movement in the ground. Fifty-one pits were dug by hand, 1 x 1 m in size and spaced at *c* 20 m intervals, and the soil was sieved through a 10 mm mesh. Finds were separated by layer, and by 0.10 m spits where layers were thicker than this.

Field survey

Non-intrusive field survey was an important tool for locating settlement sites and establishing their extent, and in detecting activities that took place away from habitation. Air photographs were scrutinised for occupation sites, and cropmarks at Worton, which include later prehistoric and Roman remains, were plotted by the (then) RCHM(E), now English Heritage.

A fieldwalking survey was undertaken in 18 fields within the extraction area and just beyond it, and 182 hectares in total were examined in this way. This work was undertaken partly to locate sites from spreads of finds on modern cultivation surfaces, but also to examine land use by identifying manuring scatters. The method of finds collection is described in more detail below (Chapter 11). Geophysical survey undertaken by Archaeometry Branch of the Ancient Monuments Laboratory (AML) covered 33 hectares of the study area. Magnetometer survey was the method most frequently used over this area (details are discussed by Neil Linford in Chapter 12) and was especially useful at Cresswell Field where the area for excavation was selected on the basis of these results.

Palaeochannel trenching

A conscious effort was made to retrieve environmental data from the wider landscape. Sampling of sections dug through palaeochannels on the Yarnton floodplain has been of vital importance in this regard. Within the waterlogged silts of the channels, pollen, waterlogged seeds, invertebrate remains and mollusca have been preserved. Radiocarbon and OSL (Chapter 13) have been used to date these sequences of deposits. These contexts acted as environmental traps from the Bronze Age to the medieval period, providing information on the conditions within the channels, land use in the fields on either side and the vegetation of the wider landscape.

At Cresswell Field two machine-excavated trenches projecting from the west edge of the site were designed to cut the adjacent palaeochannel at right angles.

Condition of archaeological features and deposits

Archaeological features were generally well preserved, the only modern disturbance being variable truncation by ploughing. The furrows associated with medieval ploughing had caused some truncation of features, particularly on Cresswell Field, but these only extended in a band running through the central-eastern area of the site, where the lowest density of features occurred. Conversely the ridges had served to protect features from modern cultivation. The existence of a buried post-medieval ploughsoil in the west of Cresswell Field and the presence of plough scars on the natural gravel surface suggested slightly more damage in this area. Fortunately, the main concentration of features had been protected from later ploughing by the greater depth of colluvial deposits towards the edge of the palaeochannel.

Although there were a large number of features on Cresswell Field there was only limited intercutting. By contrast the later occupation on the Yarnton site, in particular the Roman ditched enclosures, had destroyed many earlier features.

CHRONOLOGY AND PHASING

The complexity of some of the features, notably the Roman enclosures which saw several phases of reuse, combined with the general paucity of stratigraphic relationships between other features, has resulted in considerable reliance being placed on the pottery evidence in assigning contexts to broad chronological groups. Many of the features, particularly the Roman and later groups, contain a varying component of redeposited material. It is possible that some of the small groups of pottery consist entirely of redeposited material, and thus some caution is needed in interpreting the features from which these groups derive. This problem is particularly acute with postholes, which generally produce small quantities of material, and with the enclosures where the constant re-digging of the ditches has made it very difficult to disentangle the sequences.

The problems of phasing at Yarnton were compounded by the general paucity of finds recovered from the excavations, with the exception of pottery. Some 22,260 sherds were recovered spanning the later Bronze Age to later Roman period. A few discrete features of later Bronze Age date were identified at Cresswell Field and a small assemblage of potentially later Bronze Age pottery was recovered across both Yarnton and Cresswell Field, redeposited in later features.

The 'absolute' chronology of the early Iron Age sequence at Yarnton is based almost entirely upon the pottery. The earliest Iron Age groups in the Yarnton area can only be dated by comparison with material with similar stylistic characteristics, principally with regard to vessel form and decoration. Chronological developments in the fabric composition of assemblages are more readily dated in relative than in absolute terms.

Forty-four radiocarbon determinations were obtained on samples of Iron Age and Roman date from the Yarnton project (Chapter 13). Some of these dates have proved crucial in identifying Iron Age activity in two main areas. Eleven dates were taken from human bone from the burials found at Yarnton, proving a middle Iron Age date for the cemetery which was originally thought to be Anglo-Saxon (Hey *et al.* 1999). Eighteen dates were taken from waterlogged organic remains from Floodplain Section A, two from a palaeochannel at Oxey Mead, four from Floodplain Section B, two from Floodplain Site 2, eight from Site 9 and two from a ditch exposed in evaluation Trench 37. The stone causeway on Floodplain Site 9, thought originally to be Bronze Age on the basis of associated finds, subsequently proved to be middle Iron Age in date.

Radiocarbon dates have been calibrated using the data given by Stuiver *et al.* (1998) with the computer program OxCal (v3.5) (Bronk Ramsey 1995; 1998; 2001) and are quoted at a 95% level of confidence in the form recommended by Mook (1986), with the end points rounded outwards to 10 years. The ranges quoted in italics are *estimated date ranges* derived from mathematical modelling of archaeological problems (see below, Chapter 13).

In addition, nine optically stimulated luminescence (OSL) samples were taken from palaeochannel deposits on Yarnton floodplain and 72 archaeomagnetic samples were taken from a ditch on Floodplain Site 25 to obtain a date from an organic rich layer sealed by the overlying alluvium (see Chapter 11).

Analysis of spatial patterning provides the only effective way of phasing a large number of the excavated features. Buildings, ancillary structures, pens, enclosures and fields would seldom have been laid out randomly across the landscape, but positioned to take advantage of the natural topography and to be accessible from other contemporary features. On a settlement, for example, it would be reasonable to propose that the inhabitants would not construct their store buildings at a distance from their houses, nor would they be likely to dig a well in the middle of their main route to the neighbouring settlement. On a site which has been occupied over some time, however, modifications will have been made to the layout and, in practice, it is not easy to distinguish early from later features. In addition, it is not necessarily the case that changes would be effected at the same time across the entire site. It is more probable that alterations would be constantly undertaken, but at different times and rates in different parts of the area. The larger the settlement, the more difficult it is to make spatial links between feature groups.

In practice, analysis of the archaeological remains on rural sites is a complex process which integrates all the methods of dating and phasing outlined above, and provides a 'best fit' for the deposits encountered. In the case of Yarnton, stratigraphic relationships have been used as the foundation for providing the phasing for the site but, where features are discrete, their spatial relationship to other features and similarities/differences in deposit character have been used to develop a phase plan. This has been undertaken in conjunction with dated material. Absolute dating, from finds recovered or radiocarbon assays, has provided the chronological framework around which the phasing has been developed. The limitations of the phasing arrived at by this method are readily acknowledged.

SITE RECORDING PROCEDURES AND TERMINOLOGY

Excavation of the Yarnton and Cresswell Field sites followed slightly different recording systems. At Yarnton, the features were accorded a single number and the cuts (interventions) across them were subdivided by letter (eg 22/A; 22/C etc) from a continuous sequence starting at 1 and continuing to 2733. If more than one layer was excavated these were labelled as a further subdivision (22/C/1; 22/C/2 and so on). Numbering of features investigated in the salvage areas started at 3000. Groups of ditches which form recuts of a single enclosure or linear ditch system have been grouped together and identified using one of the ditch numbers. These are the numbers used in the text to describe these features. Other groups refer to structures or fence lines.

The system used at Cresswell Field was a single-context numbering system, regardless of feature type (whether cut or fill), with numbers starting at 7000 and continuing through to 8789.

Description of soils on site was typically quite detailed. For the purposes of site description (Chapters 5-9) these descriptions are usually omitted or highly abbreviated, though almost all fills fell within a range of sandy silt to silty or sandy loam. A simplified hierarchy of feature fill descriptions was established, based on the amount of gravel contained within the deposit, and is used in some of the descriptions below. The categories are as follows: 'gravel-free fills' – those with less than 5% gravel; 'non-gravelly fills' – those with *c* 5-15% gravel; 'silty loams' – with a variable gravel content of *c* 16-60%; 'gravelly fills' – with >60% gravel inclusions.

The main designated phases are: late Bronze Age (1100-750 BC), early Iron Age (*c* 750-400 BC), middle Iron Age (*c* 400-50 BC), Iron Age (uncertain whether early or middle), late Iron Age/early Roman (50 BC-AD 80), early Roman (*c* AD 80-250), late Roman (AD 250-410) and Roman (precise date uncertain). It should be noted that 'Roman' is used simply as a convenient chronological term. 'Romano-British' is sometimes employed when discussion of cultural aspects requires a distinction to be made between native and non-native practice.

ARCHIVE

The paper archive will be deposited with Oxfordshire County Museums Service, where it is hoped also to place the finds (accession numbers 1989.101; 1989.126; 1991.24-6; 1991.33; 1995.168-72; 1996.76) and ultimately the records that have been computerised will be available through the Archaeology Data Service. Copies of all evaluation reports and post-excavation assessments generated through the life of the project have been deposited with the Oxfordshire County Council Historic Environment Record (HER).

Chapter 2: Settlement and Landscape

by Mark Robinson and Gill Hey

INTRODUCTION

During the course of the 1st millennium BC and the first half of the 1st millennium AD, landscape and settlement in the Yarnton area underwent profound change. Settlement became permanently-sited and, for the first time, nucleated. At Yarnton, the occupation site was situated on the higher Second Gravel Terrace, in contrast to the earlier Bronze Age focus which had been on the floodplain, and it shifted gradually eastwards across the terrace over time. It changed from a settlement characterised by post-built structures and pits, to one in which enclosures dominated the settlement layout and buildings were hard to detect. At Cassington, a small nucleated settlement was established on the floodplain in the mid to late Bronze Age and appears to have been permanently occupied until the end of the Bronze Age. Settlement then seems to have moved onto the adjacent gravel terrace, where its history apparently paralleled that at Yarnton. At the same time, landscape change was underway as flooding became more common on the floodplain and the deposition of alluvial silts raised low-lying areas, clogged old river channels and, eventually, overlay earlier ploughed fields on the floodplain. Cultivation at the edge of the gravel terrace caused erosion of the terrace edge and colluviation on its lower slopes. The inhabitants developed land-use strategies to adapt to these changing environmental conditions and also to external economic and, perhaps, political pressures.

At the end of the Roman period there appears to have been a hiatus in the settlement record, with no conclusive evidence for structures of the 5th century AD; sunken-featured buildings of Anglo-Saxon type date to the late 5th century at the earliest (Hey 2004, 39). Nevertheless, the environmental evidence from the floodplain shows that there had been no regeneration of woodland, or even scrub, in these low-lying areas, demonstrating that animals had been grazing upon them throughout.

This chapter examines these changes from the end of the late Bronze Age into the 5th century AD. It draws upon the range of evidence which is described in greater detail in Chapters 5-19 of this volume, and complements the overview of social life presented in Chapter 3. Chapter 4 considers the wider implications of this evidence, Yarnton's position in its contemporary world, and how results from this study relate to modern research on the period. Full discussion of the late Bronze Age settlement and landscape and that of the 5th century AD is provided elsewhere (Hey *et al.* forthcoming; Hey 2004), but is summarised here in order to provide a meaningful context in which to understand the Iron Age and Roman evidence.

THE LANDSCAPE AND SETTLEMENT CONTEXT

The landscape context

The topography of this part of central southern Britain is dominated by the river Thames which winds through a wide floodplain with low hills rising gently from the valley bottom. The Cotswold limestone slopes lie further to the north, but are not generally visible from the valley. Landscape changes are relatively subtle (Fig. 1.2). In the Yarnton area, the Thames flows north-east around the Corallian ridge before turning south towards Oxford (Figs 1.1 and 2.1). On the south bank the terraces are fairly narrow and the edge of the ridge comparatively steep; small quantities of Corallian Rag limestone found within the most recent floodplain gravels attest erosion into the ridge in the last Ice Age (Philip Powell pers. comm.). To the north of the river there are wide river terraces and these attracted settlement from an early period, including that investigated at Yarnton.

The main Iron Age and Roman sites around Yarnton were situated on the Second (Summertown-Radley) Gravel Terrace, which lies above the floodplain and above the 60 m contour (Fig. 2.1), although some middle Iron Age sites are known on the floodplain at Cassington and in Port Meadow to the south-east and at Farmoor to the south-west. From the terrace edge there would have been an open prospect over the broad floodplain (at *c* 58 m OD), and ready access to it and the river, with Wytham Hill rising beyond. Today that hill is heavily wooded and this may have been so in the Roman period. Behind the settlements, to the north, the land rises gently onto higher gravel terraces at around 92 m OD and the clay slopes of Bladon Heath (110 m OD), which was crowned with an Iron Age hillfort. It is uncertain how extensively this part of the landscape would have been cleared, but it seems probable that some woodland would have survived, as it did at Eynsham Hall Camp which lay on similar topography 6.5 km away (Robinson and Wilson 1987; Fig. 2.1), although grazing may have begun to encroach upon it. Some woodland may

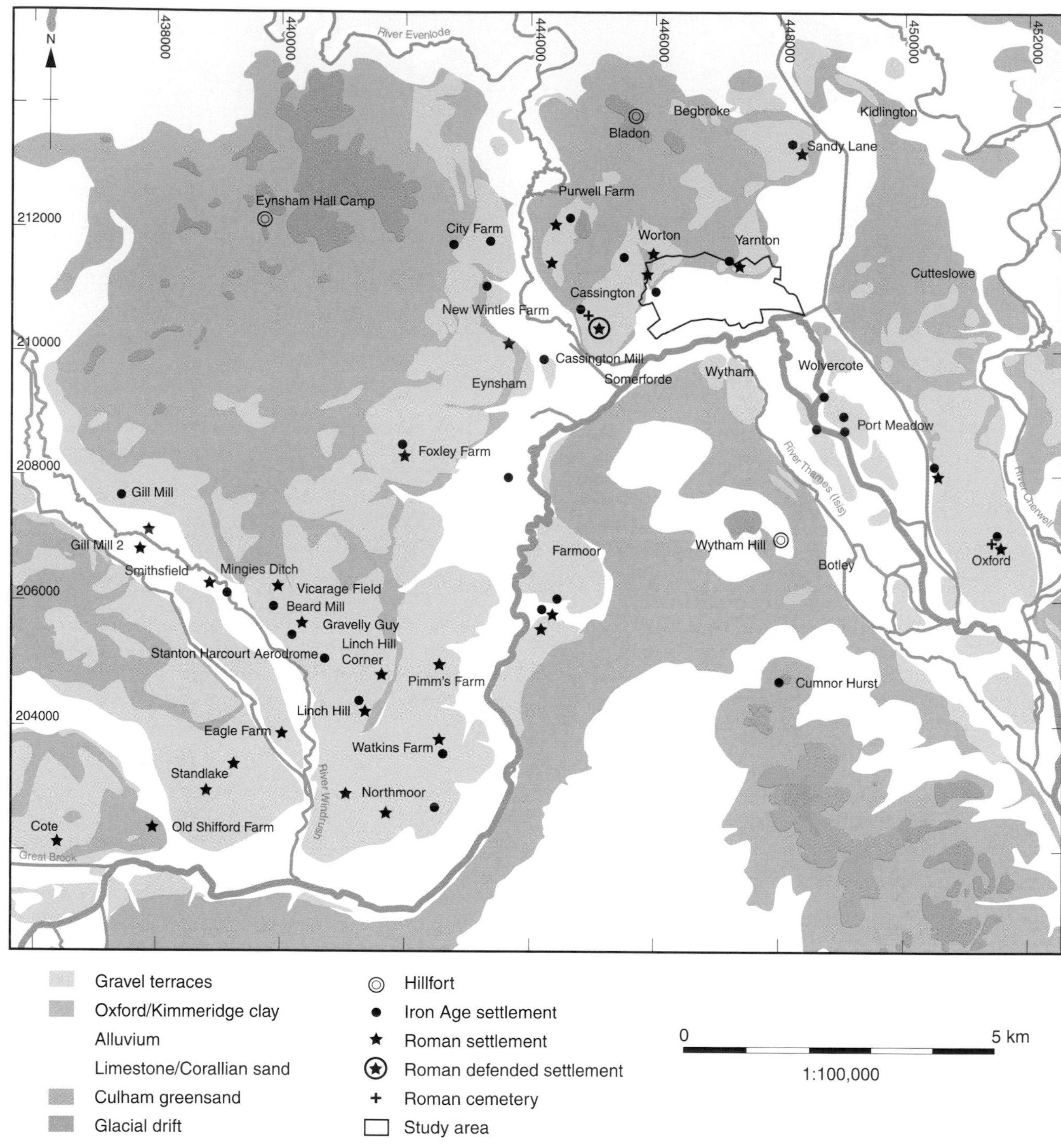

Fig. 2.1 Windrush to Cherwell confluence area: geology and principal local sites

have stretched down the sides of streams. Glacial drift lies on the highest of the slopes, and limestone outcrops beyond (Institute of Geological Sciences 1972). Views along the valley in each direction could have been wide, depending on the extent and location of tree cover.

Landscape development, geology and soils

By the end of the Bronze Age, human activity had brought major changes to the vegetation of the Yarnton-Cassington area from its mid Holocene (post-glacial) state. Hydrological changes were also occurring on the floodplain.

The gravel quarry area lay mostly on the floodplain of the river Thames, but the focus of Iron Age and Roman settlement was upon the Second Gravel Terrace, bounded to the north by Oxford Clay, at the foot of the dip slope of the Cotswolds. A minor late glacial valley dissects the terrace at Cresswell Field (Fig. 1.4), and in this gap between Cresswell Field and another area of Second Terrace at Worton Rectory Farm, loamy drift and some unbedded gravel slope down to the floodplain. Otherwise, the

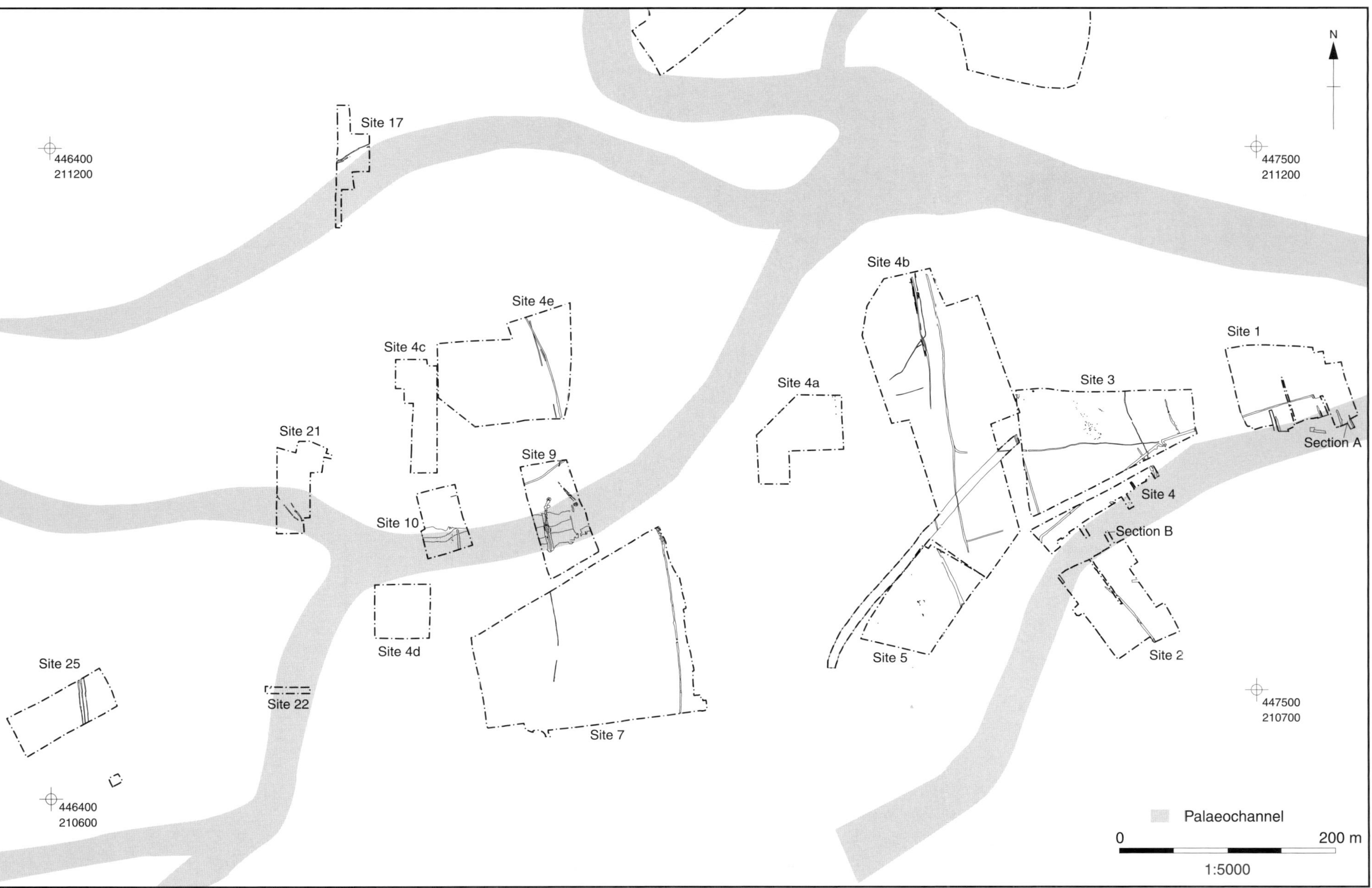

Fig. 2.2 Yarnton floodplain excavations: late Bronze Age and Iron Age-Roman features

gravels of the Second Terrace are contiguous with the gravels of the floodplain. Seasonal springs in the valley probably flowed from the base of the gravel terrace down to the northern floodplain palaeochannel. Late Bronze Age 'burnt-mound' activity at the western edge of the Cresswell Field site probably utilised this source of water, as did a pond on the north edge of Cresswell Field which was first used in the late Bronze Age (Chapter 11).

The Bronze Age soil on the Second Gravel Terrace was a stone-free non-calcareous silt loam brown earth (Robinson and Wilson 1987, 73; Robinson 1984, 4; Robinson 1992a, 53-4). It is likely that there had been at least limited cultivation of the Second Terrace in the Bronze Age, although subsequent cultivation had removed any traces. The drift between the two areas of Second Terrace gave rise to the Isle of Abbot soil series, a gleyed brown earth (Jarvis 1973, 84-5). Evesham or Denchworth series soils develop on the Oxford Clay (ibid., 72-4, 76-8). They are surface-water gleyed clay loams or clays, the Evesham series being calcareous whereas at least the A horizon of Denchworth soils is non-calcareous. Acid soil developed on glacial plateau gravels further north at Bladon Heath.

The mid Holocene floodplain consisted of flat gravel 'islands' with a thin soil covering dissected by low-lying hollows of Late Glacial palaeochannels of the River Thames. Two larger palaeochannels entered the area from the south-west (Fig. 1.4). The northern arm crossed Floodplain Sites 10 and 9 before running along the edge of the Second Gravel Terrace below the Yarnton site. The southern arm ran along the south of the study area between Floodplain Sites 2 and 4 (for these numbers see Figs 1.6 and 2.2), before joining with the northern arm at the north-west corner of Oxey Mead. The combined channel ran around the northern and eastern side of Oxey Mead before joining an extinct channel of the Thames.

Hydrological changes caused by clearance in the catchment (Robinson and Lambrick 1984; Robinson 1992b) resulted in a rise in the water table of the floodplain at Yarnton from the middle Bronze Age onwards. By the late Bronze Age, the major southern channel and that on Oxey Mead had been re-activated. No evidence was found of overbank flooding from these channels at this date but settlement was abandoned on low-lying ground at the end of the Bronze Age while continuing on the Second Gravel Terrace. Molluscan evidence suggests that there was at least a seasonal flow of water along the channels from the main channels of the Thames, but it is possible that these were stagnant and swampy during dry periods in the summer. Little sedimentation was occurring in the palaeochannels except around the obstruction created by a timber and brushwood platform on Site 1 (Fig. 2.2).

The lowest-lying areas of floodplain, such as Site 2, had a covering of about 0.2 m of circumneutral brown-earth soil of clay loam, which was never cultivated. The remainder of the floodplain was covered with 0.2 m or more of a non-calcareous brown-earth soil of silt loam to silty clay loam which had experienced some clay eluviation (the formation of a clay pan).

The late Bronze Age background

The late Bronze Age settlement pattern

Evidence of settlement dating from the earliest Neolithic to the late Bronze Age, including an early Neolithic longhouse, was uncovered on the Yarnton and Cassington floodplain during the course of the Yarnton-Cassington Project (Hey *et al.* forthcoming). This evidence suggests that the area was visited repeatedly throughout the Neolithic, but that habitation was probably quite short-lived (perhaps only a few weeks or months at a time) and was situated within woodland clearings. Circular structures were built from the early Bronze Age and perhaps indicate more long-lived occupation. These buildings lay in a much more extensively-cleared landscape.

Six late Bronze Age circular post-built structures have been identified on the Yarnton floodplain, dated mainly by pottery finds; other undated structures may also be of this period. These were found on the large central gravel island between the two main palaeochannels, on Site 5 (one structure), Site 3 (three structures) and Site 1 (two structures) (Fig. 2.2). Pits further north on Site 4e and postholes on Site 4a suggest that settlement may have been more widespread. In addition, pits, postholes and finds scatters on both the Cresswell Field and Yarnton sites indicate that there was also habitation on the Second Gravel Terrace at this time. The overall pattern is quite dispersed (Fig. 2.3). Buildings were either paired, as on Site 1 and two of the structures on Site 3, or stand as single, isolated structures. It can be proposed that these unenclosed dwellings represent single-generation households, surrounded by open grassland. There is no suggestion that settlement location was constrained by boundaries, and no indication of population pressure in the landscape.

A small settlement at Cassington, at the western limit of the study area, is of a different character. It contained the remains of several roundhouses and D-shaped, four-post and rectangular structures, as well as pits and ten waterholes (Hayden *et al.* forthcoming).

The character of late Bronze Age settlement

The single or paired late Bronze Age structures on the floodplain tended to be surrounded by a scatter of pits and postholes which might be expected in a domestic space but which do not suggest intensive occupation over a long period of time. The pits do not seem to have been used for refuse disposal, and household waste was probably either recycled or cast into the surrounding landscape. Nevertheless

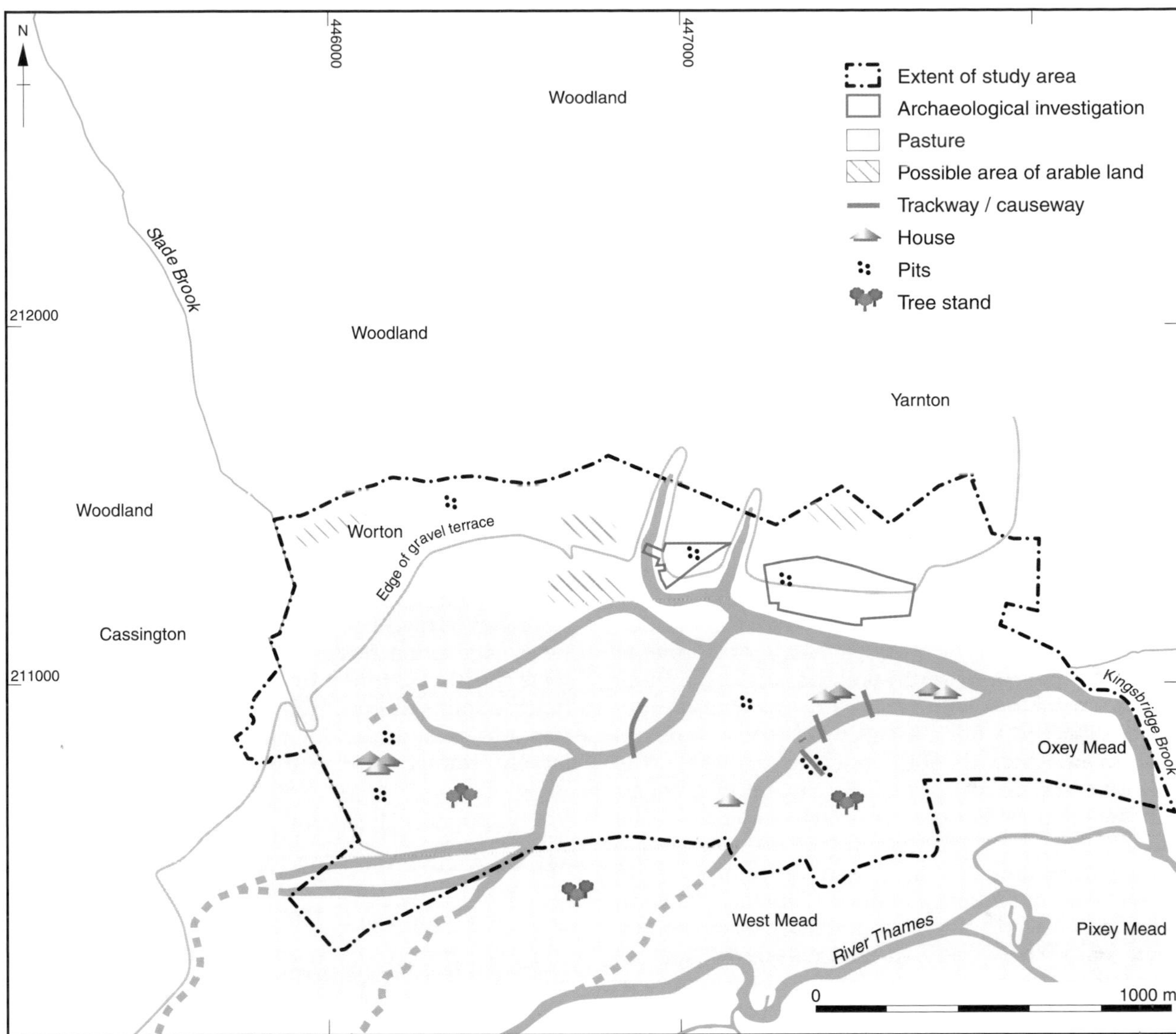

Fig. 2.3 The late Bronze Age/early Iron Age landscape

some pottery, worked stone, burnt stone, fired clay, animal bone and charred plants were recovered from the pits. Waterholes were found adjacent to some of the buildings; other waterholes appeared to lie in more open grassland settings. A limited amount of organisation within or adjacent to settlements may be indicated by the presence of fence-lines on Site 3 and Site 4a, and a late Bronze Age boundary ditch which was found running northwards from the palaeochannel on the south edge of Site 1.

At the nucleated Cassington floodplain settlement, elements of order can be detected (Hayden *et al.* forthcoming; see Lambrick 2009. fig. 4.8). These elements include fence lines and rows of four-post structures, as well as distinct groups of houses and zones of pits, waterholes and possible midden deposits.

Features or hollows packed with burnt stone and charcoal, and situated close to water sources and away from domestic structures, were a common feature in the later Neolithic and Bronze Age landscape. A number of these appear to have been of late Bronze Age date, such as the features on the bank of a palaeochannel next to the Cresswell Field site. The purpose of these features is uncertain (Hodder and Barfield 1991), but they are a phenomenon that did not persist into the early Iron Age in this area. Wooden structures within channels were preserved from around this time as a result of the rising water table, including a possible revetment in the channel next to the Site 1 Bronze Age buildings.

Although most earlier prehistoric ceremonial features were of Neolithic or earlier Bronze Age date, there is evidence of the continuing importance of ritual activity into the late Bronze Age. A linear ditch on Site 2, running NW-SE towards an earlier penannular enclosure on the channel edge and a ring ditch on the far bank, appeared to have a ceremonial purpose (see below, Chapter 11). It was cut parallel to an earlier, middle Bronze Age ditch and was associated with a series of pit and slot alignments which shared its orientation, and which appeared to have been dug from the late Bronze

Age/early Iron Age into the middle Iron Age period. Burials of this period are not common, but 27 deposits of cremated human remains were found scattered throughout the Cassington West site. Many of these were small and may have been residual, but others were large enough to suggest deliberate deposition. Many of these lay near roundhouses and other structures, but their chronological (and thus spatial) relationship with these structures is unclear.

Late Bronze Age landscape and land use

The Neolithic and early Bronze Age vegetation on the floodplain was typified by a shifting pattern of woodland clearings, but conditions were generally open by the late Bronze Age. The number of seeds of *Alnus glutinosa* (alder), possibly from trees growing along the riverbank, declined up the sediment sequence associated with the late Bronze Age platform in the palaeochannel on Site 1 Section A (Fig. 2.2) and they were virtually absent from the top. There was only a slight presence of alder pollen at the bottom of the sequences from this channel at Site 2. Total tree and shrub pollen values from these samples were low, with *Quercus* sp. (oak) best represented. The Second Gravel Terrace was perhaps completely clear of trees but the nature of the vegetation on the Oxford Clay to the north is uncertain and it possibly carried much woodland. The slopes of Wytham Hill south of the Thames, were probably wooded. The charcoal from the late Bronze Age settlements on the floodplain at Yarnton suggested mixed sources of fuel, with oak probably from woodland and thorny rosaceous species perhaps cut from scrub or hedges. One aspect to emerge from the study of macroscopic plant and insect remains from some of the late Bronze Age waterholes on the floodplain was that, upon abandonment, their immediate surrounds became overgrown with thorn scrub while the more general landscape remained open.

The pollen evidence from the waterholes and the palaeochannels suggests the presence of much grassland on the floodplain during the late Bronze Age. Values for pollen of Poaceae (Gramineae, grasses) and *Plantago lanceolata* (ribwort plantain) were generally high. The occurrence of scarabaeoid dung beetles indicates that the floodplain was being used for the grazing of domestic animals.

Charred plant remains from the late Bronze Age settlement sites included the cereals *Triticum dicoccum* (emmer wheat) and *Hordeum* sp. (barley). Concentrations of grain were low and there was a ratio of grain to nut-shell fragments of *Corylus avellana* (hazel) of about 2:1. Although *Triticum spelta* (spelt wheat) was not recorded from any later Bronze Age contexts, it was present on the site during the middle Bronze Age. Cereal cultivation was perhaps a relatively minor activity in comparison to the raising of domestic animals. Waterlogged seeds and capsules of *Linum usitatissimum* (flax) were found in some of the waterholes on the floodplain.

The results for the late Bronze Age fall into the pattern which is emerging for the Upper Thames Valley as a whole. A landscape of lightly-grazed grassland with some thorn scrub was indicated by waterlogged plant and invertebrate remains from a late Bronze Age pond at Mount Farm, Berinsfield, on the Third Gravel Terrace of the Thames (Robinson 1992a, 54). A little chaff of *Triticum* cf. *dicoccum* (emmer wheat) was also present. Evidence for thorn scrub was absent from a late Bronze Age waterhole at Eight Acre Field, Radley, but there was a strong presence of grassland (Parker 1995b; Robinson 1995). In this case, a few glumes of *Triticum spelta* (spelt wheat) were present. In contrast, there was evidence from Shorncote Quarry (Glos), on the First Gravel Terrace, for the persistence of some woodland near to the source of the Thames well into the late Bronze Age (Robinson 2002). Some agricultural intensification was probably beginning to occur during the late Bronze Age (Robinson 1999, 274), but although the gravel terraces and the floodplain alongside the Thames were mostly pasture with some arable before *c* 650 BC, the status of the other geologies remains uncertain. It is possible that areas such as the Oxford Clay largely retained their woodland cover.

EARLY AND MIDDLE IRON AGE SETTLEMENT AND LANDSCAPE (*C* 750-50 BC)

The early Iron Age (*c* 750-400 BC)

The early Iron Age settlement pattern

A small unenclosed settlement was established at Yarnton on and near the edge of the Second Gravel Terrace overlooking the floodplain of the Thames. This settlement was examined at Yarnton (in the original Yarnton Worton Rectory Farm excavations) and Cresswell Field. Before it was bisected by a railway line and shunting yards in the 19th century (see Chapter 1), these areas formed part of what had once been a continuous settlement, with a small stream running through it (Chapter 11). In all, sixteen post-built structures and numerous pits of early Iron Age date (probably around 560 pits; see Chapter 5) have been identified, stretching from the east edge of the palaeochannel in Cresswell Field into the Yarnton site where features were mostly located in the north-west and north of the excavated area. On the basis of the number of pits and the quantity of artefacts, the densest area of activity appears to have been in Cresswell Field to the west. Despite extensive survey and fieldwork in the study area, no occupation sites of this date have been found on the Yarnton floodplain.

Other excavated early Iron Age sites are not known within the study area, and no early Iron Age remains were uncovered during field evaluation on the Second Gravel Terrace at Worton. The date and extent of the earliest Iron Age settlement that was destroyed during gravel extraction in the adjacent Tuckwell's Pit on the north-west edge of the study area (Fig. 1.10) is unknown; only middle Iron Age material is noted, but very little archaeological recording was undertaken (Leeds 1935).

Iron Age sites were uncovered to the south-west of Cassington during the construction of the Oxford Northern Bypass (now the A40) and by gravel extraction up to the 1950s (Chapter 1), but archaeological investigation was extremely limited and suggested that the features uncovered were middle rather than early Iron Age in date (Leeds 1935; Harding 1972, 19-21). However, the north-south string of pits running parallel to the terrace edge, which was uncovered in the Cassington West site (Harding 1972, plate 27), is very reminiscent of other Thames Valley Iron Age sites which have their origins in the early Iron Age, such as Yarnton or nearby Gravelly Guy (Lambrick and Allen 2004; Lambrick 2009, 105-9). Similar sites were uncovered on the other side of the river Evenlode, at City Farm, Hanborough (Case *et al.* 1964-5).

The origins of the Purwell Farm and Yarnton Sandy Lane sites (Figs 1.10 and 2.1) are also uncertain, but it can be suggested on the basis of parallels with better-known sites on the Thames gravels that nucleation and the organisation of agriculture which led to the excavation of deep grain-storage pits was a phenomenon which occurred in the early Iron Age (Lambrick 1992b, 88-93; 2009, 105-9). It is interesting, in this context, that the hillfort at Bladon Castle appears to have been constructed and slighted at this time (Allen 2000, 17). The fort sits on a high point, centrally placed within the block of land on which the Yarnton, Worton, Cassington, Purwell Farm and Begbroke settlements were situated.

The character of early Iron Age settlement

The most striking difference between late Bronze Age and early Iron Age settlements is the sheer density of features associated with Iron Age occupation sites (Fig. 2.4). This partly reflects the longevity of use of these sites, but a number of new features also appear at this time, in particular deep circular pits which are believed to have been used for grain storage. At Cresswell Field, the pits ran in two distinct linear swathes, north-south parallel to a palaeochannel and then turning south-eastwards to run parallel to the edge of the Second Gravel Terrace (Figs 5.6 and 5.7). A number of placed deposits were found within these features (Chapter 3). The pits were sampled in such a way as to allow the numbers of pits by period to be extrapolated, and approximately 560 pits are likely to have been dug over the early Iron Age period. Some were small and irregular in profile. Amongst the deeper examples, it was not easy to identify the characteristic undercut profile of classic grain-storage pits since potential examples of this type had suffered from the collapse of their sides dug in loose gravel, as well as from disturbance by later settlement activity and severe truncation by ploughing (Chapter 5). George Lambrick has estimated that, at Gravelly Guy, the annual seed-grain requirement for the settlement could have been contained within a single pit (Lambrick and Allen 2004, 485), with the implication that perhaps only one grain storage pit need have been dug each year. The Yarnton evidence appears to be roughly in line with this calculation (with all the provisos above and the fact that some features undoubtedly lay beyond the excavated area and others appear to have been reused).

Seven four-post structures were also present on the Yarnton site, though not in Cresswell Field. This was initially thought to reflect a slightly later date for these structures, but recent discovery of these features on the Cassington floodplain late Bronze Age site has led us to revise this view. Four four-post structures at Yarnton had been placed within what are assumed to be earlier circular buildings, and the others lay close to the houses. It is suggested that the four-post structures were associated with the above-ground storage of cereals (Cunliffe 1991, 376).

Circular or oval post-built structures of early Iron Age date tended to be more substantial than those of the late Bronze Age, but a range of forms and sizes was present (Chapter 3). Pairs of buildings in Cresswell Field suggest domestic units (Figs 2.4 and 5.6), and three broad groupings can be also discerned on the Yarnton site, one in the north-west, one in the centre and the other in the north-east of the site (Fig. 5.7). To the west and east, small buildings were present within these domestic groups and may represent ancillary structures (the central area had been badly disturbed by later settlement activity). Within the overall broad scatter of features, pits did appear to cluster around structures.

On the evidence available it cannot be ascertained whether all these groups of buildings were established and occupied at the same time. It is not considered likely that individual buildings would have survived over the suggested, and very approximate, 350 years duration of this phase of settlement, but it is possible that some groups may have been long-lived. The buildings in the north-west of the Yarnton site may represent a sequence of structures erected within the same settlement unit, and there is good evidence to suggest that one of these structures was replaced on the same site as its predecessor (B 1474; Chapter 5). All three groupings on the Yarnton site, and the south-west pair of buildings on Cresswell Field, were in areas that were subsequently occupied in the middle Iron Age and this is highly suggestive of long-lived and discrete settlement foci which may represent household units.

The layout of the early and middle Iron Age settlement is paralleled at a number of other sites on

Fig. 2.4 Yarnton and Cresswell Field early Iron Age settlement

the Thames gravels (Lambrick 1992b) and very closely at Gravelly Guy (Lambrick and Allen 2004), which consisted of a linear scatter of post-built roundhouses and pits, partially defined on one side by a gully. The pits infilled the spaces between the buildings, but also extended beyond them on one side.

Early Iron Age landscape and land use

The pollen, macroscopic plant remains, insects and molluscs from the sediment sequence of the southern arm of the major palaeochannel on the floodplain at Yarnton (Section A, column 1 on Site 1 and Section B on Site 2; Figs 1.4 and 2.2) showed little evidence for environmental change from the late Bronze Age. Muddy bankside conditions were suggested by seeds of plants such as *Rumex maritimus* (golden dock) and *Mentha* cf. *aquatica* (water mint) and beetles such as *Platystethus cornutus* gp. The majority of the waterlogged seeds were from aquatic plants. They suggested a rich vegetation of large emergent plants, such as *Sagittaria sagittifolia* (arrowhead) and *Schoenoplectus lacustris* (bulrush). The pollen, however, gave a much better indication of the terrestrial vegetation, with evidence for open grassland on the floodplain. The occurrence of scarabaeoid dung beetles suggested grazing, continuing the pattern observed for the late Bronze Age. Animal bone from the settlement demonstrates the importance of cattle rearing at this time, although sheep were also present in quite large numbers (Chapter 17).

Organic sediment was slowly accumulating in the palaeochannel, but there was no certain evidence of early Iron Age overbank alluviation even on the lowest areas of the floodplain. However, it is possible that occasional episodes of flooding extended right onto the higher areas of floodplain.

Although it was not possible to date any cultivation soils to the early Iron Age, the quantity of charred crop-processing remains from the settlement on the Second Gravel Terrace, together with the presence of grain-storage pits, suggest a greater emphasis on arable agriculture than previously. The most numerous charred cereal remains from the early Iron Age settlement at Yarnton and Cresswell Field were of *Triticum* sp., including *T. spelta* (spelt wheat). Indeed, it is possible that all the wheat was spelt, as there were no certain identifications of *T. dicoccum* (emmer wheat). *Hordeum* sp., including possible hulled *H. vulgare*, (six-row hulled barley) was also an important crop. The remains appeared to have been derived from small-scale processing of crops which had been stored, either above ground or in pits, in their hulled state, that is the wheat as spikelets and the barley retaining the lemma and palea. Grain was probably parched, pounded, winnowed and sieved when it was needed for consumption. The remains represented processing waste, including those weed seeds which had not been removed by earlier stages of crop cleaning, and grain which had been burnt in minor accidents. The absence of flax remains was perhaps due to the fact that there were no waterlogged contexts in the settlement in which they could have been preserved. A very slight presence of nut shell fragments of *Corylus avellana* (hazel) at Cresswell Field showed that wild food plant resources were not entirely ignored, although wild animals were very rare (only 0.2% of the animal bone assemblage) and there may have been a taboo on their consumption (Mulville *et al.*, Chapter 17). No fish bones were found.

The charred weed seeds gave some indication of the conditions of cultivation. The flora was appropriate to plough cultivation of a circumneutral soil, as would have been present on the Second Gravel Terrace. Many of the seeds were from species which are members of the Polygono-Chenopodietalia (Silverside 1977, 240-3), annual weeds which tend to be favoured by spring cultivation and nitrogen-rich soil. These species included *Chenopodium album* (fat hen) and *Urtica urens* (small nettle). However, there were also a few seeds of *Galium aparine* (goosegrass), a weed which tends to be associated with autumn-sown cereals. Some of the samples contained seeds of *Eleocharis palustris* or *uniglumis* (spike rush) and other marsh plants. This suggested that the cultivated area extended beyond the edge of the gravel terrace, perhaps onto the spring line between the terrace and the Oxford Clay.

The open, mixed agricultural landscape of early Iron Age Yarnton fell into the pattern shown by other early Iron Age settlements on the gravel terraces of the Upper Thames Valley (Robinson 1992a, 56). Spelt wheat and six-row hulled barley seem to have been the main crops throughout the region. Emmer wheat became perhaps no more than a weed in spelt wheat fields.

The middle Iron Age (c 400-50 BC)

The middle Iron Age settlement pattern

The settlement site at Yarnton and Cresswell Field continued to be occupied through the middle Iron Age period, although the most densely-occupied area had by now shifted eastwards and lay in the north-west part of the Yarnton excavation site (Fig. 2.5).

Material recovered from the Tuckwell's gravel pit between Worton and Cassington shows that there was a middle Iron Age settlement located here, 1.5 km to the west of Yarnton (Leeds 1935; Harding 1972, plate 62). Further occupation of this period was recorded to the south-west of Cassington, under the present A40 and to the north of the road in the Smith's and Partridge's No. 1 pit (Chapter 1; Fig. 1.10; Leeds 1935), 1.2 km from the Tuckwell's site. Middle Iron Age occupation evidence is also present at Purwell Farm and in the Yarnton Sandy Lane/Begbroke area (Figs 1.10 and 2.1), suggesting

Fig. 2.5 Yarnton and Cresswell Field middle Iron Age settlement

settlements spaced every 1.2-2 km around the edge of this spur of Second Gravel Terrace.

Small middle Iron Age sites are also found on the floodplain. At least two discrete settlements appear to be present in the south-west of the study area south of Worton (Chapter 11), and a number of sites of this date are known on Port Meadow to the south-east (Lambrick and McDonald 1985; Fig. 2.1). These have not been fully excavated, but resemble the floodplain sites which have been examined more thoroughly upstream at Farmoor (Lambrick and Robinson 1979; Fig. 2.1) and in the Lower Windrush Valley, for example at Mingies Ditch (Allen and Robinson 1993) and Gill Mill (South Leigh, unpublished). The evidence suggests that these were pastoral settlements, in contrast to the gravel terrace sites which had a more mixed farming regime, and their presence indicates increasing settlement density and pressure on precious resources (Lambrick 1992b, 93-7). A substantial middle Iron Age ditch was dug in the south-west of the Yarnton-Cassington study area (Site 25 and evaluation trenches; Chapter 11; Fig. 11.10) between the Yarnton gravel terrace settlement and the small floodplain sites. The ditch was recut twice and silts at the base of its second cut were formed between *370-110 cal BC (95% probability)* (Chapter 13). Could this have been an attempt to define the limits of Yarnton's land? It was the first boundary ditch ever to have been dug in this area.

The character of middle Iron Age settlement

In many respects, the character of early and middle Iron Age settlement at Yarnton was similar. People still lived in circular post-built structures, and pits continued to be dug at regular and similar intervals within the settlements (Figs 6.1-3). As before, a number of these pits appear to have been used for grain storage, and special deposits were subsequently placed within some when they were backfilled (Chapter 3). Discrete groups of domestic structures and features can be seen in the south-west of the Cresswell Field site and in the west, centre and north-east of the Yarnton site perpetuating four of the household units that were suggested for the early Iron Age settlement.

There were changes in settlement appearance, however, in that many buildings were encircled by gullies or ditches, some of which lay close to house walls and may have been for drainage. Other enclosures were more substantial. A large enclosure in the south-west of the Yarnton site, which was recut on at least three occasions, accommodated a circular house at each stage, but the building only occupied approximately half of the enclosed space, the remainder allowing for domestic activities and/or the temporary penning of animals. A fence line subdivided the area. Other enclosures in the north-east of the Yarnton site and the south-west of Cresswell Field did not contain any obvious structural evidence, but the density of artefactual material suggests that they were domestic areas and it is proposed that buildings may have been constructed of mass walling such as cob or turf which do not require deep foundations and do not leave any traces on plough-damaged sites. Later Iron Age and Roman structures are equally hard to detect and may have been using similar construction techniques (Allen *et al.* 1984).

It is possible that a chronological pattern is present in the middle Iron Age settlement layout. Post-built circular buildings may have been encircled by ditched enclosures or gullies during the early part of the middle Iron Age, and a move towards mass wall construction may have occurred in its later phases. Alternatively, settlement layout may be indicating functional differences between these different buildings and enclosures. A smithy may be suggested by a D-shaped building lying within a penannular gully, which may have been an open-sided structure.

As with the early Iron Age, the Yarnton settlement is paralleled in many ways at Gravelly Guy (Lambrick and Allen 2004), although Yarnton appears to have been less constrained in terms of the layout of its domestic features. Penannular ditches surrounded some of the buildings at Gravelly Guy and other buildings were present that may have formed peripheral groups.

One unusual feature of the Yarnton settlement, however, was the presence of a middle Iron Age inhumation cemetery on its eastern side (Chapter 3 and 16; Hey *et al.* 1999). This cemetery appears to have been in use for a short period of time during the third century BC, perhaps only for one to three generations. As discussed in Chapter 13, burial started in *420-230 cal BC (95% probability)* and spanned a period of *1-220 years (95% probability)* (Fig 13.1B). It cannot be paralleled in the Thames Valley, although middle Iron Age cemeteries are occasionally coming to light in other parts of southern England, for example at Suddern Farm, Hants (Cunliffe and Poole 2000).

Middle Iron Age landscape and land use (Fig. 2.6)

The middle Iron Age saw major changes on the floodplain, while more deposits of charred plant remains in the settlements at Yarnton and Cresswell Field suggest increased arable activity. There were larger number of features in the wider landscape, particularly those associated with river channels and channel crossings. These appeared to be linked to changes that were occurring during the middle Iron Age, though they may have begun earlier.

In the south of the study area, on Site 2 (Fig. 2.2), a sand-and-gravel causeway was constructed running across the southern palaeochannel. The causeway, perhaps constructed in response to increasing wetness, sealed a soil, possibly of early Iron Age date, which only contained shells of terrestrial molluscs. In contrast, the primary fills of adjacent alignments of small pits and slots which appear to have been cut for ceremonial or ritual purposes, contained shells of the amphibious snail *Lymnaea truncatula*. Shells of the flowing-water mollusc *Bithynia* sp. were also present. This showed that at least some of these curious features were open to receive clean floodwaters before the onset of alluviation. Alluviation began to occur over the entire ground surface on the lowest areas of Site 2 during the middle Iron Age; sediment filled the tops of earlier Bronze Age ditches and some of the small pits and slots and sealed the palaeosol. The rising water table resulted in the preservation of organic remains in the alluvium, and a radiocarbon date of 440-160 cal BC (OxA-6616; 2215±45 BP) was obtained on seeds from alluvium in the top of a Bronze Age ditch while a radiocarbon date of 50 cal BC-cal AD 130 (OxA-6618; 1975±40 BP) was given by seeds from alluvium overlying the palaeosol (Chapter 13). Alluvial sediment also filled some irregular probable drainage ditches which flanked the gravel causeway and cut some of the slot alignments.

At least six causeways were constructed across the palaeochannels. These were either dated to the middle Iron Age or are believed to be of middle Iron Age date (Chapter 11). All but the causeway of Site 9 were made of sands and gravels with a mollusc content which suggested they had been dug from Holocene sediments in the bed of a river channel. The causeway on Site 9, which crossed the northern branch of the 'Oxey Mead palaeochannel', was constructed of limestone rubble and had subsequently been repaired and heightened with a narrower gravel causeway along the centre. It was constructed in *380-210 cal BC (95% probability)* (Chapter 13), and a radiocarbon date of 410-200 cal BC (OxA-9377; 2275±50) was obtained on organic material from the socket of a spear which had been placed beneath the limestone causeway. Biological evidence suggested that the causeway was constructed across an area on which rushes grew and which was perhaps flooded in winter. The causeway was the site of the deposition and,

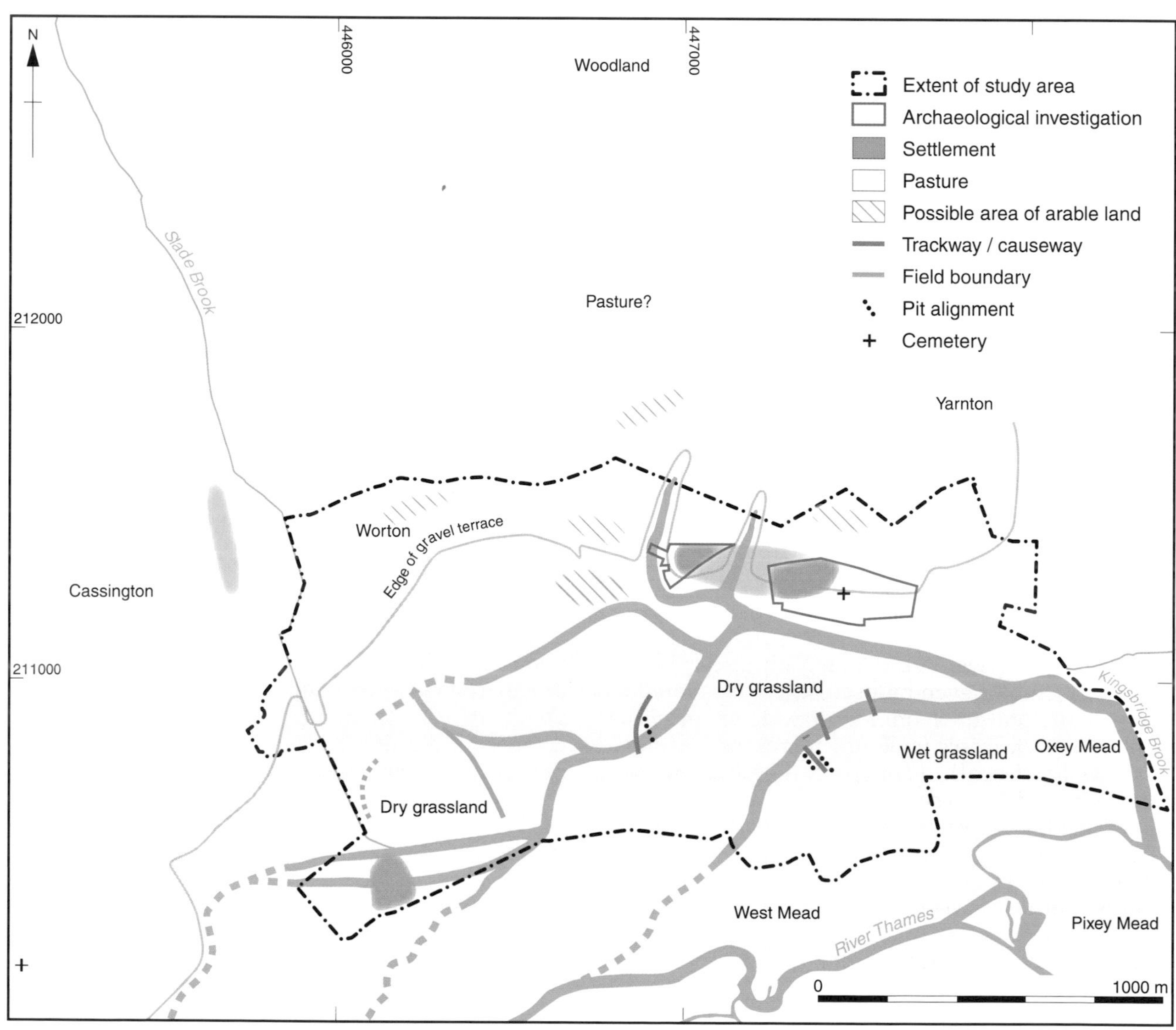

Fig. 2.6 The middle Iron Age landscape

perhaps, consumption of a very large number of animals. Parts of at least 30 cattle, five horses, three sheep, two red deer, and one roe deer, a pig and a dog were found here (Mulville *et al.*, Chapter 17). There was a strong bias towards the deposition of the right limbs of cattle, and this assemblage is not considered to be derived from mundane refuse disposal, but rather is representative of a highly symbolic act or acts which were probably attended with some ceremony. The minor presence of horse and dog and also of wild animals, which are absent from the contemporary settlement site except as antler, supports this conclusion.

Seed evidence suggests that marshy pasture grew on the bed of a minor palaeochannel between two gravel islands further west at Site 21, although the presence of a ditch on the channel bed running alongside a causeway (Chapter 11) implied that the channel did not normally hold water. The gradual rise in the water table was causing a progressive re-activation of the floodplain palaeochannels during the Iron Age. The southern arm of the 'Oxey Mead palaeochannel' probably began to experience a seasonal flow during the middle Iron Age and, as the water-depth increased, so causeways were constructed across channels in a number of places on the floodplain (Fig. 11.10) and the height of the limestone causeway on Site 9 was also increased. The minor palaeochannel at Site 21 possibly became waterlogged later. Presumably the causeways acted as fords when the river was in flood.

One result of the continuing rise in the water table was that seeds were preserved in the Iron Age palaeosol on a low-lying area of the floodplain beneath alluvium in Oxey Mead (Fig. 1.4). A sample from a floodplain sequence across the palaeo-channel at Section 3 (Sample 7) contained seeds of *Potentilla anserina* (silverweed) and *Carex* sp. (sedge), along with many seeds of *Juncus effusus* gp. (tussock rush), suggesting marshy pasture.

Pollen, seeds and insects were also identified from the middle Iron Age boundary ditch on a higher area of the floodplain at Site 25, which was probably above any contemporary flood levels. The ditch was recut twice, with the first recut beginning to silt in *370-110 cal BC (95% probability)* (Chapter 13). Conditions were very open, with no evidence for local scrub or even boundary hedges. A diverse grassland flora grew on the floodplain including *Ranunculus* cf. *repens* (creeping buttercup), *Prunella vulgaris* (self-heal), *Plantago lanceolata* (ribwort plantain) and *Leontodon* sp. (hawkbit). Scarabaeoid dung beetles, especially *Aphodius* spp., showed that grazing by domestic animals was occurring. However, the range of grassland insects, such as the plantain-feeding weevils *Ceuthorhynchidius troglodytes* and *Mecinus pyraster*, vetch and clover-feeding weevils from the genera *Apion* and *Sitona*, and the grass-feeding leaf beetle *Crepidodera ferruginea*, all suggested that the grassland was not being closely grazed. Dry, well-drained conditions were suggested by some of the ground beetles, for example *Lebia chlorocephala*, and snails such as *Vallonia excentrica*.

No evidence for middle Iron Age cultivation soils was found on the floodplain, although a very little cereal pollen, presumably from nearby cultivation, was identified from Floodplain Site 25. As with the early Iron Age, the quantity of charred crop-processing remains from the settlements and the occurrence of grain-storage pits suggested the importance of arable agriculture. Subsequent cultivation has re-worked any Iron Age soils on the Second Gravel Terrace, although evaluation trenching and test-pit sieving identified a narrow terrace lying below the edge of the Second Gravel Terrace to the west of the Cresswell Field site, which had been ploughed and subsequently sealed by colluvium of Roman date (Chapter 11). There was a scattering of weed seeds from plants of light soils, such as *Tripleurospermum inodorum* (scentless mayweed), amongst the charred weed seed assemblages from the Yarnton settlement, as might be expected from crops grown on the Second Gravel Terrace, but the majority of the seeds were undiagnostic as to soil conditions. However, the presence of charred seeds of *Eleocharis palustris* or *uniglumis* (spike rush) in some of the samples from Yarnton and Cresswell Field again suggested cultivation extending beyond the terrace edge. Some seeds of grassland plants were also present, which could have been the result of cultivation extending over what had been grassland, or of the fields being left fallow for periods of time. The weed assemblages were characteristic of fields which have undergone only short-term cultivation in order to prepare a seed bed and had only experienced limited weeding.

Triticum spelta (spelt wheat) and hulled *Hordeum vulgare* (hulled six-row barley) remained the major cereal crops processed at Yarnton throughout the middle Iron Age. The reasonably frequent occurrence of charred seeds of *Galium aparine* (goose-grass) suggested that some of the cereals were autumn-sown, while a significant presence of seeds of members of the Polygono-Chenopodietalia community pointed to relatively high levels of soil fertility. Crops were mostly harvested by cutting near ground level, resulting in the occurrence of seeds from low-growing weeds such as *Trifolium* spp. (clover) in many of the samples.

The middle Iron Age charred assemblages were rich in weed seeds and chaff, particularly glumes of hulled wheat. Such material is characteristic of processing waste. The settlement had many pits which were interpreted as being for grain storage; certainly there was no other obvious use for them. The pit-storage of grain is dependent on the grain being alive and able to respire, thus creating an atmosphere of carbon dioxide, which then induces dormancy in the grain, in the sealed pit (Reynolds 1981b, 22-4). If the grain of hulled cereals were to be de-husked before pit storage, damage to the grain would result in much of it decaying in the damp subterranean conditions. Therefore, the crop need not be fully cleaned before storage because a final cleaning will be necessary after de-husking. When a storage pit was opened for the grain to be used, the contents would have been damp. It would have been necessary to parch the grain both to make the glumes of spelt wheat or the lemma and palea of hulled barley brittle so that they could be rubbed off and to render the grain sufficiently hardened for it to be ground. Some of the debris generated by this process was probably either used to fuel the parching or burnt as waste, giving rise to much of the charred remains. Inevitably, some grain would also have become carbonised as a result of incomplete separation of grain from waste or through minor accidents.

Charcoal from the middle Iron Age settlements was not analysed in detail. Much of it was of rosaceous species, particularly Pomoideae (hawthorn etc), showing that thorn scrub or hedgerows were an important source of fuel. However, *Quercus* sp. (oak) was also well-represented, suggesting that woodland timbers were available for constructional purposes and some fuel needs.

The open, mixed agricultural landscape of middle Iron Age Yarnton very much represented a continuation of developments which began in the early Iron Age. The basic agricultural economy remained the same, with spelt wheat and six-row hulled barley the main crops and the same range of domestic animals being raised. Analysis of the animal bone assemblage indicates an increase in the importance of cattle and horse rearing (Chapter 17). However, the hydrological changes on the floodplain, which followed the general trend established for the Upper Thames Valley (Robinson 1992b), would have constrained land usage in the valley bottom. The lowest areas, which were beginning to experience seasonal flooding, would no longer have been available for winter grazing although the grass on them would have been less vulnerable to summer drought. It is possible that the higher areas of floodplain, as at Site 25, were used for the overwintering of stock. The area of floodplain experiencing inundation at Yarnton during the middle Iron Age was perhaps not as great as further upstream at Farmoor, where floodplain grazing was managed from small seasonal settlements (Lambrick and Robinson 1979). Overstocking when the ground was too wet on the floodplain at Port Meadow during the middle Iron Age resulted in damage to the pasture, with areas of mud being created (Lambrick and Robinson 1988, 65-8). At Yarnton, the scale of settlement had increased in comparison to the early Iron Age and it is possible that a greater emphasis was placed on secondary products from the domestic animals than previously. Doubtless the area under cultivation had increased but there does not seem to have been any pressure on the arable economy either, as might have been shown by evidence for declining fertility or by the expansion of cultivation onto the floodplain. There was no evidence for any limitation on the cultivation of the Second Gravel Terrace at Yarnton, unlike the area around the Neolithic and Bronze Age ceremonial complex of the Devil's Quoits, to the west of Stanton Harcourt. The setting of these monuments amidst grassland was a tradition maintained throughout the Iron Age, long after the monuments had fallen out of use (Lambrick 1992b, 90). This was so despite a shortage of land for cultivation and the fact that the Second Terrace was particularly suitable for arable. The middle Iron Age settlement at Yarnton fell into the 'open' category of settlements on the Upper Thames gravels which exploited a fully open agricultural landscape, rather than the 'enclosed' category, such as Mingies Ditch, on the floodplain of the Windrush, which was perhaps primarily related to pastoralism in a less managed landscape which retained some scrub (Allen and Robinson 1993, 149-50).

THE LATE IRON AGE TO EARLY ROMAN SETTLEMENT AND LANDSCAPE (*C* 50 BC-AD 80)

The late Iron Age/early Roman settlement pattern

It has proved difficult to attribute archaeological contexts specifically to the late pre-Roman Iron Age, as the use of the characteristic grog-tempered pottery of this period spans (perhaps) the later 1st century BC and much of the 1st century AD, and so a broader division extending into the early Roman period has been used.

The focus of late Iron Age settlement at Yarnton lay slightly to the east and south of the main middle Iron Age occupation area (Figs 2.7 and 7.1), and no settlement features of this date were found on the Cresswell Field site. Traces of late Iron Age and early Roman occupation were also uncovered during evaluation trenching over a cropmark site to the west of Worton (Chapter 10; Figs 10.1 and 10.2), and this may represent a settlement which had also moved eastwards, from the middle Iron Age site found in Tuckwell's Pit (Fig. 1.10). The settlements lay approximately 1.3 km apart. The presence of Iron Age and Roman material at Purwell Farm and Yarnton Sandy Lane/Begbroke (Fig. 1.10) also strongly suggests continuity of settlement throughout this period.

A large, late Iron Age defended enclosure was constructed above the confluence of the rivers Thames and Evenlode (Case 1982a). The 'Big Enclosure' was enclosed by a ditch and rampart. Settlement within it appeared to be mostly early Roman in date, and it is possible that occupation was still centred on the area to the north when it was first constructed. The purpose of the enclosure is uncertain, although its defences were certainly substantial and it occupied an obvious strategic position above the rivers (Allen 2000, fig. 1.14). There are no known Roman sites of the Conquest period within the immediate vicinity of Yarnton,

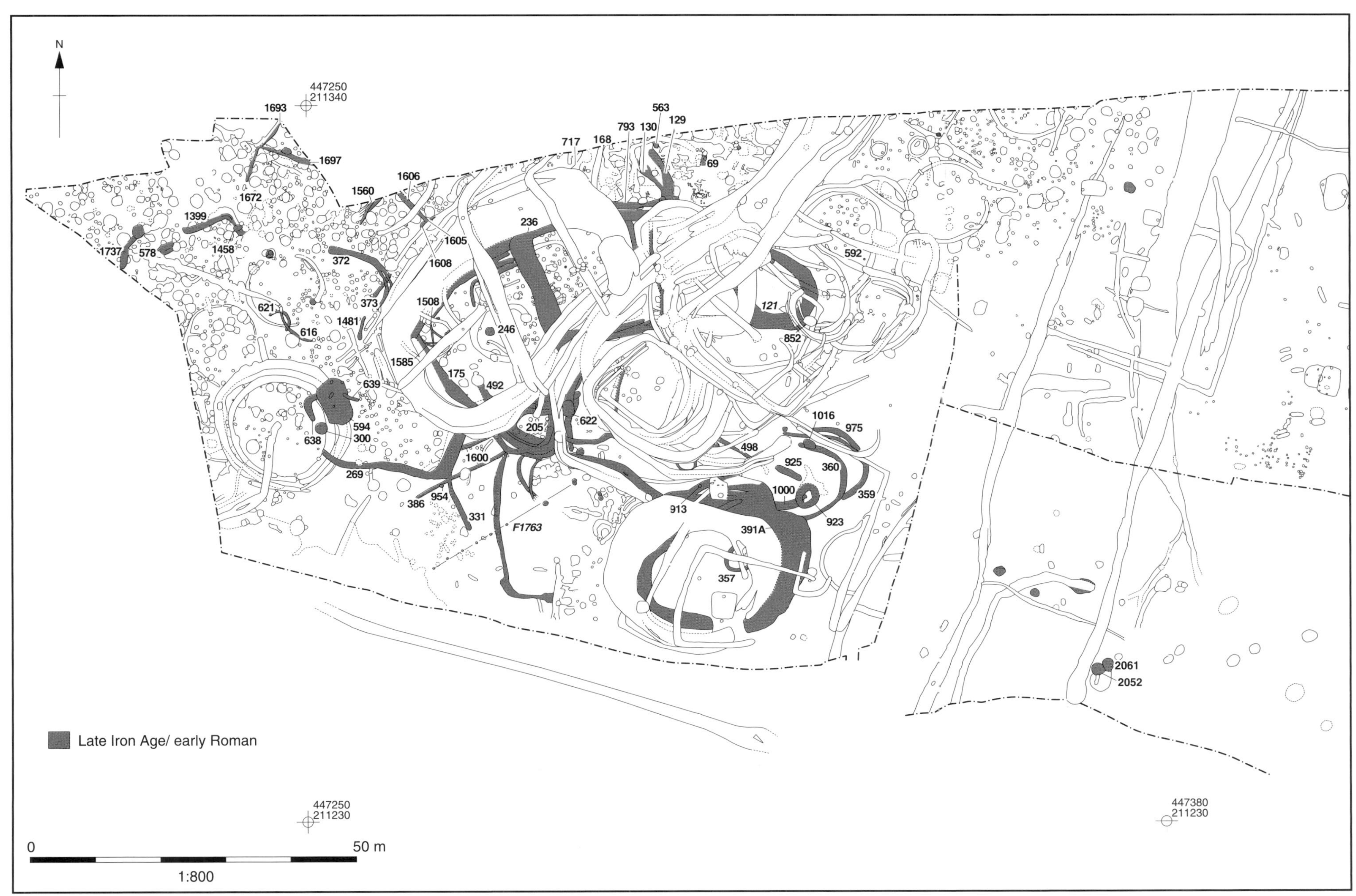

Fig. 2.7 Yarnton late Iron Age settlement

although the early Roman fort/fortress complex at Alchester (Sauer 1999; 2000; 2001; 2002; 2005) lies only 13 km to the north-east.

The character of late Iron Age/early Roman settlement

In common with other sites of the same period in the Upper Thames Valley, such as Gravelly Guy, Stanton Harcourt (Lambrick and Allen 2004), Yarnton changed from an open settlement characterised by pit scatters and circular post-built structures, to one in which ditched sub-circular and sub-rectangular enclosures and paddocks predominated (Fig. 2.7). Even though the features were of considerably greater scale than on the earlier sites, no domestic structures could be found and, as discussed above, walls were probably built of cob or turf (cf Allen *et al.* 1984, 94). The density of material within ditches, however, did indicate three possible sites where houses might have been situated and these lay in the centre, the north-east and the south-east of the site. It is possible that they represent discrete domestic areas, as in the early and middle Iron Age periods.

Such radical change in settlement layout but continuity of settlement location in this area is striking. A number of sites in the Upper Thames Valley shifted location at this time, for example Gravelly Guy, where late Iron Age to early Roman occupation was relocated to the other side of the middle Iron Age settlement boundary (Lambrick and Allen 2004). Other sites, for example Watkins Farm in the Lower Windrush Valley, were abandoned (Allen 1990a). Change in settlement layout is a common trend, however, and may be linked to widespread innovations in agricultural practice which began to take place at this time (Lambrick 1992b, 97-103). However, it is very difficult to identify a late Iron Age origin to the early Roman field system that has been exposed in the Yarnton study area, and the animal bone assemblage for this period is too small to indicate meaningful changes in husbandry.

Late Iron Age/early Roman landscape and land use

There had been little change to the reedswamp vegetation of the southern arm of the major palaeochannel to the south of the study area (Sites 1 and 2; Fig. 2.2) since the early Iron Age. There were numerous seeds of plants of emergent vegetation such as *Oenanthe aquatic* gp. (water dropwort) and *Schoenoplectus lacustris* (bulrush) along with many insects which feed on such vegetation. Shells of molluscs such as *Bithynia tentaculata* in the very organic sediments which were accumulating in the channel bed suggested at least seasonal flow to the water, but a substantial rise in numbers of the snail *Lymnaea truncatula* was perhaps a reflection of increasingly muddy conditions alongside the channel. By the late Iron Age, alluviation was occurring over a wider area of floodplain but the higher areas were still above flood levels. Most interestingly, the rising water table resulted in the preservation of the roots of an oak tree sitting within a late Neolithic/early Bronze Age penannular enclosure in the late Iron Age. Roots of oak trees were not preserved elsewhere on the floodplain, suggesting the tree to have been isolated. It is possible that the religious association of the enclosure, which was still a visible feature at this time, had become transferred to a tree growing within it, which perhaps resulted in the tree being retained when the remainder of the floodplain had long been cleared. Pollen and insect evidence from the palaeochannel on Sites 1 and 2 indicated very open conditions on the floodplain, with scarabaeoid dung beetles suggesting pasture grazed by domestic animals. The charred plant remains from the late Iron Age to earliest Roman contexts at Yarnton did not suggest any changes in cultivation practices or crop processing since the middle Iron Age, spelt wheat and six-row hulled barley remaining the only major cereal crops.

THE EARLY ROMAN PERIOD (*C* AD 80-250)

The early Roman settlement pattern and the character of settlement

The Yarnton early Roman settlement overlay that of the late Iron Age period, to the extent that a number of enclosures were retained and recut in this period (Fig. 2.8). Early Roman settlement has been more certainly identified at Worton, 1.3 km away (Chapter 10), and Roman sites are known at Purwell Farm and Yarnton Sandy Lane/Begbroke (Chapter 1; Fig. 1.10); the settlement pattern had become remarkably stable. At Cassington, however, occupation appears to have moved to within the defended space of the Big Enclosure.

A major shift in settlement location is evidenced at a number of rural sites in the Upper Thames Valley at this time (Lambrick 1992b, 82-4; Henig and Booth 2000, 106-10). This is clearly seen in the Lower Windrush Valley, for example, and seems to date to the early 2nd century AD. The late Iron Age/early Roman sites at Old Shifford Farm and Stonehenge Farm, Northmoor, for example, were abandoned and new settlements were positioned adjacent to trackways which can be traced over considerable distances, linking several settlements (Lambrick 1992b, 82-4; Hey 1995). The new sites typically had a more regular, rectilinear layout. Gravelly Guy was not reoccupied after the early 2nd century. This is a pattern which does not appear to be repeated to any extent in the Yarnton/Cassington area.

Settlement at Worton did appear to shift *c* 250 m to the north, and the new settlement was more rectilinear and lay to the north of a trackway, but the available evidence suggests that this took place in the late Roman period (Chapter 11). At Yarnton,

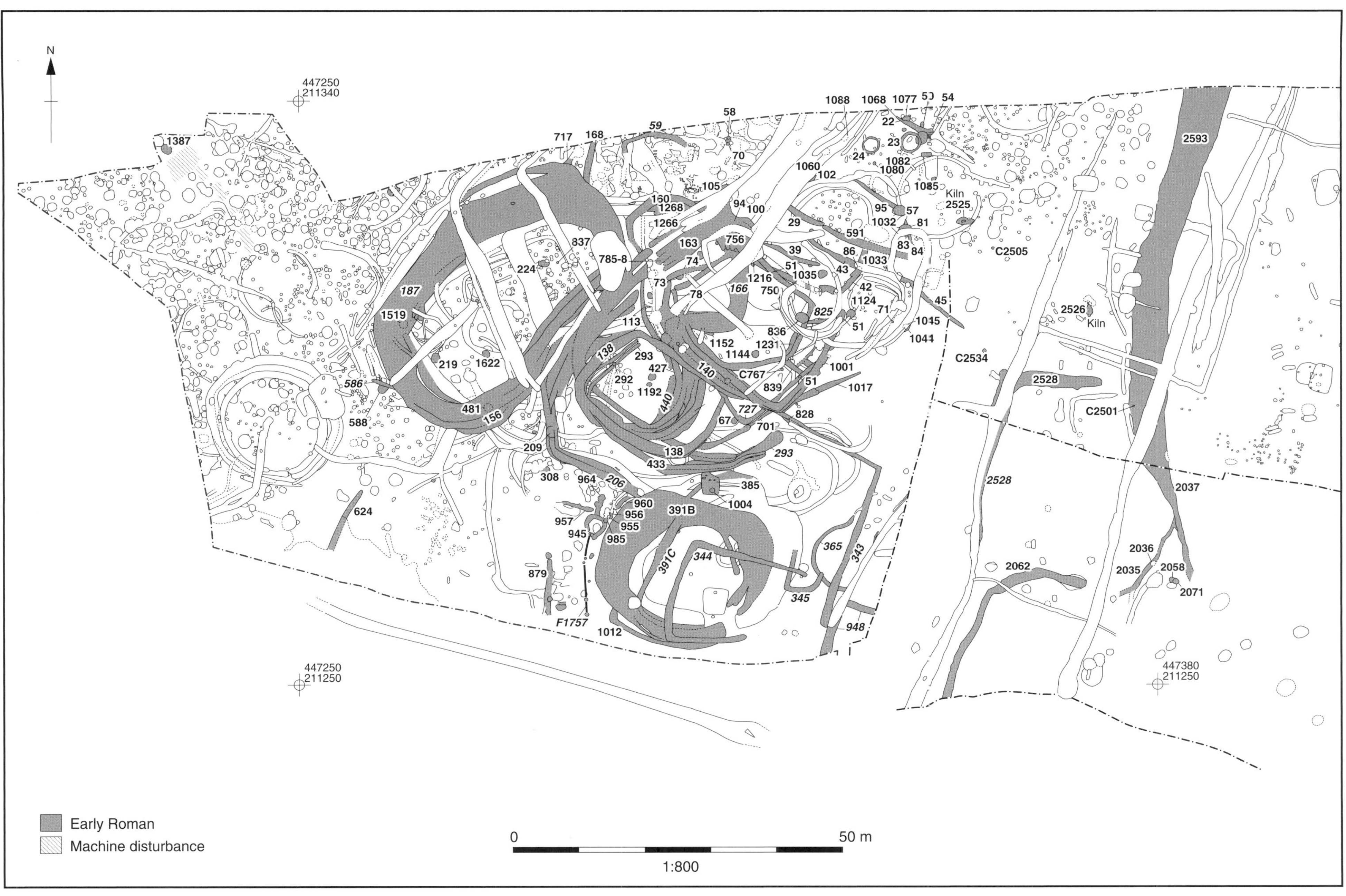

Fig. 2.8 Yarnton early Roman settlement

settlement in the early Roman period was focused in the same or similar areas to those of the 1st century AD, and four separate enclosures can be identified, surrounded by smaller paddocks, possible stack rings and, to the east, a possible boundary at the edge of the site (Fig 2.8). Gradually over this period of time, enclosures within the site became more rectilinear in shape, as new forms were laid out over earlier sub-rectangular or oval enclosures with increasing frequency, but the settlement continued to be organised around the four major enclosure areas.

No early Roman structures have been recognised within the Yarnton settlement, and it is not known whether buildings would have resembled the circular mass-wall structures of the late Iron Age or would have been rectangular buildings resting upon sill beams. The remains of houses of either type will have been destroyed by later ploughing over the settlement. It is likely, however, that the continuity of location of enclosures indicates continuity of use for purposes which included domestic occupation. This appears to be borne out by the occurrence of domestic rubbish, although the distribution of this material has not been analysed in detail. Two pottery kilns, which probably date to the end of the 1st century AD, were uncovered just to the east of the settlement.

Early Roman landscape and land use

The Roman period saw an increase in intensity of agricultural exploitation, some of the changes in land management occurring in spite of – rather than as a result of – the hydrological changes that were also happening.

Sedimentation changed in the southern arm of the major palaeochannel in the south of the study area during the Roman period, with a much higher clay content to the deposits. These sediments gave an OSL date of 160 BC-AD 140 (957b) from the base and radiocarbon dates of cal AD 130-430 (OxA-7362; 1730±50 BP) and cal AD 250-540 (OxA-7361; 1640±50 BP) on waterlogged seeds from towards the top at Section B on Site 2 (Fig. 2.2; Chapter 13). Sedimentation probably began in the palaeochannel at Oxey Mead in the Roman period, while alluvial clay in the northern arm of the major palaeochannel at Site 10 was sealed by a gravel causeway of Roman or later date. Clay alluviation would have been occurring over the lower areas of the floodplain. There were few seeds of terrestrial plants from the early Roman sediments in the palaeochannels but seeds of species such as *Potentilla anserina* (silverweed) and *Rumex conglomeratus* (sharp dock) were likely to have been from marshy pasture alongside the channels. Chafer and elaterid beetles with larvae which feed on the roots of grassland herbs, such as *Phyllopertha horticola*, from the sediments at Section B on Site 2 and at Oxey Mead confirmed the presence of grassland, while the occurrence of scarabaeoid dung beetles from the genus *Aphodius* suggested that it was being grazed.

While those areas of floodplain which were being seasonally flooded remained as pasture, the grassland on the higher areas of floodplain, such as at Site 25, was ploughed up. Indeed, an extensive Roman field system has been uncovered, with field boundaries and ploughsoils present, and droveways leading down through the cultivated fields from the settlement site to the lower-lying areas of pasture (Chapter 11; Fig. 11.44). Fields were varied in shape and size, ranging from enclosed areas of up to 3 ha to very small fields *c* 0.5 ha in size and, rather than having a regular appearance, they ran up to channels or low-lying areas, maximising the potential of the topography. Usually fields were bounded by ditches, but sometimes the cultivated areas ran up to the banks of palaeochannels and spills of ploughsoil could be observed interstratified with the channel silts (Chapter 11). These fields were manured from the settlement, as evidenced by scatters of Roman pottery recovered from the surfaces of modern fields, but also retrieved during the evaluation and excavation fieldwork. Where the sherds were datable, early Roman material predominated (compare Figs 11.4-6). On Site 3 (Fig. 2.2), an east-west field boundary ditch was dug close to the northern bank of the southern arm of the major palaeochannel, cutting through a late Neolithic/ early Bronze Age ring ditch. The upcast from the Roman ditch seems to have served as a flood protection embankment. The part of the ring ditch to the north of the boundary became filled with ploughsoil, whereas the southern part of the ring ditch eventually became filled with alluvial clay. Cultivation was also intensified on the Second Gravel Terrace, where plough-derived colluvial sediments began to fill the small valley to the west of the Cresswell Field site.

There were changes to the weed flora of the arable fields in the early Roman period. *Agrostemma githago* (corn cockle) and *Anthemis cotula* (stinking mayweed), which are both regarded as Roman introductions to the region, were represented by small quantities of seeds. (The presence of seeds of these species in Iron Age samples was thought to be the result of post-depositional contamination from late Roman or Saxon contexts, in which they were well represented). There was also a decline in the proportion of seeds of Polygono-Chenopodietalia weeds such as *Chenopodium album* (fat hen) and a substantial rise in the seeds of *Vicia* and *Lathyrus* spp. (vetches, tares etc). Members of the Polygono-Chenopodietalia favour fertile soils whereas *Vicia* and *Lathyrus* spp. are legumes which have associations with bacteria in their roots which enable them to utilise atmospheric nitrogen. One interpretation of this trend would be that soil fertility had declined since the Iron Age as a result of overcropping without sufficient manuring. However, vetches and tares would have been favoured by autumn as opposed to spring sown crops, so it is also possible that there was an increase in the proportion of land sown in autumn. On the other hand, there was no increase in the number of seeds of *Galium aparine* (goosegrass) compared with the Iron Age samples, even though this is very much associated with autumn-sown crops. A continued presence of seeds of wet-ground plants such as *Eleocharis palustris* or *uniglumis* (spike rush) was consistent with cultivation extending to the edge of the flooded area of the floodplain.

There was no change in the main cereal crops that were cultivated. Harvesting and crop-processing techniques likewise remained the same. However, pit storage of grain was no longer practised, above-ground structures presumably being used. The main source of charred non-woody plants was still likely to have been the parching of hulled cereals. Charred crop-processing waste was found in context 2537, the fill of a kiln. Chaff predominated, including glumes of *Triticum dicoccum* or *spelta* (emmer or spelt wheat) and awns of *Avena* sp. (oats). It is uncertain whether the kiln had been used for cereal processing or whether chaff was being used as fuel for another purpose. Limited scanning of charcoal in the sample flots showed that both oak and hedgerow or thorn scrub species were being used for fuel. The location of any woodland exploited by the Roman settlement is unknown, but it is plausible that there was some woodland on the plateau gravels at Bladon Heath.

The spread of cultivation onto the floodplain, despite changing hydrological conditions which made the floodplain less suitable for cultivation, also occurred at Drayton (Robinson 2003, 172). Part of the surface of a field which had been cross-ploughed with an ard-type plough had been sealed beneath the upcast from an early Roman ditch. Unfortunately there was no evidence from Yarnton for the type of plough that was used but the soil conditions on the floodplain prior to alluviation would not have been much different from those at Drayton. A rise in the proportion of *Vicia* and *Lathyrus* spp. seeds in crop weed seed assemblages was also seen at Ashville, Abingdon on the Second Gravel Terrace, where a trend already established in the Iron Age continued into the Roman period (Jones 1978, 100). At Gravelly Guy, near Stanton Harcourt, there may have been some re-organisation of the landscape which saw much more of the Second Terrace being brought into cultivation (Lambrick and Allen 2004, 482-3). These developments suggest that there could have been general pressure to increase arable production in the Upper Thames Valley during the early Roman period.

While the main arable crops at Yarnton, spelt wheat and six-row hulled barley, remained the same from the Iron Age to the Roman period, and indeed were the main crops throughout the region, it is likely that there were major changes in the other crops that were cultivated. At those Roman settlements on the Thames gravels with waterlogged evidence from the settlement features themselves, such as deep pits, wells and waterholes, there are often remains of various horticultural crops introduced by the Romans such as coriander, celery and plums (Robinson 1992a, 58). These plants were apparently cultivated and certainly used even on low-status rural settlements. It is very likely that this aspect of changing cultural practice had reached Yarnton by the early 2nd century, but remains of these plants rarely become charred so it is unsurprising that they were absent from the archaeological record of the settlement. Another arable crop, flax, tends only to be represented by waterlogged remains so its absence from the charred remains does not mean that it was not cultivated, indeed the higher areas of the floodplain would have been well-suited to spring-sown flax.

It is likely that changes also occurred in the management of domestic animals in the early Roman period. The animal bone assemblage at this time indicates that cattle were reared to a slightly greater age, allowing them to grow to full size when their meat yield would be highest (Chapter 17). In addition, some animals lived to an older age and were presumably used for traction or milk production. The loss of some floodplain grazing and the winter flooding of the remainder could perhaps have been met by increased use of pasture on the Oxford Clay, but it is possible that available land on the Clay was already fully utilised before the end of the Iron Age. Although there was no evidence of hay meadow on the floodplain at Yarnton in the early Roman period, floodplain hay meadow was established further upstream at Claydon Pike (Robinson 2007, 158) during the early-mid Roman period. It is possible that some domestic stock was overwintered in enclosures at the settlement and fed on hay along with cleanings from cereal processing. While there was insufficient evidence from the charred weed seeds to ascertain the degree to which cultivated fields were left fallow, some grazing on well-drained ground would have been available for the first half of the winter on stubble fields that were to be spring sown.

The main domestic animal species kept, cattle and sheep, along with smaller numbers of pig and horse, were typical for the Upper Thames Valley. The settlement also displayed the usual changes in the minor components of the animal part of the diet which occurred within the Roman period. Hare was eaten, which would probably have been unacceptable in the Iron Age (Mulville *et al.*, Chapter 17), and small quantities of marine oyster were imported. Evidence elsewhere shows that domestic fowl were kept and fish were being eaten.

Thus, the early Roman settlement at Yarnton seems to have fallen into what was the typical pattern for sites with access both to the Second Gravel Terrace and to the floodplain. It had a mixed agricultural economy based around both the grassland of the lower areas of the floodplain and arable fields centred on the Second Terrace.

LATE ROMAN SETTLEMENT AND LANDSCAPE (AD 250-410)

The late Roman settlement pattern

Late Roman settlement at Yarnton was mainly situated superimposed on the early Roman site and slightly to the north-east of it. A trackway ran SW-NE on its eastern boundary in the direction of Yarnton Sandy Lane. Traces of another trackway were recovered to the south of the site, leading towards Worton (Fig. 2.9).

Fieldwalking and cropmark evidence indicate that the settlement at Worton shifted slightly to the north, north of an east-west trackway which probably linked to the Yarnton trackways (Chapter 11). The Worton settlement was rectilinear and regular in layout, comprising at least ten conjoining enclosures, and overlay a Bronze Age ring ditch, which was presumably slighted by this time (Fig. 10.1; Fig. 11.1). A number of pits belonging to the settlement are visible, although some larger sub-rectangular features are Anglo-Saxon sunken-featured buildings (Hey 2004).

The longevity of the Roman settlements at Purwell Farm and Yarnton Sandy Lane/Begbroke is uncertain, although Purwell Farm at least was occupied in the early Anglo-Saxon period. At Cassington, settlement within the Big Enclosure appeared to decline in the 3rd century, but a large late Roman cemetery north of the A40, from which *c* 110 burials were recovered (Chapter 1), indicates that a substantial settlement lay in the vicinity. Three unusual burials excavated by Humphrey Case in 1950 within the southern part of the Big Enclosure were probably also late Roman in date (Kirk and Case 1950; Case 1982a, 137).

The extent of external control on the inhabitants and resources of this area is uncertain (Henig and Booth 2000, 79-82). Although no settlements within the immediate area appear to be highly Romanised, a Roman villa is known at Woodstock only 5 km to the north. The Roman road between Oxford and Akeman Street lay 10 km to the east and Akeman Street itself, with a concentration of Roman villas nearby, 8 km to the north. The impression of isolation and independence is probably more apparent than real.

The character of late Roman settlement

The final phase of Roman settlement at Yarnton was more regular in layout and rectilinear in shape than previously. A wider range of features was recognisable on the site, including buildings, corn-drying ovens, trackways and a small cemetery with both cremation and inhumation burials on the east edge of the site. The northern part of the settlement would probably have lain beneath the railway line and sidings; a large soil bund precluded examination of a 20 m strip between the line and the excavated area. The limit of occupation to the west was observed in evaluation trenches excavated in 1990, 30 m west of the modern field boundary (Hey 1991c). The layout suggests that around 70% of this *c* 2 hectare site was excavated, including the core of the settlement.

In the centre and north of the site, a long sub-rectangular enclosure, 30 m wide and in excess of 70 m long, contained postholes and post-pads of a structure forming an approximate rectangle 5 m long and 4 m wide (Figs 2.9 and 9.3), but insufficient of the plan remains for the form of the building to be at all clear. In addition, a late 3rd- to early 4th-century small circular building was uncovered further east. This was slightly sunken, with a preserved compact floor surface and external gullies. It was unusual, but resembled two buildings excavated at Cassington, which appeared to be earlier in date (Case 1982a, 136). Associated features attest to the agricultural character of the settlement, including a kidney-shaped feature which seems to have been associated with crop processing, three corn-drying ovens, small enclosures, pits and small patches of cobbling.

This was a small, rural settlement into which Roman material possessions were introduced very gradually. By the 4th century, however, the inhabitants were using the full range of Oxfordshire colour-coated wares and some pottery transported over a greater distance, but there were no signs of great personal wealth. Coins were few (43), the majority (53% of those identified) dating to the third quarter of the 4th century (Booth, Chapter 15).

Late Roman landscape and land use (Fig. 2.10)

At late Roman Yarnton mixed agriculture continued to thrive despite a crisis brought about by the early Roman arable expansion in the face of hydrological change.

Continuing alluviation and a rise in flood levels eventually forced abandonment of cultivation on the higher areas of floodplain. In the south of the floodplain area, on Site 3 (Fig. 2.2), alluvium filled the boundary ditch and although the embankment may have initially protected the cultivated areas, layers of alluvium spilled in through a gateway (Chapter 11). Alluvium sealed all the Roman ploughsoils on high areas of floodplain, and substantial bodies of alluvial clay were also deposited in all the palaeochannels. This alluviation would have had a substantial influence on the drainage pattern of the floodplain, with the low-lying parts tending to be levelled up to a height closer to that of the remainder. The southern arm of the major palaeochannel continued to flow in winter but it is possible that, because of the quantity of sediment deposited within it, it was reduced in dry summers during the late Roman period to little more than a series of discontinuous pools. The pools supported an aquatic vegetation of pondweeds (both *Potamogeton* sp. and *Zannichellia palustris*). Grazing pressure had perhaps reduced some of the

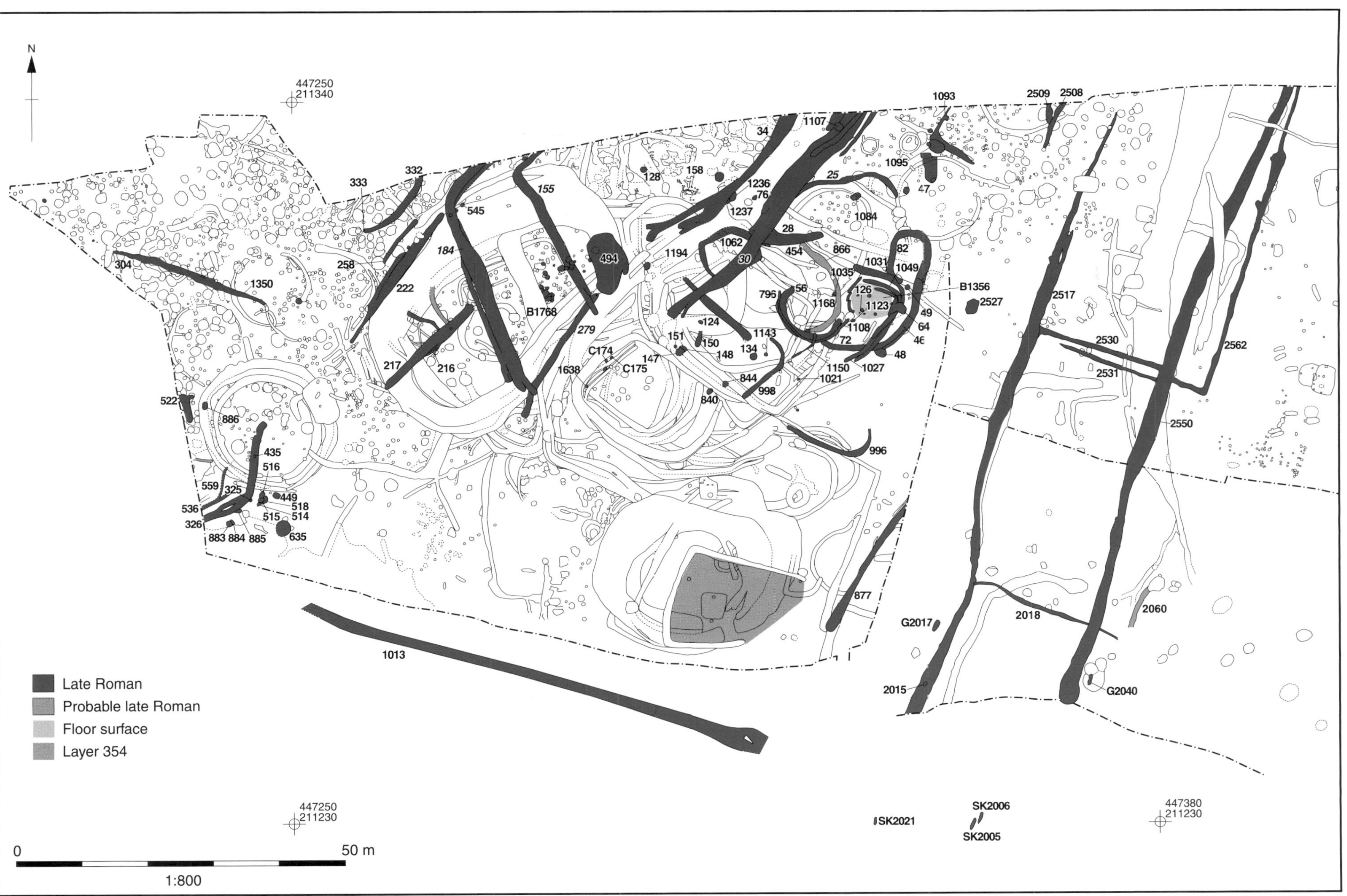

Fig. 2.9 Yarnton late Roman settlement

reedswamp species of shallower water, but deeper-water species, such as *Sagittaria sagittifolia* (arrowhead) and *Schoenoplectus lacustris* (bulrush), were well represented by seeds in the Roman channel sediments at Sites 1 and 2 and Oxey Mead.

The landscape seems to have been very open and values for tree pollen, mostly *Quercus* sp. (oak), from the Roman palaeochannel sediments were low. There was no macroscopic evidence for the proximity of woodland to the channels and unlike some Roman sites in the Thames Valley, for example Watkins Farm, Northmoor (Robinson 1990, 69), the watercourses were not lined with willows. The pollen and insect evidence from the palaeochannels suggested much grassland on the floodplain during the late Roman period. There were high values of pollen of Poaceae (Gramineae, grasses), *Plantago lanceolata* (ribwort plantain) and Chicoridoidae (Compositae-Liguliflorae, dandelions etc) from late Roman levels in the palaeochannel at Section B on Site 2 *(cal AD 250-430; at 95% probability)* and in the Oxey Mead palaeochannel (cal AD 240-540, OxA-7360; 1675±55 BP; Chapter 13). Evidence from scarabaeoid dung beetles suggested that the grassland was being grazed. In particular, in Context 3/7 from Oxey Mead, scarabaeoid dung beetles were more than twice as abundant as the clover and vetch-feeding weevils of the genera *Apion* and *Sitona*. The former are characteristic of pastureland while the latter are favoured by hay meadow conditions. If the grassland had been meadowland, the ratio between the two groups of beetles would have been expected to have been reversed. The results were consistent with a post-Roman origin for the ancient hay meadow of Oxey Mead, the flora of which has attracted much botanical interest (Tansley 1939, 568-70; Rodwell 1992, 56-9; Robinson 2004, 395-404).

Some cereal-type pollen was recorded from the Roman palaeochannel sediments but cereals (other than rye) scatter little pollen to the wind and some difficulty was experienced in differentiating between

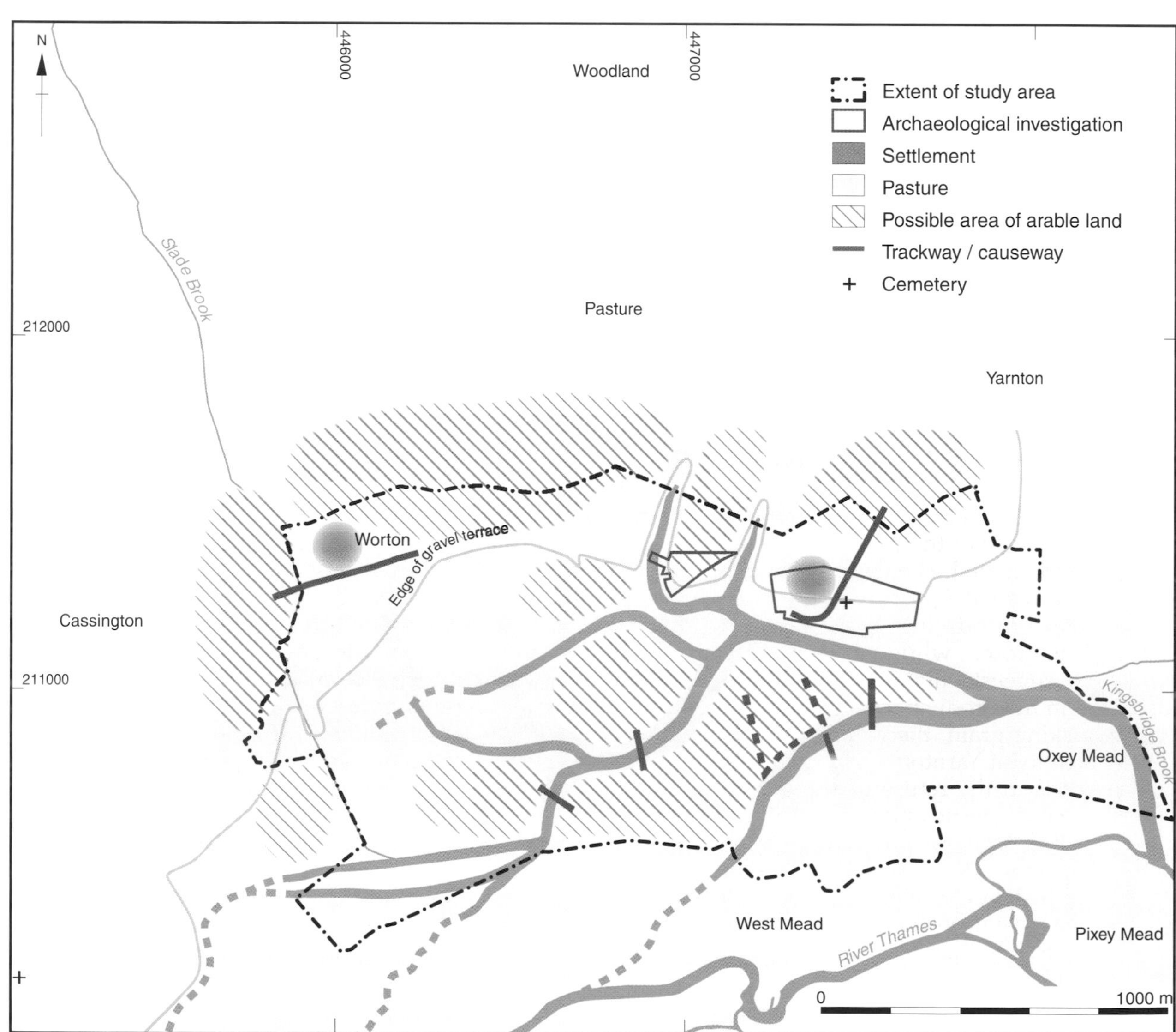

Fig. 2.10 The late Roman landscape

the reedswamp grass *Glyceria* and cereal pollen. The pollen evidence, therefore, was not very useful in providing information on the extent of the arable fields. As in the early Roman period, the main area of cultivation was probably the Second Gravel Terrace and colluvial sediments continued to accumulate in the small valley to the west of the Cresswell Field site (Chapter 11, test pitting). However, there was some evidence from the weed seeds amongst the charred crop-processing remains which suggested that cultivation spread onto or became more extensive on the Oxford Clay. There was a substantial increase in the percentage of seeds of *Anthemis cotula* (stinking mayweed), from less than 2% of the weed seeds in the early Roman period to over 8% of the weed seeds in the late Roman period. This weed favours heavy loam and clay soils which are calcareous (Kay 1971). It is not a plant of waterlogged soils, and seed numbers of plants of marshy habitats, such as Cyperaceae (sedges, spike rush etc), did not increase. However, the presence of these seeds of wet-ground species was probably an indication of some pressure to maximise the area under crops, with cultivation extending to the edge of the floodplain or into wet hollows on the Oxford Clay. The other evidence from the charred remains suggests that conditions of cultivation remained the same as in the early Roman period.

The main crops in the charred assemblages were *Triticum spelta* (spelt wheat) and hulled *Hordeum vulgare* (six-row hulled barley), although there was also a trace of free-threshing wheat. Many of the samples contained *Avena* sp. (oats) but at this date they were more likely to have been grains of wild oats growing as a weed. Crop-processing activities at the settlement were probably similar to those during the early Roman period, although three corn-drying ovens were discovered. These were likely to have provided centralised facilities for the de-husking of spelt wheat and, although charred remains were not particularly abundant in the three samples from one of these ovens, glumes of hulled wheat predominated. There were neither remains of germinated cereal grains nor detached cereal sprouts from the drying and cleaning of malted grain. Therefore, while evidence from sites elsewhere suggests that corn-drying ovens were also used in the production of spelt beer, as well as for de-husking grain, there is no indication of the former activity at Yarnton.

The bones in the refuse of the settlement were almost all of domestic animals and they suggested an interesting shift towards sheep rearing at this time (Chapter 17). A worker of *Apis mellifera* (honey bee), identified from the later Roman sediments in the Oxey Mead palaeochannel, served as a reminder that it is possible that occupants of the settlement engaged in beekeeping.

The results for the late Roman period very much fell into the pattern which has already been established for the Upper Thames Valley (Robinson 1981; 1992a, 57). The valley bottom presented an open agricultural landscape organised around the potential of the soils. The floodplain, which was experiencing extensive alluviation, was grassland (Lambrick and Robinson 1988, 68-71), mostly being used for seasonal grazing although there was some hay meadow (Robinson 1992a, 58). The First Gravel Terrace, which was not represented at Yarnton, had areas both of grassland and arable. The deep, well-drained soils of the Second Gravel Terrace were extensively cultivated. There is less evidence available for the clay hinterland. While it had previously been assumed that it was mostly grassland with some small areas of managed woodland, the results from Yarnton suggested that arable also extended over the claylands.

In that they both exploited extensive areas of alluvial grassland on the floodplain, the late Roman settlement at Yarnton was similar to the settlement a little upstream at Farmoor (Lambrick and Robinson 1979). However, there was probably a greater pastoral emphasis at Farmoor because it was situated on the First Gravel Terrace. The crops grown at Yarnton and the domestic animals that were kept were very much typical for the region. Doubtless if waterlogged deposits had been found in the Yarnton settlement, the range of cultivated plants recorded would have included fruit trees and herbs.

FIFTH-CENTURY SETTLEMENT AND LANDSCAPE

The end of Roman settlement *by Paul Booth*

The chronology of the latest Roman phases at Yarnton is imprecise owing to the difficulties of dating the available material, principally pottery. The coin evidence, though limited in quantity, is useful in indicating activity right up to the 'end' of Roman Britain, as far as this is usually indicated by coin losses, with the latest issue being of the House of Theodosius (Booth, Chapter 15). The fact that this (and a number of the other later coins from the site) is unstratified does not significantly reduce its value as evidence for late Roman activity, though it does mean that the specific location and character of this activity cannot be identified, except perhaps on the basis of ceramic evidence.

Pottery is a blunter tool. The principal components of late Roman assemblages in the region are a range of Oxford products, supplemented by Nene Valley colour-coated ware, late shell-tempered wares, most probably from the production centre of Harrold (Bedfordshire) and perhaps also by pink grogged ware which may have remained in production right to the end of the Roman period. South of Oxford, there are occasional occurrences of Alice Holt reduced ware (which is now known, from current (unpublished) work, to have been relatively abundant at Dorchester on Thames), but finds of this ware north of the city are exceptionally rare. By the last quarter of the 4th century occurrences of black-burnished ware are likely to have been residual.

As far as the Oxford products are concerned, definition of ceramic phases within the 4th century assemblage is difficult. The principal mortarium fabrics, parchment ware and colour-coated wares, have most if not all of their repertoire of forms established by the beginning of the century. A number of colour-coated forms are assigned a date after AD 350, but there are no significant additions to the range of forms thereafter (Young 1977, 240). In the case of the one form (C102) specifically dated by Young to the closing decade of the century, work on the production site of Lower Farm, Nuneham Courtenay, suggested that such an exclusively late date was questionable (Booth *et al.* 1993, 160-163). While it is thought (and it is indeed plausible) that certain characteristics of the colour-coated repertoire, such as the widespread use of painted and stamped decoration, became more common in the second half of the 4th century, there is relatively little hard evidence to support this. More to the point, the small amounts of such material in an assemblage like that from Yarnton are such that quantitative analysis cannot be used to identify the increasing importance of these types. There is still effectively no way for a meaningful distinction to be made between early and late 4th-century coarse wares from the Oxford industry. Indeed, it is not certain that all the 4th-century reduced wares from sites such as Yarnton necessarily derive from the Oxford kilns.

Subjectively, a typical late 4th-century assemblage from the region, uncontaminated by residual material (a situation which rarely prevails, adding to the difficulties already outlined), should include a relatively high proportion (probably at least 10-15%) of fine and specialist wares, even on low-status rural sites such as Yarnton (see Booth 2004). These would consist principally of Oxford colour-coated ware, including mortaria, supplemented by the Oxford (Young 1977) white-slipped form WC7, which seems to be more common at this date and may have begun to supplant the standard 4th-century white mortarium type M22, particularly in the last quarter of the century. Nene Valley colour-coated wares in utilitarian forms (jars, flanged bowls and dishes), might also be expected. The coarse wares would consist of hard-fired, moderately sandy reduced wares, often with burnished decoration, plus a range of types in ?Harrold shell-tempered fabrics. Jars from this source were perhaps present in the region by the late 3rd century, but flanged bowls and dishes seem to have arrived later, and their presence is taken to be indicative at least of a date after AD 350. Oxidised wares, if present, would include the Oxford wide mouthed jar type O27, and very large jars (and possibly other forms) in pink grogged ware, though at present there are no typological criteria to distinguish early and late 4th-century versions of these forms.

At Yarnton, no pottery assemblages of this character were identified, but this is inevitable because of problems of residuality and contamination; however most of the individual components are present here and there. There is certainly enough evidence to indicate that occupation continued after AD 350 (in any case this is demonstrated by the relatively abundant coins of the House of Valentinian), but while there is pottery which would be consistent with activity up to the end of the 4th century, there are no surviving groups which must have been of that date.

The terminal date of the Oxford industry is not known. As already indicated, it may be that one of its principal 4th-century products, the white mortarium M22, was in decline before the end of the century, and the state of coarse ware production at the very end of the 4th century is unclear. Some kilns may have ceased production before the end of the 4th century (Young 1977, 240; *cf.* Booth *et al.* 1993, 168) but since, for the most part, products of individual production sites cannot be distinguished, this process is identified only at those sites, and not at the consumer end of the market. Colour-coated ware, at least, is likely to have been produced right up to the end of the life of the industry. Its demise may be dated in line with the collapse of other major late Roman producers, most probably in the first decade or two of the 5th century. The collapse seems to have been a consequence of the end of the monetary market economy, into which the industry must have been closely tied by this time. The effective cessation of coin imports to Britain after *c* AD 402 signalled the end for these centralised industries which were unable to survive in totally changed economic conditions. This was essentially the view of Young 30 years ago (Young 1977, 241), and still seems the most likely interpretation of events.

Thus it is difficult to define with any certainty when, or even whether, the Yarnton settlement was abandoned. The status of the site was such that the general absence of coins after 375 AD would not be surprising, and need not imply that the site was not occupied. A low-status rural settlement in AD 400 (and probably in AD 425, if not later) would, in terms of its physical character and material culture, probably look very similar to one in AD 375. Evidence for continuing occupation on this site in the 5th century is most persuasively made by the environmental evidence, considered below.

The 5th-century settlement pattern

Initially there appeared to be strong links between late Roman and early Saxon occupation, in terms of the settlement pattern in general and site location in particular. At Yarnton, a sunken-featured building was located within a late Roman enclosure in a part of the site which had yielded late Roman artefacts (Hey 2004, 101-3). It seems probable that some of the deeper Roman ditches were still visible as hollows, and Saxon sherds were found in the tops of some of these. However, radiocarbon dating showed that there was no convincing evidence for settlement activity at Yarnton before the late 5th or 6th century AD, and a review of the evidence from nearby sites suggested that this was also the case in the vicinity (ibid., 37-40).

The 5th-century landscape

As there is no clear evidence for settlement at Yarnton for nearly 100 years, from the end of dated Roman occupation until late in the 5th century, there are no environmental remains associated with habitation. The only evidence for this period comes from the palaeochannel and floodplain sediments. At some stage after the end of the Roman period, mineral sedimentation in the palaeochannel at Section B (Fig. 2.2) was reduced and the subsequent deposit had a higher organic content. The organic layer gave dates of *AD 540-900* (*OSL-957c*) and *cal AD 550-760* (*OxA-7363*) (Hey 2004, fig. 13.7). The alluvial sequence on the floodplain adjacent to Section B showed a dark layer of manganese staining which was continuous with the organic layer. A similar layer, with some organic content, was recorded at Oxey Mead Sections 2 and 4 (ibid., figs 1.3 and 11.10; plate 11.2). It is assumed that this horizon represents an episode of soil development which occurred as a result of a slow-down of sedimentation. Alluviation on the floodplain of the Upper Thames valley during the Roman period has been interpreted as a consequence of extensive agriculture in the Cotswolds (Robinson and Lambrick 1984) and evidence had been found elsewhere for a slow-down in sedimentation during the early Saxon period (Robinson 1992a). This was interpreted as an agricultural collapse at the end of the Roman period, with much arable land being abandoned. Whilst the results from Yarnton do not exclude the possibility of overbank alluviation continuing for some decades into the 5th century, they do serve to provide some of the best evidence from the Upper Thames Valley for the post-Roman slow down in sedimentation, and would be consistent with this change occurring in the early 5th century AD. This supports an hypothesis of a reduction in cultivation at this time. The Abingdon Area Archaeological and Historical Society has exposed a similar alluvial sequence in a palaeochannel of the Thames at Thrupp, near Abingdon, although it has yet to be dated closely.

The pollen sequences from Oxey Mead (Section 3) and the palaeochannel at Section B, however, show that there was little woodland or scrub in the immediate surroundings of the sites throughout these periods, although there is more tree pollen from Oxey Mead than at Section B (Greig 2004). The macroscopic plant remains do not even suggest the local development of scrub (Robinson 2004). The Coleoptera show a decline in scarabaeoid dung beetles to half their previous level, suggesting a reduction in grazing pressure, but the terrestrial part of the insect fauna remained characteristic of open conditions with grassland. This would not be the case if use of the surrounding area had been abandoned.

The extent to which the Roman agricultural system survived into the 5th century at Yarnton remains unknown. There is a gap in the cereal pollen record at this stage in the Section B channel sequence, although quantities of cereal pollen are generally too small to provide conclusive evidence for a reduction in cultivation. If the Roman fields and pastures had been entirely abandoned after AD 410, rough grassland with areas of thorn scrub would have covered them by AD 450. The resolution offered by the 5 cm sample interval in the pollen sequence here may have been too coarse to record such an event, if it were brief. In addition, some thorn scrub taxa such as sloe are insect pollinated and poorly represented in pollen assemblages, although the presence of *Crataegus* at the bottom of the Oxey Mead sequence shows that they have been recorded at Yarnton. However, some oak/ash woodland would have begun to succeed the scrub before AD 500, and this should have been detected by the pollen analysis. Such evidence would also be expected from insects, mollusca and waterlogged plants.

Thus it seems probable that agricultural activity at Yarnton was greatly reduced in the early 5th century, but that there was sufficient grazing by domestic animals to maintain open conditions. Elsewhere in the Upper Thames Valley there appears to have been some agricultural continuity from the Roman to the Saxon period, for example on the Second Terrace at Barton Court Farm, Abingdon where a weed associated with flax persisted throughout this period (Robinson 1986, fiche 9E5). Gold of pleasure (*Camelina sativa* ssp. *alyssum*) is only found with flax, but it is not common. That it would independently colonise a site in the late Roman and again in the early Saxon period is considered very unlikely. However, woodland regeneration did occur over some Roman sites in the Cotswolds and the abandonment of agricultural land there was probably the cause of the reduction in alluviation in the Upper Thames Valley (Robinson and Lambrick 1984).

CONCLUSIONS

The palaeoenvironmental studies at Yarnton showed that an open agricultural landscape had been created before the start of the Iron Age. The rising water table, itself probably a consequence of large-scale clearance of the catchment, resulted in the cessation of habitation on the floodplain and the concentration of settlement around two centres on the Second Gravel Terrace by the start of the Iron Age. The Iron Age was a period of agricultural expansion reflected, for example, in the much larger assemblages of charred crop-processing remains than from the Bronze Age sites, and there was much good soil for arable on the Second Gravel Terrace. The higher areas of floodplain would have provided good winter grazing above flood levels. The lower areas of floodplain, although becoming increasingly vulnerable to seasonal flooding as the Iron Age progressed, would have had a good early summer growth of grass. With the onset of alluviation, before the end of the Iron Age, it is possible that some of the lowest areas of floodplain became muddy over-grazed pasture with rush tussocks. The economy of Iron Age Yarnton was mixed, the only specialisation perhaps being a concentration on cattle (and horses?) rather than sheep because ready supplies of water were available and the presence of the snail *Lymnaea truncatula* on the floodplain would have left sheep vulnerable to liver fluke (this snail is the intermediate host of the sheep liver fluke). However, sheep were by no means absent. Surplus production for trade or tribute could have been either in the form of grain or livestock.

These lands were being farmed from a settlement where there seem to have been between four and five household units, each living in post-built roundhouses with ancillary structures and pits, including grain-storage pits. Deliberate deposits attest to the non-mundane aspects of life within this site, and slots on the floodplain (Site 2) and activity associated with the stone causeway on Site 9, including feasting, demonstrate ritual and ceremony taking place in the wider landscape. In the middle Iron Age, some people were buried in a small cemetery.

The character of settlement changed dramatically at the very end of the Iron Age/early Roman period. Large enclosures became the major features of the occupation site, and domestic buildings were constructed without earthfast foundations. A number of structures were also built which were associated with arable agriculture, for example corn-drying ovens.

Pressure for cereal production increased in the Roman period and there was an expansion of cultivation onto the higher areas of the floodplain in the early Roman period just as increasing flood levels were creating adverse conditions in those areas. Intensified cropping was also possibly causing a reduction of soil fertility. The loss of relatively well-drained floodplain pasture was perhaps compensated for by an increasing dependence on the Oxford Clay for grazing, although there was not necessarily much woodland remaining on it which could be cleared for grassland. It is also possible that domestic stock was managed more efficiently with, for example, stubble grazing and the closing off of grassland after an episode of grazing to allow for recovery. Hay could have been used for winter fodder although there was no evidence from Yarnton for Roman hay meadows. By the late Roman period, clay alluviation was occurring on even the highest areas of floodplain, forcing the abandonment of cultivation here. There was some evidence that cultivation was extended onto or increased on the Oxford Clay to compensate for this loss. The demand for increased arable production need have been no more than a consequence of increasing population levels, although the rise of the towns would have provided a market for crops and domestic animals. Unfortunately, preservational factors did not enable the degree to which horticulture was part of the economy to be determined, but it is very likely that the changing cultural practices suggested by the keeping of domestic fowl would also have been reflected in the cultivation of orchard and garden crops. Other economic activities perhaps included beekeeping.

At the end of the Roman period, there was a decline in agricultural activity after the abandonment of the settlement. However, there appears to have been little scrub regeneration during the 5th century, so perhaps some grazing continued.

The hydrological changes during the Iron Age and Roman periods undoubtedly had a major influence on the agricultural economy of Yarnton. At the very least they created a considerable nuisance. Some pasture became marshy, vulnerable to stock damage and only seasonably available. Some cultivation was prevented by alluviation. While these changes forced agricultural re-organisation, they need have been no more than short-term upsets. The Second Terrace remained good arable land and even the wettest areas of floodplain could have been grazed in the summer.

Chapter 3: Iron Age and Roman Society at Yarnton

by Dan Stansbie, Leigh Allen, Angela Boyle, Fiona Roe, Jane Timby and Chris Hayden

INTRODUCTION

This chapter is concerned with the reconstruction of social life at Yarnton, and with the ways in which that life changed over time. It focuses on the structures recognised on the site, the processes of deposition and the distribution of finds, the burial evidence, the evidence for craft, technology and trade, and for the production and consumption of food.

There can be little doubt that throughout the Iron Age and Roman periods the settlement at Yarnton was home to a small farming community, and was comparable in many ways to numerous other settlements of similar date on the gravel terraces of the Upper Thames Valley. Although there is evidence for metalworking, pottery production (including kilns in the Roman period) and various other 'craft' activities, their economic significance was almost certainly secondary to the site's agricultural production, and they were probably directed primarily to provision for the site itself, rather than for exchange. There is, of course, evidence for exchange between the site and other areas – imported pottery, briquetage, shale, jet and stone for querns – but the quantities of material involved are not great. If the settlement was involved in more intensive exchange (and something must have been given in return for the exotic items on the site) it is perhaps most likely that this involved the pastoral products of the site, cattle in particular. Cattle dominated the animal bone assemblage until the late Roman period, when the numbers of sheep increased. Varying degrees of specialisation in agricultural economies have been suggested at other sites in the Upper Thames Valley (eg Smith and Muir 2004, 147, 153-55), albeit in contexts – of which Yarnton was probably an example – in which most production was still likely to have been for local consumption.

The interpretation of Yarnton as a small farming settlement implies that many of its features and artefacts would have been related to agricultural production as well as to the processes of everyday – and occasionally more exceptional – life. The discovery of the middle Iron Age cemetery, and of deposits of metalwork and animal bone associated with a causeway on the floodplain, serve as useful reminders that many activities took place away from the occupation site. The cemetery shows that at least the final phases of some (but not all) funerary rites were carried out outside the settlement. The presence of other human bones within the settlement suggests that distinctions were made in the way in which different categories of people were treated (or perhaps between people who had suffered different forms of death), and reminds us – as do other 'special' deposits on the settlement, and perhaps also an early Iron Age rectangular structure at Cresswell Field – that ritual will have formed a component of life within the settlement. In settlements such as Yarnton, domestic, agricultural and ritual activity would probably have been closely integrated, providing a distinctive setting for social interaction.

Clear indications of differences of status are absent from the structures of the settlement and the character of objects associated with them, perhaps because these differences did not exist on an intra-site level, or because domestic buildings did not form an appropriate sphere in which to express such distinctions. These may have been expressed in dress and/or eating practices or in other ways that leave no trace in the archaeological record. One exception may be the two sequential middle Iron Age structures lying within a ditched enclosure (390) on the Yarnton site (Fig. 6.12).

SETTLEMENT APPEARANCE AND ORGANISATION

There is little evidence for the spatial organisation of settlement by means of ditches and other linear features before the middle Iron Age at the earliest, and even then ditches and gullies appear to have been related to individual structures rather than suggesting more wide-ranging layouts. For the early and middle Iron Age, therefore, discussion of settlement appearance and organisation is largely concerned with the physical characteristics and disposition of structures and their spatial relationships with groups of pits.

Early and middle Iron Age buildings (Figs 3.1-3.6)

The principal building type at Yarnton during the early and middle Iron Age, and probably the focus of domestic activity, was earthfast post-built structures. Within this category, however, there was considerable variation in plan, with circular, slightly oval and D-shaped post-built structures all present, generally evidenced by a post-ring and, in the middle Iron Age, additionally by a penannular ditch or gully. One rectangular building was also present. Seventeen early Iron Age structures of this form were identified (including completely rebuilt structures), running along the edge of the Second Gravel Terrace broadly in a west-east band, and a further seven have been dated to the middle Iron Age. It is likely that other buildings were either not recognised or had been destroyed by subsequent Roman and medieval activity. In addition, six penannular gullies may well have contained structures (for example middle Iron Age enclosure 97 and 241 on the Yarnton site and the double enclosure 8018/8286 on Cresswell Field) but no physical traces remained; either they had been cut away subsequently or were not built with earthfast foundations (see further below).

The presence of only 24 structures from the *c* 700 years of the early and middle Iron Age occupation suggests that, at any one time, the settlement was rather small, even allowing for further unidentified posthole structures and an unknown number of structures that may never have left subsurface remains. The spatial distribution of the settlement evidence (above Chapter 2) suggests that there may have been two or three households at Yarnton and one or two at Cresswell Field. Of the identified structures, 17 were circular or slightly oval in shape (Figs 3.1. and 3.2), six were D-shaped and one sub-rectangular (Figs 3.3 and 3.4). Whilst it is assumed that the majority of these buildings were domestic, it is possible that two of the smaller early Iron Age buildings (1752 and 1482) served a function ancillary to larger round houses, and that one of the D-shaped structures (803) may have been associated with metalworking. The unusual early Iron Age sub-rectangular structure (8202) at Cresswell Field may also have served a non-domestic role (Fig. 3.4; see below).

There were very few stratigraphic relationships between the structures, so their dating is based primarily on the relative proportions of different types of pottery in their posthole fills, a process involving assumptions about the likely presence of residual and intrusive sherds. Buildings with postholes yielding a high proportion of shell-tempered pottery were interpreted as belonging to the early Iron Age, whereas those with a high proportion of sand-tempered pottery were assigned to the middle Iron Age. On this basis, the majority of the posthole buildings are believed to be early. Although only one D-shaped structure and six circular buildings, all on the Yarnton site, were dated to the middle Iron Age, it is quite possible that postholes of some middle Iron Age structures contained only early Iron Age pottery, with the result that their numbers have been underestimated. In addition, the six small penannular enclosures were all middle Iron Age in date, and parallels elsewhere (for example Mingies Ditch in the Lower Windrush Valley; Allen and Robinson 1993) suggest that these might have contained houses. Such enclosures are also paralleled at Watkins Farm and Claydon Pike (Allen 1990; Miles *et al.* 2007; Lambrick 2009, 135).

The early Iron Age buildings on the Yarnton site were all circular or slightly oval in plan, whereas D-shaped structures predominated on Cresswell Field. Although these different building shapes could suggest different functions, the features and finds surrounding them were similar in type, spatial organisation and content and there was little in the character of the two parts of the settlement that was significantly different. Both types of building seem most likely to have been in domestic use, even if they may have had a different appearance. It is possible that the Cresswell Field buildings were earlier in date than those at Yarnton, and the closest parallels for the D-shaped structures on Cresswell Field are those of middle to late Bronze Age date found *c* 500 m away on the Yarnton floodplain (Site 1; Hey *et al.* forthcoming, see Fig. 3.5). However, the impossibility of distinguishing phases within the *c* 350 year timespan of the early Iron Age means that chronological differences cannot be discerned. Alternatively, structural form may have been determined by the cultural preferences of families with different traditions of house building. The location of these different styles on either side of the stream running through the settlement may lend some substance to this suggestion but, in view of the very widespread distribution of circular building plans in the early Iron Age (and in the late Bronze Age), it is hard to see why such a tradition should have been sustained here.

Roundhouses

The circular and oval buildings were all constructed using posts set into individual postholes; there were no post trenches, and no stakeholes survived (Figs 3.1 and 3.2). Five of the middle Iron Age buildings and, possibly, one of early Iron Age date, were surrounded by penannular ditches/ gullies. In all cases, truncation through ploughing or erosion had led to the destruction of floor surfaces, hearths and any superficial internal features.

None of the buildings was particularly large. The early Iron Age roundhouses averaged 7.5 m in diameter, but were varied in size, ranging from 5 m to 10.5 m across (Fig. 3.1). The variation in size was continuous, however, and did not suggest particular size groupings or distinct structural categories. Middle Iron Age roundhouses, on the other hand, all clustered in the range between 8 m and 9 m across (Fig. 3.2). The majority of these structures were equivalent to the 'wall post ring' structures (Type 3) distinguished at Gravelly Guy (Lambrick and Allen 2004, 132). In this type of building, a single ring of posts incorporated a pair of door-posts and fulfilled the dual function of forming the outer wall and supporting the roof. Five or six buildings had door-posts which stood out from the

Fig. 3.1 (facing page) Plans of early Iron Age round and oval buildings

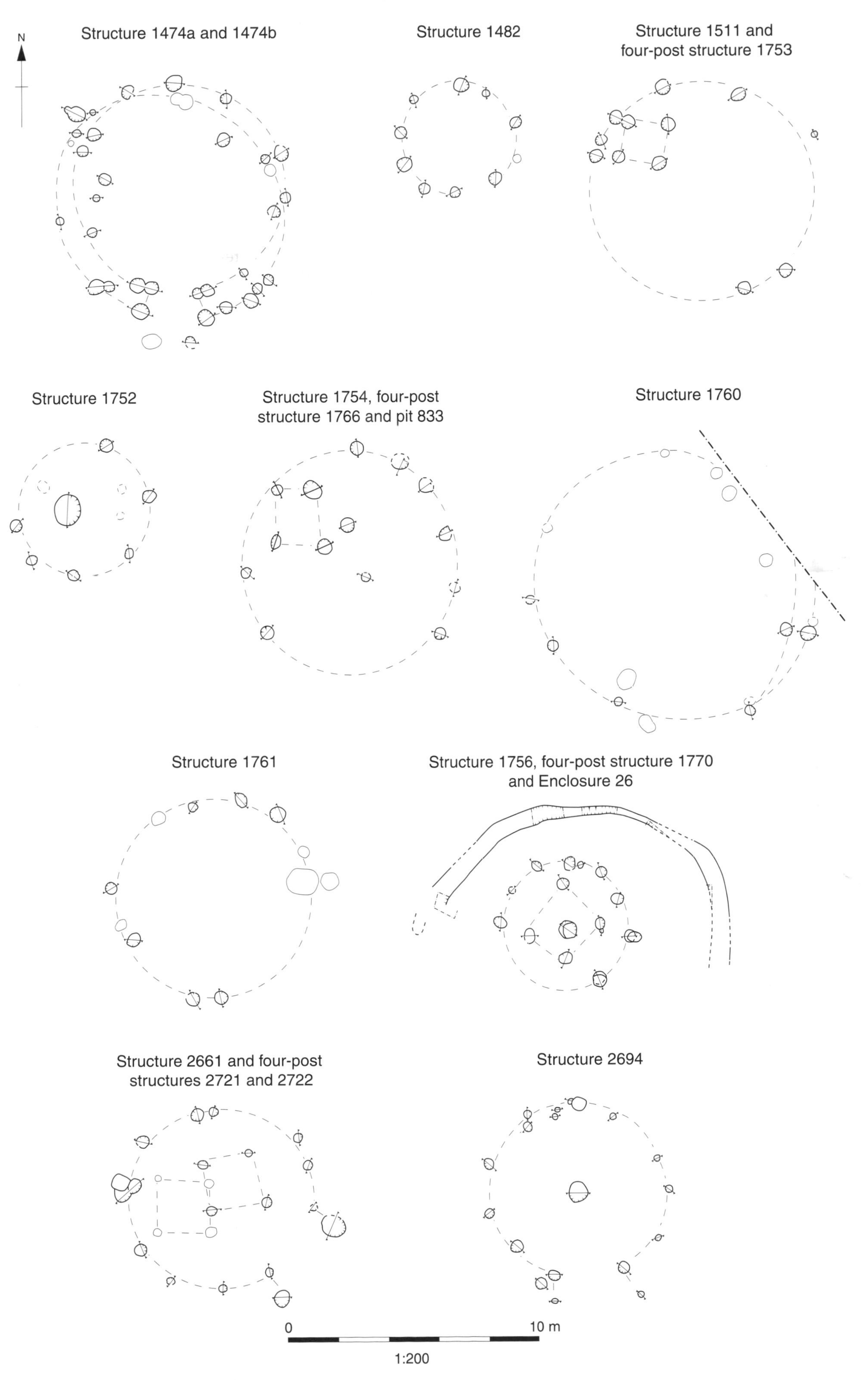

N
Structure 1474a and 1474b
Structure 1482
Structure 1511 and four-post structure 1753
Structure 1752
Structure 1754, four-post structure 1766 and pit 833
Structure 1760
Structure 1761
Structure 1756, four-post structure 1770 and Enclosure 26
Structure 2661 and four-post structures 2721 and 2722
Structure 2694
0
10 m
1:200

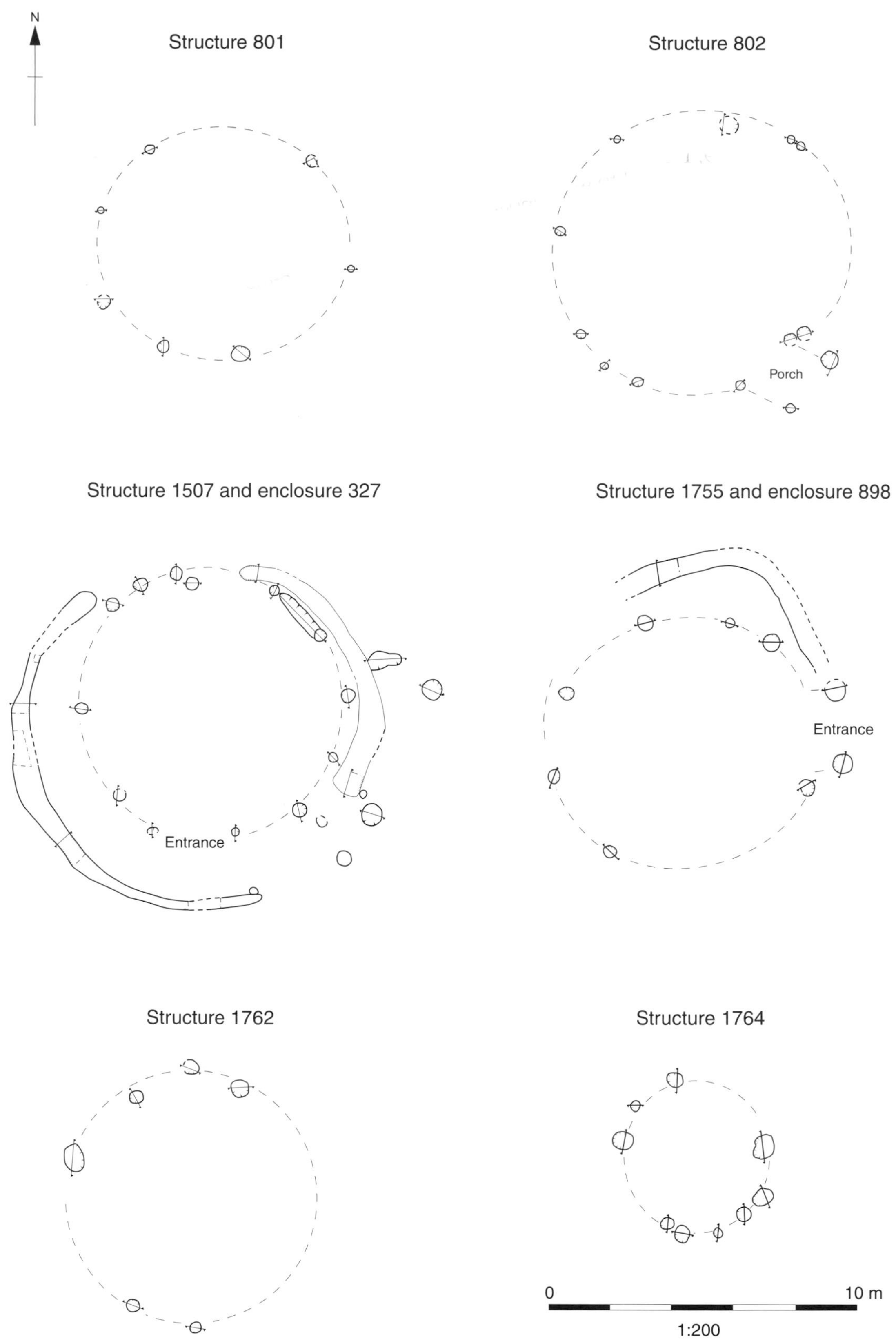

Fig. 3.2 Plans of middle Iron Age round and oval buildings

main post-ring , three or four of early Iron Age and two of middle Iron Age date. These are similar to the Gravelly Guy building Type 1 (ibid.), interpreted as comprising an inner post ring which would have carried the ring beam upon which the roof structure would have been based, and the two door posts flush with the outer wall of the building which would have had very shallow foundations, or none at all (Lambrick 2009, 135). It is possible that more structures originally conformed to this design, as postholes representing the remains of doorposts would easily have been missed amongst the morass of intercutting features that surrounded the roundhouses. The substantial porches present in these houses would have been impressive additions, providing areas for display and decoration, and a public space for meeting visitors, as well as a light space for domestic tasks (ibid., 137-42).

Where entrances are discernible (in seven cases), all faced between east and south, as is typical of Iron Age structures in southern England in general (Oswald 1997), and the Thames Valley in particular

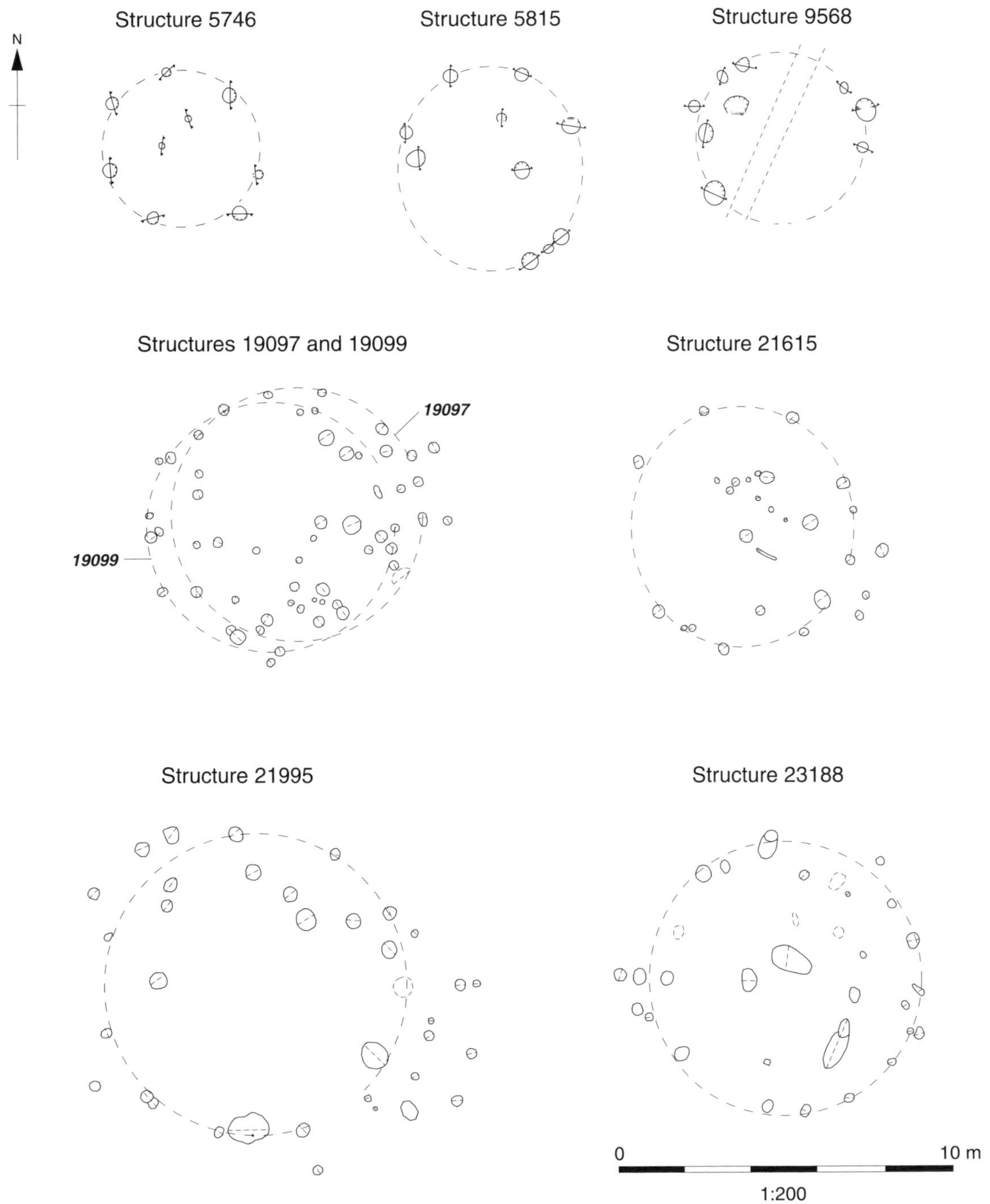

Fig. 3.3 Plans of late Bronze Age structures from Yarnton Floodplain (5746, 5815 and 9568) and Cassington (19097/19099, 23188, 21005 and 21615)

(Lambrick 2009, 142). This is likely to have been both a cultural choice (through religion, superstition or simply tradition) but also a practical one, for this is the direction that would allow most light into these buildings (Pope 2007; Lambrick 2009, 145-8, fig. 5.8).

These round to oval structures fit into a tradition of vernacular architecture that was widespread in the British Isles during the Iron Age and had well-established earlier antecedents. Examples of such post-built structures of late Bronze Age date from Yarnton Floodplain sites and from Cassington

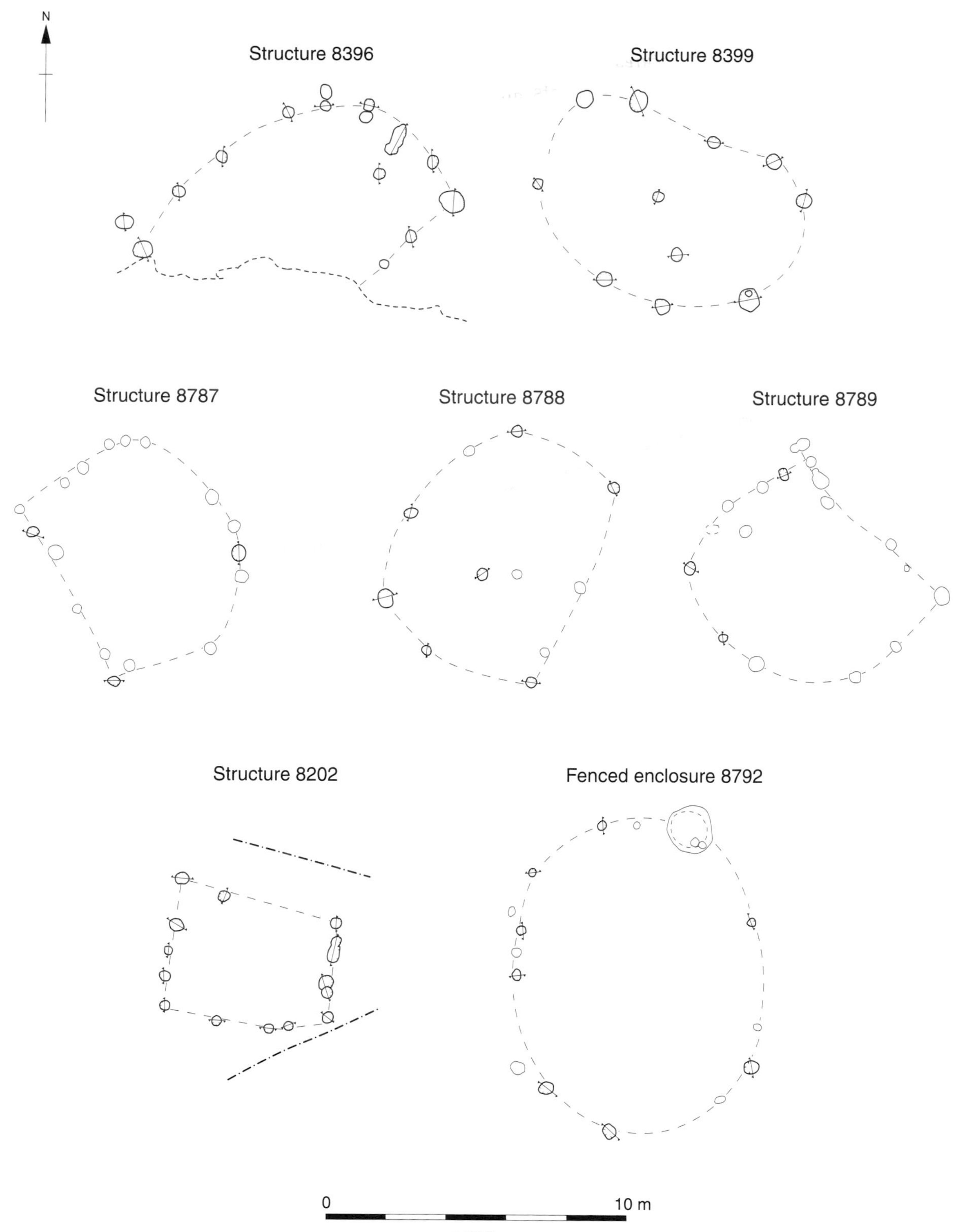

Fig. 3.4 Plans of early Iron Age D-shaped and rectangular structures and fenced enclosure from Cresswell Field

floodplain are shown in Figure 3.3. The contrast in size between the two groups of structures is very pronounced, although it is notable that both groups lie within the overall range of sizes present at Cresswell Field and Yarnton (Figs 3.1 and 3.2) and demonstrated there to constitute a continuum (see above).

The early Iron Age D-shaped structures

Five early Iron Age D-shaped post arrangements, all found on Cresswell Field, suggest a more local tradition (Fig. 3.4). Two pairs of buildings (8399 with 8787 and 8788 with 8789; were situated to the west of the main focus of early and middle Iron Age settlement. with a single structure to the south (Fig. 5.6). Their average dimensions were 7.2 m x 5.4 m, with a range of 7-8 m x 5-6 m. The internal spaces would thus have been only slightly smaller than those of the roundhouses and were more uniform in size. The above-ground appearance of these structures is uncertain. Like the more clearly-defined roundhouses described above, it is possible that the posts supported a ring beam inside the line of the wall, or they may represent the line of the wall itself.

Close local parallels are provided by six structures from Yarnton Floodplain Site 1 both in size and shape (Fig. 3.5; Hey *et al.* forthcoming) which are, as already discussed, middle to late Bronze Age in date. The best contemporary local parallel for these structures, however, was found at Beard Mill, Stanton Harcourt (Williams 1951, 10-12, fig. 6), where Williams suggested that there was evidence for a semicircular, post-built structure. It is worth noting that, like some of the structures on Cresswell Field, a shallow pit containing burnt stone and charcoal lay adjacent to the structure at Beard Mill. D-shaped houses have been identified elsewhere in the Upper Thames Valley, for example at Wyndyke Furlong, Abingdon (Muir and Roberts 1999, 62-3) and near the source of the Thames at Shorncote (Hearne and Heaton 1994; Hearne and Adam 1999) and Latton Lands (Powell *et al.* 2009) and approximately D-shaped gullies which probably surrounded houses have been recognised at other sites such as Gravelly Guy (eg Lambrick and Allen 2004, 126), giving some reason to think that the early Iron Age D-shaped structures at Cresswell Field were not as exceptional as they might at first appear.

Above ground appearance of roundhouses and D-shaped structures

All the buildings seem to have consisted of a single room. There was no evidence for internal partitions, although the presence of numerous postholes in some areas made this difficult to establish with confidence. A few early Iron Age buildings (four circular and two D-shaped) had postholes in or near their centres which could have held posts to support transverse beams for upper floors (Figs 3.1 and 3.3). Otherwise such supports appear to have been absent, if the possibility that four-post structures found within some roundhouses were contemporary is excluded (see below). Walls were probably constructed from wattle and daub attached to stakes which have left no recognisable trace (see, for example, Lambrick 2009, fig. 5.4), but the modest amount of structural daub from the site probably derived largely from ovens rather than the walls of buildings (Edwards and Barclay, Chapter 15 below). Some structures may have had walls of turf or cob, as for example at Mingies Ditch (Allen and Robinson 1993, 94-7), and this is certainly the interpretation favoured for the buildings that probably lay within the small enclosures found on both the Yarnton and Cresswell Field sites which appear to be associated with domestic activity (see Chapter 2, Fig. 2.5). Roofs were probably of thatch, as cereals seem to have been harvested low on the straw and thatching material would have been plentiful (see Pelling, Chapter 18 below; Lambrick 2009, 137). Turf roofs would probably have been too heavy to have been supported by the timber frames indicated by the evidence.

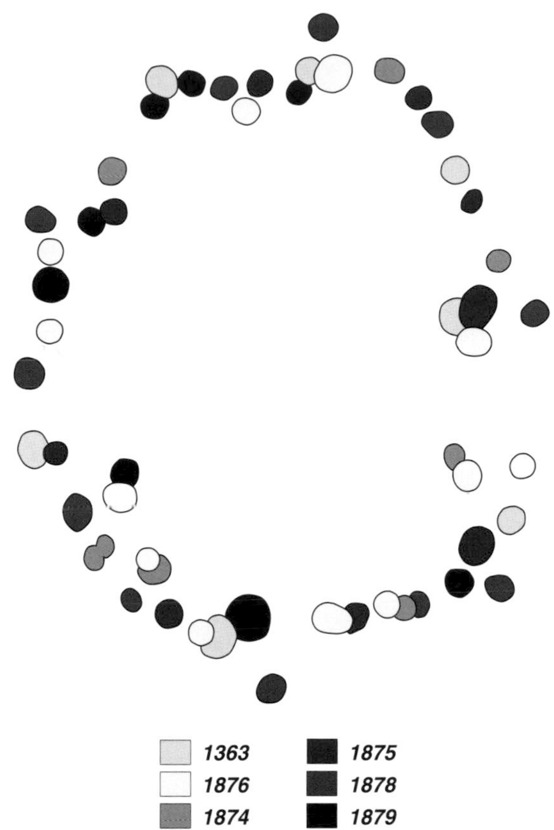

Fig. 3.5 Comparative outlines of D-shaped structures from Yarnton floodplain

The middle Iron Age D-shaped structure

The middle Iron Age D-shaped or semi-circular structure at Yarnton (803; Fig. 3.6) is a more common type than the earlier Cresswell Field examples (Lambrick 2009, 153-4). It was situated amongst the roundhouses in the west of the main focus of the middle Iron Age settlement. It was slightly larger than the early Iron Age D-shaped structures, measuring 9.8 m x 6.5 m externally, and was more clearly defined. The postholes formed two concentric D-shapes surrounded by a discontinuous penannular gully (Fig. 3.6), and it is suggested in Chapter 6 that the smaller building was replaced by a larger structure which was open to the east. The four-post setting within the structure/s is not thought to have been contemporary. Finds of metalworking debris were concentrated around this area (see below, Fig. 6.36), and it seems reasonable to suggest that this open-sided structure with protection against westerly or south-westerly winds was used for metalworking.

A possible parallel for this structure was found at Farmoor where a semicircular arrangement of postholes was identified surrounded on the curved side by a palisaded enclosure (Lambrick and Robinson 1979, fig. 4). There, the posthole structure measured approximately 8 m by 4.3 m. Again, it is worth noting that two shallow pits within the semicircle contained burnt stone and a few scraps of iron slag came from the surrounding gully (ibid., 12). Loomweight fragments were found nearby, but not in this immediate area (ibid., 57) and need not have been associated with the semicircular structure (cf Lambrick 2009, 154).

Rectangular structure

As already indicated, the early Iron Age sub-rectangular structure (8202) at Cresswell Field may also have served a non-domestic role. Fifteen postholes survived, making a slightly wedge-shaped structure

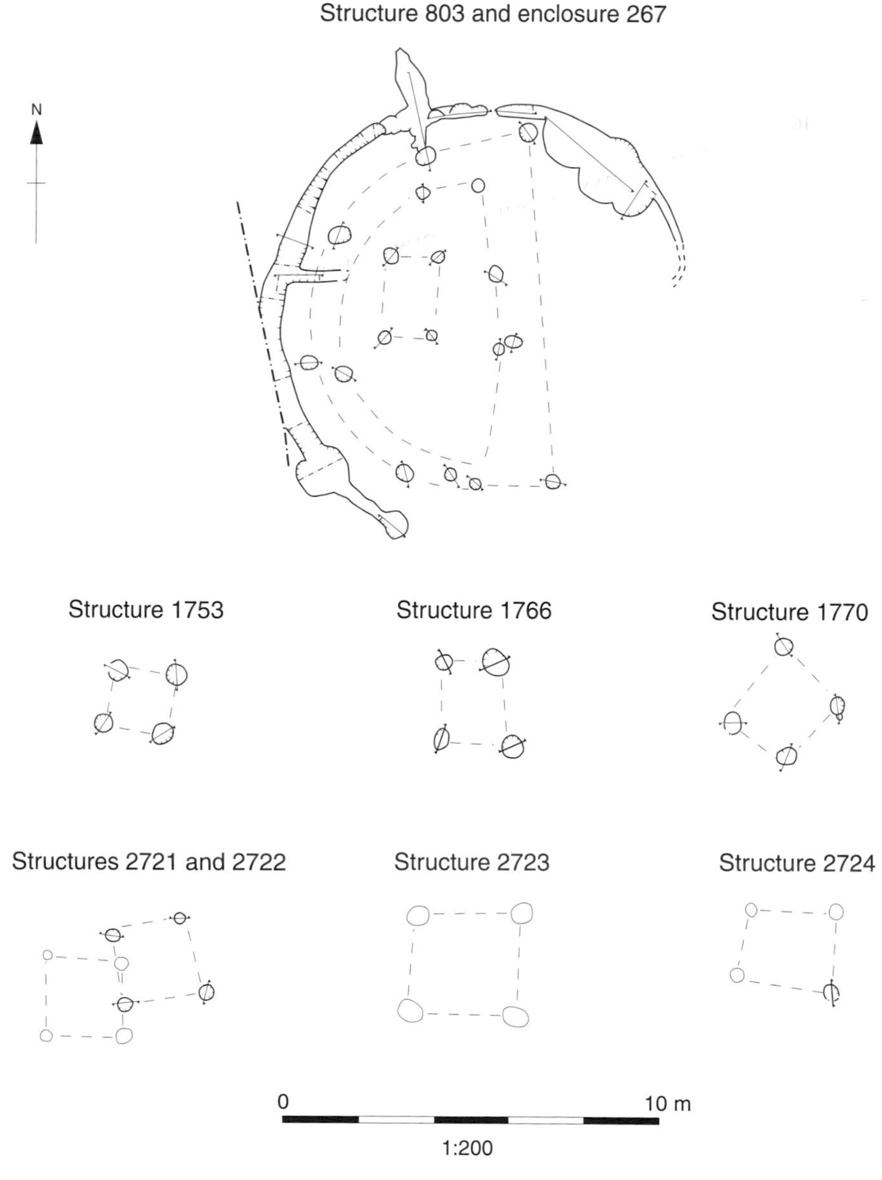

Fig. 3.6 Middle Iron Age D-shaped structure, and early and middle Iron Age four-post structures

with maximum dimensions of 5.4 m x 4.2 m (Fig. 3.4). There were few postholes along the north wall, where the entrance may have been situated. Two pits (8591 and 7029) lay nearby, which contained an inverted skull and a neonate humerus respectively, and a further fragment of probably human bone was found in one of the postholes (7018). Although only a small amount of human bone, in the context of the paucity of human bone in early Iron Age settlements generally, and Yarnton in particular, this concentration is noteworthy. It constitutes three of the four occurrences in the early Iron Age period at Cresswell Field, and the placing of the skull is striking (Fig. 5.9). Rectangular buildings elsewhere (eg Danebury, (Cunliffe 1984a, 86-7); Heathrow (Grimes and Close-Brooks 1993, 312-8) and Uley (Woodward and Leach 1993, 10)) have been interpreted as shrines. They are usually, however, more elaborate structures, often constructed using bedding trenches, and are also often later in date, while direct evidence for a religious function is not always present. Other rectangular buildings have been thought to be workshops (Lambrick 2009, 151-3, fig. 5.10). The evidence for the sub-rectangular structure at Cresswell Field is insufficient to support such a specific interpretation of its function; its position at the eastern corner of the Cresswell Field excavations makes it difficult to ascertain whether it lay apart from other buildings, and other pits excavated around it appeared little different from those elsewhere on the site. Nevertheless, the presence of the human remains in and around it suggests that it may have had ritual associations of a kind which differed from those of the other structures. Human bone is otherwise placed in pits away from buildings.

Structures and society

This evidence has a number of implications for the nature of early and middle Iron Age society at Yarnton. First there is no obvious indication in the size or shape of the buildings of any differences in status or prestige. Since no floor surfaces or internal features survived in these buildings the only finds directly associated with them were incorporated into the fills of the postholes. This could have occurred during the construction of the buildings, during their use, or after their abandonment and it is, therefore, impossible to relate the finds to specific activities or activity areas within the structures.

Contrary to what might be expected if status had been expressed through the size of buildings, there were actually fewer small structures (with diameters 5-7 m) than large structures (with diameters 8-11 m). It seems more likely that the smaller buildings were in some sense ancillary to larger structures, and hence complementary in function, rather than having been their lower-status equivalents. One possible exception is the two successive buildings (801 and 802; Fig. 3.2) found within enclosure 390 on the Yarnton site (Figs 6.3, 6.5, 6.9 and 6.11). Although the buildings themselves were no larger that the norm, they lay within just one part of an enclosure that was both larger and more substantially defined than those around the other middle Iron Age buildings. The additional space was subdivided with a fence (1758), and contained a pit (584) with a rich and interesting collection of finds, including a bone comb, a leaze rod, a bone/antler handle, loomweight fragments, quernstones and a crucible fragment. The enclosure ditch was also comparatively prolific in finds (see below, Chapter 6).

In the early Iron Age phase of the settlement it appears that eight of the roundhouses were paired, and it may be argued that a single pair of houses served as a domestic unit for an extended family. Two of these pairs comprised one smaller and one larger building and it is possible, as suggested above, that the smaller buildings served an ancillary function. In the middle Iron Age the layout of buildings in relation to each other changed and it is possible that a single building served as the domestic unit. At Gravelly Guy, Lambrick identified settlement elements each of which may have been related to extended family units (Lambrick and Allen 2004, 152-5). These were defined by boundaries marked either by a lack of features or, occasionally, by the ephemeral remains of ploughed-out ditches. No such boundaries were apparent at Yarnton, although it is possible that they simply did not survive or perhaps did not take an archaeologically recognisable physical form. As an alternative, it is possible that roundhouses did not serve as a focus for family units and that access to them was divided up rather differently, possibly along the lines of gender, or activity type. It is also possible that there was a mixture of buildings used by individual family units and buildings used for specific activities. Overall, however, what is most striking at Yarnton is the uniformity of the distribution of different kinds of features and finds. There is, for example, a very close similarity in the proportions of different kinds of pit at both Yarnton and Cresswell Field in both the early and the middle Iron Age. This supports the hypothesis of a series of household units, each undertaking a similar range of social and economic activities, comparable to the pattern suggested by Lambrick for Gravelly Guy, rather than a clustering of particular activities or categories of people in different parts of the site.

Four-post structures

Eight four-post structures were identified on the Yarnton site (Fig. 3.6). All but one of these structures were dated to the early Iron Age by the high ratio of shell-tempered pottery to sand-tempered pottery found in their posthole fills and by their spatial association with the early Iron Age roundhouses. The exception lay within the D-shaped structure 803 and is more likely to have been of middle Iron Age date than earlier. It is assumed that the posts supported a wooden frame and platform of some

Fig. 3.7 Artist's reconstruction of four-post structure

kind and they may have had roofs (Fig. 3.7) but this is not certain.

These structures were mostly closely associated with early Iron Age roundhouses, five being encircled by post-rings and two lying very close by, while the probable middle Iron Age example lay within a D-shaped structure. It seems unlikely that these structures were in contemporary use with the houses. Only one four-poster was situated centrally within the ring and even its ground plan was not completely certain. The positions of the others do not suggest structural supports (for example for an upper floor). They seem more likely to have been placed within collapsed houses, which perhaps continued to provide some protection against the elements or animals.

The function of four-post structures remains uncertain. A possibility, put forward by Knüsel and Carr (1995; Carr and Knüsel 1997), is that they were used as mortuary platforms upon which corpses were left during the process of excarnation. It could be argued that the correspondence between four-post structures and houses at Yarnton suggests that the four-posters were used for the excarnation of the houses' former occupants. There are, however, no clear parallels for this sequence of events in the Upper Thames Valley, nor was any human bone found in features associated with, or even near, the four-post structures, though such an absence is not in itself conclusive.

It seems most probable that four-post structures were used in a variety of ways. Gent's (1983) survey of the available evidence suggests that their usual interpretation as grain storage silos is amongst the most plausible. The relatively small numbers of four-post structures at Yarnton might be explained by the suggestion that alternative forms of storage (such as pits) were adopted before the end of the early Iron Age. It is, however, quite possible that such structures were used to store other materials, or were used for quite different purposes. They could, for example, have been used as racks for drying and stretching animal hides. The dating, layout and number of the four-post structures at Yarnton is very closely paralleled at Gravelly Guy where all the examples (16 certain and three possible) were of early Iron Age date (Lambrick and Allen 2004, 144-6). A small number of the Gravelly Guy four-post structures lay within penannular ring-gullies or post-rings, but none of these was centred within their respective buildings, leading Lambrick to suggest that the relationships were coincidental (ibid.). The comparative paucity of four post-structures on Iron Age sites in this part of the Upper Thames Valley was noted by Lambrick (ibid., 144), who could find only a handful of sites on the First and Second Gravel Terraces with such structures; Gravelly Guy and Yarnton were more prolific than most. A further 16 examples were identified in the late Bronze Age settlement on Cassington floodplain (Hayden *et al.* forthcoming). Further upstream, they are relatively common, however, with an exceptional group of about 150 four-post structures found at Horcott near Fairford, many arranged in regular rows (Mullin *et al.* 2009), as they are in Wessex and areas such as the Welsh Marches (Allen *et al.* 1984, 98). The significance of this extreme inter-site variability in the numbers of four-post structures is as yet unexplained.

EARLY AND MIDDLE IRON AGE FINDS DEPOSITION

Early and middle Iron Age finds came from two principal kinds of context on the settlement sites: ploughsoil layers and the fills of cut features. The material from the ploughsoil was clearly unstratified and therefore of limited use for the elucidation of patterns of finds disposal. This discussion will therefore focus on the material from cut features.

Early and middle Iron Age finds came from postholes, pits and penannular gullies/ditches, with pits providing the main source of material; very little came from postholes. This pattern reflects the relative volumes of the different feature types, but is more meaningfully related to functional differences between them. The distribution of finds within these features may be assumed to reflect both secondary deposition, through erosion into pit and ditch fills of artefacts lying on contemporary ground surfaces, and the deliberate dumping or placing of material into fills. In the case of postholes most if not all the associated finds are likely to have derived from secondary deposition, whether during their construction and use, or after the demolition of the structures of which they formed part. However, much material was dumped or placed into the fills of pits and ditches either during their use, or as part of the process of final backfilling.

The majority of finds from the early and middle Iron Age settlement comprised either pottery or animal bone, with charred plants tending to concentrate in the larger pits and penannular ditches and metalworking debris and other artefacts tending to be fairly sparsely distributed. Relatively substantial quantities of animal bone and pottery were clearly deposited in the fills of cut features either directly after processing or breakage, or from middens. The abraded state of much of this material suggests that a good deal of it also made its way into cut features from the contemporary ground surface, where it had been lying for a reasonable period of time. It is clear that plant remains were dumped into ditch and pit fills along with animal bone and pottery, as concentrations of these materials often come from the same deposits. Other finds were rare, but when they did occur it was usually with deposits of animal bone and pottery.

The majority of the pottery assemblage comprised abraded body sherds in sand and shell-tempered fabrics. Pottery was evenly distributed over the settlement in both the early Iron Age and the middle Iron Age periods. In total there were 11,540 sherds of which 2511 (22%) were stratified in contemporary deposits, 827 (32%) coming from early Iron Age and 1112 (44%) from middle Iron Age pits. Since more early Iron Age pits were excavated than middle Iron Age (early Iron Age: 195; middle Iron Age 138), this suggests a marked increase in the quantity of pottery being deposited through time. Of the rest of the pottery, 433 sherds (17%) came from middle Iron Age ring-gullies, 97 (4%) came from the early Iron Age structures and 42 (2%) from those of middle Iron Age date.

Animal bone (3090 fragments) was widely distributed across the site. Much of the material was very fragmented, and a little was burnt, gnawed or butchered. The great majority of the fragments came from pits; 886 (29%) from the early Iron Age pits and 1601 (52%) from the middle Iron Age pits. Again, given that more early than middle Iron Age pits were excavated, this suggests an increase over time in the quantities of animal bone being deposited (although it is not possible to quantify the amount of bone in middle Iron Age pits that might have been redeposited material of early Iron Age date). Many of the pits – both early and middle Iron Age – also contained bone from a variety of different domestic species. A total of 376 bone fragments (12.1%) came from the deeper and more common middle Iron Age ring-gullies, including some quite large single deposits of domestic species, but only four fragments (0.1%) were from the early Iron Age ditches. A comparatively small quantity of bone came from structures, 3% from the early Iron Age and 2% from the middle Iron Age structures. There was a very small amount of wild animal bone, including red deer and badger; this appeared to be fairly randomly distributed.

Metalworking debris occurred in a few features but only in small quantities. There were 131 fragments in total, of which 112 (85%) came from early Iron Age pits, 15 (11%) from middle Iron Age pits and 4 (3%) from middle Iron Age enclosure 390 (phases B and D) in the south-west of the Yarnton site. Even given the greater number of early Iron Age pits, there is considerably more evidence for metalworking in the early Iron Age than in the middle Iron Age. Although this material was found widely dispersed across the settlement, the vast majority was concentrated in a single pit (pit 330) in the south-west of the main Yarnton settlement area. This suggests that metalworking took place on site, but away from the main domestic buildings. No structures which may have been associated with such metalworking were identified.

Middle Iron Age pits containing metalworking debris were more restricted in their distribution, being largely confined to the western part of the Yarnton settlement, the majority clustering around structure 803, an unusual D-shaped building which may have functioned as a smithy. The few scraps of metalworking debris from the middle Iron Age ring-gullies may have been redeposited and represent residual early Iron Age material.

Inevitably, the distribution of charred plants reflects sample location, even though a range of feature types of different dates were selected for sampling. Some 3811 specimens of charred plants were recovered from the early and middle Iron Age settlement. Of these, 1807 (47%) came from early Iron Age pits, 1717 (45%) from middle Iron Age pits, and 287 (7.5%) from middle Iron Age ring-gullies. The majority of the pits with charred plants were cylindrical in profile suggesting that they were originally used for grain storage and, following the suggestion that the pits were fired after use, perhaps in order to sterilise them (Reynolds 1974, 128), some of the plant material from their fills could have been residual material left over from storage. However, much charred plant material was mixed with deposits of animal bone and pottery and must have been incorporated into dumps of rubbish or structured deposits. Both early and middle Iron Age pits with charred plants were fairly evenly distributed over the settlement. Charred plants came from the majority of the middle Iron Age ring-gullies/penannular ditches, with concentrations in the larger features, particularly in circular enclosure 390 in the south-west of Yarnton. As with the pits, this material was mixed with animal bone and pottery suggesting that it formed part of dumps of rubbish.

There were few other artefacts and where they did occur they were often found in pits and ditches associated with deposits of animal bone and pottery, suggesting that they had been incorporated into rubbish deposits. The small quantities of other artefacts such as jewellery, quernstones and decorated metalwork were not indicative of a high-status site.

The distribution of finds reflects a community which practised mixed agriculture, or had access to mixed agricultural resources. The dumping of large quantities of material into pit and ditch fills was probably occasional and much of the material probably derives from secondary deposition. In the early and middle Iron Age waste material, including animal bone, broken pottery and charred plant remains, was dumped or placed into pits, some of which may originally have been used for grain storage. The middle Iron Age penannular gullies/ditches incorporated pottery, animal bone and charred plants within their fills, but not in quantities that would suggest regular and large-scale deposition of material. The quantity of metal-working debris makes it likely that metalworking was carried out on site in both the early and middle Iron Age, though principally in the early Iron Age. For example, the concentration of slag in a pit to the south of the settlement suggests that metalworking was carried out in this area. In the middle Iron Age period metalworking debris was concentrated in pits around an unusual D-shaped structure, which may be interpreted as a smithy, although the absolute quantities of material involved were quite small.

Placed deposits

A number of early and middle Iron Age pits were singled out from the others as containing 'special' deposits. The definition of a special deposit is open to debate (eg Hill 1995, 95-101; see also Chapter 17 below). In the case of Yarnton, deposits were distinguished as special primarily on the grounds that they contained exceptional categories of material: human bone, articulated animal bone and, in one case, an exceptional artefact (an adze). A second consideration in classifying deposits as special or structured was evidence that the material had been carefully and deliberately placed. This was true in the case of the iron adze in pit 7787 at Cresswell Field. The adze had been placed on the base of the pit, and large sherds of an early Iron Age storage vessel had been laid around the northern edge of the pit. This second criterion probably also applies to pit 8127 at Cresswell Field, in which a number of vessels, including one in the All Cannings Cross style, appear to have been deliberately smashed around a large, burnt quartzite pebble which lay in the centre of the bottom of the pit (Fig. 5.4). Deliberate positioning also applies in the case of pit 8591, which contained an inverted adult female skull (and little else). Less clearly, a dog skeleton in pit 7762 had been laid on a bed of burnt stone.

It can be argued that singling out particular categories of material as special may have more to do with our preconceptions than with the beliefs of the Iron Age inhabitants of the settlement. The context, for example, of some of the human bone, deposited along with varying quantities of pottery and animal bone, much like that in other pits which do not contain human bone, could suggest that its deposition was mundane. However, until the establishment of cemetery burial in the 3rd century BC, after which accidental redeposition is always a possibility, human remains are likely to have had symbolic significance. Perhaps the most striking find associated with human bone was a miniature vessel in pit 276 at Yarnton.

There are no very consistent patterns within the categories of material distinguished as special. The pattern of human bone deposition suggests a focus on long bones and perhaps skulls, but the sample is very small. The majority of this material came from early Iron Age deposits and comprised an adult female skull (pit 8591), fragments of skull vault (pit 276), a neonate humerus (pit 7029), part of a probable adult ulna from a possible stakehole (7644), a mixed deposit of burnt animal bone with possible human bone from posthole 7017 and a human phalanx (pit 951). A number of these clustered near the rectangular building 8202 (see above). A tibia shaft (pit 248), a femur shaft and a fragment of ulna (both from pit 1189) came from middle Iron Age features at Yarnton.

Cattle, dog, horse and sheep bones were all found placed in articulation. Articulated cattle bones occurred in five pits, the largest number for any species and, like most of the sheep and horse bones, these consisted of parts of skeletons and, in particular, limbs. Pit 330, to the south-west of the Yarnton settlement, contained a more or less complete sheep skeleton, one of the front legs of which had been replaced with the limb of a different animal. Articulated dog bones were found in four pits, and in two (both early Iron Age) they consisted of almost complete skeletons. A third group of articulated dog bones, in middle Iron Age pit 1744, consisted of a less complete, but nonetheless substantial part of the skeleton, plus two separate mandibles. This apparently different treatment of dog remains compared to the other animals suggests that dogs were classified differently (cf Sahlins 1976, 169-76). It is worth noting that only dog limbs (three, from two different animals, see below) were found in pit 7762, suggesting selective deposition of dogs even when only represented by small parts of the animal.

Like most of the human bone, the articulated animal bone was associated with other material – largely pottery and other, disarticulated animal bone. The most notable associations were, in fact, other articulated animal bone remains. Three deposits with articulated animal bone contained articulated animal bone from more than one species; the 'composite' sheep in pit 330 has already been mentioned. Two pits (7590 and 7762) contained dog remains associated with articulated cattle and horse bones respectively. In pit 511, a cow torso was associated with foal limbs.

Articulated remains clearly contrast with fragmented, disarticulated bone and pot which occurred in the majority of the pits and, along with the obvious signs of special treatment in some contexts, suggests that they constitute the remains of distinct offerings or sacrifices.

LATE IRON AGE/EARLY ROMAN AND ROMAN SETTLEMENT

Late Iron Age/early Roman and Roman finds deposition

Aside from unstratified material from ploughsoil contexts, finds from these periods of occupation were recovered almost exclusively from the fills of ditches, reflecting the change in the character of settlement from posthole features and pits to one in which enclosure ditches and their banks predominated; much less material was recovered from pits and even less from postholes. The majority of finds came from the fills of the enclosure ditches situated in the main focal area of late Iron Age and Roman occupation in the Yarnton site. Less came from the outlying ditches which may have been field boundaries, and very few finds were retrieved from the substantial Roman ditches which lay to the south and east of the settlement.

The finds included pottery, animal bone, charred plant remains, metalworking debris and various other artefacts, with pottery or animal bone forming the majority. Plant remains were concentrated in the fills of the larger ditches; metalworking debris and other artefacts were generally rare. The general composition of finds assemblages in these deposits was much the same as that seen in the early and middle Iron Age, although the distribution of metalworking debris was more variable (see below).

Some 8896 sherds of pottery were recovered from features of these periods. The assemblage included a range of wares, although fine wares were limited in quantity and variety, and was widely distributed over the settlement area in this period. Ditches and pits yielded relatively large quantities of pottery, including some abraded material, although little pottery came from the boundary ditches surrounding the late Roman settlement. The pits of all three phases contained a consistently small quantity of material ranging from 5.2% in the early Roman phase to 2.5% in the late Roman phase.

Like pottery, animal bone (quantified by numbers of fragments) was widely distributed and was often found together with pottery. Animal bone from the late Iron Age/early Roman period was concentrated in the fills of sub-rectangular enclosure ditches in the centre of the site, on either side of a linear ditch which crossed the settlement area. Comparatively little material came from the fills of the rectilinear enclosures to the west. Animal bone of the early Roman period was concentrated in the fills of the enclosure ditches, which occupied the centre of the settlement area. Comparatively little material came from the smaller ditches to the south and east, or from the substantial eastern boundary ditch, but a large assemblage was recovered from the large sub-circular enclosure to the south-east of the main settlement. Animal bone belonging to the late Roman period was concentrated in the fills of enclosure ditches to the east of a trackway, which ran through the middle of the main occupation area. It was also recovered in relatively large quantities from the fills of the eastern boundary ditch of the trackway. Comparatively little material was recovered from the fills of the ditch bounding the trackway to the west, or from the fills of the settlement boundary ditches. Animal bone was common in the fills of pits of all periods, but was particularly concentrated in nine pits: 300, 563 and 1608 from the late Iron Age/early Roman period, 57, 836, 1088 and 1216 from the early Roman period and 454 and 1084 from the late Roman period. In total there were 4775 fragments of animal bone, of which 23% came from pits and 72% from enclosure and linear ditches. Much of this material was very fragmented, but little was burnt, gnawed or had butchery marks.

In the late Iron Age/early Roman period small amounts of metalworking debris were found in the fills of a few pits scattered across the site and in the fills of some of the larger enclosure ditches, but there were no significant concentrations. This suggests that metalworking was carried out off-site and that much of the material derived from secondary deposition, or was residual. The vast majority of metalworking debris from early Roman contexts came from the fill of one feature (ditch 1586), situated in the south-west corner of a large oval enclosure (187), perhaps indicating that metalworking was carried out nearby. The rest of the material from this period was dispersed among the fills of various pits and ditches. Little metalworking debris was recovered from late Roman features and, like that from late Iron Age contexts, it was scattered amongst the fills of various pits, postholes and ditches. This may suggest off-site metalworking in the late Roman period, but much of this material may have been residual.

The distribution of charred plants in this period (as in other periods) reflects sample location, but a range of feature types of possible different dates were selected for sampling. Plant remains were scarce in deposits of the late Iron Age/early Roman period. There were relatively small assemblages from the ditch fills of some major enclosures, but the most substantial assemblage came from a short section of ditch just to the west of circular enclosure 391. Plant remains from late Iron Age/early Roman pit fills, also relatively uncommon, were randomly distributed. There were some relatively large assemblages from the major Roman enclosure ditches and where these occurred they tended to be mixed with animal bone and pottery, suggesting that they formed part of rubbish deposits. Plant remains from Roman pits were mainly from cylindrical pits, which may still have been used for storage, and may represent the remains of stored grain, but none of these pit assemblages was large.

Other artefacts were relatively rare, but where they did occur they were often (as in the early and middle Iron Age) associated with deposits of animal bone and pottery. In spatial terms, other artefacts were concentrated in the main occupation areas.

The finds suggest that the community was still mainly agrarian during the late Iron Age and Roman period. There is no real evidence for industry; in fact with one exception metalworking debris was rare in features from the late Iron Age to late Roman periods. This suggests no more than low level activity of a type required by any farming community, while the demonstrable early Roman pottery production was probably at a comparable level. The distribution of ceramics and small finds does not indicate a particularly wealthy community. The concentrations of mixed deposits of animal bone, pottery and plant remains in the central enclosure ditches indicate that these enclosures were the main focus of domestic occupation, while the outlying ditches, which generally have fewer finds, were probably paddock or field boundaries.

Placed deposits

Two deposits of Roman date were found to contain whole animal skulls, or parts of animal skulls, and one contained a collection of disarticulated skulls and long bones. Roman enclosure 160 contained a horse skull and vertebrae, found lying upside down on the base of the ditch. No other finds were associated with these remains. The terminal of ditch 1350 contained two complete animal skulls, one of a cow and one of a horse, lying parallel to one another, while four sherds of late Roman pottery and a fragment of sheep/goat size bone were also recovered here. In addition, a series of disarticulated animal skulls and long bones (408) was found just within the area enclosed by middle Iron Age penannular ditch 390.

Evident care had been taken in placing the skulls within the ditch fills and this may mean that they represented structured deposits of some kind. The collection of disarticulated long bones and skulls (408) may plausibly be interpreted as butchery waste, but structured deposition should not be ruled out for this deposit either, as it clearly represents selected parts of a number of animals (Mulville *et al.*, Chapter 17). These deposits were different from animal burials in the early and middle Iron Age, in that accompanying finds were absent.

PEOPLE AND BURIALS

Iron Age and Romano-British burials

A number of burials have been uncovered in the Yarnton area over the past 150 years. In particular, 'a considerable quantity of urns and human remains' was noted in 1854 from a ballast pit in the area between Yarnton church and the railway station. However, the only 'urn' salvaged (Bradford 1942b, 55-6, fig. 12 no. 36) could as easily be of later Bronze Age date as later. In 1875-6 Rolleston visited the reopened quarry and found a number of contracted burials, near one of which a sherd of decorated Iron Age pottery was found. The date and number of these burials is thus very uncertain. Some were definitely Beaker and others Anglo-Saxon in date (Hey 2004, 10); while it is possible that Iron Age burials were present this is far from clear.

Burials more confidently attributable to the Iron Age have been found in the vicinity, however. The ditch of the Big Enclosure ditch at Cassington contained the contracted burials of a woman and child (Case 1982a, 131). An undated pit burial was also found during gravel working at Cassington (Chambers 1977; Boyle this volume). Slightly further afield middle Iron Age burials have been found at Purwell Farm, and early, middle and late Iron Age and Roman burials at Gravelly Guy and Vicarage Field gravel pit. More recently a group of three middle Iron Age inhumations, interpreted as part of a small cemetery, has been excavated at Spring Road, Abingdon (Allen and Kamash 2008, 16-18). Such sites remain rare in the region, however, and, indeed, nationally.

A cemetery was excavated at Cassington in the 1930s revealing in excess of 110 graves of Romano-British date (Anon 1936, 201; 1937, 201; 1938, 165; for a partial plan see Harding 1972, plate 27). A total of 15 skeletons had been decapitated and there were 3 cremation burials, at least one of which was urned. The decapitations suggest a late Roman date for at least part of the otherwise (on existing evidence) undated cemetery.

Burials from Worton Rectory Farm, Cresswell Field and Yarnton-Cassington evaluation

A small assemblage of human remains of late Bronze Age/early Iron Age was recovered from Cresswell Field and Yarnton, and further human bone came from middle Iron Age features at Yarnton (see above, Placed deposits).

A small inhumation burial cemetery of middle Iron Age and Roman date was discovered in the initial rescue work carried out in 1990 during stripping by the gravel company to the east of the Yarnton settlement. Six cremation burials and 46 inhumation burials were recorded, but only a single urned burial within an early Roman vessel could be securely date by conventional means. The date of the cemetery has been established through a programme of radiocarbon dating (Hey *et al.* 1999; Hey and Bayliss, Chapter 13). Of the inhumations, five, at the south of the salvage area, were extended and one of these was decapitated. Two of these have been dated to the Roman period by radiocarbon. A further six extended east-west burials date to the post-Roman period (Hey 2004, 163-5). This left 35, mainly crouched burials, which lay in three groups on the site; one group on the south and east edge of the Iron Age settlement, and a northern and southern group in the salvage area to the east. Nine of the fourteen radiocarbon dated skeletons proved to be of Iron Age date (Chapter 13; Table 13.1). On statistical grounds at least eight of the dated individuals could have died at the same time or over a relatively short period of time. A probability distribution of the dates (see Hey *et al.* 1999; Hey and Bayliss this volume) suggests that the cemetery was in use for only a short period of time.

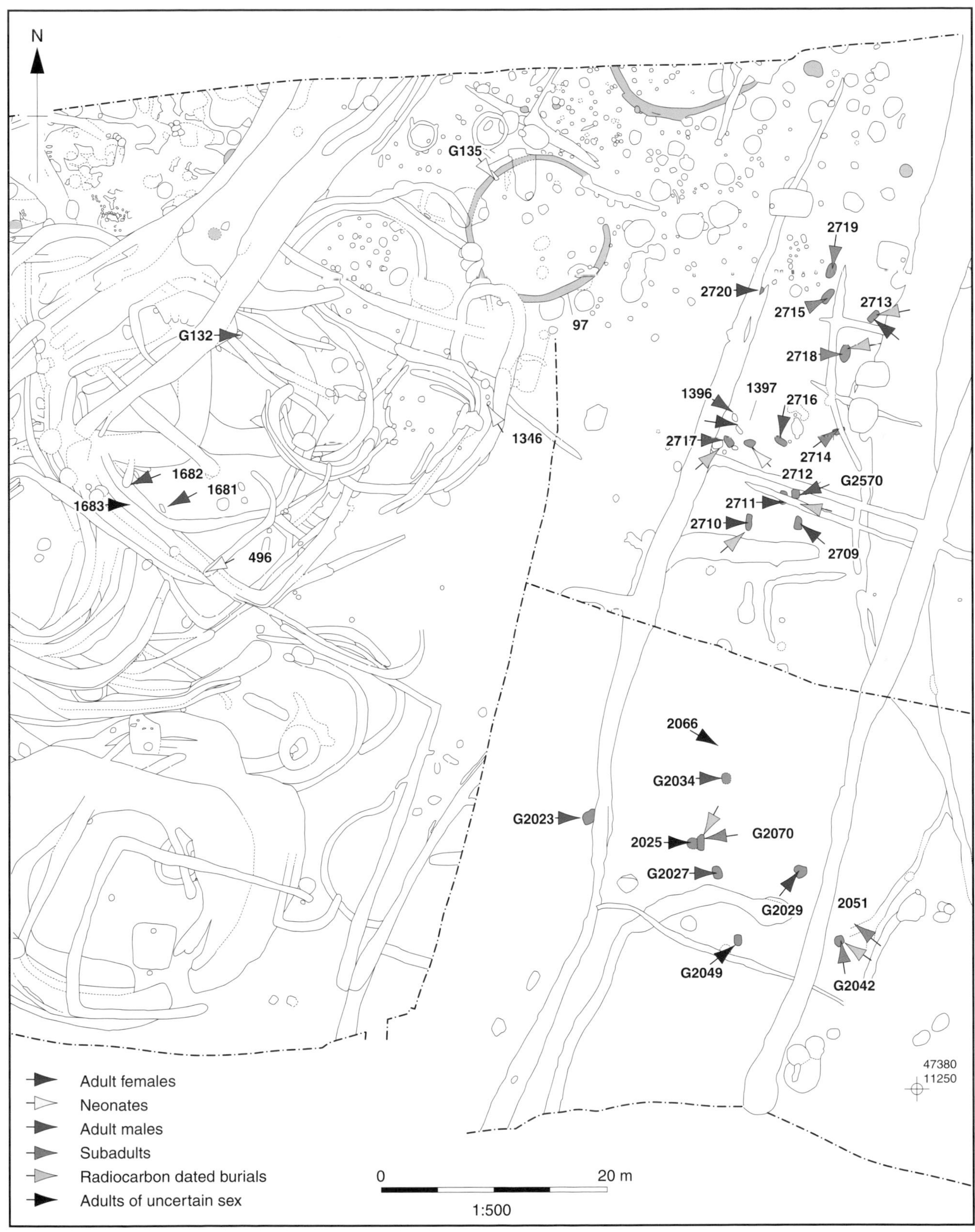

Fig. 3.8 Distribution of middle Iron Age burials at Yarnton

Cemetery layout

The cemetery appears to have comprised two distinct groups, northern and southern, of 15 and 10 individuals respectively (Fig. 3.8). The gap between the groups was only 20 m and this could partly be a result of poor retrieval in the intervening area, or could indicate that the two groups were socially distinct, perhaps two family units. A further ten inhumations have been described as outliers, scattered along the southern and eastern edge of the settlement. All the neonates in the group were buried within or adjacent to the settlement area. As none of these were radiocarbon dated and stratigraphic relationships are inconclusive it is possible that some or all of these are Roman. A further 11 deposits of disarticulated material from Roman contexts may be redeposited Iron Age material. The radiocarbon dates were obtained from five burials in the northern group, two southern burials and two outlying burials.

All of the burials were unaccompanied and burial position was predominantly crouched on the left or right hand side. It was possible to determine the orientation in 22 cases, and the majority were north-south or close to this. Three possible extended burials were identified within the northern group, but as these were recovered during machine observation it is possible that the body positions were incorrectly identified. However, the possibility that these bodies were genuinely extended cannot be discounted as this position does occur in the Iron Age. There is no indication that any of the Yarnton burials received special treatment. The skeletons were fully articulated, the shallow grave cuts appear to have been purpose dug for the burial and there were no grave goods.

The Roman burials comprised five skeletons from Yarnton and two from evaluation fieldwork at Worton, 1.5 km to the west. There were also five cremation burials. Two of the inhumations were radiocarbon dated and both are likely to date to the later Roman period. They were located to the south of the Iron Age burials.

The Roman burials were on or close to north-south or south-north alignments. Burial position was either supine extended or slightly crouched. One adult male skeleton had been laid on top of a subadult. There were no associated grave goods. One of the adult female skeletons (2016) had been decapitated, and was also partially overlain by an articulated dog.

Population

The population from the middle Iron Age cemetery comprised 22 adults (of which 12 were male, 7 female and 3 of unknown sex), 6 juveniles, 3 infants and 3 neonates. Of the 22 adults present, 2 were young adults (17-25 years), 9 were prime adults (25-40 years) and 1 an ageing adult (over 40 years). The remaining 10 could only be assigned to a broad adult category.

If the cemetery represents all the people from the settlement who died during the period of time it was in use, a good working hypothesis might be that it represents the burials from two or three nuclear families of around six to eight people. This would be consistent with the settlement evidence which suggests around three foci for the buildings. The age and sex composition suggests that, apart from the neonates, it was appropriate to bury all members of the community in the same manner.

The Roman inhumation burials from Yarnton comprised two male and two female adults and an infant. The two analysed cremation burials are those of an adult, probably female and a young child. The two burials from the evaluation at Worton were of neonatal infants.

Health

In both the Iron Age and Roman periods the skeletal pathology exhibited was mainly traumatic in origin. Twelve Iron Age skeletons and one of the Roman bodies exhibited vertebral degeneration. One male Iron Age skeleton had a benign osteochondroma on the right femur (Chapter 16).

Dental caries was seen to affect eleven of the middle Iron Age skeletons and four skeletons had dental abscesses. Eight individuals had calculus build-up and one juvenile had been affected by enamel hypoplasia. In the Roman group, four skeletons had dental caries and three had calculus. Although the sample is small, dental health in the Roman period appears to have been much poorer than in either the preceding Iron Age or succeeding Saxon period (for details of the latter see Boyle 2004).

A few skeletal anomalies were noted. Two of the Iron Age and one of the Roman skeletons exhibited the condition known as spondylolysis which may be a genetic condition or associated with a physically demanding lifestyle. Wormian bones were present on the crania of five Iron Age and one Roman skeletons, which again could suggest genetic links or be attributed to environmental or stress factors. A small number of dental anomalies were also noted in the Iron Age population.

Stature shows a marked increase from the Iron Age through into the Roman period, particularly in the male population. Five individuals amongst the Iron Age group and one Roman body exhibited cribia orbitalia, traditionally seen as a condition which arises due to iron-deficiency anaemia which can occur either as a result of disease or poor diet (Stuart-MacAdam 1989).

Jewellery, dress fittings and other personal possessions

There are few personal possessions relating to dress, jewellery or other personal adornment from the Yarnton sites throughout the Iron Age and Romano-

British periods, which may suggest that the occupants of the settlement were not wealthy. However, two fairly prestigious pieces of metalwork were found, an openwork sheet fragment possibly from a bucket of 1st-century BC date and a fibula of Aesica type of Claudio-Neronian date, the latter associated with an early Roman cremation burial. It is suggested by Henig (Chapter 15) that the former may derive from a ritual deposit or even possibly a bucket burial. In total, six other brooches were recovered, all of early Roman date. Fragments of two bracelets, a pin and a buckle represent later Roman personal ornaments.

Personal items of dress relating to the Iron Age phases of the site are even more sparse. Three fragments of shale bracelets were fund in pits, one of the early Iron Age and the others from the middle Iron Age. A polished jet earring also came from a middle Iron Age pit. A decorated bone toggle, possibly a dress accessory, was of middle Iron Age date and a single bone pin fragment was late Iron Age..

Other items, such as knives, represented by possible antler handles and iron knife blades, may also have been personal items. At least one cheek piece from a bridle came from an early Iron Age context and demonstrates the use of horses for transport.

CRAFT ACTIVITY

Textile manufacture

There are several strands of evidence pointing to textile production at Yarnton. Sheep were present in reasonably large numbers (if minimum numbers of individuals are calculated for the animal bone assemblage; Mulville *et al.*, Chapter 17), although they are less important than cattle until the late Roman period when they became the most numerous animal reared. The evidence suggests that animals were mainly reared for meat and that wool production would have been a relatively small-scale domestic activity. There are five combs, four of antler and one of bone, of early and middle Iron Age date. Although conventionally described as weaving combs, their function is by no means certain. A minimum of 26 triangular loomweights have been identified, of which around half come from middle Iron Age contexts and approximately five from early Iron Age contexts. Various bone tools such as the polished sheep/goat tarsals may also be connected with textile production. At least five spindle-whorls have been recorded from the site, dating from the early Iron Age to the early Roman period. A pair of iron shears from an unstratified context could have been used for shearing sheep or cutting cloth, but it is uncertain if they are of Iron Age or Roman (or even later) date.

In contrast to the Saxon period when there is clear evidence for the growth and processing of flax and hemp, there are no indications from the Iron Age and Roman plant or pollen records for the use of these plant materials for fibres or dyeing. However, waterlogged features of these periods, the most likely context in which they would have been discovered, have not been found on the Yarnton sites. Flax is only occasionally found as charred remains.

It is possible that some of the bone tools were used for processing animal hides, and some of the numerous postholes found on the site could have been supports for racks for stretching hides.

Bone working

There is evidence for the small-scale manufacture of tools from antler in the early Iron Age. At least three pieces of manufacturing debris or unfinished objects came from features of this period and the individuality of many of the decorated antler objects, in particular the weaving combs, suggests local manufacture.

Metallurgy and smithing

In general, only small quantities of metalworking debris were recovered from the site. However, a significant amount of this was from early and middle Iron Age contexts on Cresswell Field, pointing to small-scale iron and copper working at this time. Very little slag or other metalworking debris came from the later Iron Age or Romano-British contexts. The early Iron Age evidence includes four or five crucible fragments and 14 complete or nearly complete smithing hearth bottoms, but the relatively small amount of slag found indicates that the amount of high temperature smithing activity (welding) was very limited. Evidence for copper working came in the form of two small fragments of slag. The quantity of metalworking debris recovered from middle Iron Age contexts at Cresswell Field is considerably less than that from the Early Iron Age. This could be a reflection of the shift in the focus of activity to the east (the Yarnton site) in the middle Iron Age phase. A semi-circular post-built structure (803, see above) at the western edge of the Yarnton site may, on the basis of its unusual plan and, more particularly, finds of metalworking debris from the ditches and pits within and surrounding it, have been a smithy.

The iron-working debris from all the later contexts could well be redeposited from these earlier episodes or transported from activity further to the east as the settlement shifted. The only later material came from late Iron Age/early Roman hearth 852 where *in situ* smithing seems to be represented by a fragment of hearth lining with attached smithing slag and a fragment of tuyère block. Metallurgical analysis of four items of Romano-British date (Gilmour, Chapter 15 below) showed the use of recycled iron in at least one piece, a knife, suggesting perhaps that iron was a relatively scarce resource. Two iron punches recovered from late Romano-British contexts may have been smiths' tools.

Whetstones would have been essential implements, both for sharpening new metal tools, and for subsequently keeping any blades in trim. Later prehistoric whetstones have not been recorded very frequently in Oxfordshire, but two whetstones were found in a middle Iron Age pit (8786) at Cresswell Field. One is a slab-shaped example of imported Pennant sandstone, the other a faceted piece of sarsen. Casually-collected pebbles must also have been utilised, as for instance an example from middle/late Bronze Age pit 8031. Whetstones of Kentish Ragstone occur widely on Roman sites, and these often became worn to a rod shape, as did the example from a late Romano-British layer (354). These whetstones of calcareous sandstone may have been used for relatively fine-grained honing.

Cobbles of hard stone with battered surfaces seem best described as anvil stones, and could have been used for small-scale metalworking, particularly for hammering objects into shape since there is no evidence for processes associated with primary iron production. Both the finds from Yarnton are quartzite cobbles. One came from a late Romano-British posthole (610), but may be an Iron Age artefact re-used as post packing, while the other was from a late Bronze Age/early Iron Age pit (8127).

Pottery production and use

Traditionally, most Iron Age handmade pottery has been regarded as locally made on demand or seasonally within the domestic sphere. However, some later prehistoric pottery was part of a more complex production system and, particularly from the middle Iron Age period, there were a number of specialist production centres such as those producing Glastonbury and Malvernian wares (Peacock 1967; 1968). These particular vessels are distinctive either in terms of their fabric or style; other wares may be less distinctive but could equally have been the product of specialised potters.

The Yarnton Iron Age pottery typically comprises a diverse range of fabric types, the constituents of which are potentially available locally. A small number of vessels stand out as distinctively different and are thus likely to represent imports to the site, notably a highly-decorated vessel in the All Cannings Cross style. Although no later prehistoric pottery production sites have been identified from the immediate area it would seem likely that most of the pottery from Yarnton was locally produced. Shelly wares are the most commonly represented fabric in the early Iron Age. An analysis by Jonathan Dempsey concluded that the shell was of fossil origin and that the principal fossil type utilised was *Gryphaea*, which was readily available in the Thames gravel terraces of the Oxford region (Chapter 14). Of the other inclusions encountered, the nearest limestone source is about 8 km distant to the north-west, and greensand could be obtained from Boars Hill some 10 km south of the site, although there is some evidence from elsewhere that glauconitic sandy wares may have been the products of specialist potters and thus potentially traded items. One unusual fabric characterised by the presence of ironstone ooliths may derive from a source close to Banbury where the parent outcrop of Lower Jurassic ironstone occurs.

The only slight evidence for localised pottery production at the site in the Iron Age tenuously comes from three quartzite pebbles which were found with distinctive wear in the form of shiny, polished surfaces. One came from the fill of early Iron Age pit 7173, while a small fragment came from middle Iron Age pit 7783, both at Cresswell Field. The third example was from a late Romano-British gully (2562). There is a lesser degree of wear on part of a burnt quartzite pebble, an unstratified find (SF 3). Similar tools, utilising pebbles of quartzite and other materials, are of quite common occurrence on Iron Age and Roman sites. It has been suggested variously that they could have been used as pot-burnishers (Wainwright 1968, 137), as slickstones for leather working (Barford 1985, 130), or even as linen-smoothers (Fiona Roe pers. comm.). However two highly-polished stones found at a pottery production site at Cowley, Oxford were considered by the excavator to be pot-burnishing stones (Atkinson 1941, 15), and this may be the most likely interpretation of such wear traces.

Clay for structural use and for other fired clay objects such as the loomweights is likely to have been obtained locally and used directly on site for building or making objects or lining pits. Items such as loomweights are generally poorly fired and could have been fired in a bonfire or clamp kiln which would leave no trace.

Iron Age pottery use

Most of the pottery recorded from the Iron Age features comprised plain undecorated jars and bowls. Fine wares were the exception. A small number of decorated sherds were noted, and approximately 24.4% of the assemblage was burnished. A total of 23 sherds had a red-slipped surface finish. A range of decorative techniques was employed, including excision (of grooves), incision, finger-tipping, stabbing, impressing, stamping, rim notching and the application of cordons. In total these sherds account for only 1% of the Iron Age assemblage. In terms of vessel type, over 90% of the rims (on the basis of estimated vessel equivalents – EVE) were classified as jar forms. Identifiable bowls accounted for 4% of the assemblage and two miniature vessels were noted. Evidence for vessel use such as sooting, limescale, burnt residues was noted, but little significant patterning was observable in their occurrence in terms of form, fabric or chronology. Organic residue analysis on a selection of samples showed degraded animal fats to be the most frequently occurring lipid component, which correlates with the conclusions of animal bone analysis that there was an emphasis on meat production and consumption. Two samples produced evidence for beeswax, and leaf wax was found in a single example.

Roman pottery production

The Romano-British assemblage is by its nature more diverse, both in terms of form and fabric, and can more easily be attributed to source in terms of local, regional or continental origin. As might be expected, especially from an area where pottery production is well attested, the bulk of the wares was of local origin. Indeed, there is evidence for on-site production in the form of two kiln structures and other kilns are known in the immediate vicinity at Cassington (Case 1982a, 134, 136), Overdale (Boars Hill) (Harris and Young 1974) and Long Hanborough (Sturdy and Young 1976). The Yarnton kilns are dated to the early Roman period, but the quantity of pottery recovered was too small for precise characterisation. It appears to have been of transitional nature falling at the point of change from the later Iron Age-early post-conquest types to a more Romanised technology. The limited number of rims recovered appear to be mostly from large storage-type jar forms, with a single bowl. Burnished decoration had been employed.

The Yarnton kilns are unusual in having a twin-flue arrangement with a well-defined central pedestal. The presence of a fragment of a firebar suggests these would have been used to create a temporary floor on which to stack the vessels. The lack of wasters and other associated structures might suggest that this activity was relatively short-lived.

Roman pottery use

The dominant vessel type throughout the Roman period was the jar, accounting for 86.5% by EVE in the later Iron Age-early Roman period, 80% in the early Roman period and 72.8% in the later Roman period. Most of the jars occur in reduced wares or in the 'Belgic' range of wares. Perhaps surprisingly for an agriculturally based settlement, large storage jars only contribute 3-4% of the total jar assemblage. Although a dominance of jars is to be expected, the overall percentage of these vessels appears slightly higher at Yarnton compared to other contemporary sites in the region. Such a conservative range of material is often seen as characteristic of lower-status rural settlements.

The second most common type was the bowl, accounting for 11.2% of the pottery assemblage in the later Iron Age/early Roman period declining to 7.6% in the early Roman period, but increasing to 9.2% of the late Roman assemblage. This general trend is replicated elsewhere in the later Roman period. Table wares are almost negligible with very small quantities of flagons, no platters and very few drinking vessels such as cups, beakers or tankards. Other specialised wares such as mortaria appear in the early Roman period, showing an increase in the later Roman period to 3.4% of the assemblage. With the exception of an early Verulamium example, these are all locally-made products. A single cheese press was also found in the later Roman deposits.

TRADE AND EXTERNAL CONTACT

Evidence for trade or contact with other areas comes from a range of artefact types, including coins, pottery, briquetage, and quernstones. Some items of personal dress or adornment, in particular of metalwork, shale and jet, and other personal equipment and tools, such as a fragment of shale vessel and some of the metalwork (for example the early Iron Age adze and the later, high-quality knives) were also evidently imported to Yarnton. Nevertheless it is clear from a general scarcity of evidence for high quality finds and traded goods, and the small-scale nature of the various craft activities, that Yarnton was a relatively self-sufficient agricultural community.

The Yarnton sites have produced a total of 14 fragments of Droitwich briquetage (salt container) in contexts ranging in date from the early to middle Iron Age through to the early 2nd century, although the material from the latter is probably redeposited. These vessels demonstrate links of some 100 km to the north-west and show how important salt was as a commodity at this time. Yarnton lay, however, at the south-east margin of salt distribution from Droitwich, and salt may have reached the site from other sources as well, but these cannot be identified in the archaeological record.

Although the Roman pottery assemblage is moderately diverse, the incidence of both regional and continental imports is relatively low. Sherds of samian tableware account for less than 1% overall (by sherd count and weight). Other foreign imports represented by single sherds include North Gaulish *terra nigra* and 'Rhenish' ware. Only four sherds of amphorae were recorded; two Spanish Dressel 20 olive-oil containers, one Gallic wine amphora and one from an uncertain source. It is debatable if any of the amphorae arrived on site with their original contents, or even as complete vessels.

A variety of regional wares are present. Amongst the earlier, dating to the later Iron Age or early Roman period, are three sherds of Malvernian limestone-tempered ware and one sherd of Clee Hills dolerite-tempered ware. This material may have come along routes already established by the salt trade. Yarnton probably falls at the extreme limit of the distribution for these wares which are more frequent on contemporary sites in the Lechlade and Fairford area, such as Thornhill Farm (eg Timby 2004a, 107) and Horcott gravel pit (Timby forthcoming). Other early Roman regional imports include a small quantity of Savernake ware from Wiltshire. In the Roman period proper, Yarnton had access to a small amount of Dorset black burnished ware, constituting approximately 1.2% by weight of the total assemblage. Products from the east include those from Verulamium kilns (at least one mortarium) and some Lower Nene Valley colour-coated ware, whilst a few sherds of Severn Valley ware demonstrate some continued links to the west. In the late Roman period, a single sherd of New Forest colour-coated ware was recorded and pink-grogged ware from Buckinghamshire was present. Some of the Roman shelly wares may also potentially originate from the late Roman industry based at Harrold in Bedfordshire. Overall, whilst there is a diversity of non-local material documented, the quantities are small and perhaps obtained from a local market with a regional catchment.

Querns

Yarnton querns were made from all the main lithic materials that have been recorded in use in the Upper Thames Valley during both Iron Age and Roman times. The three main saddle quern materials that were in use during the Iron Age at Yarnton were Lower Calcareous Grit from the Corallian, Lower Greensand from around Culham, and sarsen, all available in Oxfordshire. A somewhat conservative element was involved, since all had been in use in the area since the Neolithic (Roe forthcoming a). Although the Upper Thames Valley was an area well supplied with varieties of reasonably good-quality quernstone, some saddle querns of May Hill sandstone were imported from north-west Gloucestershire, mainly during the middle Iron Age; the one Oxfordshire find of this material known to date from an early Iron Age context is from Cresswell Field. Only one saddle quern from Yarnton was made from the local Jurassic limestone. This quern material has not been often recorded, possibly because of poor survival, or poor recognition, although it may simply have been utilised less frequently than the harder sandstones.

Saddle querns seem to have continued in use in the Upper Thames Valley until quite late in the Iron Age. One possible reason could be that the local saddle quern materials were not found to be satisfactory for making rotary querns, which in this area were nearly all made from a different range of materials. It may have taken time to organise the new supplies of stone for rotary querns from outside the region. It is not easy to see when the changeover to rotary querns took place. Many sites with Iron Age occupation, including Yarnton, also have a subsequent Roman phase. As a result, many pieces of Iron Age quern, and indeed other finds, are found redeposited in Roman contexts. Just a few sites that have only Iron Age occupation demonstrate a consistent choice of saddle quern materials during this period. At Mingies Ditch, for example, occupation was restricted to the middle Iron Age, and here saddle querns of the same materials as those from Iron Age Yarnton are known to have been still in use during the 3rd century BC (Allen and Robinson 1993, 140). Often precise dating information is not available, but at Bicester Fields Farm a saddle quern of May Hill sandstone was discarded during a late middle Iron Age to late Iron Age phase (Cromarty *et al.* 1999, 198).

At Yarnton, the earliest rotary quern is one made from Lodsworth stone from a late Iron Age context. There are signs that a few querns made from this Sussex stone were beginning to arrive in Oxfordshire as early as the early Iron Age, with fragments of this date known from Gravelly Guy (Lambrick and Allen 2004, 339; Ingle 2004) and middle Iron Age examples from Abingdon Vineyard (Roe, Chapter 15 below). At the Vineyard, a high-status site by the late Iron Age, if not earlier, there was also a single rotary quern of Millstone Grit from a middle Iron Age context. The introduction of rotary querns may have been a gradual process, with the main impetus apparently coming from the Lodsworth quarries to the south-east of Oxfordshire, perhaps aided by ease of transport up the Thames. Contacts with Gloucestershire were still being maintained, however, and fragments of both May Hill sandstone and Lodsworth stone were found in the same middle Iron Age pit at Abingdon Vineyard (ibid.). The Bicester Fields Farm quern (above), may represent one of the latest of these saddle quern imports after what may have been several centuries of use in the area. Some fragments of Upper Old Red Sandstone came from early/middle Iron Age contexts at Gravelly Guy (Lambrick and Allen 2004, 372-3), but appear to have belonged to saddle querns. This quern material was to be extensively used in the area during the Roman period.

With the advent of rotary querns at Yarnton, the changeover to an almost completely different set of quern materials is striking. Here, in addition to the Lodsworth quern from a late Iron Age context, rotary querns from Romano-British contexts, or else unstratified, were all made from stone brought in from some distance away, from the Forest of Dean, the Pennines and the Rhineland. In the Upper Thames Valley generally, these sources of quernstone, as well as the Sussex source for Lodsworth greensand, were in regular use during the Roman period. Roman sites with no previous Iron Age occupation demonstrate most clearly the complete changeover to imported materials. At Asthall for example, Upper Old Red Sandstone and Millstone Grit were in use (Booth 1997a, 100), while at Mill Street, Wantage, Niedermendig lava was additionally found (Holbrook and Thomas 1996, 152). Lodsworth stone is also attested from a number of local Roman sites, including Alchester (Roe 2001, 248-50) and Dorchester-on-Thames (Frere 1962; Ashmolean Museum).

A technological innovation which arrived in the Roman period, although again it cannot be closely dated, is the use of mechanical mills, with millstones that could be up to a metre in diameter. These provided a considerably greater grinding capacity than Roman rotary querns, which average some 400 mm in diameter. The increased production of flour must have been a valuable asset at a time of growing population. One millstone fragment from Yarnton is made from Upper Old Red Sandstone quartz conglomerate, and came from a late Romano-British pit. With a diameter of *c* 750 mm and a thickness (now) of 120 mm, it would have been too heavy to work manually. The millstones from Barton Court Farm also come from a late Roman context (Miles 1986, 47 and fiche 5:A13), and were made from Millstone Grit. The same Pennine stone was used for a probable millstone found unstratified at Yarnton (SF 226). Roman mills seem to have been fairly common by the 2nd century, and the Niedermendig lava millstone from Mill Street, Wantage could be this early, with a suggested time bracket from the mid 2nd century to the mid 3rd or early 4th century (Holbrook and Thomas 1996, 152; see also Booth *et al*. 2007, 298-9).

Personal and other items: metalwork, shale and jet

A relatively high proportion of the personal items (see above) of Iron Age and Roman date are likely to have been imported. This would certainly apply to objects of shale, most likely from the Kimmeridge area of Dorset where an extensive shale industry was in operation during the Iron Age and Roman periods. As well as the shale bracelets these included a single vessel fragment, decorated with a cordon and beading below, from a middle Iron Age pit. Another certain import is a single jet earring, probably from the Whitby or York areas, found in a middle Iron Age context.

Other personal dress items unlikely to have been locally made include the seven brooches, two penannular bracelets and late Roman buckle. The latter is in a well-known style for which a number of parallels can be identified, suggesting a specialist metalworker. An openwork sheet fragment in the form of a helmet, and interpreted as a bucket fitting, is a particularly prestigious piece dating to the late Iron Age but from an early Roman context; it is also undoubtedly an import to the site. The superior quality of some of the knives (Gilmour, Chapter 15), might suggest that some of the ironwork was also imported to the site. The early Iron Age adze is also unlikely to have been a local product

Amongst the other items recovered from later phases of the site are 43 late Roman coins. Further unprovenanced coins have been recovered from the area, of which some 20 or so examples have been examined. All appear to date to the late 3rd or 4th century. The assemblage is typical of late Roman low status rural settlements in the region and indicates a low level of commerce.

FOOD PRODUCTION AND CONSUMPTION

The settlement at Yarnton was located in a landscape rich in natural resources. The floodplain and gravel terraces provided two ideal environments for the grazing of cattle and production of arable crops respectively, the two main food staples visible in the archaeological record. The environmental evidence has demonstrated cereal cultivation with the growing of barley and spelt wheat and the presence of storage pits, corn-drying ovens, quernstones and cooking vessels provides evidence for the processing and consumption of grain. The animal bone shows that cattle were dominant through most periods, with other species providing supplementary meat. In addition to meat, the animals kept are also likely to have contributed secondary products such as milk and cheese. Analysis of residues on pottery sherds has identified degraded animal fats in a number of samples. Perhaps surprisingly, in view of the proximity of the river, very little fish bone was recovered, but this is in line with a broad national trend in which fish remains are poorly-represented on lower status Roman rural sites (Locker 2007, 158) and barely at all earlier. Salt would have provided a valuable commodity for preserving perishable foodstuffs, in particular meat, and for cow licks. Imported commodities such as olive oil, wine and garum (fish sauce) popular in the Roman world and prolific at the larger Roman towns, are hardly visible at Yarnton where only four amphora sherds were recorded. It is possible that other vessels were used to transport both smaller quantities of materials normally carried in amphorae, as well as other foodstuffs.

Plant cultivation

Charred plant remains revealed the presence of wheat (*Triticum* sp.) and to a lesser extent barley (*Hordeum vulgare*). The most commonly represented species was *Triticum spelta,* one of the principal crops of the Iron Age in the Thames Valley. A number of weed seeds were identified, some of which may have been deliberately harvested, in particular the larger non-cereal grass seeds such as *Bromus*. Some oat grains were present in some of the samples but most of these are likely to be non-cultivated varieties. Other edible plants amongst the carbonised remains were limited to hazel nut. No other crop remains were recovered.

Animal husbandry

Some 38% (by NISP, see Chapter 17) of all the animal bone recovered came from early Iron Age contexts with slightly less in the middle Iron Age and still smaller but roughly equal amounts from the late Iron Age, later Iron Age/early Roman and late Roman periods. Overall the assemblage is made up of approximately one third cattle, one quarter sheep/goat and one twentieth pig if animal presence is calculated by numbers of bone fragments (NISP). Large (cattle sized) mammal and medium (sheep sized) mammal bones each represent a further 12% of the total assemblage. Other domestic species include horse and dog. Wild mammals only contribute a very small percentage to the assemblage and these include red deer, roe deer, wild pig, hare and fox. Comparison of the domestic species based on the more reliable data for the minimum number of individuals (MNI) shows a steady fall in the percentage of cattle over time from a peak of 53% in the middle Iron Age to a mere 27% in the late Roman period. The representation of sheep is more consistent at a little over one third until the later Roman period when they show an increase to 50%. Pig is present throughout but best-represented (at *c* 15%) in both early and late Roman periods, whilst records for horse peak in the late Iron Age/early Roman period. Dog is most common in the early Roman period, at 6%, whereas it never amounted to more than 3% of the assemblage in other periods, its apparently high incidence in the early Iron Age (9% of NISP) reflects the occurrence of articulated dog remains in pits at this time. Overall, the data suggest a significant increase in the importance of sheep at the expense of cattle in the later Roman period, but with neither species totally dominant in the settlement economy at any time.

The rich floodplain grass would have been ideal for the fattening of cattle, especially in the summer months when drier conditions prevailed, with animals possibly being moved to higher ground in the winter. The large number of enclosures evident, particularly in the later Iron Age and early Roman periods, were probably for stock management.

For all periods, the first peak in cattle slaughter occurs when the animals are between 8 and 30 months, when they had reached full body size. A second peak in the death rate occurs when the animals were older and were perhaps being culled. The slaughter rate for the sheep also supports a meat production model with most of the animals killed before their third year. In conclusion, the animal bone demonstrates that there is perhaps a greater emphasis on prime animals in the Roman period compared to the Iron Age. This has been observed elsewhere and interpreted as indicative of a husbandry system in the Roman period focusing on meat and wool production (King 1991).

Analysis of the skeletal elements at Yarnton showed that for cattle and pig, limb bones predominate, suggesting either the importation of joints of meat (which is very unlikely) or differential disposal of meat and waste elements. A general lack of calves and lambs on the site may perhaps be a consequence of poor preservation, but could also suggest the existence of an extensive farming system with animals breeding away from the settlement focus and only food animals brought in as required.

Food storage and processing

In the Iron Age period, large numbers of pits of various shapes and sizes were dug on the settlement sites, many of which could have been used for grain storage. Some of the four-post structures identified may also have supported above-ground granaries. By the late Iron Age/early Roman period, not only had the number of pits decreased but their size range was smaller and cylindrical pits no longer dominated, suggesting that proportionately fewer pits were used for grain storage. This probably reflects a change in storage practice from below to above ground. The evidence strongly suggests that at Yarnton the grain may have been stored as spikelets or even on the sheaf, and was processed on a regular basis, as required.

In the late Roman period, at least three 'corn-drying' ovens were built on site. These structures have traditionally been linked with the drying of grain, but it is likely that they were multi-functional structures and could have been used for the roasting of germinated grain for the production of malt (although no direct evidence for this was recovered at Yarnton) as well as for drying grain prior to grinding or storage. A T-plan corn-drying oven was excavated at Barton Court Farm, Abingdon from which a quantity of carbonised barley grain was recovered (Miles 1986). The grain had chitted (sprouted), the point at which in the malting process grain is roasted to terminate germination. Experiments carried out by Reynolds and Langley (1979) confirmed that such structures functioned more successfully as malting floors than as grain dryers. A review of the botanical evidence by Van der Veen (1989) also concludes that these structures were multi-functional.

Querns would have played an important part in daily life at Yarnton, since they would have been used to make wholemeal flour for bread, and any other food that provided the carbohydrate component of meals. Substantial food of this nature must have been part of the staple diet, and would have been especially needed by those engaged in hard agricultural work. Quernstones were found in deposits of all periods, with a change from saddle querns to rotary querns in the late Iron Age to early Roman period and the addition of millstones later in the Roman period. While the general sequence of development is clear from the point of view of technology, it is difficult to identify specific contexts of use, though it is likely that each household processed sufficient flour or meal for its own requirements, except perhaps in the later Roman period, when the likely use of a mill might imply more centralised processing of grain, whether or not each household produced its own basic material.

Butchery marks were observed on some of the animal bones, including horse, although this species is considered to be of minor importance in terms of meat production. Butchery evidence was much less common in the early and middle Iron Age periods than later, however (3-4% as opposed to *c* 10%). The body-part distribution of cattle suggests a bias towards exploitation of meat bearing elements up to the late Roman period, at which point there is a change to both prime and lesser meat bearing elements.

The preponderance of jars in the pottery assemblage is commensurate with an agriculturally-based rural society and also, in reflecting the preponderance observed in the early and middle Iron Age periods, an essentially conservative one in which traditional patterns of vessel use, favouring multi-purpose jars rather than the diversity of functionally-specific vessels available in the Roman period, were maintained to a significant degree. Residue analysis has identified the presence of fatty acids in some vessels corresponding with the evidence for a strongly meat-based diet from the animal bone, and degraded beeswax which presumably served some other purpose, perhaps sealing vessels or candles. The presence of beeswax also implies that honey was available as a foodstuff to the Iron Age occupants of Yarnton, although the first direct evidence for the honey bee is an individual recovered from middle Saxon sediments in a palaeochannel on Oxey Mead (Robinson 2004, 409).

Finally water would have been a most important commodity for drinking, food preparation and other uses. It is notable that no wells were identified within the confines of the site and it has to be deduced that water was obtained directly from the nearest natural water sources adjacent to the settlement, for example the river channels to the south. If this was the case, water carrying would have been a significant activity in the daily life of the settlement.

Chapter 4: The Wider View

by Gill Hey

INTRODUCTION

The gravels of the Upper Thames Valley have become one of the most intensively investigated areas in southern Britain, and development, principally gravel extraction, has been the catalyst behind much of this research. This was as much true in the mid 19th century, when regional studies of the Iron Age began with the pioneering work of Stephen Stone, as it is today. Atypically for his time, Stone focused his attention on ordinary settlement, attempting to understand the deep pits, postholes and ditches of an unenclosed site in the Lower Windrush Valley (Stone 1856-9) and making a scale model of the features he saw (Bradford 1942a, pl. XXIX). His work set a trend for Iron Age research in the region which has continued ever since, enabling a fairly detailed understanding to be gained of Iron Age settlement patterns and land use in some areas of the valley (eg Lambrick 1992b; Lambrick 2009). Numerous rural sites of the Roman period have also been investigated, although the details of settlement layout on some of these sites remain a little uncertain (Henig and Booth 2000, 79-82; Booth *et al*. 2007, 42-79).

The scale of development has increased dramatically since the 1960s, with ever larger sites being investigated (Miles 1997) and large tracts of the countryside have been exposed in advance of some sizeable gravel quarries, enabling the excavation of hectares of late prehistoric and Roman remains. This has encouraged a wider perspective to be taken of settlement patterns and land use; there has never been a narrow, site-based focus. In addition, there has been a long tradition of environmental archaeology in the Upper Thames Valley and the investigation of the wider landscape context of excavated archaeological sites (Robinson 1992a). Since the innovative work of Martin Jones, David Miles and Mark Robinson unravelling the villa economy at Barton Court Farm in the late 1970s (Miles 1986), there has been a conscious effort to collect environmental data from archaeological and natural features both on- and off-site, and to integrate the evidence with data from the excavations. The results of research by, for example, George Lambrick, Mark Robinson and Tim Allen in the Lower Windrush Valley have shown how successful this can be. However, much less is known about Iron Age communal or higher status sites than about ordinary settlements, and comparatively little work has been done on hillforts, especially in the area around Yarnton, although understanding of the hillforts of the Berkshire Downs has been enhanced by recent work (Miles *et al*. 2003; Gosden and Lock 2003; Lock *et al*. 2005; Allen *et al*. 2010).

The extensive excavations that have taken place have not only revealed Iron Age and Roman sites, for archaeological remains from the Neolithic to the present day have been discovered. In particular, it has been possible to observe the development of communities from the Neolithic to the Iron Age in terms of settlement type, land use, the extent to which they transformed the landscape around them and their response to changing environmental conditions. Although this pattern is more easily seen in some parts of the valley than others, it is apparent that differences can be observed along its length. These differences may be particularly revealing about mechanisms of social change and interaction in the later prehistoric period (Hey 2007).

Yarnton has a particularly complete record of settlement from the Neolithic, with a continuous history of the use of the floodplain and terraces from the beginning of the 4th millennium BC to the modern day. Similar threads of settlement continuity can be observed elsewhere in the region as demonstrated by recent work in Gloucestershire at Horcott gravel pit near Fairford (Pine and Preston 2004; Lamdin-Whymark *et al*. forthcoming) and at Cotswold Community near Shorncote (Powell *et al*. 2010).

FROM THE LATE BRONZE AGE TO THE EARLY IRON AGE: A SOCIETY IN TRANSITION

Undefended domestic settlements of the late Bronze Age are not well represented in the region, but are increasingly coming to light. Typically, such sites comprise a scatter of pits and small numbers of post-built structures, for example those excavated at Eight Acre Field, Radley (Mudd 1995), Appleford (Hinchliffe and Thomas 1980) and several sites around Lechlade, such as Butler's Field (Jennings 1998). Late Bronze Age settlement has also been uncovered in an evaluation undertaken at Mead Farm, Eynsham, close to Yarnton (Miles 1997, 10). The extent of fieldwork at Yarnton has shown that settlement in this area centred on small individual households living in sites with single or paired structures surrounded by small pits and postholes and a waterhole. These were situated in open grassland and their subsistence economy was focused on

pastoralism with only very small quantities of cereals being grown (Robinson in Hey *et al.* forthcoming). It is uncertain how long individual sites were occupied, but they may represent single generation settlements.

As elsewhere in this part of the Thames Valley, no fields or boundaries have been discovered, in contrast to many parts of Middle and Lower Thames where field systems are a feature of the Bronze Age landscape (Yates 1999). Evidence of fields is also increasingly coming to light south of Abingdon and in the area around Dorchester-on-Thames (eg Booth and Simmonds 2009, 11-20). It is suggested that in the Middle and Lower Thames these field systems were associated with high-status sites, and are a manifestation of the agricultural intensification which was linked to the conspicuous consumption that is evident on these sites (Bradley and Yates 2007). It seems probable that field systems south of Abingdon were linked to the rich river island settlement at Wallingford and the site at Castle Hill, Little Wittenham (Hingley 1980; Lambrick 1992b, 86-8). No late Bronze Age sites of this type have yet been found between Abingdon and Lechlade and the model proposed for this region is of a continuum of traditional land use based on animal herding but with settlement becoming more permanent and, perhaps, rights over grazing land becoming more firmly established.

Large numbers of early Iron Age settlement sites have been found in the region, and the contrast with the late Bronze Age pattern is dramatic, at least in terms of its representation in the archaeological record. The Yarnton evidence suggests that this may be less the result of sudden population increase and more an artefact of changes in settlement location and lifestyle. There is no reason to believe, on the basis of the archaeological evidence, that more people lived in what later became the parish of Yarnton. Rather, people chose to stay in the same settlement area for generation after generation, shifting house plots only slightly as buildings were replaced and new ones built. Other domestic features, such as pits, were dug near to their predecessors, giving an appearance of density that may not be real.

Another reason why early Iron Age sites are so visible is that they are very often located on gravel terraces, where they are more readily detectable by archaeological survey techniques and where, until recently, gravel companies have focused their extraction activities. Although less work was undertaken on gravel terraces than on the floodplain at Yarnton, it is apparent that settlement was preferentially sited on the floodplain in the Bronze Age, on what had been traditional Neolithic grazing areas, although some funerary monuments were placed on higher ground and activity does appear to have been intensified on the gravel terrace sites in the later Bronze Age. Thus, small late Bronze Age households, which are difficult to find in the settlement record at the best of times, were sealed beneath floodplain silts and ploughsoils. They were detected purely by chance.

There are other new features of the early Iron Age settlement landscape, however, and these are related to changes in agricultural practice. Grain-storage pits are a common feature of early Iron Age settlement, and are highly visible in the archaeological record (Lambrick 1992b, 89-90). Their presence is associated with a dramatic increase in the quantities of cereals recovered from occupation sites. This suggests a shift in emphasis from pastoralism to a much more mixed agricultural regime, with cultivation undertaken in what appear to have been a series of shifting fields situated on the adjacent areas of gravel terrace. Nevertheless rearing of animals, particularly cattle, was still of great importance, and Yarnton, with its wide floodplain grasslands, would have been well positioned to maintain sizeable herds. Any surplus that the occupants made would have been in stock.

Settlement shift at Yarnton has been seen as a response to increasing flooding in the valley bottom at this time, as a result of widespread forest clearance in the Upper Thames catchment (Robinson and Lambrick 1984), and a rising water table on the lowest ground is evidenced from the middle Bronze Age (Hey *et al.* forthcoming). However, the evidence for flooding on the higher gravel islands within the floodplain at this time now appears more ambiguous than it did (Chapters 11 and 18), and it may be appropriate to ask whether changes in settlement location might have been associated with a desire to increase cereal production, whilst at the same time maximising floodplain land for grazing. The degree to which social pressures and the wider political context may have influenced these changes should also be considered, as they are so widespread. The appearance of hillforts in the area at the time (Allen 2000), particularly perhaps that at Bladon which is so close to the Yarnton site and also dominates the neighbouring settlements around Cassington, Yarnton and Begbroke, may be a manifestation of these processes, although it should be noted that the chronology of this site is uncertain.

IRON AGE SETTLEMENT

Yarnton, with its post-built structures and pits, is typical of open settlements of the Iron Age in the area. A number of these sites have been excavated in advance of gravel extraction including Gravelly Guy, a settlement occupied throughout the Iron Age (Lambrick and Allen 2004), City Farm, Hanborough (Case *et al.* 1964-5), Roughground Farm, Lechlade (Allen *et al.* 1993) and Ashville/Wyndyke Furlong (Parrington 1978; Muir and Roberts 1999). As with the site at Gravelly Guy, analysis of the dense settlement features has shown that at any one time there may only have been a few families occupying the site. Settlement around Abingdon may have been more intensive. Continuity of settlement through the early and middle Iron Age is also common, for example at Gravelly Guy (Lambrick and Allen 2004), Abingdon Vineyard (Allen 1990e), Vicarage Field, Stanton Harcourt (Thomas 1955) and Mount Farm, Dorchester (Myres 1937; Lambrick 1979a; 2010).

These settlements all seem to have been small self-sufficient communities with mixed agricultural economies. Social organisation within settlements has been elucidated as a result of the very detailed excavations at Gravelly Guy, in which it was possible to excavate virtually all of the Iron Age settlement, including around 800 pits. George Lambrick has pointed out that this represents approximately one pit for every year of occupation, and has estimated that this would store enough seed for the site's arable fields (Lambrick and Allen 2004, Chapter 12). He suggests that the house areas are differentiated, and that the enclosures opening out from them indicate that each house had its own animal enclosures. Crop husbandry, however, may have been managed on a settlement level. This pattern is of interest because it suggests that arable farming, which was new on this scale, was a communal activity whereas traditional family ownership of herds may represent continuity from an earlier period.

Enclosed settlements, usually of relatively small size, appear to predominate on the upland slopes (Hingley 1984), and in the middle Iron Age they began to appear on the Thames floodplain. A number of these sites have been excavated, for example at Farmoor (Lambrick and Robinson 1979) and Mingies Ditch in the lower Windrush Valley (Allen and Robinson 1993), and have been shown to be small pastoral establishments. Their presence is widespread on the Thames floodplain from the Dorchester (Baker 2002) and Abingdon areas (Everett and Eeles 1999) to the upper reaches of the Thames, for example at Cotswold Community (Powell *et al.* 2010, 74-80). Hingley (1984) has suggested that these sites represent single family units engaging in animal herding, in contrast to open settlements which were more densely occupied and had a mixed farming regime.

A small number of these sites have been located from the air and in field evaluation in the south-west of the Yarnton-Cassington study area, and limited excavation has shown them to be middle Iron Age in date (Chapter 11). No such sites have been discovered on the Yarnton floodplain, in spite of extensive fieldwork. A substantial boundary ditch was dug across the floodplain between Yarnton and these small sites at Cassington at this time, the first such boundary to be formed in this area. It may have served to demarcate the valuable grassland resources of different communities. This is a different pattern to the one that has emerged in the Lower Windrush Valley, where there appears to have been a shared strategy for communal grazing amongst the settlements which were located on the edge of the Second Gravel Terrace surrounding the late Neolithic Devil's Quoits circle henge (Lambrick 1992b). The henge was a major ceremonial monument and, as people gathered at such sacred sites, it seems likely that a communal pattern of grazing would have become established. As communities settled permanently, traditional land-use patterns seem to have become fossilised as the agricultural pattern around intensified (Lambrick 1999). It is possible that other groups still retained access to grazing rights, even if they were not permanently settled in the immediate area, limiting options to change land use.

There is considerable evidence of Neolithic and Bronze Age activity in the Yarnton-Cassington area, but there is no major ceremonial focus. Activity was generally small in scale and, importantly, was mainly domestic in character. The evidence suggests repeated, though not permanent use of the floodplain in the Neolithic with more permanent occupation by the end of the Bronze Age in a widely cleared landscape with small patches of scrub. By that time small pastoral farms were set in grazed grassland with little evidence of cereal cultivation and no field systems, representing a more individualistic settlement pattern. Around Yarnton each habitation site seems to have developed its own strategy to cope with changing environmental circumstances and pressure on land and at Yarnton at least, it is possible to claim that the floodplain remained a critical resource, as it always had been for this community. Therefore, the pattern in the Yarnton area in the Iron Age does not resemble that in the Lower Windrush Valley, even though it was still very heavily influenced by traditional land-use patterns, in a long trajectory that first became established in the Neolithic period. Repeated, recurrent activity became gradually fossilised into permanent, settled ways of life (Hey 2007). These differences between areas with apparently similar economic and settlement patterns indicate the subtle distinctions that existed in the settlement record in the valley.

There is some evidence to suggest that agriculture intensified at this time (Chapter 2 and 18), in line with other areas of the Thames Valley (Lambrick 1992b) and southern Britain (Cunliffe 1984d). Movement across the floodplain, presumably with herds, is evidenced by a number of sand-and-gravel causeways constructed over channels as the volume of water flowing within them increased, especially in the winter months. One causeway, however, was special. A limestone causeway, constructed of several tons of stone brought from over 4 km away, was placed across one of the major channels at what had probably been an earlier crossing point (Chapter 11; Fig. 11.20). Wooden uprights seem to have formed guide markers across the causeway. A foundation deposit included a Bronze Age side-looped spearhead which had been kept as an heirloom and deposited at the same time as the stone in the period *380-210 cal BC (95% probability)* (Chapter 13; Fig. 13.6). Other metal finds were recovered from the causeway (Northover, Chapter

15 and in Hey *et al.* forthcoming), but the most surprising discovery was a large deposit of animal bone, representing over 30 cattle, as well as horse, red deer and other animals, which had been spread across the surface. There was a significant bias towards the deposition of the right limbs of these animals (Mulville *et al.*, Chapter 17). It is suggested that this was feasting debris. This site adds to the range of wet places, especially river channels, where deliberate deposits were made in the Iron Age, of which Flag Fen and Fiskerton are obvious examples (Pryor 2001; Field and Parker Pearson 2003).

Another possible indicator of variability between settlements at this time lies in the burial record. As with its counterparts in the Upper Thames Valley and in southern Britain generally (Wait 1985; Hill 1995), disarticulated human remains at Yarnton were buried within pits in the settlement, often as single bones, along with other placed deposits. Formal burial is rare and these occasional finds of human bone appear to represent the norm (Fitzpatrick 1997, 82). For a relatively short period during the third century BC (*1-220 years; 95% probability*) (Chapter 13; Fig. 13.1B), however, people in Yarnton were buried within a small cemetery on the east side of the site. Thirty-five bodies were discovered and these were generally crouched and lying on their sides, usually on a north-south alignment (eg Fig. 6.42). They had been placed in shallow graves with no accompanying grave goods, and represent a cross section of the population, with women, men and children present. This cemetery is unusual in the archaeological record, although more sites of this type are coming to light as a result of the greater tendency to investigate wider landscapes beyond settlement sites, for example at Suddern Farm near Danebury in Hampshire (Cunliffe and Poole 2000), and its significance remains uncertain. It could be argued that such cemeteries exist outside most settlement areas but that they are not usually sought. However, it seems unlikely that this could account for such a striking absence in the archaeological record. In addition, interment at Yarnton was not a long-lived practice, and through most of the Iron Age the dead of Yarnton seem to have been treated in the same way as others in southern Britain.

THE 1ST CENTURIES BC AND AD

During the late Iron Age, the settlement at Yarnton changed as did other sites in the Upper Thames Valley (Miles 1997, 16-7). The distinctive features of post-built roundhouses, sometimes encircled by gullies or ditches and always accompanied by large pits, disappear and houses are less easy to identify (Allen 2000, 20-2). This may indicate the adoption of construction materials and designs which leave little archaeological trace, for example cob or turf walls, or timber structures on sleeper beams, as has been suggested for this widespread phenomenon in southern Britain (Allen *et al.* 1984). Some houses are represented by incomplete ovals of postholes, or arcs of gully, but surviving roundhouse gullies, such as those found at Bicester Fields Farm, are generally rare in Oxfordshire (Cromarty *et al.* 1999). Rural settlement sites from the end of the Iron Age to the late Roman period at Yarnton, as elsewhere, are typified by ditched enclosures which were frequently re-dug and re-designed. It is apparent that some of these were intended to be animal enclosures, but the density of finds in others suggests that they may have been used as domestic enclosures. The extent of later settlement activity at Yarnton has made it difficult to disentangle individual phases of occupation, although three separate areas of occupation can be suggested (Chapters 7 and 8). The layout at sites like Old Shifford Farm (Hey 1995) and the first phase of occupation at Barton Court Farm, Abingdon (Miles 1986) provide clearer indications of the appearance of settlements at this time.

Unlike some other sites in the Upper Thames Valley, the settlement at Yarnton did not shift at this time (Lambrick 1992b, 82-4). At sites like Gravelly Guy, occupation continued into the late Iron Age, but was relocated onto the other side of the earlier linear pit boundaries and a gully (Lambrick and Allen 2004). Other sites in the Stanton Harcourt area underwent a similar change. At Yarnton, late Iron Age enclosures were laid out on top of middle Iron Age structures, pits and gullies, although the settlement focus shifted slightly eastwards.

The construction of large ditched enclosures may be taken to indicate intensification in animal rearing and production, with more animals being brought onto the settlement. The animal bone assemblage from the site does indeed indicate that animals were being raised for a longer period of time before being slaughtered, in order to allow them to reach their maximum meat-producing size, and it is suggested that this was an important component of the economic life of the settlement (Mulville *et al.*, Chapter 17). At the same time arable fields were laid out across the Yarnton landscape, within ditched boundaries, and the ploughsoils were being manured from the settlement. The main area of arable expansion was on the floodplain, and fieldwork has shown that all of the higher areas on the floodplain were ploughed at this time (Chapters 11 and 18); only in low-lying areas on the southern edge of the study area, on land close to the main course of the Thames, was pasture retained throughout the Roman period. Cultivation on the floodplain was undertaken in the face of deteriorating environmental conditions. As a result, ditches were dug to protect fields from flooding and alluvial silts can be seen to have filled these features and spilled through the entrances into them onto ploughed fields. The charred plant remains show that the higher gravel terraces continued to be ploughed. These two strands of evidence indicate that a considerable degree of effort was invested in increasing agricultural production, even though there are no particular signs of population increase within the Yarnton settlement itself (although it is uncertain to what extent further foci of domestic (and other) activity might have lain just to the north of the excavated area, both at this time and later in the Roman period). Animals must have been grazed on the banks of the Thames in the summer and on the clay lands north of the settlement in the winter when they were not corralled on the settlement site itself. Droveways leading through the fields from the settlement to these pastures were exposed during fieldwork.

The exact impetus behind the production of what might have been a substantial surplus is not known, but the possibilities have been discussed by Henig and Booth (2000, 79-82). The impact of taxation after the Conquest could help to explain these changes, although it has been suggested that the demands of the Roman army might have been quite easily met by the native population (cf Young 1986, 59; Millett 1990 56-9). Furthermore, the evidence suggests that the changes began in the late Iron Age (although they certainly accelerated in the early Roman period). It is possible, then, that the payment of tribute to the Iron Age elite may have been the catalyst for these developments. The artefactual record provides evidence of trade. Briquetage, for example, suggests the acquisition of salt, quernstones were imported from Sussex and Gloucestershire, and pottery may also have been imported (Morris, Roe, Chapter 15). There is, however, little to indicate that many imported or exotic objects arrived on the site in exchange for agricultural produce; quantities of traded material were always very small.

Defended sites reappear in the late Iron Age, with the refurbishment of existing defended sites and the creation of new sites such as the 'valley fort' at Cherbury close to the River Ock some 16 km south-west of Yarnton (Allen 2000, 22). Constructed some time after 200 BC, this was a multi-vallate structure with extra-mural settlement. Other similarly low-lying sites, though perhaps of rather different character, are known at Dyke Hills, Dorchester, and under modern Abingdon. The Big Enclosure at Cassington, only 2.5 km south-west of Yarnton, was also constructed at this time. It lay on a prominent ridge of Second Gravel Terrace overlooking the confluence of the Thames and the Evenlode (Case 1982a). It was only 10 ha in size and there appear to have been causeways across it which suggest that it may not have been completed, and there is little indication of contemporary activity within the enclosure, in contrast with the situation at Abingdon and perhaps also at Dyke Hills.

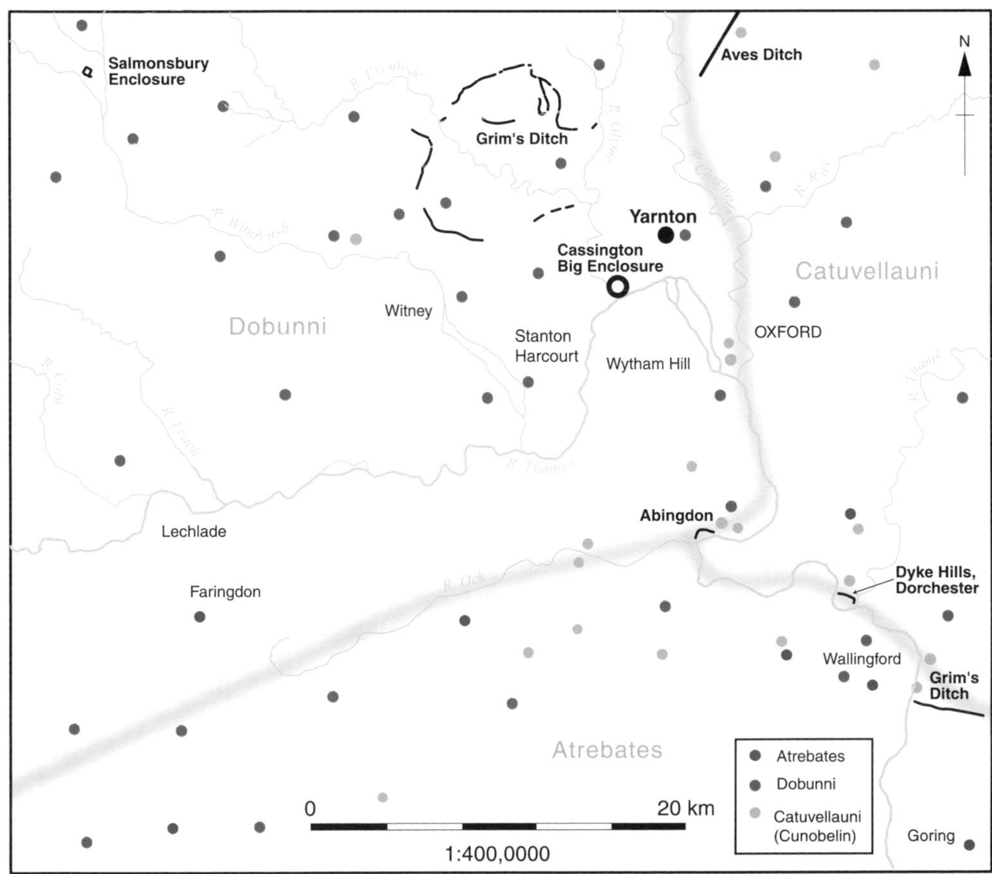

Fig. 4.1 Yarnton in relation to late Iron Age linear earthworks and coin distributions and hypothetical late Iron Age and Roman political boundaries

Nevertheless, the ditch was substantial and its position defensible. Allen has suggested that these sites were positioned to control riverine trade during the late Iron Age (Allen 2000, 24-5).

The North Oxfordshire Grim's Ditch lay 4.5 km north of Yarnton settlement, north of the confluence of the Rivers Evenlode and Glyme (Copeland 1988). It was a huge sub-circular ditch system which originally enclosed an area of 200 ha, but was later enlarged. A number of suggestions concerning its function have been put forward, including the possibility that it was associated with large-scale herding. Sauer (1999) has suggested that it might have been a Catuvellaunian stronghold lying within the territory of the Dobunni, but this is not generally accepted. Later in the Roman period, a number of wealthy villas lay within its circuit and this may indicate that it had been the location of similarly high-status settlement in the late Iron Age. The known villas include a significant proportion of those from the county with evidence for unusually early occupation, in the 1st century AD (Booth 1999a, 47-8).

Yarnton lies between the Grim's Ditch complex and the River Cherwell, the only major tributary of the Thames without a defended focus. For this reason, the river has long been seen as marking a boundary between two tribal territories, of the Dobunni and the Catuvellauni. Dobunnic coinage is generally found on the western side of its course and Catuvellaunian coinage to its east (Sellwood 1984a; fig. 4.1). Allen has pointed out that precise boundaries may be difficult to define by these means, as late Iron Age coinage may have circulated for up 30 years after it was minted, during which time boundaries may not necessarily have been static; although coins provide a general indication of the location of tribal groupings, there are a number of potential border areas where the distributions of different coinages are mixed (Allen 2000, 27-30). He suggests that Cassington may have been a Catuvellaunian fort built on the Evenlode facing the Dobunnic territory to the west. These issues are of considerable academic interest to us today, but it could be suggested that they would have been of greater concern to the inhabitants of Yarnton in the late Iron Age.

THE DEVELOPMENT OF YARNTON IN THE ROMAN PERIOD

Settlement at Yarnton changed only slowly over the period of Roman occupation. The occupation site continued to be dominated by ditched enclosures, and buildings and domestic areas were equally difficult to detect. This is a common pattern on Roman sites in this area (Henig and Booth 2000, 92-5). Enclosures became more rectangular over time, but it was only in the 3rd century AD that a system of clearly-defined, mainly rectilinear enclosures can be identified, with associated domestic and agricultural structures. A small inhumation cemetery developed to the south-east of the habitation area at this time. One of the burials, of a woman, had been decapitated and her head had been placed by her legs. A dog was placed across her knees.

Changes in potting techniques were amongst some of the more obvious developments in the early Roman period. Nevertheless the products of two small pottery kilns set up on the east edge of the settlement in the later 1st century AD, wheel-thrown wares in fabrics that were, perhaps, transitional between early post-Conquest 'Belgic types' and a more 'Romanised' (sandy grey ware) technology (Booth, Chapter 8), were recognisably grounded in late Iron Age traditions. Pottery ceased to be obtained from immediately local sources by the middle of the 2nd century at the latest, but the ceramic repertoire that was adopted, while containing occasional examples of several of the wider range of wares available in the region's markets, such as samian ware and possibly the occasional amphora (though whether with its original contents is uncertain), was conservative in character with regard to the range of preferred vessel types, remaining characteristically dominated by multi-purpose jars. Extra-regional imports were generally scarce (Booth, Chapter 14). The ceramic assemblage indicates that Yarnton remained a low-status site throughout the Roman period.

Some other material, such as Niedermendig lava as quernstone and Kentish Rag as whetstones, was imported from further afield (Roe, Chapter 15). The importance of the River Thames as a routeway is uncertain. It has been suggested that many products such as pottery would have been transported by these means (Young 1986) but other analyses do not readily support this view (Booth *et al.* 2007, 314-7) and it is clear that in strategic terms the river was of little importance (ibid., 36-7). While localised use is almost certain this is not clearly demonstrated by archaeological evidence. River transport might possibly have had a role in the transport of products acquired from the upstream direction, such as quernstones of May Hill Sandstone, Droitwich briquetage and Malvernian ware pottery, but it seems unlikely that this was on any significant scale.

Although Yarnton's economy was still based on agriculture, as in earlier periods, the late Roman period was a time of change. Fields on the floodplain suffered increasing flooding and were abandoned as arable agricultural land. The weed seeds that were found with charred cereal remains suggest that these fields were replaced by ploughlands on clay soils to the north of the site. Corn-drying ovens on the settlement site indicate some technological improvements in crop processing, as does the occurrence of millstones. The floodplain was once again used for the grazing of animals. The rearing of sheep became more important and that of cattle less so. This may indicate a more integrated agricultural strategy, as sheep are more readily folded onto stubble after harvest, and are a good source of manure for these fields (Mark Robinson pers. comm.). At the same time the range of animals consumed broadened throughout this period, with more pork being eaten along with other animals such as hare and bird. Bees were kept, although analysis of lipids in absorbed residues in pots suggests that beeswax was also available in the Iron Age (Copley *et al.*, Chapter 14). Palaeoenvironmental work at Farmoor has indicated that by the late Roman period even small rural communities would have been influenced by Roman eating habits, with herbs such as coriander and soft fruits such as plum being consumed (Lambrick and Robinson 1979, 120).

A number of Roman sites in the Lower Windrush Valley were abandoned or relocated during the course of the Roman period, and new sites were positioned on trackways that can be traced over considerable distances, connecting settlements in a manner that suggests the importance of these communication links and the more careful and intensive use of the landscape they traversed. These changes can be seen as part of a phase of more widespread changes which affected many sites in the Upper Thames Valley in the first half of the 2nd century, suggestive of extensive reallocation of landholding at this time (eg Henig and Booth 2000, 106-8). In the immediate area the location of the Worton settlement, Yarnton's neighbour to the west, shifted to the north of an east-west trackway and although this area has seen only minimal investigation the limited evidence is consistent with the view that this shift took place in the 2nd century. The Yarnton settlement did not follow this pattern, however, but remained on much the same site as in the earlier Roman period. Nevertheless, trackway ditches were laid out to the east and south of the site, suggesting the existence of routes westwards to Worton and north-eastwards to the site at Yarnton Sandy Lane (Fig. 2.1). It is apparent that these tracks, which were a particularly marked feature of the Upper Thames Valley landscape from the early 2nd century onwards, criss-crossed the Roman countryside and would ultimately have linked in to the main roadways of Roman Oxfordshire (ibid., 96-102). The north-south road from Dorchester to Alchester ran 10 km east of Yarnton, and a lesser but still important road crossing the Thames at Oxford and running north to a major settlement at Kings Sutton was only about 3 km to the east. Akeman Street lay only 8 km to the north. The nearest Roman town was at Alchester, 13 km away, but a number of other substantial roadside settlements lay on Akeman Street to the north and north-west of Yarnton, and the closest of these, at Sansom's Platt (Henig and Booth 2000, 63-4; Winton 2001), was barely 8 km distant. The status of Roman settlement at Oxford itself (eg Booth and Hayden 2000; Bradley *et al.* 2005) is uncertain, but it is possible that a minor nucleated settlement existed here as well. Connection to the wider settlement network and its markets was therefore quite possible.

The influence of villas and their inhabitants upon the rural communities close to the Thames is uncertain. A number of villas are known north of Yarnton, principally within the area of the North Oxfordshire Grim's Ditch as discussed above (Henig and Booth 2000, 90-2; fig. 4.1), and some of these may have been sufficiently close to have exerted social and economic influence, if not control, on the Yarnton inhabitants. Villas are of course rare within the Upper Thames Valley itself, the nearest known examples lying some distance upstream at Roughground Farm, Lechlade (Allen *et al.* 1993) and downstream at Barton Court Farm, Abingdon (Miles 1986). What is less certain is whether the lands of villa estates centred further north might have extended as far as the river. For Barton Court Farm, Jones (1986a) proposed a series of models for the size of the estate, ranging from 77-311 ha in area, with model C (*c* 162 ha) considered to have the best fit with the biological data (ibid., 42). The nearest known villa to the north of Yarnton is near Woodstock, some 5 km distant. Unless this or similar sites had much larger estates than that envisaged for Barton Court Farm, therefore, it is unlikely that Yarnton fell within the lands of such an estate, although the existence of separate subsidiary agricultural units within larger groups of holdings could perhaps be considered and could have made larger units viable. The presence of corn-drying ovens and millstones, both representative of crop-processing technologies of which the latter, in particular, was more commonly associated with villas than with low-status rural settlements in the Upper Thames Valley (Booth *et al.* 2007, 288-291, 298), might just provide a pointer in this direction. On balance, however, it seems as likely that the inhabitants of Yarnton belonged to a community holding land independently of what may have been quite extensive villa estates centred further north. This may have been a pattern that was widespread on the gravel terraces of the Upper Thames Valley. It is particularly notable that Yarnton, rather unusually for this area, was not obviously affected in a major way by the early 2nd century settlement pattern hiatus and reorganisation discussed above. It is not obvious why this should have been the case. It does not seem likely that the site was too insignificant to be considered worth including in this process, and it seems that settlement at nearby Worton was. Perhaps the location of the site at the very edge of the gravel terrace, and its close relationship with fields on the floodplain, gave it a particular and persistent character which meant that there was no clear advantage in relocating or reconfiguring the settlement area, though this can only be speculation.

Whatever the truth of the matter, the Yarnton settlement was at the same time linked into the wider landscape by trackways which will have provided the necessary access to appropriate local centres for purposes of Roman administration and marketing and trade, and yet only lightly impacted by the material correlates of such contact, with the partial exception of pottery and occasional other items, as discussed above. Overall the changes in material culture through the Roman period at Yarnton appear to have been both gradual and undramatic, in line with the trajectory of other sites of this general character. The incorporation of Britain into the Roman empire will undoubtedly have had direct impacts on the lives of the occupants of Yarnton, but these were not generally of a character that is directly recognisable in the archaeological record.

THE END OF ROMAN YARNTON

As discussed by Booth (Chapter 2), it is very difficult to date late Roman rural sites with any precision because of the paucity of the artefactual record. Yarnton did produce two coins which certainly post-dated AD 375 and a buckle fragment, probably of Hawkes and Dunning type IIIA, will have been of similar date. The significance of the latter is unclear, as comparable items are excessively rare in the region, being known only from Dyke Hills, Dorchester (Kirk and Leeds 1952/3, 64-6, no. 1; a second example was recovered from the Dyke Hills in 2010) with a further piece (in the Ashmolean Museum) reported to be from Oxford (Hawkes and Dunning 1961, fig. 20 f). Other late Roman quasi-official metalwork, such as buckles of Hawkes and Dunning type IB and related pieces, are more common in the area (eg Henig and Booth 2000, 181, fig. 7.1), but are not generally associated with low-status settlements. While no other clearly diagnostic material for the end of the 4th or early 5th centuries was recovered there is no reason to believe that the site was not occupied until at least the later 4th century.

The location of early Saxon settlements in the Yarnton locality within or immediately adjacent to Roman sites, and the presence of a sunken-featured structure within a late Roman enclosure, initially created considerable interest in the possibility of continuity of settlement on the site (Hey 2004, 37-40). However, analysis of the site evidence, particularly radiocarbon dating, and review of archives suggests that sites around the Yarnton, Cassington and Eynsham area seem to belong to a phase of Anglo-Saxon expansion at the end of the 5th or early in the 6th century (ibid., 40-3). It has been suggested that curious burials with late Roman finds excavated within the late Iron Age enclosure at Cassington are sub-Roman in date (Blair 1994, 11), but there is no definite dating for these and they are as likely to be late Roman, a period which sees considerable diversity in burial practice (Booth 2001), as demonstrated by the decapitated inhumation with associated dog from Yarnton itself. The Saxon grave goods at Cassington appear to date to the late 5th-7th centuries (Dickinson 1976, 65-7; Blair 1994, 11; Helena Hamerow pers. comm.). Pottery and radiocarbon assays from Yarnton suggest a late 5th- or early 6th-century date for the earliest Saxon structures (Hey 2004, chapters 1 and 5; fig. 13.1 *First start_Yarnton*) and, despite extensive excavation, there were no obvious signs of 'sub-Roman' activity on the Roman and Saxon site. No 5th-century finds have been recovered from either the Cresswell Field or Worton settlements. Recent excavations at Eynsham Abbey indicate that Saxon settlement there commenced in the 6th century (Hardy *et al.* 2003), and similar dates are suggested for occupation at New Wintles Farm and Purwell Farm (Arthur and Jope 1962-3; Hawkes and Gray 1969; fig. 1.10).

The question, however, is what form might 5th century evidence be expected to take in a region where identifiable material of the first half of the century is effectively absent. Moreover, despite the apparent absence of habitation through most of the 5th century, the environmental evidence demonstrates the presence of human occupation in the landscape around Yarnton throughout this period. The pollen record indicates that there was no regeneration of woodland, while the waterlogged plants and beetles recovered from Roman to Saxon layers in the old river channels which crossed the floodplain area do not even provide any evidence for the spread of scrub (Greig, Robinson, Chapter 18). As noted in Chapter 2, abandoned fields would rapidly acquire thorn scrub, and woodland-edge trees would be expected to have grown up by the end of the century. That this did not occur at Yarnton suggests that land was being cultivated or, more probably, grazed throughout these periods. The Upper Thames valley has not traditionally been thought to have extensive deposits suitable for pollen preservation, but recent work by Petra Day and Adrian Parker has revealed several locations with good pollen sequences. Day's work at Sidlings Copse, only 8 km east of Yarnton, also indicates no woodland regeneration in that area in the early Saxon period (Day 1991, 467); increasing woodland cover in the late Saxon or early post-Norman period probably reflects deliberate forestation of medieval Shotover Forest (Day 1989). Small quantities of pollen found in a Saxon well at Barton Court Farm, Abingdon suggested only a slight rise in tree and shrub pollen further south in the valley (Miles 1986, 52). Such evidence for the endurance rather than the collapse of agricultural systems in the 5th century is not unique to the Upper Thames valley. In East Anglia and Essex, for example, there appears to have been no woodland regeneration at this time, though there was a shift in emphasis from arable to pasture (Murphy 1994, 35-6), and a similar situation seems to have prevailed in Wessex (Bell 1989, 277-80; Higham 1992, 78-9).

At Barton Court Farm, the survival of an unusual weed occasionally found in flax fields, *Camelina allysum*, from the Roman into the Saxon period, strongly suggests continuing cultivation of flax over this period of time. At this site it was suggested that late Roman activity continued into the first half of the 5th century while early Saxon occupation may have commenced by the mid 5th century, even if this does not necessarily suggest direct contact between the British occupants and the Saxon settlers (Miles 1986, 49; see below). The material culture aspects of the late Roman part of this sequence were not significantly different from what is observed at Yarnton, only more numerous and therefore more readily identified, while the presence of stone buildings allowed destruction deposits to be isolated. The conclusions to be drawn from the Yarnton evidence, where the apparent gap in the occupation record is longer (in the middle quarters of the 5th century), are much less certain, but if the parallel with Barton Court Farm is accepted then continuation of occupation into the early 5th century, at least, can be considered likely. Presumably habitation continued somewhere in the area throughout the 5th century, if not at Yarnton itself. Reduced quantities of dung beetles in the floodplain channels suggest that grazing pressures slackened from late Roman levels. Perhaps there was a smaller population to support and/or reduced arable cultivation may have increased the area of pasture available. As Esmonde Cleary (1995) has pointed out, the collapse of Roman control would have eliminated the need to produce a surplus for taxation and also heralded the end of markets in which goods could be exchanged.

The location of early Saxon settlements in the Yarnton area within or immediately adjacent to Roman sites has been discussed above (Chapter 2). The difficulty lies in distinguishing between true continuity of settlement and the successive use of one place for habitation. At Barton Court Farm, the excavator was of the opinion that, whereas Roman and Saxon occupation was very close in date, it did not overlap (Miles 1986, 51-2), and this seems to be the best interpretation of the evidence at Shakenoak Roman Villa (Brown 1972; Blair 1994, 11). At Orton Hall Farm, near Peterborough, Saxon buildings were sited within and adjacent to the Roman enclosures in a manner suggesting close association if not contemporaneity (Mackreth 1996). These examples are all villa sites, however, which would be most seriously affected by changing economic circumstances, and where clearly-defined estate units with rich land would have been attractive locations for incoming settlers. Parallels for the shared location of ordinary Romano-British and 5th-century Saxon rural sites are less common. Higham (1992, 109-13) considers several possibilities but finds few clear-cut examples. Fieldwalking in Northamptonshire, for example, suggested that there was Saxon settlement on several Roman sites (Hall 1988, 101), but recent analysis of the data from the Raunds area survey shows that while Saxon pottery does occur on some Roman sites in this survey the correlations are not particularly strong (Parry 2006, 94-5) and the problems of dating in this period do not allow the specific identification of the earliest material (ibid., 91). Fieldwalking data from North Stoke, in South Oxfordshire, showed that the distribution of early Saxon pottery there was much more restricted than that of the prehistoric and Roman material, and also that it occurred in a relatively low lying terrace edge locale, with the principal concentration some 800 m distant from the main Roman settlement in the area (Ford and Hazell 1989, 18-20).

The interesting feature of the evidence from the Yarnton area is that continuity of site location occurred not just at Yarnton but also apparently at Worton, Cassington and Purwell Farm and, by the time records indicate the location of villages and manorial boundaries in the 10th and 11th century, settlement had moved only a short distance. The distance between contemporary sites remained fairly constant. It has been shown, however, that in the intervening period settlement was relatively mobile, shifting around the gravel terraces without a clear focus (Chapter 2). Perhaps a more plausible explanation for the permanence of settlement location through this period is the stability of land units. This is not to imply that Yarnton and the surrounding villages had well-defined estates which survived into the Saxon period, of the sort proposed for several areas, including Barton Court Farm (eg Biddle 1976, 334-5; Miles 1986; Higham 1992, 136-42). The nature of late Roman land ownership in this part of the Thames valley, where the cultural impact of incorporation into the Roman empire was relatively limited, is uncertain. But it may be that the land of an organised late Roman village, with its clearly-defined fields, woodland and pasture, would have been easier to adopt than reorganise, especially if it was of an adequate size to support the inhabitants. Field boundaries would have remained visible. A Roman bank next to a river channel on the floodplain was still an upstanding feature when a medieval boundary was dug next to it (Chapter 11, Fig. 11.47). Alternatively, the native British population may have been more vigorous than the material remains suggest.

Chapter 5: The Early Iron Age

by Chris Bell, Dan Stansbie and Gill Hey

INTRODUCTION

This chapter describes the early Iron Age settlement at Yarnton and Cresswell Field, including its earliest features which may date from the end of the late Bronze Age. As already discussed above (Chapter 1), much reliance has been placed on the pottery assemblage for assigning features to broad chronological periods as, although there is inter-cutting of pits and ditches, there are no extensive stratigraphic sequences from which to construct series of site phases.

Traces of late Bronze Age activity were identified across Cresswell Field in the form of a sparse scatter of pits and at least two burnt stone features and spreads on the edge of the palaeochannel (Fig. 5.1). In addition, a light spread of Bronze Age pottery, flintwork and fired clay (loomweights, spindlewhorls and structural fragments) found across the excavated area of both sites, largely as residual finds in later features, is clear testimony to use of the Second Gravel Terrace at this time. Four pits on Cresswell Field were identified as belonging to the late Bronze Age/early Iron Age transition.

From the early Iron Age, the Second Gravel Terrace became the focus of a small settlement with all the features typical of the period, in particular numerous pits and postholes. The early Iron Age settlement comprised a number of occupation clusters, including round houses, spread west to east along the edge of the Second Gravel Terrace for about 500 m on either side of a palaeochannel that was probably a stream at the time (Fig. 5.2). To the west, on the Cresswell Field site, were two swathes of features, mainly represented by pits, one running ESE-WNW along the gravel terrace, the other running north-south parallel to the eastern edge of a more substantial palaeochannel that delineated the western edge of the settlement. The ESE-WNW-aligned concentration of features appeared to continue eastwards into the Yarnton excavation area where clusters of settlement features were exposed in the north-west and north-east of the site. The northern extent of settlement at Yarnton was revealed during the course of small-scale fieldwork in advance of a recycling plant in 1996-7 (YRP 96-7; Fig. 5.2), where a number of north-south linear features containing early Iron Age pottery were exposed but few occupation features were evident (Bell 1997; 1998). Evaluation trenching to the south and south-west of the Yarnton site and around Cresswell Field established the limit of settlement in these directions (Fig. 1.6).

The settlement comprised 16 possible post-built circular structures and at least 560 pits. In addition, seven four-post structures, two small enclosures (one ditched and one fenced), one recognisable fence line, a small number of ditches and gullies, an isolated hearth, a midden and a myriad of postholes were all present. In the following description, the evidence is presented by feature type across the site, integrating as far as possible the evidence from the two main excavated areas of Cresswell Field and Yarnton. The main feature types identified were structures (and associated features), enclosures, boundaries (fence lines and ditches), and pits.

LATE BRONZE AGE/EARLY IRON AGE TRANSITIONAL FEATURES (Figs 5.1 and 5.3)

Four pits were identified as being particularly early in the Iron Age sequence and are regarded as belonging to the late Bronze Age/early Iron Age transition (pits 7412, 8084, 8091 and 8127; Fig. 5.3). Three of these pits (8084, 8091 and 8127) occurred in an east-west line in the north-east of the Cresswell Field site. One of these pits (8127) contained the substantial part of three whole smashed pots including one in the All Cannings Cross style (Fig. 5.4; Fig. 14.1, No. 1), along with parts of a minimum of 11 other vessels.

The three pits in the east-west alignment were circular, flat-bottomed features and fairly similar in diameter, ranging from 1.25 m to 1.5 m (Fig. 5.5). Pit 8084, with a depth of 0.8 m, was the deepest of these pits and was slightly undercut, suggesting that it may have originally been a grain-storage pit. It contained a large amount of burnt stone (750 g) but the only other finds were nine sherds of pottery. The easternmost pit, 8091, was only 0.21 m deep but, unlike the other pits in this group, it was found in an area of medieval ridge and furrow and may simply have been more truncated than the other features. It also contained burnt stone (three small slabs of burnt limestone lying on its base) and six sherds of pottery. The All Cannings Cross pottery within pit 8127 seems, in contrast, to represent a significant, placed deposit. The vessels appeared to have been deliberately smashed around a large, burnt quartzite pebble in the centre of the bottom of the pit (Figs 5.4 and 5.5). Although almost all of the pot was contained within the lower fill, several sherds from the same vessels were found in the upper fill, suggesting that the pit was deliberately backfilled in a single operation. Soil samples taken

Fig. 5.1 Yarnton and Cresswell Field early prehistoric and late Bronze Age/early Iron Age features and finds

Fig. 5.2 Yarnton and Cresswell Field early Iron Age features

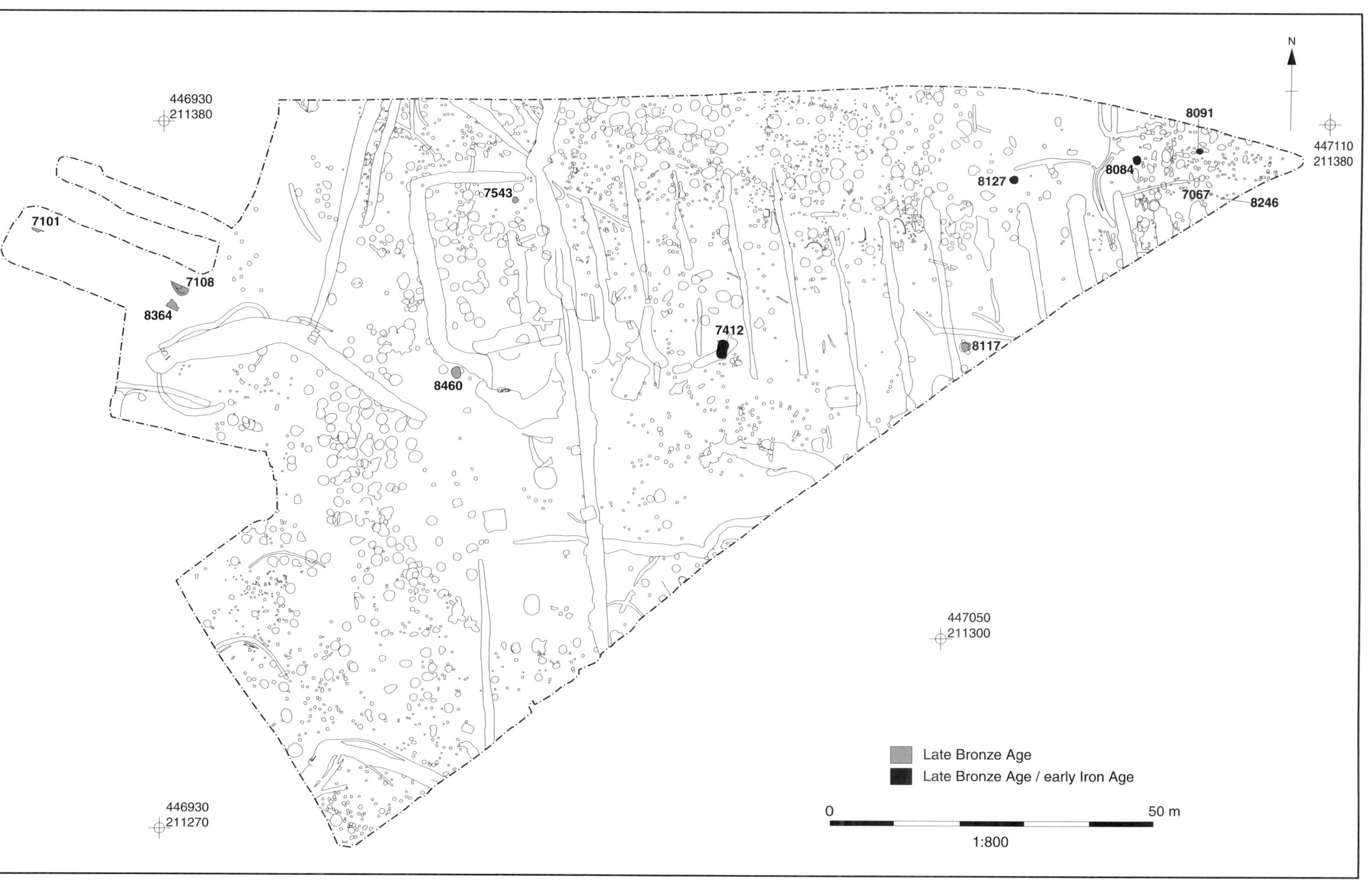

Fig. 5.3 Cresswell Field late Bronze Age and late Bronze Age/early Iron Age transitional features

from above and around the pots in the lower fill contained large quantities of charred grain and charcoal, but since the pots were broken it was impossible to determine whether the grain was originally contained within them or was deposited separately. A small amount of animal bone and a fragment of a quernstone were also found in this pit.

It is possible that this late Bronze Age/early Iron Age alignment was more extensive, since only around 45% of the pits in this area were excavated (see above, Chapter 1). It is of considerable interest that the alignment correlates well with the later orientation of early Iron Age pits, and it may have defined the area of subsequent settlement. A late Bronze Age pit, 7543, which also lay within this zone contained large quantities of refuse, including several fragments of a cylindrical loomweight (Hey *et al.* forthcoming).

The other late Bronze Age/early Iron Age pit, 7412, was found in the central part of the Cresswell Field site cut into one of the ditches of a Neolithic U-shaped enclosure, probably originally an oval barrow. This barrow may have been an upstanding feature at the time, and may have retained some significance. It seems to have been marked by an early Iron Age pit, 7365, which contained an unusual assemblage of animal bone, with fox and red deer as well as the usual domesticates and a number of amphibia (see below, Chapter 17). Pit 7412 was a slightly irregular, bath-shaped feature, very different in shape to the other late Bronze Age/early Iron Age pits. It may have been recut (Fig. 5.5) or have remained open for a time, allowing silting around the edges of the feature. It contained a small assemblage of pottery (27 sherds), 22 fragments of animal bone and pieces of burnt quartz and limestone.

Fig. 5.4 All Cannings Cross type and other pottery in pit 8127

EARLY IRON AGE STRUCTURES

Summary

Identification of structures in some parts of the Cresswell Field site was made difficult by the sheer density of features present, and was further complicated in the central northern area by both the presence of numerous postholes associated with the Saxon occupation (Hey 2004, figs 9.1-2) and the lack of time to excavate all the features. It is highly likely, therefore, that structures existed which were not recognised. The six post-built structures from this phase of occupation which were identified are also distinctly different from those at Yarnton (Fig. 5.6, see below and Chapter 3 above). One (8202) in the far north-east corner of the site, was a small, roughly rectangular structure. The others were represented by similar 'D-shaped' arrangements of postholes in the central southern part of the site (8396), in the north-west (8787 and 8399) and the south-west (8788 and 8789). Four of these structures were almost identical in size, measuring 7 m by between 5 and 5.5 m; the fifth was slightly larger at 8 m x 6 m. It is unclear whether these arrangements of posts were related to roofed structures or marked out pens or enclosures (comparable, perhaps, to the small enclosures defined by gullies in the middle Iron Age settlement).

Ten early Iron Age post-built roundhouses and seven four-post structures were recognised on the Yarnton site (Fig. 5.7). These structures were broadly divisible into three groups: a western group consisting of six circular structures (1474, 1482, 1511, 1752, 1760 and 1761) and one four-post structure (1753); a central group comprising a single roundhouse (1754) and a four-post structure (1766); and an eastern group comprising three circular structures (1756, 2661 and 2694) and five four-post structures (1770, 2721, 2722, 2723 and 2724). The settlement pattern on this site is somewhat distorted, however, by the presence of several large Roman enclosures in the middle of the site, the digging of which would have destroyed any structures between these possibly illusory groups. The presence of an isolated roundhouse (1754) within one of these large enclosures lends weight to the suggestion that occupation may once have spread across the area. All the Roman ditches contained significant quantities of Iron Age pottery (see below, Chapter 14).

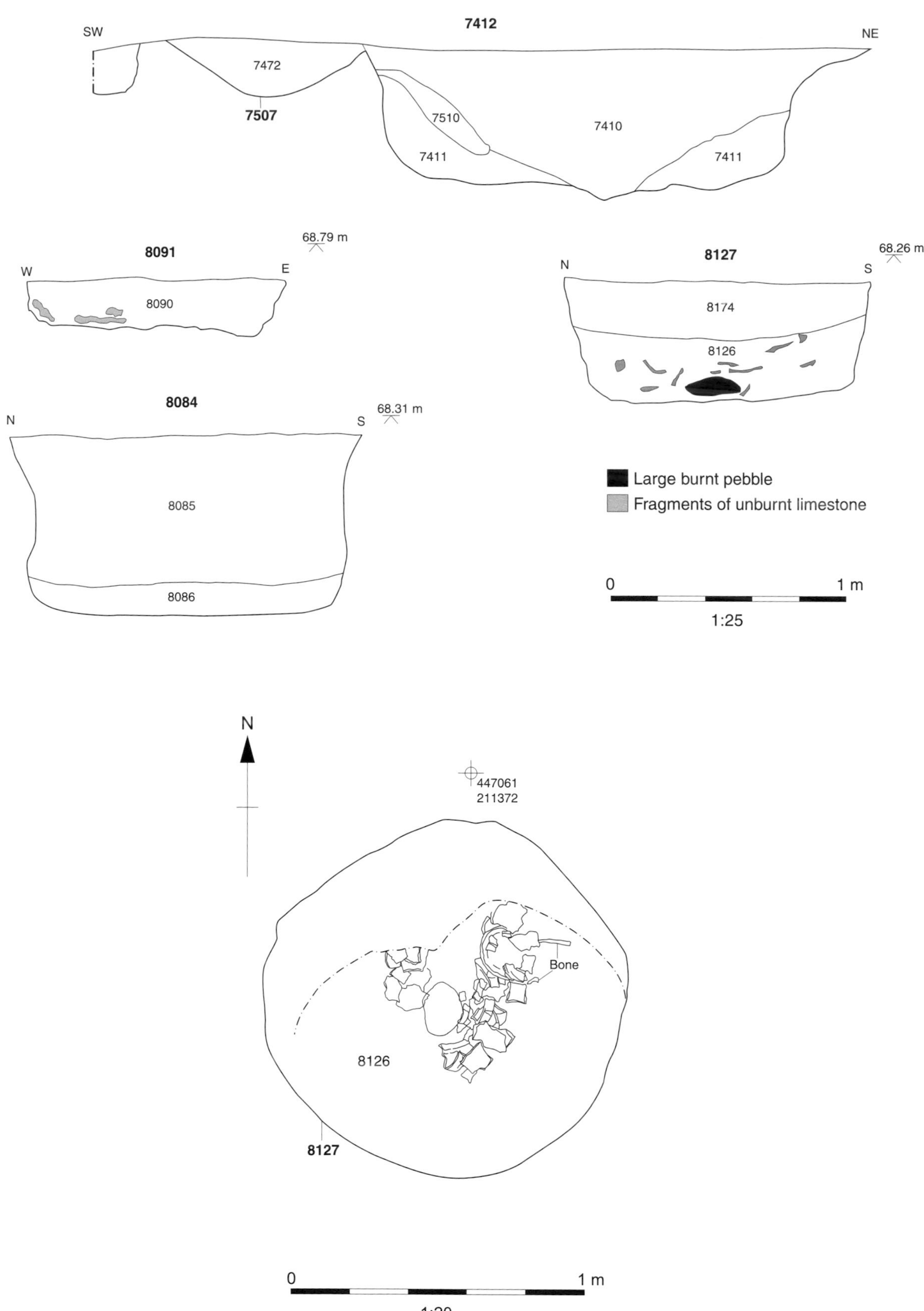

Fig. 5.5 Cresswell Field late Bronze Age/early Iron Age transitional pit sections (7412, 8091, 8127, 8084) and plan

Fig. 5.6 Cresswell Field: early Iron Age features

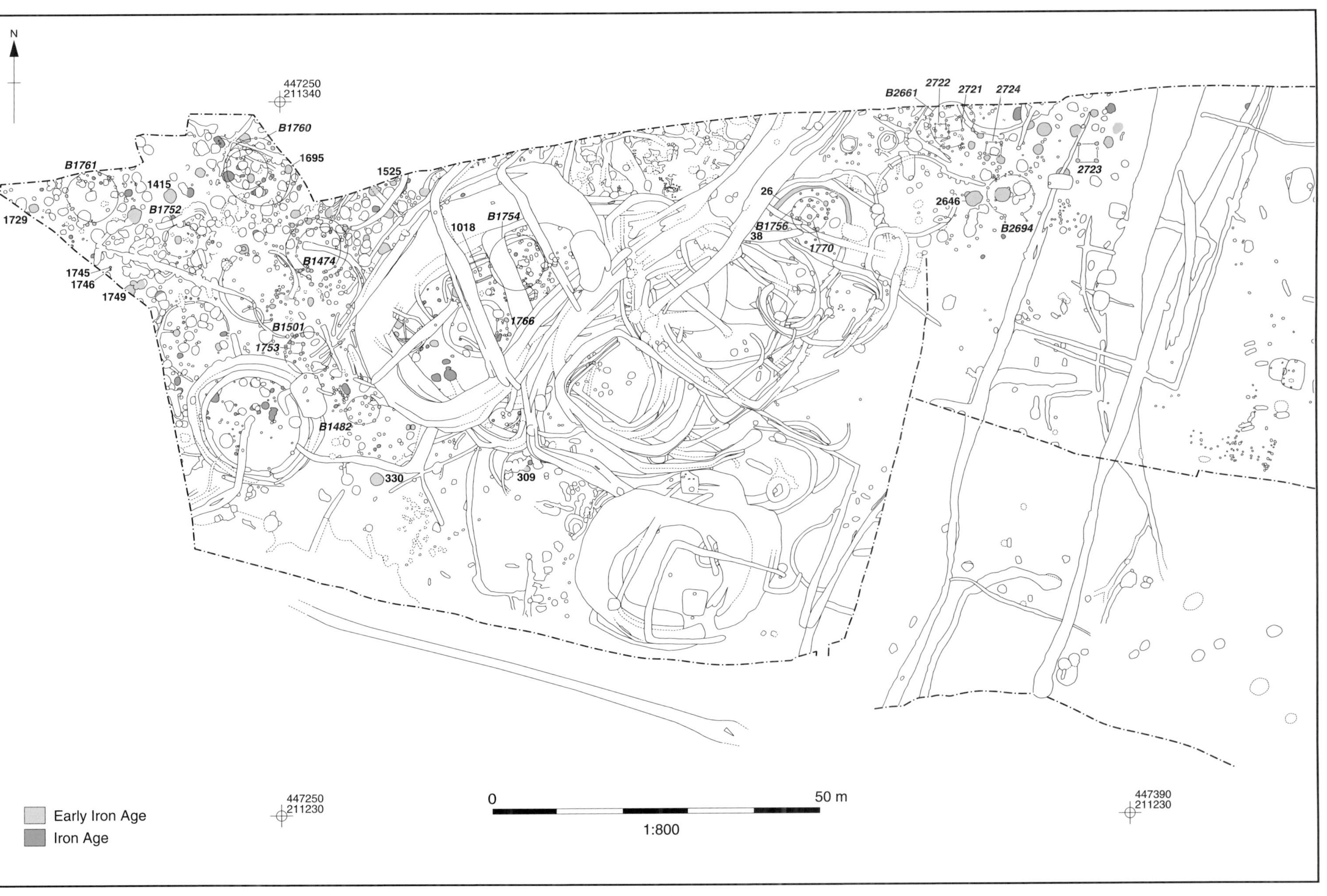

Fig. 5.7 Yarnton early Iron Age features

The buildings formed a broadly linear arrangement, on a SW-NE axis, and occupied the northern part of the excavation area. Within this known distribution they tended to occur singly or as clusters of two or three buildings associated with groups of pits which were distributed around the buildings and in the gaps between them. Once again, however, the pits shown represent only a proportion of the early Iron Age total: it was only possible to excavate a sample of those exposed (*c* 25%) and, in addition, there are a number of potentially early Iron Age pits which could not be confidently dated to this rather than the middle Iron Age period.

The diameter of the houses on the Yarnton site varied between 4.75 m and 10.9 m, and averaged 7.9 m. The four-post structures averaged 2.35 m by 2.27 m. Where entrances to the roundhouses could be discerned, they faced south or south-east.

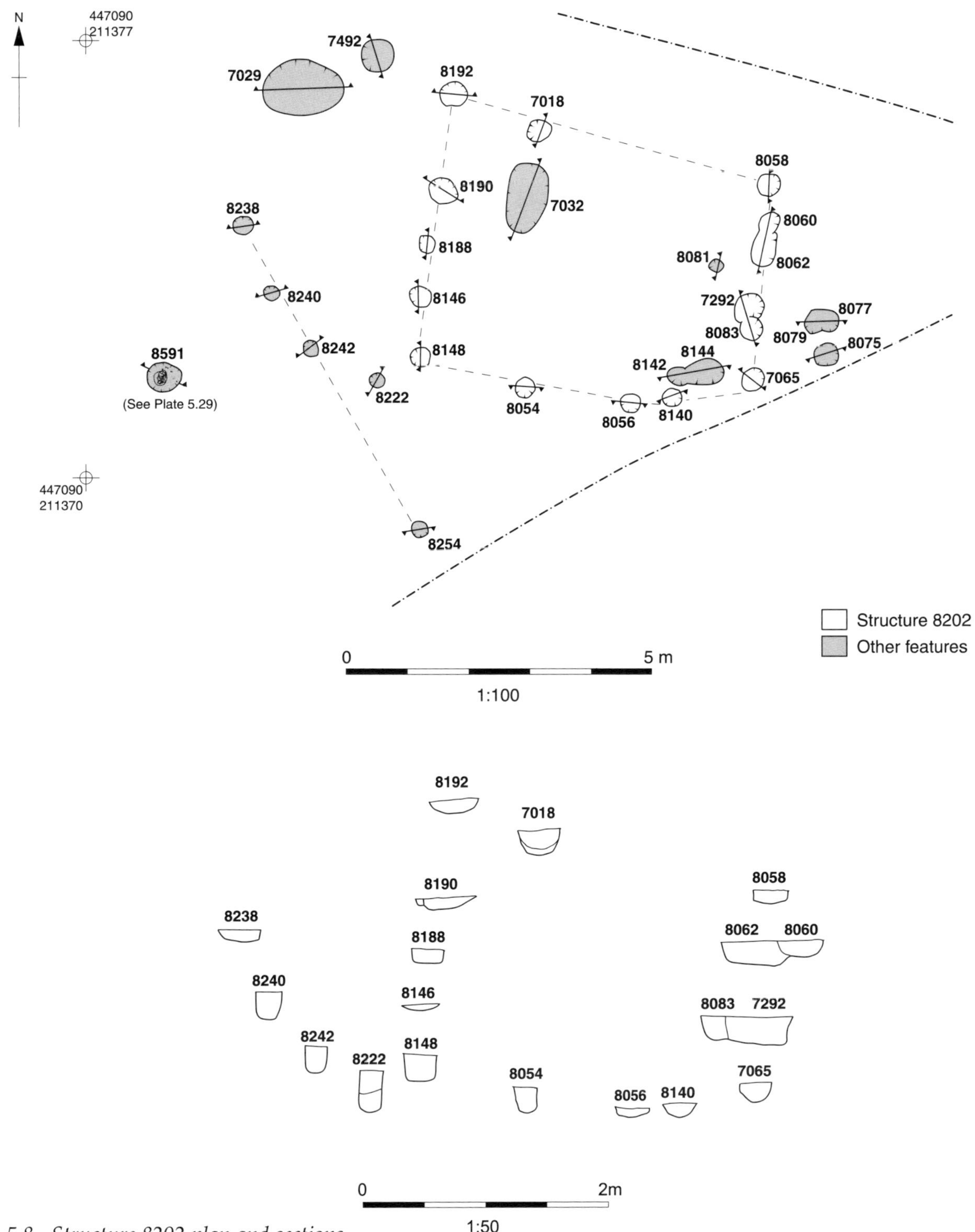

Fig. 5.8 Structure 8202 plan and sections

In general, the four-post structures appeared to be associated with individual buildings and four were actually situated within structures. The off-centre positioning of three of these four-posters indicates that they cannot have played structural roles within the buildings (ie as supports for ring-beams). Four-post structure 1770 was situated fairly centrally within roundhouse 1756, but this small building would not have required additional roof support. In all cases it seems most likely that the four-post structures and roundhouses were not contemporary.

Structures on the Cresswell Field site

Six structures were recognised at Cresswell Field: one roughly rectangular structure and five D-shaped structures. Whilst the rectangular structure perhaps stands out clearly enough from the surrounding features, some, at least, of the D-shaped structures were less obvious. Nonetheless, several of them derive from distinct clusters of features (eg structures 8396 and 8788); they were quite clearly distinguished during excavation and they appear to conform to a common pattern. Their interpretation as buildings rather than pens or small enclosures is less certain, although it can be noted that, if the latter, they would have been sturdy structures.

Rectangular Structure 8202 and associated features (Fig. 5.8)

An arrangement of sixteen postholes at the eastern extremity of the site appeared to form a roughly rectangular post-built structure with internal measurements of 5 m x 4 m. A small pit (8591), which lay 4 m south-west of the structure, contained a human skull (Fig. 5.9), and a row of three large pits further to the west (7060, 7173 and 7307) contained significant quantities of domestic refuse (Fig. 5.6). The pits are described in more detail below (see also Fig. 5.36).

The postholes which made up the structure mostly had steep-sided, conical-shaped profiles and ranged in size from 0.22-0.37 m in diameter and 0.1-0.23 m in depth (Fig. 5.8). The spacing of these features suggests that the entrance lay in the north-east of the building, and inter-cutting of postholes on the east side (7292 and 8083, and 8060 and 8062) suggests that some of the posts had been replaced. Three of the postholes (7292, 8062 and 8188) produced early Iron Age pottery (four sherds in total, weighing 25 g). However, posthole 8146, which may have been part of the structure, contained a single sherd of possibly intrusive middle Iron Age pottery. One posthole (7018) contained a deposit of cremated bone, mostly from animals but including a fragment possibly from a human femur. Another posthole (8083) contained burnt stone (1.25 kg). A further posthole packed with burnt stone (8222) lay immediately south-west of the line of ?roof-supporting posts. Small pits or postholes filled, or partly filled, with burnt stone were also found on the line of, or adjacent to, the posts of the other five identified structures (see below).

Four postholes (8238, 8240, 8242 and 8254) which lay immediately to the south-west of the structure forming a NW-SE alignment may represent part of an associated fence line. Three of these features contained early Iron Age pottery (5 sherds, 31 g in total). A further cluster of postholes (8075, 8077, 8079, 8081, 8142 and 8144), two of which were double postholes, lay within or immediately adjacent to the south-east corner of the building. Although none produced any finds it seemed likely that some or all of these features were also directly associated.

Three large pits (7060, 7307 and 7173) lay in a roughly north-south line 10 m to the west of structure 8202. All three features were slightly oval and of similar dimensions in plan, but differed in depth and profile (Fig. 5.47). Pits 7060 and 7307 were comparatively deep with undercut sides, whilst 7173 was shallower and slightly bowl-shaped (see below). The pit (8591) containing a human skull (Figs 5.9 and 5.43) is discussed below.

The distal half of a neonate humerus was found in pit 7029 which lies just outside the structure to the north-west. It was associated with six sherds (45 g) of early Iron Age pottery. Similar pottery (7 sherds, 92 g) was found in pit 7032 which lay within the structure, although the two need not be strictly contemporaneous. A further pit lying near this corner of the building (7492) contained no finds, but may belong to the same broad phase of activity.

The fact that three of the features in and around this structure – pit 8591, pit 7029 and posthole 7018 – contained human bone, suggests that this structure may have had a special, perhaps ritual, role. Rectangular buildings at other sites, albeit often more elaborate in form and often later in date, have been interpreted as shrines (Woodward 1992, 31-3). Unfortunately, the fact that this structure lay near the edge of the excavation means that it is unclear to what degree it might have been separated from other structures, as the shrines at other sites tend to

Fig. 5.9 Human skull 8592 in pit 8591

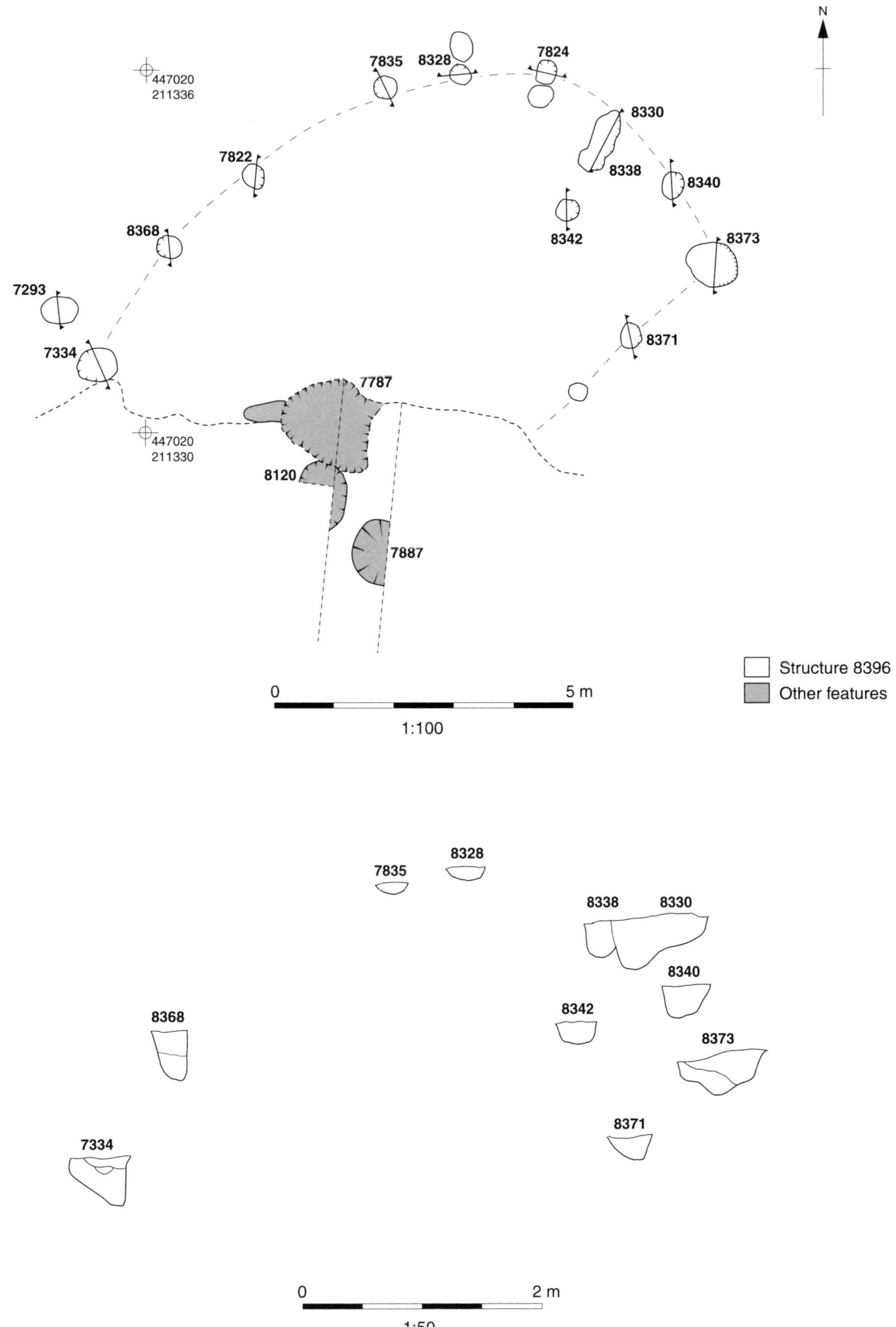

Fig. 5.10 Structure 8396 and pit 7787, plan and sections

be. The area to the west of the structure which was excavated does not, however, provide any clear indications of being different from other parts of the site. The pits forming a row to the west of the structure (7060, 7307 and 7173) contained large deposits of pottery and animal bone which are similar to those spread throughout the rest of the site.

D-shaped Structure 8396 and associated features (Fig. 5.10)

A clearly-defined cluster of twelve postholes, not all excavated, in the central southern area of the site formed a sub-oval or D-shaped arrangement to the north of a series of inter-cutting middle Iron Age ditches. What survived of the post-built structure measured 7 m x 5 m internally. Postholes along the north edge of the ditch suggest that the structure had a flatter southern side or, if the ditches cut the structure, that extra supports or internal posts existed within the structure. Several double postholes in the northern half of the structure suggest that it had undergone remodelling or rebuilding at some point.

The postholes were mostly rounded or conical in profile and ranged in size from 0.3-0.5 m in diameter and 0.1-0.4 m in depth (Fig. 5.10). They contained only one or two fills and no postpipes were visible. Two of the larger postholes, 8373 at the eastern corner and 7334 towards the western extremity, had slightly irregular V-shaped profiles with two fills.

Seven of the postholes contained early Iron Age pottery (totalling 11 sherds, weighing 73 g) and two fragments of a saddle quern were recovered from posthole 8371 near the eastern corner. Posthole 7334 also produced a small quantity of charred grain and fragments of burnt bone.

Within the linear spread of inter-cutting middle Iron Age pits and ditches in the area immediately south of the structure were pits of an earlier phase, cut by later features and containing varying quantities of early Iron Age pottery, mostly comprising large unabraded sherds. The general paucity of other early Iron Age features in this area of the site suggests that they were directly associated with structure 8396.

One of these pits, 7787 lay immediately adjacent to the southern edge of the post-ring, but within the structure if this is to be understood as D-shaped (Fig. 5.10). A complete iron adze head had been placed in the bottom of this pit (Fig. 5.11) and its northern edge had been lined with large sherds from an early Iron Age storage vessel. As a whole it contained a large quantity of pottery (72 sherds, 3921 g) and the largest deposit of daub (360 g) recovered from the site. It also contained 168 fragments of animal bone, amongst which 17 fragments of cattle femur and large numbers of fragments of sheep/goat teeth and small lower limb bones stand out. Much of the bone in its upper fill was burnt. Further fragments of burnt bone, probably derived from this pit, were found in the later ditches which cut it, suggesting that it may originally have contained a substantial quantity of this material.

Fig. 5.11 Iron adze in bottom of pit 7787. Scale 10 cm

D-Shaped Structure 8399 and associated features (Fig. 5.12)

A second roughly D-shaped structure, more or less similar in size to building 8396, was identified in the central northern area of the site. It was difficult to distinguish the plan of this structure within an area with numerous postholes and stakeholes associated with Saxon occupation, but the postholes of the latter period were smaller, mostly occurred in linear alignments and contained distinct and sterile fills. In contrast, the postholes associated with structure 8399 were more substantial and often contained finds, including pottery, burnt stone and fragments of animal bone. There was also a cluster of small pits which lay within and adjacent to this structure, several of which also contained large unabraded sherds of early Iron Age pottery.

The structure was represented by a cluster of nine postholes. However, some of the postholes on its eastern side had been partially truncated by a medieval plough furrow (as shown by the shallow depths of these features in section, Fig. 5.12), and a gap between posts on this side suggests that at least one feature may have been completely cut away. The south-west corner of the structure had also been partly cut by one of the Saxon fence lines. The postholes ranged from 0.3-0.6 m in diameter and, where unaffected by the plough furrow, survived to a depth of between 0.3-0.4 m. Only one of these features (8213) contained a visible postpipe. Two more postholes (8310 and 7261) lay within the structure. One or both of these may have been associated with internal supports; 8310 was almost centrally placed.

Three of the postholes (8213, 8216 and 8219) produced sherds of early Iron Age pottery (four sherds in total) and small pieces of animal bone, and these features and posthole 8247 also contained significant quantities of burnt stone (0.75 kg, 2.5 kg, 1.5 kg and 1 kg respectively). The quantities of stone in these small features suggest that it may have been used for post-packing.

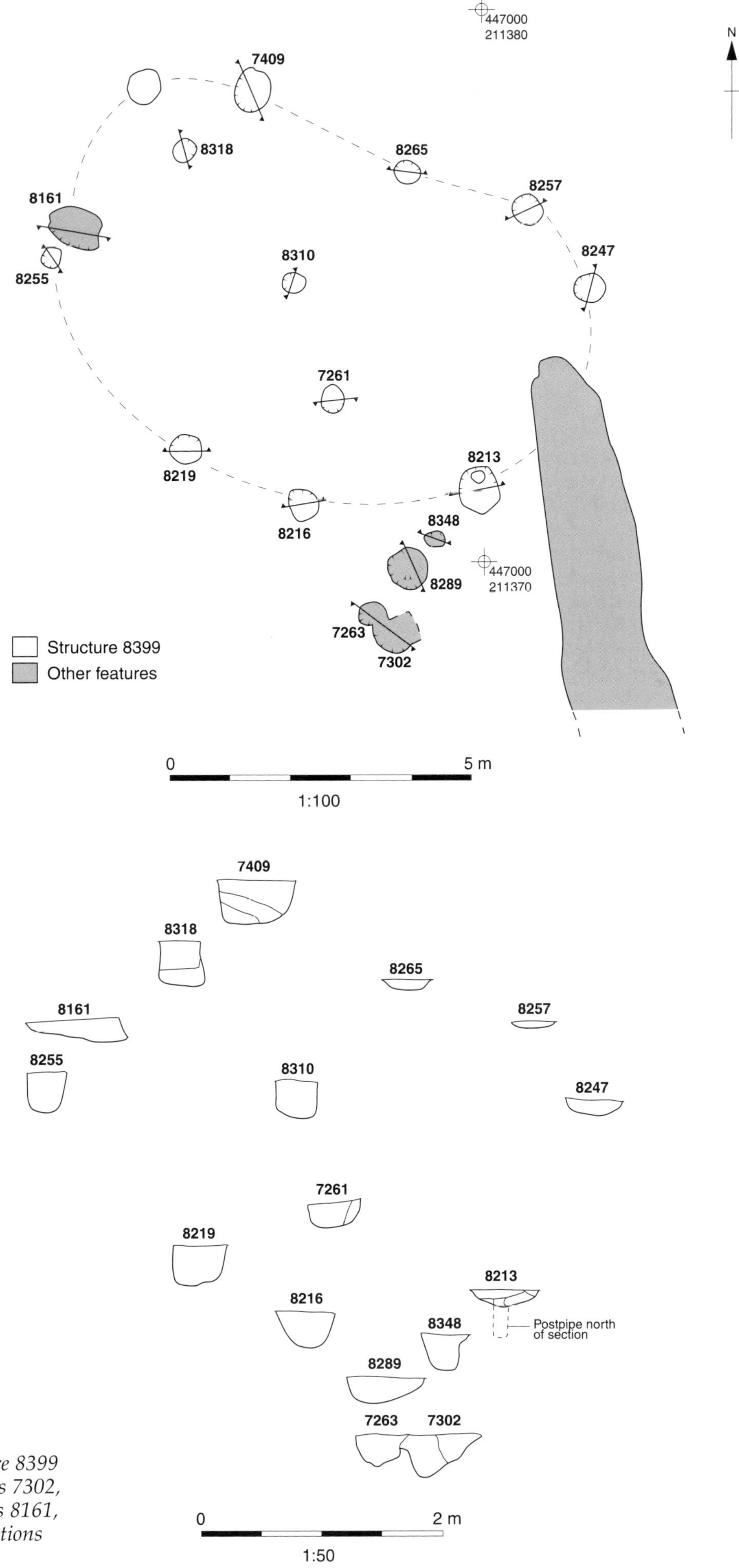

Fig. 5.12 Structure 8399 (including postholes 7302, 7263, 8348 and pits 8161, 8289), plan and sections

Clusters of further postholes and small pits lay within or immediately adjacent to the post-ring on the western edge and the south-east corner of the structure. The features by the south-east corner, comprising three postholes (7302, 7263 and 8348) and a small pit (8289), all contained large sherds of early Iron Age pottery (14 sherds in total, weighing 152 g), along with small fragments of animal bone. A shallow pit (8161) lay on the western edge of the post-ring.

D-shaped Structures 8787, 8788 and 8789 and associated features (Figs 5.13-5.15)

Structures 8787, 8788 and 8789 were identified during post-excavation analysis and consequently only a limited number of their postholes had been excavated. However, the similarity between the ground plans of these buildings, and between those of 8787 (Fig. 5.13) and 8789 (Fig. 5.15) in particular, was striking. These two structures, which lay

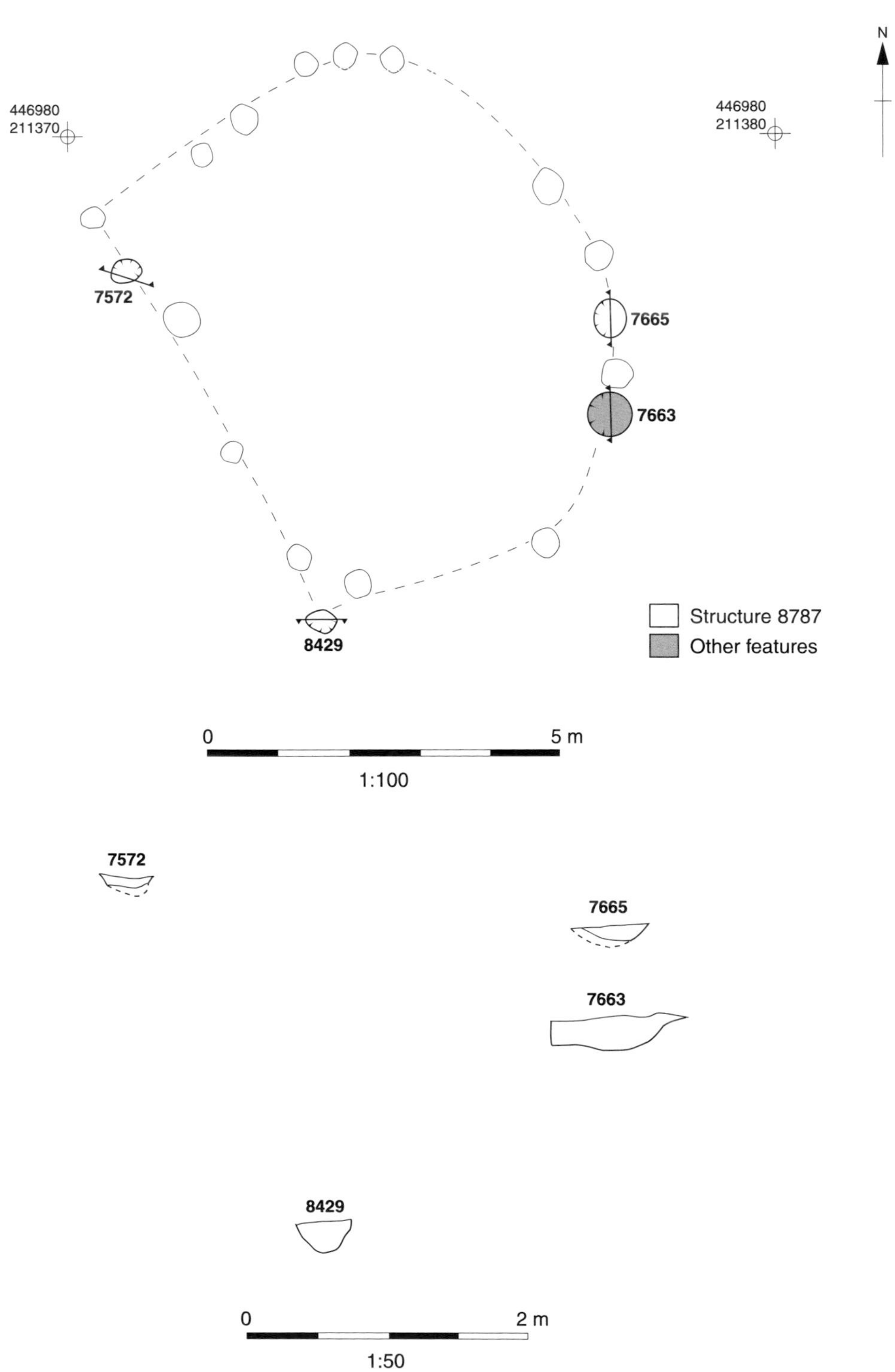

Fig. 5.13 Structure 8787 plan and sections

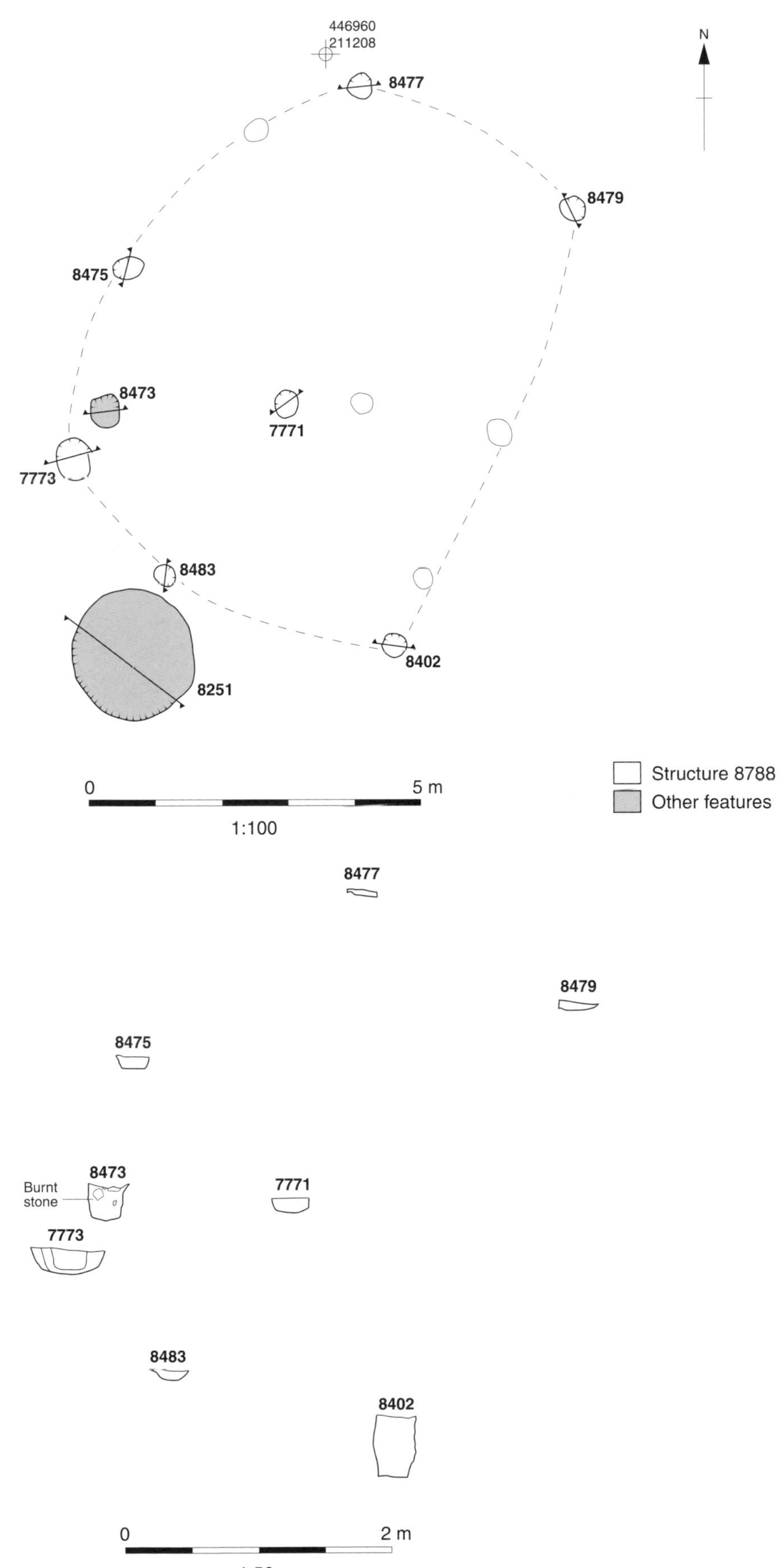

Fig. 5.14 Structure 8788 plan and sections

toward the north-west and south-west corners of the site, were both represented by a D-shaped arrangement of approximately 16 or 17 postholes with internal measurements of 7 m x 5.5 m, though their flat sides were orientated in opposite directions (to the south-west in structure 8787 and the north-east in 8789). Each of these structures also had a small pit (7663 and 7850) containing burnt stone situated in a similar position on the rounded ('back') side of the post-ring. These two features also each produced three large sherds of early Iron Age pottery.

Only three of the postholes from each of these two structures were excavated and only a single piece of animal bone was recovered from them. A large sherd of early Iron Age pottery was collected from the top of one of the unexcavated postholes, 7037, in structure 8789.

The third structure identified during post-excavation analysis, 8788 (Fig. 5.14), lay 10 m south of structure 8789, in the south-west corner of the site. It was slightly larger than 8787 and 8789, measuring 8 m x 6 m, and was represented by fewer postholes. It also had a small pit, 8473, packed with 2.5 kg of burnt stone, lying adjacent to the back edge of the structure. Eight postholes formed the post-ring, five of which were excavated. Two further postholes lay in the centre of the structure and may have been associated with central supports. Four of the postholes (7773, 8402, 8477 and 8483) and the

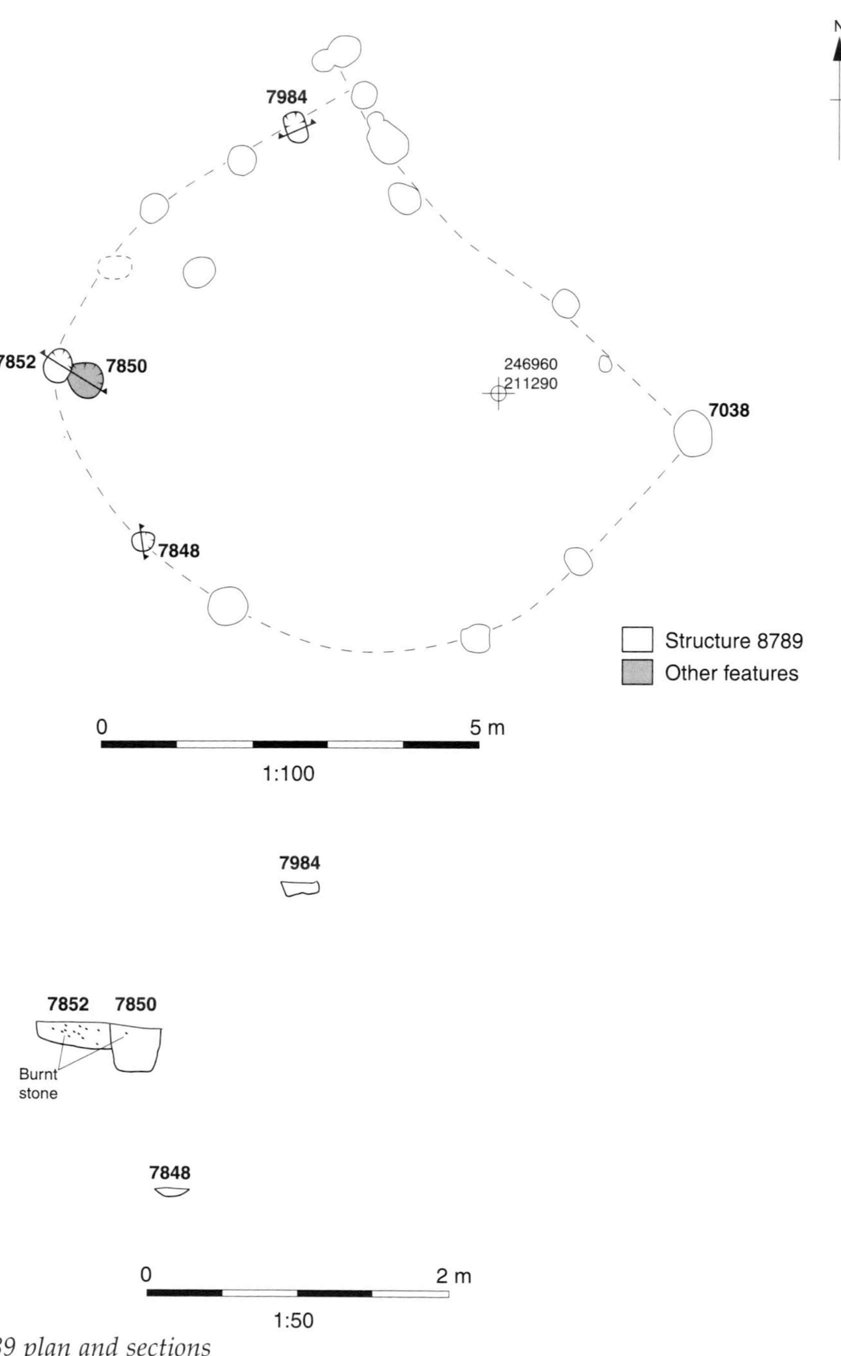

Fig. 5.15 Structure 8789 plan and sections

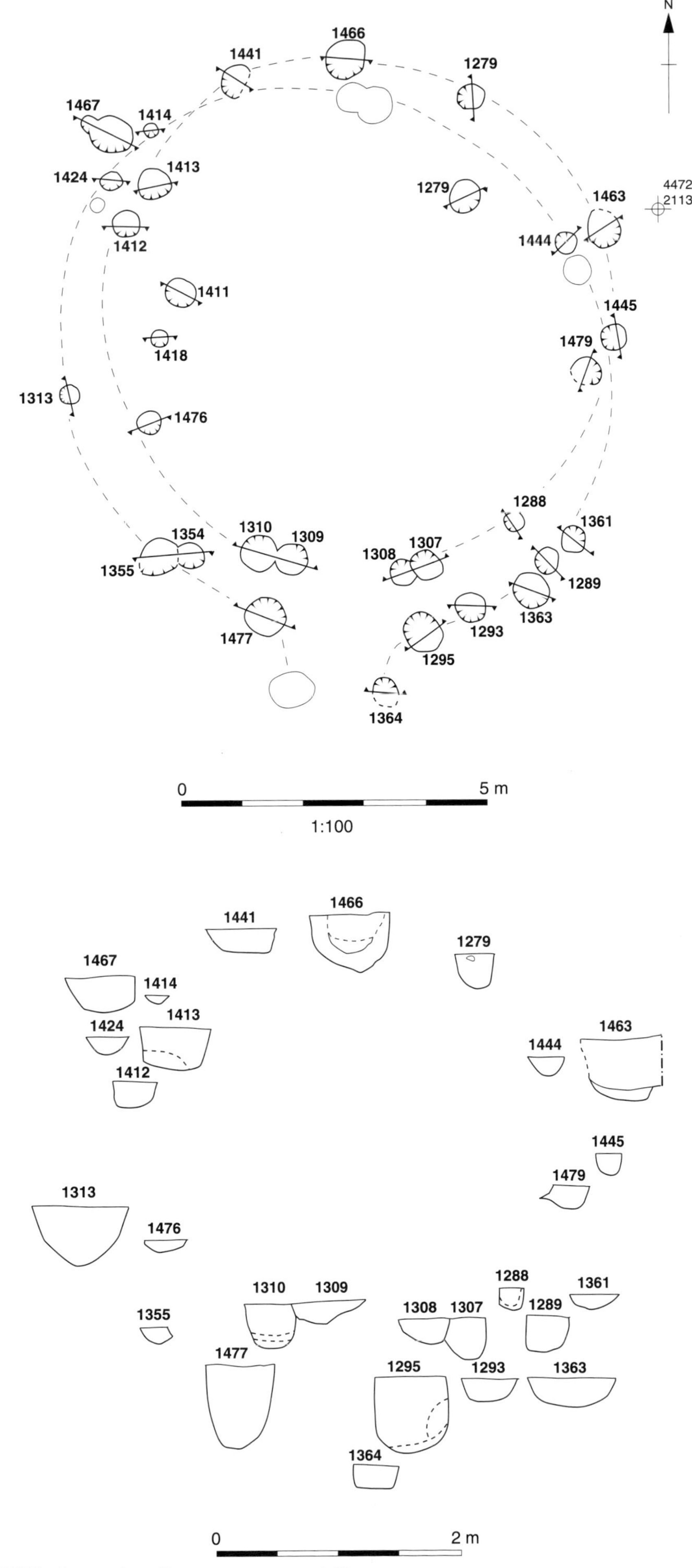

Fig. 5.16 Structure 1474 plan and sections

burnt stone pit (8473) produced early Iron Age pottery (12 sherds in total weighing 129 g) and two of these features (7773 and 8402) also contained small pieces of animal bone.

A concentration of features comprising numerous postholes and a number of pits lay in the area immediately to the west of structures 8788 and 8789 and may have been directly associated with them. Four large early Iron Age pits (7912, 7854, 8175 and 8251) in a NW-SE alignment were excavated. These finds-rich pits had similar profiles with vertical or slightly undercutting sides and flat bases, but they varied slightly in size and shape (see Figs 5.51 and 5.52 and discussion below).

The numerous postholes in this area mostly lay in a linear scatter on a similar alignment to the pits. No obvious structures or individual rows could be identified and only a limited number of these features were excavated. The small quantity of pottery recovered from these features was early Iron Age in date.

The western group of structures on the Yarnton site (Fig. 5.7)

The western group of structures on the Yarnton site comprised six roundhouses and one four-post structure which appeared to have a linear distribution, although the significance of this, given the extent of Roman ditch digging to the east, is uncertain. The buildings included three relatively large roundhouses, one of which had been replaced or formed a double ring of posts, and three smaller structures. The four-post structure was situated eccentrically within one of the circular buildings, and is not likely to have been contemporary with it, although it may have been contemporary with other roundhouses of this phase. All of the buildings were associated with pits, which mainly lay to the north.

Structure 1474 (Figs 5.16 and 5.17)

Building 1474 was a circular post-built structure in the middle of this group which was represented by circular arrangements of between 27 and 38 postholes, spaced between 1 m and 2.75 m apart, two possible interpretations of which can be put forward. The plan could show two successive and substantially overlapping structures, one 8.2 m in diameter and the other, a little further south-west, of a more oval shape (9.5 m x 8.5 m), as shown on Figure 5.16. Alternatively, this may have been a circular building 9 m in diameter, using the outer posts examined, with a much smaller structure 6.8 m in diameter which either preceded or replaced it, as shown on Figure 5.7. All these possible structures would have had a south-facing entrance, 2 m wide; two postholes external to the main body of the structure (1364 and an unexcavated feature) may have formed a porch.

Fig. 5.17 Structure 1474

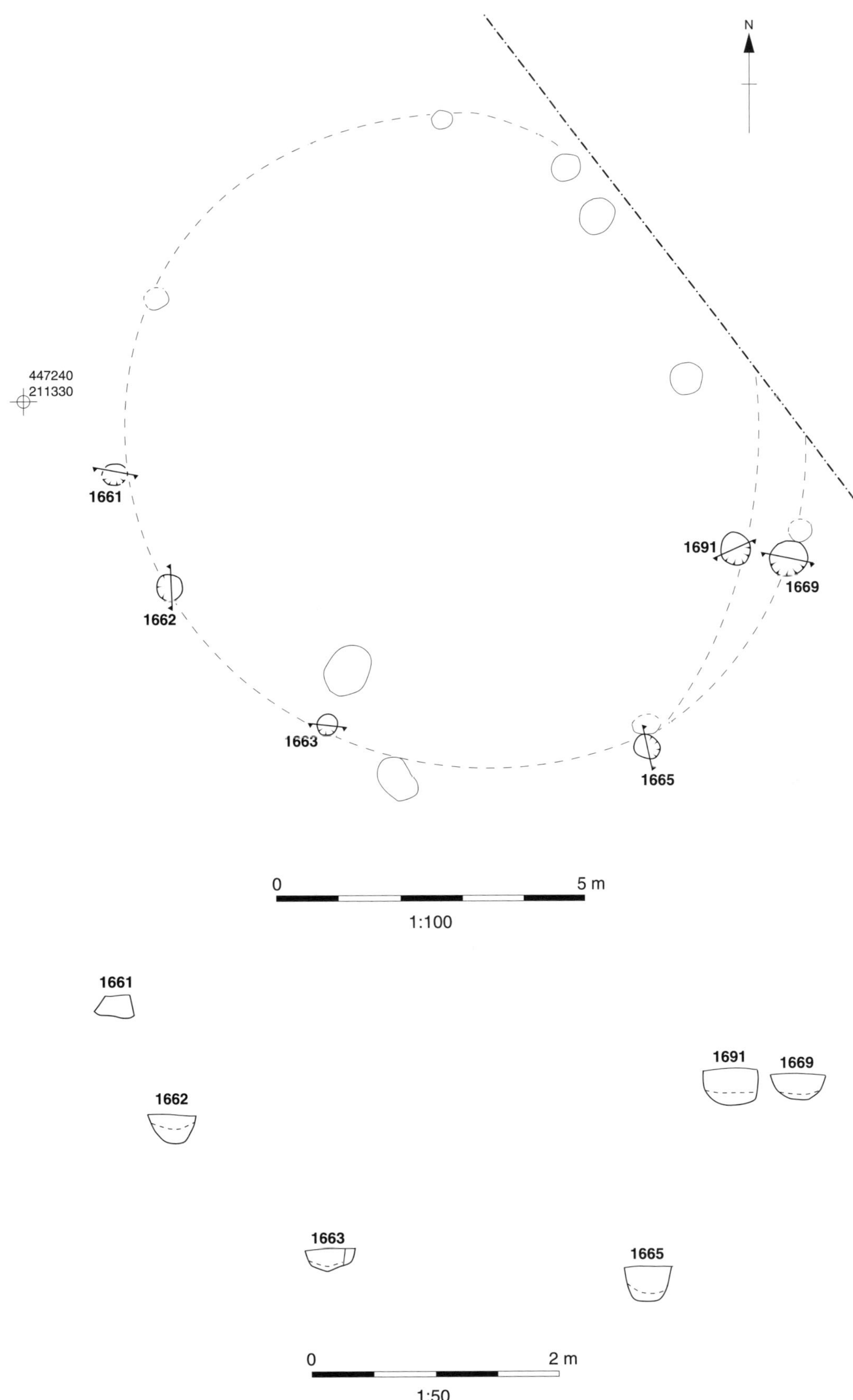

Fig. 5.18 Structure 1760 plan and sections

The postholes making up this structure/s were generally circular in plan, with diameters of between 0.3 m and 0.6 m and depths of between 0.1 m and 0.6 m (Fig. 5.16). In profile they were predominantly steep-sided with flat, round or bowl-shaped bases. Fills were grey-brown and orange silty sands containing 2-30% gravel. The fill of posthole 1479 contained occasional charcoal flecks, and postpipes were observed within postholes 1288, 1466 and possibly 1295. Postholes 1364 and 1466 showed signs of animal disturbance. Finds from the postholes include 16 sherds (170 g) of early Iron Age pottery, 15 fragments of animal bone and one vitrified clay fragment.

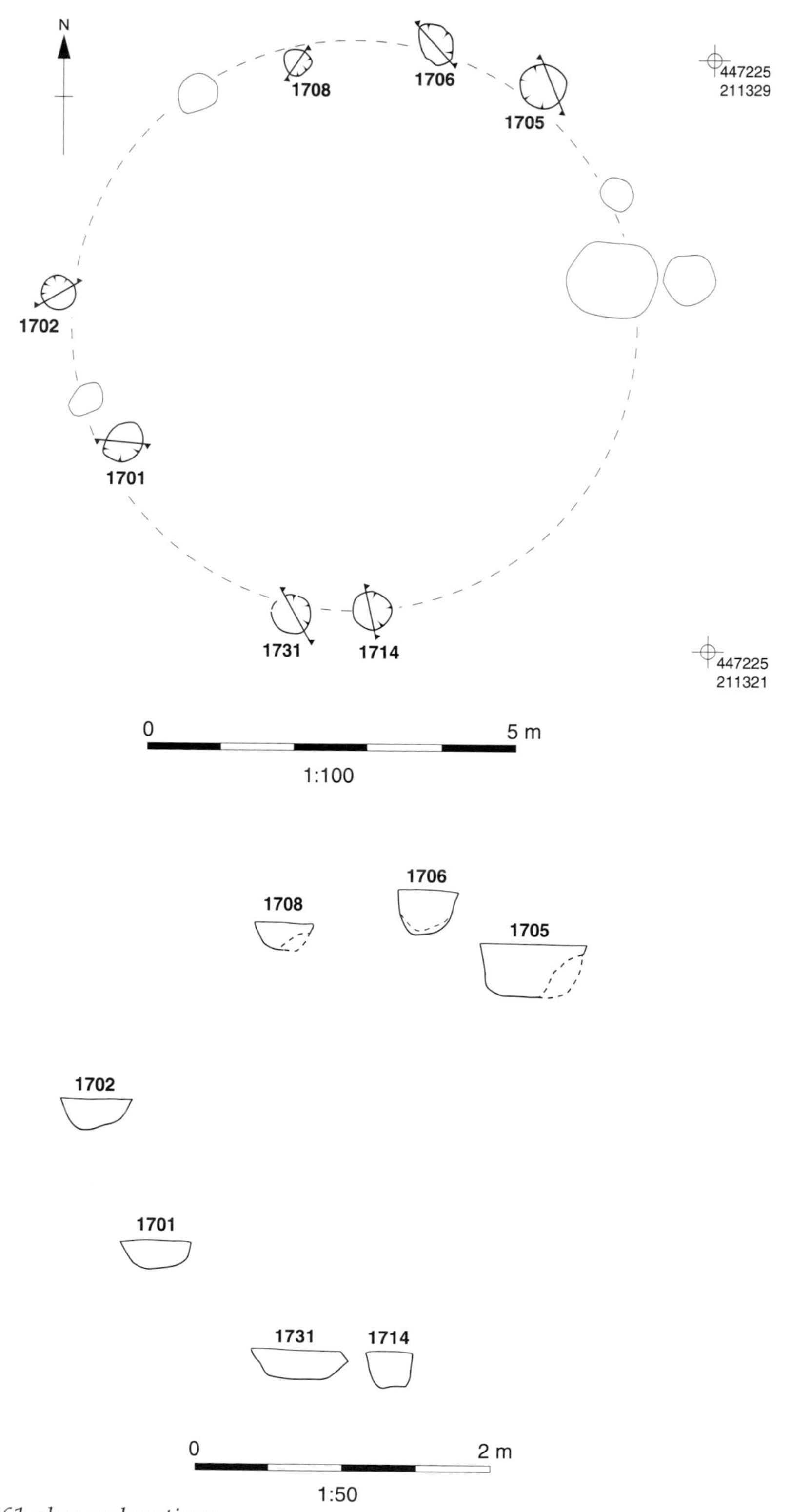

Fig. 5.19 Structure 1761 plan and sections

Structure 1760 (Fig. 5.18)

A ring of posts in the north of the site suggested a post-built structure with a ring beam 10.0-10.5 m in diameter. The presence of several later pits and ditches and the edge of the excavation made its north-eastern arc difficult to determine precisely. There is no clear indication of an entrance, though this may have been to the south, between postholes 1663 and 1665. Much of the interior was cut away by pits, postholes and gullies. The five excavated postholes of this structure were generally circular in plan, between 0.3-0.7 m in diameter, and 0.18-0.3 m in depth. Recorded profiles were bowl-shaped, and fills comprised brown silty sands containing 1-20% gravel. Charcoal was recorded from the upper fills of 1662, 1665 and 1691. Three sherds of early Iron Age pottery and four fragments of bone were found in these features.

Structure 1761 (Fig. 5.19)

A circular post-built structure measuring 7.8 m in diameter was exposed in the north-west corner of the site. Only seven postholes of this building were excavated, however, and postholes 1705 and 1708 were disturbed. There was no clear indication of where the entrance was situated. The excavated postholes were generally circular in plan, 0.45-0.6 m in diameter, and 0.2-0.4 m in depth. Posthole profiles showed some variation but were mostly bowl-shaped. Fills consisted of brown sandy silty loams, containing 2-15% gravel. Finds were limited to three animal bone fragments.

Structure 1752 (Fig. 5.20)

Between buildings 1761 and 1474 lay the remains of a small circular post-built structure comprising six postholes, with a diameter of approximately 5.5 m. There was no clearly-defined entrance. The surviving postholes were roughly circular in plan, measuring 0.3-0.6 m in diameter and up to 0.3 m in depth. In profile they were steep-sided with flat, round, or bowl-shaped bases. Fills were predominantly mid-brown silty sands containing 5-15% gravel and some features contained charcoal flecks, pebbles and pea grit. An early Iron Age pit (266) was situated close to the centre of the building, but in the absence of stratification it is impossible to say whether the pit and the building were contemporary. A single large sherd of shell-tempered early Iron Age pottery came from posthole 1369.

Structure 1511 (Fig. 5.21)

A circular post-built structure, of which eight postholes survived, was found to the south of B1474. Its south-western segment had been cut away by middle Iron Age enclosure 390. The building had an approximate diameter of 9 m and no discernible entrance. The postholes making up this structure were generally circular in plan with diameters of between 0.25 m and 0.65 m, and depths ranging between 0.08 m and 0.42 m. Profiles were either bowl-shaped and shallow or steep-sided with flat/round bases, with the exception of one (720), which had a pointed profile. Posthole 1302 had traces of a postpipe. Fills mostly comprised brown and grey silty sands and contained very variable amounts of gravel/pea grit, with some charcoal flecking; some clay or charcoal-rich fills were also noted. Posthole 1306 had been affected by animal disturbance. Finds from the postholes of structure 1511 include nine

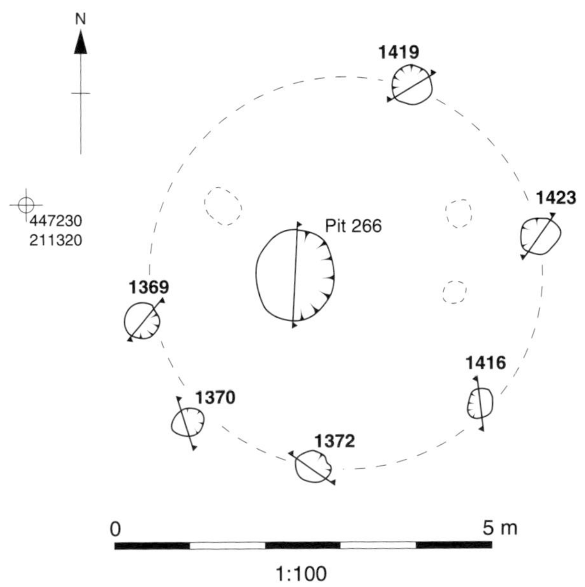

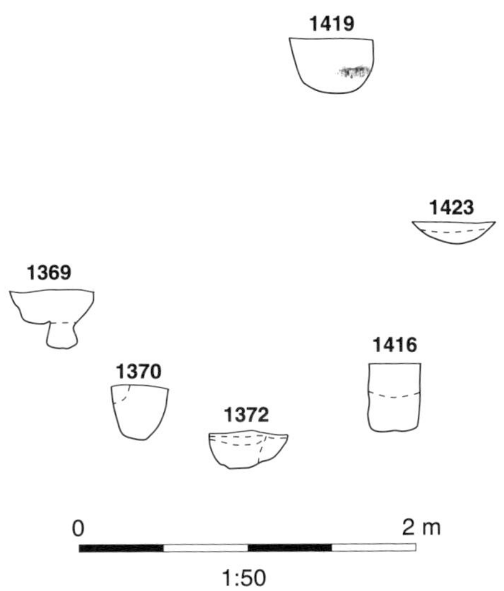

Fig. 5.20 Structure 1752 plan and sections

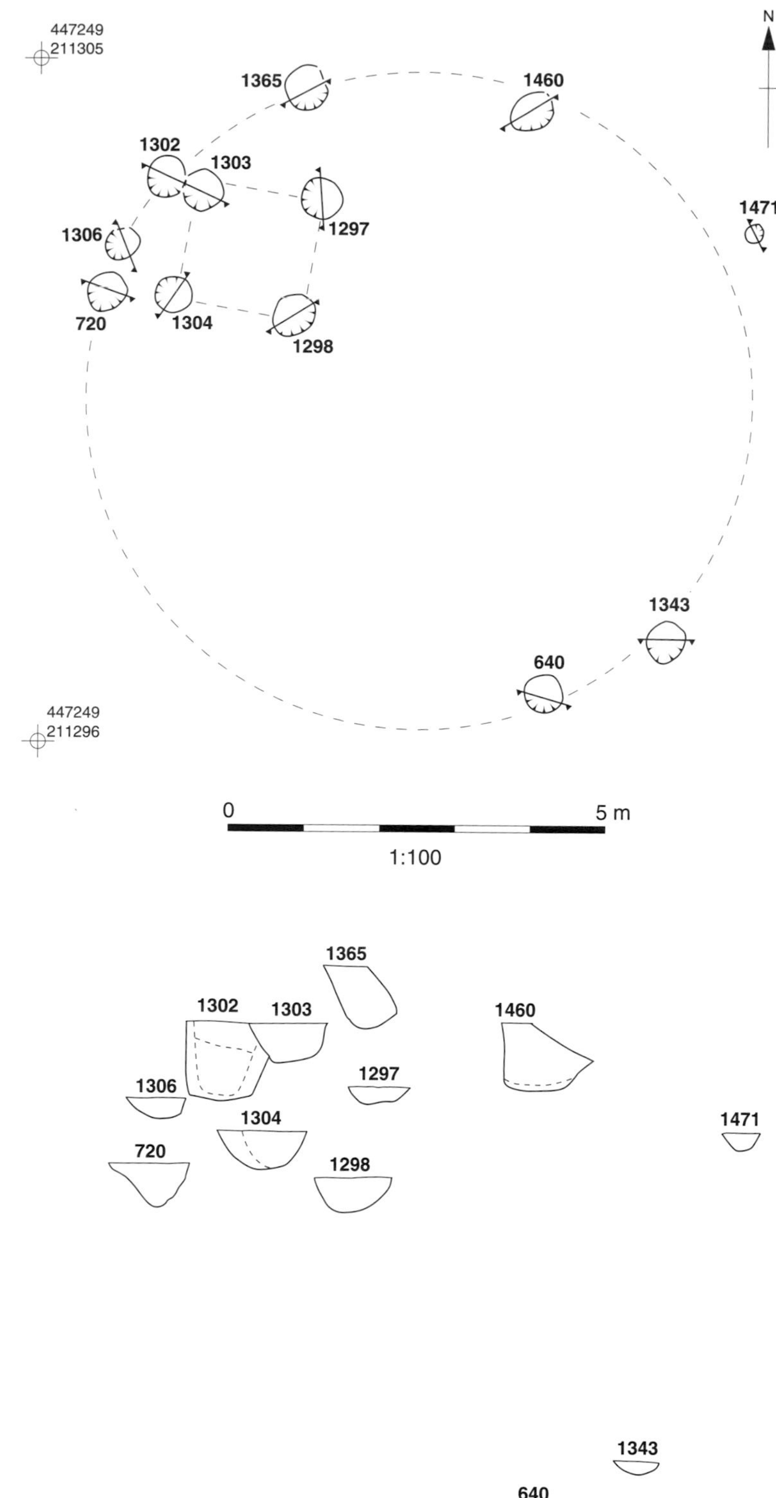

Fig. 5.21 Structure 1511 and four-post structure 1753, plan and sections

early Iron Age pottery sherds (399 g) and eleven fragments of animal bone.

Four-post structure 1753 (Fig. 5.21)

A four-post structure measuring 2.2 m by 2 m, was situated within circular structure 1511, close to the north-western side of its wall. The postholes of the four-poster were circular in plan, with diameters of 0.4-0.6 m, and depths of 0.12-0.24 m. Profiles were bowl shaped, and fills comprised brown silty sands containing 10-30% gravel. The fill of posthole 1298 contained charcoal flecks. Finds comprised four sherds of early Iron Age pottery (52 g) and five animal bone fragments It seems unlikely that the four-post structure was contemporary with building 1511 as it was placed close to the wall in the north-west. Furthermore, posthole 1303 of the four-post structure appeared to cut posthole 1302 of the circular building (Fig. 5.21).

Structure 1482 (Fig. 5.22)

To the south of this group lay a small circular post-built structure comprising ten postholes, one of which was not excavated. The ring beam would have formed a diameter of approximately 5 m and there was a convincing south-east facing entrance 1.2 m in width. The postholes were fairly substantial, generally circular in plan and with diameters of 0.3-0.6 m, and depths of 0.1-0.5 m. In profile they were steep-sided with flat or round bases, with the exceptions of 1229 and 1489, which were bowl-shaped. Fills comprised grey and brown silty sands containing 2-20% gravel. One posthole, 1199, contained flecks of charcoal. Some animal disturbance had affected postholes 1199 and 1489. Given the small size of this structure, and its position relative to structure 1511, it may be interpreted as an ancillary building of some kind, rather than a dwelling. Finds comprised only six sherds (65 g) of pottery and two animal bone fragments.

The central group of structures on the Yarnton site (Fig. 5.7)

A sizeable roundhouse and a four-post structure were found within a substantial early Roman ditched enclosure, in an area also cut by late Roman linear ditches. The early Iron Age features may, therefore, represent the surviving remains of a more extensive group of buildings. A short gully situated to the south-west of the roundhouse, and lying at right angles to it, may have been associated with the occupation of the building. A number of early Iron Age pits were also found in this area, mostly situated to the south-west of the roundhouse, and the presence of early Iron Age pottery in the Roman ditches attests to the destruction of other Iron Age features here.

Structure 1754 (Fig. 5.23)

A circular post-built structure approximately 8.6 m in diameter was found in this central area, of which eight postholes of the roof support and one internal posthole survived as well as a pit (833). Evidence for an entrance is lacking; it was probably obliterated by the many ditches and later postholes in the area, especially to the south and south-west. The postholes constituting this structure were generally circular in plan, between 0.4 to 0.7 m in diameter and up to 0.38 m in depth. Profiles were either flat-based and steep-sided, or shallow and bowl-shaped, and several contained possible postpipes. Fills comprised orange-brown and brown sandy silts containing 1-50% gravel. Charcoal flecks were recorded in the fills of postholes 861, 874 and 999.

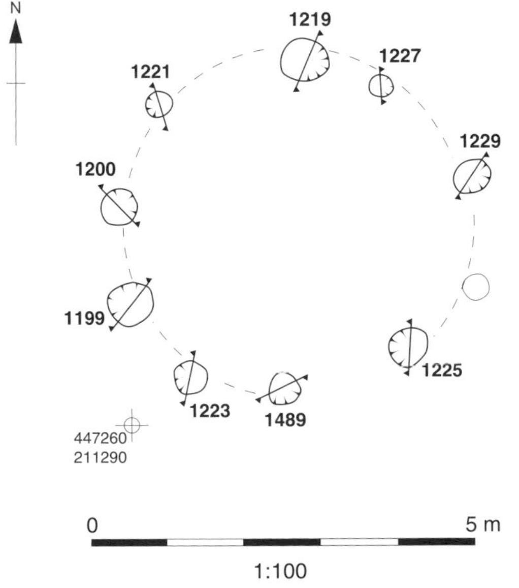

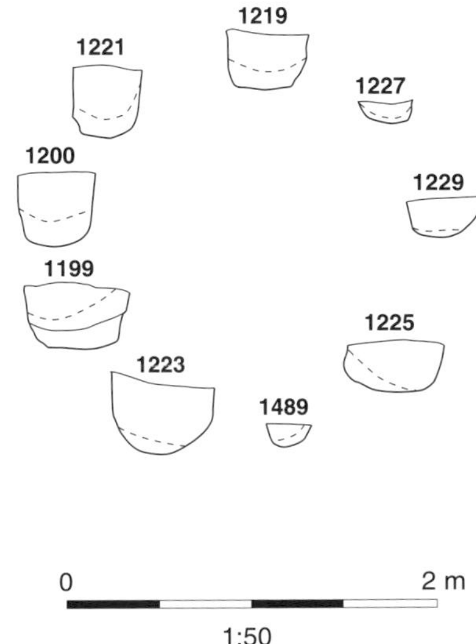

Fig. 5.22 Structure 1482 plan and sections

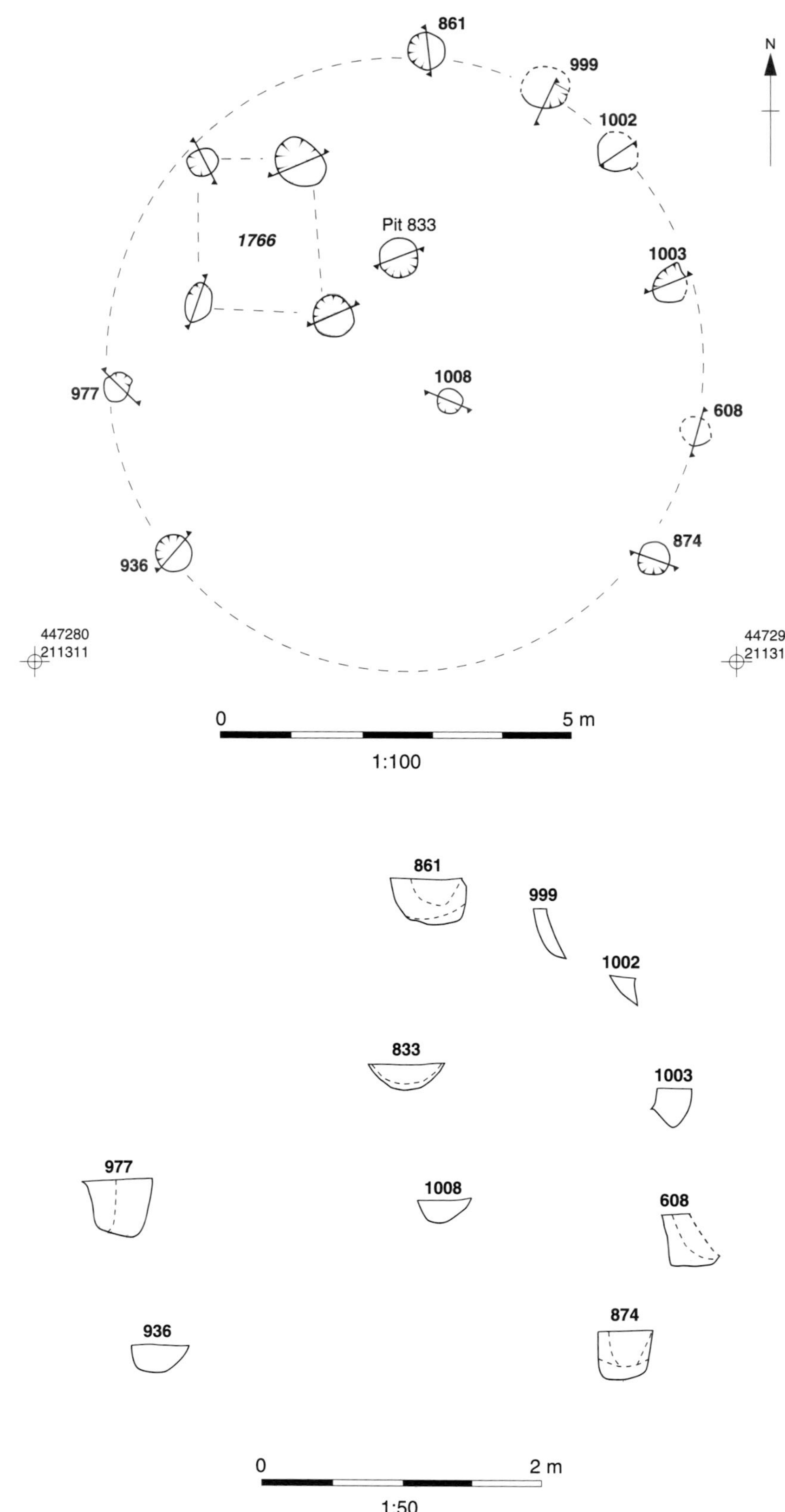

Fig. 5.23 Structure 1754 and four-post structure 1766 and pit 833, plan and sections

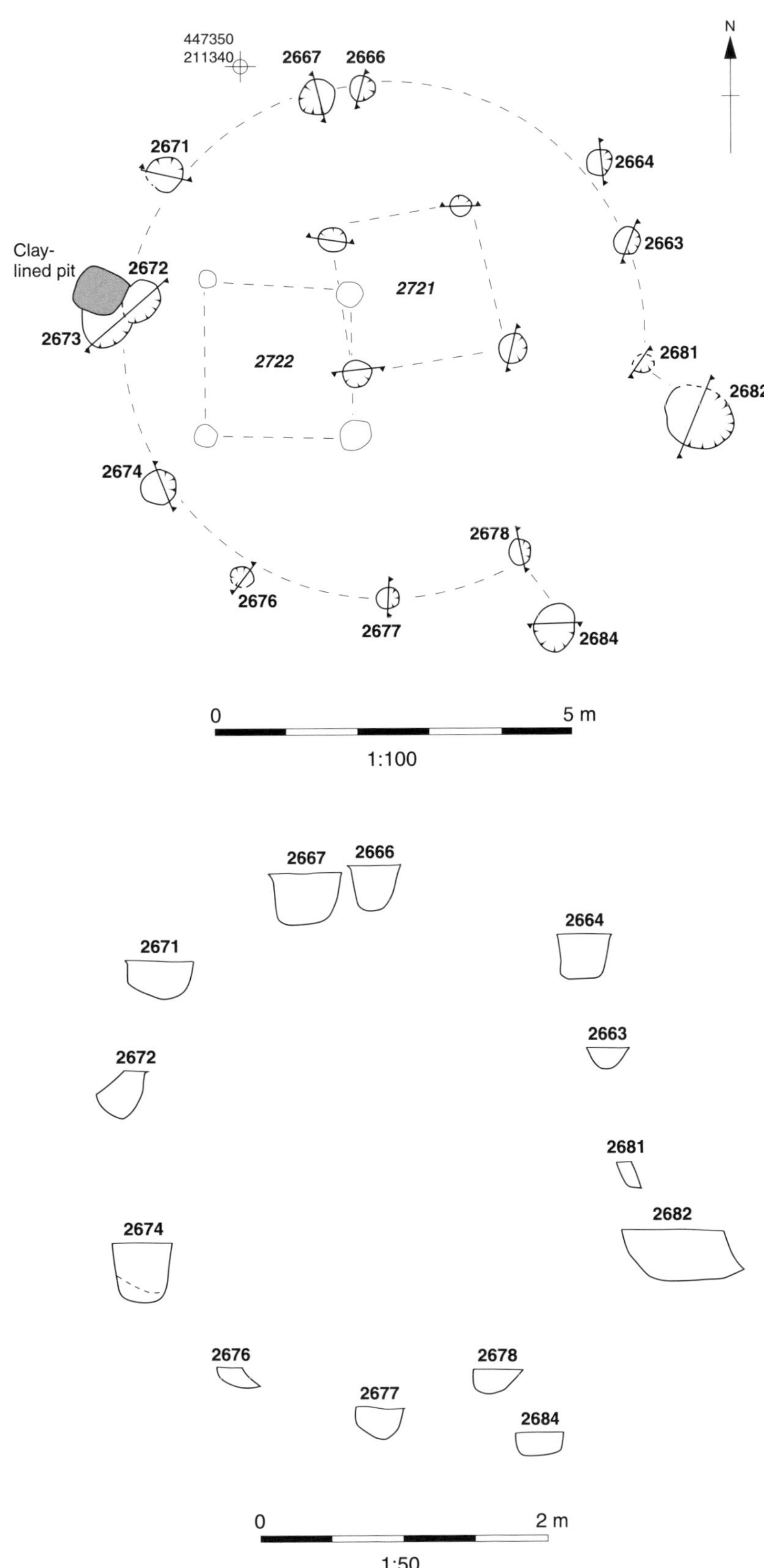

Fig. 5.24 Structure 2661 plan and sections

Finds were limited to four large sherds of early Iron Age shell-tempered pottery and four fragments of animal bone.

A clay-lined pit (833) located within the northern part of the structure may have been contemporary with the use of the building.

Four-post structure 1766 (Fig. 5.23)

A four-post structure, measuring 2 m by 1.75 m, was situated approximately 4 m south-west of circular structure 1754, in an area which later formed the entrance of a middle Iron Age enclosure (241). The postholes making up this structure were circular, measuring 0.41-0.59 m in diameter and 0.1-0.4 m in depth. Postholes 892 and 916 were substantial features with steep sides and flat, or slightly rounded bases; 919 and 980 were very shallow, probably the result of differential preservation. Fills comprised orange-brown sandy loams, with no finds.

The eastern group of structures on the Yarnton site (Fig. 5.7)

The eastern group of structures consisted of three roundhouses and five four-post structures. Two of the roundhouses were of medium size, one situated to the south-east of the other. Both of these buildings had clearly discernible entrances orientated south-east and south respectively. The third roundhouse was situated further to the west, and was bounded by an oval ditched enclosure, which had been cut away to the south by later Roman enclosures. A fragment of ditch to the south-west of the building (38) may have been part of this enclosure. This building was smaller than either of the roundhouses to its east, and probably originally had an entrance to the south or south-east which was also destroyed by the later Roman ditches. Of the five four-post structures which were found in this area, three lay within roundhouses. One of these was situated fairly centrally within the smaller building, the other two lay within the northern building and could be seen to be superimposed in plan; they cannot have been contemporary with one another and neither is likely to have been contemporary with the structure within which they lay. The remaining four-post structures lay between the larger roundhouses.

These structures were associated with a group of pits, most of which lay to the east of the roundhouses, but two of which were found within the circumference of the southern building. The two larger roundhouses, with their associated pits and four-post structures, were similar in form to the western group, and may be assumed to have had a similar function. However, the layout of the smaller roundhouse surrounded by an enclosure ditch may mark this structure out as different.

Fig. 5.25 Structure 2661 with four-post structure 2721

Structure 2661 (Figs 5.24 and 5.25)

This circular post-built structure lay on the north-east edge of the site, comprising 13 postholes, with a diameter of 7.5 m and a south-east facing entrance 3 m wide, marked by a possible entrance porch consisting of large postholes 2682 and 2684 protruding 1 m beyond the main roof-support posts. The postholes making up this structure were circular in plan, measuring 0.3-0.9 m in diameter and 0.2-0.4 m in depth. Profiles were steep-sided, with flat or rounded bases, or bowl-shaped. Fills consisted of brown and grey silty sands containing 5-10% gravel and postholes 2663, 2664 and 2666 contained charcoal flecks. Finds from the postholes comprise 31 sherds (467 g) of early Iron Age pottery.

An unexcavated clay-lined pit was situated just beyond the line of the roof-support posts. If the wall of the building lay beyond the ring beam, as seems likely, the pit may have been within the building and contemporary with its occupation. Several unexcavated postholes inside the southern part of the structure (Fig. 5.7) may have been additional roof supports or associated with smaller internal features. Two overlapping four-post structures, 2721 and 2722, were also found within the circumference of the building. Neither can be linked stratigraphically to the building itself, although it is unlikely that either was contemporary with it. Equally, they cannot have been contemporary with each other.

Structure 2694 (Figs 5.26 and 5.27)

A sub-circular post-built structure lay to the south-east with roof support-posts giving a diameter of 6.5-7 m. It had a south-facing entrance, 3 m wide, marked by porch posts protruding 1 m beyond the wall line. This structure comprised 14-17 postholes which were circular in plan, and measured 0.25-0.45 m in diameter and 0.06-0.28 m in depth. Time pressures in this watching brief area precluded the full recording of some of these features. Profiles were varied: postholes 2695, 2696, 2702, 2704 and 2705 were steep-sided with flat or slightly rounded bases; the remainder were bowl-shaped. Fills consisted of brown and grey silty sands containing 5-50% gravel/pea grit. Like structure 1756 (see below), structure 2694 contained a central posthole or small pit, 2693, which may have been contemporary with the use of the building. Finds were restricted to 12 sherds (227 g) of early Iron Age pottery. As in structure 2661, a clay-lined pit lay on the circumference of the roof supports in the north of the structure.

Structure 1756 (Fig. 5.28)

A small circular post-built structure 5.2 m in diameter and comprising 11 extant postholes lay in the west of this group of structures. It was surrounded on its northern side by a gully (26),

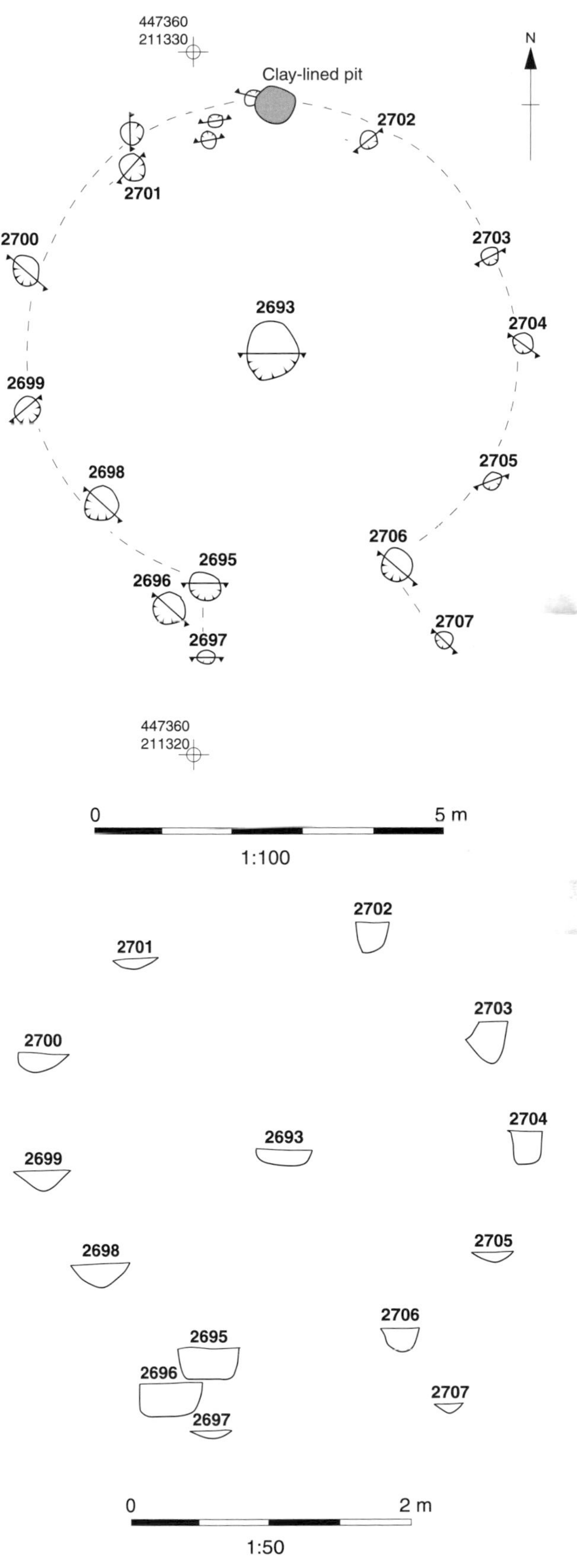

Fig. 5.26 Structure 2694 plan and sections

Fig. 5.27 Structure 2694

which was difficult to trace to the east and south because of later features (Fig. 5.7) but which may have been open on the south and south-west sides. (A possible terminal is visible in plan to the south-west, but was not examined on the ground). A cluster of pits and postholes lay to the south and a central pit or large posthole with at least two cuts (1127/1128) may have been contemporary with the use of the building. A four-post structure, 1770, was also found centrally placed within this structure (see below).

Recutting of postholes to the south-east may indicate the position of an entrance in this direction, 1.5 m wide (between postholes 1166/1167 and 1103/1178), but the building had been cut away to the south by a later ditch and an entrance could also have lain in this direction. The postholes making up this structure were roughly circular in plan, measuring 0.3-0.65 m in diameter and 0.12-0.42 m in depth. Profiles were varied, some were steep-sided with flat or rounded bases and others were bowl-shaped or shallow (Fig. 5.28). Some postholes had been partly cut away by later features, obscuring their original shapes. Fills comprised brown sandy silts containing 5-20% gravel and some charcoal and charcoal flecking was in evidence, particularly in the fills of 1109 and 1137. Animal disturbance had affected 1109, 1114 and 1208. Finds from the postholes included seven sherds of early Iron Age shell-tempered pottery and 19 fragments of animal bone. The central pit 1127 contained six large cow bones.

Four-post structures in the eastern area (Fig. 5.29)

Structure 1770

Four post structure 1770, measuring 2.1 m by 2.5 m, was found within the area enclosed by structure 1756. Although it was centrally located within that structure, the latter was so small that extra roof supports would have been unnecessary and it seems unlikely that the two structures were contemporary. The postholes were circular in plan with varied profiles; two were steep-sided with flat bases, one was bowl-shaped and the other shallow. No recuts were apparent, although postholes (1111 and 1126) contained two fills each while the other two both contained single fills. Fills consisted of brown silty sands containing 5-50% gravel. A single scrap of sand-tempered pottery and three animal bone fragments came from the fills.

Structure 2721

Four-post structure 2721, measuring 2.2 m by 2.4 m, was situated within roundhouse 2661, though it was not centrally placed. The postholes were circular in plan, with diameters of 0.3-0.4 m and depths of 0.16-0.26 m. Profiles were bowl-shaped and fills consisted of brown silty sands containing approximately 5% gravel. A single sherd of early Iron Age shell-tempered pottery came from one of the postholes.

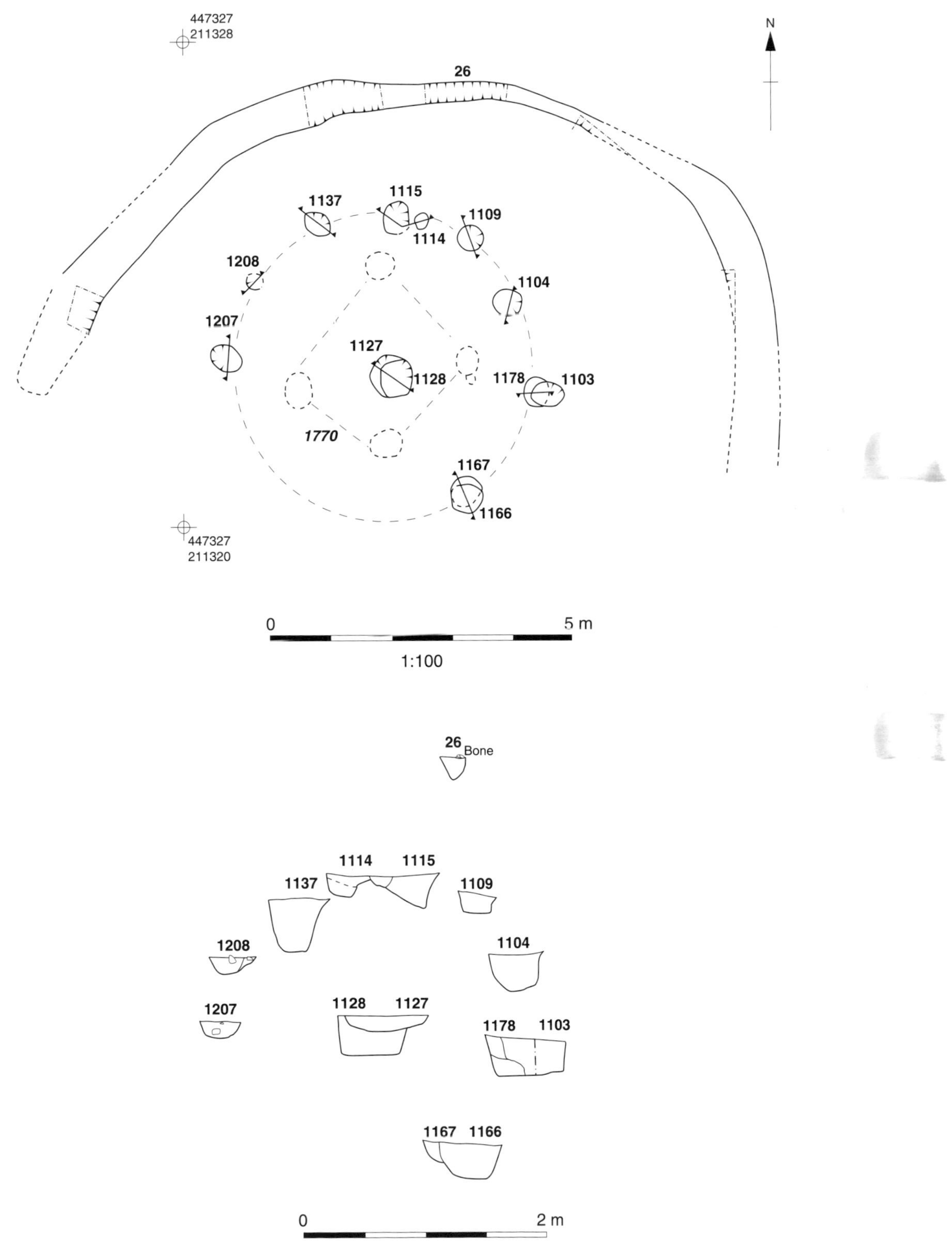

Fig. 5.28 Structure 1756, four-post structure 1770 and enclosure 26, plan and sections

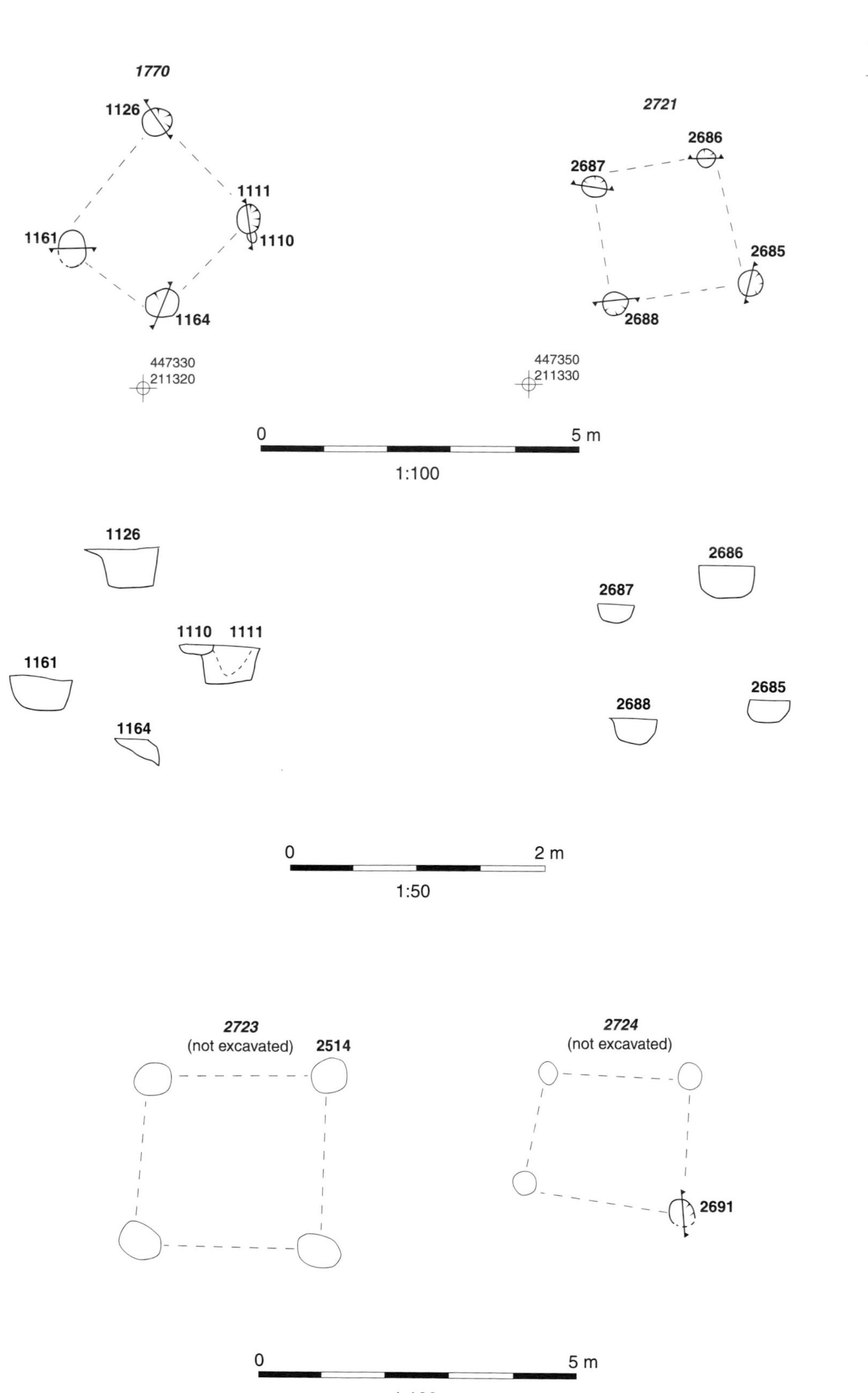

Fig. 5.29 Four-post structures 1770 and 2721, plans and sections, and 2723 and 2724 (plans only)

Structure 2722

Another probable four-post structure, 2722, measuring 2.3 m by 2.4 m, was also found within roundhouse 2661 (Fig. 5.24). The postholes making up the structure were circular in plan and 0.3-0.4 m in diameter. They were not excavated and thus there is no dating evidence to help determine its relationship to structure 2661 or adjacent four-post structure 2721.

Structure 2723

The unexcavated postholes of a four-post structure, 2723, measuring approximately 2.9 m by 2.9 m, were exposed to the east of roundhouses 2661 and 2694. The postholes making up this structure were circular in plan with diameters of approximately 0.6 m. Two sherds of early Iron Age pottery were recovered from the surface of posthole 2514.

Structure 2724

A four post structure, 2724, measuring 2.8 m by 2 m, lay south-east of circular structure 2661. The postholes were circular in plan and *c* 0.35-0.4 m in diameter. Only posthole 2691 was excavated. It was bowl-shaped in profile, measured 0.24 m in depth, and was filled with dark brown loam. No finds were recovered from this structure.

The distribution of finds from structures

Roundhouses

Finds recovered from the early Iron Age roundhouses comprised pottery and a range of animal bone fragments (Tables 5.1-2). The individual pottery assemblages were not very large, and were not evenly spread in terms of quantity or average size of sherds. Structures 1474 and 2661 had reasonably-sized collections of material, but the numbers of sherds found in the others were small or very small (Table 5.1). Similarly, the animal bone assemblage was not large and was unevenly distributed amongst the different buildings, quantities ranging from 1 to 22 fragments per structure (Table 5.2). Those buildings with larger quantities of bone were not necessarily those which produced most pottery. One of the largest groups of bone came from structure 1756 which produced relatively little pottery. The animal bone assemblage represented a range of domestic species; cattle, sheep/goat and pig occurred in that order of frequency and no wild animal bones were present. Just over half the fragments were undiagnostic, however, being classified as cow/horse size, sheep/pig size or completely unidentifiable (26 out of 73 fragments).

Table 5.1 Quantities of pottery from early Iron Age structures by broad fabric type.

Structure	*Shell-tempered*	*Sand-tempered*	*Limestone-tempered*	*Flint-tempered*	*Grog-tempered*	*Indeterminate voids*	*Rock-tempered*	*Total*
Roundhouses								
1474	11 (141 g)	3 (21 g)	1 (4 g)		1 (4 g)			16 (170 g)
1482	5 (58 g)							5 (58 g)
1511	7 (377 g)			1 (5 g)				8 (382 g)
1752	1 (98 g)							1 (98 g)
1754	4 (157 g)							4 (157 g)
1756	7 (59 g)							7 (59 g)
1760	3 (24 g)							3 (24 g)
2661	22 (385 g)	5 (40 g)	3 (32 g)			1 (10 g)		31 (467 g)
2694	7 (195 g)	3 (20 g)		1 (5 g)			1 (7 g)	12 (227 g)
Total	67 (1494 g)	11 (81 g)	4 (36 g)	2 (10 g)	1 (4 g)	1 (10 g)	1 (7 g)	87 (1642 g)
Rectangular structure								
8202	4 (25 g)							4 (25 g)
D-shaped structures								
8396	5 (26 g)							5 (26 g)
8399	3 (6 g)	1 (3 g)						4 (9 g)
8788	8 (112 g)	2 (8 g)			1 (3 g)			11 (123 g)
8789	2 (16 g)							2 (16 g)
Total	18 (160 g)	3 (11 g)			1 (3 g)			22 (174 g)
Four-post structures								
1753	3 (49 g)	1 (3 g)						4 (52 g)
1770		1 (1 g)						1 (1 g)
2721	1 (6 g)							1 (6 g)
2723	2 (46 g)							2 (46 g)
Total	6 (101 g)	2 (4 g)						8 (105 g)

The overall (small) quantity of material, and its generally undiagnostic state, would suggest that the majority represents secondary deposition which accrued in the postholes of these structures either during their construction or their use.

Four-post structures

Very little pottery was recovered from the seven four-post structures, and this was unevenly distributed amongst the different structures (Table 5.1). Similarly, little animal bone was recovered, and this was found in only two structures. The bone was mostly undiagnostic. The size and condition of the finds once again suggests secondary deposition during the construction or use of the structures.

D-shaped structures

In general, the postholes related to the D-shaped structures contained similarly small quantities of finds, if any. Pottery typically consisted of one to three sherds from each posthole, almost always weighing less than 20 g. Similarly, animal bone usually occurred only as single fragments or in very small amounts. Most of the bone could not be identified but cow and sheep/goat bone were both recognised in structure 8399. Other finds were even more scarce, although fragments of a saddle quern (in posthole 8371) and charred grain (in posthole 7334) were found in structure 8396. The most characteristic material associated with these structures was burnt stone. This occurred not only in pits which may have been associated with the structures, often in large quantities, but also in some of the postholes where its presence may simply reflect expedient use of nearby stone for post-packing. The other finds need be nothing more than stray material which has been incidentally incorporated into the postholes.

Rectangular structure 8202

The finds from rectangular structure 8202 consisted only of small quantities of pottery, animal bone and burnt stone, similar to those recovered from the other structures. The only exceptional finds were the cremated animal bone associated with a fragment of possibly human femur in posthole 7018, situated not far from the pit (8591) which contained a human skull and pit 7029 which contained part of a neonate humerus.

ENCLOSURES, DITCHES, GULLIES AND FENCE LINES

Three shallow ditches or gullies at Yarnton appeared to be associated with the structures on that site. Other postholes and shallow ditches appeared to represent traces of enclosures and fences on Cresswell Field.

Table 5.2 Quantities of animal bone (fragment count) from early Iron Age structures.

Structure	*Cattle*	*Cattle/Horse size*	*Horse*	*Sheep/goat*	*Sheep/Pig size*	*Pig*	*Unidentified*	*Total animal bone*
Roundhouses								
1474	3	1		3	2	2	6	17
1482	1					2	3	6
1511	1	3		2	2		3	11
1754				2			2	4
1756	10	2		2			8	22
1760				1	1	1	1	4
1761	2					1		3
2661				3			2	5
2694							1	1
Total	17	6		13	5	6	26	73
Rectangular structure								
8202	1			1	1		4	7
D-shaped structures								
8399	3	3		1	3		1	11
8788		4		1	2			7
8789	1			2	5			8
Total	*4*	*7*		*4*	*10*		*1*	*26*
Four-post structures								
1753		2			2	1		5
1770	1	1		1				3
Total	1	3		1	2	1		8

Ditches and gullies at Yarnton

Enclosure 26 (Fig. 5.28)

A curvilinear ditch, 35 m in length and enclosing an area of approximately 10 m by 15 m, lay around the northern side of structure 1756 in the east of the Yarnton site. No part of a southern side of this potential enclosure survived, but an entrance may have lain to the south-west where the enclosure had been cut away by later ditches, and where a possible terminal (not excavated) can be seen in plan. Five sections were excavated through the enclosure ditch, representing 15% of its total length. The ditch had a very variable profile, the average width being 0.3 m and average depth 0.15 m, and had a homogeneous and non-gravelly fill. There was no evidence of recutting. Finds from the ditch comprised three sherds of early Iron Age pottery, one piece of slag, two animal bones and charred plant remains with cereal grains and weed seeds present.

Ditch 38 (Fig. 5.7)

A short stretch of linear ditch or gully (38), 0.45 m in length and orientated NE-SW, was found to the south-west of enclosure 26, and may have been contemporary with the early Iron Age features in this area, perhaps being associated with enclosure 26. The feature was much cut away by later ditches and a single segment was excavated through all that survived of it. It was 0.55 m wide and 0.2 m deep, with an irregular base, but too little survived to provide a definable profile. Fills consisted of non-gravelly material. The only find was a single cattle bone.

Gully 1018 (Fig. 5.7)

A linear gully, 1018, ran WSW from the edge of structure 1754 in the centre of the Yarnton site for a distance of 2.65 m. Its profile was U-shaped and open, measuring 0.32 m wide and 0.12 m deep on average. There was no evidence of recutting. Fills consisted of mixed material with some primary silting. Three sherds of early Iron Age pottery and an animal bone were retrieved.

Enclosures, fences and gullies on Cresswell Field

Possible fenced enclosure 8792 (Figs 5.6 and 5.30)

An oval arrangement of fourteen postholes enclosing an area approximately 10 m x 8.5 m was located in the central area of Cresswell Field. Eight of the postholes were excavated and all of these were well defined, and of similar size and character. They appeared to be too widely spaced in comparison to the size of the area they enclosed to support a building, and it seems likely that this was a fenced enclosure, probably an animal pen. The only finds recovered from the postholes comprised a few small pieces of animal bone and burnt stone, thus dating remains uncertain. The enclosure lay just to the north of early Iron Age structure 8396 (see above), but was also in close proximity to a Saxon sunken-featured building (7325), and it could have been associated with either of these structures.

Possible fence line (Fig 5.6)

Four postholes (7146, 7380, 7382 and 7384) formed a straight north-south alignment immediately north-east of fenced enclosure 8792. They were evenly, but widely, spaced at around 5 m apart. It is possible that, as perhaps with enclosure 8792, a fence had originally been made up of larger posts interspersed with smaller uprights, traces of which have not survived later ploughing. Two of the postholes (7380 and 7382) produced sherds of early Iron Age pottery and, although there were numerous fence lines associated with the Saxon occupation in the area further to the north, they all lay on a common ESE-WNW alignment, so an early Iron Age date for this alignment seems likely.

Ditch Group 8790 (Figs 5.6 and 5.31)

An arrangement of shallow discontinuous stretches of east-west and north-south aligned gullies situated toward the north-east corner of the Cresswell Field site appeared to form part of a possible enclosure only the southern end of which (measuring approximately 20 m east-west and 10 m north-south) lay within the area of excavation.

The gullies varied between 0.45-0.7 m in width and 0.04-0.28 m in depth along their lengths. They mostly contained a single uniform fill of grey-brown sandy silt. There was some suggestion of a recut along part of one of the gullies which formed the eastern side of the enclosure (gully 7234/7238, recut 7232/7236) and also along part of the gully which appeared to form the southern edge (gully 7115, recut 7113).

A small quantity (18 sherds) of fairly mixed pottery was recovered from the gullies on all three sides of the enclosure. Most of this material was early Iron Age in date (15 sherds), though it included two possibly earlier transitional late Bronze Age/early Iron Age sherds. In addition, two sherds of middle Iron Age pottery were recovered from one of the apparent recuts 7236 (7235) and a single sherd of Romano-British pottery came from the gully which formed the western side of the enclosure (gully 7198, fill 7197). However, these three later sherds comprised only small scraps weighing a total of 9 g and were probably intrusive. The only other finds recovered consisted of a single small fragment of animal bone and a flint flake.

Although the gullies were discontinuous and slightly irregular, they appear to have defined an area, possibly an enclosure, which was then respected by the dense east-west swathe of early

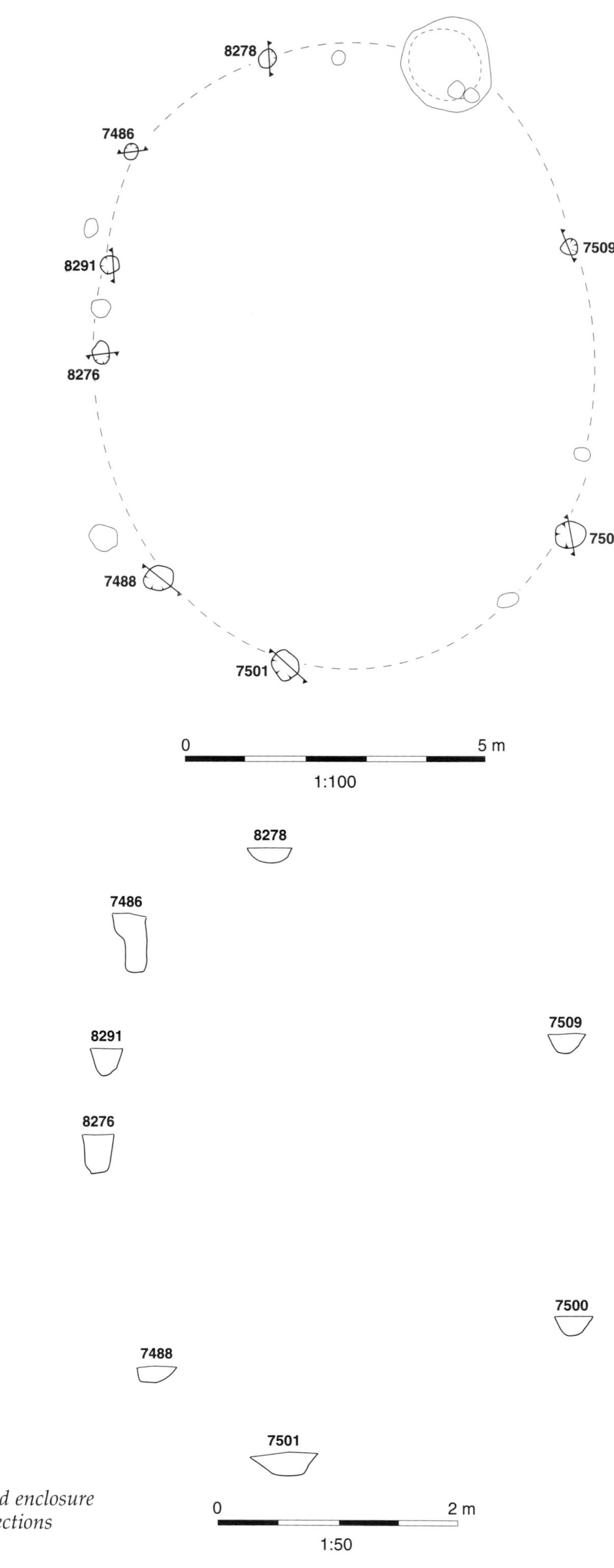

Fig. 5.30 Fenced enclosure 8792 plan and sections

Iron Age pits. Indeed, when observing the overall site plan (Fig. 5.6) the absence of features within the area of the enclosure is quite striking in comparison to the areas immediately to the east and west. It is also noticeable that there were very few features in the area to the south of the enclosure, and as some of the gullies forming its eastern boundary actually continued into this area it is possible that the enclosure may originally have extended further to the south. Alternatively, the gullies may have been associated with an access route through the area of pits and the settlement itself.

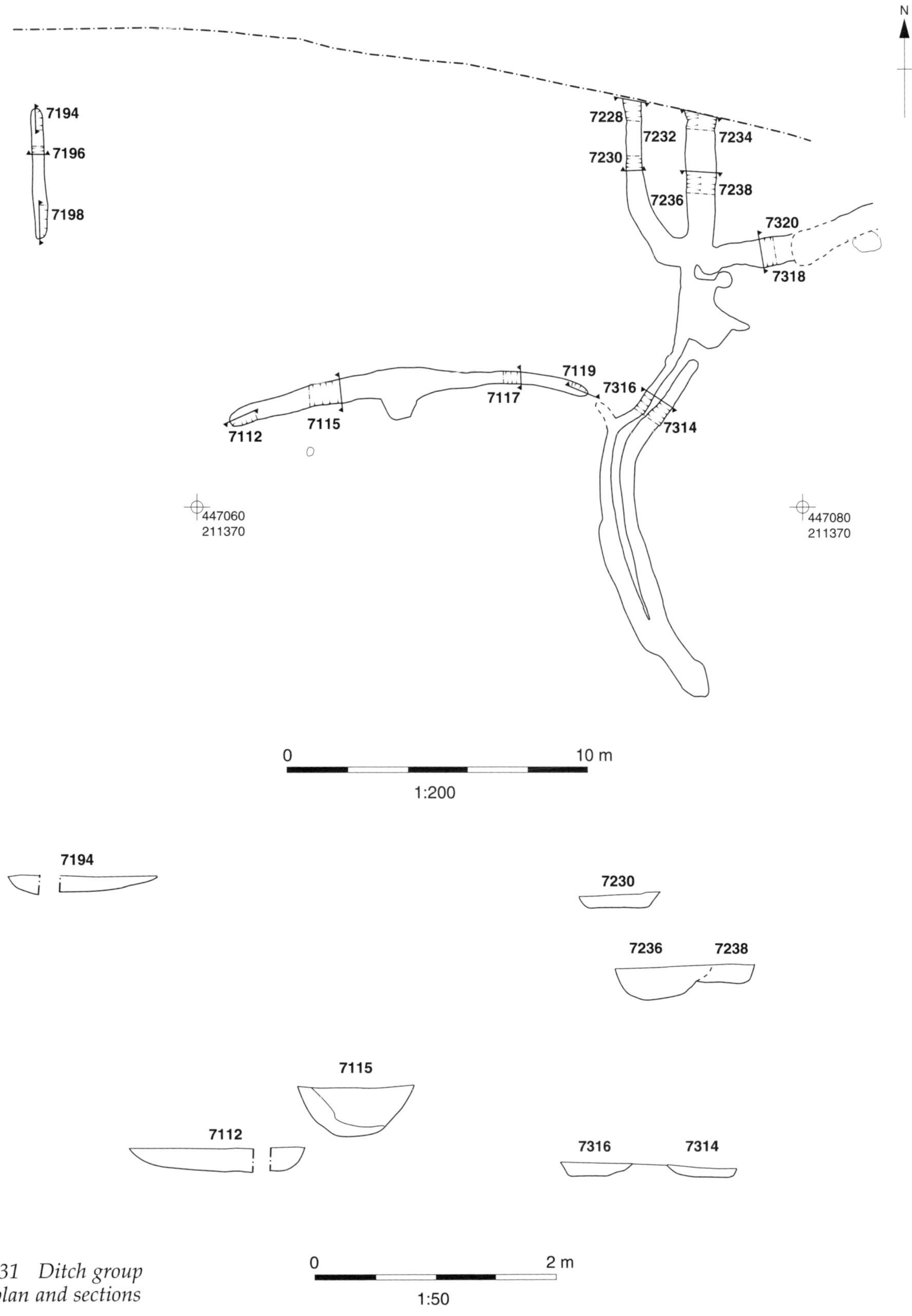

Fig. 5.31 Ditch group 8790 plan and sections

Although there has been some truncation of the gullies by later ploughing, the survival of posthole structures in the areas immediately to the east and west suggests that this has not been severe. The gullies forming this enclosure, therefore, originally appear to have been fairly shallow and defined an area that did not require a substantial boundary.

Gullies in north-west corner of Cresswell Field (Figs 5.6 and 5.32)

A group of three gullies in the north-west corner of Cresswell Field appeared to be related to some form of enclosure, only a small part of which lay within the area of excavation. The gullies comprised a fairly straight north-south aligned segment (7582/7620), with a slightly curving segment (7574) immediately to the east, and another stretch of curving gully (7540/7585/7623/7527) running roughly east-west and then curving to the south-east. The three features were fairly similar in size, varying along their lengths from 0.35 m to 0.5 m in width and 0.16 m to 0.32 m in depth, but their profiles were variable. All three gullies contained two fills of similar clay silt material.

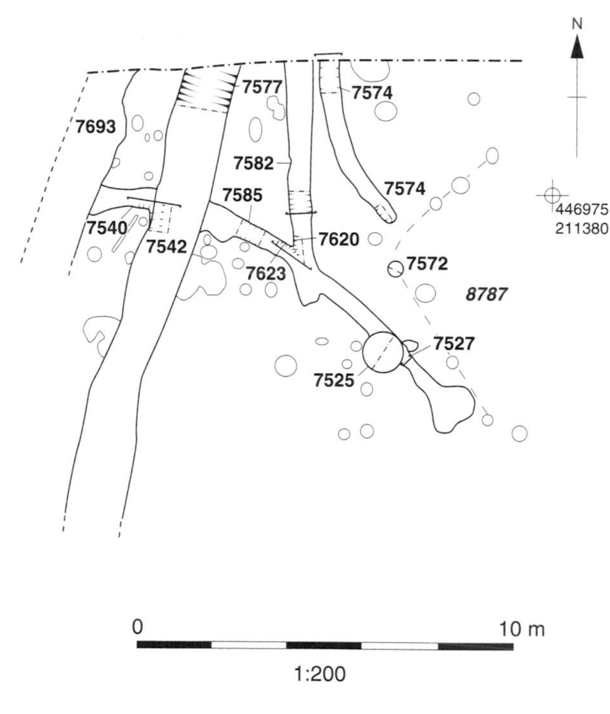

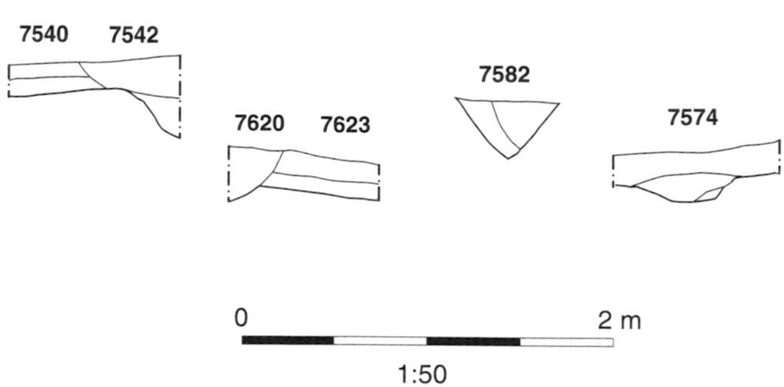

Fig. 5.32 Gullies in the north-west corner of Cresswell Field

Segment 7623 of the NW-SE gully (7540 etc) appeared to be cut by straight north-south gully 7620, but their fills were so similar that this relationship was uncertain and they may have been contemporary. The NW-SE gully was itself cut by two ditches of probable Romano-British date (7577 and 7693) and, at its eastern end, by an early Iron Age pit (7525). Both 7540 (etc) and 7574 terminated very close to the D-shaped structure 8787. The only dating evidence recovered from the gullies comprised five small sherds of early Iron Age pottery. The stratigraphic relationship with pit 7525 indicated that this possible enclosure was no later than the early Iron Age.

Other ditches and gullies in Cresswell Field (Fig. 5.6)

A 13.5 m segment of east-west ditch (7297/7474) lay close to the south edge of excavation towards the east end of Cresswell Field. The ditch, which was 0.8 m wide and up to 0.5 m deep, produced 15 sherds of early Iron Age pottery, which was mostly concentrated towards the western terminal. It also contained a single sherd of Saxon pottery, though this had almost certainly been introduced as a result of animal burrowing which was clearly visible in section. A narrow linear gully (7503) extending from the west terminal of ditch 7297/7474 appeared to be the continuation of one of the burrows. It was less certain whether a short gully (7295) to the north of 7297/7474 was also a burrow or a settlement feature.

Three shallow, slightly irregular segments of gully lay close to the south edge of the excavation (Fig. 5.6). They comprised two NE-SW segments (8385/8387 and 8413/8415), which appear originally to have been continuous, and a curving east-west segment (8409/8411) which intersected with the southern segment of NE-SW gully. The gullies were between 0.45 m and 0.6 m wide and up to 0.2 m deep. A small quantity of early Iron Age pottery and slag was recovered from these features; their function remains unclear.

The remnant of narrow curving gully (8021), 13 m in length, 0.3 m wide and up to 0.14 m deep, survived in the south-west of the site (Fig. 5.6). This feature was much truncated and it seems probable that it was once more substantial. The only find recovered was a single, but large (55 g), sherd of early Iron Age pottery.

A short stretch of east-west aligned gully (7346), 4.6 m long, 0.6 m wide and 0.4 m deep, lay north-east of the centre of the site. The clear definition of its terminals suggests that it was not originally part of a larger feature, the rest of which has been removed by truncation. It contained six sherds of early Iron Age pottery (49 g) but also a domestic fowl bone. Since the latter is perhaps most likely to be of Roman date the date of the feature is therefore uncertain.

Six other small linear features in the centre (7204, 7218 and 7322) and north-west (8152, 8036 and 8131) of the site were irregular and seem likely to have been animal burrows. No finds were recovered from them. Other narrow, irregular but deep features (including 8606) proved to be ice wedges. These features were later observed in section during gravel extraction where they could be seen tapering down several metres into the gravel terrace.

OTHER FEATURES ON CRESSWELL FIELD

Postholes in the central area of Cresswell Field (Fig. 5.6)

A sparse scatter of postholes was investigated in the central area of Cresswell Field, but no structures or alignments could be identified, not even any well-defined pairs of posts. Only five of the postholes produced any dating evidence and this all comprised small sherds of early Iron Age pottery. Two fragments representing the mid shaft of a probable human adult ulna were recovered from stakehole 7644, which cut put 7598.

These features may have been tethering or marker posts, and could have been associated with either the Iron Age or Saxon occupation.

Hearth feature 7185 (Fig. 5.33)

A shallow, irregular-shaped scoop (7185) containing large quantities of charcoal and burnt clay was located toward the northern edge of the site, to the east of structure 8399. The feature was 1.8 m x 1.1 m in plan and 0.2 m in deep and appeared to be a sunken hearth, although its function was slightly uncertain. It produced two small sherds of early Iron Age pottery, and small quantities of burnt stone, charred grain, and fragments of animal bone, three of which were burnt and another of which showed signs of gnawing.

There were no postholes in close proximity to suggest an associated structure, but the hearth lay within an area of fairly densely-concentrated early Iron Age pits. One of these pits (7149) also contained significant quantities of charcoal and charred grain and it is possible that the two features were associated in some way. Within the wider area there were also a number of fence lines associated with the Saxon occupation, and it is possible that the hearth was a Saxon feature containing redeposited pottery.

Midden deposit 7003 (Figs 5.6 and 5.34)

A layer of silty loam (7003) containing large quantities of early Iron Age pottery and other domestic refuse extended over an area approximately 20 m square at the southern edge of Cresswell Field. This deposit appeared to fill a slight hollow, and was at its thickest towards the south where it was up to 0.5 m deep. A 1 m wide section was hand dug through the deepest part of the deposit and the spoil was dry sieved to recover artefacts. This exercise produced

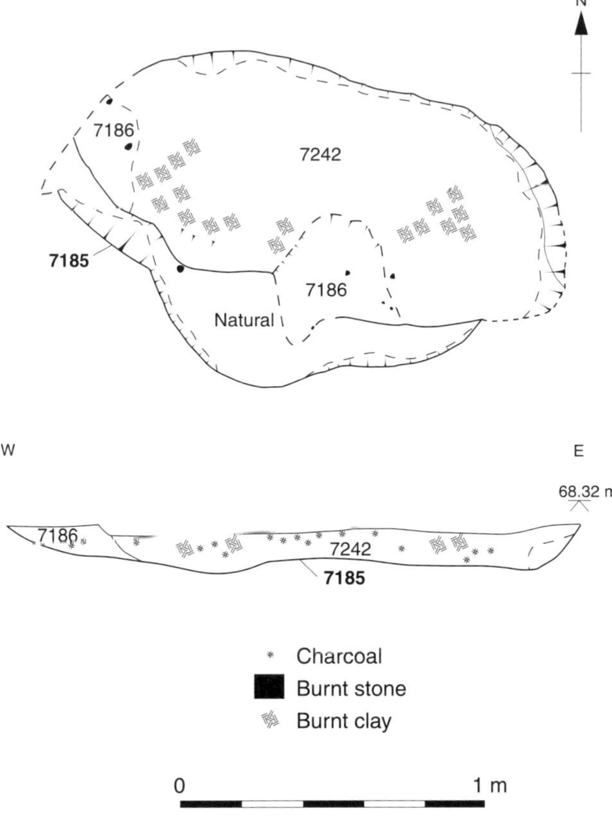

Fig. 5.33 Hearth 7185

140 sherds of early Iron Age pottery (3 kg), 85 pieces of animal bone, including a polished bone metatarsal and part of a deer antler, and a small quantity of briquetage and slag. The olive colour and character of this deposit suggested that it may also originally have contained cess or other organic matter. Further assemblages of animal bone, including an antler cheek piece (Fig. 15.8, Fig. 15.10, No. 24), an antler handle and early Iron Age pottery, were recovered from a pit (8195) which was exposed beneath this layer.

During the machine stripping of the topsoil in the area of the field overlying layer 7003, a large finds scatter was observed and 568 g of pottery (66 sherds) was collected (7016). All the pottery was early Iron Age in date and was almost certainly derived from the layer below, having been brought to the surface by ploughing. The midden would therefore appear to have originally been fairly substantial, and may have been associated with one or more of the early Iron Age dwellings which lay only a short distance to the north (8396) and west (8788 and 8789).

PITS

Summary

Pits formed a major component of the evidence for the early Iron Age settlement (Figs 5.6 and 5.7). It was not possible to excavate all these features in the

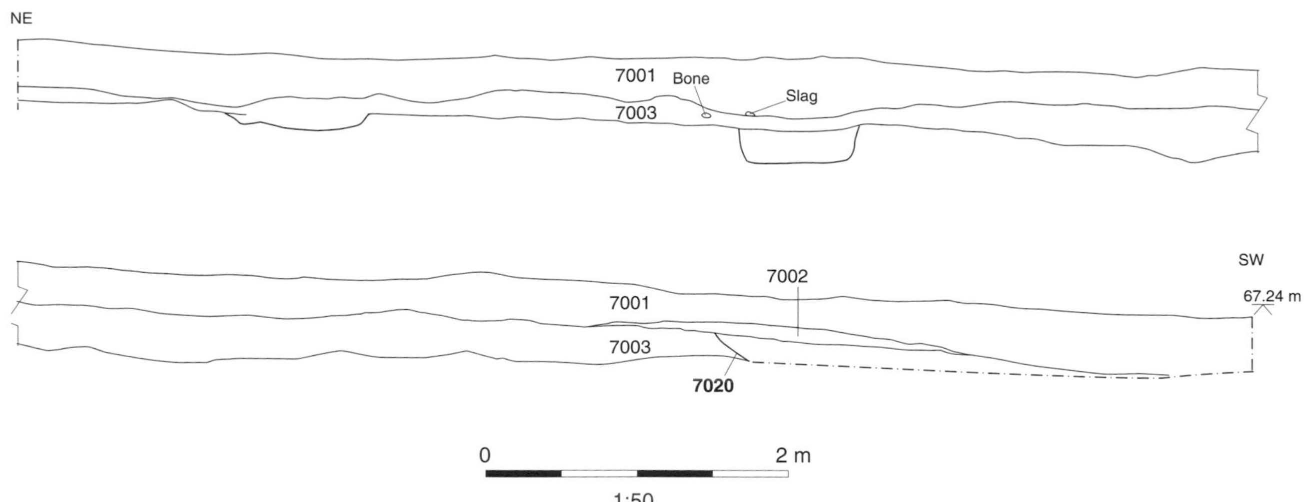

Fig. 5.34 Section through midden deposit 7003

time available, but care was taken to examine a stratified random sample of those present, as described in Chapter 1. At Yarnton only 25% of the pits were excavated, but on Cresswell Field it was possible to investigate 45% of these features.

At Cresswell Field some 253 pits were excavated, of which 132 (52%) have been assigned to the early Iron Age period, while at Yarnton 63 (16%) out of a total 384 excavated pits were dated to this phase. This suggests that there would have been approximately 293 pits of early Iron Age date on Cresswell Field and 252 at Yarnton, indicating the westerly focus of activity at this time.

Pits were usually dated by the pottery recovered from them, the dates being determined principally from the character of the fabrics, and occasional stratigraphic relationships with other dated features. Approximately 15% of the excavated pits, however, contained no clear dating evidence and these were assigned to phase on the basis of their spatial distribution.

Pit distribution

As already described, the majority of pits in Cresswell Field lay in two groups, one a broad north-south swathe, *c* 20 m wide, parallel to the palaeochannel and the other aligned WNW-ESE along the northern edge of the excavation area where they occupied an area around 25 m wide. Their extent to the north was confirmed by geophysical survey and evaluation trenching. This

Table 5.3 Numbers of early Iron Age pit types

	Undercut (GSP)	*Cylindrical*	*Bowl-shaped*	*Large shallow*	*Shallow saucer*	*Other*	*Total*
Cresswell Field	9	66	34	12	5	6	132
Yarnton	1	24	9	4	5	20	63
Total	10	90	43	16	10	26	195

GSP = 'grain storage' pit

Table 5.4 Pit dimensions (m) by type (range for those where dimensions were recorded).

Dimensions	*Undercut (GSP)*	*Cylindrical*	*Bowl-shaped*	*Large shallow*	*Shallow saucer*	*Other*
Yarnton						
Length	-	1.06-2.1	0.78	1-1.14	0.7	-
Breadth	1.65	0.5-2.56	0.5-1.5	0.6-2.0	0.7-1.2	0.4-1.8
Depth	0.9	0.24-0.45	0.24-0.45	0.21-0.45	0.14-0.25	0.15-0.92
Cresswell Field						
Length	1.09-1.52	0.34-2.18	0.46-3.0	-	-	0.46-1.5
Breadth	1.0-2.06	0.32-2.45	0.26-2.5	1-2.15	0.55-0.82	0.44-1.5
Depth	0.56-1.12	0.11-0.8	0.13-0.75	0.1-0.3	0.04-0.2	0.2-0.84

alignment lay approximately parallel to the edge of the gravel terrace, 80 m from its edge, and appeared to continue east into the Yarnton site, where the densest groups of pits lay along the northern edge of the excavation area, although much disturbed by later ditch digging. Within this broad trend, some patterning could be discerned, with some pits lying in groups which appeared to be directly associated with individual structures or house plots on both sites. There was also an impression on Cresswell Field that rows or alignments of pits occurred within the two main swathes, but too few of these were excavated to allow this issue to be clarified.

Pit morphology

Most of the pits were circular in plan with a few oval or sub-circular examples. The majority (*c* 46%) were flat-bottomed cylinders, with a smaller number of concave or bowl-shaped features and just one or two which had conical profiles. In addition, there were a number of shallow scoops and other amorphous forms, some of which were probably the result of the

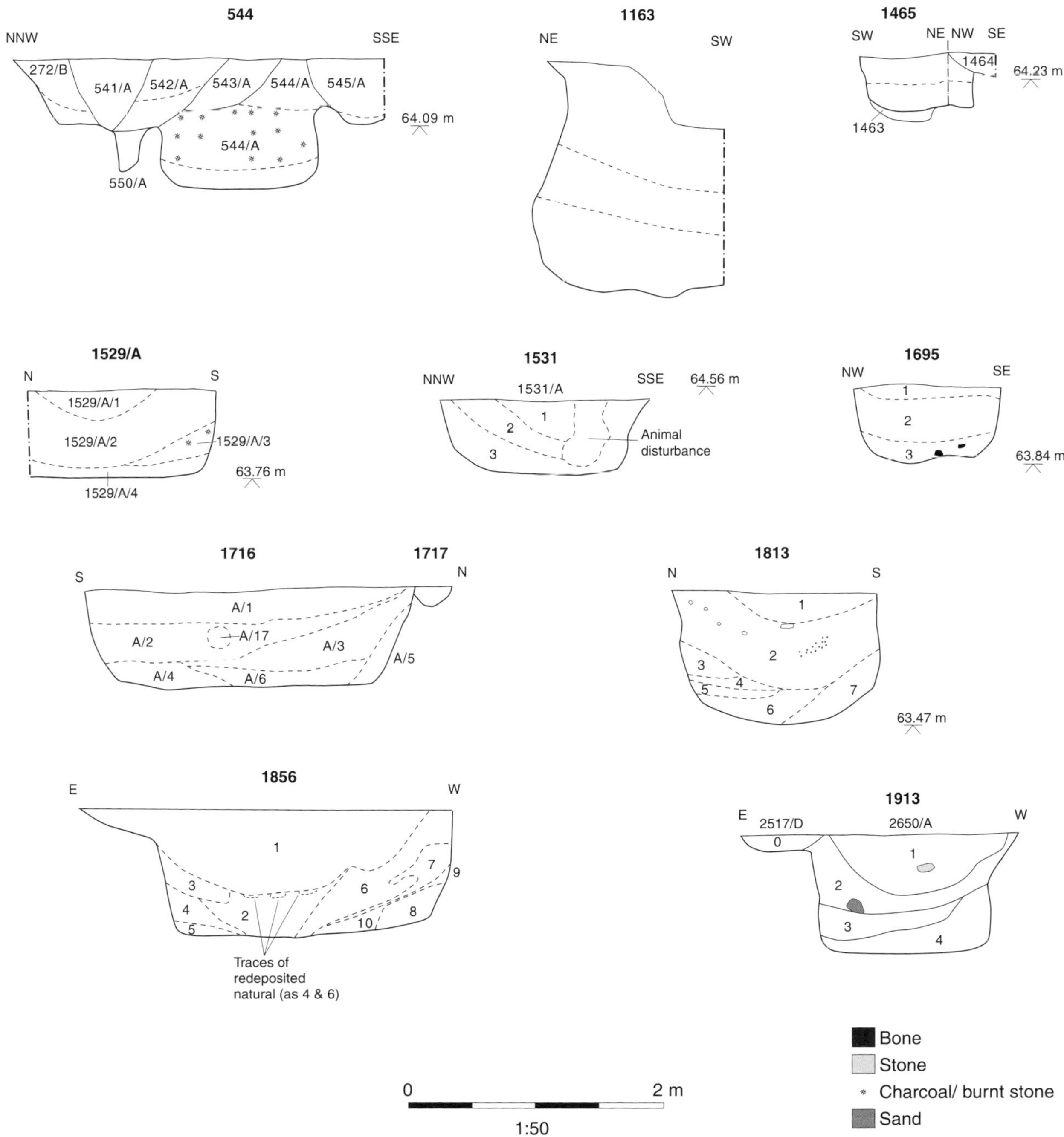

Fig. 5.35 Sections of selected grain storage pits at Yarnton: 544, 1163, 1465, 1529, 1531, 1695, 1716, 1813, 1856 and 1913

collapse of unstable and quick-weathering gravel in the sides of pits. There were no traces of gravel upcast from these features, but evidence from better-preserved sites elsewhere, such as Farmoor (Lambrick and Robinson 1979) and Mingies Ditch (Allen and Robinson 1993, 26-8) suggests that the gravel would have been used for floors, paths and tracks. It may also have been used to level off abandoned pits where the fills may have sunk.

The 63 Yarnton pits assigned to the early Iron Age were divided into six categories based on their shape in profile (Table 5.3): undercut (classic grain-storage pit shape; 1), cylindrical (24), bowl-shaped (9), shallow saucer (5) and large shallow (4). Pit diameters ranged between 0.4 m and 2.56 m (averaging 1.19 m) and depth varied from 0.14 m to 2 m (averaging 0.53 m) (Table 5.4). The variation in pit size is illustrated by the estimates for original pit volumes, which ranged between 0.03 m^3 and 1.8 m^3, averaging 0.74 m^3. The pits found in the north-east of the site contained a higher proportion of larger features.

More undercut, grain-storage pits were identified at Cresswell Field (9) but, as at Yarnton, cylinders were the most common type (66). There were also 47 bowl-shaped features, 17 shallow pits of varying sizes and four that were V-shaped (two further pits could not be classified according to these categories). Pit diameters varied from 0.26 to 3.00 m (averaging 1.20 m) and depth varied from 0.03 m to 1.12 m (averaging 0.39 m). The pit volumes ranged from 0.01 m^3 to 3.73 m^3. Not surprisingly, the grain storage pits have the highest mean volume (1.57 m^3; range from 0.57 m^3 to 3.73 m^3), followed by the cylindrical pits (0.65 m^3; range from 0.03 m^3 to 3.32 m^3). Most of the grain storage pits were 0.8-1 m deep; only two were smaller (0.56 m and 0.73 m deep) and one larger (1.12 m deep). In contrast, the largest cylindrical pit was only 0.80 m deep, and only 18 were over 0.50 m deep; around half were less than 0.40 m deep.

It is likely that many of the pits recorded as cylinders at Yarnton and Cresswell Field were once grain-storage pits, but the loose and sandy character of the gravel here probably led to the collapse of the overhanging pit sides. Disturbance by later feature digging and truncation by ploughing are additional factors that may have caused pit profiles to straighten and widen. A number of examples of cylindrical pits which seem likely to have been grain-storage pits are shown on Figures 5.35 and 5.36; amongst these only pit 1163 was categorised as 'undercut'.

Pit fills

Soils

There were normally only one to four fills within each pit, although a few pits at Yarnton contained from five to nine fills with one exceptional example containing 18 well-defined deposits. Similarly, at Cresswell Field only six pits had more than four layers of fill: three grain-storage pits and three cylindrical pits, one of which (7452) contained 12 layers of fill. The character of the fills was generally homogeneous, consisting almost entirely of non-gravelly silt-loams, and the similarity between the fills made relationships between intercutting pits difficult to establish. Thirteen of the pits from Yarnton contained identifiable evidence of primary silting, and nine showed good evidence of having been deliberately backfilled; of these six were over 0.8 m^3 in volume. At Cresswell Field, evidence of primary silting was recorded in 36 pits but deliberate backfilling was only noted in three. Of these

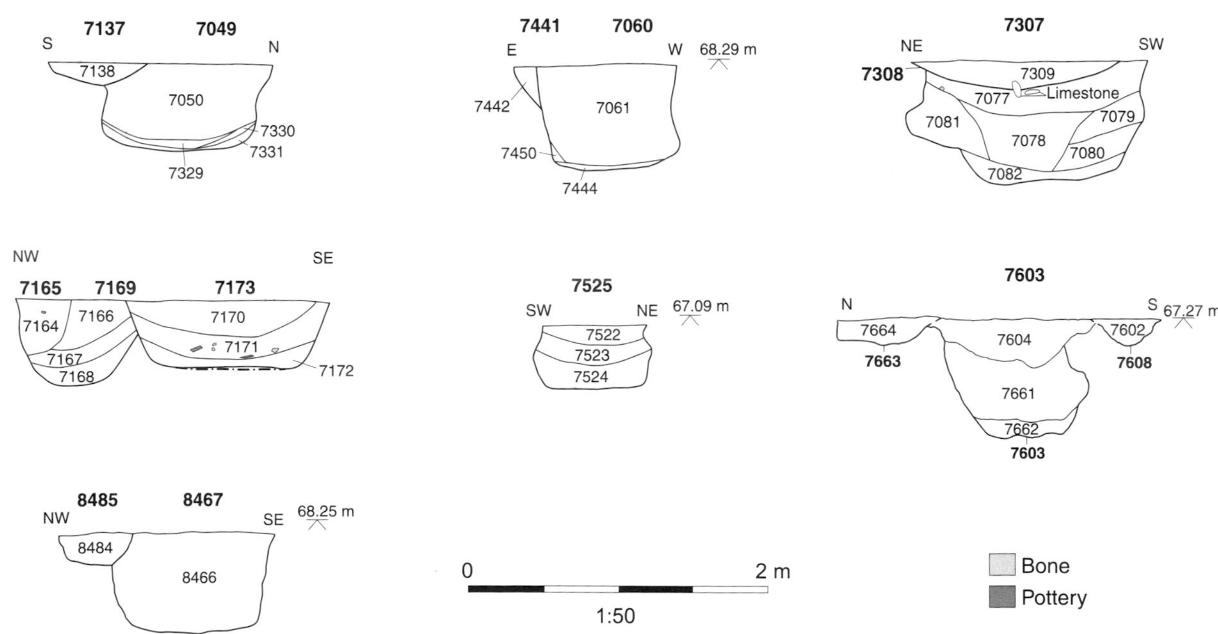

Fig. 5.36 Sections of selected grain storage pits at Cresswell Field: 7049, 7060, 7307, 7173, 7525, 7603 and 8467

three, two (7057 and 7560) were amongst the largest pits, with volumes over 3 m^3; pit 7787, however, was much smaller (0.27 m^3). Over half of the pits at Cresswell Field with evidence for primary silting had volumes over 0.80 m^3. Three pits had clay linings, two of which were associated with roundhouses 2661 and 2694 in the east of the Yarnton site, and the other lay within structure 1754.

The analysis of pits at Yarnton and Cresswell Field suggests that there was no correlation between fill types and pit shape, and it seems more likely that the general character of the soils derived principally from the geology through which the pits were cut. Recuts were rare at Yarnton (six examples with only two recut more than once) and absent on Cresswell Field.

Finds

Deposits that could be described as deliberately placed or special in some way were identified with some confidence in eleven pits, with another seven possible examples. These are discussed below. Otherwise, finds concentrations, although sometimes substantial, appeared more mundane. Finds usually occurred within the upper fills of pits, suggesting that the disposal of rubbish was very rarely the primary function of the pits even if they may ultimately have been used in this way. There was usually no clear distinction in spatial terms between pits containing deliberately-placed or special deposits and pits with more mundane finds assemblages.

One notable exception to this pattern – pit 7365 – also provides an example of a pit which cannot be very clearly categorised as either mundane or special. This feature was situated away from the main area of pits at Cresswell Field and lay at the entrance to a U-shaped barrow ditch of probable Neolithic date. The pit contained large quantities of domestic refuse, comprising over 400 pieces of animal bone and 200 sherds of early Iron Age pottery. However, mixed in with the normal domestic refuse were a fox leg bone, a deer bone, a dog bone, a bone object and large quantities of frog and toad bones. The inclusion of this material may suggest elements of deliberate selection of material and placed deposition.

Eleven pits on the Yarnton site and 34 pits on Cresswell Field contained substantial assemblages of pottery (over 25 sherds; groups of more than 50 sherds are located on Figs 5.37 and 5.38), and all of these contained animal bone of more than one species.

Finds distributions within pits

Human bone

Four early Iron Age pits (276, 951, 7029, 8591) contained human bone. The material from pit 276 comprised skull fragments. Pit 8591, however, contained a complete adult female skull which was placed upside down. The absence of the jaw suggests that the skull had been excarnated before deposition. A first phalanx and the distal half of a neonate humerus came from pits 951 and 7029 respectively (Fig. 5.43). Pits 7029 and 8591 were situated close together to the west of rectangular structure 8202 on Cresswell Field. One of the postholes associated with this structure (7018) contained what may have been a fragment of a human femur associated with cremated animal bone. It has been observed elsewhere that human remains in the early Iron Age tend to be found near or at the periphery of the settlement area (Wait 1985). This does not appear to be the case at Yarnton, but the sample is too small to make any broad generalisations. The proportion of early Iron Age pits with human remains seems, however, to be small (only 2%).

Animal bone

Of the 195 pits assigned to the early Iron Age, the majority (152) contained animal bone (104 at Cresswell Field and 48 at Yarnton), and some substantial deposits were present (Figs 5.37 and 5.38). The assemblages comprise mainly cattle and horse bones, with some sheep, pig, domestic fowl and dog. In addition to the remains of these mainstream domestic animals, a minority of pits contained the remains of wild animals such as red deer, wild bird, rabbit, and amphibians. It may be assumed that the rabbit bones are intrusive and derived from animals that died in their burrows. Amphibians may also have reached the pits by themselves. The majority of wild animal remains came from features at Cresswell Field; at Yarnton the only wild animal remains found were one red deer antler from pit 951 and one bird bone from 1684.

Seven pits (330, 371, 1163, 2646, 7057, 7598 and 7762) were found to contain whole or partial articulated animal skeletons. These included the remains of three dogs (pits 2646, 7598 and 7762); four cows (pits 371, 1163, 7057 and 7598); one horse (pit 7762) and one sheep (pit 330) (see below). In addition, these pits all contained disarticulated animal bone from at least four different species. Substantial deposits of pottery were also recovered (Table 5.5), although these were not remarkable in terms of decoration or sherd size. Four of these pits also contained small finds: copper alloy fragments, an iron nail and a cut piece of antler in pit 330, a grooved, polished metapodial in pit 371, an antler handle and the beginnings of what might have become a second in pit 7057 and a bone gouge in pit 7598. Two pits with articulated animal skeletons (330 and 7762) contained large deposits of metalworking debris, with smaller quantities coming from pits 1163, 2646 7057, 7598 and 7762. It is perhaps of interest that these pits were all sited away from identified structures. The articulated remains, the presence of quantities of other animal

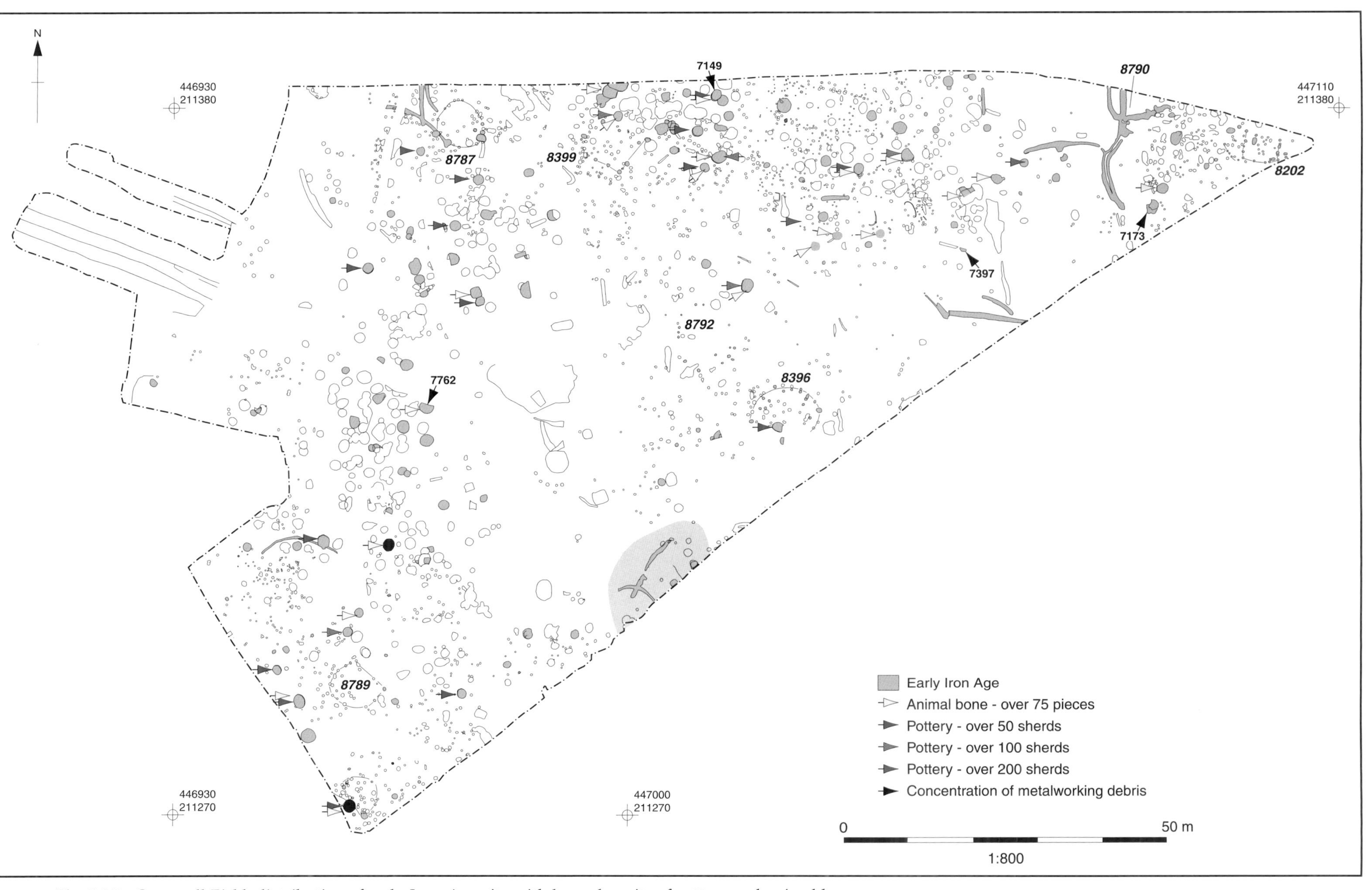

Fig. 5.37 Cresswell Field: distribution of early Iron Age pits with large deposits of pottery and animal bone

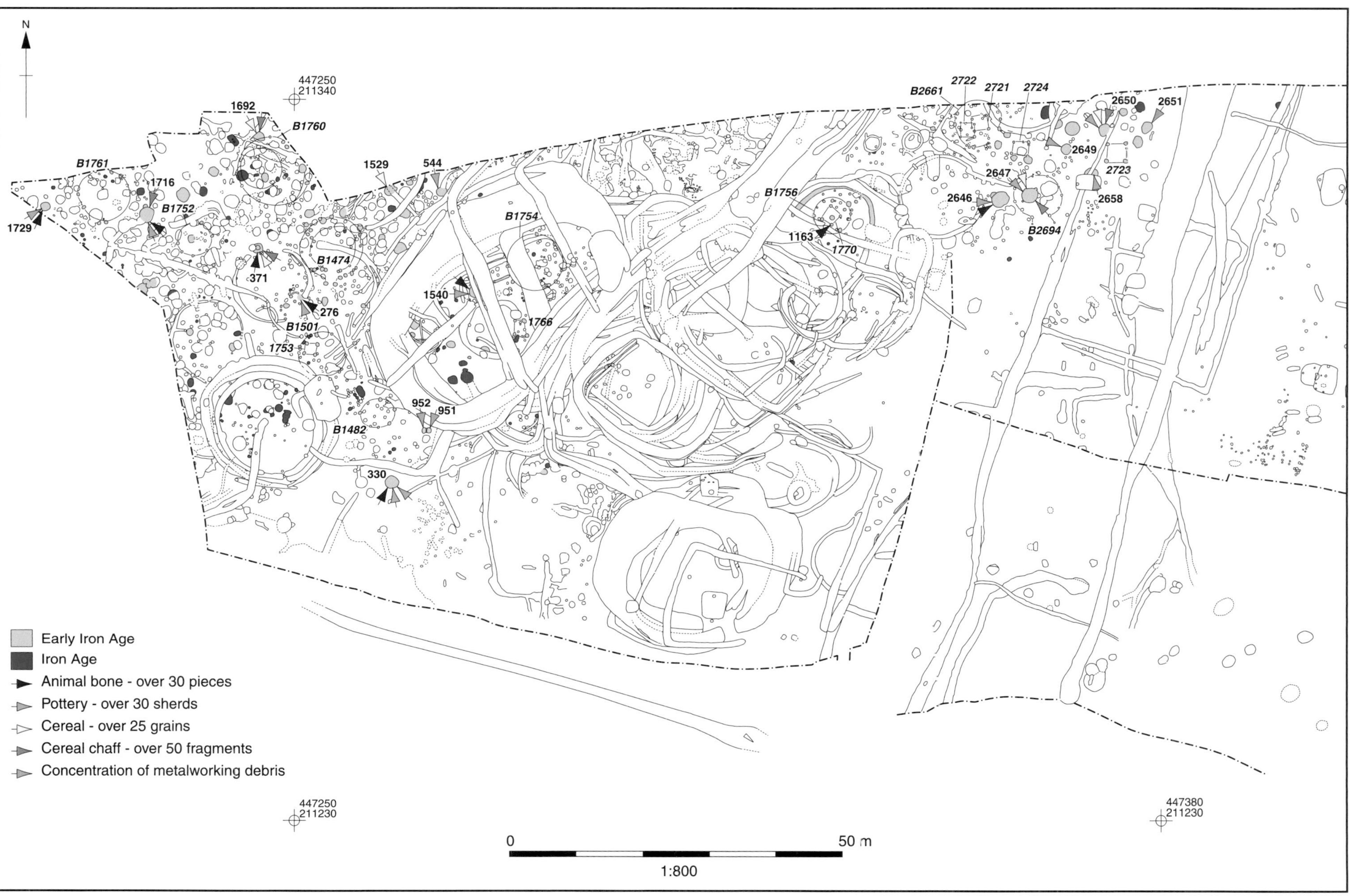

Fig. 5.38 Yarnton: distribution of early Iron Age pits with large deposits of pottery and animal bone

Table 5.5 Quantities of pottery in early Iron Age pits containing articulated animal skeletons.

Feature	*Sherd count*	*Sherd wt (g)*	*Mean sherd wt (g)*
330	53	520	9.8
371	18	430	23.8
1163	15	150	10
2646	69	1019	14.7
7057	157	3776	24.1
7598	91	1316	14.5
7762	122	2004	16.4

bone, the metalworking debris and the fairly substantial, if unremarkable, deposits of pottery all suggest that these were structured deposits of some kind, rather than mundane refuse.

Patterning in the deposition of animal bone in pits generally is not very evident. The majority of pits seem to have contained a wide variety of different species. None of the larger assemblages contained exclusively one species, and it was not uncommon to find all the major domesticates, cow, sheep/goat and to a lesser degree pig, together in one pit. One observable feature is that the pits with articulated animal bone frequently contained large assemblages of other animals comprising a mixture of species.

At Cresswell Field, the pits with the largest assemblages of animal bone lay at the north-eastern end of the east-west arc of pits crossing the site, with another small concentration at the western end (Fig. 5.37). At Yarnton, pits containing more than 30 fragments of animal bones were widely distributed over the site (Fig. 5.38). It has been observed that on some Iron Age sites cattle bone is more common in the peripheral areas, in contrast to sheep which is more centrally distributed (Wilson 1996). This does not appear to be sustained by the Yarnton evidence.

No spatial relationship was apparent between any of the pits which contained articulated skeletal remains; they were widely dispersed across the site (Figs 5.41 and 5.42).

Pottery

Of the 195 early Iron Age pits, 168 contained pottery. The total assemblage of early Iron Age pottery from pits at Yarnton comprised 826 sherds weighing 13 kg; at Cresswell Field the total assemblage was considerably larger, amounting to 2891 sherds weighing 47 kg. Sherd weight and sherd count were calculated for each of the pits at both sites and are displayed graphically in the form of an XY scatter chart (Fig. 5.39). At Yarnton this shows two distinct groups: a large group consisting of pits containing fewer than 20 sherds of pottery, and a smaller group comprising pits containing over 28 sherds of pottery. At Cresswell Field, there is a similar contrast, marked by the very low numbers of pits containing between 15 and 20 sherds. At Cresswell Field, however, there are more pits with larger numbers of sherds (between 20 and around 100, especially 20-40), as well as a few with assemblages larger than any at Yarnton (over 100 sherds). These include pit 7365 (discussed above), pit 7057, which contained articulated cow bones (discussed below), and also pits containing less exceptional, albeit substantial deposits (eg 7182, 7854 and 7912).

A second pair of plots (Fig. 5.40) displaying mean sherd weight against sherd count reveals that the majority of pits contained a small number of small abraded sherds. However, there are also pits outside this scatter, one group of which had larger or very large quantities of smallish sherds. A second, smaller group contained small quantities of large sherds. It is noticeable that although the numbers of sherds in some of the pits at Cresswell Field are much larger than those at Yarnton, even in the largest assemblages, the mean sherd weight is generally not much higher than it is in pits with many fewer sherds. At Yarnton two pits gave anomalous results. Pit 1716 had a large number of fairly large sherds, and pit 2647 contained a moderate number of very large sherds. At Cresswell Field, the anomalous pits include pit 7787 (described below) which contains large numbers of large sherds. This pit also contained an adze head and some of the pottery had probably been arranged around its base. The three pits containing small numbers of large sherds (pits 7797, 8562 and 7516) did not contain otherwise noticeable material.

Sherd weight and count were analysed by pit type. Unsurprisingly perhaps, the most common, cylindrical, pit type contained the highest overall number of sherds and the greatest overall weight of pottery (Table 5.6). At Yarnton, the cylindrical pits also contained the largest number of sherds per pit. The highest mean number of sherds per pit, however, occurred in the undercut grain storage pits at Cresswell Field. These pit groups also had one of the highest mean sherd weights. Rather surprisingly, however, high mean sherd weights were also recorded from bowl-shaped pits at Yarnton and large shallow pits at Cresswell Field, although the mean number of sherds in both is quite low. Not surprisingly, the shallow saucer-shaped pits have a much lower mean number of sherds than the larger pits, but the mean sherd weight is not correspondingly low. There is, however, little consistency between the figures for the same kinds of features between the two sites. Thus, for example, the high mean number of sherds per pit in the grain storage pits at Cresswell Field is not mirrored in high values at Yarnton, nor is the high mean sherd weight in bowl-shaped pits at Yarnton mirrored in similarly high scores in similar pits at Cresswell Field.

Following Hill (1995), it may be argued that the distinction between the two broad groups of pits indicated by the scatter charts – those containing few, small abraded sherds and those containing large groups of larger sherds – reflects a real difference between pits containing deliberate deposits of material, and pits containing redeposited or casually discarded material. At Yarnton, in particular, those pits containing over 30 sherds (features 276, 1540, 1716, 1729, 2646, 2647, 2649, 2650, 2658, 544, 330) were found to be largely the same as those pits containing dense concentrations of animal bone (Fig. 5.38). It might, therefore, be expected that pits identified as containing articulated animal remains would also be those with larger quantities of pottery. This is not always the case, as pits 371 and 1163 yielded less that 20 sherds each, although the pottery in 371 had a high mean sherd weight (Table 5.5). Nevertheless, pits with articulated animal remains tended to contain at least relatively large pottery assemblages.

The pattern that emerges from the pottery-distribution analysis is of a relatively small number of

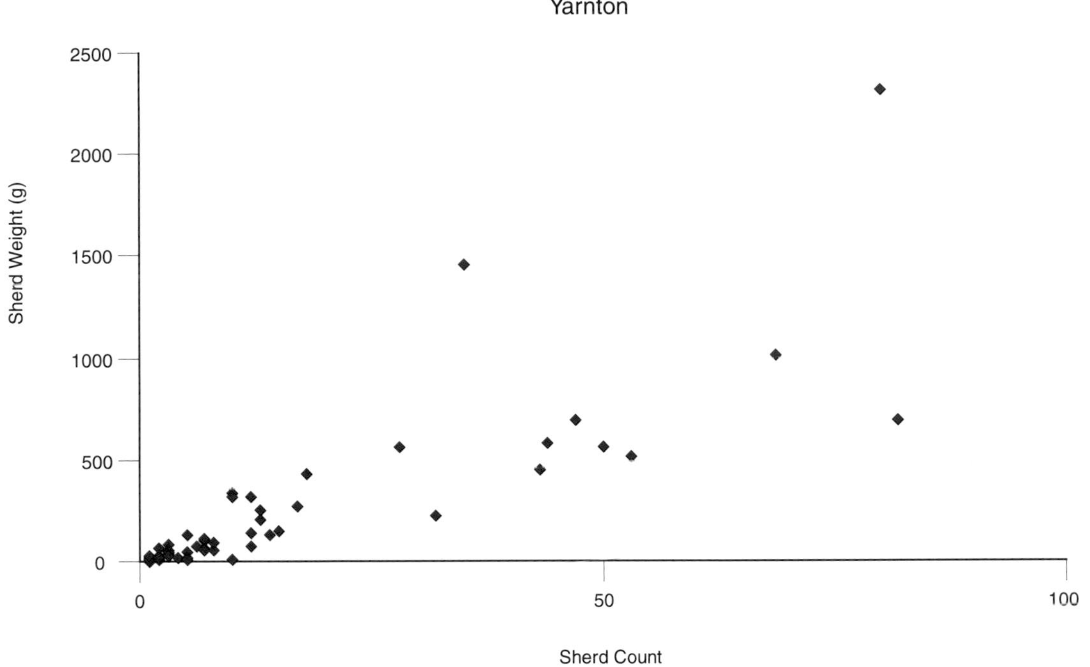

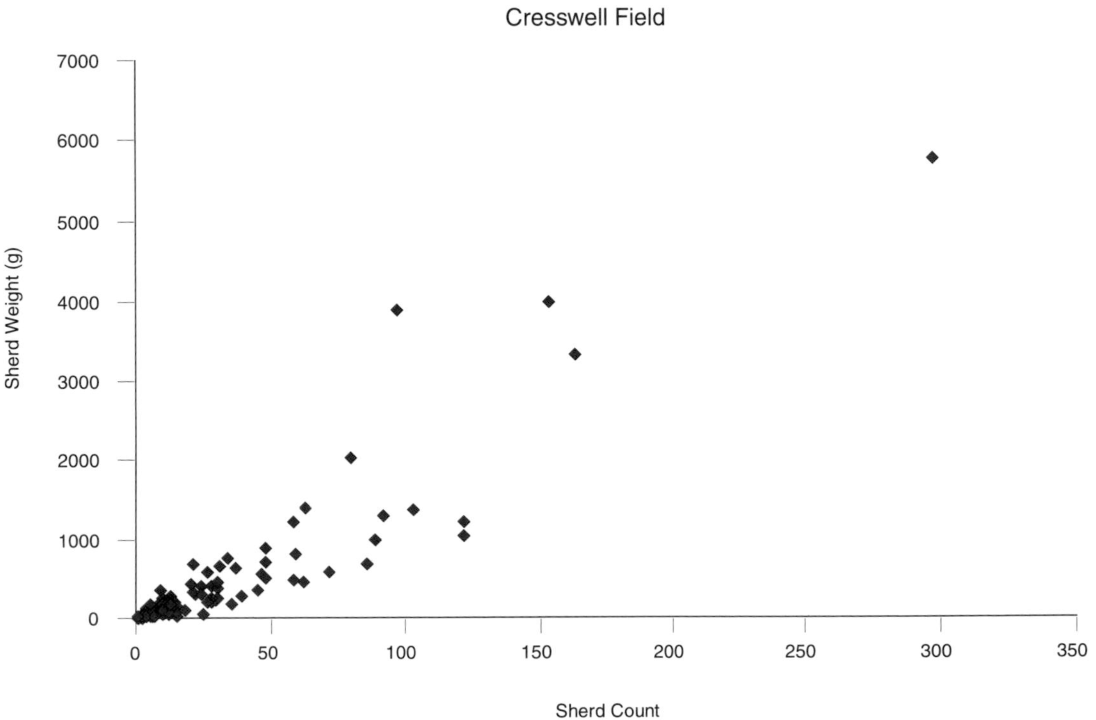

Fig. 5.39 Scatter diagram showing total sherd weight against sherd count in early Iron Age pits

pits which contained fairly substantial deposits of pottery and the majority which contained small collections of redeposited or casually-discarded material.

Plant remains

Charred plant remains were recovered from 29 early Iron Age pits. Ten of these were over 0.8 m^3 in volume, and their average original volume would have been 1.19 m^3, (ie in the large size range). The spatial distribution of these pits was similar to that of pits containing large amounts of pottery and animal bone (Figs 5.37 and 5.38). Particularly notable were pits 276, 1729, 1716, 1528, 1529, 2649 and 7149 which contained substantial quantities of plant remains, as well as concentrations of bone and pottery. The correlation between those features containing plant remains and those containing over 30 sherds of pottery was particu-

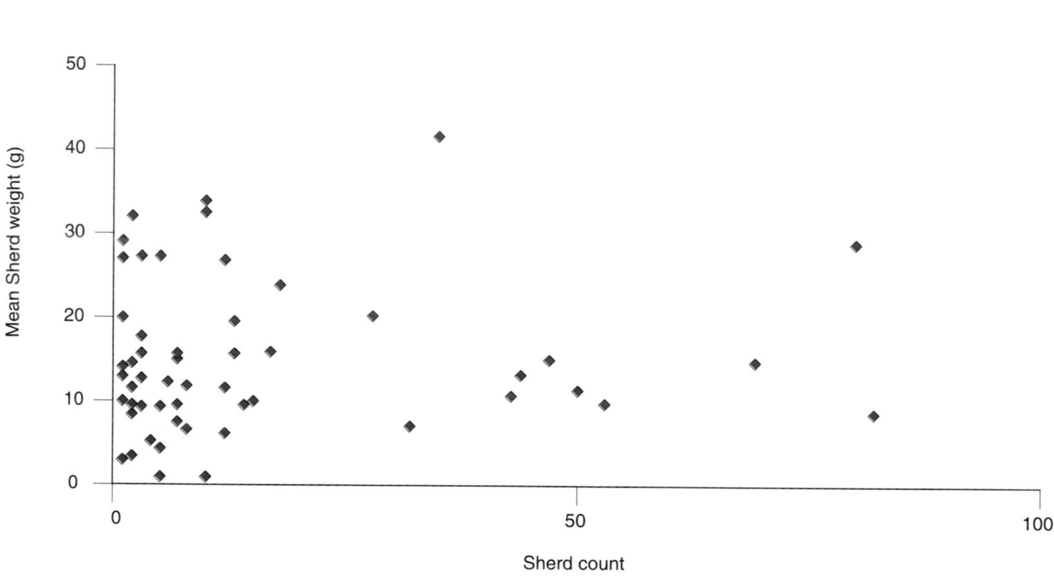

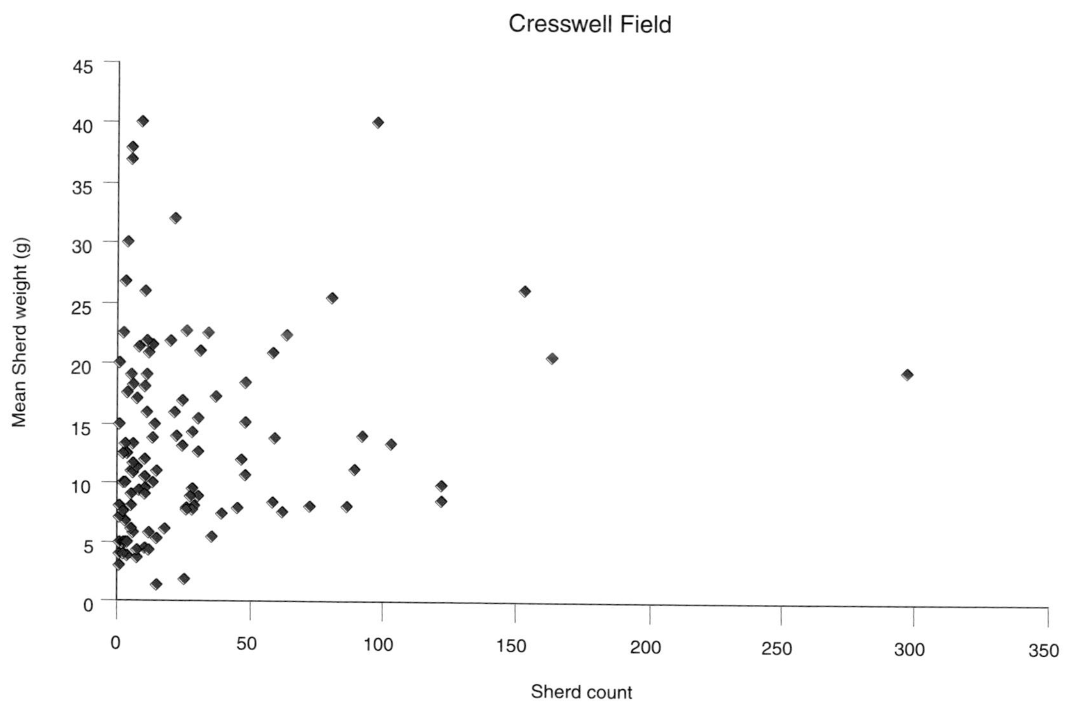

Fig. 5.40 Scatter diagram showing mean sherd weight against sherd count in early Iron Age pits

Table 5.6 Quantities of pottery by pit type.

	Pit type						
	Undercut (GSP)	Cylindrical	Bowl-shaped	Large shallow	Shallow saucer	Other	Total
Yarnton							
Count	15	556	30	25	3	197	826
Weight (g)	150	9228	592	327	44	2809	13150
Mean sherd weight (g)	10	16.5	19.7	13.8	14.6	14.25	15.9
Mean no. sherds per pit	15	23.1	3.3	6.3	0.6	9.9	13.1
Cresswell Field							
Count	438	2056	218	118	7	54	2891
Weight (g)	8335	33494	2381	2165	93	553	47021
Mean sherd weight (g)	19.0	16.3	10.9	18.3	13.3	10.2	16.3
Mean no. sherds per pit	48.7	31.2	6.4	9.8	1.4	9.0	21.9

Table 5.7 Quantities of charred plant remains by pit type.

	Pit type						
	Undercut (GSP)	Cylindrical	Bowl-shaped	Large shallow	Shallow saucer	Other	Total
Yarnton							
Cereals	5	223	13	12		32	285
Chaff	18	661	4	3		62	748
Weed seeds	14	656	45	15		44	774
Ave no. cereals per sampled pit	5	20.2	13	6		16	16.8
Cresswell Field							
Cereals	76	174	12			36	298
Chaff	61	215	15			8	299
Weed seeds	59	104	23			8	194
Ave no. cereals per sampled pit	19	35	6			36	27

larly noticeable among pits associated with the two roundhouses situated in the north-east corner of the Yarnton site.

Of the pits containing plant remains, 17 were cylindrical in shape, five were defined as undercut grain-storage pits, two were large shallow features, three were bowl shaped, one was V-shaped, and two were classified as amorphous ('Other' in Table 5.7). The cylindrical pits clearly contained the largest quantity of material, whereas the amounts found in other categories of pit were broadly comparable to each other. The composition of the charred cereals at the two sites differs. Although at Yarnton quantities of cereals were significantly smaller than those of chaff and weed seeds, at Cresswell Field the differences are less great: chaff and cereals are usually present in more or less similar quantities and weed seeds are notably rarer. This suggests that the charred cereals at Cresswell Field had been more thoroughly processed than those at Yarnton.

Analysis of the spatial distribution and context of plant remains suggests that the bulk of the material derived from large pits which may have been used for grain storage. It is tempting to infer that the plant remains at Yarnton at least were introduced during their primary use and were never recovered. However, much of this material came from deposits which also contained large amounts of pottery, animal bone and burnt charcoal, so it seems probable that the plant remains entered the pits during later episodes of deposition and backfilling.

Metalworking debris

Metalworking debris was not common in the early Iron Age pits. Fragments of slag were found in 33 pits, 23 of which were on the Cresswell Field site. Most of the Yarnton debris was concentrated in just four pits (330, 951, 952 and 2651). At Cresswell Field the larger concentrations of material came from pits 7149, 7762, 7397 and 7173.

In spatial terms the assemblage of metalworking debris was widely dispersed. On Cresswell Field, (Fig. 5.37) with the exception of pit 7149, they lay at the edge of the pit distribution away from buildings. At Yarnton (Fig. 5.38), these pits were similarly located at the edges of the pit groups. Furthermore, the three features containing the majority of the material (330, 951 and 952) were situated close together in the south of the site.

Other Finds

Other finds from early Iron Age pits were found in a fairly narrow range of features, and many of them were from the same pits as the metalworking assemblage. However, this pattern may simply be due to the general rarity of other finds. Objects of bone, antler, iron, stone, shale and jet were recovered (Table 5.8), most of which came from the Cresswell Field site. Most of the recorded structural fired clay also came from this part of the excavation, although the loomweight fragments were equally distributed across the two excavated areas.

Table 5.8 Other finds from early Iron Age pits (excluding residual flint).

Pit	Bone	Fired clay	Metal	Stone	Industrial
268	leaze rod				
330		misc	Fe nail		
371	polished metapodial SF 481				
389		loomweight			
951					furnace lining
952				misc	furnace debris
1512	polished metatarsal				
1540		daub			
1716					Slag
1749		fired clay			
2646					crucible
2646					furnace debris
2646	object				
2649					crucible
2649	gouge				
7057	antler handle, possible rough-out for a second				smithing hearth bottom
7130					
7149					Fe slag
7173	gouge			quartzite polisher	smithing hearth bottom ore slag
7182		loomweight			
7300			Cu alloy pin Fe nail/tack		Fe slag
7307				sarsen quern	
7365	sawn section of antler				
7397					smithing hearth bottom Fe slag Fe frags
7563					vitrified clay
7598	gouge				smithing hearth bottom Fe slag
7616		loomweight			
7677					vitrified clay
7707		spindle whorl			
7787			Fe adze		vitrified clay
7942	gouge				
8000					slag
8005		spindle whorl		shale armlet	Fe slag
8062					vitrified clay
8072					smithing hearth bottom
8092				Cu waste frags	Cu slag
8195	antler handle, cheek piece, awl/pin				smithing hearth bottom
8251				Cu ring	
8327	antler handle, gouge, manufacturing debris			Fe strip	ore vitrified clay
8394					slag
8517	worked bone	loomweight			slag
8537					slag
8541					slag

Selected pits

Grain-storage pits

Of the 132 early Iron Age pits excavated on Cresswell Field, only nine had forms suggesting that they were grain-storage pits (Table 5.3). This suggests that, even if all pits had been excavated, only 20 such features would have been present; this seems to be a very low number. It was noticeable that the grain storage pits tended to occur in pairs or clusters of three; even isolated pit 8005 may have been part of a group with other unexcavated features in the same area. At Yarnton, only one undercut, grain-storage pit was identified in this phase (1163; Fig. 5.35). As already suggested for both sites, however, a number of the cylindrical pits probably represent the remains of grain-storage pits which have either been truncated by later ploughing and/or whose upper sides have collapsed when still open. At least 11 further examples can be suggested for Yarnton (371, 544, 1465, 1529, 1531, 1695, 1716, 2646, 2647, 2649 and 2650; Figs 5.35 and 5.47). These features are included in the following discussion.

In general, there was nothing particularly remarkable about the fills or finds in grain-storage pits compared to the other pits. Pit 7057 was, however, exceptional (Figs 5.47 and 5.50). It was the largest pit to be excavated on the site, measuring nearly 2 m in diameter and 1.15 m in depth. Articulated cow leg bones lay in the bottom of the pit, overlain by a very large quantity of disarticulated mixed animal bone (mostly cow), which included a number of butchered bones. A polished, perforated bone object, an antler handle and what may have been the beginnings of a second, and a single piece of deer bone were also present, along with over 100 sherds of early Iron Age pottery. Pits 371 and 1163 also contained partly-articulated animal skeletons and are described below.

Pit 544 (Figs 5.7 and 5.35)

Pit 544 was a large pit measuring approximately 1.2 m in diameter and 1 m in depth located near the northern limit of excavation at Yarnton, and cut by later Roman features (541, 542 and 545). It was flat bottomed and had undercut sides. The pit had three fills, the main fill (544/A/2) containing charcoal and burnt earth flecks. Finds comprised 32 sherds of early Iron Age pottery and 16 animal bones (sheep/goat, cow and pig).

Pit 1465 (Figs 5.7 and 5.35)

This circular pit, 0.7 m in diameter and 0.4 m deep, lay on the north-east edge of structure 1474 which it post-dated as it cut one of its postholes (1463). It was in turn cut by Iron Age pit 1464 which contained no closely-datable finds. The pit had almost vertical sides and a slightly rounded base. The single fill contained just three sherds of pottery and eight animal bones, mostly cow with one pig mandible.

Pit 1529 (Figs 5.7 and 5.35)

This oval pit, 1.5 m x 2.1 m and 0.68 m deep, was located at the northern limit of excavation on Yarnton, west of pit 544. The pit had almost vertical sides with a flat base and contained four fills, largely of sandy-silty loam. Fill 1529/A/3 contained some charcoal. Ten sherds of pottery and 12 animal bones (horse, one pig mandible, sheep/goat, cow and one dog bone) were recovered.

Pit 1531 (Figs 5.7 and 5.35)

This circular flat-bottomed pit, 1.54 m in diameter and 0.57 m deep, with almost vertical sides, was found in the same area of the site as pits 1529 and 544. It was disturbed by an animal burrow, but three fills were defined, all of which contained charcoal flecking. Seventeen sherds (271 g) of pottery and 22 animal bones (cow, sheep/goat and horse) were recovered.

Pit 1695 (Figs 5.7 and 5.35)

A circular pit, 1695, 1.12 m in diameter and 0.72 m deep, located on the northern edge of the excavated area at Yarnton, east of structure 1760. The pit had near vertical sides and a slightly concave base. Three fills were present, the lowest (1695/3) containing a number of large bones, mainly of calf and horse with some sheep/goat. Ten sherds of pottery with a mixture of sandy, quartzite, shell and calcareous fabrics were found.

Pit 1716 (Figs 5.7 and 5.35)

This sub-rectangular pit, 2.1 m across and 1.2 m deep, lay in the north-west of the site where it cut early Iron Age posthole 1717. It had steep sides and a flat base. The six sandy- or silty-loam fills had charcoal flecks throughout. Finds included 80 sherds (2 kg) of well-preserved pottery (mainly sand-, shell- or limestone-tempered fabrics) and a large assemblage of 87 animal bones, including one dog and three pig mandibles, other dog and pig bones, sheep/goat and cow, and one fragment of plano-convex smithing hearth. The density of material in this feature and the mixed presence of dog and pig bone in some numbers might indicate that the deposit represents more than simple rubbish disposal.

Pits 2647, 2649 and 2650 (Fig. 5.7)

Pits 2647, 2649 and 2650 lay in the north-east of the Yarnton site. They ranged from 1.5-2.4 m in diameter and 1-2 m deep. All these pits yielded well above-average numbers of pottery sherds (35 sherds in 2647, 82 sherds in 2649 and 47 sherds from 2650), and pits 2647 and 2650 contained sizeable assemblages of charred plants with over 25 cereal grains and 50 chaff fragments from each. In addition, a bone object and a crucible fragment came from pit 2649. Numbers of animal bones were small: 12 fragments from 2647, 9 from 2650 and none from 2649.

Pit 7049 (Figs 5.6 and 5.36)

Circular pit 7049, located in the north-east of the Cresswell Field site, was 1.64 m in diameter and 0.83 m in depth, with steep sides and a flat base. It was cut by middle Iron Age pit 7137. The pit contained four fills, two of which may be the remnants of an original clay lining. The main fill, 7050, consisted of dark grey-brown clay silt with charcoal flecking and contained 31 sherds (746 g) of mainly shell-tempered pottery and 49 animal bones, with sheep/goat, cow and pig present.

Pits 7060, 7307 and 7173 (Figs 5.6 and 5.36)

Pits 7060, 7307 and 7173 formed a NNE-SSW alignment to the west of structure 8202. The two northerly pits, 7060 and 7307, both measured approximately 1.5 m x 1.35 m, and were 1 m and 0.8 m deep respectively. Both of these features had slightly under-cut sides and fairly flat bases, and their size and character suggested that they were originally grain-storage pits which had subsequently been used as refuse pits.

Pit 7060 was predominantly filled with a homogeneous deposit of sandy silt (7058). Several lenses of gravelly silt (7444, 7450, 8296 and 8297) in the base of the pit suggested an initial phase of natural silting, and one of these deposits (7444) was noticeably compacted, possibly as a result of trampling. The main fill contained frequent animal bones (74 in total), and a smaller quantity of early Iron Age pottery (22 sherds, weighing 350 g), charred grain and burnt stone. The animal bone is noteworthy in that two red deer bones were present in addition to the usual domesticates. Two antler handles were also recovered from (7058) (Fig. 15.6, Nos 21 and 22) along with a fragment of antler-manufacturing debris.

Pit 7307 contained an unusually complex sequence of fills (seven in all), representing a short phase of natural silting (7082), followed by several dumps of domestic refuse (7077, 7078, 7079, 7080 and 7081) and a final phase of silting (7309). These deposits produced just under 1 kg (87 sherds) of early Iron Age pottery, 177 pieces of animal bone and small quantities of burnt stone and charred grain. Although mainly dominated by cow and sheep/goat, the animal bone also included pig, horse and dog.

Pit 7173 was less deep than the other two pits (0.42 m), and had a slightly more bowl-shaped profile. It produced a substantial finds assemblage, consisting of 157 pieces of animal bone, 26 sherds (590 g) of early Iron Age pottery and a bone gouge-like point and just over 1 kg of burnt stone. The animal bone includes the usual domesticates along with a number of frog bones. A quantity of metal-working debris was also recovered from this feature including four pieces of ore, a fragment of a small plano-convex hearth bottom and six pieces of slag-lining reaction product.

Pit 7525 (Figs 5.6 and 5. 36)

This large circular pit with a maximum diameter of 1.14 m and a depth of 0.56 m lay near the north-east corner of the site, adjacent to structure 8787. Its sides were slightly undercut and the base was flat. The pit contained three fills. The primary fill (7524) included flecks of charcoal and produced ten fragments of animal bone and three sherds of pottery. Further finds from the upper fill (7522) comprised 18 sherds of mainly shell-tempered pottery and 21 animal bones.

Pit 7603 (Figs 5.13 and 5.36)

An oval-shaped pit with undercut sides and a slightly bowl-shaped base. The maximum width was approximately 1 m wide and the depth 0.5 m. The three fills (7604, 7762 and 7761) were all light greyish-brown sandy loams. Pottery was recovered from all three layers (36 sherds in total) in a mixture of sand-, shell- and limestone-tempered fabrics, and a total of 28 animal bones, mainly sheep/goat, was also recovered.

Clay-lined pits

Six pits were identified which appear to have had a clay lining. The three clay-lined pits at Yarnton were all apparently associated with structures. At Cresswell Field, however, no such association was apparent. Although pit 8175 lies near structures 8789 and 8788, the other two clay-lined pits on this site (7049 and 8492) were not close to any identified structure.

Only one of the clay-lined pits at Yarnton, 833, was excavated, and this was located within round-house structure 1754 (Fig. 5.23). The pit was circular, 0.53 m in diameter and 0.18 m deep, and had a shallow bowl-shaped profile. The lining was a mottled light green- to orange-brown clay, 2-5 cm thick. The upper fill of the pit comprised an almost gravel-free clay loam.

A similar, circular pit lay immediately west of the ring of postholes which defined structure 2661 (Fig. 5.24), but it was not excavated. Its position could suggest it was used to collect water from the eaves. The third example, also unexcavated, lay immediately north of structure 2694 (Fig. 5.26). A similar clay-lined pit of middle Iron Age date at Gravelly Guy was also sited in close proximity to a structure, and may have been a tank for collecting water from the roof (Lambrick and Allen 2004, 109).

One of the clay-lined pits at Cresswell Field (7049) was an undercut grain-storage pit; the other two (8175 and 8492) were cylindrical. All were amongst the largest pits on the site, measuring between 1.5 and 2.3 m wide, and 0.45-0.83 m deep. The contents of these pits – consisting of quite large quantities of pottery and animal bone – did not differ significantly from those of other pits of the same general type. The finds are, however, likely to derive from re-use of the features, rather than

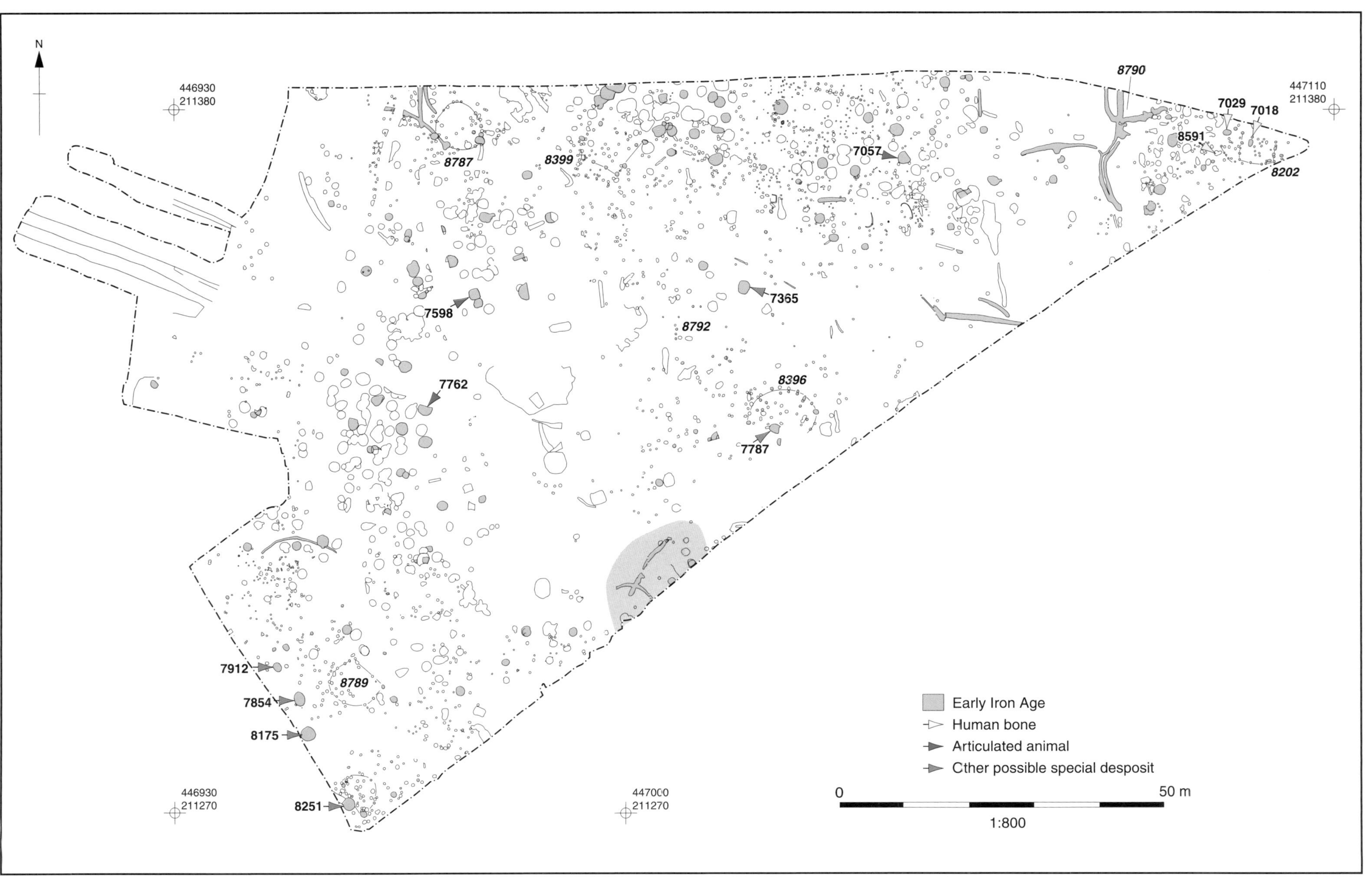

Fig. 5.41 Cresswell Field: distribution of early Iron Age articulated skeletal remains, disarticulated human bone and other special deposits

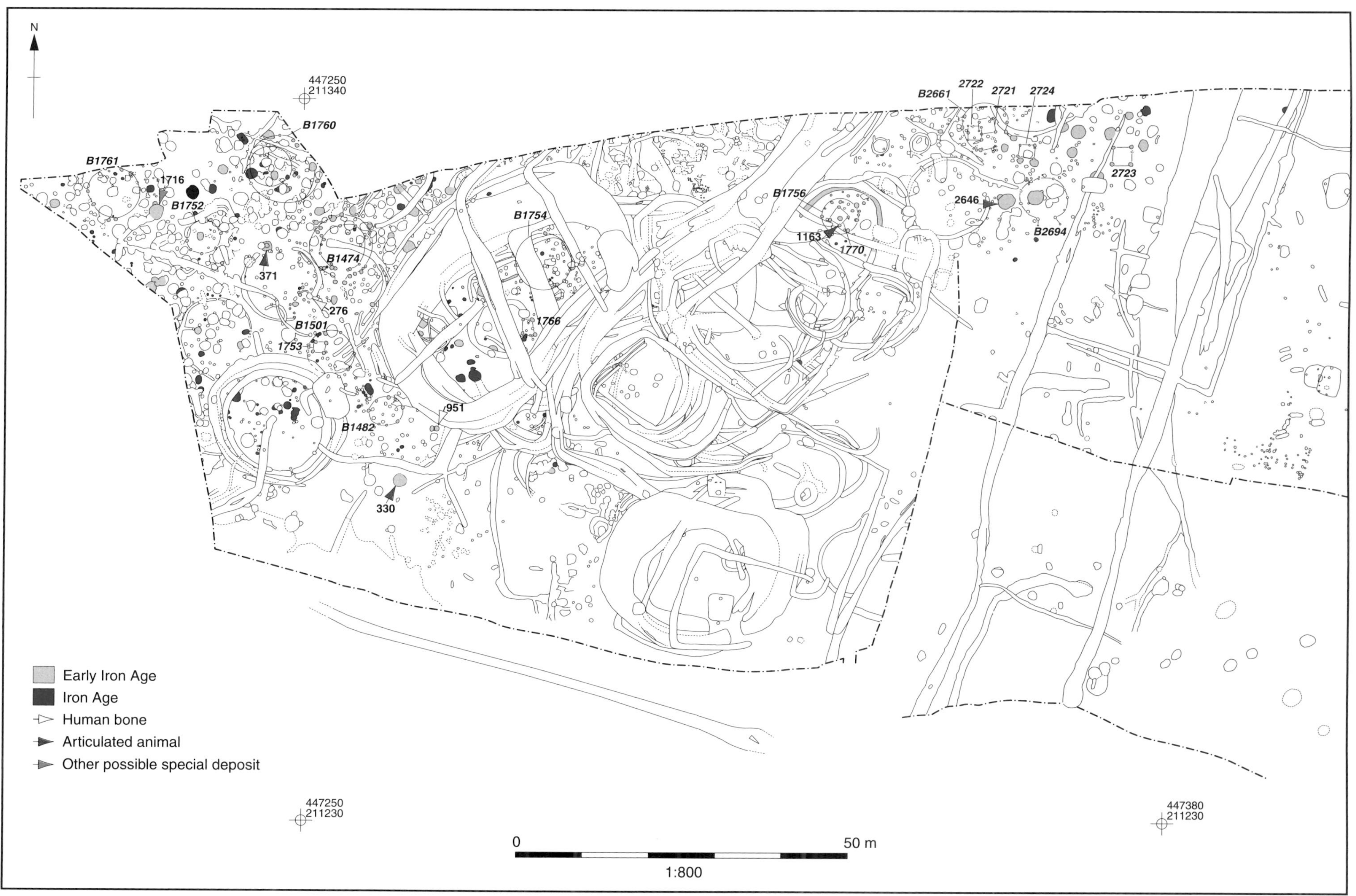

Fig. 5.42 Yarnton: distribution of early Iron Age articulated skeletal remains, disarticulated human bone and other special deposits

reflecting their primary function. The environmental samples taken from these pits were not analysed in detail.

Pits with special or deliberate deposits

A number of deposits were assessed as containing a special selection of material that was deliberately placed. Their distribution is shown in Figures 5.41 and 5.42. These deposits fall into various categories:

- Deposits with human bone (although it is accepted that in some cases individual bones may have been incorporated accidentally).
- Deposits of articulated animals or parts of animals. Some animals could have been disposed of as rubbish because they were regarded as inedible for some reason, and dogs in particular may have fallen into this category. However, it was felt that all the deposits discussed here were placed with more deliberation.
- Pits containing special artefacts, of which the pit with the iron adze is a notable example.
- Pits containing a substantial quantity of material of either a single category or with a variety of material found together.

Pits with human bone (Fig. 5.43)

Pit 8591 (Figs 5.6, 5.9 and 5.43) lying to the south-west of structure 8202, contained a human skull. The skull, which lay upside down, was that of an adult female and the absence of the mandible indicated that it was defleshed when placed in the feature. The pit itself, at 0.45 m in diameter and 0.2 m in depth, was only just large enough to contain the skull, and the only other finds present were a few small scraps of early and middle Iron Age pottery, some or all of which may have been intrusive, and 20 animal bone fragments, mainly sheep/goat sized.

Circular pit 7029 (1.18 m in diameter and 0.44 m deep; Figs 5.6 and 5.43) had near-vertical sides and a flat base. It contained four defined fills. The lower fills comprised dark-brown sandy clays with no associated finds, but the upper deposit, 7059, produced six sherds of pottery and the distal half of a neonate humerus.

Pit 276 was roughly circular (1.6 m across and 1 m deep; Figs 5.7 and 5.43) with vertical sides and a flat base. Seven fills were identified, the middle fill of which (276/A/4) contained fragments of human skull vault. Thirty-seven pottery sherds, mostly shell-tempered, were found in fills 1-6, amongst which were eight jar rims, a handled body sherd with simple geometric incised decoration (Fig. 14.5, No. 150) and a miniature vessel (Fig. 14.5, No. 151). A moderately-large animal bone assemblage (89 bones) was also recovered which includes domestic fowl and a dog mandible, as well as cow, pig, sheep/goat and horse.

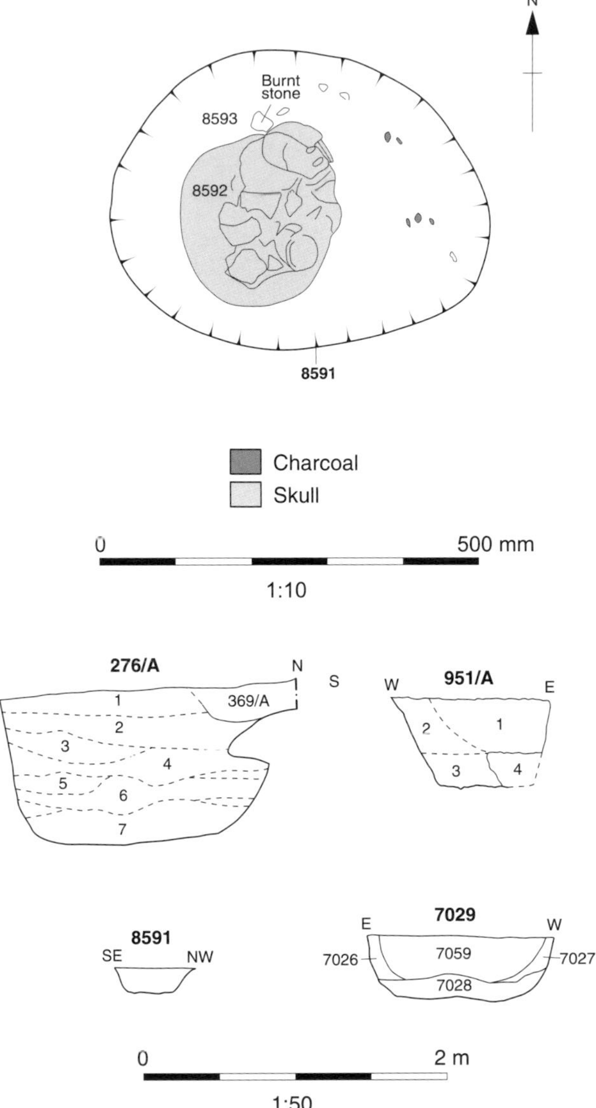

Fig. 5.43 Pits with disarticulated human bone: 276, 951, 7029 and 8591

Pit 951 was a sub-rectangular pit 1 m x 0.8 m and 0.56 m deep, with convex sides and a flat base (Fig. 5.7 and 5.43). The top fill (951/A/1) contained a human first phalanx. The pit also yielded an important assemblage of metalworking debris, including one fragment of dense slag, 24 fragments of fired clay, three fragments of vitrified clay, nine fragments of lining vitrification flow and a piece of fuel ash slag. In addition, nine animal bones were found, including red deer antler and a horse atlas along with cow and sheep/goat, and six sherds of pottery amongst which are single examples of grog-tempered and quartzite-tempered sherds alongside shelly wares.

Pits with articulated dog remains (Fig. 5.44)

Two pits (7598 and 7762), lying 25 m apart within the north-south swathe of early Iron Age pits on Cresswell Field, contained the articulated remains of dogs. Both features also contained an articulated

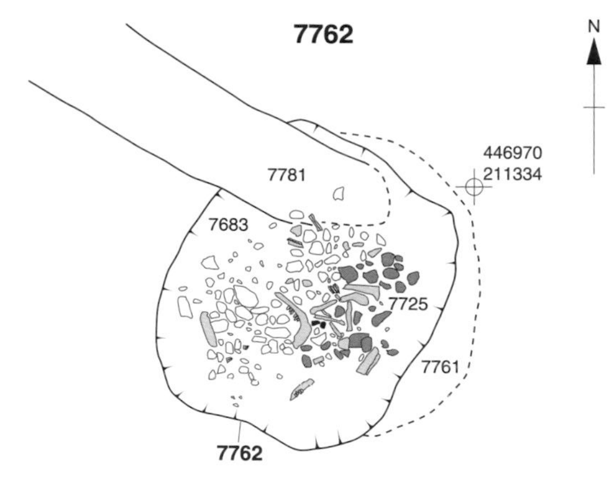

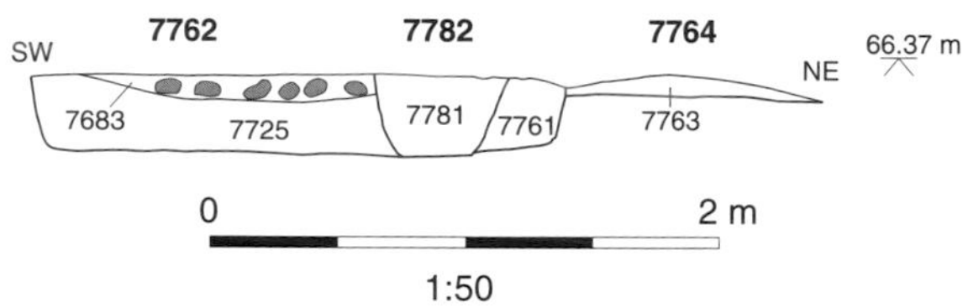

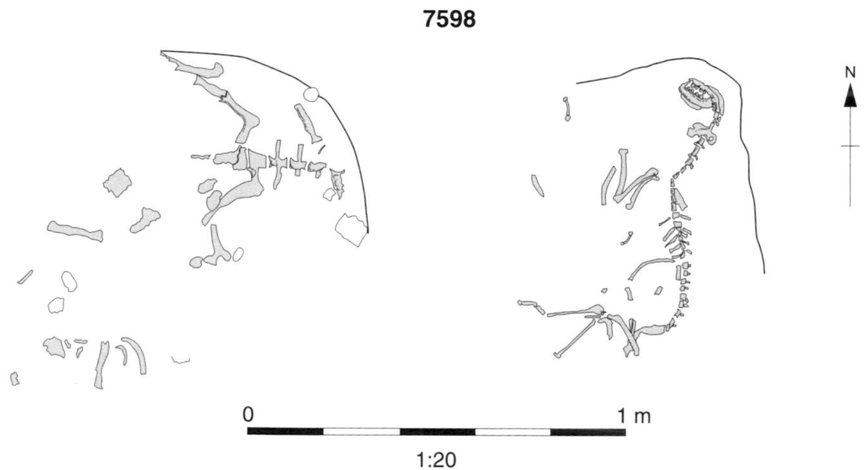

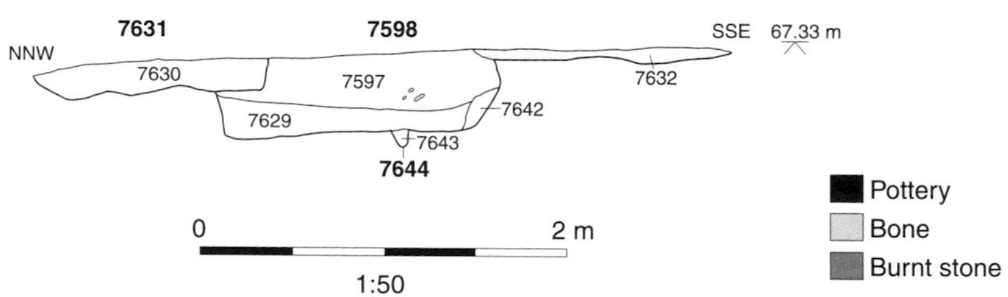

Fig. 5.44 Pits with articulated dog remains: 7598 and 7762

Fig. 5.45 Dog skeleton in pit 7598

segment of cow or horse. Articulated dog was also found in pit 2646 on the Yarnton site, along with other animal bone and finds.

Pit 7598 was oval with steep sides and a flat base, 1.49 m x 1.22 m and 0.4 m deep. It had been badly disturbed by animal burrowing (Figs 5.6, 5.44 and 5.45). Three fills were identified. A complete articulated dog skeleton, overlain by part of an articulated cow skeleton, appeared to have been placed in the top of the pit when it had already partially silted up with soil and refuse. The dog was laid out flat, centrally in the pit, and had clearly been placed. Several other animal bones were also present, notably a piece of mallard duck and a wild pig (the only example from the site). The pit also contained just over 10 kg of burnt stone, 50 sherds of early Iron Age pottery, three pieces of slag (two from sub-tuyère plates) and a bone gouge.

Circular pit 7762, 2.1 m in diameter and 0.34 m deep, had vertical sides and a flat base (Figs 5.6, 5.44 and 5.46). It had five fills, the uppermost one of which (7683) contained the disturbed remains of an articulated dog skeleton laid out on a bed of burnt stone. The dog had a healed fracture in one of its legs. Within the bed of burnt stone was part of an articulated horse leg. As in pit 7598, these deposits seem to have been placed in the top of an already partly-filled pit which contained over 100 sherds of pottery, and large quantities of disarticulated cow and horse bone. The horse bone was the largest single concentration on the site. A small quantity of metalworking debris was also found, comprising two fragments of dense iron slag, one from a small sub-tuyère plate, and a piece of copper slag.

Pit 2646 at Yarnton (Fig. 5.7) was a sub-circular, flat-bottomed pit, measuring 2 m across and 1.15 m in depth. Six distinct fills were identified in the pit which contained an articulated dog skeleton, alongside the bones of cattle, horse, pig and sheep/goat. Additionally, there were 69 sherds of pottery weighing 1019 g.

Other pits with articulated animal skeletons (Fig. 5.47)

Circular pit 330 lay on the southern edge of the Iron Age pit distribution on the Yarnton site (Fig. 5.42). It was approximately 2 m in diameter and 0.75 m deep, with vertical sides and a flat base. Six fills were identified. The articulated skeleton of a sheep was found in the lower fill lying east-west on its right side. (Figs 5.47 and 5.48). One of the front legs had been replaced by the limb of another animal. In addition, bones of cattle, goat, pig, cow/horse and some unidentifiable fragments were present. Fifty-three sherds of pottery, an iron nail, and a substantial amount of metalworking debris were also recovered. The metalworking debris comprises 43 identified fragments, including crucible, copper alloy slag and vitrified clay fragments (see Table 5.8).

Fig. 5.46 Deposit of burnt stone and animal bone (7683) in pit 7762. Scale 0.5 m

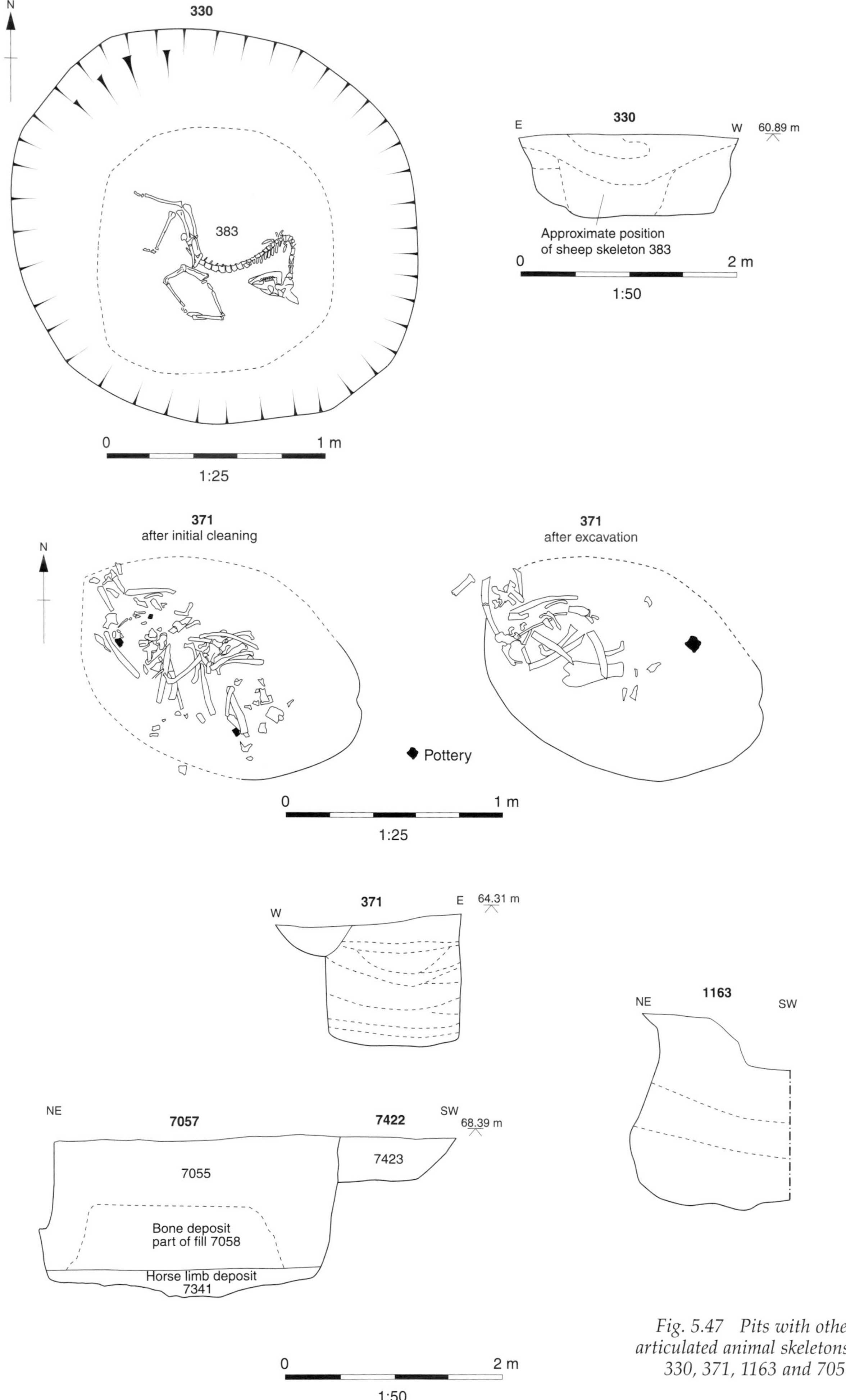

Fig. 5.47 Pits with other articulated animal skeletons: 330, 371, 1163 and 7057

Fig. 5.48 Sheep skeleton in pit 330. Scale 0.5 m

A circular grain-storage pit, 371, 1.25 m in diameter and 1.18 m deep, was equidistant from structures 1752, 1474 and 1760 to the north (Fig. 5.42). The pit had vertical sides and a flat, slightly-dished bottom and contained 14 fills. The primary fill (371/A/18) was a yellow-brown silty clay with some charcoal and ash. Remaining fills comprised various sandy-silty loams, with flecks of charcoal from layers 371/A/3 to 371/A/7. Within the upper fill (Figs 5.47 and 5.49) were the disturbed remains of an articulated cow (378), whilst further animal bone (sheep, pig, cow) came from the lower fill 371/A/17. Eighteen fragments of fairly well-preserved shell- or limestone-tempered pottery (44 g) were recovered, as well as a polished metapodial object (SF 481, Chapter 15).

Circular grain-storage pit 1163 was found within the area of structure 1756 and adjacent to four-post structure 1770 (Fig. 5.42). It had been partly cut away by an early Roman ditch (591). The pit, 1.65 m in diameter and 0.9 m deep, had an undercut north-east side but was otherwise vertical sided, with a dished base. It contained three fills, all sandy silts or loams with some charcoal. The middle fill contained moderate amounts of charcoal and substantial quantities of animal bone. Nine sherds of pottery (100 g) and one fragment of dense slag were also recovered from the fills (Fig. 5.47).

Pit 7057, already described above, contained

Fig. 5.49 Pit 371. Scale 2 m

articulated cattle limb bones placed in its base (Fig. 5.50). These were overlain by a substantial number of other, disarticulated animal bones, in which, however, cattle bones predominated. It also contained a substantial assemblage of early Iron Age pottery (153 sherds, 4000 g) as well as a polished, perforated bone object, an antler handle and what may have been the beginnings of another.

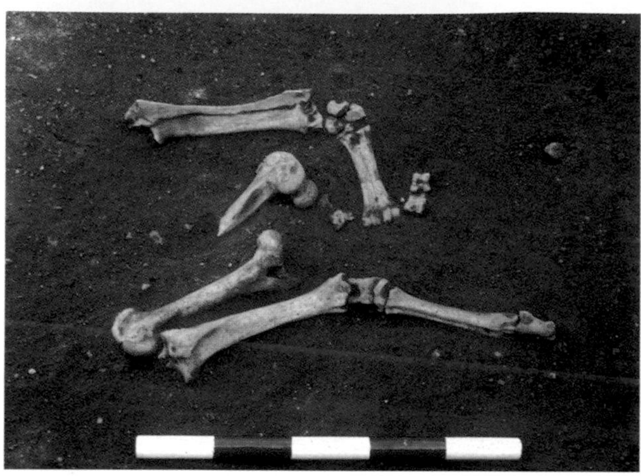

Fig. 5.50 Articulated cattle bone in pit 7057. Scale 0.5 m

Other pits with possible deliberate deposits

Pit 7787, lying immediately to the south of structure 8396 or (more likely) within it, was 1.5 m in diameter and 0.5 m in depth (Figs 5.6 and 5.10). Very large sherds of an early Iron Age storage vessel were placed around its northern edge and a complete iron adze head was recovered from its primary fill (8067; Fig. 5.11, Chapter 15, Fig.15.3, No. 6). The upper fill (7788) produced 42 sherds of pottery (3294 g in weight) of which 20 may have been from one vessel. One sherd has impressed decoration. The same fill also contained 31 animal bones, some of which were burnt, and the largest single deposit of daub recovered from the site (360 g). The top and southern half of the pit had been partly cut away by a middle Iron Age ditch, and further fragments of burnt bone occurred within a number of later ditch fills and also in upper feature fills in this general area. If, as seems likely, this material had derived from the disturbed pit, it suggests that the original quantities deposited in the pit were significantly higher than the extant sample.

Pit 8161 lay immediately to the west of structure 8399. It was a shallow, oval-shaped pit approximately 0.6 m by 0.75 m and 0.2 m deep and was packed with burnt stone (4.75 kg) and showed signs

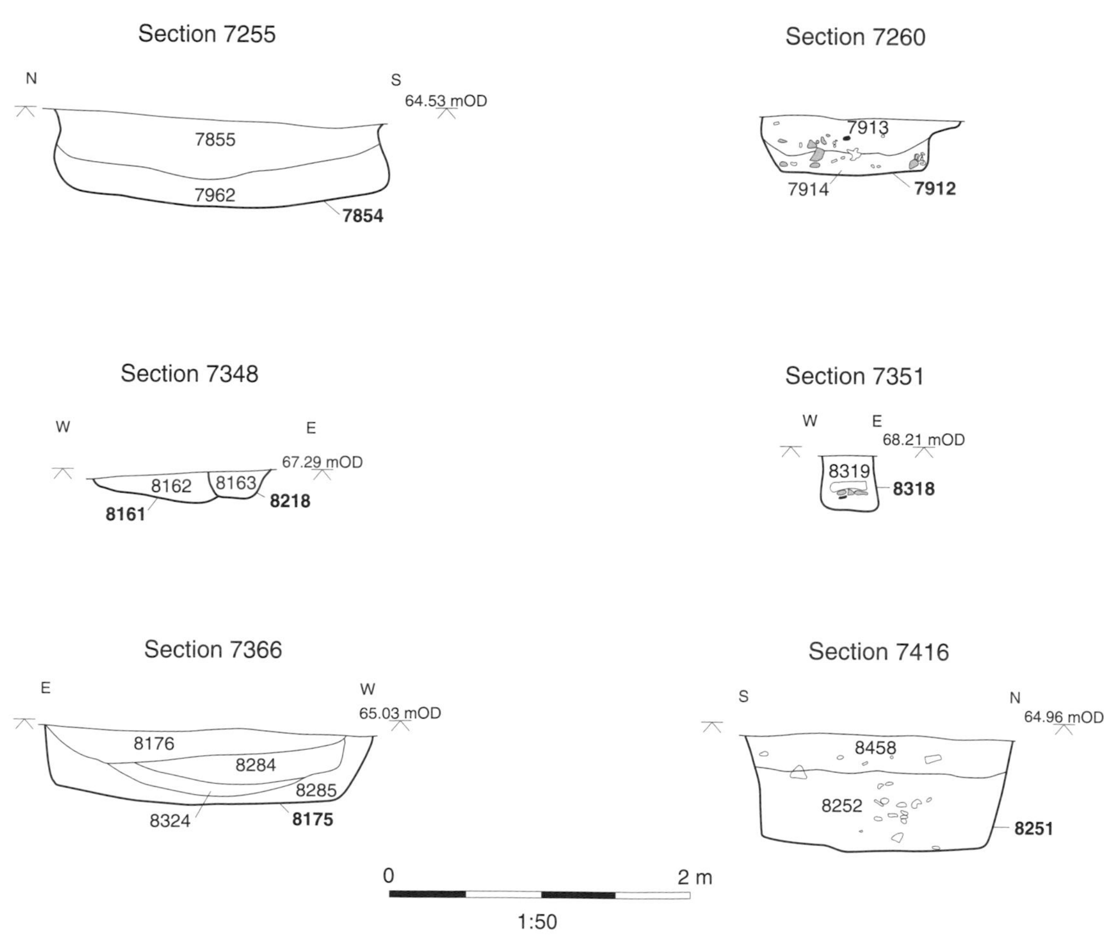

Fig. 5.51 Pits with deliberate deposits: 7854, 7912, 8161, 8175, 8251 and 8318

Fig. 5.52 Deposit of animal bone and stone in pit 7912. Scale 1 m

of fire-reddening on its sides (Figs 5.6 and 5.51). A dense deposit of charcoal was recovered from near the base. A second, circular pit, 8318, 0.34 m across and 0.34 m deep with vertical sides and a concave base, lay just north-east of 8161 within the structure (Fig. 5.51) and contained a dense deposit of burnt stone, as well as three large sherds of early Iron Age pottery and a piece of butchered cow bone.

Four finds-rich pits lay to the west of structures 8788 and 8789 (8251, 7854, 8175 and 7912; Figs 5.6, 5.51 and 5.52). The most southerly pit (8251) measured 1.8 m in diameter and 0.8 m in depth. The two central pits (7854 and 8175, which was clay-lined) were broader but shallower (2.2 m in diameter x 0.5 m in depth) and pit 7912 to the north was smaller, measuring 1.2 m in diameter and 0.4 m in depth. These features all produced similar finds assemblages, comprising large quantities of animal bone (totalling 475 pieces), early Iron Age pottery (totalling 253 sherds, weighing 2540 g) and burnt stone (over 10 kg from each feature). The bone in pit 7912 mostly lay in a dense layer in the bottom of the feature (7913) and this deposit included a high percentage of mandibles.

Other Iron Age pits

An additional 92 pits were of Iron Age date (41 at Cresswell Field and 51 at Yarnton), but could not be confidently placed in the early or the middle period. This was usually because of the small quantity of material recovered from them. The characteristics of their shapes are shown in Table 5.9, and their distribution on Figures 5.6 and 5.7.

Table 5.9 Numbers of pit types of uncertain early or middle Iron Age date.

	Undercut (GSP)	*Cylindrical*	*Bowl-shaped*	*Large shallow*	*Shallow saucer*	*Other*	*Total*
Cresswell Field	-	10	20	2	6	3	41
Yarnton	-	10	9	3	6	23	51
Total		20	29	5	12	26	92

Chapter 6: The Middle Iron Age

by Chris Bell, Dan Stansbie and Gill Hey

INTRODUCTION

The middle Iron Age occupation was concentrated toward the south-west corner of the Yarnton site, a little to the south of the early Iron Age focus, and extended north-east along the gravel terrace (Fig. 6.1). As in the earlier period, the settlement layout was much disturbed by later ditch digging. Occupation features also extended to the WNW into the Cresswell Field site, and features of this date were found amongst the northerly swathe of pits there, but the greatest levels of activity at this time appear to have been further west, in the area adjacent to the palaeochannel (Fig. 6.1). The general distribution and character of the middle Iron Age features, however, strongly suggests continuity in the settlement layout and land-use from the early to middle Iron Age.

In Cresswell Field, activity of this phase was represented by several curvilinear gullies, a regular scatter of pits, and an area of inter-cutting pits and ditches (Fig. 6.2). A curving line of pits across the northern part of the site seem to have been dug on the southern edge of the denser spread of early Iron Age pits. To the west, middle Iron Age pits occurred amongst the early features, but were more densely distributed, especially to the south. A concentration of inter-cutting pits and gullies was found along the southern edge of the excavation area, to the south of early Iron Age structure 8396.

The main occupation area excavated was in the western part of the Yarnton site, with at least six circular or semi-circular structures, three of which were surrounded by gullies, and with associated pits (Fig. 6.3). Two parallel fence lines aligned NW-SE were also present in this part of the settlement; they may have defined a trackway. As in the early Iron Age period, remains of occupation were also found in the centre and the north-east of the site although, as before, the apparently discrete nature of this distribution may be a factor of later disturbance rather than representative of separate household units in the Iron Age. In the centre of the site lay a circular structure (perhaps a direct replacement of early Iron Age structure 1754), a penannular enclosure and other gullies and pits. The eastern group consisted of two penannular gullies, one of which ran beyond the northern limit of the excavation, and a few pits.

A small middle Iron Age inhumation cemetery was found in the salvage area, on the eastern edge of the excavated settlement site (Fig. 6.3). The cemetery appears to have comprised two distinct groups of burials, northern and southern, of 15 and 10 individuals respectively. The space between the two groups was only 20 m and this could partly be a result of poorer retrieval in the intervening area (see Chapter 1 for the circumstances of their discovery and investigation), although it is possible that the two groups belong to different family units. A further ten inhumations have been described as outliers and these were scattered along the southern and eastern edge of the settlement. Nine radiocarbon dates were obtained from the burials (see Chapter 12).

There was generally very little inter-cutting between the middle and early Iron Age features, and it was observed that the small number of middle Iron Age pits scattered through the northern half of the Cresswell Field site appeared to respect the earlier swathe of features. The pits from this phase were almost identical in character to their early Iron Age counterparts and, apart from the later pottery, contained similar quantities and categories of finds. However, there were fewer deep pits and no obvious grain storage pits.

The obvious continuity in the character and layout of the settlement, and the occurrence of large quantities of early Iron Age pottery in most of the middle Iron Age features, suggests that at least some were transitional early/middle Iron Age in date. Much of the earlier pottery in these features may, therefore, not necessarily be redeposited. The imprecision of pottery dating for these features (with the exception of those with radiocarbon dates and occasional features with diagnostic small finds) makes it difficult to place many into an early or a late phase with certainty.

MIDDLE IRON AGE STRUCTURES AND ASSOCIATED ENCLOSURES

Summary

Six circular and one D-shaped post-built structures were identified from this phase of occupation, two of which (structures 801 and 802) were successive buildings on overlapping sites. A feature of the middle Iron Age occupation was the location of several of these structures within ditched enclosures or gullies, and there are five, or possibly six, additional examples of penannular ditches or gullies which appeared to have been house enclosures but within which no evidence of buildings survived. As the relationship between the structures

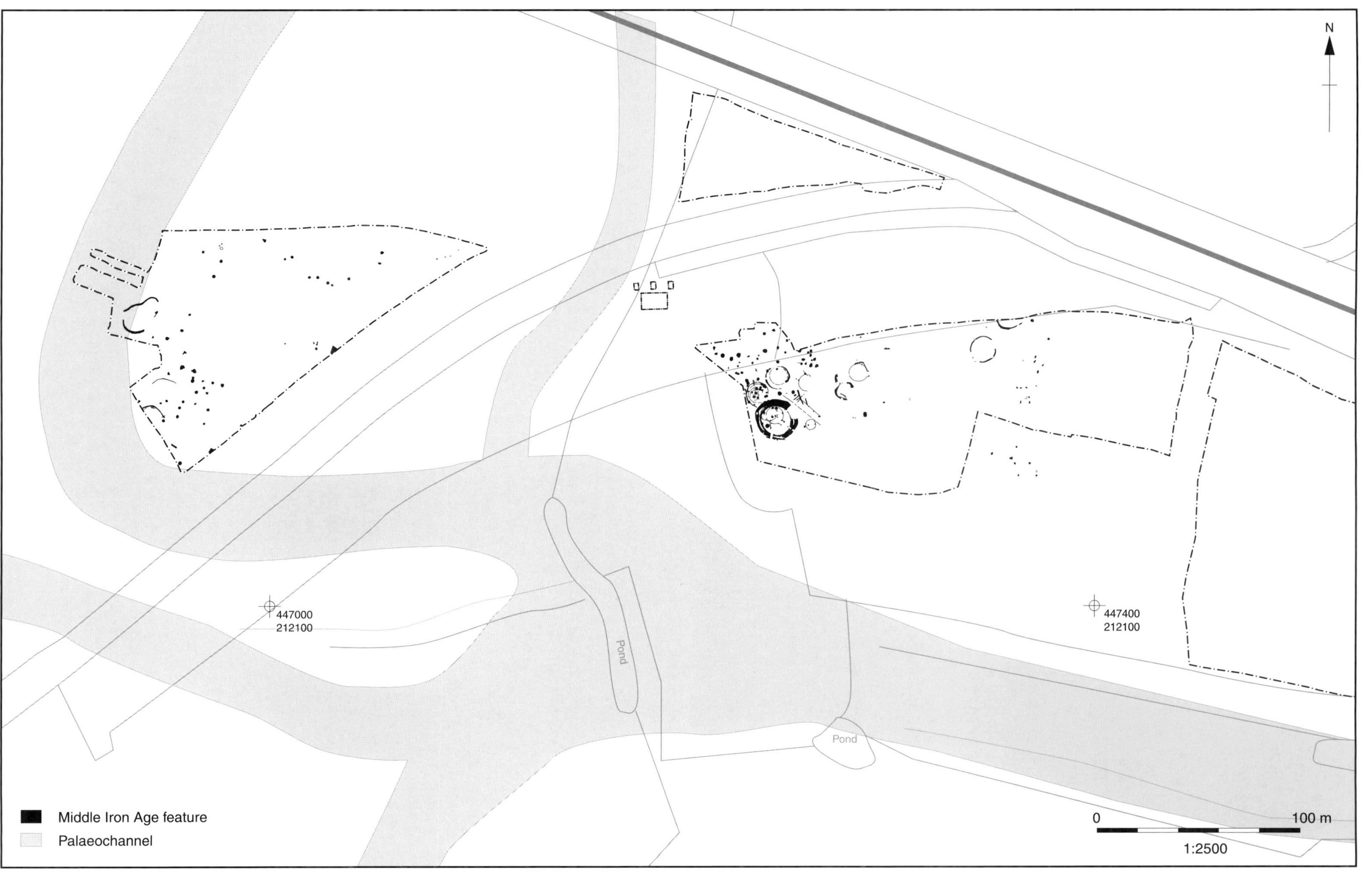

Fig. 6.1 Yarnton and Cresswell Field middle Iron Age features

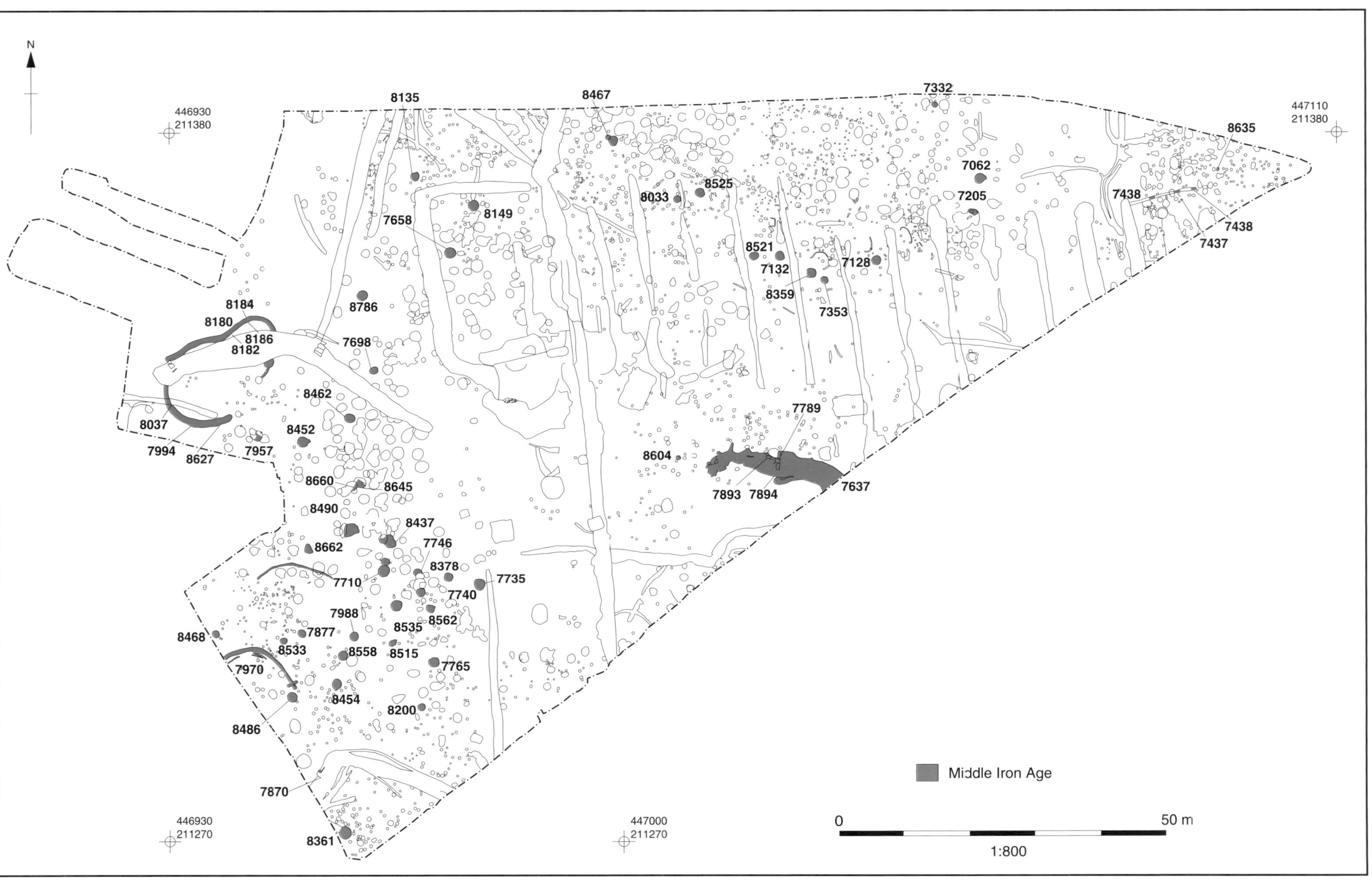

Fig. 6.2 Cresswell Field: middle Iron Age features

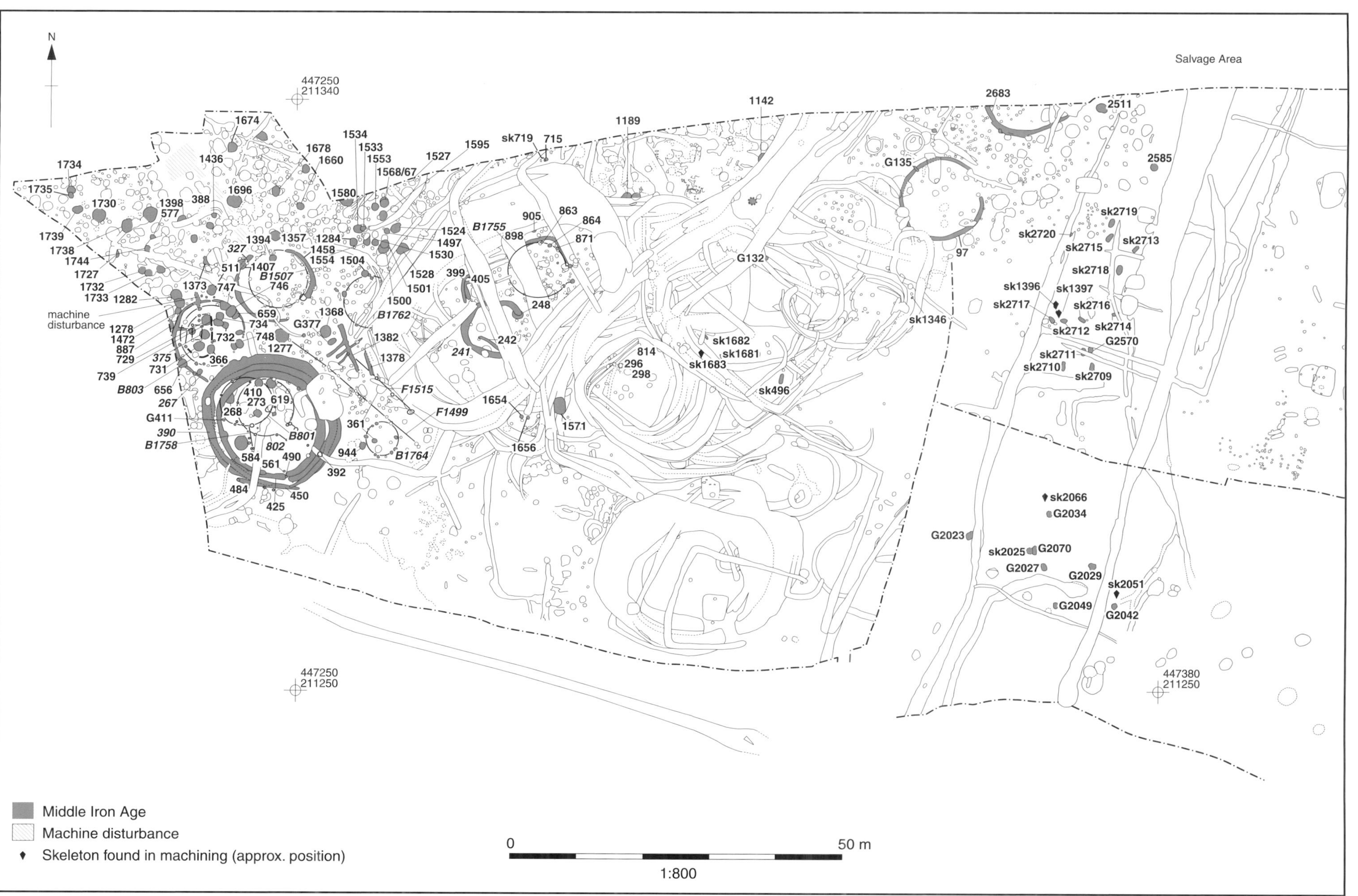

Fig. 6.3 Yarnton: middle Iron Age features

Fig. 6.4 D-shaped structure 803

Fig. 6.5 Structures 801 and 802 within enclosure 390

and the enclosures is so close they are described together in the following account.

The western group of structures and associated enclosures on the Yarnton site (Fig. 6.3)

A semi-circular or D-shaped post-built structure, 803, was situated at the western edge of the Yarnton excavation within a penannular enclosure, 267, comprising two curvilinear segments of ditch with an apparent entrance to the south-east (Figs 6.4 and 6.6). Finds of metalworking debris from the ditches and pits surrounding this unusual building suggest that it may have been a smithy. To the north-east of the D-shaped structure was another interrupted ring-gully, 327, with gaps to the north-west and south-east, which enclosed a post-built roundhouse, 1507, with an entrance to the south. A second post-built roundhouse, 1762, with no associated ring-gully, lay to the south-east of this structure. Irregular ditch arrangements were found to its south, but this complex was cut away to the east by a substantial early Roman enclosure.

South of these buildings was a substantial penannular ditch, 390, which had been recut on at least three occasions, and had several short stretches of ditch running from east to west across its entrance. A post-built roundhouse, 802, with a clearly defined entrance to the south-east, lay within the enclosed space (Fig. 6.5). This building was superimposed upon an earlier post-built roundhouse, 801, most of which also lay within the penannular ditch, but was cut by its latest recut. Abutting these structures to the south was a north-south running fence line, 1758, which was cut away by later activity to its south. It is possible that the fence formed part of a partition within the enclosure, the northern boundary of which was formed by the wall of the building itself. Outside and to the east of the large penannular ditch was a small post-built roundhouse, 1764, with a small pit lying to its west. The size and position of this structure suggest that it may have been an ancillary building, rather than a domestic structure. Directly to the north-east of the large penannular ditch and structure 1764, was a track defined by two fence lines orientated NW-SE and aligned on structure 1507. Irregular ditch arrangements lay north-east of this route, between the fence and structure 1762. They are of unknown function, but may perhaps have been associated with stock management.

Structure 803 and enclosure 267 (Figs 6.4 and 6.6)

Structure 803 comprised an outer and inner concentric D-shaped, or semi-circular, arrangement of posts, 9.3 m x 6.5 m, with an east facing entrance 1.5 m wide. A rectangular four-post structure 1.3 m x 2.1 m lay in the centre. The 18 postholes which made up this structure or structures were generally circular in plan, measuring 0.3-0.6 m in diameter and 0.12-0.28 m in depth. Their profiles had steep sides and flat or rounded, bases. The fills of the postholes consisted of brown or orange silty sands containing 10-20% gravel. Some postholes (649, 650 and 651) had been disturbed by animal activity. The only find from this structure was a single moderately-large sherd of sand-tempered pottery.

Surrounding structure 803 was enclosure 267, comprising two stretches of curvilinear gully with a diameter of 11 m, enclosing an area of *c* 85 m^2. It is uncertain whether the gap to the north was real or was the result of later truncation by ploughing or disturbance during machine stripping of the site. The presence of possible individual postholes between 267/C and 267/F, however, suggests that the gap may have been an original feature that was filled at a later stage, perhaps when the outer ring of posts of structure 803 was constructed. The gully came to a well-defined terminal in the south (267/A) and, although it became too shallow to have survived in the north-east, it is apparent that there would have been an entrance to the south-east corresponding with the entrance to the building or buildings. Twelve sections were excavated through the enclosure gully, representing 35% of its original length. In profile it was an open U-shape and showed no sign of recuts. It was, on average, 0.4 m wide and 0.14 m deep, and the single fill consisted of gravel-free material.

In contrast to the internal structure/s, the gully was relatively rich in finds, yielding 22 sherds of pottery (748 g in weight), mainly in sand-tempered fabrics, 16 fragments of animal bone and some preserved plant remains including cereal grains.

It is uncertain whether the posthole layout represents a single contemporary structure, or a sequence of buildings. The inner ring appears to have formed a D-shaped structure with a closed eastern side and a well-defined entrance between posts 297 and 711. The outer ring of posts, on the other hand, seems to have been open-sided to the east. The four-post structure, if it was formed of roof-height posts, would have cluttered the small internal space unnecessarily. Its central position within either/both D-shaped structures may be fortuitous or, more probably, suggests that it was laid out with reference to earlier buildings. It could be suggested that the earliest structure was the smaller of the two D-shaped features, which was replaced by a large, open-sided building at the same time as the possible northern entrance to the enclosure was closed off with posts. The four-post structure may have been the final component of this sequence. Its location can be paralleled by those of the four-post structures found within three early Iron Age buildings on this site (see Chapter 5 above).

Structure 1507 and enclosure 327 (Fig. 6.7)

Structure 1507, to the north-east of structure 803 and enclosure 267, was a circular post-built building with a diameter of approximately 9 m and a south facing entrance 2 m wide. The 11 postholes

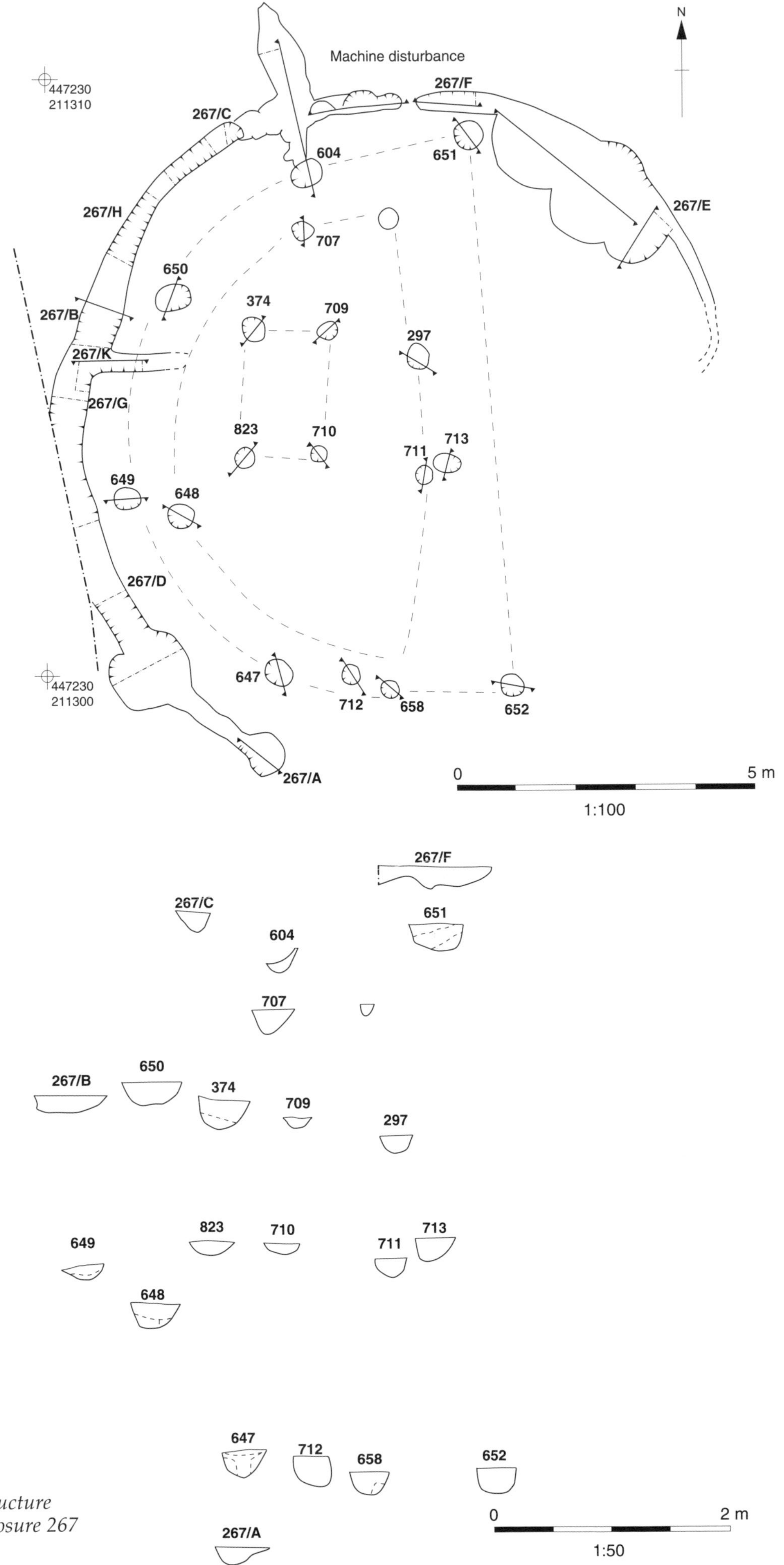

Fig. 6.6 Structure 803 and enclosure 267

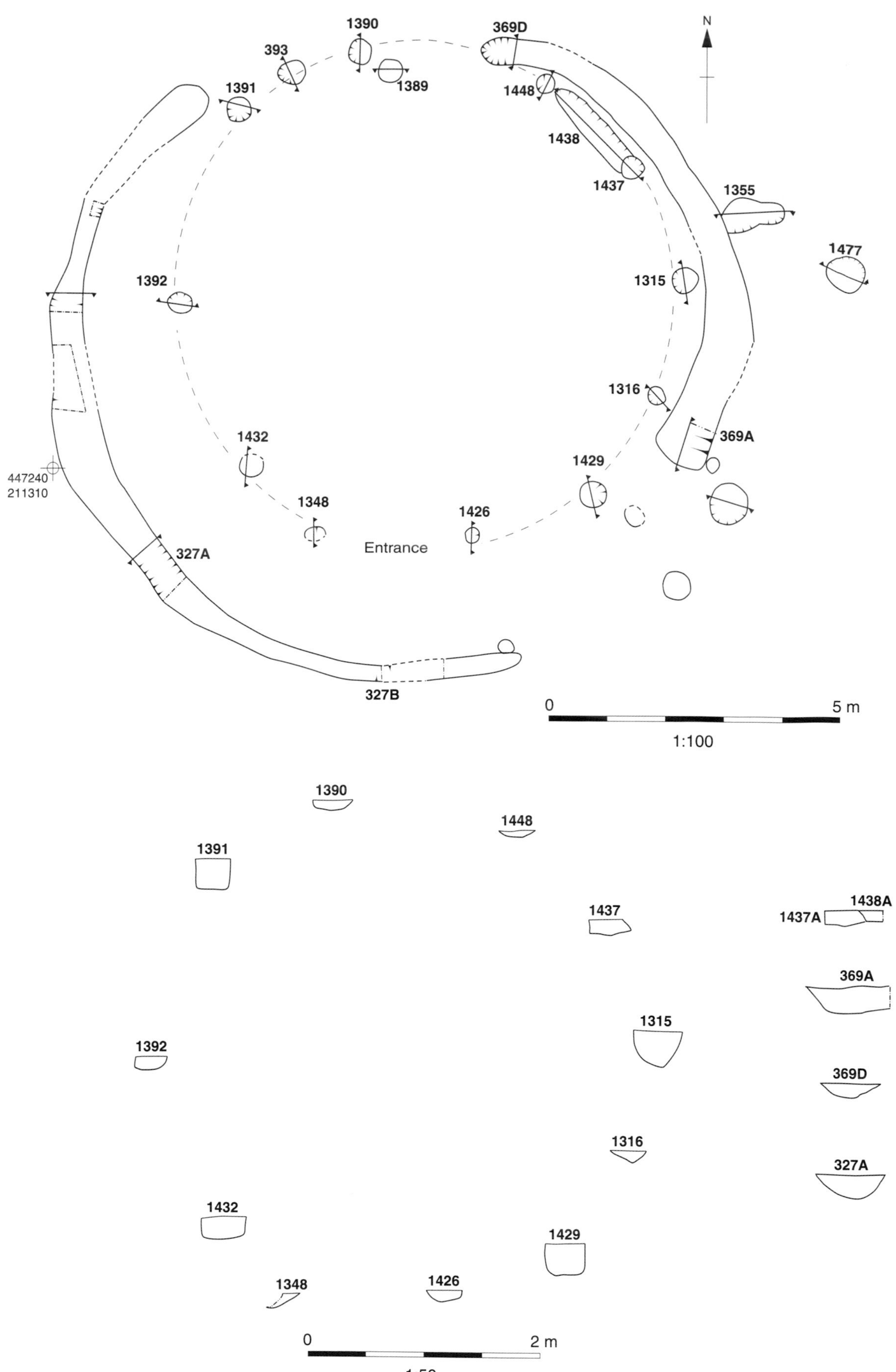

Fig. 6.7 Structure 1507 and enclosure 327

comprising this structure were circular in plan, approximately 0.3-0.6 m in diameter, and ranged in depth between 0.07 m and 0.3 m. The profiles of the postholes varied, being either U-shaped or shallow, and their fills consisted of grey and brown silty sands containing 5-20% gravel. Flecks of charcoal were recorded in the fill of 1391. Finds from the postholes included eight sherds of pottery and 14 fragments of animal bone.

Structure 1507 was surrounded by enclosure 327, an interrupted ditch/gully similar in form to enclosure 267 (see above, contexts 267, 369 and 1405). It consisted of two sections of curvilinear ditch with a diameter of 10.5 m, enclosing an area of approximately 85 m². Nine sections were excavated through these ditches, making up 10% of their original length. In profile the ditch was an open U-shape, 0.55 m wide and 0.15 m deep on average, and no recuts were apparent. There was a single principal fill of homogeneous non-gravelly soil, with some primary silting evident. The plan and section suggested that there were two possible entrances to the enclosure, one to the north and another to the south-east, with the south-east opening being more clearly defined. A number of unexcavated postholes in this area could represent a gate structure.

As with ring-gully 267, gully 327 was quite rich in artefactual material, producing 34 sherds of pottery weighing 396 g, 17 animal bone fragments and plant remains, amongst which were cereal grains, chaff and weed seeds.

The building was positioned rather eccentrically within the enclosure, closing its northern entrance and sitting close up against the north-east arc of the ditch. To the south, the probable entrance to the building did not open directly into the south-eastern enclosure entrance but to one side, with a *c* 2 m-wide space here between the building and the surrounding ditch, perhaps creating a small enclosure or activity area between the house and its ring ditch. This may have been part of the original design of this group of features, but it is also just possible that the enclosure was the earlier feature and that the building was later placed within it. A number of undated and some probably early Iron Age postholes in the area of the enclosure south-east entrance may possibly have been associated with such an early phase of use (cf Fig. 5.7). The general absence of gullies in association with early Iron Age structures makes this interpretation unlikely, however.

Structure 1762 (Figs 6.3 and 6.8)

South-east of enclosure 327 lay structure 1762, a circular building with a diameter of *c* 8 m. Only part of this structure survived, as its eastern section was cut away by an early Roman enclosure ditch. It consisted of five or six postholes (posthole 1290 being slightly inside the suggested circuit) which were generally circular in plan, measuring 0.4-0.5 m in diameter except for feature 1351, which was 0.9 m

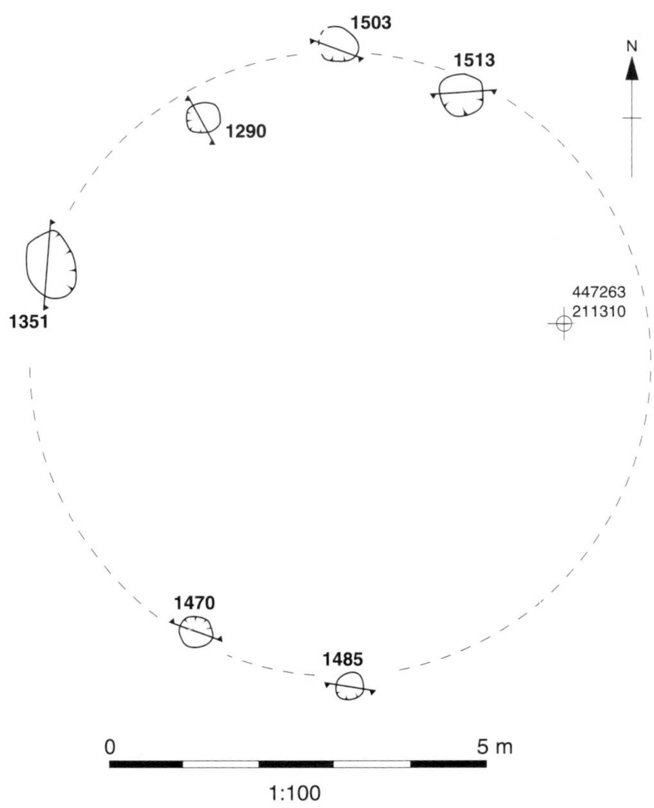

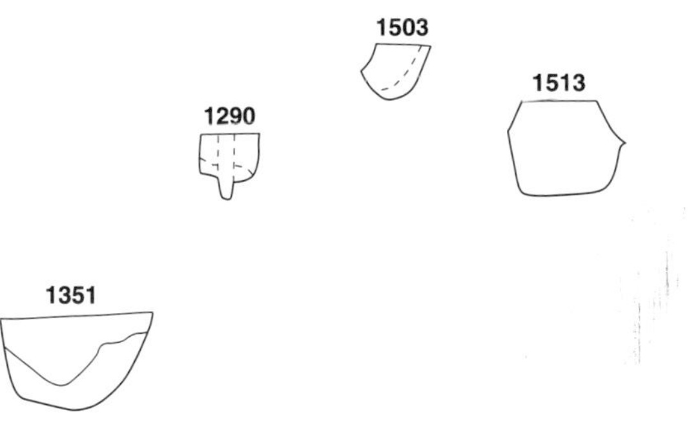

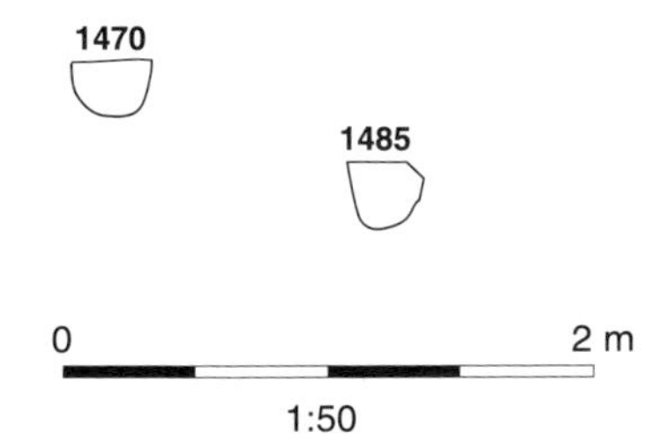

Fig. 6.8 Structure 1762

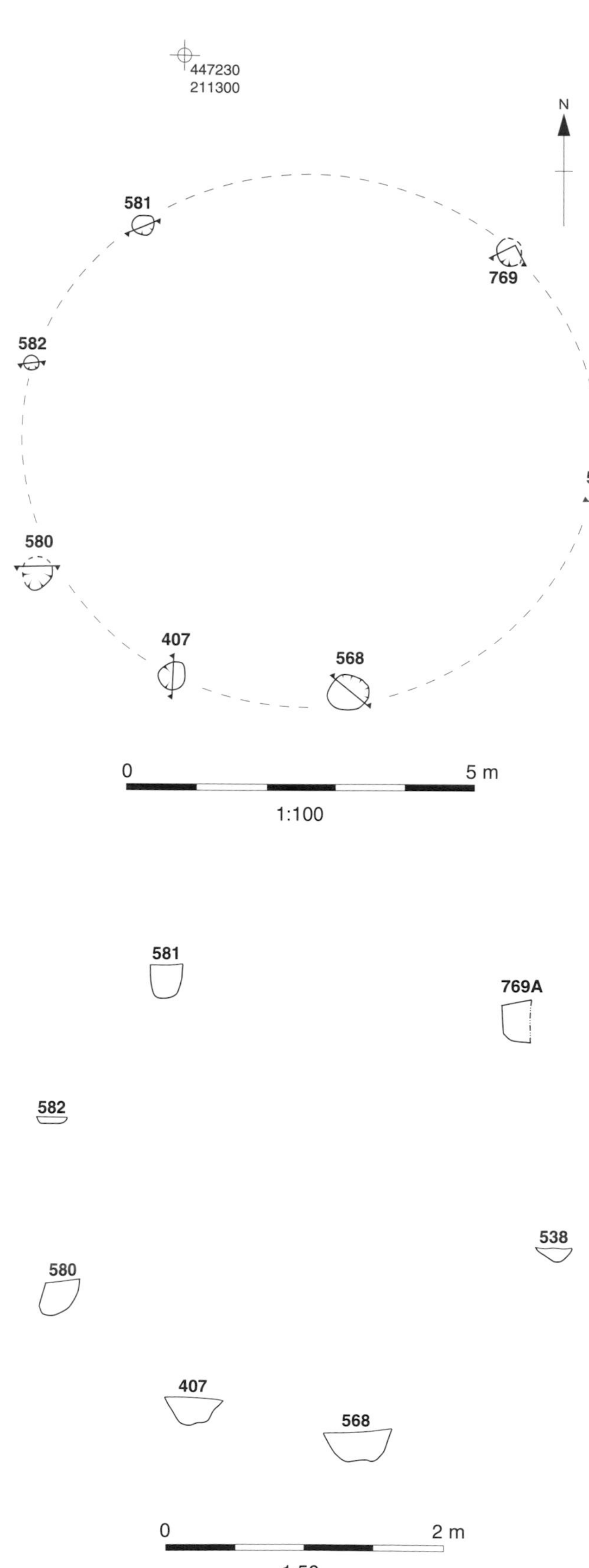

Fig. 6.9 Structure 801

across, and 0.12-0.48 m in depth. In profile they were either bowl-shaped, or steep-sided and flat-based. Their fills comprised brown silty sands containing 5-20% gravel, and possible postpipes were visible in three postholes (1351, 1290 and 1503). Finds from structure 1762 were limited to five sherds of pottery, 44 g in weight, and two animal bones.

Structures 801 and 802, enclosure 390 and fence line 1758

Structure 801 (Figs 6.3, 6.5, 6.9 and 6.11)

Two circular buildings were found lying within a large enclosure (390) in the south-west corner of the site. Enclosure 390 was dug to enclose a much larger space than an individual house and was recut on at least three separate occasions. The earlier of the two houses, 801, lay in the north-west of the enclosure close to the ditch of its first three phases. The final phase of the enclosure ditch cut through this building, and this is probably the stage at which structure 802 was constructed.

Structure 801 was a circular post-built building approximately 8 m in diameter. There was no clear indication of an entrance, but it may have been in the south-east within the wide space between postholes 568 and 538. The structure comprised seven postholes which were roughly circular in plan, and measured 0.25-0.6 m in diameter and 0.1-0.3 m in depth. When examined in section these postholes had steep sides and flat or slightly-rounded bases. Their fills consisted of brown, grey and orange sandy silts; these were generally gravel free, or contained approximately 2-5% gravel. The exception was posthole 538 which contained 25% gravel. The only finds comprised seven sherds of pottery (76 g) in sand-tempered and shell-tempered fabrics.

Structure 802 (Figs 6.3, 6.5 and 6.10)

Post-built structure 802 partly overlapped structure 801 to the south-east, and lay in the northern part of the final phase of enclosure 390. It was circular to oval in shape, measuring 8.5-9 m across, with an entrance to the south-east. The entrance was approximately 1.8 m wide, and was indicated by a porch structure comprising two door posts (525 and 558), and two porch posts (794 and 524). The surviving structure consisted of 13 postholes, circular in plan and measuring 0.18-0.45 m in diameter and 0.06-0.22 m in depth. In general the postholes were steep-sided with flat or rounded bases, and their fills consisted of grey, brown and orange silty sands containing 5-20% gravel. Animal burrows had disturbed postholes 525, 557 and 558. Finds were sparse, being limited to four small sherds of pottery (18 g) and three animal bones.

Enclosure 390 (Figs 6.5 and 6.11-6.14)

A substantial penannular ditch, 390, with an entrance to the south, lay in the south-west part of the Yarnton site. It had a maximum external

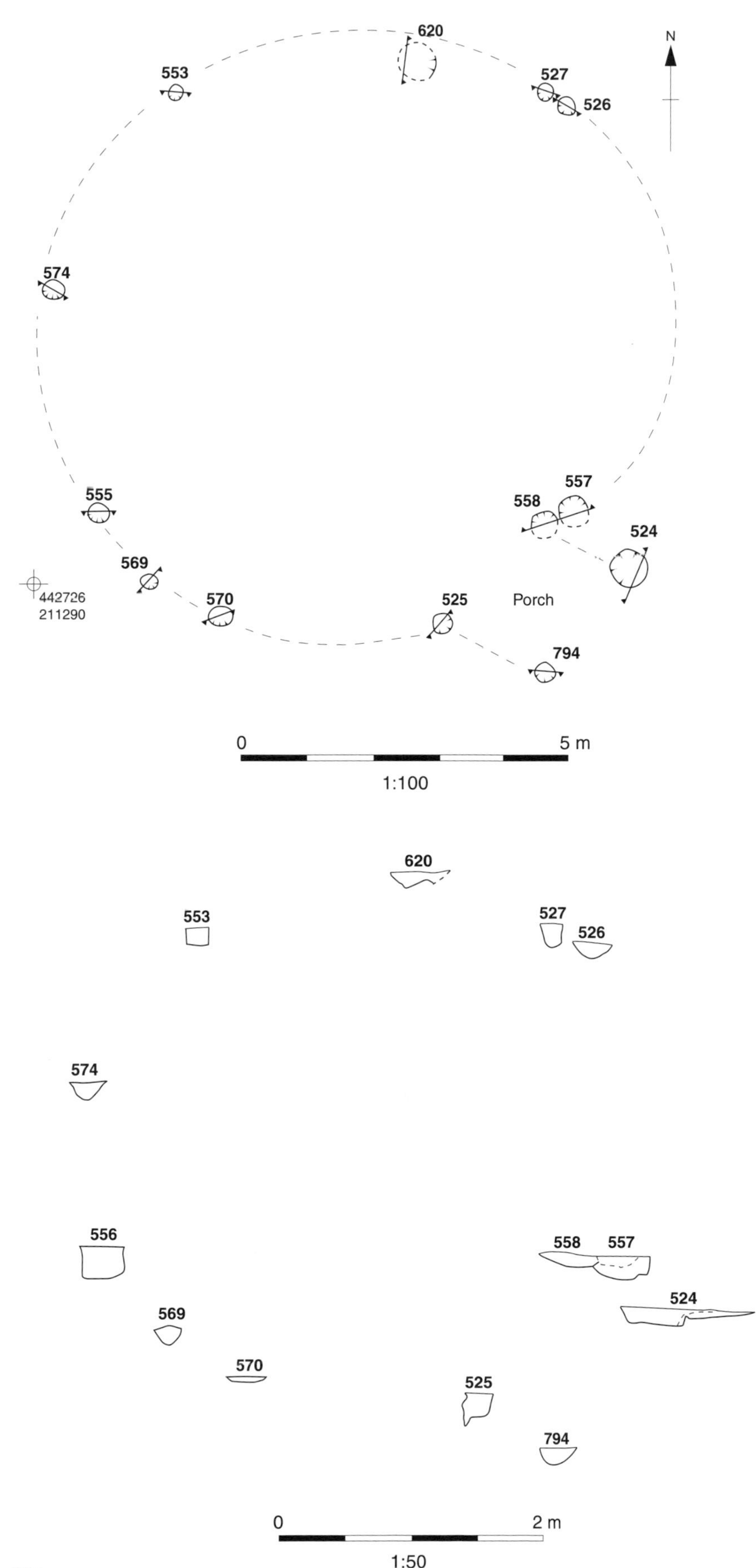

Fig. 6.10 Structure 802

diameter of approximately 20 m, delimiting an area of *c* 310 m^2 and had been recut on three separate occasions. As already described, structures 801 and 802 lay within its north-western sector, the former having been cut through by the final phase of the enclosure ditch. A short fence line (1758) running south from these structures seems most likely to have been contemporary with the earlier building, 801, and appeared to create a small enclosure or pen in the south-west of the larger enclosure. A number of postholes around the entrance suggest a gate structure associated with its final phase, and a few other postholes were found within the enclosure. Five middle Iron Age pits were also found within the enclosed space, all in the north-west, but these seemed either to pre-date the enclosure and structures (pit 268), or to post-date its use (pits 273, 410 and 619). Only pit 584, a large and shallow pit in the south-west of the enclosure, could have been contemporary with the buildings (of any phase). This pit yielded an interesting collection of finds including a bone comb and leaze rod, a bone/antler handle, several loomweight fragments, quernstones and a crucible fragment. Pottery (53 sherds; 1046 g), animal bone and charred plants, including cereals and chaff were also recovered. The enclosure ditch was comparatively prolific in finds, the densest concentrations coming from the north of the enclosure, in the area of the structures.

The sequence of enclosure development is described in stratigraphic order.

Enclosure 390A (Figs 6.13 and 6.14)

The earliest phase of enclosure 390 (390A) was defined by a slightly irregular sub-circular ditch with a diameter of 18-19 m, enclosing an area of *c* 270 m^2. The south-facing entrance to the enclosure of this initial phase was approximately 7 m wide, as indicated by a single terminal to the east, although the western terminal had been cut away by later activity. Nine percent of the total length of this ditch was excavated in five sections. In profile the ditch had irregular sides and a flat base, and averaged 0.57 m in width and 0.35 m in depth. It contained a single fill of silty loam with a little gravel and some greenish material. Finds comprise 11 sherds of pottery and 16 animal bones.

Lying across the entrance to this enclosure were two short east-west ditches, 425 and 450. Ditch 425 was at least 4 m in length. Although it was cut to the west by a Roman ditch, which obscured its relationships to the enclosure here, it may represent an eastwards extension of the west terminal of ditch 390A. It was clearly cut by the ditch of the final phase of the enclosure (390D), and probably by its second phase ditch (390B). Two sections were excavated across ditch 425, representing 30% of its extant length. No recuts were observed, and the ditch profile was varied, being U-shaped and open in one section, and irregular in the other. On average it was 0.55 m wide and 0.32 m deep. Its main fill comprised slightly gravelly silty loam with

Fig. 6.11 Enclosure 390 prior to excavation

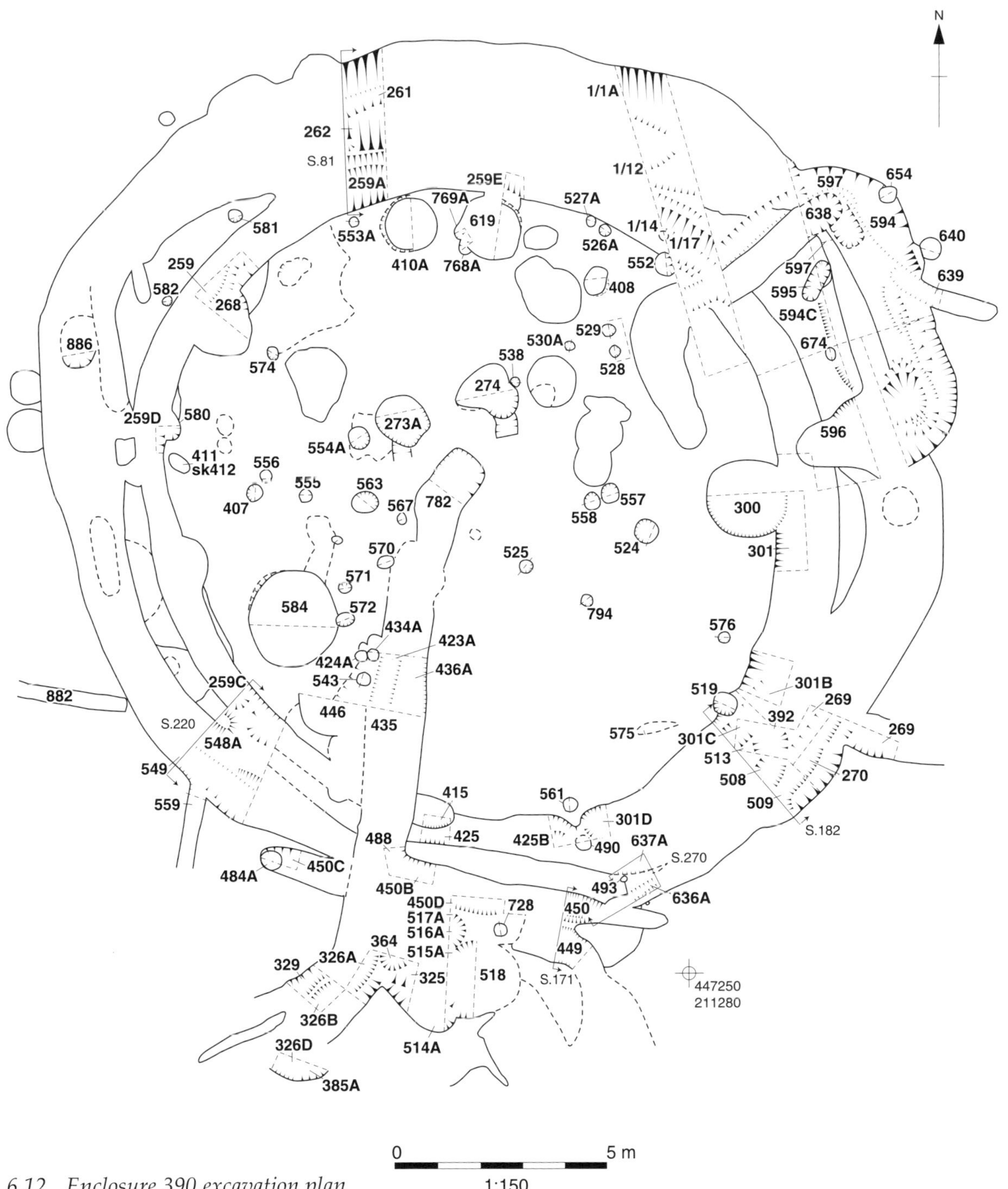

Fig. 6.12 Enclosure 390 excavation plan

some greenish material above primary silting. There were no finds.

To the south of the entrance to enclosure 390A was ditch 450, which was cut by the second phase of the enclosure (390B). The ditch was 9.6 m long and five sections were excavated across it, representing 30% of its original length. In profile it was generally an open U-shape, 0.6 m wide and 0.2 m deep on average, and there was no sign of any recuts. For the most part it had only a single fill, of slightly gravelly, silty loam, with some burnt limestone and fragments of clay present near the bottom. Six sherds of pottery (130 g) and six animal bones were recovered.

The purpose of these ditches is very unclear. They may each represent a single event when it was important to prevent ingress to or egress from the enclosure.

Enclosure 390B (Figs 6.13 and 6.14)

Enclosure 390B was circular, with a ditch 20.7 m in diameter enclosing an area of *c* 335 m. The entrance to this phase of the enclosure also faced south, and was approximately 6 m in width. The enclosure ditch appeared to cut the fills of the two ditches which blocked the entrance at the end of phase 1. Six sections were excavated through the ditch of this

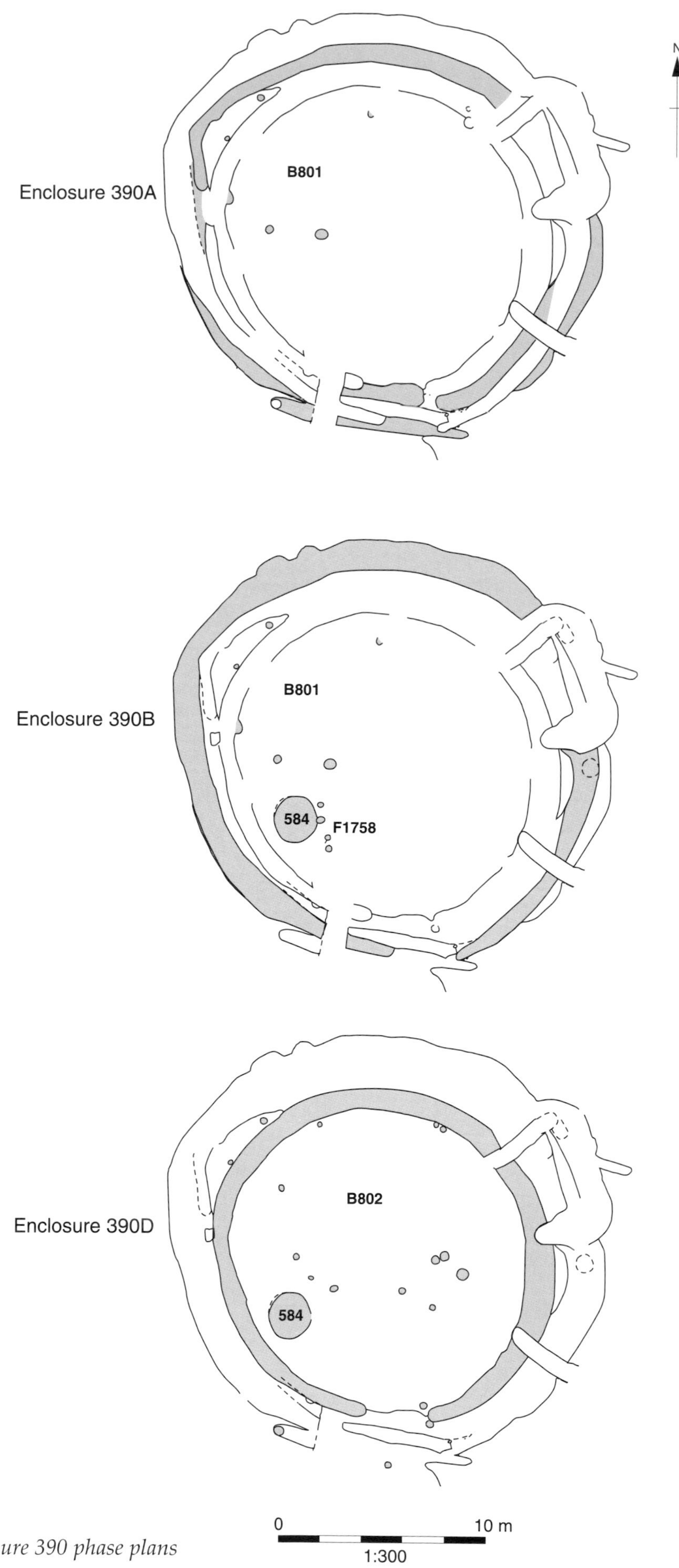

Fig. 6.13 Enclosure 390 phase plans

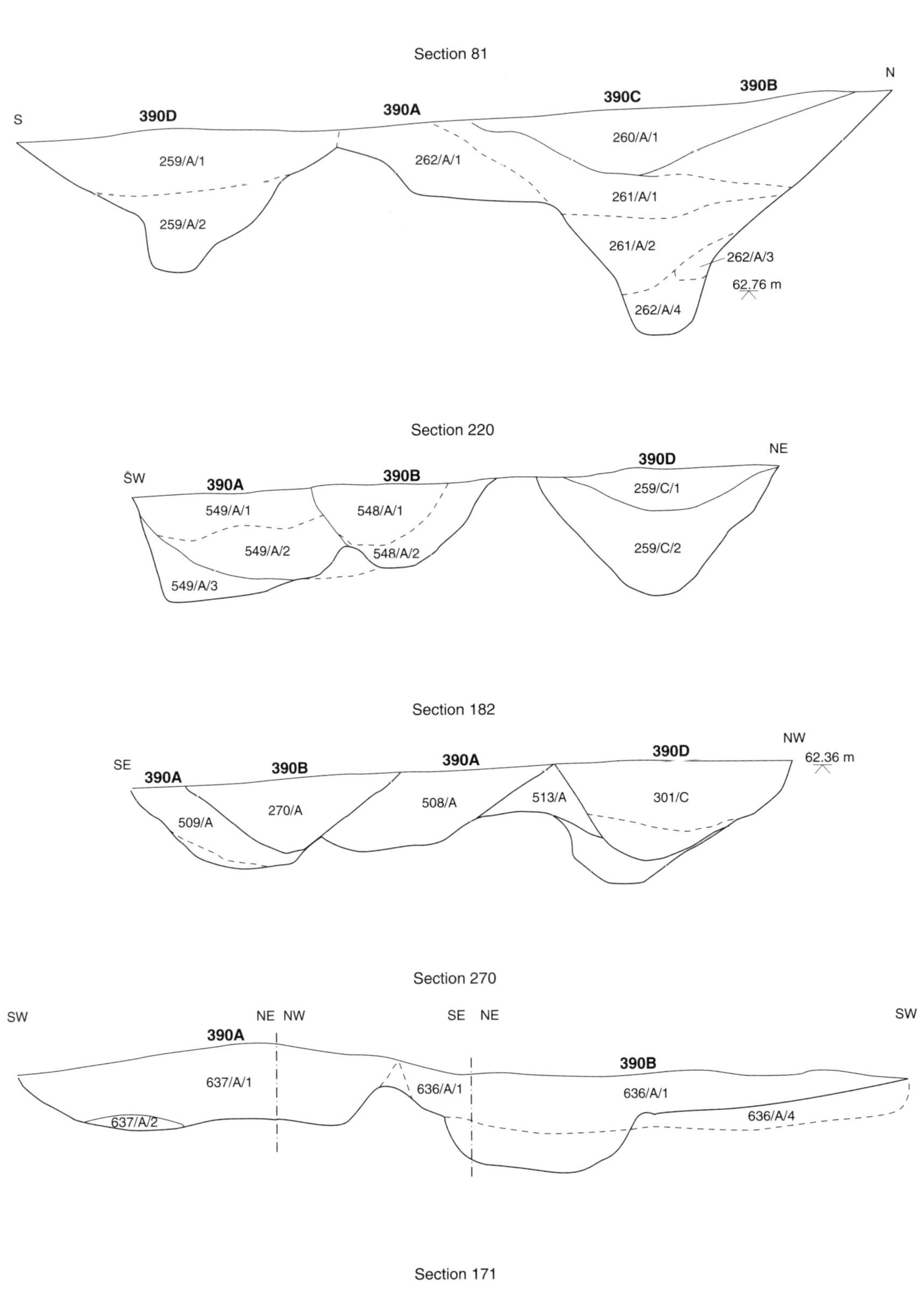

Fig. 6.14 Enclosure 390 sections

enclosure, representing 12% of its total length. In profile the ditch was varied, being an open U-shape in places, and irregular in others. On average it was 0.95 m wide and 0.57 m deep. The single fill consisted of silty loam with gravel. Finds were relatively prolific and included 39 sherds of pottery (598 g), 42 animal bones and one fragment of slag lining. Plant remains were also abundant in both the north and the south-east sectors of the enclosure ditch, with a number of cereal grains, weed seeds and evidence of crop processing in the form of chaff.

Enclosure 390C (Fig. 6.14)

A second recut of the enclosure ditch (390C) was traced over a distance of 18.2 m in the northern part of the enclosure. It then either followed an inner line and was cut away by the final phase of enclosure ditch (390D) or was perhaps only a localised recut on the northern side of the enclosure. No entrance was observed in the extant part of the ditch. Two sections were excavated through this ditch, revealing a distinctive U-shaped profile, open in one section and more narrow in the other. The ditch was, on average, 1.15 m wide and 0.29 m deep. The single fill comprised silty loam with gravel, and some greenish material. Thirty sherds of pottery (407 g) were recovered, of which at least 21 are in sand-tempered fabrics, along with 55 animal bones and two fragments of fired clay. Much of this came from a section to the north of the house structures (Fig. 6.14 Section 81).

Enclosure 390D (Figs 6.13 and 6.14)

Enclosure 390D was formed by an almost circular ditch cut within the circuit of the earlier enclosure ditches. It had a diameter of about 16 m defining an area of *c* 160 m^2. As before, the entrance to this enclosure faced south, but it was comparatively narrow at 3 m wide, suggesting more restricted access to the smaller interior space. Five postholes (561, 490, 493, 728 and 484) found in the entrance area, might possibly have related to a gateway and associated structures. Eleven sections were excavated through the ditch, representing just over 20% of its original length. The ditch profile was varied, being U-shaped and open in places and irregular in others. On average the ditch cut was 1 m wide and 0.5 m deep. Its fill consisted of silty loams with gravel, and more gravelly fills; some greenish material and ash were also present

Numerous finds were recovered from the fills of enclosure ditch 390D, including 120 sherds of pottery (1692 g), 59% of which are in sand-tempered fabrics, 101 animal bones of which over 60% were either cattle or horse, one fragment of sub-tuyère plate and two crucible fragments. Plant remains included several cereal grains and evidence of crop processing. The largest concentrations of finds of this phase came from the south-east side of the enclosure (Fig. 6.32). Fragments of a copper alloy brooch were also recovered from the final phase of the ditch on its south-east side.

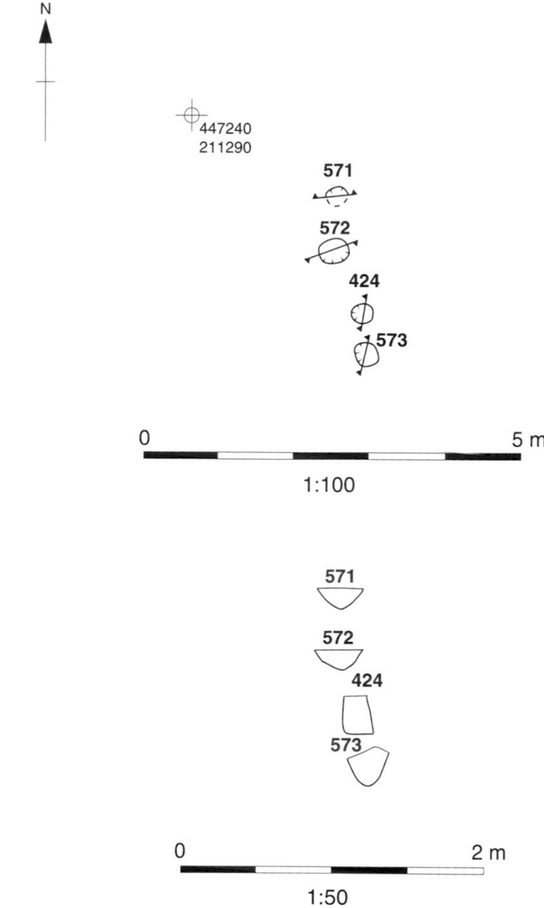

Fig. 6.15 Fence 1758

Fence line 1758 (Fig. 6.15)

Abutting structures 801 and 802 to the south was a fence line, 1758, which survived for just over 3 m but was cut away to the south by a later ditch. It consisted of four postholes which were roughly circular in plan with diameters of 0.2-0.4 m. The postholes were predominantly bowl-shaped in profile, but there was a single flat-based, steep-sided example (424). Their fills consisted of mid to dark brown silty sands containing 1% gravel. A single large sherd of shell-tempered pottery was recovered from posthole 572. This fence may have served to divide the space within the enclosure, or may have been a barrier next to pit 584 to the east.

Structure 1764 (Fig. 6.16)

Lying to the east of enclosure 390 was structure 1764, the most southerly of the buildings amongst this settlement group. It was a small, circular to oval building, *c* 5 m in diameter, of which nine postholes survived. The postholes were generally circular or slightly oval in plan, with diameters of 0.2-0.6 m, and depths of 0.1-0.34 m. In section these postholes were predominantly steep-sided and flat-based, but some examples were more bowl-shaped or shallow. Their fills consisted of brown silty sands containing 5-40% gravel, with some charcoal flecks. Animal

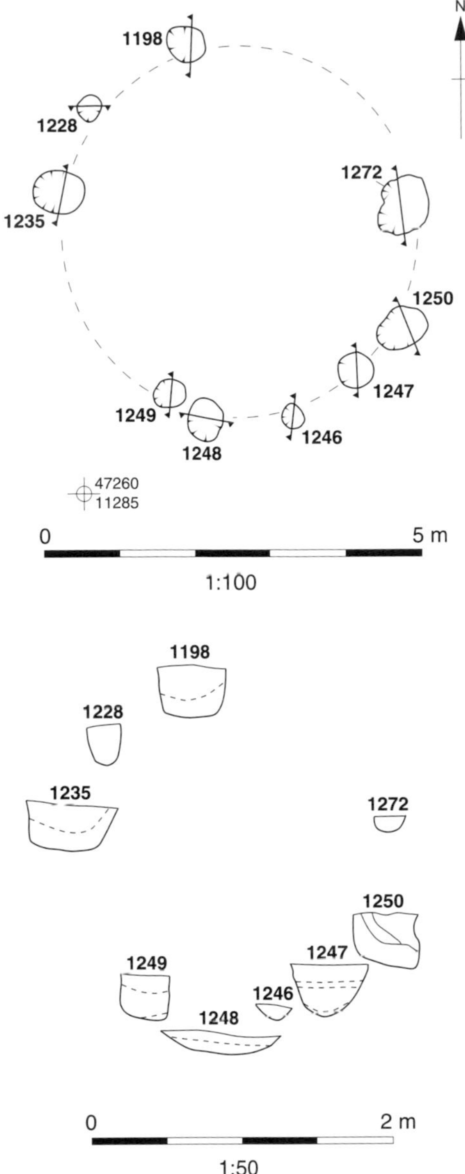

Fig. 6.16 Structure 1764

disturbance had affected postholes 1272 and 1250. The only finds were two small sherds of pottery (7 g) and five animal bones.

The central group of structures and associated enclosures on the Yarnton site (Fig 6.3)

An oval post-built structure, 1755, was situated in the centre of the site, approximately 15 m from the northern limit of the excavation (Fig. 6.3). It occupied an area that overlapped substantially with early Iron Age house 1754 (Fig. 5.7). Immediately north of structure 1755, and cutting the earlier structure, lay a short section of curvilinear gully, 898, which may be the remains of an enclosure surrounding the middle Iron Age building. South-west of the structure was a penannular ditch, 241, with an entrance to the east. A NW-SE orientated curvilinear gully, 242, lay within the penannular ditch; their relationship had been destroyed by a Roman ditch. Two parallel curvilinear gullies, 399 and 415, lay to the north of penannular ditch 241 and they seemed to belong to this phase. This group of features had been much disturbed by Roman ditch digging and it is certain that occupation would have been more extensive than now survives. In particular, it seems possible that settlement was continuous from the area to the west.

Structure 1755 and gully 898 (Fig. 6.17)

Structure 1755 was a circular post-built structure, 8.5 m in diameter, which was cut by later Roman ditches. It appeared to have had an east facing entrance 1.7 m wide, with a porch arrangement extending 1 m out from the main circuit of posts. Nine postholes survived and these were generally circular in plan, with an average diameter of 0.47 m and an average depth of 0.3 m. In profile they were either bowl-shaped, or steep-sided and flat-based. The posthole fills consisted of grey or brown sandy silts with widely varying gravel content and some charcoal flecks. Finds comprised seven sherds of pottery (81 g), two animal bones and a quern fragment.

Lying immediately to the north of structure 1755 was a short section of curvilinear ditch/gully (898), 8.5 m in length. The form and position of this feature relative to structure 1755 suggest that it may have been part of an enclosure ditch which was subsequently cut away by Roman activity. It ran SW-NE from a Roman ditch to the west and then turned to curve sharply to the south-east where it was cut by another Roman ditch. If it was indeed contemporary with structure 1755, it would have terminated to the north of outer porch posthole 611. In profile 898 was a narrow U-shape and there was no sign of recutting. It was, on average, 0.6 m wide and 0.35 m deep. Five sections excavated through the ditch, representing 20% of its extant length, revealed a single fill of gravel-free material, which was greenish in colour and contained charcoal flecks. The relatively few finds recovered from the ditch fill (13 potsherds, eight animal bones and a fragment of fired clay) show that it was not used for the dumping of material from the building.

The eastern group of possible house enclosures on the Yarnton site (Fig. 6.3)

Summary

In the eastern area of the Yarnton site a group of curvilinear features indicated the presence of small sub-circular enclosures or penannular ditches/ gullies, which were associated with several pits. The northernmost ditch, 2683, mainly lay beyond the northern limit of the excavation, but the portion that was observed formed an arc with the apex to the south-west. It was cut away by an amorphous group of pits and ditches to the east. To its south-

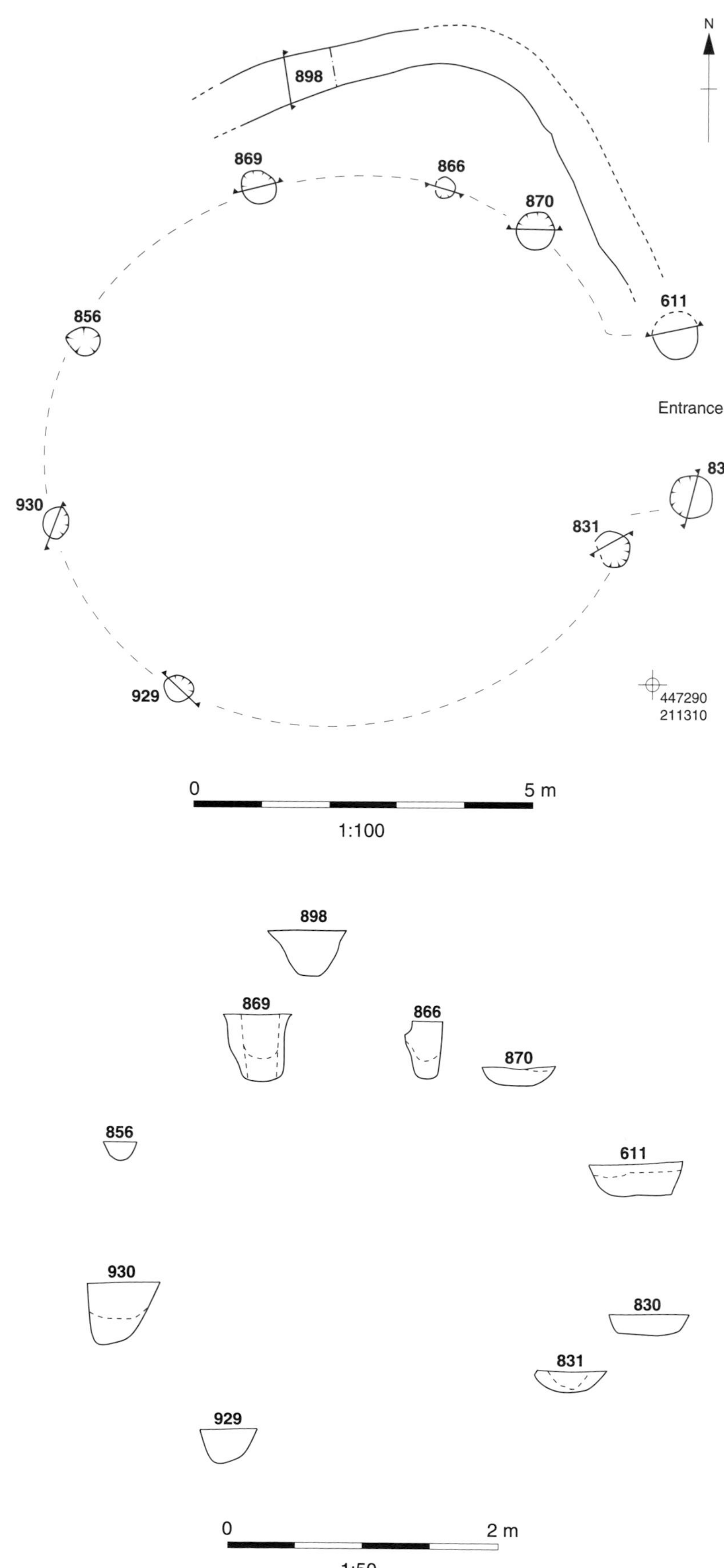

Fig. 6.17 Structure 1755 and gully 898

west were the remains of a penannular gully (97) with an entrance to the north-east.

Enclosure 2683 (Fig. 6.3)

Ditch 2683 was a curvilinear feature 14 m in length, the western end of which ran beyond the northern limit of excavation, and the eastern end of which was cut away by a cluster of pits and gullies. It cut through early Iron Age structure 2661. A few other postholes lay within the south-west of the enclosed space, but these were not excavated and it is not known whether they represent the traces of a post-built structure within the enclosure.

Three sections were excavated through the ditch, representing 5% of its exposed extent. It had a narrow U-shaped profile, 0.62 m wide and 0.4 m deep, which appeared not to have been recut, and had a single homogeneous fill of non-gravelly material. Finds from the ditch were scarce, comprising seven sherds of Iron Age pottery (130 g) in mixed, but mainly sand-tempered fabrics.

Enclosure 97 (Figs 6.3 and 6.18)

This penannular gully lay approximately 8 m south-west of ditch 2683. It was subcircular in plan, up to 13 m across, enclosing an area of *c* 110 m^2, and had an

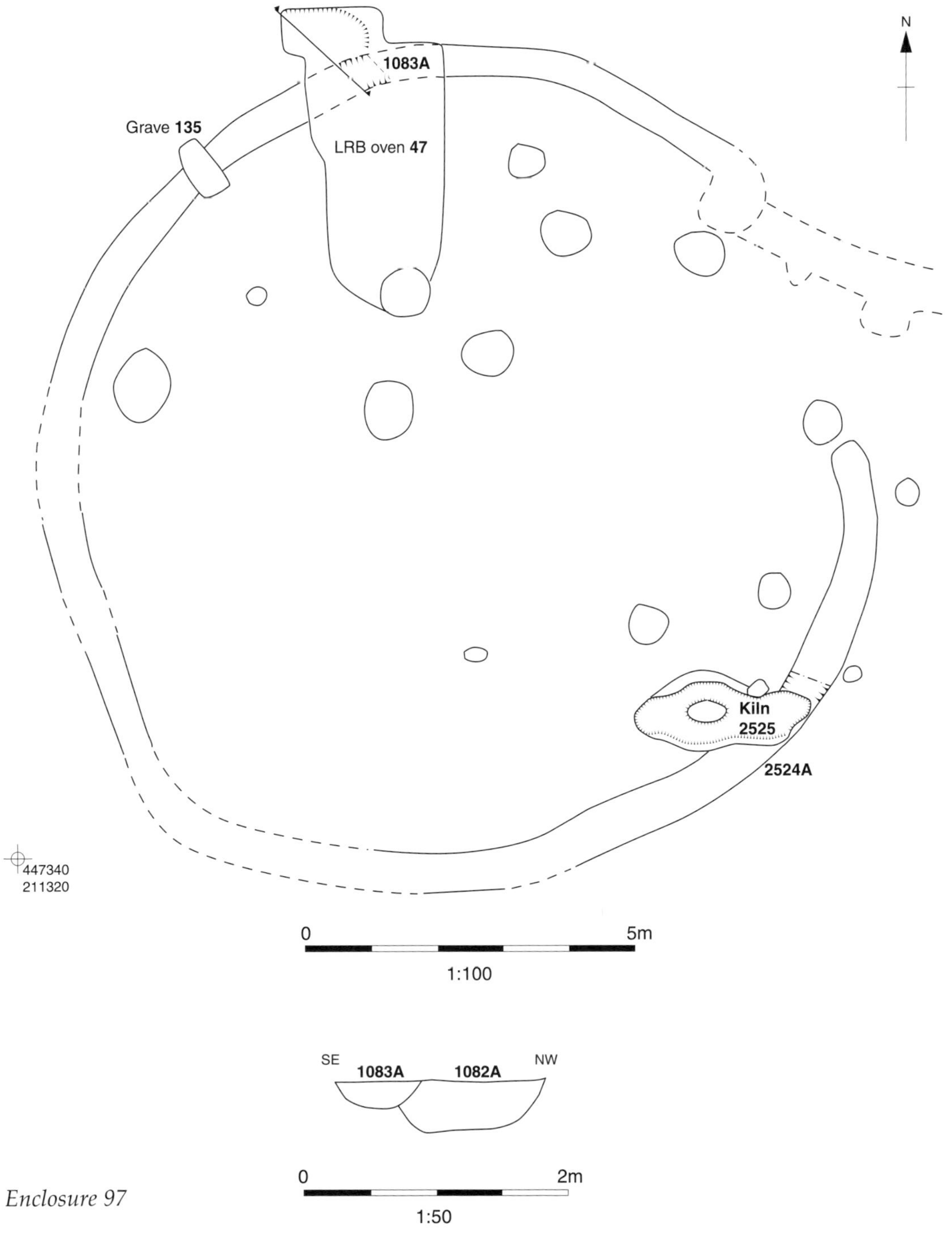

Fig. 6.18 Enclosure 97

entrance to the north-east which was 4 m wide. A number of unexcavated pits and postholes lay within the enclosure and may have been contemporary with it. The gully was much cut away by later features and grave cut 135 of middle Iron Age burial 136 lay in the top of it in the north-west sector. Both features were very shallow here and it proved impossible to ascertain their relationship with certainty.

Four sections were excavated across the gully, representing 4% of its length. The gully was an open U-shape in profile, 0.5 m wide and 0.2 m deep on average, and there was no evidence for recuts. Two fills of gravelly material were revealed, including some primary silting. The fills yielded 18 sherds of pottery (206 g) and six animal bones, principally from the east of the enclosure near its entrance.

Possible house enclosures on the Cresswell Field site (Fig. 6.2)

Double ring-gully 8018/8286 on the edge of channel (Figs 6.2 and 6.19)

Two segments of curving gullies (8018 and 8286) on the east edge of the palaeochannel in Cresswell Field appeared to be the remnants of a discontinuous oval enclosure, possibly representing a double house gully. Gully 8018 consisted of cuts 8037, 7994, 8627 and 8630, and an unnumbered section which is very probably a continuation of the same cut; 8286 comprised cuts 8230, 8180, 8182, 8184, 8186. Gully 8283 almost certainly represented a continuation of this feature. The enclosure gullies had been recut, making it appear very wide in places (eg 8180, 8184, 7994 and 8627). The gullies varied in size along their lengths, being 0.35-1.1 m wide and 0.06-0.56 m deep. This variation was mostly due to differential truncation by ploughing and other disturbance in this area of the site. The enclosure was also cut by two Romano-British ditches.

The gullies enclosed an area of approximately 20 m by 10 m, with the longest axis aligned NE-SW, with a 6 m wide gap in the south-east segment apparently representing an entrance. The gully to the west of the entrance ended in a clearly-defined terminal, but to the north-east the gully was shallow and disturbed and the entrance could have been narrower than it appeared. It is also possible that there was a small gap in the north-west segment of the enclosure; one section of gully (8230) appeared to terminate at the point where it was truncated by a later ditch (8228). This possible terminal was directed toward the channel to the west and could have been a run off point allowing rain water collecting in the gully to flow into the adjacent watercourse.

The fill of the original gully consisted of a single homogeneous layer of gravel-free sandy silt. The recut contained mostly one or two fills of similar material, but where the gully survived to its greatest depth along the southern segment (7994) six fills were present. Both the original gully and the recut contained small quantities of middle Iron Age pottery, along with larger quantities of redeposited early Iron Age material. The gully also produced a small quantity of mixed animal bone and 2.35 kg of burnt stone.

The function of this enclosure is open to question. No features survived within it to indicate the presence of structures, but its shape and size suggest the presence of two adjacent circular buildings. The level of truncation by ploughing in this particular area, and the disturbance caused by the later ditches, may have removed all traces of postholes.

House gully 7895 in south-west corner of Cresswell Field (Fig. 6.20)

A 15 m stretch of curving gully (7895, comprising cuts 7966, 7862 and 7886) containing dense concentrations of pottery and animal bone lay adjacent to the south-west edge of the Cresswell Field site. Only part of this feature lay within the area of excavation but its character suggested that it was a penannular house gully. Its continuation to the west can be seen on the geophysical survey, as can a possible entrance to the south, although a number of highly magnetic pits appear to fill this space and these may represent discontinuous sections of deeper ditch (see Chapter 12). The survey indicates that the ditch enclosed an area *c* 15 m in diameter. A small scatter of contemporary finds-rich pits lay in the area immediately to the east of this enclosure and one of these, 7988 (see Fig. 6.2), produced a jet earring.

The gully, which measured up to 0.8 m in width and 0.36 m in depth, had a variable profile, changing from an almost V-shape next to the west edge of excavation to a more flat-bottomed U-shaped profile toward its southern terminal. Although the immediate area around the house gully was relatively flat, the land generally sloped down from north to south toward the floodplain. The enclosure gully may have allowed rainwater collecting around the house to drain downslope.

The three sections excavated through the gully produced 1.5 kg of pottery, although a significant percentage of the pottery was redeposited early Iron Age material. In addition, 5 kg of burnt stone and over 220 fragments of animal bone (almost entirely sheep and cattle) were retrieved along with a fragment of briquetage and a copper-alloy ring. Soil samples taken from these sections also produced charred grain.

Close to the southern terminal was a 1.5 m-long slot, 7888, running east-west at right angles to the main gully. This feature was the same size and character as the main gully and was clearly associated, though its exact function, and the relationship of the two features, was unclear. The remnants of a posthole, 7890, lay beneath the junction of the two segments of gully.

Remnants of narrow gully (7970, 7991 and 7992) measuring only 0.2 m in width and up to 0.2 m in depth, survived in patches running parallel close to the inside the main gully. These features were possibly eaves-drip gullies.

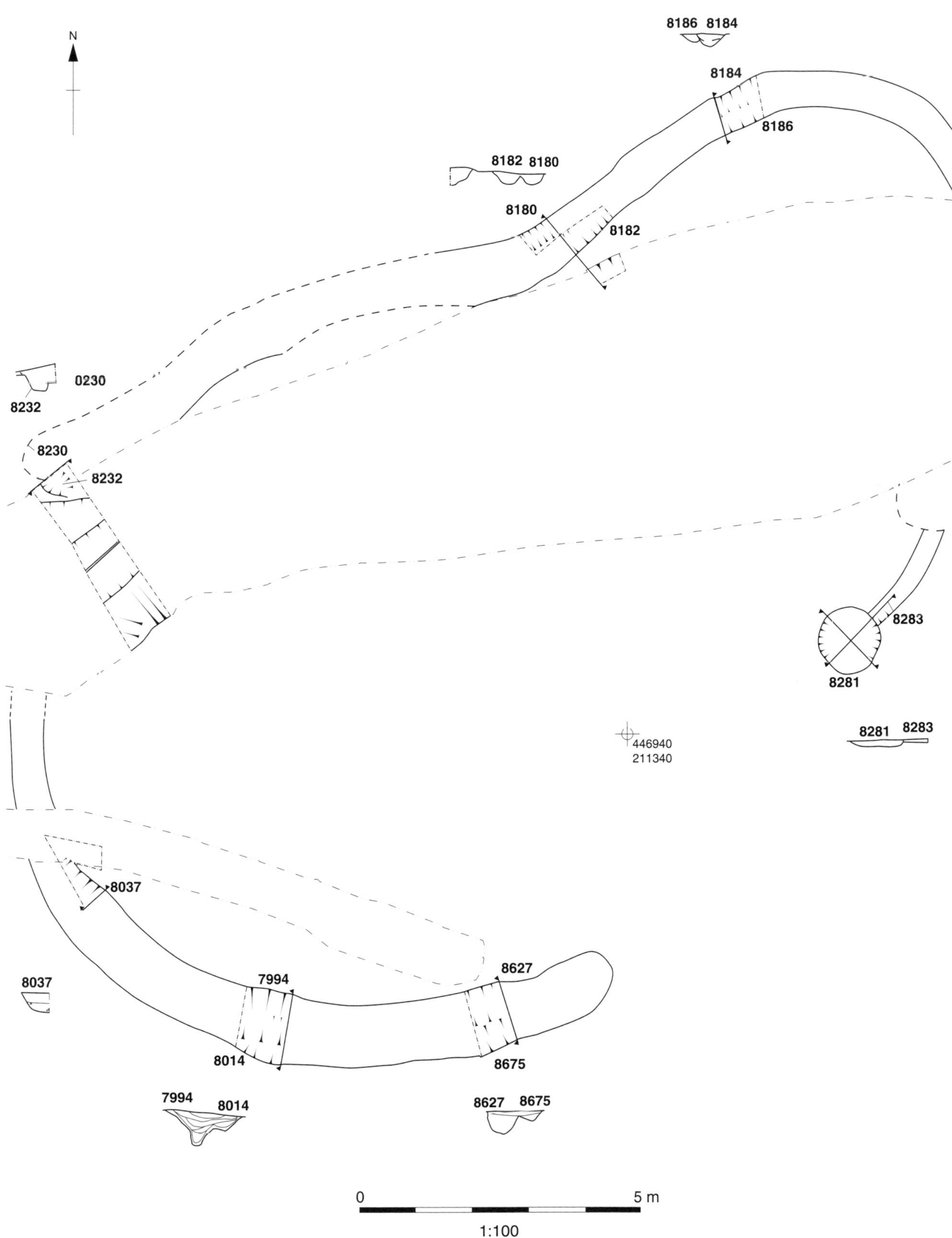

Fig. 6.19 Double ring gully enclosure 8018 and 8286 on edge of channel

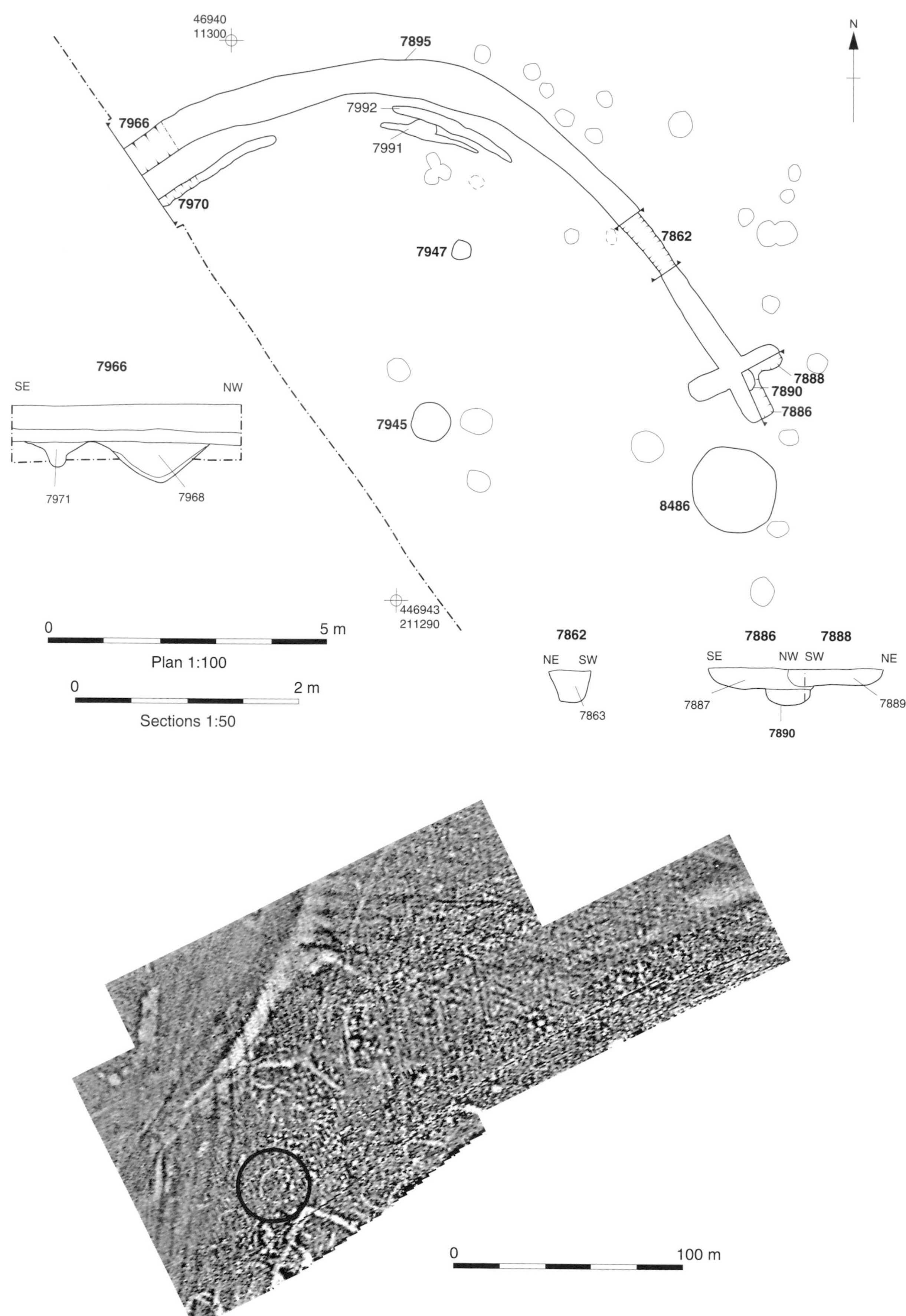

Fig. 6.20 House gully 7895 south-west corner of site

Distribution of finds from middle Iron Age structures and associated enclosures

Little pottery was found in the postholes of the middle Iron Age roundhouses, and the material that was recovered was fairly evenly spread between the different structures (Table 6.1). Similarly, there was only a small amount of animal bone, but this mostly concentrated in structure 1507. The majority of the animal bone was undiagnostic, and was identified as cow/horse size or sheep/pig size. The only other find recovered was a fragment of quernstone. The size and undiagnostic nature of the assemblage suggests that it represents secondary deposition during the construction or use of the buildings.

All the penannular ditches and gullies associated with structures contained relatively substantial assemblages of finds, mostly comprising animal bones and pottery (Table 6.1). The only gully to produce no finds at all was 425 which lay across the entrance to enclosure 390A. The quantities of animal bone and pottery from the different penannular ditches and gullies were fairly similar in the western part of the Yarnton site, with the exception of the later cuts of enclosure 390, especially 390D, which were more prolific (Table 6.1 and Fig. 6.13). The penannular gullies on the eastern side of the site, on the other hand, contained comparatively little material. Metalworking debris and other finds were generally scarce, and plant remains were mostly confined to the larger ditches of the western and central groups. The finds from the penannular features all suggest deposition of rubbish which presumably derived from the buildings which they enclosed, but there was no evidence for concentrations of artefacts in the ditch terminals at the entrances to these enclosures.

Table 6.1 Finds from middle Iron Age structures and associated enclosures.

Structures	*Pottery (no. sherds)*	*Animal bone (no. frags)*	*Other finds*
801	7	0	
802	4	3	
803	1	0	
1507	8	14	
1755	7	2	1 quern fragment
1762	5	2	
1764	2	5	
Sub-total	34	26	1
Fence line			
1758	1	0	
House enclosure and associated gullies			
267	22	16	
327	34	34	
390A	12	16	
450	6	6	
390B	39	42	1 metalworking debris
390C	30	55	1 loomweight fragment, 1 fired clay fragment
390D	120	74	3 metalworking debris; 1 brooch
898	13	8	1 fired clay fragment
97	18	6	
2683	7	0	
Sub-total	302	257	8
TOTAL	336	283	9

At Cresswell Field, there was no evidence for the presence of structures within the gullies. The finds from the gullies themselves (both 8018/8286 and 7895) include quite high proportions of residual early Iron Age pottery. It is possible that an unknown proportion of the other finds are also residual, and may not relate to the use of the gullies themselves. The southern ditch (8018) of the oval enclosure (8018/8286) contained larger quantities of pottery and animal bone than the northern ditch (8286). This may simply be because there was a greater density of early Iron Age activity in this direction. Certainly the northern ditch, which faced the palaeochannel more directly, was in an area where there was little other evidence for early or middle Iron Age activity. The largest group of pottery was found in the end of ditch 8018 (section 8267), which is the part of the enclosure which lies nearest to other early and middle Iron Age features. The animal bones consist mostly of teeth and small feet bones. However, in both enclosure 8018/8286 and gully 7895 there appeared to be significant numbers of fragments of hind limb bones (femora and tibiae) of cattle and sheep/goat, as well as of skull and mandible fragments of the same species. Burnt stone was found in both sets of features. Gully 7895 also contained a large piece of vitrified clay, probably derived from metalworking activity, and two fragments of copper alloy. Again, these may not have been related to the gully itself, since no other evidence for metalworking was recorded. Each of the three samples taken for charred plant remains contained small numbers of cereal grains associated with smaller numbers of weed seeds.

OTHER ENCLOSURES, DITCHES, GULLIES AND FENCE LINES

Cresswell Field

Area of inter-cutting pits and ditches adjacent to the central southern edge of Cresswell Field
(Figs 6.21-6.23)

What at first appeared to be a single length of irregular west-east ditch in the central southern area of Cresswell Field was in fact a dense concentration of inter-cutting pits, postholes, ditches and gullies. The fills of all these inter-cutting features were very

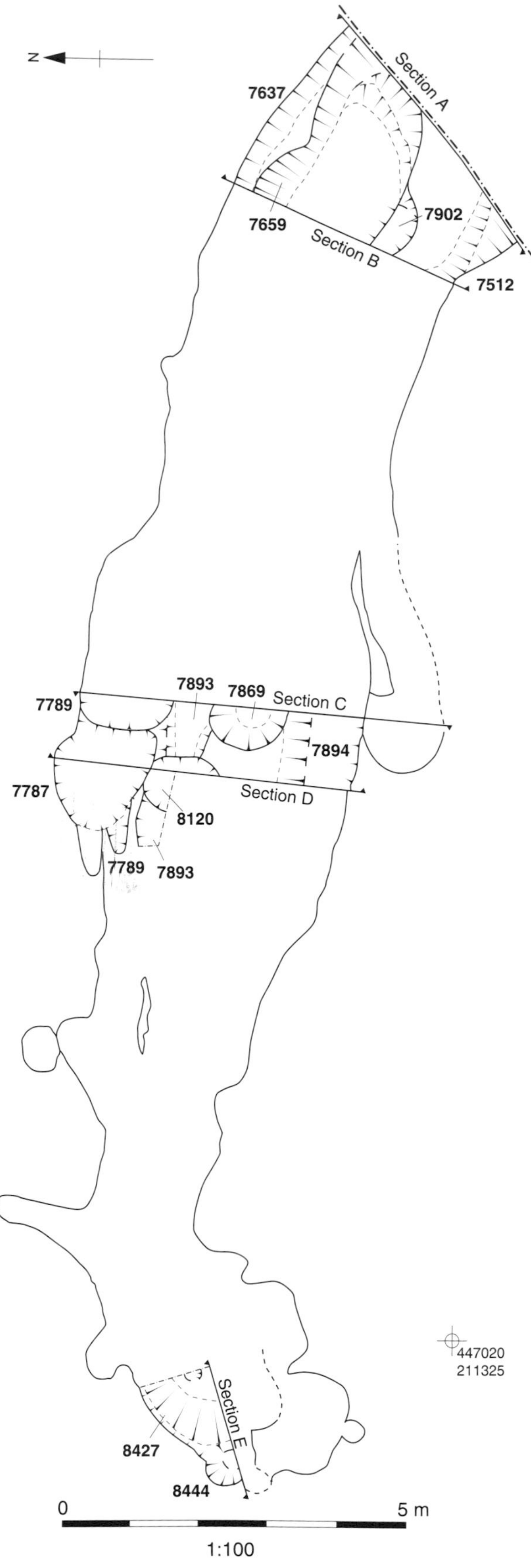

Fig. 6.21 Area of inter-cutting pits and ditches south edge of Cresswell Field

similar, consisting mostly of dark brown gravel-free silt loams, and initially this made it very difficult to establish relationships between features. It may have led to some errors in recording the stratigraphy and undoubtedly resulted in finds contamination between some features. However, the dating of the pottery assemblages suggests that this problem was fairly minimal, and once the sequence was dated and phased it could be broken down fairly simply. There appears to have been a group of early Iron Age pits which were cut by several middle Iron Age ditches and gullies. A small number of middle Iron Age pits and postholes were found to inter-cut with the linear features. Three sections were excavated across these inter-cutting features; the first against the south edge of excavation, the second half way along it, and the third at its west terminal.

In the section excavated next to the south edge of excavation (Figs 6.21 and 6.22; Sections A and B) the remains of a small pit, 7902, were cut by what appeared to be a fairly large NW-SE aligned ditch, 7659, becoming shallower and apparently terminating toward the edge of excavation. The ditch was 1.6 m wide and up to 1 m deep. This terminal was partly truncated by the terminal of a smaller ditch, 7817, coming from the opposite direction, and by a cluster of five inter-cutting pits and postholes (7599, 7732, 7783, 7785 and 7856), all of which lay along the north edge of the large ditch. These features were truncated by a wide but shallow ditch, 7512, measuring 2.4 m in width and 0.6 m in depth, which was in turn cut by another smaller NW-SE ditch, 7637, running along the northern edge of this spread of features. All of the features excavated in this section produced middle Iron Age pottery, but varying quantities of early Iron Age pottery were also present, particularly in the features with the largest assemblages of finds, ditches 7659 and 7512. These two features also contained the largest groups of animal bones and burnt stone. The animal bones consisted generally of teeth and small, lower limb bones, but ditches 7512 and 7659 were distinguished by the presence of cattle femora and, in the case of 7512, of fragments of large mammal skulls and cattle mandibles. Pit 7783 contained fragments of a quartzite polisher and of a loomweight. In addition, ditch 7637 contained a worked bone toggle.

The section excavated mid way along the linear spread of features (Figs 6.21 and 6.23; Sections C and D) revealed a cluster of four pits, the earliest of which, 8068, was undated. The other three pits (7869, 7787 and 8120) were all early Iron Age in date and produced large quantities of finds, including the iron adze head described in Chapter 5 (in structure 8396). These pits were cut by a series of three ditches (7789, 7893 and 7894) containing middle Iron Age pottery, two of which appeared to be the continuation of features 7512 and 7637 seen in Sections A and B to the east. Ditch 7789 is of partic-

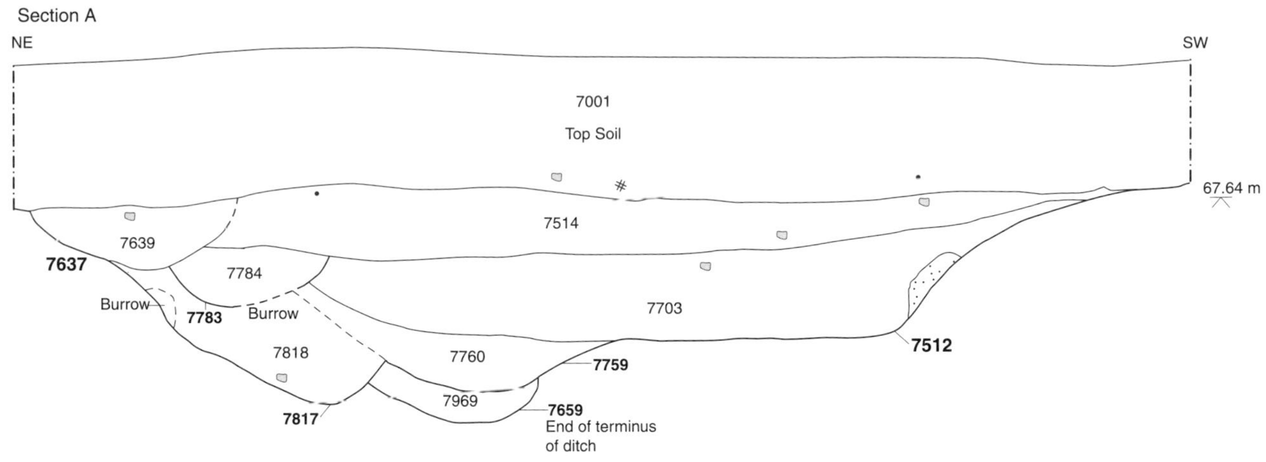

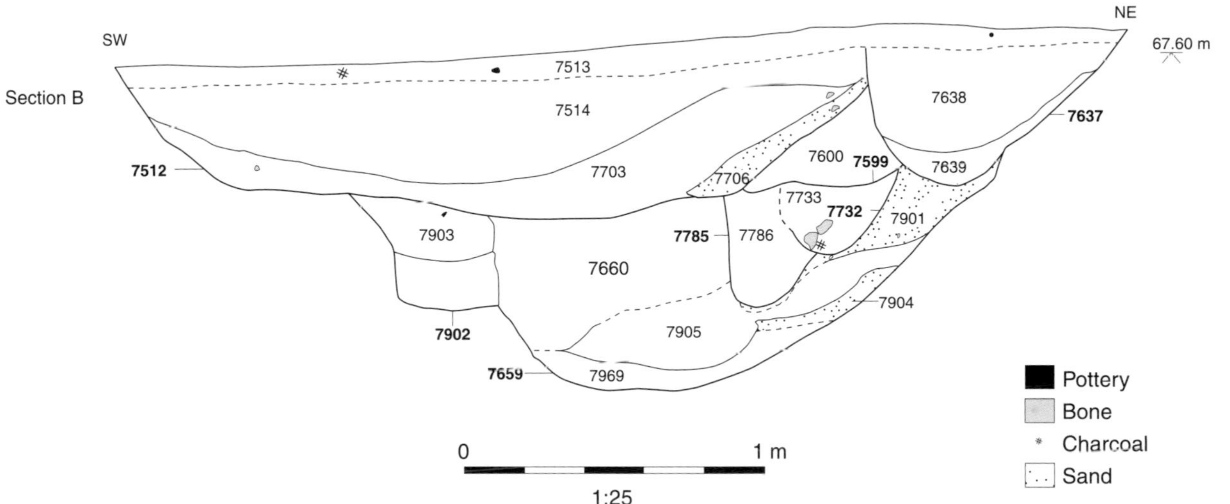

Fig. 6.22 Sections A and B through area of inter-cutting pits and ditches in south of Cresswell Field

ular note as it contained a concentration of cattle femora, similar to those in ditches 7512 and 7659 mentioned above (and see Chapter 15), along with a fragments of a bone comb and fired clay. Ditch 7893 also contained two fragments of vitrified clay, probably derived from metalworking activity.

At the west end of this linear arrangement of features was an undated posthole, 8444, cut by an early Iron Age pit, 8427 (Figs 6.21 and 6.23; Section E). All the middle Iron Age ditches had, therefore, terminated before they reached this point.

The explanation for this series of inter-cutting features remains uncertain, even though it represented one of the most concentrated areas of middle Iron Age activity on the site. It is of note that few contemporary features were found in the surrounding area. It is possible that the intercutting features defined the northern limit of an area of activity which lay south of the excavated site. The quantities of pottery and other refuse recovered from the ditches suggest that this may have included a dwelling.

Western area of Yarnton site

Fence lines 1499 and 1515 (Figs 6.3, 6.24 and 6.25)

On the Yarnton site, to the north-east of enclosure 390, were two fence lines which may have defined a trackway running SE-NW towards structure 1507 to the north and skirting structure 1764 to the south. The more westerly of these was fence line 1499, which ran for a distance of approximately 25.5 m and comprised six fairly evenly spaced postholes (except 1353) approximately 5.5 m apart. The postholes were oval to circular in plan with steep sides and flat bases and were, on average, 0.42 m in diameter and 0.38 m deep. Their fills were mid to dark brown silty sands containing 5-50% gravel. Posthole 1197 contained flecks of charcoal and posthole 1243 had suffered some animal disturbance. Finds consisted of five sherds of pottery, six animal bones and one fragment of vitrified clay.

Fence line 1515 ran approximately parallel to 1499 on its north-east side. The two fences would

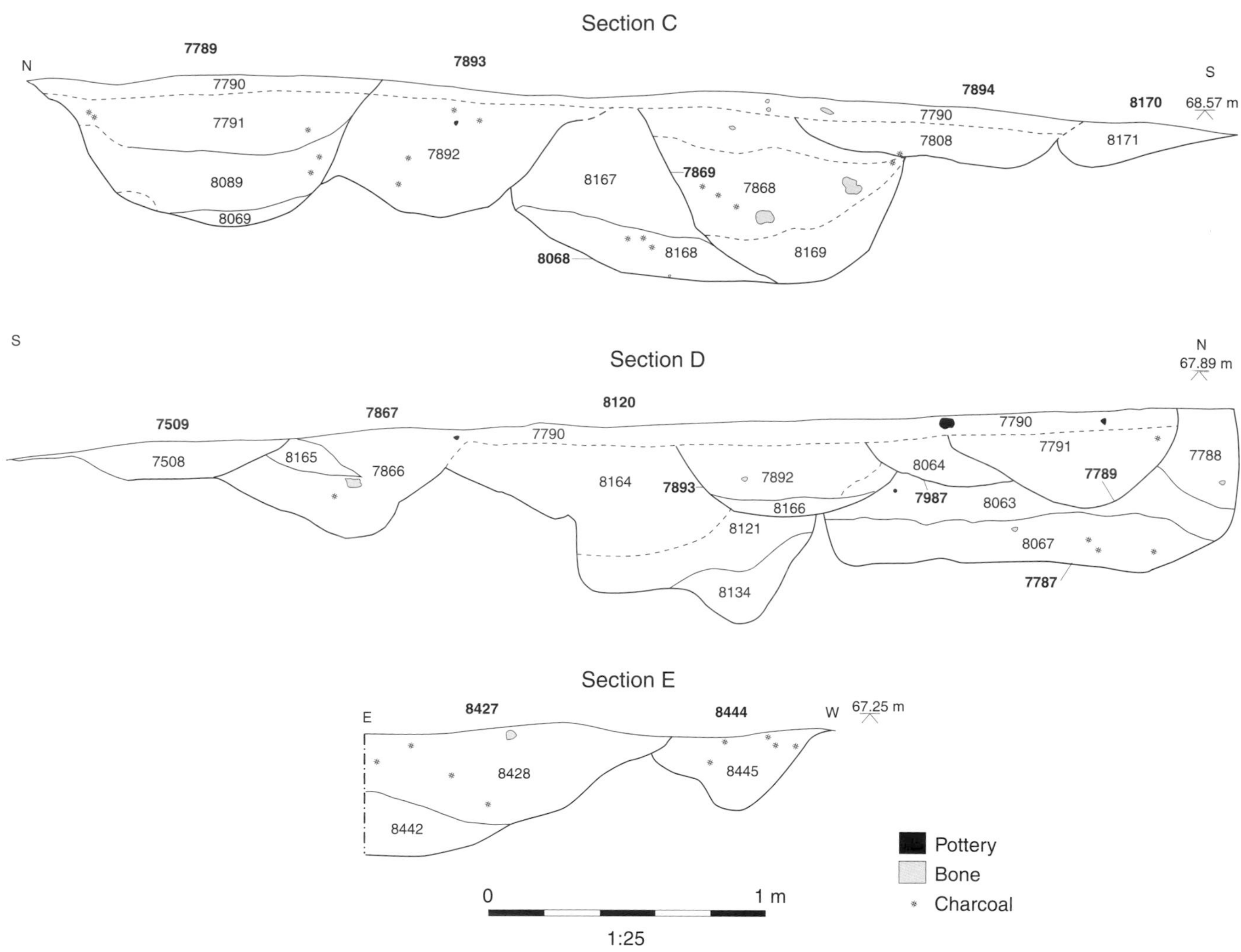

Fig. 6.23 Sections C-E through area of inter-cutting pits and ditches in south of Cresswell Field

have lain 3 m apart in the south-east and 5 m to the north-west, creating a slight funnelling effect. Fence line 1515 only survived for a length of 14 m, being made up of four postholes spaced approximately 5 m apart. A linear arrangement of gullies to the north (1382) may have provided some kind of continuation of this fence line. The postholes in the fence line were generally circular in plan with an average diameter of 0.34 m and depth of 0.18 m. They were bowl-shaped, with the exception of 1498 which was steep-sided and flat-based. Their fills comprised brown and grey silty sands containing 2-10% gravel. No finds were recovered.

Gullies 1382 and 1378 (Fig. 6.3)

Immediately to the north of fence line 1515 and south of structure 1762 were several short stretches of irregular gully. Gully 1382 ran north-west from the north end of the fence line for a distance of 7.5 m. It appeared to have been cut by one of the postholes of the fence (1383). Three other short gullies lay perpendicular to it (1384, 1385 and 1450), but their fills (mixed non-gravelly soils and silty loams with gravel) were so similar that it was impossible to establish stratigraphic relationships between them. They were probably all broadly contemporary but their function is very unclear. These gullies were open U-shaped, 0.6 m wide and 0.14 m deep. The ten sections excavated through them (45% of their length) yielded just nine sherds (121 g) of pottery and three animal bones.

East of these features, and parallel to 1482, was gully 1378 which was 6.2 m in length. It was cut away to the south, and had clearly formed part of a larger feature. In profile it was an open U-shape, 0.7 m wide and 0.25 m deep. After primary silting it had been recut four times, each recut containing a single fill of mixed silty loam with gravel. Finds from 1378 comprised 30 sherds (230 g) of pottery, 35 animal bones and one fragment of fired clay.

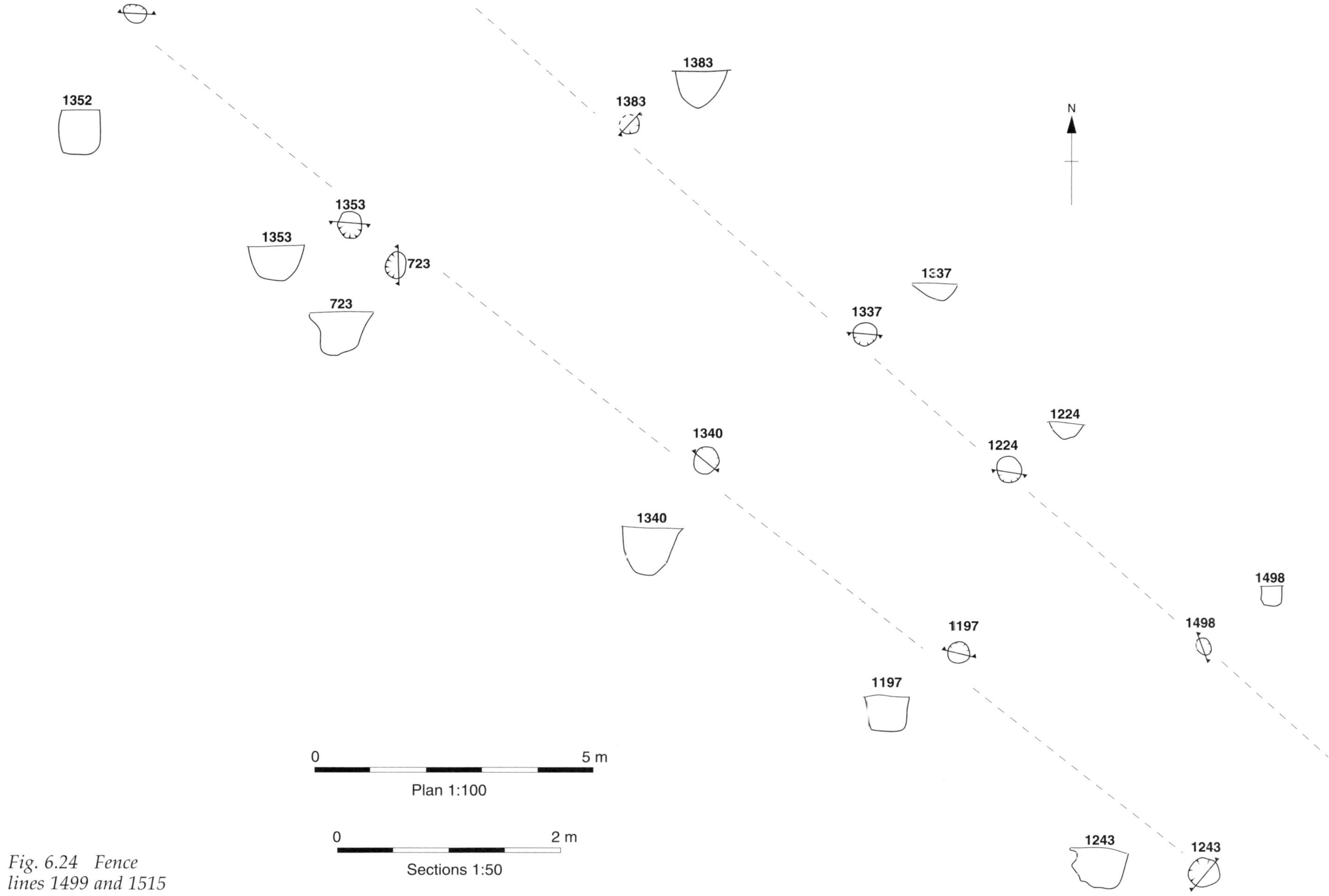

Fig. 6.24 Fence lines 1499 and 1515

Fig. 6.25 Fence lines 1499 and 1515 indicated by the red-topped pegs

Central area of Yarnton site

Enclosure 241 and gully 242 (Figs 6.3 and 6.26)

To the south-west of post-built structure 1755 was enclosure 241, a penannular ditch with a diameter of 7.5 m, which enclosed an area of *c* 40 m^2. The enclosure entrance faced east and was 4.5 m in width. It had a clear terminal to the south, while the northern one could be seen in section cutting an earlier middle Iron Age pit (248). Eight sections were excavated through the ditch circuit, representing 20% of its extant length. The ditch, which had been recut on one or two occasions, was an open U-shape in profile, averaging 0.7 m wide and 0.25 m deep. There were one to two fills per cut, which were of mixed gravelly and non-gravelly soils with some evidence of burning.

There was no evidence for a structure within the enclosure, although much of its interior had been cut away by later ditches. Postholes around the entrance included early Iron Age four-post structure 1766, but others were Iron Age of uncertain phase and these are shown on Figure 6.26. They may have been associated with a gate structure across the entrance, perhaps to enclose animals. Charcoal and a fairly dense concentration of finds from the enclosure ditch fill suggest rubbish deposition, however, possibly from adjacent structure 1755. Amongst the finds were 42 sherds (475 g) of pottery and 19 animal bones. The pottery was mostly concentrated in the western part of the ditch (Fig. 6.32). Plant remains include weed seeds and cereal grains, but no chaff.

Gully 242, a NW-SE aligned linear feature, was found within penannular ditch 241 but their stratigraphic relationship was obscured by a late Roman ditch. The surviving length of the gully was 5 m, and it ended in a terminal 1.5 m from the western, inner edge of the enclosure ditch. It was an open U-shaped feature, *c* 0.3 m wide and 0.2 m deep, which showed no signs of recutting. Three sections revealed a homogeneous gravel-free fill. Finds from the gully were scarce (three sherds of pottery and three animal bones) suggesting that it had not been used for rubbish disposal.

Gullies 399 and 405 (Fig. 6.3)

Parallel gullies 399 and 405 ran north from enclosure 241 and then turned north-east where they were cut away by a late Roman ditch. Their relationship with enclosure 241 had been destroyed by another ditch of late Roman date. Both ditches had single open U-shaped cuts, 399 being 0.6 m wide and 0.2 m deep on average, and 405 *c* 0.4 m wide by 0.1 m deep. Their fills were homogeneous non-gravelly soils. Gully 399 yielded a fairly dense concentration of finds, including 43 animal bones and 45 sherds of pottery, mainly shell-tempered. This suggests rubbish deposition, possibly from the same source as the material from enclosure 241 (ie from structure 1755). Amongst the plant remains were cereal grains, weed seeds and chaff. Gully 405 contained only a small

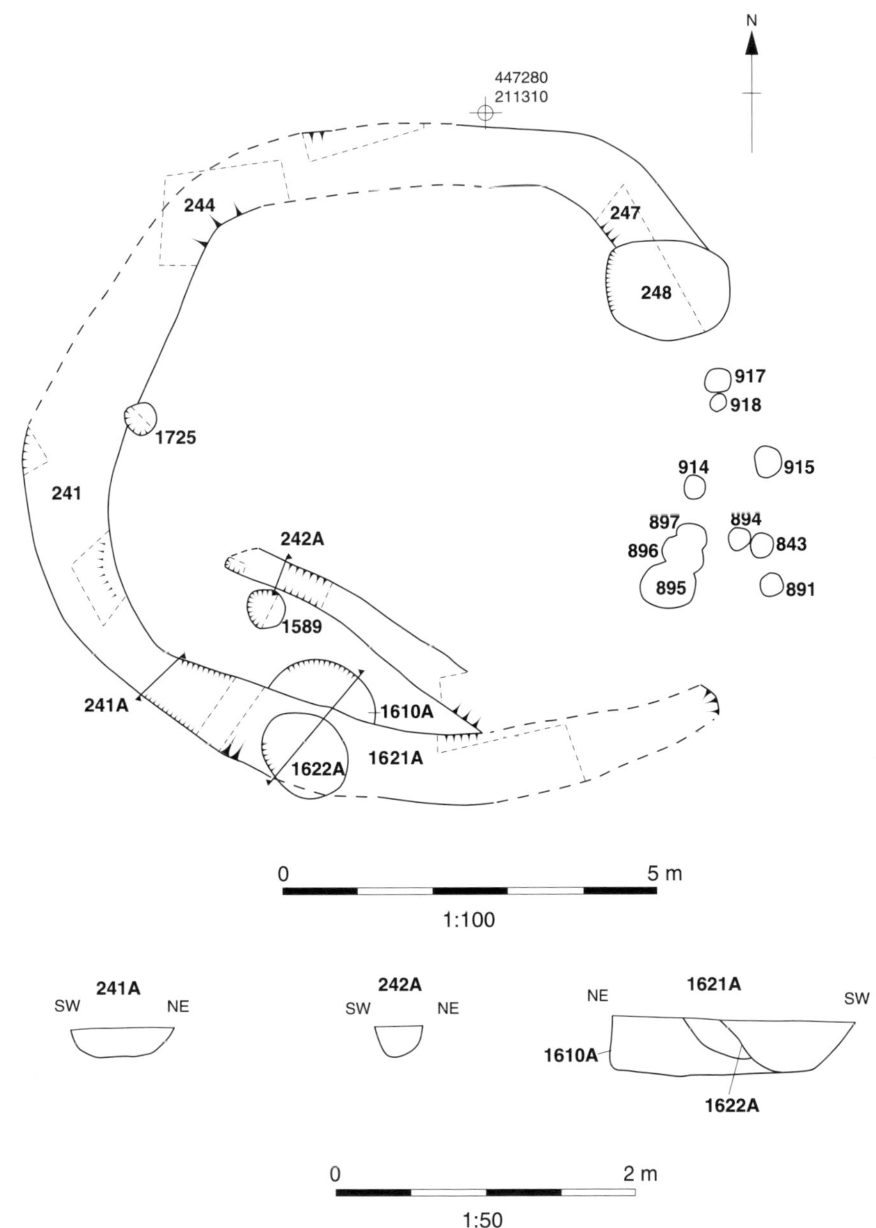

Fig. 6.26 Enclosure 241 and gully 242

number of finds, including ten animal bones, suggesting secondary deposition rather than the dumping of large quantities of rubbish.

Finds distributions from other enclosures, gullies and fence lines

Very few finds were recovered from the middle Iron Age fence lines, most of the sherds were small and the animal bone was mostly undiagnostic (Table 6.2). One fragment of fired clay was also recovered. It is probable that this material accumulated as secondary deposition during the construction and/or use of the fence lines.

Enclosure 241 yielded reasonable quantities of finds, which were generally evenly spread but included a cluster of pottery on the west side (Fig. 6.32). The quantities of material from the other gullies were generally in proportion to their size, with the exception of 399 which contained fairly large amounts of pottery and bone (Fig. 6.32) and some plant remains, and 1378 which yielded quite large amounts of pottery and bone.

The intercutting ditches and pits at Cresswell Field contained sometimes quite large assemblages of mixed early and middle Iron Age pottery and animal bone which are very similar to those found in the pits described below, and this material is likely to have been deposited in the same way as the finds from the pits. The other finds – a quartzite polisher, a loomweight, a worked bone toggle and two fragments of vitrified clay – are all isolated finds which are perhaps better regarded as stray material rather than reflecting deliberate deposition

Table 6.2 Finds from other enclosures, gullies and fencelines.

Fence lines	*Pottery (no. sherds)*	*Animal bone (no. frags)*	*Other finds*
1499	5	6	1 fired clay
1515	0	0	
Other enclosures and gullies			
1378	30	35	1 fired clay
1382	9	3	
241	42	18	
242	3	1	
399	45	43	
405	0	10	
TOTAL	134	116	2
Cresswell Field Ditches			
7895	132	265	2 fragments of copper alloy, charred grain, charred weed seeds
8095/8096	67	39	
8018/8286	96	188	charred grain, charred weed seeds
TOTAL	228	452	

or any relationship between these features and particular kinds of activity.

PITS

Summary

Some 138 pits were assigned to the middle Iron Age, 87 on the Yarnton site (23% of the excavated pits) and 51 on Cresswell Field (20% of the pits excavated there). In proportion to the total numbers of pits present, these figures suggest that there would have been approximately 348 pits of middle Iron Age date at Yarnton and 113 at Cresswell Field. This demonstrates the eastward shift of settlement from the early to the middle Iron Age (see above, Chapter 5).

Pit distribution

Pits on the Cresswell Field site were found among the broad north-south and WNW-ESE swathes of pits, but clustered in the north-south band towards the south-west of the site, near to the proposed middle Iron Age house enclosures. Pits to the north appeared to lie on the southern fringe of the WNW-ESE band of pits, and an additional cluster was found intercutting linear ditches and gullies next to the southern edge of the excavation, as already described. They may have been associated with activity to the south of the excavation area.

At Yarnton, middle Iron Age pits were distributed in a band running SW-NE across the northern

Table 6.3 Middle Iron Age pit dimensions (m) by type.

	Undercut (GSP)	*Cylindrical*	*Bowl-shaped*	*Large shallow*	*Shallow saucer*	*Amorphous*
Yarnton						
Total no.	3	34	8	22	9	12
Breadth	1.2-2.75	0.3-2.4	0.55-1.6	0.9-2.1	0.6-1.35	0.33-1.5
Depth	0.47-1.25	0.33-1.05	0.23-0.6	0.15-0.45	0.04-0.17	0.14-0.64
Length	1.2-1.2	1.3-2.1	1.1-1.4	1.4-2.4	0.92-1.2	1.3-1.7
Cresswell Field						
Total no.	1	26	14	9	1	0
Breadth	1.5	0.35-1.98	0.2-1.95	1.0-2.4	0.98	-
Depth	1.0	0.2-0.92	0.1-0.43	0.1-0.24	0.06	-
Length	-	0.6-1.8	0.35-1.75	-	-	-

Table 6.4 Percentages of pit types in the early and middle Iron Age (column %).

	Early Iron Age			*Middle Iron Age*		
	Yarnton	*Cresswell Field*	*Total*	*Yarnton*	*Cresswell Field*	*Total*
Undercut (GSP)	2	7	5	3	2	3
Cylindrical	38	50	46	39	51	43
Bowl-shaped	14	26	22	9	27	16
Large shallow	6	9	8	25	18	22
Shallow saucer	8	4	5	10	2	7
Amorphous	32	5	13	14	-	9

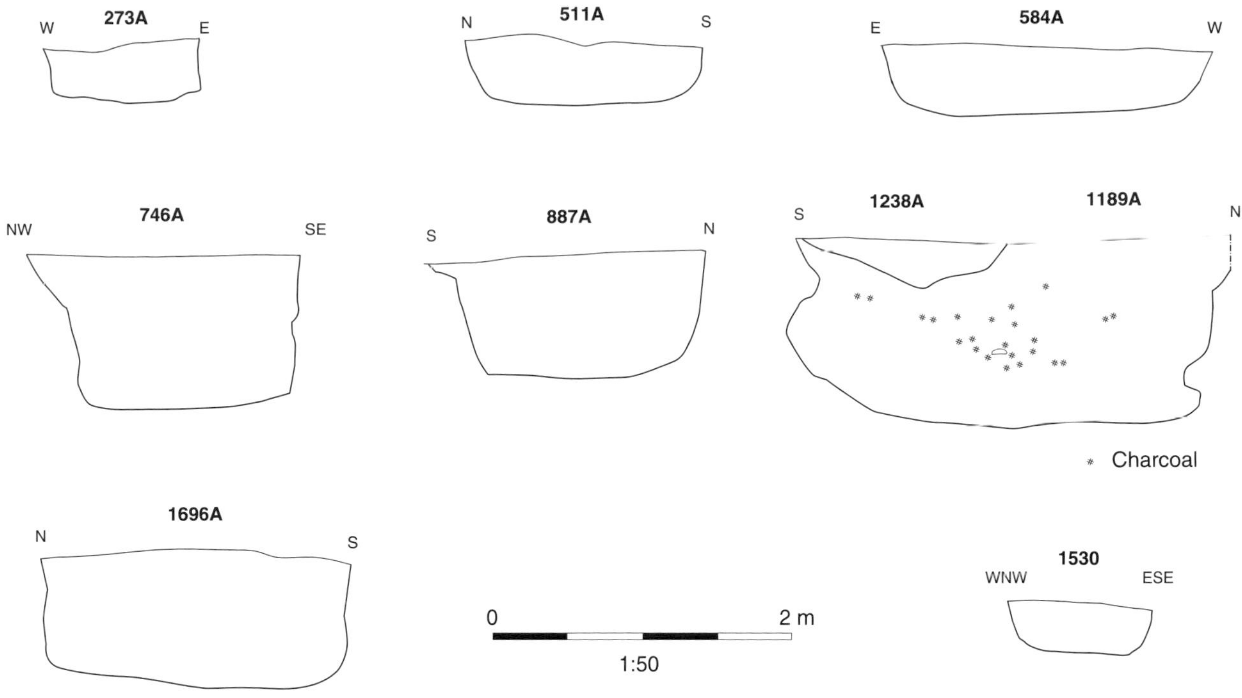

Fig. 6.27 Pits on the Yarnton site

part of the site. As already indicated, they were more numerous than early Iron Age pits, with a tendency to cluster in the west of the site, north of the middle Iron Age buildings.

Pit morphology (Figs 6.27 and 6.28)

Like those of the early Iron Age, the majority of middle Iron Age pits were circular or oval in shape, with a very few amorphous or irregular examples. The majority of pits were cylindrical in profile, although there were also substantial proportions of large shallow and bowl-shaped examples, as well as some amorphous and shallow-saucer shaped features and a very few undercut, grain-storage pits (Table 6.3). The relative proportions of all of the pit types, even within each site, are very similar to those for the early Iron Age (Table 6.4), with the exception of large shallow pits which at both sites become more common in the middle Iron Age (22% rather than 8%).

As in the early Iron Age, it is very probable that a number of larger cylindrical and bowl-shaped pits had been grain-storage pits, but their upper sides had collapsed or had been sufficiently truncated to remove their classic undercut shape. At Yarnton it is thought that 17 of the middle Iron Age pits were originally dug for grain storage.

Pit diameters on the Yarnton site ranged between 0.3 m and 2.75 m, averaging 1.28 m, and depths from 0.1 m to 1.25 m, averaging 0.45 m (Table 6.3). Estimated original pit volumes ranged between 0.03 m^3 and 7.39 m^3, and averaged 0.71 m^3. At Cresswell Field the pits were, overall, slightly smaller, ranging in diameter from 0.10 m to 2.40 m, averaging 1.15 m, in depth from 0.06 to 1.00 m, averaging 0.28 m, and

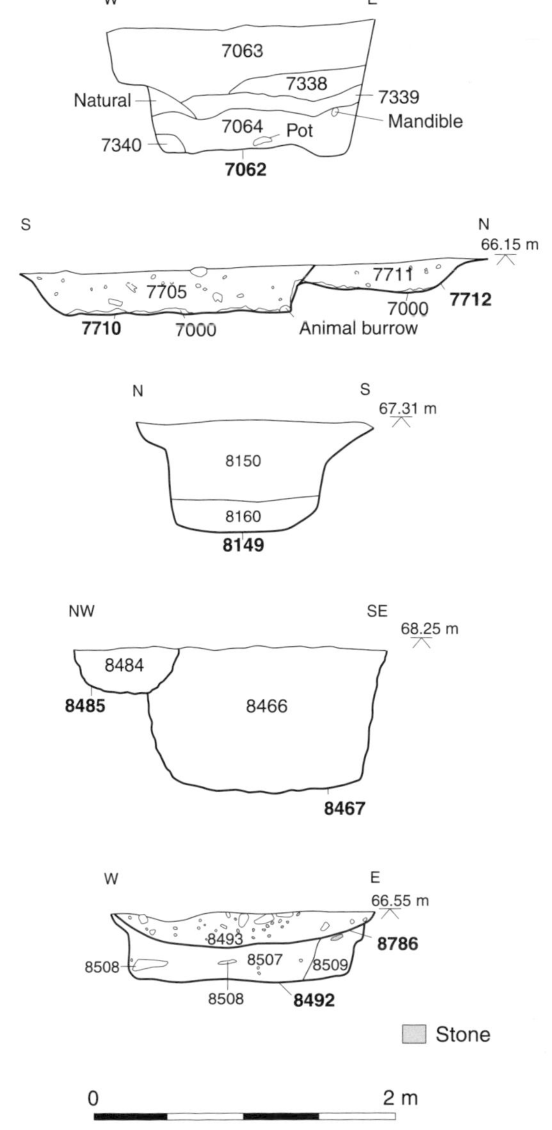

Fig. 6.28 Pits on the Cresswell Field site

in volume from 0.01 to 1.77 m^3, averaging just 0.38 m^3. The substantial variation in pit volumes reflects a few anomalous examples, and the result of severe truncation of some pits by ploughing.

Pit fills

Soils

At Yarnton, the number of separate fills per pit ranged from one to 21, but the vast majority contained from one to four fills and few had more than ten. The average (mean) number of fills was three. At Cresswell Field the pits overall contained fewer fills, ranging from one to five, most having just one (mean = 1.3). Silty loams and generally gravel-free fills predominated, although some more gravelly fills were also observed. Greenish-coloured soils were noted in four pits at Yarnton (two bowl-shaped and two cylindrical) and charcoal-rich soils were recorded in one large shallow pit and one undercut grain-storage pit. One bowl-shaped pit (1530) was packed with green-grey clay with flecks of charcoal.

Sixteen of the 87 Yarnton pits contained identifiable evidence of primary silting. This was generally present in small pits; only two were over 0.8 m^3 in volume. Seven pits had identifiable evidence of deliberate backfilling; of these two were bowl-shaped, three were cylindrical, one was undercut and one was large and shallow. Four of the deliberately-backfilled pits were over 0.8 m^3 in volume.

A rather higher proportion of the pits at Cresswell Field (16 out of 51) contained evidence of primary silting. Most of these were also small pits with volumes below 0.8 m^3. However, they also included two larger pits with volumes of 1.11 m^3 and 2.34 m^3. Only two pits, one cylindrical and one shallow, seemed to have been deliberately backfilled

Recutting of middle Iron Age pits was rare. Only eight pits on the Yarnton site had visible recuts, of which seven were recut once and a single pit was recut twice. No evidence for recutting was observed at Cresswell Field.

Finds

Deposits that could be described as deliberately placed or special in some way were observed in some of the pits (Figs 6.29 and 6.30). Articulated animal skeletons were present in five pits (273, 511, 1744, 8786 and 8149) and disarticulated human bone was found in a further three (248, 746 and 1189).These are discussed below. Two of the pits with human bone also contained substantial deposits of pottery and animal bone. Additionally, the selection and quantity of material within pit 584, which lay within enclosure 390, marked it out as a special deposit. Clay-filled pit 1530 was also believed to contain unusual deposits; it had a sheep mandible and fragments of cow skull within its clay packing.

Some middle Iron Age pits contained large concentrations of finds (Figs 6.31 and 6.32). At Yarnton these were mainly located in the north-west of the site, with just two examples to the east of the central group of structures. The distribution at Cresswell Field showed no similar pattern, the pits containing the richest assemblages being distributed across the site. At Cresswell Field, it is perhaps most notable that pits containing fewer finds occurred in the south-western corner of the site, although this may simply reflect the larger number of pits in this area. Nonetheless, the majority of pits at both sites contained some artefacts or ecofacts. No obvious correlations existed between finds and different pit types or sizes.

Finds distributions within pits

Human bone

Three middle Iron Age pits contained disarticulated human bone. A tibia shaft fragment was found in pit 248, a femur shaft in pit 746 and a proximal left ulna in pit 1189 (Fig. 6.30). These pits were spread across the site and lay away from known inhumation burials (see below). They were all large features, although they varied in depth. The human deposits were all of individual bones and, given the presence of formal burials at this time, the significance of single bones could be questioned; they may be chance deposits.

Animal Bone

Of the 87 excavated middle Iron Age pits at Yarnton, 70 contained animal bone. This assemblage mostly consisted of sheep/goat or undiagnostic bone of sheep/goat or pig size, but there was also a substan-

Table 6.5 Occurrence of animal species in Middle Iron Age pits at Yarnton.

Species	*No. of pits*
Sheep/goat	56
Sheep/pig size	49
Cattle	46
Cattle/horse size	43
Horse	15
Pig	15
Dog	6
Wild bird	5
Hare	2
Rabbit	2
Badger	1
Domestic fowl	1
Deer	1
Lizard	1
Toad	2
Rodent	2

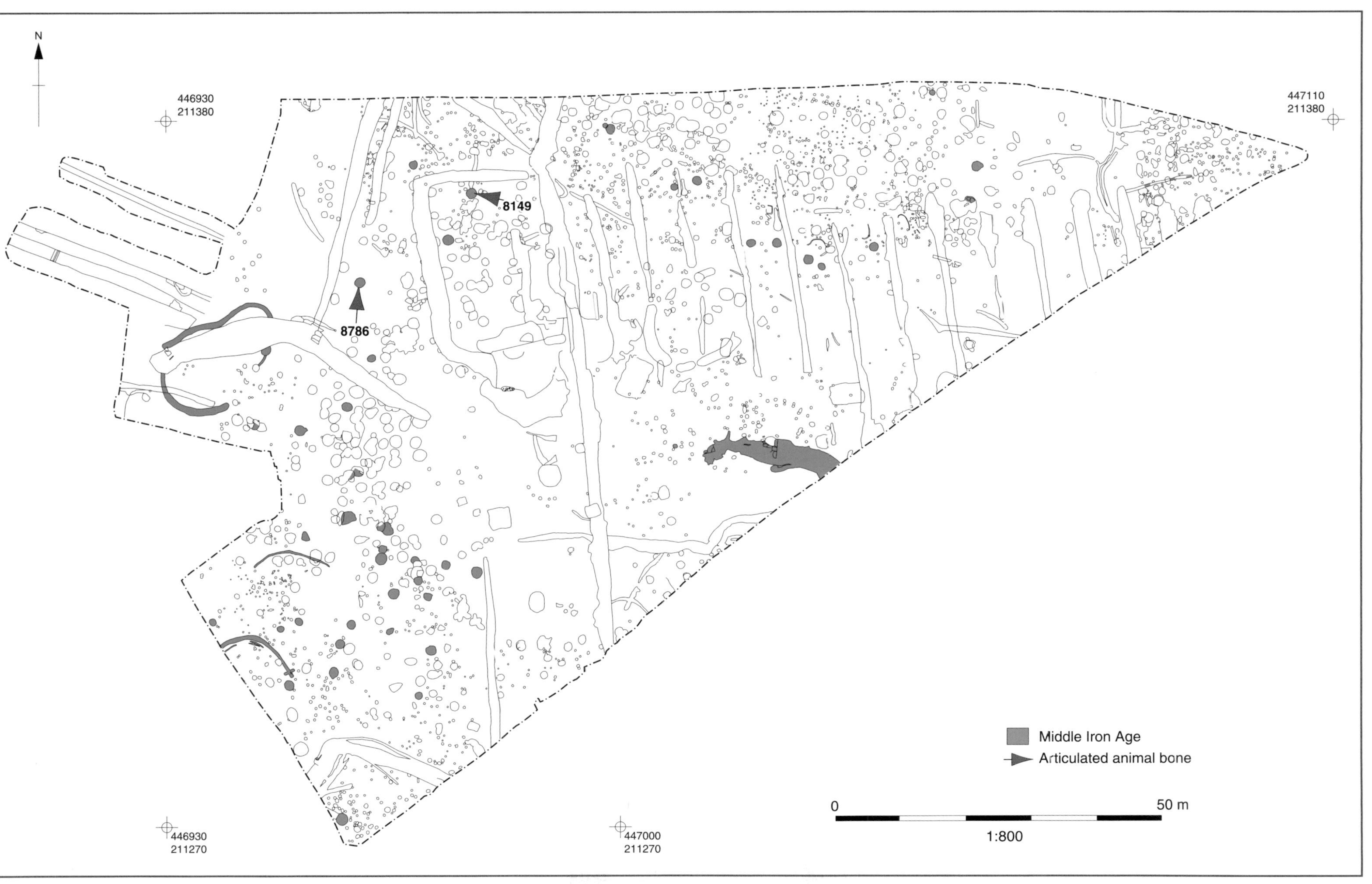

Fig. 6.29 Distribution of middle Iron Age disarticulated human bone, articulated animal bone and other possible special deposits on Cresswell Field

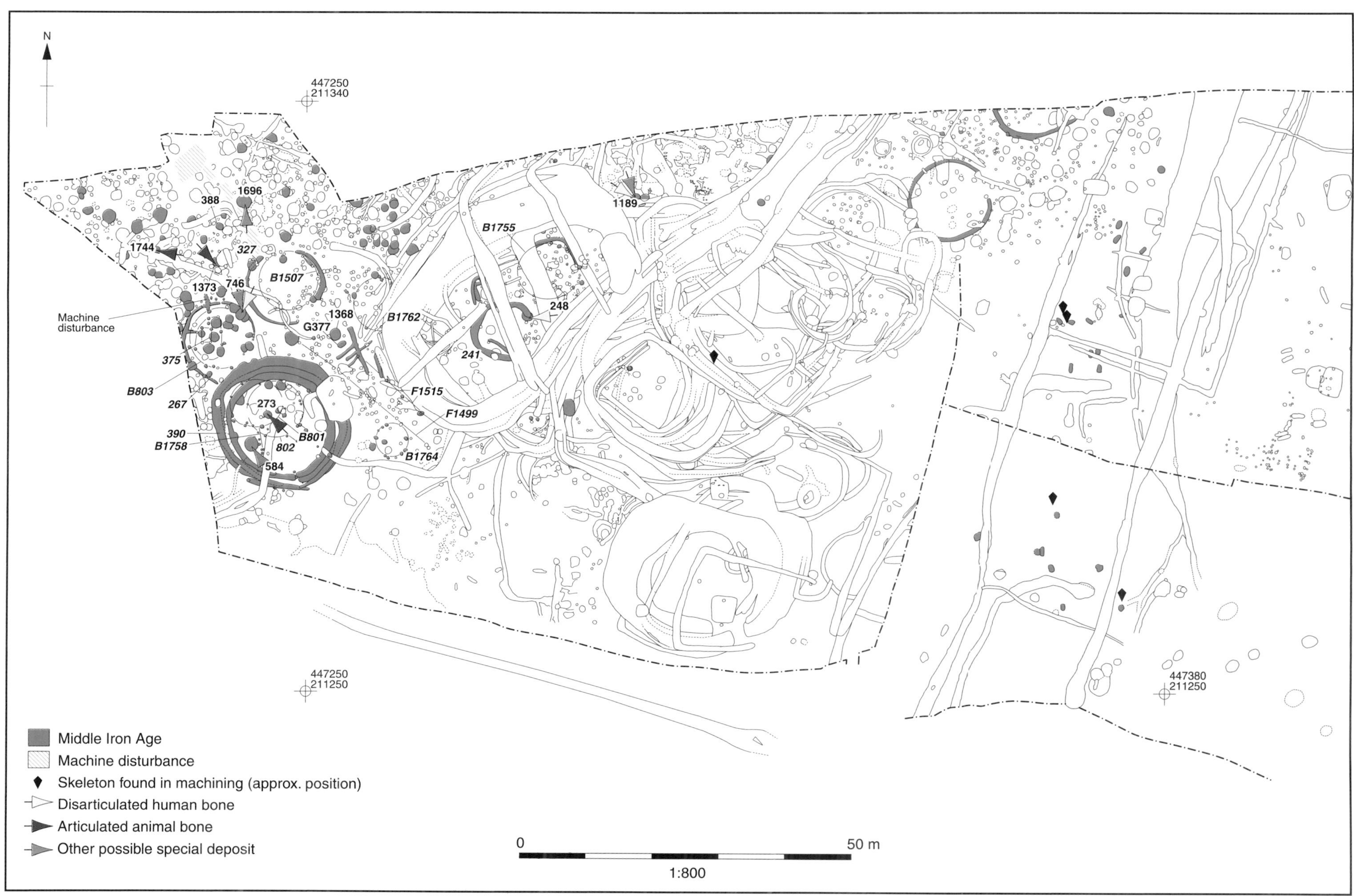

Fig. 6.30 Distribution of middle Iron Age disarticulated human bone, articulated animal bone and other possible special deposits at Yarnton

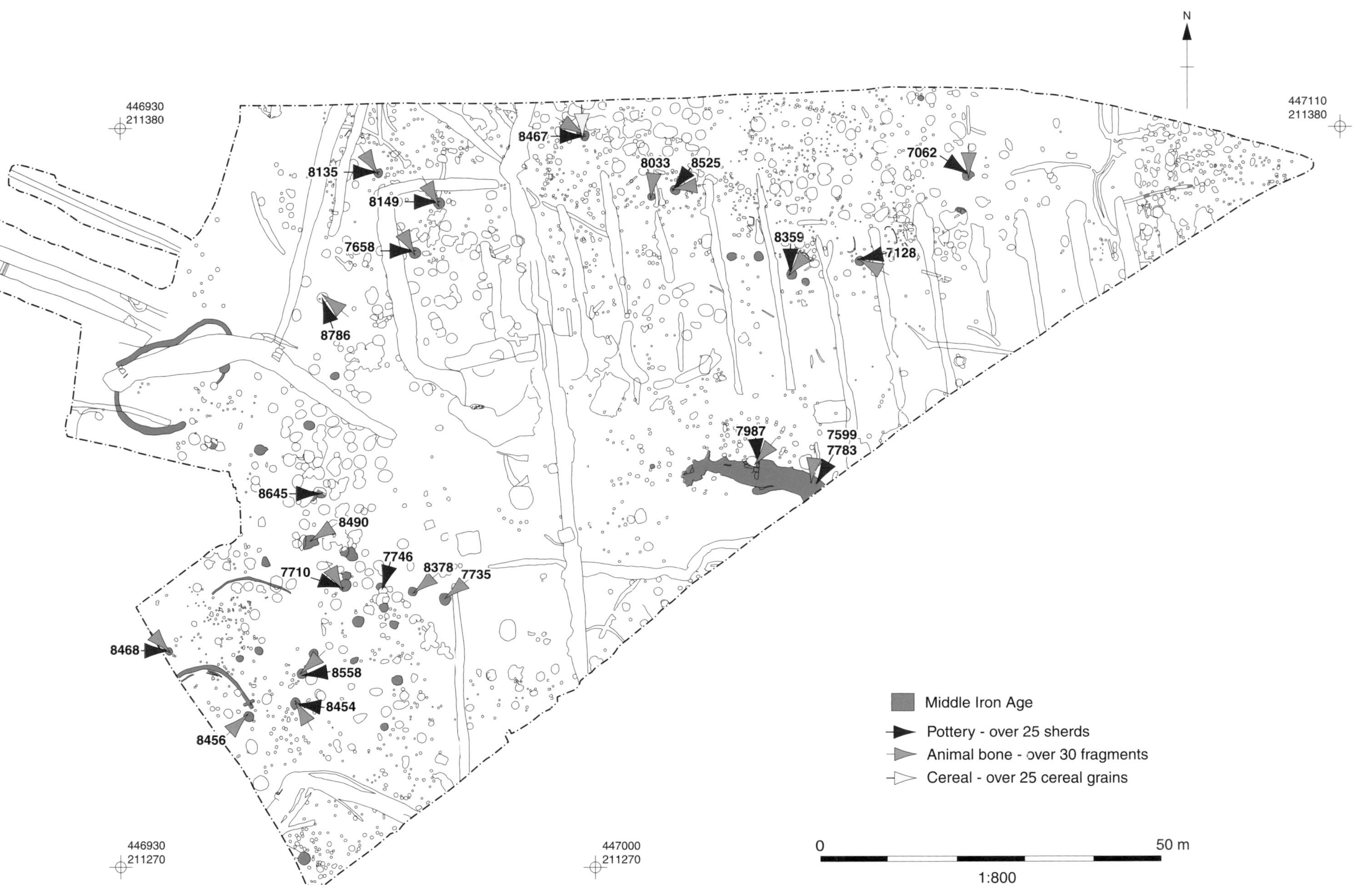

Fig. 6.31 Distribution of substantial deposits of middle Iron Age pottery, animal bone and charred plant remains on Cresswell Field

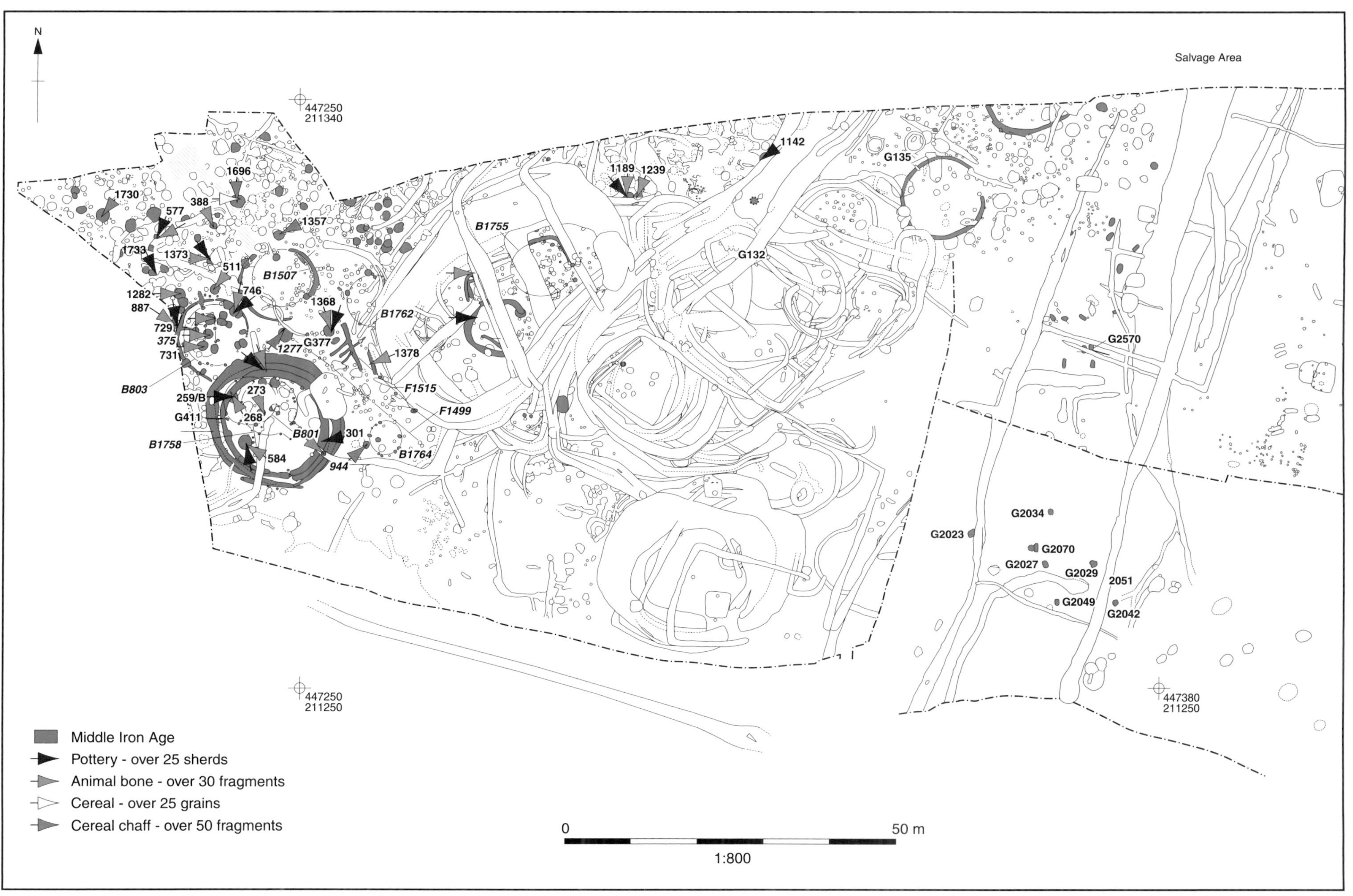

Fig. 6.32 Distribution of substantial deposits of middle Iron Age pottery, animal bone and charred plant remains at Yarnton

tial proportion of cattle bone, and undiagnostic bone of cattle/horse size (Table 6.5). Additionally, there were smaller amounts of pig, sheep, goat, horse, dog and domestic fowl bones, as well as some remains of wild animals. Plots of the spatial distribution of different animal species across the settlement site showed no marked differences between them, with the exception of dog bone which was mostly recovered from the north-west, north of the middle Iron Age buildings. The bones of wild animals were also spread thinly across the site.

As in the early Iron Age, patterning within this distribution at Yarnton is not very evident, and the majority of pits with animal bone contained a wide variety of different species. Of the 70 middle Iron Age pits containing animal bone, all had bone from at least one of the major domestic species and 29 contained bone from all of these species. Pit 273 within enclosure 390 stood out because, in addition to a sheep skeleton, there was a preponderance of other bones of this species, with only one pig and one cow bone present, and pits 1373 and 268 all had higher than normal proportions of bones of large animals within them (58% and 50% respectively). These pits all contained relatively large assemblages (Fig. 6.32). Otherwise assemblages were very mixed. Nevertheless, some interesting correlations were evident. All three pits with human remains also contained horse remains, and the significance of this is strengthened by the fact that only 15 pits contained horse bone (Table 6.5). Wild animal remains seem to be fairly randomly distributed, but pit 584, which had other interesting and substantial deposits, contained both wild bird and hare.

At Cresswell Field the animal bone is less diverse. Of the 51 excavated middle Iron Age pits, 48 contained animal bone. Here, cattle and cattle-sized bone predominated, although there was also a considerable proportion of sheep/goat and sheep/goat-sized bone. Pig bone was rare, and with the exception of some probably incidentally incorporated frog bone all of the other bone was unidentifiable. There were no very marked patterns in the distribution of the animal bone.

Five middle Iron Age pits contained what appeared to be placed deposits of articulated animal bone (273, 511, 1744, 8149 and 8786). Pit 273 contained a partial sheep skeleton. A cattle torso lay within pit 511 along with the fore and hind left limbs of a foal, the only evidence for young horses from the site (see Chapter 17) and a partial dog burial was found within pit 1744 along with a pair of mandibles from another dog. In pit 8149 were two groups of very young sheep bone: a partial skeleton and a pair of foetal tibiae. Pit 8493 contained one of the richest assemblages of artefacts other than pottery (described below) associated with articulated sheep leg bones. Although they were not articulated, it is also worth noting a concentration of cattle femora in ditch 7789.

Pottery

Of the 87 pits at Yarnton dating to the middle Iron Age period, 81 contained pottery. The assemblage comprised 1107 sherds with a mean sherd weight of 17 g, and the average number of sherds per pit was 14. Following the procedure adopted for the early Iron Age material, sherd weight, mean sherd weight and sherd count were calculated for each of the middle Iron Age pits, and these were plotted on scatter charts (Figs 6.33 and 6.34). This analysis showed that the majority of assemblages comprised small numbers of small abraded sherds. However, there was a minority of pits containing either large assemblages of small to average-sized sherds, or small assemblages of large sherds. This pattern conforms to that seen among the early Iron Age assemblages. A plot of the spatial distribution of pottery within the middle Iron Age pits shows that those with large numbers of sherds lay around and to the north-west of the main area of buildings, with only two pits in this category to the east of the area of later Roman ditch digging (Fig. 6.32). Two pits which were situated near to each other in the north-west of the site (577 and 1733) contained particularly large sherds; those from pit 577 weighed, on average, 83 g each.

The pits at Cresswell Field contained slightly larger quantities of pottery than those at Yarnton. Forty-eight of the 51 excavated middle Iron Age examples yielded some material. The assemblage comprised 1130 sherds with a mean sherd weight of 14 g, and the average number of sherds per pit was 24. Plotting mean sherd weight against sherd count shows again that most of the pits contained small numbers (less than 20) of small sherds (less than 20 g). There was also, however, an appreciable number of pits which contained larger numbers of equally small sherds and a few which contained small numbers of larger sherds. The most exceptional pit in this respect was 7712, a small shallow pit with a volume of only 0.22 m^3. Apart from the pottery, the other finds it contained – a little animal bone and burnt limestone – were quite unexceptional.

The pits with significant amounts of pottery generally also contained large groups of animal bone (Figs 6.31 and 6.32). Most of these animal bone assemblages were mixed and there appears to be no particular correlation between the deposition of large numbers of pot sherds and particular domestic animal species. It is worthy of note, however, that of the eight middle Iron Age pits at Yarnton which contained the remains of wild animals, six also contained significant quantities of pottery.

Plant remains

Sixteen of the 87 middle Iron Age pits at Yarnton were sampled and found to contain charred plant remains. Of these, nine were over 0.8 m^3 in volume (their average original volume was 1.51 m^3). As for the early Iron Age, the spatial distribution of features containing over 25 cereal grains and more than 50 fragments of cereal chaff was examined (Fig. 6.32). Only pit 1696 yielded substantial quantities of cereals (155 grains from two samples), although pit 273 within enclosure 390 yielded 20 grains. Large quantities of chaff were more common, occurring in five pits, and were distributed down the west side of the site, usually adjacent to, though not within, the house enclosures. Three of these pits (those nearest to the structures) contained only modest numbers of other finds, but the other two pits also contained large assemblages of animal bone and, in the case of pit 1696, a large quantity of cereal grain. There was no correlation with substantial groups of pottery.

Only three of the middle Iron Age pits at Cresswell Field were sampled for charred plant remains. All

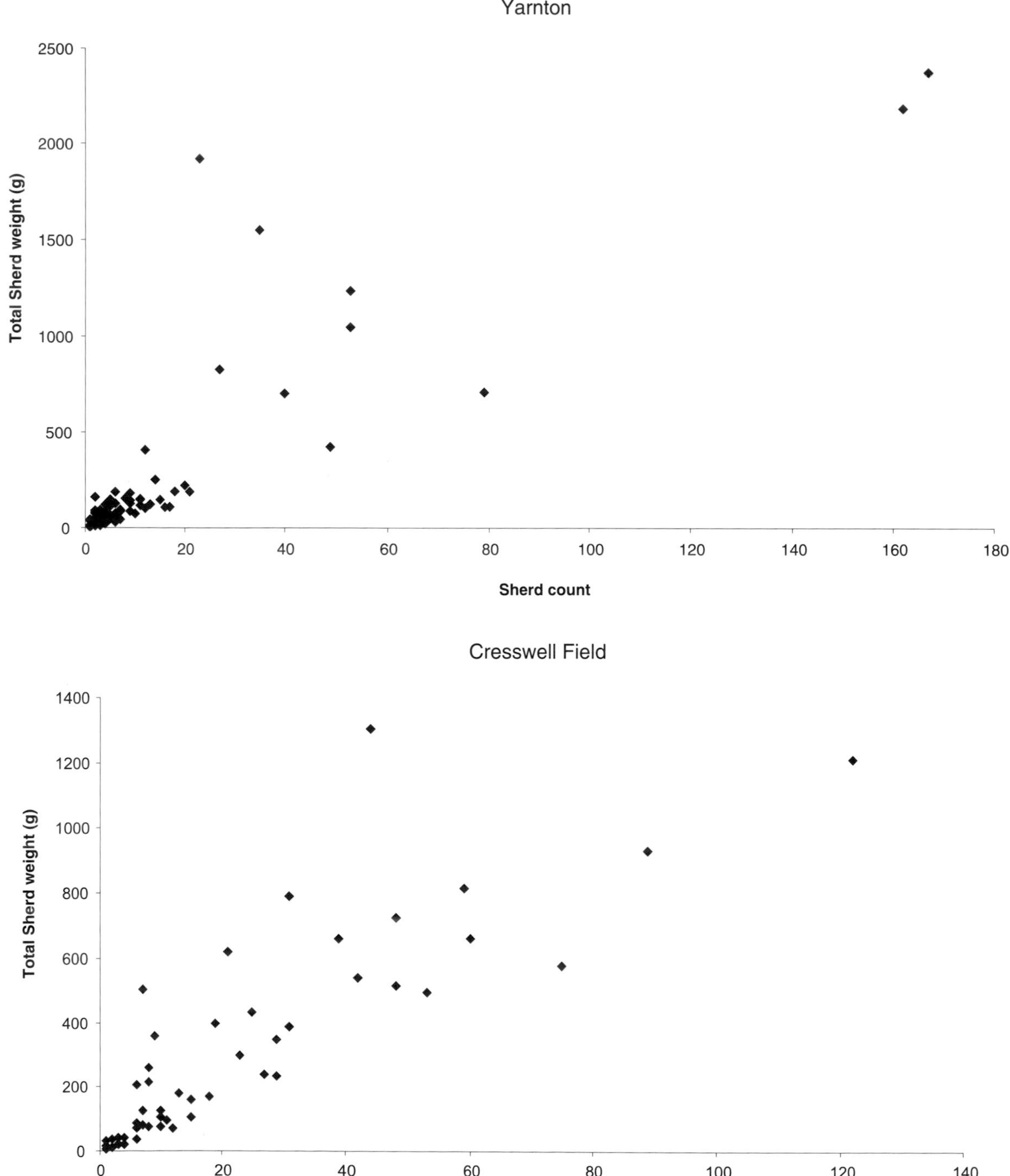

Fig. 6.33 Scatter diagram showing sherd weight against sherd count in middle Iron Age pits, Yarnton and Cresswell Field

contained small quantities of grain, the largest number (59 specimens) occurring in pit 8467 while the other two pits (7658 and 8786) contained only 19 and 14 specimens respectively. The ratio of chaff to grain differed between the pits. The two pits with smaller quantities of grain contained slightly more chaff than grain; the pit with the largest quantity of grain contained only half as much chaff as grain. Too few pit groups were analysed to establish whether or not there was any relationship between deposits of grain and deposits of other materials.

The majority of the pits from which the plant remains came were cylindrical, but bowl-shaped, undercut and large shallow features were also present (Table 6.6). As in the early Iron Age, cylindrical pits were the most prolific of plant remains. There were, however, fewer instances of pits with plant remains that also contained large quantities of charcoal.

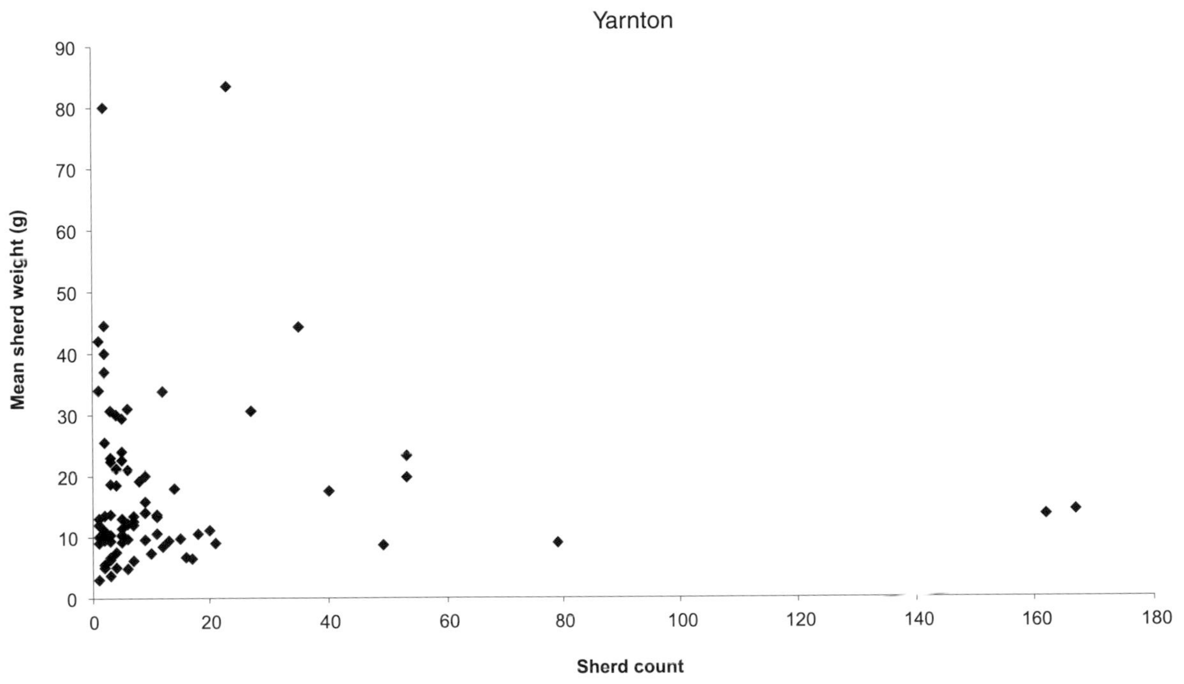

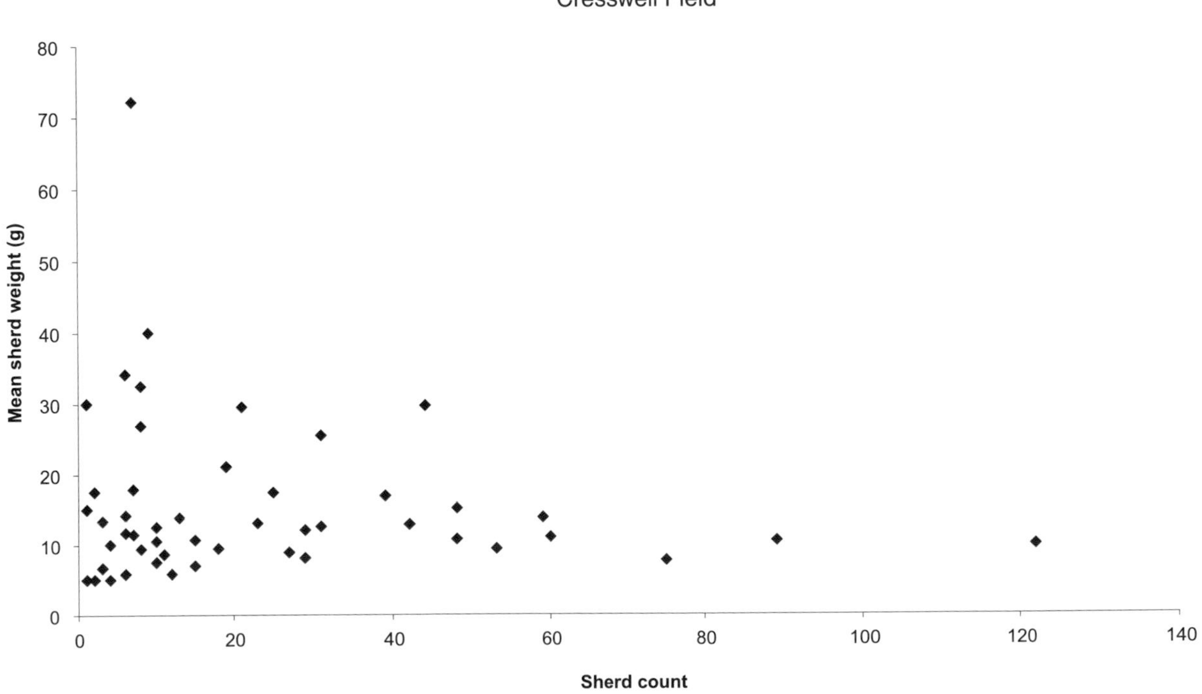

Fig. 6.34 Scatter diagram showing sherd count against mean sherd weight in middle Iron Age pits, Yarnton and Cresswell Field

Table 6.6 Charred plant remains data by pit type.

	Pit type						
	Undercut(GSP)	*Cylindrical*	*Bowl-shape d*	*Large shallow*	*Shallow saucer*	*Other*	*Total*
No. pits sampled	1	10	1	4	-	-	16
Cereals	10	245	9	20			316
Chaff	34	578	2	107			783
Weed seeds	32	572	5	103			756
Ave no. cereals per sampled pit	10	24.5	9	6.7			19.8
Cresswell Field							
No. pits sampled	1	1	1	-	-	-	3
Cereals	59	19	14				92
Chaff	36	20	26				82
Weed seeds	22	43	25				90

Metalworking debris

Metalworking debris was only found in seven middle Iron Age pits at Yarnton and eight pits at Cresswell Field (Figs 6.35 and 6.36). At Yarnton, two pieces of slag, including a hearth bottom fragment, came from pit 1189 in the north-east of the site, but otherwise evidence of metalworking was only found in the west of the area, and much of this came from pits around or within enclosure 267A and open-sided or D-shaped building 803. Middle Iron Age metalworking debris at Yarnton may therefore be seen as fairly localised, and possibly associated with structures in which metal was being worked. At Cresswell Field, the metalworking debris was less clearly localised, but only two pits (7658 and 7128) contained anything like large deposits (430 g and 120 g respectively); the others all produced less than 50 g. Much of this is likely to have been stray material which could have been incorporated into features some distance from the actual location of metalworking, or was perhaps redeposited from early Iron Age contexts.

Other Finds

At Yarnton the distribution of other finds within middle Iron Age pits was quite restricted, as all this material was contained in eleven pits. Nine of these features were cylindrical in shape and two were large shallow features, and they were mostly situated in the west of the site. One of the large shallow pits, 584, which lay within enclosure 390 to the south of the house structures, contained a particularly dense concentration of finds. In addition to large quantities of pottery and animal bone (Fig. 6.32), it was one of the few middle Iron Age pits to contain metalworking debris. It also yielded four fragments from two saddle querns (SFs 194b, 201 and SFs 194a and 199), part of a bone comb (SF 195), a worked bone textile tool (SF 464), an antler handle (SF 189) and much fired clay, including half a triangular loomweight. Loomweights were also recovered from pits 746 and 1524, and a bone point came from pit 1189. There also seems to have been a loose association between pits containing small finds and penannular ditches/gullies. Three of these pits lay within the penannular gully surrounding the D-shaped metalworking structure.

At Cresswell Field other finds were recovered from 13 pits, eight of which were cylindrical, one undercut, and the others all bowl-shaped. The richest group of finds was from pit 8786 which, alongside pottery and articulated sheep leg bones, also contained fragments of daub in which the position of interwoven wattles could be observed, two whetstones of sarsen and sandstone, a fragment of a shale bracelet and the rim of a shale vessel, and a grooved and polished metapodial. Pit 7783 was less rich but contained a spindlewhorl, a quartzite polisher and two fragments of copper alloy. The remaining pits contained fewer finds: loomweights in pits 8467, 8135, 7658 and 8525, pieces of Greensand quernstones in pits 8660 and 7353, a hollowed fragment of sandstone in pit 8454, pieces of copper alloy in pits 7987 and 7658 and of iron in pit 8525.

THE CEMETERY (Figs 6.37-6.40)

Topsoil stripping by the developer on the eastern side of the excavated area at Yarnton exposed a number of burials apparently grouped around a pair of Roman trackway ditches (Fig. 6.3). Six cremation burials and 46 inhumation burials were recorded, but only a single urned cremation burial within an early Roman vessel could be securely dated by conventional means. Fourteen skeletons were submitted for radiocarbon dating and, of these, nine were middle Iron Age in date (see Chapter 13). The spatial distribution of these burials and the form of interment indicated that, of the inhumations, 11 could be dated to the Roman or Saxon periods. Thirty-five mainly crouched burials seem to be Iron Age, including the dated examples. Analyses of the radiocarbon dates suggest that the cemetery was in use for only one or two generations (Chapter 13; Hey *et al.* 1999).

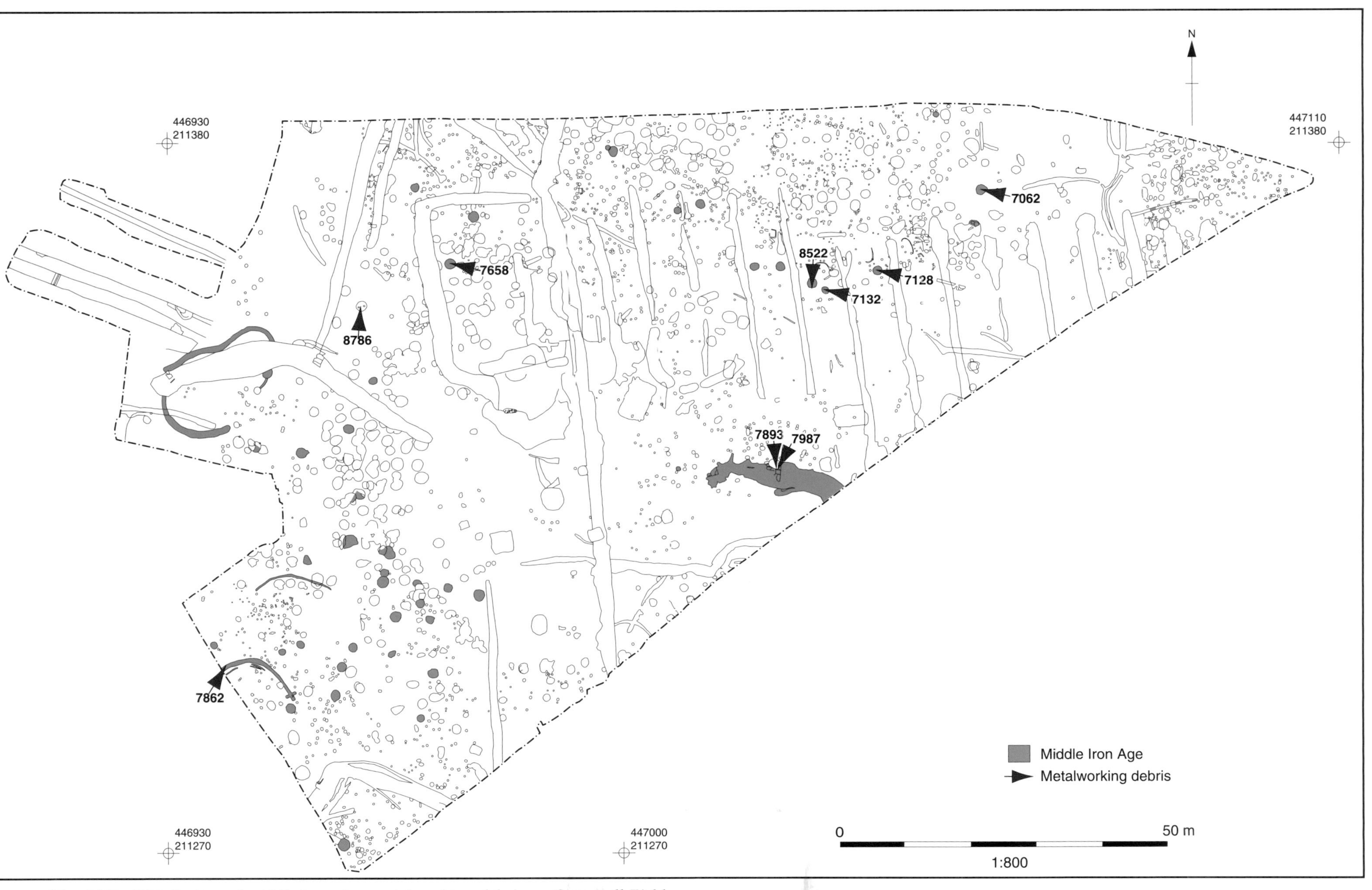

Fig. 6.35 Distribution of middle Iron Age metalworking debris on Cresswell Field

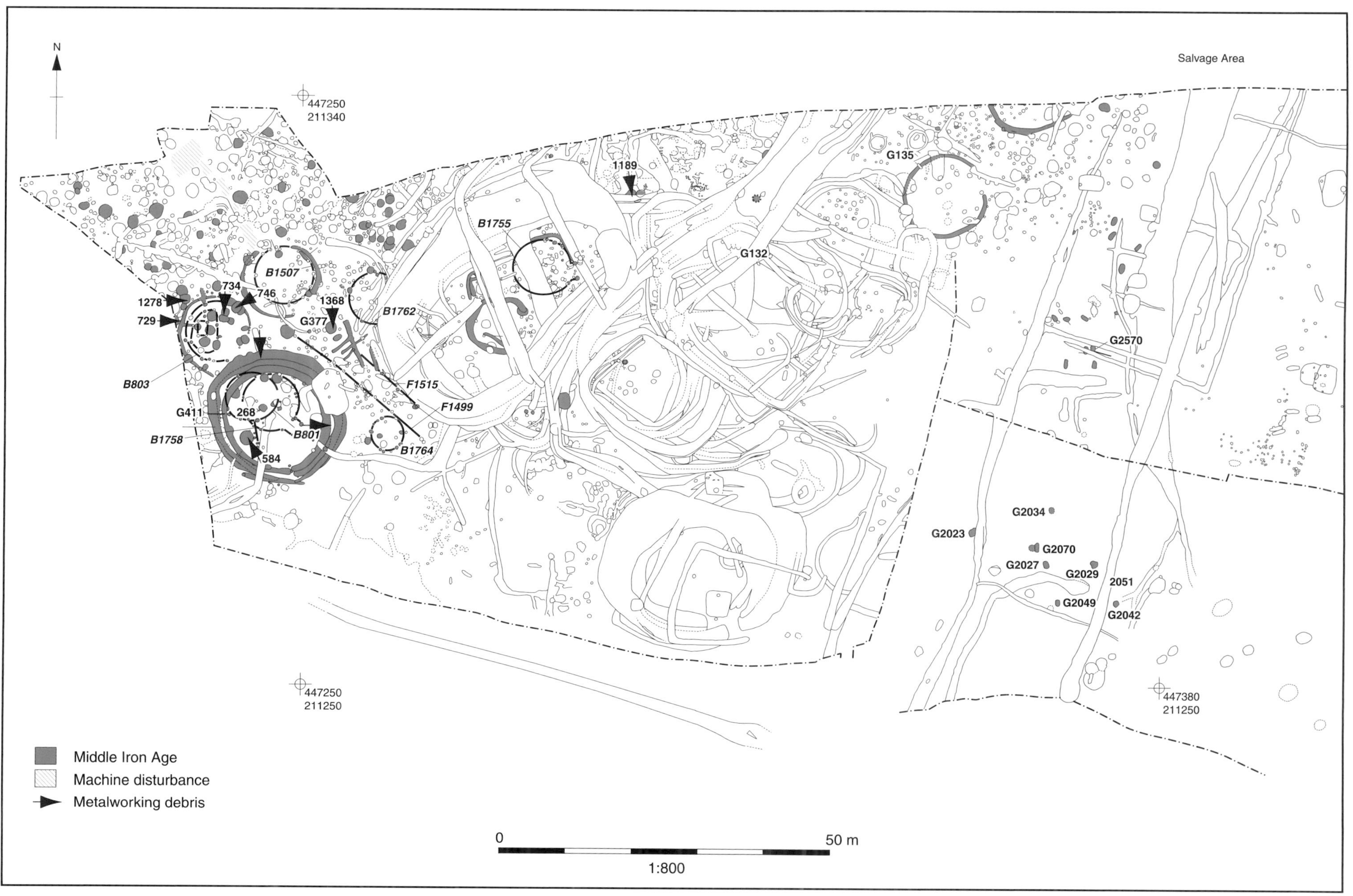

Fig. 6.36 Distribution of middle Iron Age metalworking debris at Yarnton

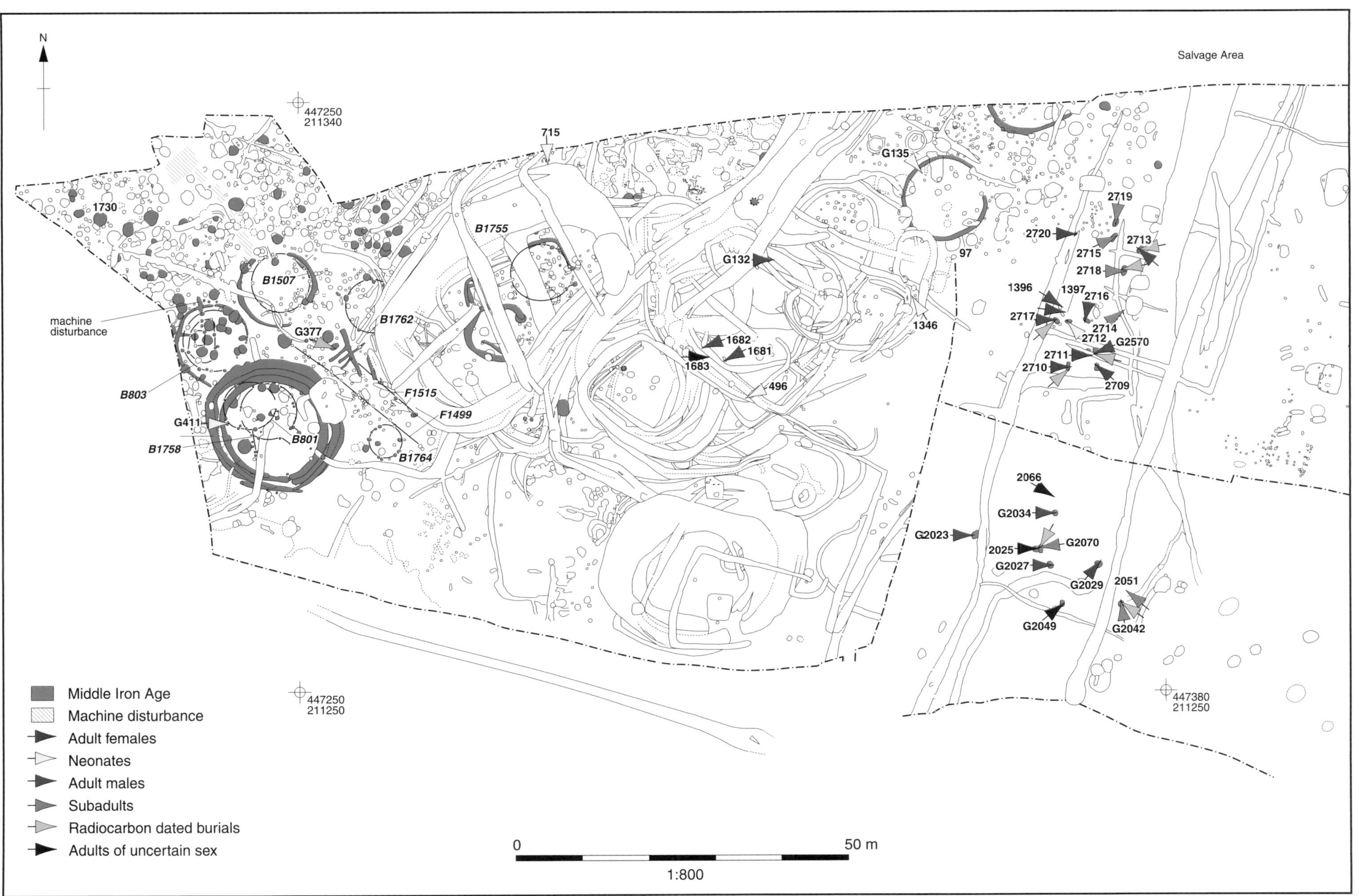

Fig. 6.37 Distribution of middle Iron Age inhumation burials

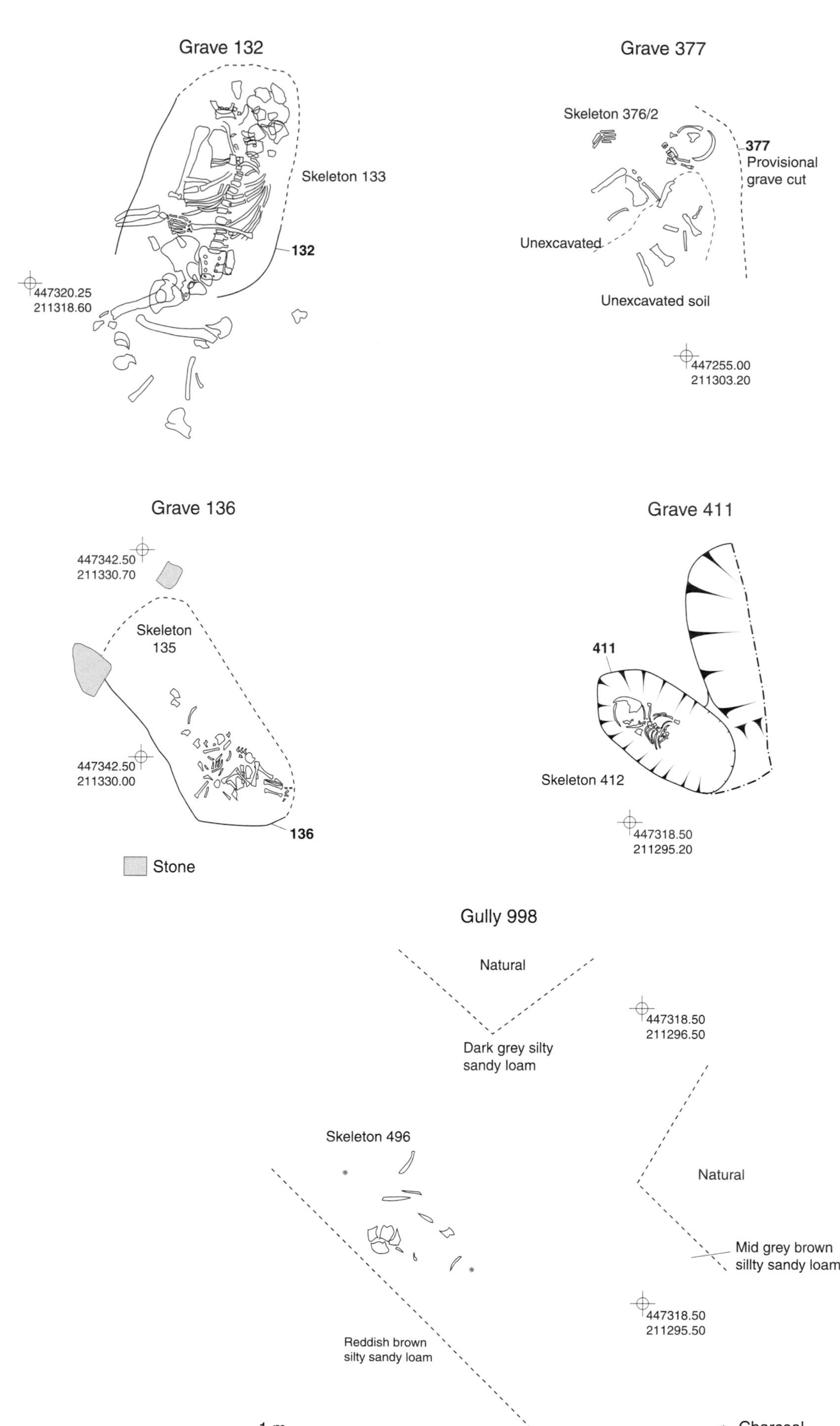
N
Grave 132
Skeleton 133
132
447320.25
211318.60
Grave 377
Skeleton 376/2
377
Provisional
grave cut
Unexcavated
Unexcavated soil
447255.00
211303.20
Grave 136
447342.50
211330.70
Skeleton
135
447342.50
211330.00
136
Stone
Grave 411
411
Skeleton 412
447318.50
211295.20
Gully 998
Natural
447318.50
211296.50
Dark grey silty
sandy loam
Skeleton 496
Natural
Mid grey brown
sillty sandy loam
447318.50
211295.50
Reddish brown
silty sandy loam
0
1 m
1:20
Charcoal

Table 6.7 Middle Iron Age inhumation burials.

	Northern Group	Southern Group	Outliers	Total
Neonates	1		5	6
Subadults	4	3		7
Adult females *	6	1		7
Adult males *	4	3	4	11
Adults of uncertain sex		3	1	4
Total	15	10	10	35
No. radiocarbon determinations **	5	2	2	9

* This is the probable sex of the individuals and does not reflect the full range of uncertainty (see Chapter 16 for details)
** See Chapter 13 for results (Table 13.1 and Fig. 13.1a)

The burials lay in three groups (Fig. 6.37, Table 6.7, for details see Chapter 16) on the site: a northern group (burials 1396, 1397, 2569 and 2709-2720) and a southern group (2021, 2022, 2025, 2026, 2028, 2033, 2041. 2048, 2051 and 2069) in the salvage area to the east, with ten individuals found on the south-east edge of the Iron Age settlement. The northern and southern groups, comprising 15 and ten individuals respectively, were only 20 m apart. The space between them could be illusory, the result of poor retrieval in the intervening area, or it is possible that the two groups belonged to different family units. A further ten inhumations (133, 135, 376/1, 376/2, 496, 719, 1346 and 1681-1683) have been described as outliers; they were scattered along the southern and eastern edges of the settlement.

The majority of these burials were recovered under salvage conditions and were in poor condition, so little information survived with regard to grave cuts and other burial details. All the graves that were recognised were very shallow, and it was apparent that many skeletons lay close to the surface and had been damaged by recent ploughing. Of the 22 individuals whose orientation could be established, the majority lay north-south and were crouched on their left or right sides (see Chapter 16); they were not tightly constricted. No burials were accompanied by grave goods.

An element of uncertainty surrounds some of the burials recovered on the edge of the settlement. These were very spread out and, as with the two main clusters, graves were very shallow and relationships hard to distinguish. Of the ten burials in this category, four were probably adult males, and two of these have been radiocarbon dated to the middle Iron Age period (skeletons 376/2 and 1681). Skeleton 376/2 was found within the centre of the middle Iron Age domestic area. One individual was an adult of unknown sex, but five were neonates

Fig. 6.39 Middle Iron Age skeleton 2022 in grave 2023

and none of these are dated. (Only one individual of this age was buried amongst the north and south cemetery groups.) Neonate 496 was discovered during the excavation of a late Roman ditch, 998, and is likely to be Roman in date. Other baby burials could also be of later date.

Discussion *by Angela Boyle*

The evidence of the burials from Yarnton strongly suggests that they formed the cemetery of the middle Iron Age settlement for a limited period in its occupation. There was nothing remarkable about the inhumations; the bodies were complete and had been predominantly laid out flexed (but not tightly constricted) in shallow graves apparently dug for the purpose. There were no grave goods and no indication of cause of death. The age and sex composition of the assemblage suggests that it was appropriate to bury all members of the community in the same manner, with the exception of neonates who were buried within the settlement. This contrasts with Iron Age funerary customs recorded elsewhere (Wait 1985; Hill 1995), where burials are found within settlements, often incomplete or apparently associated with special practices. Indeed, it has been argued (Fitzpatrick 1997, 82)

Fig. 6.38 (facing page) Plans of graves 132 (inhumation 133); 136 (inhumation 135); 377 (inhumation 376/2); 411 (inhumation 412); inhumation 496 in gully 998 and 2023 (inhumation 2022)

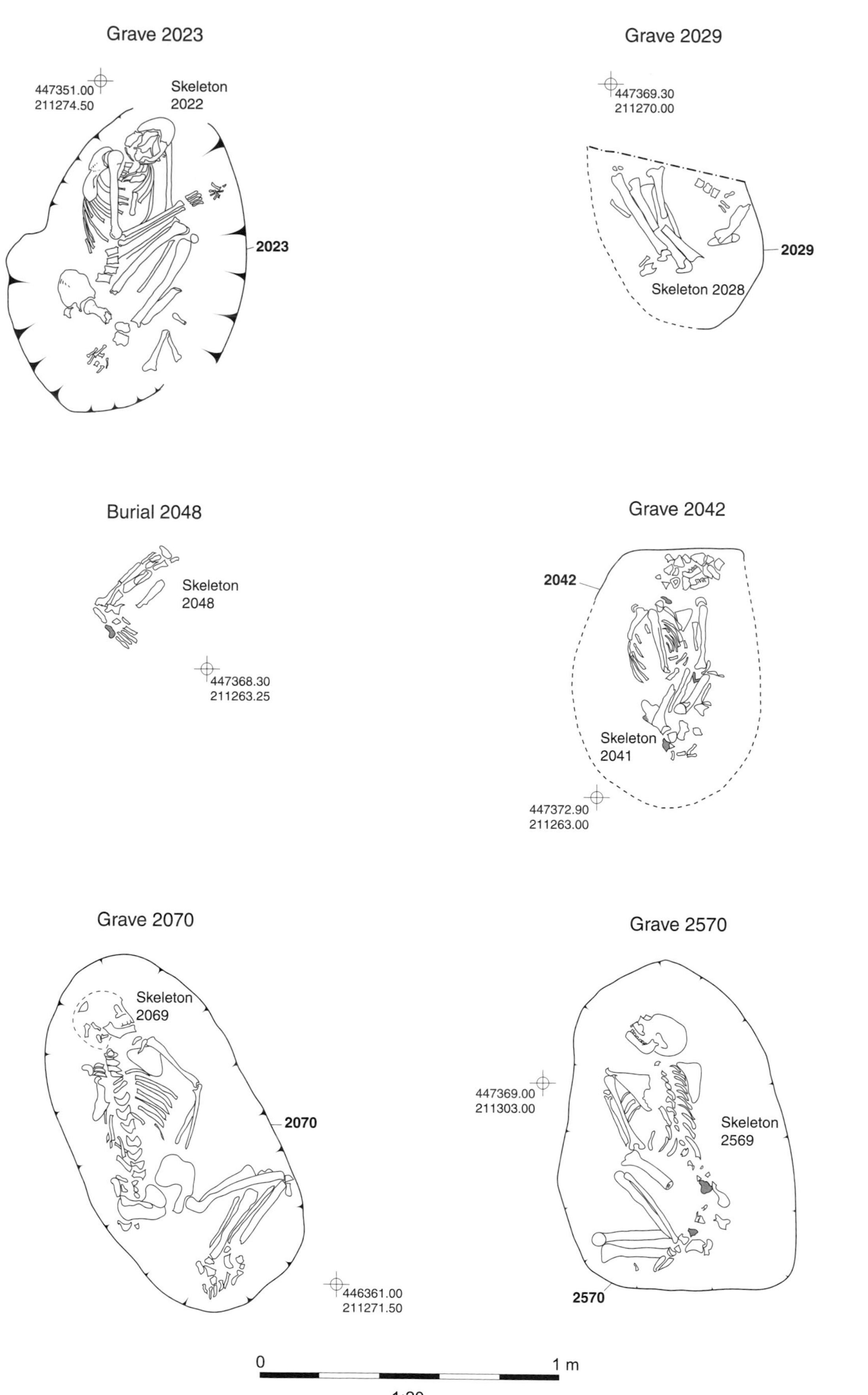

Fig. 6.40 Plans of graves 2029 (inhumation 2028); 2042 (inhumation 2041); 2048; 2070 (inhumation 2069) and 2570 (inhumation 2569)

that, since human remains in pits constitute the majority of archaeologically recoverable evidence at this time, *a priori* they represent the typical.

In 1981 Whimster wrote of southern England that 'no traces of extensive extramural cemeteries ... have ever been recorded in the region, and although the sample of isolated inhumations has increased greatly in recent years, there are still too few burials to account, in proportional terms, for the dead of what must once have been a particularly populous territory' (1981, 191), and little has changed in the interim. Given the Yarnton evidence, it is appropriate to consider whether its cemetery represents an unusual and localised Iron Age phenomenon, or whether such cemeteries exist elsewhere, but have rarely been found because of a bias in fieldwork practices toward the examination of occupation areas.

In general terms, excavations have rarely extended beyond the limits of settlements, making the detection of external cemeteries unlikely. At Owslebury, where a small number of middle Iron Age burials was recovered, including a child burial from the upper fill of an enclosure ditch, the excavator suggested that not only were such burials of an ephemeral nature but that they were located in areas rarely excavated (Collis 1994, 108). It has recently been re-emphasised that 'it is the juxtaposition of the living and dead on settlements which sets the Iron Age apart' (Fitzpatrick and Morris 1994, x) and it is perhaps this very supposition that may be leading us to look for burials within Iron Age settlements rather than on their periphery. By the same token it is possible that unaccompanied Iron Age burials may be overlooked; a survey of the Oxfordshire Sites and Monuments Record in 1993 turned up some 50 reports of finds of unidentified (ie undated) human burials (Blair 1994, 72) but it has never been considered that some may be Iron Age. Radiocarbon dating of inhumations found at Mill Hill, Deal, Kent, which were initially believed to be Anglo-Saxon gave late Iron Age and early Roman dates (Parfitt 1995, table 46). There were two distinct cemetery groups. The south-west cemetery comprised 28 burials, although an unknown number had been destroyed during 19th-century chalk quarrying. Within the central cemetery, 13 graves were classified as Iron Age in the field but the precise number is unknown because many had no grave goods and some were certainly Roman (as indicated by a radiocarbon date).

Recent discoveries of Iron Age inhumations show that the Yarnton cemetery is not unique. Excavations at Cockey Down, near Salisbury, by Wessex Archaeology, in advance of the laying of a water main in 1996, uncovered eight skeletons and disarticulated human bone lying 30 m south-west of an Iron Age and Romano-British enclosed settlement examined in 1989 (Trust for Wessex Archaeology 1996). Radiocarbon dating suggests that they are of middle Iron Age date (Andrew Fitzpatrick pers. comm.). Greater current emphasis on archaeological investigations of wider landscapes may also lead to further discoveries.

Work at Suddern Farm by the Danebury Environs Project revealed burials in an early to middle Iron Age chalk quarry just beyond the south-west corner of the settlement enclosure during the course of investigating linear ditches which ran from the enclosure (Cunliffe 2000). The suggestion that the Iron Age bodies excavated at Suddern Farm had been brought to the sites as 'bundles of bones' (Cunliffe 2000, 132), having previously been excarnated, cannot possibly be supported by the clearly articulated inhumation burials (Cunliffe and Poole 2000, vol 2, pt 3, 153-74; Hey 2001, 631). Pit deposits of human bone are few at Suddern Farm, as at Yarnton, and it is tempting to suggest that where burial proper occurs there is less emphasis on the former.

While it may appear easy to argue that many cemeteries of the type discovered at Yarnton do exist, but remain undiscovered because of excavation strategy, we should not exclude the possibility that Yarnton represents a localised tradition or preference. Although a small quantity (eight deposits) of disarticulated bone was present in the settlement features, there was considerably less than might be expected and no burials within storage pits were found. This is in marked contrast to other Iron Age sites in the region, for example Gravelly Guy, Stanton Harcourt, where 65 deposits of bone were recovered from pits, ditches, shallow scoops and a postholes (Lambrick and Allen 2004). No less than 48 of the deposits represented infants. It has been argued (Wait 1985, 94) that while the late Bronze Age and early Iron Age was characterised by the presence of single bones on both hillforts and settlements (Brück 1995), the middle Iron Age saw a significant increase in the number of formal inhumation burials on settlements, albeit in storage pits, with a corresponding decrease in the number of deposits of single bones. We might argue that the absence of burials in pits, and paucity of disarticulated fragments at Yarnton is more likely to indicate that a dedicated cemetery was in existence on the periphery of the settlement. It should not be forgotten that a skull and a small number of disarticulated fragments were deposited in settlement features at Cresswell Field.

If we accept the radiocarbon evidence, the cemetery may only have been in use for 50 years, and it is essential to consider why this was the case when settlement activity is believed to span the whole of the Iron Age. In this context, the cemetery may have been a short-lived practice against the backdrop of the normative secondary burial rite which involved excarnation. Indeed, the possibility that the inhumations from Yarnton were victims of a sudden, infectious disease and were buried differently, and over a very short period of time, cannot be discounted. Only chronic conditions and traumatic injuries will leave any indication on bone. Short-lived viral and bacterial infections would have been responsible for many deaths in antiquity (Roberts and Manchester 1995, 124-5).

Although it is not possible to draw unequivocal conclusions from the Yarnton evidence, on balance it seems probable that the cemetery represents a more common Iron Age burial custom than the current archaeological record allows. It suggests that formal inhumation burial was practised as a normative rite in some places at some time in the Iron Age and a growing awareness of the variety of locations in which Iron Age burials can be found will undoubtedly lead to further discoveries of 'extramural' cemeteries. It also demonstrates the value of radiocarbon dating of burials of uncertain age.

A range of burials of Iron Age date have been found in the vicinity of the site and these are discussed in Chapter 16 below. All appear to fall into the categories of deposits traditionally identified as 'typical' of the Iron Age in the region. The largest group, as mentioned above, is that from Gravelly Guy, Stanton Harcourt (Lambrick and Allen 2004, 221-252).

Chapter 7: The Late Iron Age and Early Roman Transition

by Dan Stansbie and Gill Hey

INTRODUCTION

The settlement spanning the late Iron Age to early Roman period (defined here as the later 1st century BC/early 1st century AD up to the early Flavian period) exhibited a marked difference in layout and structure from those that preceded it (Fig. 7.1). In common with other sites of the same period in the Upper Thames Valley, such as Gravelly Guy, Stanton Harcourt, Yarnton developed from an open settlement characterised by pit scatters and circular post-built structures to one in which ditched sub-circular and sub-rectangular enclosures and paddocks predominated. This settlement was situated mainly to the south and east of the middle Iron Age habitation site and no features of this date were identified at Cresswell Field.

LATE IRON AGE/EARLY ROMAN STRUCTURES

Summary

No late Iron Age/early Roman buildings were identified, and the only structure clearly dating to this period was a fence line, 1763, traced for a length of approximately 13 m in the southern part of the site. It is very unlikely, however, that people did not live on this site, and it is reasonable to assume that the evidence has not survived. A number of related reasons for this can be proposed. Later Roman activity, particularly the extensive ditch digging, may have removed traces of structures, but ploughing and other forms of truncation will also have removed shallow features. Structures of this period (and of the later middle Iron Age) are notoriously difficult to identify (Allen *et al.* 1984), even on sites preserved beneath alluvium, such as Mingies Ditch in the Lower Windrush Valley (Allen and Robinson 1993). Reynolds (1979) has shown that postholes need not penetrate the subsoil in order to support circular buildings, and buildings lacking substantial foundations and house gullies would not necessarily have been visible during excavation. Two methods of construction in particular would have left no structural evidence if conditions for preservation were not ideal. One is sill-beam construction, which seems unlikely to have been used for roundhouses (Allen *et al.* 1984) but may have been used for rectangular buildings, which Rodwell (1978) argues were dominant in the late Iron Age of south-eastern Britain (cf Allen *et al.* 1984), although there is no significant evidence for this technique in rural contexts within the Upper Thames Valley (cf Booth *et al.* 2007, 35-6, 60-1) Another is mass-wall construction of turf or cob, which Allen argues was used at Mingies Ditch (Allen and Robinson 1993). It is suggested that these types of buildings would have originally existed on the present site. An unusual sub-rectangular sunken feature (594) in the south-west part of the site may also represent the remains of a structure, though it is unlikely to have been domestic in character.

Fence line 1763 (Figs 7.1 and 7.2)

A 13.4 m length of a NE-SW aligned fence line was located towards the south of the site. This was represented by six postholes which were roughly circular in plan with diameters of 0.3-0.4 m, and depths of 0.08-0.2 m. Profiles were predominantly bowl-shaped, with one exception, which was flat-based and steep-sided. Fills consisted of mid or dark brown silty loams containing 2-10% gravel. The only finds recovered were a single small sherd of pottery and an animal bone fragment.

Feature 594 (Figs 7.1 and 7.3)

The sub-rectangular feature

A sub-rectangular feature *c* 7 m x 4 m and orientated NNW-SSE lay on the west side of the settlement, overlying middle Iron Age circular enclosure 390. Approximately 90% of this feature was excavated, but its function was extremely difficult to determine. The possibility that it was an Anglo-Saxon sunken-featured building was considered during excavation, especially as other Saxon features had been discovered on this site. This interpretation was abandoned, however, because of the very shallow profile of the feature sides (Fig. 7.3), the presence of quantities of late Iron Age/early Roman finds and the absence of Anglo-Saxon material of any kind. The fine, dark and friable character of the feature fill suggested that it had been exposed to a considerable degree of trampling or that it had been filled with midden material or a similar deposit. It is suggested that it was either an animal pen or byre, or possibly a smithy.

Fig. 7.1 Plan of late Iron Age/early Roman features at Yarnton

The feature sides were concave but shallow, at about 30 degrees, and it had a generally flat, though uneven base. It was 0.2 m deep on average and no recuts were apparent. Its western edge was difficult to locate as it lay within earlier ditch fills. The feature fill yielded a large quantity of finds, including some 145 animal bones, a fragment of human humerus, and 105 sherds of pottery weighing 1768 g, fired clay and six pieces of slag, including two plano-convex hearth bottom fragments. A significant number of the animal bones are of cattle, with some horse and sheep/goat. Of particular note are some fragments from a horse forelimb (see Chapter 17), and a worked piece of bone (SF 452), which shows light polish and was probably used in textile production (Allen, Chapter 15). A posthole, 654, on the north-east edge of feature 594 contained part of a cattle skull and maxilla.

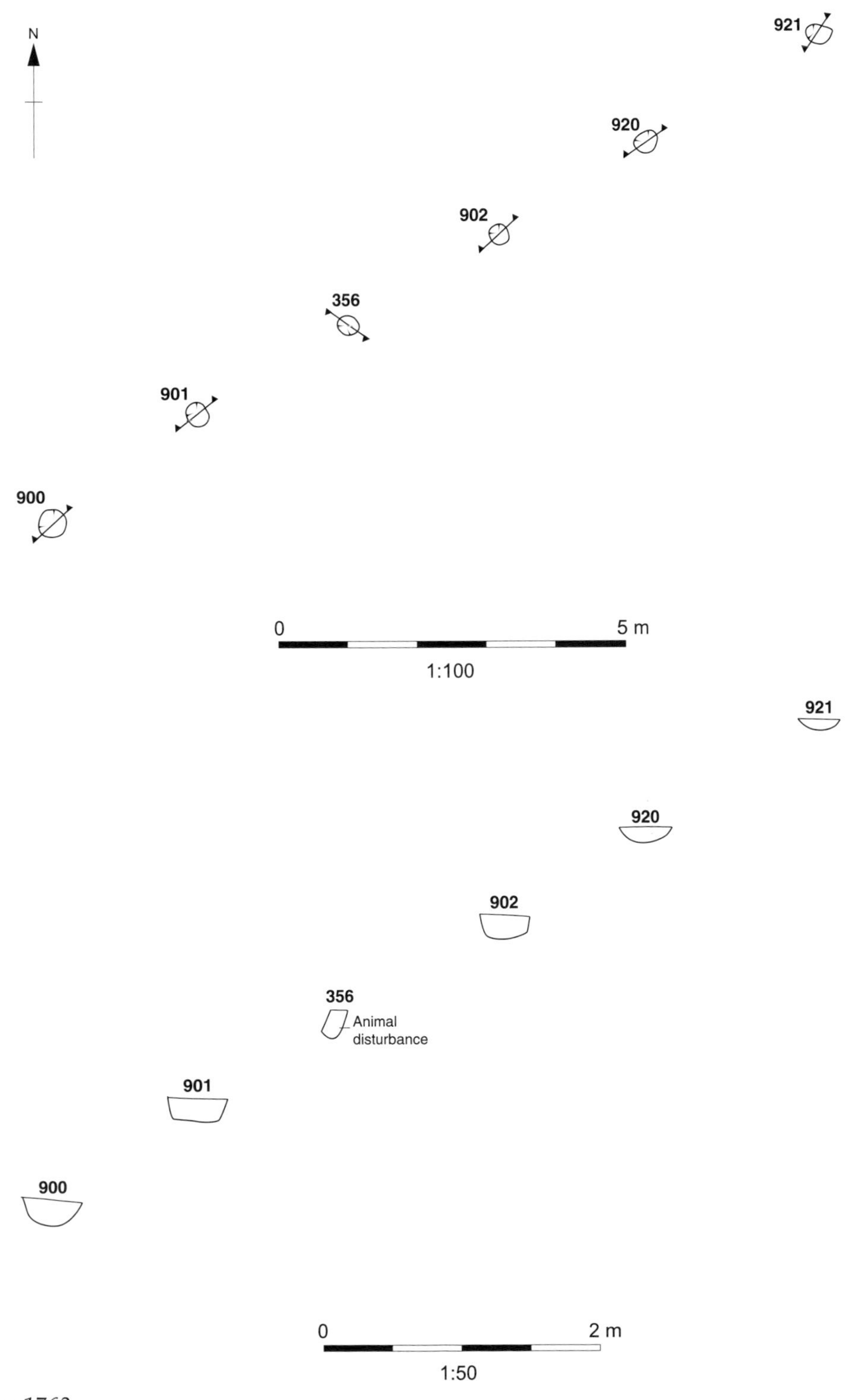

Fig. 7.2 Fence line 1763

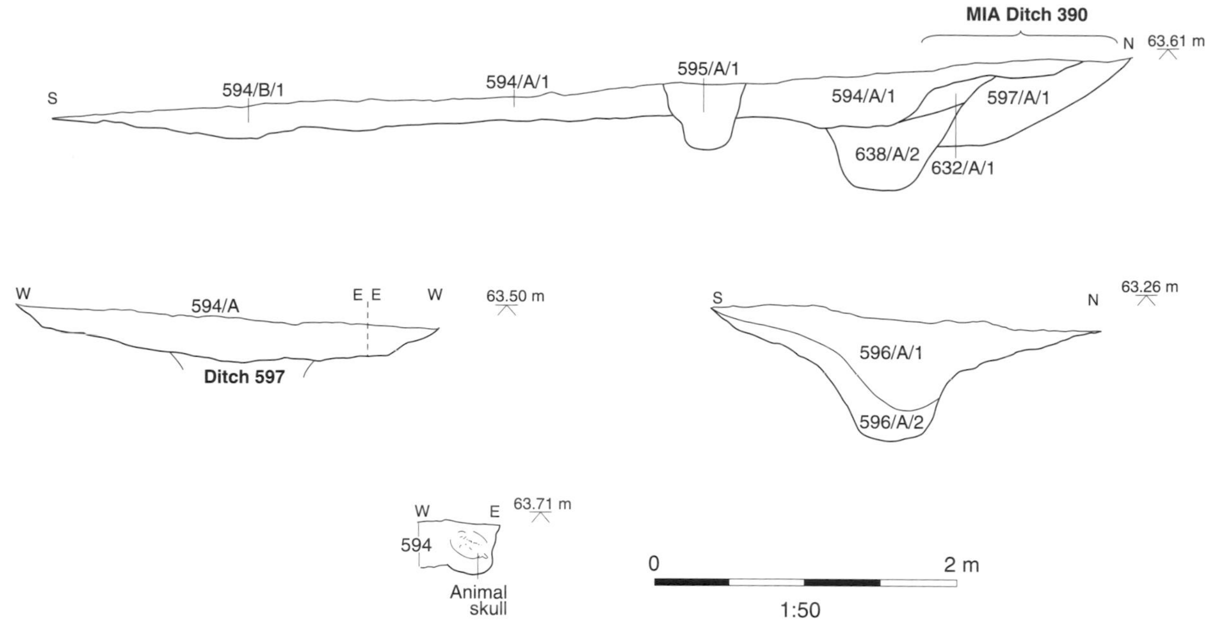

Fig. 7.3 Sections across feature 594

Ditches 596 and 638

Feature 594 appeared to cut late Iron Age ditch 638, which probably formed part of enclosure 269 (described below). Ditch 638 ran close to the northern edge of 594 and terminated within the feature near its north-east corner (Fig. 6.9). It lay parallel to and *c* 4 m from another linear ditch-like feature, 596, which lay within and on the south edge of 594. The profiles of 596 and 638 were remarkably similar, with steep lower sides, flattish bases and depths of *c* 0.8 m (Fig. 7.3) and the fills of both were overlain by that of 594. They may have defined the original extent of feature 594. Ditch 596 produced nine sherds of pottery, 21 animal bones and three fragments of small plano-convex hearth bottom from metalworking. Ditch 638 contained five animal bones and three sherds of pottery.

Features 595 and 639

The fill of 594 was cut by two features, 595 and 639, within its northern half. Feature 595 was a short linear feature, or perhaps an elongated pit, 1 m long and 0.4 m wide (Figs 6.12 and 7.3). It was steep sided, 0.4 m deep and fairly flat bottomed. It contained five grog-tempered pottery sherds and ten animal bones, mainly of cattle. Gully 639 (Fig. 6.12) was slightly curved and measured 4.2 m in length. It was orientated NW-SE and ran beyond feature 594 to the east. A single section revealed its profile to be U-shaped and narrow, *c* 0.5 m wide and 0.4 m deep. It was filled with a greenish-brown sandy loam. Five sherds of mid to late 1st century AD pottery and three animal bones were recovered. In neither case is it clear how, if at all, these features related functionally to 594.

LATE IRON AGE/EARLY ROMAN ENCLOSURES AND DITCHES

Summary

The late Iron Age/early Roman transition was defined by the laying out of a series of ditched enclosures, mainly to the south and east of the early and middle Iron Age settlement (Fig. 7.1). Like the structures in the early and middle Iron Age phases, these enclosures were broadly divisible into three groups: a central group comprising three large sub-rectangular enclosures, with several smaller circular and sub-rectangular enclosures which abutted them to the south-east; a western group consisting of linear arrangements of ditches that suggest sub-rectangular paddocks running up to the central enclosures; and a south-eastern group comprising a substantial circular enclosure with a small circular enclosure within it and several other smaller circular enclosures abutting it to the north-east.

The central group of enclosures and ditches

The central group consisted of seven enclosures or fragments of ditched enclosures, the largest of which (enclosure 175) was sub-rectangular and orientated NW-SE. Abutting this enclosure to the north-east was a second sub-rectangular enclosure (enclosure 236/793), smaller than the first, while on the south-west was a more rectilinear enclosure (enclosure 269/638), aligned east-west. These enclosures were cut away to a large extent by later Roman ditches and were difficult to trace. Remains of any structures within the compounds may have been entirely lost. Within the south-west corner of enclosure 175 was a smaller sub-circular enclosure, 205, which was probably earlier in date than 175. A second, more substantial but similar sub-circular enclosure (121) lay to the east, but was separate from the main group. A number of linear ditches, possibly the remnants of small paddocks, lay south-west of enclosure 175 (ditches 386 and 331) and fence line 1763 may have been associated with these. A further enclosure, 341, lay south of 175 and was cut by it. This enclosure seems to have formed a link between the central group of enclosures and feature 391A to the south-east (see below). Other ditches on the northern edge of the site, including 69 and 129, north of enclosure 236, suggest the existence of further enclosures in this area.

Enclosure 175 and associated features

Enclosure 175 (Figs 7.1, 7.4 and 7.5)

This wedge-shaped ditched enclosure, aligned NW-SE and measuring *c* 20 m x 17 m, lay in the centre of the site. Some 70% of the enclosure ditch was excavated in 37 segments. Excavation revealed multiple cuts and a varied profile, including flat to rounded bases, and steep to sloping concave sides (Figs 7.4 and 7.5). The maximum width of the enclosure ditch was 1.3 m, with the average width of the identified elements (mostly truncated by later features) 0.66 m. The depth ranged from 0.18 m to 0.84 m, averaging 0.48 m. The ditch fills were a mixture of gravel-free material, silty loams with gravel, and silt-sand above primary silting, with occasional white clay patches, burnt material and a possible turfline. The fills had suffered from some degree of animal disturbance. No entrance to this enclosure was identified but, given the general layout, it would most likely have been sited either to the north or the south-east. A large quantity of pottery, animal bone, finds of stone, iron and fired clay, charred plant remains and some metalworking debris were recovered from the ditch fill, suggesting rubbish deposition. Of the 399 sherds (5404 g) of pottery recorded, 50% were residual earlier Iron Age wares. The remainder were grog-tempered wares with a small proportion of Roman types, suggesting a probable date for final infilling in the later 1st century AD. A few later Roman sherds were probably intrusive, suggesting some disturbance of deposits. The 125 fragments of animal bone include the usual domesticates along with bones of dog and hare and a broken up horse mandible possibly indicative of a special deposit (see Chapter 17 below). Other finds include a saddle quern (SF 200), an iron nail, a loomweight fragment, a piece of fired clay and seven slag fragments, three from plano-convex hearth bottoms.

Gullies 1508 and 1585 in the north-west of enclosure 175 (Fig. 7.1)

Gully 1508 was a north-south aligned linear feature 3.6 m in length, located within the north-west sector of enclosure 175. It was cut away at both ends by early Roman ditches. Three sections were excavated through the gully, revealing a U-shaped profile with no visible recuts. It was 0.4 m wide and 0.25 m deep and was filled with non-gravelly material. Finds comprised nine sherds of pottery, all grog-tempered, with a mid 1st-century AD date, and ten animal bones, including red deer, horse and cattle.

Gully 1585 was a 0.85 m long fragmentary arc aligned east-west, lying immediately to the west of gully 1508. Like 1508, its ends were cut away. Two excavated sections revealed a U-shaped profile, 0.4 m wide and 0.39 m deep, with evidence of a single recut. The fills were a gravel-free material and silty-loams with gravel which produced four pottery sherds weighing 80 g and three animal bones.

Enclosure 236 (Figs 7.1, 7.4 and 7.6)

Ditched enclosure 236, contiguous with and on the north-east side of enclosure 175, was approximately square, measuring 16 m x 15 m. It lay in the centre of the site and was visible as a series of ditches extensively disturbed by later features. A gully terminal in the south-east corner may have marked one side of an entrance. Excavated segments representing *c* 35% of the surviving enclosure lengths indicated multiple recutting. The individual cuts were small; gullies rather than ditches, mostly with U-shaped profiles which were on average 0.49 m wide and 0.35 m deep, except on the south-west side, where much more substantial ditches were present. Fills were mixed, with some greenish staining present, and their formation processes were unclear. An assemblage of some 103 sherds (1343 g) of pottery, 119 animal bones, two fragments of slag and some charred plant remains were recovered from the gully fills. This material may have been the result of rubbish deposition, but the quantity is relatively small and at least 86% of the pottery sherds by count were redeposited. The contemporary assemblage suggests a mid to late 1st century AD date.

Enclosure 269 and ditch 638

Enclosure 269 (Fig. 7.1)

Ditch 269 formed the south and east sides of a roughly rectilinear enclosure, possibly linked to enclosure 175 on its west side. The extant size of the enclosure was 20 m east-west by 12 m north-south. The ditch had a clear terminal to the west, where it curved very slightly northwards towards ditch 638, possibly representing the site of an entrance. Pit 300 and feature 594 (see above) lay within the enclosed space. The ditch had a flat-based, steep-sided profile, on average 0.75 m wide and 0.41 m deep. The fills were mixed, comprising a light greenish-brown and dark brown sandy silts and a greenish-brown sandy loam. Twenty sherds of pottery, of which 12 are early or middle Iron Age, and 19

Fig. 7.4 Plan and sections of enclosures 175, 205 and 236

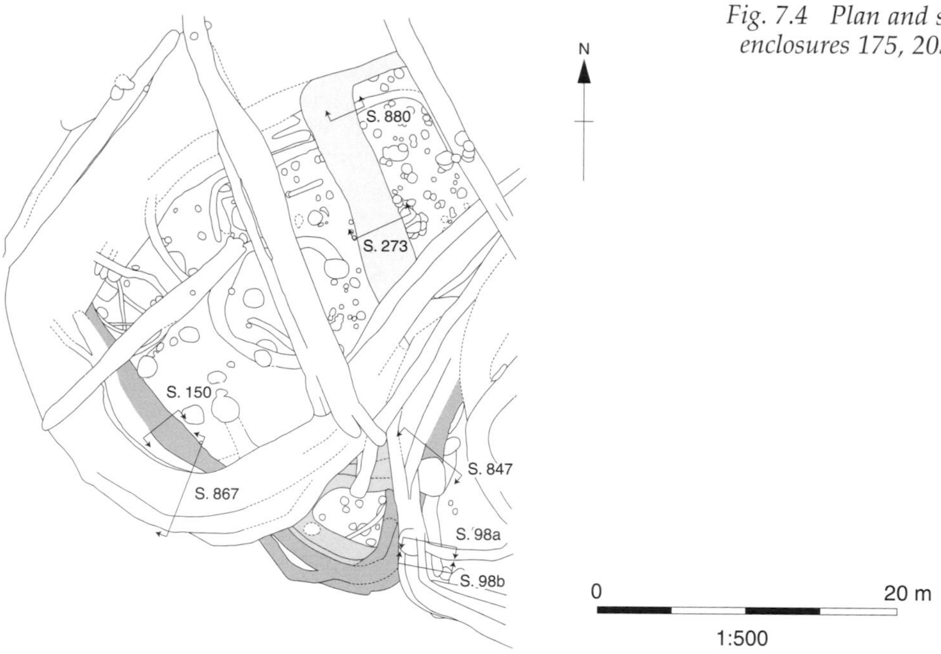

N

S. 880
S. 273
S. 150
S. 867
S. 847
S. 98a
S. 98b

0
20 m
1:500

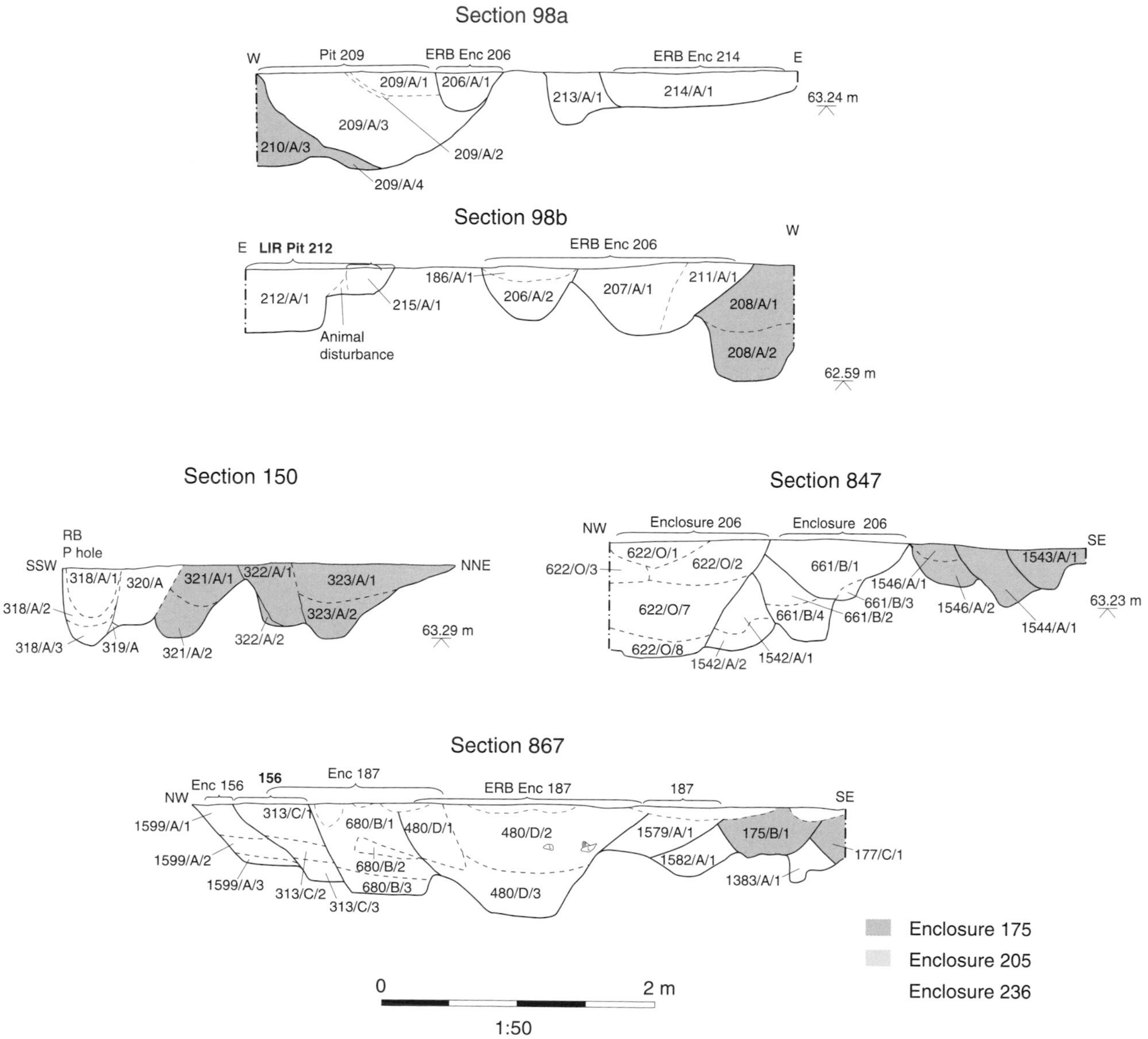

Section 98a

W
Pit 209
ERB Enc 206
ERB Enc 214
E
209/A/1
206/A/1
213/A/1
214/A/1
63.24 m
209/A/3
210/A/3
209/A/2
209/A/4

Section 98b

E
LIR Pit 212
ERB Enc 206
W
186/A/1
211/A/1
212/A/1
215/A/1
206/A/2
207/A/1
208/A/1
208/A/2
Animal disturbance
62.59 m

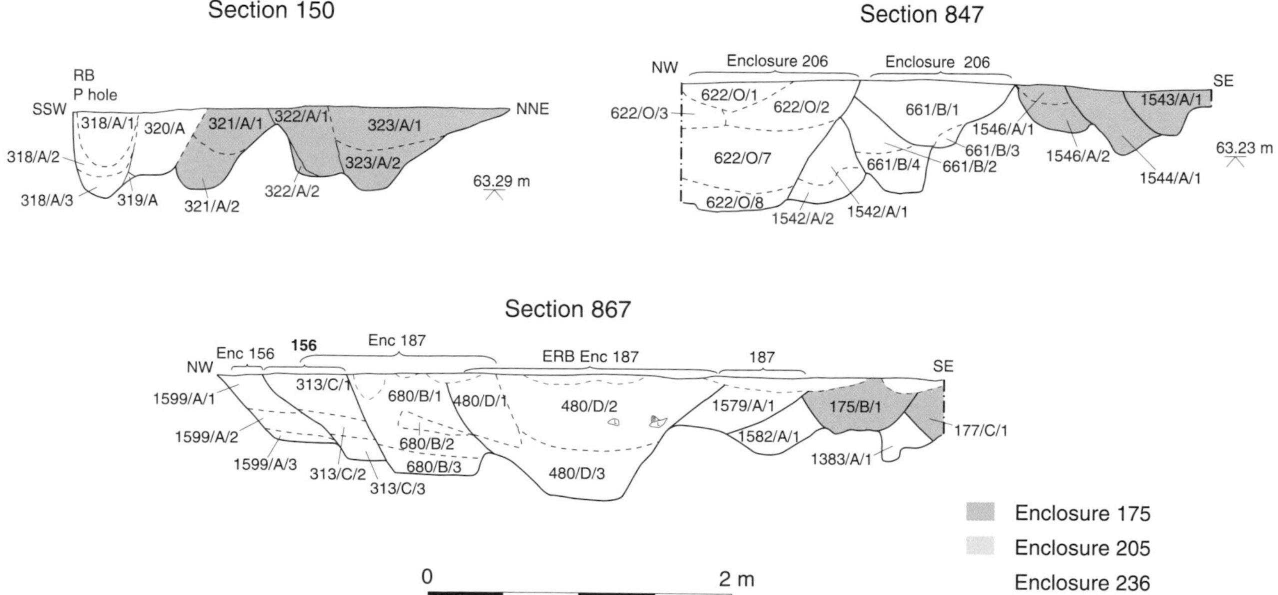

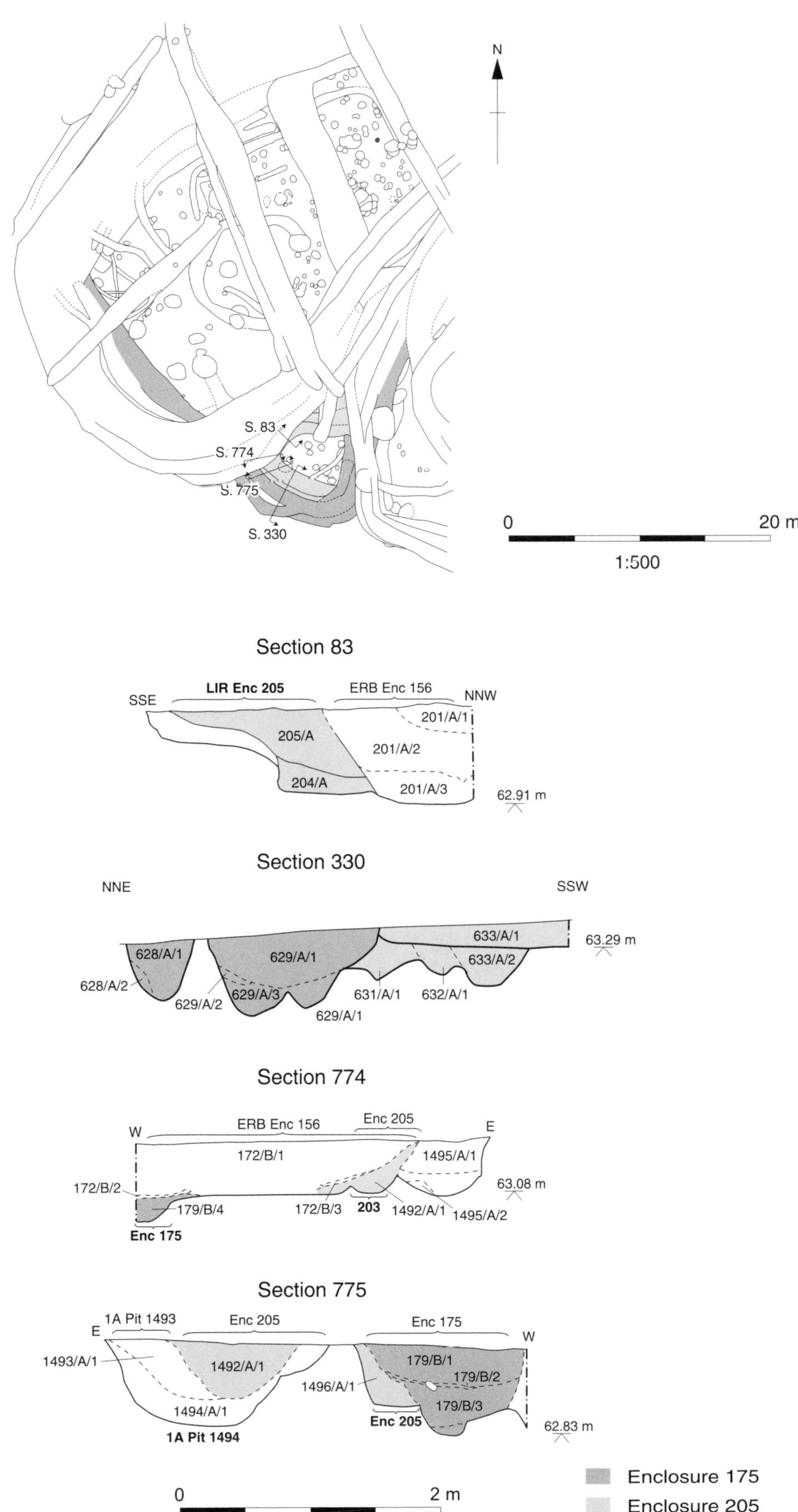

Fig. 7.5 Sections through enclosures 175 and 205

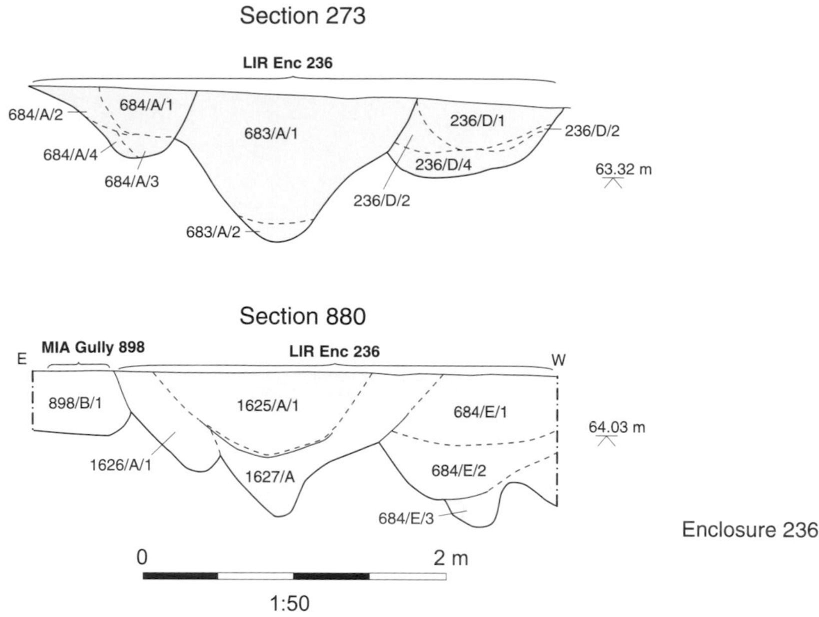

Fig. 7.6 Sections of enclosure 236

fragments of animal bone were recovered from the ditch fill and these may represent the secondary deposition of material lying on a contemporary ground surface.

Ditch 638 (Figs 7.1 and 7.3)

Ditch 638 was a right-angled feature 7.5 m in length in total, lying to the north of ditch 269. It south and east terminals were clearly identified, the latter lying within possible structure 594 as discussed above. The terminals of 269 and 638 were 5 m apart, and this gap may indicate a poorly preserved western entrance to the enclosure. The profile of 638 was U-shaped and no recuts were observed. Its average width was 0.85 m, and the average depth was 0.78 m. Two fills were noted, a yellowish-brown sandy loam with flecks of charcoal sealing a greenish-brown sandy loam. Few finds were recovered from the fill: five animal bones and three sherds of pottery, all probably derived from secondary deposition.

Enclosure 205 and associated features

Enclosure 205 (Figs 7.1, 7.4 and 7.5)

This roughly oval enclosure lay within the southern part of enclosure 175. It was extensively recut and, consequently, its original shape is difficult to determine, but it enclosed an area of approximately 8 m x 7 m. No entrance was identified but the northern and eastern sides were cut away by later features. Multiple episodes of recutting, visible in section (Fig. 7.5), made it difficult to ascertain profiles and dimensions. The gullies were on average 0.65 m wide and 0.42 m deep. Some primary silting was present in the gullies, but fills were generally mixed and it was unclear whether they formed by deliberate or natural infilling. The deposition of relatively large quantities of animal bone (80 fragments) and pottery (36 sherds, 306 g) in the fills, along with a piece of metalworking slag and a rotary quernstone (SF 210) suggest modest rubbish deposition, presumably from a nearby structure. The pottery assemblage suggests a mid 1st-century AD date.

A number of pits and postholes were exposed within the enclosure, but these contained only middle Iron Age finds. The degree of redeposition within features in this area should, however, be noted, and it is possible that some structural evidence was contemporary with the enclosure.

Gully 492 (Fig. 7.1)

A 4 m stretch of gully, aligned SE-NW, lay within enclosure 175 just to the north of enclosure 205 and may have been a continuation of one of the gullies forming part of enclosure 205, but this was uncertain. A section excavated across the gully revealed an open U-shaped profile, 0.3 m wide, with no visible recuts. The fills were a gravel-free material which produced only two Iron Age pottery sherds and three fragments of animal bone.

Possible enclosures south of enclosures 269 and 205

A number of linear ditches/gullies, together with fence line 1763, appeared to form small enclosures or paddocks to the south of the settlement.

Ditch 1600 (Fig. 7.1)

A short stretch of ditch 6.3 m long, aligned NW-SE, ran between and was cut by enclosures 269 and 205. Three sections were excavated across the ditch, representing 75% of its total length. The profile was U-shaped and open, and no recuts were observed. Its width was 0.7 m, and the average depth was 0.33 m.

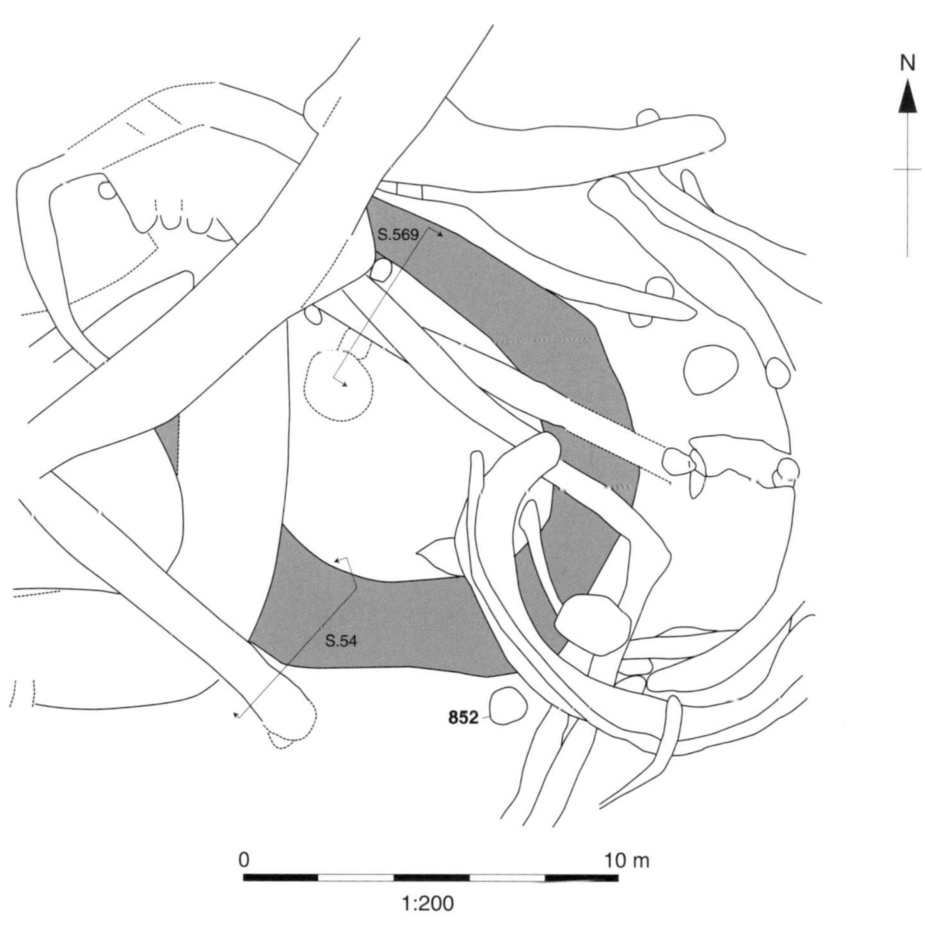

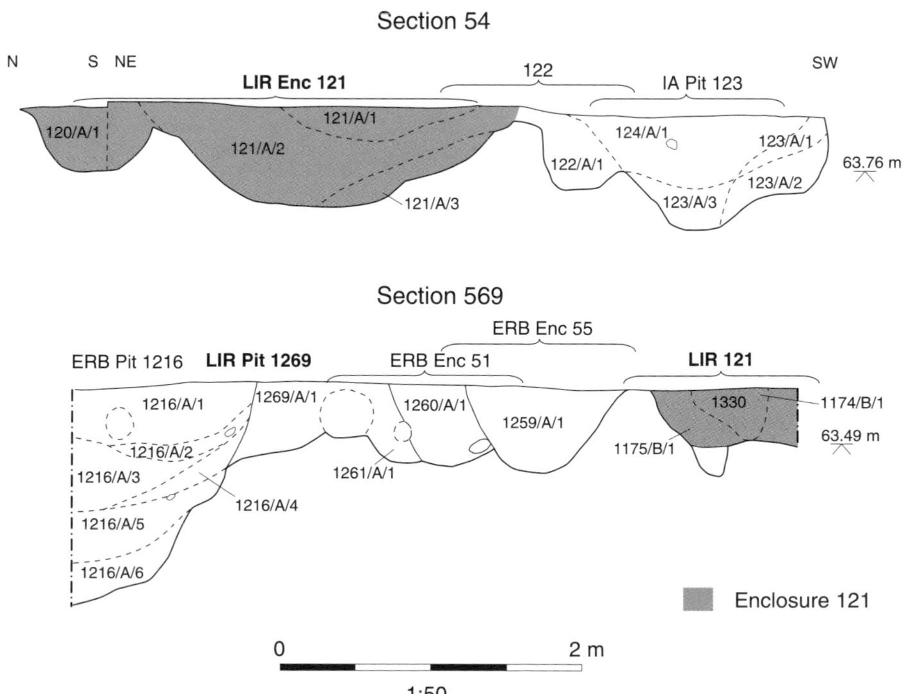

Fig. 7.7 Plan and sections of enclosure 121

Fills consisted of non-gravelly material with flecks of charcoal. A scarcity of finds from the ditch fill, one pot sherd and six animal bones, indicated that there was no concentrated rubbish deposition.

Gully 386 (Fig. 7.1)

This NE-SW aligned gully was 23.45 m long and ran parallel to ditch 1600 (above) and fence line 1763. At least four cuts were visible, showing varied profiles, including flat and rounded bases, and sloping concave or convex sides. The width was, on average, 0.29 m and the depth 0.22 m. Some primary silting was noted and fills were generally mixed. Fifteen animal bones, 17 sherds of pottery (145 g) and a single fragment of fired clay were recovered from the fill.

Ditch 331 (Fig. 7.1)

Ditch 331 ran roughly perpendicular to gully 386 towards fence line 1763. It was 9 m long, orientated NW-SE and had a varied profile which was generally U-shaped and open. The width range was 0.4-0.8 m and average width was 0.63 m. The depth range was 0.14-0.2 m and average depth was 0.17 m. Fills consisted of non-gravelly material and silty-loams with gravel with occasional charcoal flecks. A single sherd of grog-tempered late Iron Age pottery was recovered.

Enclosure 121 and associated features

Enclosure 121 (Figs 7.1 and 7.7)

Enclosure 121 was a fairly small oval enclosure with quite a substantial ditch with surviving external dimensions of *c* 12 m x 10 m. The western part of the enclosure was completely cut away by later features. Its internal area may have been no more than *c* 7 m across. Approximately 50% of the total length of the extant ditch was excavated. No entrance was observed, but it may have been sited in the truncated north-west sector. The ditch had a U-shaped profile and one episode of recutting was observed in section. The ditches were approximately 0.82 m wide on average and 0.48 m deep. A considerable quantity of material was recovered from the ditch fill, comprising 61 sherds (1043 g) of pottery, 50 animal bones and one slag fragment from a small sub-tuyère plate. Abundant plant remains, including cereals, were also present. These deposits may represent disposal of rubbish, probably from a nearby domestic source. The pottery assemblage included mostly grog-tempered wares with a small number of more Romanised wares, suggesting a date between the mid and later 1st century AD.

Hearth 852 (Figs 7.1 and 7.7)

Feature 852 may have been a small hearth, measuring 0.9 m x 1.1 m and with a depth of 0.3 m. It was exposed during section cleaning immediately south of enclosure 121. Three layers were defined, the uppermost comprising coarse gravel with silty sand, the middle fill a finer, dark brown silty loam and the lower fill a black silty loam with abundant charcoal and slag. The eight pieces of slag included fragments of a bellows protection block, two pieces of plano-convex hearth bottom and dense slag. Other finds recovered include a substantial part of a grog-tempered jar, and a flint core. The rounded shape of the feature and presence of associated metalworking debris suggest that it may have been a bowl furnace or similar structure.

Fragmentary enclosures in the north of the site

Ditch 793 (Fig. 7.1)

Ditch 793 was 5.2 m long, aligned east-west parallel to the north side of square enclosure 236. Three sections were excavated; the ditch was U-shaped and open, with one recut. Its average width was 0.63 m, and average depth 0.43 m, and fills were mixed. Fifteen sherds of pottery and 14 animal bones (excluding three rabbit bones) were found.

Gully 129 (Fig. 7.1)

Gully 129 ran roughly perpendicular to 793 and may have belonged to the same enclosure. It was aligned NNW-SSE and was over 8 m long, but its extent to the north is uncertain. It was U-shaped and the profile varied from narrow to open. The average width was 0.5 m and the average depth was 0.45 m. Fills consisted of homogeneous sandy-silt loam and the finds comprised 31 sherds (641 g) of pottery, 21 animal bones and one fragment of slag. The pottery consists of grog-tempered wares and earlier Iron Age sherds.

Gully 69 (Fig. 7.1)

This short fragment of NE-SW aligned gully was located towards the northern edge of the excavation to the east of gully 129. It was 0.4 m wide and 0.7 m deep. Fills comprised sandy-silt loams with some greenish material. The few finds from the fill, a fragment of cattle bone and a single sherd in a shell-tempered fabric, suggest secondary deposition of material deriving from the contemporary ground surface.

The western group of possible enclosures

The western group of features consisted of a series of short linear and curvilinear ditches and gullies perhaps representing the remains of several recti-linear enclosures, aligned approximately SE-NW and roughly parallel to one another. They lay north of enclosures 175 and 269, on alignments that related loosely to the orientation of both enclosures. These features did not define identifiable coherent enclosed areas, however, and the irregularity of their plan does not appear to be the result of truncation of the 'missing' parts by later features, as early and late Roman linear features are largely absent from this part of the site. Two or more possible rectilinear enclosures that extended beyond the northern edge of the site, and may have abutted the central enclosures to the east (any possible relationships with these enclosures were removed by later features), were apparent (1560, 1605, 1606, 1672, 1693 and 1697; Fig. 7.1). To the south of these enclosures was a series of sometimes ephemeral straight and curvilinear ditches and gullies (372, 373, 1481, 616, 621, 1737, 578 and 1399), which may indicate the presence of further irregular enclosures.

Ditches 1560, 1605, 1606, 1672, 1693 and 1697 (Fig. 7.1)

A number of linear ditches or gullies, possibly forming a series of WNW-ESE aligned rectilinear enclosures or paddocks, were exposed in the north-west part of the site. The principal WNW-ESE gully was 1697, abutted at its west end by 1672 which ran perpendicular to the south from this point, and by 1693, which ran to the north-east from the same point. A further possible linear feature on the same alignment as 1697 lay west of this feature junction, but was not investigated. Gully 1560 lay parallel to and about 18 m east of 1672, but its junction with 1693 lay outside the excavated area, and the relationship of 1605 and 1606 to 1697 is similarly unknown. These gullies were generally U-shaped and open in form. They varied in size from 1606, the most substantial at 0.7 m wide and 0.3 m deep, to 1605 at only 0.22 m wide and 0.13 m deep, but were on average 0.4 m wide and 0.3 m deep. The small quantities of finds recovered from the fills were in part a reflection of their small size, but also of the absence of obvious domestic activity in the vicinity. Collectively, these features produced 51 sherds (938 g) of pottery, 13 animal bones, and a bone point.

Ditches/gullies 372, 373, 616, 621 and 1481 (Fig. 7.1)

This group of features lay adjacent to the west angle of enclosure 175. The slight gullies 373 and 1481, aligned roughly NNE-SSW, may have been an extension, albeit discontinuous, of the alignment of gully 1605 further north. Gully 621, to the west, was a short semicircular feature, open to the south-west, with an external diameter of *c* 4 m, and was not clearly associated with any adjacent features. It was cut by another less sharply-curving gully (616). This feature can be tentatively associated with the more substantial curving ditch/gully 372 to the north, which itself cut the straight gully 373. Together, 372 and 616 could have been parts of a system of gullies defining a subcircular area *c* 16 m east-west by *c* 13 m north-south.

These features together produced only 13 fragments of animal bone and six sherds of pottery, insufficient to attest to domestic activity in the immediate vicinity, although gully 372 did produce a small amount of charred plant remains.

Ditches 578, 1399 and 1737 (Fig. 7.1)

This group of linear and curvilinear ditches lay west of the features just discussed. It is possible that 1399 and 1737 formed part of a discontinuous boundary, but this is far from certain, nor is it clear how they might have related to the groups of features to their east and north-east. These ditches had U-shaped profiles and were generally *c* 0.65-0.7 m wide and 0.3 m deep. A moderate quantity of pottery (92 sherds weighing 1464 g), one fragment of vitrified clay and 55 animal bones came from the fills. These quantities contrast with those from the group of features to the east and suggest a functional distinction between the two areas.

The eastern group of enclosures (Fig. 7.1)

The eastern group of enclosures was situated south-east of the central enclosures, for the most part separated from them by *c* 15-20 m, although the southern part of this space was occupied by enclosure 341. With the exception of the latter, these enclosures were broadly sub-circular in form. The southernmost enclosure, 391A, was the most substantial, and had clearly been recut a number of times. Recutting continued throughout much of the early Roman period (391B), and the division between the two phases of activity is fairly arbitrary given the potential for redeposition of finds. Within 391A lay a small ring-gully, 357. To the west of 391A, and probably laid out in relation to it, was a fairly large subrectangular enclosure, 341, the north-western corner of which was cut away by the ditches of enclosure 205 belonging to the central group of enclosures. North-east of enclosure 391A was a group of curvilinear ditches, 359, 360 and 975, indicating the presence of a further smaller sub-circular enclosure of several phases. The southernmost of these, 360, contained several lengths of linear ditch and another small oval ditch (923, 925 and 1000). The function of the sub-circular ditches is not clear, but they may have been associated with domestic activity. Their continuing use into the early Roman period is probably significant in itself.

Enclosure 391A and associated features

Enclosure 391A (Figs 7.1 and 7.8)

The early phase of this substantial sub-circular enclosure, located in the south-east corner of the site, measured 18.5 m across and had an approximate internal area of 270 m^2. An entrance was identified on the south side. Approximately 20% of this feature was excavated but multiple recutting obscured the precise sequence. At least four separate cuts appeared to belong to 391A (eg 370, 462, 463 and 464 in Fig. 7.8), but evidence of other cuts is likely to have been destroyed by remodelling during later phases. The ditches were very variable in size; their profiles were generally U-shaped with a width

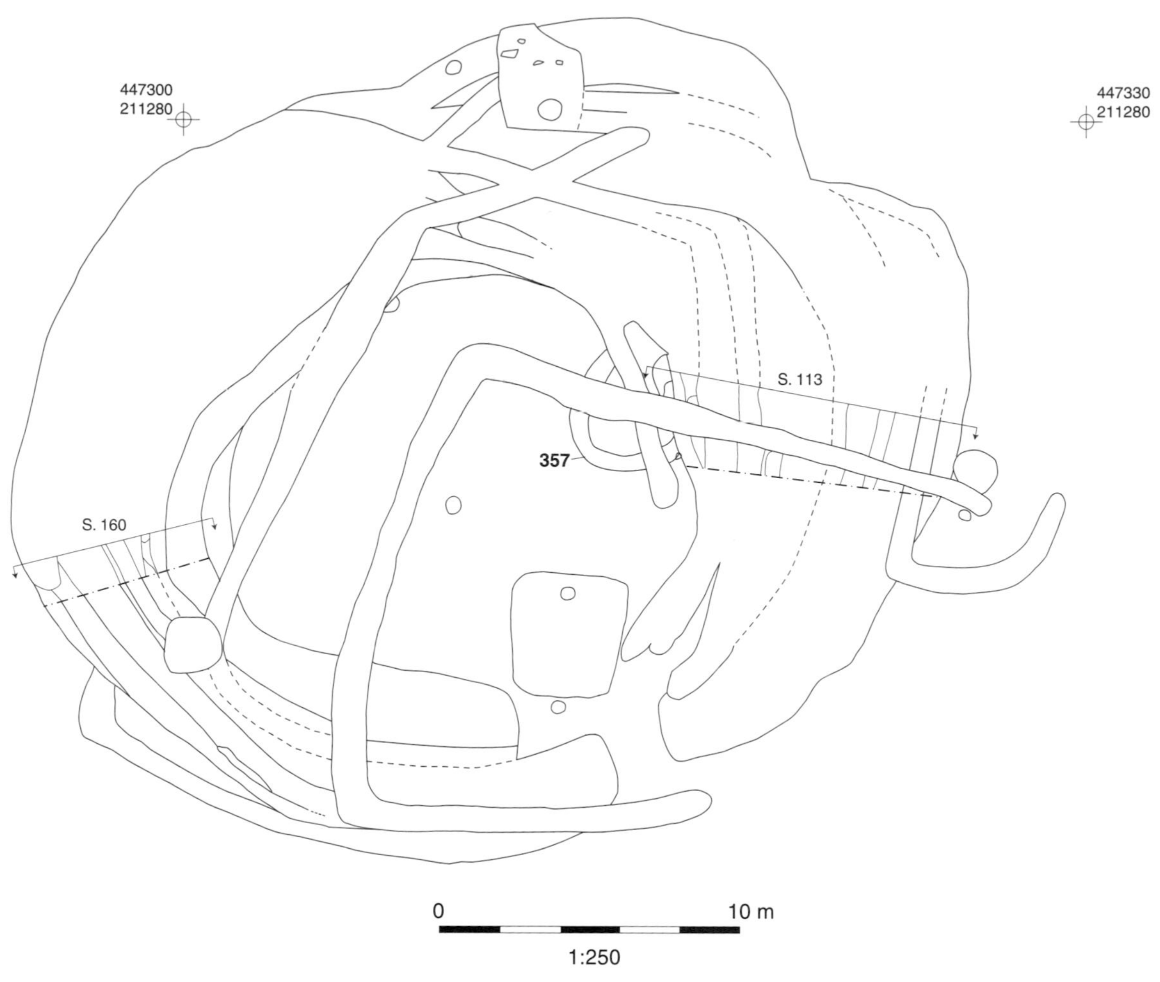

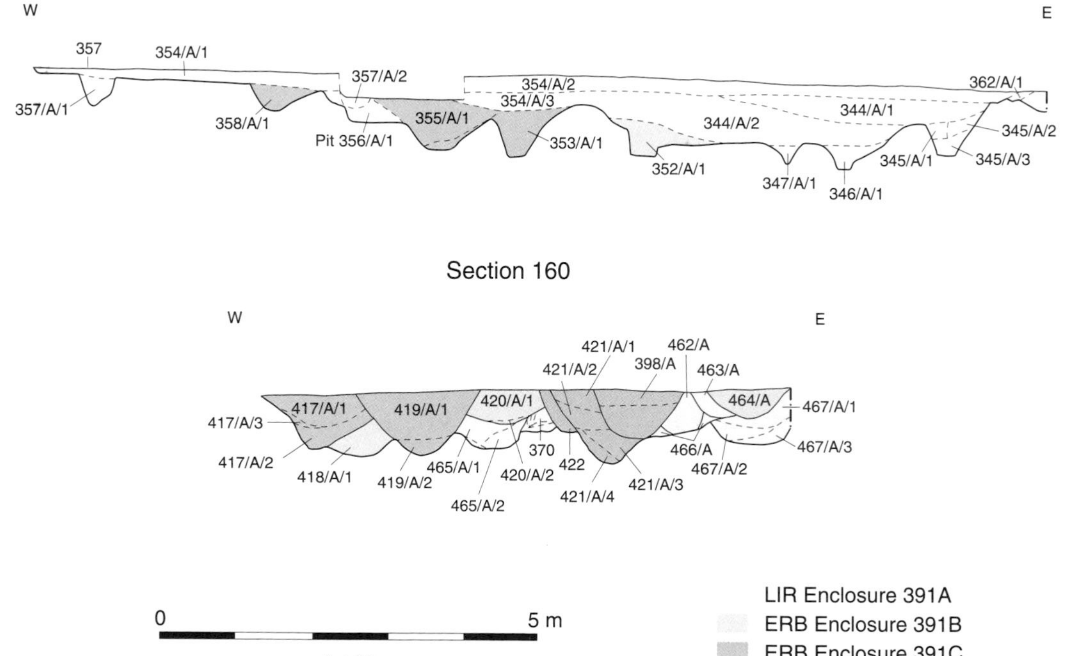

Fig. 7.8 Plan and sections of enclosure 391

range of 0.64-1.2 m and depth of 0.36-1.1 m. Fills consisted of non-gravelly material and silty-loams with gravel. There was some primary silting and burnt material was noted in the lower fill of cut 347.

Fifty-three sherds (1142 g) of pottery were recovered from the fills of 391A. The sherds were relatively well preserved and generally dominated by fabric E80 (grog-tempered) with smaller amounts of other 'Belgic' wares and early Roman types (fabrics E30, E50, C10, O18 and R10). Other finds included eight animal bones, three pieces of metalworking debris and a fragment of a saddle quern (SF 298).

Enclosure 357 (Figs 7.1 and 7.8)

A small penannular ring-gully lay within the area enclosed by enclosure 391A. It measured 4.5 m x 3.2 m and appeared to have an entrance to the north. Two segments, representing 65% of its total length, were excavated revealing a U-shaped profile 0.5 m wide and 0.45 m deep. Fills consisted of non-gravelly material and no finds were recovered.

Enclosure 341 (Fig. 7.1)

This enclosure lay immediately west of enclosure 391A and its east side was probably formed by the west side of 391A, although the precise relationship between the enclosure ditches at the north-east corner of enclosure 341 was obscured by later features. The enclosure was sub-square in plan, with maximum internal dimensions of *c* 22 m east-west and north-south. There appears to have been an opening in the south-east corner, which may have been as much as 6 m across. The enclosure ditch was relatively slight, ranging from 0.4-0.9 m across but no more than 0.38 deep at most. There was no certain evidence of recutting. The non-gravelly loam fills produced 13 sherds (194 g) of late Iron Age and early Roman pottery.

A short length of gully (644) curved north-eastwards from the northern side of enclosure 341 towards the group of ditches and gullies north of enclosure 391A (359 and 360; see below). It is possible that (as ditch 474) this feature extended as far as these ditches and gullies, but some of the pottery from 474 was of later 1st century or later date and it may, instead, have been associated with an early Roman complex of gullies in this area (feature group 293).

Curvilinear enclosures to the north of enclosure 391A

Ditches 359, 360 and 975 (Fig 7.1)

A curvilinear ditch (359), 21.5 m in length, lay north-east of the large enclosure 391A. It may have been part of a sub-circular enclosure 13 m across and open to the south-west. No recuts were observed. The ditch had a U-shaped profile and was 0.7 m wide and 0.5 m deep. Fills consisted of gravel-free material and silty loams with gravel, while some charcoal was present in the fills of the ditch terminals. Ten sherds of pottery (132 g) with a *terminus post quem* in the later 1st century AD were recovered from the fill along with 29 animal bones and three residual flints, suggesting rubbish deposition.

A second curvilinear ditch (975A), 11.5 m long, lay on the same general alignment as 359 and may have been a later recut of that feature, and itself showed evidence for at least two recuts. It was U-shaped in profile with an average width of 0.7 m and a depth of 0.34 m. Fills comprised mixed non-gravelly material, and silty loams with gravel, with some primary silting visible. Nine sherds (44 g) of pottery and eight animal bones from the fill probably represent secondary deposition.

A third curvilinear ditch (360), 20 m long, probably defined a later stage of the same sub-circular enclosure some 10 m across from north to south. The ditch profile was U-shaped and there was no evidence of recutting. The width ranged from 0.45-0.8 m and the depth from 0.31-0.54 m. Two fills were recognised: silty loam with gravel and a gravel-free silty loam. Dumped clay and burnt limestone were present in the upper fill. Seven sherds of pottery (125 g) and four animal bones were recovered.

Like feature 975, ditch 360 cut ditch 359 and, while the absolute sequence of 360 and 975 is unknown, it seems most likely that 975 was earlier than 360, giving a sequence of enclosures of similar character. All of these enclosures were either open or cut away to the west. Oval ditch 923 and several linear features (described below) lay within the enclosed area, but it is not clear to which of its several phases they related.

Other traces of ditches and small enclosures to the north of enclosure 391A

Other traces of ditches and small enclosures were located in, and adjacent to, the area of the smaller curvilinear enclosures, but their relationships with these enclosures are uncertain. On spatial grounds, it is hard to see how feature 1000 could have functioned within these enclosures, and it is suggested that it might have been slightly earlier in date. Oval ditch 923, however, could have been a contemporary internal feature related to any or all phases of the curvilinear enclosures, as could the short length of ditch 925. The more remote feature 498 might have been completely unrelated, although it was broadly contemporary.

Ditch 1000 (Figs 7.1 and 7.9)

Feature 1000 was a short stretch of a substantial east-west aligned ditch, 4 m long. It was cut by oval ditch 923 to the east and by enclosure 391A to the west. Three sections were excavated, revealing a deep and narrow U-shaped profile, 1 m wide and 0.8-1 m deep. Fills were mixed, though generally gravelly, and there was evidence of some primary silting. The fills were particularly rich in pottery,

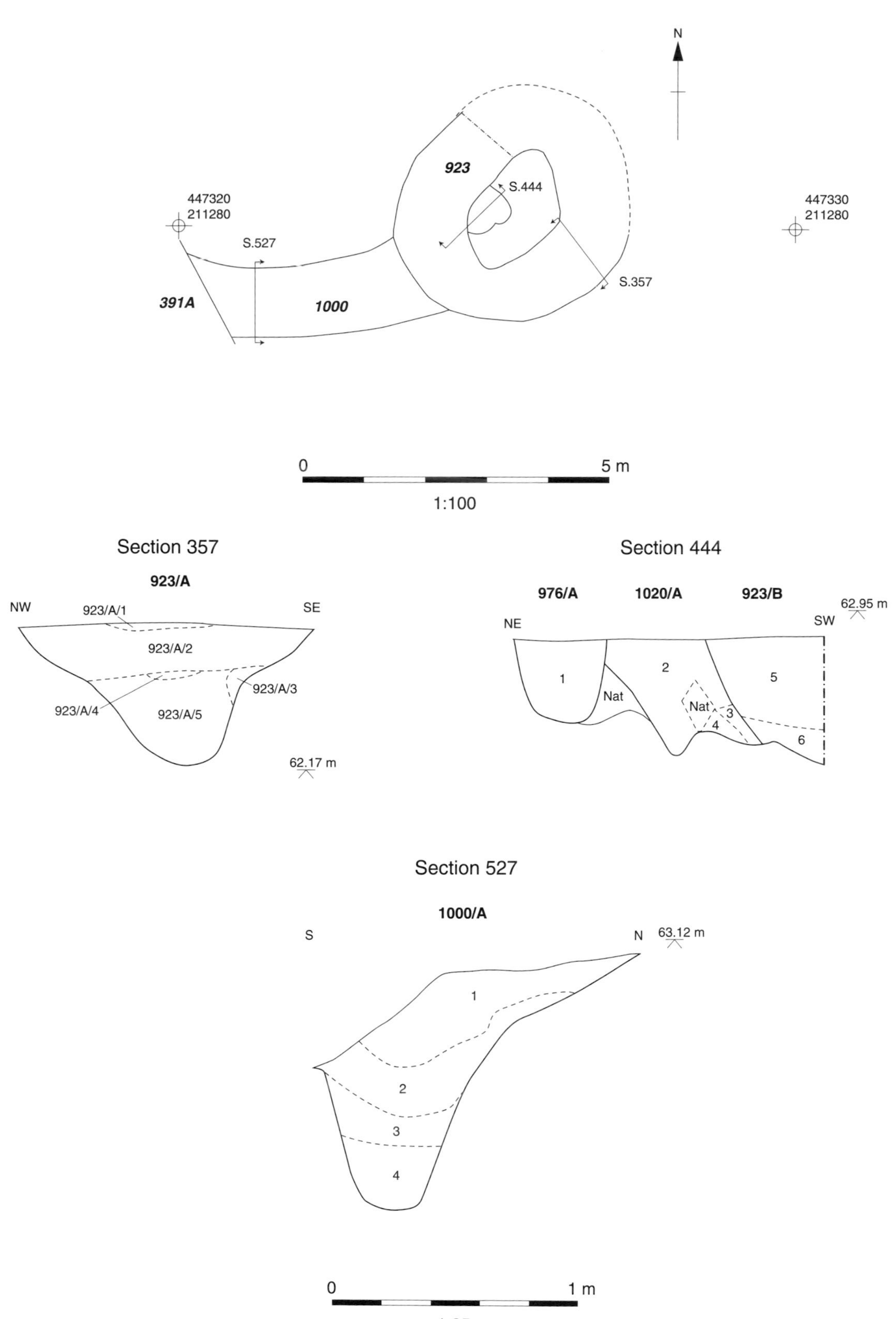

Fig. 7.9 Plan and sections of enclosure 923, associated features and ditch 1000

animal bone and charred plant remains. The 66 fragments of animal bone comprised 29% cattle bone, 20% sheep with some pig, horse and red deer. A pair of sheep mandibles was also noted, possibly part of a special deposit (see Chapter 17 below). Ninety-six sherds of pottery (1850 g) were recovered, of which 36 were earlier Iron Age and the remainder, in fabrics C10, E30, E40 and E80, typical of the late Iron Age. Other finds include several fragments of a fired clay oven plate (SF 302) and a flint arrowhead.

Oval ditch 923 (Figs 7.1 and 7.9)

Ditch 923 was a small oval feature that lay within enclosure 360 (or one of its likely predecessors) and cut linear ditch 1000 (see above). The enclosed area was only 3 m x 2.5 m, and the continuous ditch was quite substantial at 0.5 m deep and 1.1 m wide. The fills were non-gravelly material and silty loams with gravel, interspersed with lenses of ash and burnt pottery. Thirty-five moderately well-preserved sherds (621 g; fabrics C10, E30, E40, E80 and O18), 23 animal bones and a bone gouge (SF 297) from the fills suggest rubbish deposition. The pottery assemblage indicates a mid to later 1st-century AD date for the filling, with little evidence of redeposited material. The size of the ditch in relation to the area enclosed is notable, but overall this feature is closely comparable to two small ring-gullies (23 and 24) of early Roman date lying to the north and interpreted as stack rings.

Ditchs 925 and 498 (Fig. 7.1)

Ditch 925 was a shallow linear feature, 4.15 m long and aligned WNW-ESE, lying north-west of enclosure 923. Two opposing quadrants were excavated, representing 50% of its total length. No recuts were observed, and the profile was U-shaped and 0.6 m wide and 0.2 m deep. Fills consisted of silty loams with gravel containing some quartzite pebbles and limestone. A collection of 13 sherds (333 g) of pottery, mostly of earlier Iron Age date but with one transitional sherd of fabric E40, and four animal bones came from the ditch fill.

Linear ditch 498 lay a short distance to the north-west of 925, and on the same alignment. It was 3 m long and 0.4 m wide. The ditch fill was sterile, although the very disturbed remains of an animal skeleton were found on the machined surface.

Finds distributions from the ditches

The majority of the larger enclosure ditches contained relatively substantial assemblages of finds, mostly animal bone and pottery. The quantities of animal bone and pottery from these ditches were similar in many cases, but enclosure ditch 236 produced far less material than ditch 175 to its south. Both produced substantial quantities of redeposited material, presumably owing to the proximity of the Iron Age settlement and the constant recycling of material. Metalworking debris and other finds were generally scarce, and plant remains were mostly confined to the larger ditches. The smaller ditches were far less productive of finds. The pattern of deposition in some of the ditch fills is suggestive of rubbish disposal, probably deriving from adjacent buildings or activity areas. These finds dumps may indicate the location of demolished buildings. This particularly applies to the area around enclosure 205 and the south-west corner of 175; adjacent to enclosure 923 and ditches 1000 and 391A in the south-east; and the vicinity of enclosure 121 in the east. In contrast, the ditches in the north-west of the settlement, around enclosure 269, or within enclosure 391A and ring-gully 357 in the south-east, produced much smaller quantities of material, which is likely to have derived from the surrounding ground surface.

LATE IRON AGE/EARLY ROMAN PITS

Summary

Fifty pits were assigned to the late Iron Age/early Roman period and were classified, as for the early and middle Iron Age features, according to shape. The majority of the pits were circular or oval in plan, but with a higher proportion of amorphous shapes than was the case for the earlier periods.

Distribution

The spatial distribution of late Iron Age/early Roman pits differed markedly from that of the earlier phases. The pattern was much more dispersed and pits were spread out over the entire extent of the excavated area. Several truncated pits were found below Roman enclosure ditches. There was no clear evidence as to how they related to the settlement layout, nor was there a discernible pattern of clustering around particular, likely building locations.

Description

In general the late Iron Age/early Roman pits tended to be smaller than the early Iron Age and middle Iron Age examples, and the relative proportions of the different pit categories differed from those of the earlier phases. Their dimensions are summarised in Table 7.1.

The pits of this period differed from the earlier examples in that bowl-shaped pits were as common as cylindrical ones. There was also a higher proportion of unclassifiable pits for this period, partly due to extensive disturbance of the features during later periods. Large shallow and shallow saucer-shaped pits were rare. It is apparent that there was also a change in function, with only four candidates for the grain-storage category. A range of pits is illustrated in Figure 7.10.

Fills were represented by five categories of material, ranging from gravel-free to gravelly fills

Table 7.1 Pit dimensions (m) by type (range for those where dimensions were recorded).

Dimensions	*Undercut (GSP)*	*Cylindrical*	*Bowl-shaped*	*Large shallow*	*Shallow saucer*	*Other*	*Total*
Breadth	0.7-0.7	0.6-1.8	0.34-3.1	1.2-2	0.9-0.9	0.37-3	
Depth	0.96-0.96	0.4-1.4	0.15-1.2	0.15-0.35	0.2-0.2	0.16-0.9	
Length	-	1-1.8	0.78-1	-	1.9-1.9	0.3-1.6	
Number	1	13	13	2	1	20	50

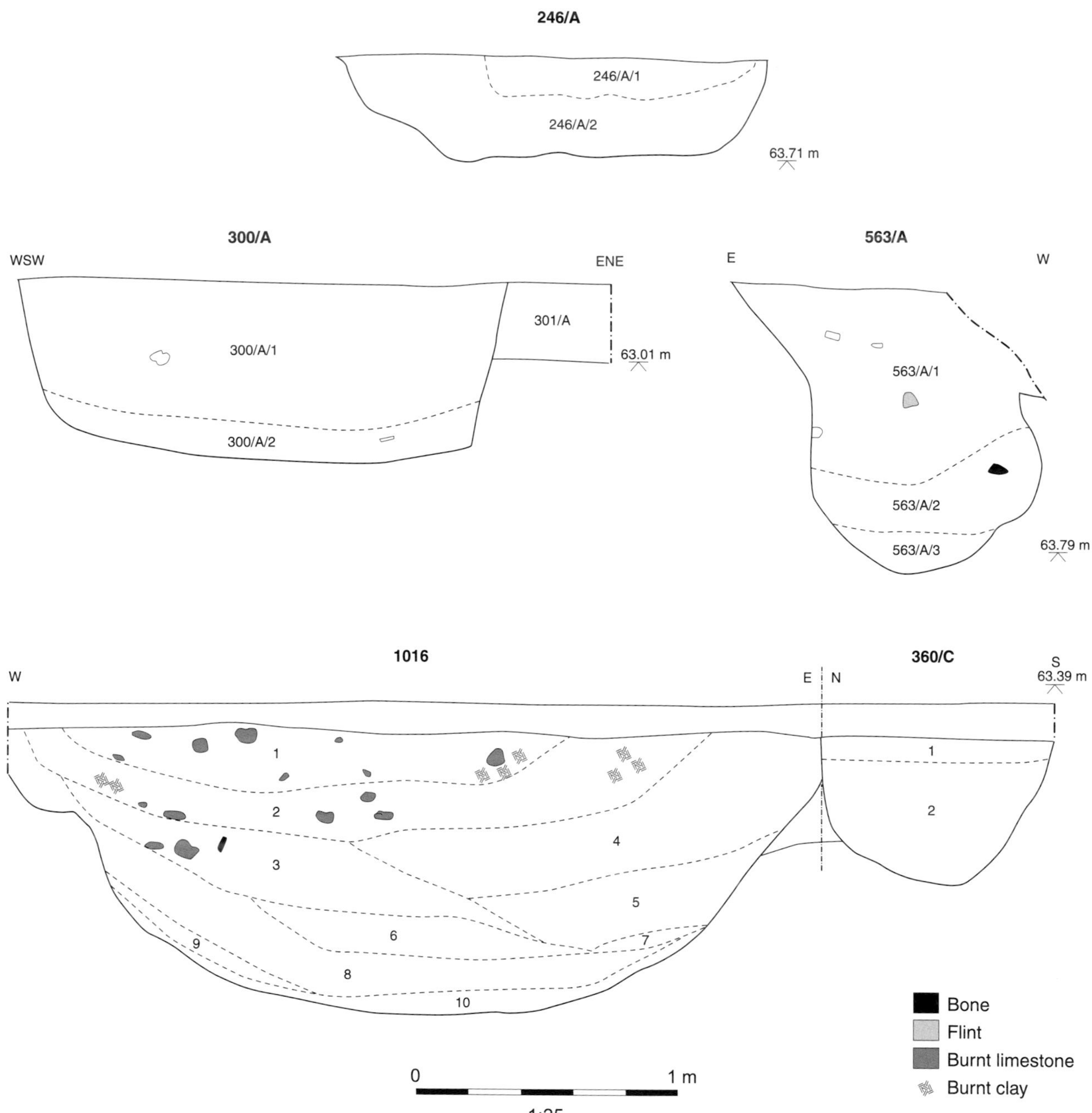

Fig. 7.10 Sections through late Iron Age/early Roman pits 246, 300, 563, 1016 and 360

Table 7.2 Numbers of pit fill types.

Silty loams	*Gravel-free fills*	*Non-gravelly fills*	*Gravelly fills*	*Other*
16	16	13	2	3

(Table 7.2). The number of fills per features ranged from one to 13, but the majority contained one to four fills. Only four pits contained more than five fills and, as in the early and middle Iron Ages, the average number of fills was three. One pit, 913, in the south of the site, was clay lined.

Recutting of late Iron Age/early Roman pits was rare compared to the early and middle Iron Age examples. Only two showed evidence of recutting, a single episode in both cases. Redeposition within pits also appeared to be rare, with 28 pits exhibiting no signs of redeposition at all. This is significant in the context of a high level of redeposition observed within the enclosure ditches and gullies over much of the site. Primary silting was found in ten pits, a figure comparable to that for the early Iron Age and middle Iron Age periods. Only three pits had evidence of deliberate backfilling, and two of these were very large, at 6.30 m^3 and 2.15 m^3 respectively. Of the six pits which were over 0.8 m^3 in volume, four contained rubbish deposits.

Artefact distributions in pits (Fig. 7.11)

Animal bone

Of the 50 pits assigned to the late Iron Age/early Roman period, 29 contained deposits of animal bone, one of which, 1016, also contained human bone (Table 7.3). The majority of pits contained the remains of one or more of the major domestic species, and two pits produced dog bones and two wild bird. The rabbit bones recovered are assumed to be intrusive. The less common species were more sparsely distributed in the late Iron Age/early Roman than in the two preceding periods, and the range of wild animal species present in this phase is also smaller. These patterns in part reflect the generally sparser distribution of bone in this period. Of note is a dog skeleton from pit 1608.

Table 7.3 Occurrence of animal bone in pits.

Species	*No. of pits*
Sheep/goat	16
Sheep/pig size	18
Cattle	20
Cattle/horse size	14
Horse	4
Pig	12
Dog	2
Wild bird	2
Rabbit	3

Late Iron Age/early Roman pits with substantial deposits of animal bones representing a wide range of species were also less common than in the earlier periods, and only 13 pits contained bones deriving from all of the major domestic species. This seems to reflect the general scarcity of bone in this period. There was no clear association between horse bone and dog bone, or between human bone and dog bone, as was the case for the earlier pit assemblages. Both dog and horse bones were generally found within pits containing a high proportion of bone of other species.

The spatial analysis of animal bone distribution indicated that there were few differences between species, and the pattern mirrored that of the distribution of the pits in general. Cattle bone, the most common type, was predominantly present in the eastern part of the site, although the pits in which it was found generally also contained bones from other species.

Pottery

Thirty-five late Iron Age/early Roman pits contained pottery. The combined pottery assemblage consisted of 331 sherds, and the average number of sherds per pit was nine. In general, pottery was relatively sparse in comparison to the earlier phases, mirroring the size of the animal bone assemblage. The plotting of mean sherd weight against sherd count revealed that the majority of pits contained small numbers of small and abraded sherds, and few pits contained either large numbers of smaller sherds or small numbers of large unabraded sherds. This suggests that few pits acted as foci of deliberate deposition.

A comparison of mean sherd weight and count with bone count suggests a disparity between contexts containing large amounts of bone and those containing large sherds or large quantities of sherds (Fig. 7.12). It seems that there were no late Iron Age/early Roman pits either with large quantities of pottery or large fresh sherds, which also contained large quantities of animal bone. Analysis of the distribution of pottery did, however, reveal some association between pits containing a wide range of animal species and significant deposits of pottery: those pits containing over 28 sherds of pottery tended also to contain bone derived from all the major domestic animals and, additionally, one contained dog bone and one contained fragments of human bone. Pits containing 10-28 sherds showed less significant associations. These data may, however, simply reflect a correlation between greater assemblage diversity and larger assemblage size.

Plant remains

Six of the 50 late Iron Age/early Roman pits, four of them cylindrical and two bowl-shaped, were

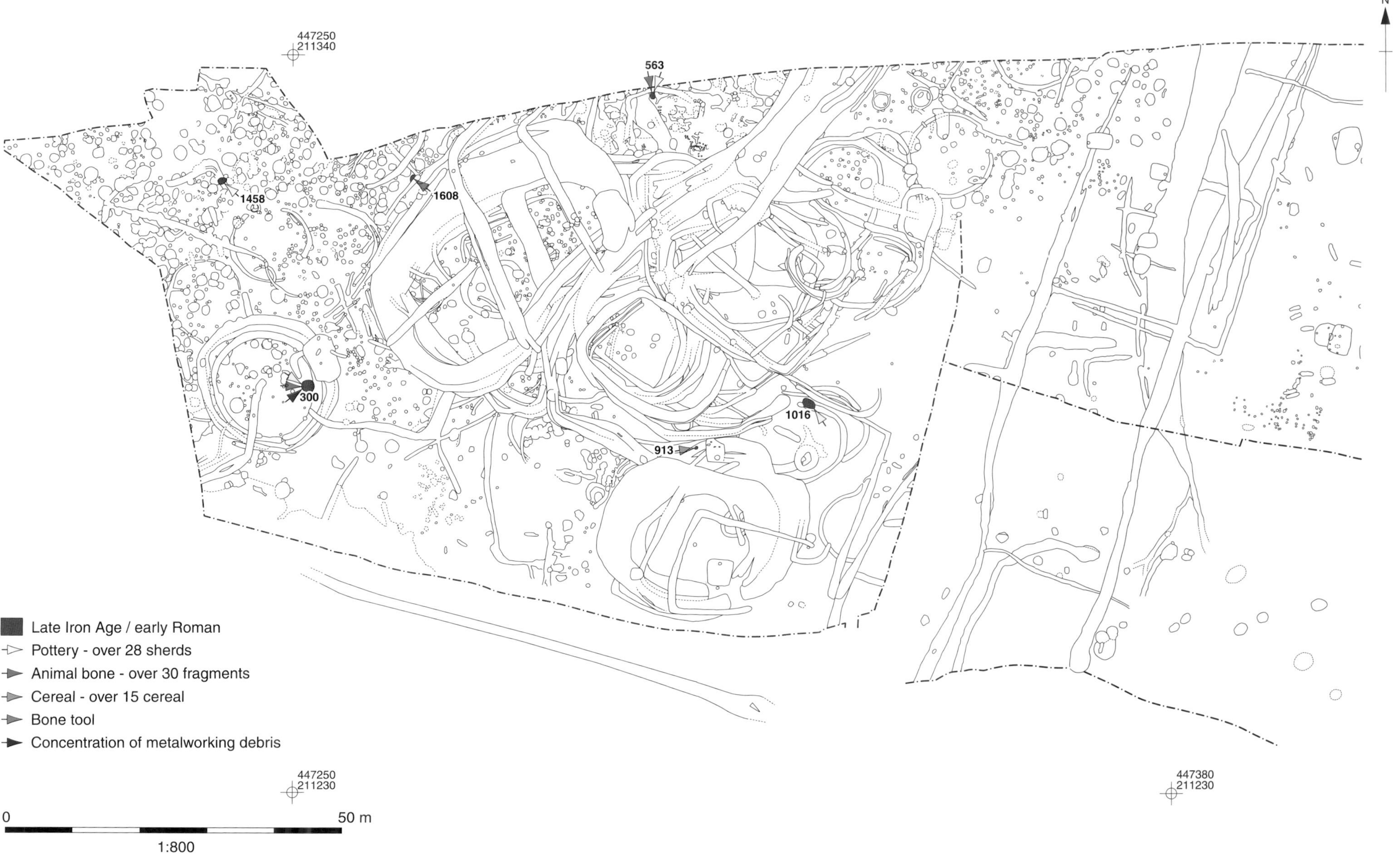

Fig. 7.11 Artefact distribution of substantial deposits and other finds in late Iron Age/early Roman pits

Table 7.4 Quantities of charred plant remains by pit type.

Pit type	*Cylindrical*	*Bowl shaped*	*Total*
No. pits sampled	4	2	6
Cereals	21	19	40
Chaff	41	9	50
Weed seeds	27	27	54
Ave no. cereals per sampled pit	5.25	9.5	6.7

sampled for plant remains. Two of the pits were over 0.80 m^3 in volume, and their average volume was 1.655 m^3 (the average original volume of all pits was 0.656 m^3). Plant remains included cereal grains, weed seeds and chaff, but the quantities were considerably smaller than for earlier periods, and weed seeds were much more uncommon. Clay-lined pit 913 was the most productive. Proportions of cereals to chaff were high in bowl-shaped features, but quantities are too small to draw useful

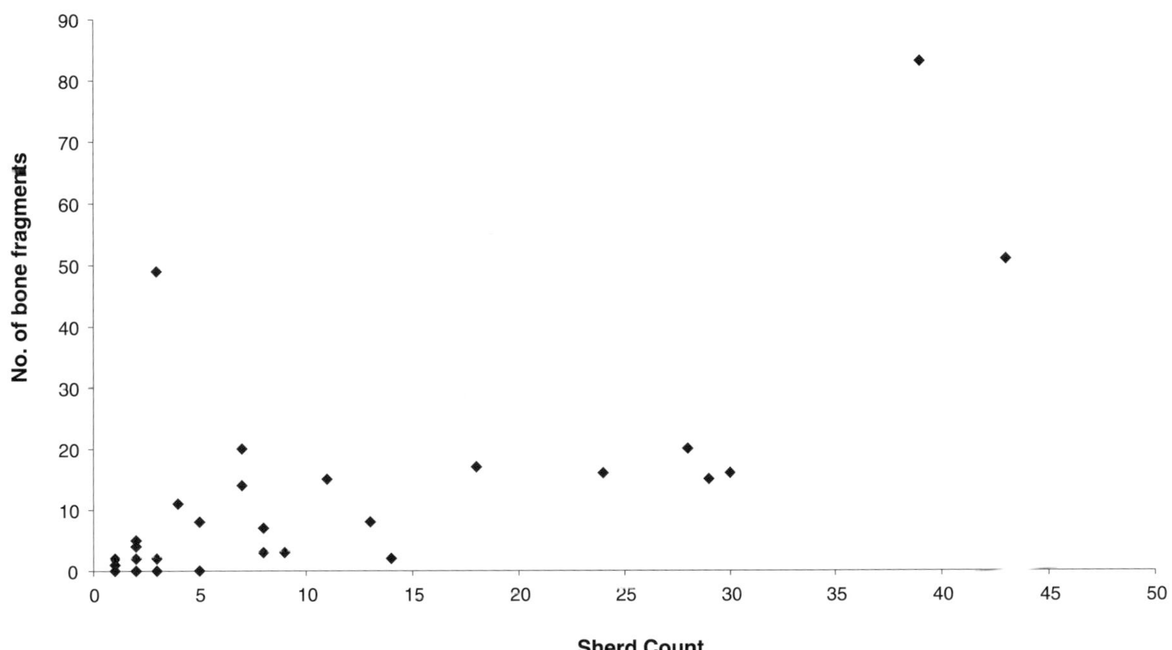

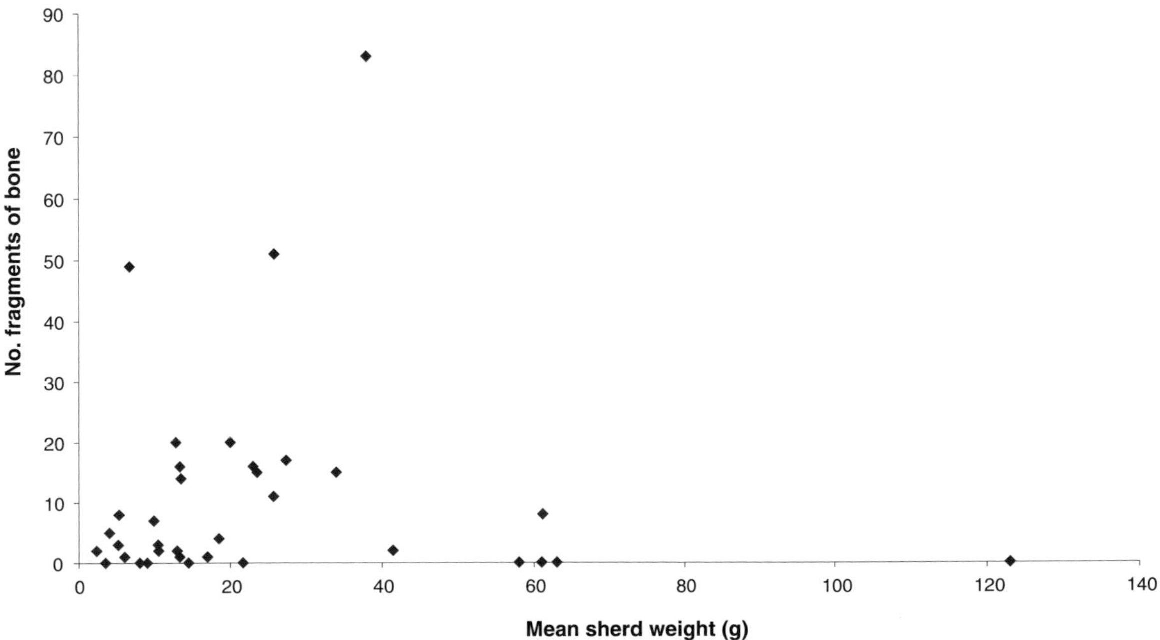

Fig. 7.12 Plot of sherd count against bone fragment count and mean sherd weight against bone fragment count in late Iron Age/early Roman pits

conclusions (Table 7.4). The plant material tended to be concentrated in pits with more varied animal remains and in pits with more substantial assemblages of pottery.

Metalworking debris

Three fragments of metalworking debris were recovered from late Iron Age/early Roman phase pits, two of unclassified dense slag and one fragment of hearth bottom. They were found in a cylindrical, a bowl-shaped and an amorphous pit (300, 662 and 954), in the south-west and south-central part of the site. One of the pits, 300, lay next to rectangular feature 594 (see above).

Other Finds

Other finds were extremely sparse. Twelve pits yielded mostly small, amorphous fragments of fired clay or redeposited flint flakes. These objects were found in both cylindrical and bowl-shaped pits, slightly more coming from cylindrical features. A bone leaze rod (SF 460), the only worked bone find, came from pit 300, which also contained metal-working debris.

Chapter 8: The Early Roman Period

by Dan Stansbie with a contribution by Paul Booth

INTRODUCTION

The early Roman period at Yarnton was characterised by the construction of more and larger ditched enclosures which became more rectilinear through time (Fig. 8.1). These can be seen to develop from the late Iron Age/early Roman layout. A large enclosure, 187, in the centre of the site encompassed two of the largest earlier (late Iron Age/early Roman) enclosures, 175 and 236, and to its east several smaller enclosures were constructed, and frequently recut on slightly different alignments (Fig. 8.2). To the south of these a large circular enclosure 391, first constructed in the late Iron Age/early Roman period, was recut on several occasions. The number of more ephemeral ditches and gullies defining ancillary enclosures also increased. To the east a substantial north-south aligned ditch, 2593, was dug which appeared to define the eastern limit of the Roman settlement. The truncated remains of two pottery kilns dated to the early Roman period. For the purposes of description the sequence of early Roman enclosures has been divided into two phases on general stratigraphic grounds, but these phases are not seen as coherent entities; rather they represent relative stages in the development of the site plan at this time. Features assigned to either of the two phases of this period in different parts of the site will not necessarily have been closely contemporary.

THE EARLY ROMAN STRUCTURES

Summary

As in the late Iron Age, there was no evidence of any domestic or other substantial structures dating to the early Roman period. The only structural evidence consisted of a small area of stone spread (385) made up of limestone blocks, situated just to the north of a substantial circular ditched enclosure which occupied the south-eastern corner of the site, and two pottery kilns lying on the east side of the settlement. The absence of buildings is surprising, given the obvious intensity of occupation shown by the numerous and frequently recut ditched enclosures dating to this period. It is probable that, as in the late Iron Age/early Roman period, buildings were of mass-wall or sill-beam construction, and therefore did not leave any trace in the archaeological record (see above, Chapter 7, for a more detailed discussion of this).

Stone Spread 385 (Figs 8.1 and 8.3)

Structure 385 consisted of a linear spread of limestone aligned east-west, measuring approximately 2.7 m by 0.9 m. It was made up of closely-packed limestone blocks, the largest of which measured approximately 0.5 m by 0.24 m, and there was a slight suggestion of an edge on the south-west side. Removal of the stones in the eastern half of the structure revealed an irregular bedding of yellow mortar. Beneath the stones in the south-east corner was a layer of reddish-brown gravel, possibly burnt. No finds were recovered.

POTTERY KILNS *by Paul Booth*

The truncated remains of two pottery kilns (2525 and 2526), broadly of early Roman date, were revealed in the course of the salvage work at Yarnton. Situated some 20 m apart at the eastern margin of the early Roman settlement (Fig. 8.1), the kilns were of similar type, with double flues/stokeholes and a large central pedestal.

Kiln 2525 (Figs 8.4-8.6)

This kiln was aligned east-west, with a maximum length of *c* 2.4 m and an internal width of *c* 0.8 m. The eastern part of the kiln, and particularly its eastern stokehole, cut a backfilled ditch (2524) of middle Iron Age date, while the remainder of the structure was set in a shallow cut in the natural gravel subsoil. The central firing chamber was oval in plan, *c* 1.05-1.2 m east-west and *c* 0.8 m north-south. Within it was a central oval pedestal of fired clay with maximum dimensions of 0.66 m x 0.42 m, surviving up to *c* 0.26 m above the level of the firing chamber floor. The pedestal was constructed above a slight rise in the natural gravel left in the base of the construction pit of the kiln. A thin band of ashy loam sandwiched between the gravel and the pedestal might just represent the remains of an earlier phase of kiln structure, but the on-site interpretation of this deposit as representing animal disturbance may be more likely.

Evidence of possible animal and/or root disturbance apart, the natural sandy gravel base of the firing chamber appears to have been lined with a thin layer of clay (poorly preserved in places) which was contiguous with the solid clay structure of the pedestal and with the clay walls of the firing chamber. The latter ranged typically from 0.16-0.22 m in thickness, of which a 15-40 mm thick surface zone

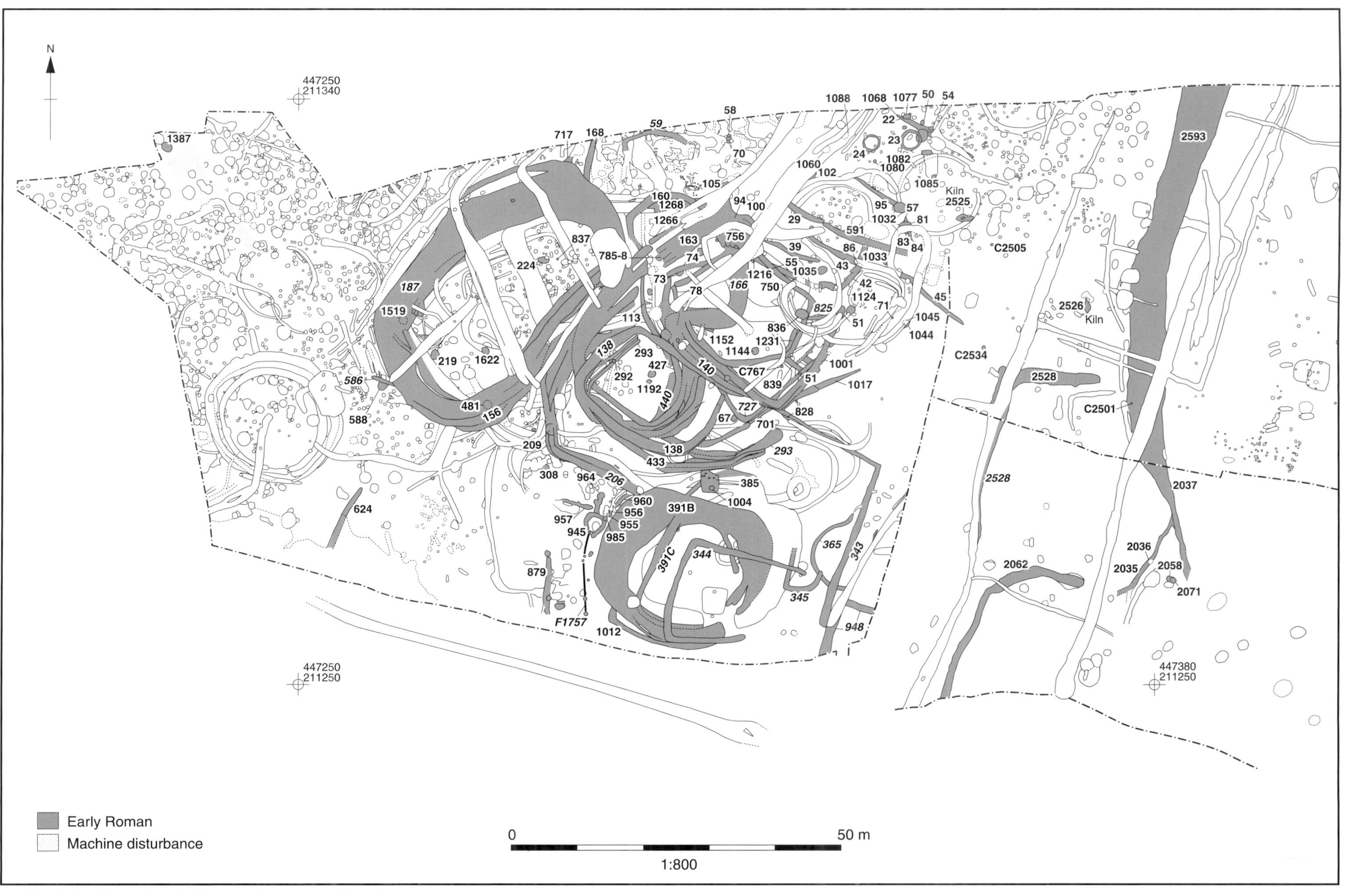

Fig. 8.1 Plan of early Roman features at Yarnton

Fig. 8.2 General view of early Roman enclosures looking north-west

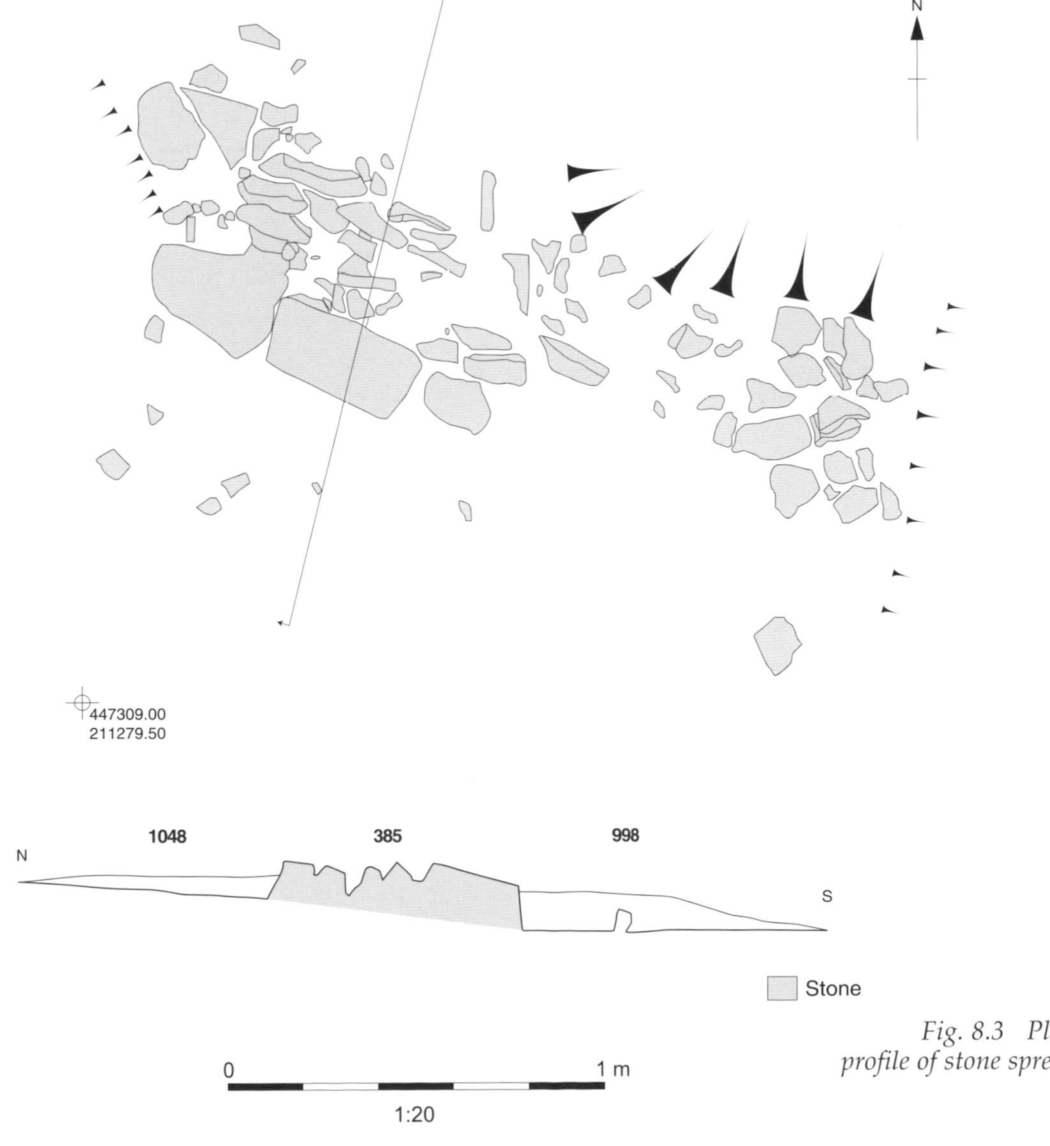

Fig. 8.3 Plan and profile of stone spread 385

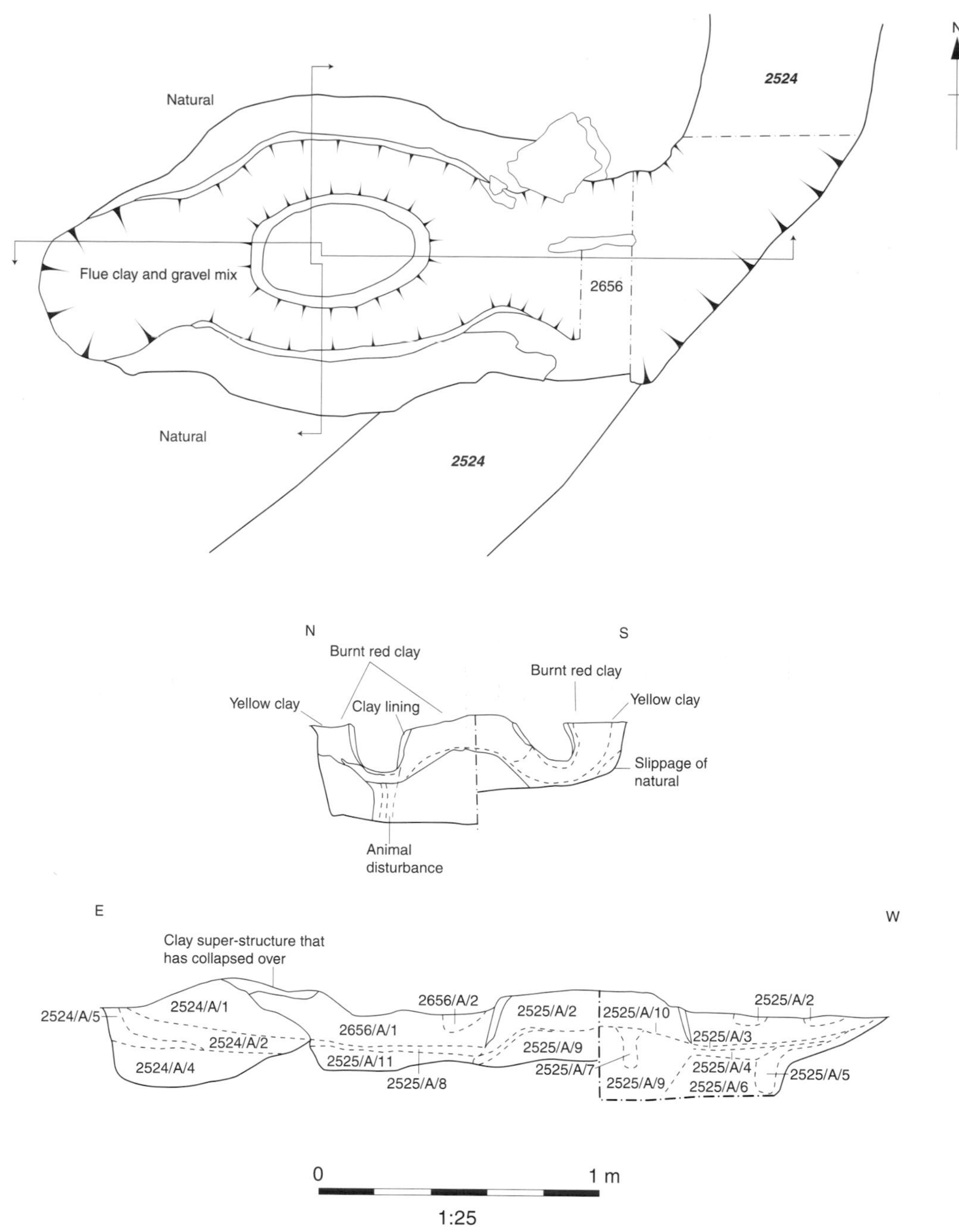

Fig. 8.4 Plan and sections of pottery kiln 2525

was characteristically reduced to a pale grey while the remainder varied from pink to yellow in colour. The surviving lower parts of the channels to north and south of the central pedestal were of irregular U-shaped section, but the sides of the pedestal itself were fairly regular, sloping slightly to give a profile tapering from base to top.

At their east and west ends the kiln walls splayed slightly, with the result that the junctions between the firing chamber and the flues were not clearly defined and any distinction between flues and stokeholes was completely unclear. It is perhaps most likely that only part of the flues survived and that the stokeholes were originally very shallow features, subsequently completely removed by plough (and perhaps other) truncation. The flues thus had the appearance (in plan) almost of apsidal projections from each end of the kiln structure. Their approximate dimensions were *c* 0.5 m x 0.5 m for the west flue and *c* 0.7 m (east-west) x 0.55 m for the east flue. Both were fairly shallow, with bases sloping up gradually from the level of the base of the firing chamber. The openings between flues and firing chamber were between 0.3 m and 0.4 m wide. While it is not particularly clear what form these openings took, some evidence for the reinforcement of the 'flue arch' is provided by the presence of two blocks of limestone up to 0.32 m x 0.24 m at the east

Fig. 8.5 Excavation of pottery kiln 2525

end of the northern side of the firing chamber wall.

The lowest fills within the kiln (2525/11 to the east and 2525/4 and 2525/5 to the west) were perhaps disturbed deposits at the interface of the natural and the base of the structure, the first two consisting of sandy gravel with an admixture of ash, while 2525/5 may have represented either further animal/root disturbance or (just possibly) the fill of a stakehole. These deposits were sealed by the mixed clay, ash and charcoal layer interpreted as the main 'floor' of the firing chamber (2525/3 and 2525/8). Above this was the principal fill of the kiln and flues, 2656/1, a layer of dark grey loam with ash, incorporating fired and unfired clay fragments (the latter defined separately as 2656/2) together with small quantities of pottery (13 sherds, 223 g). This fill had a maximum surviving depth of 0.16 m.

Some 29 fragments (991 g) of fired clay were recovered from the kiln structure and its fill. All but one of these were in heavily organic-tempered fabrics and were of variable thickness, in a range from 10-28 mm, generally with irregular surfaces. These characteristics are consistent with the use of these fragments as part of the temporary capping of the kiln structure. The one exception was a single fragment in an organic and sand-tempered fabric. This was a broken part of a squared object, with incomplete dimensions of 55 mm x 31 mm x 65 mm length. It may have been from a firebar, though its fragmentary nature makes this interpretation extremely tentative.

Kiln 2526 (Figs 8.1 and 8.7)

This kiln was aligned north-south, with a maximum length of *c* 2.25 m and a maximum internal width of *c* 0.9 m. The central firing chamber was constructed above an oval pit of irregular profile, with

Fig. 8.6 View of pottery kiln 2525 from the south

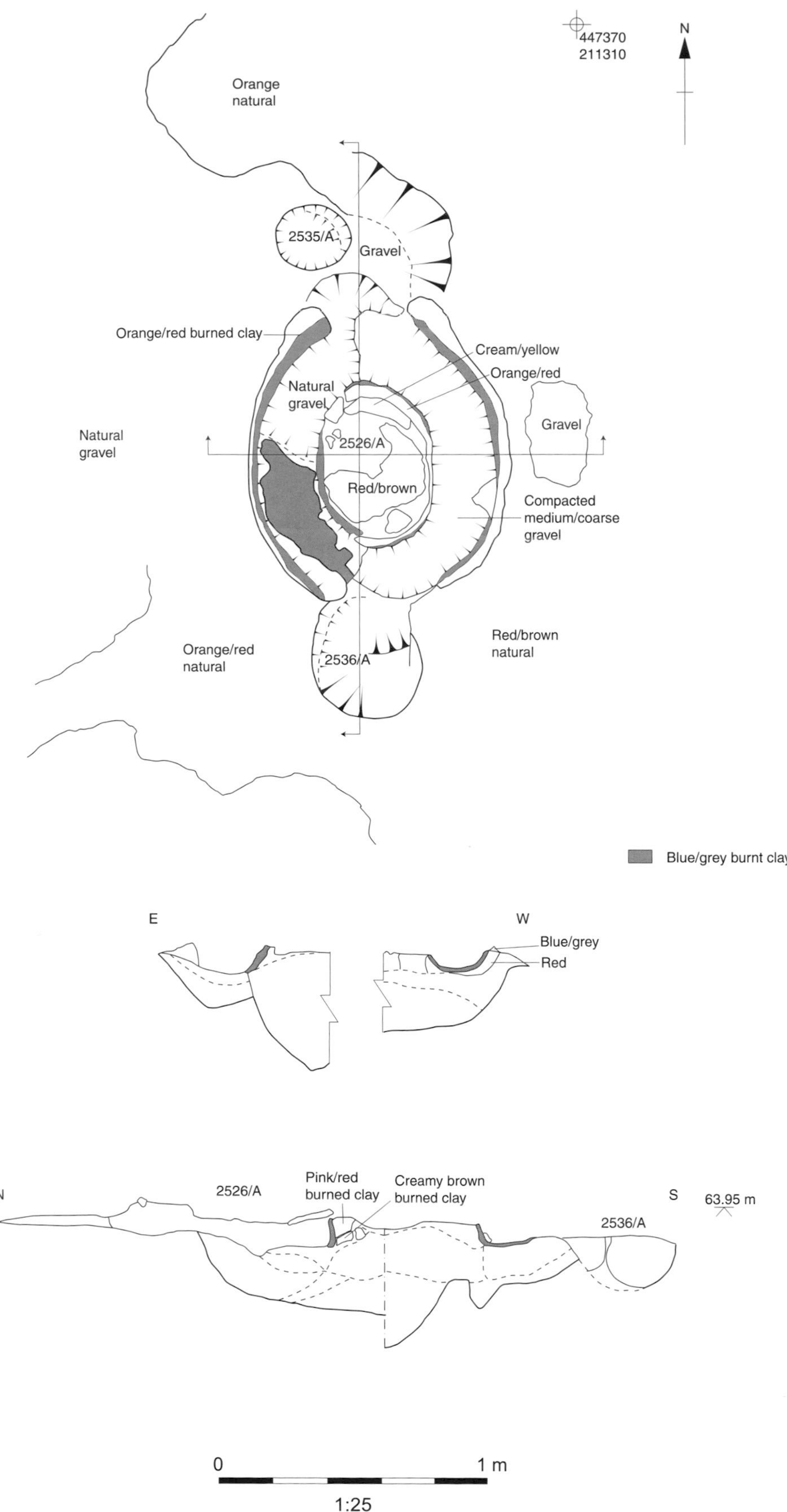

Fig. 8.7 Plan and sections of pottery kiln 2526

maximum dimensions of *c* 1.45 m x 1.15 m and up to *c* 0.3 m deep below the level of the base of the kiln structure. The sterile silty loams, sands and gravels filling this presumed feature or group of features do not shed much light on its interpretation. It is possible that the pit represented an earlier phase of kiln activity from which any structural components had been completely removed, but the clean nature of its fills does not support this suggestion.

The extant structure of the kiln only survived to a maximum depth of *c* 0.12. The firing chamber was oval in plan, with a maximum width of *c* 0.9 m and an estimated length of *c* 1.1 m. The centre of this area was occupied by a substantial oval pedestal with maximum dimensions of 0.62 m x 0.42 m. The sides of the pedestal and the base and walls of the firing chamber were lined with a thin layer of clay (rarely more than 20 mm thick) fired to a blue-grey colour. In parts of the base of the firing chamber this deposit did not survive and had presumably been worn away by repeated raking out of the kiln. At one point on the west of the firing chamber the heavily-fired lining was backed by a thicker deposit, up to *c* 40 mm, of oxidised fired clay. This indicates that the firing chamber walls were more substantially constructed than would appear. This is very likely, and it is presumed that the upper parts of these clay walls would have been quite thick, as was the case in kiln 2525. It is less clear if the upper part of the pedestal would have been entirely of clay or if this feature would simply have had a clay capping – the former is perhaps more likely but the surviving core of the pedestal was of gravelly loam. The level of truncation of the kiln is such that the profile of the firing chamber walls and pedestal are unknown. The surviving fragments mostly sloped quite gently, but again it is presumed that chamber and pedestal sides would have been approximately vertical, as is indicated by the best preserved face of the pedestal, on its north side. The height of the pedestal and chamber walls is of course unknown, though slight hints that burning extended towards the core of the pedestal might suggest that the level at which this feature was truncated was not far below its top. It might therefore not have been much more than *c* 0.2 m high.

There were small flues/stokeholes to north and south of the firing chamber, although as with kiln 2525 it is likely that the stokeholes proper were very shallow and had been completely lost. Both flues were rounded in plan, with extant diameters of approximately 0.45 m for the southern flue and 0.7 m for the northern one. The base of the northern flue sloped up very gently from the base level of the firing chamber. Its relationship to a fairly well-defined but shallow, circular feature (2535), perhaps a posthole, is unclear, but 2535 may have been later than the flue. The southern flue (2536) appeared to be deeper than the northern one and more rounded in profile (up to 0.2 m deep) with a dark grey clayey loam fill. It is possible, however, that the latter belonged to an earlier feature, though its description is the same as that of the fill of the rest of the kiln. The loam was sealed by 'a very thin crust of burnt clay', which might indicate a surviving floor sealing an earlier feature beneath the flue, but it might equally describe a smear of structural debris dragged across the kiln fill by post-Roman ploughing. If it is assumed that the deeper fill did belong to another feature, the southern flue would have been very shallow, which is consistent with its impracticably small surviving extent. In neither case was there any indication that the flue was a very substantial feature indicating a formally defined distinction between firing chamber and stokehole; in effect it is possible that both stokeholes opened almost straight from the chamber wall, the openings being roughly 0.3-0.4 m across.

The principal surviving fill of both firing chamber and flues/stokeholes (2526/A/1) was a dark grey clayey loam. This contained a mere five sherds (25 g) of pottery. The similar fill 2537/A/1, located in the eastern part of the firing chamber, produced a single sherd (27 g) of Oxford colour-coated ware that was clearly intrusive. A total of 37 fragments of fired clay, weighing 2137 g, was recovered from the fill of the kiln and from flue/stokehole 2536. Almost without exception this material was from flattish pieces of variable thickness in heavily organic-tempered fabrics. These are interpreted as deriving from temporary capping of the top of the kiln. No significant fragments of permanent kiln structure or of other moveable kiln furniture were present.

Discussion of kilns 2525 and 2526

The structures

The Yarnton kilns are very similar in their overall size, plan and details of pedestal shape and of the relationship of the small flues or flue/stokeholes to the firing chamber. In view of these similarities there can be little doubt that the kilns are relatively closely contemporary, even though precise dating evidence is lacking. On this basis the discussion of characteristics of one kiln will be assumed to apply to both.

The presence of a small fragment of a possible firebar in kiln 2525 is probably significant. This suggests that the vessels to be fired were supported on firebars that stretched from the pedestal to a ledge in the firing chamber wall. This would have been above the level at which the kilns survived. The height of the top of the pedestal above firing chamber base level can be estimated as at least 0.25 m, and could have been rather more. The height of the firing chamber walls is, of course, unknown. The upper part of the kiln structure was presumably open and the load given a temporary capping each time the kiln was fired. The characteristic remains of this process, in the form of heavily organic tempered, rough flat 'plates', formed the majority of the fired clay recovered from the kiln fills and are widely encountered in Oxford industry production sites (Young 1977, 34, 37-8; Booth *et al.* 1993, 134; Booth and Edgeley-Long 2003, 244-5).

The most striking characteristic of the Yarnton kilns is their twin flue arrangement. In the Oxford region this is unparalleled except probably at Kiln C at Overdale, Boars Hill (Harris and Young 1974, 16-17), assigned to the first half of the 2nd century, though here there does not seem to have been a well-defined central pedestal in the manner of the Yarnton kilns. Such a feature was very evident in kiln I at Hanborough (Sturdy and Young 1976, 57-8), a kiln which, apart from having only a single flue, was in other respects quite reminiscent of the Yarnton examples, both in the use of firebars to provide a temporary floor and in the relatively small size of the stokehole area. This kiln is dated to the third quarter of the 1st century AD (ibid., 63).

Single-chambered twin-flued kilns are well known in Roman Britain and occur in different places throughout the period (Swan 1984, 117-20). First- and second-century examples, however, are particularly common in Wiltshire, being found in the Savernake and North Wiltshire industries. Central pedestals are not well-evidenced in these kilns, but did occur in kiln 4 at Savernake and may also perhaps be inferred for kiln 1 there (Annable 1962; cf Anderson 1979, fig. 3). These provide some of the closest parallels for the Yarnton kilns and were probably broadly contemporary with them, being assigned to the later 1st century AD (Anderson 1979, 5).

As already mentioned it is likely that the load in the Yarnton kilns was carried on firebars. It is worth noting, however, that the only other local example of a twin flued kiln, Overdale (Boars Hill) Kiln C, is thought not to have had a raised floor, but rather the pots were stacked against the long central pedestal (Young 1977, 40-41). There is no direct evidence that this happened, but this technique had certainly been used in the adjacent Overdale Kiln B, in which the pots were recovered still stacked on the base of the firing chamber around a slight rise in the centre (Harris and Young 1974, 14-15 and plate 1). Despite the use of two flues/stokeholes, however, the Overdale C kiln is in other respects quite dissimilar to the Yarnton ones (in proportions, size of flues, pedestal form and method of load support) and is therefore of little relevance as a close parallel.

Products and date

The quantities of pottery recovered from the kilns were very small indeed and allow neither precise characterisation nor close dating of the material being produced within them. This is discussed in detail elsewhere (Booth Chapter 14). It is most likely, however, that the products were of a transitional character, falling at the point of change from the regional late Iron Age and early post-Conquest 'Belgic type' tradition to a more 'Romanised' technology, particularly with regard to fabrics. While its paucity is problematic, the material from Yarnton does have both general and specific parallels with pottery from Cassington kiln 2 (Case 1982a, 134-6) and Long Hanborough (Sturdy and Young 1976). These characteristics, together with the structural similarities noted between the Yarnton kilns and Hanborough Kiln I, and the physical proximity of these sites, suggest that they can all be placed in the same phase of the developing regional ceramic tradition. On this basis the third quarter of the 1st century AD dating applied to Hanborough Kiln I, or the slightly broader date for Cassington Kiln 2 'in the second half of the 1st century' (Young 1982, 146) may be applicable to the Yarnton kilns. While the evidence from the latter may be insufficient in itself to sustain such a close date it is, within its limitations, perfectly consistent with it.

THE EARLY ROMAN ENCLOSURES

Summary

The development of ditched enclosures, begun during the late Iron Age/early Roman period, continued and intensified in the early Roman period. These enclosures can be divided spatially and, to some extent, chronologically. The earliest, most prominent, and probably most long-lived enclosures were those modelled on late Iron Age enclosures: 156/187 in the north-west and 391B in the south-east of the Yarnton site (Fig. 8.1). Between them, and probably also forming part of this first phase of early Roman settlement layout, was enclosure 206, and enclosures 166 and 160 to the east of enclosure 187 also seem likely to have been part of this early group. They were all oval or sub-rectangular in shape and were frequently recut on the same line.

At a later stage, enclosure 206 seems to have gone out of use and been replaced by sub-oval and sub-rectangular enclosures of various sizes (440 etc and then 138), perhaps as 391B and 187 were enlarged. Enclosures 166 and 160 were also abandoned, and a series of sub-rectangular enclosures (51, 55, 74 etc) was laid out to the north of and abutting a right-angled linear ditch (343 and 828) which ran into the settlement area from the south-east corner of the main excavation area. Thus this series of enclosures, sometimes only recognised as fragments of linear ditch, defined two contiguous enclosure areas, initially represented by two linked sub-circular enclosures on the south-western side (156/187 and 391B), with a series of shifting sub-rectangular enclosures lying in and north-east of the space between these features.

Numerous stretches of linear and curvilinear ditches to the south, north and east of the central enclosures indicated ancillary enclosures or paddocks, one of which (344) cut the large sub-circular enclosure to the south-east. There were also at least two small ring-gullies (23, 24) to the north-east, possibly stack rings, and a similar though not completely closed structure to the south (945).

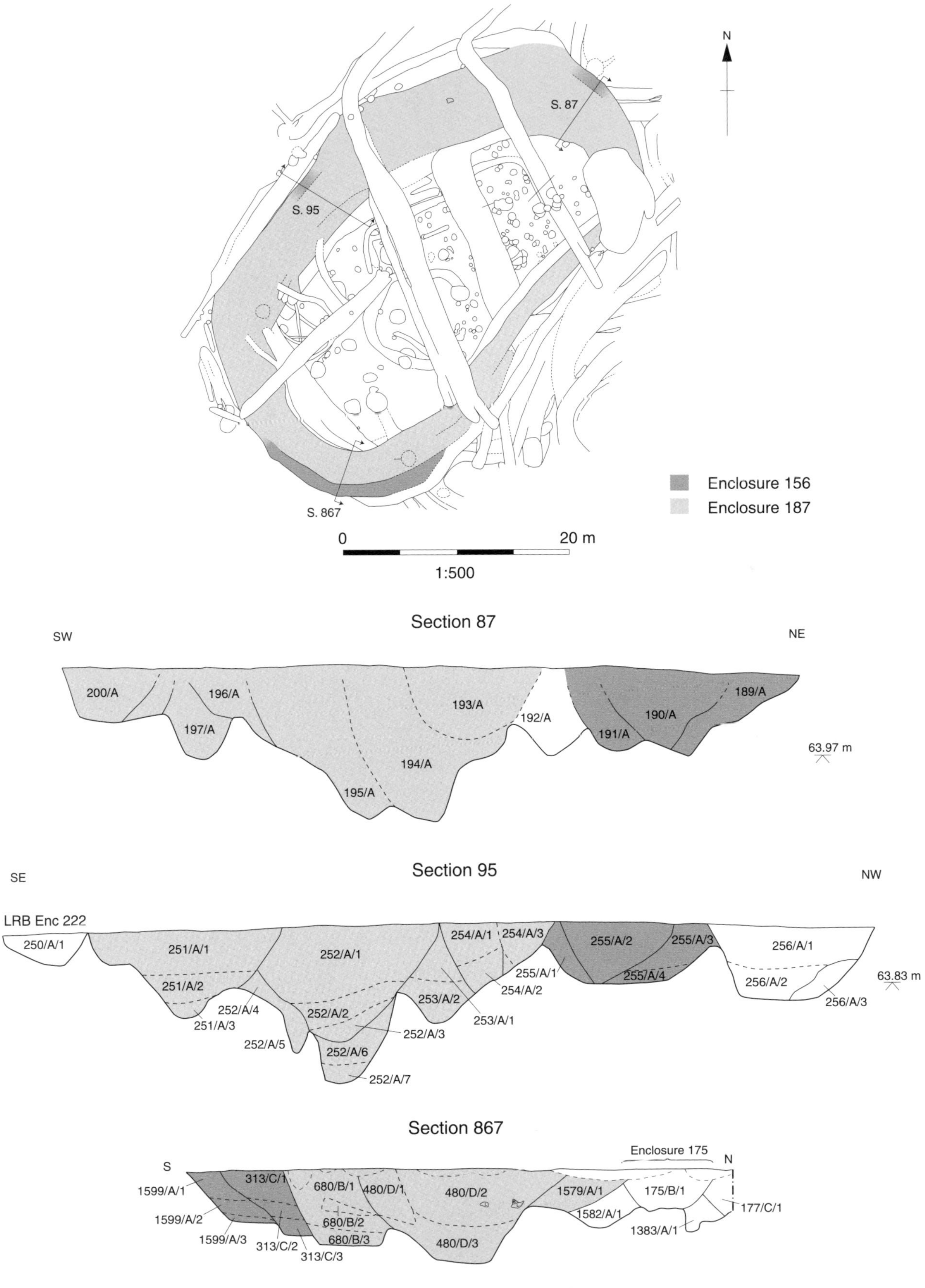

N
S. 87
S. 95
S. 867
Enclosure 156
Enclosure 187
0
20 m
1:500
Section 87
SW
NE
200/A
196/A
197/A
193/A
192/A
194/A
195/A
190/A
191/A
189/A
63.97 m
Section 95
SE
NW
LRB Enc 222
250/A/1
251/A/1
251/A/2
251/A/3
252/A/1
252/A/2
252/A/3
252/A/4
252/A/5
252/A/6
252/A/7
253/A/1
253/A/2
254/A/1
254/A/2
254/A/3
255/A/1
255/A/2
255/A/3
255/A/4
256/A/1
256/A/2
256/A/3
63.83 m
Section 867
S
N
Enclosure 175
1599/A/1
1599/A/2
1599/A/3
313/C/1
313/C/2
313/C/3
680/B/1
680/B/2
680/B/3
480/D/1
480/D/2
480/D/3
1579/A/1
1582/A/1
1383/A/1
175/B/1
177/C/1
0
2 m
1:50

Fig. 8.8 Plan and section showing sequence of ditches in enclosures 156 and 187

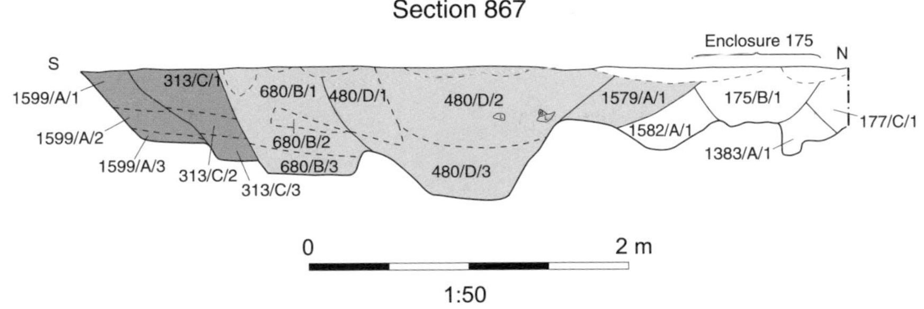

Enclosure 156/187 in the north-west of the site and associated features

Enclosures 156 and 187 (Figs 8.1 and 8.8)

Enclosure 156 was a very substantial oval enclosure in the central north area of the site which was replaced on the same line by enclosure 187 (the division between them is fairly arbitrary). Both enclosures were orientated NE-SW. The maximum area covered by the enclosure ditches was 44 m by 25 m, but because it was not possible to identify a complete ditch/gully in an individual phase the area enclosed at any one time is only known approximately.

Enclosure 156 measured *c* 33 m NE-SW by 18 m NW-SE and the area enclosed was roughly 550 m^2. No entrance was immediately apparent, but the enclosure itself was clearly the product of repeated recutting and the entrance may have shifted over time; it perhaps lay in the south-west. Thirty-four ditch/gully segments were excavated through the enclosure, representing *c* one third of its total length. The gully profiles were variable, although typically of open U-shape, on average 0.58 m wide and 0.55 m deep. The enclosure had been recut at least twice. Most gully segments had one or two fairly mixed fills; overall these comprised a wide range of gravelly and non-gravelly soils, with some primary silting, some burnt/ashy material and some greenish soils. Animal disturbance was also observed. A relatively large assemblage of pottery (136 sherds, 2023 g), animal bone (148 pieces), and charred plant remains was recovered from the ditch fill along with two human bones and a small amount of metalworking debris. The animal bone assemblage is quite diverse with examples of hare, dog, horse, pig, sheep and cattle. The cattle or cattle/horse size bones account for 39% of the bone assemblage. The finds suggests rubbish deposition, possibly from buildings contained within the enclosure.

Enclosure 187 was slightly larger, enclosing an area of *c* 36 m x 22 m. There was no clearly-defined entrance, but terminals in the south suggest that it may have lain in this area. The entrance may have shifted over time and multiple recuts have probably cut across earlier openings; a minimum of five cuts is observable in section (Fig. 8.8) and it is likely that the original number of cuts was higher. Forty sections were excavated through the enclosure ditch. The ditch/gully profiles were very variable, although broadly of open U-shape. Average cut widths and depths were 0.81 m and 0.74 m respectively, but depths varied from 0.6-1.35 m. As in enclosure 156 the number of fills per cut varied, usually from one to three. The fills were mixed, consisting of non-gravelly soils, silty loams with gravel and greenish material. A substantial finds assemblage including 280 sherds (4146 g) of pottery and 155 animal bones, charred plant remains and some metalworking debris, was recovered from the ditch fill. Just over half the pottery by sherd count (51%) is Iron Age in date, however. This high level of redeposition is reflected in the relatively low average sherd weight for the group (14 g) and is perhaps not surprising given the proximity of the Iron Age settlement to the west and beneath this enclosure, and the constant re-digging of the ditches. A Dorset black-burnished ware flat-rim bowl provides a *terminus post quem* of mid-late 2nd century. The animal bone is quite diverse with cattle, dog, goat, pig, sheep, hare and toad represented. A pair of cattle mandibles in one context might suggest a special deposit of some type (see Chapter 17 below). The cattle and cattle/horse size bones dominate the assemblage, accounting for 44.5% of the animal bone. Other finds include a quernstone, a worked bone object (SF 381) and metalworking debris. The latter comprises fragments of fuel ash slag, a small sub-tuyère plate, fragments of lining vitrification flow and a fragment of a bellows protection block. This material may indicate rubbish deposition from structures within the enclosure which did not survive at the time of excavation and also suggests that metalworking was being carried out nearby.

Gully 586 (Fig. 8.1)

A short length of gully (586) projected ESE-WNW from the southern side of enclosure 187, by which it was cut, and ended in a terminal to the west. This indicated a total length of *c* 4 m, although only the eastern end was clearly identified in excavation. The gully profile was an open U-shape. It contained three fills of homogeneous non-gravelly material which produced four sherds of pottery and thirteen animal bones.

Earliest phase of early Roman enclosures in the south and east of the site

Enclosure 391B (Figs 8.1 and 7.8)

Enclosure 391B was a substantial sub-circular enclosure in the south-east corner of the site, at its nearest point some 22 m south-east of enclosure 156/187. It retained a similar size and shape to those of its late Iron Age predecessor (enclosure 391A), with maximum dimensions of *c* 25 east-west by 22 m north-south. Although it was extremely difficult to trace the entire circuit of individual ditch cuts, the enclosure seems to have shifted slightly to the north-west over time. Its entrance remained in much the same place as in the late Iron Age period, however, and thus lay in the south-east of the 391B phase of enclosure, at which time it was *c* 2.5 m wide. Fourteen sections were excavated through the enclosure ditch, representing 20% of its original length. The profile was an open U-shape, averaging 0.8 m wide and 0.5 m deep. There were up to nine recuts (Fig. 7.8). The fills were mixed, consisting of gravel-free silty loams, silty loams with some gravel, and gravel-rich deposits, with some greenish material and some primary silting. The finds from the ditch comprise 64 sherds (1117 g) of pottery and 31 animal bones; a very modest assemblage given the size of the ditch. The pottery contained a high proportion of 'Belgic-type' grog-tempered ware and grey sandy ware (fabric R37) broadly dating to the early Roman period.

Ditch 206 in the centre of the site (Fig. 8.1)

Ditch 206 lay between enclosures 156/187 and 391B and was cut by the latter. It possibly formed part of a polygonal enclosure in an area later occupied by enclosure ditches 138, 427, 440 and 293 (see below), but there was no clear evidence for the presence of related features forming the north-east and south-east sides of such an enclosure. It is possible, therefore, that the ditch served to define a relationship between the two enclosures, 156/187 and 391B. The fact that it was aligned on and cut by the north-west corner of enclosure 391B suggests a direct link between the two. To the north-west, however, 206 ran up to rather than impinging on enclosure 156/187. It is uncertain, however, if there was a gap between the north-west arm of 206 and the adjacent enclosure, which could have provided an access between the two, or whether the spacing was deliberately intended to preclude such access. Unfortunately the extent of 206 to the north-east is also unknown. It might have reached as far as the north-east corner of the enclosure 156/187, or even further, but in this area it was completely obliterated by later features.

Thirty-five sections were cut through ditch 206. The ditch profile was predominantly an open U-shape, averaging 0.7 m in width and 0.5 m in depth. There were six or more recuts, with a corresponding number of fills which were fairly mixed with wide variation in gravel content. The fills contained some greenish material and some evidence of burning. A substantial assemblage of pottery and animal bone, along with three fragments of metalworking debris and one bone small find, were recovered from the ditch fill. The pottery comprised some 178 sherds (3448 g), including a number of residual later prehistoric sherds (42% by sherd count) alongside local Roman wares. The Roman material was dominated by native grog-tempered wares, accounting for a further 35%, with Roman wares proper forming the remaining 23%. The latter provide a *terminus post quem* for the group in the middle part of the 2nd century. The large collection of 250 animal bones was dominated by cattle but included bird, dog, horse, pig, sheep and roe deer. Amongst the other finds were a bone leaze rod (SF 454) and some fragments of fired clay. The finds probably derive from dumping of rubbish from structures to the east of the ditch, which did not survive by the time of the excavation.

Enclosure 166 and related features in the north-east of the site

Enclosure 166 – ditches 166, 94, 100, 1152 and 1268 (Figs 8.1 and 8.9)

North of ditch 206 was a substantial right-angled ditch sequence, 20 m in length. This probably formed the south-eastern corner of an enclosure (166) that was perhaps completed by ditches 94, 100 and 1268 and would therefore have measured approximately 15 m north-south x 12 m east-west. Such an enclosure would have been focused on and presumably related to the north-east corner of enclosure 156/187, and the possible extension of ditch 206 (see above) in this direction might also have been relevant to the configuration of the enclosure. Later Roman ditches obscured parts of the north and east sides. No definite entrance was observed during the course of excavation, but this may have lain to the north-west, for example between the west end of ditch 1268 and the adjacent north-east side of enclosure 156/187.

Nine sections were excavated representing 25% of the original length of the enclosure ditch. The ditch profile was an open U-shape, averaging 0.7 m wide and 0.75 m deep (Fig. 8.10, section 649).

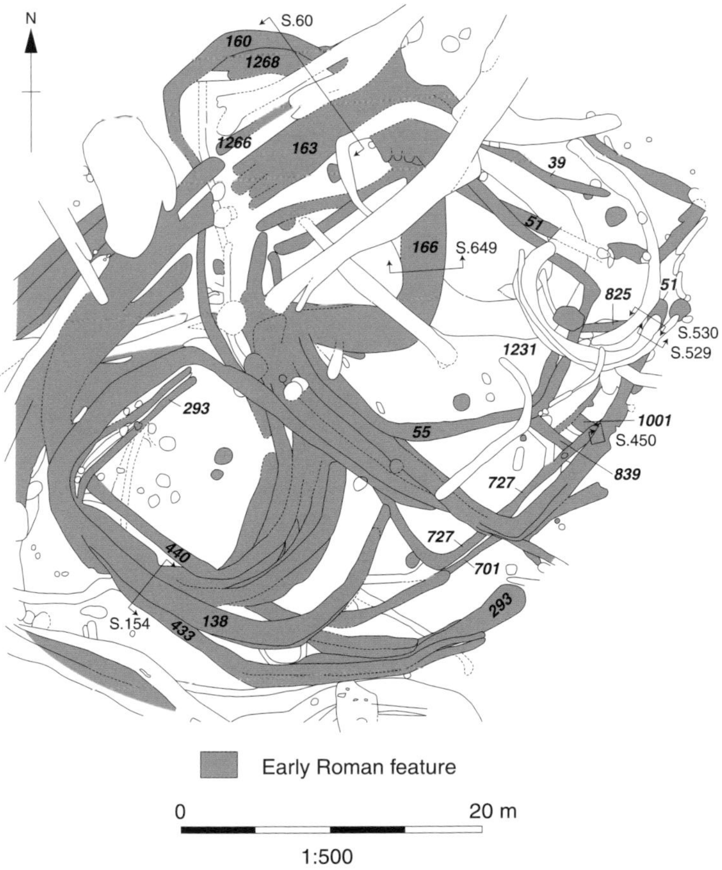

Fig. 8.9 Plan of early Roman enclosures 51, 138, 160, 163, 166, 433, 1001, 1266 and 1268 with section locations

There were up to four to five recuts, and a corresponding number of fills. The fills were generally mixed with a varying gravel content, and overlay primary silting; they also contained some greenish material. A large quantity of pottery (143 sherds, 2344 g), 130 fragments of animal bone, some charred plant remains and one fragment of metal-working debris were recovered from the ditch fills. The pottery mainly comprised local wares with grog-tempered and oxidised and reduced sandy fabrics. The only import was a sherd of a *terra nigra* cup which may have been redeposited or curated. The general *terminus post quem* for the assemblage lies somewhere in the later 1st-early 2nd century. The animal bone included examples of all the usual domesticates, cattle, pig, sheep and horse. The material may represent rubbish deposition from a nearby structure, possibly within the enclosure.

Further possible components of enclosure 166 lay to the north. Beyond the most northerly point at which ditch 166 was identified was feature 100, a 2 m long stretch of ditch aligned NW-SE (Fig. 8.1). The ditch was an open U-shape, averaging 1 m wide and 0.5 m deep, and had mixed fills of silty loams with varying quantities of gravel. It produced no finds and had suffered some animal disturbance. Ditch 100 was cut away to the north by a large pit (1147, not on plan) and to the south-east by ditch 94, which may also have formed part of the same enclosure as 166. Ditch 94 was curvilinear, 5.5 m in length, and aligned NW-SE. It was cut to the south-east by ditch 30, and its north-western end was also impossible to trace. This ditch was excavated in three sections, which represented 40% of its extant length. The profile was an open U-shape, and it averaged 1.4 m in width by 0.84 m in depth. The fill was fairly mixed and consisted of non-gravelly material, silty loams with gravel, some greenish soils and some orange/green/brown material. Pottery (24 sherds) and animal bone (11 fragments, of which four are intrusive rabbit) from the ditch fill suggested low level rubbish deposition.

West of ditches 94 and 100 was a further slightly curvilinear ditch length, 1268, aligned roughly east-west, which probably formed the northern side of enclosure 166. It was only traceable for 5.5 m but may have been cut away by later features.. Five sections excavated through this feature formed two groups; an eastern group comprising 1268/A and 1270/A, parallel to one another, of which 1.2 m lengths were recorded; and a western group comprising 765/A, 766/A, and 792/A which also lay parallel to one another and were 0.9 m in recorded length (these features certainly extended beyond the excavated interventions but their continuations could not be identified with confidence). At least one recut was observed in section, but animal disturbance to 765/A and 766/A was heavy and there may have been more recuts. The ditch profile was an open U-shape, averaging 1.1 m wide and 0.41 m deep. There were at least five fills, which consisted of non-gravelly material and silty loams with gravel above primary silting. The ditch fills contained pottery, animal bone, and fired clay, possibly from a loomweight, but the assemblage was fairly dispersed and not particularly substantial. Amongst the 27 sherds (378 g) of pottery was a scrap of Dorset black-burnished ware, several sherds of 'Belgic-type' grog-tempered ware, grey sandy wares and six redeposited Iron Age sherds. The *terminus post quem* of the group lies in the early 2nd century. The 26 animal bones include eight hare bones along with cattle, pig and sheep/goat.

A fragment of a linear feature (1152) projected from the southern margin of enclosure 166 and was cut by that ditch. It is not clear if gully 1152, with an open U-shaped profile 0.32 m wide and 0.19 m deep, formed part of the enclosure. The single fill contained two sherds of early Roman 'Belgic-type' pottery and three intrusive fragments of rabbit bone.

Enclosure 160 and related features in the north-east of the site

Enclosure 160 (Figs 8.1 and 8.9)

Feature 1268, probably the northern side of enclosure 166, was cut by ditch 160, forming the north-western half of a roughly circular enclosure the rest of which had been cut away by multiple later features to the south-east. It is not clear if further elements of this enclosure survived beneath or just south of the many cuts in ditches 785-8. Ditch 160 was curvilinear and was traced for 14.5 m. No entrance was apparent in the extant ditch, but it may have lain to the south-west or, perhaps more likely, in the missing south-eastern part.

Thirty-five percent of the enclosure was excavated in five sections. In profile the ditch was an open U-shape and there were no recuts. The ditch was 1.1 m wide on average, and 0.6 m deep. The fill was fairly mixed consisting of burnt clay, non-gravelly material and silty loams with gravel. There were also lenses of burnt ashy or charcoally loam, and some greenish material. Some 36 sherds of pottery (959 g) and 54 animal bones (excluding 19 rabbit bones) from the ditch fill may indicate rubbish deposition.

Ditch 159 lay on the outer north-east side of 160 and was cut by it, and may have been an earlier cut of the same enclosure ditch. A 5 m length survived, but most of the feature had been removed by the digging of later ditches. Two sections were excavated through this feature. The ditch profile was an open U-shape with an average width of 1 m, and an average depth of 0.6 m. The single fill comprised non-gravelly material, which produced only a small assemblage of pottery and four animal bones.

Peripheral features east of enclosure 391

Gully 365 (Fig. 8.1)

Gully 365 was a curvilinear feature 27.5 m in length, to the east of enclosure 391B. It probably defined a penannular enclosure, partly cut away to the east by late Roman ditch 877, but also bisected by a (later) early Roman ditch (343). The gully ended in a terminal to the north, which may have indicated the position of a NNE-facing enclosure entrance. The putative enclosure measured up to 10 m NNE-SSW by *c* 8 m WNW-ESE. The gully profile was an open U-shape, averaging 0.49 m wide and 0.3 m deep. The single fill was generally homogeneous and consisted of silty loam with gravel. A small amount of well-fragmented pottery (15 sherds, 82 g) and nine animal bones were recovered from the ditch fill.

Ditch 948 (Fig. 8.1)

Ditch 948 was a right-angled ditch, a 13 m length of which lay in the south-east corner of the excavated area and immediately south-east of gully 365. One arm was aligned WNW-ESE, and the other NNE-SSW. Both arms extended beyond the limits of the excavation but it is possible that the WNW-ESE aligned arm was associated with ditch 2528 further east (see below). Three segments were excavated through this ditch, representing 20% of its extant length. The profile was a narrow U-shape, averaging 1 m wide and 0.6 m deep. There were no recuts, but three fills were present, consisting of non-gravelly material and silty loams with gravel, with some primary silting. Finds comprised nine very small sherds of pottery and five animal bone fragments.

Later early Roman enclosures in the centre of the site

An extremely complex sequence of ditches and gullies, defining a succession of partly or wholly enclosed spaces, lay in the central part of the site within the area originally defined on the south-west side by ditch 206. The extent of recutting and small-scale enclosure shift means that many of these 'enclosures' are very incomplete in plan. They fall broadly into two interlocking complexes, one to the south and one to the north. The multiple cuts observed in the core of the southern complex were themselves assigned, rather arbitrarily, to two main groups, 440 and 427. Other features extending more widely both to the south-east and north-west were related, usually in rather uncertain ways, to these groupings, while a more compact enclosure, 138, was probably the latest component of the sequence. The northern complex was a little more diffuse, but at least some if not most of its components were clearly later in date than enclosure 138 to the south.

Enclosure 440 (Figs 8.1, 8.9 and 8.10)

Enclosure 440 was a sub-oval enclosure in excess of 14 m NE-SW by 12 m NW-SE. There were at least three major cuts of the enclosure ditch/gully, representing distinct changes in character. In particular the south-west side was defined by a straight length of ditch in its third main phase, whereas all the earlier ditches appeared to be more or less curvilinear. The entrance was probably to the north-west, but there seems also to have been a north-east entrance in the primary phase. Twenty-two segments were excavated through the enclosure gully, representing *c* 50% of its extant length. The gully profile was an open U-shape, averaging 0.44 m wide and 0.4 m deep. Each cut typically had only one fill, except where primary silting was identified. The fills were variable, and consisted of gravel-free and gravelly silty loams, some red/brown sand, and lenses of charcoal and some greenish material. Pottery, animal bone, charred plants and two copper alloy artefacts came from the ditch fill and probably represented deposition of rubbish within it. The 45 sherds (771 g) of pottery were quite well-preserved and were largely local early Roman types. Although 63 animal bones are recorded, 23 of these are rabbit and presumably intrusive. Of note amongst the usual complement of species are one domestic fowl bone and one hare bone. The copper alloy items were a dolphin brooch (SF 160) of Neronian-early Flavian date and an early Roman stud (SF 161).

The possible north-east entrance in the primary phase of enclosure 440 was poorly defined. The ditch that may have terminated to form the north side of this entrance extended north-westwards and then curved to the north (cut by the later enclosure 138), perhaps defining an extended entrance into the enclosure from the north-west. As ditch 113 it was traced for a distance of 10 m beyond the point at which it was cut by enclosure 138. There was no corresponding feature to the south-west.

Enclosure 427 (Figs 8.1, 8.9 and 8.10)

Curvilinear ditch/gully group 427 cut enclosure 440 on the south and east sides. It may originally have defined a replacement enclosure, roughly 16 m NW-SE by 12 m NE-SW, but there was very little evidence for any part of it except on the south-east and south-west sides. No entrance to this enclosure was observed during excavation, but one may have existed to the north-east, where the boundary ditches related to this feature were probably obliterated by later enclosures.

Eleven segments were excavated through the enclosure ditch, representing *c* 40% of its extant length. The ditch/gully profile was an open U-shape, averaging 0.5 m wide and 0.5 m deep. There were two or more recuts. The two or more fills in each cut consisted of a mixture of non-gravelly material and silty loams with gravel. There was

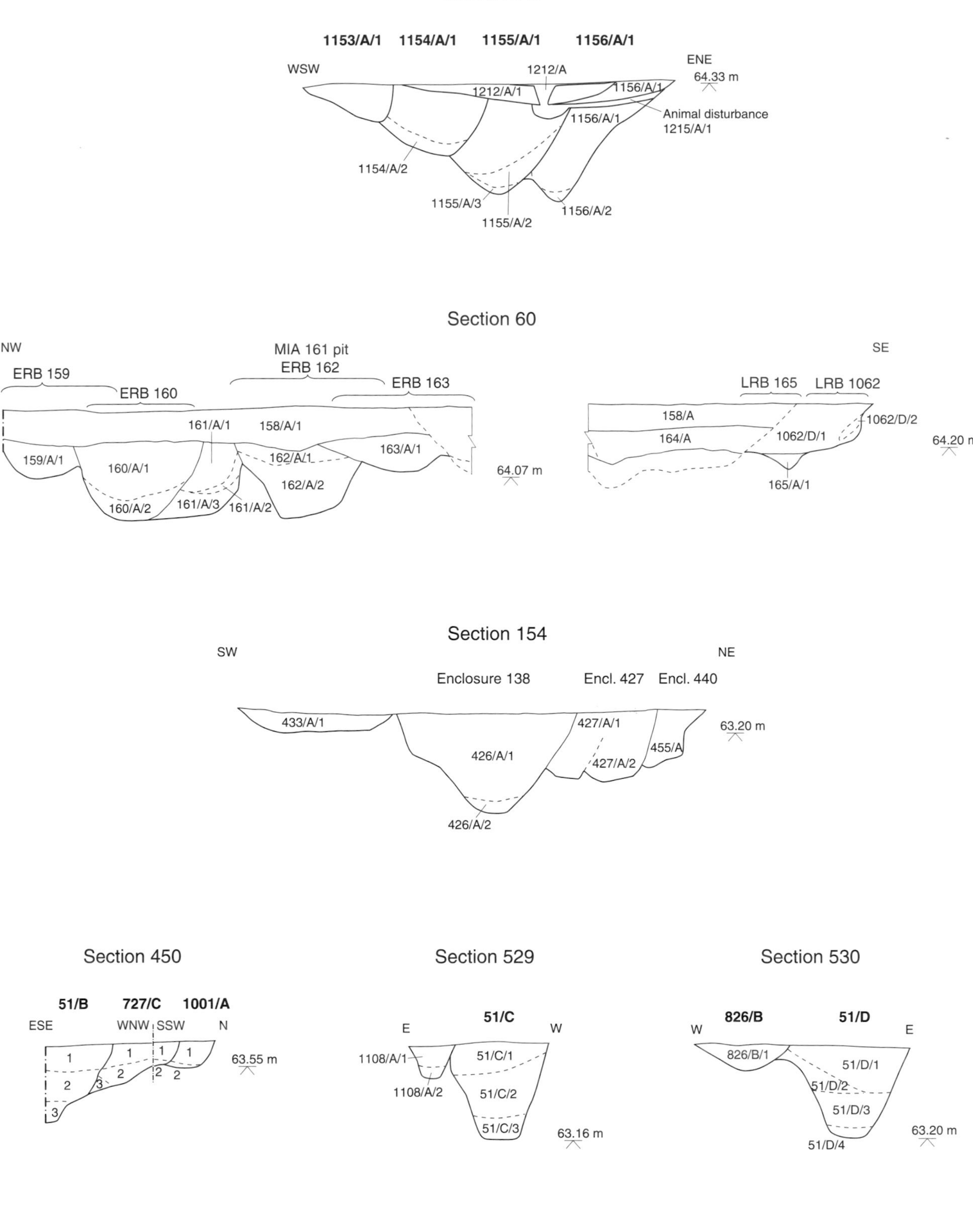

Fig. 8.10 Section of early Roman enclosure ditch sequences 51, 138, 160, 163, 166, 433, 1001, 1266 and 1268 and late Romano-British ditches 165 and 1062

some primary silting, and some animal disturbance of the fills. Pottery and animal bone mixed with charcoal and charred plant remains found in the ditch fill probably represent rubbish deposition, perhaps from structures originally located inside the enclosure. The 93 sherds (3156 g) of pottery had an average sherd weight of 34 g suggesting well-preserved material which has undergone relatively little disturbance. The assemblage was dominated by grey sandy west Oxfordshire wares (fabric R37) and grey sandy grogged ware (fabric R94) and included a white ware globular beaker (Young 1977, type W37) of 2nd-century date. The animal bone, a total of 19 fragments, included examples of the usual domesticates.

Possible enclosure 293 (Figs 8.1 and 8.9)

The features assigned to possible enclosure 293, lying north of and approximately reflecting the line of ditch 206, fall into two groups; a series of fairly straight NE-SW aligned gullies on the north-west side and more extensive curvilinear ditches and gullies along the south side with termini turning towards the north-east. Any connection between the features forming the southern and north-western ditch/gully groups had been removed, perhaps by components of enclosure 427 and certainly by the ditch of later enclosure 138. The southern side of the possible enclosure had been significantly realigned, with the better-preserved features of what is likely to have been a secondary phase lying some distance to the south of the original line. This was seen most clearly to the north-east, where ditches 397 and 474 terminated some 2.5 m apart. This spacing was not maintained consistently, however. The maximum NW-SE dimension of this 'enclosure' was *c* 26 m and a hypothetical NE-SW dimension was *c* 15 m, there being no clear evidence for a north-east side.

Eighteen sections were excavated through the ditches/gullies, representing *c* 25% of their extant length. The dimensions and profiles of the individual features were very variable. Profiles ranged from very shallow and rounded to steep-sided or V-shaped and average dimensions were 0.6 m wide and 0.35 m deep. There were up to six recuts in places. Fills were mixed and varied in number, ranging from one to six in individual cuts. They included non-gravelly material, silty-loams with gravel, and some orange/brown sand. Some coarser primary silting was also present and animal disturbance was observed in places. The fills contained a reasonable amount of pottery and a small amount of animal bone along with one iron hobnail. The pottery, comprising some 100 sherds (820 g), was quite well fragmented with a few redeposited sherds. Although the bulk of the assemblage dates to the early Roman period there are at least five Oxfordshire ware vessels (Young (1977) forms M18, P18, C22, C45 and C51) dating from the second part of the 3rd century or later. These may have been intrusive, or suggest a later phase of feature infill; with one exception they were found towards the north-eastern end of the ditch/gully complex.

Enclosure 138 and ditch 140 (Figs 8.1, 8.9 and 8.10)

Features belonging to probable or possible enclosures 440, 427 and 329 in the central area of the site were all cut by the ditches of enclosure 138. This was a sub-rectangular enclosure measuring *c* 21 m NW-SE by 16 m NE-SW overall. The entrance was situated in the north-eastern corner, where there was a gap in the circuit. The north-east arm of the enclosure extended about 2.5 m beyond the corner adjacent to the probable entrance, where it terminated. Ten segments were excavated through the ditch, representing 15% of its total length. The profile was an open U-shape, averaging 1.1 m wide and 0.6 m deep (Fig. 8.10, section 154). There were multiple recuts (4-5 or more), and the fills consisted of a mixture of silty and sandy loams with widely varying gravel content and some flecks of charcoal. Some coarser primary silting was seen in the base of the ditch. A substantial assemblage of pottery (129 sherds, 2582 g), animal bone, charred plant remains, a fragment of triangular loomweight, a brick fragment and fired clay were recovered from the ditch fill.

Most of the pottery comprises products of the local Oxfordshire industries with substantial quantities of grey ware accompanied by shelly ware and grog-tempered ware. The only fine ware is a single sherd of mica-slipped ware and the only extra-regional imports a small amount of Dorset black-burnished ware. A sherd of Oxfordshire colour-coated ware mortarium from one fill probably represents contamination. Of the 54 animal bones recovered, 39% were from cattle with lesser amounts of sheep, horse and pig. Amongst the cattle bones was a complete torso, possibly a special deposit (see Chapter 17). In general, the material suggests rubbish deposition and possibly the presence of buildings within the enclosure.

Ditch 140 cut the north-east arm of enclosure 138 for much of the length of the latter, extending slightly further east before being cut away by enclosure 51. It survived for a length of 18 m, but it is unclear what happened at its north-west end, and in particular whether it represented an isolated reworking of the north-east side of enclosure 138 or whether it formed part of one of the relatively loosely-defined enclosures to the north. Three segments were excavated through this ditch, representing *c* 15% of its original length. The ditch profile was an open U-shape, averaging 0.73 m in width and 0.47 m in depth. There was one recut, and the ditch was filled with a generally homogeneous non-gravelly material. A small amount of pottery (15 sherds weighing 823 g), was recovered from the fill.

Right-angled ditch 343 and possibly associated features (Fig. 8.1)

Ditch 343

Ditch 343, lying east of enclosures 391B and 138, was a roughly right-angled ditch measuring 44 m in length. Its southern arm, aligned SSW-NNE, terminated adjacent to and probably respected the line of enclosure ditch 948, east of the entrance to enclosure 391B (see above). The other arm was aligned SE-NW on the centre of the settlement, where it ran along the division between two groups of enclosures on a very similar alignment to the north-east arm of enclosure 138 and the later ditch 140, although it was cut away by later features (particularly enclosure 51) so it is not certain if it extended as far as these. Any association with features further north-west is speculative and it is far from certain that ditch 343 formed part of an enclosure in its own right. The ditch was excavated in 10 sections. The profile was an open, sometimes irregular U-shape, averaging 0.64 m wide and 0.46 m deep and there was no clear evidence for recutting. There were typically one or two fills per cut, consisting of silty loams with varying proportions of gravel. A small assemblage of 33 sherds (253 g) of fragmentary early Roman pottery, accompanied by 19 animal bones, charred plant remains and a piece of indeterminate fired clay came from the ditch fill.

A short length of ditch (828) projected south-east from the southern edge of ditch 343 close to the point where the latter was cut by enclosure ditch 51, and ended in a terminal to the south-east.

Later rectilinear enclosures to the north-east

Ditch 727 (Figs 8.1 and 8.9)

Most of the enclosures of the north-east group shared a common south-western limit, linking them with or separating them from the central group of enclosures and other ditch alignments just described. The clearest exception to this rule was ditch 727, perhaps one of the earliest of the features in the north-eastern group and possibly forming the south-east corner of an enclosure, but if so no other enclosure ditch elements were clearly associated with it. Feature 727 was a right-angled ditch with a surviving length of 19 m, its arms aligned NE-SW and SE-NW, cut away to the north-west by elements of enclosure 138 and to the north-east by enclosure 51. It is possible that 727 was a predecessor of the latter feature. The southern angle of 727 lay well to the south of the common boundary. One component of the central feature group 293 (ditch 397) ran up to this angle and terminated adjacent to it, respecting its location. Fourteen sections were excavated through 727. Its profile was an open U-shape and the cut was 0.56 m wide on average, and 0.34 m deep. There were at least two fills in each cut, the compositions of which were variable, including non-gravelly, gravel-free and gravelly silty loams, with some primary silting. The fills produced 43 sherds of pottery (362 g), 26 animal bones and one fragment of metalworking debris. The pottery comprises a mixture of native-type wares and Roman grey ware with a few residual Iron Age pieces.

A possible recut (701) of ditch 727 lay adjacent to its south-east side at the south angle. The association is not certain, however, and it is possible that this feature was connected with further features to the north-east.

Ditches 825, 839, 1001 and 1231 (Figs 8.1 and 8.9)

Several short lengths of ditch were located just west of the eastern arm of ditch 727. At least two of these (839 and 1001) were cut by 727 and were therefore either earlier than it or contemporary with the initial phase of its use (the fact that 839 did not project east of the line of 727 supports the latter interpretation).

Ditch 839 was aligned NW-SE and projected 3 m from the line of ditch 727. It was cut away to the north-west by enclosure 55. The ditch was excavated in two sections, which represented 50% of its extant length. The profile was an open U-shape, up to 0.8 m wide and 0.21 m deep, with no recuts. The fill was a mixture of gravelly and non-gravelly material. Ten pot sherds came from the ditch fill, along with nine fragments of animal bones and two of human bone. Ditch 1231, running SSW-NNE on the inner (west) edge of enclosure ditch 55, may have been a continuation of ditch 839, the angle made by the two having been cut away by enclosure 55. Ditch 1231 extended northwards for 5 m and then appeared to terminate. Another 3 m length of ditch, this time aligned east-west (825) lay *c* 1.5 m further north and was also cut by enclosure 55. Two sections were excavated through this ditch, representing approximately 40% of its extant length. The profile was a narrow U-shape, and there were no recuts. The ditch was 1 m wide on average, and 0.98 m deep. There were five fills which consisted of a mixture of non-gravelly and gravelly material, with charcoal flecks. Pottery (28 sherds, 624 g), 16 animal bones and a fragment of daub were found in the fill.

It is quite possible that these three ditches formed part of a small enclosure, perhaps related to ditch 727 (see above). A further short ditch length, 1001, ran parallel to and just north of ditch 839. Like 839 it was cut to the east by ditch 727, but its extent to the west was obscured, although it cut a small NNE-SSW aligned gully (1179). One section was excavated. The profile was an open U-shape, c 0.8 m wide and 0.22 m deep and there were no recuts. There were two mixed fills of silty loam with gravel and gravelly material, with some primary silting. No finds were recovered.

Enclosure 51 (Figs 8.1, 8.9 and 8.10)

Enclosure 51 overlay enclosure 727, although it was cut slightly further to the north. Ditches defined parts of three sides of a roughly rectilinear enclosure which may have been completed to the north-west by ditch(es) 163, although the presence of late Roman ditches made this difficult to ascertain and other features which might have fulfilled this role include ditch 74 (see below). The enclosure would have measured *c* 25 m NW-SE x 17 m NE-SW, and had a clear terminal in its north-east angle. This probably marked one side of an entrance, but the likely location of a corresponding terminal at the east end of the northern side of the enclosure was obscured. Twenty-seven sections were examined across this features (*c* 60% of its visible length). There was typically a minimum of three cuts in the ditch. Profiles were mostly of open U-shape, averaging 0.83 m wide and 0.79 m deep. Most cuts contained one or two fills, although three or four fills were seen occasionally. The fills consisted of non-gravelly material, silty loams with gravel, and greenish soils, with occasional charcoal. Some primary silting was recorded and animal disturbance of the fills was also noted. The fills contained a very large assemblage of pottery amounting to some 741 sherds (9915 g) and a substantial quantity of 103 animal bones, as well as an iron nail, fragments of daub, some miscellaneous fired clay and one fragment of slag. This material was mixed in with fragments of charcoal and may have been the result of rubbish deposition from structures within the enclosed area. Plant remains from the ditch included a variety of weed seeds, cereals and chaff.

Most of the pottery comprised local Roman wares with very little redeposited material evident. Of note were a sherd of Dorset black burnished ware, two sherds of Oxfordshire white ware mortaria and an Oxfordshire white ware flagon (Young 1977, form W2) amid a large quantity of grey ware. The pottery provides a broad 2nd-century date for the fill. The bone is dominated by cattle but with a range of other types including dog, pig, horse, sheep/goat and a single bird bone.

A group of closely-linked ditches, 1017 (with 1014 and 1015) projected east-north-eastwards for a distance of *c* 13.5 m from the southern corner of enclosure 51 and clearly predated it. Their function is not certain, but it is possible that they were related to gully 701 just to the south (see above).

Enclosure 55 (Figs 8.1 and 8.9)

Enclosure 55 was an irregularly polygonal successor to enclosure 51. Its ditches cut those of enclosure 51 on the north-east and south-west sides, while the south-east ditch lay some distance inside the corresponding component of enclosure 51. The relationship of their north-western sides is less certain. Enclosure 55 probably had maximum overall dimensions of *c* 20 m by 16 m. Fourteen segments were excavated through the ditch, representing *c* 40% of its extant length. The ditch profile, which appeared not to have been recut, varied from an open to a narrow U-shape, and was 0.79 m wide on average, and 0.48 m deep. There were several fills which were very mixed. Finds of pottery (76 sherds weighing 1525 g), animal bone (47 fragments), charred plant remains and a fragment of fired clay from the ditch fill indicate rubbish deposition, possibly from buildings contained in the enclosure to the west. A single human finger bone was also recovered from context 846 at the southernmost extremity of the enclosure ditch.

Ditch 74 lay within a zone of intercutting ditches to the north-west of ditch 166, and may have formed the north-western side of enclosure 55 or, perhaps more likely, of its predecessor, enclosure 51. The feature survived in a 7.5 m length aligned WSW-ENE. Two sections were excavated, revealing an open U-shaped profile with no recuts. The average width of the ditch was 0.56 m, and its average depth 0.25 m and its single fill consisted of a non-gravelly material. The ditch terminated adjacent to the northern terminus of a roughly north-south aligned ditch, 110, which was presumably related.

Ditch 78 cut ditch 74 at their respective north-eastern ends and then diverged from it, the two features terminating in line about 1.3 m apart. It is perhaps more likely than ditch 74 to have formed the north-west side of enclosure 55. Three sections were excavated through the ditch, representing *c* 20% of its extant length. The ditch was an open U-shape, averaging 0.9 m wide and 0.36 m deep, with no recuts. There was a single fill of silty loam with very variable amounts of gravel, which contained ten sherds of pottery and one cattle bone. As with ditch 74, the terminal of ditch 78 lay immediately adjacent to the northern terminal of a north-south aligned ditch, 111, although the latter could only be traced for a distance of some 2 m. For this reason it is not certain that these features related to enclosure 55. It was thought possible that one or other of the north-south ditches 110 and 111 was related to the angled ditch 727, but the distance between the extant lengths of these features is such as to render the association highly speculative, although further features (eg 841) in the NW-SE aligned mass of ditches and gullies dividing northern and southern central enclosure complexes were also assigned to 727, while in the same area gully 1050 was thought to be possibly related to enclosure 55.

Ditches 162, 163, 785-8 and 1266 (Figs 8.1, 8.9 and 8.10)

A dense cluster of NE-SW aligned ditches lay between earlier enclosures 160 and 166 and just north-west of enclosures 51 and 55. These ditches were probably related to enclosures 51 and 55, and perhaps 727; some components of the ditch group may have formed parts of some of these enclosures from time to time, but direct associations could not be established. The ditches terminated to the south-west but were only traced over a distance of 10 m as they merged with other features to the north-east. If these ditches were related to enclosures such as 51 their south-west terminals suggest the location of entrances to these enclosures at their south-west corners.

The earliest of these features was the fragment of ditch 162, of which a 4 m length was observed. Its fill contained 20 sherds of early Roman pottery (644 g), including a large proportion of 'Belgic-type' grog-tempered storage jar, and 13 animal bones along with a bone gouge (SF 350).

The ditch cuts grouped as 163, which cut ditch 162, spread out to the south-west and four individual features were present, which were excavated as 785-788. All had open U-shaped profiles. The earliest may have been 788, the furthest north-west. To the south-east ditch 786 may itself have had as many as four recuts. Ditch 787 lay between 788 and 786 and cut both, while gully 785 cut ditch 786 at the south-east edge of the complex.

Gully 785 was 0.5 m wide and 0.21 m deep. It contained a single fill of silty loam with gravel. Just three potsherds and four fragments of animal bone were recovered; two of the latter were of rabbit and thus intrusive. The average dimensions of the cuts in ditch 786 were 0.7 m (width) and 0.33 m (depth). Most contained a single fill of non-gravelly material. A modest assemblage of pottery (28 sherds) and two animal bones was recovered. Ditch 787, 0.95 m wide and 0.36-0.5 m deep, contained two fills, consisting of silty loams with gravel and non-gravelly material, from which 11 sherds of pottery and 19 animal bones were recovered. Two sections were excavated through ditch 788 which was deeper than the other ditches in this group. It was on average 0.9 m wide and 0.65 m deep. There were five fills consisting of silty-loams with gravel, with some primary silting, some greenish material, and deposits of burnt limestone. A modest assemblage of 13 pottery sherds, 19 animal bones and a fragment of metal-working debris came from the fills.

Ditch 1266 ran parallel to ditch 163/785-788 on the north-west side. It had a south-western terminus in line with those of 785-788 but only a 5 m length survived, the rest being cut away by later features. It may have been part of the same enclosure system as the adjacent ditches, but this is not demonstrable. Two sections were excavated, representing *c* 25% of its extant length. The profile was an open U-shape, and there were no recuts. The ditch was 1.1 m wide on average, and 0.4 m deep. The fill was non-gravelly with lenses of burnt material and contained three sherds of pottery, two of which were quite large and unabraded.

Ditch 756 (Fig. 8.1)

Ditch 756 was a general number (like 163) assigned to a collection of linear features traced over a distance of 4.5 m, being cut away at both ends by later Roman ditches. The alignment was NW-SE, at right angles to 163, and it is likely that at least some elements of the two groups were related, together forming the northern corner of one or more enclosures, although their relationship to enclosures to the south-east such as 51, 55 and 727 remains unclear. Two sections were excavated through this feature group. The profiles were a narrow U-shape, and there were two recuts. The average cut width was 0.5 m, and the average depth 0.4 m. There were three fills which consisted of mixed non-gravelly material, with some primary silting. Ten sherds (154 g) of pottery and five animal bones came from the fills. These modest quantities are comparable to those from feature 163/785-788 and do not suggest significant deposition of rubbish within these features.

Later early Roman rectilinear enclosures in the north-east of the site

Linear ditches to the north-east of the main enclosure groups

To the north and east of enclosures 55 and 51 etc was a series of NW-SE aligned linear ditches and associated features which suggested the presence of small paddocks and trackways on this side of the settlement.

Ditch 39 (Figs 8.1 and 8.9)

Ditch 39, 8 m in length and aligned NW-SE, lay parallel to and north of the north-east side of enclosure 51. It was cut away by late Roman features to the west, although it may originally have extended as far as the 'corner' formed by ditch groups 163 and 754, discussed above, and had a terminus to the south-east. Two segments were excavated representing *c* 30% of its total length. The ditch was an open U-shape, averaging 1 m wide and 0.41 m deep with no recuts, and was filled with a mixture of non-gravelly material and silty loam with gravel. The fill produced 17 sherds of pottery and eight animal bones, including one hare bone.

Ditches 29 and 591 (Fig. 8.1)

Some 6 m north of and parallel to ditch 39 was ditch 29, which survived for a length of 6 m. Like 39 it was cut away by a later feature to the north-west, while to the south-east it ended in a terminal respecting the terminal of ditch 591, which continued on a similar alignment further south-east. Some 15% of ditch 29 was excavated in three segments. The profile was an open U-shape, averaging 0.4 m in width and 0.24 m in depth, with no recuts. It was filled with a generally homogeneous non-gravelly material, with some coarser primary silting. The only finds were five sherds of pottery and five animal bones.

Ditch 591 extended the alignment of 29 for another 14 m to the south-east, beyond which its line was obscure. The ditch was excavated in two sections, representing 20% of its extant length. The profile was an open U-shape, with no recuts, averaging 0.75 m in width and 0.33 m in depth. There were two fills, of non-gravelly material and silty loam with gravel, with some primary silting. A fairly substantial deposit of 62 sherds (1323 g) of pottery, 17 animal bones and one fragment of fuel ash slag was recovered. Most of the pottery comprises local early Roman fabrics with marked numbers of sherds in fabrics R37 and R94.

Ditches 42 and 43 and gully 45 (Fig. 8.1)

Ditch 43, 9 m in length and aligned NW-SE, lay mid way between and parallel to ditch 39 and ditches 29/591, and was one of several short NW-SE-running ditches in this part of the site. It was cut away at either end by ditches 807 and 1031. Two segments were excavated through this feature, representing *c* 15% of its total length. The profile was an open U-shape, and the ditch averaged 1.1 m wide by 0.37 m deep. There were no recuts. The fills consisted of non-gravelly material and silty loam with gravel. There was some coarser primary silting, but no finds.

Gully 45 may have been a south-easterly continuation of ditch 43, but there was a gap of *c* 7 m between them caused by the presence of later features. The gully was 13 m long and ended in a terminal to the south-east. Five sections were excavated through this feature, showing a profile varying from an open U-shape in places to a narrow U-shape in others, but there were no recuts. The average width was 0.5 m, and the average depth 0.35 m. The single fill consisted of non-gravelly material containing 15 sherds of pottery and six animal bones.

Ditch 42 ran at right angles to the line of these features, extending *c* 7.5 m in a SSW direction from a junction with 591, which may have been the later of the two ditches. Its relationship with ditch 43 was removed by a later feature, but it is likely that 42 was broadly contemporary with the NW-SE aligned ditches described above.

Ditches 84 and 95 (Fig. 8.1)

These features lay north of the group of ditches just described. Ditch 95 was 7.45 m in length and aligned NW-SE, parallel to and *c* 6 m north of ditch 591. At its north-western end it was cut by a late Roman curvilinear ditch, and it did not appear to continue on the other side of this feature. Its south-eastern end was cut by a large pit (57), but a possible continuation towards the SSE is indicated by ditch 84. Feature 95 faded out *c* 4 m beyond pit 57 but it may originally have curved to the south to link up with ditch 84. In section ditch 95 was 0.58 m wide and 0.31 m deep with an open U-shaped profile, while ditch 84 was 0.56 m wide and 0.19 m deep, but with a more V-shaped profile. In both cases the single fill was of non-gravelly material and devoid of finds.

Possible stack rings in the north-east of the site (Fig. 8.1)

Two small ring-gullies were found in the north-east of the site. Such features are not uncommon on early Roman Thames gravels sites (eg Hey 1995), and they may have surrounded stacks for animal fodder.

Enclosure 23

Enclosure 23 was a small ring-gully in the north-east corner of the excavated area. It measured 3.1 m in external diameter and there was no visible entrance. A single segment excavated through this gully represents *c* 15% of its original length. The profile was steep-sided and flat-bottomed with no recuts, 0.35 m wide and 0.28 m deep. It contained a single fill of sterile, gravel-free material.

Enclosure 24

Enclosure 24 was a small ring-gully immediately west of enclosure 23, measuring 2.4 m in diameter. A single segment excavated through this feature represents *c* 10% of its total circumference. No entrance was apparent, there were no recuts and the gully profile was U-shaped and narrow, 0.24 m wide and 0.27 m deep, with a fill of gravel-free material. Finds comprised just five pottery sherds.

Possible enclosures to the north-east of enclosure 187

A number of ditch fragments at the northern edge of the excavation probably represent the remains of small enclosures or paddocks on this side of the site. None of the features produced large assemblages of finds suggesting the presence of domestic activity in the vicinity. In addition to the features described below, feature 58 may have been part of another ditch in this general area of the site, but insufficient was examined for meaningful interpretation.

Ditch 59 (Fig. 8.1)

Curvilinear ditch 59, located against the northern limit of the excavation, was 12 m in length and aligned roughly east-west. It appeared to turn south at each end; at the western end it was cut by an amorphous cluster of pits and at the east it ran southwards for several metres before merging with another cluster of poorly-defined features. Five sections were excavated through the ditch, representing 15% of its extant length. The profile was varied, being mostly an open U-shape but with one section which was a narrow U-shape. There was at least one and possibly two recuts. The ditch was 0.65 m wide on average, and 0.28 m deep. The number of fills in the excavated sections ranged from one to four, and these consisted of non-gravelly material and silty loams with gravel. Finds from the ditch fill comprised three sherds of pottery, 18 animal bones and two possible loomweight fragments.

Ditch 168 (Fig. 8.1)

Ditch 168, aligned almost north-south, ran between the north baulk of the excavated area and the ditches of enclosure 187 which cut away its southern end. A single section through the ditch showed an open U-shaped profile with no recuts, 0.6 m wide and 0.33 m deep. The fill was generally homogeneous and consisted of non-gravelly material which produced just two pottery sherds and six animal bones.

Ditch 717 (Fig. 8.1)

Ditch 717 was a short stretch of linear feature, 1.4 m in length and aligned WNW-ESE, which lay immediately north of enclosure 187 and ran parallel with one of its outside recuts. The profile was an open U-shape with no recuts, 0.7 m wide and 0.38 m deep. There were two fills of sandy and silty loam, which contained ten sherds (107 g) of pottery and just three fragments of bone. The pottery comprised five Iron Age sherds and five sherds of early Roman native-type wares.

Later early Roman rectilinear enclosures in the south of the site

Enclosure 391C (Figs 8.1 and 7.8)

Enclosure 391C represents the latest stages of redefinition of the large sub-circular enclosure 391 in the south-east of the site, and a change towards a more rectilinear shape. This was a substantial oval enclosure measuring *c* 15 m east-west by 18 m north-south, enclosing an area of roughly 200 m^2. The entrance, as in previous phases of the enclosure, was situated to the south-east. The ditch profile was an open U-shape, averaging 1 m in width and 0.5 m deep. The total number of recuts in this phase is uncertain, but there were at least five or six; many had one or two fills, but three or four fills were occasionally present. The fills were very mixed in character, and some had a greenish hue. Lenses of charcoal and deposits of burnt limestone were also encountered.

A substantial assemblage of 243 sherds (4526 g) of pottery and 162 animal bone fragments, along with a single human bone, a fragment of fuel ash slag, five fragments of fired clay triangular loomweight and an iron double spiked loop (SF 410) came from the ditch fills. Charred plant remains were also recovered. The pottery, despite a moderately high average sherd weight of 18.6 g, contained a high incidence (25%) of redeposited Iron Age sherds. 'Belgic-type' grog-tempered ware accounted for a further 46% and grey sandy ware (fabric R94) was also well represented. A single sherd of Oxfordshire white ware mortarium was also recorded. Although cattle again dominated the bone assemblage there was also quite a marked presence of pig bone.

Two final ditch 'cuts' constituted enclosure 391D. Since in its final form the ditch was of open rounded profile with an average width of 2.4 m and a depth of 0.41 m it is possible that these represented silting up of hollows over earlier ditches rather than distinct cuts in their own right. Each contained a single fill of non-gravelly material. A small assemblage of 25 sherds (340 g) of pottery and 17 animal bones came from these ditch fills.

Ditch 345 (Fig. 8.1)

Ditch 345 may have defined part of a small sub-rectangular enclosure lying between enclosure 391 and linear ditch 343 to the east of 391. It cut ditch 365 and was in turn cut by ditch 344. Its extent to the north is uncertain. The extant ditch was 12 m in length, and the 'enclosure' measured 3.8 m from east to west. There was a clear terminal to the eastern, curvilinear part of the ditch, possibly indicating that an entrance faced in this direction. The full extent of the western, north-south aligned side is unknown, however, nor is it clear that there was any eastward return from a north-west corner. Three sections were excavated through the ditch. The profile was a narrow U-shape, on average 0.8 m wide and 0.65 m deep with no recuts. The fill was mixed, consisting of non-gravelly material, silty loam with gravel and some coarser primary silting. A small assemblage of 25 sherds of pottery (311 g) and 20 animal bones from the ditch fill probably represented rubbish deposition.

Ditch 344 (Fig 8.1)

Ditch 344 formed three sides of a rectilinear ditched enclosure which appears to have been open ended. It may have been contemporary in terms of layout with ditch 343, which was of similar character and lay just to the east, but 344 also seemed to continue in use into the later Roman period. It cut both enclosure 391 and the small possible enclosure ditch 345. Ditch 344 was 45 m in length and defined an area with maximum internal dimensions of approximately 17.5 m east-west by 14 m north-south. The 'enclosure' was open on its east side. Some 40% of this ditch was excavated in seven segments. The ditch was 0.5 m wide on average, and 0.55 m deep with a U-shaped profile. The single fill was variable in composition, ranging from non-gravelly silty loams, through silty loams with gravel to very gravelly material, with some coarser primary silting and lenses of burning. Pottery, animal bone and one fragment of metalworking slag mixed with the burnt material suggested rubbish deposition, possibly from structures within the enclosure. The 55 sherds (1080 g) of pottery are quite well preserved with an average weight of 19.6 g. The group is dominated by grog-tempered ware (fabric E80) but also includes several local grey sandy wares, a 2nd-century Oxfordshire mortarium (Young 1977, type M6) and an oxidised bowl (ibid. form O42) of similar date. The animal bone includes the usual range of domesticates and one dog mandible.

Features in the south-west of the site

A number of early Roman features were found lying to the west of enclosure 391, towards the southern edge of the site. These were a small penannular enclosure, a group of ditches, all but one quite closely adjacent to enclosure 391, and a fence line. The general similarity of alignment suggests that many of these features were broadly contemporary.

Enclosure 945 (Fig. 8.1)

Enclosure 945 was a small irregular penannular ring-gully *c* 3.2 m across located immediately west of enclosure 391. It was excavated in five sections, which represented 30% of its original length. The entrance to this enclosure lay to the SSW, and was 0.95 m wide. Two postholes which formed part of fence line 1757 were cut into the natural between the gully terminals but had no stratigraphic relationship with the enclosure ditch (see below). The gully profile varied between an open and a narrow U-shape, and there was at least one recut, but possibly more. The average width of the cuts was 0.39 m and the average depth 0.15 m. There were four fills which varied from gravelly to gravel free. Six sherds of pottery and two animal bones were recovered from the gully. These were probably stray finds incorporated into the fill through secondary deposition.

Fence line 1757 (Fig. 8.1)

A fence line 13.2 m long lay in the south of the site just to the west of enclosure 391B. It ran from the south edge of the excavation in a northerly direction, parallel to ditch 879, but curved slightly to the north-east to run to the entrance of the penannular enclosure 945, and it is assumed that the fence and the small enclosure were in contemporary use. The fence line was made up of seven postholes (907, 908, 909, 911, 912, 946 and 947) which were circular or slightly oval in plan with diameters of 0.35-0.5 m, but were very shallow (at most 0.14 m deep). They were filled with mid to dark grey-brown silty sand with 2% gravel and contained no finds.

Ditches west of enclosure 391 (Fig. 8.1)

Several short lengths of ditch/gully were located in the vicinity of the small penannular gully 945. To the north, gully 960 was a curvilinear feature 1.65 m long that ran parallel to the outer north-west edge of enclosure 391 and was cut away at its north end by enclosure 206. To the south it merged with a group of amorphous pits. The open U-shaped gully was 0.52 m wide and 0.18 m deep. Its single, non-gravelly fill contained no finds.

Gully 964 to the west was aligned north-south. It was cut by penannular gully 945 to the south, and by a cluster of amorphous pits to the north. It was similar in profile to 960 and was 0.4 m wide and 0.24 m deep. The single, gravel-free fill was again undated by finds.

Ditch 957, 5.45 m in length and aligned east-west, was at right angles to and almost contiguous with 964, lying just north-west of penannular gully 945. This feature had very irregular edges. Its southern edge appeared to be cut by an amorphous pit, and to the east it ended in a large oval terminal while to the west it petered out. One section was excavated through this ditch, revealing an open U-shaped profile with no recuts. The ditch was 0.6 m wide and 0.22 m deep. The single fill, of gravel-free material, produced no finds.

To the south, ditch 879 was 8.75 m in length. It was aligned north-south but, like 957, had an irregular edge (on its east side), possibly caused by the difficulty of distinguishing between its fills and those of a series of pits which had been cut into it. To the north it ended in a terminal and to the south it petered out approximately 2 m short of the southern limit of excavation. Three sections were excavated representing 30% of the extant length. The ditch profile was an open U-shape, and no recuts were apparent. The average width was 0.69 m and the average depth 0.37 m. Two fills were consistently present, but they varied in composition along the length of the feature, so that gravel-free, non-gravelly and silty loam with gravel fills were all present. Two large, unabraded sherds of grog-tempered pottery were recovered from the ditch, along with two fragments of cattle bone and a single piece of sheep-goat bone.

Ditch 624 (Fig. 8.1)

Ditch 624 was an isolated stretch of linear ditch 10.4 m long and aligned NE-SW, located towards the south-west corner of the site some 30 m west of ditch 879. It terminated approximately 0.9 m short of a large pit at its north-eastern end, and was obscured by colluvium to the south. It was excavated in three sections, representing *c* 25% of its extant length. The ditch profile was an open U-shape, and no recuts were observed. The average width was 0.62 m, and average depth was 0.24 m. There was a single fill which consisted of silty loams with very variable quantities of gravel, gravel being dominant in the fill of the terminal. Pottery, nine animal bones and charred plant remains were recovered from the ditch fill. The pottery assemblage was substantial comprising some 105 sherds (1760 g). Unlike many of the other groups of this period the assemblage largely comprised 'Romanised' local reduced and oxidised wares including two examples of late 1st to early 2nd-century oxidised wall-sided carinated bowls (Young 1977, form O42) with only a single 'Belgic-type' sherd.

Boundary ditches to the east

Boundaries on the eastern edge of the settlement consisted of three substantial ditches, two of which were roughly right-angled in plan, while the third was slightly curvilinear. These ditches were recorded during salvage work to the east of the main excavated area. The most substantial of them appeared to be the curvilinear example 2593, which was aligned broadly north-south. It extended beyond the edge of the site to the north, while petering out to the south-east; its terminus was not identified. West of ditch 2593 in the space between the ditch and the main complex of settlement features were the remains of two pottery kilns (see above). The other two ditches (2062, 2035) were less substantial, and were situated to the west and south of 2593 where they apparently defined the edges of paddocks or enclosures related to the larger ditch. It seems likely that the latter formed a major boundary at the eastern margin of the settlement.

Ditch 2593 (Fig. 8.1)

Ditch 2593 was a large curvilinear ditch 92 m in length, aligned roughly north-south. The profile was mostly an open U-shape, but was narrow in places. At least two recuts were noted in a machine-dug section cut through the ditch about half way along its length, but there may have been more and it is likely that the feature represents numerous versions of a relatively slight but significant boundary, rather than a single very large feature redefined occasionally. The overall width of the ditch varied between 3 m and 6.8 m except at its southern end where it narrowed considerably; its maximum recorded depth was 0.55 m. The principal cut contained two fills of sandy loam with gravel. Fifty-two sherds of pottery (2735 g), 20 animal bones and one fragment of dense slag from metalworking came from the ditch fill. The pottery assemblage which, while not large for the size of the feature, was derived from very limited interventions, is notable for the large average sherd weight, 52 g, suggesting refuse material that had undergone little disturbance. The group comprised exclusively local wares, dominated by the grog and sand-tempered fabric R94 accompanied by fabrics R37, O11, E80 and E30. A single sherd of an Oxfordshire colour-coated mortarium (Young 1977, type C97) is presumed to be intrusive, since the assemblage otherwise suggests a date in the later 1st-2nd century for the infill of this feature.

Gully 2035 (Fig. 8.1)

Gully 2035 was 11.2 m in length and ran SSW from the southern part of 2593, by which it was cut. Since 2035 did not extend east of 2593 it is likely to have been continuous with an early component of the 2593 complex not distinguished in plan. The gully was slightly irregular in plan and faded out at its south-west end approximately 2 m east of ditch 2062. Two sections were excavated through this gully, representing *c* 10% of its extant length. The profile was an open U-shape, with an average width of 0.32 m and an average depth of 0.14 m. No recuts were observed and there was a single fill of sterile silt.

Ditch 2062 (Fig. 8.1)

Ditch 2062 was an irregular right-angled ditch with an extant length of *c* 32 m. Its eastern end terminated over a large later Iron Age pit (2063), and to the south it ran beyond the edge of the excavation. It is possible that this ditch formed part of an enclosure, perhaps a small field or paddock, with boundary ditch 2593 or 2035 to its east. The ditch profile was an open U-shape, and no recuts were observed. The average width of the ditch was 0.55 m, and its average depth was 0.23 m. The single fill of silty loam with gravel produced one sherd of coarse grey ware pottery and an ox tooth, confirming the impression that this was a field boundary unrelated to structures.

Ditch 2528 (Fig. 8.1)

Ditch 2528 was a right-angled ditch 43 m in length. Its southern terminus was not certainly located, but may have been approximately 3 m north of the corner of ditch 2062 (above). Ditch 2528 ran north from this point before turning east and terminating approximately 2 m west of ditch 2593. It was cut by a later Roman trackway ditch on the same alignment. Like feature 2062, ditch 2528 may have formed an enclosure in association with ditch 2593 and with ditch 2062 probably forming its south side. This enclosure would have been roughly 28 m north-south and almost as wide at its widest point east-west. The ditch profile was an open U-shape, and one recut was observed in section. The unexcavated east-west arm of the ditch was up to 2.3 m wide but as with 2593 this may represent the combined width of several recuts. The average depth of the two observed cuts was 0.6 m. There were two fills, both of sandy silt, which produced three sherds of pottery, including a large sherd of Dressel 20 olive-oil amphora, and three fragments of animal bone. Again this suggests that the enclosure ditches were not used for significant rubbish disposal.

Finds distributions from the ditches

The majority of the finds from the ditches comprised animal bone and abraded sherds of pottery which probably represent the dumping of rubbish into the open ditches, combined with the secondary deposition of material that had been lying around on the ground surface. Most of the material came from the larger enclosure ditches, which generally contained quantities of finds in proportion to their size. Particularly heavy concentrations of artefactual and ecofactual material in ditches 138, 51 and 391 indicate that these enclosures probably contained buildings. The smaller ditches, some of which may have represented paddock or field boundaries, generally contained less material and this is more likely to represent secondary deposition rather than dumping. However, there were some exceptions, particularly

Table 8.1 Early Roman pit dimensions (m) by type (range for those where dimensions were recorded).

Dimensions	*Undercut*	*Cylindrical*	*Bowl-shaped*	*Rectangular*	*Shallow saucer*	*Irregular*
Diameter	0.9	0.4-1.3	0.23-1.0	1.05	0.27-1.0	0.27-3.0
Depth	1.0	0.34-1.44	0.11-0.75	0.33	0.11-0.4	0.19-0.88

Table 8.2 Numbers of early Roman pits by type.

	Undercut (GSP)	*Cylindrical*	*Bowl shaped*	*Rectangular*	*Shallow saucer*	*Other*	*Total*
Yarnton	1	8	17	1	5	15	47

ditch 624, which contained a large quantity of pottery amounting to just over 100 sherds. This may represent the dumping of domestic refuse into ditches away from the site, as may have been the case with deposits found in boundary ditch 2593. A large quantity of metalworking debris including a fragment of furnace debris came from the fills of ditch 187, indicating that metalworking may have been carried out within this enclosure. Apart from this, metalworking debris and other finds were generally scarce and plant remains were mostly confined to the larger ditches.

Metal small finds were recovered from seven ditches, including a copper alloy brooch and stud from enclosure 440, an iron loop from ditch 391C and nails from enclosures 293 and 51. A worked bone artefact came from enclosure 187, which also produced a saddle quern, while part of an Old Red Sandstone rotary quern from gully 1048.

Articulated animal bone from ditch fills

Articulated animal bone was found in some of the ditches. A cattle torso lay within the ditches of enclosure 138 and articulating toes came from enclosure 187. Possible special deposits include a pair of cattle mandibles also from enclosure 187.

EARLY ROMAN PITS

Summary

A total of 47 excavated pits were attributed to the early Roman phase, suggesting that there may have been around 188 pits of this date present on site (see above Chapter 5). The early Roman pits were divided into six categories generally based on their shape in profile. These were the same as the categories used for the Iron Age period, except that rectangular pits were also present for the first time. There were no large, shallow pits. The majority of the pits were circular or oval in plan.

Distribution

The early Roman pits mainly occupied the central and north-eastern part of the settlement area, forming a relatively dispersed scatter with a NE-SW axis. This distribution coincided with the main area of early Roman enclosures and ditches, and very few pits were found beyond the settlement area.

Table 8.3 Numbers of early Roman pit fill types.

Silty loams	*Gravel-free fills*	*Non-gravelly fills*	*Gravelly fills*	*Other*
14	19	8	1	5

Description

Pit diameter ranged from 0.23 m to 3 m, averaging 0.87 m, and pit depth ranged between 0.11 m and 1.44 m averaging 0.45 m (Table 8.1). Recorded original pit volume ranged between 0.020 m^3 and 3.360 m^3, and averaged 0.354 m^3. The variation in pit size was, therefore, relatively high, although not as high as that seen in the middle Iron Age or late Iron Age/early Roman periods.

The majority of the early Roman pits were either bowl-shaped or irregular in profile, although there were relatively substantial numbers of cylindrical and shallow saucer-shaped examples (Table 8.2). It is notable that the numbers of cylindrical pits in comparison to bowl-shaped and irregular examples had declined in this period; although this trend had begun in the late Iron Age/early Roman period, it is particularly marked here. It presumably reflects a continuing (if not complete) shift away from below-ground storage of grain.

The number of fills contained within individual pits ranged from one to twenty, although the vast majority contained one to four fills and only three pits contained five or six. The average number of fills per pit was two. The majority of pit fills were gravel-free, but there were a relatively high proportion of silty loams, and some non-gravelly fills (Table 8.3). One pit contained a very gravelly fill, and the fills of five pits were very mixed.

There does not appear to have been any correlation of fill type with pit shape in the early Roman pits. In fact the most common fill in the majority of

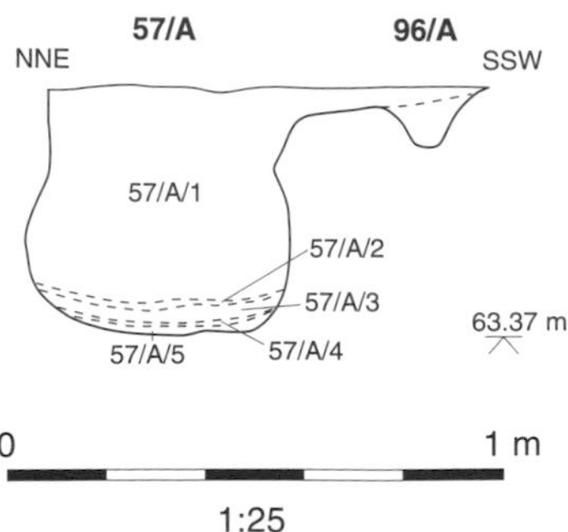

Fig. 8.11 Section through pit 57

Table 8.4 Occurrence of animal bone in early Roman pits.

Species	*No. of pits*
Cattle	19
Cattle/Horse size	14
Horse	5
Sheep/Goat	21
Sheep/Pig size	14
Pig	7
Dog	1
Wild animals	1

pit types was gravel-free, and those pit types which were not most often filled with gravel-free material were the least common categories. Recuts were very rare in the early Roman pits; only one was recorded, and it may be assumed that this represents a real pattern. Nine pits contained identifiable evidence of primary silting, and of these two were over 0.8 m^3 in volume. Four pits were recorded as deliberately backfilled, and all of these were over 0.8 m^3 in volume.

Deliberate deposits were found in five pits, none of which were over 0.8 m^3 in volume. Three of these pits were classified as storage pits on the basis of their morphology, for example pit 57 (eg Fig. 8.11). Redeposited material was commoner in the early Roman period than in the Iron Age, with only 18 out of 47 pits having no signs of redeposition (as represented by 'residual' finds), 11 with low levels of redeposition, 15 with medium levels and 4 with high levels.

Finds distributions in early Roman pits

Bone

One early Roman pit (1060), located in the north-east area of the site 5 m south of the northern limit of excavations beneath a late Roman ditch (Fig. 8.1), contained a fragment of human skull and an unusually high number of right cattle femora (a minimum of 12; Chapter 17 below). Of the 47 pits assigned to early Roman period, 30 contained animal bone (Table 8.4). The assemblage consisted mainly of cattle and horse bone, but there was some pig, sheep, goat and dog. A pair of sheep mandibles and a partial pig burial were found in pit 57 (Chapter 17). One pit contained a hare bone.

Patterning among the animal bones from early Roman pits is not very evident. All 30 of the early Roman pits containing animal bone had bones of at least one of the major domestic species, and ten contained bones of all these species. There seems to have been little differentiation between, or separation of, the different domestic species, and in these respects the distribution of bone in this phase was little different from that seen in the preceding phases. Far fewer pits contained dog and human bone than in preceding periods, particularly the middle Iron Age, and neither of these species was associated with the other. However, although horse bone, human bone and wild animal bone were not deposited within the same contexts, they was clearly deposited in the same general area; namely the north-eastern part of the site. Deposition patterns were, therefore, not entirely random.

Pottery

Of the 47 early Roman pits, 37 contained pottery. The total assemblage comprised 468 sherds, weighing 10.95 kg. The average number of sherds per pit was 13, and the average weight of pottery per pit was 283 g. Comparison of mean sherd weight against sherd count for the early Roman pits, revealed a pattern that is familiar from the preceding phases (see Chapters 5-7). On the basis of this analysis the pits were divisible into two groups, the larger group containing small quantities of small sherds, and a few pits containing either small quantities of large sherds or large quantities of small sherds.

Fig. 8.12 Pot base in pit 837

Two pits, 71 and 837, contained apparently deliberate deposits of substantial parts of pots; most of a vessel in a reduced coarse ware in pit 71 and the complete base of a large shell-tempered ware jar in pit 837 (Fig. 8.12). Clearly these deposits represent a very small proportion of the pottery deposited in this phase, and in general little patterning was evident in the distribution of pottery.

Plant remains

Five of the 47 early Roman pits contained plant remains. Two of these pits were over 0.8 m^3 in volume, and their average original volume was 1.048 m^3. One of these pits contained charcoal, two contained deliberate deposits and three contained rubbish deposits.

Of the early Roman pits containing plant remains, one was bowl-shaped, one was cylindrical and three were irregular. It is clear that plant remains were not evenly distributed through the different pit types (Table 8.5). The cylindrical pit (1088) contained the largest amount of material, and amounts in irregular pits were also substantial, but the bowl-shaped pit contained very little. The material in pit 1088 was dominated by cereal chaff, but other pits produced quite variable proportions of grain, chaff and seeds of weeds or wild plants (see Table 18.7 below).

Analysis of the spatial distribution and context of plant remains from early Roman pits is difficult, as the sample is so small and the depositional processes uncertain. However, their association with deposits of pottery and other burnt material is of interest.

Table 8.5 Quantities of early Roman charred plant remains by pit type.

Pit type	*Cylindrical*	*Bowl shaped*	*Irregular*	*Total*
No. pits sampled	1	1	3	5
Cereals	32	4	77	113
Chaff	273	1	72	346
Weed seeds	129	1	251	381
Ave. no. cereals per sampled pit	32	4	25.7	22.6

Table 8.6 Early Roman pits containing small finds.

Context	*Pit type*	*Small find*	*Material*
308	Amorphous	Brick	Fired clay
481	Amorphous	Miscellaneous	Flint
836	Amorphous	Brooch	Copper alloy
1082	Rectangular	Quern	Stone
1088	Cylindrical	Daub	Fired clay
1144	Bowl-shaped	Daub	Fired clay
1160	Shallow saucer	Miscellaneous	Fired clay
1192	Amorphous	Scythe	Iron
1192	Amorphous	Daub	Fired clay
1192	Amorphous	Flake	Flint
1192	Amorphous	Flake	Flint
1622	Bowl-shaped	Awl	Iron
2071	Bowl-shaped	Quern	Stone

Metalworking Debris

Few fragments of metalworking debris were recovered from the early Roman pits, and its distribution was consequently limited. Four pits, 1216, 1387, 1082 and 1088, contained metalworking debris, seven fragments in total, four of which were of fuel ash slag. The majority of material was recovered from cylindrical pits, two of which contained three of the slag fragments. Additionally one fragment was recovered from a rectangular pit, and one from a shallow saucer shaped pit.

Two pits containing metalworking slags were found in the north-eastern corner of the early Roman pit scatter, and one, 1387, was situated in the far north-western corner of the excavation area (Fig. 8.1). The incidence of fragments per pit was so low that it probably represents a background scatter away from the source of the metalworking.

Small Finds

Just three metal small finds and two stone quern fragments were recovered from the early Roman pits, with fragments of fired clay/daub from five pits and redeposited flints in three (Table 8.6). The majority came from pits classified as amorphous/irregular, although a substantial minority came from bowl-shaped pits. The small finds assemblage itself was more diverse than those recovered from the Iron Age pits, and included a copper alloy brooch (SF 327 from pit 836), an iron reaping hook (SF 360 from pit 1192), an iron awl (SF 402 from pit 1622) and two quernstones. Of the quernstones, one is a typical Iron Age saddle quern from pit 1082, the other is represented by fragments of Niedermendig lava in pit 2071. A possible fragment of fired clay loomweight came from pit 1160. Once again this may merely reflect a change in the kind of artefact in use, rather than a shift in deposition practices.

Distribution

Pits containing small finds were found in the eastern and southern part of the early Roman settlement, reflecting where the majority of all the pits lay. There were no obvious patterns in the deposition of different classes of artefact, and no associations between structures and small finds.

CREMATION BURIALS

Three cremation burials were uncovered to the east of the settlement, between the occupation area and its eastern boundary ditch (Fig. 8.1; Chapter 16).

Fig. 8.13 Cremation burial 2501 with urn

They all lay within the salvage area and had been badly truncated. Cremation burial 2505 was found in a small bowl-shaped pit 0.24 m in diameter and 0.18 m deep. A similar feature, 2534, 0.19 m in diameter and 0.06 m deep, contained the cremated remains of a child.

Cremation burial 2501 was found within the smashed remains of an early Roman vessel (Fig. 8.13), but was accompanied by a well-preserved copper-alloy brooch, of Aesica type (Henig, Chapter 15; Figs 15.1 and 15.2, No. 2). It survived within a very shallow scoop, 0.2 m in diameter and 0.07 m deep.

ROMAN FEATURES IN CRESSWELL FIELD

A number of features of probable or certain Roman date were located in the western part of the Cresswell Field site (Fig. 8.14). In most cases dating evidence was extremely poor, and the only pottery derived from some of these features was entirely of Iron Age date, but attribution to the Roman period is consistent with the stratigraphic relationships as well as with the limited finds. It is possible that the features described here spanned the entire period, encompassing late Iron Age/early Roman, early Roman and late Roman phases, but this cannot be demonstrated and they are treated all together for convenience.

Enclosure in the south-western corner of Creswell Field (Figs 8.14 and 8.15)

The north-west corner of a probable ditched enclosure was located in the extreme south-west corner of the site. This was of at least two main phases. The initial phase was represented by gullies 8096 and 7925 on the north-east and north-west sides respectively. These gullies were steep-sided and 7925, in particular, was V-shaped in profile. The enclosure, which had minimum dimensions of *c* 16 m (NW-SE) by 13 m (NE-SW) was slightly enlarged in a second phase, the ditch in this phase (8095 and 7870) being more substantial – still steep-sided, but wider (up to *c* 1.3 m) and flat-bottomed, with multiple fills (Fig. 6.21). Additional lengths of unexcavated gullies are visible in plan both inside and outside the alignments of the two principal phases of enclosure just described. Some may relate to other recuts of the enclosure, but others are more eccentrically aligned and their relationships to the main enclosure features are unknown.

Some 67 sherds (547 g) of Iron Age pottery, mostly of early Iron Age character, were recovered from the fills of cuts 8095 and 8096 but it seems almost certain that this material is entirely redeposited. The character of these features is very different from that of any others before the late Iron Age. The rectangular nature of the enclosure to which they relate is emphasised by the geophysical survey (eg Fig. 6.20). It is possible that this formed part of a field system (see below, Chapter 11).

Features in the north-western part of Cresswell Field (Figs 8.14 and 8.15)

North of the enclosure corner its alignment was roughly mirrored by a slightly curving feature (7920) on a broad east-west alignment. This wide feature, the result of several phases of intercutting of adjacent ditches on the same general alignment, had a total length of *c* 32 m, with well-defined terminals at each end. This sequence of ditches was cut by the southern terminal of a roughly south-north aligned ditch (7880/7693) which extended beyond the north baulk of the site. A further ditch, 7577, ran parallel to and east of this feature in its northern half, while further east again another ditch (7609) ran south-eastwards from the north baulk, approximately parallel to the eastern part of ditch complex 7920. Like the latter feature, the south-eastern terminus of 7609 lay about 15 m east of the line of north-south ditch 7693. although in the case of 7609 its alignment was continued after a short gap by a much slighter gully, 7447, of which a 7.5 m length survived.

These features may have been intended to form part of a system of paddocks or enclosures, but the complete lack of any related features on the eastern side makes such an interpretation very uncertain. The character of the more sharply-defined north-south ditches, particularly 7693, is reflected in a

Fig. 8.14 Plan of Roman features at Creswell Field

length of east-west ditch (8039), lying exactly at right angles to the line of 7693, but situated south of the west end of ditch complex 7920. 8039 extended further west than 7920 towards the line of the palaeochannel at the western margin of Cresswell Field. Two pits east of the eastern terminal of this feature included one (7961) which produced the tip of an iron knife blade of Roman type (see Allen, Chapter 15 below (No. 4); Gilmore, Chapter 15 and Fig. 15.17).

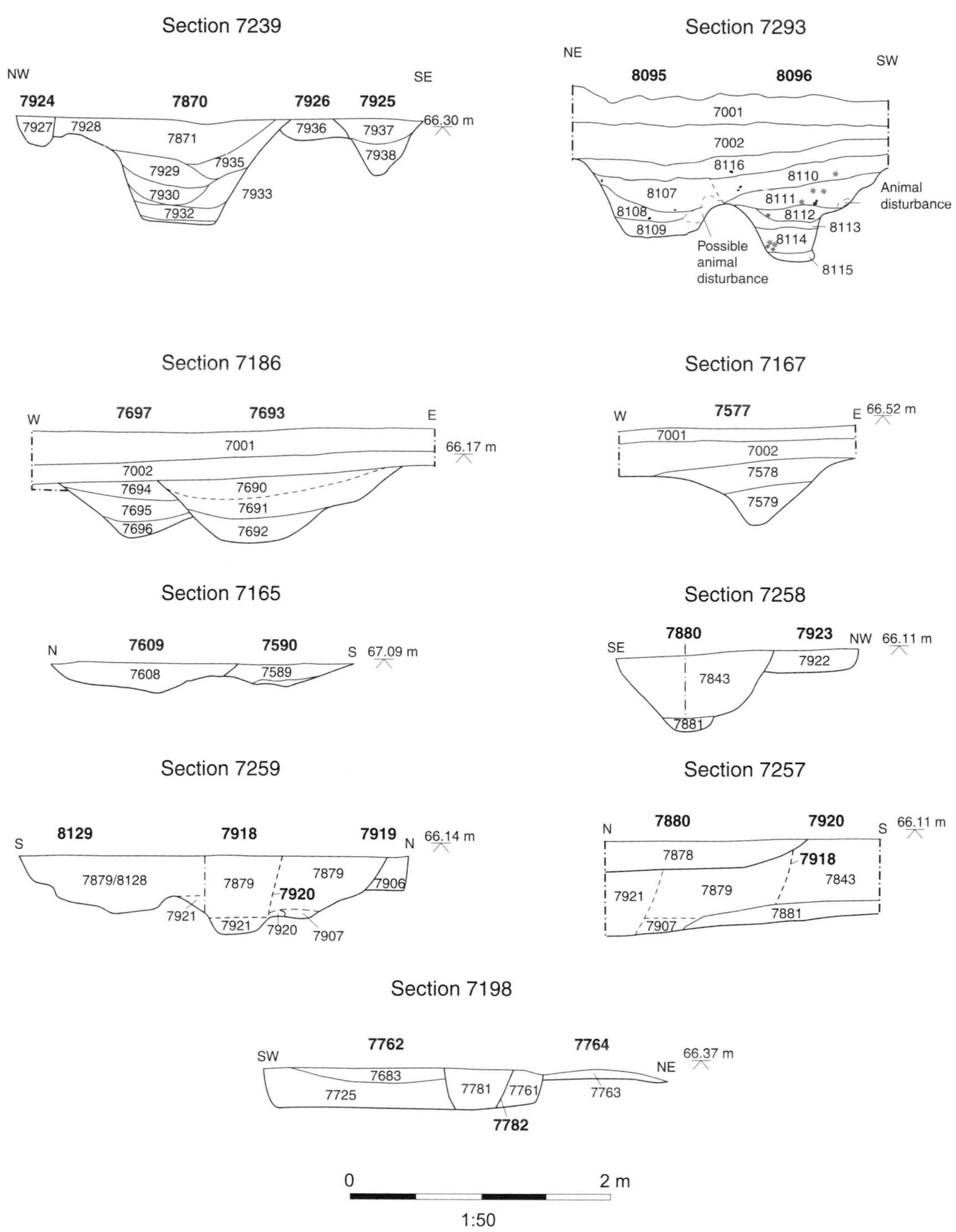

Fig. 8.15 Sections of Roman features at Cresswell Field

Chapter 9: The Late Roman Period

by Dan Stansbie and Paul Booth

INTRODUCTION

The settlement underwent considerable reorganisation at the beginning of the late Roman period. The main area of late Roman activity was situated in the northern part of the Yarnton site and probably also lay to the north of the excavation area, in an area beneath the quarry boundary that was not examined (Fig. 9.1). Three zones of activity can be identified associated with the settlement. The eastern and southern margins of settlement were defined by trackways, and inhumation burials were placed in the south-east part of the site around these features.

The large early Roman oval enclosure, 187, which had occupied the centre of the site at Yarnton was replaced with a series of rectilinear enclosures which partly extended beyond the northern limit of the excavation. A possible rectangular post-built structure lay within one of these, as did a kidney-shaped feature thought to be associated with agricultural processing. Abutting these enclosures to the east was a series of curvilinear ditches and gullies and a circular and slightly sunken building, of which the compact floor and drainage gullies survived. Two corn-drying ovens were also found in this area.

To the south-west, the eastern side of a possible rectilinear enclosure with a wide entrance at the north-east corner lay partly within the excavated area. Within it were another corn-drying oven and a number of pits. In the south-eastern part of the site the large penannular enclosure, 391, had gone out of use and had been replaced by rectangular enclosure 344 at the end of the early Roman period. A spread of dark soil and finds (354) within that enclosure included later Roman material, suggesting that while its ditch may have become infilled the enclosure was still used, if only for the deposition of refuse.

A substantial trackway ran NNE-SSW to the east of the settlement, and appeared to have overlain, or possibly originally been associated with, earlier paddocks. It was defined by two parallel ditches, approximately 20 m apart. A ditch just south of the main excavation area ran WNW-ESE, at right angles to the line of the track, and probably formed part of the same routeway. A parallel ditch is likely to have been present even further south, but it was not possible to observe more than a small part of the southern area before gravel extraction. The remains of a small inhumation cemetery were found near the suggested junction of these tracks, and six burials were examined. In addition, two cremation burials were discovered on the settlement site, cutting early Roman enclosure ditches. Their precise date is uncertain.

LATE ROMAN STRUCTURES

Summary

Six possible structures are associated with this phase of settlement. The traces of two possible buildings survive from the late Roman period, one of which was post-built, largely on postpads, and little of it survived, and the other was an unusual sunken building which was approximately circular. This appears to have been at least partly post-built and was associated with a floor surface and surrounded by short lengths of gully. An ambiguous kidney-shaped depression, lined with compact gravel and stone, was situated towards the south-east side of an irregular sub-rectangular enclosure. The remaining three structures are all thought to be corn-drying ovens, although one is only very tentatively identified as such. As in the late Iron Age and early Roman periods, it is probable that other structures would have been present, but had been built using sill-beam or mass-wall construction, leaving no archaeologically-detectable trace (see Chapter 7 for a more detailed discussion of this).

Structures

Kidney- shaped feature 491/494 (Figs 9.1 and 9.2)

This feature measured 8.6 m by 3.9 m and was filled with compact gravel and limestone, with some burnt material, 491, which principally lined its edges. It consisted of two parallel curvilinear depressions, *c* 3.5 m and 1 m wide and 0.3-0.4 m deep, which were flat bottomed and conjoined at the top. The outer and narrower feature was also shorter, terminating 3 m short of the larger depression. Its function is unknown.

A substantial amount of pottery (142 sherds, 2.7 kg), 86 animal bones, one splinter of human long bone, fragments of two quernstones (SF 224, 225 and 226), a slab of Forest Marble (SF 174) and an iron ferrule (SF 175) were recovered from the fill of this feature, suggesting that its final use was for the dumping of rubbish. The Roman pottery was

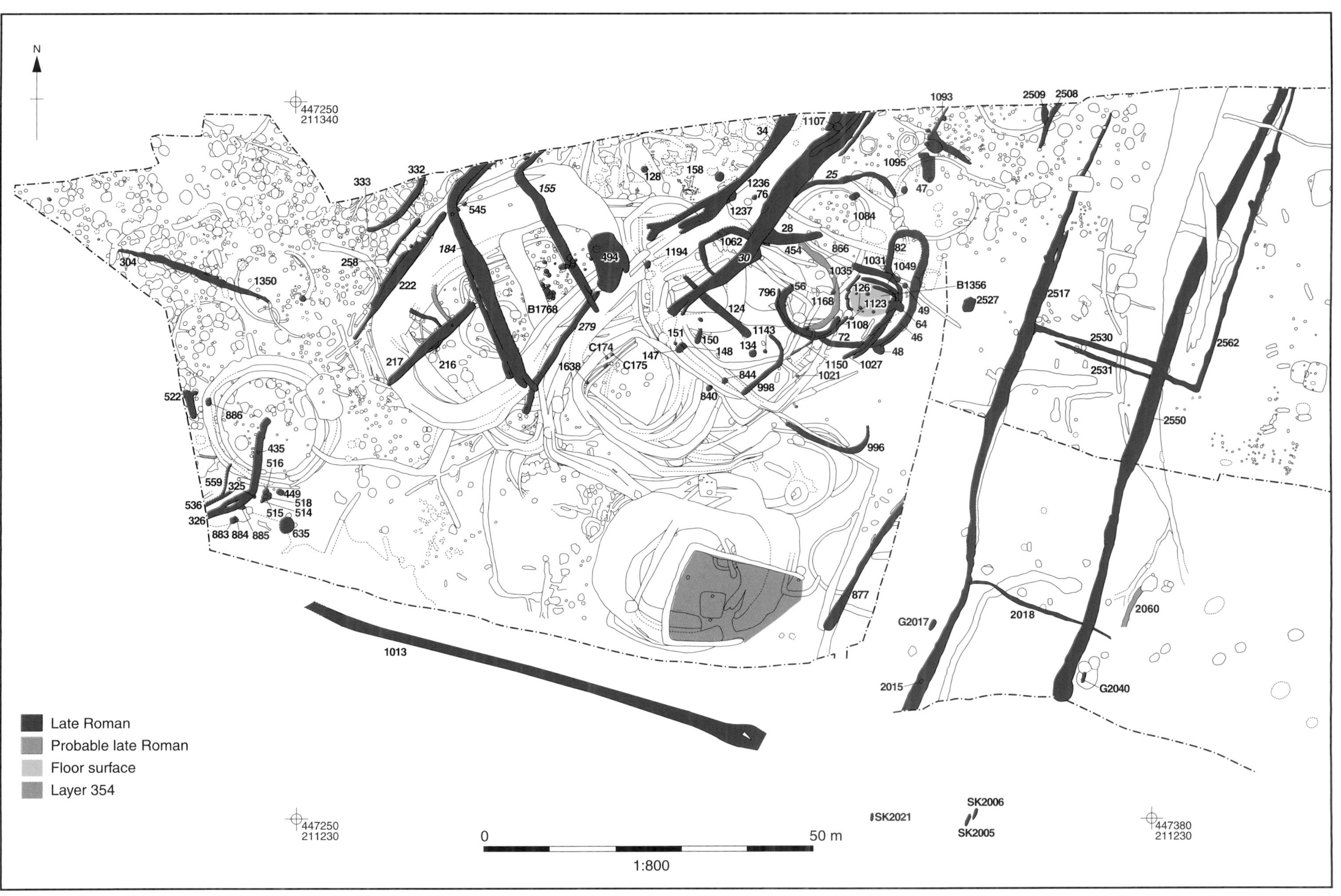

Fig. 9.1 Plan of late Roman features at Yarnton

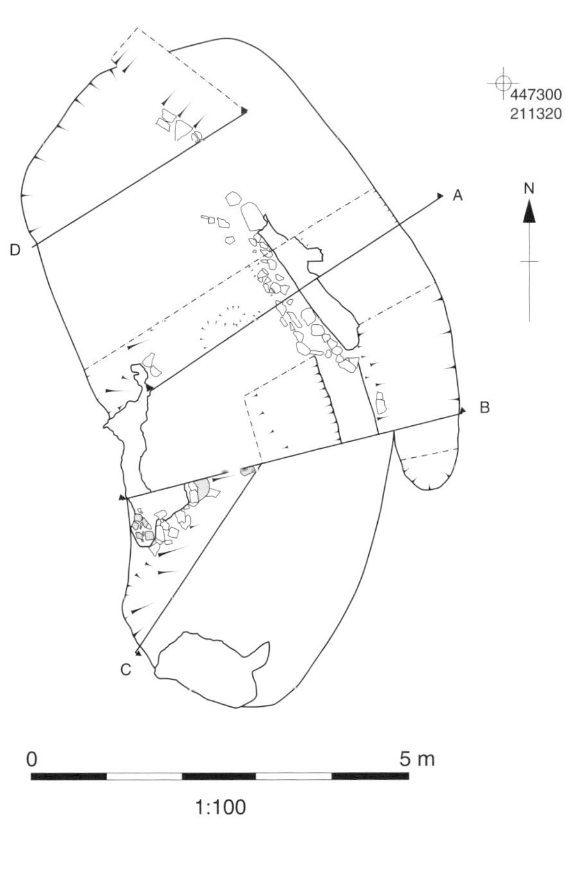

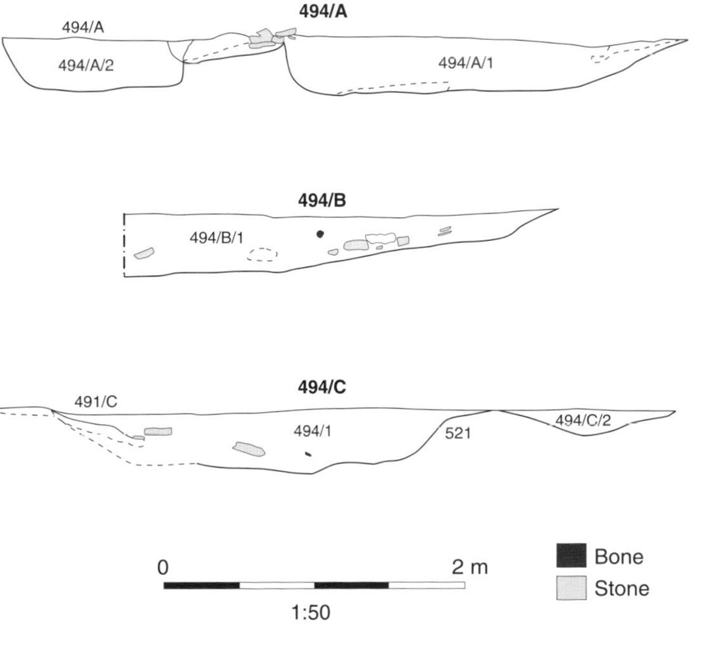

Fig. 9.2 Kidney-shaped feature 491/494

moderately well-preserved in terms of sherd size with an average weight of 19 g. A significant proportion of the assemblage comprised local grey wares but this was accompanied by Oxfordshire mortaria, (white ware, white-slipped and colour-coated examples), Oxfordshire colour-coated wares and shell-tempered wares ranging in date from the 2nd century through to the early-mid 4th century. Overall the assemblage suggests a *terminus post quem* in the 4th century. The animal bone includes a variety of animal species, notably sheep, sheep/goat, ox, cow, pig, horse, hare and rodent.

Post-built structure 1768 (Figs 9.1, 9.3 and 9.4)

Structure 1768 formed the remains of a post-built building consisting of three postpads (610, 702 and 775) and four postholes which defined a sub-rectangular area 3.5 m x 5 m. It is assumed that other related features have been destroyed. The postpads consisted of limestone blocks measuring approximately 0.25 m x 0.16 m x 0.03 m, which were set into shallow saucer-shaped hollows. Circular postholes set into the post-pads averaged 0.86 m in diameter and were between 0.08 m and 0.36 m in depth. The fills of the postpad hollows consisted of mid brown silty-loams with a 2% gravel content. A large, worn slab was recovered from post-pad 775. Five sherds of pottery came from the fills of postholes 610 and 775, with a sherd of Oxfordshire colour-coated ware from each, along with one fragment of fuel ash slag, a quartzite anvil stone (SF 193) and an iron file (SF 230).

This building lay to the west of kidney-shaped features 494, and may have been associated with it.

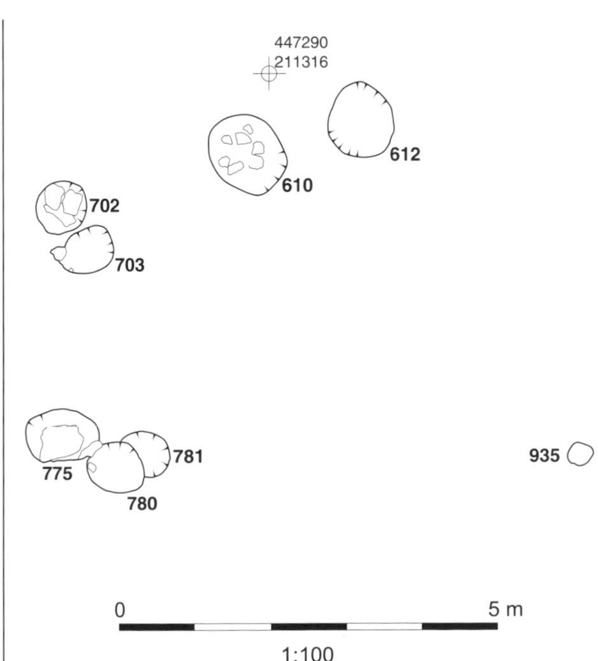

Fig. 9.3 Plan of post-built structure 1768

Fig. 9.4 Postpads and other remains of structure 1768 looking north. Scales 2 m

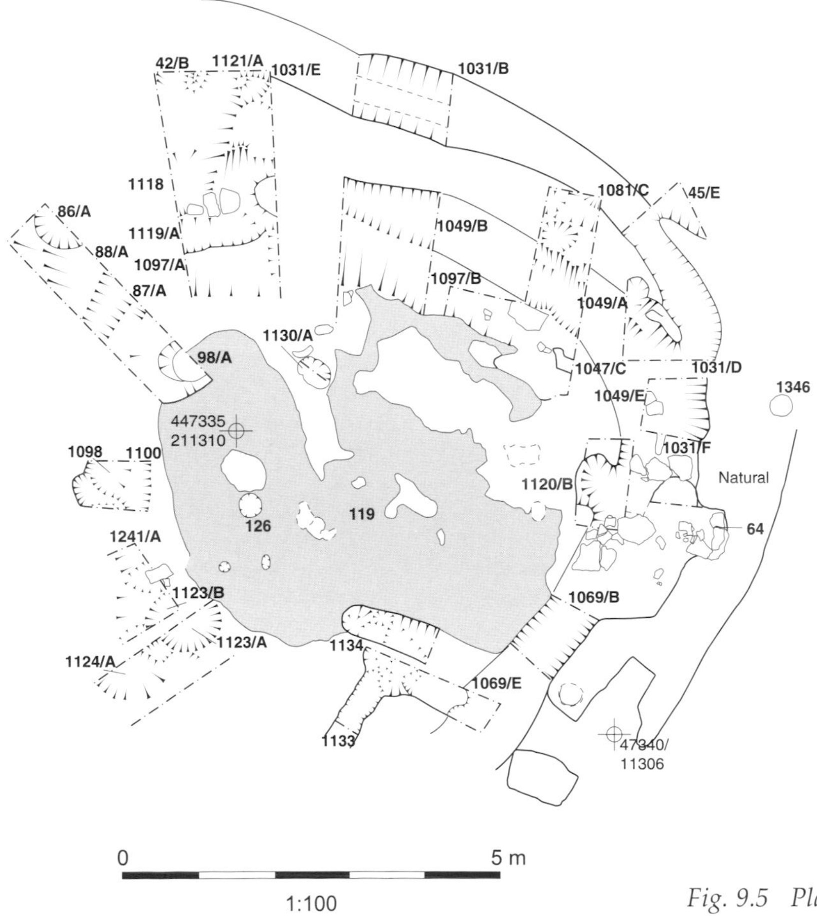

Fig. 9.5 Plan of structure 1356

Structure 1356 (Figs 9.1, 9.5 and 9.6)

The structure

This was a sub-circular structure with a diameter of 8.5 m located towards the eastern edge of the excavated area. It was defined on at least three sides by short lengths of gully, and on the fourth by postholes. Other postholes lay within the building. The entrance is thought to have lain to the south, and some limestone slabs to the east which were originally thought to represent a threshold were subsequently found to belong to a corn-drying oven inserted into the east wall of the structure. Inside the building a floor surface (119) measuring approximately 5.5 m by 6.5 m was partially preserved, and this was associated with a hearth and some pits. Concentrations of finds in the fills of the surrounding gullies support an interpretation of the structure as domestic in function although its overall form was not very coherent. While unusual, this structure does have a parallel in two earlier buildings found within the Cassington Big Enclosure (Case 1982a, 136).

Ditch 1049

A penannular enclosure ditch 16 m in circumference and comprising a series of short ditches/gullies was found around the north and east sides of floor surface 119. Approximately a third of this ditch/gully system was excavated. Profiles varied, being flat-based in places and V-shaped in others. Widths ranged from 0.3-1 m, averaging 0.7 m, and depths varied from 0.2-0.52 m, averaging 0.36 m. Fills were of gravel-free silty loam.

Ditch 1031

Outside ditch 1049 and for the most part running parallel, but eventually curving to cut it, was another curvilinear ditch (1031), 16.5 m in length, which was probably part of a sub-rectangular enclosure surrounding the area containing structure 1356 (see above). The ditch profile was U-shaped and open, and was 0.6 m wide and 0.32 m deep. Fills consisted of silty loams (some with gravel), and gravel-dominated deposits. There was some primary silting, and some fills contained flat limestone slabs.

Gully 1027

Running south-west from the south end of ditch 1031 was a gully 9 m in length. Feature 1027 may in some way have defined the north-west side of structure 1356, but its interpretation is not certain. It was 0.4 m wide and 0.2 m deep. Fills consisted of non-gravelly material and silty loams with gravel; there was some primary silting.

Finds from the ditches

Amongst the finds from the ditches were 300 pot sherds weighing 5.5 kg, 130 animal bones and two fragments of metalworking debris, one a fragment of

Fig. 9.6 Structure 1356 looking south. Scale 2 m

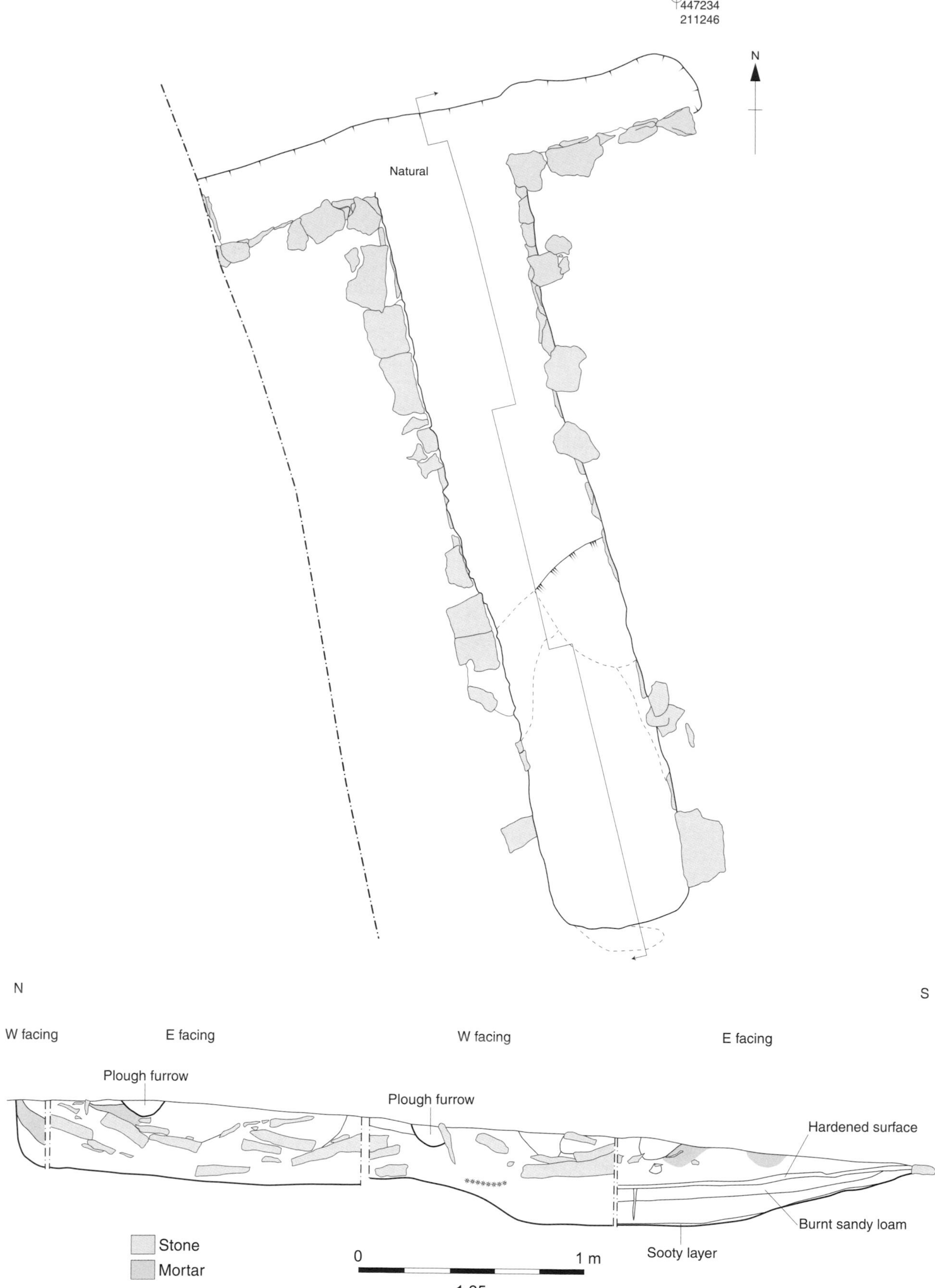

Fig. 9.7 Plan and section of corn-drying oven 522

blast furnace slag, the other a piece of fuel ash slag. The pottery was well preserved with an average sherd size of 18 g. A small amount of Oxfordshire colour-coated ware, and a sherd of Nene Valley colour-coated ware date the group overall to the later 3rd-4th centuries, while a coin dated to AD 350-60 (SF 345) came from the floor surface (119) along with an iron nail. The animal bone from the ditches includes examples of most of the main domestic species along with a single bird bone.

Other associations

Structure 1356 lay between two small curvilinear enclosures, 56 to the south-west and 82 to the north-east (see below). It is possible that all three initially formed elements of a contemporary feature complex, subsequently altered by the addition of the gullies (above) most closely associated with 1356.

Corn-drying oven 64 (Figs 9.1 and 9.5)

A probable corn-drying oven was cut into ditches 1031 and 1049 on the east side of building 1356. It had been partially robbed out but comprised a shallow east-west trench *c* 2 m x 0.8 m lined with thin flat limestone slabs of irregular shape (*c* 0.5 x 0.4 m in size and 0.07 m thick). Otherwise, the sides and bottom were defined by a thin compact orange-brown layer of sand and gravel, which was burnt natural subsoil. Three indeterminate sherds of Roman pottery and two animal bones were recovered.

It is not known whether this corn-drying oven was inserted during the use of building 1356, or whether it was a later feature. A combined domestic/-agricultural function for 1356 (see above) is plausible.

Corn-drying oven 47 (Fig. 9.1)

Structure 47, some 20 m north of corn-drying oven 64, was first exposed as a large, irregular area of dark soil and charcoal, but when excavated revealed the badly truncated remains of a north-south aligned sub-rectangular structure approximately 4.5 m by 2 m. It had a scorched natural edge to the west. The fill comprised a homogeneous dark grey-brown sandy silt containing 32 sherds of pottery, 880 g in weight, 13 animal bones and an iron knife (SF 52). The pottery includes several later Oxfordshire ware sherds suggesting a 4th-century date for the fill. The feature is interpreted as a robbed out corn-drying oven subsequently used a repository for rubbish.

Corn-drying oven 522 (Figs 9.1, 9.7 and 9.8)

A well-defined T-shaped corn-drying oven was found on the far western edge of the excavated area within an enclosure demarcated by ditches 304, 1350 and 326. The structure was constructed of flattish stones averaging 0.05 m thick and measuring 0.3 m x 0.7 m. There were three surviving courses at the southern end and six to the north. The stones were held in place with a yellow sandy mortar which had become burnt to a bright orange-red colour at the

Fig. 9.8 Corn-drying oven 522 looking south

southern end. One metre from the southern end there was a fire pit cut 0.3 m into the natural with a slightly asymmetrical profile, deeper at the north end and shallowing out to the south. Just beyond the structure to the south was a small ash deposit, possibly the result of raking out. Finds from the corn-drying oven included 17 large sherds of pottery, 654 g in weight, with examples of Dorset black burnished ware, a Midlands grogged storage jar and Oxfordshire mortaria, all indicative of a late Roman date. Nine animal bones were also recovered.

Finds from late Roman structures

The ceramic assemblage recovered from the late Roman structures is fairly extensive, especially when compared with the material from buildings of earlier phases (Table 9.1). The majority was retrieved from 491/494, which may have been used for rubbish disposal in its final stages, and from the gullies associated with structure 1356 (see above). Only five sherds were recovered from post-built structure 1768. The animal bone also mainly derived from feature 491/494, and from gullies and a floor surface within building 1356. Much of the animal bone is undiagnostic; almost half of it is classified as cow/horse size, sheep/pig size or unidentifiable. Metalworking debris and small finds were sparse but the presence of at least two quernstones in 494/491 is noteworthy. The nature of the assemblage suggests a good deal of redeposition and abrasion, but this may not have been as severe as noted in earlier structures which were mostly post-built.

LATE ROMAN ENCLOSURES (Fig. 9.1)

Summary

The enclosure system of the late Roman settlement layout appeared to have been considerably altered from the large sub-circular and rectilinear enclosures of the earlier Roman period. The enclosures of the later period can be separated into five groups, which each occupy different parts of the site and have their own characteristics:

- a series of large enclosures in the centre and north of the site. Structures 1768 and 494 lie within one of these enclosures
- smaller penannular and curvilinear enclosures in the east of the site, associated with sunken circular building 1356
- a small group of linear features in the north-east of the site which are suggestive of paddocks and extend into the unexcavated area
- a rectilinear enclosure in the south-west of the site associated with a corn-drying oven and pits
- a trackway system running around the east and south of the site, overlying earlier rectilinear enclosures, possibly paddocks

Large enclosures and trackways in the centre and north of the site

The main enclosure system to the centre north of the site is not easy to understand, even though its layout is apparently simple (Fig. 9.1). Several interpretations of both the function and the sequence of the features are possible. Originally it was thought that two trackway systems, 5 m to 10 m wide, entered the site from the north, one (30 and 34) running NE-SW, and the other (155 and 184) running roughly parallel and then turning sharply in the north of the site to run in a south-easterly direction. This proved difficult to reconcile with the settlement evidence and an alternative scheme was suggested, that two rectangular enclosures were laid out: the first defined by ditches 155 and 34, with an entrance *c* 12 m wide in the south-west angle; and then expanded by the addition of ditches 184 and 30, forming a larger enclosure in excess of 65 m long x 35 m wide. Rectangular post-built structure 1768 lay within the later enclosure and

Table 9.1 Summary of finds from late Roman structures.

			Structure			
	491/494	*1356*	*47*	*522*	*1768*	*Total*
Pottery sherds	142	300	32	17	5	496
Cattle bone	23	38	1	3	0	65
Cow/Horse size bone	20	18	5	2	0	45
Horse bone	4	3	0	0	0	7
Sheep/Goat bone	9	11	2	0	0	22
Sheep/Pig size bone	11	19	3	1	0	34
Pig bone	4	8	0	1	0	13
Wild animal	2	2	0	0	0	4
Unidentified animal bone	13	20	0	1	0	34
Total animal bone	86	119	11	8	0	224
Metalworking debris	0	2	0	0	1	3
Small finds	1	1	1	0	2	5
Stone artefacts	2	0	0	0	1	3

overlay the earlier south-western enclosure ditch. The later enclosure also cut a number of ditches associated with activity to the east.

A final interpretation, followed (tentatively) here, combines elements of both the earlier interpretations. In this view the central part of the site was divided by two NE-SW aligned trackways. The more westerly of these trackways was defined on the north-west side by ditch 332 and on the south-east by elements of ditches 222 and 184. It is suggested that this trackway was aligned on the gap at the north-east corner of enclosure 304/1350 and 326, situated at the west end of the site. Further east there seems little doubt that ditches 34 and 30 did indeed define a trackway whose ditches were recut on numerous occasions. This trackway completely disregarded some elements of the early Roman enclosure system (and cut right through the small late-Roman enclosure 1062) but its alignment may have been intended to cut between and largely respect the positions of two of the principal early Roman enclosures, 138 in the centre of the site and 187 to the north-west (Fig. 8.1). Ditch 279 was clearly a continuation of the alignment of ditch 34 on the north-west side trackway. Both of these features seem to have respected the location of the 'kidney-shaped' structure 494 and were therefore presumably broadly contemporary with its use. The absolute chronology, and some details of the relative chronology of the sequence are unclear, but it is likely that 494 lay adjacent to the trackway within a large enclosure lying between the two trackways and defined on its south-west side by an element of ditch 184. It is also likely that ditch 155, subdividing this enclosure, was a later addition, but this is not demonstrable with certainty. Structure 1768 may have belonged to this later phase of activity, while structure 494 could have remained in use throughout. A minor, sub-rectangular enclosure, open-sided to the south-west, was formed by the south-east ditch of the more westerly trackway (222) and by ditch 217, both of which were laid out with respect to the alignments established by ditch 184.

The eastern NE-SW trackway

This is likely to have been one of the earliest if not the primary component of the late Roman layout in this part of the site, although its south-eastern ditch post-dated a number of features relating to the area further east. The most significant of these was the small enclosure 1062, but the (pottery) evidence on which this feature is assigned to the late Roman period is extremely slight. Overall, the number of cuts and recuts that relate to ditches 30 and 34 suggest that the trackway was a long-established feature.

Ditch 30 (Figs 9.1 and 9.9)

Ditch group 30 consisted of a series of linear ditches 44 m in length which formed the south-eastern side of the trackway. To the north the ditches extended beyond the limit of the excavation, and to the south they could be seen to terminate. There were at least six recuts in the ditch, which were 0.7 m wide, on average, and 0.35 m deep. Fills were homogeneous and non-gravelly.

Large amounts of pottery, animal bone and some plant remains came from the ditch fills, along with some metalworking debris including a small plano-convex hearth bottom and several other finds. This probably represented rubbish dumped from structures nearby. The pottery, some 708 sherds weighing 11.8 kg, comprised a mixture of residual later prehistoric and early Roman sherds alongside

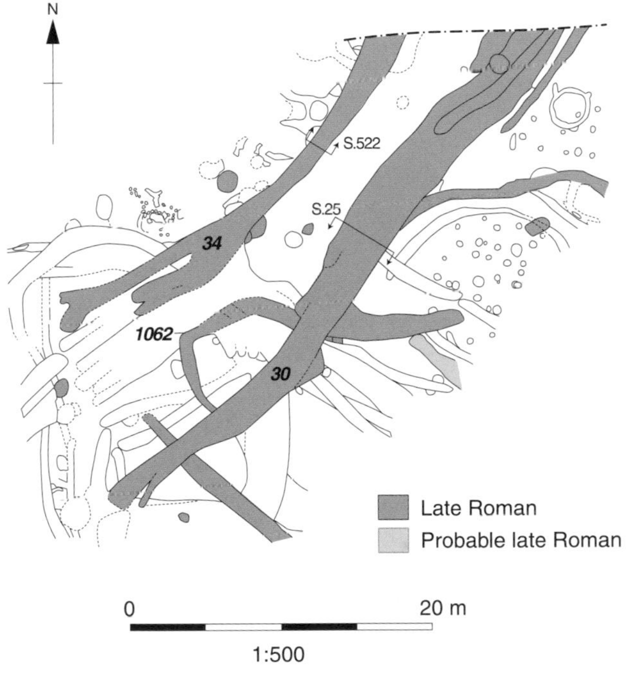

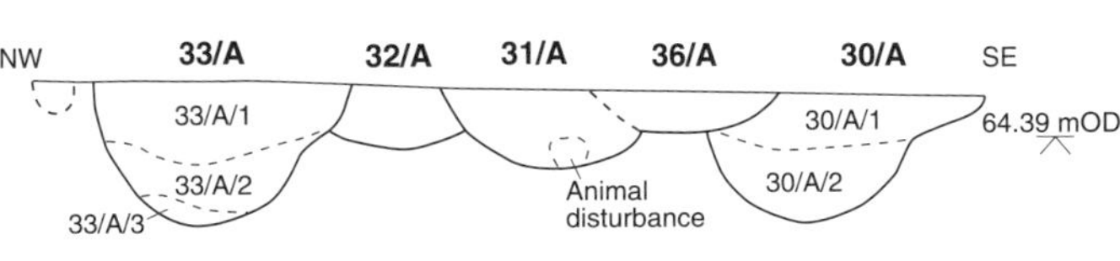

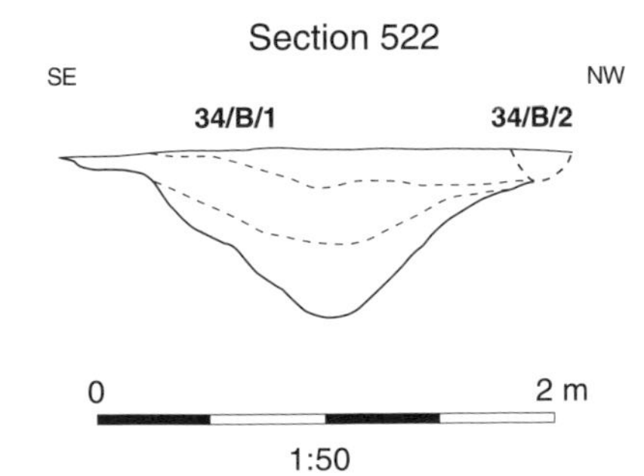

Fig. 9.9 Plan and sections of ditch groups 30 and 34

typical later Roman wares such as Oxfordshire and Nene Valley colour-coated ware, Dorset black-burnished ware and shell-tempered ware. Local grey sandy ware, in particular fabric R37, accounts for 35% of the total assemblage. The overall *terminus post quem* for the assemblage would appear to lie in the 4th century. The 150 animal bones include examples of deer, dog and hare alongside the usual domesticates. Amongst the other finds are one worked bone (SF 451), a copper alloy pin (SF 237), an iron nail, a fragment of daub and a fragment of triangular loomweight.

Ditch 34 (Figs 9.1 and 9.9)

The north-western side of the trackway, 34, extended *c* 30 m from the north baulk of the site. Ten percent of this ditch was excavated in four sections. One or two recuts, apparently mostly localised in extent, were observed in section, and the ditch profile was U-shaped-open. Its average width was 1.6 m and average depth was 0.6 m. Fills were mixed and included some primary silting and lenses of burnt/ashy or charcoal material. There was also extensive animal disturbance. Finds of pottery, 16 animal bones, and one fragment of dense slag came from the ditch fill, but this assemblage was far smaller than that from ditch 30 to the east. Over half the 44 sherds of pottery (729 g) were of Iron Age origin indicating a high level of residuality.

Ditch 279 (Fig. 9.1)

After a gap of at least 11 m at the south-west end of ditch 34 etc, largely occupied by structure 494, the roughly NE-SW alignment was resumed by ditch 279, some 21.5 m long. Its profile was varied, with flat and rounded bases and sloping concave sides. The average width was 0.65 m and the average depth was 0.73 m. The fills were mixed and produced an assemblage of 87 pottery sherds (1361 g) and 32 animal bones. These may represent deliberate rubbish deposition, although 35% of the sherds are of Iron Age origin and thus residual. The bone included hare, horse, sheep/goat and cattle. The latest pottery included an Oxfordshire colour-coated beaker, white ware mortaria and Dorset black-burnished ware.

The earliest rectangular enclosure

Ditch 184 (Fig. 9.1)

An angled ditch, 184, probably formed the south-west and north-west sides of this enclosure, the south-eastern side of which was formed by the north-west side of the more easterly trackway (ditch 34). The north-western arm of ditch 184, which extended beyond the excavated area, also served as the south-east side of the more westerly of the two NE-SW aligned trackways. In total, a 38.6 m length of this feature was exposed within the excavated area. Multiple recuts, possibly as many as 12, were observed in the ditch; its profile, including rounded bases and sloping concave sides, and size were consequently extremely varied. The average cut width was 0.66 m and the average depth 0.52 m. Fills were mixed and formation processes were uncertain.

Relatively large numbers of finds were recovered from the ditch fill, suggesting that at various times rubbish was being dumped in the ditch from structures 1768 and 494 within the enclosure. The pottery assemblage comprises some 234 sherds (3274 g) with an average weight of 14 g. This is slightly on the low side for Yarnton assemblages (see Chapter 14), indicative of disturbed material which is verified by the fact that 33% by sherd count is of Iron Age date and thus redeposited. The latest material includes wares from the Oxfordshire industry, with colour-coated vessels including a mortarium, and white ware mortaria. The animal bone assemblage, consisting of some 164 fragments, includes dog and bird alongside the usual domesticates. Other finds include two copper alloy strips (SF 99 and SF 212) and three fragments of metalworking debris, including a small plano-convex hearth bottom.

The ?secondary rectangular enclosure

Ditch 155 (Fig. 9.1)

A second angled ditch, 155, mirrored the line of ditch 184 and could have been approximately contemporary with it or perhaps a little later in date. The ditch had been recut many times; the recuts had variable profiles, including rounded to flat bases and steep to sloping concave sides. The cuts ranged from 0.4-0.68 m in width, with an average of 0.46 m, while the depth ranged from 0.44-0.82 m, with an average of 0.57 m. Fill types consisted of mixed silty loams, silty loams with gravel and greenish material. There was also evidence of some primary silting and animal disturbance. Forty-three sherds of pottery (559 g) and 52 animal bones came from the ditch fill. Characteristics of the pottery assemblage, a low average sherd weight (13 g) and a fairly high presence of redeposited material, are comparable with those of ditch 184. The presence of colour-coated wares (Oxfordshire and Nene Valley) indicates at least a 4th century date for the final infill of this feature.

Subsidiary enclosure south-west of the large enclosures

On the west side of the large enclosures lay a series of roughly parallel, NE-SW aligned ditches. Some of these ran up to the south-western arm of the enclosure and formed a subsidiary unit, while others were probably related to a trackway to the north-west..

Ditch 217 (Fig. 9.1)

Ditch 217 ran NE-SW at an angle to the line of ditch 184 but clearly respecting its position. It was 18 m long and 0.7 m wide and probably formed the south-east side of a small trapezoidal enclosure. In profile this ditch had steep sides and a flat base, with no signs of recutting. It contained a moderately substantial assemblage of 64 sherds (824 g) of pottery, 70% of which was redeposited, and some metalworking debris. The latter included a small sub-tuyère plate and a small plano-convex hearth bottom and may suggest that metalworking was carried out in a nearby area. Fifty-six animal bones were also recovered. Ditch 217 largely cut away a small curvilinear gully (216), 7.6 m in length. This had a single fill which produced 28 sherds (436 g) of pottery, 12 animal bones and plant remains.

Ditch 222 (Fig. 9.1)

Ditch 222 was a relatively substantial linear feature measuring 24.4 m in length, and aligned NE-SW, forming both the north-west side of the trapezoidal enclosure and, probably, the south-east side of an adjacent trackway. It ran at a slight angle to the line of ditch 217 and also abutted ditch 184 at the western corner of the larger enclosure, extending the alignment of the north-west side of that feature. The profile of ditch 222 was U-shaped and open, and one recut was observed. Its average width was 0.8 m, and the average depth was 0.28 m. There were two fills, which were mixed and consisted of gravel-free loams and silty loams with gravel. Pottery (27 sherds, 287 g) and 18 animal bones from the ditch fills may largely derive from secondary deposition. The latest material includes an Oxfordshire white ware mortarium dating to the later 3rd or 4th century. A single fragment of metalworking debris may derive from the same source as that in ditch 217.

Western NE-SW trackway

As discussed above, the south-east side of this probable trackway was formed by part of enclosure ditch 184 and its south-westerly continuation, ditch 222. A fragment of gully, 258, 8 m long and 0.4 m wide, ran adjacent and parallel to 222 and may have defined one edge of the trackway in one (perhaps early) phase of its existence. The sole fill yielded a single large sherd of Oxfordshire colour-coated dish, eight animal bones, including one hare bone and some plant remains.

The probable north-west side of the trackway was formed by a slightly curvilinear gully (332) measuring 13 m in length located some 4 m north of ditch 258. It ran beyond the limit of the excavation to the north but had a clear terminal at its south-western end. The gully profile was U-shaped and open and two recuts were apparent. The average width was 0.37 m and the average depth 0.25 m. There were four fills comprising gravel-free and gravelly silty loams. A fairly substantial assemblage of 89 sherds of pottery weighing 3223 g, and 47 animal bones including the usual domesticates, came from the gully fill and may indicate rubbish deposition from a nearby source, although again a significant proportion of the material derived from the underlying Iron Age deposits.

Enclosures to the east of the site

A group of straight and curvilinear ditches and gullies was exposed in the east of the site. Some of these seemed to form a series of sub-circular and curvilinear enclosures, although very few of these were apparently fully enclosed. The interpretation of some of these features is quite unclear. In general, however, they seemed to be associated with domestic activity and agricultural processing.

Ditches in the south of this group (Fig. 9.1)

Four linear features in the south of this area (124, 150, 996 and 998) shared broadly similar alignments but did not form coherent enclosures.

Ditch 124 was 13.5 m in length and aligned NW-SE, lying at right-angles to the southern end of trackway ditch group 30, by which it was cut. No recuts were observed in section, and the ditch profile was U-shaped-open with steep sides. The average width was 1.3 m and the average depth 0.6 m, and fills consisted of non-gravelly silty loams. Amongst the 58 sherds (1273 g) of pottery was a sherd of Dressel 20 olive-oil amphora as well as local grey sand- and grog-tempered wares and a small quantity of animal bone, suggesting rubbish deposition from structures to the north of the ditch.

South of the mid point of 124 and roughly at right angles to it was a short stretch of ditch/gully (150), 2.2 m in length, the full extent of which could not be traced. The profile was U-shaped and open, and no recuts were observed. The average width was 0.6 m, and the average depth was 0.25 m. There was a single fill consisting of homogeneous gravel-free material. No finds were recovered.

Just east of 124 was gully 998, with a total length of 12 m. Its longer arm was perpendicular to the alignment of 124, while to the north it curved through a rounded right angle to terminate *c* 3 m from the south-east terminal end of 124, parallel to it but offset from its line. No recuts were observed, and the profile of 998 was U-shaped to open. It was 0.4-0.65 m wide, with an average width of 0.51 m, and 0.17-0.32 m deep, with an average depth of 0.22 m. Fills consisted of non-gravelly material and silty loams with gravel; there were also some burnt/ashy or charcoal fills. Twenty-six sherds of Roman pottery (469 g) and only five animal bones were recovered. Gully 1150 continued the SW-NE alignment of 998 in a north-easterly direction, but was very fragmentary and was not excavated. Gully 1150 cut the small enclosure ditches 56 and 1108 (see below), so if contemporary with 998 this would indicate that these features were later than the group of enclosures to the north.

Feature 996, a little further to the east, was very similar in form to 998, except that the longer arm was on a WNW-ESE axis roughly parallel to the line of 124. A 15 m length of this feature survived. Its average width was 0.8 m and the average depth was 0.3 m. A substantial assemblage of pottery and animal bone from the ditch fill may suggest rubbish deposition. It was notable that the pottery recovered (206 sherds, 1695 g) was well-fragmented, with an average sherd weight of just 8 g. Grog-tempered storage jar was well-represented along with a small quantity of Oxfordshire colour-coated ware and white ware mortaria providing a *terminus post quem* for the fill of the ditch in the later 3rd or 4th centuries. The 54 animal bones are a mixture of sheep and cattle or sheep/pig sized pieces, with single examples of horse and dog.

Enclosure 1062 (Figs 9.1 and 9.9)

A small sub-rectangular enclosure was cut by the south-western end of trackway ditch 30. It was 8 m x 7 m in size, and probably had an entrance to the south-east. The ditch had been recut once. It ranged in width from 0.43-0.85 m, with an average width of 0.6 m; the depth range was 0.22-0.44 m with an average of 0.3 m. Fills consisted of non-gravelly material and silty-loams with gravel; there were some greenish fills and some animal disturbance. Sixteen sherds of pottery (481 g) and eight pieces of animal bone from the ditch fill may indicate a general lack of contemporary domestic activity. Only one very small sherd needs indicate a late Roman date for the pottery assemblage (see above).

Sub-circular enclosure 56 and associated features (Figs 9.1 and 9.10)

A semicircular ditch (56) 14 m in length, lay to the east of enclosure 1062. It was adjacent to building 1356, mirrored its enclosure ditches and was very similar in size. This 'enclosure' was 8 m x 5.5 m and was open to the north-east. No recuts were observed in section and the ditch profile was U-shaped to open, with an average width of 0.8 m and an average depth of 0.37 m. Fills comprised non-gravelly silty loams with some greenish material. Twenty-four well-preserved pottery sherds weighing 779 g and including an Oxfordshire colour-coated mortarium were recovered, along with five animal bones.

A curvilinear gully, 1108, 17.5 m in length, was a recut of enclosure 56 on the same alignment but much less wide. Gully 1108 produced 25 sherds (787 g) of pottery and 10 animal bones. The pottery comprised grog-tempered storage jar accompanied by at least one Oxfordshire colour-coated mortarium. Gully 796 seems to have been a continuation of gully 1108 at its north-west end.

Ditches to the east and north of building 1356

Enclosure 82 and related features (Figs 9.1 and 9.10)

An small oval enclosure, 82, was located immediately north-east of structure 1356. It was 7 m x 4 m and had an entrance to the south, opening into a space between the enclosure ditches around the building and near to the corn-drying oven, 64 (see Fig. 9.5). The average width of the ditch was 1 m, and its depth was 0.45 m. Fills comprised non-gravelly material. A collection of 27 large sherds of pottery (with an average sherd weight of 36.5 g) came from the ditch fill, possibly representing rubbish deposition. The pottery featured at least two Oxfordshire white ware mortaria and a Nene Valley ware colour-coated bowl.

There was no sign of contemporary features within enclosure 82. A curving ditch/gully (46/72) ran in a SSW direction from its south-eastern terminal, curving to the west and terminating adjacent to enclosure ditch 56, suggesting a close association between the latter and enclosure 82. Ditch/gully 46/72 had a total length of *c* 25 m. Eight sections were excavated through this feature. A single recut was observed in section, and the ditch profile was U-shaped to open. The width range of the recut was 0.1-0.56 m, with an average width of 0.34 m; the depth range was 0.18-0.52 m. Fills were mixed and there was some primary silting. Thirty-one sherds of pottery (391 g) and some plant remains came from the fill of feature 46, while a substantial amount of moderately well-preserved pottery, (73 sherds, 1361 g) was recovered from the fill of gully 72.

Both 46/72 and the enclosure ditch 82 were cut by the curvilinear gullies adjacent to the north and east sides of structure 1356 (see above and Fig. 9.5). Their establishment is likely (but not certain) to have precluded further use of enclosure 82. North of this feature complex were further ditches/gullies (25 and 28) that might have related to it but whose role in this context is less clear.

Ditch 28 (Fig. 9.1)

Ditch 28 was an east–west slightly curving feature 9.5 m long, projecting from beneath the trackway ditch complex 30. Widest at the west end, its width ranged from 1.08-1.4 m and the depth range was 0.2-0.38 m, with an average of 0.32 m. A single recut was observed in section, and the ditch profile was U-shaped to open. Fills consisted of non-gravelly material and silty-loams with gravel; there was also some greenish material and some primary silting. Finds comprised 21 sherds of pottery and eight animal bones. The former included several typical late wares, for example Oxfordshire colour-coated ware, pink grog-tempered ware and late Roman shell-tempered ware, alongside a number of clearly redeposited sherds.

Gully 25 (Fig. 9.1)

North of ditch 28, and also cut away at its western end by ditch complex 30, was a curvilinear gully (25) about 16 m in length. This may have served to define an outer limit to the enclosure/structure group (56, 82 and structure 1356) to the south, but it was not certainly exactly contemporary with these features. Its profile was U-shaped and open, and no

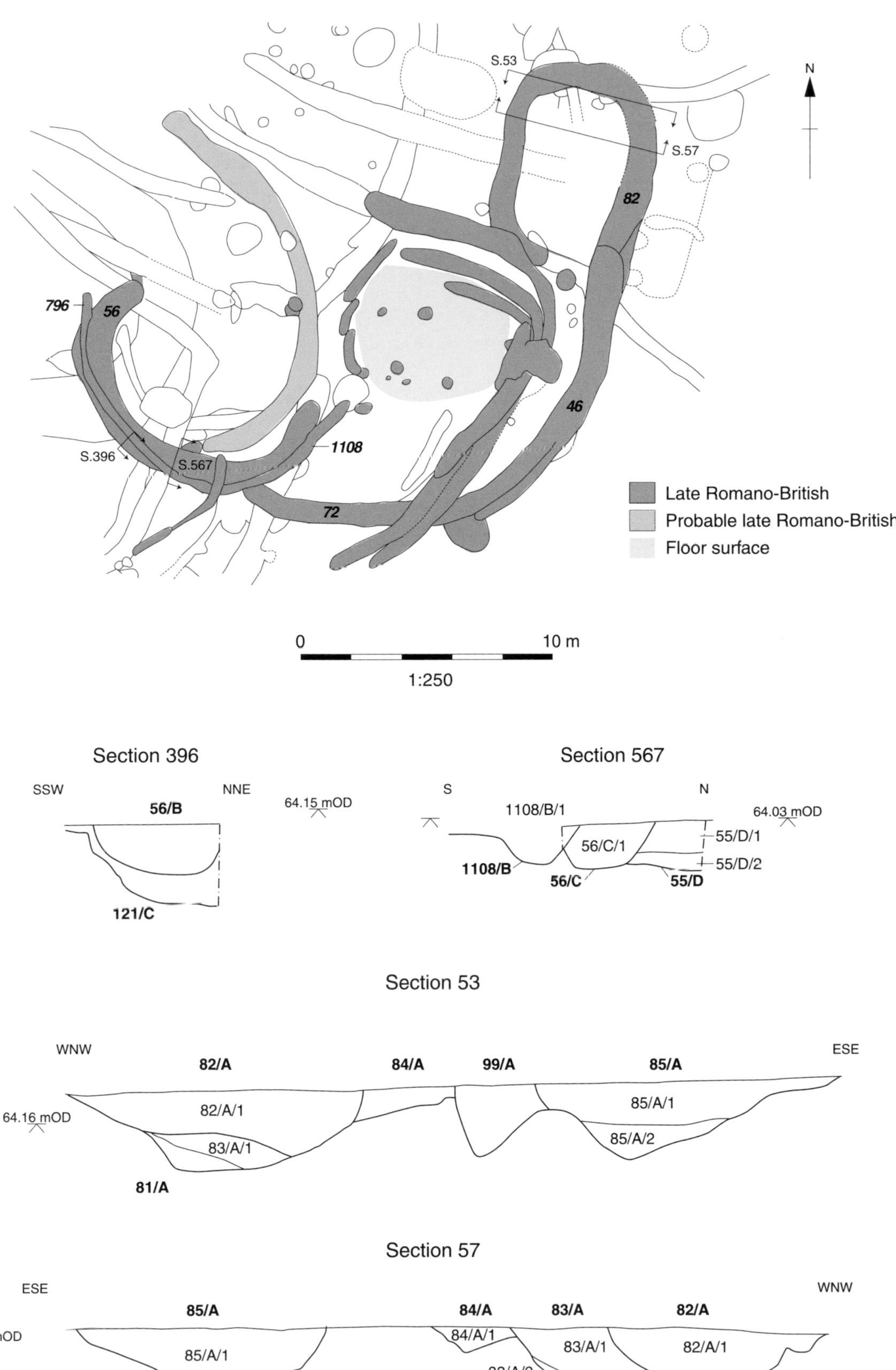

Fig. 9.10 Plan and sections of enclosures 56 and 82

recuts were apparent. The average width was 0.6 m, and the average depth was 0.5 m. There was a single homogeneous fill containing seven sherds of pottery and nine animal bones.

Possible enclosure to the north-east of the site (Fig. 9.1)

A series of ditches, 1093, 2509 and 2508 may possibly represent the remains of the southern part of a square or rectangular enclosure *c* 15 m WNW-ESE by at least 12 m SSW-NNE. The south-east corner is completely missing, however, and it is not clear if this was a functional characteristic, representing a very large entrance, or a consequence of post-Roman truncation of the relevant features.

Ditch 1093 formed the extant north-west and south-west sides of the possible enclosure, and appeared to terminate to the south-east. The ditch was excavated in three segments. No recuts were noted, and the ditch profile was U-shaped to open, 0.3-0.7 m wide with an average width of 0.55 m, and 0.1-0.3 m deep with an average depth of 0.18 m. The fill, of silty loam with gravel, produced three sherds of grey coarse ware pottery.

Ditch 2508 lay to the east and appeared to form the south-east side of the enclosure, but it also ran parallel to trackway ditch 2517 to the east and it is possible that it related to that feature. The ditch was U-shaped and open, and there were no recuts. The average width was 0.7 m, and the average depth was 0.3 m. The single fill was made up of homogeneous silty loam. Seven large, fresh sherds of pottery, along with six animal bones and a fragment of fired clay, came from the ditch.

Within the putative enclosure, ditch 2509, on a north-south alignment, lay adjacent to and was cut by 2508. It yielded a relatively substantial quantity of 35 large unabraded sherds, along with a single fragment of sheep/goat bone.

Ditch 877 (Fig. 9.1)

A 23 m length of a substantial NNE–SSW aligned ditch, 877, was located in the south-east corner of the main excavated area, its northern end falling outside that area. Its southern terminal was adjacent to the corresponding terminal of early Roman enclosure ditch 343 and cut the north-west corner of the apparently related ditch of enclosure 948, lying to the east and assigned to the early Roman period. It is likely, therefore, that 877 related to some continuation of enclosure function in this area. The ditch was 0.8-1.5 m wide and 0.3-0.66 m deep, with an average width of 1 m and average depth of 0.35 m. The profile was U-shaped to open and was filled with non-gravelly material. Some 56 sherds (416 g) of pottery and 26 animal bones from the ditch fill may represent rubbish deposition. A coin dated AD 335-41 (SF 274) also came from this feature. The pottery included a small number of redeposited sherds alongside Dorset black-burnished ware and Oxfordshire colour-coated ware, the latter providing a *terminus post quem* in the 4th century to complement the coin date. Three dog skull fragments featured amongst the animal bone.

Enclosure in the west of the site

The north-east corner of a possible subrectangular enclosure was uncovered at the west end of the site. It was in excess of 35 m x 25 m in size, and had an gap *c* 15 m wide in the north-eastern part. The enclosure was principally made up of ditches 304/1350 and 326, although a number of ditches in the south may have been predecessors of 326.

Ditches 304 and 1350 (Fig. 9.1)

Ditch 304/1349/1350, aligned WNW–ESE with a total length of 25 m, formed the northern side of the possible enclosure. The ditch profile was U-shaped to open. It was 0.4-1 m wide and narrowed markedly towards each end, but it is not clear if either had a genuine terminal. The depth ranged from 0.08-0.6 m, suggesting extreme truncation in places; there was no evidence of recutting. Fills were of silty loam, some with a gravel component, and there was some primary silting. A relatively large assemblage of 91 sherds of pottery weighing 1524 g and 102 animal bones was recovered, along with two fragment of metalworking debris (one a small sub-tuyère plate), some fired clay, a bone

Fig. 9.11 Horse and cattle skulls in the terminal of ditch 1350. Scale 0.5 m

object (SF 462) and some charred plant remains. This might suggest rubbish deposition from a nearby building, but it should be noted that *c* 65% of the pottery appeared to be redeposited Iron Age sherds. A few sherds of Dorset black-burnished ware and local grey sandy wares provide an overall late 3rd–4th century date for the fill, however. Two skulls, one cattle and one horse, lying parallel to one another probably represent a structured deposition of some sort (Fig. 9.11).

Ditch 326 (Fig. 9.1)

The eastern side of the enclosure was formed by ditch 326, the northern terminus of which lay some 18 m south of the east end of ditch 1350. A 20 m length of 326 lay within the site. It was aligned almost north-south in its northern part (*c* 11.5 m) before making an angled turn to the south-west and running beyond the limit of excavation. A single recut was noted in section and seems to have extended along most of the length of the feature. The ditch profile was open-concave. The width range was 0.6-1 m with an average of 0.65 m, while the depth range was 0.15-0.32 m with an average of 0.22 m. Fills consisted of silty loams with gravel and gravel-rich deposits. Twenty-four quite fragmented potsherds and 17 animal bones were recovered from the ditch fill. As with ditch 304/1350 at least half the pottery was redeposited Iron Age material, but a late Roman date is indicated by a large sherd from a Nene Valley colour-coated ware jar. A single fragment of vitrified clay was also recovered.

Ditches associated with 326 in the south-west of the site

A short (5 m) length of shallow ditch (536) aligned NE-SW lay immediately adjacent to ditch 326 on its north-west side. It was 0.64 m wide and 0.1 m deep with a fill of silty loam with gravel. No finds were recovered. A further gully, 559, 5.5 m long, branched off ditch 536 in a northerly direction, but the relationship between the two is not certain. A single sherd of Oxfordshire grey sand-tempered pottery and five animal bones came from the gully fill. It is not clear if these features were contemporary with the use of the possible enclosure formed by 304/1350 and 326. Their presence, together with that of corn-drying oven 522 (see above) and an adjacent pit (886) to the north, suggest that a focus of activity, perhaps including a domestic component, may have been located just west of the excavated area.

Trackway ditches to the east and south of the site and associated features

Ditch 1013 (Fig. 9.1)

Feature 1013 was a substantial ditch located in the salvage area beyond the southern limit of the main excavation area. It was traced for a distance of 69 m on a WNW-ESE alignment, but neither end was located. The ditch lay at right angles to trackway ditches 2517 and 2550 further east, and it may have formed one side of a westward return of this trackway system or a boundary on the southern edge of the settlement. Four sections were excavated through the ditch which was U-shaped and open in profile and had been recut at least once. The average width was 1.51 m and the average depth 0.64 m. There were at least two fills, consisting of gravel-free material and silty-loams with gravel. A fairly modest collection of finds was recovered from the ditch, perhaps suggesting that it was not used for direct rubbish deposition. The 56 sherds of pottery were dominated by local grey coarse wares and shell-tempered wares, with a single sherd of Oxfordshire colour-coated ware from a miniature jar giving a later 3rd century to 4th century *terminus post quem*. The animal bone comprised just 14 pieces, of which two were dog mandible fragments. In addition, one fragment of slag and a slab of Forest Marble (SF 374) were recovered.

Trackway on the east side of the site (Fig. 9.1)

A substantial track or droveway, defined by ditches (2517 and 2550) some 20-22 m apart and aligned NNE-SSW, defined the eastern limit of settlement in the late Roman period. It perpetuated the general location, but not the exact line, of the probable settlement boundary indicated by the substantial early Roman ditch 2593, which it cut. The alignment of ditch elements of possible enclosures associated with 2593 (particularly early Roman feature 2528) was maintained by one of the trackway ditches, 2517. Ditch 2517, which formed the western side of the trackway, was traced for a distance of 96.6 m on the site. It faded out to the north, probably more as a result of truncation than other factors (compare also the enclosure ditches 2508 and 1063 adjacent to the west; above), and extended beyond the limit of excavation to the south. The ditch profile was varied, being an open U-shape in places and a narrow U-shape in others. There was at least one recut. The average width was 1.3 m, and the average depth was 0.42 m. The fills consisted of silty loams with gravel and finds comprised 78 sherds (1713 g) of pottery, 27 animal bones and one human calcaneum. Ditch 2550 on the east side of the trackway had a U-shaped and open profile, and there were at least two recuts, but possibly more. The average width was 1.7 m, and the average depth was 0.42 m. There were at least three fills, which consisted of gravelly and gravel-free silty loams. Only six sherds of pottery and five animal bones were found in the ditch, although it was not extensively sampled.

An earlier paddock system? (features 2108, 2531, 2530 and 2562) (Fig. 9.1)

The trackway ditches appeared to cut across a series of linear ditches which would have formed enclosures or paddocks on a similar alignment to that of the track. Like the trackway, these features also cut the early Roman boundary ditch 2593.

Ditch/gully 2018, in the southern part of the site, was a heavily truncated slightly sinuous feature 20.2 m in length which was aligned WNW-ESE between the trackway ditches, and cut by both of them, extending east of ditch 2550. Where best-preserved the feature was up to 0.8 m deep and almost 1 m wide. The profile was U-shaped and open, and there were no recuts. The single fill consisted of silty loam with gravel and was devoid of finds.

Some 38 m north of 2018 and parallel to it, gully 2531, 16 m in length, was confined to the area between the trackway ditches, terminating or fading out 5 m short of the western ditch and at its eastern end cut by ditch 2550 which it did not appear to extend beyond. The gully profile was U-shaped and open, and there were no recuts. The average width was 0.55 m and the average depth was 0.43 m. There was a single fill of homogeneous silty loam with no finds. Immediately north of and parallel to gully 2531 was a similar gully (2530) 9.8 m in length, aligned WNW-ESE and running between (but not extending beyond) the two trackway ditches, both of which cut it. The profile was U-shaped and open, and there were no recuts. The average width was 0.5 m, and the average depth was 0.4 m. The sole fill, of homogeneous silty loam, produced a single large sherd of a pink grogged ware storage jar.

A notable characteristic of gullies 2530 and 2531 was that neither of them lined up with gully 2562, which extended east from the eastern trackway ditch 2550 on exactly the same orientation as 2530 and 2531, but splitting the distance between them. It is not clear if 2562 was cut by, or butted up to the line of ditch 2550. Five metres east of ditch 2550 the gully turned a right angle to the north and ran *c* 50 m to the north baulk of the site approximately parallel to the alignment of the trackway. Gully 2562 had a V-shaped profile with no apparent recuts and was 0.36 m wide and 0.17 m deep. There was a single fill of homogeneous pebbly silt, which produced three heavily abraded pottery sherds, three scraps of animal bone and a quartzite polisher (SF 284).

Distribution of finds from the ditches

The majority of the finds from the ditches comprised animal bone and sherds of pottery which probably represent the dumping of rubbish into the open ditches, combined with the secondary deposition of material that had been lying around on the ground surface. The majority of the material came from the ditches defining the larger enclosures in the centre and north of the site. A particularly heavy concentration of artefacts in ditch 30 could have consisted of material dumped from the buildings either to the east or the west, or both. Some of the small enclosures to the east also contained substantial assemblages, indicating domestic activity in this area. Some metalworking debris came from the fills of ditches 217 and 222, to the west of the largest enclosure, indicating that metalworking may have been carried out in the space which they defined. However, metalworking debris also came from early Roman ditches in this area and this material could have been redeposited. Perhaps of greater significance was a small concentration of metal-working slag in layer 354 (Fig. 9.1) which lay within early Roman enclosure 344 in the south-east of the site. This comprised some 13 fragments with examples of dense slag, a small sub-tuyère plate and vitrified clay. Otherwise, finds were scarce. Plant remains were mostly recovered from the larger ditches. The most notable animal bone deposit was in ditch 1318 (a component of enclosure 1350), which contained two complete animal skulls, one of a cow and one of a horse, found lying parallel to one another in the ditch terminal (Fig. 9.11).

LATE ROMAN PITS

Summary

Fifty-four pits were assigned to the late Roman period, and were categorised in terms of their morphology as for other periods. In plan these features were mostly circular to oval, with one sub-rectangular example. A complete range of profiles was present.

Distribution and description

The late Roman pits were generally well dispersed through the centre and north-east of the excavated area, with a cluster of pits in the south-west corner of the site (Fig. 9.1). Pit diameters ranged between from 0.28 m to 2.5 m and averaged 0.9 m, while depths ranged between 0.12 m and 1.15 m and averaged 0.38 m. Original recorded pit volumes were from 0.003 m^3 to 2.550 m^3 and averaged 0.378 m^3. In profile these features exhibited a degree of variation (Table 9.2). Fills were mixed (Table 9.3). The number of fills contained within individual features ranged from one to five, but there was only one feature with more than four fills and the average number of fills was two.

Table 9.2 Numbers of late Roman pits by type.

	Cylindrical	*Bowl-shaped*	*Rectangular*	*Large shallow*	*Shallow saucer*	*Other*	*Total*
Yarnton	10	13	1	4	8	19	55

Discussion

The range and greatest number of fills in pits within this period was less than in the early Roman period, but the average number of fills per pit (two) was the same in both early and late Roman periods. Nine pits contained evidence of primary silting, and three of these were over 0.8 m^3 in volume. These figures are comparable to those for earlier periods. Only two pits contained deliberate deposits of articulated animal remains, and neither of them were over 0.8 m^3 in volume. Five pits showed evidence of having been deliberately backfilled, and of these two were over 0.8 m^3 in volume. The shape of one pit suggested that it could have been used for grain storage.

Artefact distributions in late Roman pits

Bone

Of the 55 late Roman pits, 30 contained deposits of bone (Table 9.4), and one of these included human bone. Horse bone was only present in three pits. Wild animal remains were found in five features, a much greater figure than that for the earlier period. Pits containing less easily identifiable animal remains were more widespread than previously. Only four late Roman pits contained bones derived from all the major domestic species.

Animal bone was fairly randomly distributed throughout the pit scatter, with a slight concentration around the edges of the enclosures. There was no apparent spatial differentiation between the deposition of bones of domestic animals and wild animals. The one pit containing human bone lay to the east of the settlement close to the middle Iron Age cemetery and the bone is likely to have been redeposited.

Pottery

Thirty-four late Roman pits contained pottery. The assemblage comprised 228 sherds, and the average number of sherds per pit was seven. The calculation and comparison of mean sherd weight and sherd count revealed that most features contained small amounts of abraded material, but some features either contained large amounts of abraded sherds, or small numbers of unabraded sherds. Thirteen pits contained significant deposits of pottery. Only of these (1084, north of the group of curvilinear enclosures including structure 1356; Fig. 9.1) also contained an animal carcass. The pottery distribution appeared fairly random within the pit scatter, with no particular spatial concentrations of pottery-rich pits, and this pattern resembles that for the earlier Roman periods.

Plant remains

Two late Roman pits (134 and 151) were sampled for plant remains. Both were circular in plan, one was cylindrical and one was shallow saucer-shaped. The

Table 9.3 Numbers of late Roman pit fill types.

Silty loams	*Gravel-free fills*	*Non-gravelly fills*	*Other*
14	22	11	8

Table 9.4 Quantities of pottery and animal bone from late Roman pits.

Pit	*Sherd count*	*Mean sherd weight*	*Bone count*
48	8	16	2
49	7	105	3
76	3	11	9
104	1	33	0
126	1	46	0
134	2	15	38
147	4	100	1
325	7	24	3
333	1	49	0
449	12	73	1
454	22	126	7
515	4	186	1
516	2	19	0
518	5	189	1
545	2	7	3
612	13	20	1
670	8	14	5
771	3	11	1
773	1	14	1
774	2	16	1
778	3	5	3
883	4	11	3
885	5	8	2
886	6	79	1
1005	2	200	1
1035	24	35	8
1084	32	56	93
1095	19	21	15
1120	12	18	2
1123	5	23	0
1194	1	7	1
1236	5	21	0
1237	1	4	0
2527	1	26	5

Table 9.5 Summary of finds other than pottery and bone from late Roman pits.

Pit	*Pit type*	*Small find*	*Material*
134	Cylindrical	Misc	Fired clay
134	Cylindrical	Flake	Flint
147	Cylindrical	Scraper	Flint
325	Amorphous	Flake	Flint
516	Bowl-shaped	Punch	Iron
670	Cylindrical	Millstone x3 frags	Stone
1084	Rectangular	Daub	Fired clay
1095	Amorphous	Daub	Fired clay
2527	Amorphous	Quern	Stone

shallow-saucer shaped pit (151) contained charcoal and a deliberate deposit of articulated animal bone, but only a small quantity of plant remains, principally seeds of weeds and wild plants. Pit 134 contained a rubbish deposit incorporating a larger plant remains assemblage with cereal grain and weed/wild plant seeds in almost equal quantities.

Metalworking debris

Very few fragments of metalworking debris were recovered from the pits of the late Roman period. Three pits, two of which were situated to the north-east and the other more centrally located, each contained a single fragment of slag.

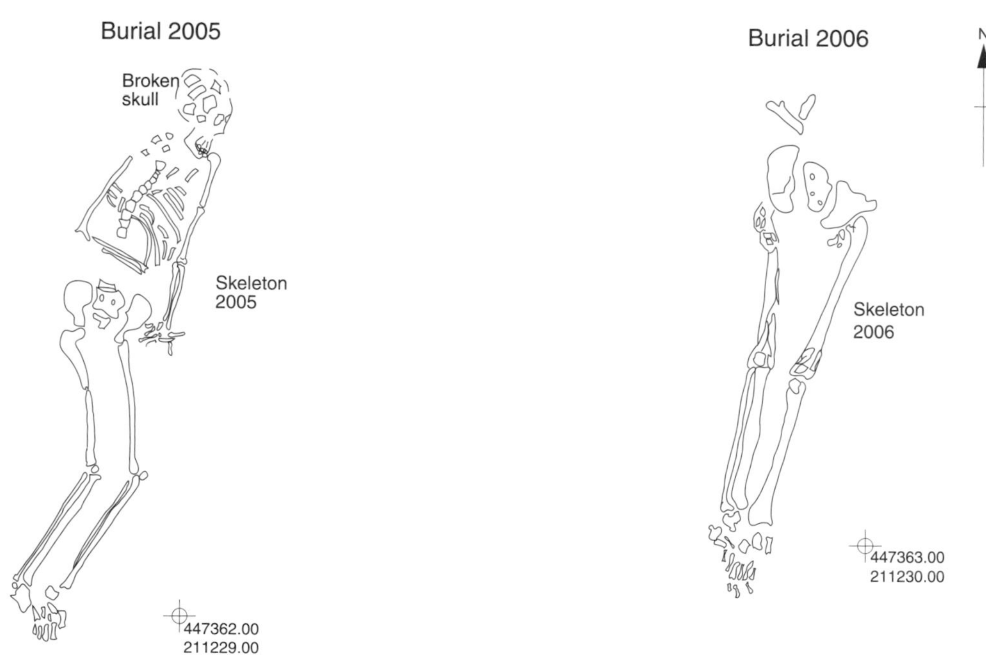

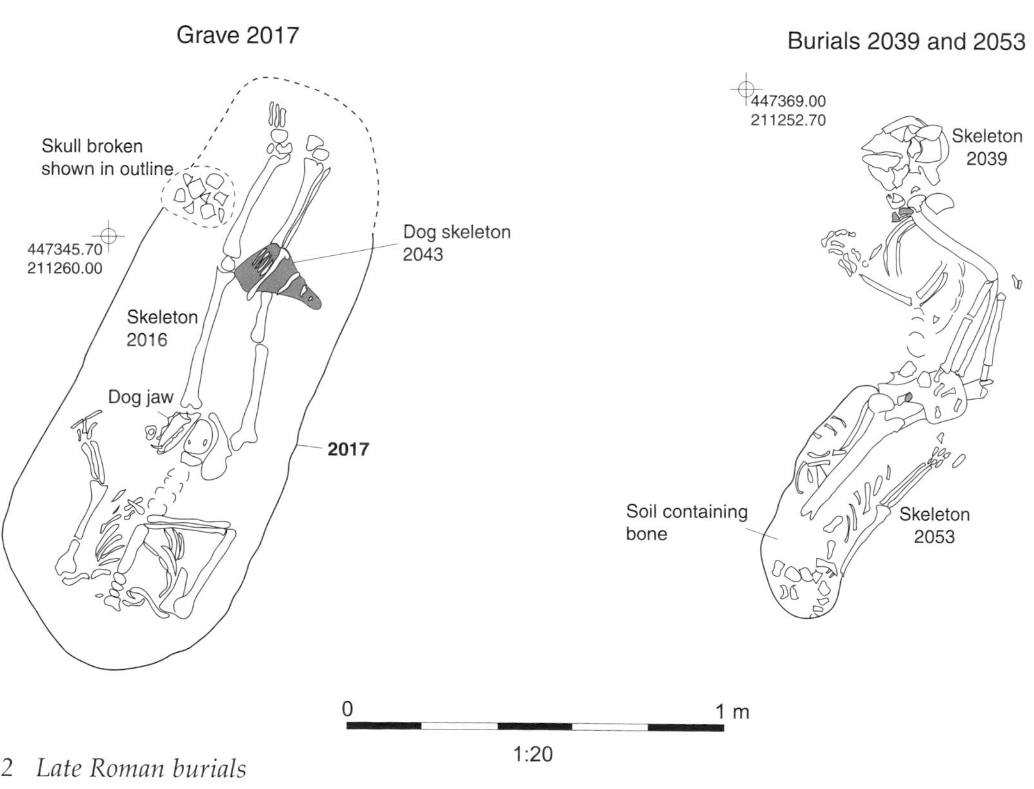

Fig. 9.12 Late Roman burials

Small finds

Only one metal small find and two stone objects were recovered from the late Roman pits (Table 9.5). These comprised an iron punch from pit 516, three fragments of Old Red Sandstone millstone from 670 and a sandstone quern from 2527. In addition, small amounts of fired clay were recovered from three pits, (134, 1084 and 1095). The majority of this material came from either cylindrical or amorphous pits, although one bowl-shaped and one rectangular pit also contained some material. Pits with small finds were distributed across the site; there was no association between small finds and structures.

LATE ROMAN BURIALS

Six inhumation burials were discovered unexpectedly in the salvage area during machine stripping by the gravel company and some had been damaged. Ploughing from the medieval period had also truncated grave cuts. Figure 9.1 shows their location and Figure 9.12 illustrates the five burials which it was possible to record. Five of the burials were of adults and one of a subadult and where it was possible to sex the individuals, two were female and two were male. The human remains are discussed in Chapter 16.

The body position of five of the burials was recorded. All were supine and extended or slightly flexed. Three individuals were aligned broadly north-south (2005, 2006 and 2039) and two others (2017 and 2053) were south-north; it was not possible to record any details of body position for skeleton 2021. Only two grave cuts were observed (2017 around skeleton 2016, and 2040 around skeletons 2039 and 2053), and both were shallow features which had been dug to a size to accommodate the burials within them.

Two of the burials (or burial groups) were unusual. Skeleton 2016, an adult female in grave 2017, had been decapitated and her head had been placed by her legs (Figs 9.12 and 9.13). The skeleton of a dog lay on her knees. The size of the grave indicates that she had been placed within the cut without her head in place. Individual 2039, an ageing adult male, had been placed on top of a subadult, 2053. They were positioned in diametrically opposite directions. As the cemetery was very dispersed and burials few in number, this is not considered to be coincidental.

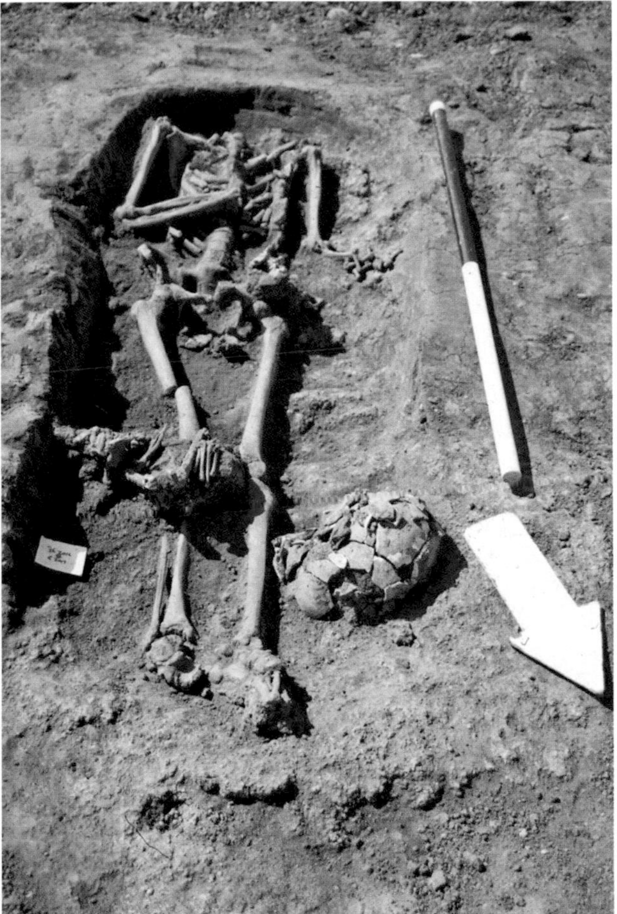

Fig. 9.13 Decapitated skeleton 2016 looking south. Scale 1 m

UNPHASED ROMAN FEATURES

As in the Iron Age, there were a number of Roman features which could not be assigned to the early or late Roman period. These comprised 23 pits, which have been divided into five categories similar to those used to define the phased examples. The proportions of the different pit types to one another were broadly comparable to those seen in other Roman phases. The pit volumes ranged between 0.006 m^3 and 2.7 m^3 and averaged 0.293 m^3. The volume range is somewhat smaller than that for the phased features, and this may have resulted in fewer finds being deposited, making these pits more difficult to date. The proportions of the different fill types to one another were generally similar to those seen among the phased pits, but with relatively few gravelly and silty loam fills.

Chapter 10: Worton in the Iron Age and Roman periods

by Jane Timby

INTRODUCTION

The modern hamlet of Worton lies on the southern edge of the Second Gravel Terrace at *c* 64 m OD overlooking the Thames floodplain (Fig. 1.3). Aerial photographs of the area to the west of the hamlet revealed a number of cropmarks including a Bronze Age ring ditch and various rectangular and curvilinear enclosure ditches typical of rural settlement of the Iron Age and Roman periods (Figs 10.1, 10.2 and 11.1). Although these areas were not directly under threat at the time, the southern part of the site lay within the original ARC application area and the western edge lay on the line of a proposed spur road for the A40 Witney-Cassington dualling scheme (now shelved). The remaining area was under cultivation during the 1990 and 1991 field seasons and the quantity of fresh pottery coming to the surface indicated active disturbance of underlying archaeological deposits. The area was thus subjected to a programme of fieldwalking in 1990-91 and to an evaluation in 1991 and 1993, to identify the nature and character of the settlements shown by the cropmarks, and to take the opportunity to compare the evidence with that being obtained from the adjacent work in Yarnton parish.

THE CROPMARK EVIDENCE

The presence of cropmarks in this location has been known about from at least 1934 from photographs taken by Allen (Ashmolean Museum, Allen Album 8, no. 259 (1934); see Fig. 11.1) and they were photographed subsequently by the Cambridge team (Fig. 10.2). A provisional interpretation was produced in Benson and Miles (1974, 52), largely of the northern group. The cropmarks were subsequently plotted by the RCHME (now English Heritage) in 1994 (Fig 10.1) (see Chapter 11, Dyer and Featherstone for details of survey). The plot suggests that there were two discrete zones of settlement approximately 120 m apart. The southern area appears to comprise a series of three or more irregular enclosures with rounded corners with associated trackways and/or droveways. The larger enclosure to the south-west of the area has within it a series of smaller conjoined oval or rounded enclosures between 10-15 m across, some of which presumably represent house enclosures whilst others may be stock enclosures. The pattern is typical of many Iron Age and early Romano-British rural settlements found across the gravels (cf Benson and Miles 1974). The cropmarks are evidently multi-period; some of the smaller pit-like structures resembled and later proved to be Saxon sunken-featured buildings and a rectangular anomaly, when excavated, was a middle Saxon timber hall (Hey 2004). The two large black maculae may be evidence of earlier gravel working. The aerial photographs also showed evidence of medieval ridge-and-furrow cultivation.

The group of cropmarks to the north shows a completely different pattern. This is much more rectilinear in layout suggesting a series of contiguous rectangular enclosed fields. A roadway runs east-west across the southern limit of the complex with at least one smaller trackway branching off this at a right angle to the north bordered on either side by fields or paddocks. A number of small maculae are scattered across the enclosed areas. A Bronze Age ring ditch with a diameter of approximately 24 m is bisected by a later linear feature on a NNW-SSE axis. Provisionally the pattern may be seen as typical of the middle to late Roman period, or later. A few discontinuous curvilinear components could suggest earlier underlying activity.

A sparse scatter of maculae occurs between the two complexes but is not associated with any obvious linear ditches. At least some of these are likely to be Saxon sunken-featured buildings, two of which were investigated as part of the evaluation across the area (Hey 2004, 189-197).

FIELDWALKING

A fieldwalking exercise, undertaken in 1966 by the Oxford University Archaeological Society, recovered a small quantity of Romano-British pottery (PRN 3746) from the locality. A further programme of fieldwalking was undertaken by OAU in 1991 across the whole Yarnton area covering a total of 18 fields. Field 6 (see Fig 10.1) coincided with the northern area of rectilinear cropmarks. This was bordered to the south by Field 8 and to the west and east by Fields 5 and 7 respectively. The northern part of Field 8 includes the southern area of cropmarks described above. The results of this

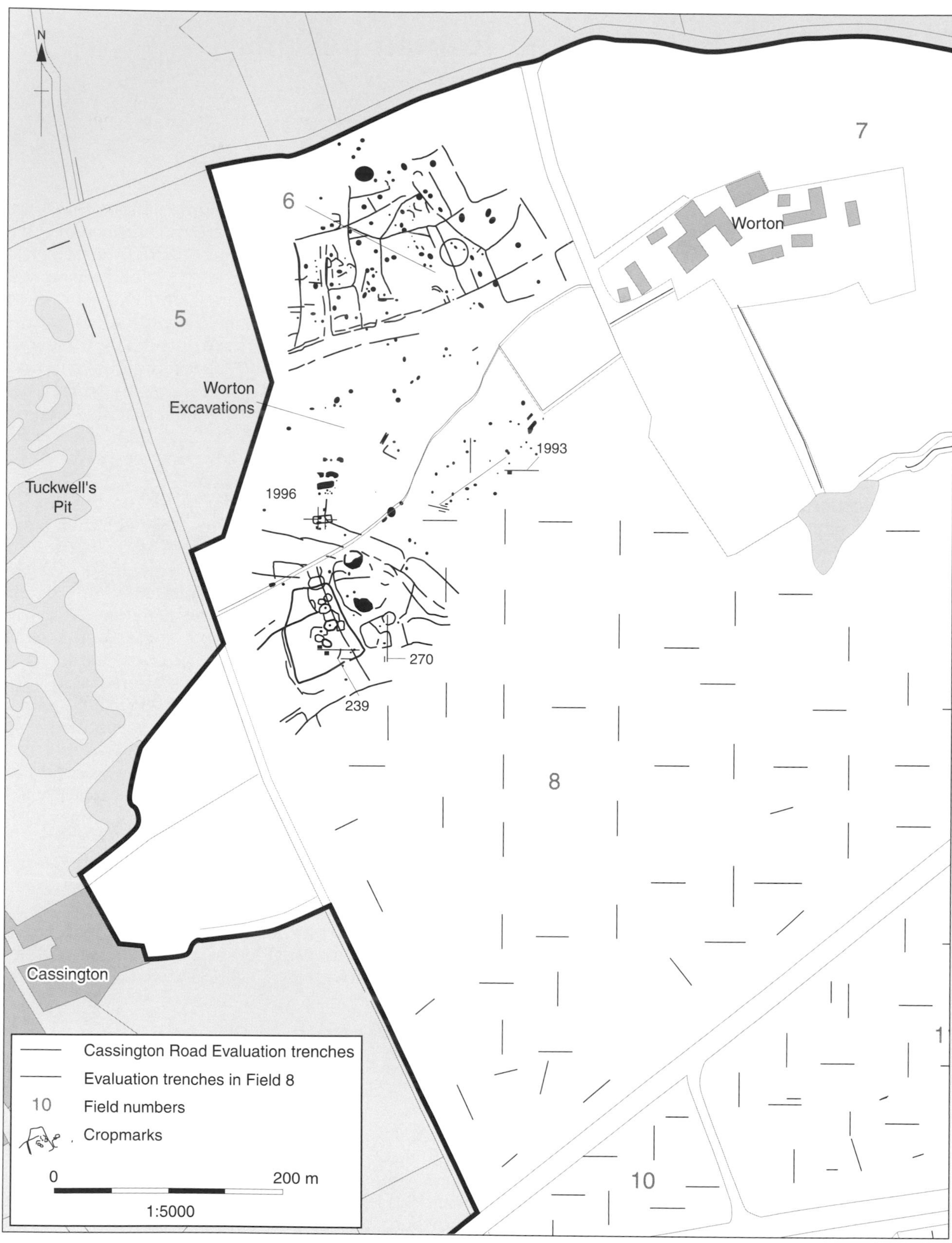

Fig. 10.1 Worton: archaeological interventions in relation to RCHME cropmark plot

survey are described in Chapter 11, but supported the observations based on cropmark morphology that earlier Roman settlement concentrated in the southern area of features visible from the air while later Roman activity was focussed to the north of the east-west trackway that appeared to define this settlement.

EVALUATION TRENCHING

In September 1991 and January 1992, OAU carried out an evaluation of the proposed route of the A40 Witney-Cassington dualling (OAU 1992b). The eastern end of this route, including the Cassington spur road, lies within the Yarnton study area. Thirteen trenches were investigated down the west side of Fields 6 and 8 adjacent to and south of Worton (Fig. 10.1). Trenches J1-7 and J10 were located along the western edge, and trenches J8, J9 and J11 in the south-west corner of the field (not numbered on Fig. 10.1). Ditches and pits were identified on the gravel terrace in trenches J1-3, and a few sherds of late Iron Age and Roman date were found in ditches in J1 and J2.

An evaluation using machine-excavated trial trenches was carried out over a 70 ha area by OAU

Fig. 10.2 Air photograph of Worton looking south showing late Iron Age/early Roman site. Cambridge University Collection of Air Photographs (AYI-95).

in 1993. This area corresponded with that threatened by gravel extraction, with the aim of examining those parts of the study area not previously investigated. Part of this evaluation exercise focused on the area of cropmarks west of Worton (Field 8). In Field 8 (Fig 10.1) where the window of opportunity between harvesting and sowing was quite short, a 2% sample was achieved in areas where the archaeological features were most dense and at least 1% of the rest of the area was sampled. In total 65 trenches, 30 m by 1.85 m in size and mostly aligned to the OS grid, were excavated across Field 8. The evaluation revealed extensive evidence of Iron Age, Roman and Saxon settlement (see also Chapter 11 and Hey 2004).

Roman settlement at Worton

A complex of intersecting enclosure and linear ditches containing several recuts was exposed in Trenches 239, 270 and 308. These were part of the enclosure system observed in the aerial photographs, A cluster of recut pits in the south of Trench 270 suggests that the dark, circular marks visible on the aerial photographs could be Roman pit groups. Trenches 239 and 270 also yielded the highest density of pottery finds of any other trenches in Field 8, along with some finds of Roman tile, contrasting with the complete lack of such material from the Yarnton settlement site. This, together with the presence of some ephemeral stone structures might hint at the presence of a higher status building(s) in the locality of Worton. The incidence of Roman pottery finds across the remainder of the field is very low and no other specifically Roman features were identified.

Trench 239 (Fig. 10.3)

Cut into the natural subsoil towards the centre of the trench was a fairly substantial NNW-SSE aligned ditch (239/19). This produced a single sherd of 1st century pottery. The ditch had been recut by a smaller ditch (239/14), the west edge of which was itself cut by a gully (239/10), set on the same alignment. The upper fill of ditch 239/14 produced 23 sherds of Roman pottery with a *terminus post quem* in the later 3rd-4th century. No dating evidence came from gully 239/10.

Running obliquely through the west end of the trench was an ENE-WSW aligned ditch, (239/24), containing pottery of late 2nd-century date. This ditch had also been recut, slightly to the north, by a shallower ditch (239/23) which contained 47 potsherds dating to the second half of the 2nd-3rd century. The similarity in shape and content suggests that 239/19 and 239/24 and their recuts may be part of the same enclosure ditch. Cut into the top of ditch 239/24 was a shallow grave (239/8) containing two neonatal skeletons (239/7) (see Boyle Chapter 16). Lying in the depression above ditches 239/24 and 239/23, and overlying the grave fill, was a deposit of dark brown silty clay (239/3) containing 50 sherds of late Roman pottery (3rd-4th century) and 17 pieces of animal bone. Two similar deposits, (239/26 and 239/27), were located in the area to the south-east of the

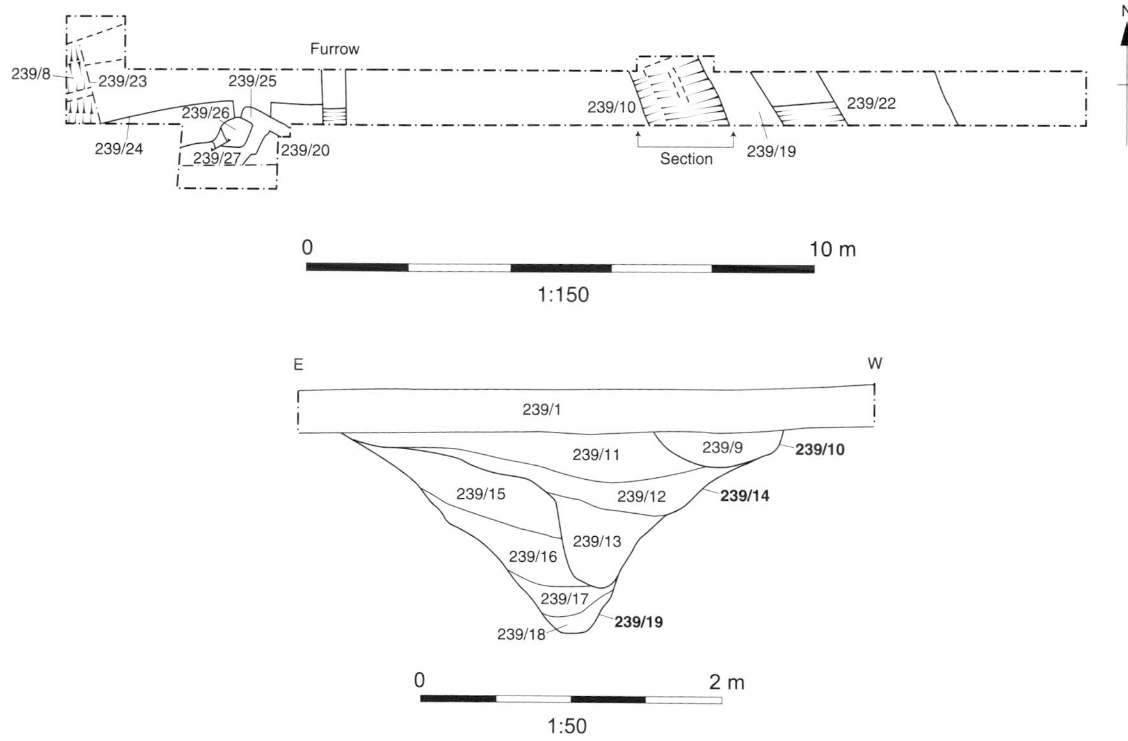

Fig. 10.3 Plan showing features in Trench 239 and ditch section

ditches and produced a further five sherds of Roman pottery which, although slightly mixed, suggest a date of around the 2nd century or possibly slightly later for these deposits.

On the north edge of, and partially cutting, layers 239/26 and 239/27, were the remains of a small T-shaped, stone lined structure (239/25), resembling a corn-drying oven or possibly a pottery-drying oven. The cropmark plot suggests that it lies within a small enclosure. The 'flue' area, however, was narrow at 0.2 m and no burnt stones were observed. A burnt deposit (239/26) was located to the south yielding burnt stone and two Roman sherds. Overlying the structure was a spread of brownish loam (239/20) containing 51 sherds of 2nd-3rd-century Roman pottery and a single radiate coin dated *c* AD 260-295 (P. Booth pers. comm.). Possible kiln debris was recovered from the adjacent enclosure ditch. Other ditches were observed at the east end of the trench but were not investigated due to lack of time.

Trench 270

Trench 270, located immediately east of Trench 239, revealed more Roman features (Fig. 10.4). Cutting into the natural gravel at the south end of the trench was a deep pit (270/13) with several fill horizons. The pit contained a small quantity of animal bone and 30 sherds of Roman pottery, including some diagnostically late Roman material in the uppermost fill, but 2nd-century sherds from further down and no datable material from lower fills. The pit had undercutting, irregular sides.

Immediately south of the deep pit was a much smaller pit (270/59), which appeared to have a NE-SW aligned gully (270/56) running from its northern edge. Some 10 m to the north of the pits was a NW-SE aligned gully (270/48), truncated by a ditch (270/50) on the same alignment. Also in the southern half of the trench were two postholes (270/44 and 270/46). None of these features produced any finds so their dates remain unknown.

Running through the centre of the trench was a fairly large NE-SW aligned ditch (270/37), recut by a later ditch (270/41) on the same alignment. The earlier ditch contained 40 sherds of late 2nd- to 3rd-century pottery. Filling the depression above these ditch fills was a layer of brown gravelly loam (270/33), overlain by a deposit of clay loam (270/24). Both these layers produced animal bone and 43 sherds of presumably redeposited 2nd-century pottery. Cutting through the top of these layers was an undated NNE-SSW aligned gully (270/53).

At the north end of the trench was a series of four intercutting ditches (270/21, 270/23, 270/18 and 270/15). All these ditches appear to be of Roman date although dating material was only recovered from 270/15, comprising 46 sherds of late Roman pottery with a possible Saxon sherd from the uppermost fill. Partially overlying one of the latest ditches, 270/15, was a small stretch of crudely built wall (270/6), running north-south. It appeared to lie in a shallow construction trench and was robbed

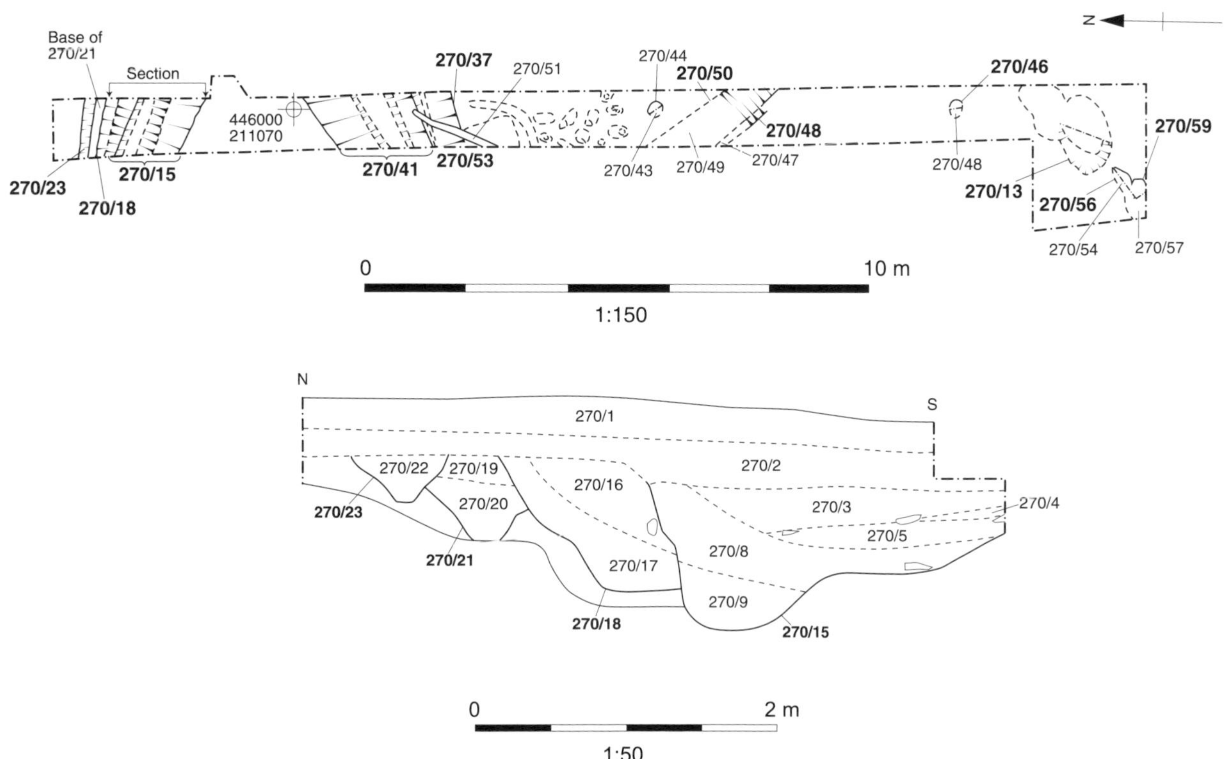

Fig. 10.4 Plan showing features in Trench 270 and ditch section

out to the north (fills 270/3, 270/4 and 270/5). Overlying the ditches and the wall, and extending throughout the northern half of the trench, was a layer of gravelly clay loam (270/2), possibly created by ploughing over the tops of the ditches.

Other features

Several probable Roman boundary ditches crossed the area along the edge of the gravel terrace. Redeposited Roman pottery was recovered from Trenches 70 and 294. A ploughsoil was observed in the zone coinciding with the floodplain gravels where the presence of a few Roman sherds from it suggests that it is of early Roman date. Several ditches and gullies probably represent Roman field boundaries and these are described in greater detail in Chapter 11.

Chapter 11: Investigation of the Wider Landscape

AIR PHOTOGRAPHIC SURVEY

English Heritage cropmark plot *by Carolyn Dyer and Roger Featherstone*

Summary

In 1994 English Heritage (then RCHME) undertook an air photographic survey of plough-levelled archaeological features in the vicinity of the hamlet of Worton in the parish of Cassington, Oxfordshire (Fig. 10.1). Photographs were examined in detail and photogrammetric plans of all the archaeological features visible were prepared at a scale of 1:2500.

Objectives

The purpose of the survey was to interpret and transcribe, at 1:2500 scale, all archaeological features showing as cropmarks (excluding ridge and furrow) on readily available aerial photographs. Rectification of the photographs was undertaken using AERIAL 4.20 (Haigh 1989). The final objective was to produce an accurate photogrammetric plan in the form of an overlay to the OS 1:2500 maps.

Definitions

For the purposes of the present survey, plough-levelled features are defined as those which have been recorded by aerial photography as differentially-coloured or textured marks in bare plough-soil, arable crops, grass or any other form of vegetation. The surviving earthworks in the area were not plotted.

Photographic sources consulted

For the purposes of this survey, all the specialist oblique air photographs in the National Monuments Record (NMR) of the survey area were consulted (eg Fig. 11.1), as well as two 1946 RAF vertical photographs. The collection held by the Cambridge University Committee for Aerial Photography (CUCAP) was also consulted (eg Fig. 1.11), and all of their relevant cover examined. Two 35 mm colour prints held by OA were also scrutinised.

It was not possible to carry out an exhaustive search for further photographs which may be held by commercial air survey companies or private individuals. Although it is possible that some such coverage exists, it is unlikely to contain significant amounts of archaeological information not already recorded on the air photographs which were available for consultation.

A listing of the oblique and vertical air photographs consulted, giving location and date for the obliques, and source, original sortie number, date and scale for the verticals is held in the project archive and by English Heritage, along with digital files created during the course of the survey.

Survey methods and techniques

Due to the need for accuracy, it was decided to produce plots of the various archaeological features using computer-aided rectification from various aerial photographs. This was achieved through the use of AERIAL software which uses plane transformation techniques offering metrical precision in the region of ±0-2 m at 1:2500. The residual errors recorded in rectification of the archaeological features were not greater than ±2 m, and were generally below ±1 m. Field control was derived mainly from current edition OS 1:2500 plans, although some control had to be taken from the earlier OS 6" maps as a result of significant changes in field boundaries.

Unfortunately, many of the photographs used were not particularly suitable for digitising. Some were very oblique, resulting in distortion of the final rectified plot in one direction. Some of the photographs also had very poor control, either due to the thickness of the field boundaries or the complete absence of control points across half of the image. In these cases, field boundaries had to be extrapolated in order to create false control points. Known boundaries and drains were digitised from the photographs and compared with the base maps, and these indicated that despite the problems of control, the resulting plots still retained an acceptable degree of accuracy (±2 m).

In the course of the survey seven separate photogrammetric plots were prepared, all of which were incorporated into the final drawing. The digital data files for these are held by English Heritage.

Description of features transcribed (Fig. 10.1)

For the purposes of this report, the archaeological features plotted have been split into five areas, based on field boundaries. Each field unit is referred to by a six figure grid reference, centred on the archaeological sites in that unit. There are obvious problems with establishing the dates of features from their morphological characteristics alone, and these are readily acknowledged. Nevertheless, only those features which may be Iron Age or Roman in date are included in any detail here. Many prehistoric and post-Roman features were observed and they are discussed in the other Yarnton publications (Hey 2004; Hey *et al* forthcoming).

Worton settlement (probably late Iron Age/early Roman)
NGR SP 459 111. NMR SP 41 SE 12;
PRN Nos: 12932 and 1346 (Fig. 10.1)

The cropmarks in this field clearly represent later prehistoric and/or early Roman settlement features, including enclosures, hut circles and pits. The large dark feature or macula at SP 4598 1108 is possibly a cropmark palimpsest of several recut hut circles, or a pit complex. At SP 4595 1105 is a large irregular rectilinear enclosure (78 m x 60 m) containing eight to ten smaller subcircular and rectilinear enclosures. On many of the photographs, the western side of this enclosure shows up as a wide ditch. However, on photograph SP4511/1 (NMR) it can clearly be seen to be double ditched. Some trenches were excavated across these settlement features as part of the 1993 evaluation programme, and these are described above (Chapter 10).

Worton settlement (probably late Roman)
NGR SP 460 114. NMR SP 41 SE 12; PRN No: 11346
(Fig. 10.1, Fig. 11.1)

As with the previous site, these cropmarks clearly represent settlement features, although the absence of hut circles perhaps suggests a later date. There are numerous pits and larger maculae across the site and many of the larger features clearly have the rectangular shape often associated with sunken-featured buildings.

Other features of note include a small rectangular enclosure at SP 45945 11155, measuring 16 m x 6 m, a rectangular macula at SP 45945 11185, 14 m x 5 m in size and, at SP 4598 1139, a large oval macula. A possible east-west trackway defined by parallel ditches *c* 14 m apart lies at the southern edge of these features.

The settlement features, which primarily consist of conjoined rectilinear enclosures, are unfortunately confused due to the presence of irregular frost cracks crossing the field at this point. The most obvious of these geological marks have not been plotted, but in the immediate vicinity of the settlement, around grid reference SP 4599 1140, it is unclear whether some features are natural or archaeological and therefore some

Fig. 11.1 Air photograph of Worton taken in 1934, looking south-east. Copyright Allen Collection, Ashmolean Museum, Allen 259

more natural-looking features have been plotted.

Cassington floodplain sites
NGR SP 461 104. PRN Nos: 10749 and 12197 (Fig. 11.2) (Not transcribed)

The cropmarks in this field unit show the remains of five, possibly six, subcircular enclosures and to the north, at SP 4613 1038, a right-angled ditch, possibly part of a large rectilinear enclosure. The subcircular features are probably settlement enclosures and one, at SP 4611 1035, is clearly double concentric, probably a hut circle and outer palisade trench.

In the north-east corner of the field at SP 4615 1036, there is a large enclosure with an entrance to the east. At this point the cropmarks are indistinct, but there appear to be curvilinear features within the outer enclosure, again probably hut circles.

To the north-east of this field at SP 4606 1045, are a number of irregular linear features. Although some appear to be fairly straight and have smooth, almost right-angled bends, they are likely to be natural frost cracks.

Other observations *by Gill Hey*

The Yarnton settlement site was first observed from the air, and a number of photographs are available which show a wide range of cropmark settlement features, especially pits and ditched enclosures (eg Fig. 1.5). These features were plotted at 1:10,000 within the Thames Valley Project which formed part of the English Heritage National Mapping Programme (RCHME 1995). Crop sensitivity to variations in the moisture of underlying soil is

Fig. 11.2 Air photograph of Cassington floodplain Iron Age settlement site looking north-east. Copyright English Heritage (SP4610/4; SF 976 Frame 146)

Fig. 11.3 Fieldwalking: distribution of all Iron Age and Roman pottery

typical of drought-influenced gravel terrace topographies. The western part of the same site in Cresswell Field, however, has never produced good cropmarks, and it was only in 1990 that features have been known to show from the air, and these were very difficult to interpret. This is probably the result of the varying drift geology in this area.

Apart from the Cassington Floodplain sites described above, no Iron Age or Roman features have ever been observed on the floodplain in this area from the air, even though a number of reasonably substantial boundary and field ditches of this date have been exposed during fieldwork. Iron Age hut circles and Bronze Age ring ditches are, however, known on nearby Port Meadow (Fig. 2.1; Lambrick and McDonald 1985).

Air photographs have also been helpful for recreating the topography of the study area before the onset of more intense arable agriculture from the Roman period, and concomitant alluviation on the floodplain as a result of the greater silt load in flood waters (Robinson and Lambrick 1984). The course of palaeochannels can be traced, as can paler areas on the floodplain indicating higher areas of gravel (eg Fig. 10.2). This information proved to be of considerable value for reconstructing patterns of land use on the floodplain through time.

FIELDWALKING *by Gill Hey*

Method

A fieldwalking programme was undertaken in autumn and winter 1990/91 over 182 hectares of arable land, both within the gravel extraction area and beyond it (Fig. 11.3). The main objective of this exercise was to assess Roman land use within the catchment of the Yarnton settlement, which was then being excavated; the catchment was defined arbitrarily as being a 1.5 km radius around the site. In practice, the area walked was dependent upon the availability of arable fields and the co-operation of farmers and landowners. Many fields to the east of Yarnton were then in pasture, and much of the land around the medieval village and north of it has been built over. These areas are, therefore, under-represented in the study. It was, however, possible to gain access to all arable fields, with the exception of two in the north-west of the site catchment.

Eighteen fields were surveyed (numbered 1–18 on Figs 11.3-11.6, over a varied topography of Fourth (Hanborough) Gravel Terrace in the north at *c* 91.4 m OD (representing 10% of the total area), clay to the south of this (29%), Second (Summertown-Radley) Gravel Terrace (16%) and floodplain between the edge of the Second Gravel Terrace and the river Thames at *c* 59 m OD (45%).

Transects were laid out at 20 m intervals on the National Grid, and finds were collected in 20 m stints (Hey 1991c; 1998). The fields were usually, but not always, walked in a north-south direction and all finds were collected, with the exception of post-medieval building material, the presence of which was noted before it was discarded. Changes within the team were minimised to reduce problems of variability in finds recognition between individual walkers (Haselgrove 1985, 21-5), and the few inexperienced members were interspersed between

Table 11.1 Quantification of pottery recovered in fieldwalking by area and period.

	YAFW N of study area (Fields 1-4)	*CWRF W of study area (Fields 5-8)*	*YWCF Cresswell Field (Field 9)*	*YWRF Floodplain (Fields 10-15)*	*YMF NE of study area (Fields 16-18)*	*Total*
Number						
IA	4	9	47	6	0	66
LIR	16	8	0	11	0	35
ERB	3	53	1	14	1	72
LRB	1	66	0	4	1	72
RB	27	862	8	72	10	979
Total	51	998	56	107	12	1224
Weight						
IA	12	63	358	53	0	486
LIR	78	47	0	63	0	188
ERB	11	462	1	190	17	681
LRB	6	461	0	32	20	519
RB	164	5466	78	680	65	6453
Total	271	6499	437	1018	102	8327
Mean sherd weight	5.3	6.5	7.8	9.5	8.5	6.8

Note: Areas with lowest mean sherd weight are those with most medieval ploughing.

experienced personnel. Ground, weather and lighting conditions were noted for every transect, and recorded on a form, with a record of finds collected and notes on geology visible. The conditions under which the survey was undertaken were generally good. The weather was mostly dry, the ground had been fairly recently ploughed and it was only towards the end of the exercise that there had been some crop growth. Even so, this did not significantly affect visibility.

Initially, finds were identified at OA and spots were plotted onto 1:2500 maps (Hey 1991c). The Iron Age and Roman pottery was subsequently identified by Paul Booth, the data were entered onto a database and distribution analysis undertaken in G-Sys (a relational-database management system). It is calculated that each walker would view an area 1 m to either side of their line, and by these means *c* 10% of the total area was seen. Densities of finds per hectare have, therefore, been calculated by multiplying actual quantities recovered by a factor of ten.

Finds of all periods from the Mesolithic to the post-medieval period were recovered during the fieldwalking survey (Hey 1991c; 1998; 2004; Hey *et al.* forthcoming). This report only considers material of Iron Age and Roman date (Figs 11.3-11.6; Table 11.1).

Results

Iron Age finds

Sixty-six sherds of Iron Age pottery were recovered during fieldwalking. The majority of these (47 sherds) came from Field 9, Cresswell Field, from the centre south of the field (Figs 11.3 and 11.4; Table 11.1). The greatest density of finds came from over and to the south-west of the settlement site, and they are likely to derive from ploughing over the occupation area which has truncated the original ground surface and also had the effect of transporting sherds downslope and over the old river channel. Iron Age sherds recovered from layers at the edge of the channel during the excavations here show that this process began at an early period (see above, Chapter 2). The pottery was mainly shell tempered (33 sherds), suggesting a predominantly early Iron Age assemblage, and corresponding to the greater level of activity of this date on the site. The relatively fresh appearance of the Cresswell Field pottery may indicate that it had only recently been brought into the ploughzone.

Smaller quantities of pottery (nine sherds) recovered from Field 6, to the north-west of Worton, are of uncertain origin. The quantity suggests that they represent much less dense settlement than at Cresswell Field, or some other kind of activity, such as manuring early fields. It is thought that the main area of Iron Age settlement lay to the west of this field, in what became Tuckwell's Gravel Extraction Pit (Leeds 1935; Harding 1972, pl. 67, A), but occasional occupation features may have spread to the east, or fields here may have received more intense manuring than elsewhere. The pottery was of mixed fabrics and undiagnostic and was fairly abraded.

A further ten sherds of pottery were mainly recovered as single finds and these were quite widely scattered (Fig. 11.4). The slight clustering apparent to the south of the old railway line some 500 m from the main Cresswell Field site (Fields 12 and 13) has no obvious cause; no Iron Age features were discovered in this area during evaluation or excavation. It is possible that these sherds derive from the 19th-century railway cutting which dug through some Iron Age features (Dawkins 1862) now known to be part of the Cresswell Field Iron Age site. However, it is also worth noting that this material lies between the occupation site and a middle Iron Age limestone causeway built across the river channel further south (in Field 14; see below) and it may, thus, genuinely represent Iron Age activity in the intervening area.

Late Iron Age and early Roman pottery

Thirty-five pottery sherds (188 g) from grog-tempered vessels were found during fieldwalking (Table 11.1). These sherds, which could be late Iron Age or early Roman in date (late 1st century BC and 1st century AD), have an entirely different spread to that of earlier Iron Age material, but share a similar distribution pattern to that of the early Roman material. They are plotted and described with these finds (Fig. 11.5).

Seventy-two sherds (681 g) could be attributed to the early Roman period (Table 11.1), and this material ranged from local coarse wares to samian ware imports. It was generally in an abraded condition, but some sherds were still quite large (average sherd weight of 9.5 g).

The late Iron Age and early Roman material appeared to cluster in three separate locations (Fig. 11.5). The densest group of material came from the north-west of the study area to the west of Worton, in the south of Field 6 and the north-west of Field 8. Much of this material was recovered from above the settlement site detected from the air, where sub-rectangular and sub-circular enclosures are visible (see above, this chapter), and evaluated during 1993. The evidence from this small settlement (described in Chapter 10) suggests that it was indeed occupied over this period of time. The east-west line of early Roman finds to the north lies approximately over the trackway seen as a cropmark (Fig. 10.1) and may suggest an early date for this presumed Roman routeway. Sherds lying south of the settlement have probably been moved downslope during ploughing.

The recovery of finds from fieldwalking on floodplain terraces is not common, but it is now well understood that these sherds do not derive from settlement, but are being brought up to the surface by modern ploughing cutting down into Roman

Fig. 11.4 Fieldwalking: distribution of Iron Age pottery

Fig. 11.5 Fieldwalking: distribution of late Iron Age and early Roman pottery

Fig. 11.6 Fieldwalking: distribution of late Roman pottery

fields (Hey 1998, 50-2). These fields, which lay on gravel islands between small river channels, were enclosed within ditches and the ploughsoils themselves can be seen when modern cultivation layers and later alluvium are removed (see below). The pottery indicates that they were fairly intensively manured during the early Roman period, their main phase of use, and possibly as early as the late Iron Age. The proximity of these spreads to the Yarnton settlement suggests that these were Yarnton's fields.

A third small cluster of late Iron Age/early Roman and early Roman sherds came from a small field to the north of the Oxford-Worcester railway line (Field 4; Fig. 11.5). This field has never been evaluated and the source of this material remains uncertain.

Late Roman

Seventy-two sherds (519 g) of diagnostic late Roman (mid 3rd-4th century) pottery were recovered in fieldwalking (Table 11.1). This material largely comprised Oxfordshire colour-coated ware and mortaria with some pink-grogged ware.

The vast majority of this pottery came from the centre and north of Field 6, to the north-west of Worton (Fig. 11.6). Cropmarks in this area indicate a settlement of rectilinear enclosures and pits, lying to the north of an east-west trackway (see above, this chapter). The pottery recovered from fieldwalking suggests that this is late Roman in date, in contrast to the earlier element of the settlement to the south of the track and modern field boundary (compare Figs 11.5 and 11.6). The Oxford University Archaeological Society walked over this field (OA Field 8) in 1970 and also reported quite dense concentrations of Romano-British pottery and tile (PRN 3746). A few sherds to the south of the late Roman cluster (in Field 8) may indicate activity spreading into this field, or pottery being transported downslope with the plough.

There is surprisingly little other diagnostically late Roman material in the wider landscape. Of particular interest is the virtual absence of late Roman material coming from the floodplain fields, presumably indicating the cessation of manuring in these areas. Whether this is the result of the abandonment of cultivation on low-lying fields at this period, or a change in crop husbandry, cannot be deduced from this evidence alone (but see Stevens below, Chapter 18).

Other Roman pottery

The majority of the Roman pottery from fieldwalking (979 sherds; 6453 g) could not be ascribed to either the early or the late Roman period. Many of these sherds were abraded and/or in fabrics that were not chronologically diagnostic. This material was found in all areas where early and late Roman clusters were present, and was recovered more generally over the wider environment in small numbers (Fig. 11.3). Its distribution adds nothing to the remarks already made about the spreads of more closely dated Roman pottery.

TEST PITS *by Gill Hey*

Method

Fifty-one test pits were excavated in three separate north-south transects across the Yarnton study area (Fig. 11.7). A long transect, Transect 1, (650 m) ran south from the top of the Second Gravel Terrace in fieldwalking Field 9 down onto the floodplain (Hey 1994a), and two shorter transects, Transects 2 and 3, (140 m and 440 m respectively) ran across areas of floodplain gravel (Field 15), one down onto a lower old ground surface where the gravel had been truncated by a migrating river channel (Hey 1992 and 1993b). Test pits 1 m x 1 m were excavated every 20 m along the transects, where this was possible. Soil was separated by layers, and by 0.10 m spits within layers, and was sieved through a 10 mm mesh. Some pits through alluvium were abandoned due to the extreme difficulty of sieving the clay soils and the fruitlessness of the search.

RESULTS

In general terms, the greatest density of finds recovered from sieving came from the Second Gravel Terrace (at *c* 65-61 m OD), and from colluvium just below this main terrace (Fig. 11.8; Transect 1, Test Pits 52-56 and Test Pits 58-64 respectively). Observation of the soils and the finds recovered indicate that there was a patchy early ploughsoil on a narrow terrace around 250 m wide, just below the main terrace at *c* 59.60 m OD, between it and a palaeochannel (Fig. 11.8, Test Pits 60-65). This layer contained flint, burnt stone, fired clay and a few late Bronze Age sherds which had been disturbed during the ploughing event (a number of Bronze Age burnt stone deposits were also discovered in this area; Hey *et al.* forthcoming). The absence of Roman material from this soil, in contrast to Roman ploughsoils elsewhere, and the proximity of this field to the Yarnton Iron Age site in Cresswell Field, may suggest that there was Iron Age arable in this area. There were no Iron Age finds from this deposit, however, but two middle Iron Age sherds were recovered from colluvium above it in Test Pit 62 and Roman sherds also came from the same layer.

Ploughsoil was also observed on the floodplain and occasional sherds of Roman pottery were retrieved from these layers in Transects 2 and 3, in addition to flint, burnt stone and very occasional prehistoric pottery sherds. Roman pottery was also found in the long Transect 1 on the gravel terrace and colluvium at its edge and on the adjacent floodplain (Figs 11.8 and 11.9), which suggests that there was more manuring in these areas than indicated by the fieldwalking results.

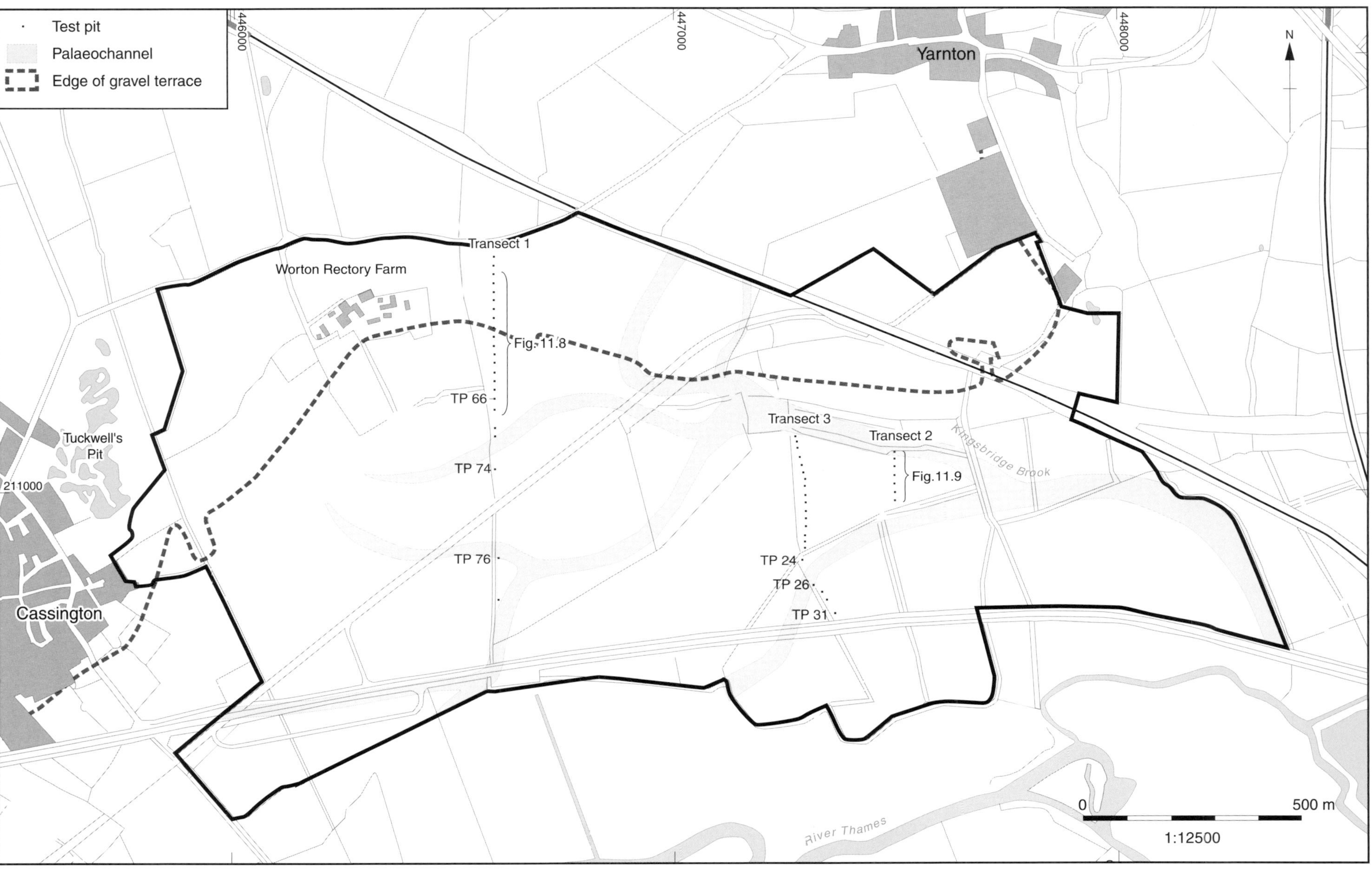

Fig. 11.7 Test pit locations

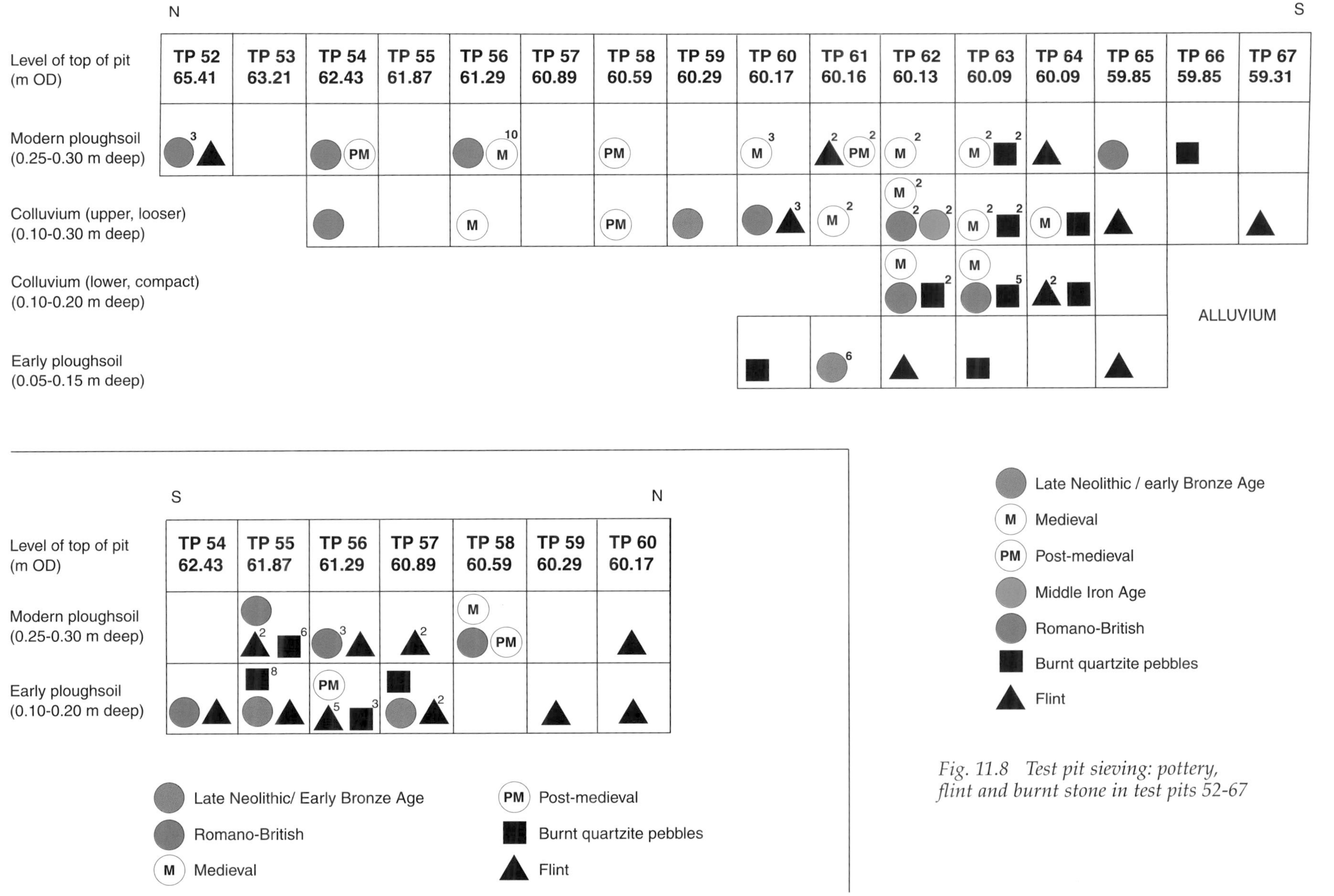

Fig. 11.8 Test pit sieving: pottery, flint and burnt stone in test pits 52-67

Fig. 11.9 Test pit sieving: pottery, flint and burnt stone in test pits 1-7

In addition to providing evidence of cultivation in the form of manuring scatters, colluvium and buried fields, the test pits provided information on the land form before and during the onset of alluviation. Palaeochannels and alluvium in low-lying adjacent areas were encountered in the southern part of Field 9 (between Test Pits 66 and 74), in Field 12 next to Test Pit 76, and along Transect 3 to the south of Field 15 between Test Pits 24 and 26. Alluvial sediment proved especially intractable to sieve. Test Pits 26-31 of Transect 3 were dug through up 0.30-0.60 m of alluvium onto a buried ground surface (on floodplain Site 2) which had been used from the early Neolithic period and crossed by a sand-and-gravel causeway in the Iron Age (see below). The test pits demonstrated both the absence of cultivated fields here throughout the Roman and medieval periods, and the effectiveness of alluvial silts for preventing the movement of finds in the soil profile where ploughing had not taken place.

EVALUATION TRENCHING AND EXCAVATION IN THE WIDER LANDSCAPE

by Gill Hey with Christopher Bell, Caroline Dennis, Grace Jones and Alex Smith

Topographical features

Evaluation trenching was of considerable assistance for reconstructing the topography of the study area during the Iron Age and Roman periods, and the picture built up largely during the 1993 evaluation has been refined by the large-scale stripping that has followed (Fig. 1.6). The edge of the gravel terrace is a noticeable feature in the modern landscape, but it is apparent that it would have been more pronounced in the Iron Age. Ploughing, especially during the medieval period, has softened the profile of the terrace edge, and the discovery of what appears to be a buried Iron Age field below the terrace in Cresswell Field has already been mentioned above. This was detected in evaluation Trenches 58, 59, 62 and 65 and Test Pits 60-65, where it was sealed beneath colluvium of medieval and possibly Roman date (Fig. 11.8).

Evaluation has been of greater importance for establishing the position of palaeochannels which flowed from the Second Gravel Terrace and across the floodplain but have largely silted up. The substantial NNE-SSW late Devensian channel that was created across the gravel terrace on Cresswell Field could be seen from the air (eg Fig. 1.2), but its course in the Iron Age and Roman periods was clarified by evaluation trenching and excavations adjacent to the Cresswell Field site. More unexpectedly, the presence of another stream course running off the gravel terrace, approximately parallel to the Cresswell Field channel, was revealed during evaluation for a recycling plant in 1996 (Figs 1.4 and 11.10). This smaller channel was obscured by a modern field boundary and the 19th-century railway line and shunting yards. It would have run through the Iron Age settlement.

A pond which appears to be Iron Age in date was found on the gravel terrace between Worton and Cresswell Field in Trench 45 (Fig. 11.10; Hey 1993b, 29-30). It lay in a natural hollow and was probably fed from a spring; modern ponds are present nearby. The lowest grey clay fill (45/17) contained late Bronze Age/early Iron Age pottery and the pond appeared to have silted up during the Iron Age; a little 1st-century AD pottery came from its upper fill (45/12).

Most of the channels that were located and examined were situated on the floodplain, and were part of the braided river system of the Thames (Fig. 1.3; see Robinson, Chapter 2). These were examined in a number of places (Figs 11.10 and 11.11) and provided important information on changing environment and land use, and evidence for the ways in which people used these channels and crossed the floodplain in the past.

The palaeochannels began to fill with silts during the Iron Age. Section B adjacent to Site 2 and Section 3 on Oxey Mead (Figs 11.10 and 11.12) show that the lowest organic sediments were still accumulating in the middle Iron Age (Oxey Mead layer 3/8 and Section B context 9; Chapter 13, Fig. 13.4 and Table 13.1), although inorganic alluvium began to accumulate in the surviving hollows over dug features on Site 2 at about this time (OxA-6616: 400-160 cal BC at 95% confidence; Fig 13.5). Inorganic alluvial sedimentation on a larger scale seems to have begun in the later Iron Age, but gained pace in the Roman period, leading to increasing overbank alluviation by the end of the period (see below). On low-lying areas next to the palaeochannel, the alluvium became trampled and mixed indicating human and animal activity, for example on Site 17 where it comprised mottled bluish-grey and yellow-brown silty clay with coarse sand, with some burnt stone trampled into the base (10168 and 10169).

The depth of silting within the channels was influenced by the presence of wooden structures and causeways nearby. These sections are discussed in greater detail below, but examples of locations where thicker alluvial deposits were found include to the west of the middle Iron Age causeway on Site 9 (Fig. 11.10; deposits 13008 (which yielded a fragment possibly of a Dressel 2-4 amphora dating to the 1st-2nd centuries AD) to 13305) and adjacent to wooden structures south of Site 1.

Overbank alluvium can be attested from the early Roman period on low-lying ground, for example on Site 2 (Chapter 13; OxA-6618: cal 50 BC-130 cal AD at 95% confidence, Fig. 13.5), but was more widespread on the higher gravel islands in the later Roman period when field boundary ditches began to clog up with alluvial silts, and spills of alluvium can even be seen in the entrances to some fields. On Site 25 the Roman alluvial layer of mid bluish-grey silty clay with rare gravel (12002 etc) overlay Roman ploughsoil (12003), and this stratigraphic

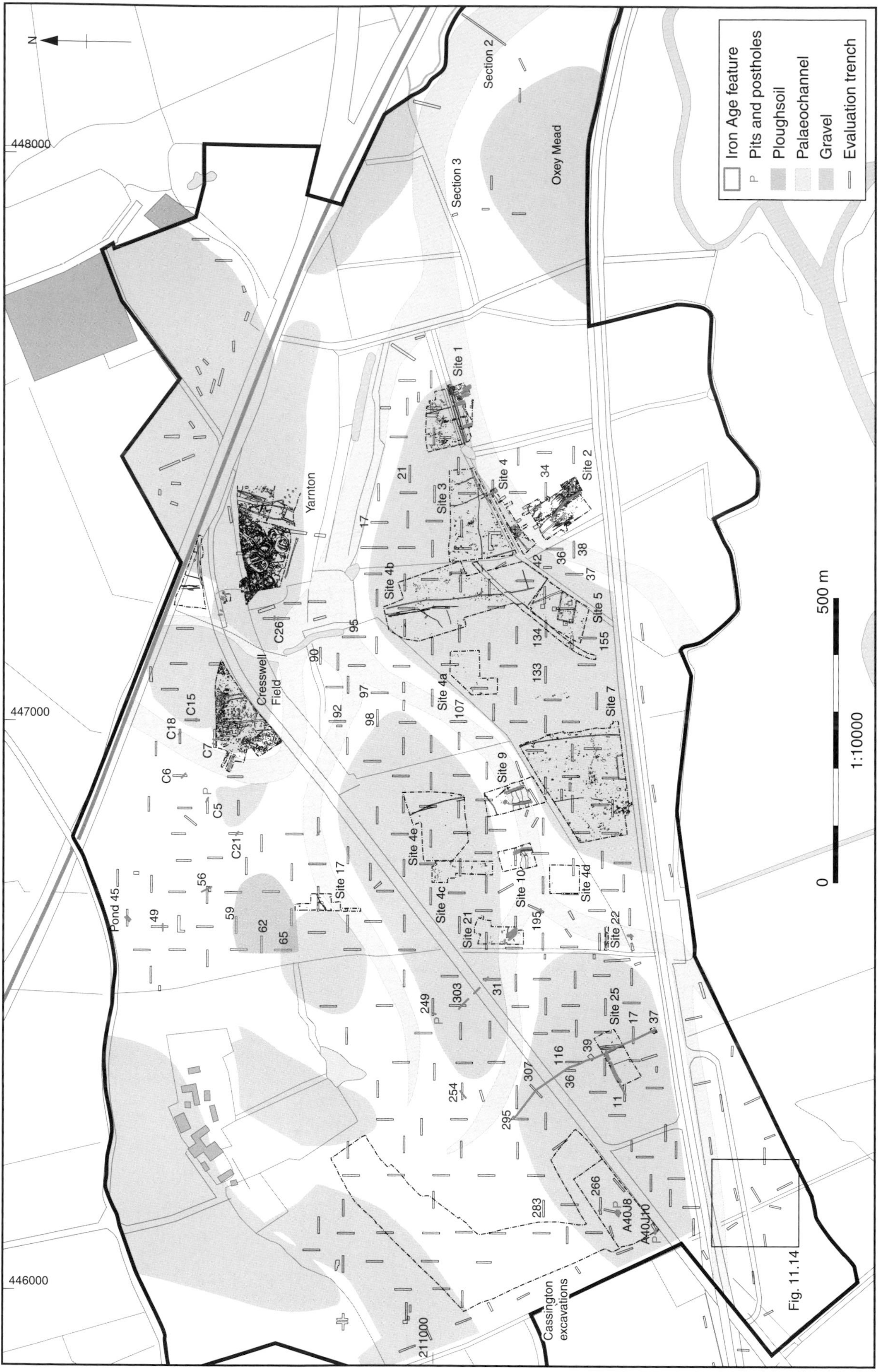

Fig. 11.10 Location of Iron Age features (in red) from excavations, evaluation trenching and floodplain work

Fig. 11.11 Palaeochannel section in evaluation Trench 215, looking north

sequence can be seen very clearly in Fig. 11.13 of the Roman field boundary ditch (5013) against the east section of Site 3. Here alluvium fills the top of the recut ditch and overlies the ploughsoil (on the left-hand side) within the field. Soil studies have shown that these deposits derive very generally from calcareous geologies (Canti 1996, 24-5).

Floodplain settlement

Iron Age

A small settlement on the floodplain to the south-east of Cassington was detected from the air in 1970 (Figs 11.2 and 11.10). The cropmarks suggest the presence of around five or six subcircular settlement enclosures, including a possible double concentric hut circle with an outer palisade trench (see above, this chapter). Rectilinear enclosures lay to the north. Part of this site was evaluated in advance of a planned A40 dualling scheme, as a roundabout junction was proposed for this area. The scheme was never developed and so no further work has been undertaken. Eight trenches (203 linear metres) were excavated over the site (Fig. 11.14; Hey 1993a) and the results suggest that there are two separate foci of activity lying either side of a palaeochannel, one of which correlates with cropmark evidence; the other was not visible from the air.

To the south, in Trench H1, a number of linear ditches and deep gullies ran east-west or NE-SW across the trench (Fig. 11.14). One seems to be part of a circular enclosure seen on the air photographs. Deep gullies, possibly house gullies, were present, as well as at least six postholes, of which two were excavated. At least some of these postholes indicated structures and a spread of clay silt with daub, burnt limestone and charcoal towards the north of the trench (H1 1/11) was interpreted as destruction debris from a house. Middle Iron Age pottery in fairly substantial quantities was retrieved from these features, including sherds with limescale and burnt residue (Barclay, note in Chapter 14; Hey 1993a). The ground shelved away to the north of the trench and no features were located in Trench H3, although a NW-SE ditch in Trench H2 produced probable middle Iron Age sherds. No features were exposed to the west, in Trench H6. This evidence indicates a discrete, enclosed occupation area focused on Trench H1.

Another dense group of occupation features was found in Trench H10, to the north of an intervening palaeochannel (Fig. 11.14). It was apparent that the site had not been detected from the air because of the depth of overburden and alluvium here. Deep ditches cut across the area, mainly in the southern part of the trench, and gullies and postholes were present suggesting domestic occupation. Once again, the majority of datable material was middle Iron Age in date, with a small earlier and probably residual component (Barclay, note in Chapter 14). Trench H13 was excavated to the east of Trench H10 to assess the extent of settlement, but no features were encountered, and an undated ditch was the

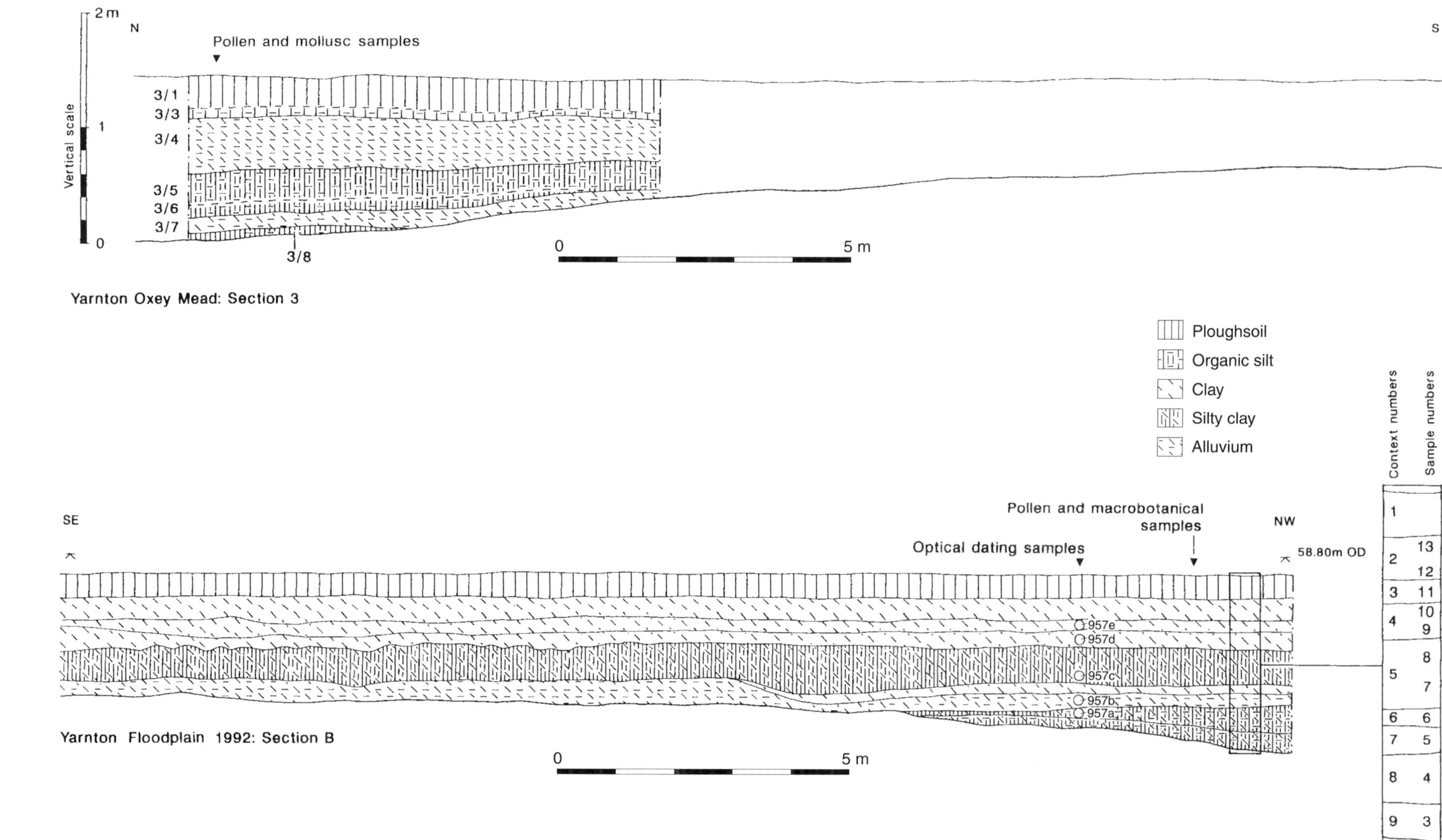

Fig. 11.12 Yarnton palaeochannel sections: Oxey Mead and Floodplain Site 2 section B

Fig. 11.13 Roman field boundary ditch 5013 in Site 3 showing ploughsoil

only feature exposed in Trench H8 to the west. As in the vicinity of Trench H1, this group of features seems to represent occupation over a very restricted area which was probably enclosed within ditches.

In conclusion, the evaluation revealed the presence of two discrete middle Iron Age settlement enclosures in this area which had been fairly intensively inhabited, though probably for a comparatively short period of time. They may not have been in contemporary use. Although the area seen was small, no deposits suggesting flooding and/or the reuse of the sites were discovered, as had been observed at the seasonally-occupied Farmoor site further upstream, also on the Thames floodplain (Lambrick and Robinson 1979). The apparent intensity of occupation at Farmoor also suggested more long-lived occupation than at Cassington. The Cassington sites appear to be more closely comparable with Mingies Ditch, a pastoral settlement situated on the floodplain of Lower Windrush Valley near Stanton Harcourt (Allen and Robinson 1993).

Other possible evidence of settlement

A small site in the south-west of the gravel extraction area was revealed during evaluation trenching in 1991/2 and again in 1994 (Hey 1993a, 15-6; 1994a, 33-4). Ditches and postholes, some of which appeared to form part of circular post-built structures, were exposed in A40 Trenches J7-11 and Yarnton-Cassington Evaluation Trenches 266 and 283 (Fig. 11.10; Hey 1993a, figs 22 and 25-6; Hey 1994a, figs 4a, 11-2). Many of the fills contained charcoal, and ploughing, possibly in the Roman period, had created a spread of burnt and mixed soils immediately above these features. The date of this site was not clear-cut in the evaluation, but on excavation in 2005 it became apparent that it was a late Bonze Age settlement and it will be reported elsewhere (Hey *et al.* forthcoming).

Evaluation trenching to the west of the Cresswell Field excavations, on the opposite side of the palaeochannel to the Iron Age occupation, revealed the possible site of a post-built structure. Four postholes were revealed in the eastern part of Trench C5, with charcoal in their fills (Fig. 11.10; Hey 1991c, 32). Ten sherds of late Bronze Age/early Iron Age pottery and one of early/middle Iron Age date came from these features. This evidence may suggest that occupation extended to the west of the excavation site, or that occasional settlement units were established on the west bank of the broad north-south channel. Features in trenches to the north of the Cresswell Field site (particularly in Trenches C15 and C16) were part of the settlement revealed in the main excavation area. The spatial spread of these features and the results of geophysical survey (see below, Chapter 12), indicate that the Iron Age settlement extended approximately 20 m north of the excavated site. This part of the settlement lies outside the gravel quarry and is not under threat.

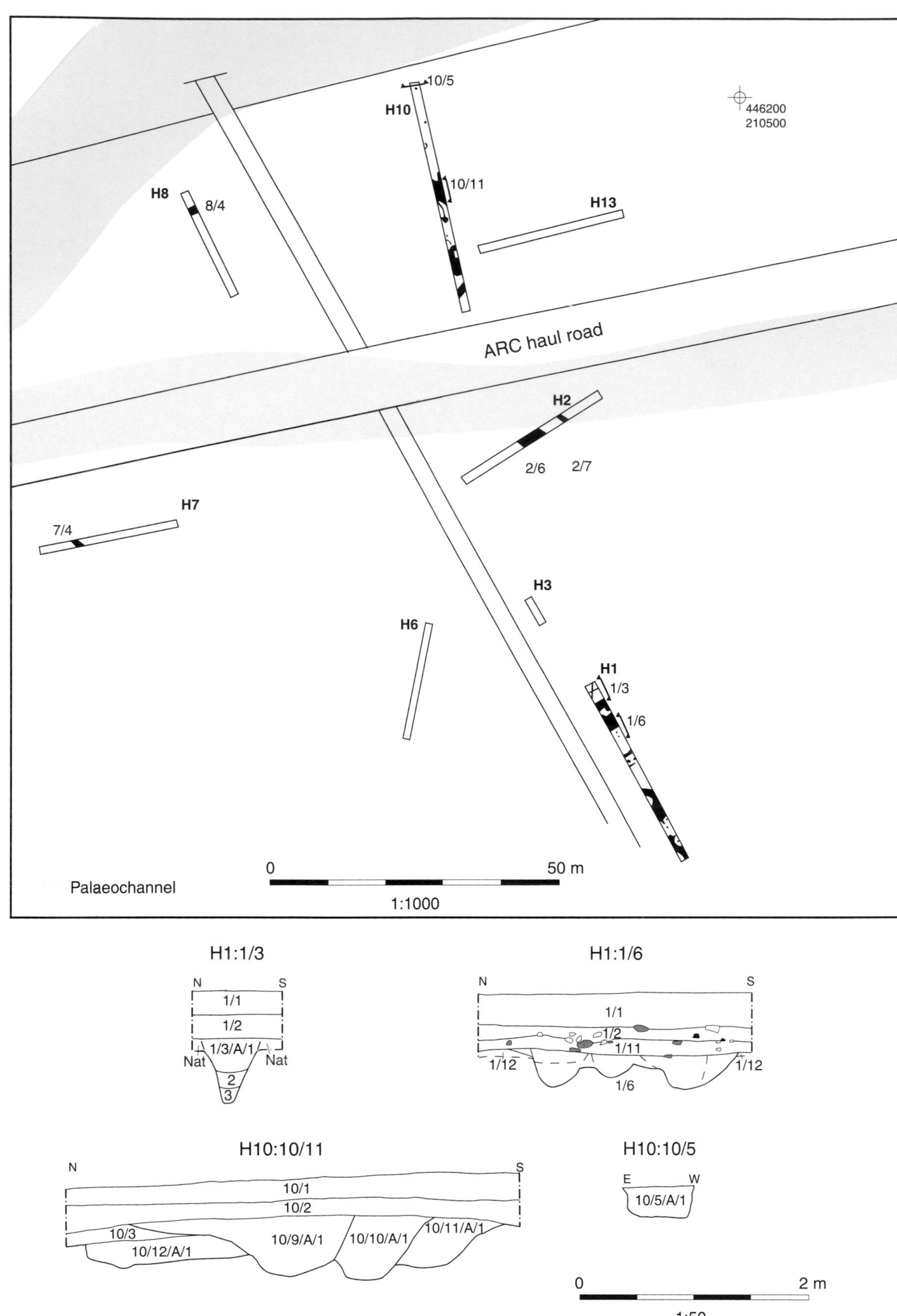

Fig. 11.14 Cassington floodplain Iron Age sites

Fig. 11.15 Middle Iron Age boundary ditch and associated gully in floodplain excavation Site 25

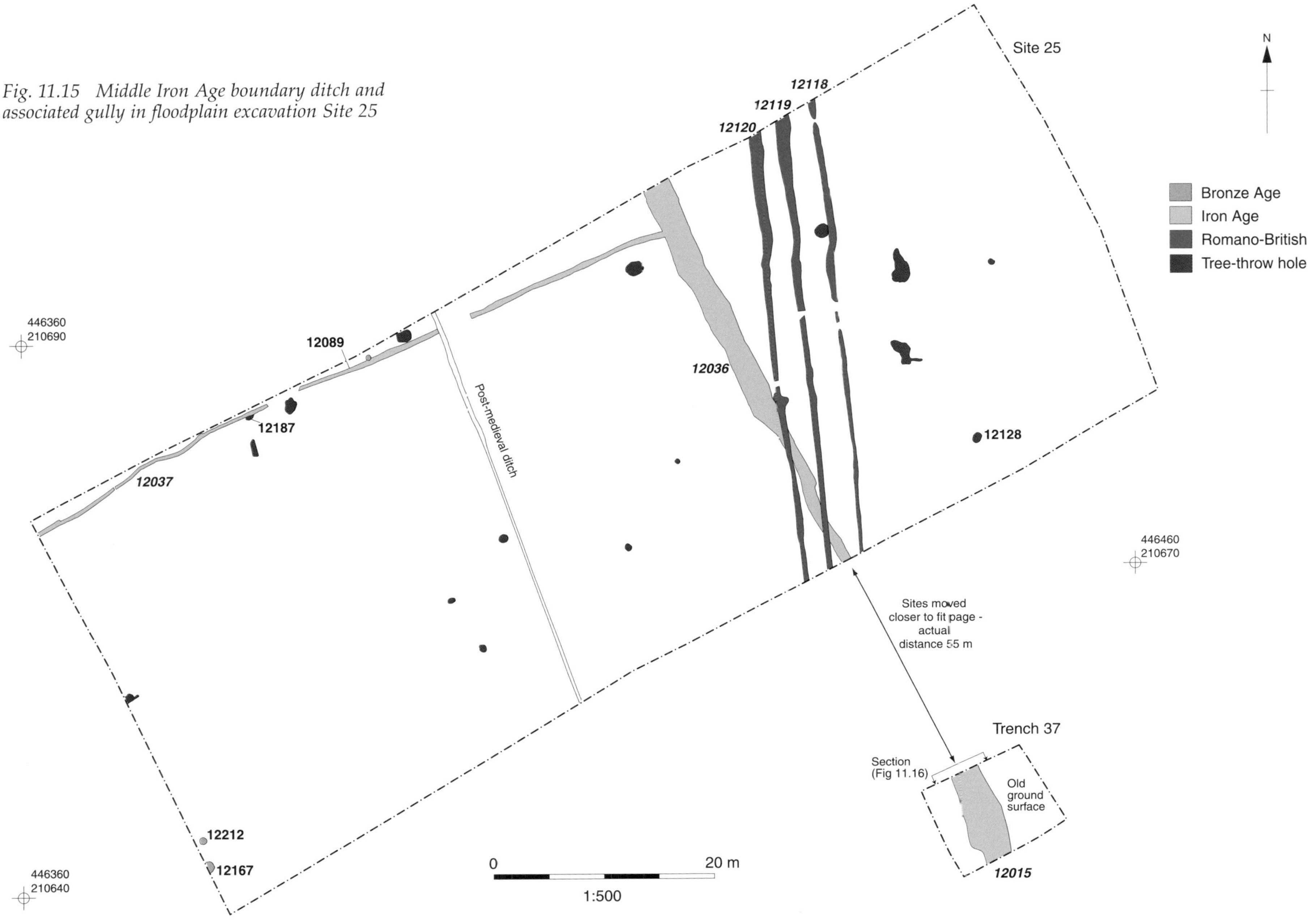

Two small evaluations were undertaken in 1996 and 1997 directly to the east of the Cresswell Field site and north of the Yarnton excavations, to assess the impact of the construction of a weighbridge for a recycling plant (Bell 1997; 1998). A group of intercutting features, including a pit and two possible postholes yielding early Iron Age pottery, were found in 1996 on the west side of a shallow palaeochannel which might have been a small stream in the Iron Age. On the other side of the stream, two postholes were also found in an area cut by Roman gullies, but no settlement features were revealed in trenches excavated to the north in the following year (Bell 1998). This evidence suggests that early Iron Age occupation was continuous from Cresswell Field to the Yarnton site and confirms its northern limit. Evidence of domestic settlement between these two sites is also supported by the observations of W B Dawkins during the construction of the railway line between the Yarnton and Cresswell Field sites in the 19th century (Dawkins 1862). In addition, middle Iron Age features were exposed, along with Roman settlement evidence, directly to the west of the Yarnton site in 1991 (Trench C26, Fig. 11.10; Hey 1991c). A decorated antler comb came from one of the small pits (Fig. 15.10, No. 24). This group of features also demonstrated the southerly extent of Iron Age settlement close to the edge of the gravel terrace.

Land boundaries

Iron Age

A substantial prehistoric ditch was revealed in the south-west of the gravel extraction area, north-east of the Cassington Iron Age floodplain sites, in evaluation Trenches 37, 17, 38, 39, 16, 36, 307 and (probably) 295, and within floodplain excavation Site 25 (Fig. 11.10). In total, a 305 m length of this ditch was traced running approximately NW-SE across the floodplain between two palaeochannels. Although originally thought to be earlier prehistoric in date, based on pottery and worked flint finds, excavation in 1997 on Site 25 (Fig. 11.15, feature 12036) and in an extension to evaluation Trench 37 near to the southern palaeochannel, produced radiocarbon and OSL dates which showed that the ditch was middle Iron Age in date and had been recut in *370-110 cal BC (95% probability)* (see Chapter 13).

As revealed in Site 25, this was a substantial ditch (12015), *c* 1.9 m wide and 0.8 m deep in its first phase of use, with moderate to steeply-sloping sides which had eroded near the top in places. It had been recut twice to the west of the first cut, each recut being more shallow and narrow than its predecessor. The surviving, primary fill of the earliest cut was a brownish-grey clay sand with moderate quantities of gravel and some organic material (12068 and 12069), but in both recuts a change to silty clay was seen, with more gravel present. A band of gravel on the eastern edge of the ditch was probably the surviving remnants of the bank, and tips of gravel were found in the ditch fills on this side. Few finds were recovered and these included a little animal bone (mostly cattle), two flint flakes and a flint chip, two pieces of burnt stone and two earlier prehistoric sherds, one of which was identified as Beaker.

The ditch became deeper further south, near the palaeochannel, where it was examined in Trenches 17 and 37 and a later extension to Trench 37 (Figs 11.15 and 11.16). A similar sequence of cuts and deposits was revealed but the lowest fills here were waterlogged bluish-grey silts. The presence of flowing-water snails in the ditch at this point may indicate that the ditch opened into the palaeochannel (see Robinson, Chapter 18). Waterlogged seeds (mixed aerial species) from the lower fills (12216 and 12181) of the first recut produced material for the radiocarbon dates referred to above (the seeds were recovered from samples taken during the evaluation: fill numbers 37/7 and 37/8, renumbered 12216 and 12181 when re-excavated). Later fills also had a more clay-silt character with moderate gravel and contained occasional manganese and charcoal flecks and sandy lenses. Alluvium was noted in the upper fills of the final recut and may indicate that the ditch remained in use for some time. Roman ploughsoil and then alluvium had slumped into the top of the ditch.

The ditch became more shallow north of Site 25, with only one or no recuts visible, and mainly gravelly fills (Hey 1994a, fig. 11). Finds were scarce in these areas too. A single sherd of late Bronze Age pottery was recovered from possibly redeposited bank material in the top of the ditch in Trench 16, along with a single middle Iron Age sherd, and another middle Iron Age sherd came from an upper fill in Trench 39. Fifteen sherds of late Bronze Age/early Iron Age pottery were found within the northernmost section examined, in Trench 295 (129505).

A linear gully (12037/12089) ran west from, and perpendicular to, this boundary ditch within Site 25 (Fig. 11.15). It was traced for 62 m within the site and continued at least as far as Trench 11, where it was cut by Roman ditches (Fig. 11.10; Hey 1994a). The gully had a clear terminal at the main boundary ditch and appeared to be contemporary with its second recut, but this could not be established with certainty. It was U-shaped in profile, 0.8 m wide and 0.2 m deep, and contained a single fill of grey clay loam with occasional gravel and pieces of burnt stone. It is uncertain whether this was a field boundary ditch, in which case it was the only Iron Age field boundary observed, or represents a property or land-use division.

On Site 2 to the east of the Yarnton floodplain, a linear NW-SE ditch (2607) was exposed on the east edge of the site. This appeared to be a replacement of a well-dated middle Bronze Age ditch (3081), one of a pair of parallel ditches on this site (Figs 11.10 and 11.39; Hey *et al.* forthcoming). It was broad (1-

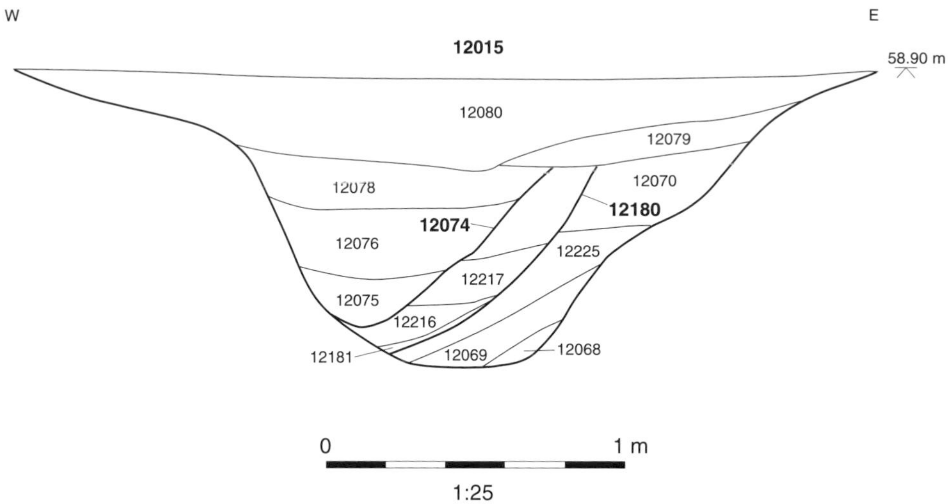

Fig. 11.16 Section through Iron Age boundary ditch 12015, Site 25

1.50 m), shallow (0.32-0.47 m) and generally flat bottomed throughout its length and it had a bank to the east. It was traced for just over 90 m from the southern limits of excavation towards a penannular enclosure on the south bank of the palaeochannel and a ring ditch on the far bank, and was associated with a series of post and slot alignments which are discussed below. The only finds from the feature were redeposited (a small sherd of late Neolithic pottery and a number of struck flints), but the palaeoenvironmental evidence suggests that this ditch was cut at a later date than the middle Bronze Age ditches (ie in the late Bronze Age or early Iron Age), when the water table had continued to rise but before the onset of alluviation (Robinson in Hey *et al.* forthcoming). On balance, this feature is most likely to be of the late Bronze Age and is described in greater detail in the volume on the Neolithic and Bronze Age discoveries at Yarnton (Hey *et al.* forthcoming). However, its alignment (following that of the middle Bronze Age ditches) influenced the position of later features in this area, and all three ditches were still slight depressions in the ground when alluvium was first deposited here in the middle Iron Age (see Chapter 13). Its function is very uncertain, but it did not appear to be part of a field or enclosure system.

Roman

No other ditches of either the Iron Age or Roman periods were encountered which were thought likely to be major boundary features, rather than field ditches. It is possible that any formal boundary between the fields of Roman Yarnton and those of the settlement at Worton would not be easily distinguished from field boundary ditches. It is also possible that they have been incorporated into later boundaries; trenching across the modern Yarnton/Cassington parish boundary revealed earlier ditches, but they could not be dated (Hey 1994a).

Iron Age tracks, causeways and other channel crossing places

Trackways

There are no known tracks or droveways of Iron Age date on the gravel terrace or gravel islands within the floodplain, but the long-lived character and permanence of settlement suggests that well-travelled routes would have lain between habitation sites. In addition, causeways found over palaeochannels on the floodplain and low-lying ground adjacent to them, including a path running for a short distance from a stone causeway towards the Yarnton site, show that people and animals traversed the floodplain using specific crossing places which were, presumably, approached by tracks either on the most direct route or bypassing fields.

Causeways across the channels

A number of causeways were constructed over palaeochannels and low lying ground during the course of the 1st centuries BC and AD. A number of these were certainly Iron Age in date. They were presumably constructed to overcome the increasing problems of crossing the floodplain at a time of rising water levels. Other causeways are less easy to date and could have been built in the Iron Age, Roman or even Anglo-Saxon periods.

Limestone and sand-and-gravel causeway on Site 9 (Figs 11.10 and 11.17-11.34)

An impressive and substantial limestone and sand-and-gravel causeway was uncovered running NNW-SSE across the palaeochannel in the western part of Site 9 (Fig. 11.17). The channel bank to the south was relatively steep, but was low-lying to the north and only gradually shelved up to a gravel island beyond the limits of the excavation (Figs 11.18 and 11.19). The causeway lay beneath Roman

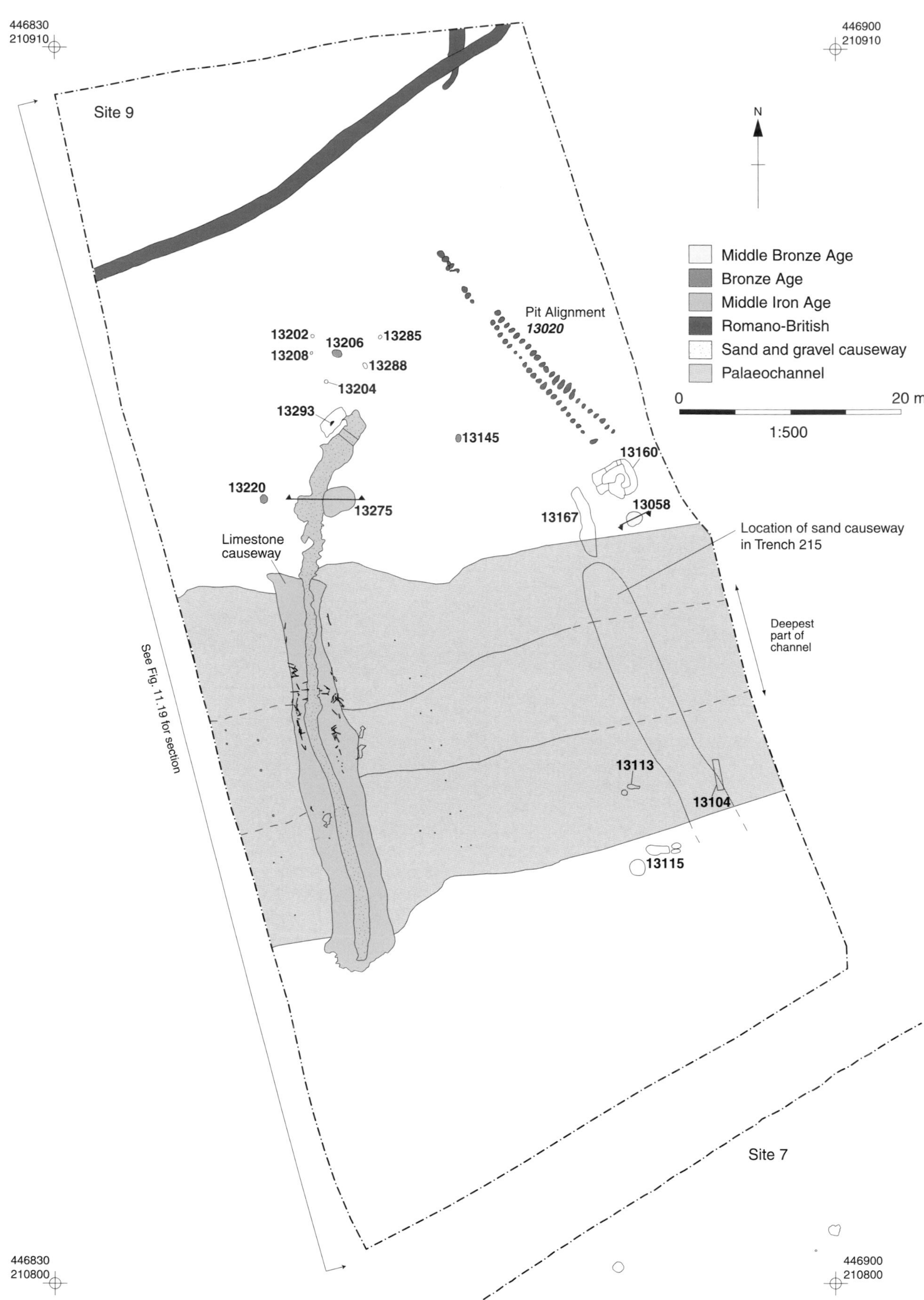

Fig. 11.17 Plan of Site 9 and the causeway

Fig. 11.18 Site 9 limestone causeway with overlying sand-and-gravel causeway removed

and later alluvium within a channel which had been actively recutting the floodplain gravel up to the early medieval period. At least three separate phases of causeway construction were present, and late Bronze Age metal finds recovered from adjacent channel silts may indicate that the crossing point was of some antiquity (Hey *at al.* forthcoming).

A possible first-phase wooden causeway

Two distinct groups of wood were found preserved under the central and southern part of the limestone causeway (13012), above a layer of animal trample (13298). These comprised a row of uprights running for 11.76 m from the southern bank of the channel NNW towards its deepest point (18128; Fig. 11.20), and a horizontal layer of small diameter roundwood to the north-west of the uprights (18192). The uprights (18128) were mostly of oak and non-oak roundwood with bark (see Chapter 19) and were irregularly spaced. Diameters ranged from 38 to 55 mm, and three of the posts were paired, possibly indicating repairs to the structure.

The horizontal wood deposit (18192) lay approximately 1.1 m west of the uprights at their northern end, and covered an area *c* 1.5 x 0.7 m. The wood, which was of small diameter (10-19 mm), had a generally north – south alignment, and is thought to be the remains of a small brushwood trackway laid down prior to the limestone causeway. Radiocarbon dating indicates, however, that the chronological gap between the two structures was small and that this wooden phase of construction dates to the middle Iron Age (*400-340 cal BC (30% probability)* or *330-230 cal BC (65% probability*; Fig. 13.6). There were no directly associated finds.

Limestone causeway (13012)

Not long after the brushwood trackway was constructed, it was replaced by a far more substantial structure built of limestone with occasional quartzite pebbles up to 50 mm in size (Figs 11.18 and 11.21). This causeway was 32.5 m long and 3.7-5 m wide and it ran north-south across the channel. Radiocarbon dating shows that it was constructed in *380-210 cal BC (95% probability)* (Fig. 13.6). The stones of which the causeway was built were generally quite flat with rounded edges, averaging 170 x 50 mm in size, and were identified by Philip Powell of the Oxford University Museum as Lower Cornbrash (a formation in the Great Oolite of the middle Jurassic). The nearest sources of this material lie at Church Hanborough, on the Evenlode *c* 6 km away, and Bladon, some 4 km distant overland, and Powell suggests that the rounded condition of the stone indicates that it may have been picked up off the surface of fields. The stone was placed onto the trampled bed of the channel (13298; Fig. 11.22) and, where it survived, on top of the earlier brushwood trackway. It also directly overlay a side-looped spearhead in a manner which suggested that the spearhead formed a foundation offering (Fig. 11.23). The spearhead is unequivocally of Bronze Age date (Northover in Hey *et al.* forthcoming), but a plug of waterlogged

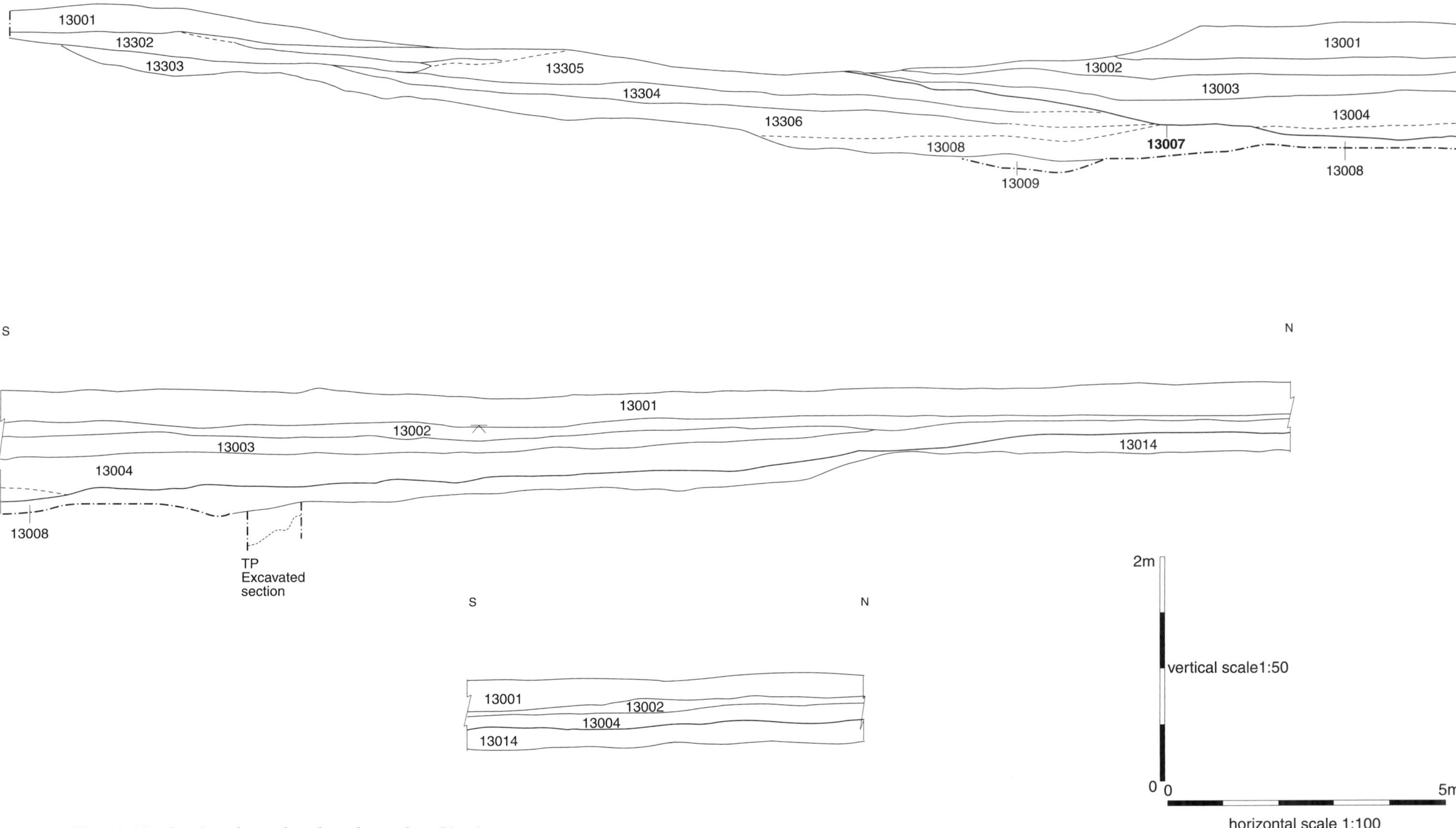

Fig. 11.19 Section through palaeochannel at Site 9

plant remains packed within the spear socket was dated to *400-340 cal BC (30% probability)* or *330-230 cal BC (65% probability*; OxA-9377) and, further inside the object, were insect remains which showed that, before the plug was inserted, it had been kept within a relatively dry environment (Robinson, Chapter 18). It is suggested that the spearhead was an heirloom which had been placed in the channel as an offering when the limestone causeway was laid down. Other datable material within or directly beneath the causeway included a small quantity of late Bronze Age/early Iron Age pottery, a Bronze Age double-pointed awl (SF13400) and some late Neolithic/early Bronze Age flint, all probably residual in this context (Northover in Hey *et al.* forthcoming).

The limestone appears to have been laid down in one to three horizontal beds (Figs 11.22, Section 18103 and 11.24), but there was no indication that these were constructed at different times. Areas of trample on the north bank of the channel (13232-3) probably relate to the movement of humans and animals crossing the causeway, and animal trample is probably represented by a layer of silt and gravel (13225) on either side of the causeway, which had a very uneven base. However, the surface of the

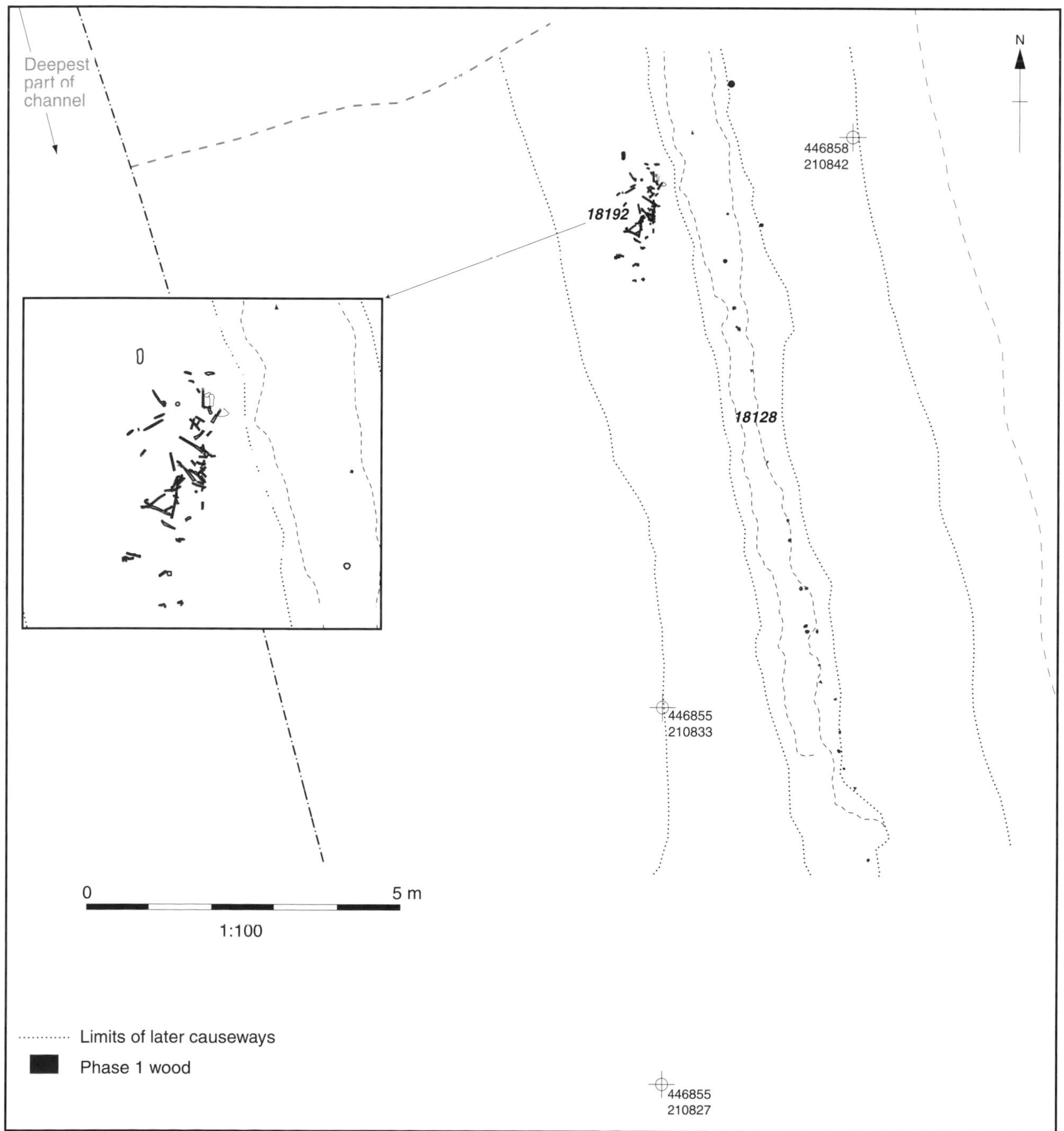

Fig. 11.20 Site 9 causeway, phase 1 wood at crossing point

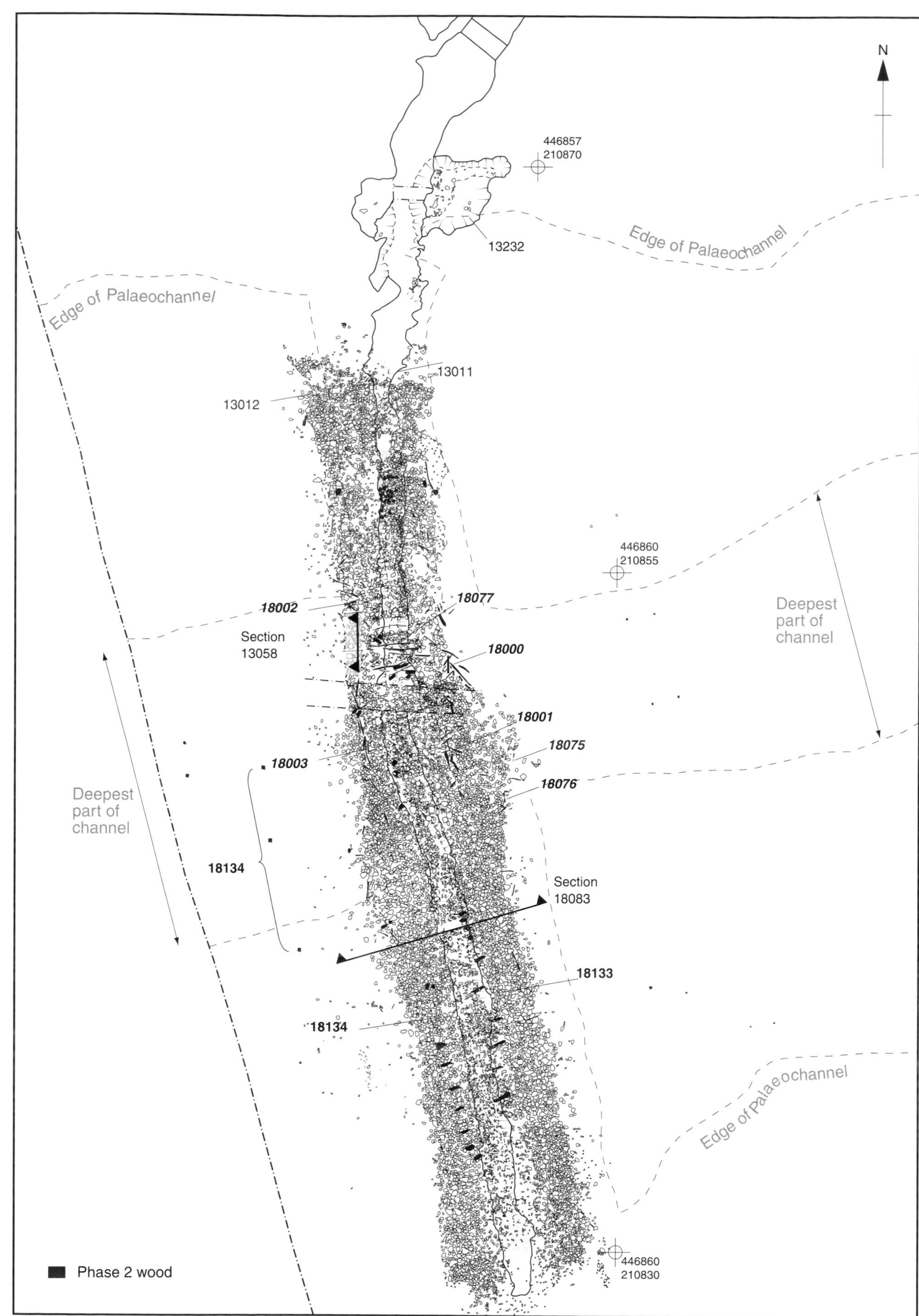

Fig. 11.21 Site 9 causeway phase 2, stone causeway and associated wood

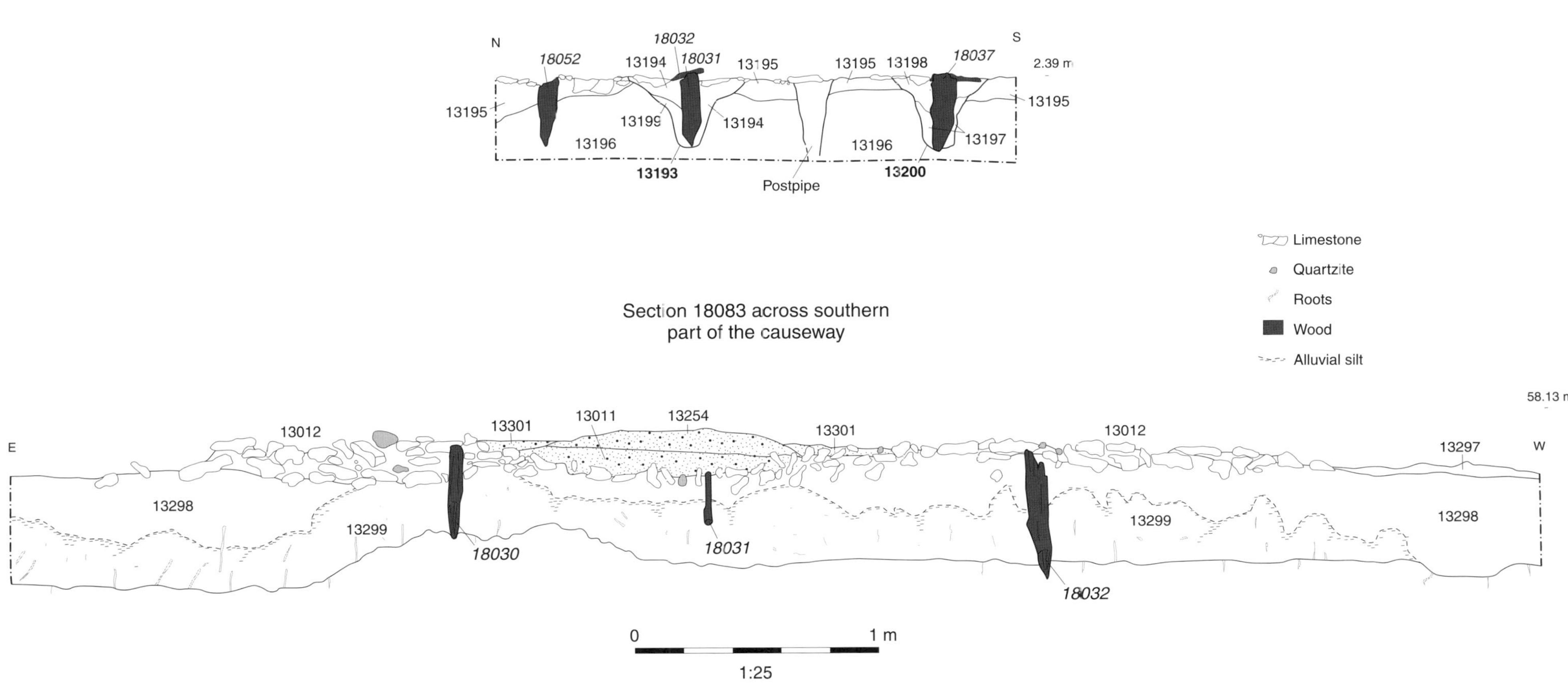

Fig. 11.22 Sections through Site 9 causeways and associated wood

Fig. 11.23 Middle Bronze Age spearhead beneath the Site 9 limestone causeway. Scale 10 cm

causeway showed differential patterns of wear. Running along the centre, the stone was worn and displaced (Figs 11.18, 11.21 and 11.22), and linear depressions in the stone mid way across the channel resembled wheel ruts (13011; Fig. 11.25). In contrast, stones on the edges of the causeway were relatively unworn, and the edge of the structure was reasonably well defined.

The worn sections of causeway lay mainly between two parallel lines of posts, 2.3 m apart, which had been driven into the underlying silts (Figs 11.22 Section 13058; 11.26 and 11.27). These were set approximately 1.10 m from each edge of the causeway (Fig. 11.21; 18002-3 to the west and 18000-1 to the east). Occasionally, however, the posts appeared to sit in dug postholes which seemed to have been overlain by the stone of the causeway, although localised patching of the surface may be difficult to detect. Although the stratigraphy was not clear cut, the radiocarbon dates from the waterlogged wooden posts were statistically indistinguishable from the causeway construction date (Chapter 13; Fig. 13.6). Horizontal and vertical pieces were present, and it was originally believed that the uprights had been linked by cross members or rails. This suggestion was supported by the recovery of small pieces of twine which may have tied the structure together. Analysis of the wood, however, and statistical work on their sizes (Chapter 19), suggests that there are no differences between the dimensions of the vertical and horizontal pieces and, on balance, it seems likely that the pieces of wood that were interpreted as horizontal on site were the upper parts of uprights which had broken and become displaced by water movement. Nevertheless, it seems probable that the posts provided both a guide across the channel, perhaps when the water in the channel was high, and a barrier to sideways movement which protected the causeway edges.

Lying within and on top of the stone causeway were a large number of animal bones (Fig. 11.28), of

Fig. 11.24 Site 9 causeway under excavation showing cross section

Fig. 11.25 Ruts in Site 9 causeway. Scale 2 m

Fig. 11.26 Line of wooden uprights on east side of Site 9 causeway

which 402 were identified to species (see Mulville, Chapter 17). The bone appears to have been spread quite evenly along the length of the causeway (13012), with the largest quantity (39%) coming from directly beneath and within the feature. It may have formed part of its construction; the radiocarbon dates from the bone indicate a statistically similar date range to those of other causeway deposits (Chapter 13; Fig. 13.6). The majority of this material was cattle bone, but with a reasonable proportion of horse and a small but significant number of deer, a species rare in Iron Age deposits at Yarnton (Mulville, Chapter 17). Of considerable interest, given the unusual nature of this structure, is a bias towards the deposition of the right sides of animals (Table 17.21). The incorporation of animal bone here appears to reflect specific depositional activities of some kind, in addition to suggesting feasting.

Lying east to west across part of the central part of the causeway were parts of nine or ten narrow timbers that would have been 1.5-2 m long (18077; Figs 11.29 and 11.30). They may represent a collapsed vertical structure, or some attempt to support carts over ruts in the stone causeway. They were directly overlain by a sand-and-gravel causeway.

Gravel causeway (13011)

A deposit of light grey silty sand and small gravel (13011) *c* 1 m wide was laid along the central strip of the causeway over its entire length (*c* 34 m), and was traced running north-eastwards on the north

Fig. 11.27 Section through wooden timbers on east side of Site 9 causeway. Scales 2 m and 0.50 m

Fig. 11.28 Bone exposed beneath Site 9 sand-and gravel causeway lying on limestone causeway (stained by sand deposits). Scale 0.20 m

bank of the channel for a further 16 m (13250) leading towards the Yarnton settlement (Figs 11.31 and 11.32). This gravel causeway was built over the worn section of the stone surface, presumably as a repair, and its width suggests that it was designed only for human traffic (Figs 11.22 and 11.24). A further well-compacted gravel layer (13254 and 13231) points to a second phase of repair. On average, the combined layers were 0.14 m in depth. Silts which had washed or worn off the crown of the surface accumulated at its edge (13301; Fig. 11.22), and into adjacent hollows on the north bank. Here, a depression in the top of an early Bronze Age pit (13275) became filled with deposits of sandy material (13239 and 13238) and these overlay what may have been an earlier attempt to metal over the depression (13240; Fig. 11.33).

Dating the gravel causeway is problematic, as it did not contain organic material for scientific dating and other finds appeared to be residual/redeposited; it probably spanned part of the middle and possibly even later Iron Age. A layer of organic silt (13009/13297) overlay the feature within the channel and presumably reflected the end of its effective use. It contained 84 g of late Bronze Age/early Iron Age pottery, in addition to a small amount of worked flint and a Bronze Age copper alloy bracelet (SF 13240; Northover in Hey *et al.* forthcoming). Animal bone was present within and over the sand deposit but this was fragmented and more eroded than that recovered from the stone causeway (62% was unidentifiable), and it, too, was probably redeposited.

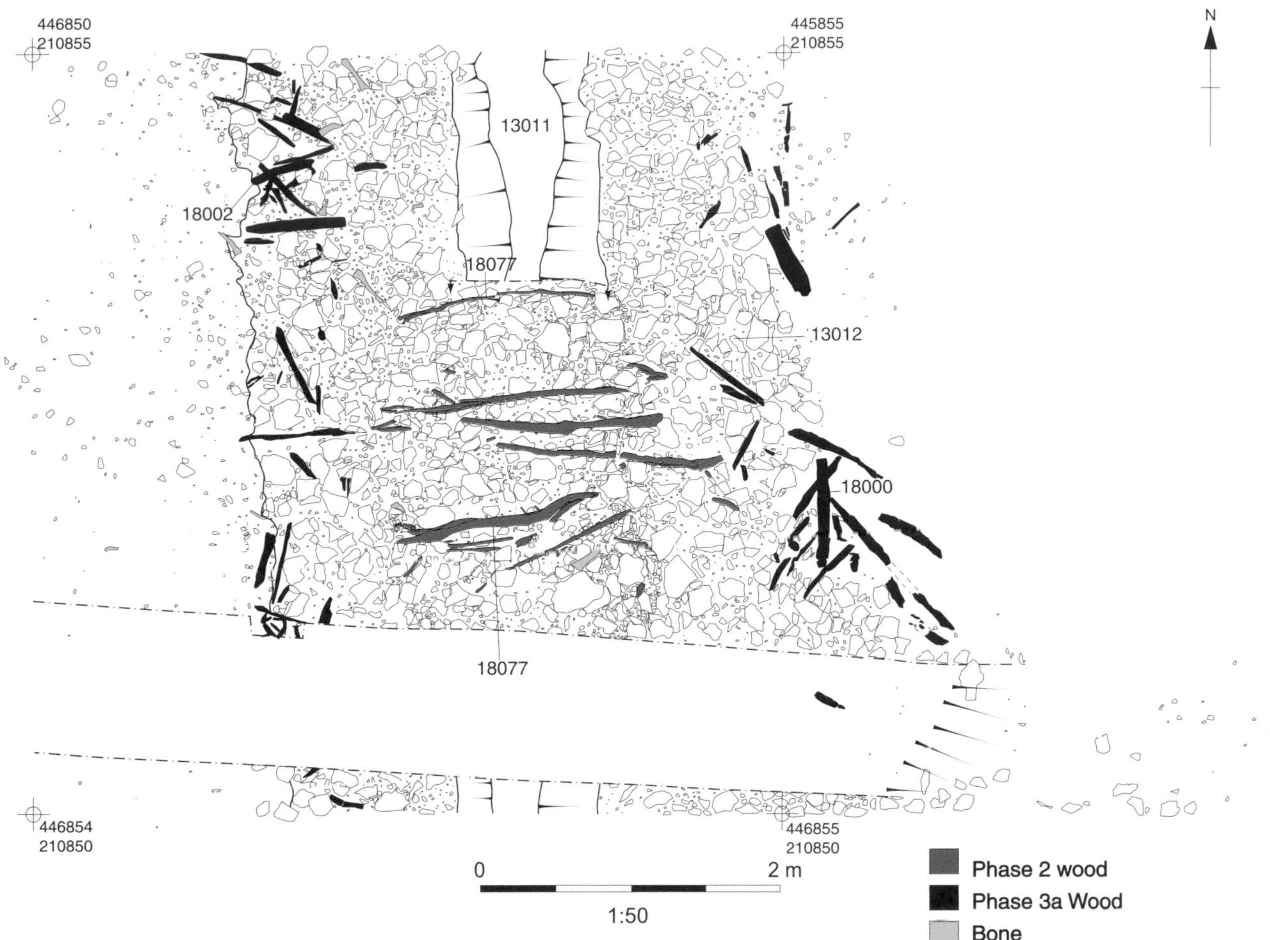

Fig. 11.29 Wood over central part of Site 9 stone causeway

Fig. 11.30 Horizontal timbers overlain by Site 9 sand-and-gravel causeway. Scale 2 m

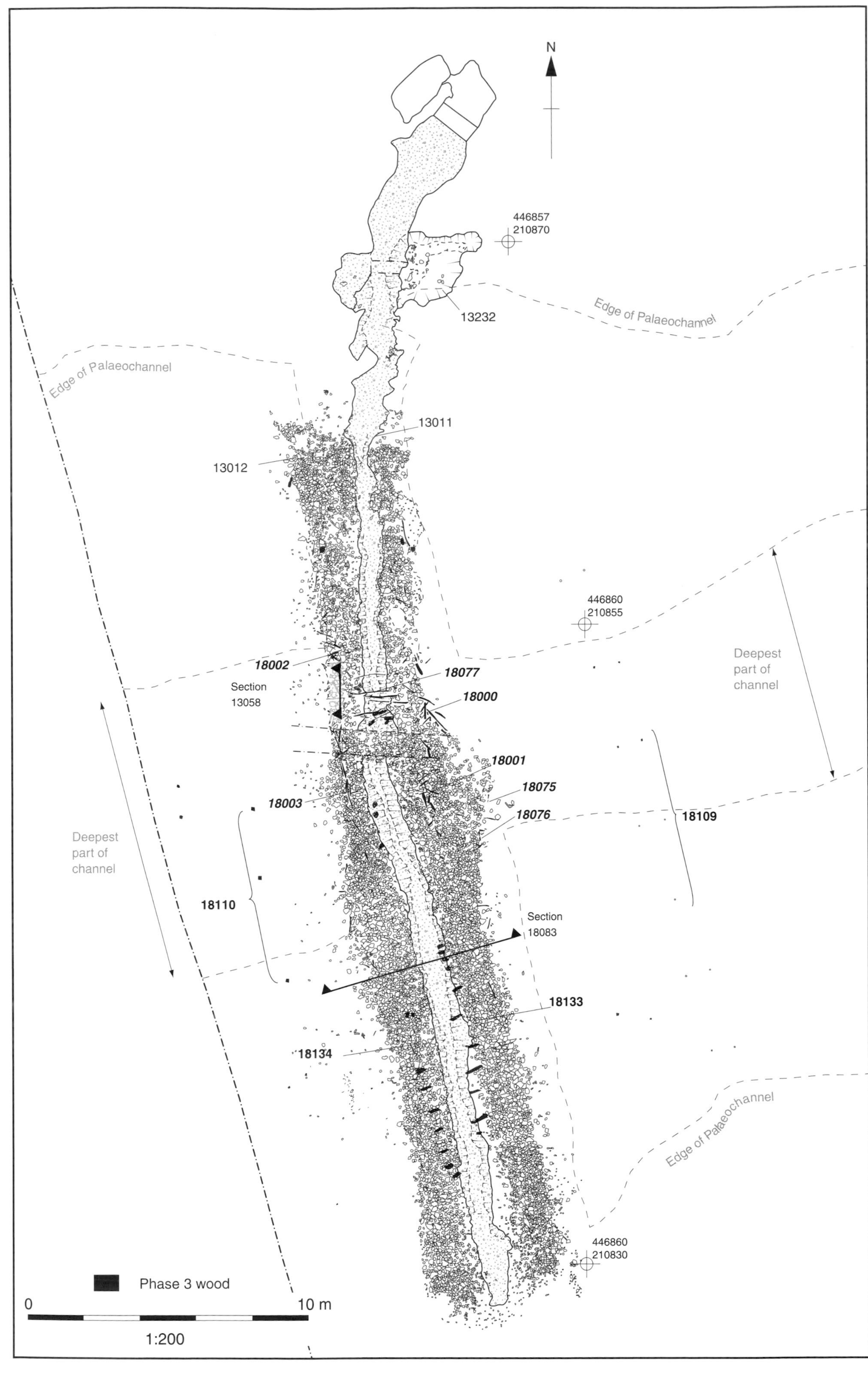
N
446857
210870
13232
Edge of Palaeochannel
Edge of Palaeochannel
13011
13012
446860
210855
Deepest
part of
channel
18002
18077
Section
13058
18000
18001
18075
18003
18076
18109
Deepest
part of
channel
18110
Section
18083
18133
18134
Edge of Palaeochannel
446860
210830
Phase 3 wood
0
10 m
1:200

Timber alignments in the channel adjacent to the causeway

To east and west of the main causeway were two double rows of timber uprights running NNW-SSE along the same alignment (18109, 18110; Fig. 11.31). The eastern row (18109) ran for 19.3 m with the posts set approximately 1 m apart, although not all of them were placed in pairs. Group 18110 was 13.1 m in length, and only two posts were paired (2.5 m apart). The date and function of these features is uncertain. The posts were not driven as deeply into the channel bed as those lining the causeway, and so it is possible that they are later features.

Fig. 11.32 Limestone causeway on Site 9 with sand-and-gravel repair

Causeway in Trenches 215, 218 and 219

Traces of another causeway of compacted silty sand were exposed only 35 m to the east of the stone causeway in evaluation Trenches 218 and 215 (218/6 and 218/5), later subsumed within the area of Site 9 (Figs 11.10 and 11.17). It was 3 m wide and appeared to have been constructed in two phases. Its outwash was first observed by Mark Robinson in evaluation Trench 215 as a thin deposit of compacted silty sand (215/11; Fig. 11.11). It was covered by layers of silt and alluvium and its date is uncertain. The only find was a single sherd of late Neolithic/early Bronze Age pottery which was probably residual or redeposited with the sand. Its proximity to the stone causeway suggests that it was not contemporary with that structure, unless it had a different, and more mundane, function.

Gravel causeway in Site 10 (Fig. 11.10)

In the south-east of Site 10, a causeway of compacted silty sand and pebbles (14012) was constructed across the palaeochannel in the area of what would seem to have been a traditional crossing point. It lay only 85 m west of the stone causeway on Site 9. It was first revealed in evaluation Trenches 184 and 216 (Fig. 11.34). It was traced running NNE-SSW for 32 m, and was approximately 2-3 m wide and 0.1-0.2 m thick, and lay upon alluvial clay. A layer of silt (14019) had built up over the causeway, possibly indicating a period of disuse, and a further sand and gravel causeway (14013) was laid down over this. There was no wood associated with this structure and no other material with which to date it. It lay beneath an alluvial deposit of reddish-brown silt (14004) and there was no determinable relationship with more general later channel silts. It may be Iron Age or Romano-British, but a Roman date is more likely.

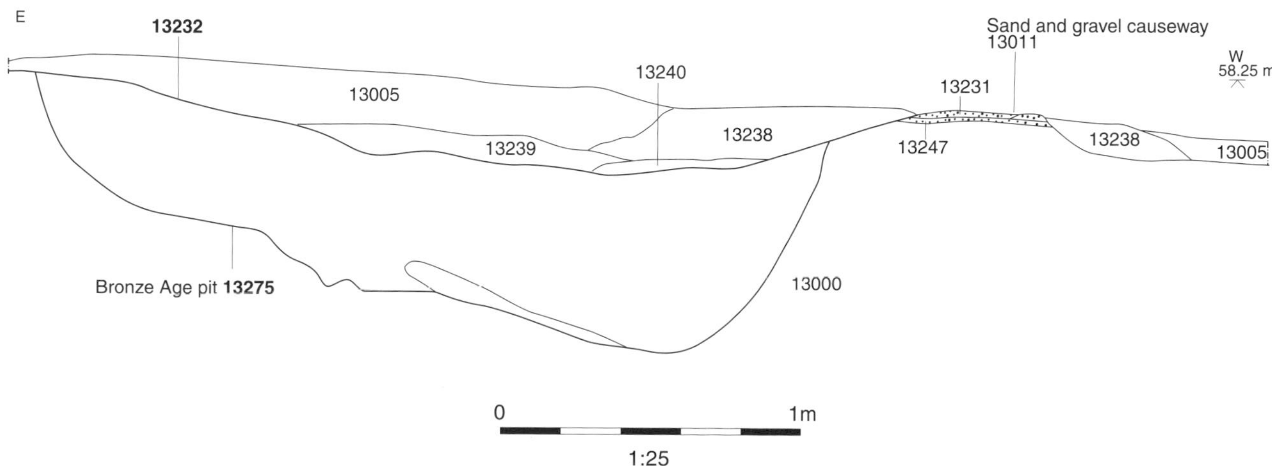

Fig. 11.33 Section through north of Site 9 sand-and-gravel causeway

Fig. 11.31 (facing page) Plan of Site 9 stone and sand-and gravel causeway

Fig. 11.34 Sand and gravel causeway on Site 10/Trench 216. Scales 2 m and 0.50 m

Gravel causeway and parallel ditch in Site 21

The fragmentary remains of a narrow causeway (15095), 0.6-0.75 m wide, were traced for *c* 30 m running NW-SE across a palaeochannel in the southern part of Site 21 (Figs 11.10 and 11.35). It was made up of two layers: a dark brown gravel (15080/15087) with a mid orange sand (15070/15086) above, but it was very thin in places, with a maximum depth of just 0.15 m. There were no associated finds, although a water-lain deposit over the causeway (15016) contained a residual Mesolithic/early Neolithic flint blade.

Parallel to the causeway, *c* 5 m to the east, was a segmented ditch (15007) running for 19 m and cutting into the earlier palaeochannel sediments. There were two visible lengths each ending in a narrow semicircular terminal, and generally having sloping concave sides and a rounded profile. The width of the feature was variable, from 0.4-0.58 m to the north and 0.6-1.2 m to the south. In most places it was only 0.2 m deep, except at the south terminal where it deepened to 0.58 m. No finds were recovered from this feature, but its alignment suggested contemporaneity with the causeway; it may have assisted with drainage off the causeway.

Causeways on Site 4

A number of causeways of probable Iron Age date were located on Site 4 (Figs 11.10 and 11.36-37), two of which were associated with Neolithic/Bronze Age ring ditch 7056, a feature later cut by a Roman field boundary ditch (7100). Causeway 7072 was aligned north-south across the southernmost part of the ring ditch and measured 2 m across at its widest part and 0.3 m in depth. It consisted of three causeway make-up layers of reddish-brown silty clay with some sand and gravel, which were sealed beneath two layers of sand forming the causeway surface (Section 7054; Fig. 11.36). A small quantity of burnt local stone and one flint flake were the only finds from this series of deposits. Alluvium accumulated up to the causeway.

On the east side of the ring ditch, another causeway (7126; Fig. 11.36), which had originally crossed the ditch, was found buried beneath alluvium within the ring ditch. It comprised two make-up layers of similar composition to those of causeway 7072 and a single layer of compacted sand, creating a total depth of 0.3 m. It was only 0.5 m wide, but appears to have been more severely eroded by use and subsequent events within the ditch. One fragment of unidentified animal bone along with a small quantity of burnt stone was found within one of the make-up layers. Both causeways clearly predated the final silting of the ring ditch, which consisted of gravel free alluvium likely to have been deposited in the late Iron Age or early Roman period.

The ring ditch lay very close to the edge of the north bank of a palaeochannel (Fig. 11.37) and still survived as a hollow which was evidently an obstacle, even though it was only *c* 0.3 m deep at this time. In the Roman period, the space between the field boundary ditch and the channel may have been used as a droveway (see below) and the causeways may be related to this activity. It is possible that, if the round barrow had been slighted (perhaps for use as causeway gravel), it may have been used to corral stock in either the Iron Age or the Roman period. Postholes found around its inner edge, and believed to be associated with its construction (Hey *et al.* forthcoming), could have been related to its later use.

Two further causeways were located on Site 4, running south across the palaeochannel (Fig. 11.37). The first (7258) was situated approximately 25 m east of the ring ditch and extended from the southern edge of excavation for 3.5 m in a south-

Fig. 11.35 Causeway and ditch on Site 21

easterly direction. It was 2.6 m wide. This causeway contained one make-up layer of gravelly silt and sand which lay above a dark grey layer of gravel and burnt stone, a layer which may have been associated with earlier activity on the river bank rather than with the causeway above. The upper surface of the causeway was an orange sand/silt with moderate gravel inclusions which had spread into alluvial layers on either side.

The second causeway (7267) ran approximately north-south at the eastern edge of Site 4 and was made up of two layers of compacted sand with some fine gravels. The exposed section of this causeway was 12 m long and approximately 2 m wide. A trampled surface of sandy gravel (7269) lay immediately to the west of this causeway and may represent associated activity. Causeway 7267 was cut by a Roman ditch on its eastern side.

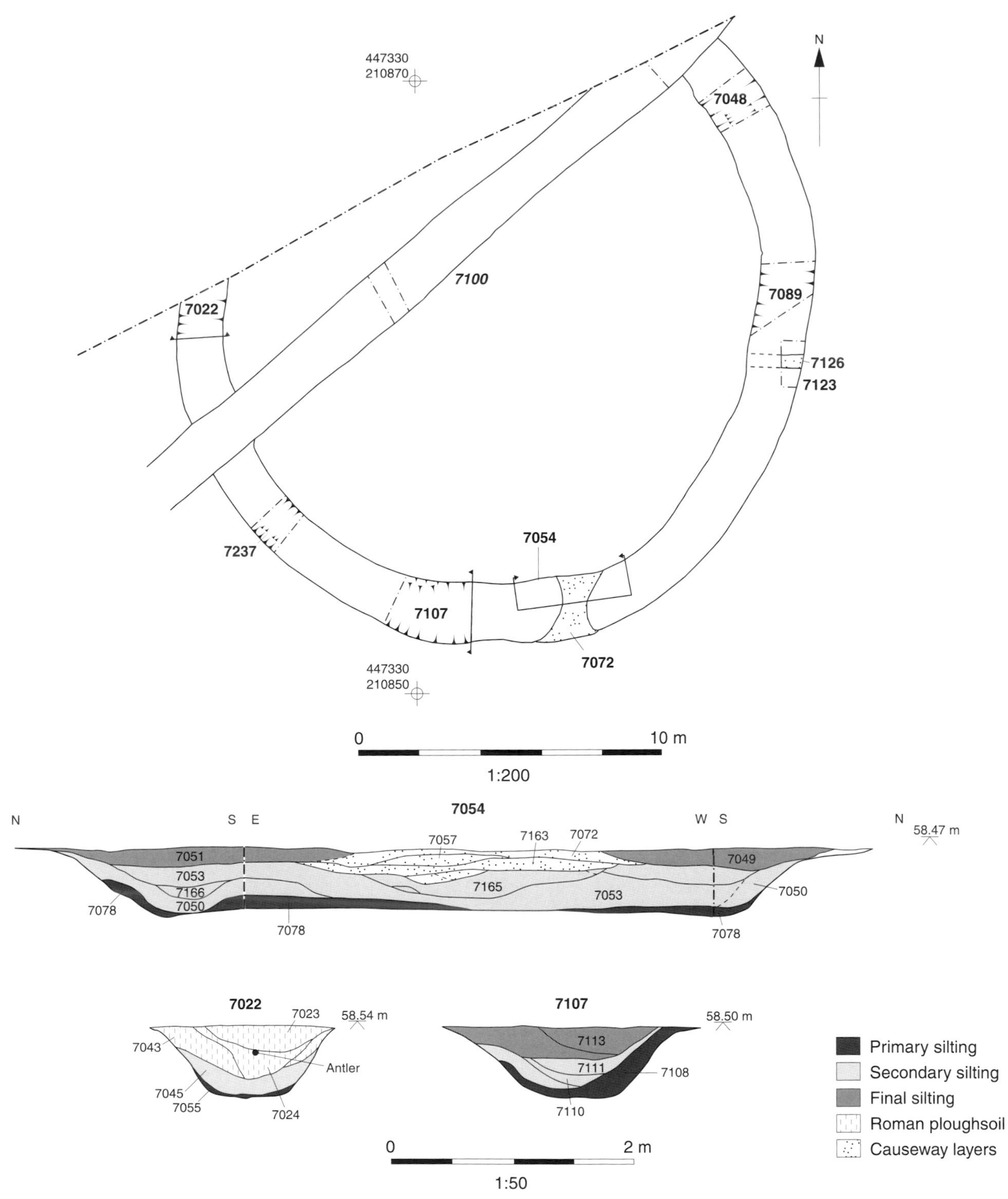

Fig. 11.36 Causeways and Roman ditch over Site 4 ring ditch 7056

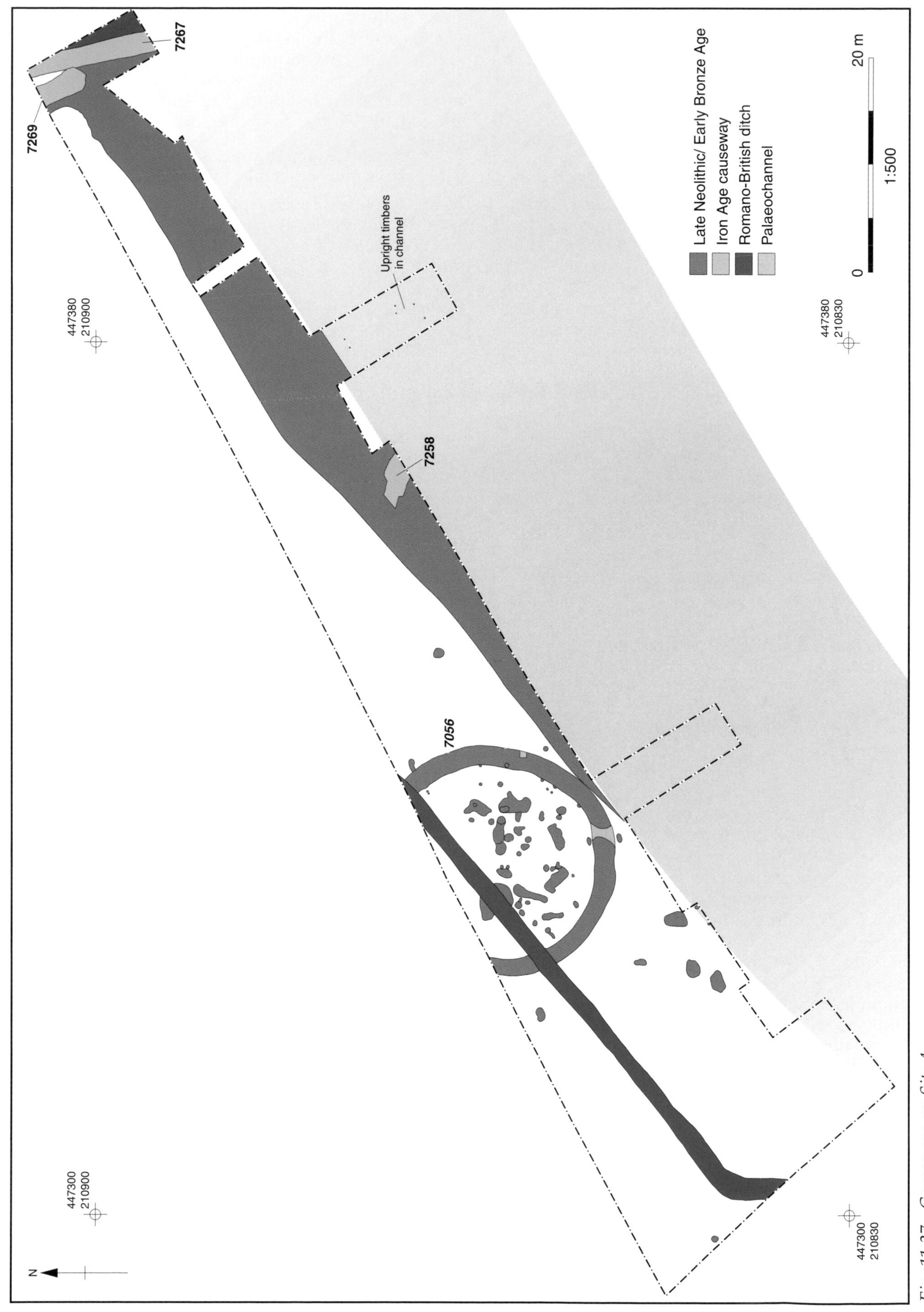

Fig. 11.37 Causeways on Site 4

Causeways on Site 2

A compacted sand-and-gravel causeway (2564/2853) ran SE-NW across Site 2, flanked by a series of dendritic gullies filled with gleyed alluvial clay (Fig. 11.38). A 70 m length of this feature was exposed, and it ran parallel to linear ditch 2607 for a distance of approximately 50 m, before running in a more westerly direction. Towards the south, a less substantial causeway diverged to the east, consisting of discontinuous (unnumbered) patches of sand and gravel extending eastwards from 3030 (Fig. 11.38). The palaeoenvironmental evidence suggests that the causeways were constructed on this low-lying area when it was at least seasonally dry (see Robinson below) and, given the middle Iron Age date for alluvial deposits within the tops of earlier ditches and the late Iron Age or early Roman date for general alluvium over the ground surface (Chapter 13; Fig. 13.5), these causeways are most likely to be early Iron Age or, possibly, middle Iron Age in date. They are later than a series of small pit and slot alignments which ran towards the channel parallel to a pair of middle Bronze Age ditches (2239 and 3081) and a later ditch (2607, ?late Bronze Age) on the same orientation.

The main causeway (2564/2853) was built up within a wide hollow, presumably a hollow way. Around 4.8 m of the causeway was excavated and it was found to consist of compact red-brown sand with gravel and occasional shell, around 1.20 m wide and 0.05 m thick, which had a cambered appearance and mainly sat on a make-up layer (*c* 0.06 m thick) of firm sand, gravel and pea-grit, though this was possibly an earlier surface. There was no evidence of alluvium beneath it. The causeway terminated in the north-west of the site, *c* 30 m south of the palaeochannel, where it appeared to have been cut by a large tree-throw hole, but possibly it had just been washed away at this end. Although the channel was examined with care at this point, no evidence of a crossing point was revealed.

Another, less substantial causeway (3030) was traced for 27 m across the south-east of the site. It had been largely destroyed by later dendritic gullies but could be seen at the east edge of the site over ditch 2607. The deposits comprising 2853 and 3030 were indistinguishable and it is likely that the two causeways were contemporary. Pale-grey, fine sand accumulated over the causeways and this deposit was seen stretching over the entire length of the main feature when it was first exposed. Finds from these features were earlier prehistoric in date and are residual or redeposited.

Depressions were present on either side of the main causeway, but it was difficult to ascertain whether these were really cut features or deposits accumulating on either side of the raised causeway. Lower fills comprised mid grey-brown clay silt with 5-10% sand and occasional charcoal. In some places these features appeared to have been cleared out at a later stage, becoming filled with more iron-stained soil with an uneven admixture of up to 20% pale brown fine sand and occasional charcoal. Darker alluvial fills with up to 60% pale brown sand, presumably washed from the surface, were found in the top.

The palaeoenvironmental context of the causeway

Mark Robinson comments that the soil sealed beneath the causeway was the brown earth soil of the floodplain which occurs beneath the alluvium. Although the soil was circumneutral, the calcareous gravel of the causeway had a buffering effect and a few mollusc shells were found in a sample from the soil surface beneath the northern end of the causeway. Although this was the closest point of the causeway to the palaeochannel, shells of marsh and aquatic species were absent. The shells identified included *Trichia hispida* gp., which occurs in a wide range of terrestrial habitats, and *Vallonia costata*, a species of dry open habitats. This suggests that the causeway was constructed when this part of the floodplain was at least seasonally dry. The sandy gravel of the causeway contained numerous shells of flowing water molluscs, suggesting it had been dug from the bed of one of the channels.

Dendritic gullies associated with Site 2 causeway

The latest features cut into the ground surface were a series of intercutting dendritic gullies which flanked the causeway (Fig. 11.38). As a group, they cut some of the pit alignment features, and also the east-west causeway. They ran from the south-east and south-west towards the shallow ditches or hollows on either side of the causeway, but although some gullies appeared to drain into these ditches, others cut them and others terminated before they reached them. Some ended in deep sumps. The gullies were irregular in width and depth, but typically they were 0.55 m wide and 0.20 m deep. The dendritic features to the west were generally narrower and shallower (*c* 0.45 m wide and 0.15 m deep). Their irregular profile suggests that they were dug in a series of scoops, perhaps when the ground was partly under water. They were filled with blue-grey clay with 5% yellow-brown silty clay, shells, and occasional stone, manganese and charcoal flecks. Occasional finds of pottery and flint were earlier in date as, presumably, were two fragments of hazelnut shell recovered from one of these features.

Mark Robinson adds that, by the time that the pattern of irregular dendritic ditches was dug, conditions on Site 2 were becoming increasingly wet, and it seems likely they were dug in response to problems with standing surface water after floods. The ditches were filled with gleyed alluvial clay but with a lower organic content than the early overbank alluvium. There were inwash bands of

Fig. 11.38 (facing page) Causeway and other features on Site 2

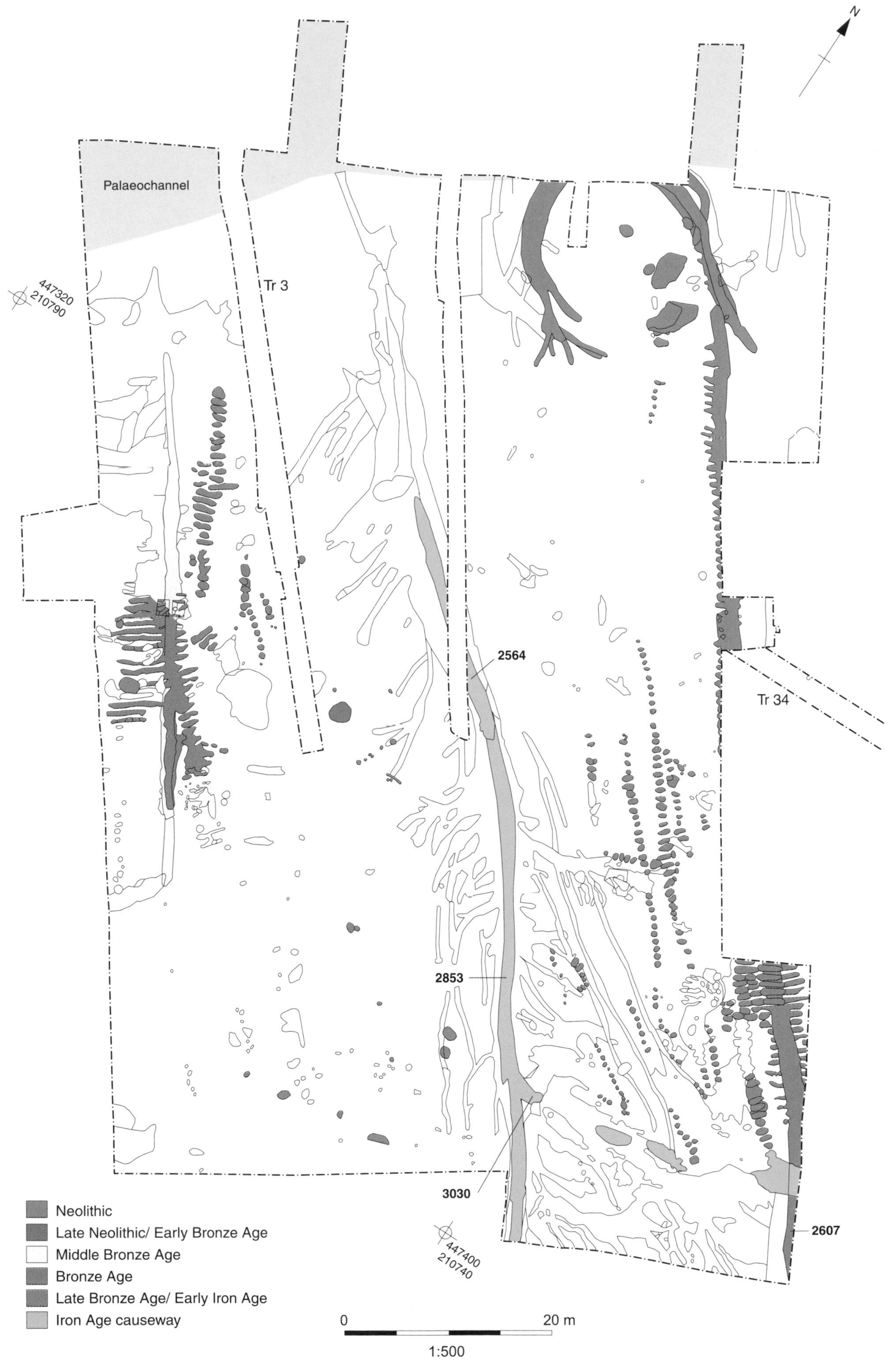

Palaeochannel
Tr 3
447320
210790
2564
Tr 34
2853
3030
2607
447400
210740
Neolithic
Late Neolithic/ Early Bronze Age
Middle Bronze Age
Bronze Age
Late Bronze Age/ Early Iron Age
Iron Age causeway
0
20 m
1:500

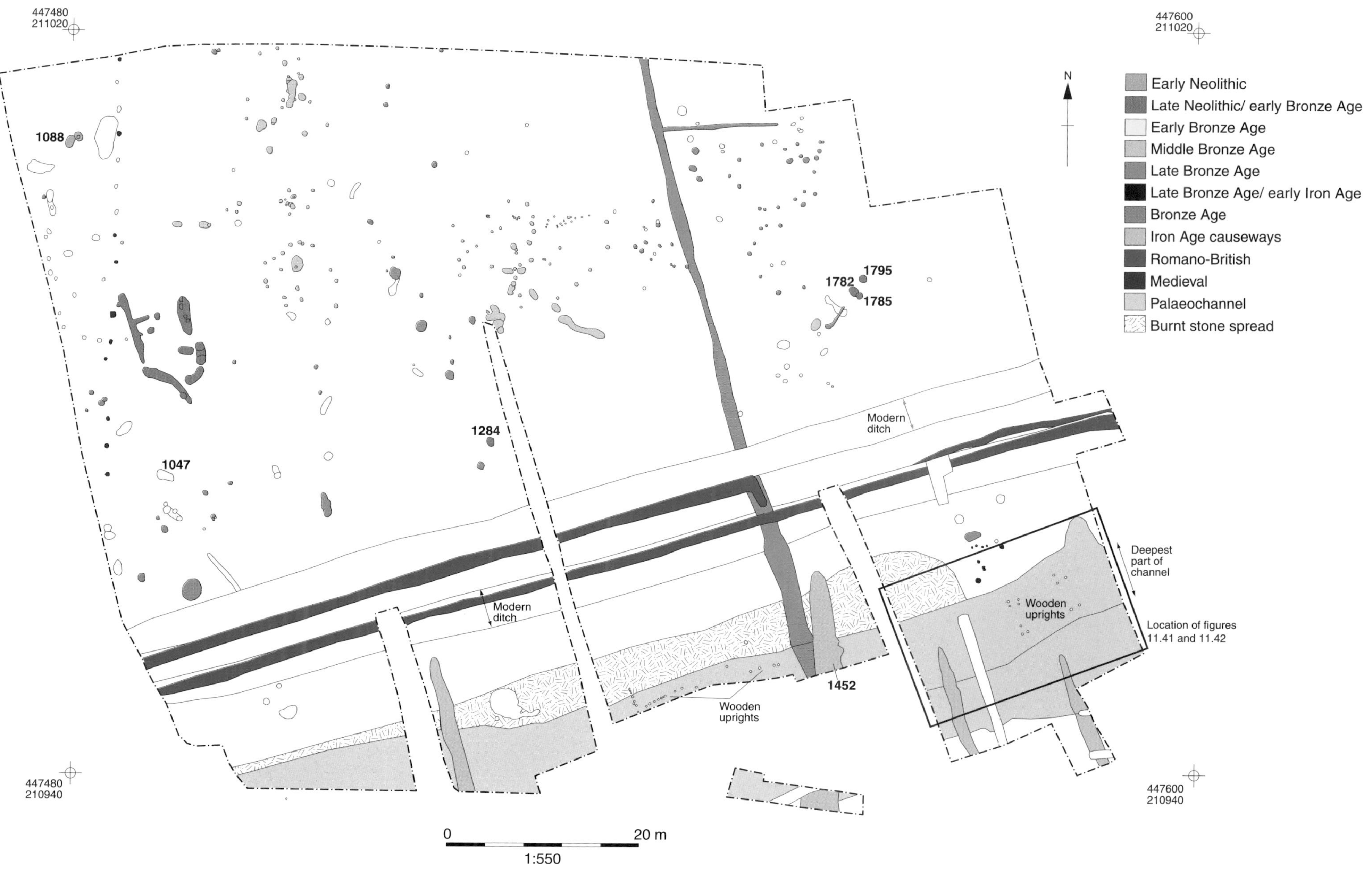

Fig. 11.39 Causeways on Site 1

sand from the causeway in the parts of the ditch system alongside the causeway itself. A sample of alluvium from the bottom of one of the deeper dendritic features contained a few shells which had presumably been deposited from the river, and some badly-preserved seeds, mostly of *Juncus* spp. (rushes). There were also many calcareous oospores of *Chara* sp. (stonewort), an aquatic algae.

Causeways crossing the channel adjacent to Site 1

Four sand-and-gravel crossing places were exposed in the southern part of Site 1, running NNW to SSE across the palaeochannel (Figs 11.10 and 11.39). The most substantial of these (1452) cut a late Bronze Age ditch and lay upon a thin organic silt layer within the channel (Fig. 11.40). It was overlain by alluvium. A row of wooden uprights ran along the north bank of the channel at right angles to the causeway and was probably contemporary with it. The other three causeways also lay above organic silts, an indication elsewhere on the floodplain of a late Iron Age or Roman date. Organic sediment began to accumulate at an earlier date in this part of the palaeochannel system, however, as early as the mid to late Bronze Age (Bayliss and Hey in Hey *et al.* forthcoming), building up against nearby wooden structures (see below) associated with settlement in the adjacent area. Nevertheless, the stratigraphy indicates that the sand-and-gravel structures were later in date, reflecting continuity of use of a traditional crossing place. The presence of an opening in the first phase of a Roman ditch system running parallel to the channel (Fig. 11.39), indicates that it was still possible to gain access between the channel here and ploughed fields beyond in the 1st millennium AD (see below).

Wooden structures across the palaeochannels

Wooden structures on Site 1

The palaeochannel adjacent to Site 1 also revealed wooden structures, some of which appeared to span the river channel (Figs 11.39, 11.41 and 11.42). These were found in an area of late Bronze Age activity associated with occupation on the floodplain nearby. An area of collapsed wattlework was discovered, which is dated to the late Bronze Age/early Iron Age (structure 119; Fig. 11.42). A deposit representing a period of ponding and silting followed (115), which included a considerable quantity of roundwood debris. This appears to be of early Iron Age date on the basis of radiocarbon determinations (Chapter 13; Fig. 13.3), and seems likely to represent the remains of a brushwood trackway thrown down for short-term use. Some of the wood was re-used and provided Bronze Age radiocarbon dates. Structure 112 was driven through these silts (Figs 11.42 and 11.43). It comprised two parallel rows of five uprights ranging from roughly 0.07-0.15 m in diameter, set approximately 1 m apart and extending 4 m across the channel from the north bank. One of these components was excavated as a posthole. The posts

Fig. 11.40 Sand-and-gravel causeway 1452 in slot to south of Site 1, looking north. Scales 2 m and 1 m

Fig. 11.41 Distribution of wood in Site 1 palaeochannel

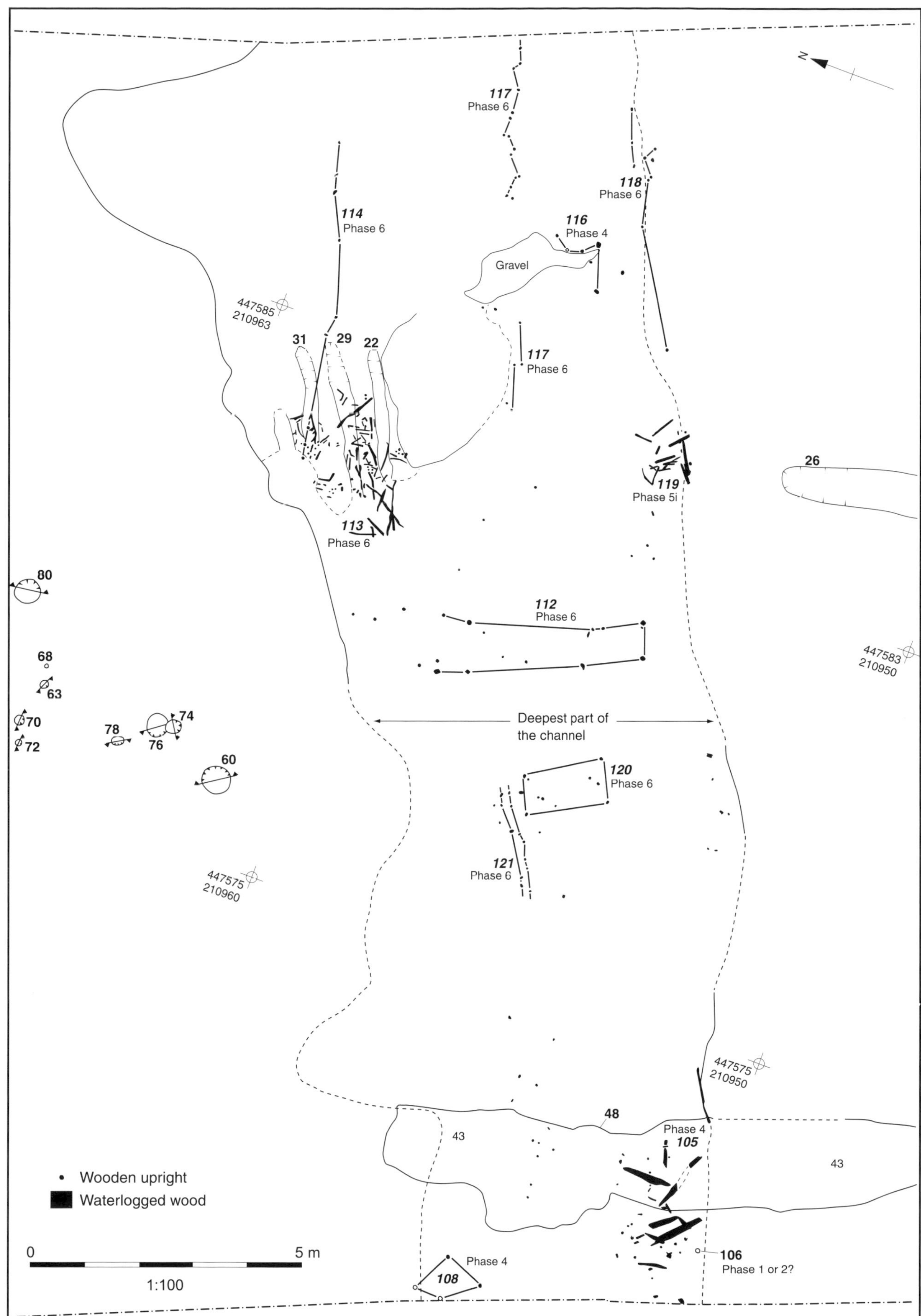

Fig. 11.42 Wooden structures in Site 1 palaeochannel

Fig. 11.43 Upright of timber structure 112 in Site 1 palaeochannel. Scale 0.30 m

were roughly paired but no pairs of verticals were of the same size, indeed there are no two pieces of wood in this structure which are of the same size. None of the uprights was substantial and, although the structure was thought in the field to be a small bridge, it is more likely to represent a boardwalk or, even, posts to retain a temporary brushwood track. The structure appears to be early Iron Age in date (Chapter 13; Fig. 13.3). Organic silts continued to accumulate in the channel through the middle Iron Age (*OxA-10711*, layer 37; *OSL-866b*, layer 11), becoming inorganic during the Roman period (*OSL-866a*, layer 10).

Possible wooden trackway in evaluation Trench 195

The remains of a possible timber jetty or trackway were found on the northern edge of the palaeochannel to the south of Site 21, in evaluation Trench 195 (Fig. 11.10). Two very large posts and two smaller posts were located in the southern part of the trench, with the edges of postholes seen around at least two of them, indicating that the posts were not simply driven in. A number of fragments of worked wood of various sizes also lay in the vicinity. The wood was sealed beneath deposits of greyish alluvium which filled the top third of the channel. This structure has not been dated.

Roman tracks and droveways

Roman tracks are more visible in the wider landscape. Cropmarks of the Worton settlement show that a track, *c* 30 m wide defined by two parallel ditches, ran from the west, past the settlement and towards Yarnton in the east (Figs 11.44 and 10.1). It may have continued to join the ditch-defined track exposed on the south and east sides of the Yarnton site (Fig. 9.1), which to the east was up to 40 m wide. It was not fully exposed to the south. This trackway may have continued to the known settlement at Sandy Lane, Yarnton.

On the floodplain, excavation and evaluation evidence demonstrated the presence of droveways between fields (Fig. 11.44); at least some of these fields had been ploughed (see below). One droveway, *c* 20 m wide, was traced for over 300 m, running roughly north-south from the south-west of the Yarnton site towards the river Thames (Fig. 11.45). It ran across a watching brief area (Site 4b) and the north-east of floodplain Site 5, where its western ditches cut a Neolithic long enclosure, and up to an adjacent palaeochannel. It was not traced south of here and it is not known if it crossed the channel, perhaps on a causeway, and continued beyond.

On its eastern side, the droveway boundary ditch was more-or-less continuous, with no obvious openings into the three or four individual fields identified (Fig. 11.45), some of which were also observed on Site 3. The ditch had, however, been truncated in the south and a field entrance may have been present here. Where it was excavated in Trench 124 (subsequently within the southern part of Site 4b), only one recut was visible (124/7 and 124/9). On the west side of the droveway, towards its northern end, a number of intercutting shallow ditches suggested modifications to the droveway and adjacent fields over time, an earlier field system being cut by later droveway ditches on a more westerly line. There were at least two separate recuts to the droveway ditch here. Where it was excavated in evaluation Trench 135 and on Site 5, it was observed to be an open U-shaped feature, 1.15 m wide on average and 0.40 m deep, which had been recut on two occasions (9088, 9495 and 9498; 135/15, 135/18 and 135/23).

It is possible that parallel ditches running NNW-SSE across Site 3 formed part of another droveway 200 m further east, although it was rather wide at 35 m and may represent small fields or a single, long field. The continuation of the western side of this possible track was probably found in Trench F18 (Fig. 11.44), and it led down to an entrance opening out onto the bank of the palaeochannel. A spill of alluvium observed in the entranceway, where flooding had occurred, overlay what appeared to be ploughsoil. However, it is apparent that two field systems are present here, with a west-east field boundary ditch being cut by the north-south trackway ditches, although both shared the

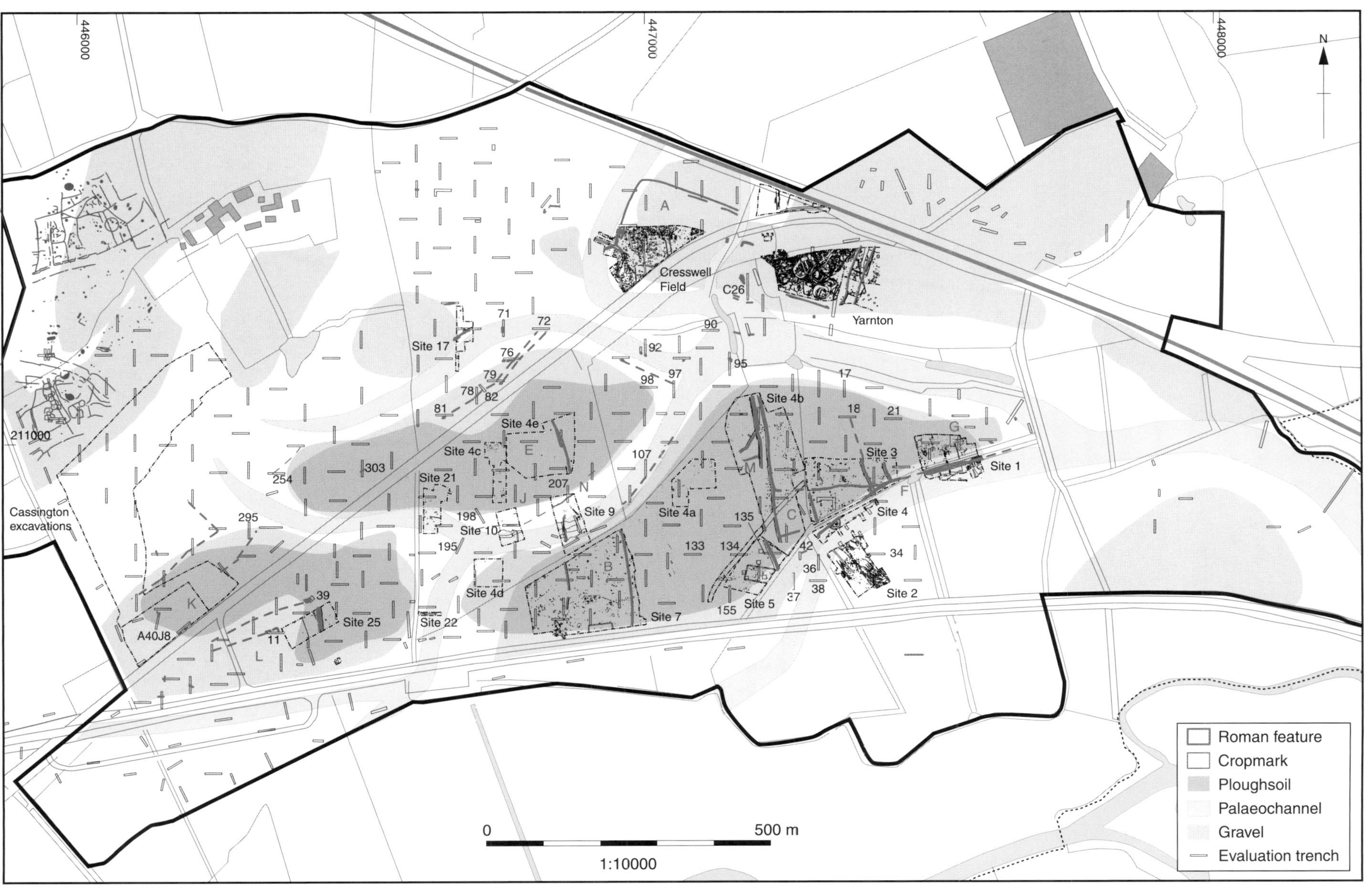

Fig. 11.44 Location of Roman features (in blue) from excavations, evaluation trenching and floodplain work

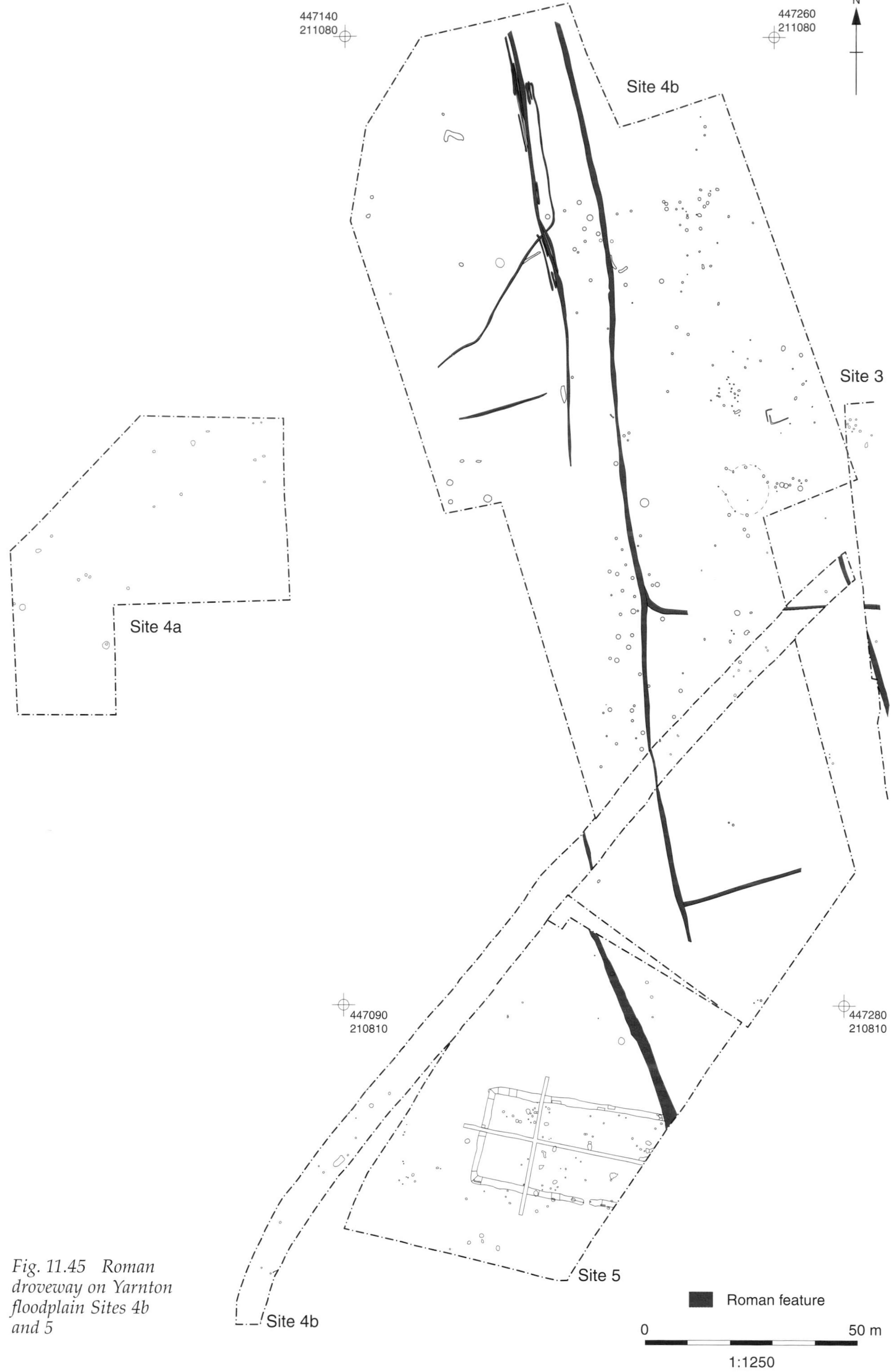

Fig. 11.45 Roman droveway on Yarnton floodplain Sites 4b and 5

entranceway. It seems most likely that a droveway was constructed over an earlier ploughed field. A row of seven small, shallow postholes was found parallel to the easternmost droveway ditch. Five similar postholes lay in a north-south line to the north-west and four were located in the south-east corner of the site around the entrance. Although they contained no finds, they were probably Roman in date. The fills of the Roman features were consistently gravel-free and clayey in nature, which set them apart from those of prehistoric date.

Both north-south droveways opened out onto the north bank of the palaeochannel and a much recut ditch seems to represent the southern boundary of the area of ploughed fields (see below). It is probable that the purpose of the droveways would have been to prevent access to arable fields whilst driving animals down onto floodplain pasture. As already described, test pitting showed that fields south of this palaeochannel had not been ploughed and their use as pasture can be proposed.

Although numerous ditches were discovered in evaluation trenches further west, especially to the south of the Worton settlement, a much smaller proportion of this area has been observed after topsoil stripping, and it is very hard to link the individual ditch sections seen. No convincing evidence of droveways or trackways on the floodplain has yet been recovered.

Field boundaries and ploughsoils

Iron Age

No field boundaries predating the Iron Age have ever been encountered in the Yarnton-Cassington study area, and evidence of ditches surrounding Iron Age fields is scant. The middle Iron Age gully (12037) running south-west from the land boundary ditch within Site 25 has already been mentioned (above) and it may have defined the edge of a field adjacent to the land boundary, but no other ditches were detected in this area. Further to the north, one middle Iron Age sherd was retrieved from a shallow SW-NE gully in Trench 254 (Fig. 11.10). One middle Iron Age pottery sherd also came from a shallow NW-SE ditch (31/10) in Trench 31 (Fig. 11.10) which appeared to follow the same alignment as the sand causeway and parallel discontinuous ditch crossing the palaeochannel on Site 21 already described (above). Further north-west, a ditch on the same alignment in Trench 303 (303/5) yielded two Iron Age sherds but a late Iron Age or early Roman grog-tempered sherd was also present. It is possible that the broad outline of a field system was present here, parallel to the boundary ditch, but the dating evidence is very slight and the problem of the occurrence of residual pottery in later ditches is a well-recognised phenomenon on the floodplain.

Upon the Second Gravel Terrace, to the north-west of the Cresswell Field excavation area, three ditches which contained middle Iron Age pottery were revealed during evaluation trenching (21/5 in Trench C21, 56/15 in Trench 56 and 49/6 in Trench 49; Fig. 11.10). A late Bronze Age/early Iron Age sherd came from ditch 6/4 in Trench C6. These features may represent the traces of defined fields of the Iron Age period, and it is possible that most field ditches of this date would have been comparatively shallow and would have been destroyed by later ploughing, or fields may have been defined by hedges. Alternatively, until later in the Iron Age, there may have been a pattern of shifting fields which did not possess formal boundaries.

Roman: Second Gravel Terrace

Excavations on the Cresswell Field site, evaluation for the recycling plant in 1996 and geophysical survey beyond, revealed a number of ditches which appear to have formed a large field of approximately 3 ha to the west of the Yarnton site (Figs 8.14, 11.44 and 12.2; Chapter 8). On the west side, an apparent opening led down to the palaeochannel that ran through Cresswell Field, but it is uncertain how the field would have been enclosed to the south-west. The north-west corner of an enclosure on a similar alignment was exposed in the south-west corner of the excavation area. Otherwise, occasional ditches which appeared to be of Roman date were found between the Cresswell Field excavations and Worton, but no field plan could be discerned.

Roman: floodplain

The layout of a field system on the Yarnton floodplain was more readily apparent. Alluviation in the later Roman and medieval periods led to the preservation of earlier Roman field boundary ditches and ploughsoils, and in some cases it is possible to identify individual fields with their entrances, and the droveways which led through them (Fig. 11.44). It is of note that the substantial Iron Age boundary discussed above (12036) was not respected by the Roman field layout; three parallel Roman field ditches on Site 25 cut on a north-south orientation across the NNW-SSE aligned earlier ditch and its bank (Fig. 11.15). Other monuments on the floodplain may have been used as markers for field boundaries but, where the evidence survived, they were cut through by Roman ditches. This is true of the south end of the droveway on Site 5 which cut through a Neolithic enclosure ditch, and on Site 4 where the ditch ran across the middle of a Bronze Age barrow (Figs 11.36 and 11.37). A Roman field boundary on Site 7 appeared to be aligned between the middle Iron Age stone causeway on Site 9 and a ring ditch at the southern edge of Site 7 (Fig. 11.44), although it did not survive as far as the barrow ditch.

The sizes of fields were quite variable. On Site 7, for example, in which preservation of remains was good, a field 100 m wide was over 150 m long, ie more than 1.5 ha in area (B on Fig. 11.44). As mentioned, its western boundary appeared to be aligned on the Bronze Age barrow and there was a possible entrance to the field on its west side. A much smaller field (C on Fig. 11.44), 75 m x 65 m (*c* 0.5 ha) survived between Sites 3 and 5, where parts of all four boundaries were detected, and there are suggestions that the field to the north of it (D) was 95 m x 60 m. Elsewhere, subdivisions of what appear to have been very large fields (for example E on the central gravel island on which Sites 21, 4c and 4e were excavated) were represented by ditches observed in some evaluation trenches. It can be concluded, however, that the fields did not have a regular layout, but rather fitted in to the topography, maximising the potential of the higher and dryer gravel islands.

Where the fields lay adjacent to palaeochannels, they were sometimes bounded by well-defined ditches running parallel to the water courses. A good example of this is the ditch system which was found in the south-east part of the floodplain, adjacent to Site 5 and crossing Sites 4, 3 and 1 (Figs 11.44 and 11.37). In Site 4, it cut across a late Neolithic/early Bronze Age ring ditch (Figs 11.36 and 11.37), and two entrances through it were observed: in Site 3 (F) it appeared to have been approached by the droveway discussed above, and in Site 1 (G) it led on to a sand-and-gravel causeway (Figs 11.39, 11.44 and 11.46). The entrance in the latter case was subsequently closed by a continuous ditch. It is possible that this long ditch bounded the area between arable fields to the north and pasture to the south (as indicated by ploughsoils) and a *c* 10 m gap between the field ditch and the channel may have enabled animals to be driven along the bank (I am grateful to Mark Robinson for this observation). This interpretation is supported by the presence of Roman ploughsoil in the top of the late Neolithic/early Bronze Age ring ditch on Site 4, to the north of the field boundary, whilst being absent to the south (compare Sections 7022 and 7107 on Fig. 11.36; see Robinson below).

A similar set of ditches appeared to have been present further to the north, on each side of the palaeochannel which ran adjacent to the edge of the gravel terrace (on Site 17 and in Trenches 71, 72, 76, 78, 79, 81 and 82; H and I on Fig. 11.44), although this suggestion is tentative as much less ground has been observed here. Field ditches also seem to have fringed the edges of the rest of this central gravel island, as shown for example by the field ditch examined in the north of Site 9 which was also traced in Site 10 and Trench 198 (J on Fig. 11.44).

In other places, however, there do not seem to have been ditches between the channels and the fields. No ditches were exposed in the south side of the channel on Site 9 (the north side of field B), and what appears to have been a spill of Roman ploughsoil into the channel on this site (13302; Fig. 11.19) and further north-east in Trench 107 (107/3; Fig.

Fig. 11.46 Entrance of Roman field in Site 1, with gravel causeway to right, looking east. Scale 2 m

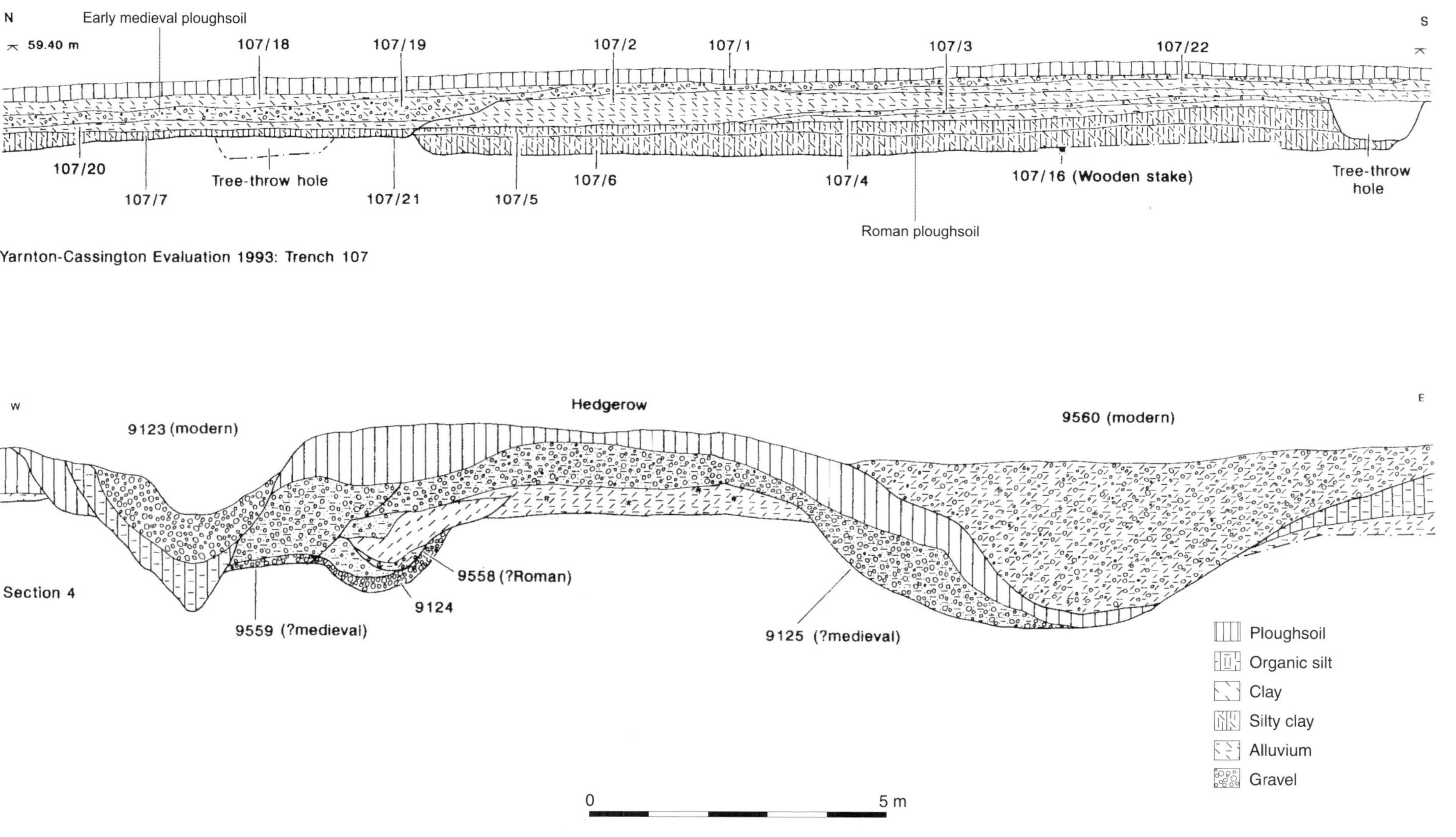

Fig. 11.47 Field boundary ditch sections, evaluation Trench 107 and Site 9

11.47) supports this evidence. Further west, and south of the Worton settlement, the field system is much less clear. Evaluation work in the south of Field 8 and in Field 6 led to impression that there may have been a number of small fields or paddocks there (K on Fig. 11.44). The possible fields associated with the ditches cutting across the Iron Age boundary ditch on Site 25 (L) have already been mentioned.

It is apparent that, in some places, the Yarnton field system was modified and field ditches were re-aligned. This is particularly the case around field entrances, for example at the southern edges of Sites 1 and 3 (F and G; Fig. 11.44), and next to droveways (eg M on Site 4b, Fig. 11.44; Fig. 11.45). Occasionally ditches were cut parallel and close to their predecessors. Ditches to north and south of the northern palaeochannel which ran parallel to the terrace edge (H and I) appear to have been recut on two or three occasions, each time further away from the channel, and the quantities of alluvium in the fills suggest that this was probably caused by increasing flooding in this area. The three parallel and presumably successive ditches, approximately 2 m apart, which ran north-south across Site 25 and were also detected in Trench 39 (field at L), lay on the gravel island, however.

Recutting of ditches on a similar alignment is evidenced in a number of other places, for example on Site 4e (E), and other ditches showed evidence of recutting within the same ditch line (eg Fig. 11.13). On the other hand, some field ditches, such as the western north-south ditch on Site 7, showed no evidence of having been re-dug, but it is not clear in these cases whether this indicates a shorter life for the field edge, or the more permanent use of adjacent fields for the same purpose. There was no evidence for hedges next to these ditches, but it is possible that more long-lived fields may have been bounded in this way.

Field ditches were similar in profile, being open U-shapes with steep or moderately-steep sides and rounded bases (eg Figs 11.13 and 11.46), and individual cuts were from 0.5 m to 0.8 m wide. Depths varied from 0.06 m to 0.5 m, depending on the state of preservation of the ditches and the topography through which they were cut. An average depth was approximately 0.3 m. Fills also differed according to the soils through which the features were cut, but tended to be brown silty or sandy clays with some gravel. A number of the ditches had indications of collapsed banks within their upper fills. Where fills were close to palaeochannels, or the latest in a sequence, however, upper fills tended to be grey alluvial deposits with only occasional gravel (eg Fig. 11.13). The two earliest of the three parallel ditches on Site 25, for example (12118 and 12119), had single fills of dark reddish-brown silty clay, with lenses of sandy gravel and rare manganese flecks, but grey-brown silty alluvial clay lay within the third ditch (12120). The latest recuts on Site 9 were filled with Roman alluvium (Fig. 11.48).

Finds within these features were rare, and tended to consist of redeposited earlier prehistoric material. A single worn sherd of samian ware was recovered from the more southerly ditch on Site 17, and 20 sherds of late Iron Age/early Roman pottery and four indeterminate Roman sherds were retrieved from the field boundary ditches on Site 7, providing some of the best dating for the layout of these fields.

Fig. 11.48 Alluvium-filled Roman field boundary ditch in evaluation Trench 207. Scales 2 m and 1 m

Ploughsoils

A mixed soil within the fields demonstrates that many of these were used for arable, at least periodically, and the presence of early Roman sherds from this layer indicates the date of this activity, and that these fields were regularly manured from the settlement site. Some of this material has been brought to the modern surface by 20th-century ploughing (see fieldwalking above). The Roman ploughsoil varied from 0.02-0.3 m in depth. On Site 25, for example, it covered the whole site and was a mid yellow- or red-brown sandy clay with rare manganese flecks. It was overlain by an alluvial layer. This relationship between ploughsoil and alluvium was seen frequently near palaeochannels (eg Fig. 11.13) and in more generally low-lying areas.

Boundaries at the channel edge

Stake alignment in Trench 107

A row of seven preserved wooden stakes was aligned NE-SW towards the southern edge of the palaeochannel within Trench 107 (107/7 Figs 11.44 and 11.47). The stakes were 0.06 m x 0.08 m in size and ran parallel to the channel bank. They may have been part of a revetment at the edge of the channel or may have been intended to prevent animals moving into or across the channel here. The upper parts of the posts had rotted and it was difficult to establish the level from which they had been driven. A single sherd of middle Iron Age pottery was recovered from the alluvium overlying the stakes.

Wooden alignments and other structures in the Site 1 channel

A number of east-west rows of small roundwood uprights were found running parallel to the channel on Site 1 (114, 117, 118, 121). These appeared to be remnants of some form of fencing or revetment (Fig. 11.42). However, the stakes were mostly only 20-40 mm in diameter, and therefore represented fairly insubstantial structures.

Structure 120, which lay to the west of structure 112 (see above), comprised a sub-rectangular arrangement of wooden uprights, enclosing an area approximately 1.5 m x 1 m, in the deepest part of the channel (Fig. 11.42). The range of diameters of the timbers within this structure tended to be larger than those of fence lines 114, 117 and 118, but the structure is too small to enable any comparison. The function of this structure was unclear and it is possible that these posts were all that survived of a more extensive feature, similar in character to structure 112 which spanned the channel. Alternatively this could have been the frame of a revetted waterhole or wattle tank (for soaking, flax retting, holding fish etc). An east-west row of smaller wooden uprights (121) immediately to the north may represent an associated fence line. The size of wood employed is similar to that used in the other 'fence' structures in the channel.

Other floodplain activity

Double 'pit' alignment on Site 9

A double row of shallow concave features ran NW-SE for *c* 15 m in the eastern part of Site 9 to the north of the palaeochannel (13020; Figs 11.44 (N), 11.17 and 11.49). They had been observed in 1993 Trench 207. The two rows diverged slightly in alignment, suggesting that they were not directly contemporary. The features were quite varied in size and profile, ranging from 0.3 m to 1 m in length and 0.03 m to 0.24 m in depth (Fig. 11.50). In one of the features (13042), charcoal timber was found in the base, possibly indicating the remains of a post. Their function is unclear. It is possible that the alignments represent a boundary connecting the ditch in the north (on the south edge of J in Fig. 11.44) to the palaeochannel in the south. Finds from these features include three sherds of pottery dating to the late 1st-2nd century AD, confirming a Roman date. Additionally, most of the features were filled with Roman alluvium. Other alluvium-filled

Fig. 11.49 Pit alignment 13020 in Site 9, looking north-west. Scale 2 m

Fig. 11.50 Pit alignment features in Site 9 half-sectioned

features to the west of the alignments comprised four postholes in no recognisable pattern. These may also have been Roman in date.

Pit and slot alignments on Site 2

One of the most striking and enigmatic groups of features on the floodplain was a series of parallel rows of slots and small pits or postholes which were found in the south-west, on Site 2 (Figs 11.10 and 11.38). They cannot be conclusively dated, and the degree of recutting indicates that they represent many individual acts or events, perhaps conducted over some considerable period of time. They share the same or a similar alignment as the middle Bronze Age linear ditches on this site, leading down to the palaeochannel and a penannular enclosure, with a ring ditch on the far bank (both monuments of probable late Neolithic/early Bronze Age date). As already described (above) the eastern linear ditch was replaced by ditch 2607, probably in the late Bronze Age, and the earliest pits and slots are associated with this ditch and were dug after it had started to silt up but before it had fully filled. Some of these curious features were open to receive clean floodwaters before the onset of alluviation (see Robinson, below) and held temporary puddles of water, but many were still hollow at the onset of alluviation in the middle Iron Age and had filled with alluvial grey clay-silt. Some slots were cut across the top fill of ditch 2607 in the south and through earlier slots. They are described in greater detail in the volume on the Neolithic and Bronze Age discoveries at Yarnton (Hey *et al.* forthcoming).

Initially these features were categorised separately as slots and postholes, for the features near to the ditches were considerably more elongated (*c* 2-2.5 m x 0.45 m) than the small, circular features away from the ditches (0.4-0.5 m in diameter; Fig. 11.38). Analysis showed, however, that between these two extremes there was a continuum of sizes and that features further away from the ditches were generally smaller and more circular than those nearby. The features were generally concave or U-shaped in profile with concave bottoms, though some had flat bases.

The length of the alignments varied considerably, though many were not fully exposed. The longer rows were between 30 m and 40 m long, and comprised 31-44 individual features. Some short 'rows' were made up of only a few slots/postholes. The majority of these features were discrete, especially those further away from the ditches. Some rows, which appeared to form continuous corrugated lines, were found on excavation to be discrete features lying in a slight depression later filled with alluvium.

In the south and centre of the site, the slots had a lower fill of brown silt with patches of sand, occasional gravel and charcoal flecks and manganese and, sometimes in the south, an upper fill of greyer clay alluvium. Further north, fills became darker and more clayey except next to the channel where fills were more brown and friable with occasional small pebbles. A small quantity of pottery was recovered from these features, including Peterborough Ware and Beaker pottery which is believed to have been redeposited from a Neolithic ground surface scatter.

Mark Robinson comments that the small pits and slots presented particular problems of interpretation. They were features within the floodplain soil which had not been cut into the underlying gravel. They could be discerned easily on the excavated surface of the soil because they were still hollow at the onset of alluviation in the middle Iron Age, and had filled with this distinctive grey clay-silt. However, they were extremely difficult to detect as features below the alluvial interface with the soil because their pre-alluvial fills were so similar to the material of the old ground surface. There were only a few examples where it proved possible to excavate convincingly a pre-alluvial fill in any of them and, in most instances, these were entirely devoid of biological remains. However, a slot which joined the later eastern ditch had a lower fill which appeared to be continuous with the ditch fill and contained a similar range of shells. *Lymnaea truncatula* predominated but the flowing water species *Valvata costata* and *Bithynia* sp. were also present. A single, badly-preserved waterlogged seed of *Mentha* sp. was also found. The results showed that at least some of these curious features were open to receive clean floodwaters before the onset of alluviation. They also possibly had the snail *Lymnaea truncatula* living in temporary puddles of water in the bottom of them.

Discussion

The function of these features remains enigmatic. The possibility that the slots were cultivation furrows was considered, but their close spacing and the absence of friable soil within them, makes this explanation implausible. They seem unlikely to be associated with drainage as the majority were discrete slots, they ran across the lie of the land and would have retained water. The shape of the longer slots could suggest the presence of logs or half-logs, but if the features had held timbers, they must have remained open after the timbers decayed or had been removed, before being filled with alluvium; none contained organic material. The circular features also presented problems of interpretation. They were initially described as postholes but may be small pits. The features were generally shallow (0.15 m on average) and would have been unable to support a post of any height. On the other hand, some of these features appeared to contain postpipes, though none had any organic content. The survival of badly-preserved organic remains in samples which were from a relatively high area of Site 2, suggests that traces of decayed wood could have been expected from the features on the lowest part of the site if they had held timbers. Even the mineral staining, which sometimes results from the decay of organic material, was not present. On the other hand, some of the pits and slots were sufficiently shallow that they need not even have been cut features. They could have resulted from earthworm action undermining timbers which had been placed on the ground.

In conclusion, the slots could represent the positions of timbers placed upon the ground forming corduroy trackways, although timbers from such tracks tend to be set closer than the Yarnton slots. The circular features could have been to support small marker posts, possibly designed to be visible above shallow water but, in this case, the posts had been later removed. Perhaps more convincingly, these features could have been dug and left open for ceremonial purposes at a time of increasing wetness on the site, shortly before the onset of alluviation. They may be paralleled by pit alignments in other parts of the Upper Thames Valley. The close spatial relationship of these features to the linear ditches and their alignment on the penannular enclosure and ring ditch strongly indicate a ceremonial rather than a practical purpose. It seems possible that these features represent activity that spanned the late Bronze Age to middle Iron Age.

Chapter 12: Geophysical Survey

by Neil Linford

INTRODUCTION

A range of geophysical methodologies has been applied at Yarnton and of these, magnetic survey has proved to be most fruitful with approximately 29 ha of the project area covered with this technique. As discussed in the previous volume (Linford 2004) interpretation of geophysical results within a period-based volume is often complicated by the palimpsest of multi-phase anomalies that must, individually, be identified and separated during the discussion. This is certainly the case with the current report, although the interpretation presented here has benefited greatly from comparison with the excavation results; these have informed the identification of Iron Age and Roman activity within the geophysical survey data.

BACKGROUND

Despite the application of a range of geophysical techniques, including magnetic, earth resistance and GPR survey, initial results from the Yarnton project area proved disappointing. This was, perhaps, unsurprising given the acknowledged difficulties presented by the alluvial conditions thought to dominate much of the site (Clark 1992). However, perseverance with mainly magnetic survey techniques was eventually rewarded at Cresswell Field where a wealth of geophysical anomalies, related mainly to Iron Age and Roman settlement activity at the site, was revealed (Linford 1995).

The success of this latter survey reinvigorated the campaign of geophysical survey to investigate how the substantial variation in the quality of results might be explained, particularly with regard to the influence of local geology and the phases of archaeological settlement under scrutiny. Whilst not all of the geophysical surveys have proved as successful as that at Cresswell Field, anomalies related to a continuum of activity from the mid-Neolithic to the post-medieval have been recorded and proved by excavation throughout the study area. Indeed, geological variation appears to be far more crucial when determining the quality of expected geophysical survey results and this is very much reflected by the number of successful surveys conducted on the Second Gravel Terrace sites, above the alluviated flood plain (see below).

The influence of geology and soils

The project area lies over a substrate of Oxford Clay and Kellaways Beds that outcrop between deposits of glacial river gravels and more recent alluvium (Institute of Geological Sciences 1972). Throughout this region the gravels are arranged in a series of terraces along the sides of the river valleys of which, following the classification by Sandford (1924), the floodplain deposits and Second (Summertown-Radley) Terrace occur within the project area (see also Chapters 1 and 2 above). Due to the lateral movement of the Thames southward down the dip-slope of the underlying Jurassic strata, the Summertown-Radley Terrace covers a large, gently sloping surface to the north of the current river course (Richardson *et al.* 1946, 118-9). As a result, the boundary between the Summertown-Radley and floodplain gravel is often indistinct, although in the Yarnton-Cassington area it would appear to follow the 60 m OD contour (Fig. 12.1).

The floodplain gravel terrace is cut by a number of buried channels that, in part, are visible during periods of wet weather as linear depressions in which water collects. Alluvium extends gradually from these channels, tending to form lake-like expanses rather than following the course of the channels, with the floodplain gravel deposits occurring as slightly raised islands.

A variety of soils are found over the project area (Soil Survey of England and Wales 1983) but are mainly clayey soils belonging to the Thames and Kelmscott Associations with finer loamy soils of the Badsey 1 Association developed over the floodplain river alluvium affected by groundwater and seasonal waterlogging. Soils of the Badsey Sutton Series are found over the Second Gravel Terrace deposits surrounding the village of Cassington.

Despite the generally low magnetic susceptibility of both the terrace gravels and the underlying clay, results from a number of topsoil susceptibility surveys over the Second Gravel Terrace demonstrate that, under suitable conditions, sufficient iron minerals are available for significant magnetic enhancement to occur. Much lower susceptibilities have been recorded from the soils developed over the floodplain and it is likely that the seasonally waterlogged nature of these soils has led to considerable gleying of constituent iron minerals.

As noted in the previous volume (Linford 2004) a far greater impediment to magnetic survey has been

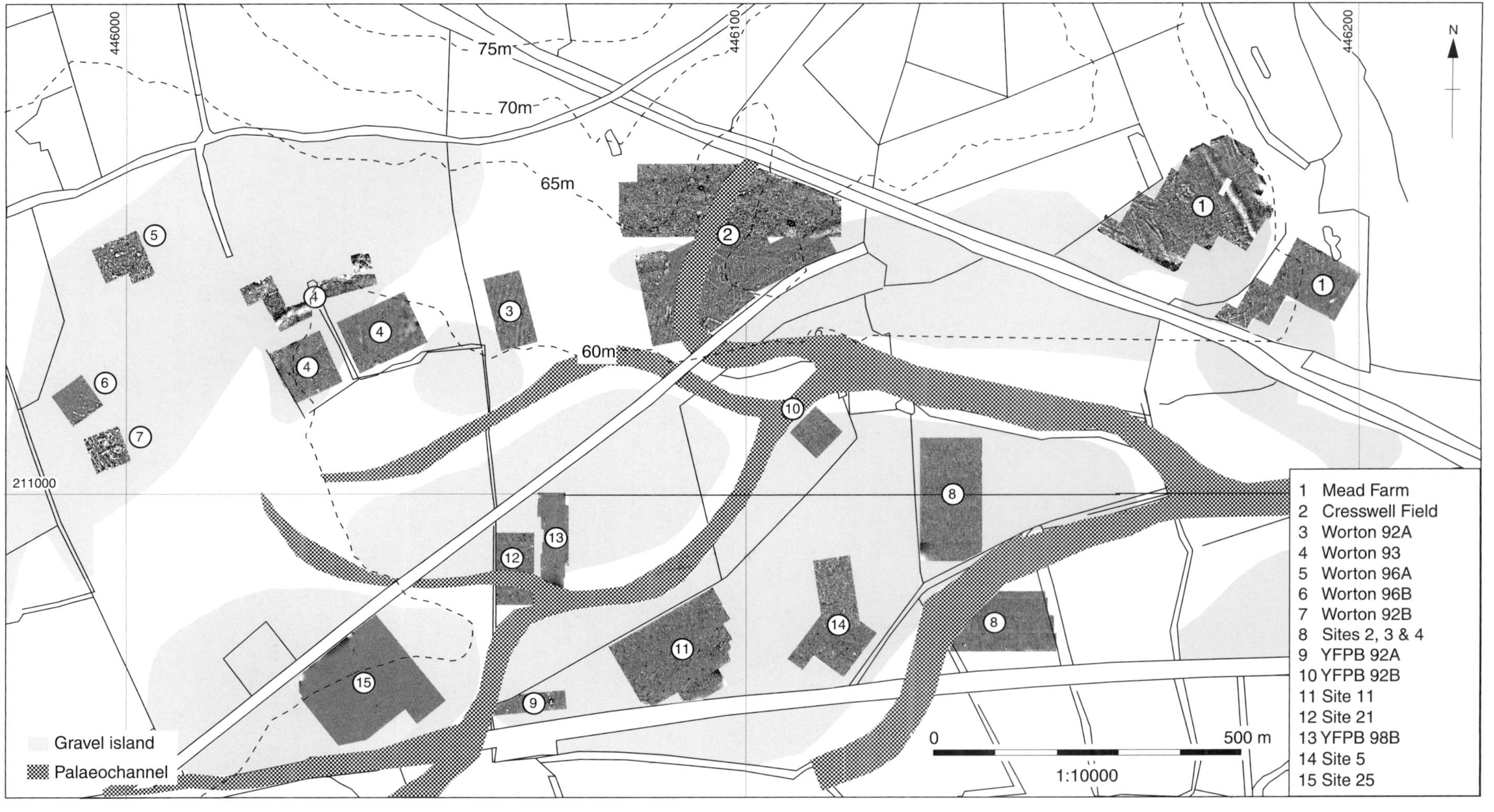

Fig. 12.1 Plan of the study area showing the location of the geophysical surveys and geomorphology.

the wide scatter of ferrous detritus found principally upon the floodplain. This would appear to emanate from a combination of highly magnetic ballast used for track bedding of the former railway line crossing the site and ferrous material derived from a commercial composting facility. Fortunately, the density of this ferrous detritus was not too great to adversely effect the quality of detailed recorded survey over the project area, but it did hamper the use of unrecorded scanning to locate potential areas of archaeological activity.

METHODOLOGY

The majority of geophysical results discussed in the current chapter were magnetic surveys conducted with Geoscan FM36 fluxgate gradiometers. These instruments are ideally suited to recording the variation in the vertical component of the Earth's magnetic field due to the presence of magnetically enhanced, near-surface features. Unless stated otherwise, the fluxgate gradiometer surveys were conducted over 30 m grid squares utilising a sample interval of 0.25 m along north-south orientated traverses separated by 1 m east-west.

Geophysical survey on the floodplain presented more particular problems due to the expectation of weak magnetic anomalies generated by more deeply buried target features sealed by alluvial overburden. Under such conditions more highly sensitive, non-differential magnetometers should improve the identification of subtle anomalies, particularly if the data are recorded at a high sample density. Suitable instrumentation was not readily available within the UK during the programme of field work at Yarnton, but a limited number of sites were surveyed in conjunction with Dr Jörg Faßbinder, Bayerisches Landesamt für Denkmalpflege, München, Germany, as part of a wider research project examining the applicability of high-resolution magnetometry to a variety of English sites (Cole *et al.* 1999). The high-resolution surveys were conducted with a pair of Scintrex CS-2 optically-pumped caesium vapour magnetometers collecting total magnetic field measurements from parallel sondes separated by 0.5 m (Becker 1995). All high-resolution data were collected at an enhanced sample interval of 0.25 m by 0.5 m, with comparative fluxgate surveys conducted over the same areas at an identical sample interval.

In addition, topsoil magnetic susceptibility values were determined either from recovered soil samples or from *in situ* measurements made with a contact field coil. All measurements were made with a Bartington MS2 susceptibility meter with a MS2B dual frequency, 10 cc laboratory coil or MS2D 20 cm diameter field coil. Laboratory measurements were made at two frequencies (470Hz and 4700Hz) on fresh samples subsequently air-dried to determine the dry mass used for the calculation of mass specific magnetic susceptibility (Thompson and Oldfield 1986). It was hoped that the susceptibility data would assist with the interpretation of the detailed magnetometer results, particularly in areas containing weakly magnetic topsoil.

RESULTS

Processed geophysical survey results from the individual sites are presented as linear greytone images at an appropriate scale for each data set. The statistical distribution of data values for each plot is shown as a histogram with a corresponding graphical key detailing the mapping of data values to subsequent shades of grey between extremes of black (low) and white (high). Additional representations of the results, including the analysis of the raw data, are not included but were employed during the interpretation of the data. A graphical summary of significant anomalies is included with each data plot. Figure 12.1 shows the distribution of geophysical survey sites throughout the project area in relation to the approximate divide between the floodplain and the Second Gravel terrace, following the 60 m contour.

Cresswell Field

Prior to excavation a gradiometer survey was conducted over an area of indistinct cropmark evidence occurring on a slight rise within Cresswell Field (Linford 1995). Further gradiometer survey was conducted following the excavation, but these data were compromised by the development of the site for gravel working and an increased concentration of ferrous disturbance hampering the identification of subtle magnetic anomalies. The contrast between the two data sets was so great that an additional area of fallow land encompassing part of the original survey area was resurveyed to examine the extent of the ferrous disturbance. This produced almost identical results to the original data set and confirmed that the ferrous litter must have been introduced since the date of that survey; possibly as a by-product from the adjacent organic waste processing activity. Fluxgate gradiometer data from all three surveys are shown in Fig. 12.2 together with a graphical summary of significant magnetic anomalies.

Superficial anomalies within the data include the response to both the modern plough pattern (extant at the time of the 1995 survey) and underlying evidence for a system of former ridge and furrow agriculture [CW1] which corroborates the north-south orientation of former agricultural patterns determined through aerial photography.

Additional recent disturbance is associated with the telegraph poles crossing the survey area [CW2] to the north and a highly magnetic response [CW3] located within the apparent course of the palaeochannel [CW4]. The intense nature of [CW3] suggests that it represents buried ferrous material, possibly abandoned agricultural machinery.

The palaeochannel [CW4] appears to represent a boundary to the excavated multi-period settlement

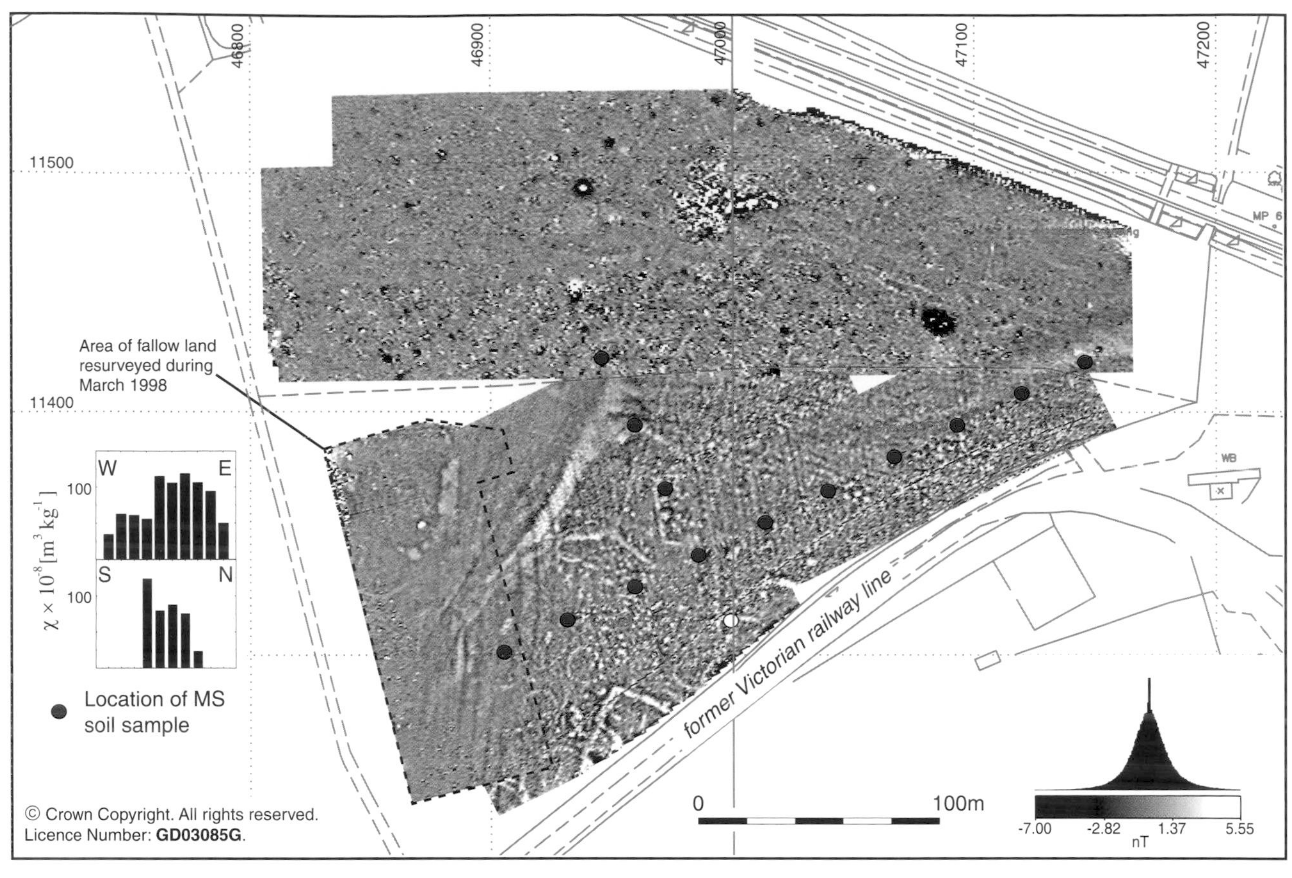

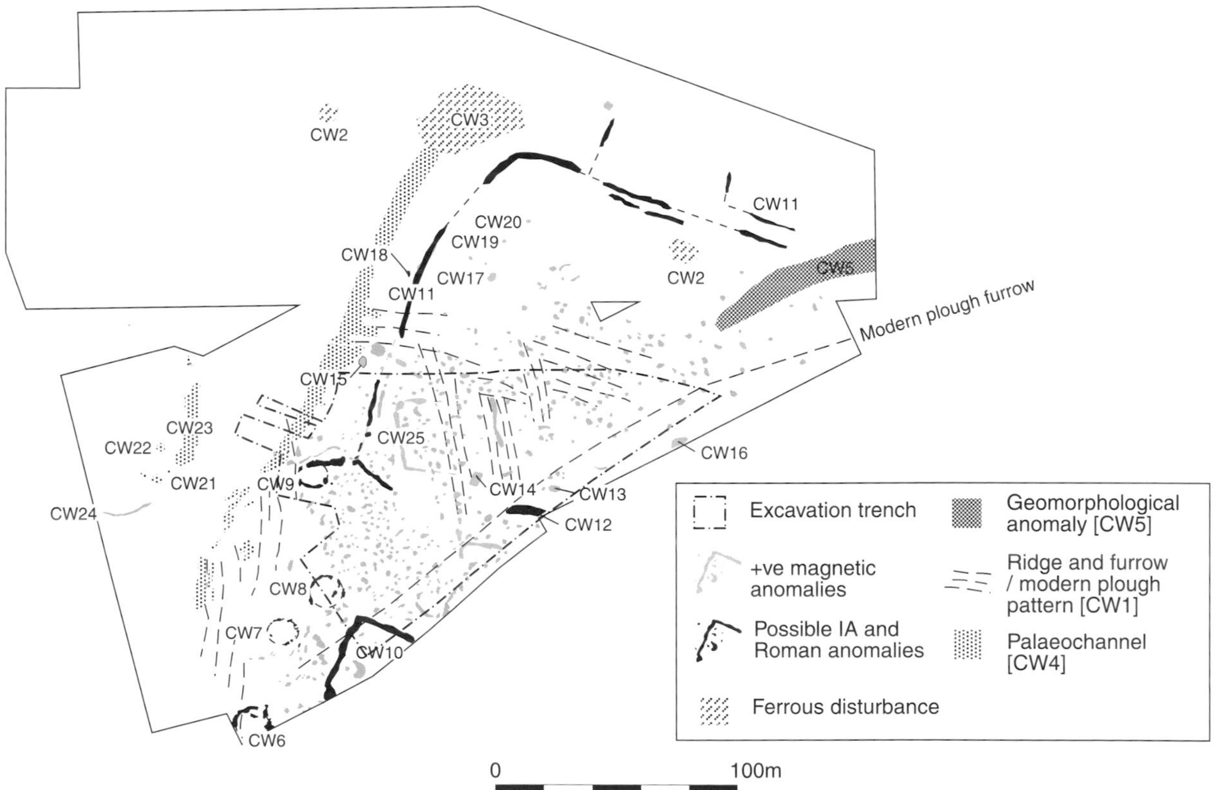

Fig. 12.2 (A) Greytone image of the fluxgate gradiometer data and topsoil susceptibility measurements from Cresswell Field together with (B) a graphical summary of significant geophysical anomalies showing possible Iron Age and Roman activity shaded black.

that is respected by all anomalies, with the exception of the presumed medieval ridge and furrow ploughing. Similar anomalies have been recorded throughout the project area and at other fluvial sites in association with former river channels, although determining the precise cause of the response has often proved elusive (eg Linford 1994; Cole 1995). Possible explanations for these anomalies include the accumulation of sediment with a high magnetic susceptibility within the channel or the development of a (p)DRM as water-borne magnetic minerals settle from suspension and align themselves with the ambient magnetic field (Butler 1992, 66-74).

The proximity of the settlement activity to the most pronounced anomaly associated with the palaeochannel may well account for the local concentration of enhanced magnetic material, reflecting the deposition of material derived from the occupation into the channel depression. Alternatively, this section of the channel may have offered more suitable, lower energy, conditions for the formation of a (p)DRM. This latter mechanism may explain the intermittent nature of these anomalies through varying turbidity conditions, which appear to affect the stability of the (p)DRM formation process (cf Ellis and Brown 1998; Rees 1961). Certainly, geophysical survey results from the floodplain suggest that the magnetic anomalies associated with palaeochannels at this site form along the edges rather than in the more deeply scoured centre of the former channel.

A diffuse magnetic anomaly [CW5] is found at the east of the site where the degree of settlement activity is apparently much reduced. On the basis of the surrounding topography this anomaly is unlikely to represent a former palaeochannel and no corroborative evidence is found in the aerial photographic record. However, it is possible that [CW5] represents a geomorphological feature, possibly a discontinuity between the gravel and underlying clay.

A series of more significant anomalies [CW6-10] represent a number of enclosure ditches and hut circles that, with the exception of [CW6] and [CW7], were all confirmed through subsequent excavation to be of Iron Age date. The largest of these [CW10] appears to form part of a rectangular enclosure continuing beyond the survey area into the course of the Victorian railway line. Note the significant magnitude of response (approximately 10nT) arising from the north-eastern section of this [CW10], suggesting the inclusion of highly enhanced material from a semi-industrial process, such as pottery production or metal working (cf David and Payne 1993).

A linear ditch-type anomaly [CW11] apparently forms part of a field system or an incomplete enclosure extending to the north where it continues as a more subtle response. Along elements of its course [CW11] appears as a double linear anomaly although it is difficult to determine whether this represents a more significant causative feature, such as the drainage ditches surrounding a former trackway, or a recut of the original ditch system.

Anomaly [CW12] was revealed to be a Roman ditch infilled with later Saxon occupation debris possibly associated with [CW13 and CW14] that were identified as sunken-featured buildings of the same period. A further sunken-featured building was identified at [CW15] although this anomaly is confused by the superposition of the response from the adjacent palaeochannel. Given the distinctive response of the sunken-featured buildings the location of further similar features may be tentatively proposed beyond the excavation area at the location of anomalies [CW16-19]. One of these responses [CW18] lies beyond the postulated enclosure ditch [CW11] together with [CW15], which suggests that [CW11] predates the Saxon activity, possibly representing a Roman field boundary.

A further group of diffuse magnetic anomalies [CW21-23] west of the palaeochannel may also be indicative of settlement activity related to a subtle curvilinear response [CW24]. However, the presence of the diffuse anomaly [CW23] is more suggestive of a geomorphological origin.

Anomaly [CW25] was found to represent a rectangular post-medieval enclosure abutting a north-south field boundary that failed to produce a discernible magnetic response. Again, the palimpsest of superimposed strongly magnetic anomalies both within and surrounding the enclosure, together with the orientation of the field boundary along the same alignment as the ridge and furrow, may have obscured the identification of significant anomalies related to this phase of activity.

Topsoil samples were recovered at 30 m intervals along the two orthogonal traverses (Fig. 12.2(A) inset bar graphs). There is little apparent correlation between the values of enhanced topsoil magnetic susceptibility and the concentration of magnetic anomalies revealed by the magnetometer survey. However, the values do appear to fall over areas associated with the palaeochannel to the north and west of the site. Overall, the topsoil susceptibility values are high with respect to those recorded on the floodplain, which may well be due to the influence of recent ploughing redistributing occupation enhanced material into the modern plough soil.

Worton settlement

Further evidence for Iron Age and Roman settlement on the Second Gravel Terrace was found east of Worton Rectory Farm, where three separate magnetometer surveys were conducted to elucidate the aerial photographic record from this area (Fig.12.3, cf Figs 10.1 and 10.2). Two of these surveys were undertaken during June 1996 as part of an ongoing collaborative research project comparing high sensitivity caesium magnetometer data to the results from more routinely applied fluxgate instrumentation. It was hoped that the application of high

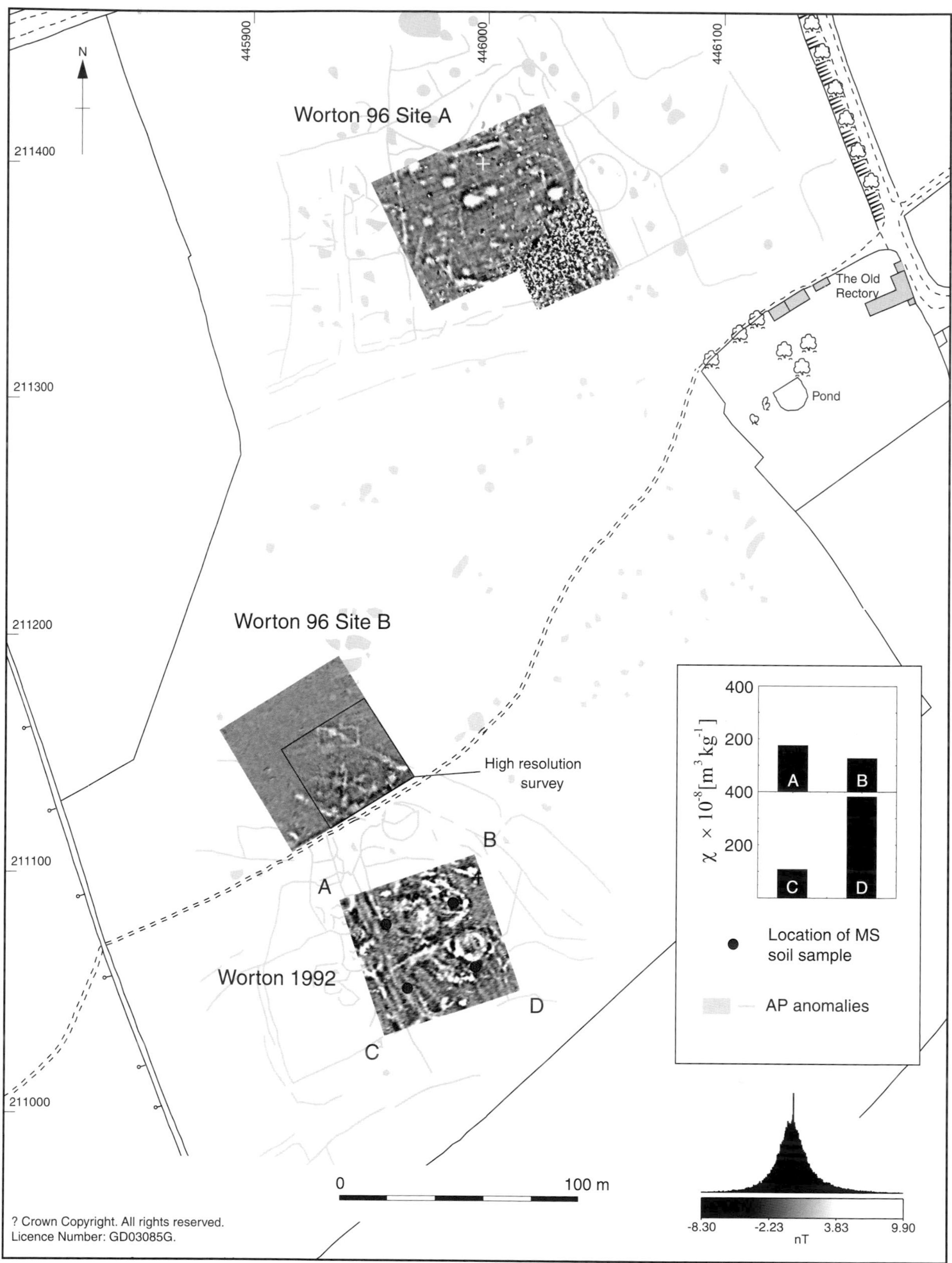

Fig. 12.3 Greytone images of the fluxgate gradiometer data from Worton Rectory Farm superimposed over the crop mark anomalies identified from aerial photography.

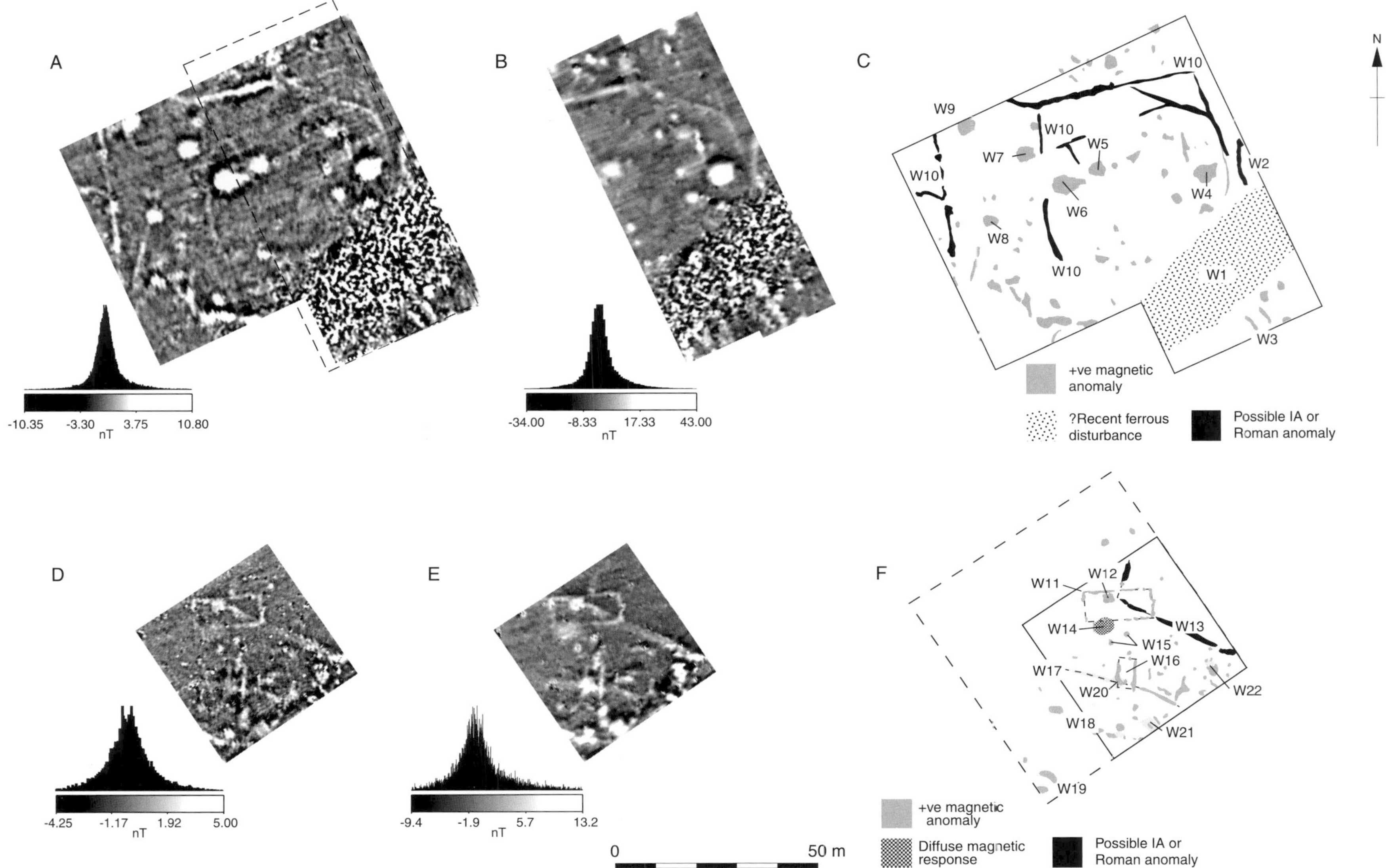

Fig. 12.4 (A) High resolution fluxgate gradiometer data from Worton 1996 Site A with (B) the corresponding high sensitivity caesium data and (C) a graphical summary of significant geophysical anomalies showing possible Iron Age and Roman activity shaded black. Results from Worton 1996 Site B are shown in the lower part of the Fig. (D) high resolution fluxgate gradiometer data, (E) corresponding caesium data and (F) a graphical summary of significant geophysical anomalies.

sensitivity magnetometers would aid the identification of anomalies from weakly magnetic features such as the Anglo-Saxon timber buildings revealed during excavation at both the Yarnton site and Cresswell Field.

Just such a feature was suspected due east of Worton Rectory Farm where aerial photography (Featherstone and Dyer 1994) located a rectilinear anomaly with similar dimensions to the other timber buildings surrounded by an extensive palimpsest of additional cropmarks. An initial fluxgate gradiometer survey in the vicinity of the rectangular cropmark (Site B) successfully located a corroborative magnetic anomaly, although the quality of the data was impaired by the over-grown nature of the site (Fig. 12.3). The landowner kindly agreed to remove this vegetation and also allowed an additional survey to be conducted over more open ground to the north used as horse paddocks (Site A) whilst the clearance work was in progress. This latter area also contains an extensive pattern of cropmarks.

Site A

The results from this area (Figs 12.3 and 12.4) are dominated by a 20 m wide band of intense disturbance running approximately NE-SW through the south-east corner of the survey [W1]. Analysis of a stacked XY traceplot representation of these data suggests that this disturbance is caused by a quantity of near-surface ferrous material that may possibly represent a recent rubbish dump. However, no evidence of surface disturbance was observed in the paddock during the survey and no cropmark anomaly is discernible in aerial photographs taken in 1968. This would suggest that the disturbance is relatively recent.

Additional linear anomalies within this area correspond to the pattern of cropmarks recorded by the 1968 aerial photograph and include a curvilinear portion of the distinctive circular cropmark [W2] of possible Iron Age date which is, unfortunately, affected by the band of disturbance [W1]. A portion of the double linear anomaly [W3] is also visible south of [W1] although the change in orientation evident in the aerial photograph data is masked by this latter disturbance. A distribution of discrete positive anomalies is also found to correlate with a number of sub-rectangular cropmark patterns identified from the air photograph. Whilst the smaller of these may represent a scatter of pits, the magnitude of response demonstrated by several of the anomalies [W4-9] is reminiscent of results recorded over sunken-featured buildings at Barrow Hills, Radley (Bartlett 1999, 11). A discontinuous series of linear ditches [W10] may form a larger enclosure that is only partially described within the limited survey area. Whilst [W10] has been identified from the geophysical data as a possible Iron Age or Roman enclosure, these anomalies may well relate to later activity associated with the Saxon settlement of the site and the interpretation must remain highly tentative.

Site B

The initial survey of this site (Fig. 12.3) covered a 60 m x 60 m area prior to the removal of the vegetation and readings were collected at a standard sample resolution of 0.25 m x 1.0 m. The results of this survey have been severely curtailed by the much denser population of thistles to the north of the area which required the magnetometer to be elevated above the height of the vegetation, attenuating the magnetic response of the data to the north. However, despite these constraints the survey successfully located a number of significant anomalies including [W10], that appears to be half of the rectilinear cropmark identified in the aerial photographs.

Once the precise location of the cropmark had been established on the ground a more detailed survey was conducted over a 40 m x 40 m area from which the vegetation had been cleared. This latter area was surveyed with both a fluxgate gradiometer and a high sensitivity Scintrex CS-2 caesium magnetometer at an identical sample interval of 0.25 m x 0.5 m. Results from the two detailed surveys are shown in Fig. 12.4 (D-F) and demonstrate a broad agreement between the two instrument types with the outline of the Saxon building appearing as a rectangular anomaly [W11] in both data sets. The outline of the ditch in the high-resolution data suggests a less continuous response with some correlation between discrete magnetic pit-type anomalies and the location of excavated post pits.

The building also contains an additional pit-type response [W12] and a linear ditch-type anomaly [W13] that enters from the south-east corner of the survey and appears to alter direction as it exits to the north. Subsequent evaluation trenching revealed that [W12] corresponds to the location of a large pit, post-dating the construction of the timber building and [W13] to the course of a Roman field boundary ditch, not associated with the later Saxon activity.

A diffuse area of magnetic disturbance [W14] appears on both plots producing a greater magnitude of response in the total field data and is related to an earlier sunken-featured building cut by the timber building. Two pit-type anomalies [W15] to the south are prominent in both the detailed data shown in Fig. 12.4 and in the initial data shown in Fig. 12.3 and are likely to contain a highly enhanced magnetic fill. Further activity is evident in the south of the survey and the faint outline of a second rectangular anomaly [W16] may be tentatively proposed. This latter anomaly coincides with a presumably Roman ditch-type response [W17] running roughly parallel to [W13], which is replicated in the aerial photographic evidence. Additional cropmark anomalies correlate with indistinct magnetic responses [W18] and [W19] in the south of the survey area.

Anomalies [W20], [W21] and [W22] all demonstrate a strong response, particularly evident within the total field data. Whilst these anomalies may well represent a series of pits an interpretation as further sunken-featured buildings cannot be entirely discounted.

Worton 1992

During March 1992 a 60 m x 60 m trial fluxgate gradiometer survey was conducted over the agricultural land to the south of Worton 1996 Site B to assess the geophysical response of this area (Fig.12.5). Although this area has never been tested through excavation the survey reveals a palimpsest of strong magnetic anomalies which replicate the fine detail evident in the cropmark data (Fig.12.3). A circular anomaly [W23] is adjacent to a series of pit type responses [W24] that correlate with the position of an apparent enclosure within the cropmark data. Two sides of a larger enclosure [W25] are found to the west where they adjoin a number of linear anomalies [W26] forming a large rectangular enclosure revealed by the cropmark data beyond the limit of the geophysical survey.

A third enclosure evident in the cropmark data to the north correlates with anomaly [W27]. Both the data sets show a large sub-circular anomaly within the enclosure. The magnetic data resolve this into a pit-type anomaly surrounded by a more diffuse magnetic response [W28]. Whilst there are no excavation data available to confirm the origin of these anomalies, the morphology of the apparent enclosures [W23], [W25] and [W27] revealed by this survey are reminiscent of Iron Age settlement activity and may be cautiously interpreted as such.

Four topsoil samples were recovered from the centre of each 30 m survey square for the laboratory determination of magnetic susceptibility. This showed some variation in magnetic susceptibility and, in particular, considerable enhancement within the square containing [W23], suggesting more intense occupation activity within this area.

Geophysical evidence for Iron Age and Roman activity on the floodplain

There is a marked contrast between the results from magnetic survey over the floodplain and those sites investigated on the Second Gravel Terrace. In general, the magnitude of magnetic response is far lower over the floodplain, resulting in a much reduced density of recorded anomalies. Curiously, only Neolithic and Bronze Age features on the floodplain appear to have retained a sufficient magnetic contrast from the surrounding subsoil to be detectable as positive magnetic anomalies. Later occupation, whilst certainly present, has failed to produce a consistent geophysical response, despite the often obvious magnetic contrast between such features and subsoil revealed during excavation.

Site 5

The only geophysical evidence for Iron Age or Roman activity to be revealed during fluxgate magnetometer survey over the floodplain appeared in the vicinity of a Neolithic enclosure, subsequently excavated as Site 5. Sections of this enclo-

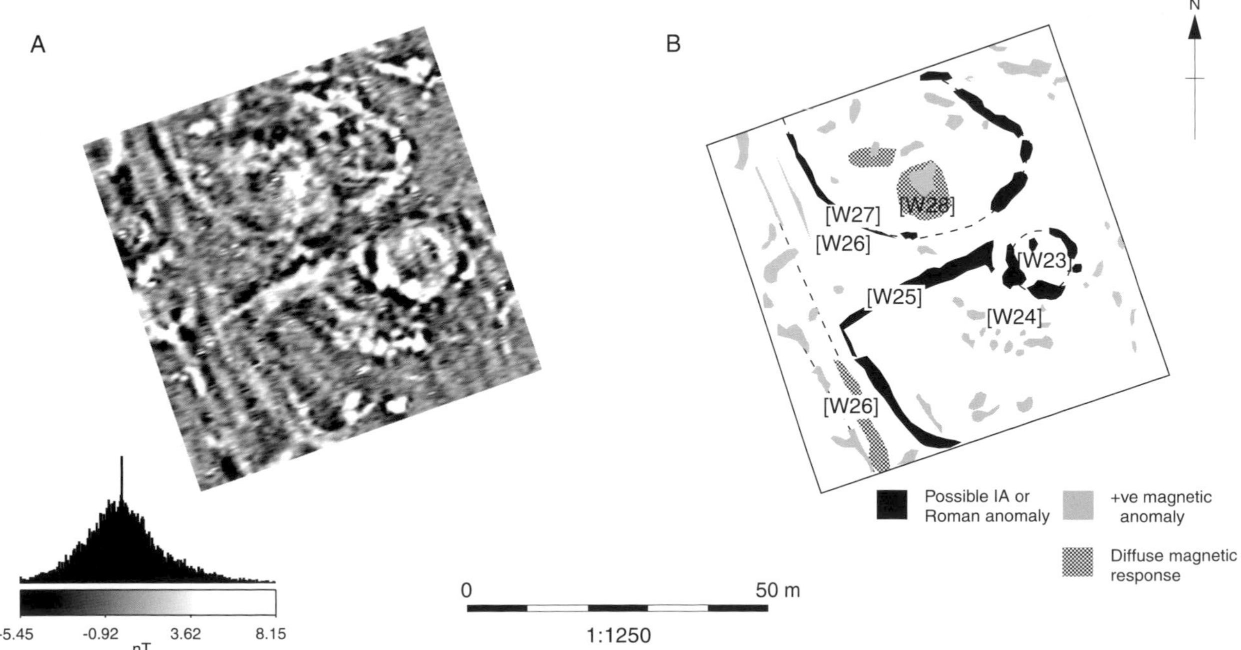

Fig. 12.5 (A) Greytone image of the fluxgate gradiometer data from Worton 1992 together with (B) a graphical summary of significant geophysical anomalies showing possible Iron Age and Roman activity shaded black.

Fig. 12.6 (A) Greytone image of the fluxgate gradiometer data from Site 5 together with (B) a graphical summary of significant geophysical anomalies showing possible Iron Age and Roman activity shaded black.

sure ditch were first discovered during the invasive 2% trial trenching evaluation and subsequent magnetic survey (Fig. 12.6) of this area revealed a rectilinear anomaly [NE1] truncated by the modern field boundary to the east. Interpretation of the data from this site is hampered by the extremely weak magnetic response of the feature and the plethora of ferrous detritus incorporated into the topsoil from the organic waste processing site. Thus, it is impossible to discern whether discontinuities along the course of [NE1] represent entrances into the enclosure or a variation in the magnetic response.

Few significant anomalies have been identified within the enclosure other than a group of pit-type responses [NE2] obscured by more recent ferrous litter. A tentative linear anomaly [NE3] is found just beyond the enclosure to the north running parallel to the course of the enclosure ditch that may, possibly, represent a recut of this feature. Activity beyond the enclosure is limited to a scatter of possible pit-type anomalies to the north ([NE4] and [NE5]) and south ([NE6] and [NE7]). However, no morphological identity is suggested by these groups and it seems equally likely that these anomalies may relate to less significant geomorphological or tree-throw features.

The single Roman feature located through geophysical survey was, ironically, found during an earlier attempt to locate the Neolithic enclosure following the trial trenching evaluation. This initial survey was erroneously positioned to the north of the Neolithic enclosure but revealed a negative linear anomaly [NE8] that correlates with the location of an alluvium filled, Roman field boundary ditch.

Magnetic susceptibility survey of the Site 5 excavation surface

The magnetic response of the archaeological features was further investigated through a magnetic susceptibility survey conducted over the topsoil stripped excavation surface. The survey, shown in Fig. 12.7, was conducted with a Randall susceptibility meter at a 0.5 m _ 0.5 m sample interval (Challands 1995).

Due to extremely dry weather conditions difficulty was encountered with evenly removing topsoil from the site and some areas of enhanced A/B horizon soils remained in place, producing enhanced readings in the magnetic susceptibility survey ([MS1], [MS2]). However, in general the excavation surface was successfully stripped back to the natural sand and gravel. This latter substrate has extremely low susceptibility in contrast to the fill of the Neolithic enclosure ditch that has produced the highest readings recorded in the survey area. The magnetic enhancement appears to be concentrated in the north-west part of the ditch, possibly suggesting a focus of activity within the enclosure. The ditch terminals found at the apparent entrance to the enclosure [MS3] also demonstrate an enhanced susceptibility as do the remains of a pit-feature [MS4] cut into the southern course of the ditch. The magnetic response of other cut features is more

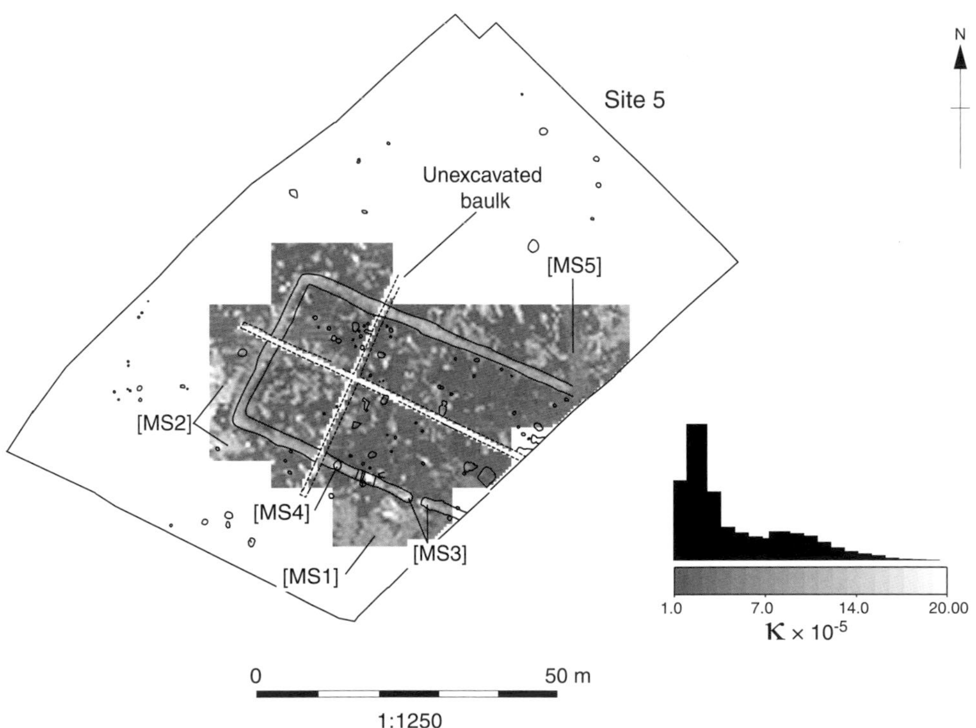

Fig. 12.7 Magnetic susceptibility survey conducted over the topsoil stripped excavation surface at Site 5. The Fig. also shows archaeological features subsequently revealed through excavation including the location of the Neolithic enclosure ditch.

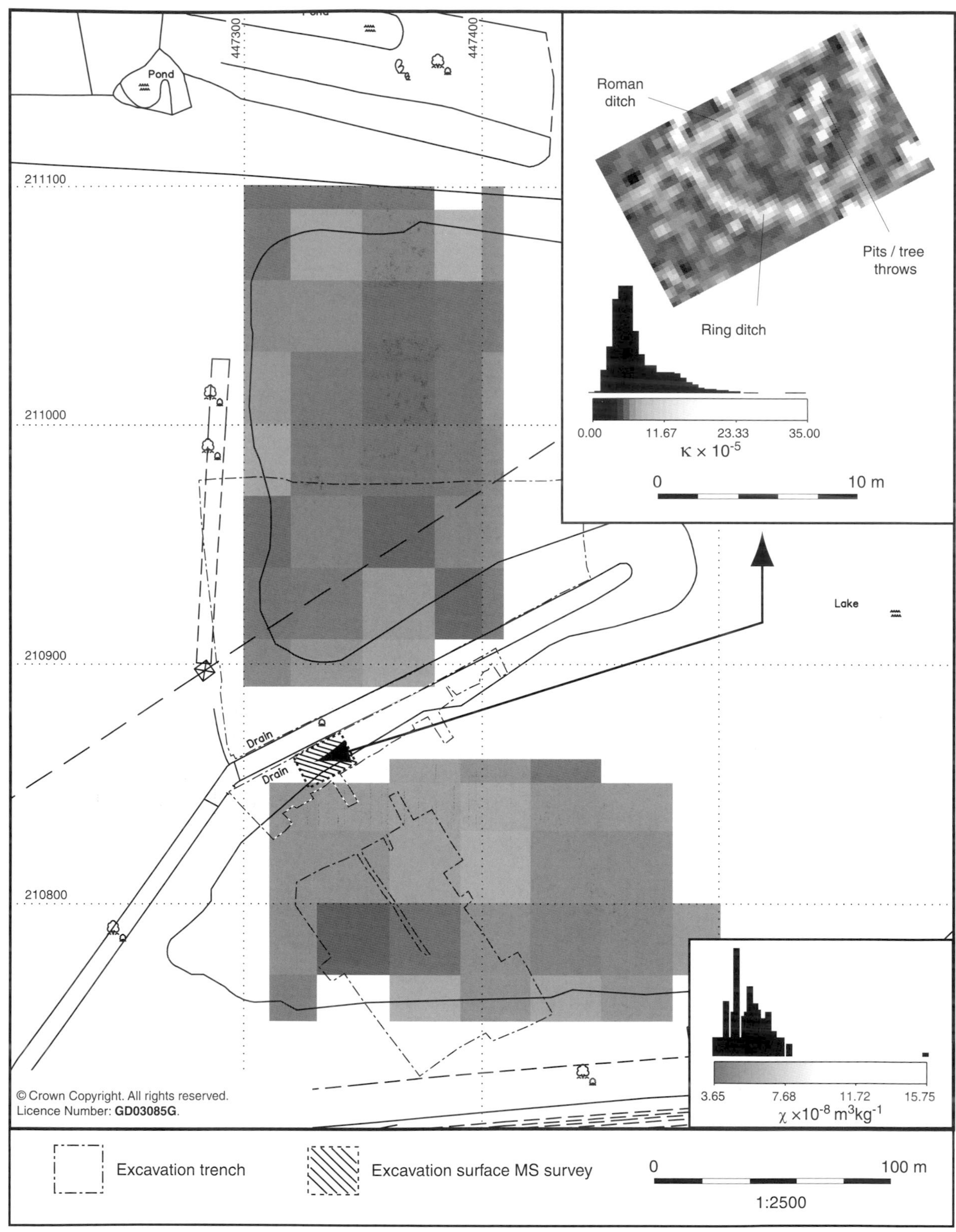

Fig. 12.8 (A) Topsoil magnetic susceptibility values for Sites 2, 3 and 4. The inset greytone image (B) shows the results of a high resolution susceptibility survey conducted over part of the stripped excavation surface of Site 4

variable, with little obvious correlation between their location and areas of enhanced susceptibility.

A north-south aligned section of Roman ditch [MS5] was detected with a low susceptibility fill cut into an area of magnetically enhanced, possibly burnt, sand and gravel. Unfortunately, the magnetic susceptibility survey does not extend to overlap with the original fluxgate magnetometer survey that revealed the negative anomaly [NE8] related to the course of the north-south Roman field boundary. However, it seems reasonable from the low susceptibility of [MS5] to suggest that this may represent a continuation of [NE8] to the south.

Magnetic susceptibility survey of the Site 4 excavation surface

Figure 12.8(B) shows results from a similar magnetic susceptibility survey conducted over the location of a Bronze Age ring ditch identified in the Site 4 stripped excavation surface. Unfortunately, the initial fluxgate gradiometer survey did not extend over the majority of this site. However, as the gradiometer survey failed to produce any significant magnetic anomalies related to underlying archaeological features, it seems unlikely that the ring ditch would have produced an identifiable response. This may, in part, be explained by the very low values of topsoil magnetic susceptibility recorded over the area covered by the fluxgate gradiometer survey (Fig. 12.8(A)).

The magnetic susceptibility survey conducted over the excavation surface did, however, reveal a degree of magnetic enhancement associated with the archaeological features in comparison to the sand and gravel substrate. The Bronze Age ring ditch is clearly defined and also contains a number of pits and tree-throw features. A single linear Roman ditch cuts through the ring ditch and this too exhibits a slightly enhanced magnetic susceptibility (k = ~10 to 20 x 10-5). The survey clearly identifies the majority of the features located during excavation.

Geophysical survey of the Site 21 excavation surface

This site, located on the edge of a palaeochannel, revealed the remains of a late Bronze Age/early Iron Age gravel causeway. Again, no indication of this feature appeared within the initial fluxgate gradiometer survey of the site conducted prior to the excavation. However, both fluxgate gradiometer and magnetic susceptibility survey (Challands 1998) conducted over the stripped excavation surface successfully recorded an anomaly derived from a gravel causeway (Fig.12.9).

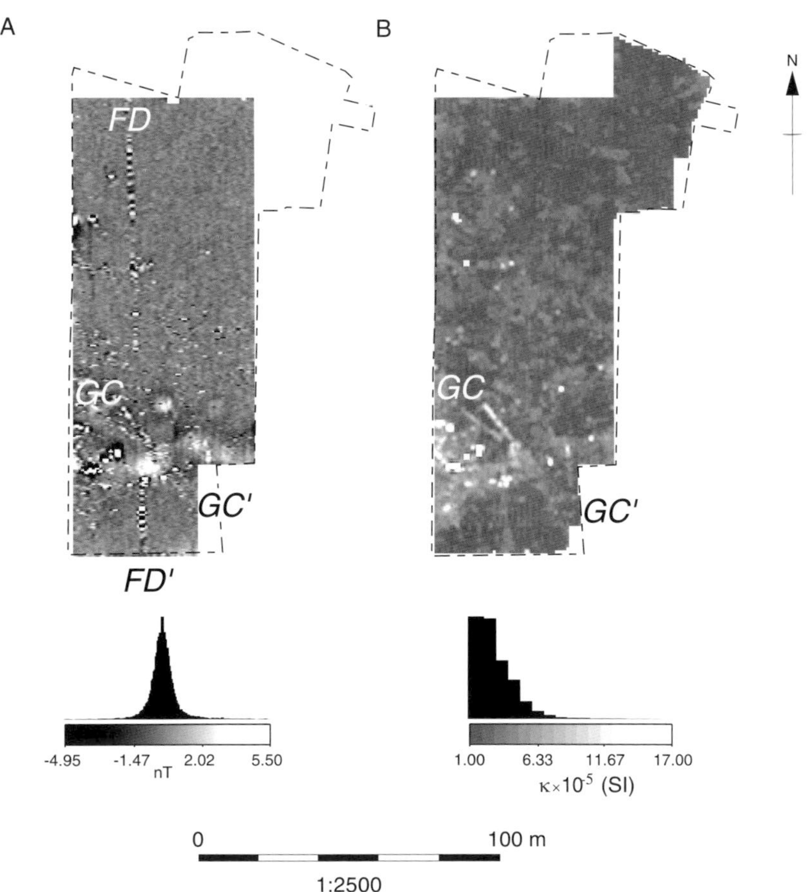

Fig. 12.9 Greytone images of (A) the fluxgate gradiometer data and (B) the magnetic susceptibility survey both conducted over the stripped excavation surface of Site 21.

The fluxgate data (Fig. 12.9(A)) reveal a number of anomalies that were not evident in the surface survey, including responses associated with the gravel causeway and a modern ceramic field drain running north-south across the length of the site (marked *GC-GC′* and *FD-FD′* respectively on Fig. 12.9(A)). Comparison of these data with the susceptibility results (Fig.12.9(B)) suggests that many of the magnetometer anomalies are produced by the remanent magnetisation of the features rather than an induced magnetisation arising from the susceptibility of the sediments. For example, neither the field drain nor the alluvium along the course of the palaeochannel produce a distinct susceptibility contrast in Fig. 12.9(B), although both are easily discernible in the fluxgate data (Fig. 12.9(A)). The magnetic response of the gravel causeway is of interest as it would appear to be either constructed from a higher susceptibility material than the channel deposits or to have had magnetically enhanced topsoil compacted along its course during use. Furthermore, both surveys provide evidence for a second, slightly weaker, linear anomaly to the west of the excavated gravel causeway, suggesting a previous alignment of the crossing.

DISCUSSION

Geophysical survey throughout the Yarnton project area has undoubtedly been influenced by the gradual environmental change to floodplain conditions on the lower lying ground. This change appears to be particularly acute during the Iron Age/Roman transition and may well explain the high degree of variability within the geophysical survey results. For example, Roman field boundary ditches have been revealed through excavation to form an extensive agricultural landscape over both the higher ground and the floodplain. The physical dimensions and the depth of overburden are also largely similar for many of these features, yet it is only on the Second Gravel Terrace that these have produced identifiable magnetic anomalies.

In part, this may reflect a shift in the density of permanent settlement to the higher ground as the floodplain develops. By the Roman period use of the floodplain may well have become seasonal, with the focus of settlement activity located on the Second Gravel Terrace on dry land immune from winter flooding. As concentrated settlement activity is associated with a local increase in the magnetic susceptibility of the topsoil, the identification through magnetic survey of cut features, where such enhanced material accumulates, will often diminish at a distance from the focus of occupation (eg Cole 1995, fig. 1).

Geophysical results from the floodplain suggest an additional constraint on the location of anomalies related to Iron Age and Roman activity. In general, geophysical survey over floodplains is hampered due to the increased depth of alluvial overburden and the leaching of magnetic iron minerals from waterlogged archaeological features. Curiously, neither process seems to be overbearing on the Yarnton floodplain. The alluvial overburden, recorded during topsoil stripping prior to gravel extraction, was found to be quite variable and only reached an excessive depth in isolated "lakes" in the south of the project area. The majority of the archaeological activity, however, was focused on raised gravel terraces within the floodplain and these areas were covered with a minimal overburden.

In addition, magnetic survey over the floodplain did successfully detect anomalies related to a number of prehistoric features including a possible Neolithic enclosure, a Bronze Age barrow and the remains of burnt tree-throw holes. Given that these features would have been established before the transition to a floodplain, in theory, they should also have been subjected to the most prolonged leaching of iron minerals during the subsequent waterlogged conditions. The survival of these magnetically enhanced prehistoric features suggests a more complex magnetisation process, particularly in the period following the onset of floodplain conditions.

This is partly illustrated through the geophysical results from Site 5 where a single Roman ditch was detected as a "negative" magnetic anomaly with respect to the response of the weakly magnetic sand and gravel substrate. The subsequent magnetic susceptibility survey over the stripped excavation surface confirmed the very low susceptibility of the alluvium filling this cut feature. It would appear that rapid alluviation during this period may well account for the absence of other similar cut features within the geophysical survey data, instantly erasing the magnetic finger print that might otherwise survive within the archaeological record.

Not all of the Iron Age and Roman features on the floodplain failed to develop an enhanced magnetisation. Both the linear Roman ditch in Site 4 and the possible Iron Age gravel causeway found in Site 21 exhibit a higher magnetic susceptibility than the surrounding sand and gravel substrate. However, this enhanced magnetisation was only proved during geophysical survey over the stripped excavation surface when the features themselves were all clearly visible. It is possible that such weakly magnetic archaeological features would still be detectable through surface geophysical survey, providing that suitable high sensitivity instrumentation was available. Comparative magnetic surveys, conducted within the project area between fluxgate gradiometers and a high sensitivity caesium magnetometer, produced encouraging results, although the limited availability of the high sensitivity instrumentation precluded a thorough test of this equipment over the floodplain sites.

In conclusion, a degree of caution must be urged when interpreting the Iron Age and Roman landscape at Yarnton from the geophysical survey results alone. The strong magnetic response to this phase of activity over the Second Gravel Terrace sites confirms the high fidelity that may often be expected from geophysical data to complement the available aerial photographic record in this area. However, the more variable magnetic response exhibited over the floodplain restricts the interpretation of the geophysical data set. Indeed, the apparent absence of fluxgate gradiometer anomalies associated with Iron Age or Roman activity over the floodplain fails to accurately reflect the archaeological record established through subsequent excavation. Currently, the complex processes of magnetisation on the floodplain are not fully understood and it is hoped that further research into the magnetic properties of excavated features may improve this situation. This research, together with the deployment of more highly sensitive geophysical instrumentation, may well extend the application and interpretation of magnetic survey results over similar floodplain environments.

Chapter 13: Absolute chronology

by Alex Bayliss and Gill Hey

The principal aim of the scientific dating programme was to identify which parts of the environmental sequences from the floodplain could be related to the Roman and Iron Age archaeological sequences reported elsewhere in this volume, but other considerations included the chronology of human burials in and adjacent to the Second Gravel Terrace settlement areas. Rather more Iron Age activity was identified than initially envisaged. For example, the middle Iron Age cemetery was originally thought to be Anglo-Saxon in date (Hey *et al.* 1999), and the stone causeway on Site 9 was thought to be Bronze Age on the basis of the associated finds (Hey 1993b).

RADIOCARBON DATING *by Alex Bayliss, Chris Bronk Ramsey, Gordon Cook and Gerry McCormac*

Forty-four radiocarbon determinations have been obtained on samples of Iron Age and Roman date from Yarnton.

Sample preparation and measurement

Sixteen samples were processed by the Radiocarbon Dating Laboratory of the Queen's University, Belfast between 1994 and 2001, according to methods outlined in Longin (1971), Pearson (1984), and McCormac (1992), and measured using Liquid Scintillation Counting (Noakes *et al.* 1965). Nine samples were processed by the Scottish Universities Research and Reactor Centre at East Kilbride between 1998 and 2002. These were prepared using the methods outlined in Stenhouse and Baxter (1983) and also measured using liquid scintillation spectrometry (Noakes *et al.* 1965). Nineteen samples were dated by the Oxford Radiocarbon Accelerator Unit between 1992 and 2001. These were prepared and measured using methods outlined in Hedges *et al.* (1989) and Bronk Ramsey and Hedges (1997). The pre-treatment method used for bone samples was a collagen extraction (Law and Hedges 1989; Hedges *et al.* 1989) followed by gelatinisation and separation by filtration (Bronk Ramsey *et al.* 2000).

Quality Assurance

All three laboratories maintain continual programmes of quality assurance procedures, in addition to participation in international intercomparisons (Rozanski *et al.* 1992; Scott *et al.* 1998). These tests indicate no laboratory offsets and demonstrate the validity of the precision quoted.

Results

The results are given in Table 13.1, and are quoted in accordance with the international standard known as the Trondheim convention (Stuiver and Kra 1986). They are conventional radiocarbon ages (Stuiver and Polach 1977).

Calibration

The calibrations of these results, relating the radiocarbon measurements directly to calendar dates, are given in Table 13.1 and in outline in Figures 13.1–13.7. All have been calculated using the calibration curve of Stuiver *et al.* (1998) and the computer program OxCal (v3.5) (Bronk Ramsey 1995; 1998; 2001). The calibrated date ranges cited in the text are those for 95% confidence. They are quoted in the form recommended by Mook (1986), with the end points rounded outwards to 10 years. The ranges quoted in italics are *estimated date ranges* derived from mathematical modelling of archaeological problems (see below). The ranges in Table 13.1 have been calculated according to the maximum intercept method (Stuiver and Reimer 1986); all other ranges are derived from the probability method (Stuiver and Reimer 1993).

OPTICALLY STIMULATED LUMINESCENCE (OSL) ANALYSIS *by Julie Rees-Jones*

Nine OSL samples were taken from palaeochannel deposits on Yarnton floodplain (Yarnton Floodplain sections A and B) and analysed as part of a doctoral thesis at the Oxford University Research Laboratory (Rees-Jones 1995). Five of the resulting dates have been integrated with the results of other scientific dating methods.

Optical dating can be used to determine the time elapsed since a buried sedimentary context was last exposed to light by using measurements of the optically stimulated luminescence signal from crystals in the sediments to calculate the radiation dose received since zeroing (Huntley *et al* 1985). Optically stimulated luminescence (OSL) is the light given out by crystals on exposure to a standard light source, due to the release of stored energy resulting from prior exposure to ionising radiation (alpha and beta particles of gamma rays). The intensity of the OSL signal is proportional to the radiation dose that the crystals have received since the stored energy was last set to zero by exposure to daylight.

Table 13.1 Radiocarbon determinations.

Site	*Lab no.*	*Context no*	*Radiocarbon Age BP*	$\delta^{13}C$ *(‰)*	*Material*	*Context type*	*Calibrated date range (95% confidence)*
Worton Rectory Farm Cemetery	UB-3777	SK 2076	1743 ± 21	-20.1±0.2	human bone	articulated skeleton 2016	cal AD 240 – 385
	UB-3921	SK 2005	1796 ± 21	-19.7±0.2	human bone	articulated skeleton 2005	cal AD 130 – 325
	UB-3776	SK 1681	2250 ± 21	-20.6±0.2	human bone	articulated skeleton 1681	cal BC 390 – 205
	UB-3778	SK 2717	2207 ± 21	-20.3±0.2	human bone	articulated skeleton 2717	cal BC 380 – 175
	UB-3779	SK 2713	2224 ± 21	-20.0±0.2	human bone	articulated skeleton 2713	cal BC 385 – 200
	UB-3782	SK 376/2	2237 ± 20	-20.0±0.2	human bone	articulated skeleton 376/2	cal BC 390 – 200
	UB-3919	SK 2710	2168 ± 21	-20.0±0.2	human bone	articulated skeleton 2710	cal BC 355 – 165
	UB-3920	SK 2718	2234 ± 20	-19.9±0.2	human bone	articulated skeleton 2718	cal BC 385 – 200
	UB-3922	SK 2069	2268 ± 20	-20.0±0.2	human bone	articulated skeleton 2069	cal BC 400 – 210
	UB-3923	SK 2041	2267 ± 22	-19.9±0.2	human bone	articulated skeleton 2041	cal BC 385 – 200
	UB-3924	SK 2569	2220 ± 23	-20.0±0.2	human bone	articulated skeleton 2569	cal BC 385 – 200
Oxey Mead	OxA-10690	YOM90 3/8	2082 ± 37	-25.9	waterlogged seeds (mixed aerial species)	from basal sediment	cal BC 200 – 10 cal AD
	OxA-7360	YOM90 3/7	1675 ± 55	-24.5	waterlogged aerial plant macrofossils		cal AD 240 - 540
Floodplain Section A	OxA-3644	YFP CC/2	2585 ± 75	-27.3	wood, *Quercus* sp.	post in structure 112	cal BC 900 – 410
	UB-4060	YFP92 W63 (C112)	2465 ± 18	-26.7±0.2	wood, *Quercus* sp. sapwood	post in structure 112	cal BC 765 – 410
	GU-5715	YFP92 115a (W24)	2600 ± 60	-27.8	wood, *Quercus* sp. roundwood	from layer 115	cal BC 900 – 540
	GU-5716	YFP92 115b (W34)	2520 ± 50	-26.0	wood, *Quercus* sp. roundwood	from layer 115	cal BC 800 – 410
	GU-5717	YFP92 119a (W76)	2520 ± 50	-25.9	wood, *Quercus* sp. sapwood	post in collapsed wattling 119	cal BC 800 – 410
	GU-5718	YFP92 119b (W77)	2570 ± 60	-25.1	wood, *Quercus* sp. roundwood	post in collapsed wattling 119	cal BC 830 – 520
	UB-4061	YFP92 W126 (C116)	3646 ± 19	-28.1±0.2	wood, Pomoideae	post in structure 116	cal BC 2125 – 1940
	OxA-10711	YFP92A 37	2098 ± 39	-25.8	waterlogged seeds (mixed aerial species)	from layer 37	cal BC 350 – 1
	UB-4062	YFP92 W125 (C116)	2567 ± 18	-27.0±0.2	wood, *Corylus* sp.	post in structure 116	cal BC 800 – 670
	OxA-10709	YFP92A 32a	2995 ± 45	-26.4	waterlogged seeds, from layer 32 *Alnus glutinosa*	cal BC 1390 – 1050	
	OxA-10710	YFP92A 32b	3145 ± 45	-26.0	waterlogged seeds (mixed aerial species)	from layer 32	cal BC 1520 – 1310
	GU-5850	YFP92 109 W99	2970 ± 50	-26.3	wood, *Quercus* sp. bark and sapwood	from layer 109	cal BC 1380 – 1000
	GU-5855	YFP92 109 W39	3340 ± 50	-26.2	wood, *Quercus* sp. (21 heartwood rings), probably centre of a short-lived tree with just the sapwood trimmed off or eroded	from layer 109	cal BC 1750 – 1510
	UB-4676	W64	2424 ± 16	-27.7±0.2	wood, *Quercus* sp. roundwood (including sapwood)	post in structure 112	cal BC 760 – 400

Table 13.1 Radiocarbon determinations.

Site	*Lab no.*	*Context no*	*Radiocarbon Age BP*	*$\delta^{13}C$ (‰)*	*Material*	*Context type*	*Calibrated date range (95% confidence)*
	UB-4677	W70	2654 ± 16	-26.6±0.2	wood, *Quercus* sp. roundwood (including sapwood)	post in structure 112	cal BC 830 – 790
Floodplain Section B	OxA-10691	YFP92 B/9	2257 ± 37	-25.8	waterlogged seeds (mixed aerial species)	from base of section (layer 9)	cal BC 400 – 200
	OxA-4816	YFP sample 5	1835 ± 55	-27.6	plant macrofossil	from layer 7	30 – 340 cal AD
	OxA-7361	YFP sample 6a	1640 ± 50	-25.6	waterlogged plant remains (mixed aerial species)	from layer 6	250 – 540 cal AD
	OxA-7362	YFP sample 6b	1730 ± 50	-27.0	waterlogged plant remains (mixed aerial species)	from layer 6	130 – 430 cal AD
Site 2 (alluviation)	OxA-6616	YFP 2835a	2215 ± 45	-27.0	waterlogged seeds (mixed aerial species)	uppermost fill of ditch 2832	cal BC 400 – 160
	OxA-6618	YFP 2004a	1975 ± 40	-26.5	waterlogged seeds (mixed aerial species)	overbank alluvium	cal BC 50 – 130 cal AD
Causeways: Site 9	OxA-8703	YFPB98 13263	2175 ± 35	-20.8	animal bone, cattle humerus	bone between stone and gravel causeways	cal BC 370 – 110
	OxA-8704	YFPB98 13221	2185 ± 40	-21.2	animal bone, cattle radius	bone between stone and gravel causeways	cal BC 390 – 110
	OxA-10628	YFPB98 18192a	2256 ± 35	-26.0	wood, *Salix/Populus* sp.	brushwood beneath the stone causeway	cal BC 400 – 200
	OxA-10629	YFPB98 18136 W168	2198 ± 35	-27.2	wood, *Alnus glutinosa*	stake forming part of a row beneath the stone causeway	cal BC 390 – 160
	GU-5852	YFPB98 18006 W2/1	2300 ± 60	-27.1	wood, *Quercus* sp. (82 rings including 25 sapwood rings)	collapsed handrail lying between stone and gravel causeways	cal BC 490 – 200
	GU-5853	YFPB98 18031 W26	2330 ± 60	-25.7	wood, *Quercus* sp (50 rings including 31 sapwood rings and bark)	upright post driven through stone causeway, beneath gravel causeway	cal BC 490 – 200
	OxA-9377	YFPB98 13266	2275 ±50	-26.6	waterlogged plant remains	bronze spearhead from beneath stone causeway	cal BC 410 – 200
	GU-5883	YFPB98 18105 W36	2240 ± 50	-26.7	wood, *Quercus* sp. sapwood and bark	upright post driven through stone causeway, beneath gravel causeway	cal BC 400 – 170
Trench 37	OxA-10707	YCE93 37/7	2120 ± 45	-27.4	waterlogged seeds (mixed aerial species)	from lower fill of ditch (context 7)	cal BC 360 – 1
	OxA-10708	YCE93 37/8	2180 ± 45	-27.1	waterlogged seeds (mixed aerial species)	from basal fill of ditch (context 8)	cal BC 390 – 90

This can be used to date sediments as they contain crystals of quartz and feldspar which have a luminescence signal that will be zeroed when exposed to sunlight, thus at deposition of the sediment the luminescence signal is set to zero. The sediment then becomes buried and is kept dark. During burial the sediment is exposed to naturally occurring radiation and the luminescence signal grows; this can be measured in the laboratory.

Measurement procedures

The samples were collected so as to minimise light exposure, by driving a steel core into a section face. The ends of the sediment cores that were exposed to light at collection were discarded in the laboratory, where sample preparation took place under restricted lighting conditions. The samples were treated with dilute hydrochloric acid and hydrogen peroxide, rinsed in distilled water and methanol and the 4–11mm grains separated by their settling time in acetone.

The luminescence signal from the samples was measured by exposure to infrared light (IRSL) using an Elsec optical dating system (Spooner *et al.* 1990), with aliquots normalised by the counts produced from a short infrared shine applied to the natural signal.

The first stage was to estimate the preheat time at 160°C appropriate for dating each sample. Preheating is required, as laboratory irradiation fills unstable traps not present in the natural signal due to fading over the burial period. Determining the appropriate preheat involved irradiating aliquots

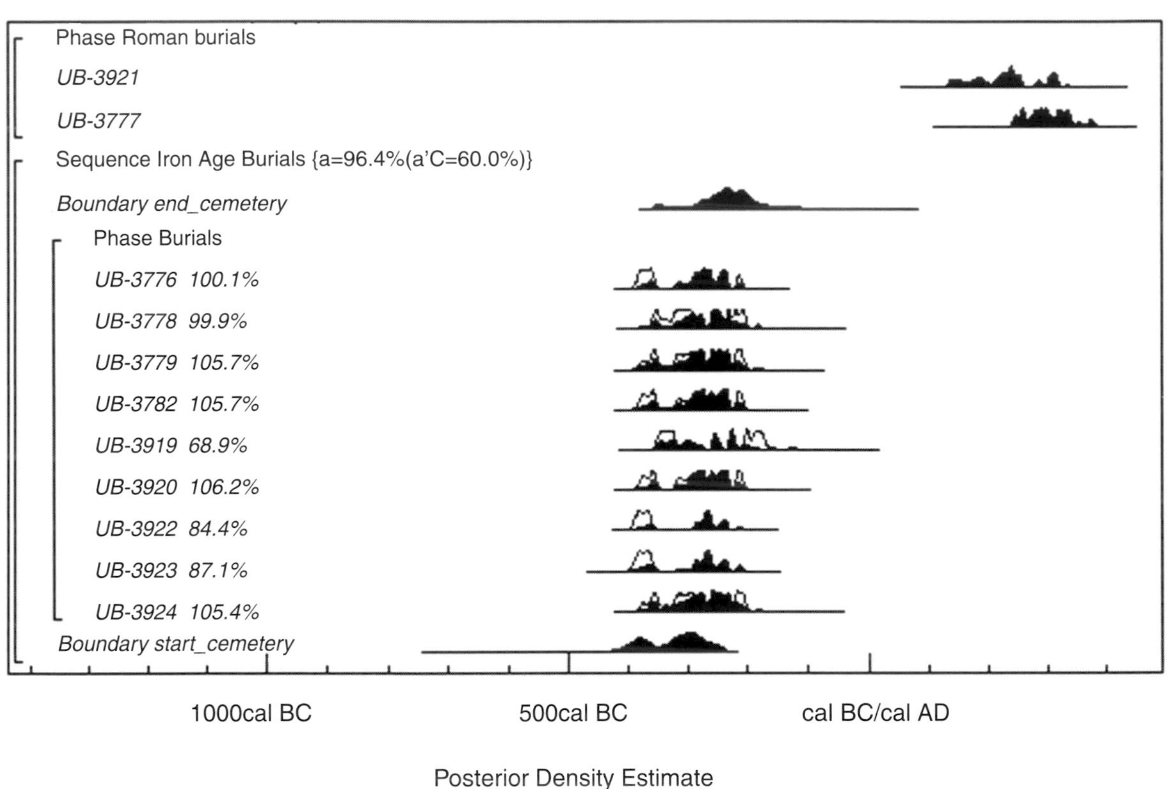

Fig. 13.1A Probability distributions of dates from the Worton Rectory Farm cemetery. Each distribution represents the relative probability that an event occurred at a particular time. For each of the dates two distributions have been plotted, one in outline, which is the result produced by the scientific evidence alone, and a solid one, which is based on the chronological model used. The large square brackets down the left-hand side along with the OxCal keywords define the overall model exactly.

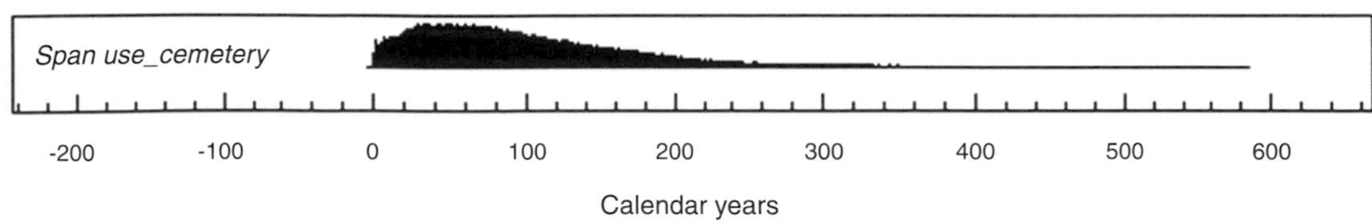

Fig. 13.1B Probability distribution of the number of years during which the cemetery was in use, derived from the model shown in Fig. 13.1A.

Phase Oxey Mead channel
OxA - 10690
OxA - 7360
500cal BC
cal BC/cal AD
500calAD
Calibrated date

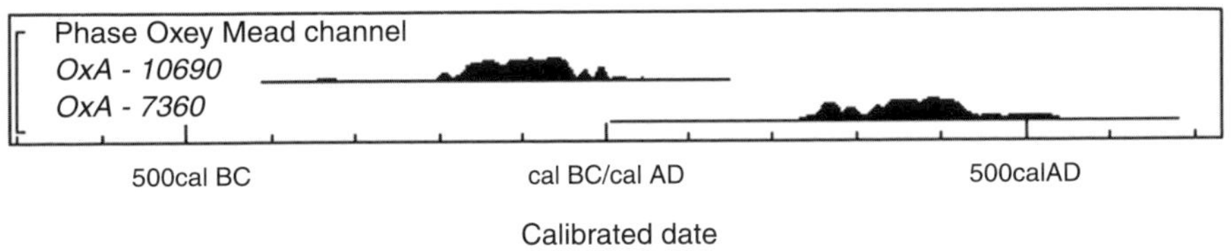

Fig. 13.2 Probability distributions of dates from Oxey Mead channel. The format is identical to Fig.13.1A. The large square brackets down the left-hand side along with the OxCal keywords define the overall model exactly.

Phase Floodplain Section A {A=96.4% (A'c=60%)}
Sequence
Boundary start_A
Phase sediments
Sequence infill
C_Date OSL-866a 105.1%
C_Date OSL-866b 100.1%
OxA-107111 100.3%
Phase S112
OxA-3644 67.4%
UB-4060 87.0%
UB-4676 112.7%
UB-4677? 0.0%
Phase L109
GU-5850? 0.0%
GU-5855? 0.0%
Phase L115
GU-5715 59.9%
GU-5716 113.7%
Phase S119
GU-5717 103.4%
GU-5718 114.4%
Phase S116
UB-4061? 0.0%
UB4062 117.2%
Phase L32
C_Date OSL-866c 116.3%
OxA-107109 100.3%
OxA-107110 95.4%
Boundary end_A
Phase trees in base of channel
OxA-10713
OxA-10739
6000calBC
4000calBC
2000calBC
cal BC/cal AD
Posterior density estimate

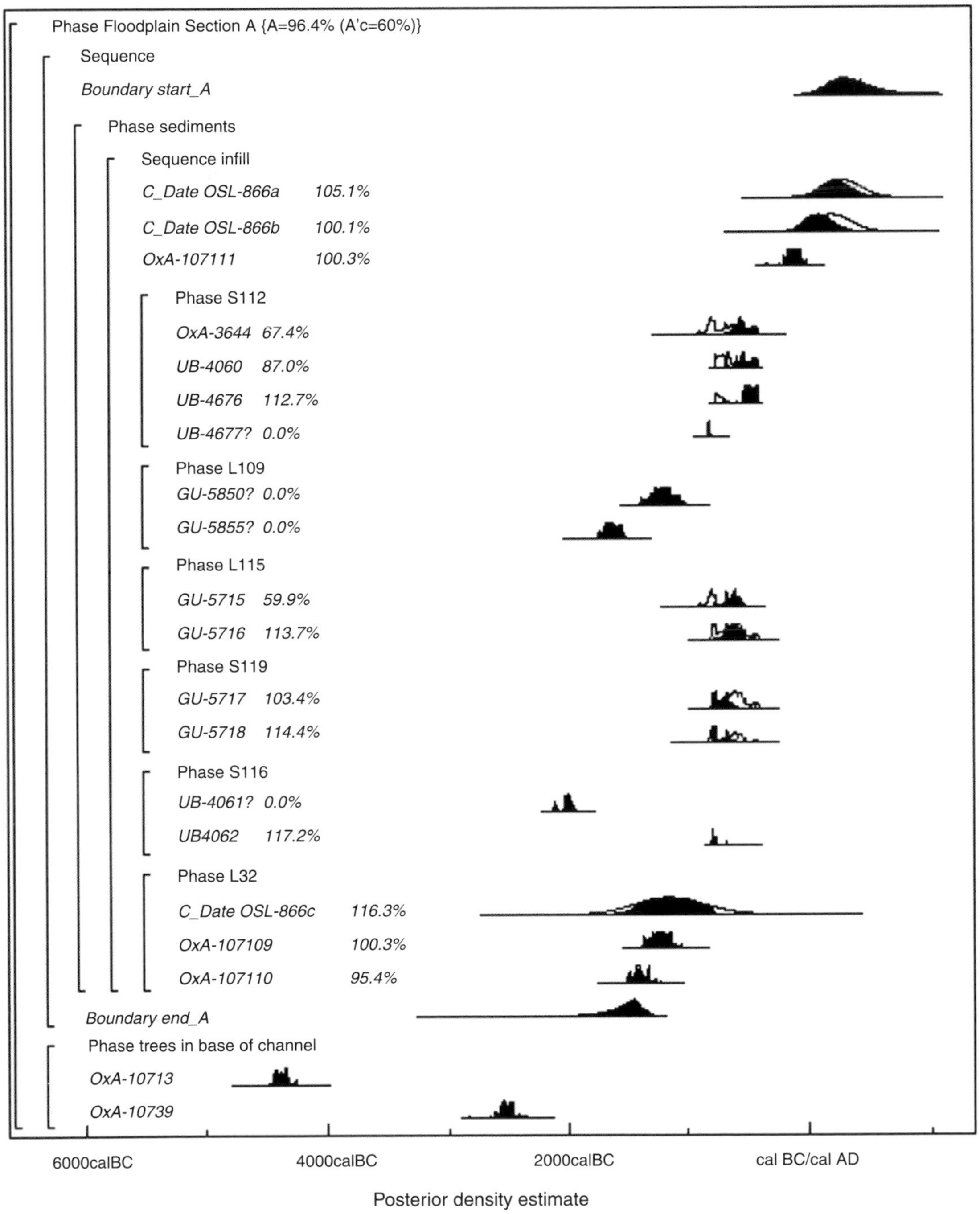

Fig. 13.3 Probability distributions of dates from Floodplain Section A. The format is identical to Fig. 13.1A. Dates followed by question mark have been calibrated (Stuiver and Reimer 1993), but not included in the chronological model for reasons explained in the text. The large square brackets down the left-hand side along with the OxCal keywords define the overall model exactly.

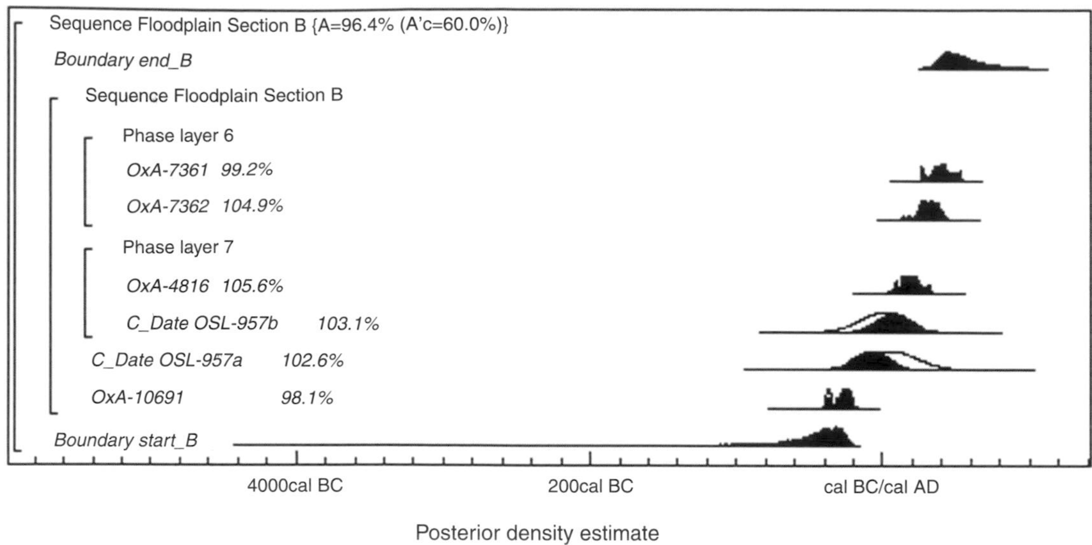

Fig. 13.4 Probability distributions of dates from Floodplain Section B. The format is identical to Fig.13.1A. The large square brackets down the left-hand side along with the OxCal keywords define the overall model exactly.

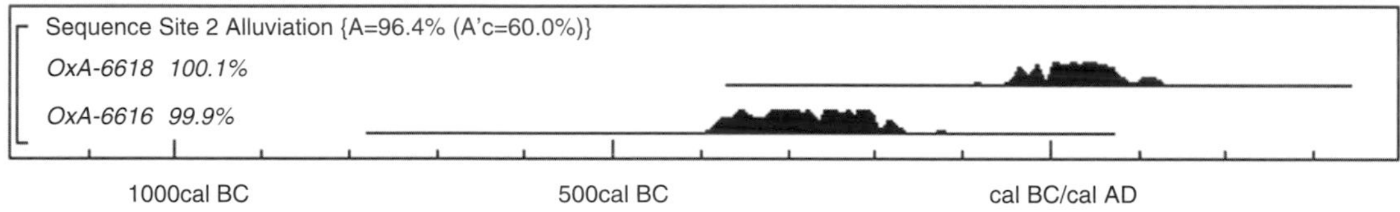

Fig. 13.5. Probability distributions of dates from the floodplain alluvium over Site 2. The format is identical to Fig. 13.1A. The large square brackets down the left-hand side along with the OxCal keywords define the overall model exactly

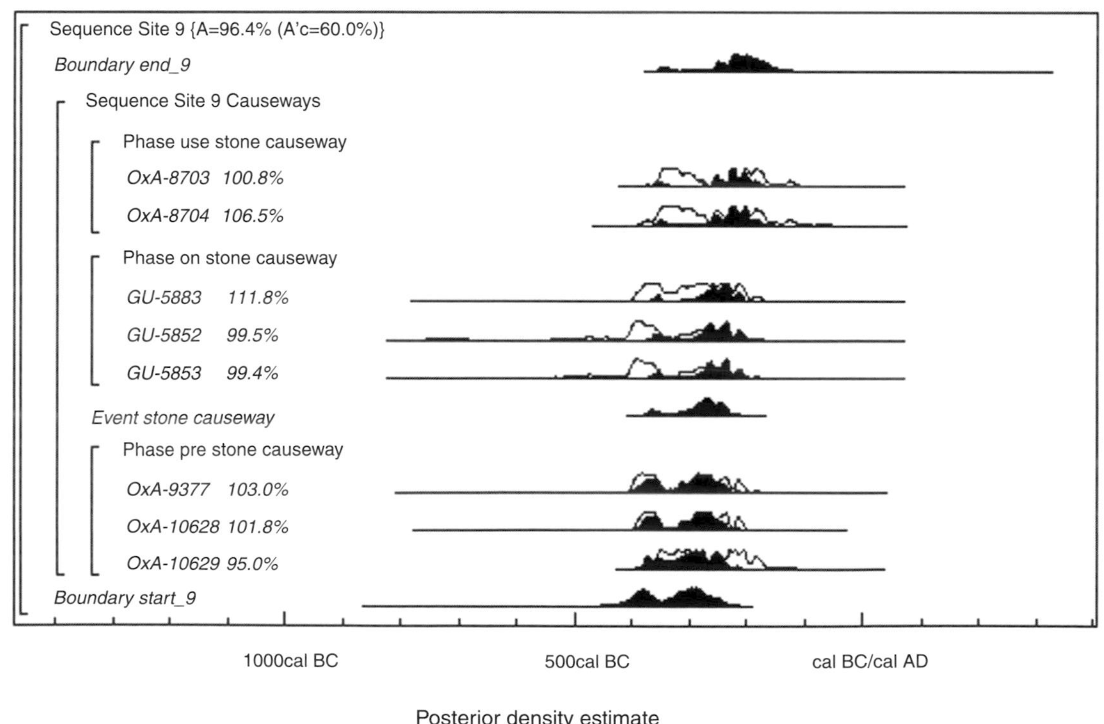

Fig. 13.6 Probability distributions of dates from the causeways on Site 9. The format is identical to Fig.13.1A. The large square brackets down the left-hand side along with the OxCal keywords define the overall model exactly.

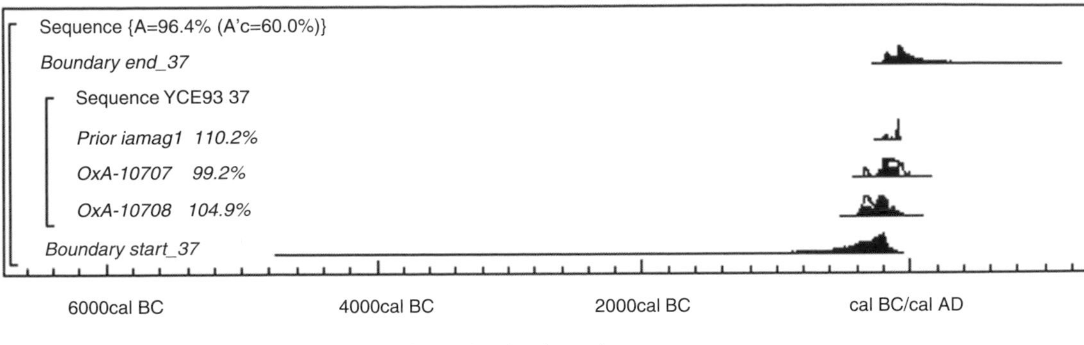

Fig. 13.7 Probability distributions of dates from Trench 37. The format is identical to Fig. 13.1A. The large square brackets down the left-hand side along with the OxCal keywords define the overall model exactly.

Table 13.2 Optically-Stimulated Luminescence measurements.

Sample number	*Context number*	*Palaeodose (Gy)*	*a-value*	*Total dose rate (Gy/ka)*	*Date (calendar years) (68% confidence)*	*Estimated date range (95% probability)*
Floodplain Section B						
957a	7	4.48 ± 0.29	0.105 ± 0.004	2.01 ± 0.14	130 BC – AD 230	
957b	8	4.47 ± 0.30	0.081 ± 0.004	2.24 ± 0.13	160 BC – AD 140	
Floodplain Section A						
866a	2/15 10	3.92 ± 0.22	0.073 ± 0.004	2.29 ± 0.15	AD 140 – 440	
866b	2/5 11	4.06 ± 0.18	0.086 ± 0.006	2.27 ± 0.16	AD 40 – 360	
866c	2/6 ?	6.27 ± 0.14	0.069 ±0.002	2.00 ± 0.16	1440 – 860 BC	

with various beta doses (90Sr–90Y source) and making short shine measurements (0.2s) after preheats of increasing duration. For each preheat time an additive growth curve was constructed and an equivalent dose (the beta dose giving rise to a luminescence signal equivalent to that of the natural signal) calculated. These equivalent doses or EDs increase in value with preheat time until the time is sufficient to remove all charge unstable over burial time. The results showed that a preheat of 4 h at 160°C was required for most samples, with sample 957b requiring only 2 h and 957e requiring 6 h.

Further aliquots were then used to construct an additive beta growth curve and a similar additive alpha growth curve (using an 241Am foil source), the previously determined preheat at 160°C being used. The beta and alpha EDs were determined by a linear fit to the growth curves. The alpha ED was used to calculate alpha particle effectiveness at creating a luminescence signal (a-value), as alpha radiation is less effective than beta.

The preheating procedure can cause transfer of charge from unbleachable to bleachable traps, which results in additional OSL signal, which must be corrected for. This is achieved by bleaching the beta growth curve aliquots then re-dosing and preheating them to construct a second growth curve from which an intercept correction is determined (Rees-Jones and Tite 1994). This correction also allows for any residual, hard to bleach signal. The intercept correction was subtracted from the ED to give the palaeodose, the radiation dose the sample has received since last bleached.

The radioactive dose received by the samples was determined by on-site gamma spectrometry, as problems were experienced in calculating the water contents of the sediments due to their high clay contents.

Results

The measured values for the palaeodose (P), a-value, and dose rate are shown in Table 13.2 together with the dates calculated. The errors quoted are at the 68% confidence level and include both random and systematic errors (Aitken 1985).

NATURAL REMANENT MAGNETISATION

by Neil Linford and Paul Linford

Sampling and measurement

Forty orientated 10 cc samples were initially recovered from the section of a heavily alluviated ditch where an organic rich black layer had accumulated at the base of the feature (Site 25, ditch segment 12012, part of ditch group 12036) (see Fig. 13.8) to investigate the magnetic properties of sediments from the site (cf Linford 1994; Linford *et al.* 2005). Measurements on these samples confirmed that, in contrast to the overlying alluvium, the organic rich layer at the base of the ditch contained a significant concentration of magnetic minerals and also retained a stable Natural Remanent Magnetisation (NRM). In an attempt to obtain a statistically more valid archaeomagnetic date from this organic rich layer a second archaeological section through the feature was cut and an additional 32 samples recovered.

The NRM of each sample was measured with a Geofysika JR5A automated spinner magnetometer. Repeat measurements were then made following the progressive removal of the NRM through triple axis AF field demagnetisation using a DTech D2000 AF demagnetiser to maximum peak field of 100mT.

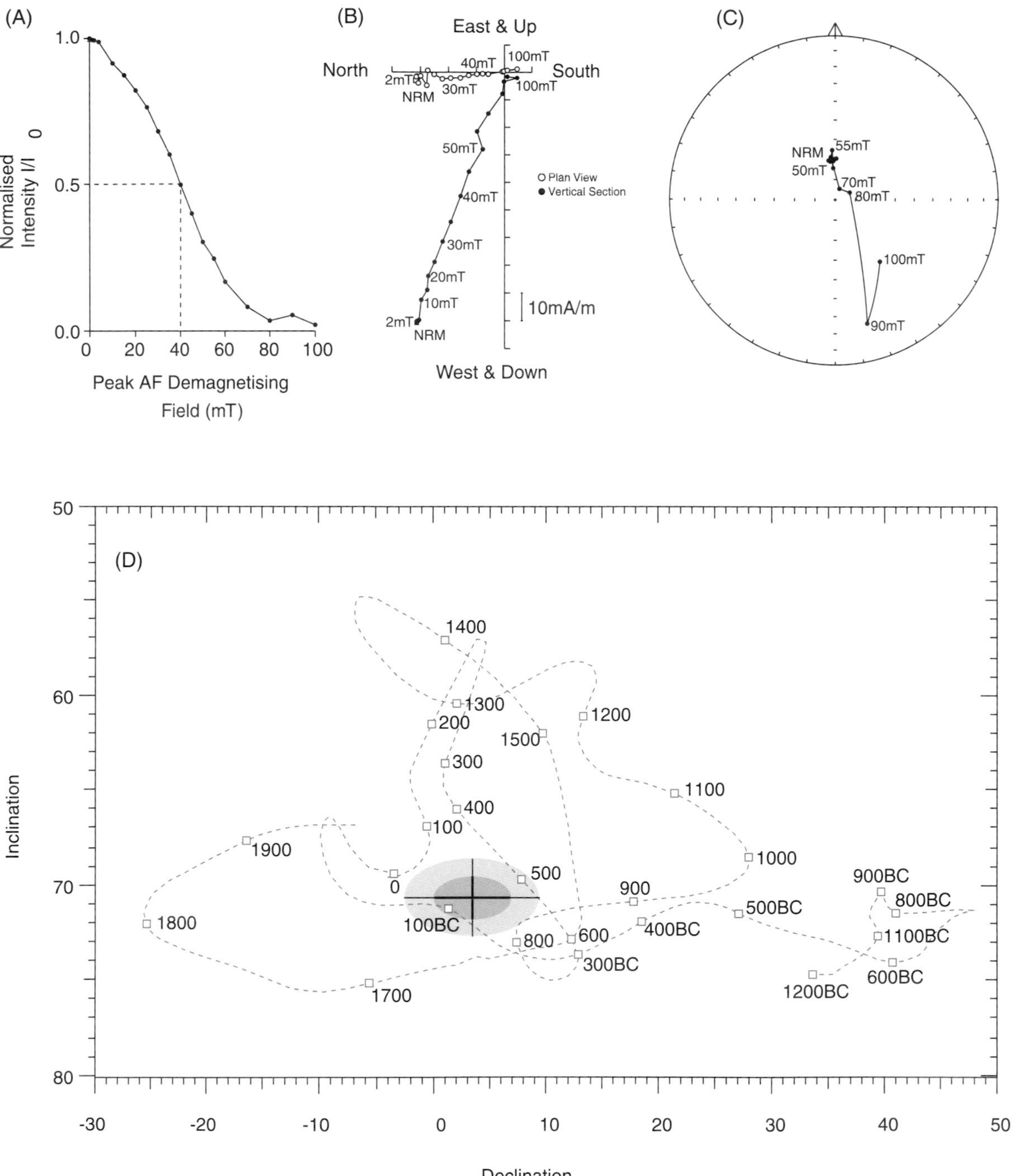

Fig. 13.8 NRM data for samples collected from the organic rich layer at the base of the alluviated ditch (section 12036). AF demagnetisation behaviour is shown for a single representative sample (BAS230) including (A) the loss of intensity and stability of remanence represented as both Zijderveld (B) and stereonet (C) projections. The lower Fig. (D) shows a graphical representation of the mean calculated from all samples superimposed over the UK archaeomagnetic calibration curve. The data suggests a date of 185 cal BC to 95cal BC at 63% confidence (215 cal BC to 85 cal BC at 95% confidence).

Determination of the archaeomagnetic date

Figure 13.8 shows the progressive demagnetisation of a representative sample (BAS230) and demonstrates the presence of a single, stable magnetisation vector. A mean direction for the magnetisation of the sediment was then calculated from similar measurements made on a total of 20 samples from ditch 12036 that were found to retain a stable magnetisation. The mean direction is shown graphically superimposed over the archaeomagnetic calibration curve for the United Kingdom (Fig 13.8 (D)) and suggests a date of 185-95 cal BC at 63% confidence (215-85 cal BC at 95% confidence).

Significance of the magnetic remanence carrier

Generally, the remanence carriers within a sediment are derived from translocated magnetic minerals from geological and soil units within the local catchment, as opposed to the formation of new magnetic material within the sediment itself. The preferential alignment of these magnetic minerals with the ambient magnetic field can certainly produce a stable NRM even under relatively turbid fluvial conditions (eg Ellis and Brown 1998).

In this case, however, additional analysis confirms the dominant NRM carriers to be a mixture of iron sulphide (most probably greigite) and bacterially derived magnetite. As the formation of both of these magnetic phases occurs only under microaerobic conditions, and usually in close association with organic matter, it is proposed that the resultant NRM is entirely post-depositional. Unlike archaeomagnetic dates derived from thermoremanent features the NRM recorded from the formation of *in situ* magnetic minerals may not, necessarily, be related to the construction or use of the feature in which the sediment has formed. In addition, the survival of greigite indicates that the sediment has been deoxygenated since the formation of the NRM, suggesting that this event was, perhaps, precipitated by a rapid change of environmental conditions, such as the onset of floodplain conditions and the sealing of the ditch cut by alluvium.

ANALYSIS AND INTERPRETATION

General approach

The approach to chronology adopted here is unashamedly interpretative. The simple date ranges provided by the various scientific dating methods are accurate estimates of the dates of the samples processed, but it is the dates of the archaeological events represented by those samples which are significant. Methodology is now available which allows us to combine the results of the scientific analyses with other information, such as stratigraphy, to produce realistic estimates of dates of archaeological interest. It should be emphasised that these distributions and ranges are not absolute, they are interpretative *estimates*, which can and will change as further data become available and as other researchers choose to model the existing data from different perspectives. These *estimated date ranges* (posterior density estimates), which combine the scientific and archaeological information, are given *in italics* to distinguish them from date ranges dependent on scientific information alone.

The technique used is a form of Markov Chain Monte Carlo sampling, and has been applied using the program OxCal v3.5 (http://units.ox.ac.uk/departments/rlaha/), which uses a mixture of the Metropolis-Hastings algorithm and the more specific Gibbs sampler (Gilks *et al.* 1996; Gelfand and Smith 1990). Details of the algorithms employed by this program are available from the on-line manual or in Bronk Ramsey (1995; 1998; 2001), and fully worked examples are given in the series of papers by Buck *et al.* (1991; 1992; 1994). The algorithms used in the models described below can be derived from the structure shown in Figures 13.1–13.7.

Specific sites

Yarnton (YWRF) cemetery

High-precision radiocarbon measurements are available from nine articulated skeletons from across the middle Iron Age inhumation cemetery, located to the east of the Iron Age settlement (Fig 13.1A). The cemetery appears to comprise two distinct groups: a northern group of fifteen individuals (of which five were dated), and a southern group with ten bodies (of which two were sampled; Hey *et al* 1999; see also Chapter 6 above). In addition, ten inhumations were 'outliers' which were scattered along the southern and eastern edge of the settlement, and two samples were derived from this group. For the purposes of the chronological model discussed here, all these burials are treated as a single group. The introduction of MCMC sampling, in particular the Metropolis-Hastings algorithm, and improved procedures for converging models since v2.18 of OxCal (Bronk Ramsey 1998; 2001), means that we have been able to remodel these data to produce absolute estimates for the date of the cemetery.

This model suggests that burial started in *420-230 cal BC (95% probability)* and ended in *290-150 cal BC (95% probability)*, spanning a period of *1-220 years (95% probability)* (Fig 13.1B; it is important to note that the chronological range in this figure is not an absolute one). It is most likely, however, that this cemetery was used for a relatively short period during the third century BC (Fig 13.1A).

Two Roman burials were also dated; one, a south-north extended inhumation of a decapitated woman, the other an extended north-south young female. Both of these were located to the south-east of the Roman settlement, and date to cal AD 240-385 (95% confidence; UB-3777) and cal AD 130-325 (95% confidence; UB-3921).

Oxey Mead

A palaeochannel sequence on Oxey Mead was dated (Section 3; Fig 13.2). The lowest organic deposit within the channel yielded a radiocarbon date of 200 cal BC-10 cal AD (95% confidence; OxA-10690). Above was greenish-brown inorganic silt (layer 3/7), which dated to the later Roman or early Saxon period (OxA-7360).

Floodplain Section A

A sequence of organic silts containing structural and dumped wood was excavated adjacent to, and south of, Yarnton Floodplain Site 1 (Figs 11.10, 11.41 and 11.42). The absolute dating information relating to the Iron Age and Roman deposits in this channel is shown in Table 13.1 and Figure 13.3.

The earliest organic silts within the channel dated to the mid to late Bronze Age (layer 32). A small wooden revetment on the southern side of the channel (structure 116) is dated to *800-760 cal BC* (*UB-4062*). A second post from this structure yielded a late Neolithic/early Bronze Age date, but must be reused in this context. On the south side of the channel, an area of collapsed wattle work was discovered, which is dated to the late Bronze Age/early Iron Age (structure 119). A period of ponding and silting followed, which appears to be of early Iron Age date on the basis of radiocarbon determinations from roundwood debris deposited in the sediments (layer 115). Further silting appears to contain redeposited wood, as GU-5850 and GU-5855 both have poor agreement with their stratigraphic positions (A=0.0% and A=0.0%; Fig 13.3; Bronk Ramsey 1995). Structure 112 was driven through these silts and has produced four statistically inconsistent radiocarbon determinations (T'=116.9; T'(5%)=7.8; df=3; Ward and Wilson 1978). UB-4677 is significantly earlier than the other three posts and is in poor agreement with its stratigraphic position (A=0.0%); it was probably reused. OxA-3644 is also slightly earlier than UB-4060 and UB-4676 (which are statistically consistent; T'=2.9; T'(5%)=3.8; df=1), and this may also have been reused, although there could be an old-wood offset as it is not known which part of the oak tree was dated. The structure appears to be early Iron Age in date. Organic silts continued to accumulate in the channel from the middle Iron Age (*OxA-10711*, layer 37; *OSL-866b*, layer 11), becoming inorganic during the Roman period (*OSL-866a*, layer 10).

The quantity of redeposited Bronze Age wood must reflect activity within this channel associated with the settlement of this date on the north bank (Site 2; Hey *et al.* forthcoming).

Floodplain Section B

The same palaeochannel was sectioned further to the west, between Floodplain Sites 2 and 4 (Figs 11.10 and 11.12). One of these sections was dated (Table 13.1; Fig 13.4). Organic sediment began to accumulate in the middle Iron Age (*OxA-10691*), and continued to build up into the early Roman period (layers 8 and 7; *OSL-957a*, *OSL-957b*, and *OxA-4816*). Slightly organic alluvium was deposited in the later Roman and, possibly, post-Roman periods (layer 6).

Site 2 (alluviation)

Inorganic alluvium began to accumulate in the surviving hollows over cut features on Site 2 in the middle Iron Age (*OxA-6616*; Fig 13.5). Overbank alluvium was deposited from the late Iron Age/early Roman period (*OxA-6618*).

Causeways: Site 9

A sequence of deposits located on Site 9 seem to represent crossing places of a palaeochannel, replaced and repaired over time. The chronological model for this activity is shown in Figure 13.6.

The earliest structure recorded here is represented by a row of stakes (OxA-10629) and associated brushwood debris (OxA-10628). This is dated to *400-340 cal BC (30% probability)* or *330-230 cal BC (65% probability)*. This was sealed by a substantial limestone causeway. A middle Bronze Age side-looped spearhead (Northover, Chapter 15) was recovered from beneath the stone of the causeway. Waterlogged plant remains packed within the socket of this spearhead were dated to *400-340 cal BC (30% probability)* or *330-230 cal BC (65% probability*; OxA-9377).

Parallel uprights and horizontal pieces were assembled along the length of the stone causeway, probably as part of its initial construction. Three samples were submitted from this structure (GU-5852; GU-5853; and GU-5883), dating it to *370-340 cal BC (10% probability)* or *320-200 cal BC (85% probability)*. A deposit of animal bone, much of which was butchered, was recovered on top of the stone causeway (OxA-8703–4). These samples produced sufficient collagen for dating, unlike all other bone so far submitted from the floodplain at Yarnton. This is probably because of the localised effect of the limestone of the causeway. They show that this activity took place between *360-320 cal BC (9% probability)* or *310-160 cal BC (86% probability)*.

It appears that this causeway was in use during the middle Iron Age, and was constructed in *380-210 cal BC (95% probability)*.

Trench 37

A boundary ditch was uncovered crossing the Cassington floodplain for a distance of some 300 m. It was recut on two occasions, and towards its southern end it approached a palaeochannel. Lower fill deposits within each cut were organic, containing waterlogged seeds. Inorganic silts and alluvium filled the upper parts of the ditch, which was sealed by Roman ploughsoil. The chronological model for this ditch is shown in Figure 13.7.

Two plant macrofossils were submitted for radiocarbon dating from successive fills of the first recut of the ditch (OxA-10708 and OxA-10707). These suggest that this recut occurred in *370-110 cal BC (95% probability)*. At this time conditions in the ditch, although waterlogged, were slightly aerobic (as shown by snails of flowing water species). The formation of greigite, dated by the NRM (see Linford and Linford above), demonstrates that these deposits had become deoxygenated by *205-105 cal BC (42% probability)* or *95-75 cal BC (53% probability)*. It seems most likely that the creation of the greigite occurred when the deposits in the ditch became compressed as a result of alluviation in this area.

It should be noted that this alluviation probably occurred slightly later than the earliest alluviation on Site 2 (see above). This is to be expected as Site 2 is more low lying.

Chapter 14: The Iron Age and Roman Pottery

by Paul Booth with contributions by Edward Biddulph, Alistair Barclay and M S Copley, R Berstan, S N Dudd and R P Evershed

GENERAL INTRODUCTION

The excavations and other fieldwork in the Yarnton area produced some 361.5 kg of Iron Age and Roman pottery, principally from the two major excavated sites of Cresswell Field and Yarnton (Worton Rectory Farm). Small amounts of pottery were recovered from a number of other locations within the Yarnton project area, some of which are referred to individually below (Table 14.1).

Analysis focused on the two main assemblages. These were recorded separately, all the material, including unstratified sherds but excluding the fieldwalking material, being quantified. The pottery from Yarnton was subject to a fairly detailed post-excavation assessment in 1991 in which all the later prehistoric and Roman pottery from the site was examined. The material covered a wide chronological range, with important early, middle and late Iron Age and Roman groups, the Roman material covering the entire period. The pottery from Cresswell Field was scanned much more briefly

Table 14.1 Summary of pottery recovered across the various Yarnton interventions.

Site	Iron Age No.	Iron Age Wt (g.)	Roman No.	Roman Wt (g.)
Fieldwalking				
YAFW90	4	12	47	269
CWRF90	10	64	992	6442
YWCF90	47	449	9	79
YWRF90	5	44	102	974
YMF90	-	-	12	102
Evaluation (except Yarnton and Cresswell Field)				
YRCA90	-	-	3	266
A40 90 and 91	249	2981	13	88
YCE93	42	226	507	6180
YRP96	171	3129	8	378
Floodplain sites				
All sites	6	32	96	989
Main excavations				
Cresswell Field	6240	95,330	32	432
Yarnton	4766	72,108	8896	170,953
TOTAL	11,540	174,375	10,717	187,152

prior to detailed recording. The majority of this material was of early Iron Age date, with a smaller middle Iron Age component. Late Iron Age and Roman activity was essentially lacking here. The late Bronze Age material was recorded by Alistair Barclay. The slightly arbitrary nature of this division, particularly with regard to the distinction between late Bronze Age and early Iron Age material, is acknowledged, but reflects the division of work on the overall Yarnton project between the Neolithic and Bronze Age components, focused largely on the floodplain (Hey *et al.* forthcoming), and the Iron Age and later elements located mainly on the Second Gravel Terrace. Material related to those earlier periods is not considered here. The Iron Age and Roman pottery was recorded using a unified system for such material routinely employed by OA on a variety of sites since 1990. The object of such a recording system is to allow comparability of results between different assemblages through the use of standardised codes for fabrics, wares, vessel types and other characteristics. Such an approach is particularly applicable in the Roman period, with its more standardised products, but also has some validity for the Iron Age.

The pottery from the two principal site assemblages was recorded by individual context group. Details of fabric, ware (for the Roman period), vessel type, rim form and surface treatment/ decoration were all recorded using standardised codes. Manufacture was not considered in detail beyond the simple division between wheelthrown and handmade fabrics. Information relating to condition, sooting, reuse and repair etc was also noted. Quantification was by sherd count and weight, rim count (eliminating duplicate rims of a single vessel where these could be identified) and rim percent (EVEs – strictly rim equivalents). The records were entered onto a DBase database. Detailed recording of the Yarnton pottery was carried out in 1993, and that for Cresswell Field in 1996. Attempts were made to ensure consistency of recording between the two assemblages, but given the time lag between the two phases of work there were inevitably some differences of emphasis in recording. Where significant these are referred to below.

As noted above, all the pottery from the two main excavated areas was recorded at the same level of detail regardless of the nature of its context or the size of the context assemblage. This contrasts for example with the approach followed within the region at Gravelly Guy (Stanton Harcourt), where the pottery was divided into three levels for analysis, dependent largely on group size (Duncan *et al.* 2004). The combined Yarnton and Cresswell Field assemblage was considerably smaller than that from Gravelly Guy and its constituent groups were also generally smaller (see below), so that exclusion of small groups from consideration would have seriously compromised understanding of the assemblage as a whole (to which even unstratified material can contribute significantly) and would have made phasing of many features, already problematical, effectively impossible.

Certain aspects of the pottery, such as fabric types, are treated on a project wide basis. Elsewhere, aspects of the analysis depend on the contrast between the Cresswell Field and Yarnton assemblages, particularly with regard to discussion of the chronology of the Iron Age phases of the site.

Pottery from components of the Yarnton project such as fieldwalking (see Chapter 11 above) is not treated in detail here. Some of the material from the evaluation at Cassington West and the floodplain site excavations is noted briefly below by Alistair Barclay, but most of this material will be presented in detail in the report on the earlier prehistoric parts of the project (Hey *et al.* forthcoming).

Recovery

In both Yarnton and Cresswell Field assemblages the recorded material included pottery from evaluation trenches dug across these sites. The Yarnton assemblage also included pottery from a gridded surface collection carried out during initial hand cleaning of the site, whereas material derived from the comparable stage of work at Cresswell Field was assigned to general collection numbers or, more commonly, associated with the discrete features from which much of this material could be seen to be derived. Additionally, pottery recovered from sieved soil samples at Yarnton was recorded and included in the main database for this site, while this was not done for Cresswell Field. The material from the Yarnton samples amounted to 213 early-middle Iron Age sherds (2247 g) and 115 late Iron Age and Roman sherds (749 g). While the average sherd weights for these groups are rather less than those for the site as a whole it is clear that more than just very small sherds were present in these samples. Hand recovery of sherds from the material selected for sampling was therefore not rigorous prior to sieving here (though it was in contexts which were not sieved), whereas in the material examined from Cresswell Field (but not recorded in detail and added to the database) sherds from sieved residues were almost invariably small fragments, many of which would have eluded normal recovery by hand on site. No contexts were sieved specifically to examine the question of recovery rates of artefacts. The inclusion of data from sieved residues from Yarnton and its exclusion at Cresswell Field is not considered (in view of the relatively small quantities involved, see above) to have produced significant disparities in the two data sets.

Assemblage size

As already noted, most of the individual context assemblages were quite small. Of some 2375 context groups containing Iron Age and Roman pottery from the two areas (some of which were of post-Roman date), *c* 1590 (almost 67%) weighed less than 100 g. Although some interventions in features generated multiple context groups from the same feature, many features produced relatively small quantities of pottery, and only rarely was it possible to augment particular assemblages by complete excavation of fills. Therefore, in contrast to sites such as Gravelly Guy, where most pits were completely excavated and feature assemblages were thus often larger, there was very little scope for selectivity in terms of prioritisation of groups for examination. Only 154 context groups (6.5% of the total) were of more than 500 g, the cut-off point defined at Gravelly Guy for those Iron Age groups meriting full scale recording (Duncan *et al.* 2004). More groups from Cresswell Field (9.2%) fell into this category than from Yarnton (only 5.7%). It is recognised that the small group sizes pose problems for accurate assessment of the date of such groups in the study area sites, particularly with regard to the possibility that small groups could consist entirely of residual material and thus provide misleadingly early dates for some features. This presents a particular problem in the Iron Age, where questions of dating can hinge on the relative proportions of specific fabric types (see further below). The relative scarcity of statistically viable groups has meant that a number of assemblages could not be assigned specifically to the early or middle Iron Age with confidence. This problem has been considered carefully, however, and stratigraphic and spatial information has been widely used in determining the phasing of the site. While there are almost certainly instances where discrete features have been assigned on ceramic evidence to an earlier phase than should have been the case, it is believed that the broad phasing of both Yarnton and Cresswell Field can be regarded with reasonable confidence.

One further characteristic of the group sizes from Cresswell Field and Yarnton merits comment. It can be seen from Table 14.2 that the cumulative frequency of different group sizes for the two sites is almost identical. At the top of the size range, however, it is notable that more very large groups occurred at Cresswell Field, despite the fact that this site had substantially fewer individual groups (the differences between the recording systems employed in the excavation of the two sites cannot be invoked to explain this). More significantly, while the few large groups at Yarnton were all of early Roman date, the six largest context groups

Table 14.2 Size of Iron Age and later pottery context groups in the main Yarnton sites.

	Yarnton		Cresswell Field		TOTAL	
Context assemblage wt (g)	No. contexts with pottery	% contexts with pottery	No. contexts with pottery	% contexts with pottery	No. contexts with pottery	% contexts with pottery
1-99	1245	67.1	345	66.5	1590	66.9
100-199	278	15.0	66	12.7	344	14.5
200-299	121	6.5	31	6.0	152	6.4
300-399	65	3.5	16	3.1	77	3.2
400-499	41	2.2	13	2.5	54	2.3
500-599	28	1.5	11	2.1	39	1.6
600-699	22	1.2	8	1.5	30	1.3
700-799	14	0.8	7	1.3	21	0.9
800-899	6	0.3	3	0.6	9	0.4
900-999	7	0.4	2	0.4	9	0.4
1000-1099	7	0.4	1	0.2	8	0.3
1100-1199	2	0.1	1	0.2	3	0.1
1200-1299	6	0.3	2	0.4	8	0.3
1300-1399	2	0.1	3	0.6	5	0.2
1400-1499	4	0.2			4	0.2
1500-1599	1	0.1	3	0.6	4	0.2
1600-1699	2	0.1			2	0.1
1700-1799	1	0.1	1	0.2	2	0.1
1800-1899						
1900-1999	1	0.1			1	+
2000-2999	2	0.1	2	0.4	4	0.2
3000-3999			2	0.4	2	0.1
4000-4999	1	0.1	2	0.4	3	0.1
TOTAL	1856		519		2375	

from Cresswell Field, ranging from 2.7-4.2 kg, were all of the early Iron Age and appear to indicate a distinct category of deposition, with abnormally large amounts of pottery. These groups are discussed further below.

Condition

The soil types in feature fills were generally fairly light, which aided pottery recovery, and were also conducive to the preservation of sherds. The pottery was therefore for the most part in good condition, with surfaces quite well-preserved and with relatively little abrasion. This was often the case regardless of sherd size, so that small sherds were typically very similar in appearance to larger ones. While it is evident that redeposition did occur widely on the site, particularly at Yarnton, where intercutting features were more prevalent, there was little clear evidence that presumed or definitely residual material was significantly more worn than that considered to be contemporary with the fills of particular features. Increased wear was not, therefore, a helpful guide in determining the degree of residuality. The reasons for this are not clear, but it may be that redeposition, while widespread, was in most cases an occasional rather than a continual process. In a limited number of cases a marked difference in the degree of wear within individual contexts was seen, but in almost all of these examples the heavily worn sherd or sherds were *later* in date than the context group in question and had clearly become worn and been deposited in the tops of feature fills as a result of plough action, probably of relatively recent date.

Fabrics and wares

Two distinct methods of categorisation of fabrics are employed side by side in the OA system. For prehistoric material, definition of fabrics is in terms of the two most common inclusion types (for which alphabetic codes are used, eg AS for quartz sand and shell), in order of importance, with a numeric indicator of the coarseness of the fabric (on a scale of 1 (very fine) to 5 (very coarse)).

Ware codes, which can act as labels rather than being strictly descriptive, are more appropriate to the standardised Romanised products of the late 1st century AD onwards and provide a convenient method of grouping fabrics by common major characteristics which are defined by a letter (eg S = samian ware, F = fine wares, O = oxidised coarse wares etc). These major ware groups are then divided numerically into subgroups and individual wares (eg major British colour-coated fine wares would be F50; within that group Oxfordshire colour-coated ware would be F51). The advantage of this system is that wares with common characteristics can be grouped together easily for the purposes of analysis, and definition can operate hierarchically at one of a number of levels of precision, as appropriate.

The use of fabric and ware codes side by side allows flexibility in examining multi-period assemblages. The Roman ware coding system relies in part on the recognition of well known products, some of which may incorporate a wider range of material than would strictly share the same fabric definition. In contrast the fabric coding system used here is most appropriate for pottery whose production was less standardised than in the later Roman period. The two classification systems can be used side by side, however, with useful results. This approach has been followed at Yarnton for the pottery of the late Iron Age/early Roman period, which marks an important ceramic transition from traditions of generally quite localised and ill-defined production to the appearance of more clearly centralised sources with definable products. The implementation of this system was helpful in terms of understanding developing trends in fabrics in this period, a problem of particular significance for the Oxford region.

Initial sorting of fabrics/wares was done by eye, with subsequent use of a binocular microscope at x20 magnification to define the inclusion types of individual sherds and allow comparison with type sherds in the Roman ware type series. In effect, all pre-Roman and many of the Roman sherds were checked under the microscope. For the purposes of presentation of the results the later prehistoric and Roman pottery was divided into two groups; early-middle Iron Age ('Iron Age') and late Iron Age-Roman ('Roman').

IRON AGE POTTERY

Some 11,006 sherds (167.438 kg, 1127 'vessels', 57.93 EVEs) of Iron Age date were recovered from the excavations. Of this total, 4766 sherds were from Yarnton. In a number of respects the Cresswell Field and Yarnton assemblages were very similar, despite their different chronological emphases and the greater degree of redeposition evident at Yarnton. The latter assemblage formed a remarkably consistent proportion of the whole, by all measures (43.3% sherd count, 43.1% weight, 43.1% vessel count (based on rim sherds) and 43.7% EVEs). The Yarnton and Cresswell Field average sherd weights (15.1 g and 15.3 g respectively) and average representation of rim circumference per vessel (ie EVEs divided by vessel count, 5.2% and 5.1% respectively) were also very close. This suggests that the patterns of use, discard and subsequent fragmentation were very similar in the two halves of the site, which is surprising in view of their rather different characters. This question is considered further below in relation to the types of contexts from which the pottery derived.

Fabrics

Fabrics were defined in terms of the two most common inclusion types and an indicator of fineness, as mentioned above. The definition of fabrics using this system does not necessarily serve to identify production sources, since these are generally unknown for Iron Age material within the region. Nor does it automatically follow that identically coded sherds were from the same (unknown) source, merely that their makers exploited very similar clay and tempering resources, indicating a uniformity of potting tradition. The range of inclusion types utilised was broad, but most would have been widely available or have occurred naturally in common clay sources in the region. Few, therefore, and none of the most commonly occurring ones, are diagnostic of specific source areas within or outside the Upper Thames region. The range of inclusion types present, and their identifying letters, were as follows:

A – quartz sand.
B – glauconitic sand.
C – calcareous sand/grit.
F – flint.
G – grog.
I – oxide minerals, mainly iron oxides.
L – limestone.
M – mica.
N – none visible.
P – clay pellets.
Q – large angular quartz(ite).
R – rock – various (includes igneous etc).
S – shell (usually fossil).
U – ironstone ooliths.
V – vegetable/organic (sometimes voids).
W – uncertain white inclusions.
X – bone.
Z – indeterminate voids.

A substantial number of fabrics contained more than two inclusion types, but it was only rarely felt that these were particularly significant in terms of characterisation of the fabric, in which cases additional inclusion types were noted. Such occurrences were most common in the early Iron Age.

All the material recorded here was handmade, wheel throwing being introduced in the late Iron Age/early Roman phase of the site. Details of manufacture and surface treatment (apart from decoration) were not systematically recorded, but the only building technique noted frequently was coil or ring construction. Smoothing and knife trimming were occasionally employed as finishing techniques, but only those techniques with a decorative aspect (including burnishing) were recorded systematically. These are discussed further below.

Full quantification of the Iron Age fabrics is presented in Table 14.3, together with an indication of the vessel types present in each fabric. Separate quantification of the pottery from the two component sites can be found in the project archive.

Table 14.3 Quantification of Iron Age fabrics (Yarnton and Cresswell Field combined)

Fabric	No.sh	.%	Wt. (g.)	%	MV - rims	%	EVEs	%	TYPES
AA4*	1	+	4	+					
AC2*	1	+	6	+					
AC3	41	0.4	726	0.4	5	0.4	0.18	0.3	C, **CA**, **CB (3)**
AC4*	3	+	41	+	1	0.1	0.03	0.1	C
AF3	6	0.1	25	+					
AF4*	2	+	8	+					
AG2#	3	+	14	+	1	0.1	0.06	0.1	C
AG3	79	0.7	827	0.5	6	0.5	0.26	0.4	C **(6)**, CS, CT
AG4	20	0.2	249	0.1	3	0.3	0.27	0.5	C **(2)**, **CB**
AI2	12	0.1	64	+	1	0.1	0.02	+	C, CT
AI3	19	0.2	255	0.2	4	0.4	0.25	0.4	C **(2)**, **CB (2)**
AI4*	3	+	25	+					
AL3	20	0.2	322	0.2	2	0.2	0.09	0.2	**CB**, **Z**
AL4	28	0.3	431	0.3	3	0.3	0.09	0.2	C **(2)**, **CB**
AM2	9	0.1	55	+					
AM3	9	0.1	140	0.1	1	0.1	0.07	0.1	C, CT
AM4*	1	+	19	+					
AN2	200	1.8	2146	1.3	25	2.2	0.92	1.6	**C (14)**, **CB (4)**, **CG**, CS, **CT**, **D (3)**, **H**, **Z**
AN3	360	3.3	6612	3.9	39	3.5	2.69	4.6	**C (8)**, **CB (20)**, **CS**, **CT**, **D (5)**, **HC**, **HG (3)**
AN4*	4	+	23	+					
AP2	73	0.7	812	0.5	9	0.8	0.37	0.6	**C (7)**, **CB (2)**, CS
AP3	220	2.0	3273	2.0	28	2.5	1.63	2.8	**C (17)**, **CA**, **CB (4)**, CS, **CT**, **D (2)**, **HC**, **HG**, **Z**
AP4*	2	+	53	+	1	0.1	0.09	0.2	**C**
AP5*	3	+	61	+					
AQ3	14	0.1	102	0.1					
AQ4*	9	0.1	120	0.1	1	0.1	0.02	+	**CB**
AR4*	1	+	4	+					
AS2	38	0.3	291	0.2	4	0.4	0.10	0.2	**C (3)**, **CB**, CT
AS3	517	4.7	6883	4.1	61	5.4	2.92	5.0	**C (36)**, **CB (10)**, **CH**, **CS**, **CT (7)**, **D (2)**, **HD**, **HG**, **Z (2)**
AS4	76	0.7	1097	0.7	6	0.5	0.57	1.0	C, CA, **CB (4)**, CT
AS5*	2	+	15	+					
AU3#	4	+	42	+					
AV2	47	0.4	427	0.3	4	0.4	0.18	0.3	**C (2)**, **CB**, **D**
AV3	394	3.6	7484	4.5	47	4.2	3.01	5.2	**C (20)**, **CA**, **CB (19)**, **CT**, **D (3)**, **HC**, **HG (2)**
AV4	15	0.1	262	0.2	1	0.1	0.05	0.1	**C**
AV5	2	+	71	+					
AW2*	1	+	4	+					
AW3*	2	+	17	+					
AZ2	5	+	52	+					
AZ3	55	0.5	674	0.4	3	0.3	0.15	0.3	**CB**, **CS**, **I**
AZ4*	5	+	35	+					
A SUBTOTAL	2306	21.0	33771	20.2	256	22.7	14.02	24.2	
BM3*	1	+	8	+					
CA3	38	0.3	331	0.2	4	0.4	0.13	0.2	**C (3)**, CS, **CT**
CA4	56	0.5	782	0.5	2	0.2	0.06	0.1	**CB**, HG, **Z**
CA5*	2	+	24	+					
CG3#	11	0.1	202	0.1					
CG4	76	0.7	134	0.1	1	0.1	0.07	0.1	**CB**
CL3#	1	+	10	+					
CM3*	1	+	14	+	1	0.1	0.08	0.1	**CB**
CM4*	2	+	14	+					
CN3	15	0.1	99	0.1	3	0.3	0.07	0.1	**C (3)**
CN4	90	0.8	1355	0.8	13	1.2	0.77	1.3	**C (4)**, **CB (8)**, **D**
CN5*	6	0.1	142	0.1	2	0.2	0.14	0.2	**CB (2)**

Table 14.3 Quantification of Iron Age fabrics (Yarnton and Cresswell Field combined) (continued)

Fabric	*No.sh*	*.%*	*Wt. (g.)*	*%*	*MV - rims*	*%*	*EVEs*	*%*	*TYPES*
CP3#	4	+	249	0.1	1	0.1	0.07	0.1	**CG**
CP4	5	+	59	+					
CQ3#	1	+	10	+	1	0.1	0.03	0.1	C
CR4*	1	+	6	+					
CS3	22	0.2	216	0.1	4	0.4	0.16	0.3	**C (4)**
CS4	86	0.8	1266	0.8	10	0.9	0.43	0.7	**C (4), CB (5)**, CT, **D**
CS5	16	0.1	252	0.2	1	0.1	0.07	0.1	**C**
CV3	8	0.1	126	0.1	1	0.1	0.03	0.1	**C**, CT
CV4	25	0.2	288	0.2	2	0.2	0.08	0.1	**C (2)**
CV5	5	+	121	0.1	3	0.3	0.18	0.3	**CB (2), HG**
CZ3#	1	+	3	+					
CZ4	11	0.1	77	+					
CZ5*	1	+	10	+					
C SUBTOTAL	415	3.8	5790	3.5	49	4.3	2.37	4.1	
FA4	5	+	69	+	1	0.1	0.04	0.1	C
FM4*	3	+	15	+					
FN4*	3	+	29	+					
FQ5*	1	+	4	+	1	0.1	0.03	0.1	C
FV4	3	+	19	+					
FV5*	1	+	4	+					
F SUBTOTAL	16	0.1	140	0.1	2	0.2	0.07	0.1	
GA3	21	0.2	160	0.1	7	0.6	0.30	0.5	**C (5)**, CS, **I, Z**
GA4	25	0.2	287	0.2	2	0.2	0.09	0.2	**C, CS**
GA5*	2	+	65	+					
GF4#	1	+	7	+					
GI4#	1	+	4	+					
GL4#	2	+	11	+					
GL5*	1	+	27	+	1	0.1	0.09	0.2	**CB**
GM4#	1	+	9	+					
GN4*	1	+	7	+					
GP3#	1	+	3	+					
GQ4*	1	+	2	+					
GQ5*	1	+	5	+					
GS3	38	0.3	258	0.2	9	0.8	0.34	0.6	**C (6), CB, CS, CT**
GS4	92	0.8	2981	1.8	10	0.9	1.78	3.1	**C (3), CB, CS (4), CT, HD**
GS5	4	+	97	0.1					
GV3	6	0.1	81	+	1	0.1	0.02	+	**CB**
GV4	4	+	53	+	1	0.1	0.08	0.1	
GV5*	3	+	27	+					
GZ3#	21	0.2	188	0.1	2	0.2	0.12	0.2	CS, **CT, HC**
GZ4#	7	0.1	58	+					
G SUBTOTAL	233	2.1	945	0.6	33	2.9	2.82	4.9	
LA3	32	0.3	276	0.2	5	0.4	0.29	0.5	**C (3), CB (2)**, CS, CT
LA4	120	1.1	1612	1.0	10	0.9	0.61	1.1	**C (2), CB (6), CS, Z**
LA5	28	0.3	428	0.3	5	0.4	0.13	0.2	**C (3), CB (2)**
LC4	10	0.1	198	0.1	1	0.1	0.03	0.1	**C**
LC5*	2	+	19	+					
LG3#	10	0.1	141	0.1	1	0.1	0.10	0.2	**CB**, CT
LG4	14	0.1	196	0.1	2	0.2	0.03	0.1	**C, CB**
LN3#	2	+	10	+	1	0.1	0.02	+	**C**
LN4	31	0.3	242	0.1	3	0.3	0.10	0.2	**C, CB (2)**
LN5*	9	0.1	254	0.2	2	0.2	0.14	0.2	**C, CB**
LP3#	1	+	2	+					

Table 14.3 Quantification of Iron Age fabrics (Yarnton and Cresswell Field combined) (continued)

Fabric	No.sh	.%	Wt. (g.)	%	MV - rims	%	EVEs	%	TYPES
LP4	8	0.1	160	0.1	1	0.1	0.05	0.1	C, CS
LP5*	3	+	60	+					
LS3	29	0.3	280	0.2	1	0.1	0.04	0.1	C, CT
LS4	62	0.6	889	0.5	5	0.4	0.18	0.3	C (3), CB, CS, CT
LS5	32	0.3	803	0.5	5	0.4	0.33	0.6	C, CB (4)
LV3#	4	+	30	+	2	0.2	0.09	0.2	C, CB
LV4	44	0.4	631	0.4	3	0.3	0.10	0.2	C, CB (2)
LV5	22	0.2	357	0.2	2	0.2	0.36	0.6	CA, HG
LZ3#	2	+	10	+	1	0.1	0.03	0.1	C
LZ4	7	0.1	139	0.1					
L SUBTOTAL	472	4.3	6737	4.0	50	4.4	2.65	4.6	
PA3	10	0.1	125	0.1	1	0.1	0.03	0.1	C
PA4	4	+	31	+	1	0.1	0.01	+	CB
PS3*	1	+	6	+					
PS4	3	+	35	+	1	0.1	0.03	0.1	C
PS5*	2	+	22	+					
PV4*	1	+	6	+	1	0.1	0.05	0.1	D
PZ3#	2	+	6	+					
PZ4	3	+	21	+					
P SUBTOTAL	26	0.2	252	0.2	4	0.4	0.12	0.2	
QA3	3	+	11	+					
QA4	5	+	32	+	1	0.1	0.07	0.1	C
QA5*	1	+	9	+					
QG3#	1	+	4	+					
QG4*	1	+	8	+					
QP4*	1	+	2	+					
QR4*	1	+	6	+					
QS3#	5	+	39	+					
QS4*	1	+	15	+					
QS5*	1	+	8	+					
QV4*	1	+	3	+	1	0.1	0.01	+	Z
QZ4*	1	+	2	+					
QZ5*	1	+	5	+					
Q SUBTOTAL	23	0.2	144	0.1	2	0.2	0.08	0.1	
RA4*	1	+	11	+					
SA3	598	5.4	5351	3.2	83	7.4	3.76	6.5	C (64), CA, CB (9), CS (2), CT (6), MD
SA4	1556	14.1	23928	14.3	142	12.6	6.99	12.1	C (95), CB (21), CS (9), CT (8), D, H, HC (3), HG, MD, Z
SA5	862	7.8	21085	12.6	67	5.9	3.68	6.4	C (45), CA (4), CB (12), CS (4), CT, D, Z
SC3	28	0.3	240	0.1	6	0.5	0.34	0.6	C (4), CT, D
SC4	150	1.4	1537	0.9	22	2.0	0.77	1.3	C (4), CB (6), CS, D (2)
SC5	138	1.3	2570	1.5	18	1.6	0.79	1.3	C (11), CB (5), CS, D
SF3#	1	+	5	+					
SG3	438	4.8	4067	2.4	64	5.7	3.28	5.7	C (46), CB, CS (6), CT (9), Z (2)
SG4	1064	9.7	13721	8.2	84	7.5	4.26	7.4	C (63), CB (5), CG, CS (8), CT (4), D, Z (2)
SG5	262	2.4	5253	3.1	12	1.1	0.49	0.8	C (11), CB, CS, CT
SI3#	2	+	7	+					
SI4	11	0.1	160	0.1	1	0.1	0.02	+	C
SI5	5	+	91	0.1					
SL3#	13	0.1	94	0.1	5	0.4	0.18	0.3	C (3), CS, CT
SL4	115	1.0	1382	0.8	12	1.1	0.40	0.7	C (11), CS, CT
SL5	199	1.8	3911	2.3	18	1.6	1.35	2.3	C (12), CA, CB (3), CE

Table 14.3 Quantification of Iron Age fabrics (Yarnton and Cresswell Field combined) (continued)

Fabric	*No.sh*	*.%*	*Wt. (g.)*	*%*	*MV - rims*	*%*	*EVEs*	*%*	*TYPES*
SN3#	3	+	11	+					
SN4	136	1.3	1674	1.0	12	1.1	0.55	0.9	**C (11), CB,** CS
SN5	352	3.2	6823	4.1	21	1.9	1.19	2.1	**C (16), CS (4), Z**
SP3	81	0.7	651	0.4	9	0.8	0.38	0.7	**C (7),** CS, **CT (2)**
SP4	514	4.7	7308	4.4	68	6.0	2.90	5.0	**C (54), CB (3), CS (2), CT (5), Z (4)**
SP5	582	5.3	11705	7.00	54	4.8	2.60	4.5	**C (46), CA, CB (2), CS (3), H, Z**
SQ3#	1	+	13	+					
SQ4	4	+	31	+					
SQ5*	5	+	33	+					
SU5#	1	+	5	+					
SV3	20	0.2	109	0.1	2	0.2	0.05	0.1	C, CS, **Z**
SV4	91	0.8	968	0.6	7	0.6	0.28	0.5	**C (5), CS, Z**
SV5	99	0.9	1591	1.0	11	1.0	0.49	0.8	**C (9), CB, Z**
SZ3#	5	+	69	+	1	0.1	0.02	+	**CB**
SZ4	32	0.3	310	0.2	2	0.2	0.03	0.1	**C (2)**
SZ5	18	0.2	420	0.3	1	0.1	0.06	0.1	**C,** CT
S SUBTOTAL	7386	67.1	115123	68.8	722	64.1	34.35	59.3	
VA3*	2	+	46	+					
VA4	5	+	128	0.1	1	0.1	0.38	0.7	**CB**
VA5*	59	0.5	478	0.3	3	0.3	0.35	0.6	**C (3)**
VG4*	1	+	4	+					
VL4#	1	+	4	+					
VN4*	1	+	2	+					
VP3*	1	+	3	+					
VS3*	1	+	4	+	1	0.1	0.03	0.1	**C**
VS4*	1	+	3	+					
VS5	4	+	61	+					
VW4*	1	+	3	+					
V SUBTOTAL	77	0.7	736	0.4	5	0.4	0.76	1.3	
XG4#	5	+	48	+					
ZA3	5	+	52	+					
ZA4	15	0.1	107	0.1					
ZA5*	2	+	7	+					
ZC4#	2	+	14	+	1	0.1	0.03	0.1	C, CS
ZG3#	2	+	9	+					
ZG4#	3	+	13	+	1	0.1	0.03	0.1	**C**
ZG5#	1	+	8	+					
ZL4*	1	+	5	+					
ZM2*	1	+	5	+	1	0.1	0.07	0.1	**C**
ZN5*	1	+	4	+					
ZP3#	1	+	16	+					
ZP4	5	+	49	+					
ZP5*	1	+	5	+					
ZQ4*	1	+	7	+					
ZS4	3	+	30	+	1	0.1	0.05	0.1	**C**
ZS5*	1	+	17	+					
Z SUBTOTAL	45	0.4	348	0.2	4	0.4	0.18	0.3	
TOTAL	11,006		**167,438**		**1127**		**57.93**		

Note: * indicates fabric present only at Yarnton, # indicates fabric present only at Cresswell Field. Vessel types and numbers represented by rims are shown in **bold**, vessel types represented only by body sherds (etc) in ordinary type. For vessel type codes see below.

Tables 14.4-5 show clearly the principal inclusion type combinations. The two main local tempering traditions in the Iron Age were shell and quartz sand, the former broadly characteristic of the early Iron Age and the latter of the middle Iron Age. Together these accounted for over 85% of all the sherds from Yarnton and over 90% of sherds at Cresswell Field. Subsidiary traditions are indicated by dominant calcareous grit and limestone tempering, both of which amounted to over 5% of the Yarnton assemblage but were only half as common at Cresswell Field, suggesting that these were essentially middle Iron Age traditions. A small, but perhaps significant, proportion of the mainly early Iron Age assemblage from Cresswell Field comprised fabrics tempered primarily with grog. This fabric group was important in what appeared to be some of the earliest Iron Age or later Bronze Age-early Iron Age transitional features at Cresswell Field. After consideration of some individual fabric types the chronological development of the assemblage in fabric terms is discussed in greater detail below.

As already indicated, the great majority of inclusion types were potentially available quite locally. Shell, the most common inclusion type, was mostly, if not entirely, fossil-derived. A number of samples from shell-tempered vessels were analysed by Jonathan Dempsey (full report in archive) who concluded that the principal fossil type utilised (at several different periods in the history of Yarnton) was *Gryphaea*, which was readily available in the Thames gravel terraces of the Oxford region. Non-shell inclusions in these fabrics suggested that the associated clay was much more likely to have been of alluvial than fossil origin, the latter being much harder to work. The shell-tempered fabrics were therefore essentially composed of recent (alluvial) clay with the deliberate admixture of broken fossil shell as a tempering agent. The materials for production of shell-tempered fabrics were therefore probably readily to hand in the immediate vicinity of Yarnton. The nearest limestone source is about 8 km distant to the north-west, but this material was in any case brought to the site for other purposes and could have been exploited in this way by locally based potters. A very small number of sherds contained unidentified rock (R) inclusions. These were so scarce, however, that there was little justification for pursuing their identification. Less common inclusion types included probable Greensand (B), which could have derived from Boars Hill only a little to the south of the site. This inclusion type may have been under-represented in recording of the pottery, but the great majority of the quartz sand observed in the Yarnton pottery appeared to be typical of the gravel terraces of the Thames. Another unusual fabric component was ironstone ooliths (U), which occurred very occasionally as a secondary inclusion type at Cresswell Field (and at Yarnton in a few late Iron Age sherds). The frequency of ironstone ooliths in these sherds was relatively low, however, and might have been consistent with their secondary derivation from alluvial clays. Elsewhere within the region fabrics with a much higher representation of this inclusion type have been noted at Gravelly Guy, in south-east Oxford at the Rover Paint Shop (unpublished, see

Table 14.4 Yarnton: Quantification of Iron Age inclusion type combinations (sherd count).

Minor inclusion type	*Major inclusion type*												
	A	*B*	*C*	*F*	*G*	*L*	*P*	*Q*	*R*	*S*	*V*	*Z*	*TOTAL*
A	1		69	1	21	127	3	6	1	1043	64	10	1346
C	40					3				85			128
F	7												7
G	32		6			7		1		403	1		450
I	19									8			27
L	45				1					199		1	246
M	7	1	3	3								1	15
N	338		81	3	1	33				243	1	1	701
P	162		3			5		1		555	1	3	730
Q	13			1	2					7		1	24
R	1		1					1					3
S	275		45		18	60	5	2			5	3	413
V	371		24	3	6	53	1	1		152			611
W	3										1		4
Z	33		4			4	2	2		16			61
TOTAL	1347	1	236	11	49	292	11	14	1	2711	73	20	4766
%	28.3	+	5.0	0.2	1.0	6.1	0.2	0.3	+	56.9	1.5	0.4	

Table 14.5 Cresswell Field: Quantification of Iron Age inclusion type combinations (sherd count).

Minor inclusion type						*Major inclusion type*					
	A	*C*	*F*	*G*	*L*	*P*	*Q*	*S*	*V*	*X*	*Z*	*TOTAL*
A		27	4	27	53	11	3	1973	2		12	2112
C	5				9			231			2	247
F	1			1				1				3
G	70	12			17		1	1361		5	6	1472
I	15			1				10				26
L	3	1		2				128	1			135
M	12			1								13
N	226	30			9			248				513
P	136	6		1	7			622			4	776
Q	10	1						3				14
S	358	79		116	63	1	5		1		1	624
U	4							1				5
V	87	14	1	7	17			58				184
Z	32	9		28	5	3		39				116
TOTAL	959	179	5	184	180	15	9	4675	4	5	25	6240
%	15.4	2.9	0.1	1.5	2.9	0.2	0.1	74.9	0.1	0.1	0.4	

Keevill and Durden 1997, 89, note 1), and also at Abingdon Business Park (Muir and Roberts 1999, 68). In these cases a clay source close to the parent Banbury outcrop of the Lower Jurassic ironstone seems to be implied (Chris Doherty pers. comm).

Bone was also used as an inclusion type, though only identified in a small number of sherds from a single feature, posthole 8147 at Cresswell Field. The frequency of bone inclusions in these sherds indicates that its use was quite deliberate. No close parallels for such usage are known within the region in this period, though bone was sometimes used as a tempering agent in earlier periods and has been observed in early Iron Age pottery from Tusmore, Northamptonshire (J. Timby pers. comm.).

A very wide range of inclusion type combinations was noted, particularly when these were amplified with the fineness/coarseness indicator. The significance of these variations is debatable. Many inclusion type combinations could have been produced by a single potter, depending on the precise mixture of clay and inclusion types, and some combinations, as would be expected, were clearly functionally determined, with coarsely tempered fabrics commonly used for large vessels and finer fabrics for smaller, thin-walled vessels. These again could all have been produced at a single source.

Chronology of Iron Age fabrics

The general predominance of shell-tempering in the early Iron Age is well established within the region. In the Yarnton area and at Eynsham, for example, there is evidence that shell-tempering was in use in the middle Bronze Age and perhaps into the beginning of the late Bronze Age, but the most distinctive fabrics of the later Bronze Age within the region were tempered with large angular quartz or quartzite or with flint. The great majority of pottery assigned to the late Bronze Age at Yarnton was in these fabrics (flint-tempering being less common) and characteristic forms were basically bipartite. These fabrics occurred in small but significant quantities at both Cresswell Field and Yarnton. Since many of the sherds in these fabrics were small, undiagnostic fragments, however, it was not possible to assign all of them to the late Bronze Age with certainty.

Limited, but significant evidence suggests that after the middle Bronze Age the earliest use of shell tempering is encountered in vessels which may genuinely be considered to be transitional between established late Bronze Age and early Iron Age pottery styles. A bipartite vessel form typical of the late Bronze Age was found in ditch 664/A, part of early Roman enclosure 187, in a fabric tempered with shell and quartzite, an inclusion type combination which is extremely rare. There are, however, no clearly stratified occurrences of shell and quartzite fabrics in the Yarnton sites which would demonstrate conclusively their position in an evolutionary sequence of fabrics from quartzite to shell-tempered traditions. The existence of such a sequence, while plausible, remains speculative, therefore.

It is thus unclear whether the major early Iron Age shell-tempered tradition represented, with the grog-tempered fabrics already mentioned and with a few sand- (often sand and shell) tempered fine wares, the full range of early Iron Age tempering traditions. While most quartz(ite) and flint-tempered sherds have been presumed to be of late

Bronze Age date and have generally been recorded as such, a few such small sherds lacking in other diagnostic characteristics have been retained within the record of the early Iron Age material. These may well have been residual late Bronze Age pieces.

The 'absolute' chronology of the early Iron Age sequence is based almost entirely upon the pottery. The earliest Iron Age groups can in turn only be dated by comparison with material with similar stylistic characteristics, principally with regard to vessel form and decoration. Chronological developments in the fabric composition of assemblages are more readily dated in relative than in absolute terms.

It has long been recognised within the region that the proportion of Iron Age pottery assemblages constituted by shell-tempered fabrics declines through the period. This decline appears to have been gradual (Lambrick 1984). On continuously occupied sites, at least, there is no clear horizon at or after which assemblages are completely dominated by sand-tempered fabrics, though at some sites where occupation appears to begin in the middle Iron Age shell-tempered material is rare, for example, at Watkins Farm (Allen 1990b, 32). The problems have always been a) to determine the point (if any) at which shell-tempered material can be regarded as residual in middle Iron Age assemblages on continuously occupied sites and b) to determine the start date of middle Iron Age sites at which shell-tempered material is essentially lacking – did these sites in fact originate in the later middle Iron Age, as suggested by Allen (ibid.) in the case of Watkins Farm?

At Yarnton this problem has been approached from the starting point of the Cresswell Field assemblage. Here the great majority of the material, and by implication the feature groups, appears to have been of early Iron Age date, with shell-tempered fabrics amounting to 75% of the total sherds.

The most distinctive early Iron Age assemblage is from pit 8127 at Cresswell Field. The principal fill of this feature (8126) contained very substantial parts of three vessels (Fig. 14.1, Nos 1, 2 and 7) and rim sherds from a minimum of 11 additional vessels (total sherds/wt. 135/4038 g). The upper fill (8174 – 42 sherds/526 g) produced a further eight rims. Four vessels (and a body sherd of a fifth) in the lower fill had excised grooves typical of the early Iron Age material from New Wintles Farm, Hanborough (eg Harding 1972, pl. 49 B, E and K) and one of these vessels bore complex incised and impressed white-infilled decoration characteristic of the early All Cannings Cross group dated 9th-8th centuries BC (cf Cunliffe 2005, 613). The form of this vessel, while having a number of recognisable early Iron Age characteristics such as a simple straight upright rim and a slightly omphalos base, both noticeable on vessels from Long Wittenham, for example (Harding 1972, pl. 50, Q and N respectively), is not precisely paralleled either in the region or at other sites where the early All Cannings Cross decorative style occurs. The most unusual aspect of this vessel is the very rounded shoulder. While this is occasionally seen in jar-like forms at All Cannings Cross (eg Cunnington 1923, pl. 29 no. 1) this feature does not seem to occur on wider (?bowl) forms of this date, which tend to be at least slightly angled or carinated at the shoulder/girth. The transformation of this aspect into a sharply angled tripartite profile, as for example at Long Wittenham (eg Savory 1937, 5), is seen by Harding (1972, 86-90) as marking a secondary phase in the early Iron Age pottery of the region. Cunliffe suggests that vessels of this type, assigned to what he calls the 'Long Wittenham-Allen's Pit group', may have overlapped with the early All Cannings Cross style in the late 6th century and continued to develop down to the 3rd century (Cunliffe 1991, 73-5; but cf Cunliffe 2005, 101).

The group from pit 8127 includes a tiny fragment apparently of an angled (tripartite) form in fabric SG3 from the upper fill, but otherwise sherds of this type are absent and more slack-profiled forms dominate the group. The character of the initial early Iron Age pottery at Yarnton is thus reasonably clear. Its affinities are with a group from Standlake (Harding 1972, pl. 47), which includes pieces with complex decoration, slack profiled jars with fingertip impressions on the shoulder and a plain bowl (ibid., pl. 47 A) which provides a generalised parallel for the decorated vessel from (8126) in terms of size (it was noted by Harding (ibid., 82) as "by far the largest of the fine ware bowls from the region" – it is a little smaller than the Cresswell Field vessel) and its orange-brown finish. Further close parallels for components of the 8127 assemblage are found at New Wintles Farm, Hanborough (see above) and at Kirtlington (Harding 1966), where slack profiled jars were characteristic. All of these groups were assigned by Harding to the primary phase of the early Iron Age. They all have slightly different characteristics, and overall the Yarnton group is closest to that from New Wintles, also the nearest geographically, but there is no difficulty in seeing all these groups as broadly contemporary. A single pit group at Gravelly Guy (Duncan *et al.* 2004, 291, 293, group LBA/EIA I) may also possibly belong to this group of assemblages, though the decorated sherds here are not so clearly in a style related to All Cannings Cross. No other feature assemblages (as opposed to individual pieces) have been identified as assignable to this primary phase of the early Iron Age and these thus remain scarce within the region.

In terms of broad fabric groupings the breakdown of the pit 8127 assemblage (both fills combined) is shown in Table 14.6. These figures are skewed somewhat by the presence of abnormally large portions of three vessels in (8126), two in fabric GS4 and one in SG4, which together account for 33% of the sherds and 60% of the weight of all the pottery in the feature. Discounting these vessels, which may have constituted a special deposit, does not particularly alter the apparently very early Iron Age character of the group, however. The main features of the range of fabrics in this pit are the absence (except as a subsidiary component in one sand-tempered sherd) of flint or quartzite, the presence of moderate quantities of sand-tempered fabrics (see further below) and the importance of both shell- and grog-tempered groups. The great majority of sherds in the grog-tempered fabric group had shell as the secondary inclusion type. The converse was true up to a point, but sand was also an important subsidiary element in shell-tempered fabrics, and was indeed present as a further component in most of the GS4 sherds in this group. The great majority of sherds making up this group were therefore in fabrics containing a combination of grog (or clay pellets), shell and sand, in varying proportions. This broadly applies also to the fabrics of some of the finer sherds in the group. These were principally sand-tempered, the sand occurring with grog or shell (and, in a single case, with uncertain voids) in the main fill of the pit, with additional (scarce) instances of fabrics AN, AP and AV, all small, fine sherds, in the uppermost fill 8174. In summary, no sherds in the group were tempered primarily with inclusions other than sand, grog/clay pellets or shell, and sherds with other inclusion types as their *minor* component accounted for just under 10% of the sherd total and less than 2% of the total weight of the group. It is important to note that the use of sand as the principal tempering agent (usually with shell or grog/clay pellets as the secondary inclusion type) in the fabric of some fine vessels was established at the beginning of the Iron Age. This appears to have remained the case throughout the early Iron Age and later, but while sand-tempered fabrics amounted to 16.4% of the sherd total they only constituted 6.6% of weight.

The other most substantial early Iron Age groups at Cresswell Field were from pits 7057, 7787 and ditch 7346, midden 7003 and a finds reference context 7269. The presence of a small intrusive Roman sherd in 7003 may mean that it was less reliable than the other groups. These groups were dominated consistently by shell-tempered fabrics, which generally comprised between 80% and 90% of sherd count and (usually) a slightly higher proportion of the total weight (Table 14.7). The group from pit 7787 was slightly anomalous in that it was dominated by 19 sherds (3007 g) from a single vessel in fabric SA5, but it still falls recognisably within the group of early Iron Age assemblages. Sand tempering was another consistent component of these early Iron Age groups and grog tempering also occurred regularly but in small quantities. Other inclusion types were less regular components of these assemblages. The slightly higher representation of calcareous gravel (C) and limestone (L) fabrics in midden 7003 might suggest that this assemblage is slightly later in date, or could reflect possible contamination in this group (see above). Certainly these two inclusion types were very rare in the primary early Iron Age group (pit 8127, see above) and were more common in the middle Iron Age.

Table 14.6 Cresswell Field: Quantification of pottery from early Iron Age pit 8127.

Fabric group	*No. sherds*	*% sherds*	*Wt. (g)*	*% weight*	*Rims*	*% rims*
A (sand)	29	16.4	301	6.6	4	18.2
G (grog)	56	31.6	2397	52.5	7	31.8
P (clay pellets)	6	3.4	88	1.9	0	-
S (shell)	86	48.6	1678	36.8	11	50.0
TOTAL	177		4564		22	

Table 14.7 Quantification of major fabric groups from the largest early Iron Age assemblages at Cresswell Field.

Context	*Pit 7057 (7058)*		*Pit 7365 (7364)*		*Pit 7787 (7788)*		*Midden 7003*		*Finds ref. 7269*	
Fabric group	*% no*	*% wt*	*% no*	*% wt*	*% no*	*% wt*	*% no*	*% wt*	*% no*	*% wt*
A (sand)	7.6	2.3	5.1	4.9	7.3	0.6	7.8	4.9	8.3	12.9
C (calcareous)	1.9	0.4					4.3	5.7		
G (grog)	1.9	2.0	5.1	3.9			2.1	0.8	1.4	0.3
L (limestone)	2.5	2.1					6.4	10.3	2.1	4.9
Q (quartzite)	0.6	0.2								
P (clay pellets)			1.5	0.7						
S (shell)	85.4	93.0	88.2	90.4	92.7	99.4	79.4	78.3	88.3	81.9
Z (voids)			1.5	0.9			0.7	0.1		
TOTALS	157	3776 g	195	4297 g	41	3294 g	141	2841 g	145	2744 g

The vessel forms from these features (in all, 77 vessels identified on the basis of rim sherds) represent a slight development in the early Iron Age form repertoire from that seen in the 'All Cannings Cross pit' group. While most rim sherds (51) were not large enough for the specific form to be determined, vessels in forms CA (bucket shaped jars – 3), CB (barrel shaped jars – 6), CS ('slack-profiled' jars – 6), CT (tripartite jars – 7) and HC (curving sided bowls – 2) were identified. Amongst this material the consistent, if relatively low-level, presence of angular tripartite forms (CT) is significant. Examples of this form were found in each group except that from pit 7787, in which there were only four rim sherds. Type CB is particularly characteristic of the middle Iron Age, but is also found in early Iron Age contexts, as here.

In order to trace the chronological development of the balance of fabrics further, a comparison was made between the pottery from the pits in Cresswell Field and Yarnton, contrasting the material in the features assigned to early and middle Iron Age phases (Table 14.8). Pit assemblages were selected for examination since these were thought less likely to have suffered from intrusive material through extensive recutting, as is seen in some of the ditch contexts (in any case, ditch groups were rare, particularly at Cresswell Field). Some intrusive material was evident in the Yarnton sample, but this was not thought to invalidate the general conclusions drawn from this analysis. It was inevitable that since in some cases the phasing was based entirely on ceramic criteria, there was a danger of a circular argument resulting. Again this was not thought to compromise the results significantly.

Table 14.8 Quantification of major Iron Age fabric groups from pits by period.

Fabric Group	*Cresswell Field* % Sherds	*Cresswell Field* % Wt (g)	*Yarnton* % Sherds	*Yarnton* % Wt (g)
EARLY IRON AGE				
A (sand)	9.4	5.8	7.5	4.1
C (calcareous grit)	2.0	1.7	0.6	0.8
G (grog)	2.5	1.9	0.5	0.2
L (limestone)	2.4	1.8	3.5	4.4
S (shell)	82.8	88.0	84.4	88.1
Other Iron Age	1.0	0.7	0.7	0.4
Roman (intrusive)			2.7	2.0
Totals	2690	45275	986	14851
MIDDLE IRON AGE				
A (sand)	23.0	19.6	39.7	52.5
C (calcareous grit)	3.0	4.5	6.9	5.9
G (grog)	0.9	0.9	0.8	0.5
L (limestone)	4.2	5.7	6.4	4.4
S (shell)	68.4	69.1	36.0	28.8
V (organic)			5.7	3.0
Other Iron Age	0.5	0.2	0.9	0.3
Roman (intrusive)			3.3	4.8
Totals	1089 sherds	15845 g	1087 sherds	18542 g

The figures show very close similarity between the early Iron Age pit assemblages in the two halves of the site, allowing for the exclusion of the earliest Iron Age group at Cresswell Field (8127) from the table, and the presence of intrusive Roman material at Yarnton. The figures for the combined pit groups from Cresswell Field are close to those for the selected largest early Iron Age groups discussed above, although the combined figures suggest a slightly higher representation of sand-tempered fabrics at the expense of shell-tempered ones than is implied in some of the largest individual groups; nevertheless these figures are closely comparable. The picture for the middle Iron Age is significantly different, however. Here the fabric proportions at Cresswell Field, while showing development of the assemblage from the early Iron Age, do not depart radically from the pattern established in that period. An increase in the proportion of sand-tempered fabrics, and a corresponding decrease in shell-tempered fabrics, is noticeable, along with increases in the proportion of C (calcareous sand) and L (limestone) fabric groups (these increases being more prominent in terms of weight than of sherd count). In the Yarnton middle Iron Age pits, however, sand-tempered fabrics have increased in importance over their early Iron Age counterparts by a factor of five (sherd count) and shell-tempered fabrics have declined to well under half their previous level. The increase in C and L fabric groups noted in the Cresswell Field assemblage is also present here, though it is much more prominent in the former group. Organic-tempered (V) sherds were also relatively significant at this time, whereas they were absent at Cresswell Field in the middle Iron Age and present on both sites in very small quantities in the early Iron Age. The significance of this is uncertain. An examination of the pottery from the middle Iron Age ditch groups at Yarnton produces a comparable picture to that from the pit groups in the same site (there were insufficient early Iron Age ditch groups here to provide meaningful comparanda). In these groups the representation of sand- and shell-tempered fabrics was fairly similar in terms of sherd count (41.7% and 44.7% respectively of sherds, with a total of 1467 sherds considered), but as with the pits, sand-tempered fabrics were much better represented than shell in terms of weight (58.1% and 32.1% respectively).

In broader terms, the contrast between the middle Iron Age assemblages at Cresswell Field and Yarnton is most likely to reflect chronology rather than other factors. In essence the pattern seen at Yarnton shows a later stage in the evolution of the shell:sand-tempering ratio than is seen at Cresswell Field. The simplest explanation of this is that activity at Cresswell Field terminated or (more likely) was reduced to a very low level at a relatively early stage in the middle Iron Age, whereas at Yarnton it is likely that there was continuous occupation through the middle Iron Age. The minimal level of late Iron Age and Roman activity found at Cresswell Field is therefore unlikely to have been a new development at that time, but simply indicated low-level use of the site following a pattern already established for perhaps as much as two centuries.

Decoration

A variety of finishing/decorative techniques was employed, though most of these were only found rarely. The most common technique was zone burnishing, which was encountered on some 2682 (24.4%) of the total Iron Age sherds, and can be regarded as a finishing technique rather than a decorative one (linear burnished decoration is considered separately). Detailed analysis of decoration in relation to fabrics and forms is not attempted here, although the data upon which such an analysis could be based exist in the pottery archive. The incidence of zone or area burnishing in relation to fabric does merit further consideration, however, in view of its frequency, and is summarised in Table 14.9 below.

These figures, which simply record numbers of sherds with burnishing, disregarding details of the location of the burnishing, show a greater incidence in what may be considered the 'finer' fabrics (particularly sand-tempered ones). The technique was quite common in limestone (L) and grog (G) groups amongst the most important major fabric groupings, though its relatively high representation in G fabrics owes much to the concentration of burnished sherds in fabric GS4 in the 'All Cannings Cross' pit 8127, including sherds from the large decorated bowl. It occurred less frequently in C and S fabric groups – it was almost exactly half as common in shell as in sand-tempered fabrics. Of the principal sand-tempered fabrics, AN2, AN3, AS2 and AS3 were most commonly treated with burnished zones, usually covering the entire vessel. In some cases there was partial or overall burnish of the interior of vessels, usually, but not always, complementary to exterior burnish.

Table 14.9 Incidence of burnishing in Iron Age fabric groups.

Fabric group	*Total sherds*	*Sherds with burnished zone decoration*	*Burnished sherds as % of fabric group total sherds*
A	2306	904	39.2
B	1	1	100
C	415	97	23.4
F	16	0	-
G	233	70	30.0
L	472	163	34.5
P	26	3	11.5
Q	23	5	21.7
R	1	0	-
S	7386	1428	19.3
V	77	3	3.9
X	5	5	100
Z	45	3	6.7
TOTAL	11006	2682	24.4

The only other overall surface finish/decorative technique employed was that of red-coating. A total of 23 sherds, 10 in sand-tempered (AN2, AN3 (2), AP3 (2), AS3 (4) and AS4) and 13 in shell-tempered fabrics (SA3 (2), SA4 (8), SG4, SP3 and SP4) had such a finish. The material in question was not analysed so its constituent(s) are not known. It is assumed not to have been haematite, however (cf Middleton 1987). Only four of the sherds with this technique came from Cresswell Field. The significance of this is not certain, since such decoration is usually characteristic of the early Iron Age, which was particularly well-represented there. It is perhaps possible that red-coated vessels were treasured for their rarity value and remained in circulation longer than other vessels, which might account for their more frequent occurrence in the later, Yarnton assemblage.

Linear burnishing, essentially a decorative feature rather than potentially combining this aspect with a functional role as in 'zone' burnish, was much less common than zone burnish, being recorded on only 20 sherds from the site (9 in A fabrics, 1 in C and 10 in S fabrics). On five sherds (from two vessels, in fabrics AN2 and AS3) this took the form of curvilinear motifs, otherwise simple vertical, horizontal or oblique lines predominated.

Other decorative techniques employed were excision/tooling (of grooves), incision (lines etc), impressing and stamping, frilling or notching of features such as rims and the application of cordons. Grooving was relatively rare, occurring on 93 sherds (0.8%), in A (26 sherds), C (1 sherd), G (34 sherds), L (11 sherds) and S fabrics (21 sherds). In most cases grooves were apparently horizontal, on the shoulder (or more rarely at the girth) of vessels or, most commonly, on body sherds uncertainly located in relation to the vessel profile. The relatively high incidence of grooving on G fabric sherds (14.6% of all sherds in these fabrics had grooves), particularly on fabric GS4 (30 grooved sherds) reflects the importance of this technique in the earliest Iron Age, all these sherds occurring on vessels in pit 8127 at Cresswell Field.

Incised decoration occurred on 115 sherds. A number of subtypes of this technique were identified and are quantified by fabric in Table 14.10.

The level of confidence of the identification of some motifs is variable. In some cases, types B, C and G incised decoration recorded on small sherds may have formed parts of more complex motifs or schemes, eg of types I and J. The most common form of such motifs, rough triangles, were frequently

Table 14.10 Incidence of Iron Age incised decoration

Incised decoration subtype	*Description*	*Fabric (number of sherds in brackets)*	*Total examples of type*
B	Horizontal incised line(s)	LN4, SA4, SN5	3
C	Vertical incised line(s)	AS3 (2), SA3, SC4, SP4?, SV4	6
F	Incised and infilled line(s)	AN2, SL4, SP4	3
G	Oblique incised line(s)	AS3 (2), CN5 (2: on rim), CS4 (2: 1 on rim), GS3, GZ3, LP4, QS3, SA3 (3), SA4 (8), SA5, SG3 (3), SG4 (9), SG5, SL4, SN4, SP3, SP4 (2), SP5, SV4	42
H	Zigzag incised line(s)	SA4, SP3, SP4	3
I	Simple geometric motifs	AS3 (4), GL5, SA3 (2), SA4 (3), SA5, SG3, SG5, SL4, SP5	15
J	Complex geometric motifs	AC3, AS3, SP5, SV4	4
L	Simple curvilinear motifs	AN2 (2), AP2, AS3, LV5 (2), SA4, SP3	8
M	Complex curvilinear motifs	see Y	-
W	Stabbed dots/ovals/triangles	AV3	1
Y	Composite (of above elements)	GS4 (24: M and W, with white infill), LV5 (4: B, C and L (arcades)), SA3 (C and roughly executed +)	29
Z	Other	ZA3 (?lattice)	1

infilled with multiple lines. The type Z (broad lattice) decoration could also have formed part of the infill of such a motif. Infill of linear patterns with other decorative types was rare, but was evident on the large 'All Cannings Cross' bowl, where complex curvilinear patterns were infilled with small roughly triangular incisions or impressions, both these and the lines having white inlay. The inlay was examined by Chris Doherty (Oxford University Research Laboratory for Archaeology and the History of Art) and shown to be of bone, whereas a body sherd of an angled tripartite jar in fabric SA3 from pit 8525 (Fig. 14.5, No. 136) had crudely executed incised decoration inlaid with calcite (chalk or limestone).

The importance of the technique in the early Iron Age is reflected in its occurrence in the 'All Cannings Cross' pit 8127 (the 24 sherds of fabric GS4 with composite incised decoration were from the highly decorated bowl (Fig. 14.1, No.1)). Shell-tempered fabrics, however, only accounted for half of all the incised sherds, despite the predominance of these fabrics in the early Iron Age. This is partly explained by the skewing effect of the decorated vessel and also by the more frequent occurrence of incised decoration on finer fabrics (though a number of coarsely-tempered fabrics did have incised decoration), with the result that there was a higher percentage of incised sherds in sand-tempered than in shell-tempered fabrics, *vis-a-vis* their relative representation in the early Iron Age. Thus using the 'average' figures established from examination of the early Iron Age pit groups at Cresswell Field (see above), shell-tempered fabrics amounted to roughly 85-90% of sherds and sand-tempered ones *c* 5-8%, while their respective contributions of incised sherds were 54.7% and 14.2% (discounting nine incised sherds of middle Iron Age date discussed below). While incised decoration did occur in the middle Iron Age it was uncommon then, the only certain middle Iron Age examples at Cresswell Field being on a globular bowl in fabric LV5 (Fig. 14.5, No. 145) and a body sherd of fabric AP2 (Fig. 14.5, No. 146) both from pit 8786. An incised rim in fabric CN5 from Yarnton (Fig. 14.8, No. 244) was probably also of middle Iron Age date. Where the vessel form could be determined the association of incised-decorated sherds with form at Cresswell Field was as follows: form C (2 sherds), form CS (18 sherds), form CT (7 sherds), form HD – (vessel Fig. 14.1, No.1) – (24 sherds) and form HG – the middle Iron Age bowl (Fig. 14.5, No. 145) (4 sherds). With the exception of this last vessel the correlation of incised decoration with specifically or predominantly early Iron Age forms is clear. The limited evidence from Yarnton is more equivocal, associations of incised sherds being with form CB (Fig. 14.8, No. 244, see above) and with forms C (2 sherds), D and H, all but form CB being in shell-tempered fabrics.

Impressed decoration also tends to be characteristic of the early Iron Age, and unlike incised decoration was found as commonly on coarsely-tempered fabrics as on finer ones, thus 72.9% of the 251 sherds with impressed decoration were in shell-tempered fabrics. The principal manifestations of the technique were as finger-tip or similar impressions on the shoulder of vessels, or less commonly on the rim or both rim and shoulder. Such instances accounted for almost 80% of all impressed decoration, of which the great majority were on vessels in shell-tempered fabrics, although the technique did also occur in A, C, G, L, P and V fabric groups, albeit very rarely in most. More carefully-impressed dimples were found on vessel (Fig. 14.5, No. 1) and small impressed oval shapes occurred rarely in sand-tempered and shell-tempered fabrics. Simple ring impressions occurred on seven sherds in sand-tempered fabrics, two in LV5 and one in SA3. These, and three sherds with white infilled dots in fabric AS3, differ in character from the cruder fingertip impressions, and may all have been of middle Iron Age date. The character of the infilled dot sherds, for example, is very similar to that of a loosely saucepan-like vessel from Compton Beauchamps, Berks (Harding 1972, 101-2 and pl. 65 F). Only three sherds were recorded as having 'stamped' as opposed to impressed decoration (ie probably involving the use of a specially made die). Two of the stamps were small penannular ones. These were in fabric SG4 on a type CB jar (Fig. 14.2, No. 42) with a very similar stamp on a sherd in fabric AQ3 (not illustrated), while a different, more linear, stamp type occurred on a bowl form in fabric AN2 from Yarnton (Fig. 14.3, No. 82). This last example was certainly of middle Iron Age date, but the penannular stamps, both from Cresswell Field, could have been earlier.

Finally, there were a few examples of more plastic decoration. Frilling or notching of the vessel rim, as opposed to fingertip impression on the outer edge of the rim, or fine diagonal incision, both referred to above, occurred on 35 shell-tempered sherds (30 from Cresswell Field) and one sherd each in A, C and F fabrics. The distribution of this characteristic was closely mirrored by that of cordons, although these were less common. There was a single example at Yarnton of a notched cordon in fabric AV2, the other ten examples of cordons were from Cresswell Field, all in shell-tempered fabrics, seven of these being notched or having indentations. The preponderance of this early Iron Age technique at Cresswell Field is consistent with the early emphasis of that assemblage.

Vessel Types (Table 14.11)

Some 1127 vessels were counted on the basis of rim sherds (discounting multiple sherds from the same vessel). These were also quantified by EVEs (measurement of rim percentage), which was felt to give a useful check on other measures despite the difficulties inherent in producing accurate rim percentage figures from irregular, hand-made vessels.

The definition of vessel types is based on the fairly broad classification scheme used for Roman as well as pre-Roman vessels. In this scheme the generalised form of vessels, which may be related to functional considerations, is considered to be of greater significance than minor variations in form. Nevertheless, a system of rim type classification, not dissimilar to that used for Gravelly Guy, was also employed to provide more detailed definition of rim shape which could be used in discussing certain aspects of the assemblage (data in archive).

The majority of the vessels were of simple forms. In many cases, despite the good condition of the sherds and the reasonably large average sherd weight, insufficient of a rim survived to allow a detailed assessment of its form, so that often only generalised form categories could be used. The average representation of rim circumference per vessel (ie EVEs divided by vessel count) was about 5.1%. When it is considered that the duplicate rim sherds of a single vessel did not appear in the vessel count figure, it is clear that the average representation of rim circumference *per rim sherd* would have been considerably less than 5%. The degree of brokenness of the assemblage suggested by these figures helps to explain why more rim sherds were not assigned to specific vessel types.

The vessels present were almost all assigned to one of two general classes, jars and bowls, the difference between these being defined principally on the basis of the ratio of height to rim diameter. Where this was more than 1:1 the vessel was usually defined as a jar (vessel class C); where this ratio was

Table 14.11 Quantification of Iron Age vessel forms.

Form code	*Description*	*Rim count*	*% rim count*	*EVEs*	*% EVEs*
C	jar (unspecified)	732	65.0	28.64	49.4
CA	bucket shaped jar	12	1.1	1.24	2.1
CB	barrel shaped jar	192	17.0	13.16	22.7
CG	globular jar	3	0.3	0.22	0.4
CH	bead-rimmed jar	1	0.1	0.03	0.1
CS	slack-profiled jar with slight shoulder	54	4.8	5.36	9.3
CT	tripartite angled-profiled jar	57	5.1	4.14	7.1
D	uncertain jar/bowl	25	2.2	1.05	1.8
H	bowl (unspecified)	3	0.3	0.10	0.2
HC	curving-sided bowl	7	0.6	1.05	1.8
HD	necked bowl	2	0.2	0.59	1.0
HG	globular bowl	10	0.9	1.05	1.8
I	uncertain bowl/dish	2	0.2	0.16	0.3
MD	(miscellaneous) miniature vessel	2	0.2	0.41	0.7
Z	form unknown	25	2.2	0.72	1.2
TOTAL		1127		57.93	

less than 1:1 it was defined as a bowl (vessel class H). Certainty of attribution even to these generalised classes was not always possible, however, since this depends on the presence of a substantial part of the vessel profile. In some instances, therefore, attribution was to an 'uncertain' jar/bowl category (vessel class D), though this was only used where there was genuine doubt about the form. In the majority of cases the 'default' option was to record rims as class C (jars) with no attempt at subdivision. This approach was felt to be justified on the basis of the known character of Iron Age vessel forms in the region, in which bowls (defined on the criteria outlined above) appear to be relatively rare. It is accepted, however, that some uncertainty may attach to the identification of some rim sherds as class C jars. Small rim sherds were assigned to an 'unknown' category (vessel class Z).

Comparison of the data for vessel count and EVEs reveals, as would be expected, that most of the more generalised form classes are represented by smaller sherds (ie the EVEs values per sherd are lower) than more closely defined types. Thus, for example, while otherwise undefined C class jars amounted to 65% of rim sherds, they totalled under 50% of EVEs, whereas type CS jars constituted 4.8% of the total rims but 9.3% of EVEs. The quantified breakdown of vessel forms by major fabric groups is presented in Tables 14.12-13

In order to emphasise the comparisons and contrasts between the Cresswell Field and Yarnton assemblages these data are then presented in terms of percentages of the EVEs figures for the two sites in Tables 14.14-15.

Table 14.12 Cresswell Field: Iron Age vessel forms by major fabric group. Quantification by rim count/EVEs.

	Fabric group							
Form	*A*	*C*	*G*	*L*	*S*	*V*	*Z*	*TOTAL*
C	56/1.92	14/0.52	14/0.52	13/0.51	335/13.35		2/0.06	434/16.88
CA					4/0.41			4/0.41
CB	21/1.09	4/0.38	2/0.13	8/0.56	36/2.29	1/0.38		72/4.83
CG	1/0.03	1/0.07						2/0.10
CS	3/0.26		7/0.98	1/0.17	34/3.21			45/4.62
CT	10/0.66	1/0.05	3/0.55	1/0.07	38/2.29			53/3.62
D	7/0.24	1/0.02			3/0.08			11/0.34
HC			1/0.02		3/0.38			4/0.40
HD	1/0.23		1/0.36					2/0.59
HG				1/0.24	1/0.05			2/0.29
I			1/0.10					1/0.10
MD					1/0.19			1/0.19
Z	1/0.05				7/0.24			8/0.29
TOTAL	100/4.48	21/1.04	29/2.66	24/1.55	462/22.49	1/0.38	2/0.06	639/32.66

Table 14.13 Yarnton: Iron Age vessel forms by major fabric group. Quantification by rim count/EVEs.

	Fabric group										
Form	*A*	*C*	*F*	*G*	*L*	*P*	*Q*	*S*	*V*	*Z*	*TOTAL*
C	72/3.08	9/0.34	2/0.07	1/0.04	9/0.26	2/0.06	2/0.08	195/7.33	4/0.38	2/0.12	298/11.76
CA	4/0.42				1/0.12			3/0.29			8/0.83
CB	53/3.89	16/0.82		2/0.11	15/0.69	1/0.01		33/2.81			120/8.33
CG								1/0.12			1/0.12
CH	1/0.03										1/0.03
CS								9/0.74			9/0.74
CT	1/0.10							3/0.42			4/0.52
D	9/0.54	1/0.02				1/0.05		3/0.10			14/0.71
H	1/0.01							2/0.09			3/0.10
HC	3/0.65										3/0.65
HG	7/0.64	1/0.12									8/0.76
I	1/0.06										1/0.06
MD								1/0.22			1/0.22
Z	4/0.12	1/0.03		1/0.01	1/0.03			10/0.24			17/0.43
TOTAL	156/9.54	28/1.33	2/0.07	4/0.16	26/1.10	4/0.12	2/0.08	260/12.37	4/0.38	2/0.12	488/25.27

The data in these tables show that both assemblages were dominated by jars, which were slightly more important at Cresswell Field than at Yarnton (93.3% and 88.4% respectively). The former site had a slightly higher representation of unspecified jar forms (class C), but in both cases these vessels amounted to roughly half of the entire assemblage. There were distinct differences between the sites regarding the remainder of the range of jar forms, however. At Cresswell Field, characteristic early Iron Age forms such as the slack profiled, slightly shouldered, jar (CS) and the tripartite angular form CT amounted to 25% of the total assemblage while the barrel-shaped jar form (CB) comprised 14.8% of EVEs here. At Yarnton, in contrast, CS and CT were both poorly represented, together totalling only 5% of EVEs, whereas form CB was much more common, at 33% of the assemblage. The simple slightly open bucket-shaped form CA was also more common at Yarnton, with the majority of occurrences in sandy fabrics, indicating that this was predominantly a middle Iron Age form, though early Iron Age examples are known. Other jar forms were globular jars (CG), very scarce at both sites, and a single example of a bead rim jar (CH), presumably of later middle Iron Age date, from Yarnton.

Bowls were more common at Yarnton than at Cresswell Field (6% as opposed to 3.9%), and the single 'All Cannings Cross' bowl from Cresswell

Table 14.14 Cresswell Field: Iron Age vessel forms by major fabric group. Percentage of EVEs (column% / row%).

	Fabric group								
Form	*A*	*C*	*G*	*L*	*S*	*V*	*Z*	*Total EVEs*	*% EVEs*
C	42.9/11.4	50.0/3.1	19.5/3.1	32.9/3.0	59.4/79.1		100/0.4	16.88	51.7
CA					1.8/100			0.41	1.3
CB	24.3/22.6	36.5/7.9	4.9/2.7	36.1/11.6	10.2/47.4	100/7.9		4.83	14.8
CG	0.7/30.0	6.7/70.0						0.10	0.3
CS	5.8/5.6		36.8/21.2	11.0/3.7	14.3/69.5			4.62	14.1
CT	14.7/18.2	4.8/1.4	20.7/15.2	4.5/1.9	10.2/63.3			3.62	11.1
D	5.4/70.6	1.9/5.9			0.4/23.5			0.34	1.0
HC			0.8/5.0		1.7/95.0			0.40	1.2
HD	5.1/39.0		13.5/61.0					0.59	1.8
HG				15.5/82.8	0.2/17.2			0.29	0.9
I			3.8/100					0.10	0.3
MD					0.8/100			0.19	0.6
Z	1.1/17.2				1.1/82.8			0.29	0.9
Total EVEs	4.48	1.04	2.66	1.55	22.49	0.38	0.06	32.66	
% EVEs	13.7	3.2	8.1	4.7	68.9	1.2	0.2		

Table 14.15 Yarnton: Iron Age vessel forms by major fabric group. Percentage of EVEs (column% / row%).

	Fabric group											
Form	*A*	*C*	*F*	*G*	*L*	*P*	*Q*	*S*	*V*	*Z*	*Total EVEs*	*% EVEs*
C	32.3/26.28	25.6/2.9	100/0.6	25.0/0.3	23.6/2.2	50.0/0.5	100/0.7	59.3/62.3	100/3.2	100/1.0	11.76	46.5
CA	4.4/50.6				10.9/14.5			2.3/34.9			0.83	3.3
CB	40.8/46.7	61.7/9.8		68.8/1.3	62.7/8.3	8.3/0.1		33.0/33.7			8.33	33.0
CG								1.0/100			0.12	0.5
CH	0.3/100										0.03	0.1
CS								6.0/100			0.74	2.9
CT	1.0/19.2							3.4/80.8			0.52	2.1
D	5.7/76.1	1.5/2.8				41.7/7.0		0.8/14.1			0.71	2.8
H	0.1/10.0							0.7/90.0			0.10	0.4
HC	6.8/100										0.65	2.6
HG	6.7/84.2	9.0/15.8									0.76	3.0
I	0.6/100										0.06	0.2
MD								1.8/100			0.22	0.9
Z	1.3/27.9	2.3/7.0		6.2/2.3	2.7/7.0			1.9/55.8			0.43	1.7
Total EVEs	9.54	1.33	0.07	0.16	1.10	0.12	0.08	12.37	0.38	0.12	25.27	
% EVEs	37.8	5.3	0.3	0.6	4.4	0.5	0.3	49.0	1.5	0.5		

Field formed a substantial component of the bowl total from that site (expressed as EVEs). Uncertain jar/bowl types (class D) were also more common at Yarnton. Each site produced a single example of an uncertain bowl/dish (class I) and a miniature vessel (class MD).

In terms of the correlation of vessel form with fabric, shell-tempered fabrics had the highest representation of unspecified jar types amongst the commonest fabric groupings in both Cresswell Field and Yarnton assemblages. There was a clear association of the early Iron Age vessel forms CS and CT with the fabrics considered most typical of this period. This is particularly noticeable at Yarnton, where all examples of the former and over 80% of EVEs of the latter form were in shell-tempered fabrics. At Cresswell Field the representation of these vessels in shell-tempered fabrics was no more than average, but was augmented by a significantly above-average representation of these forms in grog-tempered fabrics, forms CS and CT constituting well over half of the total EVEs in grog-tempered fabrics. The relatively high incidence of form CT in sand-tempered fabrics should also be noted. This reflects the use of sand-tempering for fine ware forms in the early Iron Age (generally, form CT was the only early Iron Age form to be consistently well-finished), and the majority of the sand-tempered examples of this form (7 out of 11 vessels represented by rims) were in the sand and shell fabric AS3.

It is a commonplace in the region that the middle Iron Age has fewer characteristic vessel forms than the early Iron Age, the most distinctive forms being the relatively scarce globular bowls, often distinguished by elaborate decoration as well as by their form. Such types occurred only rarely in the Yarnton sites (amounting to 1.8% of EVEs). The barrel-shaped jar (CB) was the form most characteristic of the middle Iron Age here, although, as already noted, it does appear to have been present in the early Iron Age as well, at least in small numbers. The greater prominence of this form at Yarnton as opposed to Cresswell Field has been referred to above, and is likely to represent a chronological trend rather than a functional distinction between the two assemblages. The form was always common in sand-tempered fabrics, and amounted to more than 40% of the total EVEs in these fabrics at Yarnton, but it was relatively common in shell-tempered fabrics as well, and while at Cresswell Field it only comprised 10% of all EVEs in these fabrics, these vessels nevertheless amounted to almost half the total representation of the form on this site. More striking, however, is the very clear association of this form with some of the less common fabric groups, particularly C and L fabrics. It amounted to over 36% of EVEs in both these groups at Cresswell Field, but then rose to 61.7% and 62.7% of their respective outputs (EVEs) at Yarnton. Together with single examples of (perhaps related) globular bowls in fabric LV5 at Cresswell Field and in fabric CV5 at Yarnton, form CB jars constituted the major part of the output of the C and L fabric groups.

The relative scarcity of bowls makes it difficult to draw general conclusions about the relationships of form and fabric in this vessel class. The majority of examples from Yarnton were in sand-tempered fabrics, exceptions being two unspecific (ie class H) bowls in shell (S) fabrics and the single type HG bowl in the surprisingly coarse fabric CV5 already mentioned. Even including the single class I bowl/dish, however, there were only 12 bowls in sand-tempered fabrics at Yarnton, although there were a further nine uncertain jar/bowl forms in these fabrics. Three quite small vessels were assigned to form HC, a slightly curving sided type defined as a bowl because its diameter was greater than its height. These vessels appear to be typologically the closest in the study area assemblages to saucepan pots and occurred in fabrics AN3, AP3 and AV3 (one each).

Aspects of vessel use

Evidence for characteristics which might have a bearing on vessel use, such as sooting, were recorded, with some 593 sherds noted as having relevant evidence, which occurred on sherds of all the major fabric groupings. This is summarised in Table 14.16.

The figures exclude instances of simple burning, which were not recorded sufficiently systematically

Table 14.16 Iron Age use characteristics by fabric. Quantification by sherd count.

Fabric group	*Soot*	*Burnt residue (internal)*	*Limescale and soot*	*Limescale*	*Composite/ other*	*TOTAL*
A (sand)	23	43	1	47	4	118
C (calcareous grit)	4	17	2	6	-	29
G (grog)	-	16	-	1	-	17
L (limestone)	10	11	-	7	2	30
S (shell)	82	219	9	84	1	395
V (organic)	3	1	-	-	-	4
TOTAL	122	307	12	145	7	593

to produce meaningful data and which in any case probably relate largely to events subsequent to the primary use of most vessels. The breakdown of use evidence in relation to fabric groups reflects very closely the relative importance of those groups across the site – in other words, use evidence is found uniformly on just over 5% of the sherds in all the major fabric groups, suggesting that there may have been little significant variation in the way in which these were used. All the categories of deposits recorded presumably relate to cooking. External soot and internal burnt residues occur fairly consistently across most of the major fabric types, again in patterns which broadly reflect their relative importance in the assemblage as a whole. There is a suggestion, however, that limescale deposits, indicating the use of vessels for heating or holding water, are relatively more common in sand-tempered vessels, almost 30% of all incidences of limescale occurring on fabrics of this type, but they are still well-represented on shell-tempered fabrics too. A small number of sherds produced both burnt food remains and limescale (a pattern also observed in some early Roman material on the site). It is not clear whether these figures indicate that the dual use of vessels for heating food and water was uncommon, or that vessels were usually well cleaned before being put to slightly different use – the identified sherds being the exceptions that proved the rule. Overall the evidence suggests that fabric was not necessarily an important criterion in the selection of vessels for general cooking use, though sand-tempered vessels, generally with a fairly smooth interior, might have been slightly favoured for heating water.

The correlation of use characteristics with vessel type (Table 14.17) perhaps produces more insights into the functions of the Iron Age assemblage. The relative incidence of the characteristics is rather different from that shown in the assemblage overall, because the concentration on rim sherds tends to emphasise particular types of use. Limescale and burnt internal residues are therefore less frequent because they tend to occur in the lower parts of vessels which may not be represented by rims unless very large parts of the profile are present. Sooting, in contrast, tends to occur most commonly around the vessel shoulder and is thus well-represented on rim sherds. Type CB (barrel-shaped) jars feature particularly strongly in these figures, particularly from Yarnton, where 21 of the 33 rims included in the table are of this type. External sooting is the most common use indicator seen on rims from Yarnton (24 out of 33 examples) whereas at Cresswell Field sooting and internal burnt residues are equally common, each occurring on 41.5% of the rims with use indicators. A relatively higher proportion of external sooting at Yarnton is also recorded in the overall sherd figures (Table 14.16) – 28.6% of sherds with use indication there had external sooting, as against only 16.3% at Cresswell Field. It is possible that

Table 14.17 Iron Age use characteristics by vessel type. Quantification by rim count.

Vessel type	*Soot*	*Burnt residue (internal)*	*Limescale and soot*	*Lime-scale*	*Composite/ other*	*TOTAL*
C	11	9	1	3	-	24
CA	3	1	1	-	-	5
CB	21	6	-	3	2	32
CG	2	-	-	-	-	2
CS	4	5	-	-	-	9
CT	-	1	-	-	-	1
D	-	1	-	-	-	1
TOTAL	41	23	2	6	2	74

this represents a slight change in cooking practice from the early to the middle Iron Age, though the nature of this change is hard to judge. Two globular jars from Yarnton also had external sooting, showing that relatively fine vessels could be used for culinary purposes in the middle Iron Age.

Other potentially significant information on vessel use emerges in relation to the early Iron Age vessel types CS and CT. Rims of the former type occur with sooting and burnt internal residues in roughly equal quantities (although the overall numbers are small), but the tripartite jar type CT is hardly represented in Table 14.17 at all. One rim had limescale, and a further body sherd attributable to this type had a burnt internal deposit, but there is otherwise no indication of use on this important and relatively numerous type. Since base and body sherds, which might carry internal deposits, can often be attributed to this type even in the absence of the rim, the scarcity of such evidence from this type is particularly significant. The relative absence of deposits does therefore tend to suggest that this vessel type was not generally used for cooking purposes. Examples at the lower end of the size range in this form might perhaps have been drinking vessels, but while examination of the occurrence of particular vessel diameters reveals some clustering for this type, it is in the middle rather than at the lower end of the diameter range (see below), suggesting no clearly-defined functional differentiation based on size.

The data on vessel diameters for selected types from Cresswell Field show relatively little significant patterning (Table 14.18). The three main types considered (CB, CS and CT) all had diameter ranges mainly from *c* 100-225 mm, a range reflected by the unspecified jars (C). Within these ranges there was a clear concentration of examples of type CT between 140 and 190 mm in diameter (69% of all examples) and of type CB jars in a similar 140 to 170 mm range (56% of all examples). It may be noted that these preferred diameter ranges are also very close to those for typical Romano-British 'cooking pot-type'

Table 14.18 Cresswell Field: Rim diameter ranges for selected Iron Age vessel types. Quantification by number of vessels.

Vessel Type	*Diameter in 2 cm increments (eg 8 = 8-9 etc)*															*Total rims with known diameter*
	8	10	12	14	16	18	20	22	24	26	28	30	32	34	36	Unknown	
C general		6	10	18	12	10	14	4	10	2	1	3	5		1	341	96
CB	2	1	3	10	8	2		2	3						1	40	32
CS	2	4	6	4	4	3	2	3	3							14	31
CT		1	2	8	5	7	2	3	1							24	29

jars. Continuity of function to those vessels from type CB is very likely on the basis of the general similarity of vessel body shape, but the relevance of this to type CT is less clear.

A little additional light is shed on vessel use by organic residue analysis (see report by Copley *et al.* below). The most frequently occurring lipid components in the 28 of the 49 submitted samples which yielded residues were degraded animal fats. *Inter alia* these were a feature of samples taken from the 'All Cannings Cross' pit group (feature 8127) but occurred in other early and middle Iron Age groups. Two samples produced evidence for beeswax, but leaf wax components were only detected in a single sample, from a sherd also from pit 8127.

LATE IRON AGE AND ROMAN POTTERY

Some 8896 sherds (170.95 kg) of late Iron Age and Roman pottery were recovered from Yarnton, with a further 32 sherds (432 g) from Cresswell Field. The latter are dealt with separately below. The following discussion is based entirely on the Yarnton material

Fabrics/wares

The pottery was divided initially into major ware groups, defined on the basis of significant common characteristics. These ware groups can be combined to constitute two main classes of material, fine and specialist wares on the one hand, and on the other the rest of the coarse wares (cf Booth 1991b; 2004a). The fine and specialist ware groups (identified by the initial letter of the fabric code) are: samian ware (S); fine wares – colour-coated, lead glazed, mica coated etc – (F); amphorae (A); mortaria (M); white wares – other than mortaria – (W); and white slipped wares (Q). The remaining ware groups are: 'Belgic type' (in the sense of Thompson 1982, 4-5), usually grog-tempered, fabrics (E); 'Romanised' oxidised coarse wares (O); 'Romanised' reduced coarse wares (R); black-burnished ware (B); and calcareous- (particularly shell-) tempered wares (C). An additional ware category (G) has been used for distinctive coarse gritted fabrics in middle-late Iron Age traditions which occur very occasionally within the region.

Within these classes there are hierarchically arranged subgroups, usually defined on the basis of inclusion type, and individual fabrics/wares are then indicated at a third level of precision, both levels of subdivision being expressed by numeric codes. Thus R20 is a general code for sandy reduced coarse wares, while R21 is a specific sandy reduced Oxfordshire product. For the bulk of the present assemblage fabric identification was at the intermediate level of precision. Most of the material was in fabrics the sources of which are unknown and detailed assignment to specific fabric codes did not seem to be warranted. Fabrics assigned to the E ware group, however, were subdivided further in terms of their principal inclusion types. This procedure was also employed for a relatively small quantity of handmade pottery of middle Iron Age character (but not necessarily of middle Iron Age date).

Quantities of the identified wares or ware groups, using all the measures employed, are presented in Table 14.19. Individual wares are not described in detail. Well-known wares are simply referred to by their common names without further reference and other wares are given summary descriptions, sufficient to define their general characteristics. Further description of some important fabrics is given here, otherwise it is contained in the project archive. In referring to products of the Oxford industry the fabric/ware types are those of the OA system, while the vessel types quoted are those of Young's (1977) corpus (it should be noted that, coincidentally, M22 is both the fabric code for Oxford white ware mortaria and one the commonest vessel types in that fabric in Young's typology, but the text clarifies which is meant in every case).

For the most part the figures indicate a reasonable degree of consistency between the different measures used. The occurrence of ceramic classes which would produce systemic biases, such as the over-representation of amphorae when recorded by weight as opposed to sherd count, was at a very low level, so such biases were not usually significant (mortaria provide a minor instance, however, being significantly less well-represented by sherd count than by other measures). Notable characteristics of the assemblage are the generally low representation of fine and specialist wares, the importance of the 1st-century material (indicated principally by 'E' wares) and the domination of the remainder of the material by reduced coarse wares, supplemented to a lesser extent by shell-tempered wares. The ware groups are discussed in the sequence in which they appear in Table 14.19.

Table 14.19 Quantification of late Iron Age and Roman wares from Yarnton.

Ware	*Description*	*No.*	*%*	*Wt. (g.)*	*%*	*MV – rims*	*%*	*EVEs*	*%*
S	Samian ware (source uncertain)	1	+	3	+	-	-	-	-
S20	South Gaulish samian ware	10	0.1	70	+	1	0.1	0.15	0.1
S30	Central Gaulish samian ware	50	0.6	1029	0.6	17	1.3	1.28	0.9
S	Subtotal	61	0.7	1102	0.6	18	1.4	1.43	1.0
F11	Terra nigra	1	+	3	+	1	0.1	0.08	0.1
F34	Mica dusted ware, fine sandy oxidised	2	+	14	+	-	-	-	-
F35	Mica dusted ware, oxidised, ?Lower Farm product	1	+	4	+	-	-	-	-
F36	Mica dusted ware, very fine reduced	1	+	5	+	-	-	-	-
F43	Central Gaulish 'Rhenish' type ware	1	+	3	+	-	-	-	-
F50	Oxidised colour-coated wares (uncertain)	5	0.1	22	+	-	-	-	-
F51	Oxford red-brown colour-coated ware	215	2.4	3564	2.1	53	4.0	4.29	2.9
F52	Nene Valley colour-coated ware	13	0.1	350	0.2	2	0.2	0.35	0.2
F53	New Forest colour-coated ware	1	+	31	+	-	-	-	-
F59	Red-brown colour-coated ware, Lower Farm	1	+	2	+	1	0.1	0.08	0.1
F61	'South-western brown slip ware'	2	+	6	+	-	-	-	-
F	Subtotal	243	2.7	4004	2.3	57	4.3	4.80	3.2
A10	Amphora (uncertain)	1	+	4	+	-	-	-	-
A11	S. Spanish amphora (Dressel 20 etc)	2	+	242	0.1	-	-	-	-
A13	S. Gaulish amphora	1	+	18	+	-	-	-	-
A	Subtotal	4	+	264	0.2	-	-	-	-
M21	Verulamium region white mortarium	1	+	26	+	-	-	-	-
M22	Oxford white mortarium	48	0.5	3268	1.9	23	1.8	2.33	1.6
M31	Oxford white-coated mortarium	3	+	73	+	2	0.2	0.13	0.1
M41	Oxford red colour-coated mortarium	16	0.2	401	0.2	8	0.6	0.54	0.4
M	Subtotal	68	0.8	3768	2.2	33	2.5	3.00	2.0
W10	Fine white wares (uncertain)	8	0.1	78	+	3	0.2	0.19	0.1
W11	Oxford parchment ware	5	0.1	110	0.1	5	0.4	0.54	0.4
W12	Oxford fine white ware	40	0.4	598	0.3	3	0.2	1.50	1.0
W20	Sandy white wares (uncertain)	29	0.3	639	0.4	5	0.4	0.63	0.4
W21	Verulamium sandy white ware	1	+	23	+	-	-	-	-
W22	Oxford sandy white ware	1	+	12	+	-	-	-	-
W23	Oxford burnt white ware	1	+	45	+	1	0.1	0.32	0.2
W35	Fine white fabric with very fine sand	3	+	69	+	1	0.1	0.22	0.1
W	Subtotal	88	1.0	1574	0.9	18	1.4	3.40	2.3
Q11	Fine oxidised white slipped fabric	2	+	7	+	-	-	-	-
Q21	Oxford oxidised white slipped ware	11	0.1	97	0.1	-	-	-	-
Q25	?Verulamium sandy oxidised white slipped ware	1	+	9	+	-	-	-	-
Q26	Moderately sandy oxidised fabric with off-white slip	2	+	31	+	-	-	-	-
Q30	Reduced white-slipped wares	1	+	3	+	-	-	-	-
Q	Subtotal	17	0.2	147	0.1	-	-	-	-
E	'Belgic type' wares (general)	1	+	3	+	-	-	-	-
E10	'Belgic type' wares, organic-tempered	8	0.1	70	+	1	0.1	0.09	0.1
E20	'Belgic type' wares, fine sand-tempered	75	0.8	948	0.6	11	0.8	1.70	1.1
E30	'Belgic type' wares, coarse sand-tempered	305	3.4	4983	2.9	44	3.4	4.82	3.2
E40	'Belgic type' wares, shell-tempered	105	1.2	1279	0.7	9	0.7	1.44	1.0

Table 14.19 Quantification of late Iron Age and Roman wares from Yarnton (continued).

Ware	Description	No.	%	Wt. (g.)	%	MV – rims	%	EVEs	%
E50	'Belgic type' wares, limestone-tempered	183	2.1	4199	2.4	43	3.3	4.03	2.7
E60	'Belgic type' wares, flint-tempered	7	0.1	145	0.1	1	0.1	0.05	+
E70	'Belgic type' wares, 'rock'-tempered	2	+	12	+	-	-	-	-
E75	'Belgic type' wares, angular quartzite-tempered	13	0.1	163	0.1	2	0.2	0.05	+
E80	'Belgic type' wares, grog-tempered	1938	21.8	42270	24.7	241	18.4	26.49	17.7
E	Subtotal	2637	29.6	54072	31.5	352	26.8	38.67	25.8
O10	Fine oxidised 'coarse' wares	69	0.8	718	0.4	8	0.6	0.54	0.4
O11	Fine oxidised Oxford ware	240	2.7	4724	2.8	48	3.7	6.63	4.4
O15	Fine oxidised fabric	1	+	8	+	-	-	-	-
O18	Fine oxidised fabric with very fine sand inclusions	23	0.2	94	0.1	1	0.1	0.04	+
O20	Coarse sandy oxidised wares	34	0.4	394	0.2	4	0.3	0.35	0.2
O21	Coarse sandy Oxford oxidised ware	2	+	32	+	1	0.1	0.09	0.1
O30	Moderately sandy oxidised wares	3	+	39	+	1	0.1	0.09	0.1
O32	Fine oxidised fabric with common sand	2	+	100	0.1	-	-	-	-
O40	Severn Valley wares	4	+	46	+	2	0.2	0.17	0.1
O80	Coarse (grog etc) tempered oxidised wares	28	0.3	1446	0.8	3	0.2	0.28	0.2
O81	Pink grogged ware	55	0.6	3211	1.9	9	0.7	1.34	0.9
O	Subtotal	461	5.2	10812	6.3	77	5.9	9.53	6.4
R10	Fine reduced 'coarse' wares	497	5.6	5762	3.4	80	6.1	9.36	6.3
R11	Fine reduced Oxford ware	105	1.2	1204	0.7	16	1.2	2.78	1.9
R18	Fine reduced fabric as O18	7	0.1	94	0.1	1	0.1	0.29	0.2
R20	Coarse sandy reduced wares	260	2.9	3437	2.0	31	2.4	2.91	1.9
R21	Coarse sandy Oxford reduced ware	43	0.5	1017	0.6	1	0.1	0.03	+
R30	Moderately sandy reduced wares	605	6.8	11268	6.6	107	8.2	11.03	7.4
R37	Moderately fine reduced fabric with common sand inclusions	1749	19.7	27523	16.1	232	17.7	27.33	18.3
R50	Moderately fine reduced wares, black surfaces	1	+	13	+	-	-	-	-
R90	Coarse (grog etc) tempered reduced wares	87	1.0	4203	2.5	9	0.7	1.02	0.7
R94	Reduced fabric with grog etc tempering	818	9.2	19177	11.2	111	8.5	15.13	10.1
R95	Savernake ware	28	0.3	1151	0.7	7	0.5	0.80	0.5
R	Subtotal	4200	47.2	74849	43.7	595	45.3	70.68	47.2
B10	Black-burnished wares (uncertain)	5	0.1	130	0.1	4	0.3	0.28	0.2
B11	Dorset black-burnished ware (BB1)	154	1.7	1998	1.2	45	3.4	3.03	2.0
B20	Wheel-thrown black-burnished type wares	1	+	3	+	-	-	-	-
B	Subtotal	160	1.8	2131	1.2	49	3.7	3.31	2.2
C10	Shell-tempered wares	231	2.6	3264	1.9	20	1.5	1.30	0.9
C11	Medium shell-tempered fabric(s) includes Harrold products	704	7.9	14679	8.6	91	6.9	11.92	8.0
C12	Very coarse shell-tempered fabric	20	0.2	591	0.3	3	0.2	0.61	0.4
C	Subtotal	955	10.7	18534	10.8	114	8.7	13.83	9.2
G25	Malvernian limestone-tempered ware	3	+	188	0.1	-	-	-	-
G31	Clee Hills dolerite tempered fabric	1	+	14	+	-	-	-	-
G	Subtotal	4	+	202	0.1	-	-	-	-
Total		8898		171459		1313		148.65	

+ indicates value of less than 0.1%

S Samian ware

Overall quantities of samian ware were small and consisted mostly of Central Gaulish (Lezoux) wares, with a low representation of South Gaulish material. No East Gaulish sherds were confidently identified. The South Gaulish sherds include a tiny decorated fragment and a body sherd of Drag. 27. The only rim was from a bowl or dish of uncertain form. These sherds were generally significantly smaller (average weight 7 g) than the Central Gaulish ones. The higher weights of the latter (average 20.6 g) reflect their occurrence in robust forms such as the bowl Drag. 31, which accounted for 10 of the 17 rims in this fabric, along with three form 33 cups, single examples of forms 36 and 38 and two unspecified bowl types represented by small rim sherds. The Central Gaulish material also included two very small decorated fragments. The balance of fabrics and vessel types, and the relative absence of decorated material, are all indicators of the impoverished nature of the samian assemblage which reflect its rural character and generally late date – ie that the majority of the material is probably of Antonine date. This material is an extreme example of a type of collection noted in the much larger assemblage from the northern suburbs of Alchester (Dickinson 2001), which was interpreted as being of semi-rural character and in which the representation of decorated material (at *c* 6% of the assemblage) was noted as particularly low. At Yarnton the three decorated sherds amounted to just under 5% of the samian ware total.

F Fine wares

The quantity and range of fine wares at Yarnton was unremarkable. A single *terra nigra* sherd was noteworthy as it was of a cup, Camulodunum type 56 (Hawkes and Hull 1947, 226). Sherds in three distinct mica-dusted fabrics were recorded, of which F34 and F36 are unsourced, but one of which (F35) can be matched at the Oxford production site of Lower Farm, Nuneham Courtenay (Booth *et al.* 1993, 138), where it is tentatively assigned to the early 2nd century. Another 2nd-century Lower Farm product to occur at Yarnton was F59, a colour-coated fabric visually very similar to the later Oxford colour-coated ware but used for bag-shaped beakers of typical 2nd-century form (ibid., 140). Late Oxford products, and small quantities of sherds from their principal contemporary regional competitors, the Nene Valley (F52), the New Forest (F53, Fulford 1975, 24-5 fabric 1a), and a probable Gloucestershire source (F61, sometimes known as 'South-western brown slipped ware', for which see Young 1980; Keely 1986, 160-1, fabric 105), accounted for almost all the remaining material. A few small oxidised colour-coated sherds were not certainly attributable to any of these sources and were assigned to a general code (F50). It is possible, but by no means certain, that these were atypical Oxford products. Discounting these, only seven of the 243 fine ware sherds are attributable to the 1st-2nd centuries. Of the remaining material even the Nene Valley products, which could have appeared on the site as early as the later 2nd century, appear all to be later (and probably all 4th century) on the basis of the vessel forms represented (an indented beaker (body sherd only), a jar and a flanged bowl). The Oxford vessel types were mostly bowls, with the two most common forms (C45 and C51) dominant (14 and 15 vessels respectively).

A Amphorae

Amphorae were very rare, the three principal sherds representing the two most common sources of such material (South Spain and (probably) Southern Gaul) found in the region. A fourth fragment was too small to be confidently assigned to a source. It is worth noting here that a further amphora sherd in an oxidised fabric (A22), possibly of South Gaulish origin and perhaps from a handle of type Dressel 2-4, came from context (13308) on the floodplain. This presumably derived from the Yarnton settlement but the fabric was not represented there.

M Mortaria

Mortaria were not particularly common at Yarnton, though they were better-represented in terms of weight, vessel count and EVEs than by sherd count. With the exception of a single body sherd from the Verulamium region industry these vessels derived entirely from the Oxford kilns, with all three main fabrics (white, white-coated and red colour-coated) represented, though the second of these was scarce. The dominance of Oxford fabrics indicates that mortarium use on the site was almost non-existent before the 2nd century, the Verulamium sherd being the only one potentially datable before c AD 100, the earliest date for the production of Oxford white ware mortaria. The Oxford products cover most of the period from the 2nd to the 4th century, but later 3rd and 4th-century types are much better-represented than earlier vessels, with only single examples of types M2, M6 and an uncertain hook-rimmed form assignable to the 2nd century. White ware mortaria (fabric M22) were most common in forms dated AD 240-300 (types M17 (9), M18 (4) and M20 (1)) with six vessels of type M22 with a date range from AD 240-400. Fourth century mortaria representation may have been boosted by vessels in fabrics M31 and M41, in which fabrics types WC7 and C100 (4) are thought to be exclusively of this date. A further fragment of an unidentifiable type in fabric M31 may also have been of 4th-century date, since this fabric appears generally to have been more common at this time than earlier, despite having been in production from about the middle of the 3rd century. Four vessels of type C97 in fabric M41, however, are not so clearly of the 4th century.

The type is thought to have been in production from *c* AD 240-400, and at sites such as Lower Farm appears to have been particularly common in the later 3rd century, though it is not certain that this trend was followed across the industry as a whole. The period of use of C97 at Yarnton is therefore uncertain, but is perhaps as likely to have been in the later 3rd century as later, in which case mortarium use at the site will have been much greater at this time than in any earlier or later period.

W White wares

White wares only totalled 1% of sherds from Yarnton. Almost all are likely to have derived from the Oxford region, with only a single sherd attributed, somewhat tentatively, to the Verulamium region kilns. In view of the importance of Verulamium potters in establishing production of white ware mortaria (and presumably other forms) in the Oxford region in the early 2nd century it is not surprising that products of the two industries can be difficult to distinguish. There seems to have been a regional tradition of production of sandy white and grey/white fabrics, most noticeable in the Abingdon area, in the later 1st century, however, arguably predating Verulamium input into the Oxford region, so the exact extent of Verulamium influence in the production of sandy white wares after AD 100 is uncertain. This difficulty is reflected in the attribution of sherds to a general code W20 for sandy white wares of uncertain source, though an Oxford region origin is (subjectively) preferred. The great majority of the sandy white wares are likely to be of 1st to 2nd-century date, the exception being the single sherd of Oxford burnt white ware (W23), for which a date range of 240-400 is proposed (Young 1977, 113).

Fine white wares are in two, probably related, traditions. One of these is represented by fabric W35, a distinctive fabric with common very fine sand temper, used for butt beakers and other forms. This fabric is found in small quantities across the region but is most common in the Abingdon area. At Abingdon itself it seems to be associated with comparable fine sandy oxidised and reduced fabrics (of which O18 and R18 are also present at Yarnton) with broadly similar ranges of vessel types. These are apparently confined to post-conquest but pre-Flavian contexts, and are currently thought to represent fine ware production, based in the Abingdon/Dorchester-on-Thames area and with parallels to similar industries at Chichester and Silchester (Timby *et al.* 1997). Here fabric W35 occurs as a two-handled flagon. It is possible that other sherds assigned to the general fine white ware group W10 are also in this tradition, but the two bowls assigned to the W10 group are not typical forms in the repertoire of this industry as understood at present. The Oxford fine white fabric W12 (to which the majority of W10 sherds may in fact be attributable) probably developed out of this early tradition. It is quite well-represented at Yarnton, though boosted by the occurrence of a number of sherds of a single vessel of Young's type W37. Again most examples are likely to be of late 1st to 2nd-century date, while Oxford parchment ware sherds (fabric W11) can be assigned to the period 240-400. These were scarce, though it is possible that a few sherds assigned to the W10 ware group were in fact parchment ware. The W11 sherds were notable in including a rim of the rare bowl form Young (1977) P18.

Q White-slipped wares

Very few white-slipped sherds were encountered. Given the soil conditions on the site, with generally good preservation of sherd surfaces, the rarity of this ware group is likely to be a genuine phenomenon rather than an accident of preservation. Most of the sherds were in the Oxford white-coated fabric (Q21; Young 1977, fabric WC), and a sherd of Verulamium sandy oxidised white-slipped ware (see Davies *et al.* 1994, 54-5) was tentatively identified. Other fabrics in this group could not be assigned to known sources. Within the region fabric Q26 has only been noted at Yarnton. No vessels were represented by rim sherds in these fabrics, but the majority of sherds are likely to have been from flagons.

E Early Roman 'Belgic type' wares

These wares formed a major component of the Yarnton assemblage – just under and a little over 30% by sherd count and weight respectively, and a little less by other measures. The term 'Belgic type' wares (broadly in the sense of Thompson 1982, 4-5) refers to vessels in a common stylistic tradition but produced in this region in a wide range of fabrics and as both wheelthrown and handmade forms. The principal sub-groups of the E ware class are defined in terms of major inclusion type. None of the material can be attributed to known sources, so further codes defining individual fabrics within the subgroups have not been used. Instead, most sherds were recorded in terms of their principal fabric components in the same way as was done for the prehistoric material. In practice this showed that there was a considerable variation of fabric within some of the sub-groups, particularly amongst the grog-tempered fabrics. There were numerous combinations of grog with a very wide range of secondary materials, of which organic, sand and shell inclusions (respectively in *c* 47%, 36% and 5% of E80 sherds) were the most common, and a continuum of degrees of fineness. Well-defined combinations of inclusions and fineness groupings were not particularly apparent, however, though it would be anticipated that such groupings were significant in indicating local variations in a much wider potting tradition. In a small assemblage from Oxford Road, Bicester, for example, grog and organic tempered fabrics were again the most common (*c* 73% of E80 sherds) with grog and sand fabrics accounting for 14% of E80 sherds and grog and shell tempering 4% (Booth 1996, 78).

In view of the uncertainty about the significance of fabric variations within the broader fabric sub-groups of the E ware class the majority of the discussion is at the level of those sub-groups. Grog-tempered fabrics (E80) dominated the group, amounting to 73.5% of all E ware sherds (78.2% by weight), but sand, shell and limestone tempering were also regularly encountered. It was the sand-tempered aspect of this tradition which eventually developed into the typical 'Romanised' reduced wares which dominated the coarse pottery of the region from the later 1st century AD. On this basis it would be expected that the proportion of E20 and E30 wares would rise at the expense of E80 wares in the later stages of the late Iron Age/early Roman phase on the site, but the nature of the site sequence, and the paucity of good sized groups, makes it impossible to demonstrate any such development with confidence.

Jars or probable jar types formed the majority of the output in E wares, amounting to some 85% of rims in these wares, though bowls (mostly carinated), dishes and the occasional lid were also present. Three butt beakers, a girth beaker and a possible cup also occurred in E80 fabrics. The distribution of vessel types was broadly comparable across the main E ware sub classes, except that an unusually high proportion of the vessels in E20 (4 out of 11) were straight sided dishes. The numbers are perhaps too small to be significant, but they suggest a correlation between this relatively fine fabric group and the form, which was presumably intended for table use.

The main question relating to this ware group is that of chronology, since it spans the period of the Roman conquest. The appearance of E wares is the principal artefactual marker for the beginning of the late Iron Age in the region, in the almost total absence of alternative dating media. Harding's chronology, which pushed the introduction of this pottery back into the 1st century BC (1972, 129) is not readily supported by the results of recent work, for example at sites such as Abingdon Vineyard (unpublished), Stanton Harcourt (Gravelly Guy; Green *et al.* 2004), and Hatford (Booth 2000). At Linch Hill Corner, Stanton Harcourt (Grimes 1943), one of the key sites for Harding's late Iron Age phase in the region, examination of the material in the Ashmolean Museum shows that the 'Belgic' pottery is associated from the beginning of the sequence with Savernake ware. While the chronology of Savernake ware is itself open to debate, with an entirely post-conquest date range suggested by Swan (1975, 40) but not universally accepted (cf. Timby 2001a, 78-83), it is nevertheless hard to see how the date range of this material could be pushed back before the beginning of the 1st century AD, even if a pre-conquest origin were accepted. The current view in the region thus tends to see the appearance of E ware fabrics within the 1st century AD (cf. Booth 1996, 81-2), though this position is not yet conclusively established. A recent radiocarbon date from Bicester Fields, Bicester, centres in the 1st century BC (NZA 9634, calibrated to 171-2 BC at 1 sigma, but 190-30 BC using Oxcal v2.18, Cromarty *et al.* 1999, 223). This date, from a site producing some middle Iron Age pottery but with the assemblage principally composed of E wares, unfortunately comes from an isolated feature within the site, so its exact significance for the chronology of the E wares is uncertain. More work is clearly needed. E ware fabrics were in common use into the Flavian period on some sites at least, but not usually beyond, except as large storage jars, which continued to be manufactured in these fabrics through much of the Roman period and are recorded here under ware code R90 (see below and Young 1977, 202).

O Oxidised coarse wares

Oxidised wares formed a minor component of the Yarnton assemblage throughout the Roman period. The great majority of these wares were certainly or probably of local origin, most being assigned to the Oxford industry itself. Oxford products included not only O11 but also very likely most of the sherds assigned to the general subgroups O10, O20 and O80. The finer oxidised wares O10 and O11 were used for a wide range of forms, while the coarser O20/O21 fabrics occurred only as jars and bowls. Much the most common individual form in fabric O11, however, was the wide necked jar, Young type O27, of later Roman date. Fabrics O15 and O18 belonged to the early Roman regional fine ware tradition discussed above which included fabrics W35 and R18, to which O18 was equivalent. The one rim sherd in fabric O18 was of a characteristic butt beaker.

Non-local oxidised wares mostly occurred in small quantities, with North Wiltshire sources probably represented by fabrics O30 and O32 and Severn Valley ware (not more closely assigned) by fabric group O40. Identification of the latter was aided by its occurrence in characteristic straight sided tankard forms of 2nd-century date, this type being absent from the Oxford repertoire, and it is possible that undiagnostic Severn Valley ware body sherds are under-represented here, though the Oxford area is very much at the limit of the south-easterly distribution of these wares (they occur, for example, in very small quantities in the northern suburbs of Alchester). The only significant non-local oxidised fabric was O81, pink grogged ware (Booth and Green 1989), which occurs regularly across the region, principally in the 3rd and 4th centuries as large jars. At Yarnton this fabric was present exclusively as jar forms, though the characteristic very large vessels were supplemented by other types, such as a narrow mouthed jar. A source for this fabric, though not necessarily the only one, is now known at Stowe Park, Buckinghamshire (Booth 1999b).

R Reduced coarse wares

Reduced fabrics constituted the most numerous ware group at Yarnton, amounting to almost half of all the late Iron Age and Roman pottery. Replacing E wares as the principal coarse ware group, they dominated assemblages from the later 1st century onwards. For the most part these wares originated within the region, but in contrast to the oxidised wares, included a substantial component not derived from the mainstream Oxford industry. Both components were present at Yarnton from early in the Roman period.

The earliest Oxford products included very small quantities of the fine fabric R18 and probably vessels in the sandy fabric R21. The more numerous R20 fabric group probably consisted very largely of Oxford sandy wares, but these sherds could only be assigned to a general fabric category. These fabrics were essentially of 1st to 2nd-century date and as already indicated developed out of the E30 ware tradition. The 'Belgic' tradition was also the basis of the R90 group, made up of coarsely tempered fabrics which were used for large jars of a type established in the late Iron Age but which apparently continued to be produced through the Roman period (Young 1977, 202). Two further aspects of Oxford production are represented by the R10 and R30 fabric groups. The former consisted of generic fine fabrics, with low levels of sand inclusions. These occurred throughout the Roman period, but a chronologically much more restricted sub-variant is the very fine fabric R11, generally assigned a date range of *c* AD 70-150 (ibid., 203 fabric 4). Despite the fineness of the fabric, however, it was used for a wide range of non-specialist forms, jars, bowls and dishes, though two beakers of Young type R31 also occurred. The most distinctive products in this fabric, poppy head beakers and imitations of samian ware forms Drag. 29, 30 and 37, were only represented at Yarnton by occasional body sherds.

Like the R10 group, R30 fabrics were not chronologically diagnostic, but represent a continuing tradition of production of moderately sandy wares through from at least the beginning of the 2nd to the 4th century inclusive. At least some minor variations within the R30 fabric group may ultimately prove to be of chronological significance, but on present evidence the grey ware output of most of the main Oxford production sites cannot be readily distinguished and detailed subdivision of these wares could not be justified within the scope of the Yarnton project. R30 did, however, appear to be the most important coarse ware grouping in the 4th century. Inevitably R30 was used for a wide range of vessel types, but these were still dominated by jars, which amounted to *c* 70% of all rims in this group.

The most distinctive non-local reduced fabric was R95, Savernake ware from North Wiltshire (Hodder 1974; Swan 1975). This occurred in small quantities at Yarnton in the 1st and 2nd centuries. The identification of this fabric was complicated, however, by the presence of another fabric of quite similar characteristically lumpy surface appearance, R94, which was used for a number of the same forms as Savernake ware, in particular bead rim jars, though no examples of this type found at Yarnton were in fact attributed to the Savernake industry. R94 is mid to dark grey in colour and characteristically hard fired. It is tempered with moderate quantities of sub-rounded quartz sand, black sub-angular grog and distinctive sub-rounded white inclusions, perhaps limestone. This corresponds tolerably well with the published description of the products of kiln 2 excavated at Smiths Pit II at Cassington in 1947 (Young 1982, 146), while examination of some of the Cassington material in the Ashmolean Museum demonstrates that the fabrics appear to be identical. The range of forms found at Yarnton is also consistent with the published material (ibid., 145, nos 112-25), with angled everted rim jars, in particular, being common to both (cf. ibid., nos 112-13). These occurred alongside bead rimmed, medium necked and storage jars, with jars altogether accounting for 104 of the 110 rim sherds in this fabric. At Yarnton, fabric R94 was an important component of the early Roman assemblage, not surprisingly in view of the proximity of the likely source, and its occurrence broadly bears out the second half of 1st century AD date originally assigned to the kiln (ibid., 146), which is also supported by the evidence of the forms, the concentration on jars to the almost total exclusion of other forms being a distinctive early Roman characteristic.

There may have been some connection between fabric R94 and the most important individual fabric at Yarnton, R37, a reduced ware with a range of surface colours from light grey to very dark grey/black, characterised by common fine sand tempering with occasional black iron and organic inclusions. This and related fabrics dominated the assemblages at Asthall (Booth 1997a, 117-19) and at nearby Wilcote (Hands 1993, 77, fabric 2), both north-west of Yarnton, though they only formed a small part of the material from Alchester, further east (Evans 2001a, 352-4). This distribution pattern prompted the suggestion of a source relatively local to Asthall and Wilcote (Booth 1997a, 117), particularly as the character of the fine sandy fabric has something in common with north Wiltshire industries (ibid.). R37, however, is at one end of a continuum of fabrics with R94 (or R95) at the other, the intermediate stage being occupied by fabric R38, recognised at Asthall (subsequent to the processing of the Yarnton pottery) as similar to R37 but containing sparse to moderate grog inclusions as well as sand. Sherds of R38 at Yarnton would have been subsumed under fabric R37. Such sherds also occur among the Cassington material in the

Ashmolean Museum, but in this case it is less clear that these are associated with the excavated kilns. One vessel, apparently in fabric R37/R38, is a 'second', however, so the possibility of production of these fabrics in this area cannot be completely ruled out. Sherds from kiln 3 at Cassington, while clearly of general R30 character, are insufficiently close for this kiln to be regarded as the source of R37 or R38, though it may of course account for some of the other R30 material from Yarnton, and on the basis of the published description the material from kiln 1 (Young 1982, 146; not located in the Ashmolean at the time that this research was undertaken) was very similar to that of kiln 3. Either way, the distribution of fabric R37 indicates a source north-west of Oxford and a tradition which is in a number of respects distinct from that of mainstream Oxford coarse wares. R37 was certainly in production by the later 1st century if not rather earlier and continued to be important through the 3rd century, but may not have been made significantly into the 4th, when it was supplanted at Yarnton by the generalised R30 fabric group. The range of forms in fabric R37 was quite wide, though still dominated by jars (78% of 230 rims, but nearly 88% by EVEs); beakers, tankards, bowls, dishes and lids all being present in small numbers.

B Black-burnished ware

Black-burnished ware only formed a small proportion of the Yarnton assemblage, the great majority of the material being attributed to the standard Dorset source (BB1). The fabric was probably present throughout its main period of export, ie from *c* AD 120 to the mid 4th century. The main forms were all present (plus a single example of a handled beaker), but bowls were relatively much less common than 'cooking pot' jars and dishes, the majority of the latter being typical 3rd-4th-century simple straight-sided types. While these were twice as numerous as jars in terms of rim count (24 to 12) the jars were in fact better represented by EVEs, which provide a more realistic guide to the relative importance of these types.

C Calcareous (shell) tempered wares

These formed a significant part of the Yarnton assemblage – almost 11% by sherd count and weight. Three sub headings of this group were used, of which C10 was a general group for sherds with no particularly diagnostic characteristics except the presence of shell, a point indicated by the significantly lower representation of these sherds by weight than by sherd count in comparison to the principal grouping, C11. Given the importance of shell-tempering in the early Iron Age and (to a lesser extent) in the late Iron Age-early Roman period (ware group E40) the purpose of the C10 group was to allow separation of material belonging to later Roman traditions but about which little else could be said.

Fabric C11 contained moderate-abundant shell-tempering, with the shell inclusions varying considerably in size. A few sherds with very coarse shell inclusions (commonly 10 mm + in length) were separated and recorded as fabric C12, but it is uncertain if this distinction had any particular significance. Sherds assigned to C11 certainly represented more than one ceramic tradition, however, though separation of these on fabric criteria alone was not possible (see below). A substantial number, perhaps a large majority, of these sherds were probably of relatively local origin, occurring exclusively as jars, all of which, where the sub-type was identifiable, were of typical 'cooking pot' form. Such vessels seem to have been particularly common at Yarnton perhaps in the late 1st and certainly in the 2nd century. Some, at least, were handmade. This fabric/form combination is quite distinct from the earlier E40 material, which consisted of a more heterogeneous group of fabrics, in which shell could be combined with sand, grog, organic material and possibly limestone, in a manner reminiscent of earlier Iron Age fabric groupings. Moreover, there was a wider variety of jar forms in E40 fabrics, and a carinated bowl was also present. There seems therefore to be no direct development of the early Roman shell-tempered tradition from the late Iron Age one.

A quite different tradition is represented by probable products of the late Roman production centre of Harrold, Bedfordshire (Brown 1994). The fabric, however, is also essentially tempered with fossil shell and was not readily distinguished macroscopically from sherds of the probable local C11 discussed above, despite the fact that the composition of Harrold fabrics (of Middle Jurassic clays in which fossil fragments were already incorporated, (ibid., 99)), was rather different. In some cases potential Harrold products could be identified on the basis of characteristic vessel forms or thin, rilled body sherds, but body sherds not treated in this way could not be separated systematically from other C11 sherds, so they were not assigned a different code. It should be noted, however, that Harrold was not the only source even of these distinctive pieces, since material from Towcester with rilled surfaces has been shown to be from an unknown source distinct from Harrold (ibid., 105). The number of sherds potentially assigned to 'Harrold' is quite small, however, including 25 sherds with rilling on the surfaces, and consisted entirely of jars, the flanged bowls and simple dishes from this source which are found in the region in the second half of the 4th century being absent here. On this basis it may be estimated that non-local shell-tempered wares amounted to 10% at most of the C11 sherd total, and may have accounted for as little as 5% of this material, probably first appearing in the region in the late 3rd century.

G Coarse gritted wares of Iron Age type

Fabrics in this ware class, consisting of sources generally located to the west of the region, are only rarely present in the Upper Thames. As far as is known the single sherd of fabric G31, Clee Hills dolerite-tempered ware (Gelling and Peacock 1970), a hard fired, very dark grey-black handmade fabric with sparse-moderate sub-angular rock fragments up to *c* 1 mm in size, sparse subrounded white inclusions *c* 0.1-0.2 mm in size and occasional mica flecks, is the first from this source to have been noted in the region. Malvernian wares do occur more commonly, though only ever in very small quantities in the Oxfordshire part of the Upper Thames. Their arrival is likely to have been associated with the transport of salt in briquetage of Droitwich origin. It is possible that fabric G25, the limestone tempered Malvernian fabric (Peacock 1968, 421-2, Group B1), is under-represented at Yarnton. It is certain, however, that the igneous rock-tempered Malvernian fabric (ibid., 415-21, Group A) was not present at Yarnton.

Chronology of wares

The incidence of wares in terms of the main late Iron Age and Roman phases is shown in Table 14.20. The data there demonstrate the problems of phasing on the site, with regard to the presence of both intrusive and residual material, although only certainly intrusive wares are indicated as such in the table. The late Iron Age/early Roman (LIR) phase was dominated by E wares, the presence of which is, indeed, its defining ceramic characteristic. This phase spans approximately the first three quarters of the 1st century AD. It is possible that E wares continued in use for some time into the Flavian period, as seems likely for example at Gravelly Guy. This is not demonstrable clearly at Yarnton, but the present evidence does not contradict the proposition. In the inevitable absence of a very closely defined cut off point between the LIR and ERB phases issues of intrusive material, particularly with regard to reduced wares, are difficult to resolve. Early fine oxidised and reduced wares (O15, O18, R18 and also W35) would all have been current in the pre-Flavian period and were very likely only produced at that time. The occurrence of O18 in phase LIR is therefore as would be expected, and later appearances of O15 and R18 probably represent entirely residual material. Other fine oxidised and reduced wares (particularly O11 and R11) are generally assigned by Young to a Flavian-mid 2nd-century date range (eg Young 1977, 203). Again in view of the lack of real precision in defining such ranges the appearance of these wares in phase LIR may be 'real'. The character of fabric R94, discussed above, means that it too is very likely to have been current before AD 70 and its appearance here is unproblematic, as is that of R37, since the evidence from Asthall (eg Booth 1997a, 117) and particularly from Wilcote indicates that it too was in use before the Flavian period (eg Hands 1993, 11-12, cf 82-83 nos 41-47). Some reduced coarse wares, such as R30, however, are likely to have been intrusive at this time, and it is quite possible that the same is true of some sherds of R37. Colour-coated and Central Gaulish samian wares were much more clearly intrusive. These sherds were generally small and abraded (see above), but one Drag. 31 rim was more substantial. Equally, therefore, condition could not always be used as a guide to identification of other less certainly intrusive pieces.

The reduced wares in phase LIR totalled 8.4% of sherds, many of which may therefore have been securely stratified in contemporary contexts. In addition to these and E wares, shell tempered (C) fabrics formed a significant component of the assemblage, consisting mainly of fabric C11 (in its 'early' form) and sherds not certainly assigned to that specific fabric (C10). These fabrics probably remained important at least into the early 2nd century and as such were the only ware group to span the LIR to ERB progression in quantity. E wares were abundant in the ERB phase – in absolute terms they were much more common than in the LIR phase – but proportionally they were more than halved, though still comprising a third of the assemblage. Amongst the E wares the E20 (fine sand-tempered) subgroup was significantly more common in this phase than earlier. This could have been fortuitous, but this group (and perhaps also the coarse sand-tempered E30 group) may represent a transitional stage in the development of regional fabric traditions, from a grog-dominated (E80) phase of the 'Belgic' tradition to a new emphasis on sand tempering. E20 fabrics could thus have become relatively more important in the early part of the ERB phase. Sand-tempered reduced wares of more obviously 'Romanised' character (particularly in terms of firing technology) became the dominant group at this time, with R37 and R94 the principal individual contributors, although the latter of these is unlikely to have been in production after the early 2nd century. Other aspects of the expansion of the range of fabrics in use include the appearance of black-burnished ware, albeit at a low level, and the occurrence of fine and specialist wares, although the most numerous element of these was Oxford colour-coated ware (F51, plus fabrics M41 and W11), which must again have been intrusive at this time. Many of these, and presumably other less readily identifiable intrusive pieces, may have come from the upper parts of ditch fill sequences which had accumulated substantially later than the original date of excavation and main infilling of the features concerned, but were not necessarily isolated as such during fieldwork.

Non-intrusive components of the ERB assemblage attributed to the Oxford industry include white wares (particularly W12) and fine oxidised and reduced wares (O10, O11, R10 and R11). It is likely that many R20 and R30 sherds were also of Oxford origin, but these fabrics are insufficiently

Table 14.20 Quantification (by sherd count) of late Iron Age and Roman wares by phase.

Ware	Description	LIR	%	Phase ERB	%	LRB	%	Total incl. unphased material	%
S	Samian ware (source uncertain)					1	+	1	+
S20	South Gaulish samian ware			1	+	9	0.3	10	0.1
S30	Central Gaulish samian ware	2*	0.3	9	0.3	25	0.8	50	0.6
S	Subtotal	2*	0.3	10	0.3	35	1.1	61	0.7
F11	Terra nigra			1	+			1	+
F34	Mica dusted ware, fine sandy oxidised			1	+	1	+	2	+
F35	Mica dusted ware, oxidised, ?Lower Farm product					1	+	1	+
F36	Mica dusted ware, very fine reduced							1	+
F43	Central Gaulish 'Rhenish' type ware			1	+			1	+
F50	Oxidised colour-coated wares (uncertain)	1*	0.1	1	+	2	0.1	5	0.1
F51	Oxford red-brown colour-coated ware	3*	0.4	27*	0.8	104	3.4	215	2.4
F52	Nene Valley colour-coated ware	1*	0.1			8	0.3	13	0.1
F53	New Forest colour-coated ware					1	+	1	+
F59	Red-brown colour-coated ware, Lower Farm					1	+	1	+
F61	'South-western brown slip ware'					2	0.1	2	+
F	Subtotal	5*	0.7	31	0.9	120	3.9	243	2.7
A10	Amphora (uncertain)			1	+			1	+
A11	S. Spanish amphora (Dressel 20 etc)			1	+	1	+	2	+
A13	S. Gaulish amphora							1	+
A	Subtotal	-		2	0.1	1	+	4	+
M21	Verulamium region white mortarium							1	+
M22	Oxford white mortarium			7	0.2	26	0.8	48	0.5
M31	Oxford white-coated mortarium					2	0.1	3	+
M41	Oxford red colour-coated mortarium			2*	0.1	9	0.3	16	0.2
M	Subtotal			9	0.3	37	1.2	68	0.8
W10	Fine white wares (uncertain)			6	0.2	2	0.1	8	0.1
W11	Oxford parchment ware			3*	0.1			5	0.1
W12	Oxford fine white ware			26	0.7	8	0.3	40	0.4
W20	Sandy white wares (uncertain)			13	0.4	13	0.4	29	0.3
W21	Verulamium sandy white ware			1	+			1	+
W22	Oxford sandy white ware					1	+	1	+
W23	Oxford burnt white ware					1	+	1	+
W35	Fine white fabric with very fine sand			3	0.1			3	+
W	Subtotal	-		52	1.5	25	0.8	88	1.0
Q11	Fine oxidised white slipped fabric			2	0.1			2	+
Q21	Oxford oxidised white slipped ware	1*	0.1	1	+	6	0.2	11	0.1
Q25	?Verulamium sandy oxidised white slipped ware			1	+			1	+
Q26	Moderately sandy oxidised fabric with off-white slip			2	0.1			2	+
Q30	Reduced white-slipped wares							1	+
Q	Subtotal	1*	0.1	6	0.2	6	0.2	17	0.2
E	'Belgic type' wares (general)							1	+
E10	'Belgic type' wares, organic tempered	2	0.3	4	0.1	1	+	8	0.1
E20	'Belgic type' wares, fine sand tempered	4	0.5	40	1.2	25	0.8	75	0.8
E30	'Belgic type' wares, coarse sand tempered	33	4.5	108	3.1	91	3.0	305	3.4

Table 14.20 Quantification (by sherd count) of late Iron Age and Roman wares by phase (continued).

Ware	*Description*	*LIR*	*%*	*Phase* *ERB*	*%*	*LRB*	*%*	*Total incl. unphased material*	*%*
E40	'Belgic type' wares, shell tempered	21	2.9	56	1.6	11	0.4	105	1.2
E50	'Belgic type' wares, limestone tempered	38	5.2	56	1.6	11	0.4	183	2.1
E60	'Belgic type' wares, flint tempered	4	0.5	2	0.1			7	0.1
E70	'Belgic type' wares, 'rock' tempered			1	+			2	+
E75	'Belgic type' wares, angular quartzite tempered	3	0.4	8	0.2	2	0.1	13	0.1
E80	'Belgic type' wares, grog tempered	450	61.8	881	25.1	311	10.1	1938	21.8
E	Subtotal	555	76.2	1187	33.8	454	14.7	2637	29.6
O10	Fine oxidised 'coarse' wares			30	0.9	30	1.0	69	0.8
O11	Fine oxidised Oxford ware	6	0.8	72	2.1	113	3.7	240	2.7
O15	Fine oxidised fabric			1	+			1	+
O18	Fine oxidised fabric with very fine sand inclusions	3	0.4	16	0.5	2	0.1	23	0.2
O20	Coarse sandy oxidised wares			9	0.3	20	0.6	34	0.4
O21	Coarse sandy Oxford oxidised ware			2	0.1			2	+
O30	Moderately sandy oxidised wares					3	0.1	3	+
O32	Fine oxidised fabric with common sand					2	0.1	2	+
O40	Severn Valley wares					3	0.1	4	+
O80	Coarse (grog etc) tempered oxidised wares			4	0.1	15	0.5	28	0.3
O81	Pink grogged ware			7	0.2	27	0.9	55	0.6
O	Subtotal	9	1.2	141	4.0	205	6.6	461	5.2
R10	Fine reduced 'coarse' wares	5	0.7	176	5.0	253	8.2	497	5.6
R11	Fine reduced Oxford ware	4	0.5	49	1.4	39	1.3	105	1.2
R18	Fine reduced fabric as O18					7	0.2	7	0.1
R20	Coarse sandy reduced wares	1	0.1	122	3.5	76	2.5	260	2.9
R21	Coarse sandy Oxford reduced ware			34	1.0	7	0.2	43	0.5
R30	Moderately sandy reduced wares	5*	0.7	183	5.2	238	7.7	605	6.8
R37	Moderately fine reduced fabric with common sand inclusions	16	2.2	701	20.0	778	25.2	1749	19.7
R50	Moderately fine reduced wares, black surfaces					1	+	1	+
R90	Coarse (grog etc) tempered reduced wares	3	0.4	38	1.1	34	1.1	87	1.0
R94	Reduced fabric with grog etc tempering	25	3.4	447	12.7	212	6.9	818	9.2
R95	Savernake ware			13	0.4	8	0.3	28	0.3
R	Subtotal	61	8.4	1763	50.2	1653	53.5	4200	47.2
B10	Black-burnished wares (uncertain)					2	0.1	5	0.1
B11	Dorset black-burnished ware (BB1)	3*	0.4	38	1.1	34	1.1	154	1.7
B20	Wheel-thrown black-burnished type wares					1	+	1	+
B	Subtotal	3*	0.4	23	0.7	103	3.3	160	1.8
C10	Shell-tempered wares	37	5.1	79	2.2	77	2.5	231	2.6
C11	Medium shell-tempered fabric(s) includes Harrold products	54	7.4	192	5.5	373	12.1	704	7.9
C12	Very coarse shell-tempered fabric	1	0.1	17	0.5	1	+	20	0.2
C	Subtotal	92	12.6	288	8.2	451	14.6	955	10.7
G25	Malvernian limestone-tempered ware							3	+
G31	Clee Hills dolerite tempered fabric							1	+
G	Subtotal	-		-		-		4	+
Total		728		3512		3090		8898	

+ indicates value of less than 0.1%. * indicates fabric intrusive in this phase

diagnostic for this to be certain. Savernake ware (R95) appeared in small quantities for the first time in this phase.

In terms of absolute chronology the transition from the early Roman to the late Roman phase is less clearly defined than that from LIR to ERB. The late Roman phase is most obviously characterised by the (non-intrusive) appearance of the standard suite of late Oxford products, but may have commenced rather before the mid 3rd century date of that development. The expansion of the Oxford repertoire was the principal reason for the slight but significant increase in the proportion of fine and specialist wares (to 7.2% of sherds) in this phase, although it is notable that samian ware was also much better represented now than earlier. Residual material may account for some of this increase, but the continued use of at least some samian ware into the later Roman period also seems likely. Minor contributors to the range of late Roman fine wares were the Nene Valley and New Forest industries and the producers of fabric F61, with an unknown source perhaps in the Cirencester area.

Reduced wares remained the dominant group, although the slight increase in their representation, to 53.5% of sherds, might reflect the continuing decline of E wares (which still accounted for 14.7% of sherds, although entirely residual by this time) as much as any real increase in the importance of reduced wares. It is notable that quantities of fabric R37 increased from 20% to 25% of the assemblage in this phase, despite the fact that production of this fabric is not likely to have extended far into the 4th century, if at all. R37 must have been the dominant coarse ware fabric in the 3rd century assemblage, but was presumably in decline after that time. Oxidised coarse wares and black-burnished ware were both more important than before, and shell-tempered (C) wares recovered from their reduced level in the ERB phase to be the second most important ware class. This group must have incorporated some residual material, but late Roman shell-tempered ware accounted for a significant (but unfortunately not precisely quantifiable) proportion of the sherds assigned to C11. These would have included Harrold (Beds) products but also vessels in a fabric more recently isolated (subsequent to the recording of the Yarnton pottery) as C13, representing a sub-regional tradition of early Roman origin but continuing through into the late Roman period (see Evans 2001a, 367-8).

Vessel types

The late Iron Age and Roman pottery assemblage included some 1313 rim sherds comprising 148.65 EVEs. Discussion of the vessel types present in the assemblage is based almost entirely on the EVEs data. The types are divided into major classes (in 14 groups, including one (Z) for unclassified vessels), extending the classification used for Iron Age vessels (see above). One vessel class, amphorae (A), was only represented by body sherds. The sequence of classes, many of which are subdivided, runs broadly from closed to open forms, and is based principally on general similarities of shape, though 'functional' labels have been applied where these are widely current. The use of such labels, for example 'beaker', 'cooking pot' or 'storage jar', should not be taken automatically as a definition of function. Many vessels could have been multifunctional and their use(s) need not have included that implied by the traditional label. In the absence of more specific data, however, these labels will be used as a matter of convenience. A rigorous distinction between the principal classes based on vessel proportions was followed as far as possible, particularly with regard to definition of the most common classes, jars, bowls and dishes. Jars were usually defined as having a height:rim diameter ratio in excess of 1:1, while bowls fell in the range of 1:1-1:3 and dishes had a height:diameter ratio of less than 1:3. Some sub-classes, particularly CE jars, do not always follow these criteria strictly and it is accepted that some type CE jars could be described as necked bowls, but the definitions followed here generally have internal consistency. Two intermediate classes (D and I – jars/bowls and bowls/dishes respectively) are used for vessels which were insufficiently complete to allow confident attribution to specific classes on the basis of the height:rim diameter ratio.

Quantification of all the vessel classes and subclasses is presented in terms of major phase in Table 14.21 (residual early and middle Iron Age material is excluded). Tables 14.22-3 show the correlation of wares with the major vessel classes, expressed as the percentage of vessels in each ware represented by individual classes (row percent, Table 14.22) and as the percentage of each vessel class comprised by individual wares and ware groups (column percent, Table 14.23). These data show that the assemblage was dominated by jars (76.2% of all vessels). While the representation of jars declined gradually through time, from 86.5% in the late Iron Age/early Roman phase, they still formed a very high proportion (72.8%) of the late Roman assemblage.

The great majority of jars were in E and R wares, with a significant contribution also in shell-tempered (C) wares (12.1%). It is notable that black-burnished ware comprised only a very small proportion of jars (1.2%), although these were the dominant vessel class amongst the black-burnished ware reaching the site. Ware groups whose output was largely dominated by jar production were the three main ones already mentioned (jars comprised 85.6% of all E ware vessels, 82.5% of all R wares and 98.9% of C ware vessels), but jar production was also significant in oxidised wares (55.5% of these) and to a lesser extent in black-burnished (42.6%) and white wares (36.5%).

Definition of jar sub-classes was rather restricted; 40% of jars could only be ascribed to the general class. The sub-classes are largely defined on the

Table 14.21 Quantification (by EVEs) of late Iron Age and Roman vessel type by phase.

Type		LIA/LIR	%	ERB	%	LRB	%	EVE Total includes unphased vessels	%
					Phase				
B	Flagons			1.00	1.8			1.35	0.9
BA	'small'			0.04	0.1			0.04	+
BB	'large'			0.22	0.4			0.22	0.1
BC	jugs					0.16	0.3	0.16	0.1
B subtotal				1.26	2.3	0.16	0.3	1.77	1.2
C	Jars	2.13	17.0	15.71	28.5	18.57	36.4	46.18	31.1
CA	'mIA' open					0.11	0.2	0.11	0.1
CB	'mIA' barrel	0.03	0.2	0.11	0.2	0.05	0.1	0.55	0.4
CC	narrow mouthed			1.52	2.8	1.51	3.0	4.73	3.2
CD	medium mouthed	2.58	20.6	11.34	20.5	6.06	11.9	23.00	15.5
CE	high shouldered	2.89	23.0	4.58	8.3	2.14	4.2	11.87	8.0
CG	globular			0.06	0.1			0.17	0.1
CH	bead rimmed	0.94	7.5	2.37	4.3	0.38	0.7	4.22	2.8
CI	angled everted rim	0.57	4.5	1.53	2.8	1.22	2.4	3.55	2.4
CK	'cooking pot'	1.27	10.1	4.10	7.4	5.07	9.9	11.48	7.7
CM	wide mouthed			0.63	1.1	0.64	1.3	1.90	1.3
CN	large 'storage'	0.45	3.6	2.23	4.0	1.40	2.7	5.51	3.7
C subtotal		10.86	86.5	44.18	80.0	37.15	72.8	113.27	76.2
D all	Jar/bowls			1.47	2.7	0.83	1.6	3.11	2.1
E	Beakers			0.33	0.6	0.44	0.9	0.81	0.5
EA	butt beaker			0.36	0.7	0.30	0.6	0.70	0.5
EC	bag shaped					0.20	0.4	0.20	0.1
ED	upright neck			0.30	0.5			0.47	0.3
EE	folded/indented					0.05	0.1	0.05	+
EF	poppyhead							0.05	+
EG	carinated							0.19	0.1
EH	'jar' beaker			0.12	0.2	0.70	1.4	1.26	0.8
E subtotal				1.11	2.0	1.69	3.3	3.73	2.5
F	Cups					0.06	0.1	0.06	+
FC	conical			0.08	0.1	0.10	0.2	0.31	0.2
FD	carinated			0.08	0.1			0.08	0.1
F subtotal				0.16	0.3	0.16	0.3	0.45	0.3
G	Tankards								
GA	handled			0.11	0.2	0.42	0.8	0.53	0.4
G subtotal				0.11	0.2	0.42	0.8	0.53	0.4
H	Bowls	0.01	0.1	0.56	1.0	0.44	0.8	1.29	0.9
HA	carinated	1.20	9.6	1.66	3.0			3.14	2.1
HB	straight sided			0.81	1.5	1.05	2.1	1.98	1.3
HC	curving sided	0.14	1.1	0.50	0.9	1.29	2.5	4.46	3.0
HD	necked	0.06	0.5	0.66	1.2	1.90	3.7	3.16	2.1
H subtotal		1.41	11.2	4.19	7.6	4.68	9.2	14.03	9.4
I	Bowl/dishes	0.14	1.1	0.59	1.1	0.52	1.0	1.37	0.9
IA	straight sided			0.40	0.7	0.49	1.0	1.22	0.8
I subtotal		0.14	1.1	0.99	1.8	1.01	2.0	2.59	1.7

Table 14.21 Quantification (by EVEs) of late Iron Age and Roman vessel type by phase (continued).

Type		*Phase* LIA/LIR	*%*	*ERB*	*%*	*LRB*	*%*	*EVE Total includes unphased vessels*	*%*
J	Dishes								
JA	straight sided			0.75	1.4	2.22	4.4	3.95	2.7
JB	curving sided			0.17	0.3	0.07	0.1	0.66	0.4
J subtotal				0.92	1.7	2.29	4.5	4.61	3.1
K	Mortaria					0.02	+	0.02	+
KA	hook rimmed			0.13	0.2			0.20	0.1
KD	wall sided			0.11	0.2	0.19	0.4	0.30	0.2
KE	tall bead			0.12	0.2	1.51	3.0	2.48	1.7
K subtotal				0.36	0.7	1.72	3.4	3.00	2.0
L all	Lids	0.07	0.6	0.15	0.3	0.40	0.8	0.62	0.4
MF	'Cheese press'					0.15	0.3	0.15	0.1
Z all	Unknown	0.07	0.6	0.31	0.6	0.37	0.7	0.79	0.5
TOTAL		12.55	(8.4)	55.21	(37.1)	51.03	(34.3)	148.65	%

Table 14.22 Vessel class as % of EVE totals per fabric (row %).

Fabric	*A*	*B*	*C*	*D*	*E*	*F*	*G*	*Vessel Class* H	*I*	*J*	*K*	*L*	*M*	*Z*	*EVE Total*	*%*
S																
S20								100							0.15	0.1
S30						24.2		71.1		4.7					1.28	0.9
Subtotal						21.7		74.1		4.2					1.43	1.0
F																
F11						100									0.08	0.1
F51		4.7	1.9	1.2	9.3			79.0		3.3				0.7	4.29	2.9
F52			48.6					51.4							0.35	0.2
F59					100										0.08	0.1
Subtotal		4.2	5.2	1.0	10.0	1.7		74.4		2.9				0.6	4.80	3.2
M																
M22											100				2.33	1.6
M31											100				0.13	0.1
M41											100				0.54	0.4
Subtotal											100				3.00	2.0
W																
W10								94.7						5.3	0.19	0.1
W11			37.0					48.1	14.8						0.54	0.4
W12		66.7	13.3		20.0										1.50	1.0
W20			82.5					3.2		14.3					0.63	0.4
W23			100												0.32	0.2
W35		100													0.22	0.1

Table 14.22 Vessel class as % of EVE totals per fabric (row %) (continued).

									Vessel Class							
Fabric	*A*	*B*	*C*	*D*	*E*	*F*	*G*	*H*	*I*	*J*	*K*	*L*	*M*	*Z*	*EVE Total*	*%*
Subtotal		35.9	36.5		8.8			13.5	2.4	2.6				0.3	3.40	2.3
E																
E10				199											0.09	0.1
E20			84.1							9.4				6.5	1.70	1.1
E30			85.5	7.7				1.7		1.5		1.9		1.9	4.82	3.2
E40			74.3					25.7							1.44	1.0
E50			79.9	2.2				11.2	2.0					4.7	4.03	2.7
E60			100												0.05	+
E75			100												0.05	+
E80			87.4	1.7	2.1	0.2		5.8	1.7	0.8		0.1		0.2	26.49	17.7
Subtotal			85.6	2.6	1.4	0.2		6.3	1.3	1.2		0.3		1.2	38.67	25.8
O																
O10			63.0		22.2					14.8					0.54	0.4
O11			49.5	2.6	4.4			42.5	1.1						6.63	4.4
O18					100										0.04	+
O20			14.3	20.0				40.0	25.7						0.35	0.2
O21								100							0.09	0.1
O30									100						0.09	0.1
O40							100								0.17	0.1
O80			100												0.28	0.2
O81			100												1.34	0.9
Subtotal			55.5	2.5	4.7		1.8	32.0	2.6	0.8					9.53	6.4
R																
R10			78.5	4.9	5.4			5.3	3.5	1.7				0.5	9.36	6.3
R11			55.8	5.8	17.6			6.8		14.0					2.78	1.9
R18					100										0.29	0.2
R20			75.9							13.1		2.7	5.2	3.1	2.91	1.9
R21				100											0.03	+
R30		3.2	76.8	1.5	0.8			5.7	3.0	9.1					11.03	7.4
R37			82.5	3.1	1.0		1.3	5.2	2.9	2.2		1.3		0.5	27.33	18.3
R90			100												1.02	0.7
R94			94.8	1.0	1.9			1.2	0.6			0.5			15.13	10.1
R95			100												0.80	0.5
Subtotal		0.5	82.5	2.6	2.7		0.5	4.1	2.2	3.6		0.7	0.2	0.4	70.68	47.2
B																
B10								75.0		25.0					0.28	0.2
B11			46.5		1.0			10.9	5.0	36.6					3.03	2.0
Subtotal			42.6		0.9			16.3	4.5	35.6					3.31	2.2
C																
C10			88.5						3.1	6.9				1.5	1.30	0.9
C11			100												11.92	8.0
C12			100												0.61	0.4
Subtotal			98.9						0.3	0.7				0.1	13.83	9.2
TOTAL		1.77	113.27	3.11	3.73	0.45	0.53	14.03	2.59	4.61	3.00	0.62	0.15	0.79	148.65	
%		1.2	76.2	2.1	2.5	0.3	0.4	9.4	1.7	3.1	2.0	0.4	0.1	0.5		

basis of characteristics of shape, some of which, such as CE, CH and CI, are chronologically diagnostic, the first two generally indicative of a 1st century AD date and the last characteristic of the period AD 70-150, although not exclusively confined to that range. The middle Iron Age derived types CA and CB would also be expected to be of 1st century date, but while the latter was found exclusively in E80 and shell-tempered wares, consistent with such a date, the former occurred in a fine reduced ware (R10). The occasional occurrence of anomalous 'Iron Age' forms in later contexts is illustrated for example at Alchester by a type CB jar in fabric R30 probably of late Roman date (Evans 2001a, 344-5, CB1.4). The 'cooking pot' type (CK), particularly characteristic of black-burnished ware, was also found in C and other ware groups.

There was a strikingly low correlation between the very high incidence of jars and a very small number of lids (only 0.4% of EVEs). It is uncertain if the use of organic vessel covers should be inferred, but this seems likely.

The second most important vessel class was bowls (class H), which constituted 9.4% of the assemblage. This heterogeneous class was encountered within most ware groups (it was not certainly present in C wares), but was distributed principally (and fairly evenly) between F, E, O and R wares. Fine wares accounted for 25.4% of all bowls, the great majority of these being in Oxford colour-coated ware. Fine and samian wares were the only ware groups in which bowls formed a dominant part of production (74% of vessels in both groups). Other individual fabrics in which the class was well represented were not generally sufficiently common for high figures to be meaningful. The only exception to this was fabric O11, in which 42.5% of vessels were bowls, but this was a slightly special case as the great majority of the vessels in question were of Young type O27, forming the bulk of the otherwise scarce necked bowl category HD (together with a single example of the corresponding reduced Oxford form R38).

The other main bowl sub-classes were carinated (HA), straight-sided (HB) and curving-sided (HC) types. The first were present from the late Iron Age onwards, occurring occasionally in E wares as well as forming a distinctive component of late 1st-mid 2nd century Oxford coarse ware production (eg

Table 14.23 Fabric as % of EVE totals per vessel class (column %).

Vessel Class *Fabric*	*A*	*B*	*C*	*D*	*E*	*F*	*G*	*H*	*I*	*J*	*K*	*L*	*M*	*Z*	*EVE Total*	*%*
S																
S20								1.1							0.15	0.1
S30						68.9		6.5		1.3					1.28	0.9
Subtotal						68.9		7.6		1.3					1.43	1.0
F																
F11						17.8									0.08	0.1
F51		11.3	0.1	1.6	10.7			24.2		3.0				3.8	4.29	2.9
F52			0.2					1.3							0.35	0.2
F59					2.1										0.08	0.1
Subtotal		11.3	0.2	1.6	12.9	17.8		25.4		3.0				3.8	4.80	3.2
M																
M22											77.7				2.33	1.6
M31											4.3				0.13	0.1
M41											18.0				0.54	0.4
Subtotal											100				3.00	2.0
W																
W10								1.3						1.3	0.19	0.1
W11			0.2					1.9	3.1						0.54	0.4
W12		56.5	0.2		8.0										1.50	1.0
W20			0.5					0.1		2.0					0.63	0.4
W23			0.3												0.32	0.2
W35		12.4													0.22	0.1
Subtotal		68.9	1.1		8.0			3.3	3.1	2.0				1.3	3.40	2.3

Table 14.23 Fabric as % of EVE totals per vessel class (column %) (continued).

Vessel Class																
Fabric	*A*	*B*	*C*	*D*	*E*	*F*	*G*	*H*	*I*	*J*	*K*	*L*	*M*	*Z*	*EVE Total*	*%*
E																
E10				2.9											0.09	0.1
E20			1.3							3.5				13.9	1.70	1.1
E30			3.6	11.9				0.6		1.5		14.5		11.4	4.82	3.2
E40			0.9					2.6							1.44	1.0
E50			2.8	2.9				3.2	3.1					24.1	4.03	2.7
E60			+												0.05	+
E75			+												0.05	+
E80			20.4	14.5	14.7	13.3		10.9	17.0	4.8		3.2		7.6	26.49	17.7
Subtotal			29.2	32.2	14.7	13.3		17.4	20.1	9.8		17.7		57.0	38.67	25.8
O																
O10			0.3		3.2					1.7					0.54	0.4
O11			2.9	5.5	7.8			20.1	2.7						6.63	4.4
O18					1.1										0.04	+
O20			+	2.3				1.0	3.5						0.35	0.2
O21								0.6							0.09	0.1
O30									3.5						0.09	0.1
O40							32.1								0.17	0.1
O80			0.2												0.28	0.2
O81			1.2												1.34	0.9
Subtotal			4.7	7.7	12.1		32.1	21.7	9.7	1.7					9.53	6.4
R																
R10			6.5	14.8	13.7			3.6	12.7	3.5				6.3	9.36	6.3
R11			1.4	5.1	13.1			1.4		8.5					2.78	1.9
R18					7.8										0.29	0.2
R20			2.0							8.2		12.9	100	11.4	2.91	1.9
R21				1.0											0.03	+
R30		19.8	7.5	5.1	2.4			4.5	12.7	21.7					11.03	7.4
R37			19.9	27.7	7.0		67.9	10.0	30.9	12.8		56.5		28.6	27.33	18.3
R90			0.9												1.02	0.7
R94			12.7	4.8	7.5			1.3	3.5			12.9			15.13	10.1
R95			0.7												0.80	0.5
Subtotal		19.8	51.5	58.5	51.5		67.9	20.7	59.8	54.7		82.3	100	35.4	70.68	47.2
B																
B10								1.5		1.5					0.28	0.2
B11			1.2		0.8			2.4	5.8	24.1					3.03	2.0
Subtotal			1.2		0.8			3.8	5.8	25.6					3.31	2.2
C																
C10			1.0						1.5	2.0				2.5	1.30	0.9
C11			10.5												11.92	8.0
C12			0.5												0.61	0.4
Subtotal			12.1						1.5	2.0				2.5	13.83	9.2
TOTAL		1.77	113.27	3.11	3.73	0.45	0.53	14.03	2.59	4.61	3.00	0.62	0.15	0.79	148.65	
%		1.2	76.2	2.1	2.5	0.3	0.4	9.4	1.7	3.1	2.0	0.4	0.1	0.5		

Young type O42). Late Roman examples of the type were confined entirely to parchment ware form P24, though all three such vessels were unstratified – colour-coated ware carinated types in the C81-C85 range were conspicuously absent and the great majority of the Oxford colour-coated ware bowls were HC types, particularly C45 (but see below) and C51. The relative paucity of HB types is quite striking. Such vessels were part of the black-burnished ware repertoire as well as occurring (principally) in reduced coarse wares, but at Yarnton black-burnished ware bowls were relatively much less common than cooking pots and dishes in the same fabric.

Dishes, here, as elsewhere, the third most important component of the assemblage, were nevertheless very poorly represented at only 3.1% of all vessels. The great majority were of simple rimmed straight sided types (in sub-class JA) with a wide chronological range from late Iron Age to late Roman periods with relatively little typological development. These occurred almost entirely in E wares (9.8% of all dishes), black-burnished wares (25.6%) and reduced coarse wares (54.7%). Curving sided (JB) dishes included rare examples in Central Gaulish samian and Oxford colour-coated wares, in the Drag. 36 and related C47 range (although it is arguable that Drag. 31 and the corresponding Oxford type, C45, categorised here as bowls, should be included with dishes).

The minor types are mostly remarkable for their relative scarcity. Amphorae, as already indicated, were represented by body sherds alone and flagons (class B) were also rare, particularly as over half of the EVEs total was made up by a complete rim from a single vessel. Only four vessels were present, two in white wares, one in reduced ware and an example of Young type C4. White slipped (Q) sherds were rare and, while characteristically used very commonly for flagons, no rims were present in these fabrics.

Beakers were another relatively scarce class, and there was no evident correlation of the type with particular fabrics. A wide variety of beaker types was present, including butt beakers and 'jar' beakers – usually small jars in coarse ware fabrics for which a function as drinking vessels is possible (although this interpretation needs to be treated with caution, see above). It is notable that fine wares did not comprise a large proportion of beakers – forms in Oxford colour-coated ware (F51) and a single vessel in the early Oxford (Lower Farm, Nuneham Courtenay) fabric (F59) being the only examples. The only rims in Nene Valley colour-coated ware, for example, were of a jar and a straight sided bowl, both of characteristic late types. Another specialised drinking vessel class, the cup (F), was very scarce indeed, being represented by a few examples of samian ware (all Drag. 33 – Drag. 27 was present only as an occasional body sherd), a single example of Camulodunum form 56 in *terra nigra*, remarkable in the context of the character of the rest of the assemblage, and a single fragment of an uncertain cup type in fabric E80 and therefore of 1st-century date. A very different drinking tradition was represented by another scarce vessel class, tankards (G). This type did not form part of the Oxford repertoire at all, and the few examples present derived from two sources, both located west of Oxford. The precise source of fabric R37 is unknown, but the possibility that it derives from the Witney area has been discussed above, while the Severn Valley tradition was rooted much further west. It is notable that tankards from the North Wiltshire industry, rather closer to Yarnton than the Severn Valley, are absent.

Mortaria, in contrast to these various drinking vessel types, show an overwhelming dependence upon the Oxford industry. A single body sherd from the Verulamium industry presumably represents the principal regional supplier of these vessels before the initiation of Oxford mortarium production *c* AD 100. Thereafter, Oxford was the only source, though the great majority of identifiable types are dated after AD 240. Earlier forms were single examples of M2, M6 and an uncertain hook-rimmed type, while the post AD 240 period was represented by M17 (9), M18 (4), M20, M22 (5), C97 (4) and C100 (4).

Only one 'miscellaneous' (M) type was represented by a rim, this being a single 'cheese press' (type MF) in fabric R20. Body/base fragments of strainers (type MG) were noted in fabrics R21, R30 and R37. Unsurprisingly, more 'Romanised' special types such as tazze, candlesticks, lamps and triple vases, were completely absent.

In terms of chronological development the main trends in the evolution of the vessel type assemblage are clear. The Late Iron Age/early Roman assemblage was relatively small (12.55 EVEs) and was dominated entirely by jars (86.5%) and bowls (11.2%). Characteristic early types such as the high shouldered jar (CE) were particularly well-represented in this phase. It is likely, however, that some other types such as butt beakers and the *terra nigra* cup were in use at this time although they were only recovered in later contexts, but the addition of these would have made little difference to the general character of the assemblage at this time.

The early Roman assemblage was larger and more diverse, but still comprised 80% jars. Bowls, however, had also declined as a proportion of the assemblage (to 7.6%), with a marked drop in the proportion of carinated bowls which were well-represented in E wares in the late Iron Age/early Roman phase; it is unclear if this shortfall was made up by dishes and indeterminate bowl/dishes. The full range of minor types was now present, amongst which flagons, totalling 2.3%, were relatively well-represented. Some of the vessels in these categories were intrusive in contexts of early Roman date, however. In particular, two of the three mortarium rims in contexts assigned to this phase were from Young (1977) types M18 and C97, both dated after AD 240.

The late Roman assemblage demonstrates the continuation of established regional trends. Jars declined further in importance. At 72.8% they still dominated the assemblage, but exactly half were not assignable to a specific sub-class – a proportion which had increased steadily from the earliest phase. Medium mouthed and 'cooking pot type' jars were the most important identifiable sub-classes present. Bowls comprised 9.2% of the assemblage, a slight increase on the early Roman phase, and the representation of most other classes also increased slightly at this time, the main exception being flagons, which formed only 0.3% of the assemblage, significantly less than in the early Roman phase. Overall, however, it is clear that some of the sub-classes present in the late Roman phase, such as butt beakers, were largely if not entirely residual by this time, but in other cases the position may have been less clear-cut than appears at first sight. For example, the cups present in this phase include a grog-tempered vessel of probable 1st century date, but the type FC cups, samian ware form Drag. 33, could have remained in use right through the 3rd century if not later, despite the fact that they were produced in the 2nd century. There is ample evidence for long term curation of Antonine samian ware in the region and beyond, particularly on lower status rural settlement sites.

Increases in the representation of beakers, tankards, bowls, dishes and mortaria all seem likely to reflect genuine trends in the evolution of the assemblage, corresponding with the decline in numbers of jars. The level of the latter, however, remained high in comparison with other contemporary assemblages in the region, although comparable quantified data are still relatively scarce (but see now Booth 2007, 331-4). For example at the small town of Asthall jars formed less than 60% of the 3rd and 4th century assemblages (Booth 1997a, 122) while at Alchester jars were only just over 50% of the assemblage by the early 3rd century and had declined further to roughly 43% in the 4th century phases (Evans 2001a, 373). A 2nd-mid 4th century villa assemblage from Roughground Farm, Lechlade, contained 55.4% of jars (Green and Booth 1993, 136). It is unfortunate that there are no comparable data for the rural settlement at Old Shifford Farm (Timby 1995a, 129). At a broadly similar site at Mansfield College, Oxford, however, jars comprised 54.2% of a small assemblage (14.42 EVEs). This quantity was not divided by phase, but the assemblage was principally of late Roman date and can be compared with the late Roman phase data at Yarnton (Booth and Hayden 2000, 310).

Late Iron Age and Roman pottery from Cresswell Field

A mere 32 sherds (432 g) of pottery from Cresswell Field were assigned to the late Iron Age-Roman periods. The breakdown of this material by ware groups can be found in Table 14.24.

Table 14.24 Quantification of late Iron Age and Roman pottery from Cresswell Field.

Ware	*No. sherds*	*Wt. (g)*	*Rim count*	*EVEs*
F51	6	96	2	0.16
M41	1	4	-	-
E30	1	1	-	-
E80	7	170	2	0.16
O10	2	22	1	0.08
R10	3	31	-	-
R30	4	46	1	0.13
R37	3	15	1	0.06
R60	1	17	-	-
R95	1	11	-	-
B11	1	4	-	-
B30	1	8	1	0.02
TOTAL	32	432	8	0.61

Vessel types represented were C (jars) in E80 (2, 1 a type CN storage jar), O10 and R30, IA (bowl/dish) in R37 and JF ('fish dish') in B30. Bowls of Young's (1977) types C45 and C55 were present in fabric F51, and flagons and a type C51 bowl occurred as body sherds in the same fabric.

Eighteen of these sherds (232 g) were from the fills of Anglo-Saxon sunken featured buildings. Significantly, these included all the Oxford colour-coated ware sherds (F51 and M41), the relatively substantial average weight of which suggests that these may have been deliberately collected, as is seen at other sites within the region (cf Booth 2004b, 275). It was not possible to determine if this had been the case with any of the other Roman material. A very small quantity of late Iron Age/early Roman pottery (E wares) probably came from contemporary features, but no features assigned to the Roman period (see Chapter 8 above) produced contemporary pottery. Occasional sherds of Roman date not within Anglo-Saxon features were poorly stratified or introduced into the tops of feature fills by ploughing.

Pottery from the Kilns

The quantity of pottery recovered from the two kilns excavated in the site (see Chapter 9) is very small, but for the most part the material from component contexts of the two kilns, which is quantified in Table 14.25, was quite consistent. Apart from a single clearly intrusive sherd of Oxford colour-coated ware in fill 2527 of kiln 2526 all the material was assignable to the 1st, or at the very latest early 2nd, century. The distinctions between the recorded fabrics were less clear cut than might at first appear, so in fill 2525/A/1 one sherd of fabric R94 was close to E80 in character and one E30 sherd was equally close to R20, while in context 2526/A one R20 sherd was a hybrid with R94.

Table 14.25 Pottery from Yarnton kilns 2525 and 2526; fabric quantities by number of sherds/weight (g), followed by vessel type where appropriate.

Fabric/ware *Context*	*E30*	*E50*	*E80*	*R20*	*R94*	*F51*	*Total*	*Comment*
2525								
2525/A/1	2/16, CH	-	8/160, CN*	-	3/43, H	-	13/219	
2525/A/10	-	-	-	-	1/3	-	1/3	
2656/A	2/20	-	3/23, (CN)*				5/43	Sample 69
2656/A/1	1/5	2/49, CN	4/123, CN*	-	1/3	-	8/180	
2526								
2526/A/1	-	2/12	-	2/9	1/4	-	5/25	
2527/A/1	-	-	-	-	-	1/27	1/27	Young type C51 intrusive

* = joining sherds

The hybrid nature of some of the fabrics suggests that they belong to the period when 'Belgic type' wares were beginning to be replaced by more 'Romanised' fabrics. This is regardless of whether or not these fabrics were being produced in the kilns, though it is very likely that they were. The limited number of rim sherds present, all from kiln 2525, belonged to jars – mostly thick walled vessels of storage jar type, though a bead rim jar was present in fabric E30 – and a single small bowl with a slightly beaded rim in hybrid fabric R94/E80. Decoration on these sherds consisted of overall or zone burnishing, the use of which was quite common, with occasional horizontal burnished lines (one example each on fabrics E30 and R94) and grooves.

The kiln products have broad parallels in the region at Cassington (Case 1982a, 134-6 – three kilns were discovered but only kiln 2 is directly relevant) and at Hanborough (Sturdy and Young 1976) and the Yarnton fabrics are also in the same broad traditions represented by those kilns. The two Hanborough kilns were associated with six pottery fabrics, five of which 'belong to the heavily tempered pre-Roman tradition' (Sturdy and Young 1976, 64) while the sixth was 'a typical Roman sandy grey ware' (ibid.). This parallels the situation at Yarnton quite closely, with fabric R20 falling into the latter category, though the Yarnton sample is too small for detailed comparison of the fabrics to be meaningful. The similarity of some of the Cassington kiln 2 material to fabric R94 has already been noted above and again broad comparability of tradition is certain. The published vessels from Cassington kiln 2 include forms which are entirely consistent with the repertoire of vessels in R94 and other early Roman fabrics from Yarnton (Young 1982, 145-6).

General discussion *by Edward Biddulph*

Weighing some 167 kg and totalling over 11,000 sherds, the early and middle Iron Age assemblage from Yarnton is among the largest of its period recovered from the region. While smaller than the massive Gravelly Guy assemblage (40,000 sherds, Duncan *et al.* 2004), it rivals that from Ashville, Abingdon, which, combining the pottery from the Ashville and Wyndyke Furlong sites, totals in excess of 13,000 sherds (De Roche 1978; Timby 1999). Smaller, but still valuable, assemblages have been recovered at Hardwick (3100 sherds, D Wilson 1993), Watkins Farm, Northmoor (1450 sherds, Allen 1990b), Farmoor (1275 sherds, Lambrick 1979b), Whitehouse Road, Oxford (630 sherds, Timby 1993), and Witney (366 sherds, Timby 1995b) among others. The late Iron Age and Roman assemblage was equally large; almost 9000 sherds, weighing 171 kg, were recovered. This total is not too far behind the 14,500 sherds (207 kg) from Gravelly Guy, but is in any case well ahead of many other sites within the region. From Watkins Farm, Northmoor, just over 3,000 sherds, weighing 34 kg were recovered (Raven 1990); Old Shifford Farm, Standlake yielded 4,000 sherds (58 kg) (Timby 1995a), while 1,000 sherds (16 kg) were found at Oxford Road, Bicester (Booth 1996). The Bicester Fields Farm assemblage of middle to (mostly) late Iron Age material totalled 3750 sherds (Brown 1999), while the largest fully published Roman assemblage from the region is that from the A421 sites at Alchester (36,800 sherds, Evans 2001a). Together, the Iron Age pottery from Cresswell Field and Yarnton forms an enviable collection, not least because it is one of the largest assemblages from the region to be comprehensively recorded. This allows comparison, not only with contemporaneous pottery, but also with late Iron Age and Roman groups, and provides a complete overview encompassing both the Iron Age and Roman period. This greatly enhances the understanding of the development and use of ceramics at the site and within the wider region.

Though the size of the pottery assemblage allows broad chronological trends to be identified, continuous occupation evident at Yarnton means that a certain amount of the Iron Age assemblage must be redeposited and residual. The problem that redeposition causes in terms of establishing a reliable chronology is one that is widely recognised. Occasionally, where the focus of early Iron Age occupation is away from that of the middle Iron Age, as at Farmoor or Watkins Farm, the extent of redeposition can be determined clearly. Otherwise, an assessment must be made internally on the basis of group composition. Well preserved pottery in reasonably large and undisturbed groups is essential. This problem of redeposition is discussed with reference to discussion of the chronology below.

Yarnton was occupied throughout the Iron Age. The early Iron Age pottery is typical of the region. Angular and slack-profiled types in shelly fabrics predominate. These fabrics contributed up to 75% by sherd count of early Iron Age pottery. This conforms to the regional pattern, though variations are evident. Limestone and fossiliferous fabrics took a large share of the early Iron Age pottery from Groundwell West, Wiltshire (Timby 2001b, 20), for example, and are also characteristic of middle Iron Age assemblages in the Gloucestershire part of the Upper Thames Valley. Yarnton was more closely comparable to assemblages such as Farmoor, where invariably 80% or above of pottery in groups by sherd count was shell-tempered (Lambrick 1979b, fig. 20). Such pottery takes the largest share of early Iron Age assemblages at Abingdon and Gravelly Guy, but at both the proportions are slightly lower: 66% by sherd count at the former (De Roche 1978, table IV), and 58% by weight at Gravelly Guy (Duncan *et al.* 2004). A chronological explanation may be sought for these differences, though they are almost impossible to tease out given the necessarily broad dating of early Iron Age pottery and the paucity of large well-dated groups at some sites, including Yarnton. Given the slight reduction in the level of activity during the middle Iron Age (see below), the high proportion of shelly fabrics in part reflects the site's early Iron Age emphasis, particularly at Cresswell Field. Of additional interest, though, it was observed at Gravelly Guy that the highest proportion of shell-tempered fabrics occurred in the 'middle' period of the early Iron Age, with larger levels of sandy fabrics in the 'early' and 'late' periods. Certainly, pottery dated to the late Bronze Age/early Iron Age transition was present at Yarnton, but limited in quantity, suggesting that activity levels were not as high at the beginning of the early Iron Age compared with later in the period. The vessels associated with this early phase were in mixed fabrics of which shell was not a totally dominant component. As at Gravelly Guy the shell-tempered early Iron Age fabrics characteristic of the region were probably later in date than these 'earliest' mixed fabrics.

The distribution of pottery slightly favoured Cresswell Field during the early Iron Age. Of the Iron Age and Roman assemblage from this site, the early Iron Age contributed 68% by weight, compared with 31% for the middle Iron Age. At Worton Rectory Farm, the distribution is reversed; this site has a middle Iron Age emphasis, with 11% of the total pottery dated to the period, against 8% for the early Iron Age. Overall, a slight decline in the level of activity during the middle Iron Age is evident. This has not had an obvious effect on the range of pottery present. Following the regional trend, sand-tempered fabrics gain in importance to the detriment of shell-tempered pottery, though the latter remains a strong element of the middle Iron Age assemblage. The range of forms is wide and includes bowls as well as jars. However, globular jars (CG) were poorly represented, possibly due to a chronological, or even regional variation. The type is absent from the 'earliest' middle Iron Age groups at Gravelly Guy, and tends to be associated with the later middle Iron and late Iron Age at Watkins Farm and Ashville, Abingdon (Allen 1990b, 45). However, it is by no means certain that the scarcity of the type at Yarnton confirms an early Iron Age and earlier middle Iron Age emphasis.

Despite the paucity of large, well-dated groups, a significant degree of redeposition occurred during the middle Iron Age. Assessed by vessel forms, however, the level of residual pottery appears to be minimal. Standard early Iron Age forms – principally slack-profiled and angular jar types (CS and CT types, respectively) – were replaced by middle Iron Age types during the 'earliest' middle Iron Age. This is evident at Gravelly Guy (Duncan *et al.* 2004) and Abingdon (De Roche 1978, table IV) where the proportions of such types fall dramatically during this period. At sites where no occupation is attested before the middle Iron Age, for example Watkins Farm (Allen 1990a) and Mingies Ditch (D Wilson 1993, 71), such forms are absent. It is reasonable to suggest, then, that typically early Iron Age forms in middle Iron Age contexts are likely to be residual. On this basis, Yarnton offers a mixed picture. At Worton Rectory Farm, just 3% of pottery (by EVEs) in middle Iron Age contexts was residual. Cresswell Field appears to have suffered from greater redeposition: it attains a level of 13%. In one respect, form is perhaps an unsatisfactory indicator of residuality. The process of redeposition causes the pottery to fragment further, resulting in a mass of small body sherds and few large rim sherds, inevitably making identification difficult. Residual pottery is, if anything, under-represented. Fabric may be deemed to be more reliable, either using sherd count or weight, so long as the fabric is unquestionably out of use in the period concerned. But again problems are encountered, since shell-tempered fabrics, while of predominantly early Iron Age manufacture, continued to be used to a lesser extent into the middle Iron Age. Mingies Ditch and Watkins Farm, both without early Iron Age precursors, yielded shelly fabrics. At Yarnton, barrel-shaped jars (CB), though not globular vessels (CG), perhaps reflecting a later introduction, were available in these fabrics. Moreover, just to the north of the Thames Valley, there is evidence to suggest that shell-tempered fabrics remained in use through the middle Iron Age (Booth 1997c, 105-7). This characteristic should serve to distinguish between the ceramic traditions of the Thames Valley and north Oxfordshire, but the point at which these traditions met and overlapped remains to be defined.

Assuming continuous occupation, one might expect to encounter a visible transition between the middle and late Iron Ages which might, for example, manifest itself through the production of forms of one period in fabrics characteristic of the other. Such evidence is, however, scarce within the region. Something of the sort can be seen at Bicester Fields Farm, where forms ubiquitous in the middle Iron Age, notably CB and CG types, were available in fabric E80, albeit in small quantities. Conversely, typical late Iron Age types CD and CE were produced in 'middle Iron Age' fabrics (Brown 1999, tables 4 and 5). A similar observation was made at Gravelly Guy, where, in 'latest' middle Iron Age contexts, late Iron Age-type necked jars were produced in middle Iron Age fabrics, though it was noted that a marked changeover period was absent (Duncan *et al.* 2004). This is particularly striking, given the size of the Gravelly Guy assemblage and the level of detail at which it was studied. In view of this the limited indications of the same pattern at Yarnton are exactly what might be expected. Typical late Iron Age forms – namely necked jars and storage jars – were available in middle Iron Age (ie generally sand-tempered) fabrics as well as in grog-tempered fabrics. However, although a small amount of 'Belgic' E wares was present in middle Iron Age contexts, none was in middle Iron Age forms, and much if not all of this material may have been intrusive. Likewise, in contexts containing mainly E wares in association with a small amount of middle Iron Age fabrics, forms typical of each period were restricted to the fabrics of those periods.

Evidently, then, pottery specifically indicative of a change from middle to late Iron Age traditions, the latter represented essentially by the south-eastern 'Belgic type ware' tradition, was scarce. None is represented at Cresswell Field, while Worton Rectory Farm yielded less than 1%. However, although most contexts lacked particularly diagnostic pottery, a small number contained 'Belgic' E wares, either alone, or in association with small amounts of middle Iron Age fabrics. These are perhaps the best candidates for a late Iron Age date. Around 5% of contexts (some 56 out of 1131 deposits with pottery) can thus be dated to the late Iron Age. That the majority of the E wares was found in association with post-conquest Roman wares seems to confirm the notion that E wares were essentially a 1st century AD tradition, and supports the chronology of those fabrics suggested in the discussion of E wares above.

This evidence does not, however, provide any support for the view that there was a hiatus in the occupation sequence at Yarnton in the late Iron Age (and there is no clear indication of such a hiatus in the stratigraphic sequence). Where middle and late Iron Age activity occurs in the same locations in the region, the ceramic evidence, as at Yarnton, suggests that the transition between the two was generally short. It is notable that the site with the best evidence for this transition, Bicester Fields Farm, lies in the eastern part of the region in territory that may reasonably be assigned to the Catuvellauni in the late Iron Age, territory in which the 'Belgic' ceramic tradition was relatively better established before the Roman conquest. Here the processes of transition from middle to late Iron Age, in ceramic terms, may have taken a different course from those seen further west in the Upper Thames, arguably in Dobunnic territory.

At Yarnton, as at some other sites in the region, the definition of a 'late Iron Age' phase rests very largely upon the presence of the distinctive ceramic tradition (which was then maintained into the early Roman period – the events of AD 43 are invisible in ceramic terms) rather than upon other clear indicators of change in settlement morphology and other characteristics. What is striking is the sheer volume of pottery – late Iron Age or earliest Roman period pottery accounted for 13% of the assemblage by weight; Cresswell Field contributed just 2%. From then on, activity was restricted to Worton Rectory Farm, and Cresswell Field virtually ceased to be occupied.

Early Roman pottery (late 1st and 2nd century) accounted for 38% of the assemblage. The chronology of Worton Rectory Farm within this period is somewhat ill-defined. The lack of well-dated, large groups makes it difficult to trace the changing levels of occupation through time. There are indications, however, that the settlement declined during the later 2nd century or early 3rd century, or at least shifted away from the early Roman focus. That activity continued into the mid 2nd century is indicated most clearly by the presence of Central Gaulish samian ware (S30), which forms the largest proportion of samian from the site (82% of all samian sherds, but 93% by weight). Earlier-dated South Gaulish samian (S20) was poorly represented, while East Gaulish material, imported into Britain from the middle of the 2nd century and the first half of the 3rd and replacing the declining Central Gaulish industry, was apparently entirely absent. Supporting evidence comes in the form of a 'Rhenish' ware beaker, again from Central Gaul. Arrivals from this source tended to appear from the mid 2nd century. The corresponding East Gaulish Moselkeramik was again absent from the assemblage. Some of the earliest black-burnished ware (B11) products are also present, including so-called 'jar-beakers' (EH), which probably arrived during the first half of the 2nd century.

Although a chronological gap is difficult to identify, pottery potentially available during the late

2nd century is all likely to be late 3rd or 4th century in date. Oxfordshire white ware mortaria and Nene Valley colour-coated ware forms, for example, are consistent with a late, rather than mid, Roman date. A mid Roman hiatus at Yarnton, while not entirely proven, is nevertheless a distinct possibility. Termination of or breaks in the sequence of activity in the 2nd century, can be seen at a large number of rural settlement sites in the region (Henig and Booth 2000, 106-8). Sites in the vicinity of Yarnton affected by this phenomenon include Gravelly Guy, Linch Hill (Stanton Harcourt) and Old Shifford Farm (Hey 1995, 171). A hiatus need not mean abandonment, albeit temporary, but rather the less drastic option of a shift of settlement focus. Such a shift is evidenced at Oxford, where 1st and early 2nd century settlement centred at Mansfield College relocated a short distance to the north, with occupation resuming after the late 3rd century (Booth and Hayden 2000, 311-312; Biddulph 2005). If a break or decline in occupation can be demonstrated at Yarnton, however, then a shift of focus is probably unlikely, as no other site in the immediate Yarnton area has yielded large quantities of 3rd and 4th century pottery. It must be emphasised, however, that the existence for such a break at Yarnton is still rather speculative and the evidence is much less clear than at other sites in the area where a hiatus is observed. In these cases the break almost invariably fell within the first half of the 2nd century AD and typically resulted in complete abandonment of settlement, with relocation elsewhere, or in a major reconfiguration of the site. Neither of these characteristics is evident at Yarnton.

Late Roman pottery, dating to the 3rd and 4th century, accounts for 30% of the Worton Rectory Farm assemblage. Most of it is likely to date from the late 3rd century onwards, given the possibility of a mid Roman hiatus and the predominance of late Roman forms, especially in Oxfordshire wares.

Most pottery throughout the period of occupation at the Worton Rectory Farm site was deposited into pits and ditches. Overall, ditches yielded more pottery, though a clear chronological distinction is apparent: pit assemblages dominated the Iron Age, while ditches yielded most of the late Iron Age and Roman pottery. The proportion of pottery recovered from pits declined rapidly. From a high point in the early Iron Age, where 83% of pottery by weight was from this feature type, the proportion drops to just 16% by the late Iron Age/early Roman period. Conversely, the proportion of pottery from linear features rises from 10% by weight in the middle Iron Age to 60% by the late Roman period.

This mirrors the general distribution of features, in which fewer pits are dated to the Roman period than the Iron Age, the converse being true for ditches. If this relates to a shift in settlement focus, with the Roman-period focus moving away from the Iron Age one, then it follows a similar pattern observed at Cresswell Field. The decline apparent in the quantities of pottery at this site is supported by the range of features from which the pottery was recovered. Early Iron Age pits yielded 90% of the pottery. This subsequently declined to the extent that, by the late Iron Age/early Roman period, no pottery was recovered from pits. Ditches became more important as places of final deposition in later periods. This may relate to a shift in the settlement, with the Roman focus moving away from the Iron Age one, but also reflects fundamental changes in the physical characteristics of the site, with a greatly increased emphasis on the use of ditches, particularly from the late Iron Age onwards.

There is no major difference in the condition of pottery between feature types, or over time. Overall, the mean sherd weight for pottery from pits is 17 g, and 16 g from ditches. The sherd weights for individual phases only deviate slightly from these averages. The 'completeness', or average rim representation, of the pottery reveals a similar picture. Rims from pits were an average of 8% complete; rims from ditches were 9% complete. Again, the deviation per individual phase is slight.

The average sherd weight of the late Iron Age and Roman assemblage, 19.3 g, is notable. It is rather higher than the figure for early and middle Iron Age pottery (*c* 15.2 g), despite the generally more substantial character of the fabrics of those periods and an absence of 'massive' fabrics (such as amphorae) which can inflate Roman period average weight figures. Comparative average sherd weight figures from other major mostly late Iron Age to Roman or solely Roman assemblages in the region include 16.3 g at Gravelly Guy and 12.2 g at Claydon Pike, Fairford, 12.6 g at Asthall (Booth 1997a, 105), 13.5 g at Alchester (Evans 2001a, 263), 13.4 g at Hatford (Booth 2000, 25), *c* 14.5 at Old Shifford Farm (Timby 1995a, 124) and 18.6 g at Wantage (data from Timby 1996, 135). The last of these is close to the Yarnton figure, but the other values are below and typically no more than two thirds of the figure for Yarnton. The significance of this is uncertain. The amount of redeposition at Yarnton indicated by extensive recutting of features, and by the relatively high incidences of residual material in the later phase assemblages, certainly does not suggest that general site formation factors would have favoured the relatively good preservation of pottery. Equally there is no indication that the average sherd weight was inflated as a consequence of a 'coarse' level of recovery of hand excavated material. Amongst the most important ware groups E wares have a high average weight (20.5 g), which might suggest that some particular characteristic of the late Iron Age assemblage resulted in an overall higher than normal average weight across the site as a whole. It is not clear, however, what such a characteristic might have been.

Pottery is perhaps an imprecise indicator of status during the early and middle Iron Age. Occasionally, a vessel is sufficiently different from the majority of the assemblage to suggest a source of manufacture away from that of the remaining pottery. This may indicate trade or social contacts beyond the local area, thus giving that settlement a degree of regional pre-eminence. Some evidence for imported pottery was observed in the assemblage from pit 8127 from Cresswell Field. Among the group of some 14 vessels is one not readily paralleled within the region, both in terms of form and decoration. A south-western source is possible, but not established. The level of decorated pottery may have some bearing on status, though, again, a link between the two cannot be confirmed. Whatever the significance, Yarnton has a comparatively large proportion of decorated pottery. As observed at Gravelly Guy, Farmoor and Watkins Farm, among others, burnishing was the commonest form of decoration, particularly on the finer fabrics. The incidence of the treatment slightly favours the early Iron Age overall, though Worton Rectory Farm had a greater frequency during the middle Iron Age. Burnished sherds accounted for 24% of the early and middle Iron Age pottery at Yarnton. By comparison, 5.5% of sherds from Gravelly Guy were similarly treated (Duncan *et al.* 2004). Some fabric groups from Watkins Farm also had high levels of burnishing (Allen 1990b, table 4), though on the whole, the site is more comparable with Gravelly Guy. A virtual absence of burnished pottery was recorded among the middle Iron Age assemblage at Mingies Ditch (D Wilson 1993, 72). Chronology might not be a strong factor in determining the level of burnishing, since such treatment was not a notable aspect of the early Iron Age pottery from Groundwell West, Wiltshire (Timby 2001b, 21). It should also be noted that in some cases variation in soil conditions may have had a significant effect on the preservation of sherd surfaces (and hence of the survival of burnishing). This was certainly a factor at sites such as Mingies Ditch (T Allen pers. comm.).

During the late Iron Age and Roman period, Yarnton was demonstrably a low-status settlement in terms of its ceramic assemblages. This can be assessed in terms of the ceramic types collectively identified as fine and specialist wares (Booth 1991b; 2004a). Overall, a level of 5.4% by sherd count is achieved, but this can be better understood by consideration of the chronological development of Roman pottery assemblages in the region, and in particular the effects of the expansion of Oxfordshire production of fine wares and other products in the period after *c* AD 240 (see Booth 2004a for detailed discussion). A simple division into early and late Roman assemblages gives a fine and specialist ware figure of 2.8% of sherds for Yarnton in the early Roman period. This places Yarnton right in the middle of a group of settlement sites in the bottom half of the fine and specialist ware spectrum (cf ibid., 43-46, 50, fig. 2). These sites range from those with less than 1% of fine and specialist wares, including Old Shifford and Gravelly Guy, up to Hatford, with 5.1%. Early Roman sites with slightly higher fine and specialist ware levels are generally morphologically distinct (eg the 'small towns'). Interestingly, the sites with the highest fine and specialist ware levels at this time (17-21%) are all rural settlements, either of villa or proto-villa character, with the exception of the settlement at Watkins Farm (Raven 1990, 49) which did not on present evidence have high status structural correlates. This apparent anomaly remains unexplained (Booth 2004a, 45).

Low status notwithstanding, the range of imports arriving at Yarnton – albeit in small quantities – was relatively wide. The 1st and 2nd century saw the arrival of *terra nigra* from Gallia Belgica, 'Rhenish' ware from central Gaul, white and white slipped ware from the Verulamium region, and, more locally, fine wares from Nuneham Courtenay. By comparison, Bicester received all of its fine and specialist wares, with the exception of the ubiquitous samian and an amphora sherd, from the Oxford kilns, together taking a 3.9% share of the assemblage (Booth 1996, 77, table 1). Indeed, expressed in terms of a simple list of sources, Yarnton resembles the Roman small town at Asthall: products from Verulamium, Spain and Gaul are represented at both. Given the quantities of such wares recovered from Yarnton, however, it is most unlikely that the pottery arrived directly from the source, but rather was acquired through regional market centres, either Alchester or perhaps a more local centre.

Perhaps the most notable import is the *terra nigra* cup. Such pottery is rare within the region. Conquest period fine wares tend to found at defended, high-status, sites, such as Dorchester-on-Thames, Abingdon and Bagendon. The appearance of *terra nigra* at Yarnton, a low-status rural settlement, is certainly unusual and might be seen as a one-off. Even so, the cup, and perhaps others like it, may have impacted upon the repertoire of local potters. A grog-tempered cup, albeit residual in a late Roman context, provided some relief from the usual repertoire of jars and bowls produced during the late Iron Age and earliest Roman period. However, the adoption of Romanised eating and drinking habits, as these cups seem to indicate, can only have been gradual at best. The late Iron Age/earliest Roman assemblage, while showing a wider range of forms than the middle/late Iron Age, remains almost exclusively jar and bowl orientated, suggesting little change in overall habits of food preparation and consumption (cf Meadows 1999). Only in the later 1st century do dishes, beakers and flagons appear, and even then their total numbers are not large. Indeed, the *terra nigra* cup was deposited at this time, and it is not clear whether its rarity caused the cup to be curated from the late Iron Age, or whether it made a belated arrival to the site in the later 1st century, though the former seems more likely.

The sources of the coarse ware fabrics used at Yarnton are of some interest. Oxford products were inevitably important, as would be expected from the proximity of their production sites, and the majority of sherds in O10, O11, R10, R11 and R30, for example, can probably be attributed to this source, but they by no means dominated the assemblage. It is probable that very local kilns were responsible for fabric R94, while the industry producing fabrics R37 and R38, perhaps in the Witney area, was clearly of considerable importance in sub-regional terms. The similarity of these fabrics to those produced in the North Wiltshire industry may mean that occasional products of the latter have been overlooked, but this is thought to be a minor problem at most. A connection between the two industries is quite likely, however, on the basis of similarities both of fabrics and also of some aspects of the form repertoire. A direct Wiltshire connection was represented at Yarnton by Savernake ware, but in small quantities only. A more distant western source was the Severn Valley industry – it has already been noted that tankards (apart from those in fabric R37) were drawn from this industry rather than from North Wiltshire. It is possible that the occurrence of Severn Valley wares, beyond the normal south-easterly limit of their distribution, provides residual evidence of the links between the Upper Thames and the Severn region indicated in earlier periods by the presence of Droitwich briquetage and Malvernian pottery, though the quantities are very small in both cases. It is notable, however, that Severn Valley ware is only recorded at Yarnton in the late Roman phase, and further east, at Alchester, it is noted from the mid 2nd century onwards (Evans 2001a, 326-328).

As expected, the proportion of fine and specialist wares rose in the late Roman period, now accounting for 13.3% of the assemblage (by sherd count – but only 6.1% by weight). This reflects the increase in the baseline level of fine and specialist wares on sites in the region as a result of the expansion of the Oxfordshire pottery industry and does not represent any clear change in status. Relatively, Yarnton remained at the lower end of the regional spectrum of late Roman sites considered in these terms (Booth 2004a, 46-49, 51 fig. 3). By way of comparison, higher status sites such as villas and nucleated settlements tended to have 20-30% fine and specialist wares, but one villa assemblage (from Roughground Farm, Lechlade) and one 'small town' group (from Asthall) had low fine and specialist ware levels (11.1% and 15.6% respectively). These values, from sites well to the west of Oxford, may suggest that in the later Roman period the relative levels of fine and specialist wares are much more dependent upon marketing factors (and reflect an aspect of Oxford distribution), whereas the variation seen in the early Roman assemblages does appear to reflect a pattern directly linked to perceived social status rather than other factors.

Another general feature of the Yarnton assemblage, its domination by jars at the expense of other vessel forms, is also demonstrably a characteristic of lower status rural settlements, as shown in evidence presented by Evans (2001a, 376), though without chronological definition. These ideas have been developed further by Evans (2001b, 27-31). The broad regional trend across sites of most types is that jar representation is high in the early Roman period and declines thereafter. The rate and extent of the decline tend to correlate with site type, and by the late Roman period assemblage compositions with less than 50% of jars are common (see above). Even in a fairly typical rural settlement context at Mansfield College, Oxford, jars accounted for little more than half the vessels, although it is possible that the figures here were skewed by the proximity of the Oxford industry with its high output of bowls and mortaria (the latter were unusually well-represented at Mansfield College; Booth and Hayden 2000, 310). The maintenance of the very high jar levels seen at Yarnton may owe something to the occurrence of residual material in the late groups, but generally it appears to reflect a characteristic conservative rural pattern of jar use.

CATALOGUE OF ILLUSTRATED VESSELS

Vessels are illustrated in a sequence of broad chronological periods, within which they are presented as individual feature groups, where appropriate, or in composite groups made up of material from related features. In each entry fabric is given first, followed by details of type and decoration. Reference is occasionally made to Young's corpus of Oxfordshire types (1977). Colour is only described where it is particularly remarkable and is typically dark grey-brown for the Iron Age pottery. Zones of burnishing are shown with a tone. Selected residual/redeposited pieces are illustrated to complement the range of material in use in a given period as demonstrated by pieces stratified in contexts of that period. The context number (in brackets) at the end of each entry is the specific deposit from which the vessel derives.

Cresswell Field

Early Iron Age

1. Fabric GSA4, type HD. The vessel is burnished overall and also elaborately decorated with rows of tooled-line festoons infilled with triangular stabbed impressions. These were filled with white bone (apatite) inlay (analysis by Chris Doherty). Pit 8127 (8126).
2. Fabric GSA4, type CS, burnished overall with tooled lines on shoulder and at base of rim. Pit 8127 (8126).
3. Fabric GSA4, type CS with tooled lines on shoulder and at base of rim. Internal burnt residue. Pit 8127 (8126).
4. Fabric AS3, type CS with tooled lines on shoulder and at base of rim and fine vertical ?fingernail impressions on rim. External sooting. Pit 8127 (8126).
5. Fabric SGA4, possibly type CS but more angular, burnished on the shoulder and with grooves at

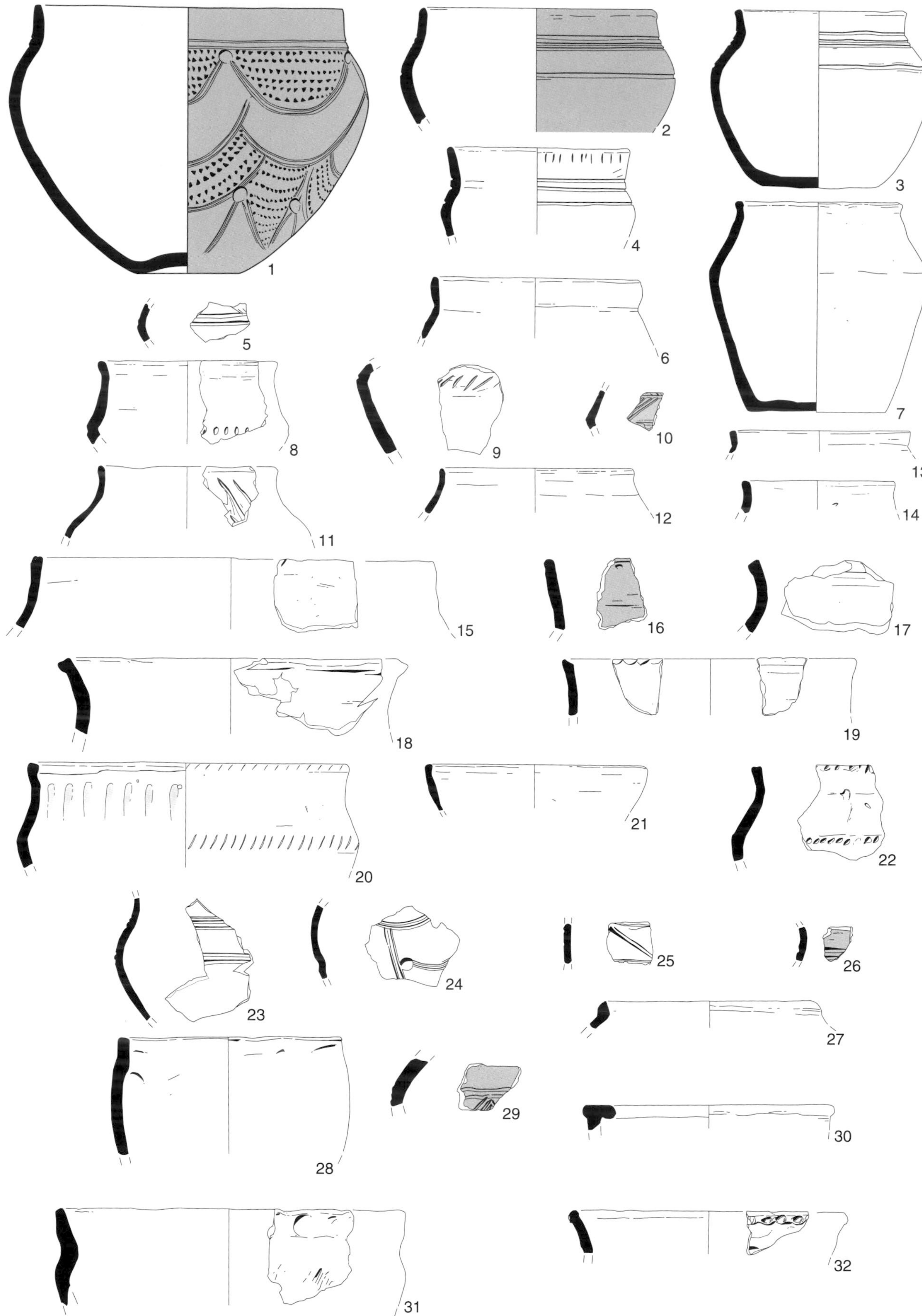

Fig. 14.1 Cresswell Field, pottery from early Iron Age contexts, Nos 1-32

carination. Pit 8127 (8126).

6. Fabric GAS3, jar (type C) but specific type uncertain. Burnished overall internally and externally. Pit 8127 (8126).
7. Fabric SGA4, type CS, though almost bipartite. Internal burnt residue. Pit 8127 (8126).
8. Fabric GSA4, type CS, with small indentations at the angle. Pit 8127 (8126).
9. Fabric SG4, ?type CS, angled sherd with oblique incised lines at the angle. Pit 8127 (8126).
10. Fabric GZ3, ?type CT. Fine angled sherd, burnished overall and with incised line decoration – paired horizontal lines at the carination and on upper body, linked by paired oblique lines. Pit 8127 (8126).
11. Fabric SA4, ?type CS. Pit 8127 (8126 and 8174).
12. Fabric AG3, jar, specific type uncertain. Burnished overall. Pit 8127 (8126 and 8174).
13. Fabric SGA4, small jar? burnished overall. Pit 8127 (8126).
14. Fabric SGA4, small jar? Pit 8127 (8126).
15. Fabric SG4, large jar? Pit 8127 (8174).
16. Fabric GSA4, type CA? The angle is uncertain and may be slightly more vertical than shown. Burnished overall. Pit 8127 (8126).
17. Fabric SAG4, large jar? Pit 8127 (8126).
18. Fabric AS3, large jar. Pit 8127 (8174).
19. Fabric SA4, jar? with internally bevelled top of upright rim, decorated with fingertip impressions. Pit 8127 (8174).
20. Fabric SGA4, type CS?, but might be wide enough in relation to its (unknown) height to be classified as a bowl. Fine oblique incised lines on the outer face of the rim and on the slightly angled 'shoulder'. Pit 8127 (8126).
21. Fabric GSA4, type uncertain but possibly a small bowl? Pit 8127 (8126).
22. Fabric SN5, type CS with rows of small oblique indentations at shoulder angle and on rim. Internal burnt residue. Pit 7412 (7410).
23. Fabric SP4, type CS, shoulder sherd with horizontal grooves cf Nos 2 and 3 above. Pit 7412 (7410).
24. Fabric SPG3, body sherd of fine ?bowl with curvilinear multiple grooved decoration and an impressed dimple at the intersection of two groups of lines in the style of No 1 above. Pit 7412 (7410).
25. Fabric SA4, body sherd with incised decoration similar to No 10 above, but the angle of this sherd is less certain. Pit 7412 (7410).
26. Fabric GS3, type ?CS. Burnished overall and with grooves on shoulder. Posthole 8254 (8253) associated with structure 8202.
27. Fabric SV5 ?jar of uncertain type with fingertip impressions on rim. Pit 7060 (7061) adjacent to structure 8202.
28. Fabric LS5, type CB. External sooting. Pit 7060 (7061) adjacent to structure 8202.
29. Fabric SA5, shoulder sherd, burnished overall and with horizontal grooves above top of triangular arrangement of incised lines. Pit 7060 (7061) adjacent to structure 8202.
30. Fabric SG5, internally expanded rim of large jar with impressed decoration on rim. Pit 7307 (7077), adjacent to structure 8202.
31. Fabric SA4, type CS with fingertip impressions on shoulder. Pit 7307 (7080), adjacent to structure 8202.
32. Fabric SG4, jar with fingertip 'frilling' of outer face of rim. Posthole 8330 (8331), part of structure 8396.
33. Fabric SA5, type CS. Expanded rim has notching on the external lip and there are large finger indentations on the shoulder. Pit 7787 (7788, 7790), associated with structure 8396.
34. Fabric AN2, fragment of burnished and decorated ?globular bowl of middle Iron Age type presumably intrusive in this feature. Pit 7787 (7788), associated with structure 8396.
35. Fabric SN5, heavy cordon with oblique incised decoration, from large jar. Pit 7869 (7868) associated with structure 8396.
36. Fabric SV4, jar with remnant of attachment for a handle on the shoulder. Pit 8175 (8176), associated with structures 8787-9.
37. Fabric SC5, possibly a bipartite form, slightly angled at the girth, with fingertip impressions there. Pit 7912 (7913, 7914), associated with structures 8787-9.
38. Fabric SC3, simple ?jar. Pit 7365 (7364).
39. Fabric SC5, type CS with fingertip impressions on shoulder. Pit 7365 (7364).
40. Fabric GS4, type CT. Burnished overall. Pit 7365 (7364).
41. Fabric AS3, type CT. Burnished overall internally and externally. Pit 7365 (7364).
42. Fabric SG4, type uncertain – everted rim with small penannular stamp impressions below tip of rim. Pit 7365 (7480).
43. Fabric SA5, everted rim of ?large jar with closely spaced fingertip impressions below rim. Pit 7365 (7364).
44. Fabric AG3, type ?CS with fingertip impressions at the girth. Pit 7365 (7364).
45. Fabric SA3, base of uncertain jar form. Pit 7365 (7480).
46. Fabric SA5, type CS/CT. The shoulder is still rounded but the angle at the base of the rim is well-defined. Burnished on shoulder. Pit 8005 (7915).
47. Fabric SP5, type CB. Pit 8005 (7915).
48. Fabric SA3,type CB. Pit 8005 (7915).
49. Fabric SG5, base of large jar with hole drilled through after firing. This practice, particularly common in the region in the late Iron Age, clearly commenced much earlier. Pit 8005 (7915).
50. Fabric SA5, type CA. Pit 7057 (7058).
51. Fabric SG4, type CS. Internal burnt residue. Pit 7057 (7058).
52. Fabric LP4, large jar of uncertain type. External sooting. Pit 7057 (7058).
53. Fabric GA4, large jar, possibly type CS. Burnished overall. Pit 7057 (7058).
54. Fabric SG3, shoulder of ?type CS jar with oblique incised lines on the shoulder. Internal burnt residue. Pit 7057 (7058).
55. Fabric SG3, type CT, burnished overall internally and externally and with incised zig-zag decoration. Pit 7057 (7058).
56. Fabric SA5, ?type CB. Pit 7598 (7597).
57. Fabric SA4, type CS. External sooting. Pit 7598 (7597).
58. Fabric AS3, type CT. Burnished overall internally and externally. Pit 7598 (7597).
59. Fabric AP2, ?type CT. Burnished overall internally and externally and with stamped ring decoration on rim. Pit 7598 (7597).

Fig. 14.2 Cresswell Field, pottery from early Iron Age contexts, Nos 33-60

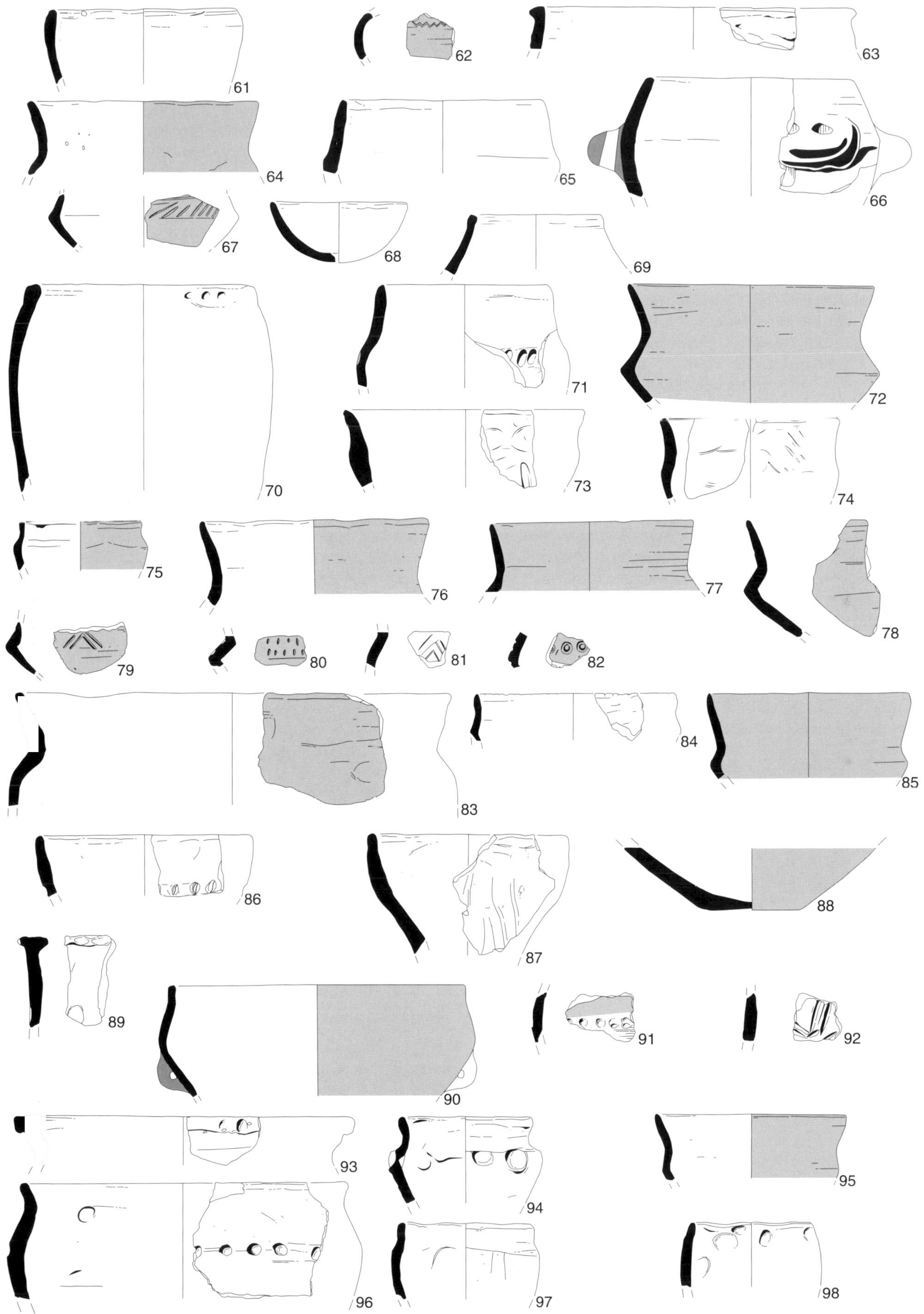

Fig. 14.3 Cresswell Field, pottery from early Iron Age contexts, Nos 61-98

60. Fabric CV3, jar of uncertain type. Notching on rim. Pit 7762 (7683).
61. Fabric SG4, type CB. Internal burnt residue. Pit 7762 (7683).
62. Fabric SA4, shoulder of ?jar burnished overall internally and externally and with incised fine zig-zag decoration. Pit 7762 (7725).
63. Fabric SP4, jar of uncertain form. External sooting. Pit 8195 (8196).
64. Fabric SP3, type CS/CT with burnished red 'haematite' coating. Pit 8195 (8196).
65. Fabric SA3, jar of uncertain form, perhaps bipartite. Midden 7003.
66. Fabric LA4, ?type CB with large lug with two vertical perforations. Midden 7003.
67. Fabric LS3, type CT, burnished overall and with oblique incised line decoration above the carination. Midden 7003.
68. Fabric SA4, type HC small rounded bowl or cup. Midden 7003.
69. Fabric SA3, jar of uncertain type. Pit 7039 (7040).
70. Fabric SC5, large type CB. Pit 7039 (7040).
71. Fabric SA4, type CS with finger tip impressions on shoulder. Internal burnt residue. Pit 7049 (7050).
72. Fabric SG3, type CT. Burnished overall internally and externally. Pit 7147 (7148).
73. Fabric SG4, ?jar of uncertain form, possibly type ?CS. Pit 7181 (7180).
74. Fabric SG3, type CS. Pit 7182 (7184).
75. Fabric SG3, type CS. Burnished overall. Pit 7182 (7184).
76. Fabric SG3, type CT. Burnished overall. Internal limescale deposit. Pit 7182 (7184).
77. Fabric SG3, type CT. Burnished overall internally and externally. Pit 7182 (7184).
78. Fabric AS3, type CT. Burnished overall. Pit 7182 (7184).
79. Fabric SG3, type CT. Burnished overall and with oblique incised line decoration. Pit 7182 (7184).
80. Fabric SA3, type CT, burnished overall. Two rows of fine, vertical oval impressions with white inlay above carination. Pit 7182 (7184).
81. Fabric SA3, ?type CS body sherd with incised line decoration. Pit 7182 (7183).
82. Fabric SA3, ?shoulder sherd burnished overall and with groove and impressed ring stamp decoration. Pit 7187 (7190).
83. Fabric LA4, large jar. Burnished overall externally and partly on the interior. Pit 7268 (7269).
84. Fabric SL3, ?type CS jar with notching on rim. Pit 7268 (7269).
85. Fabric SP4, type CT. Burnished overall internally and externally. Pit 7268 (7269).
86. Fabric SA4, ?jar type uncertain, but perhaps a bowl. Finger tip impressions on upper body wall. Pit 7268 (7269).
87. Fabric SA4, type HC. Pit 7268 (7269).
88. Fabric SA3, base, possibly of bowl form. Burnished overall. Pit 7268 (7269).
89. Fabric SI4, large jar with T-shaped rim. Fingertip impressions on outer face of rim and on neck. Pit 7397 (7473).
90. Fabric SG3, ?type CS jar with handle/perforated lug below girth. Burnished overall. Internal burnt residue. Pit 7397 (7398).
91. Fabric SG4, body sherd, burnished on shoulder and with rounded impressions on shoulder. Internal burnt residue. Pit 7397 (7398).
92. Fabric SN5, body sherd with tooled linear decoration. Pit 7397 (7398).
93. Fabric SC5, large jar of uncertain form. Pit 8023 (8022).
94. Fabric GS4, type CS jar with pronounced fingertip impressions on shoulder. Pit 8023 (8022).
95. Fabric SG3, type CS. Burnished overall. Pit 8025 (8024).
96. Fabric SP4, type CS, with fingertip impressions at girth. Pit 8327 (8326).
97. Fabric SA5, ?type CB. Pit 8327 (8326).
98. Fabric VA4, type CB. External sooting. Pit 8327 (8326).
99. Fabric SL5, type CB. Pit 8327 (8326).
100. Fabric SP5, type CA with notching on rim. External sooting. Pit 8327 (8326).
101. Fabric SG4, type CS/CT. Pit 8327 (8326).
102. Fabric AN3, type CT. Burnished overall externally and partly on interior. Pit 8327 (8326).
103. Fabric SG3, type CS with handle. Burnished on shoulder and with oblique incised lines near handle attachment. Pit 8389 (8390).
104. Fabric SA4, type CT. Burnished overall. Pit 7516 (7517).
105. Fabric SA4, ?type HC. Pit 7603 (7661).
106. Fabric SA3, type CB. Burnished overall externally and partly on interior. Pit 7742 (7743).
107. Fabric SA4, type CT. Burnished overall externally and internally. Pit 7742 (7743).
108. Fabric CN4, ?type CB. Pit 7997 (7995).
109. Fabric SP5, ?large jar with expanded rim with fingertip impressions on outer edge. Pit 7997 (7995).
110. Fabric SG4, neck of large jar with internal ledge and two pre-firing perforations through wall above the ledge. Burnished overall. Pit 7997 (7995).
111. Fabric SA4, ?type CS with handle at shoulder. Pit 8251 (8252).
112. Fabric LA4, type CS/CT. Pit 8427 (8428).
113. Fabric SA4, vertical cordon from neck of large jar, with oblique incised decoration. Ditch 8287 (8288).
114. Fabric SC3, type CT. Burnished overall externally and internally. U/S. Finds reference (7036).
115. Fabric SA4, type CT. Burnished overall externally and partly on interior and with fingertip impressions at carination. Surface (8455).
116. 638 Fabric SG4, large jar of uncertain type with internally expanded rim. Surface (8455).

Middle Iron Age

117. Fabric SG4, type CS. Burnished overall externally and partly on interior. Gully 8182 (8181).
118. Fabric AN3, type CB. Gully 7862 (7863).
119. Fabric SA4, ?type CB or bipartite form, with fingertip impression at girth. External sooting. Gully 7862 (7863).
120. Fabric AS3, body sherd burnished overall externally and internally and with incised triangle decoration. Gully 7862 (7863).
121. Fabric AN2, type CB. External sooting. Pit 7988 (7986).
122. Fabric SA3, small pedestal base with out-turned foot. Burnished overall. Ditch 7659 (7969).
123. Fabric SA5, decorated cordon from ?large jar. Ditch 7659 (7660).
124. Fabric SA3, type CB. Burnished overall externally and internally. Ditch 7512 (7514).

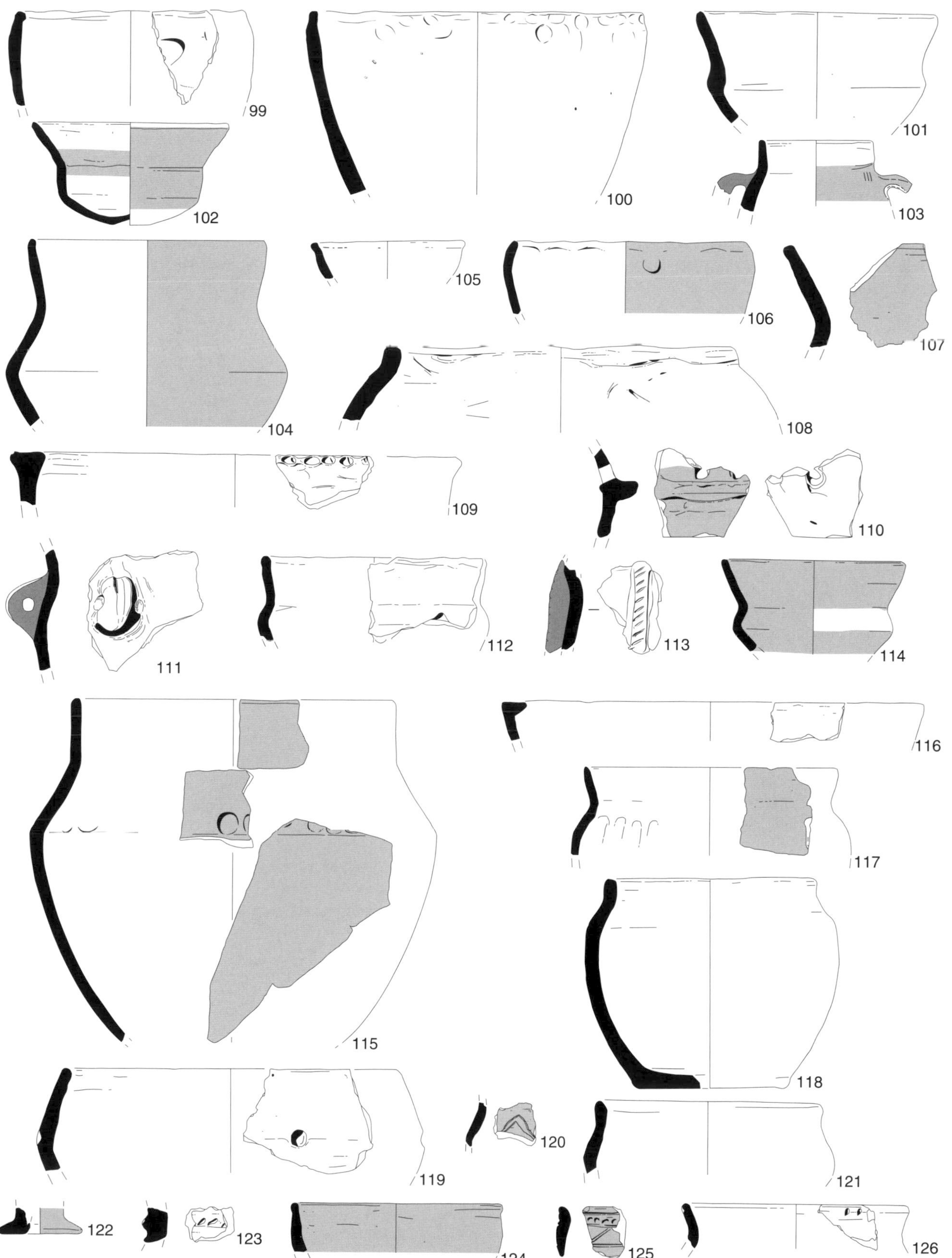

Fig. 14.4 Cresswell Field, pottery from early Iron Age (Nos 99-116) and middle Iron Age contexts (Nos 117-126)

125. Fabric AN2, shoulder of jar or bowl burnished externally and with row of stabbed impressions between grooves, and oblique and horizontal incised lines below. Ditch 7637 (7638).
126. Fabric CS4, jar of uncertain form with incised notches on rim. Internal burnt residue. Gully 7893 (7892).
127. Fabric SA4, type HG. Burnished overall. Pit 7062 (7064).
128. Fabric CP3, type CG. Burnished overall. Pit 7353 (7352).
129. Fabric AS3, type D (uncertain jar/bowl). Burnished overall. Pit 8033 (8034).
130. Fabric AV3, type CB. Pit 8359 (8358).
131. Fabric LV3, ?type CB. Pit 8359 (8358).
132. Fabric GV4, ?type CS with fingertip impressions on the shoulder. Pit 8359 (8358).
133. Fabric SL5, type CB. Pit 8359 (8358).
134. Fabric SA3, type CB. Burnished overall. Pit 8467 (8466).
135. Fabric SN5, large jar with internally expanded rim. Pit 8525 (8526).
136. Fabric SA3, body sherd burnished overall externally and partly on interior and with incised decoration with a white calcite (limestone/chalk) inlay (analysis by Chris Doherty). Pit 8525 (8526).
137. Fabric SN4, large jar with internally expanded rim and rough vertical cordon on outer face of rim. Pit 7710 (7709).
138. Fabric LA5, type CB. Pit 8149 (8150).
139. Fabric AS3, type CB with fingertip impression on shoulder. Another sherd from this vessel appeared to have an oblique burnished line, and yet others had internal limescale deposits. The decoration might suggest an early rather than a middle Iron Age date. Pit 8437 (8436).
140. Fabric AP2, type CB. Pit 8468 (8469).
141. Fabric AV3, ?type CB. External sooting and internal burnt residue. Pit 8468 (8469).
142. Fabric LA3, type CB. Burnished overall externally and internally. Pit 8533 (8516).
143. Fabric CS4, type CB. Burnished overall externally and internally. The fabric might suggest an early Iron Age date. Pit 8533 (8516).
144. Fabric AS3, type HD burnished overall externally and partly on interior and with lightly tooled grooves under rim and linear pendant swag or festoon decoration. Pit 8645 (8644).
145. Fabric LV5, type HG burnished overall and with elaborate impressed and tooled decoration. Pit 8786 (8493).
146. Fabric AP2, ?type HG burnished overall and with poorly preserved linear tooled and ring stamp decoration. Pit 8786 (8493).

Miscellaneous post-Roman contexts

147. Fabric SA4, jar with notches on outer lip of rim. Quarry 7276.
148. Fabric SA5, jar of uncertain form with roughly T-shaped rim. SFB 8634.
149. Fabric QS3, body sherd with horizontal incised line decoration above and below rows of small oblique impressions. Ditch 7538.

All these vessels are probably early Iron Age, though the ?quartzite inclusions in No. 149 might indicate a slightly earlier (late Bronze Age) date.

Yarnton

Late Bronze Age/early Iron Age and early Iron Age

150. Fabric SA5, type D. Handled body sherd with simple geometric incised decoration. Burnished overall externally. Pit 276.
151. Fabric SA3, type MD. Pit 276.
152. Fabric SP5, type CB. Combed decoration. Pit 371.
153. Fabric AP3, type D. Burnished overall externally and internally. Pit 371.
154. Fabric SA5, type C. Fingertip impressions on rim. Pit 389.
155. Fabric SA5, type C. Pit 770.
156. Fabric SA3, type CA. Pit 857.
157. Fabric SA4, type H. Pit 1465.
158. Fabric AS4, type CA. Internal burnt residue. Pit 1529.
159. Fabric SP4, type C. Pit 1540.
160. Fabric SP5, type H. Complex geometric incised decoration. Pit 1540.
161. Fabric SP5, type CB. Pit 1561.
162. Fabric SN5, type CS. Pit 1684.
163. Fabric SP4, type CT. Burnished overall externally. Pit 1695.
164. Fabric AC3. Body sherd with impressed decoration. Pit 1695.
165. Fabric SA5, type CS. Pit 1716.
166. Fabric SA5, type C. Pit 1716.
167. Fabric SA5, type C. Fingertip impressions on rim. Pit 1716.
168. Fabric SC5, type C. Fingertip impressions on rim and shoulder. Pit 1716.
169. Fabric SL5, type C. Pit 1716.
170. Fabric SN5, type C. Pit 1716.
171. Fabric SP5, type C. Pit 1716.
172. Fabric LS5, type CB. External sooting. Pit 1750.
173. Fabric SV5, type C. Pit 2515.
174. Fabric SA4, type CT. Burnished overall externally and internally. Pit 2649.
175. Fabric SP5, type CS. Grooved on rim and fingertip impressions on shoulder. Pit 2692.

Middle Iron Age

176. Fabric AN3, type HC. Enclosure 267.
177. Fabric CN4, type CB. External sooting. Enclosure 327 (369).
178. Fabric SG5, type C. Fingertip impressions on shoulder. Enclosure 327 (369).
179. Fabric AP4, type C. Enclosure 390 (549).
180. Fabric AP3, type HC. Burnished overall externally and internally. Enclosure 390 (549).
181. Fabric AN3, type HG. Burnished overall externally. Enclosure 390 (301).
182. Fabric AV3. Externally burnished body sherd with impressed, grooved, and stabbed dot decoration. Enclosure 390 (260).
183. Fabric AV2. Internally and externally burnished body sherd with grooves and a roped cordon. Ditch 450.

Late Iron Age/early Roman transition

184. Fabric GL5, type CB. Simple geometric decoration and burnished zone on shoulder. Enclosure 121.
185. Fabric CN4, type CB. Enclosure 121.
186. Fabric E80, type CD. Burnished overall externally. Enclosure 175 (386).
187. Fabric E80, type CD. Cordon at base of neck and

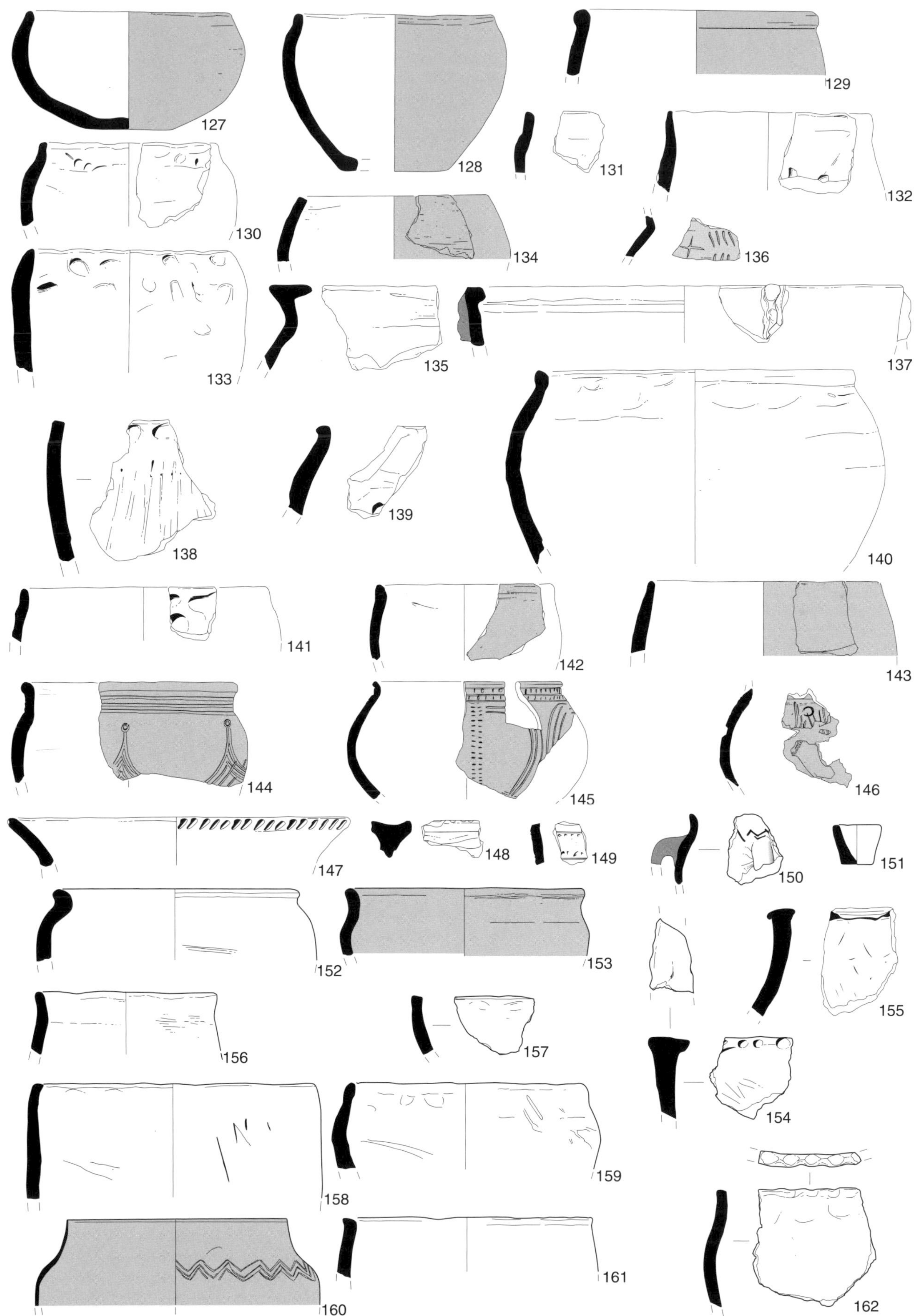

Fig. 14.5 Cresswell Field, pottery from middle Iron Age contexts (Nos 127-146) and Iron Age pottery from post-Roman contexts (Nos 147-149). Yarnton, pottery from late Bronze Age/early Iron Age contexts, Nos 150-162

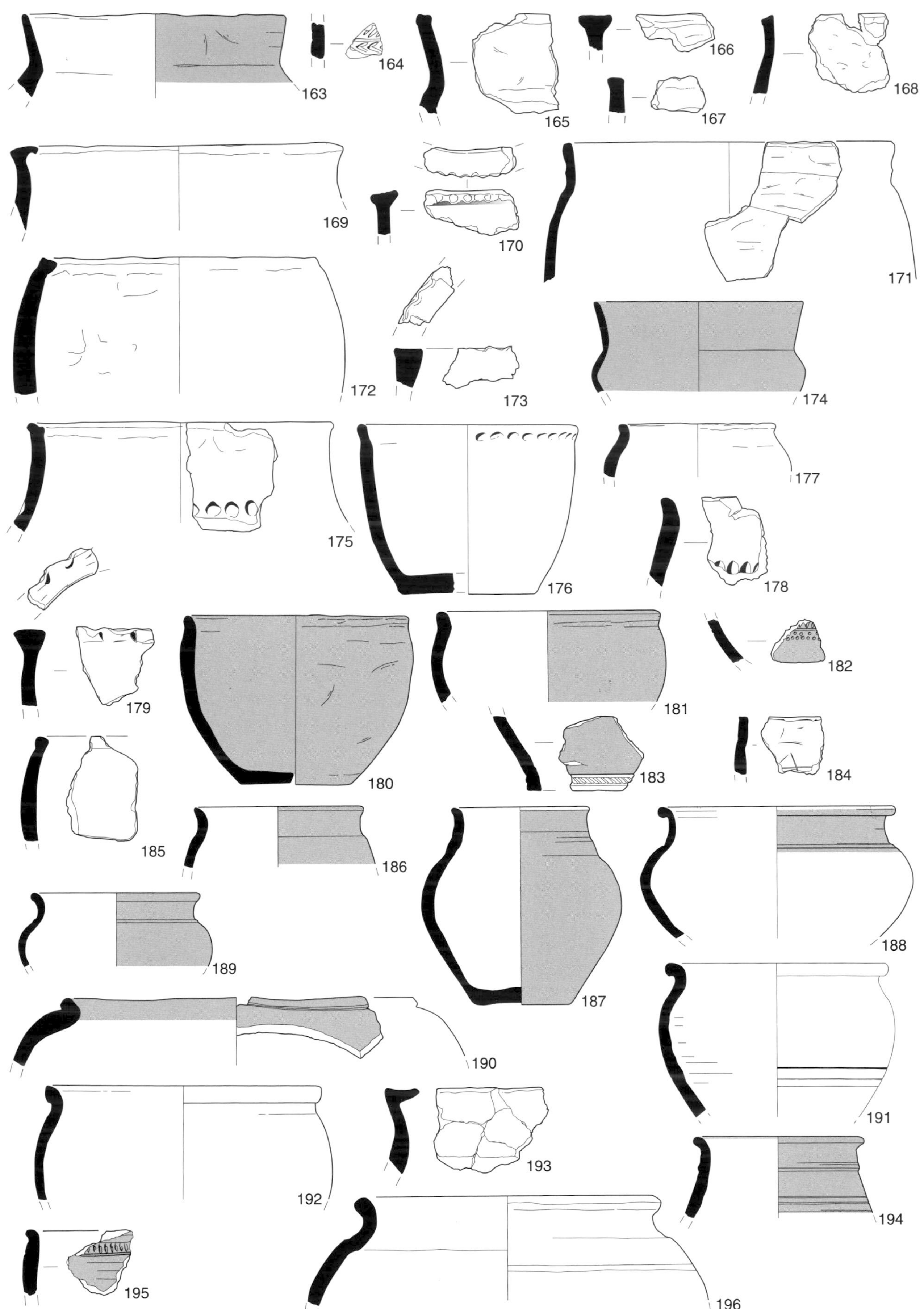

Fig. 14.6 Yarnton, pottery from late Bronze Age/early Iron Age (Nos 163-175), middle Iron Age (Nos 176-183) and late Iron Age/early Roman (Nos 184-196) contexts

burnished overall externally. Enclosure 175 (622).
188. Fabric E80, type CE. Enclosure 175 (208).
189. Fabric E80, type CE. Cordon at base of neck and burnished overall externally. Enclosure 175 (210).
190. Fabric R94, type CH. Burnished on shoulder and rim. Enclosure 175 (622).
191. Fabric C11, type CK. External sooting. Enclosure 175 (210).
192. Fabric C11, type CK. Enclosure 175 (210).
193. Fabric SP5. Jar with internally expanded rim. Early Iron Age. Enclosure 175 (622).
194. Fabric E80, type HA. Externally burnished bowl with cordon on body. Enclosure 175 (622).
195. Fabric AN2. Burnished rim sherd of bowl decorated with row of short incised lines on shoulder bordered by grooves. Middle Iron Age. Enclosure 236 (428).
196. Fabric E50, type CN. Groove on shoulder. Ditch 1606.
197. Fabric E40, type HA. Burnished overall externally. Ditch 616.
198. Fabric E50, type HA. Burnished externally. Ditch 359.
199. Fabric E80, type CD. Burnished overall externally. Enclosure 391A (995).
200. Fabric E80, type CE. Burnished overall externally. Enclosure 391A (973).
201. Fabric C10, type CK. External sooting. Enclosure 391A (995).
202. Fabric O18, type EA. Body sherd with notched scroll decoration and grooves around girth. Copy of *terra rubra* butt-beaker. Enclosure 391A (995).
203. Fabric E80, type HA. Externally burnished bowl with cordons on neck. Enclosure 391A (995).
204. Fabric E80, type CD. Enclosure 923.
205. Fabric E80, type CH. Burnished externally on top of and below rim. Enclosure 923 (926).
206. Fabric SA4, type CB. Middle Iron Age. Enclosure 925.
207. Fabric AS4, type CB. Middle Iron Age. Ditch 1000.
208. Fabric SA4, type CB. Exterior sooting and overall burnish. Middle Iron Age. Ditch 1000.
209. Fabric E80, type CE. Burnished jar with cordon at base of neck. Ditch 1000.
210. Fabric E80, type CH. Ditch 1000.
211. Fabric E80, type HA. Burnished bowl with cordons on body. Ditch 1000.
212. Fabric QA4. Jar with fingertip impressions on rim and shoulder. Early Iron Age. Ditch 1000.
213. Fabric SA4, type CB. Middle Iron Age. Pit 300.
214. Fabric AV3, type CT. Jar burnished overall. Early Iron Age. Pit 404.
215. Fabric E80, type CE. Burnished overall externally and at the rim internally. Pit 563.
216. Fabric E80, type CE. Pit 563.
217. Fabric R94, type CI. External sooting. Pit 662.
218. Fabric R94, type CI. External sooting. Pit 662.
219. Fabric R94, type CI. External sooting. Pit 662.
220. Fabric E80, type HA. Groove on carination and burnished on rim and neck externally and at the rim internally. Pit 697.
221. Fabric E80, type CE. Burnished overall externally. Pit 1016.

Early Roman

222. Fabric R11, type CM. Burnished externally; grooves at girth and base of neck. Ditch 45.
223. Fabric O11, Young type O27. Necked bowl with grooves on girth. Ditch 45.
224. Fabric R94, type CC. Externally burnished jar with rippled shoulder. Ditch 51.
225. Fabric E20, type CD. Externally burnished jar with grooved shoulder. Ditch 51.
226. Fabric O11, type CD. Ditch 51.
227. Fabric R11, type CD. Jar burnished overall externally and on rim internally. Ditch 51.
228. Fabric R37, type CD. Grooves on shoulder. Ditch 51.
229. Fabric R94, type CD. Ditch 51.
230. Fabric R94, type CD. Ditch 51.
231. Fabric R94, type CD. Ditch 51.
232. Fabric R94, type CD. Ditch 51.
233. Fabric R10, type CE. Ditch 51.
234. Fabric R37, type CE. Externally burnished jar with grooved girth. Ditch 51.
235. Fabric R37, type CE. Burnished externally on rim and neck. Ditch 51.
236. Fabric R94, type CI. Ditch 51.
237. Fabric R94, type CK. Ditch 51.
238. Fabric C11, type CK. Ditch 51.
239. Fabric C11, type CK. External sooting. Ditch 51.
240. Fabric C11, type CK. External sooting. Ditch 51.
241. Fabric C11, type CK Burnt deposits and sooting. Ditch 51.
242. Fabric R37. Jar or bowl burnished externally on shoulder and on rim internally. Ditch 51.
243. Fabric E80, type CD. Ditch 55.
244. Fabric CN5, type CB. Oblique incisions on rim. Middle Iron Age. Enclosure 138 (426).
245. Fabric E80, type CN. Large storage jar burnished on rim and neck. Enclosure 138 (426).
246. Fabric R11, Young type R31. Jar-beaker with rouletted decoration. Enclosure 138 (426).
247. Fabric E80, type CN. Burnished shoulder. Ditch group 140.
248. Fabric R94, type CD. 313. Enclosure 156.
249. Fabric SV4. Burnished body sherd decorated with complex geometric motifs. Early Iron Age. Enclosure 156 (1647).
250. Fabric E80, type CG. 90. Enclosure 160.
251. Fabric SA4. Slack-profiled jar. Early Iron Age. Enclosure 187 (664).
252. Fabric E80, type HD. Bowl with rippled and burnished shoulder. Enclosure 187 (706).
253. Fabric SL2. Externally burnished body sherd decorated with simple geometric motifs. Early Iron Age. Enclosure 187 (666).
254. Fabric E50, type CH. Ditch 344.
255. Fabric E80, type CH. Ditch 344.
256. Fabric R37. Body sherd with burnished zones and motifs. Ditch 344.
257. Fabric E80, type CH. External sooting. Enclosure 391B (418).
258. Fabric E80, type CH. Burnished externally on rim and shoulder and internally on rim. Enclosure 391B (987).
259. Fabric W35, type BB. Burnished externally. Enclosure 391C (419).
260. Fabric E50, type CD. Burnished externally. Enclosure 391C (693).
261. Fabric E80, type CD. Enclosure 391C (417).
262. Fabric E80, type CD. Burnished on rim, neck and shoulder with wavy line decoration on girth. Enclosure 391C (966).
263. Fabric E40, type CE. Burnished externally on neck and shoulder and internally on rim. Cordon on

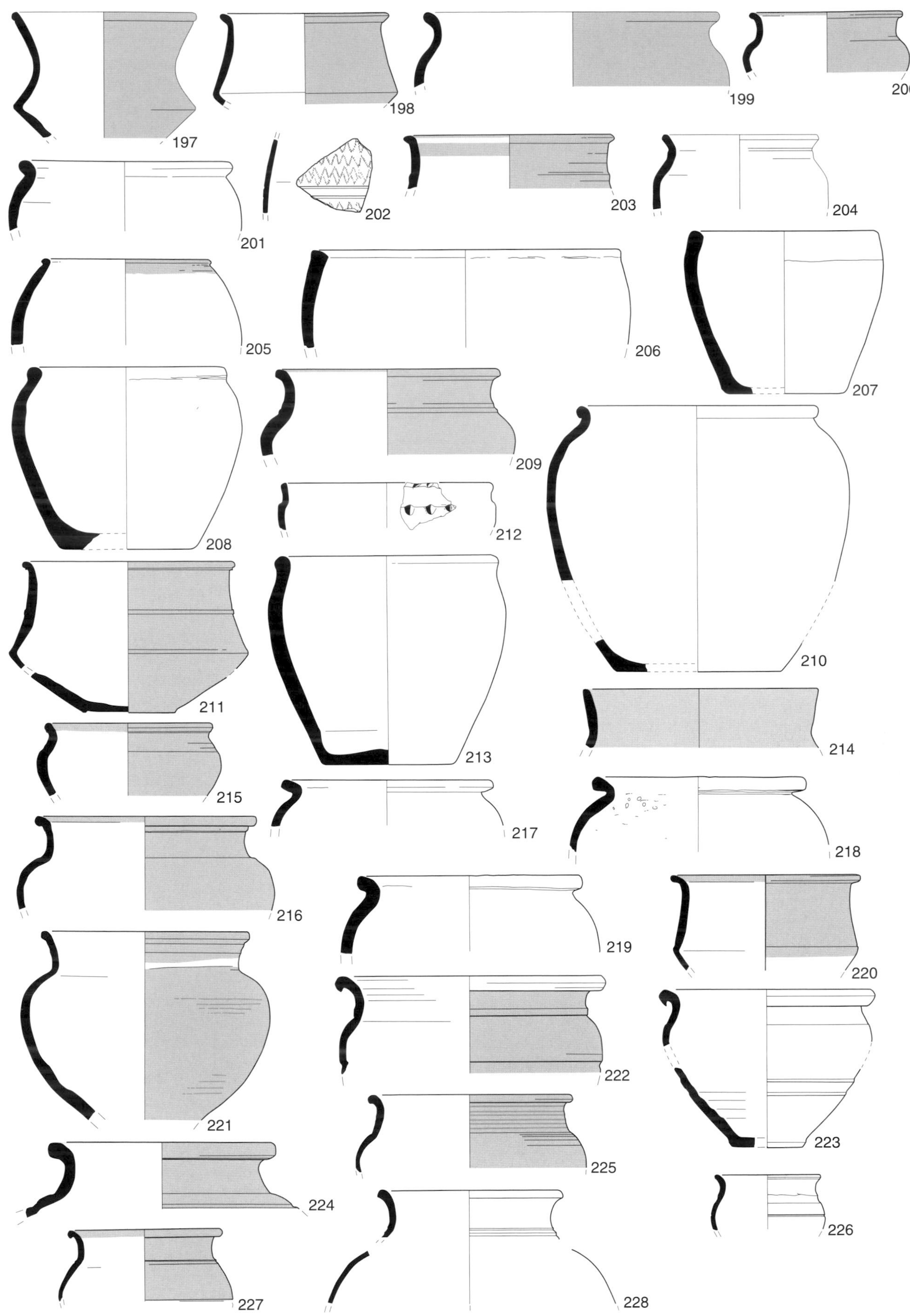

Fig. 14.7 Yarnton, pottery from late Iron Age/early Roman (Nos 197-221) and early Roman contexts (Nos 222-228)

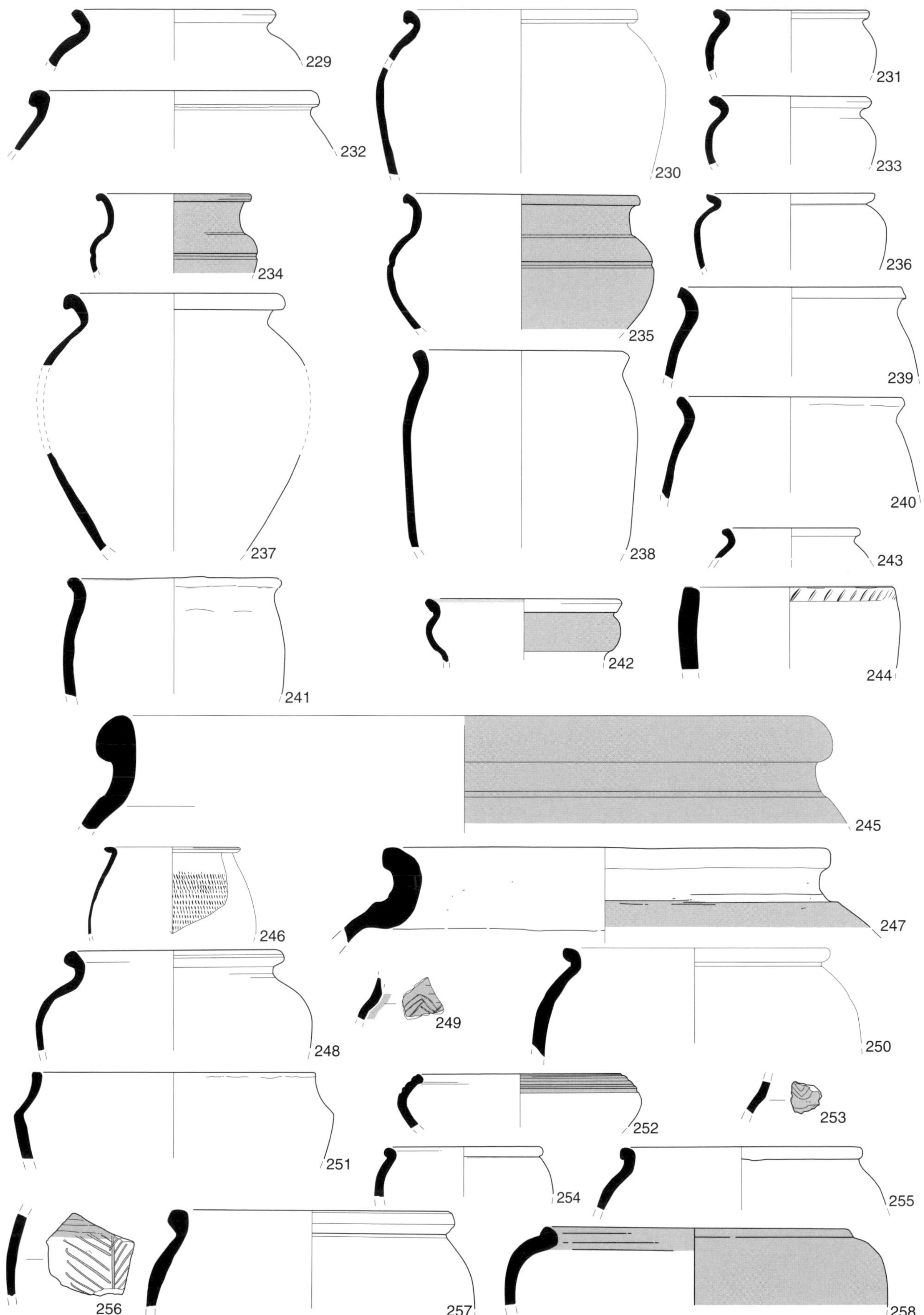

Fig. 14.8 Yarnton, pottery from early Roman contexts, Nos 229-258

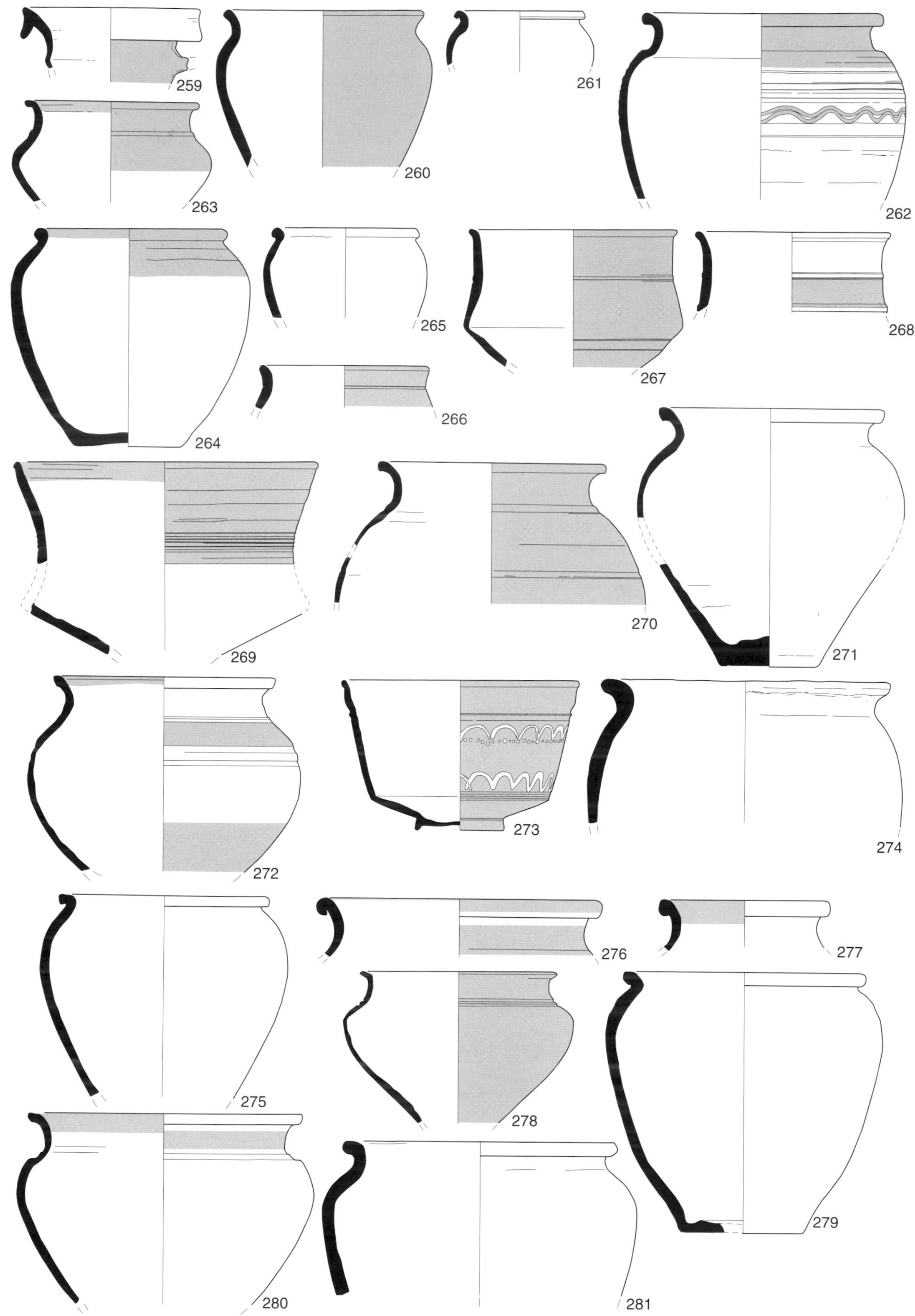

Fig. 14.9 Yarnton, pottery from early Roman contexts, Nos 259-281

neck. Enclosure 391C (693).
264. Fabric E80, type CH. Burnished externally on neck and shoulder and internally on rim. Enclosure 391C (695).
265. Fabric R94, type CH. External sooting. Enclosure 391C (419).
266. Fabric E50, type HA. Burnished overall. Groove on neck. Enclosure 391C (693).
267. Fabric E80, type HA. Externally burnished jar with cordon on girth. Enclosure 391C (353).
268. Fabric E80, type HA. Enclosure 391C (421).
269. Fabric E80, type HA. Enclosure 391C (1073).
270. Fabric R37, type CD. Externally burnished overall. Cordons on neck and girth. Ditch 591.
271. Fabric R94, type CD. External sooting. Ditch 591.
272. Fabric R37, type CD. External and internal zones of burnishing; grooves and cordons on neck and shoulder. Ditch 624.
273. Fabric O11, Young type O42. Carinated bowl, burnished overall with white dot and arc painted decoration. Ditch 624.
274. Fabric C11, type CK. Ditch 813.
275. Fabric C11, type CK. Ditch 813.
276. Fabric R37. Jar burnished on shoulder and rim. Ditch 813.
277. Fabric R37, type C. Rim burnished internally. Ditch 813.
278. Fabric O11, type CE. Externally burnished jar with cordons on neck. Ditch 859.
279. Fabric R94, type CI. Ditch 859.
280. Fabric E80, type CE. Burnished externally on neck and internally on rim. Ditch 1067.
281. Fabric R94, type CD. External sooting. Ditch 2593.
282. Fabric R94, type CD. External sooting. Ditch 2593.
283. Fabric R94, type CH. Ditch 2593.
284. Fabric E80, type CN. Ditch 2593.
285. Fabric E20, type JA. Burnished internally. Pit 57.
286. Fabric E20, type JA. Pit 86.
287. Fabric E80, type CD. Pit 209.
288. Fabric R94, type CD. Pit 209.
289. Fabric R94, type CE. Externally burnished overall. Pit 209.
290. Fabric R94, type CD. Groove on girth. External sooting. Pit 308.
291. Fabric R21, type MG. Pit 308.
292. Fabric R90, type CD. Pit 816.
293. Fabric E50, type CD. Pit 836.
294. Fabric E80, type CD. Pit 836.
295. Fabric E80, type JB. Burnished overall. Pit 836.
296. Fabric R37, type GA. Burnished zone below rim and above lattice. Joining sherds in Pit 1033 and ditch Group 140.
297. Fabric SC4, type CB. ?Middle Iron Age. Pit 1082.
298. Fabric SN5, type CS. Fingertip impressions on shoulder. Early Iron Age. Pit 1082.
299. Fabric R37, type CC. Overall external burnish. Pit 1088.
300. Fabric R11, Young type R57. Carinated bowl with overall external burnish. Pit 1088.
301. Fabric R10, type CD. Burnished and grooved on shoulder. Pit 1144.
302. Fabric E30, type CN. Burnished externally on body and internally on rim; grooved on neck and girth. Pit 1192.
303. Fabric E80, type CK. Pit 1216.
304. Fabric R37, type GA. Burnished zone below rim overlain by lattice that extends towards base. Pit 1387.
305. Fabric O11, type HC. Burnished zone above flange. Pit 1387.

Late Roman

306. Fabric M41, Young type C97. Vertical impressions on flange. Kidney-shaped feature 491/494.
307. Fabric R37, type CD. Burnished overall. Structure 1356 (1069).
308. Fabric B11, form CK. Structure 1356 (1098)
309. Fabric O81, form CN. Structure 1356 (87)
310. Fabric R30, type HB. Flanged bowl with exterior burnish. Structure 1356 (87).
311. Fabric R37, type C. Burnish on top of rim. Ditch 25.
312. Fabric R94, type CD. External sooting. Ditches 1181 and 1182, ditch Group 30.
313. Fabric E30, type CE. Burnished zone on girth below shoulder cordon. Late Iron Age/early Roman. Ditches 106 and 1181, ditch Group 30.
314. Fabric R37, type CE. Burnished externally overall and internally on rim. Ditch 1061, ditch Group 30.
315. Fabric C11, type CK. External sooting and internal lime scale. Ditch 1061, ditch Group 30.
316. Fabric C11, type CK. External sooting. Ditch 1061, ditch Group 30.
317. Fabric C11, type CK. Lime scale and sooting. Ditch 1061, ditch Group 30.
318. Fabric R37, type CK. Burnished zone on shoulder above wavy line. External sooting. Ditch 1061, ditch Group 30.
319. Fabric C11, type CN. Ditch 1061, ditch Group 30.
320. Fabric R37, type C. Burnished overall externally. Ditch 115, ditch Group 30.
321. Fabric R18, type EA. Early Roman. Ditch 115, ditch Group 30.
322. Fabric O11, Young type O27. Externally burnished bowl with cordon on neck. Ditch 103, ditch Group 30.
323. Fabric O11, Young type O27. Burnished on shoulder; grooved and cordoned on neck and body. Ditch 1181, ditch Group 30.
324. Fabric R30, type JA. Burnished overall; intersecting arcs on exterior. Ditch 762, ditch Group 30.
325. Fabric C10, type CD. Burnished overall externally. Ditch 34.
326. Fabric LN5, type CB. External sooting. ?Middle Iron Age. Ditch 46.
327. Fabric R37, type CD. Ditch 56.
328. Fabric R94, type CD. Ditch 56.
329. Fabric R94. Narrow-necked jar. Burnished on rim and neck; cordon on shoulder. Enclosure 82 (85).
330. Fabric O11, type EC. Large beaker with roughcast decoration. Enclosure 82.
331. Fabric F52, type HB. Flanged bowl. Enclosure 82 (85).
332. Fabric R30, type JA. Burnished on top of rim and with horizontal lines on walls. Enclosure 82 (85).
333. Fabric M22, Young type M17. Enclosure 82 (85).
334. Fabric M22, Young type M22. Enclosure 82 (85).
335. Fabric C11, type CD. Ditch 155.
336. Fabric C11. Body sherd with incised festoons and border. Ditch 155.
337. Fabric E80, type CH. Late Iron Age/early Roman Ditch 162.
338. Fabric C11. Jar base, trimmed around the break. External sooting. Enclosure 279 (505).
339. Fabric E80, type CD. External sooting. Late Iron Age/early Roman. Ditch 332.
340. Fabric E30, type CE. Overall external burnish.

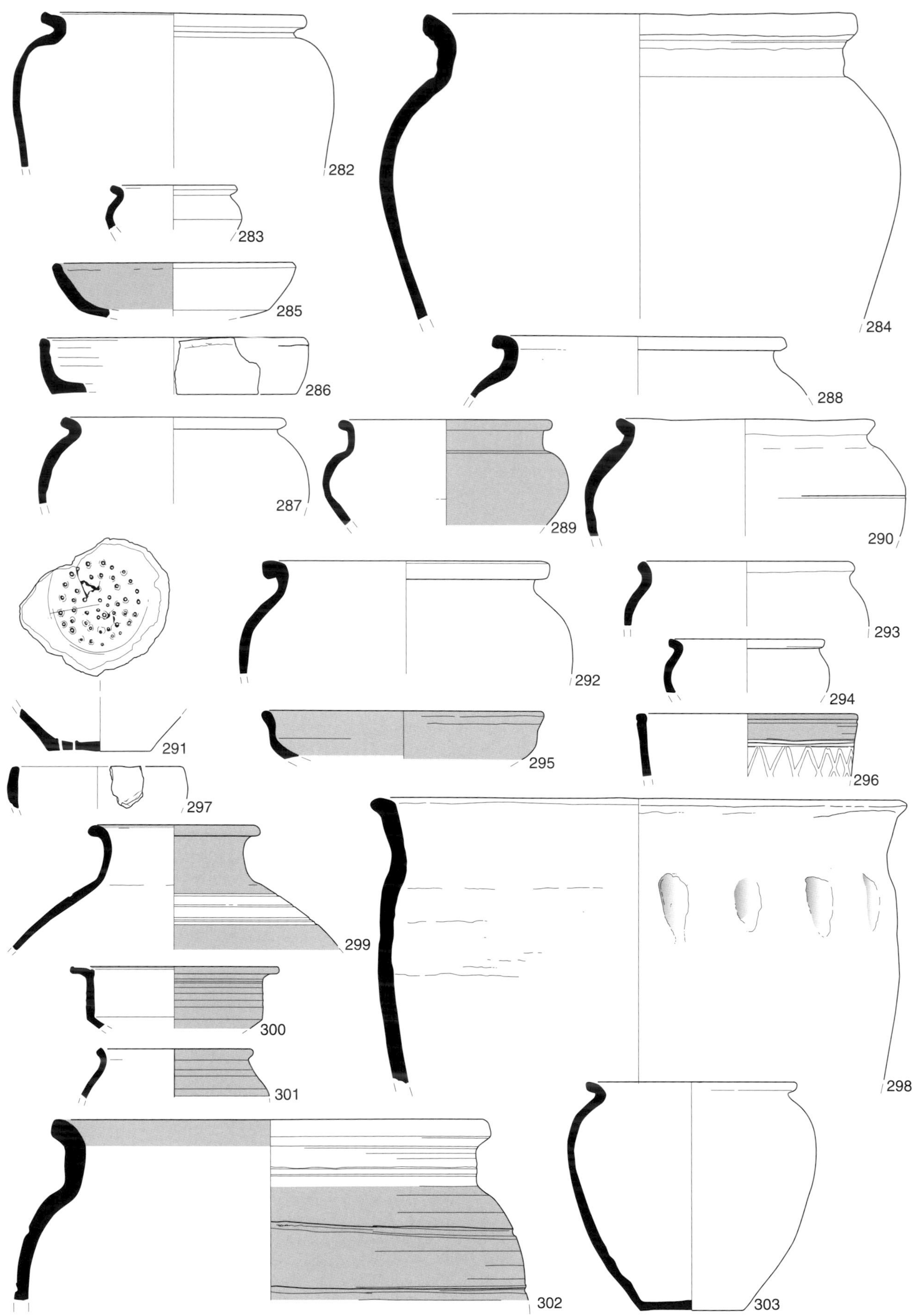

Fig. 14.10 Yarnton, pottery from early Roman contexts, Nos 282-303

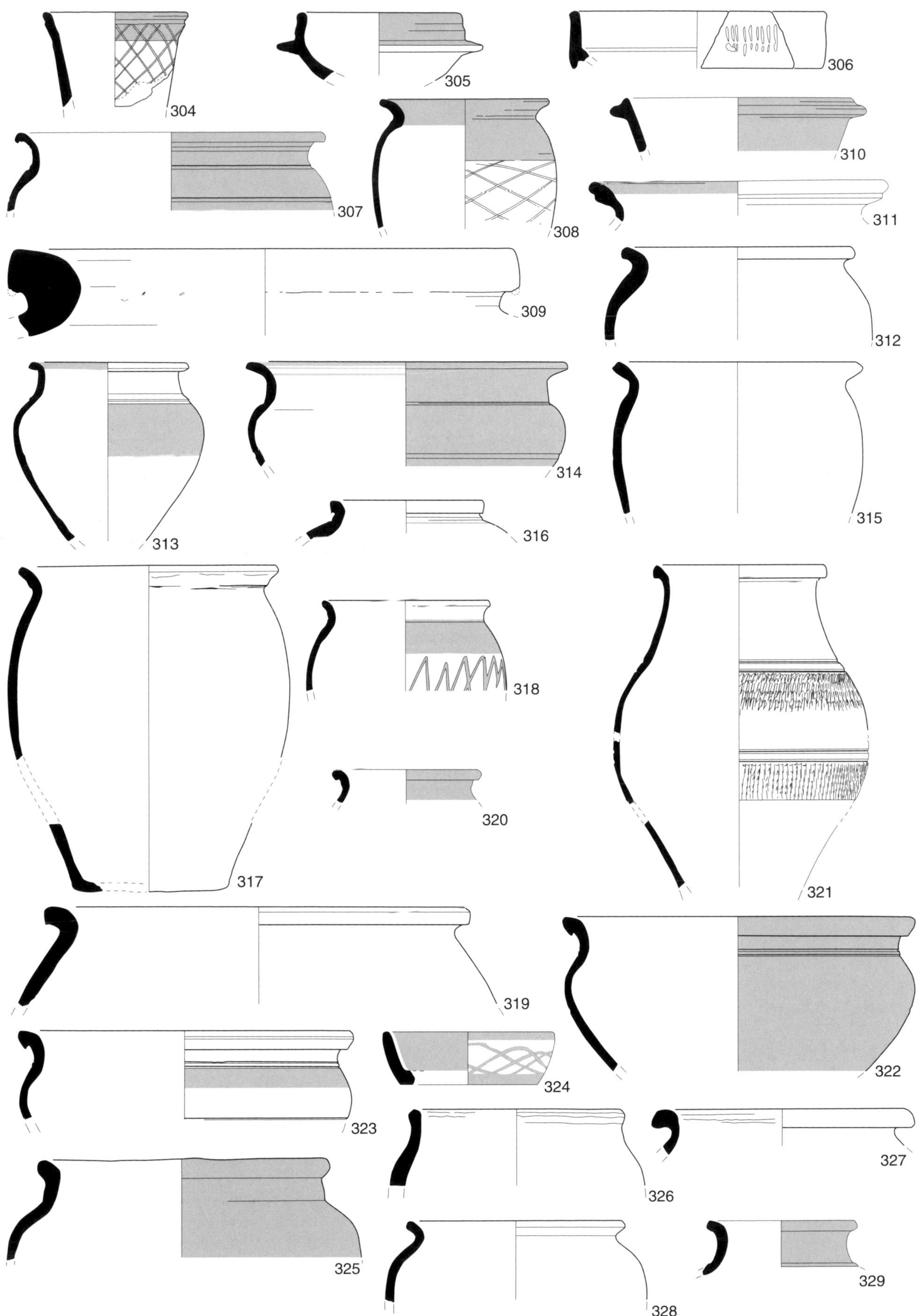

Fig. 14.11 Yarnton, pottery from early Roman (Nos 304-5) and late Roman contexts (Nos 306-329)

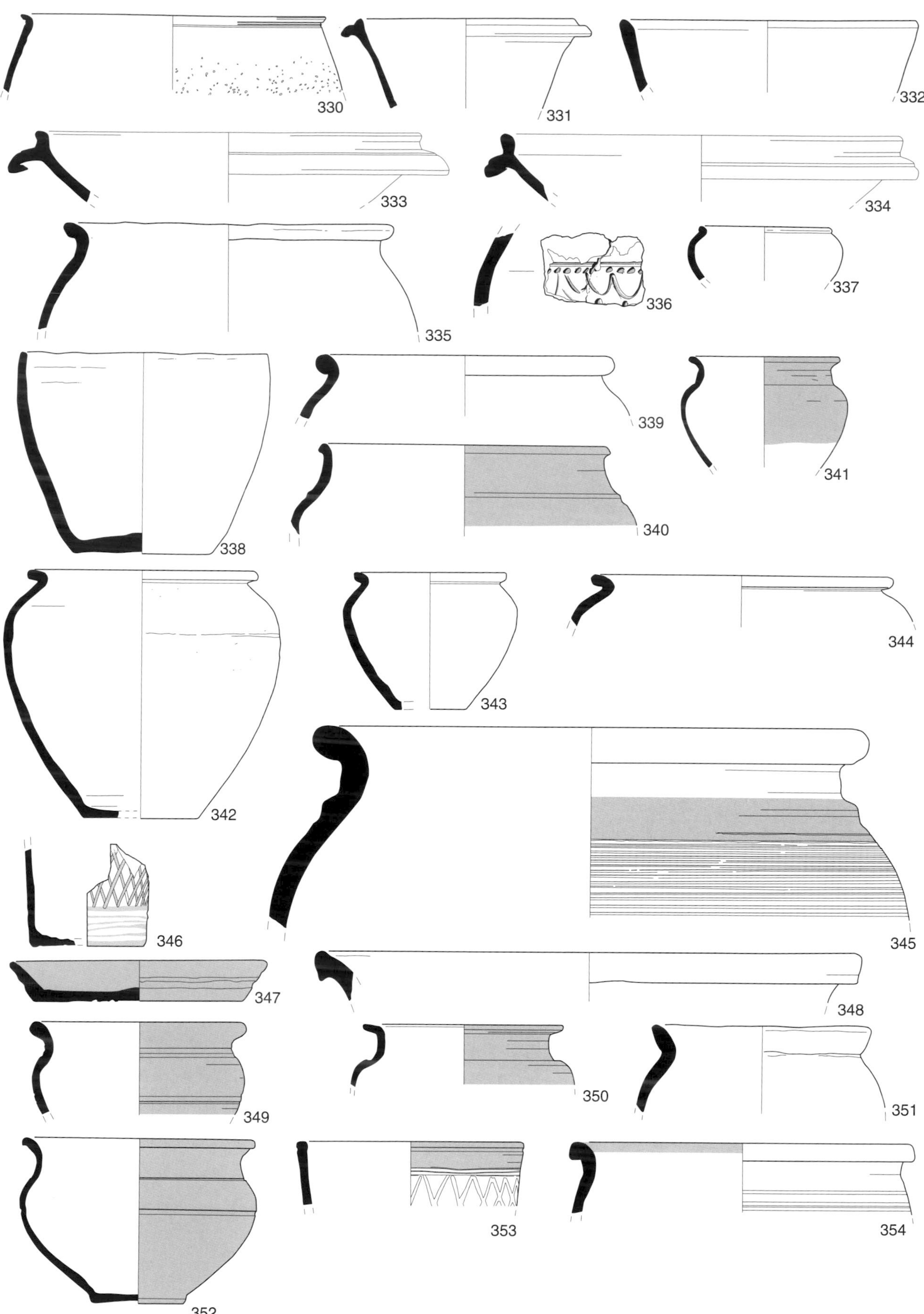

Fig. 14.12 Yarnton, pottery from late Roman contexts, Nos 330-354

Cordon on shoulder. Late Iron Age/early Roman. Ditch 332.

341. Fabric R37, type CE. Overall external burnish; grooves on rim. Ditch 332.
342. Fabric R94, type CI. Internal burnt residue. Ditch 332.
343. Fabric R94, type CI. External sooting. Ditch 332.
344. Fabric R94, type CI. External sooting. Ditch 332.
345. Fabric E80, type CN. Storage jar with burnished zone and cordons on shoulder and decorated with white paint. Late Iron Age/early Roman. Ditch 332.
346. Fabric R37, type GA. Base of tankard decorated with lattice above horizontal line burnish. Ditch 332.
347. Fabric R20, type JA. Burnished overall. Ditch 332.
348. Fabric C11, type CN. Ditch 471.
349. Fabric R37, type HD. Overall exterior burnish. Grooves on neck and girth. Enclosure 996.
350. Fabric R37, type CD. Overall exterior burnish. Ditch 1013.
351. Fabric C12, type CK. Ditch 1027.
352. Fabric E20, type CE. Overall interior burnish. Late Iron Age/early Roman. Ditch 1031.
353. Fabric R37, type GA. Possibly the same vessel as No. 296 above. Ditch 1031.
354. Fabric R37, type H. Burnished on top of rim and with horizontal lines. Ditch 1031.
355. Fabric C11, type CK. Rilling on shoulder. External sooting. Enclosure 1049.
356. Fabric O11, type HB. Burnished overall internally and externally with horizontal lines. Enclosure 1049.
357. Fabric R37, Young type R53. Straight-sided bowl with overall interior burnish. Enclosure 1049.
358. Fabric W20, type CC. Burnished on neck and rim. Neck cordon and shoulder groove. External sooting. Enclosure 1062.
359. Fabric R37, type CD. Burnished neck and rim. Neck cordon and grooves on girth. Ditch 2509.
360. Fabric R37, Young type R38. Burnished shoulder, neck and rim. Neck cordon and groove on girth. Lime scale. Ditch 2509.
361. Fabric R37, type EE. Burnished rim and neck; shoulder groove. Ditch 2517.
362. Fabric O81, type CC. Overall exterior burnish. Pit 48.
363. Fabric C11, type CB. Pit 49.
364. Fabric E80, type CH. Overall exterior burnish. Late Iron Age/early Roman. Pit 101.
365. Fabric E80, type CN. Overall exterior burnish. Late Iron Age/early Roman. Pit 101.
366. Fabric E80, type CD. Late Iron Age/early Roman. Pit 147
367. Fabric R37, Young type R51. Dish with overall internal and external burnish. Pit 1084.
368. Fabric O40, type GA. Overall exterior burnish. Pit 1095.
369. Fabric E30, type HD. Overall exterior burnish. Late Iron Age/early Roman. Pit 1318.

Other pottery from Worton Rectory Farm

(Unstratified or residual material arranged chronologically by type)

Early Iron Age

370. Fabric SP5, type CB. Pit 371.
371. Fabric SP5, type CB. Internal burnt residue. Pit 1561.
372. Fabric SP5, type CS. Fingertip impressions on shoulder. Posthole 999, Structure 1754.

Middle Iron Age

373. Fabric AP3, type CA. External sooting. Pit 1142.
374. Fabric AV3, type CB. Handled jar. Pit 577.
375. Fabric AV3, type CB. Burnished overall. Pit 1142.
376. Fabric AV3, type CB. Pit 1142.
377. Fabric SP4, type CB. Fingertip impressions on shoulder. Pit 1407.
378. Fabric AG4, type CB. Exterior sooting and overall burnish. Pit 2585.
379. Fabric SA5. Large jar. External sooting. ?Residual. Pit 1189.
380. Fabric AN3. Jar/bowl. Pit 1357.
381. Fabric CA4, type HG. Perforated base. Pit 746.
382. Fabric AP3, type HG. Burnished overall. Impressed ovals bordered by horizontal grooves on shoulder. Pit 1282.
383. Fabric AS3, type HG. Burnished externally overall and internally on rim. ?Middle Iron Age. Finds reference 20.
384. Fabric SA5. Lower body sherd with roughly combed decoration. Pit 584.

Late Iron Age/early Roman

385. Fabric E50, type CD. Burnished exterior. Rippled shoulders. Pit 1458.
386. Fabric E80, type CN. Fabric E80, type CN. Burnished externally on shoulder and internally on rim. Grooves on neck and base. Finds reference 592.
387. Fabric E80, type CE. Perforated base. Pit 1189.
388. Fabric E30, type CE. Layer 116.
389. Fabric E80, type CE. Finds reference 602.
390. Fabric E30, type CE. Pit 328.
391. Fabric E80, type EG. Overall burnish. Finds reference 566.
392. Fabric E80, type HA. Exterior burnish. Finds reference 20.

Early Roman

393. Fabric E80, type CD. Externally burnished on rim, neck and shoulder and internally on rim. Rilled body. Ditch 564, Enclosure 129.
394. Fabric E30, type CD. Burnished on neck. Ditch 565, Enclosure 59.
395. Fabric E80, type CD. Jar with perforated base. Ditch 1154, Enclosure 166.
396. Fabric R37, type CD. Externally burnished on rim, neck and shoulder and internally on rim. Rilled body. External sooting. Ditch 1157, Enclosure 427.
397. Fabric R37, type CD. External sooting. Ditch 1157, Enclosure 427.
398. Fabric R94, type CD. Overall exterior burnish. Ditch 1157, Enclosure 427.
399. Fabric R94, type CE. Overall exterior burnish. Ditch 280, Enclosure 206.
400. Fabric R30, type CE. Externally burnished on rim, neck and shoulder and internally on rim. Grooves on body. Ditch 821, Enclosure 51.
401. Fabric E20, type CE. Externally burnished on rim, neck and shoulder. Cremation burial 2501 (associated with brooch Fig. 15.2, No. 2).
402. Fabric E80, type CH. Externally burnished on rim,

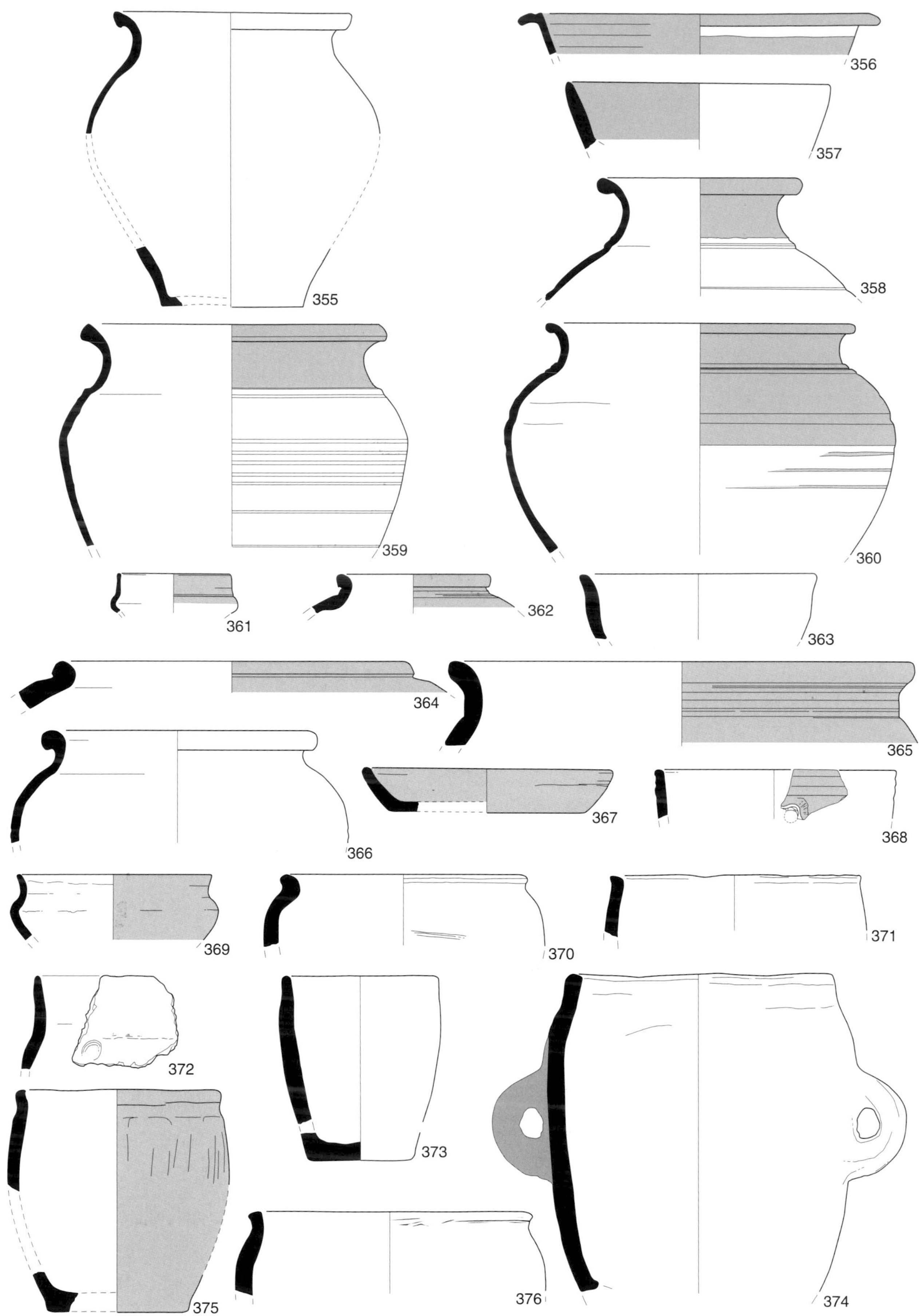

Fig. 14.13 Yarnton, pottery from late Roman contexts (Nos 355-369) and miscellaneous unstratified or residual vessels arranged chronologically by type (Nos 370-376)

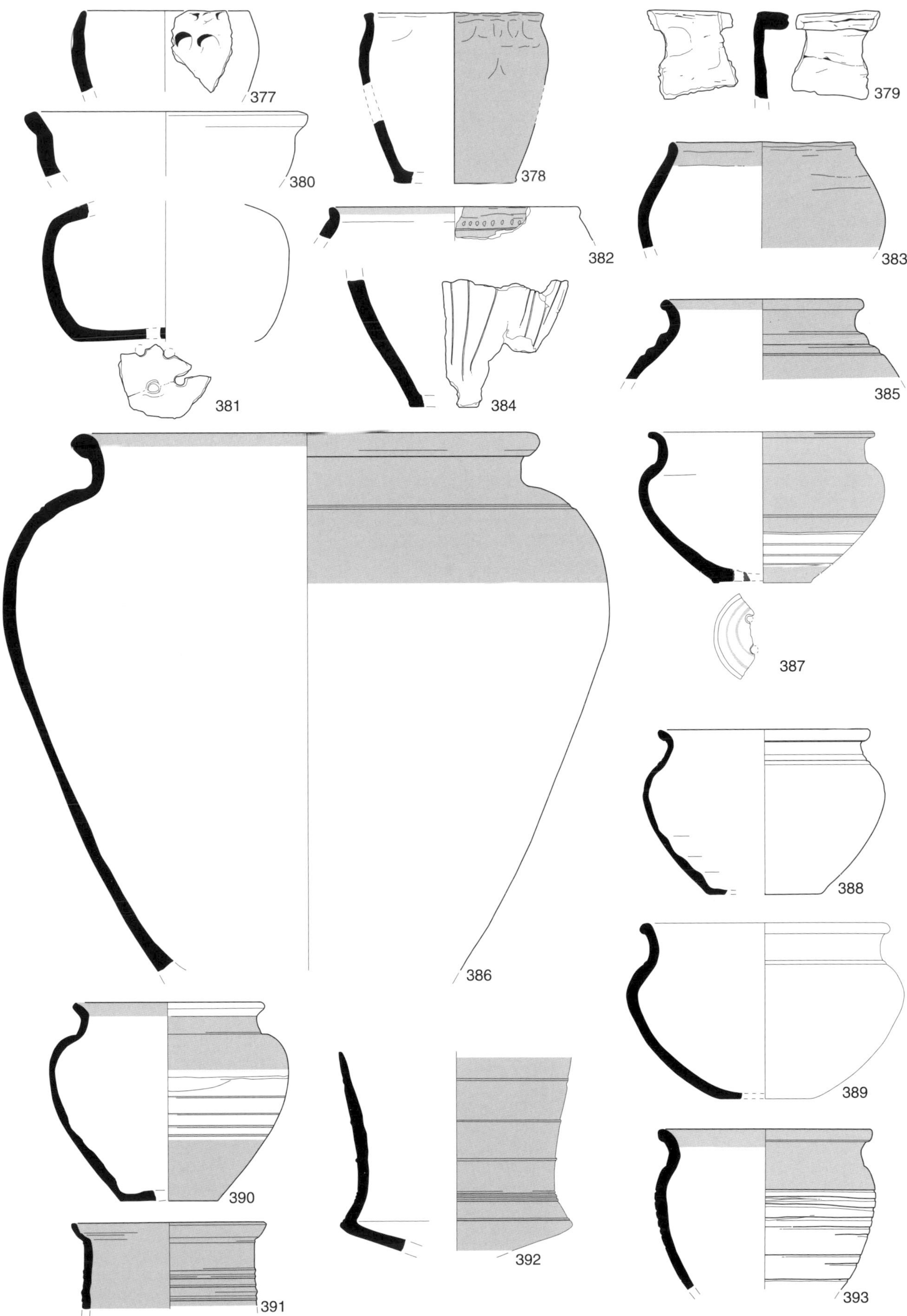

Fig. 14.14 Yarnton, unstratified/residual Iron Age and early Roman pottery, Nos 377-393

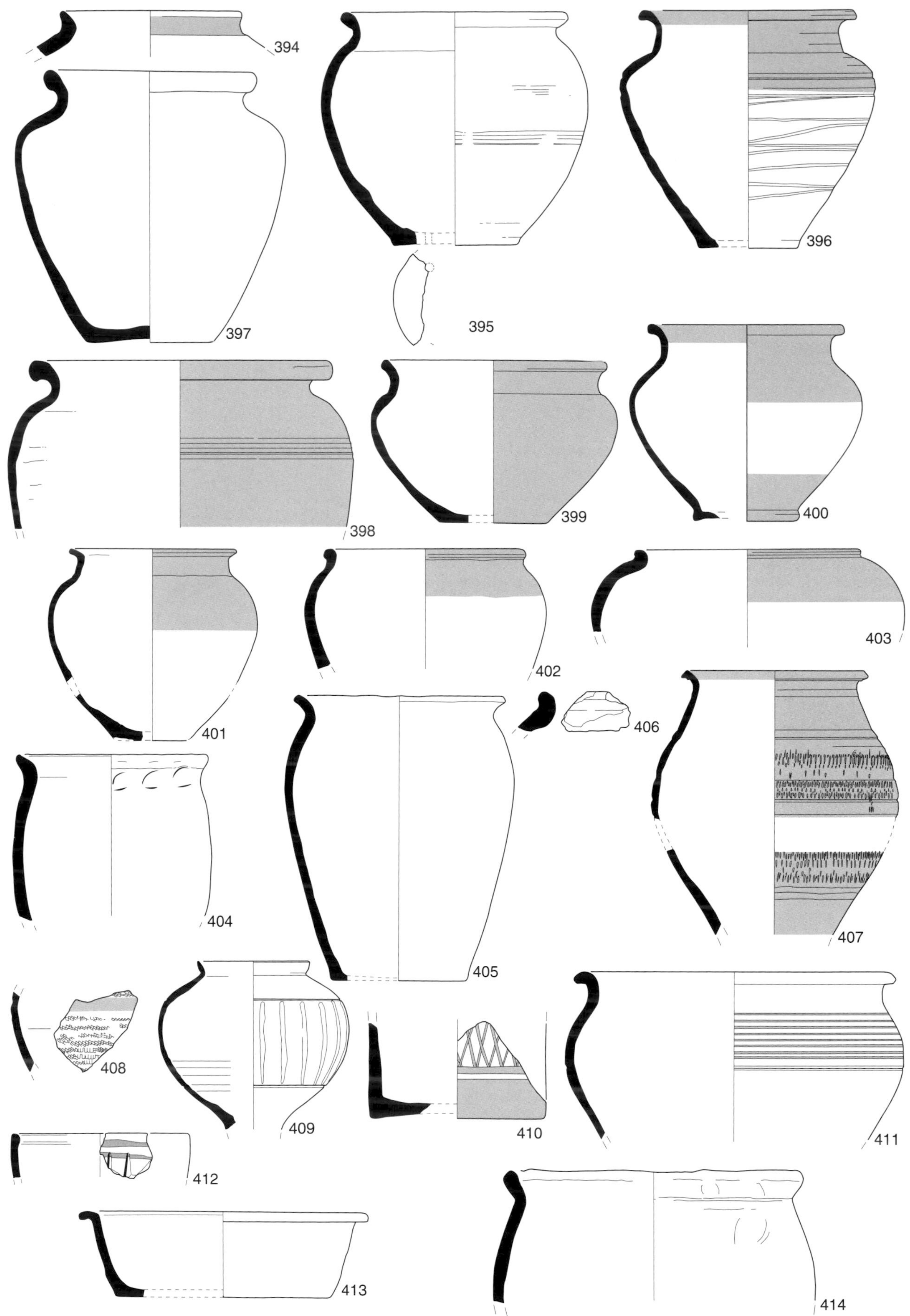

Fig. 14.15 Yarnton, unstratified/residual Iron Age and early Roman pottery, Nos 394-414

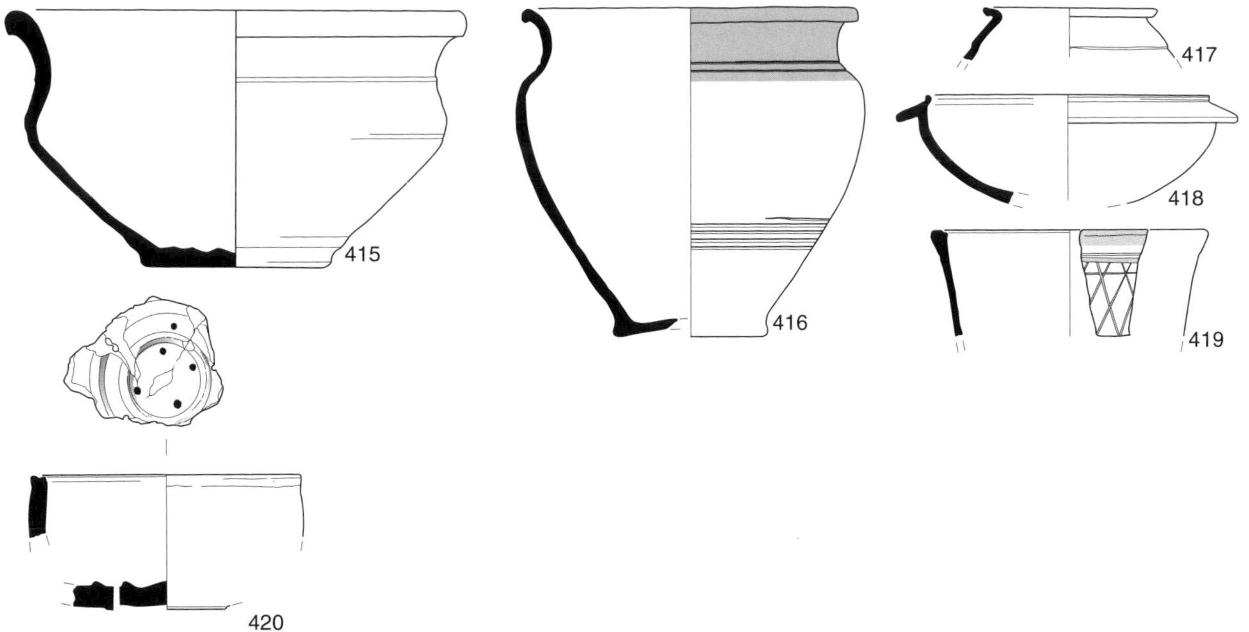

Fig. 14.16 Yarnton, unstratified/residual Roman pottery, Nos 415-420

neck and shoulder. Ditch 355, Enclosure 391C.

403. Fabric R94, type CH. Burnished rim and shoulder. ?Early Roman. Finds reference 607.
404. Fabric C12, type CK. Lime scale and sooting present. Pit 83.
405. Fabric C11, type CK. Ditch 726, Enclosure 51.
406. Fabric E75. Large jar. Ditch 145, Enclosure 55.
407. Fabric E80, type EA. Rouletted beaker with overall exterior burnish. Ditch 1154, Enclosure 166.
408. Fabric E80. Body sherd of ?butt-beaker with rouletted decoration. Ditch 645, Enclosure 206.
409. Fabric W12, Young type W37. Globular beaker decorated with red painted lines. Ditch 1157, Enclosure 427.
410. Fabric R37, type GA. Base of tankard decorated with lattice above burnished zone. Ditch 821, Enclosure 51.
411. Fabric R37, type HD. Jar with rilling on shoulder. Ditch 821, Enclosure 51.
412. Fabric W11, Young type P18. Dish or bowl with bands of red painted decoration. Gully 641, Enclosure 293.
413. Fabric R37, type JA. 2nd/3rd century. Topsoil.

Middle-late Roman

414. Fabric C11, type CK. Probably late Roman. U/S finds reference 20.
415. Fabric O81, type CM. Probably late Roman. U/S finds reference 20.
416. Fabric O81. Wide-mouthed jar. Probably late Roman. U/S finds reference 20.
417. Fabric R37, type EH. Groove on shoulder. U/S 829.
418. Fabric R11, Young type R48. U/S finds reference 20.
419. Fabric R37, type GA. Burnished zone on rim above lattice. Layer 354.
420. Fabric R20, type MF. Cheese-strainer. ?Residual. Pit 1628.

ORGANIC RESIDUE ANALYSIS OF POTSHERDS FROM YARNTON CRESSWELL FIELD *by M.S. Copley, R. Berstan, S.N. Dudd and R.P. Evershed*

Introduction

Lipids are a major constituent of living organisms and are therefore present in appreciable abundances in foodstuffs. During the processing of animal and plant products in unglazed pottery vessels, lipids are absorbed into the vessel wall due to their hydrophobic properties (ie they are not soluble in water) and the use of heat during cooking. These absorbed lipids may survive thousands of years, often without any structural changes having occurred, and are thus amenable to solvent extraction and characterisation using modern analytical techniques (Evershed *et al.* 1999; Evershed *et al.*, 2002).

The identification of ancient commodities based on lipid residues extracted from pottery is inevitably complicated by the degradative processes occurring during vessel use and burial (Evershed 1993). Some identifications can be made based on the structures of individual components and comparison of lipid profiles with modern reference samples and degraded materials produced in laboratory simulation experiments (Dudd *et al.* 1998). However, knowledge of how specific lipid compounds degrade/survive is an important part of organic residue analysis. Degraded animal fats are by far the most commonly identified residues found in association with pottery vessels, and are characterised by a readily recognisable distribution of free fatty acids, monoacylglycerols, diacylglycerols and intact triacylglycerols. However, identification of the particular type of animal from which the fat is derived is much less straightforward, and is complicated to some extent by chemical and micro-biological alteration (Evershed *et al.* 1992; Dudd *et al.* 1998).

Although bulk stable isotope values have been utilised for a number of years in archaeology, recently the determination of compound-specific stable carbon isotope values ($\delta^{13}C$ values) has proven to be vital in any assessment of the origins of the fat/oil (Evershed *et al.* 1994; Mottram *et al.* 1999; Copley *et al.* 2003). This latter approach determines the $\delta^{13}C$ values of the principal fatty acids ($C_{16:0}$ and $C_{18:0}$) present in animal fats. Due to differences in the metabolism of different species, fat-types display specific $\delta^{13}C_{16:0}$ and $\delta^{13}C_{18:0}$ values thus enabling the origin animal to be distinguished. Importantly, the $\delta^{13}C$ values are very robust and are unaffected by decay during burial/vessel use.

Aims and objectives

The initial objective of this investigation was to screen a group of selected sherds from the Cresswell Field site in order to determine the lipid composition of the organic residues. Here we report the results of chemical analyses of these lipid extracts. This work forms part of a larger study into dairying during British prehistory, which investigated the persistence of organic residues obtained from pottery vessels from a total of 14 sites ranging from Neolithic to Iron Age (Copley *et al.* 2003). As part of a later study, a further 91 sherds were selected from the Neolithic phase of occupation at Yarnton Floodplain, and will be the subject of a later publication.

Where degraded animal fat residues have been detected, further analyses comprising a combination of criteria have been considered in the determination of origin, including the characterisation of solvent extractable lipid components by high temperature gas chromatography (HTGC) and GC/mass spectrometry (GC/MS) and the application of compound-specific stable carbon isotope analysis to measure $\delta^{13}C$ values of the major *n*-alkanoic acids ($C_{16:0}$ and $C_{18:0}$).

The analysis of the Cresswell Field assemblage constitutes the most comprehensive study performed to date of organic residues in Iron Age pottery. The Iron Age features are believed to be predominantly related to domestic activity but due to the fragmentary nature of the pottery assemblage in most cases the exact form of the vessel from which the sherds derive is not known. However, two vessel types from context 8126 have been identified, with one sherd deriving from a bowl form (sherd no. CF126; Fig. 14.1, No. 1 above) which is very unusual for this region, both in form and decoration (but not in fabric). It may originally have come from Wessex and not the Thames Valley where it was found. The un-specified base and body sherds from the second vessel are thought to be almost certainly derived from one of the common forms, ie barrel-shaped jar, slack shouldered jar or tripartite jar (Paul Booth pers. comm.). These vessel forms are potentially multi-functional domestic wares, although the smaller tripartite jars are often made of slightly finer fabrics and better finished than other vessels and conceivably represent 'table ware' in the early Iron Age. The vessels are considered to be significant since they were recovered from the fill of one of the earliest Iron Age features on the site which contained an unusually large group of pottery dating to approximately the 7th century BC.

The Cresswell Field site lay on calcareous gravel of the Second Gravel Terrace which affords good preservation to bone, and thus an abundance of animal bone has been recovered in excellent condition, comprising mainly cattle (64%) but also sheep and goat (27%), pig (7%) and horse (2%), but very few wild animals (see Chapter 17 below). Butchery marks were visible on some bone.

Analytical methods

Lipid analyses were performed using our established protocols which are described in detail in earlier publications (Evershed *et al.* 1990; Charters *et al.* 1993; Copley *et al.* 2003). Analyses proceeded as described below.

Solvent extraction of lipid residues

Approximately 2 g samples were taken and their surfaces cleaned using a modelling drill to remove any exogenous lipids (eg soil or finger lipids due to handling). The samples were then ground to a fine powder, accurately weighed and a known amount (20 μg) of internal standard (*n*-tetratriacontane) added. The lipids were extracted with a mixture of chloroform and methanol (2:1 v/v). Following separation from the ground potsherd the solvent was evaporated under a gentle stream of nitrogen to obtain the total lipid extract (TLE). Portions (generally one fifth aliquots) of the extracts were then trimethylsilylated and submitted directly to analysis by gas chromatography (GC). Where necessary combined gas chromatography/mass spectrometry (GC/MS) analyses were also performed on trimethylsilylated aliquots of the lipid extracts to enable the elucidation of structures of components not identifiable on the basis of GC retention time alone.

Preparation of trimethylsilyl derivatives

Portions of the total lipid extracts were derivatised using *N,O*-bis(trimethylsilyl) trifluoroacetamide (30 μl; 70°C; 20 min; Sigma-Aldrich Company Ltd., Gillingham, UK) and analysed by gas chromatography (GC) and gas chromatography-mass spectrometry (GC-MS).

Saponification of total lipid extracts

A methanolic sodium hydroxide (0.5M) and water solution (9:1 v/v) was added to the TLE and heated at 70°C for 1 hour. Following neutralisation, lipids were extracted into hexane and the solvent reduced by rotary evaporation.

Preparation of methyl ester derivatives (FAMEs)

FAMEs were prepared by reaction with BF_3-methanol (14% w/v; 200 µl; Sigma-Aldrich, Gillingham, UK) at 70°C for 1 hour. The methyl ester derivatives were extracted with diethyl ether and the solvent removed under nitrogen. The FAMEs were re-dissolved into hexane for analysis by GC and gas chromatography-combustion-isotope ratio mass spectrometry (GC-C-IRMS).

The pottery samples

A total of 49 sherds were provided from the Cresswell Field Iron Age assemblage with a range of fabric types represented. Several of the sherds were assigned to either jar or bowl forms, although the majority cannot be classified to form. Table 14.26 details the fabric type and description of the sherds submitted for organic residue analyses.

Results

GC analyses were performed on the solvent extracts of a sub-sample of each pot sherd, totalling 49 analyses of this type. The results of screening by GC are summarised in Table 14.26 on a sample-by-sample basis, giving the total lipid concentration per gramme of powdered sherd, a brief description of the lipid distributions and, where known, the commodities from which they originate. Extracts selected for further analysis by GC-C-IRMS are indicated by an asterisk in column 1.

Twenty-eight of the 49 sherds analysed yielded lipid residues, which ranged in concentrations of between 0.43 mg g^{-1} to 2.11 mg g^{-1} of lipid. Preservation of the extracts from Yarnton Cresswell Field is extremely variable but comparable with extracts from Yarnton Flood Plain, with 5 extracts (ie CF101, CF108, CF117, CF138 and CF147) comprising only free fatty acid components (Table 14.26). Conversely, excellent preservation of intact triacylglycerols is seen in samples CF112, CF126, CF127, CF129, CF137 and CF146.

Mid-chain ketones (C_{31}, C_{33} and C_{35}) were detected in sherds CF101, CF105, CF118, CF142 and CF149. These components have been shown to form *via* a condensation reaction which occurs when fats are heated in the presence of fired clay at temperatures in excess of 300°C (Evershed *et al.* 1995; Raven *et al.* 1997). The distributions of lipid components in sherd CF142 (a barrel-shaped jar) are characteristic of degraded beeswax, comprising a series of diagnostic palmitic acid wax esters. Components characteristic of degraded animal fats and mid-chain ketones (C_{31}, C_{33} and C_{35}) were also detected, indicating that this

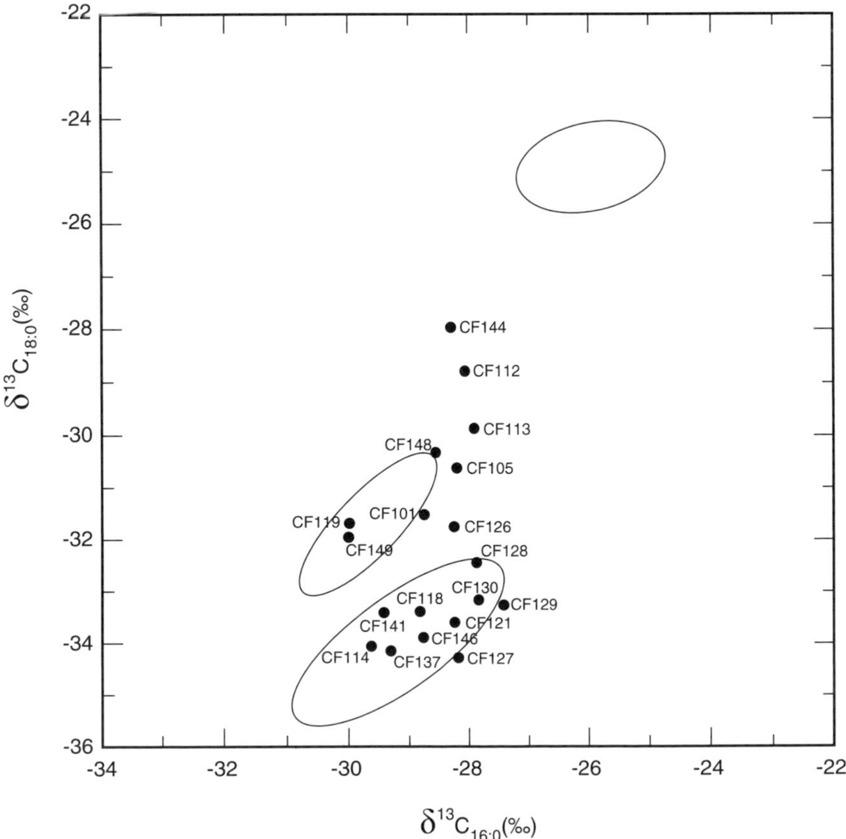

Fig. 14.17 Plot of $\delta^{13}C$ values for Cresswell Field sherds sampled for residues

Table 14.26 Iron Age vessels from Cresswell Field submitted to organic residue analysis.

Sherd no.	*Context*	*Fabric type*	*Description*	*Lipid content (Ìg g-1)*	*Lipid components present*
CF101*	7180	SG4	Lower body wall	288	FFA, K
CF102	7180	SA4	Body sherd	trace	nd
CF103	7180	SA4	Lower body wall	trace	nd
CF104	7180	SA3/4	Rim-type, slack shouldered jar?	13	DAF
CF105*	7180	SN5	Rim-type, slack shouldered jar?	50	FFA, K
CF106	7184	SP3	Rim-type, tripartite jar	trace	nd
CF107	7184	SP4	Body sherd	trace	nd
CF108	7184	LS4	Body sherd-limescale	21	FFA
CF109	7184	SA4	Body sherd-limescale	trace	nd
CF110	8174	AS3	Body/base	trace	nd
CF111	8174	AS4	Body	8	DAF, WE, ALC
CF112*	8174	GS4	Body	130	DAF
CF113*	7986	SC5	Rim, barrel-shaped jar	85	DAF
CF114*	7986	AG3	Body	11	DAF
CF115	7986	SG5	Body	trace	nd
CF116	7986	SP4	Body/base	trace	nd
CF117	8428	SG4	Rim, slack shouldered jar	6	FFA
CF118*	8428	SA5	Body	105	DAF K
CF119*	8428	SL4	Body	15	DAF
CF120	7863	SG4	Body/base	trace	nd
CF121*	7863	AN3	Body	41	DAF
CF122	7863	AI3	Body	trace	nd
CF123	7863	AP3	Rim, barrel-shaped jar	trace	nd
CF124	8628	AN3	Body/base	trace	nd
CF125	8628	SA4	Handle/shoulder	trace	nd
CF126*	8126	GSA4	Body, bowl	161	DAF
CF127*	8126	GSA4	Base, slack shouldered jar	44	DAF
CF128*	8126	GSA4	Body, slack shouldered jar	15	DAF
CF129*	8126	GSA4	Rim, slack shouldered jar	142	DAF
CF130*	8126	SG4	Base	61	DAF
CF131	8126	PAS3	Body	trace	nd
CF132	7150	CS3	Rim, jar	trace	nd
CF133	7150	CQ3	Rim, jar	trace	nd
CF134	7150	SG4	Body	trace	nd
CF135	7150	SA4	Body FT DEC	6	Beeswax?
CF136	7150	SP4	Body	8	DAF
CF137*	7176	SG3	Rim	411	DAF
CF138	7176	SA5	Rim, slack shouldered jar	5	FFA
CF139	7176	LS4	Body	trace	nd
CF140	7176	CS3	Body	trace	nd
CF141*	7176	AN3	Body	75	DAF
CF142	8326	SN4	Rim, barrel-shaped jar	41	Beeswax?, DAF, K
CF143	8326	SA4	Shoulder, slack shouldered jar	trace	nd
CF144*	8326	SP4	Shoulder	28	DAF
CF145	8326	SG3	Body	trace	
CF146*	8064	SG3	Rim, tripartite jar	211	DAF
CF147	8064	AN2	Body	5	FFA
CF148*	8064	AN2	Body	27	DAF
CF149*	8064	AN2	Body	114	DAF, K

* Extracts analysed by GC-C-IRMS. FFA are free fatty acids; DAF are degraded animal fats (comprising distributions of FFA, monoacylglycerols, diacylglycerols and triacylglycerols); K are mid-chain ketones; WE are wax esters and ALC are n-alcohols, nd = not detected.

vessel was also utilised in the heating of fats/oils to temperatures exceeding 300°C.

It was possible to take samples along the profile of some of the vessels. For example, the slack-shouldered jar CF127, CF128 and CF129, which contained lipid concentrations of 44 $\mu g\ g^{-1}$ in the base, 15 $\mu g\ g^{-1}$ in the body and 142 $\mu g\ g^{-1}$ in the rim. This illustrates a phenomenon detectable in many archaeological pottery cooking vessels (eg Charters *et al.* 1995); namely that due to their hydrophobic nature, fats and oils are more concentrated towards the top of the vessel where the water-level would have been. Indeed, this has been demonstrated experimentally (Charters *et al.* 1997).

The $\delta^{13}C$ values for the Cresswell Field sherds (Fig. 14.17) indicate that the majority of extracts plot in the region of the ruminant adipose and dairy fats, with the remainder plotting between the ruminant and non-ruminant reference fats. Table 14.27 summarises the commodities detected in the potsherds. None of the remnant fats plot close to the range for the modern reference porcine fats. Approximately half of the archaeological extracts plot within the range of the modern reference cow's milk. The triacylglycerol distributions illustrated in histograms in Figure 14.18 show that a number of these extracts comprise the lower molecular weight triacylglycerols found in dairy fats. It is clear that the archaeological extracts with a higher abundance of lower molecular weight components exhibit more depleted $\delta^{13}C$ values, and hence reflect trends seen in the reference ruminant dairy fats. Furthermore, no

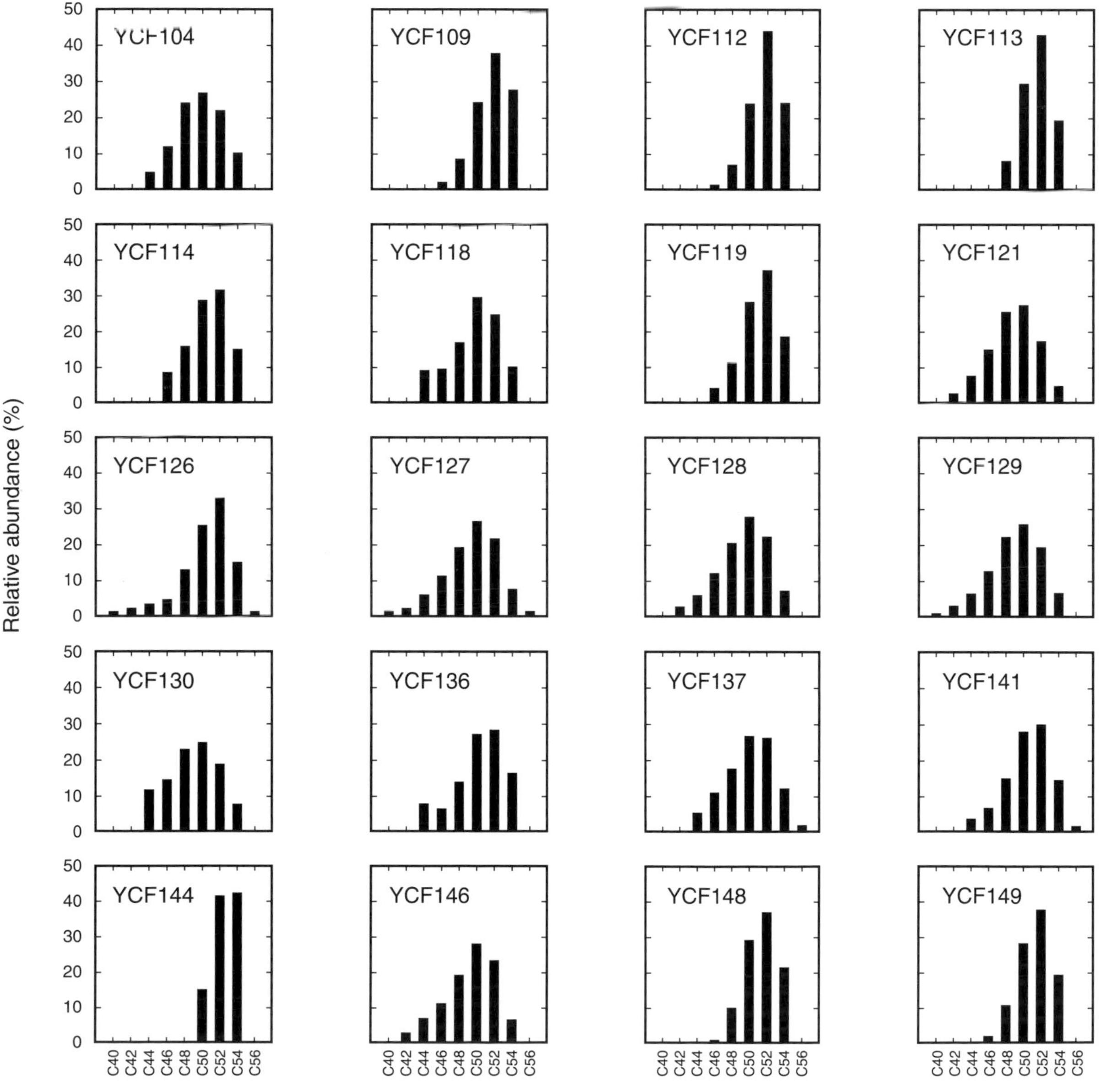

Fig. 14.18 Triacylglycerol distributions for sampled Cresswell Field sherds

Table 14.27 The commodities detected absorbed in Cresswell Field pottery.

Sherd number	*Assignment based on lipid distributions and fatty acid $\delta^{13}C$ values*
CF101	Ruminant adipose fats
CF102	
CF103	
CF104	
CF105	Ruminant adipose fats
CF106	
CF107	
CF108	
CF109	
CF110	
CF111	
CF112	Mixed ruminant / non-ruminant adipose fats
CF113	Mixed ruminant / non-ruminant adipose fats
CF114	Dairy fats
CF115	
CF116	
CF117	
CF118	Dairy fats
CF119	Ruminant adipose fats
CF120	
CF121	Dairy fats
CF122	
CF123	
CF124	
CF125	
CF126	Dairy fats
CF127	Dairy fats
CF128	Dairy fats
CF129	Dairy fats
CF130	Dairy fats
CF131	
CF132	
CF133	
CF134	
CF135	Beeswax?
CF136	
CF137	Dairy fats
CF138	
CF139	
CF140	
CF141	Dairy fats
CF142	Beeswax?
CF143	
CF144	Mixed ruminant / non-ruminant adipose fats
CF145	
CF146	
CF147	
CF148	
CF149	

apparent correlation exists between the relative abundances of the $C_{16:0}$ and $C_{18:0}$ fatty acids and other chemical characteristics of the lipid extracts. This was also seen in the extracts from Yarnton Floodplain assemblage (and other lipid extracts derived from prehistoric pottery) and suggests that the distributions of fatty acids are unreliable indicators of animal origin due to their greater natural variability and susceptibility to decay and leaching of the shorter chain components, resulting in enhanced relative abundances of the longer chain fatty acids (to unpredictable degrees, depending upon the extent of diagenesis).

Discussion

In general, the sherds comprising higher concentrations (>100 $\mu g\ g^{-1}$) of absorbed lipid also exhibited more depleted $\delta^{13}C$ values (ie resembling dairy fats), possibly reflecting the way in which the vessels were used and the ease with which certain fats are absorbed within the porous pottery. There is no clear correlation between fabric types from Cresswell Field and $\delta^{13}C$ values of the fatty acids, but the majority of the GSA4 and SG3 types plot within the range for reference dairy fats, as does sherd CF114 (fabric type AG3). Sherd CF144 (fabric type SP4) contains remnant fats with the least depleted $\delta^{13}C$ values in the entire assemblage.

Lipid residues from Cresswell Field consist of predominantly remnant animal fat residues. The use of a combination of criteria including compound-specific stable isotope determinations and distributions of triacylglycerol components has enabled distinctions to be drawn between ruminant and porcine (non-ruminant) fats, and different types of ruminant fats (ie dairy and adipose fats). Five of the sherds (26%) yielded fatty acids with $\delta^{13}C$ values indicative of predominantly ruminant adipose fats, and a further three sherds (16%) contained mixtures of ruminant and porcine adipose fats. Furthermore, ruminant dairy fats have been clearly detected in 11 of the extracts (equivalent to 39% of the lipid-containing sherds and 22% of all of the sherds). Although a large proportion of the lower molecular weight triacylglycerols originally present in the dairy fats have been degraded, resulting in a profile similar to degraded adipose fats, the stable isotope values provide a robust chemical signal apparently unaffected by decay.

A further two vessels were also found to contain degraded beeswax residues which were not detected in sherds from the earlier Bronze Age vessels at Yarnton; these two vessels were quite distinctive, one being decorated and the other a barrel-shaped jar. In general, no distinctions were apparent between vessel type/form and commodity detected. None of the sherds contained any plant-derived lipid components (such as *n*-alkanes, *n*-alcohols or ketones). These latter components are present in relatively high abundances in the epicuticular leaf waxes, on the stems and on the outer coating of seeds. The fact that these commodities were not present in detectable quantities suggests that the processing (ie cooking) of leafy vegetables is unlikely to have occurred in these vessels to any great extent.

The proportion of sherds containing substantial lipid concentrations (ie >5 μg of lipid per gram of potsherd) from Creswell Field was higher (59%) than at Yarnton Floodplain (29%). It is likely that this may in part relate to the burial time, but it is also likely to be a function of burial conditions. The results from Cresswell Field contrast with those obtained from pottery vessels from Yarnton Floodplain (Neolithic), where dairy fats were detected in only 13% of the sherds (equivalent to 26% of the extracts). This may suggest that although dairying was an important component in local farming practices at both sites, it is during the Iron Age that either (i) dairy products become an even more important commodity, or (ii) the processing of dairy products in pottery vessels became a more important activity.

A NOTE ON IRON AGE POTTERY FROM CASSINGTON FLOODPLAIN SITES

by Alistair Barclay

Iron Age pottery was excavated from five trenches in the area of the Cassington floodplain sites (H1, H2, H9, H10 and H13), examined after the reports on the main Cresswell Field and Yarnton assemblages had been completed (see Fig. 11.14). This material will be considered in more detail alongside the earlier pottery from this and other component sites of the Yarnton project, all recorded by the writer, in the report on the earlier prehistoric components of the project (Hey *et al.* forthcoming). The purpose of the present note is to draw attention to the existence of further material of this period that can be compared with the Cresswell Field and Yarnton assemblages.

Ten contexts within trench H1 produced a significant assemblage of middle Iron Age sherds. The material was characterised by rounded forms, simple rims, burnishing, absence of decoration and the predominance of sandy fabrics. A small proportion of early Iron Age sherds may be present in features H/1/8 and H/1/9 and a possible late Iron Age sherd in H/1/3.

Ditch H/1/10 produced the largest quantity of middle Iron Age material (54 sherds, 561 g), although a small proportion of this is hard to characterise. Five sherds from the rim, body and pedestal base of a vessel in sandy- and/or organic-tempered fabrics are more typical of early Saxon ceramics but would not be out of place in the middle Iron Age (G Lambrick pers. comm.). Ditch H/1/4 produced 28 sherds (330 g) of middle Iron Age pottery, including two rim fragments from barrel and globular-shaped jars. Ditch H/1/5 also produced middle Iron Age material (8 sherds, 190 g) which included three fragments from globular vessels. Limescale and burnt residues were noted on a number of middle Iron Age sherds and fired clay (daub) and possible crucible fragments were also seen (in H/1/8 and H/1/10).

A ditch in trench H2 (H/2/7) produced a few middle Iron Age sherds, as did ploughsoil above this (H/2/5). The latter also contained two possible Roman sherds.

In trench H10, middle Iron Age pottery was recovered from a layer (H/10/3), two ditches (H/10/8 and H/10/25), a gully (H/10/14) and a pit (H/10/15), although a few sherds could be early Iron Age in date. Two possible late Iron Age sherds came from the surface above possible postholes, and earlier prehistoric pottery was retrieved from a ditch and the disturbed layer above the Iron Age features, along with middle Iron Age pottery (H/10/2).

A single post-medieval sherd was recovered from the topsoil in trench H9, and a post-medieval sherd and possible middle Iron Age sherd from the top of trench H13.

Chapter 15: Artefacts

by Leigh Allen, Alistair Barclay, Paul Booth, Philippa Bradley, Roger Doonan, Emily Edwards, Brian Gilmour, Vanessa Fell, Martin Henig, Elaine Morris, Peter Northover, Fiona Roe, Chris Salter, Jane Timby and Jonathan Wallis

INTRODUCTION *by Jane Timby*

This chapter describes and discusses the finds from the Iron Age and Roman features at Yarnton. Reports are, as originally prepared, based on material/artefact types and within each report the material is presented in a broadly chronological manner. In many instances datable finds occur in later contexts, either as redeposited or curated finds, thus the presentation of the finds reflects the occupation of the site and not necessarily the context in which they were found. Personal fashion items such as brooches are far more datable than perhaps tools which are adapted to a longer period of use. In the following chapter the detailed reports and catalogues are preceded by a more synthetic discussion based on the distribution of artefacts through time and through the functional categories represented, to shed more light on the nature of the activities being carried out on the site. More detailed descriptions of the incidence and distribution of finds in general alongside other material such as animal bone and plant remains can be found in Chapters 5-9. The specialist reports found below start with the metal finds: copper alloy artefacts (Martin Henig), coins (Paul Booth) followed by iron-work (Leigh Allen, Vanessa Fell and Alistair Barclay). These are followed by reports of the worked antler/bone (Jonathan Wallis and Leigh Allen), jet and shale (Philippa Bradley) and worked stone by Fiona Roe. The next section deals with briquetage (Elaine Morris) and fired clay (Emily Edwards and Alistair Barclay), and the final section catalogues and discusses the metalworking debris (Roger Doonan and Chris Salter) with analyses of selected items (Peter Northover and Brian Gilmour).

DISTRIBUTION AND FUNCTION

The finds assemblage recovered from Yarnton overall is generally extremely poor considering the size of the areas investigated and the duration of occupation. It must be presumed that a significant amount of the cultural assemblage comprised organic materials such as wood and leather and that metal, as a valued resource, was recycled. Despite this the quality of some the items is of note. Table 15.1 shows the distribution by material type across the three main excavated areas: Cresswell Field, Yarnton and the floodplain sites. In total 212 individual artefacts have been catalogued of which 158 came from Yarnton, 51 from Cresswell Field and just three from the floodplain sites. Most of the non-ferrous and ferrous finds come from Yarnton, which produced a total of 17 and 31 individual pieces respectively, compared to a single piece of iron from Cresswell Field and single pieces of each from the floodplain. Similarly, all the coins came from the Yarnton site, which reflects the different chronological emphasis of occupation with most of the Roman activity focussed at Yarnton. The numbers even out slightly for the bone and stone categories with 16 stone items and 20 bone/antler objects from Cresswell Field and 27 stone and 21 bone pieces from Yarnton. One Iron Age bone artefact came from the floodplain. Four items of jet/shale all came from Cresswell Field. In terms of fired clay objects, namely loomweights and spindlewhorls, Cresswell Field produced approximately 10 examples and Yarnton 19, although estimating the exact number from fragments can only be approximate.

Table 15.2 summarises the artefacts by material type and the period from which they were recovered. Some pieces, where they can be dated, are clearly redeposited or curated. In terms of the contexts from which they were recovered the highest incidence of finds is in the early Iron Age, 45 in total. Thirty-two pieces came from late Roman contexts closely followed by the middle Iron Age with 31 finds. The late Iron Age and late Iron Age/early Roman phases show the greatest dearth of pieces (though they are also of the shortest duration), and early Roman

Table 15.1 Quantification of small finds by site and material type.

Material	*Cresswell Field*	*Yarnton*	*Floodplain*	*Total*
Non-ferrous metal	-	17	1	18
Iron	1	31	1	33
Jet/shale	4	-	-	4
Stone	16	27	-	43
Bone	20	21	1	42
Glass	-	-	-	-
Coins	-	43	-	43
Fired clay objects	10	19	-	29
Total	51	158	3	212

Table 15.2 Quantification of small finds by period.

Material	Period								
	EIA	MIA	LIA	LIR	ERB	LRB	RB	US	Total
Non-ferrous metal	1	1	0	0	5	4	0	7	18
Iron	2	2	0	1	5	10	2	11	33
Jet/shale	1	3	0	0	0	0	0	0	4
Stone	8	11	1	2	4	8	0	9	43
Bone	21	7	1	4	3	3	1	2	42
Coins	0	0	0	0	0	5	0	38	43
Fired clay objects	8	10	0	1	6	2	2	0	29
Total	45	31	2	8	22	32	5	67	212

features produced 22 items. Where datable most of the finds appear to belong to the Iron Age, early Roman or late Roman periods. The later 2nd-3rd century is often a difficult period to identify from a small finds assemblage (Cool 1998, 222). More reliable evidence for this period can come from glass or pottery, but the evidence from the pottery assemblage at Yarnton may also suggest a decrease in activity on the site in the mid Roman period.

Table 15.2 complements Table 15.1 insofar as the greater number of metal pieces come from contexts dated to the Roman period and thus by default from the Yarnton site. The early Iron Age produced just one non-ferrous piece, a copper alloy strip (SF 390) from a posthole, and two iron objects, a nail from pit 330 and an adze from pit 7787. In addition a fragment of copper alloy slag came from early Iron Age pit 8092 and various traces of metal-working debris, crucible and hearth bottoms, attest to both non-ferrous and ferrous working not really substantiated by the artefacts. The middle Iron Age phase was similarly poorly represented in terms of artefact recovery, although again there are traces of metal-working debris indicating that such activity was taking place in the locality. The middle Iron Age metalwork is restricted to three items. Two were recovered from the surface of the causeway on the floodplain, a riveted copper alloy ring (SF 13089) and a composite piece, a copper-alloy coated iron ring (SF 13087). An iron ring came from pit 729 at Yarnton. There are no late Iron Age examples of metalwork and just a single iron nail from the late Iron Age/early Roman phase, from ditch 175. Numbers start to increase from the early Roman period with five non-ferrous and five ferrous pieces all from the Yarnton site. The non-ferrous items include three brooches (SF 128, 160-1) and a stud, two of which came from enclosure 440, one from pit 836 and one from layer 152. The iron items comprise two nails, one a hobnail, a double-spiked loop (SF 110) an awl (SF 402) and a hook-shaped cutting tool (SF 360). A further increase occurs in the late Roman period with four non-ferrous finds and ten ferrous items. The non-ferrous items comprise a brooch of early Roman date (SF 276), two strips (SF 99, 212) and a pin (SF 762). The ferrous objects include four nails (one a hobnail), two ferrules (SF175, 469), two punches (SF 178, -), a file (SF 230) and a knife (SF 52). Two further iron items, a nail and a knife, are simply dated as Roman, and seven copper-alloy and eleven iron finds constitute unstratified finds. Of the 43 coins recorded from the site just five came from stratified contexts, all late Roman, the remainder being unstratified.

One jet and three shale objects were recovered from the site, one from an early Iron Age context, pit 8005 and the remaining three from middle Iron Age features, in particular pits 7988 and 8786. Most of the stone and bone artefacts similarly come from Iron Age contexts. Eight stone objects were recovered from early Iron Age features and eleven from the middle Iron Age. The early Iron Age (or late Bronze Age/early Iron Age) finds comprise saddle querns or rubbers, one polisher, two whetstones and one anvil. The middle Iron Age finds similarly comprise saddle querns, rubbers, one polisher and two fragments of indeterminate function. Only three stone items came from late Iron Age or late Iron Age/early Roman contexts, two saddle querns (SF 200, 298) and one rotary quern (SF 210), the latter from enclosure 205. Four querns (SF 313, 319, 382, 606), including examples in Old Red Sandstone and Niedermendig lava, were recovered from early Roman contexts and eight stone items came from late Roman contexts; two querns, one millstone, one anvil stone, one polisher, one whetstone and two slabs.

The bone/antler objects show a very clear bias towards the early Iron Age with 20 recorded items. The range of objects is quite diverse with four antler handles, a cheek piece, two combs, three gouges, three polished metapodials, one awl/pin, three undefined objects and three pieces of manufacturing debris. There is a marked drop off to just eight objects from middle Iron Age contexts, in which four polished metapodials, two combs, one toggle and one undefined object are recorded. In the late Iron Age and early Roman periods a further seven objects, five metapodials, one gouge and one point, were recovered, and in the late Roman period just three items, two polished metapodials and one gouge. Of note amongst the unstratified finds are a further weaving comb and a pin.

Table 15.3 Quantification of small finds by functional categories (after Crummy 1993).

Functional Category	*Cresswell Field*	*Yarnton*	*Floodplain*	*Total*
1. Personal ornaments	3	12	0	15
3. Textile manufacture	13	38	1	52
4. Household	9	20	0	29
8. Transport	1	0	0	1
10. Tools	13	10	0	23
11. Fasteners and fittings	3	26	2	31
14. Objects associated with religious beliefs	0	1	0	1
15. Objects associated with metal working	3	2	0	5
16. Antler/bone manufacturing debris	3	0	0	3
Total	48	109	3	160

The final category of finds in Table 15.2 is the fired clay. In terms of loomweights and spindle whorls there are approximately eight objects from early Iron Age contexts, two of which are spindle-whorls, and ten from the middle Iron Age with just one spindlewhorl, the remainder being triangular loomweights. These numbers exclude the cylindrical late Bronze Age fragments recovered from the site. A further six loomweights and one spindle-whorl came from late Iron Age or early Roman contexts and two loomweights from late Roman features. Also excluded from the table is briquetage (salt container), recovered largely from early and middle Iron Age features.

Table 15.3 divides the finds assemblages into functional categories as defined by Crummy (1983) irrespective of material type. Nine individual categories can be defined for the Yarnton material. The first is that of personal adornment or dress, to which a total of 15 pieces can be attributed. These include seven brooches, one pin, one earring (jet), one stud, four bracelets (two of shale and two of copper alloy) and a buckle. No items were identified which can be specifically associated with Crummy's category 2, toilet, surgical or pharmaceutical instruments. Category 3, objects used in the manufacture or working of textiles, is well subscribed, however, with a total of 52 pieces. These include the polished bone metapodials, five weaving combs, loomweights and spindlewhorls which are moderately well represented at both Cresswell Field and Yarnton and particularly associated with the early and middle Iron Age phases of occupation. These objects strongly suggest the presence of on-site textile manufacture, albeit on a small scale.

A number of finds can be placed in Crummy's category 4, household utensils. These are objects used in the preparation, cooking and serving of food (other than pottery vessels) and objects associated with lighting or furniture. The latter two functions cannot be identified from the finds here but in the former are items like the shale vessel and all the quernstones, giving a total of 29 finds. No items were identified relating to recreation, weighing or measuring or written communication (categories 5-7), and just a single find, an antler cheek piece from a bridle, could be construed as connected with transport (category 8). At least 23 tools (category 10) were recovered from the sites, largely in iron, stone and bone. The iron tools include an adze, two knives, an awl, a cutting tool, two punches and some shears. The stone objects include anvil stones and whetstones whilst the bone tools include an awl and gouges.

The number of items that can be placed into category 11, fasteners and fittings, is perhaps surprisingly low, at 31 finds. These are mainly nails, ferrules, cleats, copper-alloy strips, iron rings and a bone toggle. This is probably a reflection of the lack of structures attributable to the Roman period, the structural techniques used in the Iron Age not requiring many metal fittings. One item, a bucket fitting, has been classified as possibly religious in function (category 14) as it may have originally derived from a burial.

The remaining two categories represented amongst the Yarnton finds are objects and waste material associated with metal working (category 15) and waste associated with bone or antler working (category 16). Table 15.3 only itemises the crucibles for category 15, but there is in addition a quantity of other evidence attesting to small scale copper and iron working from the early Iron Age onwards. The iron punches (category 10) may also be linked with metalworking. Antler working is demonstrated by the recovery of three pieces of manufacturing debris, all from early Iron Age contexts at Cresswell Field.

COPPER ALLOY *by Martin Henig*

Introduction

Only seventeen copper alloy objects were recovered from the Yarnton and Cresswell Field sites but several of them are of considerable interest. A further three items (reported on by Peter Northover below) were recovered from the Iron Age causeway on the floodplain (Floodplain Site B). The gravel terrace sites produced a small fragment of what may have been an ornate anthropomorphic bucket mount, originally dating to the Iron Age, hinting at high status activity, possibly funerary. This is also true of another piece of metalwork, early Roman in date, but native in its aesthetic affinities, the Aesica brooch associated with a cremation burial.

The other six brooches form a small but remarkably consistent group; all the fibulae are early Roman and none needs be later than the reign of Nero. The assemblage contains an interesting Hod Hill variant. As is so often the case with assemblages of finds, brooches do not date the life of the site. There are two later Roman bracelet fragments, and an important find (alas fragmentary), a buckle dating from the very end of the Roman period and perhaps not lost until the later 5th century to judge from its abraded surface.

Bucket fitting (Fig 15.2, No. 1)

1. The ornate bucket fitting consists of a fragment of open-work sheet with crescentic aperture and circular terminal on the left side (half remains); it is ornamented on the front with a wide hatched band but is plain and unworked on the back. It has the appearance of being part of the crest of a helmet and can, indeed, be matched by the crests on the two helmeted heads which form the escutcheons of the Aylesford bucket (Stead 1971, 261-3, fig. 4). These have opposed crescentic openings and circular terminals and are embellished with cross-hatched decoration and are almost exactly the same size (width 60 mm) as the Yarnton crest would have been when complete. Unfortunately only about half of the Yarnton crest remains (surviving width 30 mm) but it is nevertheless of considerable importance. It was recovered from an early Roman ditch (context 1268) where it was clearly residual. The presence of such a high status object at Yarnton is interesting. Was it derived from a similar bucket burial or was it from a ritual deposit? It probably dates to the 1st century BC. SF 379. Enclosure ditch 1268. Early Roman.

Miscellaneous

2. A strip with a roughly rectangular section, grooved on one side. Length 30 mm. Probably scrap, but possibly binding as used for shields (see Stead 1991, 20-1, fig. 22). SF 390. Posthole 1452. Early Iron Age.

Brooches (Fig. 15.2, Nos 2-5)

3. Fig. 15.1; Fig. 15.2, No. 2. The fibula of Aesica type was recovered from context 2501, an early Roman cremation burial found in the salvage area. The brooch has a spring, its external chord held in place by a forward hook. The body of the brooch is in two parts, an arched bow with swept-back fins and a lozenge-shaped plate with a fan-tail, which bears the catch-plate on its underside. The bow is riveted to the lower plate in the middle of the lozenge. The pin is present but is broken off from the spring. Both the bow and plate of the brooch still retain their covering of thin sheet ornamented en repoussé in insular La Tène style. On the bow the decoration is disposed symmetrically on either side of a central beaded band. It consists of eye-like motifs with lids highly curved on the inner side but somewhat more angular on the outer edge where there is a pronounced carination beside each of the knobs which terminate the side fins; from here the ornament curves away along the narrowing line of the bow. The foot, which is beaded along its end with simple bands of repoussé along its other sides, has two triple-lobed 'flowers' one on each side of a thin central band but joined to one another by the curved device which balances a similar arc that demarcates the point of junction with the bow.

Fig. 15.1 Roman brooch SF 276 (context 2501)

Aesica brooches are named after the finest and largest known, a gilded specimen buried in the later (3rd century AD) cache of jewellery in the strong room at the headquarters at the Hadrian's Wall fort of Great Chesters (Aesica) (Charlesworth 1973, 226-8). Although the shape of these brooches may be partially derived from a continental prototype, the type is unique to Britain in form and decoration, which, as in the cases both of the type example from Great Chesters and the present Yarnton fibula, is worked en repoussé in insular La Tène style.

The Yarnton brooch can be closely compared with a well-known example from Hook Norton in Oxfordshire (Ashmolean Museum) which is similarly constructed with a single rivet attaching bow and plate and a near identical motif on the sheet covering the foot. The ornament on the bow is largely lacking but the remaining piece of sheet preserves part of the central beaded band (Harden and Taylor 1939, 338-9, fig. 42; Collingwood and Richmond 1969, fig. 105 no. 92). The two brooches were surely made in the same workshop. Other Aesica brooches constructed in the same way are recorded from Winterbourne Bassett, Wiltshire (Cunnington and Goddard 1911, 40-1, no. 306, pl. xxi), from near Winchester, Hampshire (Hattatt

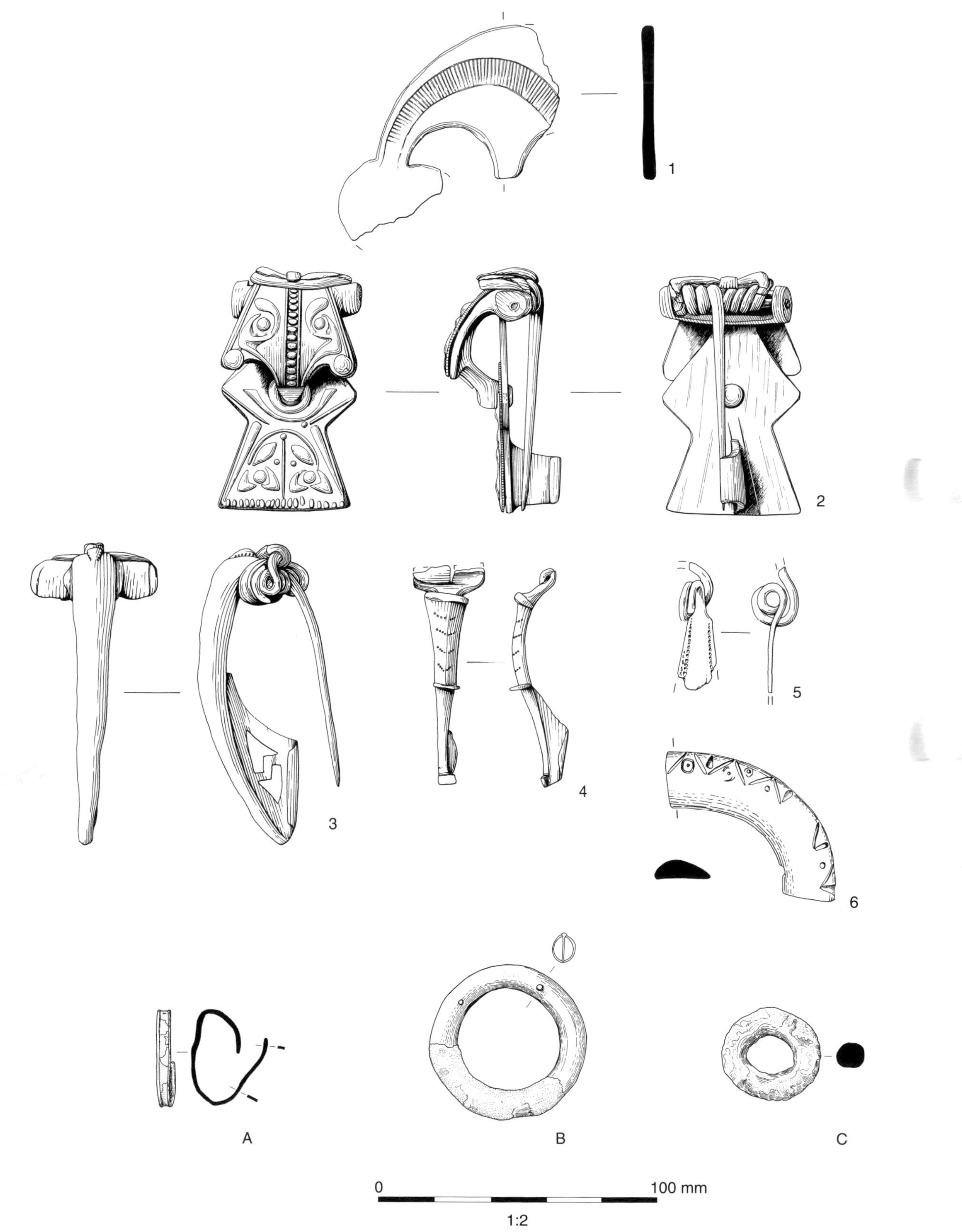

Fig. 15.2 Objects of copper alloy, Nos 1-6 and A-C

1987, 58 no. 800, fig. 21) and from Shakenoak Farm near Wilcote, Oxfordshire (Mackreth 1973, 114-5, fig. 53 no. 176), though the repoussé sheet in these cases is largely (or in the case of the Shakenoak brooch, completely) lacking. Another example, from Usk, was also covered with repoussé sheet ornament, though the structure of the brooch is different, and the riveting was designed to hold the sheet in place (Webster 1995, 72-3 no. 26). It is dated to the Neronian occupation of the fortress, and in fact all Aesica brooches would seem to belong to the Claudio-Neronian period. Further, Hattatt shows that the type is concentrated in Gloucestershire, Wiltshire and Oxfordshire (Hattatt 1989, 38-41, fig. 18).

Although only 40 mm in length the subtle, elusive patterns of this brooch place it amongst the masterpieces of Celtic art from Britain, as has already been recognised in an earlier publication (Henig and Booth 2000, 134-5, fig. 5.19). It is suggested that as the best specimen of these smaller Aesica brooches, this should henceforth be known as the Yarnton type. SF 276. Cremation burial 2501. Early Roman, associated with a pottery jar (cf. Fig. 14.15, No. 401).

4. Fig. 15.2, No. 3. A Colchester two-piece brooch (Colchester B). It has two piercings on the catch-plate separated by a zig-zag. The external chord of the spring passes through a lug at the head above which is a short triangular crest edged with hatching. For the form see Hod Hill (Brailsford 1962, 7 and fig. 6 no. C10), though the catch-plate is not pierced. Examples from Colchester (Crummy 1983, 11-12 no. 48, fig. 6) and Brooke, Norfolk (Hattatt 1989, 26-7 no. 1459, fig. 11) do have openwork catch-plates, though that of the Yarnton brooch is best paralleled by examples from Newstead (Collingwood and Richmond 1969, 294 and fig. 102, no. 7), the east Midlands (Hattatt 1985, 82-3, no. 374) and Usk (Webster 1995, 75-6, fig. 24, no. 28) all related to the 'Polden Hill' series. In any case the brooch should be dated *c* AD 50-70. SF 327. Pit 836. Early Roman.
5. A Dolphin brooch with a spring and ornamented with a beaded moulding running down the spine of the bow and at the ends of side wings. The brooch is somewhat corroded. Compare Hattatt 1989, 70 no. 1509, fig. 33 (find spot not known) and Webster 1995, 70-1 no. 23 (Usk). Claudio Neronian. SF 72. Finds reference context 20. Unphased.
6. A second Dolphin brooch. Bow of D-shaped section (convex on underside), rather less humped than usual though the head approximates to the usual dolphin form; there is a beaded moulding running down the spine as on SF 72 (No. 5 above). Length 45 mm. Probably hinged. The brooch is badly corroded, the pin is missing as is the catch plate. Compare Hattatt 1985, 76 no. 360 (unknown provenance) with similar moulding; Brailsford 1962, 7 and fig.6. C12 (Hod Hill); also (for the shape) Hattatt 1987, 94 no. 889 (Dorset/Wiltshire border). Neronian-early Flavian. SF 160. Ditch 442, part of enclosure 440. Early Roman.
7. Fig. 15.2, No. 4. A hinged Hod Hill brooch. This specimen, which has lost its pin, is of a rare variant form of class A. The brooch has a cross-rib below the head and another at the junction with the foot. Between these the bow has a pronounced spine and is decorated with four Vs composed of closely spaced punched dots. The foot is plain and terminates in a pronounced kick. Length 37 mm. For the form in general see Brailsford 1962, 9 and fig. 8 nos C53-C56 (Hod Hill). Compare Hattatt 1989, 60 no.1498, fig. 30 (Bergh Apton, Norfolk) with similar decoration. Note also plain examples: Mackreth 1982, 92 and fig. 25 no. 13 (Cirencester) and Lloyd-Morgan 1997, 78-9 no. 2 fig. 4.1 (Asthall, Oxfordshire). Claudio-Neronian. SF 128. Layer 152. Early Roman.
8. Fig. 15.2, No. 5. A brooch of Atrebatic (formerly 'Nauheim derivative') type; spring and part of bow remaining. The bow has ornamentation of punched dots down sides. Surviving length 22 mm. Compare Brailsford 1962, 7 and fig. 7 nos C22-C25 (Hod Hill); for local examples note Mackreth 1993, 30-1 nos 14-16, fig. 24 where no. 14 has similar decoration (Wilcote, Oxfordshire), as does Lloyd-Morgan 1997, 78-9 no. 1, fig. 4.1 (Asthall, Oxfordshire). Mid 1st century AD. SF 673. Unstratified.
9. Brooch of Langton Down type. The foot of the brooch with its catch plate remains. The form is discussed in Wheeler and Wheeler 1932, 71-4 with fig. 10, citing on p. 73 no. 31 an example from the site of the Natural History Museum, Oxford (in Ashmolean). Cf. also Brailsford 1962, 8 and fig. 7 nos C29-C31 (Hod Hill). *c* AD 43-75. SF 675. Unstratified.

Stud

10. Stud with a domed head, originally flanged though only a small portion of this remains. Diameter 15 mm. SF 161. Ditch 443, part of enclosure 440. Early Roman.

Pin

11. Pin, with a moulding towards the head ornamented with diagonal grooves. The head itself seems to be lost as is the lower part of the shaft with the point. Surviving length 48 mm. It probably dates to the 3rd or 4th century. SF 237. Ditch 762, part of ditch group 30. Late Roman.

Bracelets

12. Segment of penannular bracelet of circular section, expanding towards terminal which is embellished with a pair of notches. About one third remains. Diameter 45 mm. Compare Lloyd-Morgan 1997, 78-9 no. 8 (Asthall, from a 3rd century context) which is flatter and has a pair of notches. SF 77. Context 19. Unstratified.
13. Segment of penannular bracelet, flat on the underside but slightly convex above though flattened at the terminal which is ornamented with ten notches. Bent, *c* 45 mm in length. Compare Brodribb *et al.* 1971, 110, fig. 48 no.75 (Shakenoak Farm, near Wilcote). Third/fourth century. SF 256. Context 19. Unstratified.

Buckle (Fig. 15.2, No. 6)

14. Segment of the loop of a buckle, plano-convex in section and embellished on the upper edge with ring-and-dot within a zig-zag. On the underside is a notch, probably a casting flaw which may have

been responsible for the break at this point. Length of fragment 37 mm. The loop probably comes from a buckle of Hawkes and Dunning type IIIA with animal terminals like the well known (but otherwise plain) example from the male warrior grave found in 1874 at Dyke Hills, Dorchester, Oxfordshire (Hawkes and Dunning 1961, 58-60, especially no. 2, fig. 1.1) and another larger and more highly decorated example (unpublished) from a closely adjacent location recovered in 2010. These buckles seem to have come into fashion on the continent by *c* 370 (Böhme 1986) and an example from grave 376 at Lankhills Winchester (Clarke 1979, 277 no. 498), was probably buried before the end of the 4th century. The decoration of the Yarnton fragment, related to chip carving, can be noted on other buckles of the type like one from Icklingham, Suffolk (Hawkes and Dunning 1961, no. 6, fig. 20d) and even more closely on the buckle of the related type IVA from Richborough (ibid., 62, no. 1 and fig. 21).

Notching and ring and dot are entirely characteristic of the increasing use of geometric ornament in Late Antiquity, especially around the North West part of the Empire. In Britain, where it was associated with the Quoit brooch Style (see Henig 1995, 170-3), this type of decoration seems to have remained common, at least in the Upper Thames region, well into the post-Roman period, hinting at stylistic continuity in the metalwork (Blair 1994, 12-13; Henig and Booth 2000, 195-8). Although the object was probably manufactured in the late 4th or early 5th century AD, the worn state of the fragment suggests a later final deposition. SF 10. Topsoil, unstratified.

Other objects

15. Narrow strip with a D-shaped section. Probably part of a flattened segment of flimsy finger-ring. Length 14 mm. SF 184. Tree-hole 535. Unstratified.
16. Strip of metal, square section with chisel-like end. Length 38 mm. Probably scrap. SF 212. Ditch 655, part of enclosure 184. Late Roman.
17. Strip of metal, now corroded and broken into two pieces. Length 44 mm. Probably scrap. SF 99. Ditch 185, part of enclosure 184. Late Roman.
18. Fig. 15.2.A. Thin rectangular section strip with slight edge ridges and tapered ends; possible unwound spiral ring fragment; dull blue-green patina. Width 4 mm; total length 95 mm. SF 13392. YFPB Site 9, 13249 (see Northover below for analysis).
19. Fig. 15.2.B. A hollow ring made of two U-shaped strips riveted together. Two pin rivets are visible, others may be buried under encrustations. There is no sign of any filling in the ring. The ring is badly corroded and fragile with some metal loss. Parallels suggest that this is an Iron Age type, parallels for sheet copper alloy claddings for rings of other materials coming from Llyn Cerrig Bach, Ynys Môn deposit (Savory 1976; Lynch 1991) and Danebury (Cunliffe and Poole 1991b, 329, 332, no. 1.95). SF 13089. YFPB Site 9, 13321, from the palaeochannel silts adjacent to the stone causeway (see Northover below for analysis).
20. Fig. 15.2.C. Thick steel penannular ring, hot-dipped in bronze to close ring and plate it; surface now has a rusty patina. SF 13087. YFPB Site 9, 13221 (see Northover below for analysis).

COINS *by Paul Booth*

Introduction

Forty-three Roman coins which could be assigned to the late 3rd and 4th centuries were recovered during the excavation. All but five of the coins from the excavation were recovered from topsoil or unstratified contexts, most with the aid of a metal-detector (two small metal detected collections of a total of 19 coins of less certain provenance are also discussed below). The condition of the coins is variable; many are worn and/or encrusted. Fourteen coins were subject to mechanical cleaning at the Ancient Monuments Laboratory in order to facilitate identification, but in some cases the coins in question were still not legible after treatment. The generally poor condition of the material precluded detailed identification (eg of mint marks) in some cases, and also made it difficult to distinguish imitation from regular issues. It is likely that imitations are better represented in the assemblage than is suggested by the listings below. All the coins are of copper-alloy and the 4th-century pieces are all either AE3 or AE4.

Yarnton coins

The coins are listed in approximate chronological order in Table 15.4. Coins are identified by small find numbers, supplemented by context numbers (in brackets) where stratified. References are quoted only where fairly precise identification is possible. Probable irregular issues are indicated with an asterisk.

Unprovenanced collections

Two small collections of poorly provenanced material were presented by local metal detector users to the excavators in the course of fieldwork. Both groups of material probably derived from the Yarnton site and/or its immediate vicinity.

Collection 1 'Yarnton' (ten coins)

This group consists entirely of 4th-century coins. The condition is variable and as with Collection 2 no specific identifications are possible (ie there are no fully legible mintmarks, though one of the Sarmatia Devicta coins was certainly a Trier piece). The following types are identified:

SARMATIA DEVICTA	2	AD 323-4
GLORIA EXERCITUS (2 standards)	3	AD 330-5
GLORIA EXERCITUS (1 standard)	1	AD 335-41

Table 15.4 Coins recovered from the excavations.

PERIOD/TYPE	*No.*	*Small Find*	*Context*	*Comment/ Reference*
Period c AD 270-296				
Uncertain radiate copies, Gallic Emperors	4	93*;202*; 247*; 250*	u/s	
Period AD 330-335				
Mint of Trier				
CONSTANTINOPOLIS	1	14	u/s	?LRBCI, 52
Mint of Arles				
GLORIA EXERCITVS (2 standards), Constantine I	1	274	Ditch 877A	RIC VII, 341
VRBS ROMA	2	155, 78		as LRBCI, 355; 382
Uncertain mints				
VRBS ROMA	3	51*;69*; 677		
Period AD 335-341				
Mint of Rome				
CONSTANTINOPOLIS	1	74		cf LRBCI, 595
Uncertain mints				
GLORIA EXERCITVS (1 standard)	3	79; 565; 674	3287/B/2 (SF 565)	
Period AD 341-348				
Uncertain mint				
?VICTORIAE DD AVGG Q NN, Constans	1	337		
Period AD 351-353				
Mint of Trier				
VICTORIAE DD NN AVG ET CAE, Magnentius	2	16, 75		?LRBCII, 56 (x2)
Period AD 350-360				
Mint of Lyons				
FEL TEMP REPARATIO (fallen horseman), Constantius II	1	154		LRBCII 253 or 256
Mint of Constantinople?				
FEL TEMP REPARATIO (fallen horseman)	1	83		mint mark uncertain
Irregular issues				
FEL TEMP REPARATIO (fallen horseman)	4	15*; 57*; 248*; 345*	119 - Building 1356 (SF 345)	all except 248 much reduced
Period AD 364-378				
Mint of Lyons				
GLORIA ROMANORVM, Valentinian	2	6; 676		mint mark incomplete; cf LRBCII, 321
GLORIA ROMANORVM uncertain Emperor		1	87	mint mark incomplete
SECVRITAS REIPVBLICAE, Valens	1	84		LRBCII, 340
Mint of Arles				
GLORIA ROMANORVM, Valentinian	2	260; 678		?as LRBCII, 479 (x2)
GLORIA ROMANORVM, Valens	2	68; 339		mint mark incomplete
SECVRITAS REIPVBLICAE, Valentinian	1	959		mint mark incomplete
SECVRITAS REIPVBLICAE, Valens	1	9		mint mark incomplete
GLORIA NOVI SAECVLI, Gratian	2	81; 249		?LRBCII, 523a; mint mark incomplete
Uncertain mints				
SECVRITAS REIPVBLICAE, Valens	1	85		
?Period AD 378-388				
Uncertain mint				
?Maximus	1	11		uncertain
Period AD 388-402				
Uncertain mint				
SALVS REIPVBLICAE, victory, captive and chi-rho	1	170	471 - unphased layer	
General 4th century				
4th century not closely identifiable AE3	1	82		
4th century not closely identifiable AE4	3	61; 70; 386	1401/A (SF 386)	

FEL TEMP REPARATIO (fallen horseman)	2	AD 353-60
SALUS REIPUBLICAE (victory and captive)	1	AD 388-402
Uncertain (??victory facing left)	1	4th century

Collection 2 'Worton' (nine coins and coin fragments)

This group contains one worn and unidentifiable coin (head facing left) which from its general character may be of 3rd-century date. The remainder, including fragmentary and damaged pieces, are certainly or probably of 4th-century date. None is sufficiently well-preserved to permit precise identification (no mint marks were fully discernible, though the Securitas Reipublicae issue was from Arles), but the following types are identified (in some cases very tentatively):

URBS ROMA (wolf and twins)	2	AD 330-5
??GLORIA EXERCITUS (2 standards)	1	AD 330-5
?VICTORIAE DD AUGG Q NN	1	AD 341-48
?GLORIA ROMANORUM (emperor and captive)	1	AD 364-78
?SECURITAS REIPUBLICAE	1	AD 364-78
VICTORIA AUGGG	1	AD 388-402
Uncertain (figure advancing left)	1	?4th century

General discussion

The chronological breakdown of all the coins from the site in terms of the issue periods defined by Reece (1972) is summarised in Table 15.5.

The collection contains no numismatic surprises and requires little comment. It is characteristic of low status rural settlement assemblages in having no early Roman coins whatsoever, despite intensive settlement at that time, and in showing a very heavy emphasis on coin loss (and therefore presumably usage) in the 4th century. The earliest 4th-century pieces, two Sarmatia Devicta issues in the 'Yarnton' collection, may represent the last phase of coin production at London, but the mint marks are not legible. Thereafter coins cover the whole of the 4th century and the range of mints represented, where identifiable, is standard. A single coin (probably) of Magnus Maximus (AD 383-8) is a relative rarity, as this period is often unrepresented in small site assemblages. The material from the final period of introduction of coins to Britain supports the view that occupation at Yarnton continued to the very end of the Roman period. The two smaller collections are useful here in producing coins of this period to supplement the single piece from the main excavation.

Table 15.5 Numbers of Roman coins by Reece periods.

Reece Period	*Date range*	*Assemblage* YWRF	'Yarnton'	'Worton'	*TOTAL*
1-13	-275	-	-	-	-
14	275-296	4	-	-	4
15	296-317	-	-	-	-
16	317-330	-	2	-	2
17	330-348	12	4	4	20
18	348-364	8	2	-	10
19	364-378	13	-	2	15
20	378-388	1	-	-	1
21	388-402	1	1	1	3
3rd century uncertain		-	-	1	1
4th century uncertain		4	1	1	6
TOTAL		43	10	9	62

IRON OBJECTS *by Leigh Allen*

Introduction

The iron assemblage, like the copper alloy one, is small but includes a number of notable items. A complete adze head recovered from the base of an early Iron Age pit appears to have been deliberately placed there. Tools including punches, an awl and a file recovered from Roman contexts indicate craft activities taking place on the site. A number of the objects have undergone metallurgical analysis adding valuable information about their manufacture (see B Gilmour and P Northover below). The majority of the identifiable objects are early or late Roman in date.

Adze head *by Alistair Barclay and Vanessa Fell*

1. Fig. 15.3, No.7; Fig. 15.4. A complete iron adze head was recovered from the base of pit 7787 (context 8067) and is considered to be a placed deposit. Its relative position within the pit stratified with part of an early Iron Age jar and other contemporary sherds provides a securely dated context. Similar adze heads are less well dated; some come from middle or late Iron Age sites, although few are from secure contexts (Table 15.6).

The object has a blade, a blade shaft, an oval shaft hole and a hammer head. There is no surviving evidence for the haft. The chisel-like blade is square in section, concave in length and tapers to a flared, convex cutting edge approximately 51 mm in width. The cutting edge is slightly distorted and asymmetrical with part of one corner missing. Here the blade edge appears to be blunt, while at the opposite corner edge the blade is bevelled to a point. The shaft hole is oval in plan (36 mm x 26 mm) and has a slightly conical profile. The hammer head protrudes approximately 7 mm and has a convex surface.

The adze head was metallographically examined to investigate the method of manufacture. Samples

Table 15.6 Comparanda of adzeheads

Site	*Reference*	*Context*	*Date*	*Metallurgy*
Bigbury, Kent	Jessup1932, pl. iA	ironwork hoard	1C BC	
Blewburton Hill, Berks	Collins 1953, fig. 17, 1		MIA	
Bury Hill, Hampshire	Cunliffe and Poole 2000, fig. 2.30, no. 2.7		cp7	
Danebury, Hampshire (x3)	Sellwood 1984b, fig. 7.12, no. 2.49; Cunliffe and Poole 1991b, fig. 7.14, nos 2.248 & 2.249		cp7	Salter 1984, Mf Table 122, D164
Glastonbury lake village, Somerset	Bulleid and Gray 1917, 386-7, pl. lx, I.50, I.51			
Ham Hill, Somerset	Walter 1923, 149	cremation pit-burial	LIA	
Hod Hill, Dorset	Brailsford 1962			
Hunsbury, Northants (x5)	Fell 1936, 66; Northampton City Museum D319/1956-7, D.320/1956-7, D.321/ 1956-7, D322/1956-7, D323/1956-7	gravel quarrying		Ehrenreich 1985, HYN4b, HYN53b, HYN54a,HYN54b, HYN55a
Meare Village East, Somerset	Coles 1987, fig. 3.52, I.57			
Waltham Abbey, Essex	Manning 1985, 17, pl. 8, B11	hoard of tools	1C AD	J Lang in Manning 1985, 17, B11

through the blade and near the eye revealed low-carbon steel with a small amount of non-metallic inclusion particles. Hardness in the blade was 126 HV. Near the eye there were several weld lines resulting from forging the iron during the later stages of manufacture, possibly in forming the eye. After forging, the adze head was left in the air-cooled and annealed, soft condition.

The metal structure of this adze head is similar in carbon composition and microstructure to other Iron Age adze heads which have been examined. These have small or variable amounts of carbon and all had been air-cooled, giving low to moderate hardness values. The significance of these results is that none appears to have been deliberately hardened, and like axe heads of the Iron Age, perhaps resilience and toughness were sought as qualities of the metal rather than hardness (Fell and Salter 1998). However, unlike several of the axe heads, there was no evidence of surface carburisation, although this may not have survived due to corrosion.

Other Tools

2. Fig. 15.3, No. 8. A hook-shaped cutting tool. Curved blade (the tip of which is missing) with a shallow lentoid cross-section which runs for a short way down towards the socket. The socket appears to have been twisted open with some force and there is a bent headless nail through it. Classified as Manning type 2 this type of blade is found on Iron Age and Roman sites and it is a tool of this type that is depicted in the foraging scene on Trajan's column (Manning 1985, 53). At Danebury it has been suggested that tools such as these with relatively short curved blades would have been more suited to pruning rather than reaping (Sellwood 1984b, 346-9). SF 360. Pit 1192. Early Roman.
3. Fig. 15.3, No. 9. A small awl with a pyramidal tang and a slender circular cross-section point. There is evidence of minerally-preserved wood on three faces of the tang. The point is perfectly preserved and may have been used for piercing holes in leather. A similar example from London is dated to the 1st-2nd centuries AD (Manning 1985, 40, plate 16, no. E9). SF 402. Pit 1622/A/1. Early Roman.
4. A whittle tang knife, incomplete. A centrally placed tang and a blade that would originally have been triangular. Both the blade edge and the back are practically straight, tapering towards the tip. Unfortunately in this case the end of the blade has snapped off and the blade edge is worn. The knife conforms to Manning type 16 (Manning 1985, 116) and is probably a long-lived form. The blade was metallographically examined and appears to be made from a re-used piece of an earlier knife blade and a recycled composite piece that has been hammer-welded to it. The steel cutting edge has then been added, after which the complete piece would have been forged to produce the later knife. It is quite likely that this later knife broke along a flaw left in the blade during the welding together of re-cycled bits of earlier objects (see B Gilmour below). Pit 7960. Roman.
5. Fig. 15.3, No. 10. A second whittle tang knife. Fragment from a larger knife, and as with the previous example the knife has snapped at right-angles across the blade. The tang has traces of organic material adhering to it indicating that it would originally have had a horn handle. The blade back and the edge run parallel, the tang is set slightly below the back of the blade. There are two shallow grooves that run parallel with and just below the back with what appears to be a corresponding, slightly wider, single groove on the other side. It is not a common type but it appears to have had a long life (Manning (1985, 116) type 17). Metallographic analysis (see B Gilmour below) revealed that the knife was made from good quality metal but that imperfect heat treatment had resulted in a blade that was very brittle and therefore easily broken. SF 52. Corn-drying oven, context 47. Late Roman.

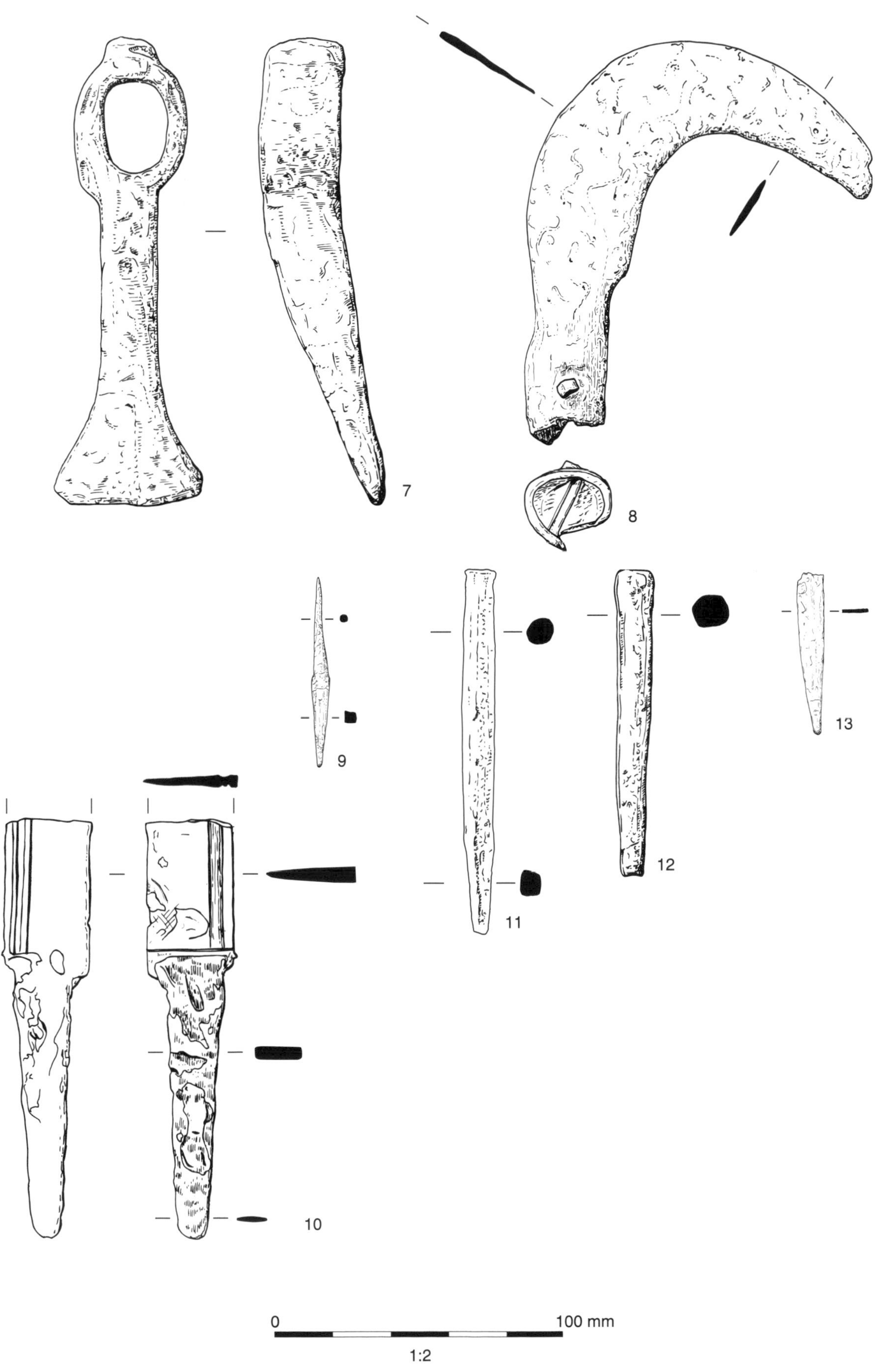

Fig. 15.3 Objects of iron, Nos 7-13

Fig. 15.4 Iron adze 8067 from pit 7787

6. Fig. 15.3, No. 11. Punch. Largely complete punch, with the tip missing, most probably broken off during use. For most of its length the shank of this tool is parallel-sided (roughly square in section, but with chamfered corners) before tapering down towards the broken end. The wider end is slightly splayed out from being struck with a hammer during use. Metallographic analysis (see B Gilmour below) indicated that the whole surviving length of the punch is made of just one piece of metal, and that it probably had a steel tip welded on. SF 178. Pit 516A/1. Late Roman.
7. Fig. 15.3, No. 12. Punch of similar construction to No. 6 above. It has a square section, chamfered at the corners and tapers towards the tip which is now missing. Again the wide end is slightly splayed out from being struck with a hammer during use. The way it has corroded suggests that the tip broke off during use and the tool was put to one side or discarded without being re-tipped. The reason for the failure of this punch is now difficult to judge, but perhaps is most likely to have been the result of defective welding. SF 192. Posthole 609A/1. Late Roman.
8. Fig. 15.3, No. 13. File. A fragment from a single cut file comprising tapering tang and part of the blade. Slender rectangular section blade with teeth visible on one narrow edge. The teeth are shallow cut with a spacing of *c* 10 per 10 mm. This type of file with fine shallow teeth could have been used for finishing slots or small perforations in sheet metal. Examples of this type of file are known from the late 4th century BC through to the Roman period. SF 230. Context 775, part of structure 1768. Late Roman.

Structural ironwork

Much of the remaining ironwork comprises structural items including a double spiked loop, rings and nails. The spiked loop was recovered from ditch 355 (enclosure 391C) dating to the early Roman period. Two large rings with circular sections were recovered, SF 228 from middle Iron Age pit 729 and SF 328 unstratified. A third ring was recovered from the palaeochannel silts adjacent to the causeway. This is a copper or copper alloy-plated iron ring probably dating to the later part of the pre-Roman Iron Age (SF 13087). Such rings are extremely common and could have had many functions. Even their size is little guide to their probable use, for rings of widely varying dimensions may have had the same function. Obvious uses are as harness or trace fittings, the rings from horse bits or as fastening or tethering rings, but other possibilities abound. All the major collections contain such rings and they appear in almost all large published groups of ironwork (Manning 1985, 140). A number of structural nails were recovered from across the site, a full list is provided in the archive. Complete nails include examples of Manning type 1A nails (ibid., 134) with pyramidal heads and square sectioned shanks; Manning type 3 (ibid., 135) with a T-shaped head and stout arms and Manning type 4 (ibid.) nails with an L-shaped head and a square sectioned shank the same width as the head.

Hobnails and cleats

A small number of hobnails and a single cleat were recovered from Roman contexts. The hobnails were found individually or in pairs and are probably only stray finds. The cleat (SF 35, unstratified) is incomplete with only one of the tangs remaining. The latter is rather long in relation to the size of the plate and the object could possibly be a small staple for fastening wood rather than from a shoe.

Ferrules

Two ferrules (SF 469 and SF 175) were recovered from late Roman ditch 1624 (enclosure 826) and kidney-shaped feature 494. These conical sockets, formed from a sheet of iron rolled to form an open ended cone, were used to protect the end of a staff or spear (Manning 1985, 140-1).

JET AND SHALE *by Philippa Bradley*

Three fragments of shale and one jet object were recovered from early to middle Iron Age contexts. The shale consists of a vessel fragment, a bracelet fragment, and another possible bracelet or ring fragment. The jet item is an almost complete penannular earring. The shale is generally in good condition but some lamination was noted. The Kimmeridge area of Dorset is the most likely source for the shale, where an extensive shale-working industry was in operation during the Iron Age and Roman periods (Calkin 1953; Sunter and Woodward 1987). It is likely that the objects came to the site in a finished form as there is no evidence for the manufacture or finishing of shale objects on the site

Iron Age shale working is well documented (see for example Cunliffe 1984c; Laws 1991c). Shale objects are known from Iron Age contexts in the region, but are probably more common from Roman sites. Shale bracelet fragments have been found at Gravelly Guy, Stanton Harcourt in early and middle Iron Age contexts (Boyle and Wait 2004). A bracelet fragment came from the early Iron Age camp at Bozedown, Whitchurch (Wood 1954, 11, fig. 4) and a fragment came from an Iron Age ditch at the Ashville Trading Estate (Parrington 1978, 80-1, fig. 59, no. 21).

Catalogue

1. Fig. 15.5, No. 14. Object, shale. Fragment with one carefully worked end, curved interior face and slightly domed exterior face. Dark brown in colour and heavily laminating. Length 26 mm, breadth 12 mm, thickness 8 mm (maximum surviving dimensions). ?Bracelet, ring or other decorative fitting. The surviving end is curved suggesting a ring or bracelet of penannular form. Pit 8005, 7915. Early Iron Age.
2. Fig. 15.5, No. 15. Bracelet fragment, shale. Laminating but consolidated; black and glossy appearance. Irregular in plan, broken at both ends and through the back of the object. Tool marks indicate lathe turning. Slight grooving can be seen on its upper face and internally. The bracelet has a round or oval cross-section and there is one flattened area. Too irregular to measure the internal diameter. Length 53 mm, breadth 17 mm, thickness 11 mm (maximum surviving dimensions). Pit 8786 (8493). Middle Iron Age.
3. Fig. 15.5, No. 16. Vessel fragment, shale. Laminating but consolidated; black and glossy appearance. Rounded upright rim, broken at one end. Decorated with a cordon and beading below, the vessel is broken below the beading. Length 31 mm, breadth 21 mm, thickness 8 mm (maximum surviving dimensions). Pit 8786 (8493). Middle Iron Age.
4. Fig. 15.5, No. 17. Earring, jet. Almost complete, one slight break to left-hand side. Penannular in shape with slight internal bevel, oval cross-section. Right-hand side has been cut flat to form an end. Similar to a jet earring from Kirkburn, Yorkshire (Stead 1991, 92-3, fig. 69). The jet is likely to have come from the Whitby or York areas (Allason-Jones 1996). Length 13 mm, breadth 14 mm, thickness 4 mm maximum, 2 mm minimum. Pit 7988 (7986). Middle Iron Age.

WORKED BONE AND ANTLER *by Leigh Allen and Jonathan Wallis*

Introduction

A large number of bone and antler objects was recovered from the site, ranging from the utilitarian to the highly crafted. Alongside the points, gouges and large collection of grooved and polished metapodials there are decorated weaving combs, antler tine handles and a highly polished bridle cheek piece. Several pieces of antler manufacturing debris indicate that antler working was taking place on the site.

Objects of bone

Gouges

Six bone gouges were recovered from the site. In general gouges are tools fashioned from the long bones of sheep which have an oblique diagonal cut across the shaft in a longitudinal direction, exposing the medullary canal. The tip is nearly always sharply pointed but may be worn to a variety of shapes according to use. The butt of the tool is formed by the distal or proximal end of the bone that is sometimes left intact or may have been trimmed. Classification of the Yarnton gouges has followed that of Danebury where the tools were classified according to the form of their point and any wear patterns (Sellwood 1984c, 382-7), rather than by the form of the butt end which had been the traditional method up until that time.

1-4. Four of the gouges have been classified as of Sellwood (1984c) Class 1. They have long pointed terminals with raised flanges at either side. The extreme tip of the point is a thin, flat point. All four gouges are formed from a sheep or goat tibia. Despite being of the same class the four gouges exhibit different wear patterns. SF 350 from late Roman gully 764/A (enclosure 162), has a light polish over the shaft and point; the tip of the gouge was broken in antiquity and then continued to be used as the polish extends over the broken edge. The butt is formed from the proximal end of the tibia which has been sawn. The gouge from pit 7942 (7941), dating to the early Iron Age, also has a light polish over the shaft. The tip is broken (probably recently) and the butt which is formed from the distal end of the tibia has been sawn. The two

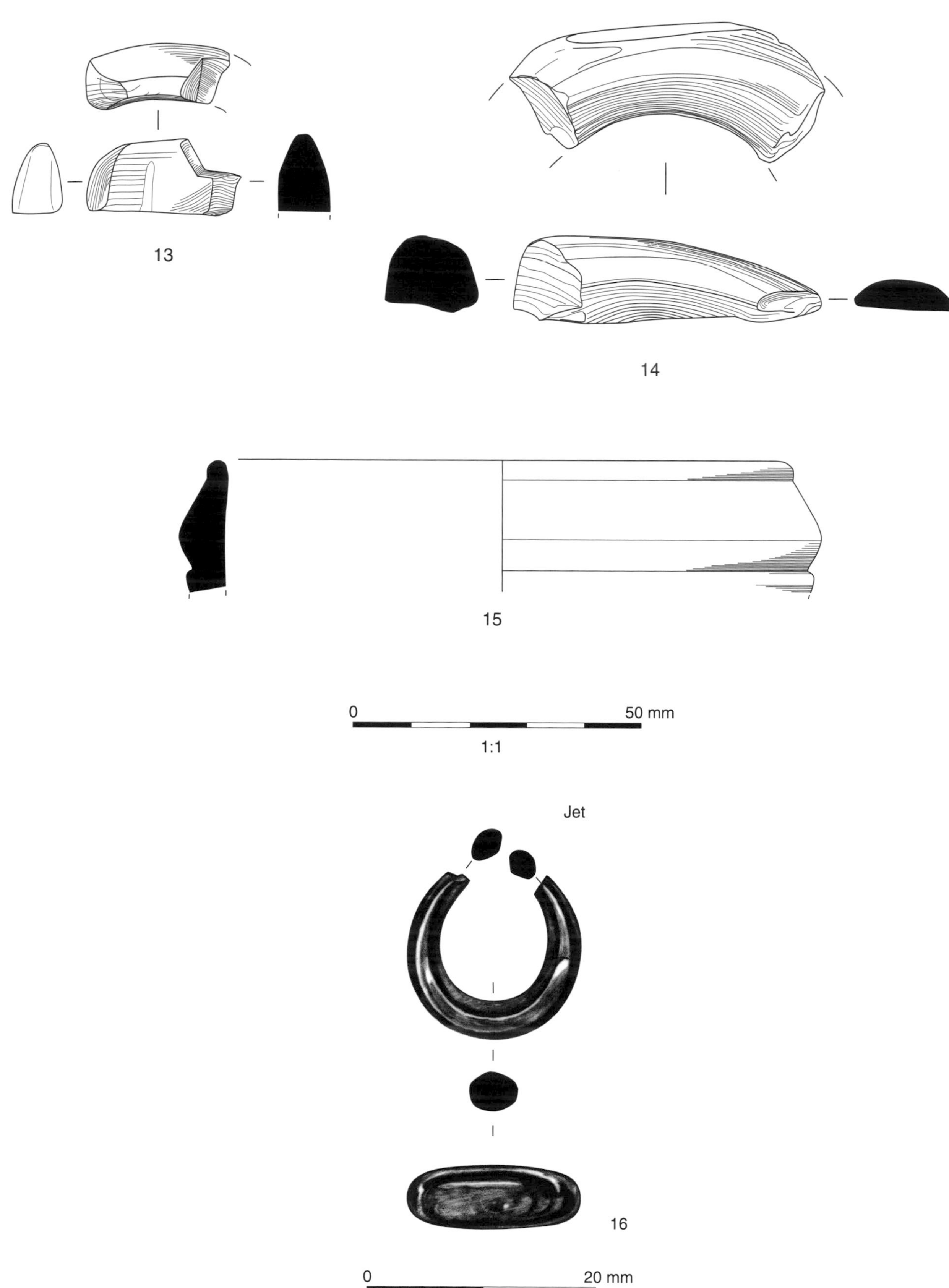

Fig. 15.5 Objects of shale and jet, Nos 14-17

remaining gouges, SF 349 from a late Iron Age/early Roman posthole (406/A) and the other from early Iron Age pit 8327 (8326) have a high polish all over the shaft and point. SF 349 has also been decorated, there are 18 fine incised grooves running nearly all the way round the upper part of the shaft (Fig. 15.6, No. 18). Decoration on this type of tool is rare.

5. There is a single example of a short squat gouge, Sellwood Class 3, with a sharp point from pit 7598, context 7597, dated to the early Iron Age.

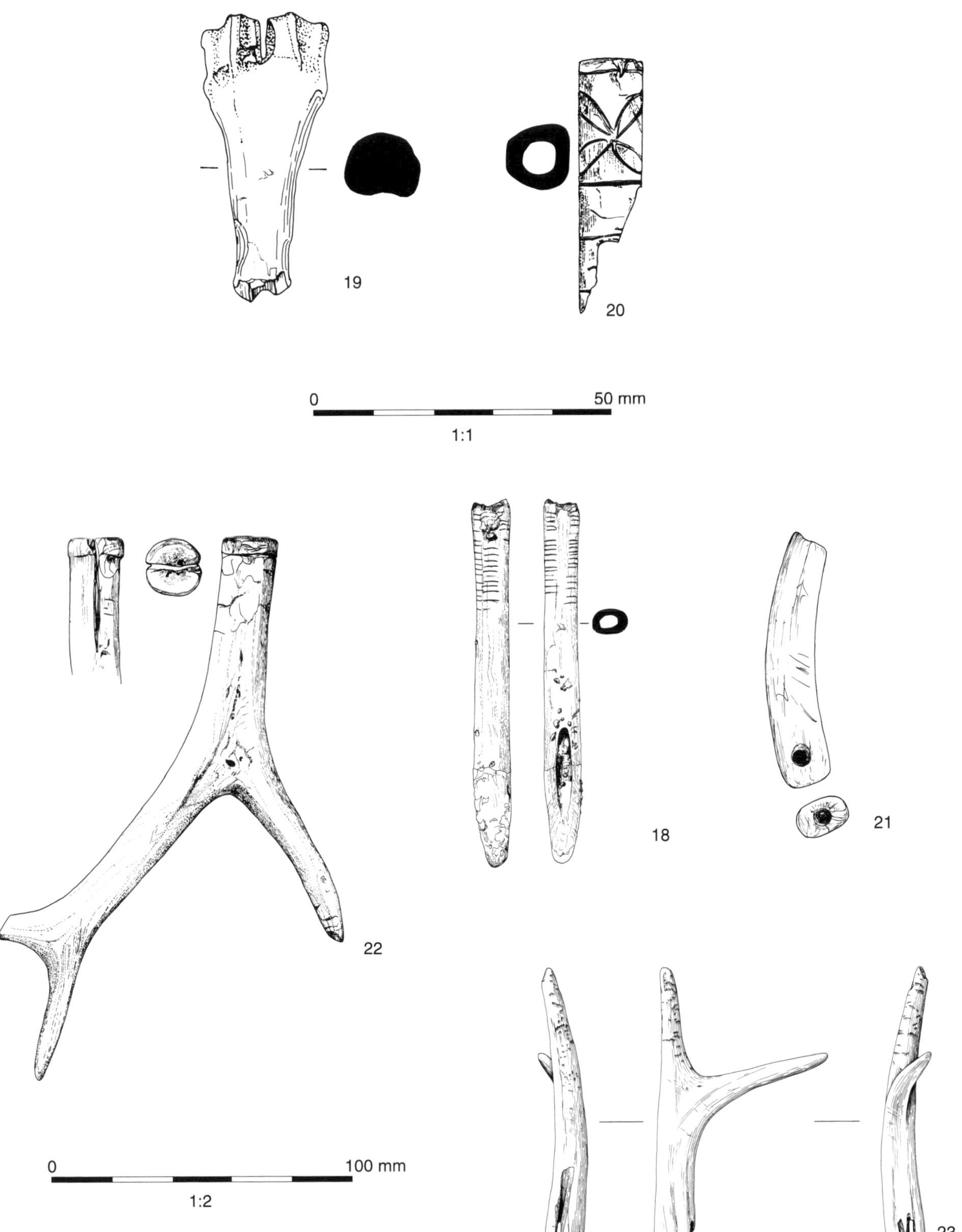

Fig. 15.6 Objects of worked bone and antler, Nos 18-23

The gouge has a high polish over the shaft and tip.

6. Gouge SF 446, from early Iron Age pit 2649/A/1, is only a fragment. The lower part of the shank is missing and the tool cannot be classified. It has, however, been burnt and highly polished and there is a perforation through the butt end, the latter being the distal end of the tibia. Below the perforation there are very fine horizontal striations, these could be have been formed during the manufacture or the use of the tool.

There has been much discussion regarding the use of tools such as these, one of the most detailed being in the All Canning's Cross report (Cunnington 1923, 86) where various interpretations were suggested, including pins, skewers, weaving equipment and tools for dressing reindeer hide. The variation in the wear patterns and the shape of the points suggest that they could have had a number of different uses.

Points

Three further gouge-like points were recovered from the site, they are dealt with separately as they do not fall into any of the classes identified by Sellwood (1984c) at Danebury.

7. A large gouge-like object was recovered from early Iron Age pit 7173 (7171), made from the distal end of a bovine long bone. In common with the gouges described above this long bone has an oblique diagonal cut across the shaft in a longitudinal direction and a rounded tip. The object displays a general sheen over the whole of the shaft and a high degree of polish on the obliquely-cut edge, especially at the tip and on the top where the thumb rests when the object is held in the hand. A fairly robust object, it could have been used with a certain degree of force, perhaps in the preparation of hides.
8. A second point, SF 297 from context 923/C/1, a late Iron Age/early Roman enclosure ditch, is fashioned from a sheep or goat tibia. Right at the tip there is an oblique diagonal cut across the shaft, forming a very short gouge end to the tool. The whole of the shaft and the tip are highly polished and there are very fine diagonal striations along one side that could be have been formed during manufacture or use. The object could well be another type of gouge, although not paralleled amongst the groups identified by Sellwood at Danebury.
9. Point SF 367, from context 1189, a middle Iron Age pit, is fashioned from a red deer antler tine. This highly-polished and obviously well-used object curves naturally along its length and has the beginnings of a perforation just below the bulbous end. The tip of the object is missing.

Awl

10. A possible awl, SF 363, was recovered from late Roman gully 1180. It has been manufactured from a splinter of shaft bone, probably from a sheep. The pointed end of the tool is sharp (although in this case the very tip is missing), but widens quite quickly. There is a fairly high polish over the whole of the upper surface of the fragment. Similar awls (or splinters with worked points) have been found at Danebury (Sellwood 1984c, 387-9, class 3). Awls such as these would have been used to pierce or bore holes in material such as leather.

Tools manufactured from sheep long bones (Fig. 15.7)

Sixteen grooved and polished sheep metatarsals were recovered from the site, from contexts dating from the early Iron Age through to the late Roman period. A further example was recovered from the Floodplain.

Six metatarsals have distinctive grooves in two places along the shaft dividing it into three roughly equal zones. The grooves appear on either side of the shaft and in two of the three examples there are additional transverse striations either side of the groove that are probably also a result of wear (Fig. 15.7, top). All of the shafts are very highly polished. Similar bone tools with two zones of wear have been recovered from Meare Lake Village East (Coles 1987, 145, fig. 3.61) and also from a number of sites in Oxfordshire, at Whitehouse Road, Oxford (Underwood Keevill 1993), Old Shifford Farm, Standlake (Allen 1995, 146), Ashville Trading Estate (Parrington 1978, fig. 61), Watkins Farm (Allen 1990a, fig. 28.7) and Farmoor (Lambrick and Robinson 1979, fig. 29.3). The grooved and polished metapodials may have been used in textile production, possibly as spindles or bobbins (cf Sellwood 1984c, 387).

Catalogue

11. Context 7003, early Iron Age plough soil.
12. SF 457 from middle Iron Age pit 268/A/1.
13. SF 454 from early Roman ditch 282/A/1, enclosure 206.
14. Fig. 15.6, No. 19. SF 13327. Grooved and polished metapodial. Chop marks visible at one end. Two side grooves are highly polished and there are other areas of polishing along the shaft of the bone. L 48 mm, B 21 mm (maximum), Th 12 mm (maximum). Species: sheep/goat metatarsal right side. Context 13221 (Finds reference layer over middle Iron Age causeway). YFPB 46860.91/10830.57.
15. SF 462 from late Roman ditch 304/A, enclosure 1350.
16. SF 456 from an unstratified context.

There are a further five examples where there are very shallow opposing grooves towards the distal end of the shaft but no trace of any grooves at all at the proximal end. These metatarsals have less of a polish than the previous group. Tools characterised by a single zone of wear have been recovered from Danebury (Sellwood 1984c, 392).

Catalogue

17. SF 481 from early Iron Age pit 371.
18. SF 464 from middle Iron Age pit 584/A.
19. SF 347 from late Iron Age gully 622/C/1, enclosure 175.
20. SF 460A and 460B, two examples from late Iron Age/early Roman pit 300.
21. SF 455 from early Roman ditch 987/A/1, enclosure 391B.

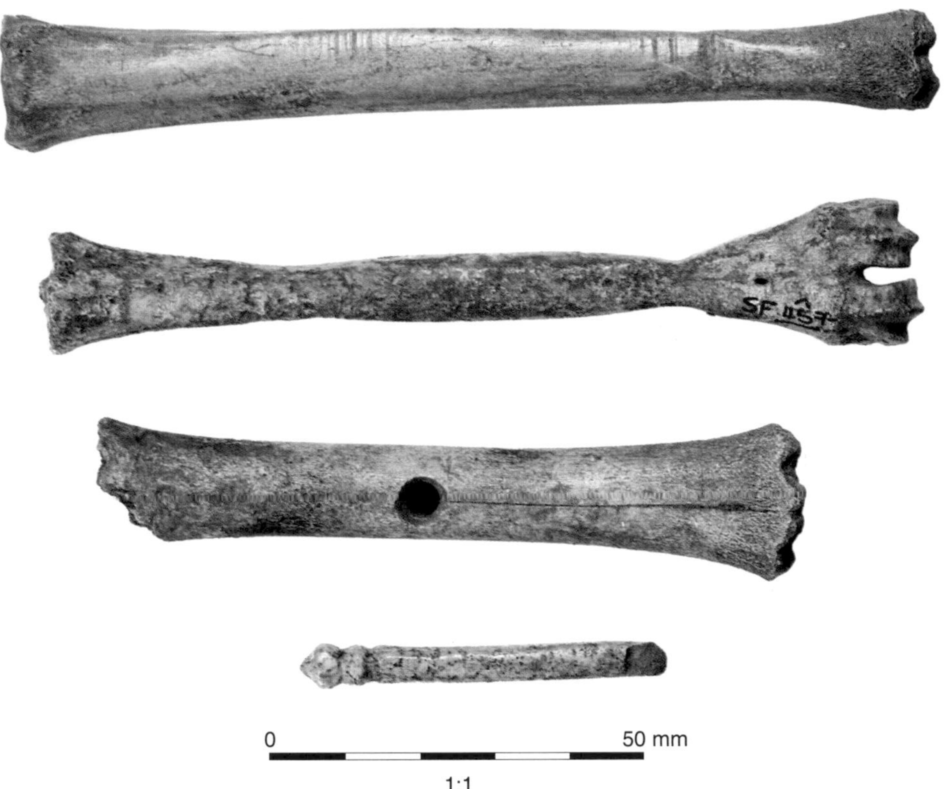

Fig. 15.7 Iron Age bone objects from the Yarnton site: tools made from sheep long bones, from top to bottom SF 457, SF 462, SF 356 and SF 480

The remaining five metatarsals do not show any trace of grooves at either end but they do have a light polish over the whole of the shaft.

Catalogue

22. SF 395 a fragment from early Iron Age pit 1512.
23. Context 8493, the fill of middle Iron Age pit 8786.
24. SF 452 from late Iron Age/early Roman ditch 594/C.
25. SF 381 from early Roman ditch 1326, enclosure 187.
26. SF 451 an unstratified fragment.

The use of these tools is still a matter of conjecture, but a function related to textile production is the most likely. The wear marks on the sides of the shafts are suggestive of repeated rubbing between threads, yarn, thongs or other similar material. This sort of tool is often referred to as a bobbin or spindle. Coles (1987) suggests uses in textile production, hide or leather production and fabrication, or for holding sacks or bags and helping in lathe work. Viner (1996) also suggests use as a fastener for personal dress, although it is unclear how this would work in practice.

27. Fig. 15.7, centre. Another tool, SF 356 fashioned from a sheep metacarpal has a transverse perforation bored through the centre of the shaft. It was recovered from context 662/A, a late Iron Age/early Roman pit. In common with similar tools recovered from Danebury the metacarpal has an unfused distal end. There is a slight sheen over the whole of the surface but this could be natural rather than a result of wear. This object could have functioned as a toggle but it has also been suggested that such pieces were used in the textile production process, possibly as bobbins, 'to hold spun yarn..,.. the thread could be fastened through the central hole' (Wild 1970, 34).

Toggle

28. Fig. 15.6, No. 20; 15.8 lower right. A decorated toggle was recovered from middle Iron Age ditch 7637 (7639). The toggle comprises a hollow tube with a rectangular transverse perforation through it. Unfortunately the object is incomplete, but presumably the perforation would have been through its centre. It is decorated with fine incised grooves running around the tube dividing the toggle into fields, the end one of which contains an incised four petalled flower. Toggles are not uncommon on Iron Age sites but this form with this decoration is thought to be without parallel. The form is similar to that of three bone and one antler toggle from Meare Lake Village East (Coles 1987, 12, B55, B64 and H81). The flower motif is found on early Iron Age pottery from Allen's Pit (Dorchester on Thames) and Blewburton (Lambrick 1984, 172).

Pins

29-30 Fragments from two pins were recovered. One, from late Iron Age gully 1562/B/1, is the lower half of the shaft tapering to a point, the head is missing. The shaft fragment is very slender and has a flattened oval section. The second fragment, SF 480 from Roman layer 473/A/1, is from the upper

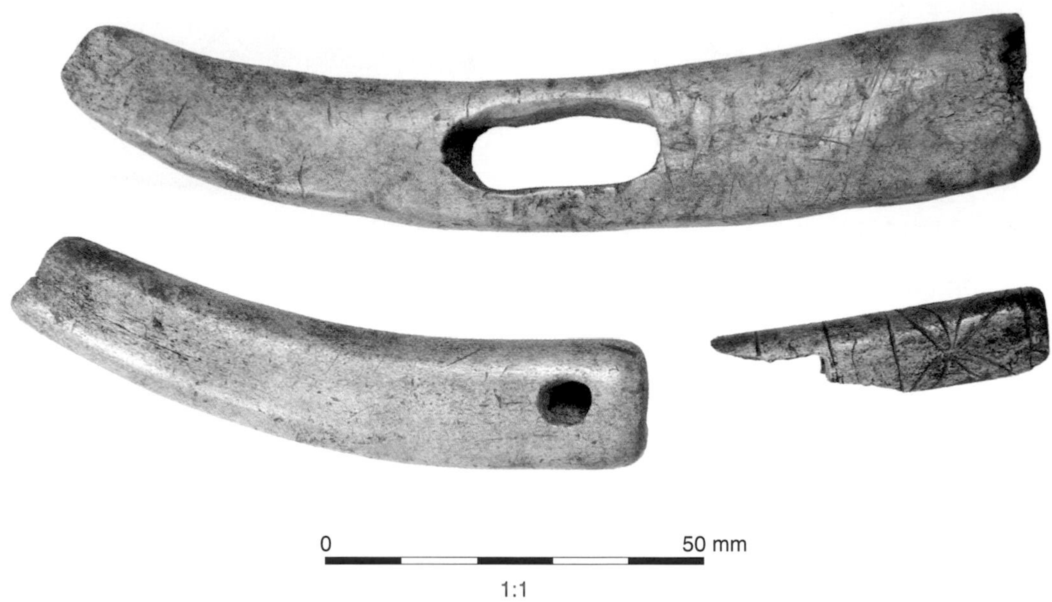

Fig. 15.8 Iron Age bone objects from Cresswell Field: cheek piece 8196 from pit 8195 (top), handle 7058 (bottom left) and decorated toggle 7639 from ditch 7637 (bottom right)

section of a pin (Fig. 15.7, bottom) with a conical head with two transverse grooves below. The head is hand carved and the whole fragment is highly polished. At Colchester similar pins have been classified as type 2 pins with a date range of *c* AD 50-200 (Crummy 1983, 21).

Handle

Antler objects were found in the same pit fill (see below).

Objects of antler

All of the antler from the site comes from red deer (*Cervus elaphus* L). The assemblage comprises handles, a cheek piece, combs, and various fragments of manufacturing debris.

Handles

31-3. Three antler handles were found. One (Fig. 15.6, No. 21, Fig. 15.8 bottom left) was highly polished with a transverse hole at the finished end and a further hole drilled into the same end of the piece. It came from fill 7058 of early Iron Age pit 7057, the same context as the better example of two handles manufactured from the crown of a red deer antler. This piece (Fig. 15.6, No. 22) has three tines still present, although the tip of one tine is missing. The lower end of the handle is worked to form a collar and transversely cut to take a blade. Similar handles from Meare Lake Village East are made either from single red deer tines or whole roe deer antlers (Coles 1987, 88); one example has an iron blade still *in situ* (ibid., 93, fig. 3.28, H137). The third handle (SF 189), from context 584/A/1, a middle Iron Age pit, is smaller and made from only the top two tines of the crown. It is also split to receive an implement. (Fig. 15.6, No. 23).

Cheek piece

34. Fig. 15.8, top; 15.10, No. 24). A complete cheek piece from a bridle from context 8196, the fill of early Iron Age pit 8195 at Cresswell Field. The check piece is highly polished with a large sub-rectangular perforation through the centre. Similar cheek pieces have been recovered from Meare Lake Village East (Coles 1987, 88). The use of these objects as bridle fittings is discussed by Britnell (1976) who catalogues seven similar examples of late Bronze Age date.

Manufacturing debris

35-9. Five unfinished antler objects were recovered, all but one from Creswell Field, indicating small scale antler working there. An object from fill 7058 of early Iron Age pit 7057, is possibly the beginnings of another antler handle with two tines (see also Nos 31 and 32 above from the same pit fill). A single polished tine from context 8326, a fill in early Iron Age pit 8327, is possibly another blank for a handle. The remaining three objects are sawn sections of red deer antler that show very little trace of any other working.

Catalogue

37. Context 7364, a fill of early Iron Age pit 7365.
38. Context 8326, a fill of early Iron Age pit 8327.
39. SF 132 from late Iron Age/early Roman pit 330/B/2.

Combs (Figs 15.9 and 15.10)

There were five combs from the site, four made from antler and the fifth from bone. Two of the combs are complete and four out of the five are

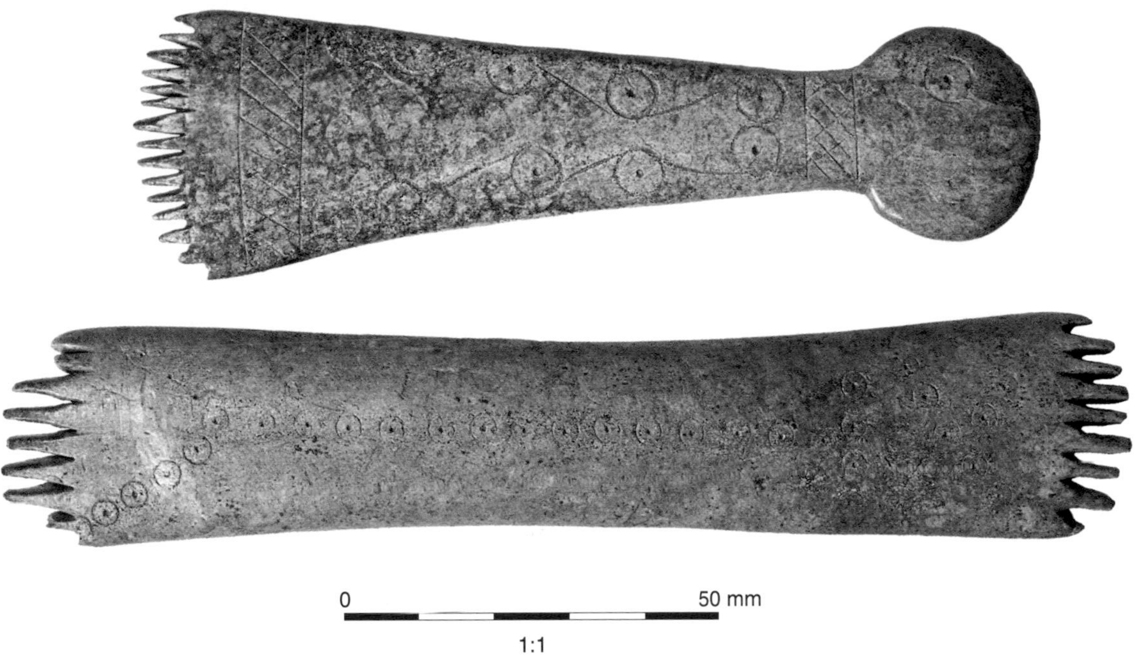

Fig. 15.9 Iron Age antler combs: SF 385 (top) and SF 605 (bottom)

decorated. Two of the three fragmentary combs are decorated and are almost certainly from single-ended combs as they both taper along the length of the shaft. Neither fragment has any surviving teeth nor any indication of the form of the butt end.

40. Fig. 15.9, lower; 15.10, No. 25. SF 605. A complete double-ended weaving comb from context 4006/A/1 (unphased). The comb is made from a section of red deer antler, with nine teeth at either end cut parallel with the long axis of the comb. The teeth are rectangular in section at the base where they join the shaft, tapering towards the apices; the inter-dentate notches are V-shaped. The teeth towards the centre of the comb are distinctly longer than those at the edges, but it is not clear whether this results from design or wear. The shaft of the comb is wider at the dentate ends and has a plano-convex section. The whole comb is highly polished and decorated with ring-and-dot motifs which have grown faint with wear. The ring-and-dot motifs form a line down the centre of the comb and then split to form a V-shape towards the dentate ends. One of the ring-and-dots is cut by the inter-dentate notch which may indicate that the comb teeth have been re-cut at some point. This type of comb conforms to Hodder and Hedges type Sh I, a common type in south-west England (Hodder and Hedges 1977, 20).
41. Fig. 15.9, upper; 15.10, No. 26. SF 385. A complete single-ended weaving comb with a circular butt, from context 1402/A/1, an Iron Age posthole. Manufactured from red deer antler it has 13 teeth cut parallel with the long axis of the comb. The teeth are rectangular in section at the base where they join the shaft, tapering towards the apices, the inter-dentate notches are V-shaped. All the teeth appear to be of a fairly consistent length with the exception of the ones on the very edge that are very worn. There is a fine incised transverse groove cutting across the base of the inter-dentate notches, the outer two teeth on the left hand side have been worn down to below this groove. This type of wear was evident on five examples at Danebury (Sellwood 1984c, 375). The comb is decorated with transverse bands of criss-cross lines just below the butt and just above the dentate end. In between these two bands there are ring and dot motifs joined by delicately curving lines. The circular butt is decorated with four ring-and-dot motifs. The form of the comb conforms to Hodder and Hedges type Sh F, a common type in central and southern England, while the decoration with its mixture of ring-and-dot and linear pattern is their decoration Jiii (Hodder and Hedges 1977, 23).
42. Fig. 15.10, No. 27, from context 7791, the fill of a middle Iron Age ditch. Shaft fragment decorated with pairs of incised straight lines running transversely across the comb, with pairs of crossed lines in between. An almost identical decoration appears on a comb at Danebury (Sellwood 1984c, fig. 7.27, no. 3.1) and is classified by Hodder and Hedges (1977, 21) as decoration B.
43. Fig. 15.10, No. 28 from context 1679/A/1, an early Iron Age posthole. Shaft fragment, highly polished and with a pattern of irregularly shaped loops running down each edge, these loops are in-filled with radiating lines and dots. This unusual form of decoration is not classified by Hodder and Hedges (1977).
44. SF 195 (Fig. 15.10, No. 29) from context 584/A, a middle Iron Age pit. This is the only comb fragment manufactured from bone, in this case the proximal half of a red deer femur. The fragment is from the dentate end of a comb which could be either single or double-ended. It is highly polished with only one

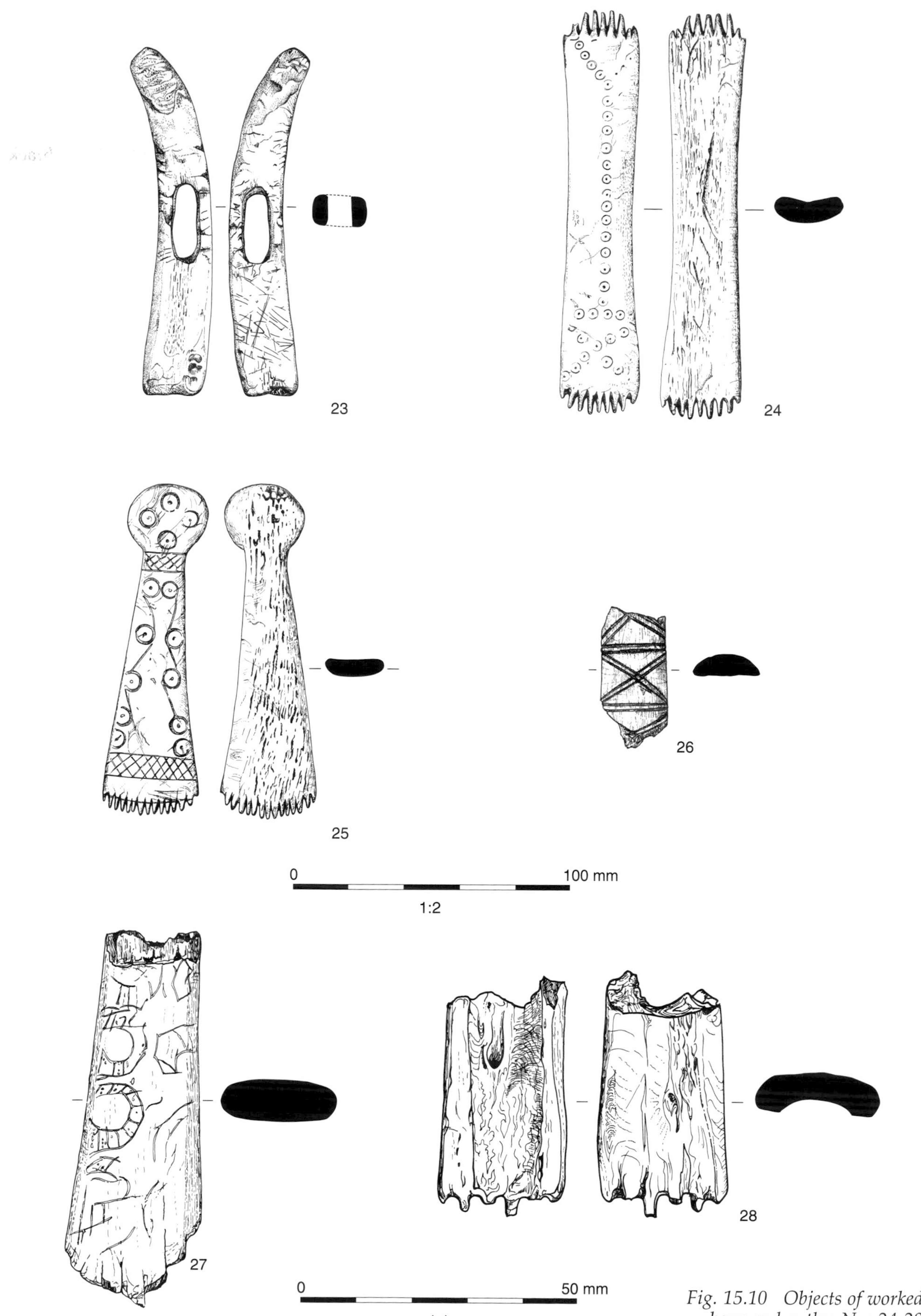

Fig. 15.10 Objects of worked bone and antler, Nos 24-29

complete tooth remaining; the other five teeth survive only as stumps. The inter-dentate notches appear to have originally been V-shaped. The one complete tooth has a transverse groove across it on the reverse side. Similar grooves have been noted on combs from Danebury (Sellwood 1984c, 377) and Meare Lake Village East (Coles 1987).

The possible function of these combs has been discussed by Hodder and Hedges (1977) who suggest that their use as weaving combs would only work with a two beamed vertical loom. Experiments using the combs for weaving demonstrated their impracticability for such a use, so their function is by no means completely understood. A typological analysis of the combs and the compilation of distribution maps of the defined types shows some to be extremely localised, suggesting local manufacture for these, whilst other types are more widespread. The classified Yarnton examples fall into the latter pattern, Hodder and Hedges decoration type B and type ShF being two of the more widespread types occurring across southern England, from Somerset to Kent for the former and from Somerset through to East Anglia (crossing Oxfordshire) for the latter.

WORKED STONE *by Fiona Roe*

Cresswell Field

Introduction

The worked stone from Cresswell Field comes from 17 contexts, and ranges from the middle/late Bronze Age until the middle Iron Age, with just one find of lava fragments of Roman (or possibly later) date. The later prehistoric pieces, summarised in Table 15.7, amount to eight fragments from saddle querns or their rubbers, and three whetstones, one a dual-purpose implement also used as a smoother. There is also a second probable smoother, an anvil stone and a hollowed fragment containing a black deposit.

Materials

The varieties of stone used at Cresswell Field during later prehistoric times are nearly all materials obtainable locally or from up to about 24 km (15 miles) distant. However two finds are of interest since they had been acquired from outside the Oxford region. A saddle quern (context 8372) was made from May Hill sandstone, a Silurian Grit from the Gloucestershire/Herefordshire border some 76 km (47 miles) away (Lawson 1955). A whetstone of Pennant Sandstone had travelled a little further, with a probable source in the Forest of Dean (Welch and Trotter 1961, 86).

Just two varieties of stone were brought to the site over medium distances of up to about 24 km (15 miles). Culham Greensand was recorded in middle Iron Age contexts, and was brought from around Culham, some 17 km (10.5 miles) from Yarnton by a direct route, although it could be reached more easily by a longer, winding journey along the river Thames. Three pieces of Sarsen, from late Bronze Age to middle Iron Age contexts, may have come from the chalk downs between Wantage and Wallingford. As with the Culham Greensand,

Table 15.7 Summary of later prehistoric worked stone from Cresswell Field.

Context	*Phase*	*Description*	*Stone*
Stone imported over long distances			
8372	EIA	Saddle quern	May Hill sandstone
8493	MIA	Whetstone	Pennant Sandstone
Stone imported over medium distances			
7352	MIA	Fragment, probably quern	Culham Greensand
8659	MIA	Saddle quern	Culham Greensand
7080	EIA	Quern fragment	Sarsen
7875	LBA	Fragment, quern or rubber?	Sarsen?
8493	MIA	Whetstone	Sarsen
Local stone			
8174	LB/EIA	Quern fragment	Lower Calcareous Grit
7172	EIA	Polisher fragment	Quartzite, from gravels
7784	MIA	Polisher, small fragment	Quartzite, from gravels
8126	LB/EIA	Anvil	Quartzite, from gravels
7107	LBA	Rubber fragment	Quartzitic sandstone, from gravels
8469	MIA	Fragment	Quartzitic sandstone, from gravels
8661	MIA	Rubber for quern	Quartzitic sandstone, from gravels
8032	M/LBA	Smoother/whetstone	Sandstone, from gravels?
8405	MIA	Hollowed fragment	Calcareous sandstone, from gravels?

Sarsen could conveniently have been brought to Yarnton by boat up the Thames. It is also possible, however, that some Sarsen could have been available more locally, since scattered boulders are known to have occurred in Oxfordshire Pleistocene deposits (Arkell 1947). Both these sources of Sarsen may have been utilised.

Materials that were chosen from entirely local sources are of two kinds. Lower Calcareous Grit came possibly from Wytham Hill, only 3.6 km (2.2 miles) from the site, or else from between Cumnor and Marcham a little further away (Arkell 1947, 88). Either source area could conveniently have been reached along the Thames. At Cresswell Field this material came from a late Bronze Age/early Iron Age pit 8127 (8174). The local gravels were mainly a source for hard pebbles, and quartzite was again used for polishers, from Iron Age pits 7173 (7172) and 7783 (7784), and an anvil stone, again from late Bronze Age/early Iron Age pit 8127 (8126). Quartzitic sandstone and further miscellaneous materials from the gravels were used for another five pieces ranging from late Bronze Age to middle Iron Age in date. Small fragments of Niedermendig lava from ditch 7920 (7921) represent Romano-British activity.

Disturbance at Cresswell Field appears to have been considerably less than at Yarnton, and there are no unstratified finds. Nearly all the late Bronze Age-Iron Age worked stone came from pits, while one rubber (8661) was from a depression 8662. The two fragments of May Hill sandstone (8372) were from a posthole 8371, where they no doubt had been reused as post packing.

The burnt stone from Cresswell Field amounted to 12.303 kg, nearly all of it from Iron Age contexts. There were numerous small broken pieces of quartzite pebbles, with a total weight of 5.413 kg. Some relatively large pieces of burnt limestone had survived, giving a total weight of 5.618 kg, while further miscellaneous burnt flint and sandstone amounted to 947 g. The same range of materials was recovered from three late Bronze Age contexts.

Yarnton (Worton Rectory Farm)

Introduction

There are 32 pieces of worked stone from Worton Rectory Farm, about one third of which were unstratified. However, analogies with other sites have enabled both unstratified and redeposited pieces to be placed with some confidence within either an early-middle Iron Age date bracket (Table 15.8) or a late Iron Age-Roman one (Table 15.9). Pieces from nine saddle querns and an anvil stone are considered to be of Iron Age date. The finds listed as late Iron Age-Roman in date consist of about 11 rotary querns, two probable millstones and a whetstone. Two quartzite polishers could be either of Iron Age or Roman date, while three pieces of Jurassic limestone could be Roman building material. Only one item (SF 4), an unstratified whetstone of post-medieval type, is likely to be later.

Materials

Table 15.8 demonstrates that only three of the saddle querns of probable Iron Age date came from middle Iron Age contexts. Two materials were used for the dated querns. Three saddle querns of Lower Greensand from around Culham include a complete middle Iron Age example (SF 229; Fig 15.13, No. 30). The more local Lower Calcareous Grit seems to have been preferred, with a possible total of five saddle querns. Just one saddle quern was made from Jurassic limestone, a shelly and oolitic variety (Bladon stone) from the Forest Marble. This was

Table 15.8 Summary of Iron Age worked stone from Yarnton.

Context	*Phase*	*SF*	*Description*	*Stone*
Stone imported over medium distances				
0	u/s	196	Saddle quern	Culham Greensand
584	MIA	194(a)	Fragment, fits	Culham Greensand
		199	Saddle quern	
746	MIA	229	Saddle quern	Culham Greensand
Local Stone				
19	u/s	50	Saddle quern	Forest Marble (Bladon)
384	LIA/ER	200	Saddle quern	Lower Calcareous Grit
521	ERB	382	Saddle quern	Lower Calcareous Grit
584	MIA	194(b)	Fragment, fits	Lower Calcareous Grit
		201	Saddle quern	
995	LIA/ER	298	Saddle quern	Lower Calcareous Grit
1082	ERB	319	Saddle quern	Lower Calcareous Grit
610	LRB	193	Anvil stone	Quartzite, from gravels

probably obtained from around Long Hanborough or Bladon, at a maximum distance of about 5 km (3 miles) from the site (Richardson *et al.* 1946, 62). The quern is one of the unstratified finds, but seems likely also to be middle Iron Age in date. The local gravels supplied quartzite pebbles, and a battered cobble seems likely to be Iron Age in date, while two pebbles utilised as polishers could be either Iron Age or Roman.

The attested middle Iron Age quern fragments came from two pits (584, 746), and the anvil stone was from a posthole. The other pieces were either from later ditches, or else unstratified.

The querns and millstones of late Iron Age-Roman date listed in Table 15.9 are very different in character, with five materials that were brought in from over 80 km (50 miles) away. The single quern from a late Iron Age context (SF 210; Fig. 15.13, No. 31) is a rotary quern made of the Lodsworth Greensand from Sussex, where known quarries are located some 100 km (62 miles) from Yarnton (Peacock 1987).

A further six pieces of rotary quern and millstone came from Roman contexts, together with another seven unstratified quern and millstone finds. The main corn-grinding material was Upper Old Red Sandstone, which was brought some 92 km (57 miles) from the Forest of Dean or south Wales (Welch and Trotter 1961, 49), and used for eight quern or millstone fragments (eg Fig 15.14, No. 32, context 472 SF 211 and context 670 SF 214). A millstone (pit 670) has been identified by its diameter of *c* 750 mm. A quern fragment that is probably of Drybrook sandstone from the Carboniferous Limestone would also have come from the Forest of Dean (ibid., 64). Other grinding materials had travelled considerably further. Millstone Grit from the Pennines was used for an unstratified quern or millstone (SF 226), while Niedermendig lava was found in an early Roman pit (2071), with further unstratified fragments. The querns or millstones of lava could have reached Yarnton by boat across the North Sea and then up the Thames, and the Millstone Grit may have arrived much the same way, via an east coast route. There is also a whetstone of Kentish Rag, which probably came from near Maidstone. However this, being small, was more easily transported long distance.

A few finds from the later contexts were made from local materials. Two quartzite polishers, one from a late Roman context, the other unstratified, could be either Iron Age or Roman in date. The local Jurassic limestone, in the form of Bladon stone, was possibly utilised for Roman paving stones and building blocks, although the evidence is slight. The context types for this later worked stone are varied, and eight pieces are unstratified. Three fragments that probably belong to the same millstone were found in pit 670.

There is a small quantity of burnt stone from Yarnton, and it is probably all of Iron Age date, though some must have been redeposited. Burnt quartzite pebbles amount to 1.274 kg, with additional small amounts of burnt limestone and other materials.

Table 15.9 Summary of late Iron Age to Roman worked stone from Yarnton.

Context	*Phase*	*SF*	*Description*	*Stone*
Stone imported over long distances				
633	LIA	210	Rotary quern	Lodsworth Greensand
-	u/s	224	Rotary quern	Old Red Sandstone
-	u/s	225	Rotary quern, same stone as SF 224?	Old Red Sandstone
-	u/s	278	Quern	Old Red Sandstone
472	u/s	211	Rotary quern	Old Red Sandstone
670	LRB	214	Millstone	Old Red Sandstone
"	"	215	Fragment of same stone?	" " " "
"	"	216	Fragment of same stone?	" " " "
1048	ERB	313	Rotary quern	Old Red Sandstone
2527	LRB	236	Quern	Drybrook sandstone?
-	u/s	226	Rotary quern or millstone	Millstone Grit
-	u/s	790	Fragments	Niedermendig lava
-	u/s	795	Rotary quern	Niedermendig lava
2071	ERB	606	Fragments	Niedermendig lava
354	LRB	163	Whetstone	Kentish Rag
Local stone				
-	u/s	3	Polisher	Quartzite, from gravels
2562	LRB	284	Polisher	Quartzite, from gravels
19	u/s	71	Block	Forest Marble (Bladon)
494	LRB	174	Slab	Forest Marble (Bladon)
2031	LRB	374	Slab	Forest Marble (Bladon)

Maps showing the regional distributions of objects in the stone types found at Yarnton are presented as Figures 15.11 (for later prehistoric periods) and 15.12 (late Iron Age and Roman periods).

Catalogue

Cresswell Field

Later Bronze Age

1. Fragment. Quartzitic sandstone. Small, burnt fragment with one flat, worn surface, possibly from rubber; 28 x 26 x 15 mm, 10 g. Late Bronze Age pit 7108 (7107).
2. Fragment. Sarsen? Small burnt fragment with one flat, worn surface, could be from a quern or rubber; 28 x 24 x 19 mm, 7 g. Late Bronze Age pit 7874 (7875).
3. Smoother/whetstone. Sandstone, fine-grained, brown, slightly micaceous. Part of thin, flat slab with one worn, slightly concave surface from possible use as smoother. A little wear on one edge from possible use as whetstone; 91 x 66.5 x 11 mm, 90 g. Middle/late Bronze Age pit 8031 (8032).

Late Bronze Age/early Iron Age

4. Anvil stone. Quartzite. Cobble with battered surface, slightly burnt; 205 x 154 x 89 mm, 2.9 kg. Early Iron Age pit 8127 (8126).

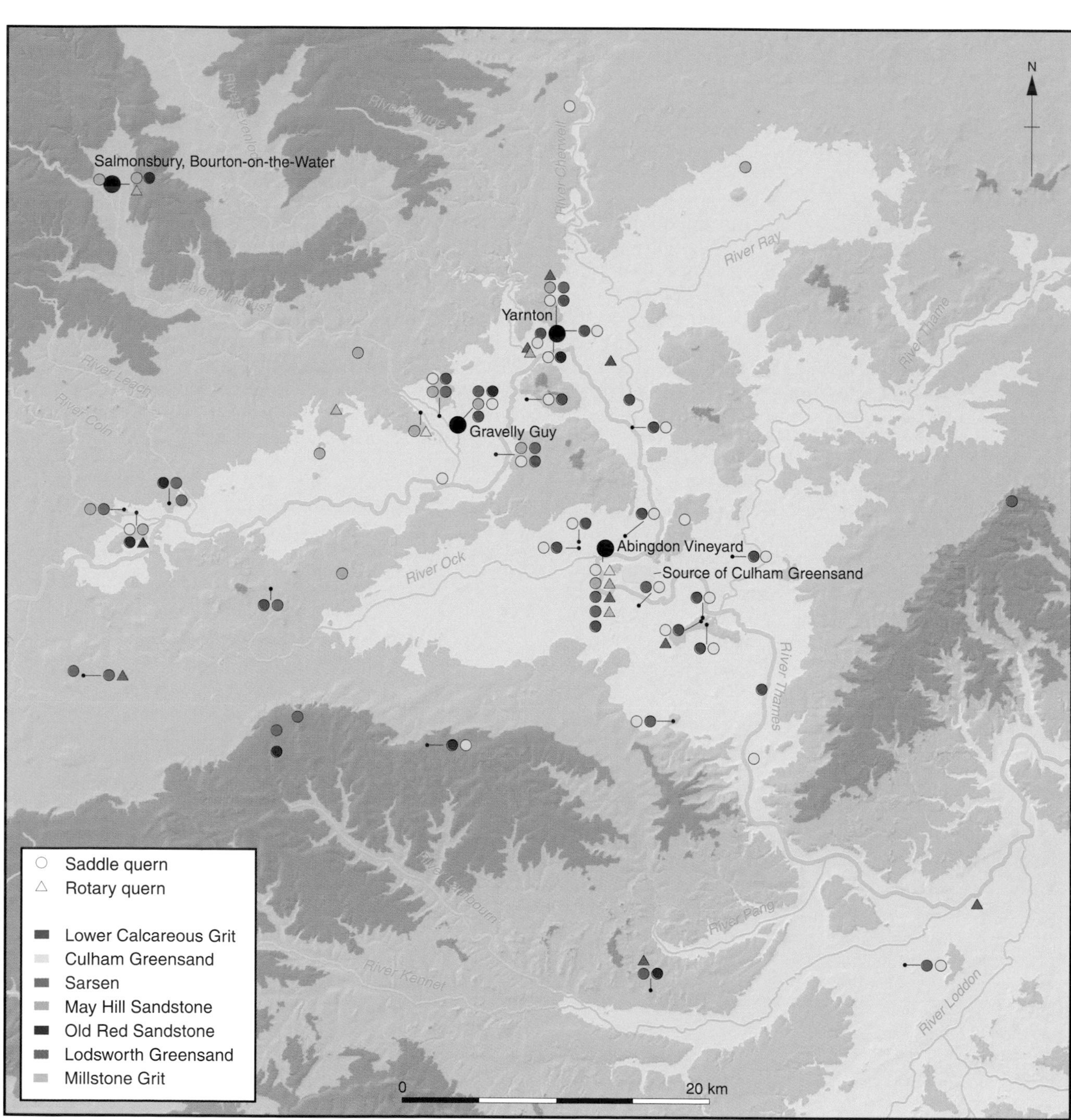

Fig. 15.11 Regional distribution of late Bronze Age and Iron Age quern stone materials by source

5. Fragment. Lower Calcareous Grit, shelly. Fragment, burnt, with a slightly convex worn surface, possibly a rubber for saddle quern; 84 x 63 x 39 mm, 160 g. Early Iron Age pit 8127 (8174).

Early Iron Age

6. Fragment. Sarsen. Burnt, with one flat, worn surface, could be from saddle quern or rubber; 62 x 49 x 44 mm, 100 g. Pit 7307 (7080).
7. Polisher. Quartzite. Part of semi-rectangular, fairly flat pebble with a glossy surface on one flat side; 64 x 49 x 31 mm, 120 g. Pit 7173 (7172).
8. Saddle quern. May Hill sandstone. Two matching fragments, burnt, one with slightly concave grinding surface; largest now 104 x 88 x 73 mm, together 1.290 kg. Posthole 8371 (8372).

Middle Iron Age

9. Whetstone. Fig. 15.15, No. 34. Pennant sandstone. Half slab type with several worn areas. Thin section R286; 62 x 48.5 x 14 mm. Pit 8786 (8493).
10. Fragment. Lower Greensand, Culham. Weathered and burnt fragment with one possibly worked surface, likely to be part of saddle quern; 97 x 89 x 97 mm, 1.340 kg. Pit 7353 (7352).
11. Fragment. Quartzite. Very small, burnt fragment with one flat, shiny surface, possibly from use as polisher; 25 x 14 x 11 mm, 5 g. Pit 7783 (7784).

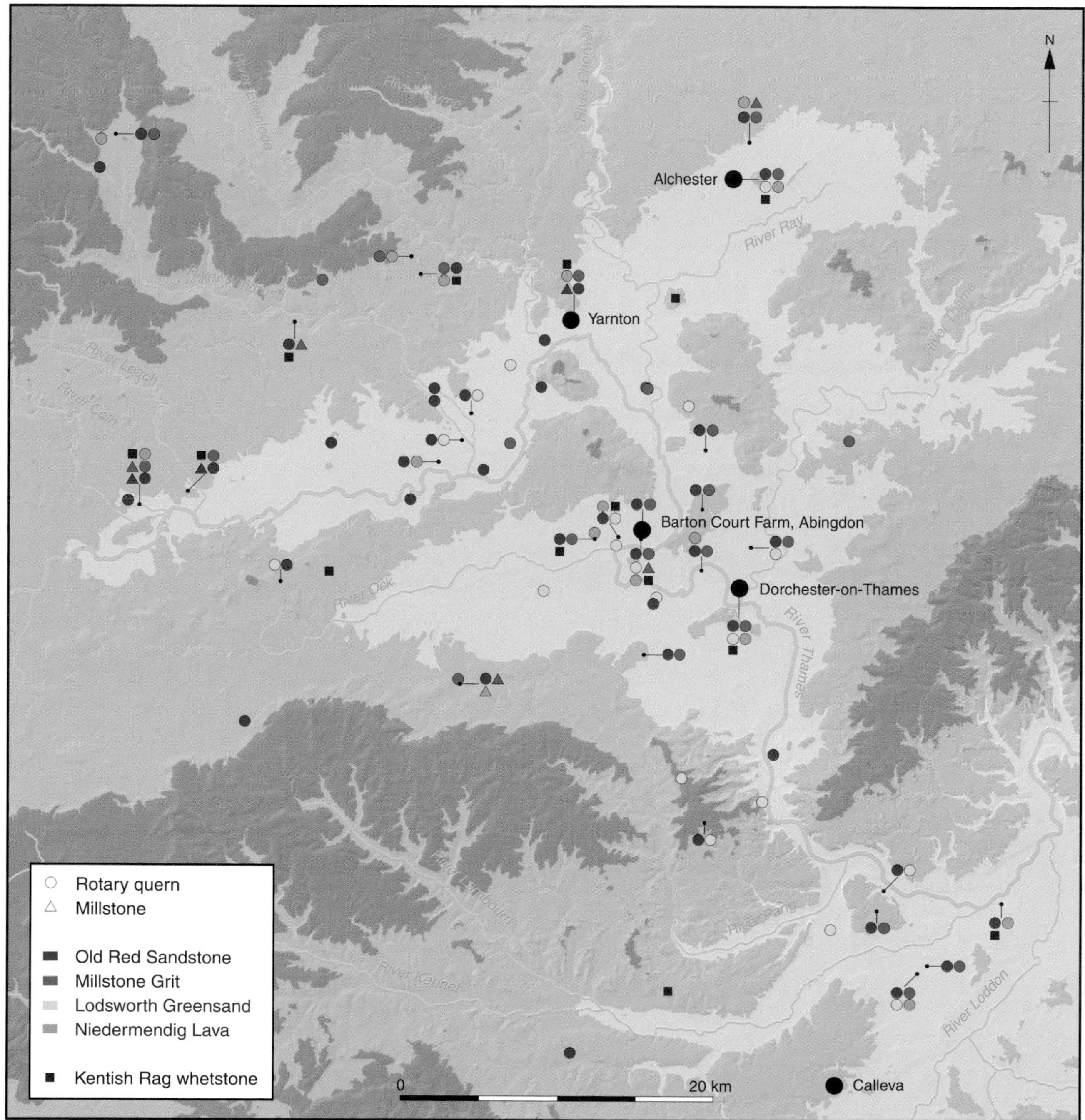

Fig. 15.12 Regional distribution of late Iron Age and Roman quern stone and whetstone materials by source

12. Fragment. Calcareous sandstone. Small burnt fragment with a hollowed surface and parts of a black deposit; 37 x 29 x 15 mm, 15 g. Pit 8454 (8405).
13. Fragment. Quartzitic sandstone, slightly micaceous. Fragment from slab, burnt, smooth flat surface, possibly utilised; 60 x 48 x 12 mm, 40 g. Pit 8468 (8469).
14. Whetstone. Sarsen, fairly fine-grained. Fragment, burnt, worn into three facets, probably from use as whetstone; 44 x 40 x 32 mm, 40 g. Pit 8786 (8493).
15. Saddle quern. Lower Greensand, Culham. Fragment with slightly concave grinding surface; 110 x 94 x 130 mm, 1.820 kg. Pit 8660 (8659).
16. Rubber. Quartzitic sandstone. Part of rubber for

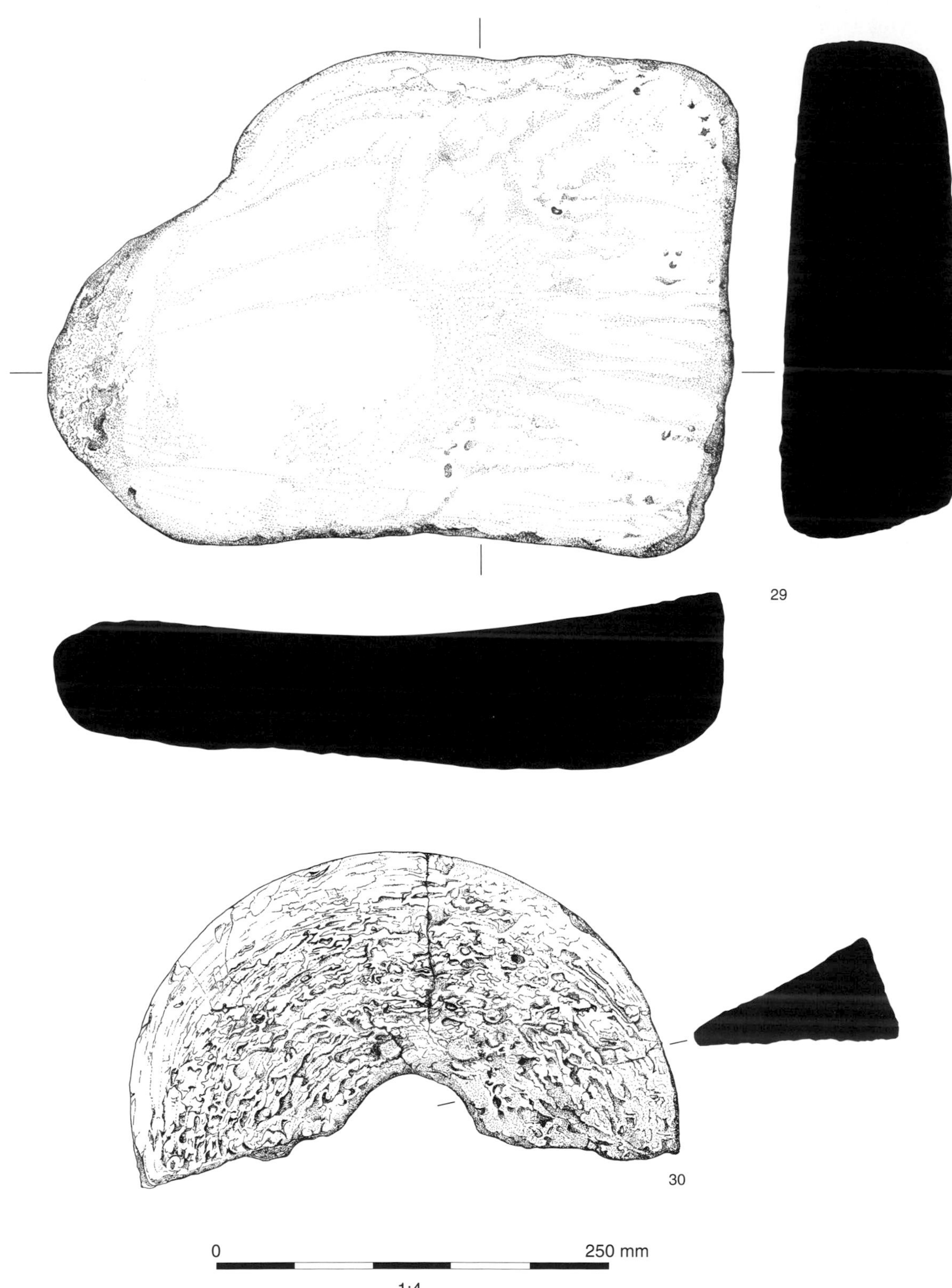

Fig. 15.13 Greensand and Lodsworth Greensand querns, Nos 30 and 31

saddle quern, made from cobble, convex grinding surface which has been dressed by pecking and then partly worn smooth; 167 x 132 x 47 mm, 1.160 g. Depression 8662 (8661).

Roman

17. Fragments. Niedermendig lava. About a dozen small fragments, likely to be from rotary quern or millstone; 60 g. Ditch 7920 (7921).

Yarnton (Worton Rectory Farm)

Middle Iron Age

18. Saddle quern. Fig. 15.13, No. 30. Lower Greensand, Culham. Nearly complete, probably made from a boulder, concave grinding surface, worn smooth in places; L 435 mm, B 308 mm, D 123 mm. SF 229, Pit 746.

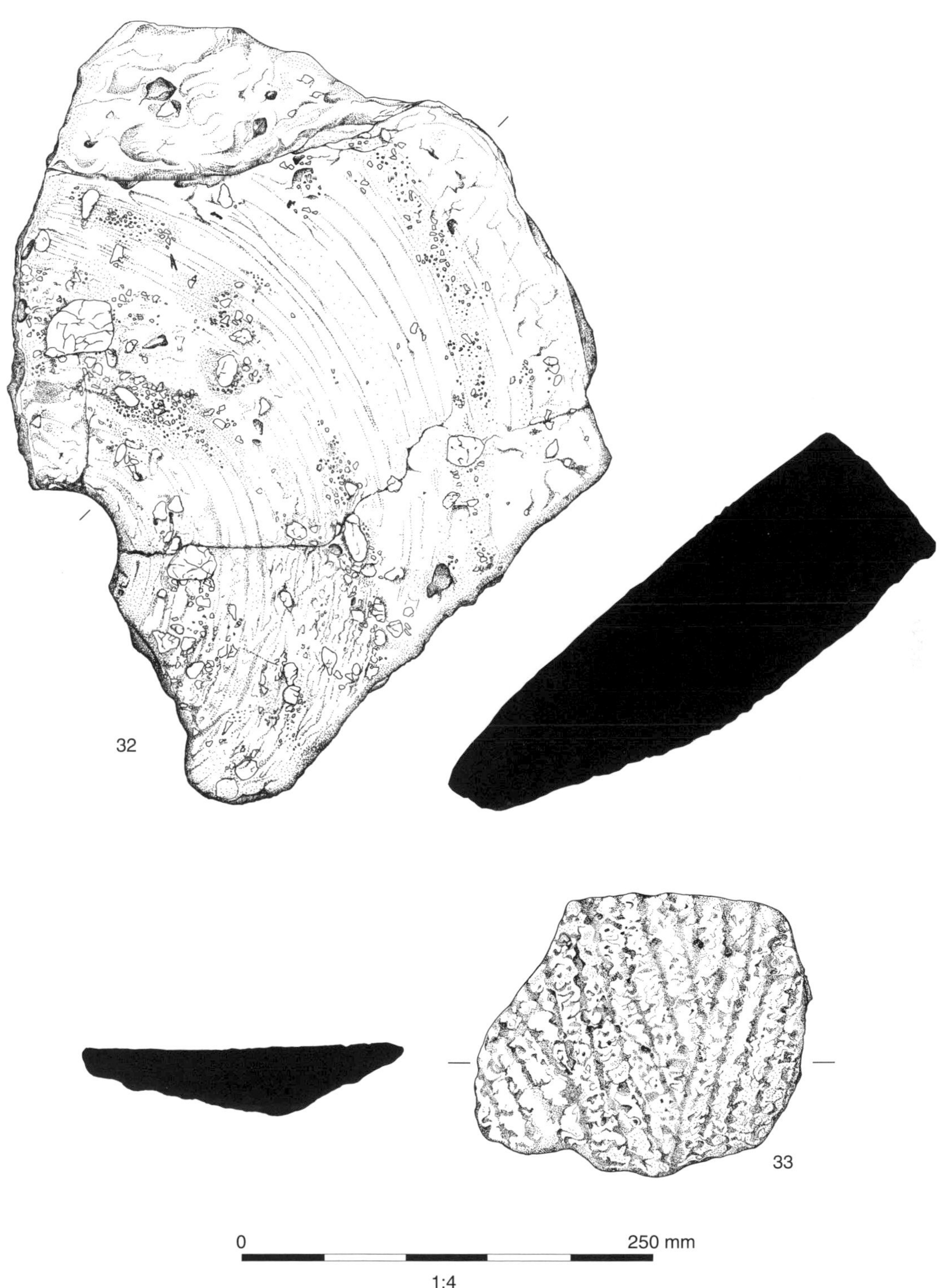

Fig. 15.14 Old Red Sandstone querns, Nos 32 and 33

19. Saddle quern. Lower Greensand, Culham. Fragment with part of grinding surface, fits SF 199; 76.5 x 53 x 42mm. SF 194(a). Pit 584.
20. Saddle quern. Lower Calcareous Grit. Burnt fragment with part of grinding surface, fits SF 201; 63.5 x 36.5 x 26 mm. SF 194(b). Pit 584.
21. Saddle quern. Lower Greensand, Culham. Fragment with part of grinding surface, fits SF 194(a); 92 x 58.5 x 49.5 mm. SF 199. Pit 584.
22. Saddle quern. Lower Calcareous Grit. Part of saddle quern, burnt, with concave grinding surface, fits SF 194(b); 170 x 115 x 69 mm. SF 201. Pit 584.

Late Iron Age/early Roman

23. Rotary quern. Fig. 15.13, No. 31. Lower Greensand, Lodsworth. Half upper stone, disc type, concave grinding surface worn smooth round outer edge; Dia *c* 350 mm, Th 78 mm. Late Iron Age. SF 210. Ditch 633, enclosure 205.
24. Saddle quern. Lower Calcareous Grit. Burnt fragment with concave grinding surface, likely to be a redeposited middle Iron Age quern; 167 x 150 x 63 mm. SF 200 Ditch 384, enclosure 175.
25. Saddle quern. Lower Calcareous Grit. Fragment, slightly burnt, flat grinding surface, likely to be a redeposited middle Iron Age quern; 182 x 120 x 73 mm. SF 298. Ditch 995, enclosure 391A.

Early Roman

26. Saddle quern. Lower Calcareous Grit. Burnt fragment with slightly convex grinding surface, possibly from rubber, likely to be a redeposited middle Iron Age quern; 166 x 107 x 76 mm. SF 382. Ditch 521, enclosure 187.
27. Rotary quern. Upper Old Red Sandstone, quartz conglomerate. Fragment of disc type quern with worn grinding surface and part of shaped rim; now 137 x 125 mm, Th 35 mm. SF 313. Gully 1048, enclosure 293.
28. Saddle quern. Lower Calcareous Grit. Part with concave grinding surface, likely to be a redeposited Middle Iron Age quern; 230 x 166 x 55 mm. SF 319. Pit 1082.
29. Fragments. Niedermendig lava. Five small fragments; 5 g. SF 606. Pit 2071.

Late Roman

30. Millstone. Fig. 15.14, No. 32. Upper Old Red Sandstone, quartz conglomerate. Fragment, grinding surface worn into rings; original dia *c* 750 mm, Th at hole *c* 120 mm. SF 214. Pit 670.
31. Whetstone. Fig. 15.15, No. 35. Kentish Rag. Complete, rod type; 91 x 26.5 x 15 mm. SF 163. Layer 354.
32. Slab. Jurassic limestone, shelly and oolitic (Forest Marble). Part of flat slab with two worn surfaces, possible paving stone or perhaps smoother; 153 x 67 x 39 mm. SF 174. Kidney-shaped feature 494.
33. Anvil Stone. Quartzite. Cobble with a heavily battered surface, might be Iron Age or Roman; 187 x 131 x 66 mm. SF 193. Posthole 610.
34. Fragment. Upper Old Red Sandstone, pebbly sandstone. Slightly burnt, part of grinding surface, may belong with millstone SF 214 (No. 30 above); 56 x 56 x 37 mm. SF 215. Pit 670.
35. Fragment. Upper Old Red Sandstone, pebbly sandstone. Part of rim and grinding surface, with secondary point sharpening groove, may belong with millstone SF 214 (No. 30 above); 152 x 103 x 64 mm. SF216. Pit 670.

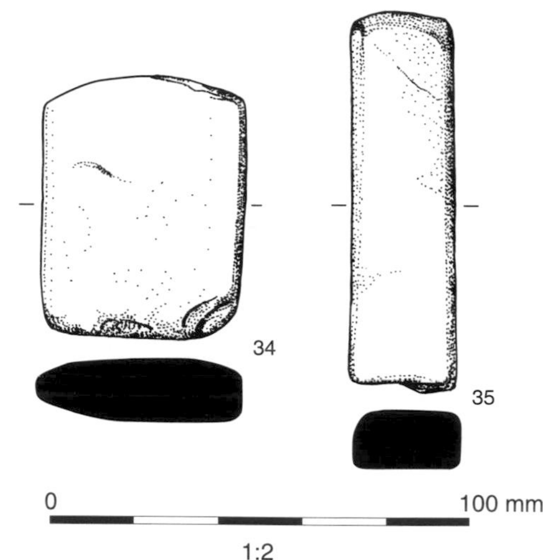

Fig. 15.15 Whetstones, Nos 34 and 35

36. Slab. Jurassic limestone, shelly and oolitic (Forest Marble). Part of flat slab with a worn surface, possible paving stone, or perhaps smoother; 118 x 107.5 x 31 mm. SF 374. Ditch 2031, enclosure 1013.
37. Fragment. Feldspathic sandstone with some mica, could be Drybrook sandstone. Part of grinding surface and rim from possible rotary quern; now 71 x 71 x 40.5 mm. SF 236. Pit 2527.
38. Polisher. Quartzite. Part of pebble with two flat sides, each worn to a glossy surface. Could be Iron Age or Roman; 75 x 67 x 17 mm. SF 284. Gully 2562, enclosure 2562.

Unstratified

39. Rotary quern. Fig. 15.14, No. 33. Upper Old Red Sandstone, sandstone. Part of Roman disc type quern with grooved grinding surface; 200 x 170 mm, Th 53 mm. SF 211. Layer 472.
40. Polisher. Quartzite. Fragment from large pebble, burnt, one side worn smooth; small area of battering also suggests slight use as hammerstone. Could be Iron Age or Roman; 102 x 65 x 56.5 mm. SF 3.
41. Whetstone. Fine-grained dark grey sandstone, slightly micaceous. Complete, post-medieval type, well worn; 265 x 36 x 24mm. SF 4.
42. Saddle quern. Lower Greensand, Culham. Fragment from thick quern with part of grinding surface, likely to be Iron Age. 175 x 125 x 130 mm. SF 196.
43. Quern or Millstone. Millstone Grit. 6+ fragments from rotary quern or millstone with pitted grinding surface, likely to be Roman; largest fragment 148 x 140 x 55 mm. SF 226.
44. Rotary quern. Upper Old Red Sandstone quartz conglomerate. Part of upper stone with trace of handle slot, may belong with SF225, likely to be Roman; Dia *c* 400 mm, Th at rim 52 mm. SF 224.
45. Rotary quern. Upper Old Red Sandstone quartz conglomerate. About half lower stone with small hole for spindle, may belong with SF 224, likely to be Roman; Dia *c* 360 mm, Th in centre 64.5 mm, at rim 28-52 mm. SF 225.

46. Quern. Upper Old Red Sandstone quartz conglomerate. Fragment, slightly burnt, part of grinding surface, probably from rotary quern and likely to be Roman; now 120.5 x 101 x 61 mm. SF 278 (surface).
47. Fragments. Niedermendig lava. Four small fragments, probably from quern or millstone, likely to be Roman; 110 g. SF 790 (surface).
48. Rotary quern. Niedermendig lava. Small fragment with part of grinding surface, likely to be Roman; 60.5 x 58.5 x 25 mm. SF 795 (surface).
49. Saddle quern. Jurassic limestone, shelly and oolitic (Forest Marble). Part of quern with concave grinding surface, likely to be Iron Age; 210 x 195 x 54 mm. SF 50, context 19 (ploughsoil).
50. Block. Jurassic limestone, shelly and oolitic (Forest Marble). Part of block, no working traces but possible Roman building stone; 191 x 122 x 51 mm. SF 71, context 19 (ploughsoil).

SALT CONTAINER OR BRIQUETAGE *by Elaine L Morris*

A total of 24 pieces (133 g) of unusual ceramic material was recovered from six different contexts from Worton Rectory Farm with a further ten sherds (284 g) from Cresswell Field. (Table 15.10). All of these pieces have been identified as sherds from Droitwich salt containers or briquetage vessels – ceramic pots used to dry and transport salt from the brine springs source to settlements in the lower Severn-Warwickshire Avon valleys, the Cotswolds and the Upper Thames area during the Iron Age (Morris 1985).

Fabrics and form

Both major Droitwich fabric types (Fabrics I and II) are represented in this small collection. Thirteen sherds were made from Fabric I, characterised by the presence of a sandy clay matrix which may be blocky in texture due to the marly clays utilised and the absence or near absence of organic matter, and the remaining eleven fragments from Fabric II, which must have more than a rare to sparse (>5%) amount of organic matter in the clay matrix. The evidence from Gravelly Guy (Morris 2004) has demonstrated that both fabrics can occur in early Iron Age contexts but that Fabric II increases in frequency during the later Iron Age period and Fabric I becomes less common. The fragments from Yarnton concur with this pattern since the pieces of Fabric I material were found in pits dated to the early-middle and the middle Iron Age phases (Table 15.10).

All of the pieces are body sherds which range from 9 mm to 27 mm in thickness, with the majority greater than 13 mm. The interiors of several sherds display the characteristic irregular relief of rounded folds and diagonal, collar construction breaks typical of this rough industrial material (Morris 1985, figs 3-4). The exterior surfaces have been vertically smoothed with a rapid technique to seal the collar joins.

Surface deposit

Two fragments displayed a patch of white deposit on the exterior surface, a characteristic of the

Table 15.10 Quantification of briquetage by context.

Context	*Context type*	*SF no.*	*Fabric*	*No. frags*	*Weight (g)*	*Thickness*	*Comment*	*Date of associated pottery*
Cresswell Field								
7003	ploughsoil layer		I	1	26	16-18 mm	oxidised through	EIA
			II	1	6	12-15 mm	oxidised/ext.; unoxidised/int.	
7150	pit 7149		I	1	10	11-13 mm	oxidised through	EIA
7344	gully 7346		I	1	25	>24 mm	several joining flakes; oxidised through; white deposit	EIA
7364	pit 7365		I	1	32	16-18 mm	oxidised through	EIA
7683	pit 7762		I	1	52	15-23 mm	oxidised through	E/MIA?
7741	pit 7740		II	1	108	13-27 mm	oxidised/ext.; irregularly-fired/int.; unoxid./core; deep fingering on interior	MIA
(8521)	pit 8521		I	1	13	11-13 mm	oxidised/ext. & int.; unoxidised/core	?MIA
8559	pit		I	2	12	14-17 mm	oxidised through	MIA
Yarnton								
746/A/2	pit	488	II	1	27	9-19 mm		MIA
835/B	ditch	491	II	6	40	11-17 mm	from one vessel	M-LIA/ERB
330/B/2	pit	495	I	4	6	15-16 mm	from one vessel	E-MIA
2050/B	pit (post-Roman)	514	II	1	23	16-22 mm	white deposit	IA and EAS
584/B/2	pit	534	I	1	12	14-20 mm	1% organic matter in fabric	MIA
394/A/4	pit	944	II	1	25	15-19 mm		LIR
TOTAL				24	417			

Droitwich salt containers. This deposit is produced by a reaction between the salt water and the slightly calcareous Mercia Mudstone clay used to make the containers. Whether this reaction occurs as a result of the original firing of the containers to produce hard ceramic vessels or during the use of the hard vessels for salt making is uncertain.

Discussion

Fragments of Droitwich salt vessels were recovered from pits containing pottery ranging in date from the early-middle Iron Age to the mid-1st century AD, and also from a ditch of late 1st to early 2nd-century date which contained much redeposited later Iron Age pottery. Three of the pits (7740, 7762, and 8558) are located in the vicinity of two possible middle Iron Age house gullies on the western edge of the excavated area on Cresswell Field, with one sherd from the ploughsoil deposit to the east of these features.

The presence of this material in the area to the north-west of the Thames during the early-middle Iron Age is being increasingly recognised due to the ongoing excavation and analysis of sites of this date range in Oxfordshire. Prior to this work, Droitwich salt container material was not thought to occur in the wider Upper Thames area (Morris 1985, fig. 6) until the later middle Iron Age, as at Watkins Farm, Northmoor (Allen 1990c). The confirmation of salt container fragments in an earlier Iron Age deposit at Yarnton was the first firm recognition of the trade in salt from Droitwich into the Stanton Harcourt-Cassington area of Oxfordshire prior to the later Iron Age. The distribution of this material now includes Gravelly Guy (Morris 2004) where numerous sherds have been recovered from early Iron Age pits.

The significance of this trade in salt is emphasized by the absence of Malvernian pottery (Peacock 1968; Morris 1981) from Watkins Farm, Yarnton and Gravelly Guy. If both the salt vessels and this distinctive pottery were found in the same phases on these sites, then a joint trade of these containers could have been suggested, a form of piggy-back relationship. However, it is now evident that the salt was being exchanged beyond the distribution of the pottery, which highlights the importance of this commodity during the Iron Age.

FIRED CLAY *by Emily Edwards and Alistair Barclay*

Introduction

A total of 42 fragments (1778 g) of fired clay was recovered from excavated Bronze Age contexts from Cresswell Field. The assemblage includes a small number of cylindrical loomweight fragments, spindlewhorls, oven fragments, structural clay with wattle impressions and amorphous material. The Iron Age and Roman contexts yielded a total of 1656 fragments (28.5 kg) of fired clay, mainly from pits. The assemblage includes a small number of loomweight fragments mainly of triangular form, spindlewhorls, oven fragments, structural clay with wattle impressions and amorphous material.

Methodology

The fired clay was sorted into eight basic fabrics (A-H) on the basis of the principal inclusions present. Table 15.11 summarises the material recovered from the Bronze Age contexts whilst Table 15.12 gives a summary quantification by number of fragments and weight from the Iron Age and Roman contexts. The fired clay was examined for evidence of wattle or other impressions, possible objects and structural pieces.

Description of fabrics

A Fine, silty clay with rare inclusions (Bronze Age structural clay and miscellaneous).

B Fine, sandy clay with fine shell inclusions (structural clay fabric).

C Fine, silty clay with rare inclusions (structural clay; miscellaneous).

D Clay with limestone gravel inclusions and shell (loomweight fabric).

E Clay with organic matter, burnt out grass stems etc, and small rounded gravel (loomweight fabric; miscellaneous).

F Clay with ferruginous pellets and sparse organic matter (structural clay; miscellaneous).

G Clay with coarse quartz sand (miscellaneous).

H Clay with quartz sand and coarse gravel (miscellaneous).

None of the fabrics appeared to involve any form of clay preparation, with many of the inclusions representing naturally occurring materials rather than deliberately added temper. The two exceptions to this rule are spindlewhorls 1201/A and 385/A, which appear to have been made from reused potsherds. The fired clay includes triangular loomweights, spindlewhorls and structural clay. Fabrics A, B and E were used for structural clay, while

Table 15.11 Summary of fired clay from Bronze Age contexts

Type	*Date*	*No*	*Wt (g)*	*Comments*
Loomweights	LBA	21	1532	
Structural clay	E-MBA	7	24	flat surface
Structural clay	LBA	1	90	burnt daub
Structural clay	LBA-EIA	1	20	smoothed concave surface
Miscellaneous	LNE-BA	5	44	
Miscellaneous	LBA	7	68	

Table 15.12 Quantified summary of fired clay from Iron Age and Roman contexts.

Type	*Date*	*No.*	*Wt. (g)*	*Comments*
Structural clay	IA	25	200	
Structural clay	EIA	89	1715	Fragments with wattle impressions
Structural clay	MIA	135	1555	
Structural clay	LIR & ERB	60	2514	
Structural clay	LRB	8	164	
Structural clay	RB	8	43	
Loomweight fragments	EIA	31	1143	Triangular
Loomweight fragments	MIA	34	4813	Triangular
Loomweight fragments	ER	20	331	Triangular
Loomweight fragments	LR	10	106	Triangular
Spindlewhorl	EIA	2	47	Two whole spindlewhorls
Spindlewhorl	MIA	1	13	One whole spindlewhorl
Spindlewhorl	ERB/RB	2	22	One only 50% complete
Miscellaneous		1231	15888	Mostly amorphous fragments
Total		1656	28554	

fabrics C and D were used to manufacture triangular loomweights. Spindlewhorls were made from fabrics A and B. All the fabrics could be of local origin.

The Bronze Age fired clay

This material will be discussed in more detail in another volume (Hey *et al* forthcoming). The pieces recovered from the Second Gravel Terrace sites comprise a small amount of structural clay, 21 fragments of loomweight, representing a minimum of three late Bronze Age cylindrical weights and seven pieces of miscellaneous fired clay of indeterminate character. The cylindrical loomweights were recovered from pit 7543 with a possible fragment from pit 7712 (Table 15.11).

Iron Age and Roman fired clay

Structural clay

A total of 325 fragments (6.91 kg) was recovered from 51 contexts (Table 15.13). Both rods (vertical) and sails (horizontal) were recorded although rods were more common, some fragments clearly showing interwoven wattles. Details of surfaces were also recorded where noteworthy, as in the case of wiped or convex surfaces. Rather than originating from burnt daub walls, these pieces mostly derive from clay ovens. Most of the pieces were recovered from pits or from the Iron Age midden horizon (7003). In addition to the fragments detailed in Table 15.13 the fired clay floor of an early Roman oven was recovered from layer 186/A, (SF 205) within enclosure 206. The pattern of oxidation on the floor fragments shows an unoxidised, grey underside with gradating degrees of red oxidisation through the core and topside. There were also several wall pieces, including one fingertip moulded fragment.

Fragments of an oven, or of a clay plate which would have fitted into an oven structure, were recovered from later Iron Age enclosure ditch 1000/B with further oven fragments from 1000/C.

Loomweights

The excavations produced 95 (6.93 kg) fragments of loomweights, representing a minimum of 15 individual weights (Table 15.14). Where possible the types were classified following a system devised for the material recovered from Gravelly Guy (Barclay and Wait 2004). The Yarnton assemblage includes examples of type A/B, possibly C, and F. Types D and E, medium triangular with rounded corners and pyramidal with a single perforation were not recognised at Yarnton.

Types

Type A Large triangular loomweight measuring 170 x 170 x 170 x 80 mm with one to three perforated corners. Weight 1750-2100 g.

Type B Medium sized triangular loomweight with dimensions of 150 mm on each axis by 60/70 mm depth and one to three perforated corners. Weight 1375-1500 g.

Type C Small triangular weight measuring 90 mm on each axis by 35 mm depth and with two perforated corners. Average weight 300 g.

Type F Indeterminate fragments

Recognisable triangular loomweights (19 fragments) occur in 15 contexts, representing 15 objects of mostly middle Iron Age date. The most substantial piece came from middle Iron Age pit 584/A and is 50% complete. The weights from pits 8518 and 7657 are 30% complete. The majority, however, are relatively fragmented.

Table 15.13 Summary of structural clay by context and period.

Context	Type	Date	No. fragments	Wt (g)	Comments
7922	Pit 7923	IA	13	88	One fragment with rods and sails and outer surface
8455	Layer	IA	12	112	Outer surface
1749/A/1	Pit	EIA	2	15	Lumps of daub
7003	Ploughsoil	EIA	39	394	
7047	Pit 7051	EIA	2	85	
7052	Pit 7051	EIA	1	24	Probable daub
7190	Pit 7187	EIA	3	65	Very black around rod impression
7192	Pit 7191	EIA	12	208	
7364	Pit 7365	EIA	7	30	
7662	Pit 7603	EIA	1	470	Surface. 60 mm thick
7706	Pit 7705	EIA	1	7	Burnt daub
7816	Pit 7814	EIA	1	11	
7868	Pit 7869	EIA	2	14	Rods on both fragments
7788	Pit 7787	EIA	8	314	
8063	Pit 7787	EIA	1	9	
8067	Pit 7787	EIA	7	49	Some fragments with flat or concave surfaces
7915	Pit 8005	EIA	1	7	Smoothed surface
8193	Pit 8194	EIA	1	13	Flat surface
1189/A/20	Pit	MIA	2	15	Daub
1282/A/1	Pit	MIA	4	18	
1380/A/4	Gully encl 1378	MIA	2	7	Daub. Lump.
1524/A	Pit	MIA	28	255	Rods
584/A/1	Pit	MIA	1	14	Lump daub
7063	Pit 7062	MIA	1	44	Two worn surfaces
731/A/1	Pit	MIA	2	10	Lumps of daub
7352	Pit	MIA	1	30	Burnt daub
7734	Cremation pit	MIA	1	94	Smoothed surface. Daub or fired clay plate
7790	Layer	MIA	15	322	One fragment with three rods and another with one
7791	Ditch 7789	MIA	1	10	
7986	Pit 7988	MIA	11	27	One fragment with rods, sails and outer surface
8064	Pit 7987	MIA	10	157	Flat surface
8136	Pit 8135	MIA	1	26	
8466	Pit 8467	MIA	3	206	Wiped lumpy surface
8493	Pit 8786	MIA	45	223	Burnt daub with interwoven wattles
8659	Pit 8660	MIA	6	86	Fragments refit to make convex surface 120 mm dia.
898/B/1	Gully	MIA	1	11	Lump daub
1000/B/2	Ditch	LIR	20	750	Plate-disc with smoothed surf; central large perforation
1042/A/1	Pit	LIR	25	1308	"Brick" -lump, traces of a smoothed surface
7879	Surface	RB	3	16	One fragment with rods and sails
7881	Ditch 7908	RB	4	22	Squared wattles
7921	Ditch 7920	RB	1	5	
2062/A	Gully	ERB	1	4	Lumps of daub
289	Ditch encl 440	ERB	14	452	Rods and sails, red-brown and small surfaces
1181/A/1	Ditch encl 30	LRB	1	20	Lump daub
594/A/1	Feature	LRB	1	110	Rods. Large wattle burnt out black
621/A	Gully	LRB	5	13	Daub rods
683/C/2	Ditch encl 236	LRB	1	21	Daub, one rod

Spindlewhorls

Five spindlewhorls (Table 15.15) were recovered, one of which was very unusual, being of sub-square shape (7915) and concave in section. The example from pit 7707 was cylindrical, 27 mm thick and 30 mm in diameter. Those from pit 1201/A and surface 385/A appear to have been made from reused potsherds.

Miscellaneous

Most of the fired clay (74% by fragment count, 56% by weight) comprises amorphous lumps of no discernible form or function but undoubtedly derives from ovens and hearths used for domestic and industrial activities. Most, if not all of this material is fired a reddish-brown colour. Rare fragments with curved or flat surfaces and one piece of vitrified clay could derive from oven linings.

Table 15.14 Summary of loomweights by context and period.

Context	Type	Date	No.	Wt.(g)	Type	Comments
389	Pit	EIA	25	614	LW?	Loomweight frags ?lumps
389/A/1	Pit	EIA	1	224	TLW	Type A/B. One perf. Corner 70 mm wide
1540/B/1	Pit	EIA	2	164	TLW	Type A/B. One perforation
7184	Pit 7182	EIA	1	15	LW	
7614	Pit 7616	EIA	1	22	LW	
8518	Pit 8517	EIA	1	104	TLW	Corner
8466	Pit 8467	MIA	1	41	TLW	Edge fragment
260/A/1	Ditch encl 390	MIA	1	20	TLW	Type A/B. One perforation
584/A	Pit	MIA	1	508	TLW	Type A/B. Two perfs. 50 mm wide
584/A/3	Pit	MIA	20	720	TLW	Type A/B
584/B/4	Pit	MIA	2	3254	TLW	Type A/B. One perforation
8136	Pit 8135	MIA	1	19	TLW	Side edge fragment
8526	Pit 8525	MIA	3	39	TLW	
7657	Pit 7658	MIA	4	182	TLW	Fragments
260/A/1	Encl ditch 390	MIA	1	30	TLW	Type A/B. One perforation.
681/A/1	Ditch encl 175	LIR	1	58	LW	Fragments
395/A/3	Ditch encl 138	ERB	1	29	TLW	Fragment
565/A/1	Ditch encl 59	ERB	2	30	LW?	Fragments
693/C/1	Ditch encl 391C	ERB	5	50	LW	Fragments; One perforation
792/A	Ditch encl 1268	ERB	10	12	LW?	Fragments
1160/A/1	Pit	ERB	1	152	LW?	Fragment
409	Posthole	LRB	7	48	TLW	Type C? One perforation. Small.
106/A	Finds ref	LRB	1	35	TLW	
403/A/3	Ditch	RB	2	23	LW	Fragments

TLW = triangular loomweight

Table 15.15 Summary of spindlewhorls.

Context	Type	Date	No. fragments	Wt. (g)	Comments
7708	Pit 7707	EIA	1	19	Cylindrical. Dia 38 mm, th 27 mm. Unoxidised brownish-black
7915	Pit 8005	EIA	1	28	Spindlewhorl? Sub-square perforated plate. ?Dia 60 mm, th 18 mm
7784	Pit 7783	MIA	1	13	Spindlewhorl? Fragment, th 15 mm (+)
1201/A	Pit	RB	1	8	Half. Dia 40 mm, th 7mm.
385/A	Surface	ERB	1	14	Dia 38 mm, th 8 mm. Recent break

Unfired clay

Three contexts, late Bronze Age/early Iron Age pit 8127 (8126), early Iron Age pit 8394 (8403) and context 7810, contained deposits of unfired clay. All of this material was recovered as lumps.

Discussion

The fired clay finds appear to be fairly evenly distributed across the site. Most of the early Iron Age finds came from Cresswell Field, largely from pits scattered across the northern half of the site. The middle Iron Age finds came from both Cresswell Field and the Yarnton site, with a slightly higher concentration in the western part of the Yarnton site in the area of the roundhouses. At least two, possibly more middle Iron Age loomweights came from enclosure 390. One loomweight was recovered from the ditch of the enclosure whilst pit 584, located within this enclosure, produced one of the highest concentrations of loomweight material with 23 fragments (4.48 kg in weight) and one lump of daub. Most of the loomweights from early Roman contexts came from the central area of the Yarnton site and were presumably largely redeposited as a result of the ongoing disturbance in the area at this time with the digging of various enclosure ditches. All the fired clay finds in Roman contexts came from the Yarnton site, reflecting the shift in the focus of activity at this time.

The quantity and range of fired clay recovered from Yarnton appears fairly typical for a site of this type and location and is broadly similar to that recorded from Gravelly Guy (Barclay and Wait 2004), Wyndyke Furlong, Abingdon (Barclay 1999) and Thornhill Farm (Timby 2004b). The assemblage from Gravelly Guy, although it showed the same

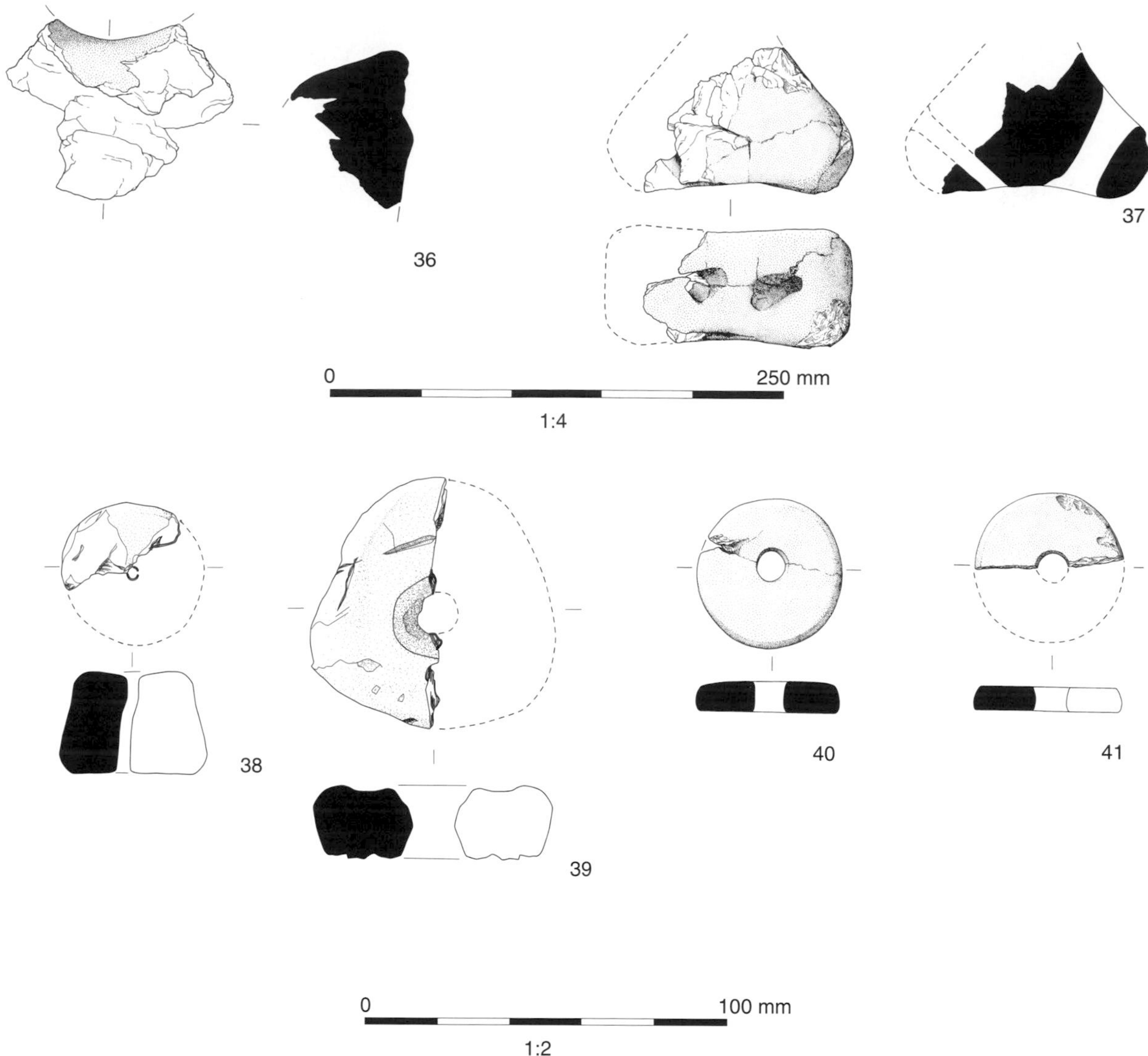

Fig. 15.16 Objects of fired clay

diversity and range of material, was considerably larger. There was a comparable number of spindlewhorls, but substantially more loomweight fragments; nearly 50 kg compared to the 6.4 kg from Yarnton. Triangular loomweights also featured at the Iron Age settlement at Wyndyke Furlong, Abingdon (Barclay 1999, 42) where 23 fragments from a minimum of nine weights were recorded, and at Thornhill Farm, Fairford where a minimum of nine triangular weights were also recorded (Timby 2004b) and Farmoor where some 16 triangular weights or fragments of weights were found (Lambrick 1979b, 57). Triangular loomweights have also been noted in small quantities on many other sites in the Thames Valley in early, middle and late Iron Age context, for example, Watkins Farm (Allen 1990d, 53), Mingies Ditch (Allen 1993, 78), Old Shifford (Barclay *et al.* 1995, 136), Deer Park Road, Witney (Timby 1995b, 81) and Whitehouse Road, Oxford (Underwood-Keevill 1993, 64). None of these occurrences would suggest anything other than low level domestic production.

Yarnton, unlike many of the other contemporary sites in the Thames Valley, did not produce any portable plate-like objects in fired clay. Gravelly Guy produced at least 13 circular plates of uncertain function and fragments have also been noted at Abingdon (Barclay 1999, 43) and Old Shifford (Barclay *et al* 1995, 137) and at a number of other sites in the region (see Booth 2009; 2010 with further references). As with loomweights, the amount of structural daub from Gravelly Guy is rather larger than from Yarnton, with 17.7 kg compared to 6.2 kg (Table 15.12) from the latter site. Most of this material was probably from ovens, though the only distinctive fragment came from late Iron Age/early Roman context 1000/B/2 at Yarnton (Fig. 15.16, No. 36). Substantially less structural clay was recovered from Wyndyke Furlong with just under 1 kg, but just over 2 kg of miscellaneous indeterminate fragments were noted

(Barclay 1999, 43). Most of the amorphous fired clay fragments from Yarnton probably originated in structures, Many of these, and of the identified structural pieces, are likely to be in secondary contexts, however.

Catalogue of illustrated material (Fig. 15.16)

1. Fig. 15.16, No. 36. Oven plate or floor fragment with large perforation. Two pieces, 369 g. Late Iron Age/early Roman enclosure ditch 1000/B.
2. Fig. 15.16, No. 37. Triangular loomweight. Several fragments, 508 g. Middle Iron Age pit 584/A.
3. Fig. 15.16, No. 38. Spindlewhorl fragment, 19 g. Early Iron Age pit 7707 (7708).
4. Fig. 15.16, No. 39. Irregular ?spindlewhorl fragment, 28 g. Early Iron Age pit 8005 (7915).
5. Fig. 15.16, No. 40. Spindlewhorl, 13 g. Early Roman surface 385/A.
6. Fig, 15.16, No. 41. Spindlewhorl fragment, 8 g. Roman pit 1201/A.

METALWORKING DEBRIS

Note: The following text has been taken from the assessment report and identification catalogue produced for Cresswell Field and Yarnton respectively by Chris Sulter. Unfortunately a full publication report was not submitted or the material recovered for further detailed analysis during the post-excavation programme. The tables for the two sites differ slightly in construction, reflecting the original recording.

Introduction

Most of the recorded metallurgical debris was recovered from the Yarnton site, a total of 8.57 kg in weight, with a significantly smaller amount of just under 3.4 kg from Cresswell Field, including small fragments of burnt and unburnt ironstone weighing a little over 60 g. In the case of Cresswell Field the majority of the material came from early and middle Iron Age contexts with very little slag or other metalworking debris from the later Iron Age or Roman contexts, reflecting the chronological development of the site. The largest amount of material came from the wide band of pits associated with domestic activity in the northern part of the site. The Yarnton site had a more even spread of material across Iron Age and Roman features, with the greatest weight coming from late Iron Age/early Roman contexts, followed by the early Iron Age and then the later Roman period. The smallest quantity came from Middle Iron Age contexts.

Early Iron Age(Tables 15.16-17)

A little under 6 kg of possible metalworking debris came from early Iron Age contexts, 1.8 kg from Cresswell Field and 3.95 kg from Yarnton. A single crucible came from Cresswell Field and four or five fragments from Yarnton. On Cresswell Field the largest weight of debris was in the form of complete and fragmented smithing hearth bottoms. The range of material from early Iron Age contexts showed the greatest diversity and included 13 complete or nearly complete hearth bottoms. However, the relatively small amount of slag found indicates that the amount of high temperature smithing activity (welding) was very limited. By contrast, Yarnton only produced three hearth bottoms and 29 fragments of dense slag. Some pieces of hearth lining along with a crucible fragment came from pit 2649 whilst pit 2646 also produced two or three crucible fragments along with some pieces of tuyère.

The presence of vitrified hearth lining is only indicative of some sort of high temperature process, not necessarily metalworking, whereas the low density slags are most likely to have been generated by a metalworking process, be it copper or iron-working. Quite a significant quantity of vitrified clay was recovered from Yarnton. However, on some Iron Age sites it has been concluded that similar material was produced by cremation or pottery firing.

The presence of iron ore, or even heated iron ore, cannot be considered as important for Thames Valley sites when the quantities are small, as they are in this case. The gravels contains many fragments of transported Jurassic ironstone. Some of these may be roasted by accidental association with a hearth.

Evidence for copper working from Cresswell Field came in the form of two small fragments of slag with the normal appearance of iron-smithing slag except for a small amount of copper staining. This copper corrosion was due to the corrosion of internal copper prills. Thus it is likely that these samples are examples of crucible slags. Eight fragments of copper alloy metal were recorded from Yarnton, seven from pit 330.

Four pits in particular can be singled out as having a relatively high incidence of metalworking debris; pits 330, 951 and 952 on the Yarnton site and pit 7173 in the north-east apex of Cresswell Field. Pit 330 stands out in that it is located on the periphery of the occupation area where there is a relatively low density of features. In total it produced 43 items weighing 797 g, including the crucible fragment, a hearth bottom, several fragments of dense slag, and vitrified clay possibly indicative of small scale metalworking in the immediate area. Pits 951 and 952 are located some 10 m north-east of 330 and may relate to the same episode of activity. Collectively these adjacent pits yielded 46 fragments weighing 745 g, amongst which is dense slag, fuel ash slag and vitrified clay.

Middle Iron Age (Tables 15.18-19)

The quantity of metalworking debris recovered from middle Iron Age contexts is considerably less than for the Early Iron Age, some 0.74 kg in total from Cresswell Field and 0.64 kg from Yarnton. In all seven

Table 15.16: Catalogue of metalworking debris from early Iron Age contexts at Cresswell Field.

Context	*Wt (g)*	*No.*	*Class code*	*Description*	*Slag description*
Type of debris: crucible or mould debris					
Pit 8393 (8394)	4.5	1	CC	Crucible – undefined	A fragment of clay with a vitrified surface, possible a crucible fragment
Type of debris: vitrified clay/hearth lining					
Pit 8326 (8326)	8.9	1	CV-B	Vitrified clay – moderate vitrification	
Pit 7677 (7775)	1.8	1	CV-A	Vitrified clay – thin surface vitrification	A thin layer of vitrification over a clay fabric. This could simply be hearth lining, but the form is unusual in that it has both a front and back surface. The back surface has what appears to be a small amount of vitrification present. The fabric is fine grain or pure clay, with a few fine vesicles, and has been fired under reducing conditions throughout the sample. Thus there is the possibility that this is either an overfired pot or crucible
Pit 8062 (8061)	7.6	1	CV-D	Vitrified clay – full vitrification beginning to soften	A fragment of vitrified hearth lining, but the vitrification has gone to greater depth (>20 mm)
Pit 7787 (8067)	3.2	1	CV-D	Vitrified clay – full vitrification beginning to soften	Unusual surface colouring – suggestive of a more calcic composition than is usual
Type of debris: slag - low density probably iron-working					
Pit 7173 (7171)	39.4	46	SB-SLV	Slag-lining reaction product	Fragments from the core of a small smithing hearth bottom. All probably from a single piece
Pit 7173 (7171)	5.7	1	SB-LSR	Lining-slag reaction product	
Pit 7173 (7171)	2.4	4	SB-SLR	Slag-lining reaction product	
Pit 8000 (7999)	3.5	1	SB-FAS	Fuel ash slag	Light coloured form of fuel ash slag. It is not clear whether this sample is true fuel ash slag or vitrified hearth lining
Pit 8541 (8543)	7.5	1	SB-LSR	Lining-slag reaction product	
Pit 8537 (8536)	16.3	2	SB-LSR	Lining-slag reaction product	
Pit 7397 (7398)	5.3	1	SB-SLR	Slag-lining reaction product	Unusual in that this piece has the sort of colours associated with cold-blown coke-fired blast furnace slag
Stakehole 7644	13.8	1	SB-SLR	Slag-lining reaction product	
Pit 8517 (8518)	68.0	5	SB-LSR	Lining-slag reaction product	It is not clear if this is simply a fragment of very deeply vitrified hearth lining or a vitrification flow
Type of debris: ironworking slag - general					
Ploughsoil 7003	5.2	1	SD-Frag	Dense slag – fragment unclassified	
Pit 7149 (7176)	59.2	40	SD-Frag	Dense slag – fragment unclassified	Fragments from the break up of a small smithing hearth bottom or the like
Gully 7297 (7298)	2.9	3	SD-Frag	Dense slag – fragment unclassified	
Pit 7300 (7299)	10.4	1	SD-Frag	Dense slag – fragment unclassified	
Pit 7397 (7398)	17.3	1	SD-Frag	Dense slag – fragment unclassified	
Pit 7598 (7643)	13.2	1	SD-Frag	Dense slag – fragment unclassified	
Pit 8005 (7915)	15.9	1	SD-1	Dense slag – irregular – semi-flow	Rather glassy flow
Type of debris: iron-working - smithing hearth bottoms					
Pit 7058 (7057)	418.0	1	SD-4	Dense slag – small/medium plano-convex hearth bottom	
Pit 7397 (7398)	102.0	1	SD-3	Dense slag – small sub-tuyère plate	
Pit 7397 (7398)	18.9	3	SD-Fr C	Dense slag –fragment probably from SD 3, 4, 5	
Pit 7762 (7683)	70.0	1	SD-3	Dense slag – small sub-tuyère plate	
Pit 7762 (7683)	20.4	1	SD Fr C	Dense slag –fragment probably from SD 3, 4, 5	
Pit 7598 (7629)	74.0	1	SD-3	Dense slag – small sub-tuyère plate	Fragmented sub-tuyère smithing slag plate
Pit 7170 (7173)	428.0	1	SD-4	Dense slag – small/medium plano-convex hearth bottom	
Pit 8072 (8073)	31.7	1	SD-Fr C	Dense slag – fragment probably from SD 3,4,5	
Pit 8072 (8073)	52.4	1	SD-3	Dense slag – small sub-tuyère plate	Part of a small smithing hearth bottom
Pit 7598 (7629)	74.0	1	SD-3	Dense slag – small sub-tuyère plate	Fragmented sub-tuyère smithing slag plate

Table 15.16: Catalogue of metalworking debris from early Iron Age contexts at Cresswell Field (continued).

Context	Wt (g)	No.	Class code	Description	Slag description
Pit 8195 (8196)	56.4	1	SD-Fr C	Dense slag – fragment probably from SD 3,4,5	Broken fragment of smithing hearth bottom, still disintegrating due to the corrosion of metallic iron within the slag
Gully 8387 (8388)	40.4	1	SD-4 Fr	Dense slag – small/medium plano-convex hearth bottom – fragment	
Pit 8428 (8428)	30.3	1	SD-3 Fr	Dense slag – small sub-tuyère plate	A fragment of smithing slag, probably from a smithing hearth bottom
Type of debris: metallic iron					
Pit 7397 (7473)	19.2	1	MI	Metal – iron alloy	
Pit 8447	34.2	1	MI	Metal – iron alloy	
Type of debris: ore					
Pit 8327 (8326)	6.1	1	N-R/O		
Pit 7173 (7171)	20.3	1	N-R/O		
Pit 7173 (7170)	11.7	3	N/R/O		
Phole 8373 (8374)	5.6	2	N-OH	Natural – iron ore heated	
Type of debris: copper-alloy working					
Gully 7297 (7298)	2.2	2	MC-SS	Copper slag – normal looking slags containing copper alloy prill	Slag with copper stains
Pit 7762 (7683)	4.7	1	MC-SS	Copper slag – normal looking slag containing copper-alloy prills	External morphology small piece of copper stained slag. Internally – a small piece of slag-like material with copper-alloy prills visible in polished section

Table 15.17 Catalogue of metalworking debris from early Iron Age contexts at Yarnton.

Context	Type	Wt (g)	No.	Class code	Description
276A/1	Pit	6.4	1	CF	Fired clay
330A/1	Pit	110.2	8	SD-Frag	Dense slag - fragment unclassified
330A/1	Pit	9.1	2	CV-C	Vitrified clay - full vitrification
330A/2	Pit	8.6	1	MC	Metal - copper alloy
330A/2	Pit	23.9	1	SB-LSR	Lining-slag reaction product
330A/2	Pit	33.8	5	CF	Fired clay
330A/2	Pit	4.4	1	CV-C	Vitrified clay - full vitrification
330A/2	Pit	18.0	1	SD-Frag	Dense slag - fragment unclassified
330A/2	Pit	3.5	1	SD-1	Dense slag - small flow/drip
330A/2	Pit	21.3	6	SB-SLR	Slag-lining reaction product
330A/2	Pit	6.1	1	CC-CB	Crucible - body fragment
330A/2	Pit	8.5	1	SD-Frag	Dense slag - fragment unclassified
330A/2	Pit	116.0	1	SD-4	Dense slag - small plano-convex hearth bottom - fragment
330A/2	Pit	234.0	1	CV-TuyH	Vitrified clay - tuyère, air-hole type
330A/2	Pit	30.4	1	CV-C	Vitrified clay - full vitrification
330B/1	Pit	14.8	2	CV-D	Vitrified clay - full vitrification beginning to flow
330B/2	Pit	1.9	7	MC	Metal - copper alloy
330B/2	Pit	15.7	1	SB-LVF	Lining vitrification flow
330B/2	Pit	7.2	1	CV-D	Vitrified clay - full vitrification beginning to flow
330B/2	Pit	10.7	1	CV-A	Vitrified clay - thin surface vitrification
857A/1	Pit	6.2	1	CV-D/E	Vitrified clay - full vitrification beginning to flow
857A/2	Pit	32.8	1	SD-Frag	Dense slag - fragment unclassified
857A/5	Pit	69.2	1	SD-Frag	Dense slag - fragment unclassified
951A	Pit	333.0	24	CF	Fired clay
951A	Pit	116.6	3	CV-D	Vitrified clay - full vitrification beginning to flow
951A	Pit	18.7	1	SB-LVF	Lining vitrification flow
951A	Pit	12.3	8	SB-LVF	Lining vitrification flow, fragments
951A	Pit	188.0	1	SB-FAS	Fuel ash slag
951A	Pit	7.4	1	SD-Frag	Dense slag - fragment unclassified
952A	Pit	18.4	1	CV-D	Vitrified clay - full vitrification beginning to flow

Table 15.17 Catalogue of metalworking debris from early Iron Age contexts at Yarnton (continued).

Context	Type	Wt (g)	No.	Class code	Description
952A	Pit	2.3	1	CV-D/E	Vitrified clay - full vitrification beginning to flow
952A	Pit	11.5	5	SB-LSR	Lining-slag reaction product
952A	Pit	36.8	1	SD-I	Dense slag - irregular - semi-flow
1163A/3	Pit	2.1	1	SD-Frag	Dense slag - fragment unclassified
1477A	B 1474	8.5	1	CV-C	Vitrified clay - full vitrification
1540A/1	Pit	230.0	1	SD-4	Dense slag - small plano-convex hearth bottom
1716A/2	Pit	230.0	1	SD-4	Dense slag - small plano-convex hearth bottom
2649A/7	Pit	60.4	1	CV-D	Vitrified clay - full vitrification beginning to flow
2651A/1	Pit	70.4	13	SD-Frag	Dense slag - fragment unclassified
2651A/1	Pit	6.8	1	SB-LSR	Lining-slag reaction product
TOTAL		2145.9	112		

Table 15.18 Catalogue of metalworking debris from middle Iron Age contexts at Cresswell Field.

Context	Wt (g)	No.	Class code	Description	Slag description
Type of debris : vitrified clay/hearth lining					
Pit 8786 (8493)	2.1	1	CV-D	Vitrified clay – full vitrification beginning to soften	Vitrification is a light colour on oolite
Ditch 7660 (7560)	7.3	1	CV-A	Vitrified clay – thin surface vitrification	
Ditch 7660 (7560)	9.3	1	CV-D	Vitrified clay – full vitrification beginning to soften	
Pit 7658 (7657)	9.3	2	CV-D/E	Vitrified clay – full vitrification beginning to flow	
Gully 7862 (7863)	1.7	1	CV-D	Vitrified clay – full vitrification beginning to soften	
Ditch 7893 (7892)	27.9	2	CV-D/E	Vitrified clay – full vitrification beginning to flow	
Type of debris: slag - low density probably iron-working					
Pit 7132 (7131)	33.3	1	SB-FAS	Fuel ash slag	Possibly bone type fuel ash slag
Pit 7658 (7657)	3.5	1	SB-FAS	Fuel ash slag	Possibly copper working or burnt bone sub-type fuel ash slag
Pit 7658 (7657)	4.9	3	SB-LSR	Lining-slag reaction product	Three small fragments of vitrified hearth lining reacting with slag
Pit 8522 (8521)	9.1	3	SB-SLR	Slag-lining reaction product	
Type of debris: slag - low density probably ironworking					
Ditch 7870	13.1	1	SB-LSR	Lining-slag reaction product	
Ditch 7870	6.0	2	SB-SLR	Lining-slag reaction product	
Ditch 7870	0.6	1	SB-FAS	Fuel ash slag	
Pit 7062 (7064)	27.4	1	SB-FSS	Fused/sintered soil/clay	
Type of debris: ironworking slag - general					
Pit 7062 (7064)	20.6	1	SD-2	Dense slag - flow	Flat form
Pit 7658 (7657)	8.0	2	SD-Frag	Dense slag – fragment unclassified	
Pit 7856	36.4	1	SD-I	Dense slag – irregular – semi-flow	
Type of debris: ironworking - smithing hearth bottoms					
Pit 7127 (7128)	120.0	1	SD-3	Dense slag – small sub-tuyère plate	
Pit 7658 (7657)	158.0	1	SD-4	Dense slag – small/medium plano-convex hearth bottom	
Pit 7658 (7657)	106.0	1	SD-4 Fr	Dense slag – small/medium plano-convex hearth bottom - fragment	Part of a small smithing hearth bottom
Pit 7658 (7657)	80.2	1	SD-3	Dense slag – small sub-tuyère plate	Fragmented sub-tuyère smithing slag plate
Pit 7658 (7657)	59.6	1	SD-3	Dense slag – small sub-tuyère plate	Broken fragment of smithing hearth bottom, still disintegrating due to the corrosion of metallic iron within the slag

Table 15.19 Catalogue of metalworking debris from middle Iron Age contexts at Yarnton.

Context	*Location/type*	*Wt (g)*	*No.*	*Code*	*Description*
261A/1	Enclosure 390B	71.0	1	SB-SLR	Slag-lining reaction product
262	Enclosure 390A	42.4	2	SB-FAS	Fuel ash slag
301A/1	Enclosure 390D	26.4	1	SD-3	Dense slag - small sub-tuyère plate
301A/1	Enclosure 390D	1.6	1	CC-CB	Crucible - body fragment
301A/1	Enclosure 390D	1.2	1	CC-CB	Crucible - body fragment
584B/4	pit	4.5	1	CV-D	Vitrified clay - full vitrification beginning to flow
734A/1	pit	2.6	1	CF-HFR	Fired clay - high reducing fired
746A/2	pit	6.2	1	SB-SLR	Slag-lining reaction product
887A/1	pit	19.9	1		
887A/4	pit	110.0	1	SD-3	Dense slag - small sub-tuyère plate
1189A/12	pit	69.8	1	SD-4	Dense slag - small plano-convex hearth bottom- fragment
1189A/13	pit	37.0	1	SD-Frag	Dense slag - fragment unclassified
1278A/1	pit	1.0	1	SB-FAS	Fuel ash slag
1368A/1	pit	2.9	1	CV-C	Vitrified clay - full vitrification
1368A/1	pit	37.1	1	SD-Frag	Dense slag - fragment unclassified
1603A/2	Enclosure 399	40.5	1	SD-I	Dense slag - irregular - semi-flow
1656A/1	posthole	130.7	1	SD-Frag	Dense slag - fragment unclassified
2551B/1	grave	37.6	1	SD-Frag	Dense slag - fragment unclassified
TOTAL		642.4	19		

Table 15.20 Catalogue of metalworking debris from late Iron Age/early Roman contexts at Yarnton.

Context	*Type*	*Wt (g)*	*No.*	*Code*	*Description*
1458A/2	LIA pit	3.7	1	SB-FAS	Fuel ash slag
121A	Enclosure 121	33.7	1	SD-3	Dense slag - small sub-tuyère plate
564A/1	Enclosure 129	22.7	1	SB-LVF	Lining vitrification flow
239A/1	Enclosure 175	118.0	1	SD-4	Dense slag - small plano-convex hearth bottom
622C/3	Enclosure 175	234.0	1	SD-4	Dense slag - small plano-convex hearth bottom
629A/1	Enclosure 175	266.0	1	SD-4	Dense slag - small plano-convex hearth bottom
629B/1	Enclosure 175	7.9	1	SD-Frag	Dense slag - fragment unclassified
478A/1	Enclosure 175	19.5	1	SD-Frag	Dense slag - fragment unclassified
671A/2	Enclosure 175	51.0	1	SD-I	Dense slag - Irregular - semi-flow.
1492B/1	Enclosure 205	16.8	1	SD-Frag	Dense slag - fragment unclassified
683C/1	Enclosure 236	79.6	1	SD-Frag	Dense slag - fragment unclassified
288A/1	Enclosure 236	41.2	1	SB-LVF	Lining vitrification flow
346B/1	Enclosure 391A	13.9	1	SD-2	Dense slag - flow, flattened form
346B/1	Enclosure 391A	3.9	2	SB-LSR	Lining-slag reaction product, plus some charcoal.
596A/1	Enclosure 596	35.7	1	SD-4	Dense slag - small plano-convex hearth bottom, frag
596A/1	Enclosure 596	138.0	1	SD-4	Dense slag - small plano-convex hearth bottom
596A/1	Enclosure 596	298.0	1	SD-4	Dense slag - small plano-convex hearth bottom
1433A/1	Enclosure 1399	11.3	1	CV-C	Vitrified clay - full vitrification
594A/1	Feature	19.6	1	CF	Fired clay
594A/1	Feature	204.0	1	SD-4	Dense slag - small plano-convex hearth bottom
594B/1	Feature	63.4	4	SD-Frag	Dense slag - fragment unclassified
594C/1	Feature	392.0	1	SD-4	Dense slag - small plano-convex hearth bottom
852	Hearth	34.4	1	CV-D	Vitrified clay - full vitrification beginning to flow
852	Hearth	87.2	1	CV-TBPB	Vitrified clay - bellows protection block
852	Hearth	132.0	1	CV-TBPB	Vitrified clay - bellows protection block
852	Hearth	5.1	1	CV-D	Vitrified clay - full vitrification beginning to flow
852	Hearth	62.3	2	SD-Frag	Dense slag - fragments unclassified
852	Hearth	122.0	1	SD-4	Dense slag - small plano-convex hearth bottom
852	Hearth	222.0	1	SD-4	Dense slag - small plano-convex hearth bottom
300A/1	Pit	20.0	1	SD-Frag	Dense slag - fragment unclassified
662A/3	Pit	700.0	1	SD-5	Dense slag - medium-sized hearth bottom
954A	Pit	13.1	1	SD-Frag	Dense slag - fragment unclassified
TOTAL		3472.0	37		

Table 15.21 Catalogue of metalworking debris from early Roman contexts at Yarnton.

Context	Type	Wt (g)	No.	Code	Description
93B	Ditch	26.3	2	SD-Frag	Dense slag - fragment unclassified
726B/1	Enclosure 51	4.3	1	SD-Frag	Dense slag - fragment unclassified
821D/1	Enclosure 51	5.2	1	SD-Frag	Dense slag - fragment unclassified
172A/2	Enclosure 156	9.0	1	SD-Frag	Dense slag - fragment unclassified
589A/1	Enclosure 156	4.6	1	CV-D/E	Vitrified clay - full vitrification beginning to flow
835B	Enclosure 166	17.3	4	SB-LSR	Lining-slag reaction product
835B	Enclosure 166	8.0	1	N-O	Natural - iron ore
223A/1	Enclosure 187	144.0	1	SD-3	Dense slag - small sub-tuyère plate
264B/1	Enclosure 187	4.4	4	SD-Frag	Dense slag - fragment unclassified
480A/3	Enclosure 187	37.0	1	CV-TBPB	Vitrified clay - bellows protection block fragment
480A/3	Enclosure 187	47.5	1	SB-LVF	Lining vitrification flow
480B/1	Enclosure 187	10.6	1	SB-LVF	Lining vitrification flow
521A/4	Enclosure 187	2.2	1	SB-LVF	Lining vitrification flow
1324A/1	Enclosure 187	25.4	1	SB-FAS	Fuel ash slag
433A/1	Enclosure 206	1.5	1	SB-LVF	Lining vitrification flow
280B/2	Enclosure 206	45.9	3	SD-Frag	Dense slag - fragment unclassified
622D/6	Enclosure 206	4.2	1	SD-Frag	Dense slag - fragment unclassified
343B/1	Enclosure 343	7.0	1	CF	Fired clay
344D/1	Enclosure 344	8.4	1	SB-LSR	Lining-slag reaction product
348C	Enclosure 348	27.9	1	SB-LVF	Lining vitrification flow
365A/1	Enclosure 365	65.4	1	SD-2	Dense slag - flow
693C/1	Enclosure 391C	22.6	1	SB-FAS	Fuel ash slag
591A	Enclosure 591	12.8	1	SB-FAS	Fuel ash slag/lining vitrification flow
727A/1	Enclosure 727	12.5	1	SD-Frag	Dense slag - fragment unclassified
788A/1	Enclosure 788	3.0	1	SB-SLR	Slag-lining reaction product
2593C/1	Enclosure 2593	56.2	1	SD-I	Dense slag - irregular - semi-flow
1082A/3	Pit	22.1	1	SD-Frag	Dense slag - fragment unclassified
1088A/1	Pit	23.6	2	SB-FAS	Fuel ash slag
1216A/2	Pit	274.0	1	SB-FAS	Fuel ash slag
1216A/2	Pit	7.0	2	CF-HFR	Fired clay - high reducing fired
1387A/1	Pit	4.8	1	SB-SLR	Slag-lining reaction product
TOTAL		944.7	42		

relatively complete smithing hearth bottoms were recovered, five from Cresswell Field, less than half the number recovered from early Iron Age contexts. Two crucible body fragments along with a small sub-tuyère plate came from ditch 301, part of enclosure 390D at Yarnton. Fuel ash slag from Cresswell Field might suggest some copper working there.

Evidence from elsewhere has suggested an increased use of iron in the middle Iron Age (Salter and Ehrenreich 1984). If this is the case here it would suggest either that any metalworking activity was taking place well away from the site or that finished items were being brought to the site. Only one iron artefact, an iron ring, was recovered from the middle Iron Age features, suggesting either a general dearth of metal artefacts in circulation at Yarnton or a very efficient recycling system.

Roman (Tables 15.20-23)

The higher level of activity on the Yarnton site in the later Iron Age and Roman periods led to the recovery of quite a large quantity of metalworking debris, although how much of this was redeposited from early or middle Iron Age activity is impossible to say. In total 5.8 kg of material was recorded; some 111 pieces, of which 60% came from late Iron Age/early Roman levels, 16.5% from early Roman contexts and 23.5% from late Roman features. The quantity of metalworking debris recovered from Roman contexts on Cresswell Field was very small, some 0.215 kg (Table 15.23). The very worn state of the smithing hearth bottom from ditch 8266 indicates that the sample was almost certainly derived from earlier metalworking activity. Again this is likely to be the result of the shift in settlement location at this time.

The later Iron Age/early Roman group of material (Table 15.20) includes 11 small plano-convex hearth bottoms, three from enclosure 596, the same general zone as the concentration of early Iron Age material. A further two fragments with associated dense slag and vitrified clay, including a bellows protection block, came from 'hearth' 852 immediately south of late Iron Age/early Roman enclosure 121. The pit-like shape of this feature suggests that it is the remains of a furnace structure (cf. Fig. 7.7); certainly *in situ* smithing seems to be represented by a fragment of hearth lining with attached smithing slag and a fragment of tuyère block. Six pieces of metalworking debris were associated with enclosure 175, two of which are plano-convex smithing hearths possibly hinting at some metalworking activity within the enclosure.

The early Roman finds are scattered across the central zone of the Yarnton site but are noticeably absent from the Iron Age settlement area in the western part of the site. In total just under 1 kg of material came from this phase, the greatest concentration coming from features associated with

Table 15.22 Catalogue of metalworking debris from late Roman contexts at Yarnton.

Context	*Type*	*Wt (g)*	*No.*	*Code*	*Description*
1031A/2	Building 1356	7.6	1	ST-BC	Blast furnace slag - tapped - Blue-green-series
1123A/1	Building 1356	27.2	1	SB-FAS	Fuel Ash Slag
775A/1	Building 1768	33.2	1	SB-FAS	Fuel Ash Slag
1061B	Enclosure 30	136.0	1	SD-4	Dense slag - small plano-convex hearth bottom
1182A/4	Enclosure 30	3.0	1	SB-FSS	Fused/sintered soil/clay
1135A	Enclosure 34	16.2	1	SD-Frag	Dense slag - fragment unclassified
379A/1	Enclosure 184	18.1	1	SD-Frag	Dense slag - fragment unclassified
655A/2	Enclosure 184	42.0	1	SB-LSR	Lining-slag reaction product
655B/2	Enclosure 184	94.8	1	SD-4	Dense slag - small plano-convex hearth bottom
217C/1	Enclosure 217	80.8	1	SD-3	Dense slag - small sub-tuyère plate
217E/1	Enclosure 217	125.7	1	SD-4	Dense slag - small plano-convex hearth bottom
1645A/2	Enclosure 222	46.4	2	CV-D	Vitrified clay - full vitrification beginning to flow
326	Enclosure 326B	3.6	1	N-Ch	Charcoal
2031A/1	Enclosure 1013	2.6	1	SB-LSR	Lining-slag reaction product
304A/1	Enclosure 1350	160.0	1	SD-3	Dense slag - small sub-tuyère plate
304B	Enclosure 1350	144.5	1	SD-3	Dense slag - small sub-tuyère plate
354B/1	Layer	91.3	2	SD-I	Dense slag - irregular - semi-flow
354B/1	Layer	57.2	1	SB-LSR	Lining-slag reaction product
354B/1	Layer	56.8	1	SD-3	Dense slag - small sub-tuyère plate
354B/1	Layer	25.6	4	CV-D	Vitrified clay - full vitrification beginning to flow
354D/1	Layer	93.4	2	SD-FS1	Dense slag - inter-fuel slag flow
354D/1	Layer	35.4	2	SD-Frag	Dense slag - fragment unclassified
354D/1	Layer	13.8	1	SB-SLR	Slag-lining reaction product
1095A/2	Pit	39.1	1	SB-FAS	Fuel ash slag
1194A/1	Pit	7.8	1	CV-D	Vitrified clay - full vitrification beginning to flow
TOTAL		1362.1	32		

Table 15.23 Catalogue of metalworking debris from Roman features at Cresswell Field.

Context	*Wt (g)*	*No.*	*Class code*	*Description*	*Slag description*
Type of debris: ore - heated					
Ditch 8129 (8128)	6.1	1	N-OH	Natural – iron ore heated	
Type of debris: slag - low density probably iron-working					
Ditch 7920 (7921)	3.6	3	SB-Fr	Low density slag fragment too small to identify	
Type of debris: ironworking slag - general					
Ditch 8129 (8128)	2.2	1	SD-Frag	Dense slag – fragment unclassified	
Type of debris: ironworking - smithing hearth bottoms					
Ditch 7920 (7921)	44.5	1	SD-4 Fr	Dense slag – small/medium plano-convex hearth bottom - fragment	Core fragment of a plano-convex smithing hearth bottom. Dense with long zone of direction crystallisation
Ditch 8226 (8223)	159.0	1	SD-4	Dense slag – small/medium plano-convex hearth bottom	A badly worn smithing hearth bottom with edges missing and corroded iron on top surface

enclosure 187. These totalled ten pieces, mostly comprising lining vitrification but including a fragment of bellows protection block.

The late Roman features on the Yarnton site produced some 1.36 kg of metalworking debris, 32 pieces. Building 1356 produced one fragment of blast furnace slag and some fuel ash slag. Layer 354 located within the interior of enclosure 391 in the south-east area of the site produced 13 fragments of dense slag, lining slag and vitrified clay. Three plano-convex hearth bottoms and four sub-tuyère plates also feature amongst the material from these late Roman contexts.

Conclusions

The quantity of slag recovered from Cresswell Field was small and dispersed across the site. The material recovered from the early and middle Iron Age periods represents a minimum of 6 days smithing involving welding. The iron-working debris from all the later contexts could well be redeposited from these earlier episodes or transported from activity further to the east as the settlement shifted. There is the possibility of some copper working in the early Iron Age, based on the presence of a single crucible fragment and two pieces of slag.

The Yarnton site produced significantly more material but this was spread across a greater timespan. It is unclear how much of the later material is redeposited from earlier activity during the digging of the various late Iron Age and Roman enclosure ditches. A concentration of material from three pits in one location in the early Iron Age may suggest a focus of metalworking activity in this area, while a possible furnace site or *in situ* smithing was identified from the late Iron Age/early Roman phase on the eastern side of the site. The evidence seems to suggest very small-scale metalworking (both ferrous and non-ferrous) in the Iron Age and Roman periods, presumably for local domestic or agricultural purposes. Similar hints of small-scale metalworking in the region have been noted at Ashville (Cleere 1978, 88), Gravelly Guy (Salter and Wait 2004) and Mingies Ditch (Salter 1993, 77).

ANALYSIS OF COPPER ALLOY MATERIAL FROM CRESSWELL FIELD *by Roger Doonan*

Two pieces of copper alloy material were submitted for analysis. One was recovered from early Iron Age pit 8092 (8093), the other from middle Iron Age pit 7783 (7784). The material had been incorrectly identified as 'slag'. This is quite understandable since the resemblance to slag is very strong.

The copper alloy fragment from pit 7783 weighs 207 g. It has large vesicles and is covered with green corrosion products. Qualitative XRF analysis shows that this material is not slag but in fact metallic copper with small amounts of lead and tin. The shape of the fragment is clearly plano-convex and strongly suggests that it is an ingot fragment. The whole ingot would have originally measured 12-18 cm in diameter. The identification of an ingot is in itself interesting and may, depending on the depositional context, be used as evidence to support hypotheses relating to exchange of materials or social attitudes to metal. The small amounts of lead and tin detected are also noteworthy as they provide information on the nature of the ingot. Generally it is thought that ingots are only produced at two opportunities. Firstly, at the refining of 'black copper' subsequent to its production in the smelting furnace, and secondly, in the remelting of scrap to consolidate it into a single ingot. The small amount of tin detected in this ingot suggests that it was produced by the melting down of scrap, some of which would have been tin-bronze. Primary ingots would not contain such levels of tin because, in general, copper ores contain very low levels of tin and derive from geographically distinct mining locations.

The copper alloy fragment from pit 8092 is quite different. It weighs 2 g, is covered in green corrosion products and has an irregular form. Its form strongly suggests that it is the result of a spillage which occurred whilst handling molten copper alloy. Qualitative XRF analysis shows that the fragment is composed of a high tin bronze. Without quantitative analysis it is not possible to say what the exact percentage of tin is, although the relative heights of the copper and tin peaks suggests that the alloy contains a substantial amount of tin.

ANALYSIS OF IRON AGE METALWORK FROM YARNTON FLOODPLAIN (YFPB)

by Peter Northover

Three objects were examined. All analyses were made on drilled samples with the exception of a section cut from the bronze-coated iron ring; the samples were hot-mounted in a carbon-filled thermosetting resin, ground and polished to a 1 μm diamond finish. Analysis was by electron probe microanalysis using wavelength dispersive spectrometry; the details of the method have been published several times (see for example Northover 1989).

Floodplain Site 9 context 13249, SF 13392

(Fig. 15.2, A)

Thin rectangular section copper alloy strip with slight edge ridges and tapered ends; possible unwound spiral ring fragment; dull blue green patina with some earth adhering. Width 4 mm; total length 95 mm.

Composition: 0.07% Fe; 0.20% Co; 0.07% Ni; 0.02% Zn; 0.41% As; 0.04% Sb; 12.44% Sn; 0.01% Bi; 0.18% Pb; 0.14% S.

If this bronze strip is regarded as being an unwound spiral ring, a length of 95 mm is equal to two turns of a spiral 45 mm in circumference and 15 mm in diameter. To take just a single example, there is at Flag Fen (Coombs 2001, fig. 10.10, no. 243) a spiral ring of about $1^1/_2$ turns, 18 mm diameter and 9 mm wide at its broadest and 2.6-2.8 mm at the terminals; unwound the length is about 80 mm. Thus the characterisation of the strip as an unwound ring is plausible.

This piece of bronze can be classified as Iron Age on the basis of it composition. An impurity pattern with arsenic but low antimony, and with more cobalt than nickel has been shown to be characteristic of the Iron Age in central southern and south-western Britain (eg Northover 1991a; 1991b). The type does appear in the middle Bronze Age but then is localised in the far south-west, in Devon and Cornwall. In the Iron Age it first appears in the earliest La Tène phase (cp4 at Danebury) and goes out of use during the 1st century BC. The Flag Fen ring also falls into this group with 0.11% cobalt, 0.03% nickel and 12.42% tin, but the antimony content is higher at 0.09%.

Floodplain Site 9 context 13321, SF 13089
(Fig. 15.2, B)

Hollow copper alloy ring; made of two U-shaped strips riveted together; despite the effects of metal wastage on one side and encrustations on the other the plan of the ring is asymmetrical. Two pin rivets are visible, others may be buried under the encrustations. There is no sign of any filling in the ring. The ring is badly corroded and fragile with some metal loss. About a quarter of the circumference is thickly encrusted with iron-rich material with a 'dried mud' surface over a thin layer of copper and tin compounds. Outer diameter 53 mm; inner 37 mm; section 8-10 mm.
Composition: 0.02% Fe; 0.02% Co; 0.17% Ni; 88.49% Cu; 0.34% As; 0.54% Sb; 8.14% Sn; 0.12% Ag; 0.01% Bi; 1.68% Pb; 0.46% S.

It was initially hoped that this ring could have been sampled in such a way that the microstructure could have been recorded, as well as the composition of the ring and the rivets. In the end the piece proved too fragile for this, so only the composition of one section of the ring was recorded.

Generically hollow rings could be a product of either the late Bronze Age or the Iron Age. Late Bronze Age rings, though, are most likely to have been cast in one piece and retain either their core or be filled with another material, now corroded, such as lead. Examples are the hollow rings in the Parc-y-meirch (Abergele), Clwyd, hoard (Savory 1976). Hollow rings made either from sheet rolled into a tube or in two halves riveted or crimped together seem much more of an Iron Age phenomenon. Where a filling survives it tends to be corroded iron; where a filling is absent it could be that it was organic and has rotted away, or even that there was never a filling at all. Examples of both can be found in the Llyn Cerrig Bach, Ynys Môn deposit (Savory 1976; Lynch 1991), and at Danebury (Cunliffe and Poole 1991b, 329, 332, no. 1.95).

However, the Yarnton hollow ring is of a very specific type widely paralleled on the Continent. The type as a whole has been catalogued by Raftery (1988) who recorded around 200 examples around Europe, but there are only five other examples from the British Isles. Raftery divides the rings into Type 1, in which the two halves are riveted together with three (sometimes two) rivets, while Type 2 has no rivets, the two parts perhaps being glued together with an organic core. The Yarnton ring is of Type 1 and almost certainly had three rivets. Raftery shows that the rings can be dated to the middle La Tène period, in Continental terms from late La Tène A through to La Tène C. Towards the end of this period the unriveted form becomes dominant. Raftery (1984; 1988) showed that these hollow rings are, on the Continent, most frequently found in graves where their association is often with the belt. It could be that the rings are connected with the suspension of a scabbard but some seem too fragile for that.

Among the examples from these Islands, a group of three Type 1 rings was found at Lisnacrogher, Co. Antrim, Ireland, one with three rivets, and two smaller ones with two. As the area of Lisnacrogher has also yielded four scabbards there may be some support for the idea of the scabbard connection (Raftery 1984, 105-7). In England one was found in a female grave at Kirkburn, East Yorkshire (Stead 1991, 92, 224 and fig. 69). The woman was found to be 17-25 years old and buried with the remains of a new-born baby. The grave goods comprised a copper alloy stud, a jet bead and an amber bead, as well as the hollow ring. All were found around the neck or head. A 3rd century BC date is given for the grave, which fits with the Continental chronology. The final example from England is from the eastern plateau in the hillfort at South Cadbury, Somerset in a context roughly contemporary with the Kirkburn ring (O'Connor and Foster 2000, 194-6, fig. 99.11).

The South Cadbury example has been analysed (Northover 2000) and was found to be made of a similar bronze (with an As>Co>Ni impurity pattern) to the bronze strip discussed above. This could be used to argue that the ring was made in Britain, while Raftery (1984) sees the Lisnacrogher rings as direct imports from the Continent to Ireland. Although the composition is certainly strong support for British manufacture of the South Cadbury ring it should be noted that the same type of bronze was found in sheet form in middle Iron Age cauldrons from La Tène itself. The Yarnton ring is different and has an impurity pattern with Sb>As and a small percentage of lead, indeed very similar to the late Bronze Age awl from the same feature (Northover forthcoming). This pattern does occur in the Iron Age as well, with examples mainly in East Anglia and Essex (eg Snettisham, Sheepen (Stone 1987)) and southern England (eg Danebury), with a scatter of examples further west. The date range would appear to be 3rd-1st century BC, and the closest parallels are from Sheepen, Colchester, Essex, and Snettisham, Norfolk. In those contexts the metal could well be imported from the Continent.

Floodplain Site 9 context 13221, SF 13087
(Fig. 15.2, C)

Thick steel penannular ring hot-dipped in bronze to close ring and to plate it; surface now has a rusty patina. Diameter 33 mm, thickness 10 mm.
Composition (bronze coat) 0.96% Fe; 0.01% Co; 0.05% Ni; 85.17% Cu; 0.06% Zn; 0.44% As; 0.06% Sb; 12.45% Sn; 0.07% Ag; 0.01% Bi; 0.11% Pb; 0.03% S.

The core of the ring was largely composed of a well-made slightly hypoeutectoid steel with some Widmannstätten ferrite and a rather low slag content. The round-section steel bar was forged into a penannular ring with the two ends close together. The ring was then hot-dipped in molten bronze: molten bronze very readily reacts with the iron, being a strong solvent for it. When removed from the molten bronze, the bronze not only coated the entire surface but has brazed the open ends of the ring together. The bronze/steel interface has the classic outline of a hot-dipped structure.

Hot-dipping iron or steel in bronze is now well-attested in Iron Age metalwork in Britain. The structure of one example, from Maiden Castle, has been analysed in detail and published (Northover and Salter 1990). Excellent examples can be found at sites ranging from Llyn Cerrig Bach, Ynys Môn to Bury Hill, Hampshire (Northover unpublished). There is no clear pattern to the contexts in which bronzed iron objects are deposited. There is a strong element of ritual at Llyn Cerrig Bach, but deposition at a site like Bury Hill or Danebury does not offer us that sense.

Discussion

The Iron Age causeway produced three metal objects each of Bronze Age and Iron Age date, the latter of which have been identified and characterised above. They include one weapon, a side-looped spearhead, one tool, an awl, and four ornaments in different materials. It is no coincidence that the site most often put forward as offering parallels for the Yarnton objects is Flag Fen, Peterborough (Pryor 2001). There the vast majority of a wide range of objects from the middle Bronze Age through to the end of the pre-Roman Iron Age was deposited in wet ground or open water around a post alignment and walkway across open water to a large timber platform.

Most of the metalwork was found to the southern side of the post alignment between the platform and dry land on the Fengate side. There is some patterning with both time and type of object with, for example pins being strongly biased towards drier ground. Most importantly, Flag Fen shows an even more catholic range of objects with tools, weapons, ornaments and possibly votives as well. A striking difference, however, is how much more the late Bronze Age is represented at Flag Fen; at Yarnton the latest Bronze Age objects, the awl and the tin strap-end, need be no later than the beginning of the 10th century BC, after which there is a gap until perhaps as late as the 3rd century BC. Flag Fen has pieces which fill much of that gap.

Two of the Yarnton objects, one Bronze Age – the tin alloy strap-end, and one Iron Age – the hollow ring, have the potential to be exotics imported from the continent. This can be seen at Flag Fen with a French-style scabbard chape (Coombs 2001, no. 38) and the tin objects. It can also be seen at another wetland site with a tin object, Caldicot Castle, where there is an Urnfield scabbard chape, unique for Britain (Northover 1997). Both utilitarian and ornamental, we can see the Yarnton bronzes as deliberately deposited (despite the lack of clear contexts for three of them). They relate to activity at the site from the middle of the middle Bronze Age into the beginning of the late Bronze Age (using traditional British chronology), and in the middle Iron Age. What importance the site had in the full late Bronze Age and the earliest Iron Age, the metalwork cannot tell us.

TECHNOLOGICAL INVESTIGATION OF ROMAN IRONWORK *by Brian Gilmour*

Introduction

Four objects from the Roman phases of two Yarnton sites were examined using metallographic analysis to determine how they were made, to identify the type of iron or steel used, and to give an assessment of their quality and condition when lost or discarded, assuming they were not intentionally placed where they were found (as seems likely for the much earlier Iron Age adze described above). In general the ironwork from these two sites did not survive in very good condition. The objects featured in this investigation were some of the more notable exceptions, separated from the rest mainly by X-ray study. First to be examined was a small broken knife from Cresswell Field and then three objects from Yarnton (YWRF), the broken hilt end of a larger knife and two punches. The structures of the knife blades were compared to a previously published series of knife blade construction types (Tylecote and Gilmour 1986, 6, fig. 1).

Metallographic Analysis

Knife. Pit 7961 (7960), late Roman

The surviving fragment of this small knife (see Allen ('Ironwork' above) No. 4; Fig. 15.17) measured 82 mm in length and consisted of the tang (32 mm long)

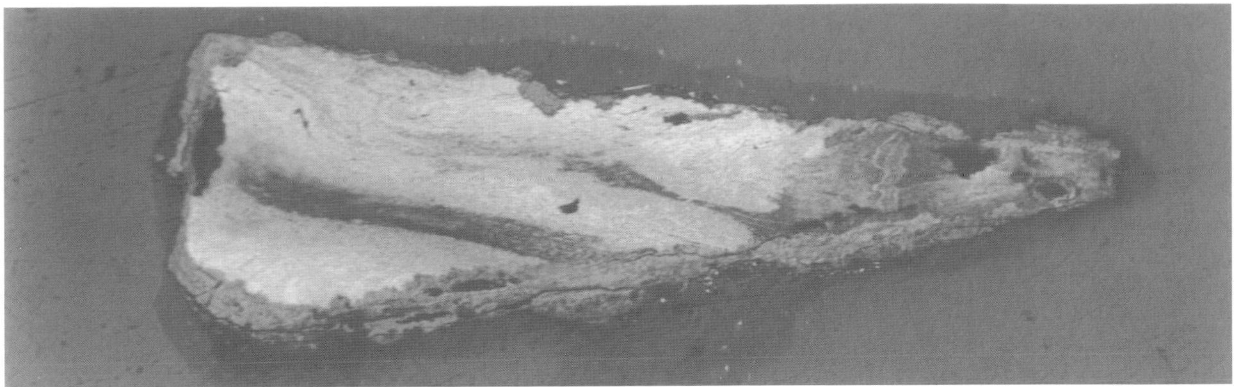

Fig. 15.17 Metallographic analysis; photograph of transverse section of iron knife tip from late Roman pit 7961

and approximately two thirds to three quarters of the original, plain, undecorated blade. This blade fragment survived in relatively good condition under what appeared to be generally surface corrosion with some heavier pitting. As far as could be seen from what survived it would appear that the end of the blade snapped off in use and the remainder of the knife was discarded. A complete transverse section (HM 75) was cut from the broken end and this was mounted for metallographic analysis.

Analysis showed the knife blade overall to be a fairly clear example of a Type 2a blade with a medium to high (0.5-0.8%) carbon steel cutting edge tip butt-welded (ie with weld at right angles to each side of the blade) to an iron back (Figs 15.17 and 15.18). This method for incorporating steel to form the cutting edge of an iron blade is more economical than most but has the disadvantage that the blade becomes virtually useless once the narrow, butt-welded steel strip has been abraded away. However, that point does not seem to have been reached on this blade, which appears to have broken beforehand. The dark-etched martensitic structure of the welded-on steel part shows that the blade was quenched, probably in cold water, and lightly tempered (gently re-heated to relieve stresses in the quenched steel), or that quenching was incompletely carried out in the first place. If this was the case then the red hot blade would just have been lightly dipped in water, possibly just along the cutting edge, allowing residual heat from the thicker back part to flow back into the cutting edge part. This may well have been a commonly preferred method (?of this smith) of ensuring a hardened but not too brittle cutting edge.

In this case, however, the larger back part of the blade did not just consist of a low carbon or plain iron but presented a much more complex and confusing structure, suggesting that a fragment of an earlier small knife (or perhaps a piece of blade from a pair of shears) was incorporated into this part of the later knife. This is visible here as a wedge shape in the lower left part of the section (Fig. 15.17) and as shown in the diagrammatic view of the section (Fig. 15.18). The earlier blade would appear to have been a Type 1a blade made by welding a

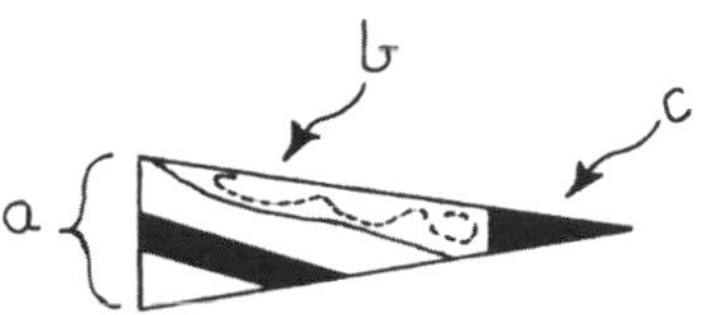

Fig. 15.18 Metallographic analysis; interpretative drawing of transverse section of iron knife tip from late Roman pit 7961

comparatively narrow steel strip (the thicker dark band in the lower left part of Fig. 15.17) between two thicker pieces of plain iron. It would appear to have previously been rendered useless as a knife blade by having been worn away unevenly – too much on one side – probably by ill-judged sharpening, so that the steel in the middle no longer formed the cutting edge.

The very convoluted and mixed structure of other half of the back of the later knife blade suggests that this part too consists of re-cycled iron, although not reused in quite the same way. Here it would appear that a piece of iron containing some steel (possibly something like another small knife or shears blade) was re-forged into a small bar which was then welded to a thin bar of steel which would eventually form the cutting edge. The reworking of the metal used for the back of the blade has resulted in extensive carbon diffusion from the steel to the iron parts. The re-used piece of earlier knife blade and the rest of this recycled composite piece appears to have been hammer-welded together, then the steel cutting edge added, after which the complete piece would have been forged out to give the shape of the later knife. It is quite likely that this later knife broke along a flaw left in the blade during the welding together of re-cycled bits of earlier objects.

Knife. SF 52, corn-drying oven 47, late Roman

All that remained of this once large knife was a single fragment consisting of the tang (92 mm in length) and a short (50 mm) length of what had been a much longer blade measuring 30 mm in

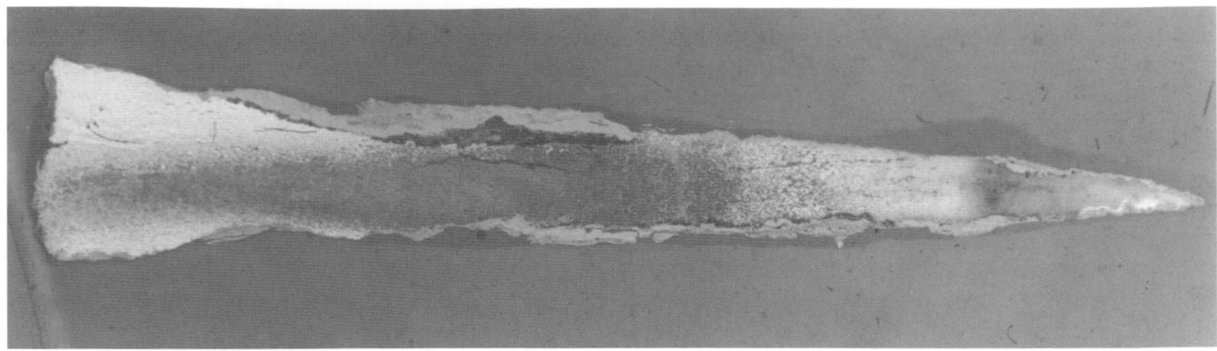

Fig. 15.19 Metallographic analysis; photograph of transverse section of iron knife SF 52 from late Roman corn drier 47

width towards the tang (Fig. 15.3, No. 10). Like the previous example this knife was broken, snapped at right angles across the blade, before it was lost or discarded. From X-ray it was clear that the core metal of this blade survived quite well, although the surface was fairly heavily corroded on both sides. On both X-ray and on the corroded surface, traces of a narrow double groove were visible running down the blade near the back on one side, with what appeared to be a corresponding, slightly wider, single groove on the other side.

A complete transverse section (HM 76) cut from the broken end of the blade was mounted for metallographic examination. This showed the blade to be a clear example of a Type 1 construction, with a larger central piece, probably of medium carbon steel, sandwiched between two smaller pieces of iron (Figs 15.19 and 15.20). Although they have partly corroded away it is clear that these outer iron pieces were only welded to the steel central piece along the back half of the blade. Extensive carbon diffusion outwards across the welds with the central steel part means that it is now difficult to gauge to what extent the outer pieces were originally relatively carbon-free plain iron.

The even appearance of both the iron and steel parts, as well as the orientation and distribution of the slag present, suggests that none of the metal of this blade is recycled. It is clear from the section that at least two thirds of the original knife was made of good quality medium carbon steel (with a carbon content estimated at approximately 0.5-0.6%). The iron of the outer parts also appears to have been of good quality with its relatively low and well distributed content of slag as well as its overall even structure, apart from the effects of carbon diffusion which would not have affected the properties in any deleterious way. If only good quality iron and steel had been used one might ask why this knife snapped off near the hilt, especially when the quality appears to have been good?

Almost certainly this was the result of inadequate heat-treatment for the proportion of steel used. Towards the tip of the cutting edge the steel part of the blade shows a pale martensitic, as-quenched structure indicating that the blade was quenched in water but not subsequently tempered. Approximately two fifths of the central steel portion of the blade shows up as this very hard, brittle martensitic structure. Further towards the back of the blade the martensitic structure gives way progressively to a very dark etching structure with the distinctive appearance of radial pearlite, inevitable where the central part of a blade like this cools at a slightly, but critically, slower rate that the thinner parts. However, there is no evidence of auto-tempering, indicating that quenching was complete, (ie no subsequent transfer of residual heat was possible between the thicker and thinner parts of the blade). It would appear likely that in this case the blade broke as a direct result of imperfect heat treatment, ie the blade was quenched but not tempered, to relieve internal stress in the steel. This would have been critical given the high proportion of steel used for the blade. The end result would have left the blade very brittle and liable to break, perhaps even if dropped.

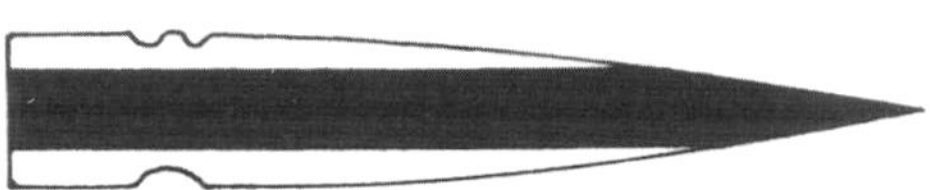

Fig. 15.20 Metallographic analysis; interpretative drawing of transverse section of iron knife SF 52 from late Roman corn drier 47

Punch. SF 178, pit 516, late Roman

This largely complete punch measured 122 mm in length although the irregular shape of the narrow end suggests that about 10 mm or so of the tip is missing, most probably broken off during use. For most of its length the shank of this tool is parallel-sided (roughly square in section measuring 9 mm across, but with chamfered corners) before tapering down towards the broken end. The wider end is slightly splayed out from being struck with a hammer during use (Fig. 15.3, No. 11). Two longitudinal sections (HM 77) were cut from this punch, the main one (about 20 mm long) from the tip end, plus a shorter second section cut from the thicker striking end to check for consistency of structure along the whole length. Metallographic analysis on

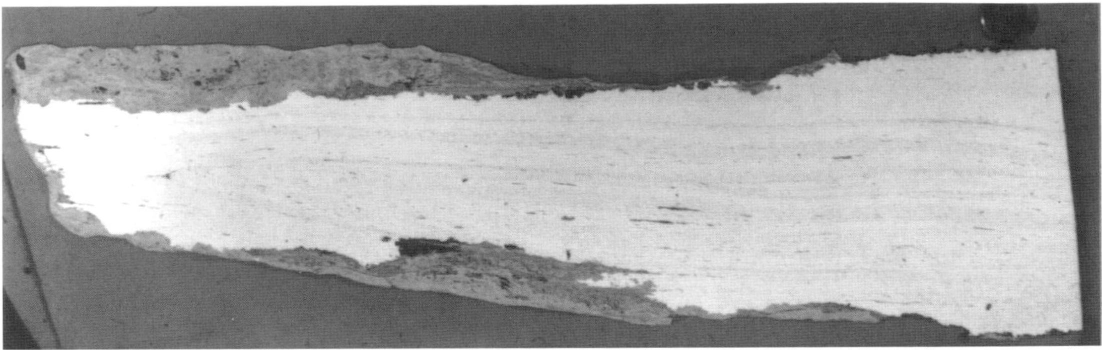

Fig. 15.21 Metallographic analysis; photograph of transverse section of iron punch SF 178 from late Roman pit 516

Fig. 15.22 Metallographic analysis; interpretative drawing of transverse section of iron punch SF 178 from late Roman pit 516

these showed the whole surviving length of the punch to have been made of just one piece of metal. In section this gave a very distinctive striated appearance with narrow, longitudinal grey bands interleaved between similarly narrow, very pale bands (Fig 15.21).

Over much of the length this striated structure is divided into three bands by welds just visible in section as slightly increased concentrations of entrapped slag particles. The central band, however, tapers so that the outer two bands meet just short of the surviving tip of the punch. In section this junction is marked by a tell-tale, larger triangular shaped entrapped slag inclusion. In addition to the striated appearance most of the entrapped slag present in the metal is very elongated in appearance and the overall concentration quite low. These factors indicate that the iron used for the punch was extensively forged before, probably, being folded along its length from both ends and the whole piece welded back together.

The use of this technique is suggested by the greater elongation of some of the slag. It is less likely that the welds simply represented internal welds within a rather less extensively forged piece of consolidated bloom iron. Either way the striated appearance is not the result of piling (the repeated folding and forging to give a multi-layered appearance, erroneously suggested for objects with this appearance even where there is no evidence for welds). Most probably the striated appearance is due to the use of iron from a bloom with an irregular, but locally relatively high, phosphorus content. In many parts of the bloom the phosphorus content was clearly low enough to allow some carburisation in those areas.

A bloom of such irregular composition would, when consolidated and forged out, give much the kind of structure seen here. Phosphorus enrichment in parts of the original bloom would have prevented carbon absorption in those areas, and would also have prevented carbon diffusion during later heating and forging of the metal. A striated appearance like the one seen here could not exist without the presence of phosphorus-rich areas which would yield a banded appearance when forged out mainly in one direction. The presence of phosphorus in these bands would subsequently prevent carbon diffusion from the adjacent carbon-containing bands. The carbon content of the bands, with their grey appearance in section, was quite low, not much more than approximately 0.1% at most, but evenly distributed, again indicating fairly extensive heating and forging since the bloom stage.

The surviving punch has clearly corroded this way and not been broken since. Equally clearly the iron from which the punch is made would not have been much use for the tip end which would have bent or blunted quickly or easily. In its present form the punch would have been useless for work on any hard materials for which an iron-shanked tool like this would seem most likely. This and the irregular broken appearance of the tip end of this punch suggest that a welded-on steel tip is missing. This is likely to have broken off along a defective scarf weld attaching it to the shank, as shown in Figure 15.22.

Punch. SF 192, Posthole 609, late Roman

This more-or-less complete punch measured 103 mm in length but in this case about 20 to 30 mm is estimated to have been lost, broken off from the narrower end (Fig. 15.3, No. 12). The shank was again parallel sided along much of its length (again with a square section, chamfered at the corners, but

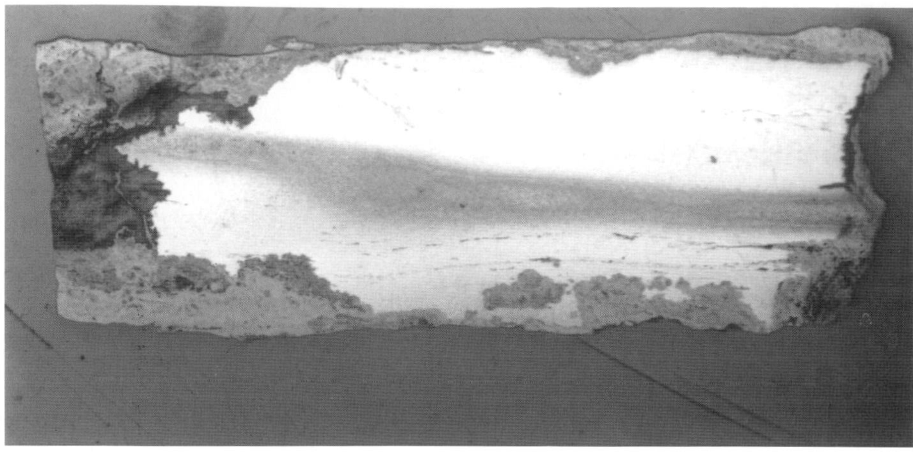

Fig. 15.23 Metallographic analysis; photographs of longditudinal and transverse sections of iron punch SF 192 from late Roman posthole 609

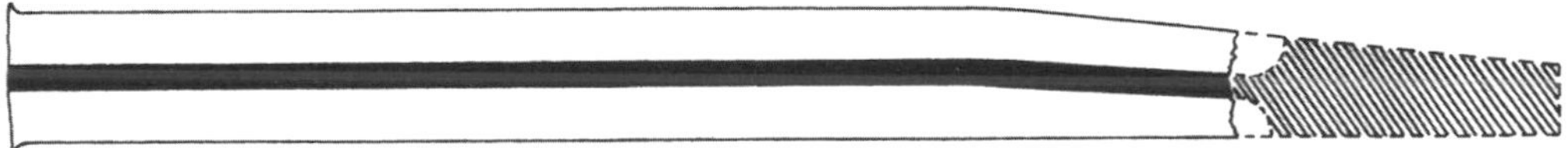

Fig. 15.24 Metallographic analysis; interpretative drawing of transverse section of iron punch SF 192 from late Roman posthole 609

this time measuring approximately 11 mm across) tapering towards the broken end. Again the wide end is slightly splayed out from being struck with a hammer during use. As before, two longitudinal sections (HM 78) were cut from this punch, the main one (approximately 15 mm long) from the tip end, plus a shorter second section cut from the thicker striking end to check for consistency of structure along the whole length. Metallographic analysis showed a structure rather different from that seen in the previous punch. Here the structure was of two pieces of plain iron for the most part with a very little, irregularly dispersed carbon. Between these two pieces of iron had been welded a narrow strip of high carbon steel (Fig. 15.23).

The iron used for this punch is quite different in character to that used for the previous punch, SF 178, the main difference being that the phosphorus content in SF 192 appears to be very low. This is indicated by the generally uneven distribution of what little carbon there is across the iron parts – no striated appearance this time – as well as the considerable carbon diffusion outwards across the welds between the central steel strip and the iron pieces on either side, the welds being marked by narrow white lines, possibly the result of arsenic enrichment during welding.

Much of the steel shows a nearly eutectoid, lamellar pearlite structure from which a slightly varying carbon content (0.7-0.9%) can be estimated. This structure also shows no evidence for any heat treatment having been used on this punch. As it stands the narrow central band of high carbon steel makes little sense in terms of this having been a practical tool, unless this simply is all that remains of a piece of steel that would have thickened out further down to form a high carbon steel tip, now missing (as suggested in the reconstruction diagram, Fig. 15.24). The way the object has corroded suggests that the tip broke off during use and the tool was put on one side or discarded without being re-tipped. If a repair of this kind was intended it clearly never happened. The reason for the failure of this punch is now difficult to judge, but perhaps is most likely to have been the result of defective welding.

Discussion and conclusions

The two knives featured in this report contrast greatly both in terms of their size, and in the way both iron and steel has been used in their construction. Both knives were provided with at least a hardened steel tip to the cutting edge that would therefore hold its sharpened edge better. The small knife from Cresswell Field is very interesting and unusual in that the back of the blade, to which the steel forming the tip of the cutting edge was welded, appears to be a very clear example of the use of recycled iron, into which has been incorporated at least a fragment of an earlier small knife (or shears) blade. The steel tip, butt-welded to the rest of the blade, is almost certainly not recycled, but does represent very economical use of an expensive stock metal.

In contrast the (?later) large knife from Yarnton (Worton Rectory Farm) showed no sign of any recycled iron having been used. The almost excessive use of steel for this much larger knife may suggest that steel was much more readily available or affordable on this site at this time, or this knife may simply just be a higher status product, even if the final smithing work (the heat-treatment of the blade) may have been defective. In the 14th century steel in this country may generally have been around five times as expensive as (plain or low carbon) iron, this being the case at least for metal imported into Britain from Spain in this period (Salzman 1952, 286 and 288). No comparable estimates have been made for late Roman Britain, but similar figures may well hold good as steel must always have been a much more specialised product and hence much more expensive.

Although the two punches were found in different contexts at Yarnton, the similarity in the way the shanks of these two tools have been shaped, especially their cross-sectional profile, suggests either that this was a common form for (late) Romano-British smith's punches, or that these two punches originally belonged to the same tool-kit. The overall dimensions are similar to those of other known metalworking punches (as in Manning 1985, A29, 10 and pl. 6). Given the nature of the site they are probably to be identified as smith's rather than stone mason's punches. However, it seems highly unlikely that they would have been effective as tools of this kind without steel tips, and – even allowing for subsequent corrosion – the ragged appearance of the narrower ends strongly suggests they would originally have been longer. It seems highly probable that both punches were lost, possibly simply discarded, as a consequence of the tips having broken off during use.

It seems clear that at one time all four of these objects are likely to have been serviceable tools and all four have been rendered useless by being broken. This was not the case, however, for the early Iron Age (probable wood-working) adze head described in the report above. It appears to have been placed intentionally, as a complete object, (though whether with or without its haft is unclear) as a votive offering at the base of a pit. The particularly soft iron from which this adze was made would not have provided at all a serviceable cutting edge. It would soon have blunted even when used on wood. Clearly no attempt had been made to provide any form of steel cutting edge, nor was there any evidence that the iron at the edge had been work hardened. This raises the possibility that this could be an example of a tool made as a votive offering rather than a working tool, using soft iron in the correct shape for an adze, but not provided with any durable working edge. Only further technological work on tools like this, and of this period, is likely to shed light on this problem.

Chapter 16: Human Remains

by Angela Boyle

INTRODUCTION

The human remains range in date from the late Bronze Age through to the Roman period, though the bulk of the material is of Iron Age date. The assemblage is dealt with chronologically in this chapter.

A small assemblage of material of early Iron Age date was recovered during excavations at Cresswell Field in 1995. The assemblage comprised an adult female skull aged 26-35 years with caries and an associated abscess from pit 8591 (8592), the distal half of a neonate humerus from pit 7029 (7059), the midshaft of a probable adult ulna from stakehole 7644, and a mixed deposit of burnt animal and well-calcined possible human bone from posthole 7018 (7017) within which a single fragment of probable human femur was identified. The skull is an interesting addition to the emerging picture of Iron Age burial practices in the Thames valley. There is some suggestion that the cremated bone may actually derive from Iron Age rather than Bronze Age contexts. This would be significant as Iron Age cremations are largely unknown in the Thames valley.

The middle Iron Age assemblage comprised a total of 34 individuals from Yarnton (YWRF). A further two skeletons (Group A: 412 and 1683) were lost prior to skeletal analysis. The cemetery appears to comprise two distinct groups, northern (Group B) and southern (Group C) respectively. The gap between the groups was only 20 m and this could partly be a result of poor retrieval in the intervening area, although it is also possible that the two groups belonged to different family units. A further 10 inhumations have been described as 'outliers' (Group A) and these were scattered along the southern and eastern edge of the settlement. In addition there were seven deposits of disarticulated bone from Iron Age contexts (summarised in Table 16.7).

Radiocarbon dates were obtained from five burials in the northern group (Group B: 2569, 2710, 2713, 2717 and 2718), two southern burials (Group C: 2041 and 2069) and two from outlying burials (Group A: 376 and 1681). A detailed discussion of the radiocarbon dates which appear in Table 16.1 has already been published elsewhere (Hey *et al.* 1999; see Chapter 13 above).

The Roman assemblage comprised five skeletons from Yarnton (2005, 2006, 2016, 2039 and 2053) and two from the Yarnton-Cassington evaluation (239/5, 239/7). There were also two cremation burials (767 and 2534). Material from a further three cremation burials (173, 174 and 2501) could not be located during analysis. The cremated Roman material is summarised in Table 16.10. Two of the adult skeletons from Yarnton were radiocarbon dated. Skeleton 2005 produced a date of cal AD 130-325 (UB-3921; 95% confidence) and skeleton 2016 (grave 2017) produced a date of cal AD 240-385 (UB-3777; 95% confidence). The burials were located in the same area as the southern group of Iron Age burials. A further 11 deposits of disarticulated material from Roman contexts (Table 16.14) may be redeposited Iron Age material.

METHODOLOGY

Adult individuals were aged by combining a number of different methods: pubic symphyseal ageing (Katz and Suchey 1986, 69), auricular surface ageing (Lovejoy *et al.* 1985) and dental

Table 16.1: Radiocarbon results and calibrated date ranges for Iron Age burials.

Laboratory number	*Context number*	*Context description*	*Radiocarbon age (BP)*	*$\delta^{13}C$ ( )*	*Calibrated date range (95% confidence)*
UB-3776	SK 1681	Unknown position & orientation, E outlier	2250±21	-20.6±0.2	395-240 cal BC
UB-3778	SK 2717	Crouched, E-W orientated, N group	2207±21	-20.3±0.2	380-195 cal BC
UB-3779	SK 2713	Unknown position, N-S orientated, N group	2224±21	-20.0±0.2	385-200 cal BC
UB-3782	SK 376/2	Crouched, N-S orientated, E outlier	2237±20	-20.0±0.2	390-205 cal BC
UB-3919	SK 2710	Extended, N-S orientated, N group	2168±21	-20.0±0.2	360-165 cal BC
UB-3920	SK 2718	Crouched, N-S orientated, N group	2234±20	-19.9±0.2	390-205 cal BC
UB-3922	SK 2069	Crouched, NNW-SSE orientated, S group	2268±20	-20.0±0.2	395-260 cal BC
UB-3923	SK 2041	Crouched, N-S orientated, S group	2267±22	-19.9±0.2	395-255 cal BC
UB-3924	SK 2569	Crouched, N-S orientated, N group	2220±23	-20.0±0.2	385-195 cal BC

Table 16.2: Summary of Iron Age burials. Skeleton numbers in ***bold*** *are those that have been radiocarbon dated*

Grave group	*Skeleton no*	*Sex*	*Age*	*Stature*	*Caries*	*Abscess*	*Ante-mortem tooth loss*	*Vertebral osteo-arthritis*	*Meric index*	*Cnemic index*	*Non-metric variation*	*Other dental anomaly*	*Other pathology*
A	133	M	prime adult (26-35 y)	1.593	0/5	0/8	1/8					calculus, mild attrition	healed fracture of right radius and ulna; benign osteochondroma
A	135	-	40.5107+/-1.87 weeks										
A	376/1	M	prime adult (26-35 y)					X					
A	**376/2**	M?	adult (18+ y)	1.724	0/14	0/22	2/22		71.85	80.6		mild calculus, moderate alveolar recession	?localised infection of right calcaneus, could be trauma, ?crush fracture
A	412	-	infant										
A	496	-	40.9004+/-1.87 weeks										
A	719	-	neonate										
A	1346	-	child 1 (1-5 y)										
B	1396	M?	prime adult (26-35 y)					X	68.75	70.96	lambdoid wormian		
B	1397	F	prime adult (26-35 y)	1.583	0/3	0/4	1/4					impaction, abscess	sacro-iliac ankylosis, right side only
A	**1681**	M	ageing adult (45+ y)	1.674	1/7	1/20	11/20		78.1			moderate alveolar recession	healed fracture of right scapula
A	1682	M	adult (18+ y)	1.780	1/7	0/15	5/15	X				marked alveolar recession	
A	1683 missing												
C	2021	?	adult (18+ y)					X		75			
C	2022	M	prime adult (26-35 y)	1.639	2/30	0/32	1/32	X	68.57	55.5	lambdoid wormians parietal foramen, septal aperture	mild calculus	exostosis on right tibia
C	2025	?	prime adult (26-35 y)	1.655 M 1.625 F									lipping of right femoral head
C	2026	M	adult (18+ y)		2/7	0/10	3/10	X	62.5				
C	2028	F?	adult (18+ y)	1.543				X	75 R 70 L				
C	2033	M?	adult (18+ y)										
C	**2041**	-	juvenile (13-15 y)		0/16	0/22	0/22	X				mild calculus, impaction, splaying, microdontia	
C	2048	?	?adult (18+ y)										
C	2051	-	child 2 (6-11 y)		0/4	0/4	0/4						
C	**2069**	-	juvenile (13-14 y)		1/28	0/32	0/32					retarded eruption, impaction, crowding, rotation	
B	**2569**	M?	young adult (18-25 y)	1.695	2/27	1/28	0/28	X	64.7 R	67.74 R			

B	2709	F?	adult (18+)		3/19	1/23	0/23			64.7 L	lambdoid x wormians, sagittal wormians	heavy attrition	
B	**2710**	F	young adult (18-25 y)	1.601	0/7	0/8	0/8		74.35 R	65.51 R	lambdoid wormians, partial sacralisation of lv5, lv3 has separate neural arch		cribra orbitalia
B	2711	F?	prime adult (26-35 y)	1.573	0/7	0/7	0/7	X				moderate calculus	
B	2712	-	child 2 (5-7 y)		0/20	0/?	0/20						cribra orbitalia
B	**2713**	F	prime adult (26-35 y)	1.616	2/22	0/30	3/30					mild calculus	
B	2714	-	juvenile (12-13 y)		1/11	0/16	0/16				lambdoid wormians	mild calculus, enamel hypoplasia	cribra orbitalia
B	2715	-	juvenile (13-15 y)		0/4	0/4	0/4					mild calculus	
B	2716	M	adult (18+ y)					X		52.5 R			
B	**2717**	M	adult (18+ y)		3/14	1/32	14/32					marked alveolar recession	cribra orbitalia, osteo-arthritis affecting left wrist
B	**2718**	-	juvenile (14-17 y)		0/30	0/30	0/30						
B	2719	-	juvenile (13-17 y)		1/17	0/20	0/20						
B	2720	F?	prime adult (26-35 y)					X					healed fracture of right clavicle

attrition (Brothwell 1981, 72). Ribs did not tend to survive well so ageing by examination of sternal rib end morphology (Iscan and Loth 1986) was not used. Subadults were aged according to degree of epiphyseal fusion, long bone length (Scheuer *et al.* 1980; Workshop 1980; Brothwell 1981; Bass 1987), dental development and eruption (van Beek 1983). The sexing of adult individuals was based on pelvic and skull morphology and metric data (Workshop 1980). In keeping with standard practice no attempt was made to sex subadults. Age estimation of the very young infants from the evaluation was based on a combination of methods (Fazekas and Kosa 1966; Scheuer *et al.* 1980; Scheuer and MacLauglin-Black 1994; Black and Scheuer 1996). The regression equations of Scheuer *et al.* (1980) allow the gestational age (from the first day of the last menstrual period) of perinatal infants to be estimated to within about two weeks using long bone lengths. The ages of both the Iron Age and Roman infants from Yarnton were all within 38-40 weeks. It has been argued elsewhere that where such a pattern occurs infanticide is the most probable explanation as it was generally carried out immediately after birth (Smith and Kahila 1992; Mays 1993). Analysis of a small group of seven infants from Stanwick Roman villa, Northants. revealed a similar pattern (Boyle 2001b). In contrast the infant burials from excavations at Springhead Roman small town, Kent, ranged in age from approximately 30-44 weeks (Boyle nd.). Stature of adults was calculated using the regression formulae of Trotter and Gleser (1952, 1958; reproduced in Brothwell 1981, 101). The dental notation employed was as follows:

/	post mortem loss	x	ante mortem loss
c	caries	a	abscess
np	not present	u	unerupted
e	erupting	pe	pulp exposed
k	calculus	-	alveolus and tooth absent

Cremated bone

The cremated bone from each context was passed through a sieve stack of 10, 5 and 2 mm mesh size. In each of the sieved groups, the bones were examined in detail and where possible sorted into identifiable bone groups, which were defined as skull (including mandible and dentition), axial (clavicle, scapula, ribs, vertebra and pelvic elements), lower limb and upper limb. This may elucidate any deliberate bias in the skeletal elements collected for burial. Each of the samples was weighed on digital scales and details of colour and largest fragment were recorded. Where possible, the presence of individual bones within each of the groups was noted.

Estimate of adult age has been based on cranial suture closure (Meindl and Lovejoy 1985), degenerative changes to the auricular surface (Lovejoy *et al.* 1985) and pubic symphysis (Brooks and Suchey

1990). Estimation of sex is based on isolated features and should therefore be viewed as tentative. In the case of cremation burial 767 the sexually dimorphic traits are contradictory: the surviving portion of the pubic symphysis appears female while the skull is more masculine. The age estimate for cremation burial 2534 is based on the surviving dentition (van Beek 1983).

IRON AGE HUMAN SKELETAL MATERIAL

Assemblage composition

Assemblage composition is summarised in Tables 16.2-3. It was possible to assign sex to 18 of the 22 adults: there were 8 males, 4 possible males, 3 females and 3 possible females. The age breakdown was: 3 neonates, 3 infants, 6 juveniles, 2 young adults, 9 prime adults and 1 ageing adult. A further 10 individuals could only be assigned to a broad adult category (18+ years). Subadult mortality does not appear to have been particularly high. Other fragmentary human bone from Iron Age contexts is listed in Table 16.7 at the end of the catalogue.

The radiocarbon dates (Table 16.1) suggest that the Iron Age cemetery at Yarnton was in use for a relatively restricted period, perhaps up to 50 years, or two generations. If the cemetery represents a cross-section of the population, and if over this period of time all dead people were buried here, a good working hypothesis might be that it represents the burials from two or three families of around six to eight people. This would certainly be consistent with the archaeological evidence which indicated two or three foci for buildings within the settlement area excavated. At Owslebury, where 70 burials ranging in date from middle Iron Age to early post-conquest (just over 150 years) were excavated, it has been suggested that no more than two nuclear families were represented (Collis 1994, 108).

Table 16.3: Iron Age skeletons: age and sex composition

Age range	*Male*	*Male?*	*Female*	*Female?*	*Uncertain*	*Total*
foetus (before birth)						
neonate (birth-11 m)						3
child 1 (1-5 y)						1
child 2 (6-11 y)						2
juvenile (12-17 y)						5
young adult (18-25 y)		1	1			2
prime adult (26-35 y)	3	1	2	2	1	9
mature adult (36-45 y)						
ageing adult (45+ y)	1					1
adult (18+ y)	4	2		2	2	10
Total	8	4	3	4	3	33

Stature

It was possible to calculate stature for 11 adults. The average for six male skeletons was 1.684 m with a range of 1.593-1.780 m; the average for five female skeletons was 1.583 with a range of 1.543-1.616 m. The results have been compared with data from Danebury (Hooper 1984), Poundbury (Molleson 1992), Wetwang Slack (Dawes unpublished), Maiden Castle (Goodman and Morant 1940), Deal (Anderson 1995), various Yorkshire Sites (Stead 1991) and Suddern Farm (Hooper 2000) (see Tables 16.4-5). Male height at Yarnton compares most favourably with Maiden Castle while females compare well with Suddern Farm and with Deal. Roberts and Cox (2003) do not provide data on stature for the Iron Age.

Table 16.4: Adult male stature in Iron Age Britain

Mean Stature	*Range*	*Site*	*Source*
1.645 (n=15) 5′5″	1.570-1.750 5′2″-5′9″	Danebury	Hooper (1984)
1.660 (n=??)	???-1.712 ???-5′7.5″	Poundbury	Molleson (1992)
1.678 (n=122) 5′6.25″	???-???	Wetwang Slack	Dawes (unpub.)
1.686 (n=26) 5′6.5″	1.572-1.812 5′2″-5′11.5″	Maiden Castle	Goodman and Morant (1940)
1.700 (n=8) 5′7″	1.605-1.792 5′3.25″-5′10.75″	Mill Hill, Deal	Anderson (1995)
1.707 (n=23) 5′7″	1.605-1.799 5′2.75″-5′11″	East Yorkshire sites	Stead (1991)
1.684 (n=6) 5′5.2″	1.593-1.780 5′2.3″-5′8.4″	Yarnton	Present report
1.657 (n=8) 5′4.4″	1.527-1.759 5′0.1″-5′7.7″	Suddern Farm	Hooper (2000)

Table 16.5: Adult female stature in Iron Age Britain

Mean Stature	*Range*	*Site*	*Source*
1.564 (n=7) 5′1.75″	1.504-1.602 4′11.75″-5′3.75″	Danebury	Hooper (1984)
1.623 (n=6) 5′4″	1.552-1.686 5′1.25-5′6.5″	Poundbury	Molleson (1992)
1.562 (n=168) 5′1.25″	???-???	Wetwang Slack	Dawes (unpub.)
1.567 (n=16) 5′1.75″	1.450-1.677 4′9″-5′6″	Maiden Castle	Goodman and Morant (1940)
1.580 (n=8) 5′2.25″	1.500-1.610 4′11.25-5′3.5″	Mill Hill, Deal	Anderson (1995)
1.582 (n=49) 5′2.5″	1.499-1.712 4′11.25″-5′7.5″	East Yorkshire sites	Stead (1991)
158.3 (n=5) 5′1.9″	1.513 1.616 5′0.6″-5′3″	Yarnton	Present report
1.568 (n=4) 5′1.4″	1.509-1.607 4′9.5″-5′2.7″	Suddern Farm	Hooper (2000)

Skeletal pathology

Benign osteochondroma

Skeleton 133, an adult male aged 26-35 years, exhibits a benign osteochondroma located on the proximal right femur. Osteochondromas are most commonly benign and primarily occur in people of 10-25 years without any apparent sex prediliction. They are usually located in proximity to the growth plate on the metaphyseal surface of long bones and more than 50% of cases involve the femur or the tibia (Steinbock 1976, 319-22; Ortner and Putschar 1985, 380). An osteochondroma is an ossified exostosis capped by a large layer of cartilage which is undergoing calcification (obviously not evident in archaeological specimens). The osteochondroma stops growing around the end of an individual's growth period. The lesion begins as a rounded outgrowth on the periosteal surface although the final shape is greatly modified by mechanical stress (muscle pull and tendon insertions) in the affected area. In this example the shaft is slightly bent in an anterior direction. The lesion causes functional and cosmetic change; in addition there is the possibility of eventual transformation into a malignant chondrosarcoma. Roberts and Cox (2003, 93) reported a total of four individuals with neoplastic disease in the Iron Age. An adult male from the Isle of Lewis at Galston had an ivory osteoma (Bruce 1986) as did a female from Maiden Castle, Dorset (Goodman and Morant 1940). A meningioma is reported in a female from Mill Hill, Deal (Anderson 1995, fig. 2.20) and another in a female from the east Yorkshire Iron Age sites (Stead 1991).

Sacro-iliac ankylosis

The sacrum of skeleton 1397, an adult female aged 26-35 years, has fused to the right ilium; the ankylosis is unilateral and the left sacro-iliac joint is completely normal. No vertebrae or legs survived and it is therefore not possible to link the ankylosis to a specific pathological condition.

Trauma

Fractures

Skeleton 133, an adult male aged 26-35 years, has a healed midshaft fracture of the right radius and ulna. This is the only example cited by Roberts and Cox (2003, table 2.45) for the Iron Age. The fracture is well remodelled with very little callus surviving; it is most likely to have been a simple fracture. Skeleton 1681, an ageing adult male (45+ years) has a healed fracture of the right scapula. Again, this is the only example cited by Roberts and Cox (ibid.). Skeleton 2720, a very poorly preserved adult aged upwards of 18 years, and very tentatively identified as female, has a healed fracture of the right clavicle close to the medial end. The bone is much shortened and deformed with a maximum length of 118 mm in contrast to the left clavicle which measures 142 mm. A total of 5 individuals out of 252 (CPR 2%) from the East Yorkshire cemeteries had fractured clavicles (Stead 1991). Roberts and Cox reported a total of 28 individuals with fractures which at 4.7% is a decrease on the Bronze Age of 8.6% (2003, 99, table 2.45).

Soft tissue trauma (myositis ossificans traumatica)

An exostosis on the right tibia of skeleton 2022, an adult male aged upwards of 18 years is probably ossified muscle which is the result of localised trauma. The skeletal evidence for trauma is only a very small proportion of the total range of injury that would have affected the population, such as cuts, abrasions and bruises. For the recognition of soft-tissue injury in skeletal remains, it is necessary for calcification or new bone formation to have occurred within the soft tissue (Roberts and Manchester 1995, 66-67). Tendons and muscle attachments to the bones may occasionally ossify as a result of trauma, for example where a haematoma has been generated in the proximity of the injured periosteum (Aufderheide and Rodriguez-Martin 1998, 26). The resulting mass of woven bone is known as myositis ossificans traumatica. It may occur without obvious skeletal injury and after only minor muscle trauma.

Joint disease

Extra-spinal joint disease

Slight osteophytic lipping is present on the right femoral head of skeleton 2025, an unsexed adult aged upwards of 18 years. Roberts and Cox recorded a total of 11 out of 326 afflicted hip joints (2003, table 2.38) in addition to the example from Yarnton.

Osteo-arthritis

Skeleton 2717, an adult male aged upwards of 18 years has mild porosity and eburnation with associated deformation of the distal articular surface of the left ulna. One other example was identified in the East Yorkshire individuals (Stead 1991). Very slight eburnation is also present on the proximal surface of the left radial head of this individual.

Spinal joint disease

Twelve adult skeletons (367/1, 1396, 1682, 2021, 2022, 2026, 2028, 2041, 2569, 2711, 2716 and 2720) exhibit vertebral degeneration in the form of Schmorl's nodes and osteophytes (12/22, TPR 54.5%). This rate is higher than reported by Roberts and Cox (2003, table 2.37). A CPR of 32.8% (137/418, 39 males and 91 females) was given. This is largely comprised of the East Yorkshire group with 25 males and 86 females affected (ibid.).

Metabolic

Cribra orbitalia

Four skeletons (2710, 2712, 2714, 2717) have cribra orbitalia. Skeletons 2710 and 2717 were adults (2/22, CPR 9%) while 2712 was a child and 2714 was a juvenile (2/12, CPR 16.7%). A much higher CPR of 19% for adults in the Iron Age is quoted by Roberts and Cox (2003, table 2.52).

Cribra orbitalia is identified on dry bone as thinning of the compact bone of the orbital roof (the eye socket) in combination with increased porosity. These lesions are believed to reflect the presence of iron deficiency anaemia (Stuart Macadam 1991). Iron deficiency may arise as a result of a number of factors including a lack of iron in the diet, the inability to absorb the iron in the diet (for example a lack of vitamin C makes it harder to absorb iron), parasitic infestation in the gut, malaria, and lead poisoning (*ibid.*).

Dental pathology (Table 16.6)

The prevalence of dental pathology at Yarnton is compared with selected other Iron Age sites (see Table 16.6). The prevalence rates are extremely variable across the sites and for different pathologies. The rates for the East Yorkshire sites are very low (Stead 1991) while those for Gussage All Saints are extremely high (Keepax 1990).

Dental caries

Dental caries was seen to affect the dentition of 11 skeletons (1681, 1682, 2022, 2026, 2069, 2569, 2709, 2713, 2714, 2717 and 2719). Dental caries is a destruction of enamel, dentine and cement resulting from acid production by bacteria in dental plaque, ultimately leading to the formation of a cavity in the crown or root surface. Usually caries progresses slowly (chronic caries) and arrested or remineralizing phases alternate with more active phases, so that a cavity may remain stable for months or years (arrested caries). Rapidly progressive destruction (rampant caries) is rare and characteristically results in the loss of most erupted tooth crowns in a child's mouth (Hillson 1996, 269).

At Yarnton 16 out 169 teeth were affected giving a TPR of 9.5% which is higher than all the sites considered with the exception of Gussage All Saints (54/220 teeth, TPR 24.5%.

Dental abscess

Four skeletons each had a single dental abscess (1681, 2569, 2709 and 2717). The TPR was 1.7% (4

Table 16.6: Prevalence of dental pathology (Iron Age adults only)

	Ante mortem loss			*Caries*			*Abscess*		
Site	*No. affected*	*No. observed*	*TPR%*	*No. affected*	*No. observed*	*TPR%*	*No. affected*	*No. observed*	*TPR%*
Yarnton	39	239	16.3	16	169	9.5	4	239	1.7
Mill Hill, Deal	85	675	12.6	65	521	12.5	25	675	3.7
East Yorkshire	175	8290	2.1	161	7611	2.1	49	8290	0.6
Suddern Farm	53	442	12.0	26	333	7.8	9	442	2.0
Gussage All Saints	75	308	24.3	54	220	24.5	20	308	6.5

out of 239 observable sockets), a rate which is broadly comparable with Suddern Farm (9/442 observable sockets, TPR 2%).

Calculus

Calculus was present on the dentition of eight individuals (133, 376/2, 2022, 2041, 2711, 2713, 2714 and 2715). Calculus is mineralized dental plaque, which accumulates at the base of a living plaque deposit, and is attached to the surface of the tooth. The mineral is deposited from plaque fluid, but ultimately derives from the saliva, and the sites closest to the ducts of the salivary glands – lingual surfaces of anterior teeth and buccal surfaces of molars – show the most abundant calculus formation. It is still unclear how plaque mineralisation is initiated, although bacteria probably have an important role (Hillson 1996, 255-6).

The CPR was 36.4% (8 out of 22 adult individuals). This compares well with the figures provided by Roberts and Cox (2003, table 2.47) which give a CPR of 35.2% (32 out of 91 individuals reported.

Enamel hypoplasia

Enamel hypoplasia affected the dentition of skeleton 2714. The condition is a developmental defect in the enamel of the dentition which can be related to generalised disturbances during the growth period. Although a number of workers have defined methods for estimating the timing of enamel defects (eg Schultz and McHenry 1975; Goodman *et al.* 1980) there are drawbacks and these are discussed elsewhere (Goodman and Rose 1990; Hillson 1996, 172-6).

Ante mortem tooth loss

A total of 9 adults exhibit ante-mortem tooth loss (39/239 teeth, TPR 16.3%). Ageing adult male skeleton 1681 has lost 11 out of 20 while adult male 2717 has lost 14 out of 30. This rate is higher than all the sites considered with the exception of Gussage All Saints (75/308 teeth, TPR 24.4%).

Skeletal anomalies

Spondylolysis and sacralisation

The third lumbar vertebra of skeleton 2710, a young adult female aged 18-25 years, had a separate neural arch (the condition known as spondylolysis). In addition the fifth lumbar vertebra was partially sacralised.

The overall prevalence of spondyloysis in modern populations is 3-7% (Resnick and Niwayama 1981, 2253). The incidence among the Iron Age population at Yarnton is 4.5%. This contrasts with Mill Hill, Deal where two males and two females displayed neural arch separation giving an overall prevalence of 18.2% (Anderson 1995, 121). The favoured interpretation of the defect is as a stress or fatigue fracture that fails to heal (Resnick and Niwayama 1981, 2253), although it may also be caused by a genetic weakness (Hensinger 1989). There is no doubt that genetic influence is important and there are families in which a quarter of the members have spondylolysis, frequently associated with other congenital abnormalities of the spine such as transitional vertebrae or spina bifida (Shahriaree *et al.* 1979; Frederickson *et al.* 1984). Skeleton 2710 conforms with this pattern by exhibiting a combination of spondylolysis and a transitional vertebra. Clinical and experimental evidence, however, tends to support the view that these lesions are acquired as the result of trauma sustained between infancy and early adult life (Waldron 1991, 64). In his comparison of Roman and Anglo-Saxon groups with the 18th- and 19th-century assemblage from Christ Church, Spitalfields, Waldron (ibid.) found that the condition was much less prevalent in the latter group and suggested that this may be one indication of a lifestyle that was much less arduous or physically demanding as compared with earlier populations in Britain. There is no evidence for spondylolisthesis, which is the term used for displacement of the affected bones.

Wormian bones

Wormian bones were present on the crania of skeletons 1396, 2022, 2569, 2710 and 2714. They are extra bones which can occur in the suture line between two cranial bones. It has been argued that this characteristic is inherited (El-Najjar and Dawson 1977) while others have argued (Bennett 1965) that their occurrence is purely related to environmental or stress factors. Skeleton 2022 also had parietal foramina and a septal aperture.

Dental anomalies

Impaction and rotation

The dentition of skeleton 2041 exhibits a number of anomalies; the mandibular canines are congenitally absent; the first left mandibular premolar is impacted and the mandibular incisors are splayed. The upper right first maxillary incisor of skeleton 1397 is impacted. Skeleton 2069 has crowding of the upper left canine, premolars and first molar, retarded eruption of the mandibular canines and rotation of upper left second incisor, upper right first and second incisor and canine.

Irregularity and overlapping of anterior teeth is so common as to be almost normal. Some are merely twisted out of position, but others are wholly displaced to lingual or to labial (Hillson 1996, 112). Any tooth may erupt in such a way that it fails to occlude with teeth in the opposing jaw. Properly, impaction implies that the tooth remains inside the jaw and does not emerge into the mouth at all, but there are many variations and a tooth may erupt sideways into its neighbour, presenting one of its crown sides uppermost. The most commonly impacted tooth is the third molar, especially the lower, followed by the upper canine (Hillson 1996, 113).

Meric and cnemic indices

The shape of the proximal shaft of the femur is expressed as an index calculated from the antero-posterior and transverse diameters. This index, known as the meric index, is a measure of the antero-posterior flattening of the bone below the subtrochanteric portion of the shaft. An index of above 85.0 indicates eumeria; from 75.0-84.9 indicates platymeria, a flattening frequently noted in earlier populations (Hooper 2000, 169), and an index of below 74.9 is indicative of hyperplatymeria, a more extreme antero-posterior flattening. At Yarnton the majority of adults are platymeric or hyperplatymeric.

With the tibia, the transverse flattening of the bone at the level of the nutrient foramen is indicated by the cnemic index calculated from the projective transverse and maximum antero-posterior diameters. An index of above 70.0 indicates eurycnemia; from 63.0-69.9 indicates mesocnemia; from 55.0-62.9 indicates platycnemia, a condition also found frequently in earlier populations sometimes in association with platymeria; and an index of below 54.9 is indicative of hyperplatycnemia. At Yarnton there is a range of variation: hyperplatycnemic, platycnemic, mesocnemic and eurocnemic.

Platymeria has been ascribed to a number of different causes, including excess mechanical stresses upon the bone during childhood and adolescence and as a physiological response to calcium or vitamin deficiencies in the diet. Various explanations have also been advanced for platycnemia, including as a response to habitual squatting.

Discussion

Burial practice

All of the burials were unaccompanied and burial position was predominantly crouched on the left or right side. It was possible to determine orientation in 22 cases, and the majority were north-south or very close to north-south. This conforms to the pattern Whimster observed for central southern England and seems to represent a "powerful and influential body of common tradition" in formal Iron Age burials throughout the country (Whimster 1981, 194). Three possible extended burials were identified, all from the northern group, but as these were recovered during machine observation it is conceivable that the body positions of these individuals were wrongly identified. However, the possibility that these burials genuinely were extended should not be completely discounted as this position does occur in the Iron Age. Examples include certain of the cart burials of east Yorkshire (Dent 1982; 1985) and the cist burials from Birdlip and Hailes, Glos. (Whimster 1981, 16) although these have been dated to the later Iron Age. Stead (1991, 180) has noted that extended burials (his 'type B') only occurred on certain of the cemeteries in east Yorkshire and were of a later date. There is no indication that any of the Yarnton burials received special treatment. The skeletons were fully articulated, the shallow grave cuts appeared to have no other purpose than to contain a burial, and there were no grave goods.

As one might expect, all three neonates in the group were buried within the settlement area. This is in marked contrast to the 'cemetery' excavated, for example, at Winnall Down which comprised 18 individuals, of which 10 were infants and two were children (Fasham 1985). None of the neonates at Yarnton have been radiocarbon dated and stratigraphic relationships are inconclusive so it is possible that some or all are Roman in date. They would not be out of place on a Roman settlement. The demography of the burials from Yarnton is suggestive of a representative cross-section of the population.

Local Iron Age burial traditions

The wider context of the Yarnton burials has been discussed above (Chapter 6), but the local setting is also important. A range of burials of Iron Age date have been found in the vicinity of the site and these are summarised below. It is fair to say that all fall into the categories of deposits traditionally identified as 'typical' of the Iron Age in the region. A left radius encircled by a bronze bracelet was disturbed by a mechanical excavator at Cassington (PRN 3356; SP 4499 0999). The complete fusion of the epiphyses indicates that this individual was fully mature. Since the bone is light, of small proportions, and the muscle markings are not heavily developed it is suggested that this individual was an adult female, probably about 5 ft in stature. The bronze bracelet had stained the bone, it had butting terminals and linear decoration; and is probably pre-Roman (Kirk and Case 1950, 106).

Excavations adjacent to the gap in the Big Enclosure ditch leading down to the ford over the river Evenlode just downstream from the present mill at Cassington revealed contracted burials of a woman and a child in the lowest ditch fills along with a few pieces of the latest non-Belgic local Iron Age pottery; stratified above was Belgic pottery (PRN 3359; SP 448 100). The adult female was aged between 22 and 28 years. The skeleton had been badly damaged, the skull as reconstructed is reasonably complete. The child was aged approximately 1.5-2.5 years. The skeleton of the child is in the British Museum (BMNH SK2071) (Case 1982a, 131, 148).

At Purwell Farm (PRN 3880, SP 445 119) five gullies and 14 pits were excavated in an area roughly 30 ft by 75 ft; two of the pits (4 and 5) contained human remains. The site was dated (by pottery) to the late 3rd to 2nd century BC. Pit 4 contained a human skeleton on its side in a crouched position. In pit 5 another skeleton was removed before the excavation and a third, complete down to the waist, was lying on its back with its arms by its sides. The individual in pit 4 was a male, adult, probably in his middle thirties, of slight build. Stature was 5ft 5ins-5ft 6ins. The fragmentary skeleton from pit 5 was an adult male with remarkably pronounced platymeria. The second skeleton from pit 5 was again a fragmentary adult male of much more robust build than the other skeletons (Dawson 1961-?)

Gravel digging at Cassington (PRN 8052, SP 4481 1001) disturbed a crouched inhumation at the bottom of a pit. The grave was that of a young woman laid supine with arms folded over the abdomen and legs hunched up left over right. An extremely thin layer of charcoal covered the feet and the lower legs and traces extended westwards over the bottom of the pit. The charcoal layer is perhaps suggestive of a wooden coffin. A tiny fragment of bronze wire came from above the hip and two small, broken flint blades, one with secondary working, were found beneath the abdomen. The skeleton was extremely well preserved and almost complete. The conformation of the skull and pelvic girdle and the size of the bones indicate that the skeleton is that of a female. Light wear on the teeth and the fact that the epiphyseal fusion line is still visible on the proximal end of the tibia suggest an age between 20 and 25 years. The woman's height was calculated from the length of the humerus, femur and tibia to be 5 ft 2.25 ins (158.1 cm). Dental health was excellent, all the teeth in the upper jaw being present, with no sign of caries or abscessing of the bone. There was no evidence of a date for the burial but it might be compared with other pit burials in the Upper Thames Valley (Chambers 1977, 256).

At Gravelly Guy, Stanton Harcourt, 40 inhumations and 1 cremation were identified as burials (as opposed to 'odd bones', which were noted in a further 46 contexts) and assigned to the Iron Age and Roman periods (Harman 2004). The majority (28) of the inhumation burials were of infants. Twenty-nine of the individuals were assigned to the early and middle Iron Age period, ten were of late Iron Age or Romano-British date (two late Roman) and one was unstratified. The number of burials represents only a small proportion of the real population of the settlement over the centuries.

Most of the burials from the early and middle Iron Age periods at Gravelly Guy can be attributed to the pit burial tradition, though in some cases the burials were not found in large 'storage' pits but in shallow bowl- and saucer-shaped pits. Where the burials were complete or partially so the remains were of infants or neonates that had been placed in shallow scoops or hollows, which may possibly have been purposely dug graves. Many of the burials were associated with artefacts and/or animal bones.

Several of the early to middle Iron Age burials at Gravelly Guy occurred with objects that in other circumstances would be called grave goods. These artefacts comprise an iron spearhead found with a disarticulated 3-4 year old child, a perforated dog tooth found with the disarticulated bones of an infant, a shale spindle whorl with an adult female and a bone toggle found behind the head of an adult male. Iron Age burials with grave goods are rare in the pit burial tradition.

Three of the discrete neonate burials contained objects which may have been placed with the bodies. A baby in scoop 2062 was not only accompanied by foetal sheep or goats and juxtaposed to an adult goat but was overlain by a piece of fired clay. The original plan of a neonate in scoop 2477 shows three large sherds close to its hands and a large animal bone at its feet, the animal bone may possibly be the cattle femur subsequently assigned to this context. A neonate in cylindrical pit 2404 seemed to have been grouped with animal bone and a fragment of burnt stone. The possibility of coincidence rather than deliberate association in these three burials is real, but not overwhelming.

Grave goods were also associated with some of the late Iron Age and early Romano-British burials at Gravelly Guy. The child in grave 409 was accompanied by the corroded fragment of an iron brooch at one shoulder and what may have been the pin of a second brooch at the other. Infant bones from immediately beside pit 441, recorded as from 441 and 463, may have been associated with a complete pot, the plough-truncated lower part of which occupied most of the pit. Cremation deposit 466 consisted of oak charcoal mixed with cremated human and animal bone and 93 sherds/1900 g of 1st-century pottery which was burnt; some of the pottery lay to one side of the deposit. Within the deposit were eleven nails, most of them fragmentary. Almost all of these were recovered during the sieving of samples from the deposit, so that their precise positions were unknown. They may have derived from a wooden box; Roman cremations are sometimes found in these, though there is nothing in the plan or section to suggest this. Alternatively they may have been present in some of the wood used to fuel the pyre. The underlying layers included lenses of charcoal and contained relatively small quantities of pottery and bone. A human phalanx came from low down in the pit and a fired clay plate and quern fragment from the basal layer.

Excavations at the Vicarage Field gravel pit, site A (PRN 8302, SP 4017 0573) in 1944 revealed a number of rubbish pits which contained potsherds and animal bones. Human bones were found in Pit 25, at about 12 inches down from the top filling. The skeleton was incomplete; the foot bones were found articulated but placed on top of a couple of rib bones; arm and leg bones lay above the badly damaged cranium. Because many of the bones were missing it was not possible to determine the age and sex of the burial (Williams 1951, 14).

CATALOGUE

Yarnton

Group A

Inhumation 133 (Grave 132)

47321/11315, NNE-SSW, 0.9 x 0.5 x 0.15 m.
Skeleton probably crouched on right side, hands clasped in front of body, head facing W though slightly displaced. Within unclear grave cut 132 which cut a series of ditches. Prime adult male (26-35 years). Most bones of skeleton present though fragmentary. Pathology includes benign osteochondroma at neck of right femur adjacent to lesser trochanter, midshaft fracture of right lower arm affecting radius and ulna, poorly aligned, small exostosis present, mild attrition and calculus. Most attrition appears anteriorly which may be indicative of an edge to edge bite.
Stature 159.3 cm.

- - - - - - - - I - - - - - - - -
8 7 x 5 4 / 2 / I - - - - - - - -
k k k k   k

Inhumation 135 (Grave 136)

47343/11330, NW-SE, 1 x 0.5 x 0.15 m.
Position of skeleton unclear. Within shallow oval-shaped grave 136 which cut ditch 339. Burial clearly disturbed. The grave is unnecessarily large for the burial of an infant which was confined wholly to the S half of the grave.
A well preserved neonate infant. Dentition and bones of the hands and feet are missing.
Age calculated using regression equations for long bone lengths (Scheuer *et al.* 1980, 260) at 40.51+/-1.87 weeks.

Inhumation 376/1

47255/11303.7, 1.5 x 0.86 x 0.2 m.
Orientation and body position unknown. Disarticulated skeleton recovered from fill of grave 377 which cuts pit 389. An early/middle Iron Age sherd and a late Romano-British sherd were recovered from the fill of the grave which appeared as a roughly circular pit. The upper grave fill was removed during machining. Burial 376/1 may have been buried first and subsequently disturbed by the interment of 376/2 which was found in an articulated state.
Adult male (26-35 years). Missing skull and mandible, right arm and both legs. There are no complete long bones. Notable pathology includes mild degeneration of vertebrae. CV 6 and CV 7 have mild osteophytes, porosity affecting bodies, Schmorl's nodes affect lower thoracic bodies.

Inhumation 376/2

47255/11303, NE-SW, 1.5 x 0.86 x 0.2 m.
Skeleton probably crouched on right side in grave 377 which cuts pit 389. An early/middle Iron Age sherd and a late Romano-British sherd were recovered from the fill of the grave. The burial of this individual is likely to have caused the disarticulation of 376/1.
Adult (18+ years) ?male. Missing scapulae, clavicles and vertebrae. Notable pathology includes ?possible crush fracture of right calcaneus, mild calculus, moderate alveolar recession.
Stature 172.4 cm.
Cnemic index 80.6 – eurycnemic.

8 7 x 5 4 3 / / I - - - - / 6 7 8
8 7 x 5 4 3 2 / I / / - - - - - -
k k k k k k

Inhumation 412

47238/11292, NW-SE, 0.55 x 0.3 x 0.13 m.
Skeleton possibly lying in supine extended position with head turned slightly to the SE. Grave 411 was sub-rectangular in shape. It was located within a middle Iron Age house enclosure and the two may have been associated.
Infant. Missing pelvis and part of mandible, also metapodials.

Inhumation 496=998/A

47317.80/11295.90.
No visible grave cut. Orientation and position unclear. Some baby bones were located at SW end of gully 998/A at a depth of 0.28 m. The gully is late Romano-British in date. Charcoal flecks appear to have been associated. Possible animal disturbance.
Neonate infant. Condition fair, largely complete. 40.90+/-1.87 weeks

Inhumation 719

47292/11331.
Orientation and position unclear. Disturbed infant burial within ?posthole 714 which contained one middle/late Iron Age sherd and one flint flake.
Neonate. Some long bones and torso, all fragmented.

Inhumation 1346

47343.15/11310.30.
No visible grave cut. Orientation and position unclear.
Infant (1-5 years). Unfused vertebral arches only.

Inhumation 1396

47365/11308 (approximate).
Orientation and position unclear. Skeleton recovered during gravel extraction. No apparent grave cut.
Adult male? (26-35 years). Missing right arm and most of torso; moderate degeneration of vertebrae. Porosity of bodies. One lambdoid wormian bone.
Meric index 68.75 – platymeric.
Cnemic index 70.96 – eurycnemic.

Inhumation 1397

47365/11388 (approximate).
Orientation and position unclear. Skeleton recovered during machine excavation. No apparent grave cut.
Adult female (26-35 years). Missing mandible, all vertebrae and both legs; sacro-iliac ankylosis right side only,

left is completely normal. Abscess, impaction of maxillary left first incisor.
Stature 158.3 cm.

```
                    a k k
- - - - - - - - | 1 - x 4 5 6 - -
- - - - - - - - | - - - - - - - -
```

Inhumation 1681

47310/11300 (approximate), in area between 47310/11300 and 47330/11330.
Orientation and position unclear, recovered during gravel extraction. It appeared to overlie late Romano-British ditches 150 and 145.
Ageing adult male (45+ years). Missing arms and lower legs; healed fracture of right scapula, abscess, caries, moderate alveolar recession. Slight porosity of cervical bodies.
Stature 167.4 cm.

```
   pe             a
- - 6 / x x x x | x x 3 4 - - - -
8 7 x - - - - - | - / 3 4 x x x x
c
```

Inhumation 1682

47310/11300 (approximate) in area between 47310/11300 and 47330/11330.
Orientation and position unclear, recovered during machining in an area which overlay late Romano-British ditches 150 and 145.
Adult male (18+ years). Missing left arm, legs and most of vertebrae; Schmorl's nodes on bodies of thoracic vertebrae, marked alveolar recession
Stature 178.0 cm.

```
- x x 5 4 - - - | - - - - - - - -
8 7 x 5 x - - - | - - 3 4 5 x 7 8
ue                    c
```

Inhumation 1683

47310/11300 (approximate), in area between 47310/11300 and 47330/11330.
Orientation and position unclear, recovered during machining in an area which overlay late Romano-British ditches.
Skeleton missing.

Inhumation 2021

47247/11230 (approximate).
Orientation and position unclear. Extremely disturbed skeleton found during machine excavation of south-east corner of salvage area. Date uncertain
Adult (18+ years) Only lower vertebrae, legs and lower arms survive, rib fragments, metacarpals and metatarsals; mild vertebral osteophytes.

Inhumation 2022

47351/11274, N-S, 1.05 x 0.8 x 0.15 m.
Skeleton crouched on left side, head facing downwards, arms folded across lower rib cage. Within a particularly small, oval grave 2023 with gently sloping sides. Crouched position dictated by size of grave.
Adult male (26-35 years). Virtually complete; Schmorl's nodes affect superior body of S1, exostosis on right tibia (posterio-lateral surface, immediately below articulation for fibula), caries.
Lambdoid wormian bones, left parietal foramen, left septal aperture, right calcaneal facet double.
Stature 163.9 cm.

```
                                ue
8 7 6 5 4 3 / 1 | 1 2 3 4 5 x 7 8
8 7 6 5 4 3 2 1 | 1 2 3 4 5 6 7 8
      c                 c
k k k k k k k k   k k k k k k k k
```

Inhumation 2025

47359/11271.5 (approximate).
Orientation and position unclear. Skeleton recovered during machine excavation. No visible grave cut.
Adult (26-35 years). Missing most of vertebrae, hands and feet; osteophytes on right femur head.
Stature 162.5 cm (F) or 165.5 cm (M).

Inhumation 2026 (grave 2027)

47362/11269.5 (approximate), ? x ? x 0.15 m.
Skeleton recovered during machine excavation, badly disturbed.
Adult male (18+ years). Missing hands and feet, surviving bones fragmented; vertebral degeneration, caries.

```
8 - - - - - - - | - - - - - - - -
- - - - - - - - | x x 3 4 5 6 7 x
                            c c
```

Inhumation 2028 (grave 2029)

47369.5/11269.5, 0.65 x 0.5 x 0.1 m.
Skeleton recovered during machine excavation. Damaged.
Adult female? (18+ years) Missing upper body, surviving bone fragmented; marked vertebral degeneration.
Stature 154.3 cm.

Inhumation 2033 (grave 2034)

47363.5/11278, ?N-S.
Skeleton possibly crouched. Skeleton recovered during machine excavation, badly disturbed.
Adult male? (18+ years). Missing skull, hands and feet, surviving bone fragmented.

Inhumation 2041 (grave 2042)

47373.5/11264, ?N-S, 0.85 x 0.65 x 0.15 m.
Skeleton crouched, damaged during machine excavation. Within small oval grave.
Juvenile (13-15 years). Missing most of vertebrae, surviving bones are fragmented; dental anomalies include splaying, rotation and impaction.

```
ue                e
8 7 6 / - - - - | / / 3 4 5 6 - -
8 7 6 5 - - 2 1 | / 2 - - 5 6 7 /
```

Inhumation 2048 (grave 2049)

47366.8/11262.9.
Orientation and position unclear. Skeleton recovered during machine excavation.

?Adult (18+ years). Only very fragmentary lower legs survive.

Inhumation 2051

47374.2/11264.2.
Finds reference for bone located 1.5 m to W of 2041.
Child (6-11 years). Skull and femur fragments only.

```
- - - - - 2 1 | 1 2 - - - - -
- - - - - - - | - - - - - - -
```

Inhumation 2069 (grave 2070)

47360/11271.8, NW-SE, 1.25 x 0.7 x 0.09 m.
Skeleton crouched on left side, head facing E, hands under body, legs bent towards E. Within small grave cut 2070, rectangular with rounded ends.
Juvenile (13-14 years). Virtually complete; caries, rotation and crowding, retarded eruption, impaction.

```
ue                ue
8 7 6 5 4 3 2 1 | 1 2 3 4 5 6 7 8
8 7 6 5 4 3 2 1 | 1 2 3 4 5 6 7 8
ue     e       e     ue
  c
```

Inhumation 2569 (grave 2570)

47369/11303.4, N-S, 1.09 x 0.8 x ? m.
Skeleton crouched on right side with legs bent at knees, skull is facing NW, upwards and away from body. Skeleton recovered during machine excavation. Damaged. Within small irregular ovoid grave. One Romano-British sherd recovered from grave fill.
Young adult male? (18-25 years). Virtually complete; vertebral degeneration, extreme attrition. Partial union of clavicle.
Stature 168.6-169.5 cm.

```
  a         c
- 7 6 5 4 3 2 - | 1 2 3 / 5 6 7 -
- 7 6 5 4 3 2 1 | 1 2 3 4 5 6 7 8
```

Inhumation 2709

47370/11300.
Orientation and position unclear (possibly NE-SW). Skeleton recovered during machine excavation.
Young adult ?female (18-25 years). Missing most of lower body; caries.

```
    a
    c
8 7 6 5 4 3 / / | - - - - - - - -
8 7 6 5 4 3 / - | / 2 3 4 5 6 7 8
c                     c
```

Inhumation 2710

47365/11300, N-S.
Skeleton is supine extended, excavated by machine.
Young adult (18-25 years) female. Virtually complete; cribra orbitalia; partial sacralisation of fifth lumbar vertebra, third lumbar vertebra has separate neural arch.
Stature 160.1 cm.

```
8 7 6 5 4 3 2 / | - - - - - - - -
- - - - - - - - | - - - - - - - -
```

Inhumation 2711

47368.5/11302, N-S.
Skeleton is crouched, excavated by machine.
Adult (26-35 years) ?female. Missing mandible and legs; moderate calculus.
Stature 157.3 cm.

```
k k k k k k k
- - - - - - - - | 1 2 3 4 5 6 7 -
- - - - - - - - | - - - - - - - -
```

Inhumation 2712

47365/11306.5, W-E.
Skeleton is ?supine with legs flexed, excavated by machine.
Child (5-7 years). Missing left leg; cribra orbitalia.

```
7     3     1 2 3     7
 6 e d c 2 1 | / / c d e 6
 6 e d c / 1 | 1 2 c d e
7     3            6 7
```

Inhumation 2713

47376/11308.
Orientation and position unclear, excavated by machine.
Adult (26-35 years) female. Virtually complete though many bones fragmented; caries, mild calculus.
Stature 161.56 cm.

```
np 7 6 5 4 / 2 1 | 1 2 3 4 5 6 - -
np 7 6 x x 3 2 1 | 1 2 3 4 x 6 / np
```

Inhumation 2714

47373/11308, W-E.
Skeleton is crouched, excavated by machine.
Juvenile (12-13 years). Virtually complete; mild cribra orbitalia, mild calculus, enamel hypoplasia.

```
- - - - - - - - | - - - - - - - -
ue 7 6 5 4 / 2 / | / 2 3 4 5 6 7 ue
      c
```

Inhumation 2715

47372/11318.
Orientation and position unclear (possibly NE-SW), excavated by machine.
Juvenile (13-14 years). Missing skull, mild calculus.

```
- - - - - - - | - - - - - - -
7 6 5 4 - - - | - - - - - - -
```

Inhumation 2716

47368/11307.
Orientation unclear (possibly NE-SW). Skeleton supine, recovered during machine excavation.
Adult male (18+ years). Missing skull and mandible; vertebral degeneration.

Inhumation 2717

47362.5/11306.5, NW-SE.
Skeleton is crouched on left side, excavated by machine.
Adult male (18+years). Virtually complete; cribra orbitalia, arthritic left wrist and elbow, marked alveolar recession.

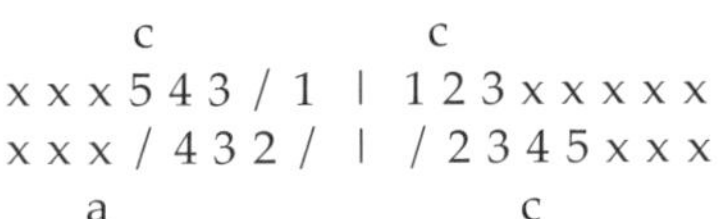

Inhumation 2718

47373/11315, N-S.
Skeleton is crouched on left side, excavated by machine.
Juvenile (14-17 years). Virtually complete.

e 7 6 5 4 3 / / | / 2 3 4 5 6 7 e
? 7 6 5 4 / / / | / / / 4 5 6 7 ?

Inhumation 2719

47372.2/11322, S-N.
Skeleton is crouched on left side. Badly damaged by machine.
Juvenile (13-17 years). Missing upper torso; caries.

? 7 6 5 4 3 - 1 | 1 2 - - - - - ?
? 7 6 5 4 3 2 1 | / 2 3 - - - -
c

Inhumation 2720

47365.8/11320, N-S.
Skeleton is supine extended, arms by sides. Skeleton damaged during machine excavation.
Adult (26-35 years) ??female. Missing legs, surviving bones fragmentary; vertebral degeneration, healed fracture of clavicle.

Disarticulated fragments

Deposit 58/A/2

47315/11334.
An incomplete adult mandible with two surviving teeth which show moderate wear and some alveolar recession. Possible female. Within early Roman ditch 58 which runs in a NW-SE direction.

- - - - - - - - | - - - - - - - -
- - - - - - - - | x / / / / x 7 8
pe

Deposit 521

Subadult? One incompletely formed permanent incisor. Possibly 8-10 years. From early Romano-British ditch 521, enclosure 187.

Deposit 846/C/1

47319.5/11300
Human bone recovered from E-W running ditch 846, part of early Roman enclosure 55. Animal bone was also present.
Adult? (18+ years). Fragmentary right ulna and left proximal tibia.

Deposit 1060/A/2

47332/11334, 1 x 0.95 x 0.71 m.
Human bone from early Roman pit 1060. Animal bone was also present.
Adult (18+ years). Skull vault only. Two lambdoid wormian bones

Deposit 1420

Human bone from Iron Age/early Roman posthole 1420 which cuts late Iron Age ditch 1399.
Adult? (18+ years). Fragmentary sacrum.

Deposit 2000

Unstratified human bone, lying within salvage area to S and SE of excavation, found during removal of topsoil and hillwash

Deposit 2020

47247/11230 (approximate).
This is a finds reference for loose bone recovered during machine excavation. Missing.

Deposit 2066

47364/11282.
Finds reference for quantity of loose bone located 4 m N of skeleton 2033 during machine excavation.
Adult? (18+ years). Right arm and rib fragments only.

Deposit 3043

47583/11205, 2 x 2.2 x 1.35 m.
Roughly circular pit with steep sides and a flat base. Waterlogged wood and leather in base, pit cuts an earlier pit, 3044.
One mature thoracic vertebrae; vertebral degeneration.

Yarnton Cresswell Field

Deposit 8592

Skull only, placed in a pit of late Bronze Age or Iron Age date.
Preservation and completeness: skull only, condition fair
Adult female 26-35 years. Dental pathology: caries, ?abscess
Discontinuous traits: metopism, parietal foramen, lambdoid wormians
Dental anomalies: third molar agenesis
Cephalic index: mesocephalic

Age estimation is based on the degree of dental attrition (Brothwell 1981). Gross caries affected the left maxillary first molar and only the roots survived. The bone around the tooth socket may be affected and it is possible that an internal draining abscess is present.

Deposit 7059

The distal half of a neonate humerus was recovered from the fill of a pit (7029) of Bronze Age or Iron Age date.

Deposit 7644

Two fragments representing the midshaft of a probable adult ulna were recovered from the fill of a stakehole of probable Iron Age date.

Table 16.7: Fragments of human bone recovered from other Iron Age contexts at Yarnton

Context no.	Context type	Context date	Identification
27/A	posthole	IA	?adult male skull vault
248/A/1	pit	IA	tibia shaft fragment
276/A/4	pit	MIA	skull vault fragments??
594/A/1	feature	LIA	lower right humerus, probably adult
746/A/1	pit	MIA	femur shaft
951/A/1	pit	M-LIA	phalange
1016/3	pit	LIA	fragment of pelvis
1420	posthole	IA	sacrum

Deposit 8774

A small quantity of human bone was recovered during sieving of the contents of sample 7127, of early Bronze Age date. Identifiable bones were skull vault, rib shaft and a fragment of scapula, in extremely poor condition. Possible adult (18+ years).

Deposit 7017

Animal bone (47 g), largely unburnt, a few pieces are charred black; a further 17 g is white and well calcined, one fragment may be human femur. From the fill of a possible posthole of early Iron Age date.

ROMANO-BRITISH SKELETAL MATERIAL

Detailed descriptions and aetiology of pathologies, discussion of conditions and of skeletal metric indices are as given above in relation to the Iron Age burials and are not repeated here.

Assemblage composition

The group of seven inhumations is summarised in Table 16.8. It was possible to assign sex to all four of the adults: there were two males and two females. Two of the skeletons could only be assigned to broad adult categories (18+ years), one was a young adult (18-25 years) and one was an ageing adult (45+ years). The only child in the group was aged 9-11 years. Both skeletons from the Yarnton-Cassington evaluation were neonatal infants.

Cremation deposit 767 was an adult of uncertain sex. The pelvis appeared female while the skull was more masculine; on balance therefore this is more likely to be female. Cremation deposit 2534 was a young child aged 3-4 years. In neither case were they representative of a complete deposit (Tables

Table 16.8: Summary of Roman burials

Grave group	Context no.	Sex	Age	Stature	Caries	Abscess	AM loss	Vertebral osteo-arthritis	Meric index	Cnemic index
Yarnton										
C	2005	F	young adult (18-25 y)	1.581	5/23	0/23	3/30		80 L	
C	2006	M?	adult (18+ y)	1.736						72.97
C	2016	F	adult (18+ y)	1.521	1/13	0/13	9/23		78.57 L 79.16 R	79.16 R
C	2039	M	ageing adult (45+ y)	1.756	3/11	0/31	18/31	X	76.3	
C	2053	-	child 2 (9-11 y)		2/10	0/10	0/10			
YCE										
	239/5	-	39.26174+/-1.87 weeks							
	239/7	-	39.36259+/-1.87 weeks							

Table 16.10: Weights (g) of cremated bone within anatomical categories and size ranges

Context	Skull	Axial	10 mm sieve fraction Upper limb	Lower limb	Not identified	Skull	Axial	5 mm sieve fraction Upper limb	Lower limb	Not identified	Skull
767	46	3	5	2	59	6	2	0	2	203	
2534	6	1	0	2	2	7	1	0	0	16	

Table 16.9: Summary of cremated bones

Context	Weight	MNI	Age	Sex	Identifiable bone
767	588 g	1	adult	?	skull vault, pubic symphysis, humerus, ulna, femur, tibia
2534	51 g	1	3-4 y	-	skull vault, maxilla, dentition, rib shaft, vertebral arch fragment, femur

16.9-10). The expected weight for a complete cremation, derived from known weights of adult cremated remains from modern crematoria has been found to range between 1001.5 g and 2422.5 g, with an average of 1625 g (McKinley 1993). While a range of reasons for potential loss of material need to be considered (incomplete recovery, disintegration related to soil type and truncation due to ploughing), this can be suggestive of deliberate selection and burial of a token deposit (Boyle 1999, 176).

Stature

It was possible to calculate stature for all four of the adults. Both females were considerably shorter than the males and this applies to females from all the Roman sites considered (Tables 16.11-12). Males compared well with the single skeleton for whom stature could be calculated at Asthall (Boyle 1997, 136), though it should be borne in mind that the numbers concerned are very small.

Non-metric variation	Other dental anomaly	Other pathology
moderate-heavy alveolar recession, crowding of mandibular incisors and canines, rotation of mandibular canines. calculus		
2 sagittal wormian bones	calculus	cribra orbitalia, healed rib fracture
cv1 has incompletely fused neural arch	mild calculus	arthritis of left and right shoulders, multiple rib fractures

	2 mm sieve fraction			
Axial	Upper limb	Lower limb	Not identified	Total weight
			60	588
			16	51

Skeletal pathology

Osteo-arthritis

Ageing adult skeleton 2039 exhibits marked vertebral degeneration particularly affecting the cervical vertebrae in the form of osteophytes, porosity and eburnation of bodies and facets.

Osteo-arthritis affects both shoulder joints of skeleton 2039. False joint surfaces have formed on the left and right acromion with associated porosity and eburnation, representing a possible persistent dislocation. The right humeral head has quite extensive lipping, porosity and eburnation while the surviving fragment of the left humeral head is involved to a lesser degree. The surviving fragment of the left humeral head is involved to a lesser degree.

Trauma

Skeletons 2016 and 2039 both have healed rib fractures. A small exostosis is present on the medial surface of the shaft of the right humerus of skeleton 2039. This is likely to be myositis ossificans traumatica (see above).

Table 16.11: Roman adult male stature: local comparanda

Mean Stature	Range	Site	Source
1.746 (n=2)	1.736-1.756	Yarnton	this report
1.665 (n=2)	1.660-1.670	Alchester	Boyle (2001)
1.752 (n=1)	1.752	Asthall	Boyle (1997)
1.650 (n=1)	1.650	Alcester	Boyle (2000)
1.708 (n=5)	1.630-1.820	Crowmarsh	Boyle unpublished manuscript

Table 16.12: Roman adult female stature: local comparanda

Mean Stature	Range	Site	Source
1.551 (n=2)	1.521-1.581	Yarnton	this report
1.530 (n=1)	1.530	Alchester	Boyle (2001)
1.599 (n=3)	1.554-1.663	Asthall	Boyle (1997)
1.565 (n=2)	1.550-1.580	Alcester	Boyle (2000)
1.588 (n=5)	1.490-1.680	Crowmarsh	Boyle unpublished manuscript

Table 16.13: Prevalence of dental pathology (Roman adults only)

	Ante mortem loss			*Caries*			*Abscess*		
	No. affected	*No. observed*	*% rate*	*No. affected*	*No. observed*	*% rate*	*No. affected*	*No. observed*	*% rate*
Yarnton	30	84	35.7	9	67	13.4	0	67	0
Alchester	24	382	6.3	5	348	1.4	0	375	0
Asthall	28	143	19.6	8	104	7.7	1	143	0.7
Alcester	1	96	1.0	2	91	2.2	0	94	0
Crowmarsh	73	542	13.5	24	424	5.7	4	542	0.7

Dental pathology

Skeletons 2005, 2016, 2039 and 2053 all had carious cavities (Table 16.13). The caries rate at Yarnton is much higher than that of the comparable groups (see Table 16.13) and this is also the case for ante-mortem tooth loss. Calculus was present on the dentition of three individuals (2005, 2016, 2039). All three adults with surviving dentition had lost teeth ante-mortem. Ageing adult 2039 had lost 18 out of 31 teeth (TPR 58.1%).

Dental anomalies

Skeleton 2005 exhibited crowding and rotation of the mandibular incisors and canines.

Skeletal anomalies

The first cervical vertebra of skeleton 2039 has an incompletely fused vertebral arch. Skeleton 2039 has two sagittal wormian bones.

Meric and cnemic indices

Measurements of the proximal shaft of the femur showed that all the adults of Roman date at Yarnton were platymeric. The cnemic index (for the tibia) could be calculated for two adults, who were both eurycnemic.

Discussion

The burials were variously orientated north-south (2006, 2039), NE-SW (2005) and SW-NE (2053). Burial position was either supine extended or slightly crouched. Skeletons 2039 and 2053 may have been laid one on top of the other although this cannot be said with certainty as no grave cuts were visible. There were no associated grave goods. A small number of pottery sherds were recovered from the grave fills of skeletons 2016, 2039 and 2053.

Decapitation

The adult female skeleton 2016 had been decapitated; the skull and a single cervical vertebrae (C1?) lay to the left of the left tibia, facing towards the body. No skeletal evidence of decapitation was present. The base of the skull had not survived and the axis, which was missing both transverse processes, was the only cervical vertebra to survive. There would have been insufficient space at the head end of the grave for the skull. The burial was overlaid by the partial skeleton of a dog (2043).

Decapitated burials have been identified at a number of rural cemeteries in Oxfordshire including Barrow Hills, Radley (Atkinson 1952-3; Chambers and Boyle 2007) and Crowmarsh, Wallingford (Boyle unpublished; see also Booth 2001). In contrast, with the exception of Alchester (Boyle 2001a) decapitations have not been identified at any of the urban cemeteries excavated in the region, these being Queensford Farm, Dorchester-on-Thames (Chambers 1987) and Asthall (Booth 1997a).

Decapitation, a rural practice of native origin, seems to have developed by the last decade of the 3rd century becoming more common in the 4th, although early Roman examples of the rite are also known in Britain. Where decapitations are associated with dateable artefacts in urban cemeteries most can be placed in the second half of the 4th century, and Clarke concluded that the rite spread from rural to urban sites during the 4th century (Clarke 1979, 374).

This type of burial does not appear to be confined to any particular age or sex group (Philpott 1991, 79): at Barrow Hills the decapitated burials were both males and females aged from 17 to 50 years (Chambers and Boyle 2007); at Lankhills men, women and children were affected (Watt 1979, 344) and the same pattern is seen for example at Melford Meadows, Brettenham, Norfolk (Boyle 2002, 37-43).

A survey of the practice in the Oxfordshire region (Harman *et al.* 1981) has shown that decapitation and prone burial were not uncommon amongst the late Romano-British cemeteries of the Upper Thames. Four recently excavated 4th-century Roman burials from Abingdon included a decapitation within a lead coffin. The individual had been buried with six coins dated AD 348-60. It is clear then that whatever the reasons for decapitation, the individuals involved in a number of cases often appear to have retained the right to an otherwise outwardly normal burial, if not one of considerable status. Philpott (1991, 73) comments that although grave furniture is not common in decapitation burials, where it does occur it is broadly consistent with the wider patterns of 4th-century grave furnishings.

Dogs occur in a number of graves which often display ritually unusual burial treatment such as decapitation (*ibid.*, 204). In Roman practice pets were sometimes killed to accompany the dead (Toynbee 1971, 50). They were also used for hunting or herding and may have been considered a sign of status. A dog accompanied a decapitated burial at Cassington (Harman *et al.* 1981, 160). The latter cemetery was excavated (PRN 1266; SP 4493 1030) by Captain Musgrave for the Department of Human Anatomy at Oxford University. The cemetery contained upwards of 110 graves, there was no evidence for coffins and no grave goods were found. A total of 15 skeletons had been decapitated and there were three cremation burials (at least one of which was in an urn). At Asthall the body in grave 1157 of probable 4th-century date, appears to have been wrapped in the skin of a large dog prior to burial (Powell *et al.* 1997, 145).

CATALOGUE

Yarnton

Inhumation 2005

47361.5/11230, NE-SW
No visible grave cut. Skeleton slightly crouched on left side, head facing east, legs bent slightly at knees. Badly damaged during machine excavation.
Young adult female (18-25 years). Virtually complete; dental anomalies include crowding and rotation; caries and calculus, alveolar recession.
Stature 1.581 m.

```
c c c
8 7 6 5 4 x 2 x  | / / 3 4 5 6 7 ?
/ 7 x 5 4 3 2 1  | 1 2 3 4 5 6 / ?
  c   k k k k k    k k k k k c
```

Inhumation 2006

47362.5/11230, N-S
No visible grave cut. Skeleton probably supine and extended, most of upper body cut away.
Adult male? (18+years). Missing dentition and humeri.
Stature 1.736 m.
Eurycnemic.

Inhumation 2016 (grave 2017)

47346/11260, S-N, 1.65 x 0.65 x 0.10 m
Skeleton supine and extended, decapitated; the skull and a single cervical vertebra lay to the left of the left tibia, facing towards the body. The base of the skull had not survived and the axis, which was missing both transverse processes, was the only cervical vertebra to survive. No cut marks were identified. There would have been insufficient space for the skull at the head end of the grave. Skeleton is overlaid by the burial of a dog, 2043, which is incomplete. Both appear to be within the grave, from the fill of which two sherds of early Romano-British pottery were recovered.
Adult female (18+ years). Virtually complete; cribra orbitalia, healed rib fracture, heavy calculus, caries, marked alveolar recession. Two sagittal wormian bones.
Stature 1.521 m.
Platymeric – 78.57
Eurycnemic – 79.16

```
                 c c   k k c
 - - 6 / / 3 / / | 1 2 3 x 5 6 7 np
x x x x 4 3 2 /  | / 2 / 4 x x x x
        k   k      k
```

Inhumation 2039 (grave 2040)

47369.4/11252.7 N-S
Skeleton crouched on right side, head facing W. Overlies skeleton 2053. Grave, which cut pit 2052, contained two Romano-British sherds, one of which was late.
Ageing adult male (45+ years). Missing most of legs; severe vertebral degeneration, arthritic shoulders, multiple rib fractures, caries. Very poor survival of vertebrae, though marked degeneration particularly affects cervical vertebrae in the form of osteophytes, porosity and eburnation of bodies and facets. False joint surfaces have formed on the left and right acromions with associated porosity and eburnation, the result of a possible persistent dislocation. Right humeral head has lipping, porosity and extensive eburnation, small exostosis on medial surface of shaft, lipping is quite extensive. Surviving fragment of left humeral head is involved to a lesser degree.
Stature 1.756 m
Platymeric – 76.3

```
      c
np x x 5 x 3 x x | x x x x 5 x x 8
 8 x x 5 x 3 / / | 1 2 3 x x x x 8
 c                 c
                   k k
```

Inhumation 2053 (?grave 2040)

47369/11251, SW-NE
Skeleton possibly crouched on right side. Recovered during machine excavation, overlain by 2039 (see above).

Table 16.14: Fragments of human bone recovered from other Roman contexts

Context no.	*Context type*	*Date*	*Identification*
58/A/2	ditch	ERB	adult mandible
166/A	pit	ERB	distal right tibia, ?adult
209/A/3	pit	LRB	humerus shaft fragment, ?subadult
355/B/1	ditch	ERB	humerus shaft
521/A/2	ditch	ERB	subadult tooth bud
839/A	ditch	ERB	humerus
839/A	ditch	ERB	infant radius
846/B/1	ditch	ERB	phalange
846/C/1	ditch	ERB	tibia and ulna fragments
1060/A/2	pit	ERB	adult skull vault
1189/A/15	pit	LRB	proximal left ulna
2066	finds reference	RB	right humerus and scapula, left ulna

As no cuts are visible it is impossible to determine whether or not the individuals are within one grave cut or two. Two Romano-British sherds (one late) were recovered from the grave fill.
Child (9-11 years). Virtually complete; caries.

```
ue 5 e 3
    c
7 6 e 4 c b 1 | - - - - - - -
7 6 e d - - -  |          6
ue 5 4 3              4    c    7
```

Cremation 767

Within oval pit. Roman
Weight 476 g. Identifiable bones include skull vault, long bones and pelvis of an adult. Animal bone fragments.

Cremation 2534

Within irregular feature. Early Roman.
Weight 55 g. Identifiable bones include skull, maxilla and dentition of an infant.

Yarnton Cassington Evaluation 1993

Two neonates of Roman date were recovered from feature 239/8 cut into the top of ditch 239/24.

Inhumation 239/5

Condition excellent, legs and skull fragments only. 39.26+/-1.87 weeks

Inhumation 239/7

Condition excellent, virtually complete. 39.36+/-1.87 weeks

```
        u     u u
- - - - a  |  a b - - -
- - - - -  |  - - - - -
```

Chapter 17: The Animal Bone

by Jacqui Mulville, Kathy Ayres and Pippa Smith

METHODOLOGY

Excavation, sampling and recovery

The majority of the animal bone was retrieved by hand, with a small quantity of bone recovered from sieved samples at Cresswell Field. The identified fragments from the latter came from large early Iron Age and middle Iron Age assemblages and accounted for less than 0.3% of the total assemblage. As these samples were small and mostly contained species and elements represented in the remainder of the assemblage they have been incorporated with the hand-collected assemblage.

Identification and recording

The animal bone was identified using the reference collection at the Faunal Remains Unit, University of Southampton. The Cresswell Field material was recorded by Kathy Ayres and the Yarnton (Worton Rectory Farm) material by Pippa Smith; the floodplain causeway material was recorded and the resulting databases were analysed and reported on by Jacqui Mulville.

When possible, sheep and goat were distinguished (Boessneck 1969) but where diagnostic features were not present due to fragmentation or poor preservation, they were classified under a single heading. Those fragments which could not be identified to species level were classified as 'cattle-size', 'sheep-size' or 'unidentified'.

Fragments were recorded using a zoning method following Serjeantson (1991), zones being recorded when over 50% present. Not all recorded elements were included in the analysis – carpals and tarsals, apart from the magnum and the navicular cuboid were excluded, as were loose upper teeth (apart from canines), lower incisors, premolars (apart from dP4), lateral metapodials and skull fragments, apart from the occipital condyles, zygomatic arch and nasal bone. Ribs were recorded when the head was present and vertebrae (except axis and atlas) when over 50% of the centrum was present. Rib and vertebral fragments are excluded from calculations. The site archive contains the full record of all the fragments of bone from the site.

Quantification

The total number of fragments (NISP) was calculated for all species, whilst the minimum number of elements (MNE) and the minimum number of individuals (MNI) were calculated for the most common taxa. As the recording method indicates the zones present on each bone, the minimum number of each element present (MNE) could be calculated. From this it was possible to estimate the minimum number of individuals (MNI) which must have been present on site to form the bone assemblage recovered. NISP counts tend to be biased towards the larger species as larger bones suffer greater fragmentation and produce higher counts. MNI counts were therefore calculated to reduce this bias. The percentage survival of each element was also calculated following Brain (1981) and Binford (1978) where the number of each element present is expressed as a percentage of the most frequently occurring element (ie the number expected if the entire skeleton was present).

Ageing and sexing

Wear stages were recorded for dP4s, P4s and lower permanent molars of the domestic species using Grant (1982) and grouped into age stages following the methods of Halstead (1985), Payne (1973) and O'Connor (1988). The fusion stage of post-cranial bones was recorded and related age ranges taken from Getty (1975).

It was only possible to separate the sexes using morphological characteristics of the pelvis and skull, and for pigs the canines. Although it is possible to detect the sexual composition of a population through metrical analysis the number of measurements produced for individual bones and species was small at these sites and precluded any conclusions using such data.

Measurements

Measurements were taken on cattle, sheep/goat, pig and horse bones, following von den Driesch (1976), Davis (1992) and Payne (1969). Those taken on pig teeth followed Payne and Bull (1986) and for horse teeth followed Levine (1982). Withers heights were calculated from formulae in von den Driesch and Boessneck (1974) and Teichert (1975). Measure-

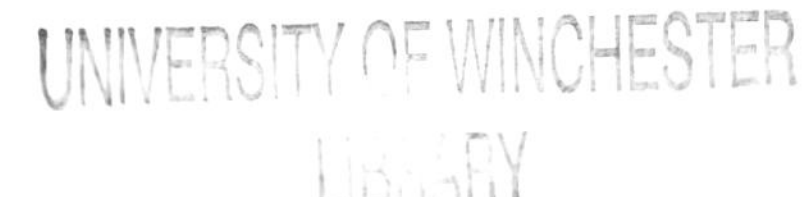

ments were compared with the measurements listed in publications of other contemporary sites and with those from Saxon Yarnton (Mulville and Ayres 2004).

Gnawing, butchery and burning

Gnawing and butchery marks were recorded for all identified bones. Butchery marks were described as "chop" or "cut" marks. There were no bones which had been sawn. Their position was only recorded if considered particularly meaningful, but was not used for quantitative purposes. Gnawing marks made by carnivores and rodents were noted. Burning on bones was simply recorded as either present or absent.

Preservation

The material from Yarnton as a whole was in very good condition, resulting in a high proportion of identified bone. Evidence for burning, gnawing and butchery can be seen in Table 17.1. The proportion of burnt bone in all phases was low (1 to 3%).

An increasing proportion of bone showed evidence of canid gnawing; rising from 4% in the early Iron Age, to 8% in the middle Iron Age and reaching over 16% from the LIR onwards. The presence of gnawing marks generally attests to the dispersal of the animal bones as a result of scavenger activity. The lower incidence of gnawing in the early Iron Age is probably a reflection of the fact that the material comes from contexts associated with organised disposal practices.

The proportion of butchered bone in each of the phases also shows an increase over time, from 3% in the early Iron Age to over 10% from the LIR onwards. The presence and identification of butchery marks is related to differential taphonomic processes and on-site practices. It is likely that even more butchery marks were present on bones, but were obscured by the high proportion of gnawing. This higher incidence of butchery marks through time suggests an increase in the rate of butchery and availability of butchery tools in the Roman phases (Peck 1986).

Table 17.1 Percentage of bone modified by taphonomic processes by phase.

Phase	*Burning*	*Gnawing*	*Butchery*
EIA	1	4	3
MIA	2	8	4
LIA/LIR	3	17	11
ERB	3	17	10
LRB	2	16	10

Analysis

Although excavated and recorded as three separate sites the material from Cresswell Field, Worton Rectory Farm and Yarnton Floodplain has been combined for the purposes of this report. The material from these sites is divided into five major phases; the early Iron Age, the middle Iron Age, the late Iron Age/Roman transition, the early Roman and the late Roman.

Comparable Iron Age and Roman Thames Valley sites are Appleford (Wilson 1980), Ashville (Wilson *et al.* 1978), Barton Court Farm (Wilson 1986), Ditches Hillfort (Reilly 1988), Farmoor (Wilson 1979), Gravelly Guy (Mulville and Levitan 2004), Mingies Ditch (Wilson 1993a; 1993b), Thornhill Farm (Levine 2004), Watkins Farm (Wilson and Allison 1990) and Whitehouse Road (Hamilton-Dyer 1993). There have been a number of reviews of Thames Valley husbandry data (Grant 1984; Hambleton 1999; Lambrick 1992b; King 1978; 1991) allowing Yarnton to be set in a regional context.

RESULTS

A total of 10,560 fragments was analysed (Table 17.2). These were identified as twelve different species of mammal, in addition to birds, amphibians and rodents. The majority of the assemblage is derived from early Iron Age contexts (38%) with slightly less in the middle Iron Age (27%) (Table 17.2). The late Iron Age/early Roman, early Roman and late Roman phases all contain roughly equal, smaller amounts of material making up about 10-14% each of the total assemblage.

Table 17.2 NISP for each species by phase.

Phase	*Cattle*	*Sheep/Goat*	*Sheep**	*Goat**	*Pig*	*Horse*	*Dog*	*Red deer*	*Roe deer*	*Wild pig*
EIA	1343	890	61	3	148	45	226	7	2	1
MIA	1374	802	20	3	106	77	43	10	2	
LIA/LIR	380	232	18	2	40	41	38	1	1	
ERB	501	383			173	46	11		2	
LRB	390	364	82	1	55	45	11	1		
Total	3988	2671	181	9	522	254	329	19	7	1
%	38%	25%	2%	<1%	5%	2%	3%	<1%	<1%	<1%

* Sheep and goat are included in the sheep/goat figure

Relative abundance of species

Based on the number of identifiable specimens (NISP) the assemblage overall is made up of over one third cattle, one quarter sheep/goat and less than one twentieth pig (Table 17.2). Other domestic species, goat, horse and dog, are present in small amounts. There is more dog than horse in the early Iron Age, but there is a large increase in the number of horse bones present in the middle Iron Age and it remains more abundant than dog in the following phases. The small amount of goat is present in similar proportions in each phase, apart from the early Roman where it is absent; at such low levels of abundance this absence is not significant. Only about 7% of the sheep/goat bone can be identified as either sheep or goat. In further analysis the goat, sheep and sheep/goat bones are all incorporated within a single group referred to as sheep, due to their greater abundance.

Wild mammals make up only a small proportion of the total assemblage, rising from about 0.2% in the Iron Age to around 1.7% in the Roman period (Table 17.3). The species present are red deer, roe deer, wild pig, hare and fox. The most abundant species is the hare; absent from the earliest periods, its numbers increase throughout time.

The major domestic species

A careful comparison of the most numerous domestic species (cattle, sheep/goat, pig, horse and dog) reveals a fall in cattle NISP over time, from above 50% in the Iron Age to about 45% in the Roman period (Table 17.4). Sheep make up about one third of the assemblage until the late Roman, when their numbers increase slightly. The number of pig bones is consistent at around 5-6%, but demonstrates a short lived increase in the early Roman period to 16%. As noted above the number of horse bones increases over the Iron Age to peak in the late Iron Age, from 2% to 6%, whilst over time the amount of dog falls from 9% to 1%.

Using the MNI calculation the contribution that cattle make to the assemblage decreases and the change over time from a cattle- to a sheep-dominated economy is clearly demonstrated (Table 17.4). The numbers of cattle fall from about one half to less than one third of the assemblage. The changes over time are complex, cattle increase in importance from the early to middle Iron Age, and then gradually decrease in importance. Sheep on the other hand only show a major change in the late Roman, when their numbers increase to account for about half of the assemblage. The MNI calculation increases the proportion of pig in the assemblage overall, and demonstrates a growth in the importance of pig in the Roman phases. This suggests that, over time, meat production is becoming more important than the secondary products that cattle, for example, could produce.

There is little change in the contribution that the horse makes to the assemblage when calculated using MNI; although their proportion increases earlier, in the middle Iron Age. The quantity of dog becomes more uniform with only 2% found in all

Table 17.3 Quantification of wild mammals by phase.

Phase	*No.*	*%*
EIA	11	0.3
MIA	11	0.4
LIA/LIR	2	0.2
ERB	22	1.5
LRB	19	1.7

Table 17. 4 Relative abundance of major domestic species by phase.

		Percentage				
	Phase	*Cattle*	*Sheep/Goat*	*Pig*	*Horse*	*Dog*
NISP	EIA	51	34	6	2	9
	MIA	57	33	4	3	2
	LIA/LIR	52	32	5	6	5
	ERB	45	34	16	4	1
	LRB	45	42	6	5	1
MNI	EIA	46	38	10	3	3
	MIA	53	32	8	5	2
	LIA/LIR	41	39	11	7	2
	ERB	34	38	16	6	6
	LRB	27	50	15	6	2

Hare	*Fox*	*Bird*	*Frog*	*Toad*	*Amphibian*	*Rodent*	*Cow/Horse*	*Sheep/Pig*	*Total*	*%*
	1	3	46	40		6	551	584	3893	38%
3		5	39	3	1	10	292	321	3088	27%
			24				126	114	997	10%
20						1	165	165	1467	14%
18						1	126	104	1115	11%
41	1	8	109	43	1	18	1260	1288	10560	
<1%	<1%	<1%	<1%	<1%	<1%	<1%	12%	12%		

phases, apart from the early Roman. This fall in the relative abundance of dog represented by MNI compared to the NISP calculation, suggests that there are many parts of a small number of dogs on site, whilst for horses the bones represent different individual animals.

The relative proportions of the three main food animals can be compared to those of other British Iron Age and Roman sites. In general, the Yarnton NISP and MNI data are similar to the Iron Age patterns described by Hambleton (1999). For NISP data, cattle and sheep are found in roughly equal proportions with a lower incidence of pig, whilst using MNI data sheep and pig represent a larger proportion of the assemblage. To examine the Yarnton assemblage in more detail a comparison can be made with the NISP data from eleven other Thames Valley data sets (Table 17.5). The data are presented as groups of material from the different phases, if a phase spans two archaeological periods it is placed with the later period. The data within each group are ordered from lowest to the highest NISP for cattle.

Overall no distinct pattern over time can be seen (see also Hambleton 1999, 88); but if we compare the average results for each phase we can describe the general trends. In the early Iron Age cattle and sheep are present in similar amounts, then during the middle Iron Age sheep become more important but by the late Iron Age this pattern reverses with cattle more abundant. In the Roman period cattle are still the dominant species, but their importance is declining whilst pigs become more abundant. The amount of pig present varies at each site, and never accounts for more than 15% of any assemblage. Within the general trends, individual sites have different trajectories. For example, over time Yarnton and Thornhill Farm have a higher proportion of cattle present than the average, whilst Ashville, Gravelly Guy and Claydon Pike always have more sheep. The assemblage from Thornhill Farm in particular has exceptionally high proportions of cattle present and the large size of this assemblage significantly alters the overall percentage abundance for the Roman period material.

Table 17.5 Comparative Thames Valley major domesticates NISP data by period

			NISP				*%*	
Site	*Phase*	*Cattle*	*Sheep/Goat*	*Pig*	*Total*	*Cattle*	*Sheep/Goat*	*Pig*
Ashville	EIA	157	242	47	446	35	54	11
Gravelly Guy	EIA	733	1066	223	2022	36	53	11
Yarnton	EIA	1342	890	148	2380	56	37	6
	Total	2232	2198	418	4848	46	45	9
Ashville	MIA	366	727	112	1205	30	60	9
Mingies Ditch	MIA	521	914	103	1538	34	59	7
Gravelly Guy	MIA	2910	3966	669	7545	39	53	9
Watkins Farm	MIA	405	429	87	921	44	47	9
Claydon Pike	MIA	270	258	26	554	49	47	5
Whitehouse Road	MIA	86	56	14	156	55	36	9
Appleford	EIA/MIA	198	99	43	340	58	29	13
Yarnton	MIA	1374	802	106	2282	60	35	5
Thornhill Farm	MIA	74	25	14	113	65	22	12
	Total	6204	7276	1174	14654	42	50	8
Claydon Pike	MIA/LIA	294	271	28	593	50	46	5
Ashville	LIA	290	334	86	710	41	47	12
Barton Court Farm	LIA	443	415	93	951	47	44	10
Yarnton	LIA/LIR	380	232	40	652	58	36	6
	Total	1407	1252	247	2906	48	43	8
Yarnton	ERB	501	383	173	1057	47	36	16
Gravelly Guy	LIR/RB	1470	1674	362	3506	42	48	10
Ditches Hillfort	LIA/ERB	2028	1644	668	4340	47	38	15
Yarnton	LRB	390	364	55	809	48	45	7
Thornhill Farm	LIA/ERB	1806	442	128	2376	76	19	5
	Total	6195	4507	1386	12088	51	37	11

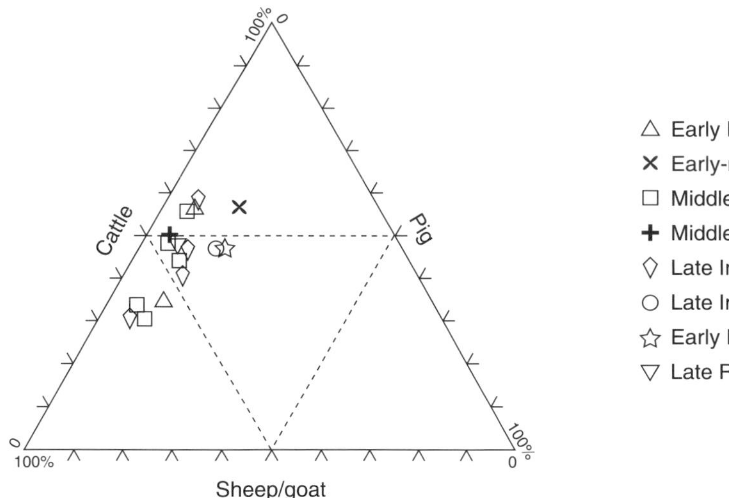

Fig. 17.1 Comparison of the relative abundance of principal domesticated species in the Upper Thames Valley

Another way of looking at the data is presented in Fig 17.1. The Yarnton Iron Age sites form a tight cluster with their higher proportion of cattle and lie closest to the sites at Thornhill Farm and Appleford. As a group the Yarnton data correspond with Hambleton's conclusion that the Upper Thames Valley Iron Age sites do not have the high percentages of sheep seen in the Wessex Iron Age assemblages (19-60% sheep, opposed to 40-70% in Wessex).

The fall in the proportion of cattle at Yarnton in the Roman period is also visible. There are few Roman sites plotted; at Thornhill Farm and Gravelly Guy the amount of cattle increases in the Roman period, whilst at Yarnton it falls to a level similar to that found at Ditches hillfort (Reilly 1988). The decrease in cattle is contrary to the conclusions of King (1978; 1991), who demonstrated an increase in the amount of cattle in the Roman period. The percentage of pig at Roman sites can be seen to be higher than in Iron Age samples.

Ageing data

The ageing data are presented in Tables 17.6-11 and Figures 17.2-3. No neonatal bones or jaws were recorded from the main food animals. There is, however, evidence for young cattle and sheep, aged between 1 and 6 months, but no young pigs. This suggests that at least cattle and sheep were breeding at or near the site but that preservation conditions were not appropriate for the survival of the fragile bones and teeth of newly born animals.

Cattle

Dentition

Overall the early and middle Iron Age phases demonstrate a higher rate of slaughter compared to the Roman phases (Table 17.6, Fig. 17.2). There is a general trend for the number of animals killed at any stage to increase between the early and middle Iron Age. Animals survive longer in the LIR and early Roman phases, but in the late Roman phase there is a return to a higher rate of slaughter, although this does not quite return to the Iron Age levels.

Whilst the proportion of animals dying at each stage differs between the phases, there is little variation in the timing of death. With no evidence for neonatal dentition, the youngest cattle die aged between one and eight months. For all phases the first peak in slaughter occurs between 8 and 30 months, probably focused on animals of full body size attained at around two years; between a third

Table 17 6 Mandibular ageing - Cattle (after Halstead 1985).

	Stage/age range									
	A	*B*	*C*	*D*	*E*	*F*	*G*	*H*	*I*	
Phase	*0-1 months*	*1-8 months*	*8-18 months*	*18-30 months*	*30-36 months*	*Young adult*	*Adult*	*Old adult*	*Senile*	*Total*
EIA		6	1	6	1	2	8	3	8	35
MIA		2	2	6		2	5	3	4	24
LIR				4	2		8	2	2	18
ERB		1		3	3	1	6	3	3	20
LRB		2		3		1	6	1	3	16
		11	3	22	6	6	33	12	20	

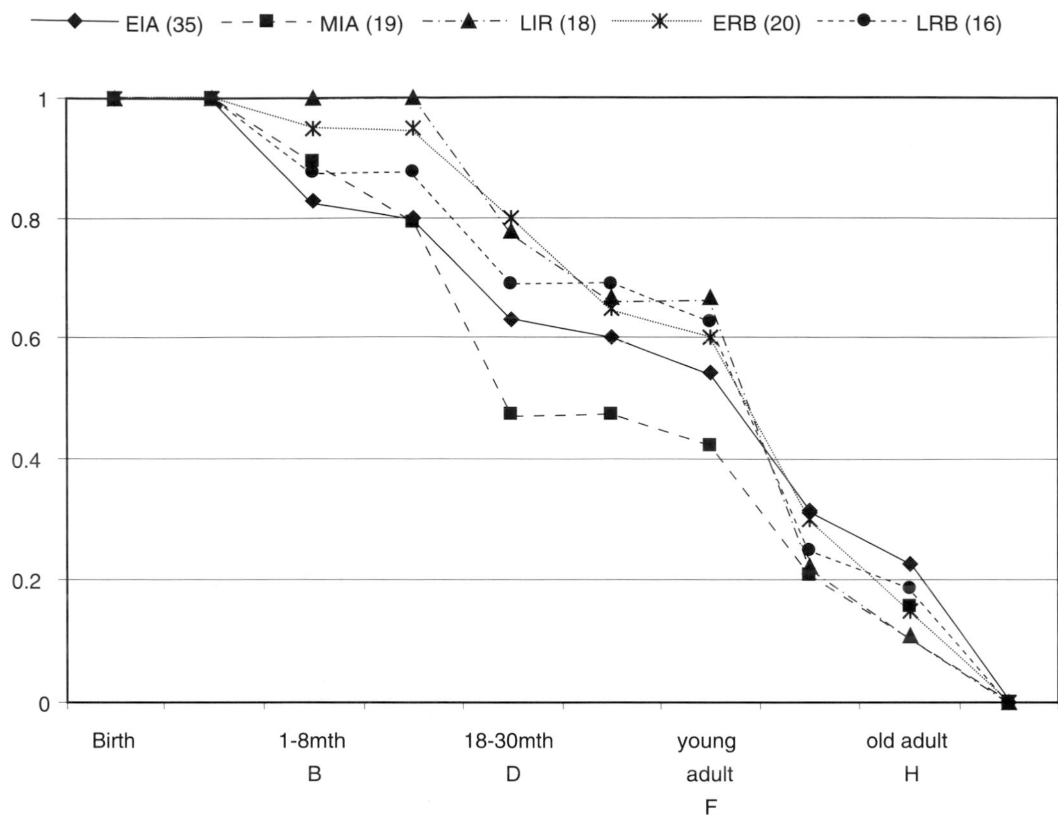

Fig. 17.2 Yarnton cattle dentition after Halstead (1985)

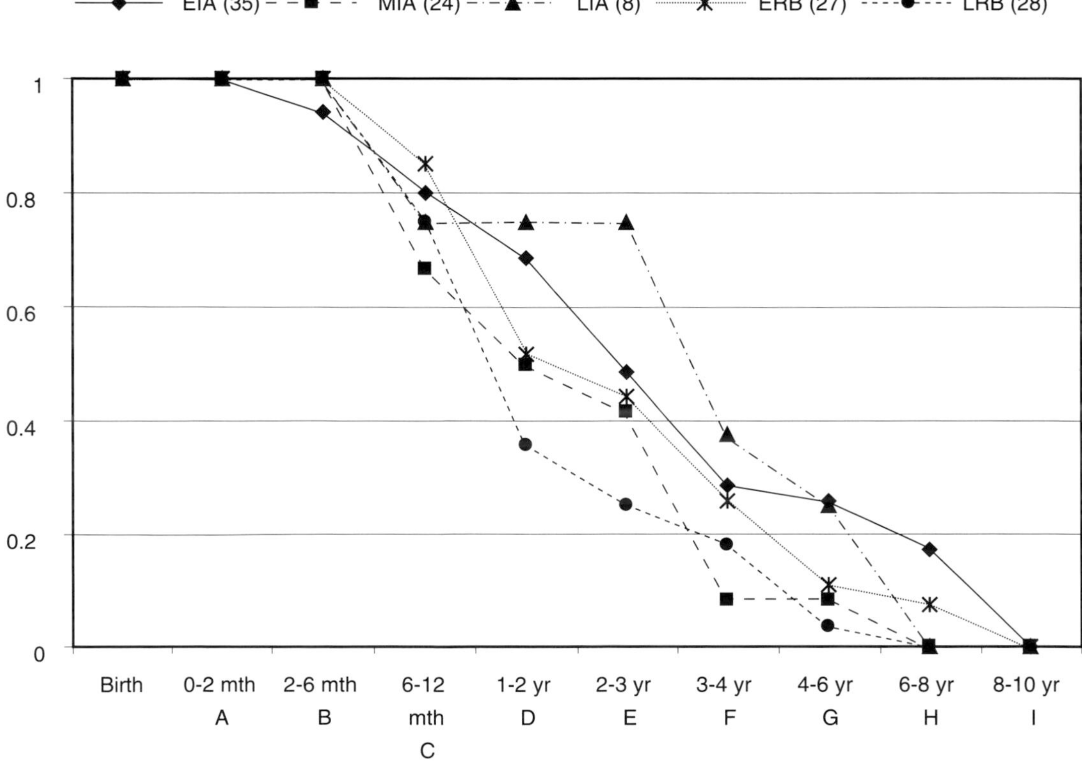

Fig. 17.3 Yarnton sheep dentition after Payne (1973)

Table 17.7 Cattle fusion data.

	Element	EIA Fused	EIA Unfused	EIA % unfused	MIA Fused	MIA Unfused	MIA % unfused	LIA/LIR Fused	LIA/LIR Unfused	LIA/LIR % unfused	ERB Fused	ERB Unfused	ERB % unfused	LRB Fused	LRB Unfused	LRB % unfused
	Scapula	8	1		16	3		15	1		12			9		
	Pelvis	2	1		12	2		13	0		17	1		18		
Subtotal <1 year		10	2	17%	28	5	15%	28	1	3%	29	1	3%	27	0	0%
	Humerus d.	18	12		26	7		15	2		21	3		1	1	
	Radius p.	26	4		45	3		20	0		24	0		13		
Subtotal <2 year		44	16	27%	71	10	12%	35	2	5%	45	3	6%	14	1	7%
	Tibia d.	31	11		21	4		0	5		8	5		11	5	
	Metacarpal d.	18	7		14	4		4	1		8	1		4	3	
	Metatarsal d.	10	2		5	6		4	0		4	1		3	3	
	Metapodial d.					1										
	Calcaneum	5	13		2	5		1	3		1	4		2	1	
Subtotal <3 year		64	33	34%	42	20	32%	9	9	50%	21	11	34%	20	12	38%
	Femur p.	16	22		12	31		3	3		5	15		1		
	Femur d.	16	28		17	22		1	1		4	12		7	1	
	Ulna p.	1	1		4	1		0	1		2	0		0	2	
	Radius d.	6	5		5	2		4	0		4	4		2	3	
	Tibia p.	9	13		8	9		0	5		3	3		3	4	
	Humerus p.	2	6		0	2		4	0		2	2		1	1	
Subtotal <4 year		119	121	50%	90	92	51%	22	22	50%	42	51	55%	36	24	40%

Based on shaft fusion evidence

Loose epiphyses not included in this calculation

and a quarter of animals die at this time. There is a second peak in the death rate occurring later with many individual cattle culled as young adults or older.

Fusion

The fusion evidence supports that from the dentition, demonstrating a higher mortality rate in the Iron Age compared to the Roman phases (Table 17.7). There are numerous unfused bones in the youngest fusing categories, indicating an early death for a large number of animals. There is a distinct change between the late Iron Age and Roman phases with a much smaller amount of unfused bone from younger animals present in the latter; indicating that fewer animals die in the first two years. Instead animals begin to be slaughtered in larger numbers from their second year onwards.

Sheep/goat

Dentition

Table 17.8 and Figure 17.3 compare the dental data from the different phases at Yarnton. The small sample from the late Iron Age is included for completeness, but with only eight dental records these results are not discussed.

Very few animals die before the age of 6 to 12 months. These are only present in the early Iron Age, and the lack of infant material may indicate an extensive husbandry system with lambing taking place away from the occupation sites. The dental evidence suggests that there is a slight increase in the rate of slaughter for sheep/goat over time; animals in the early Iron Age live longer than those in succeeding phases. For example the middle Iron Age and early Roman periods have a similar, slightly earlier, age of slaughter compared to the early Iron Age. This can be best demonstrated by comparing the number of animals surviving to stage D (1 to 2 years); in the early Iron Age 69% survive, whilst by the late Roman this falls to 36%.

As well as differences in the rate of slaughter there is a change in emphasis over time. The early Iron Age and middle Iron Age data indicate a fairly constant cull rate over the early stages of life, until the animals reach three to four years when the rate falls. In the later periods the peak in slaughter occurs in animals between 6 months and two years; at the prime age for meat production.

Fusion

The fusion data demonstrate a changing rate of slaughter over the different periods (Table 17.9). In general, few animals die in their first year, except in the middle Iron Age when 30% of unfused bones come from very young animals, suggesting that many die in their first year. For all phases there is a peak in slaughter between one and two years, the time of prime meat production, and the rate of slaughter declines in the third year. In the early Iron Age, late Iron Age, and early Roman almost 40% of fused bone is from animals over three years of age. Thus in these phases there is a peak in slaughter at around two years, but with many older animals kept to produce fleeces and possibly milk.

For the remaining two phases, middle Iron Age and late Roman, only breeding stock survive to over three years. In the middle Iron Age sheep are slaughtered very early, probably in the autumn of their first year, and few survived to old age. This would fit a meat production model, possibly in an environment where pasture was limited. For the late Roman phase we again see a meat emphasis, but although animals do not begin to be slaughtered in large numbers until their second year, this slaughter continues, leaving few older animals.

These data generally support the dental data; the earlier age of slaughter in the middle Iron Age is demonstrable, although the increase in the rate of slaughter and decrease in age of slaughter over time is not as clear.

Pig

Dentition

The small sample of pig jaws demonstrates that the majority of animals died as sub-adults (Table 17.10). Few adult animals were recorded overall, although there was an almost equal number of sub-adults and adults in the late Iron Age.

Table 17.8 Mandibular ageing - Sheep/goat (after Payne 1973).

	Stage/age range									
	A	*B*	*C*	*D*	*E*	*F*	*G*	*H*	*I*	
Phase	*0-2 months*	*2-6 months*	*6-12 months*	*1-2 years*	*2-3 years*	*3-4 years*	*4-6 years*	*6-8 years*	*8-10 years*	*Total*
EIA		2	5	4	7	7	1	3	6	35
MIA			8	4	3	8		2		25
LIR			2			3	1	2		8
ERB			4	9	2	5	4	1	2	27
LRB			7	11	3	2	4	1		28
		2	26	28	15	25	10	9	8	

Table 17.9 Sheep fusion data.

	Element	*EIA* *Fused*	*EIA* *Unfused*	*EIA* *% unfused*	*MIA* *Fused*	*MIA* *Unfused*	*MIA* *% unfused*	*LIA/LIR* *Fused*	*LIA/LIR* *Unfused*	*LIA/LIR* *% unfused*	*ERB* *Fused*	*ERB* *Unfused*	*ERB* *% unfused*	*LRB* *Fused*	*LRB* *Unfused*	*LRB* *% unfused*
Humerus d.		27	3		12	11		10	1		9	3		5	1	
	Radius p.	18	4		15	2		8	2		12	0		7	1	
	Scapula	3	1		5	1		4	0		7	0		3	2	
	Pelvis	5	1		4	1		2	1		12	1		13	0	
Subtotal <1 year		53	9	15%	36	15	29%	24	4	14%	40	4	9%	28	4	13%
	Tibia d.	20	9		12	20		5	6		7	3		5	7	
	Metacarpal d.	3	11		2	11		1	2		2	3		2	2	
	Metatarsal d.	4	7		2	10		2	1		1	5		4	1	
	Metapodial d.															
Subtotal <2 yrs		27	27	50%	16	41	72%	8	9	53%	10	11	52%	11	10	48%
	Calcaneum	2	2		1	1		3	2		2	0		0	1	
	Femur p.	3	6		2	7		0	3		1	3		0	3	
	Radius d.	4	12		2	11		2	5		2	6		0	3	
	Ulna p.	4	1		1	5		0	1		1	0		0	2	
	Humerus p.	2	6		1	6		0	2		0	1		0	2	
	Tibia p.	4	8		0	6		1	2		0	3		3	4	
	Femur d.	2	7		3	2		1	0		1	2		0	0	
Subtotal <3.5 yrs		21	42	67%	10	38	79%	7	15	68%	7	15	68%	3	15	83%

Based on shaft fusion evidence

Loose epiphyses not included in this calculation

Table 17.10 Pig mandibular ageing

Phase	Subadult	Adult	Total
EIA	4		4
MIA	1		1
LIA/LIR	4	3	7
ERB	3		3
LRB	3	1	4
Total	15	4	19

Fusion

The sample of ageable material for pigs is rather small (Table 17.11), and as a result only the percentage of unfused bone overall has been calculated. The late Iron Age sample is small and excluded from this discussion. Over time we see an increase in the proportion of unfused bone, from 54% to 77%, indicating a younger age of slaughter. There is a large increase between the first three phases, early Iron Age to early Roman, with a smaller increase between the early and late Roman phases. The increasingly young age of slaughter suggests intensification in meat production.

Comparison

We can compare the dental evidence from Iron Age and Roman Yarnton with grouped data from the other Upper Thames Valley Iron Age sites (Ashville, Barton Court Farm, Mingies Ditch, Claydon Pike, Watkins Farm and Farmoor). Yarnton is also considered within Hambleton's more detailed study of the Thames Valley data.

Yarnton Iron Age cattle are dying at similar ages and at a similar rate to the other Thames Valley sites of this period (Fig. 17.4), although a slightly larger number of animals die in the first few months of life. Hambleton (1999) found that the majority of Upper Thames Valley sites showed extremely heavy mortality during stages C, D, or E. Yarnton has a small peak in mortality occurring in stage C, the younger range for beef animals, and falls in Hambleton's group of sites with about half of the animals surviving until stage E (3-3.5 years). This suggests a concentration on beef production with sufficient older animals kept for secondary products. The Roman period shows an increase in the age at which animals are slaughtered compared to the Iron Age. More animals are surviving until 8-18 months but then the rate of slaughter is similar to that for the Iron Age.

Sheep at Yarnton have a similar mortality profile to that found on other Thames Valley sites (Fig. 17.5). Lambs are generally absent from Thames Valley sites, suggesting that lambing took place away from the majority of sites. Most animals survived the first 2-6 months, and were steadily culled from that point onward. At Iron Age Yarnton there are fewer animals dying between their first and third years than in the grouped Thames Valley data, but after this the mortality rate is very similar. Hambleton identified two different groups of Thames Valley sites characterised by low (40-45%) and high (60-80%) percentage survival at the end of stage C. Yarnton falls into the latter group, and is amongst the sites interpreted as lacking a deliberate cull of yearlings, focusing on the exploitation of slightly older sheep for food, rather than younger sheep for manure.

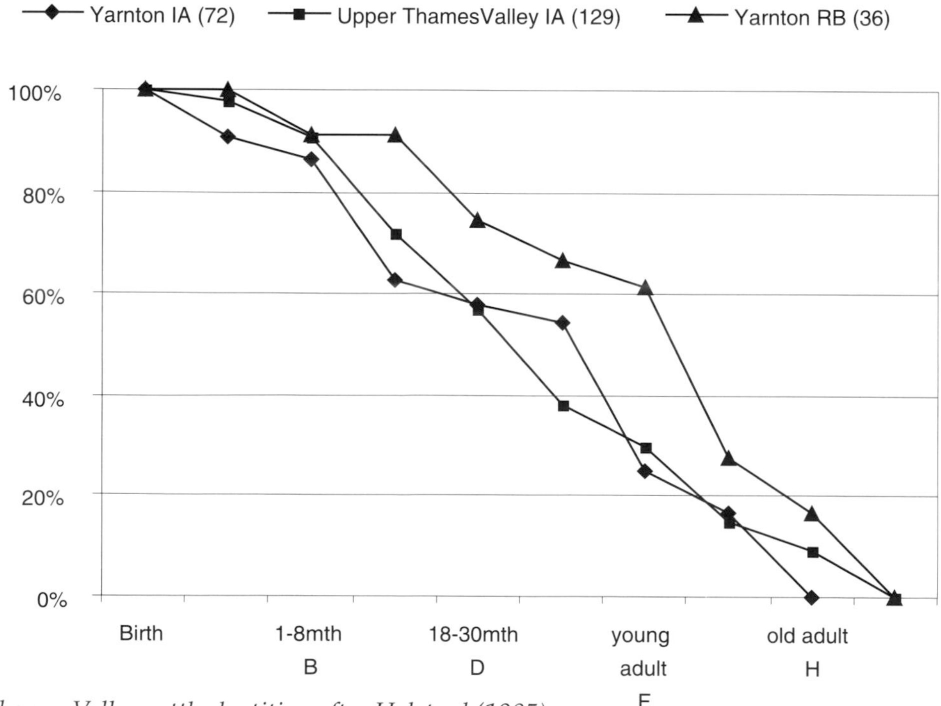

Fig. 17.4 Thames Valley cattle dentition after Halstead (1985)

Table 17.11 *Pig fusion data.*

Element	EIA Fused	EIA Unfused	EIA % unfused	MIA Fused	MIA Unfused	MIA % unfused	LIA/LIR Fused	LIA/LIR Unfused	LIA/LIR % unfused	ERB Fused	ERB Unfused	ERB % unfused	LRB Fused	LRB Unfused	LRB % unfused
Humerus d.	1	3		1	3		0	1		2	4		0	0	
Radius p.	4	0		3	1		3	1		4	3		0	0	
Scapula	6	3		1	1		0	0		4	2		1	0	
Pelvis	1	1		2	1		3	0		3	2		1	0	
Metacarpal d.	2	5		0	4		1	0		1	5		0	1	
Metatarsal d.	2	3		1	1		0	0		1	4		0	2	
Tibia d.	0	1		0	2		0	0		0	3		0	2	
Calcaneum	0	1		0	0		0	1		1	3		1	1	
Femur p.	0	1		0	0		0	0		0	2		0	1	
Femur d.	0	0		0	0		0	0		0	2		0	1	
Ulna p.	0	0		0	2		0	0		0	6		0	1	
Radius d.	0	1		0	1		0	1		1	4		0	1	
Humerus p.	0	0		0	0		0	1		1	3		0	0	
Tibia p.	1	1		1	0		0	0		0	4		0	0	
	17	20	54%	9	16	64%	7	1	13%	18	47	72%	3	10	77%

Based on shaft fusion evidence

Loose epiphyses not included in this calculation

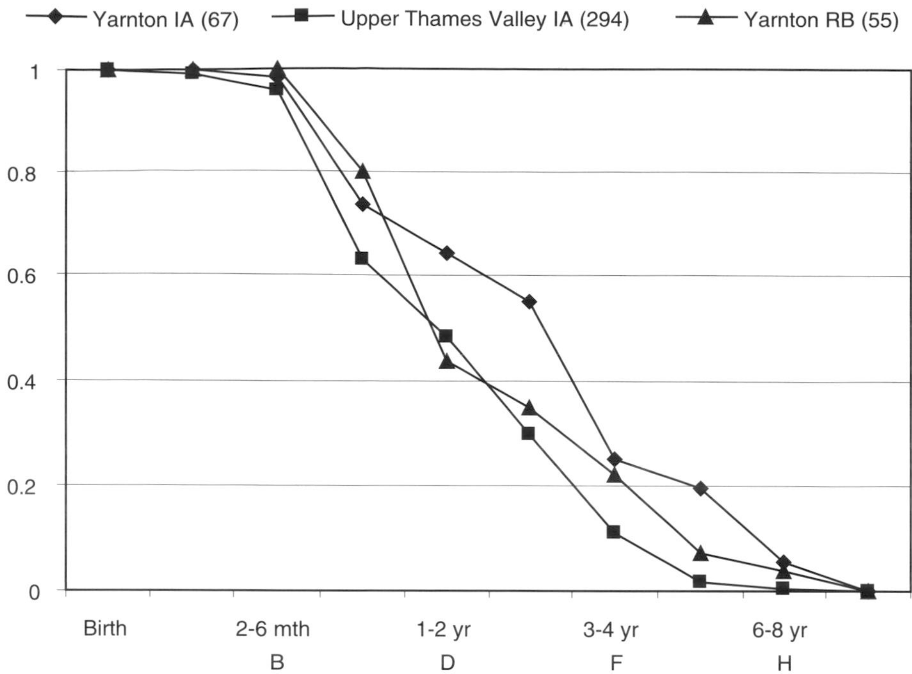

Fig. 17.5 Thames Valley sheep dentition after Payne (1973)

Hambleton found that mortality in general was higher in stage C than was the case in Wessex. The intensity of the seasonal cull of yearlings may be exaggerated due to the seasonal nature of some of the Thames Valley floodplain sites such as Farmoor (Lambrick and Robinson 1979), with the highest stage C mortality on alluvium and peat sites. The low mortality at Yarnton therefore suggests a more permanent occupation of the site. The Roman mortality profile is very similar to that of the Thames Valley Iron Age sites; there is no change in emphasis and sheep exploitation is mainly for meat at all times.

The small amount of Yarnton pig data can also be compared with Thames Valley data. The comparison demonstrates that the Yarnton animals are initially slaughtered at an older age than on the other Thames Valley sites, and then rapidly culled leaving no adult or older animals. Hambleton records that the majority of animals in the Thames Valley were killed between 6 months and 2.5 years and suggests that killing in the second and third years indicates the intense exploitation of the pig population for meat. Pigs can breed in their first year and there is no need to keep older individuals as breeding stock; at Yarnton they were killed upon reaching adult weight and in the Thames Valley assemblages no pig survived beyond 4 years.

At Yarnton there seems to be a focus on meat production for all species throughout time, although there is a greater emphasis on prime animals in the Roman period compared to the Iron Age. This compares well with King's (1991) conclusions that more Roman animals are killed when adult or sub-adult than in the Iron Age, suggesting a husbandry system that emphasised meat and wool production. King also concluded that Romano-British farming communities in general must have been richer as more live animals were occupying the land at the same time, consuming valuable pasture and fodder.

Overall, the pattern of sheep exploitation is similar to that on other Iron Age sites in the region, but the cattle found at Yarnton are being kept until a slightly older age and culled at two specific times, at 8-18 months and as adults. This slight increase in age is consistent with the culling of animals at the age of prime meat production. This could demonstrate that Yarnton was a consumer site where meat is imported or, more likely, that it was one with abundant pasture allowing animals to be kept to an older age. The lack of very young or old pigs is again consistent with prime meat production.

Body part analysis

The relative abundance of body parts for each phase is demonstrated in Figures 17.6-8. The Minimum Number of Elements was calculated for each element. In the case of elements recorded using zones, this was the most abundant left or right zone. For those elements not recorded by zones, eg astragalus, the maximum number of left or right records was taken to represent the MNE. For repeating elements, such as phalanges, the NISP was divided by their abundance in the skeleton. The highest MNE represents the Minimum Number of Individuals for a particular species. The relative abundance for each element was calculated as the MNE divided by the MNI expressed as a percentage.

Cattle

All parts of the cattle skeleton are present in all periods (Fig. 17.6), from the skull to the feet; indicating that entire animals are being bought to the site and slaughtered. Only small amounts of cattle phalanges were recorded. These are smaller bones and their absence along with that of the patella and navicular cuboid, suggests that taphonomic factors are biasing the results. It is only in the last phase, late Roman, that the quantity of the smaller bones increases.

The different phases demonstrate a difference in body part abundance. The early and middle Iron Age distribution indicates that the majority of elements are from the back leg, in particular the femur and tibia, with a smaller but significant number from the front leg. This suggests a focus on meat bearing elements. By the late Iron Age/LIR the emphasis now moves onto the forelimb, although the hind limb is still abundant. There is an increase in the numbers of metapodia, suggesting that fewer deposits were made up of prime meat elements and that more comprised waste bones. In the early Roman period both fore and hind limb dominate. The relative numbers of metapodia fall again, and the deposits return to a meat emphasis. In the late Roman the pattern changes completely; there is a much more even distribution of all the elements, both prime and lesser meat bearing. This can be seen in the predominance of mandibles in the late Roman assemblage.

The body part distribution overall suggests a bias towards meat bearing elements in the assemblage, in all but the late Roman period. This may indicate the importation of meat to the site or that the bones in the Iron Age and early Roman periods derive from contexts associated with the disposal of food, rather than butchery waste. In the late Roman it appears that importation ceases, or that all types of waste were being deposited in the excavated contexts.

Sheep/goat

As with cattle, some elements of all parts of the body are present from the head to the hooves (Fig.17.7). There are only small amounts of the smaller bones, such as phalanges, navicular cuboid and patella; this again suggests a taphonomic bias.

For each phase the same pattern of elemental abundance is seen. Tibiae are the most common bones, with large numbers of radii and mandibles. These are not the prime meat bearing elements (which are femora, humeri and scapulae), and may demonstrate the removal of these body parts elsewhere, or the preferential destruction of these elements into unidentifiable fragments during the cooking/consumption process. The lesser meat bearing elements such as metapodia are also fairly rare, suggesting that the deposits are not made up of waste bone. The only exception is in the late Roman period, when metapodia are relatively common. As for cattle this suggests that deposits of this date were made up of a mixture of waste material.

Pig

The small assemblage of pig bone shows a more uneven distribution in all phases (Fig. 17.8). Bone from all the extremities is present, although the small quantities of metapodia and phalanges suggest that some lower limbs are missing. The high number of mandibles present in most phases suggests that the heads are present, despite the lack of skull or neck bones. There is a predominance of front limb bones, particularly the scapula, which may indicate the importation of front limb joints. There is little difference in the elemental abundance over time.

Comparison

Hambleton (1999) considered that the lack of comparable body part data for the British Iron Age in published reports precluded any significant discussion of this aspect. Only three of the sites she examined utilised Binford's MNI method and only a further six sites produced data of sufficient quality to allow the calculation of skeletal representation by this method. She did, however, describe the overall pattern observed at these sites, and these can be compared with Yarnton.

For cattle the mandible was nearly always the most abundant element. The remaining elements generally had similar levels of abundance, although upper limbs were slightly more common. In the Iron Age Yarnton does not fit this pattern, with femora dominating over mandibles, whilst later in the Roman phases, they are not as predominant as at other sites.

Sheep also demonstrated a predominance of mandibles, along with tibiae and radii, and this pattern is reflected at Yarnton. The proximal radius (fusing at under 1 year) and distal tibia (fusing at under 2 years) are both early fusing bones. These elements would be fused by the time the majority of animals are slaughtered and their persistence is probably a function of their resulting robusticity.

The relative abundance of pig skeletal elements indicates a predominance of mandibles at most site, with other elements substantially less well represented. Again Yarnton differs from this pattern, for in the Iron Age the upper forelimb bones predominate, and whilst mandibles become more common in the Roman phases, they are not always dominant.

The skeletal element representation found at Yarnton indicates a site that differs from those described by Hambleton (1999); although none of these are Thames Valley sites. Yarnton is unusual in that, for cattle and pigs at least, limb bones are more common than at other Iron Age sites. This could demonstrate the importation of joints of meat or differential disposal of meat and waste elements.

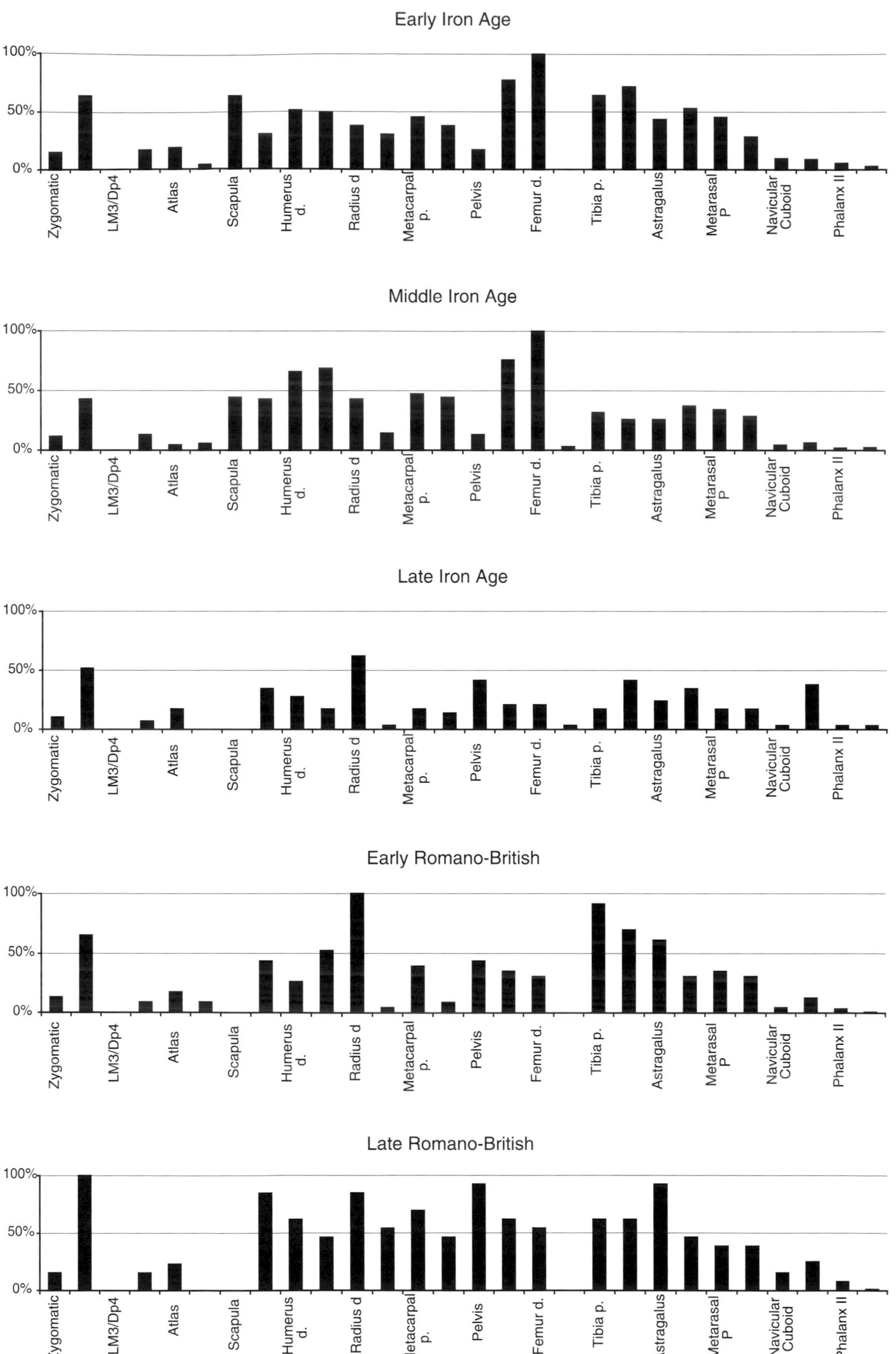

Fig. 17.6 Cattle - relative abundance of elements

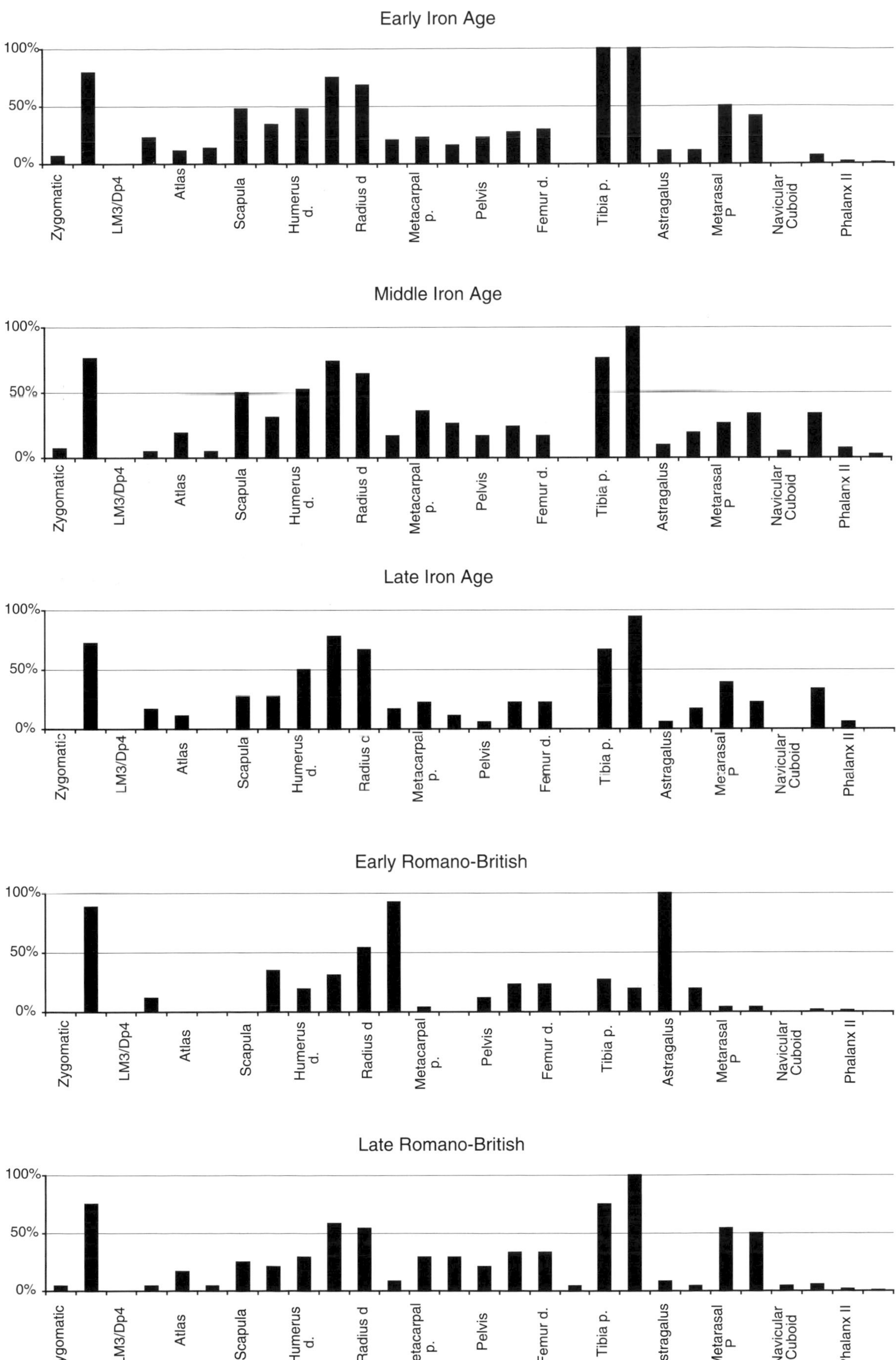

Fig. 17.7 Sheep/goat - relative abundance of elements

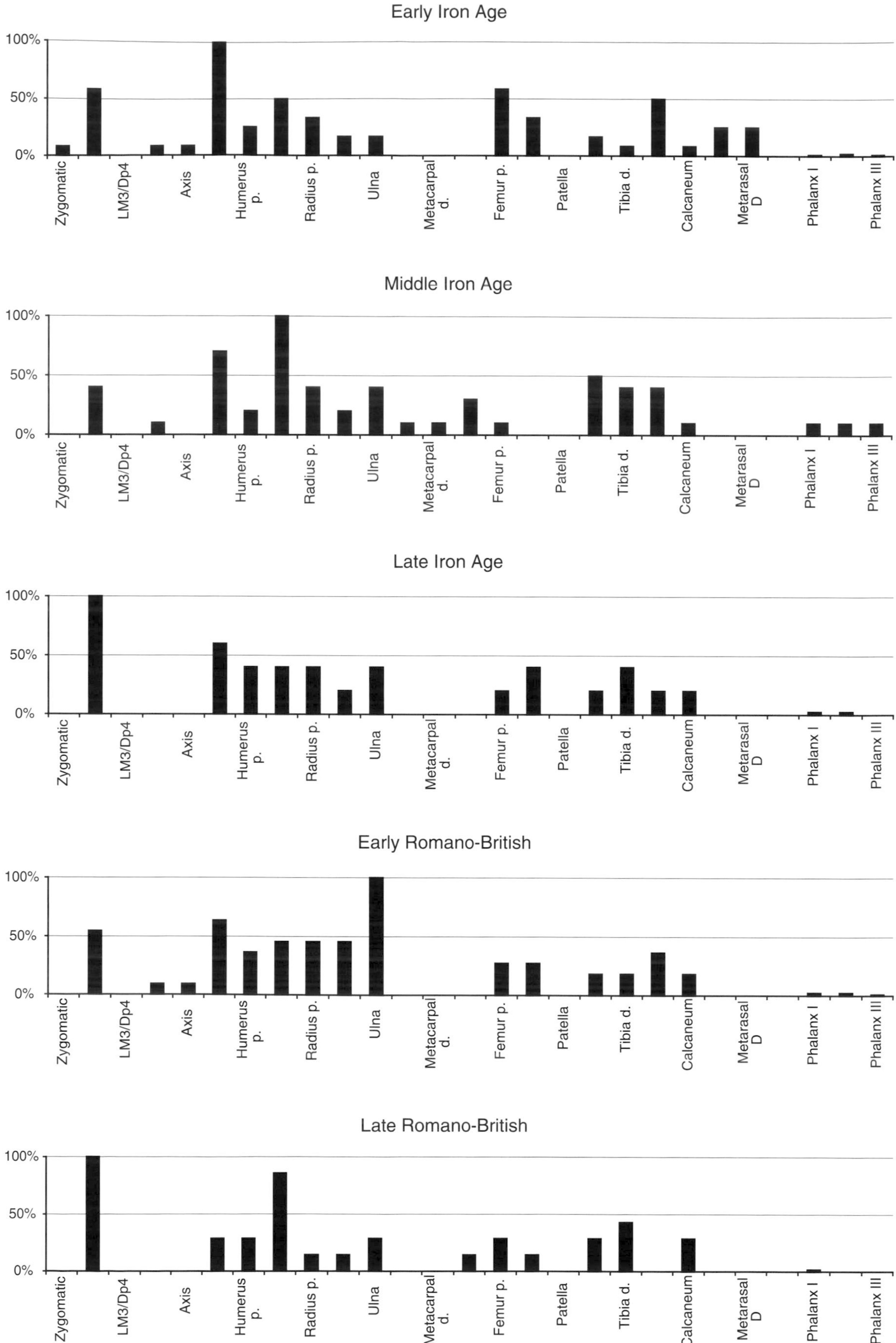

Fig. 17.8 Pig - relative abundance of elements

Table 17.12 Males and females of the main domestic species.

Species	*Phase*	*Element*	*Male*	*Female*	*Male :female ratio*
Cattle	EIA	Pelvis	1		
	LIR	Pelvis	1	3	1:3
	ERB	Pelvis	2	7	1:3.5
	LRB	Pelvis	3	7	1:2.3
Sheep/Goat	EIA	Pelvis	1	1	1:1
	ERB	Pelvis	1	3	1:3
	LRB	Pelvis	3	3	1:1
Pig	EIA	Lower canine	4		
	MIA	Lower canine	6	1	
		Mandible		1	
			6	2	1:0.3
	LIR	Lower canine		2	
	ERB	Lower canine	1		
		Mandible	1	2	
		Pelvis	1		
			3	2	1:0.6
	LRB	Lower canine	2		
		Mandible	1		
			3	0	

Table 17.13 Males, females and castrates of the main domestic species in the Thames Valley.

Sheep	*Male*	*Prob male*	*Female*	*Prob female*	*Castrates*	*Ratio**
Ashville	4		5	4	1	
Appleford			1	1	1	
Barton Court Farm	1		1			
Guiting Power			2			
	5	0	9	5	2	1:2.2
Cattle						
Ashville	1	3	1	4	1	
Appleford					1	
Farmoor			1	1		
Barton Court Farm			1		3	
Guiting Power					1	
	1	3	3	5	6	1:2.3

* Male to female ratio includes probable males and females

Sex ratios

The available information on the numbers of males and females present is shown in Table 17.12. For cattle and sheep this is based on pelves. For pigs both upper and lower teeth were sexed but the information has been reduced to the most abundant lower or upper tooth data in order to avoid counting the same individual twice. The small sample demonstrates a male to female ratio of between 1:1 and 1:3. As cattle pelves fuse at 7 months and sheep at 5 months, this ratio is a reflection of the sex ratio of animals over this age, and suggests that more females that males survive to this age, although any selection for meat/breeding and working animals is probably made slightly later. The male to female ratio recorded at a number of other Iron Age sites (Table 17.13) is very similar, with just over twice as many female sheep and cattle to males recorded. No castrates were noted at Yarnton.

For pigs the result is very different, with males more abundant than females (Table 17.12). The higher number of males is thought to reflect preferential use of the larger males in meat production.

Minor domestic species

Goat

Goat is present from the early Iron Age and is found in all phases in very small numbers. It is slightly more common in the Iron Age than in the Roman period, and a range of elements is identified, all from different contexts. In the early Iron Age a butchered horncore (pit 330) and two right scapulae, one unfused (pit 7268 (7269), Iron Age ploughsoil 7003), were recovered. The middle Iron Age has a second horncore (pit 1730), a humerus (pit 1394) and metacarpal (ditch 1621, part of enclosure 241). All were left hand side elements. Another left horncore and a proximally butchered (cut) left humerus were recorded from an LIR period deposit whilst the only Roman record was a late Roman proximal fused right radius and ulna.

Few goats are recorded in Iron Age assemblages. In the Thames Valley goat is only recorded at Mingies Ditch, Watkins Farm and Gravelly Guy in small quantities. Further afield at the Danebury environs sites, goat is only recorded at Danebury and Suddern Farm and at the latter only horncores were recorded. At Mingies Ditch goat are thought to make up about 8% of the total ovicaprid assemblage based on the identification of goat dp4s (Wilson 1993b, 190). At Yarnton this figure is much lower, and no goats were identified from dental information. A metrical analysis of the metapodia data suggests that no unidentified goats were present in the sample. The goat humerus was measurable.

Horse

The fusion information for horses is sparse (Table 17.14). Few unfused bones were recovered and the majority of these came from a single middle Iron Age foal burial (aged under 9-12 months). There is only one other bone from an animal of less than three years old in the early Roman phase. There is a gradual increase in the proportion of unfused bone over time, demonstrating an earlier age of death for horses in the Roman phases. The general lack of young animals suggests they were not used in meat production, when an early age of death would be most economical. The presence of a foal indicates that horses were breeding on or near the site.

Horse bone revealed evidence of butchery marks with a small number of bones in each phase demonstrating cut and chop marks (Table 17.15). The majority of marks were knife cuts, and bones of the forelimb were more often butchered than those of the hind limb. Horse butchery is relatively common on Iron Age sites and is generally consistent with their use for meat. King (1991, 17) noted an 'apparent ending of consumption of horse meat as butchery marks are not found on horse bones' by the early Roman period, a statement which cannot be supported here. At Yarnton the percentage of bone butchered lies between 5 and 11% in all phases with the largest proportion in the late Roman. The lack of butchery marks is ambiguous evidence, and the evidence from Yarnton and Gravelly Guy (Mulville and Levitan 2004) demonstrates that for these rural settlements horse consumption, as evidenced by the butchery, continued.

Table 17.14 Horse fusion data by phase.

Phase	*Fused*	*Unfused*	*%fused*
EIA	21	14	60%
MIA	37	12	76%
LIR/ERB	17	1	94%
ERB	29	3	91%
LRB	26	2	93%

Table 17.15 Horse butchery data.

Phase	*Element*	*Butchery type* Cut	Chop	Cut and chop	*Total*	*% butchered*
EIA	Scapula	1			1	
	Metacarpal	1			1	
	Tibia		1		1	
	Total	2	1		3	7%
MIA	Radius	2	1		3	
	Metacarpal	1			1	
	Pelvis	1			1	
	Metatarsal	1		1	2	
	Total	5	1	1	7	9%
LIR	Scapula	1			1	
	Pelvis	1			1	
	Total	2			2	5%
ERB	Radius	1			1	
	Tibia	2			2	
	Total	3			3	7%
LRB	Humerus	1			1	
	Radius	2			2	
	Radius and Ulna		1		1	
	Femur		1		1	
	Total	3	2		5	11%

There is a range of horse elements present, and Table 17.16 shows the MNE for each of the phases. It is difficult to discern a pattern in such small samples and the distribution of elements appears fairly even. However, it is interesting to note that nearly half of the horse bone recovered from the middle Iron Age period is derived from the causeway deposits (33 of the 77 fragments), and this represents five of the six individuals identified.

A comparison of the relative abundance of horses at other sites in the region is shown in Table 17.17. At Thames Valley sites the proportion of horse varies from 4% to 20% (expressed as the percentage of cattle, sheep/goat, pig and horse). If the average for each period is calculated the middle Iron Age has the highest percentage and the late Iron Age the lowest.

It has to be considered that the analysis of the role of horses (and dogs) is complicated by their method of disposal. Horses are often found in articulated/associated animal bone groups (ABGs; Hill 1995, 27) and disposed of in contexts away from the usual domestic debris. Different authors deal with ABGs in various ways and this can lead to problems in comparisons. For example, at Watkins Farm, where horses are 20% of the domestic animals, the bones from (unknown numbers of) partial skeletons were included with the totals, as they were at Yarnton. On the other hand, at Gravelly Guy the articulated bones from eleven incidents of special deposits (isolated skulls, a single complete burial and two sets of articulated limbs) were excluded. It is also interesting to note that at many of the sites

Table 17.16 Horse MNE.

Element	*EIA*	*MIA*	*Phase* LIA/RB	*ERB*	*LRB*
Mandible		1	2	2	1
Scapula	3	1	1	4	3
Humerus p.	1	1	3	1	1
Humerus d.	2	1	3	1	2
Radius p.		6	2	1	2
Radius d	2	5	1	3	2
Ulna	1	1			2
Metacarpal p.	1	1	1	1	2
Metacarpal d.	1	1	1	1	1
Pelvis	1	4	1	1	1
Femur p.	1	2			3
Femur d.	2	3		1	2
Tibia p.	2	3	2	3	2
Tibia d.	3	2	2	3	2
Astragalus	2			1	
Calcaneum	2		1		
Metatarsal P	3			2	1
Metatarsal D	2			2	1
MNI	3	6	3	4	3

Table 17.17 *Thames Valley minor mammalian species NISP data.*

Site	Phase	NISP Horse	Domesticates NISP Total*	% Horse	Dog	Cat	Red deer	Roe deer	Wild species Wild pig	Hare	Fox	Badger	Weasel	No. wild spp	Comments
Ashville	EIA	19	465	4	7										excl sheep/goat skeleton
Gravelly Guy	EIA	162	2184	7	80		18	1					18	37	
Yarnton	EIA	45	2425	2	226		7	2	1		1			11	
Farmoor	IA	3	46	7	2		2P							2	excl antler frags and dog part skeleton
Whitehouse Road	IA	29	185	16	1										excl piglet burial
Appleford	EIA/MIA	53	393	13	10		1							1	3 shed red antler excluded, dog skeleton and a hedgehog
Ashville	MIA	47	1252	4	7		A							A	
Mingies Ditch	MIA	203	1741	12	5		2A							2	excl 2 piglet part burials, and puppy burial
Gravelly Guy	MIA	618	8163	8	145	3	20 (1A)	6(1A)					2	28	
Watkins Farm	MIA	237	1158	20	34	2	2A							2	
Yarnton	MIA	77	2359	3	38		10	2		3				15	
Thornhill Farm	MIA	30	143	21	1										incl ass and equids
Ashville	LIA	37	747	5			A							A	excl dog part skel (x2)
Yarnton	LIA/LIR	41	693	6	38		1	1						2	
Thornhill Farm	LIA/ERB	308	2684	11	5										incl ass and equids
Gravelly Guy	LIR/RB	242	3748	6	87		1	1		1	1	4		8	
Yarnton	ERB	46	1103	4	11			2		20				22	
Watkins Farm	ERB	138	540	26	40		2			2				4	possible roe deer A, excl dog skeleton
Ashville	RB	10	183	5	6	4				1				1	
Appleford	RB	18	272	7	8		1							1	
Farmoor	RB	31	357	9	2		4							4	excl 2 sheep and a horse part skeleton
														0	
Watkins Farm	LRB?	53	245	22	1		A								
Watkins Farm	LRB site B	55	191	29	15										
Thornhill Farm	LRB	9	34	26	55										incl ass and equids
Yarnton	LRB	45	854	5	11		1			18				19	

* Total NISP for Cattle, Sheep/Goat, Pig and Horse

A = antler; P = antler pedicles

with a high percentage of horse, eg Thornhill Farm, Appleford and Mingies Ditch, no horse ABGs are recorded.

Although it is difficult to compare the ageing information (many different techniques are used in different sites) the age range of horses at a number of Iron Age/Roman sites can be estimated from the percentage of fused bone (Table 17.18; cf Wilson 1979, 130). The majority of sites have animals dying slightly younger in the Iron Age; although Yarnton has a higher percentage of unfused horse bone than most other sites.

At the horse-dominated site of Bury Hill, Hampshire, Hamilton (2000b) concluded that the lack of perinatal and juvenile mortality indicates the absence of breeding population in the Iron Age. Potentially similar sites in the region include Farmoor, where no animals aged under 1.5 years were identified, and Whitehouse Road (Oxford) and Ditches, where only mature specimens were recorded. One possible explanation for this is that horses were not kept permanently at the sites, but were semi-feral, living and breeding in independent herds. The absence of infants and juveniles at Gussage All Saints has been adduced to support this view (Harcourt 1979).

On-site breeding is, however, demonstrated at a number of sites including Gravelly Guy, Thornhill Farm and Yarnton. At Thornhill Farm 3% of mandibles came from animals under 1 year, and at Gravelly Guy one or two infant/juveniles were found, and one third of all animals identified as under 2.5 years due to their deciduous dentition. Other evidence includes a single 9-12 month old foal at Yarnton, one immature animal from Mingies Ditch, unfused bone from an animal under 12-18 months at Watkins Farm (and three in the Roman period there), and at Ashville four mandibles came from animals under 2.5 years. This sparse evidence for foals suggests that occasionally horses were breeding on site or were captured young.

There is also little evidence that horses were being exploited mainly for meat, when a peak in slaughter at around 2 years would be expected. Despite the evidence for horse butchery at Yarnton, the management of horses best fits Levine's (1982; 1999) general attritional model where meat production is of secondary importance. The only sites with sexing information (Thornhill Farm and Bury Hill) demonstrate a large proportion of males; these would be surplus in a purely breeding herd where a ratio of 1:50 of males to females is sufficient (Levine 1999).

There is no evidence to indicate the presence of specialised horse breeding centres, although at Gravelly Guy and at Bury Hill, where large number of younger animals and few older animals have been found, it is possible that young horses were trained and then exported. At Gravelly Guy the only older animals present derive from the isolated horse skull burials, where they make up half of the ten specimens. This suggests that the disposal of adult horses was through a distinct burial practice, as younger individuals were disposed of within the general refuse (Mulville and Levitan 2004; Morris 2008).

Levine (2004) undertook a detailed analysis of the equid species present at Thornhill Farm and found both *Equus caballus* (the true horse) and *Equus asinus* (the ass) present. No other site has seen a similar level of analysis, but it is feasible that both horse and ass are present elsewhere.

Table 17.18 Percentage of horse bone fused on Thames Valley sites.

	Site	*% horse bone fused*
Early Iron Age	Appleford	75
	Ashville	100
	Barton Court Farm	90
	Farmoor	76
	Yarnton EIA	60
Middle/late Iron Age	Yarnton MIA	76
	Gravelly Guy	60*
	Thornhill Farm LIA/RB	85*
	Bury Hill LIA	90
	Watkins Farm	93
Romano-British	Ashville RB	100
	Barton Court Farm RB	94
	Farmoor RB	95
	Yarnton ERB	91
	Yarnton LRB	93
	Appleford RB	100
	Watkins Farm RB	90

*estimated from mandibles

Dog

The evidence for dogs is mostly derived from three early Iron Age burials, and a single late Iron Age burial, all of which are of adult animals. There are only four unfused dog bones; a distal metatarsal (early Iron Age), a proximal radius (late Iron Age), a proximal humerus (early Roman), and a distal femur (late Roman). The absence of young dogs may be due to the disposal of their bodies outside the excavated area, or the importation of older animals. The latter seems unlikely as dogs are best trained as puppies.

Dog bones are present at all Iron Age sites in small quantities; only appearing in large quantities in burials. Gravelly Guy, for example, has 27 dog burials; the majority were adult skeletons, although some foetal/infant burials and isolated skulls were found. Dog burials were also found at Iron Age Farmoor and in Roman deposits at Appleford, Farmoor and Watkins Farm. Thornhill Farm has an unphased dog burial (148 bones) in a pit cut by a late Roman trackway.

Only one fragment of dog bone, a skull fragment associated with a right mandible from the late

Roman enclosure ditch 877, was butchered; it bore both a chop and cut mark. Butchery marks on the skulls of smaller animals are usually associated with skinning.

Cat

Cat bones were not present in any phase. They are generally rare in the Iron Age, but have been recorded from a few sites, for example Gussage All Saints, Balksbury and Danebury. The presence of a number of juvenile remains has led to the conclusion that the domestic cat was present in Britain from the Iron Age, (Harcourt 1979; Grant 1984, Kitchener and O'Connor 2010). The few cat remains recovered from the Thames Valley, at Gravelly Guy and Watkins Farm, have not been firmly identified as domestic.

Wild mammals

Wild mammals comprise only a small part of the assemblage at Yarnton (see above). The most commonly hunted species at Yarnton are deer, hare and wild boar. None is present in large amounts in any phase. There is a very low incidence of wild mammals in most British Iron Age faunal assemblages (Hambleton 1999) and various authors have suggested that there was a proscription against the exploitation of wild animals in the Iron Age (Hill 1995) and early Roman (King 1991) periods. King (ibid.) identified an increase in the significance of wild species at late Roman sites and suggested this change may have a religious dimension and could be linked to a decline of any taboos that may have existed about the consumption of certain animals.

Table 17.17 also summarises the evidence for the larger wild species in the Thames Valley (rodents and amphibia are excluded as their bones do not occur as a result of direct anthropogenic action), and a change in wild animal exploitation is not apparent. The number of wild species shows no overall increase and the only species showing any significant change is the hare. Gravelly Guy produced the widest range of wild species in the region, but there they make up only 2% of the middle Iron Age assemblage and less in every other phase

Red deer

Of the 19 fragments of red deer recovered at Yarnton, the majority are found in the early Iron Age pit groups and the middle Iron Age causeway deposits. Only one fragment was recovered from Roman period deposits, suggesting that deer played a more important role in the Iron Age.

On the settlement sites deer bones are generally deposited as single occurrences within a feature, with a range of elements represented. The causeway deposits on the other hand, are made up of a range of bones with fragments from a left jaw and scapula and parts of two right humeri and two right tibiae. There is a lack of prime meat bones outside the causeway deposits, with only one fragment of gnawed humerus recovered from a late Iron Age/early Roman context. This is at odds with the distribution of cattle, the other large mammal found on site, whose meat bones are recovered in the settlements, and the presence of the majority of red deer meat bones in the channel suggests this species was treated differently from other animals.

The most abundant element overall is antler, with five fragments recovered, two of which are shed. One of the shed antlers from the causeway deposits has chop marks around the pedicle, and shows some signs of wear on the base of the pedicle.

A review of the Thames Valley sites reveals that a small number of red deer antler fragments were found on many sites; this material can be collected once shed, and was probably traded due to its utility. Red deer bone was only found at one other site, Gravelly Guy; where a humerus and radius were present but the majority of bone was from skull fragments, metapodials and toes. The general lack of deer remains at Thames Valley sites could indicate an absence of deer in the area, but this is at odds with the presence of their butchered bones on some sites. If venison was being traded why do we find so few meat bones? The presence of waste bones strongly suggests a local population; but why trade waste material? Wherever the deer are derived from, the general lack of meat bearing waste on settlement sites is perplexing and leads us to the conclusion that the prime meat bones were deposited elsewhere on the site or that deer were caught and consumed off-site with only parts of their carcasses returned. The causeway deposits at Yarnton (see below) provide evidence for the off-site disposal of deer bone, and suggest that this sometimes took place in watercourses.

Roe deer

Roe deer are rarer than red deer in all Iron Age assemblages. At Yarnton metapodia were recovered from two different early Iron Age pits; an almost complete metacarpal fragment from pit 8071, and a small fragment of metapodia from pit 8075, both bones were fused. In the middle Iron Age a roe deer radius and tibia were recovered from causeway deposits 13221 and 13012 (see below). The only other evidence for roe deer consist of fragments of humerus and tibia, recovered from an early Roman enclosure ditch (ditch 474, part of enclosure 206). The latter had been chopped through the distal shaft.

As with red deer, the only other site in the area with roe deer is Gravelly Guy, with a fragment of metacarpal and a phalange from middle Iron Age deposits. A possible roe deer antler was recorded from Watkins Farm (Wilson and Allison 1990). Roe deer remains are similar to those of red deer in that fragments of waste bone are the most commonly reported bones and the presence of small amounts of roe deer again raises the question of locally hunted or traded animals.

Hare

Hare increases in abundance over time. A small amount of bone was recovered from the middle Iron Age and the late Iron Age/early Roman periods, with the remainder recovered from Roman contexts (Table 17.2). This is the only wild species that increases in frequency in the Roman period compared to the Iron Age; the other common wild species, red deer, decreases at this time.

All elements of the skeleton are present but there are no groups of articulated bone found in any one context. There is no butchery recorded on any of this material, but it is likely that these animals were consumed. The rise in the quantity of hare bone is not a factor of increased sample size; the later phases contain smaller quantities of bone. Their relative absence in Iron Age contexts may have been due to a proscription against hare consumption (King 1991). The 'Celts' are said to have worshipped hares for their speed and fertility, whilst Boudica reportedly released a hare prior to battle for good luck. Caesar wrote:

> *'leporem et gallinam et anserem gustare fas non putant; haec tamen alunt animi voluptatisque causa'*
> (*De Bello Gallico*, V.12.6)

This extract states that the people of Britain do not eat hares, chicken and geese but like to keep them for pleasure and amusement. Alternatively there are many Roman references to the methods of cooking and keeping of hares in hutches and enclosures (Grant 1996), demonstrating that for the Romans hare consumption was common.

Fox

The distal half of an adult fox humerus was recovered from an early Iron Age pit, 7365 (7364). Gravelly Guy also produced evidence for fox, but from the Roman period.

Wild pig

One fragment of possible foetal wild pig left pelvis was identified by P. Smith in an early Iron Age oval pit 7598 (7597). There are no other records of fox or wild pig on sites in the Thames Valley.

Amphibia

Yarnton boasts a large collection of amphibians. The vast majority are derived from the Iron Age when it is likely they fell, or chose to hibernate, in open pits. The large numbers of bone present is a result of the deposition of a number of entire skeletons. In general only a single individual was recovered from each pit. Individual frogs are found in three early Iron Age pits (7057, 7173 and 7365) and a posthole (7065). Toads were also recovered from early Iron Age pits 7057 and 7365, with more individuals found in single contexts.

Rodents

Overall forty rodent bones were recovered. Many of these were individual finds, but a number of vole-size long bones were recovered from the early Iron Age pit 7057 (7058), and the partial skeleton of a single water vole (identified from its skull/teeth) came from the middle Iron Age pit 887.

Bird

Few bird bones were identified to species. In the early Iron Age there was a single domestic fowl tibia and a mallard metatarsal and clavicle. A goose tibia and ulna, a bantam metatarsal and a raven metacarpal from middle Iron Age contexts were the only bird bones identified to species.

Fish

Forty fragments of unidentifiable fish bone were recovered from the limestone causeway 13012 (13260), all from sieved samples. The material consists of the vertebra and skull of a fish, probably not present as a result of human activity. Its presence is, however, of note as it demonstrates that the lack of fish bone in the majority of dryland contexts at Yarnton cannot be attributed to recovery or sampling problems.

'Special' deposits

As the assemblage was recorded all bones that articulated or matched as pairs were noted. Also identified during recording were large associations of single elements, skulls and any side preferences in patterning (ie an abundance of lefts or rights). These groupings embrace and extended the special deposits identified by Grant (1984); animal burials, skulls or articulated legs and the articulated or associated animal bone groups (ABGs) highlighted by Hill (1995, 27). At Danebury, the study undertaken by Poole (1995) noted that some individual bones, for example the mandibles of horse, cattle and sheep, seem to have been selected for special treatment and also that long bones and pelves were sometimes placed in contexts suggestive of deliberation. The study of the animal bone at Yarnton does not consider all these categories; mandibles have been recorded when found in pairs but the significance of single long bones or pelves can only be demonstrated in conjunction with other contextual information. All the special deposits at Yarnton are referred to as ABGs. The recording of all articulated bones, including those expected to be deposited together during butchery, for example the calcaneum and astragalus of the hock joint, allows an assessment of the frequency of any 'waste' associations in the assemblage.

In total, 45 incidents of articulating elements, skulls, pairs or repeating elements/sides were identified in this assemblage (Table 17.19). These were classified as skeletons (limbs and torso and/or head), torsos (vertebral columns with or without ribs), limbs (fore and/or hind), repeating elements, mandible pairs and waste (articulations of the lower limbs, eg the hock joint and/or metatarsal, articulating phalanges or associations between the radius and ulna). Of the total number of ABGs, sixteen groups of waste elements (Table 17.19) were identified. Of these a number are found within pits containing other ABGs material, raising the possibility that these elements are part of a broader depositional pattern. The low incidence of waste associations highlights the unusual nature of the other ABGs. The majority of ABGs (including 'waste' groups) were found in the early Iron Age assemblage, with 23 records. There were smaller numbers in the subsequent periods. Detailed description of articulated bone and special deposits follow below.

Early Iron Age

The complete skeleton of a sheep was laid out in the bottom of a partially eroded pit 330 (383) (see Fig. 5.38). The animal was lying on its right side, with its head turned to face backwards and the front legs above the pelvis (Fig. 17.9). There were no ribs, but most of the other bones were present. This skeleton is a composite of at least two animals as both the front legs were from the right-hand side. The removal and repositioning of the front legs could indicate that both forelimbs came from other animals. However it is only possible to identify one introduced limb, which has a fusion stage at odds with the rest of the skeleton. The majority of bone is fused indicating an adult animal of over three and a half years, and is consistent with the mandibular evidence for an animal of around 8-10 years. The second right forelimb is from a younger animal; the unfused distal radius suggests an animal less than three and a half years of age.

Posthole 1314 contained the partial burial of a lamb (aged under 3-4 months) with only left hand limb elements present; the scapula, radius, pelvis, tibia and a fragment of metacarpal. Pit 1675 contained a young, less than 12-15 months old, cattle articulated left upper forelimb. The humerus, radius and ulna were present and part of the right scapula of the same animal. In structure 1756 a cattle torso made up of the cervical and thoracic vertebra and ribs was inserted into a posthole. Pit 2646 contained an adult dog skeleton; only the phalanges and left mandible were missing.

Pit 7057 contained articulated cattle limbs. One context (7341) within the pit held the right lower fore and hind limbs of a single adult individual. A second context (7058) contained a cattle jaw and a set of articulating first and second phalanges. An adult dog skeleton lay within pit 7598; most elements were present including its head and phalanges. This dog was found in association with a second pair of dog pelves. The contents of pit 7762 included a pair of dog hind limbs, on the left side from the femur to the metatarsals, and on the right from the tibia downwards. This was an adult animal with all elements fused; it had suffered a fracture of the right tibia which had healed. Also within this pit, in a different context, were a fused

Fig. 17.9 Articulated sheep in pit 330. Scale 0.5 m

Table 17.19 Articulated bone groups

Phase	*ABG no.*	*Site*	*Context . no.*	*Feature no.*	*Type*	*Species*	*Description*	*Elements*
EIA	14	YWRF	383	330	pit	Sheep	Skeleton	Skeleton
	12	YWRF	1101		scoop	Cattle	Waste	Hock
	7	YWRF	1127	B1756	feature	Cattle	Waste	Calcaneus & astragalus
	2	YWRF	1167	B1756	posthole	Cattle	Torso	Torso
	6	YWRF	1314		posthole	Sheep	F/H limbs	Part burial
	1	YWRF	1695		pit	Cattle	Fore limb	Forelimb
	25	YWRF	2646		pit	Cattle	Waste	Radius & ulna
	24	YWRF	2646		pit	Dog	Skeleton	Skeleton
	28	YCF	7058	7057	pit	Cattle	Jaw	Pair mandible
	43	YCF	7058	7057	pit	Cattle	Waste	Toes
	29	YCF	7341	7057	pit	Cattle	F/H limbs	Lower fore and hind limb
	48	YCF	7078	7307		Cattle	Waste	Tibia & astragalus
	26	YCF	7171	7173		Cattle	Waste	Radius & ulna
	27	YCF	7171	7173	pit	Cattle	Waste	Calcaneus & astragalus
	46	YCF	7298	7297	gully	Cattle	Waste	Toes
	37	YCF	7597	7598	pit	Dog	Skeleton	Skeleton
	50	YCF	7683	7762	pit	Dog	Waste	Forelimb
	38	YCF	7723	7762	pit	Dog	Hind limb	Hind limb
	38	YCF	7723	7762	pit	Dog	Hind limb	Hind limb
	39	YCF	7724	7762	pit	Horse	Hind limb	Lower hind limb
	35	YCF	8196	8195	pit	Horse	Hind limb	Lower hind limb
	34	YCF	8390	8289	pit	Sheep	Waste	Radius & ulna
	32	YCF	8425	8426	pit	Cattle	Waste	Toes
MIA	49	YWRF	7791			Cattle	Repeating elements	Femur
	5	YWRF	511			Cattle	Torso	4 VC/4VT
	42	YCF	8150	8149	pit	Sheep	F/H Limb	Skeleton
	41	YCF	8150	8149	pit	Sheep	Pair	Tibia
	3	YWRF	273			Sheep	Skeleton	Skeleton
	33	YCF	8466	8467	pit	Sheep	Waste	NQ/MT/P1
	44	YWRF	1744		pit	Dog	Skeleton	Part skeleton
	22	YWRF	510	511	pit	Horse	F/H limb	Part skeleton
LIR	10	YWRF	1000		ditch	Sheep	Jaw	Mandible
	9	YWRF	1608		pit	Dog	Skeleton	Skeleton
	15	YWRF	594		pit feature	Horse	Fore limb	Fore limb
	8	YWRF	1634		ditch	Horse	Jaw	Mandible
ERB	18	YWRF	1060		pit	Cattle	Repeating elements	Femur
	4	YWRF	51	Encl 187	ditch	Cattle	Jaw	Mandible
	19	YWRF	416	Encl 138	ditch	Cattle	Torso	Torso
	16	YWRF	264	Encl 279	ditch	Cattle	Waste	Toes
	17	YWRF	1082		pit	Sheep	Jaw	Jaw
	13	YWRF	251			Horse	Waste	MT/LMT
	11	YWRF	171	57	pit	Pig	Fore Limb	Front limbs/torso
LRB	21	YWRF	505	Encl 279	ditch	Cattle	Waste	P1/P2
	47	YWRF	332		ditch	Cattle	Waste	NQ/MT
	20	YWRF	1084		pit	Sheep	Skeleton	Skeleton

Side	*Comments*	*Age*
R	2 right forelimbs, no left	>42 months skel, forelimb <42 months
L	Ast/Cal/NQ	>3 years
R		
	3 VC, 6 VT, 1 VL (path), 15 ribs	
L	Scap/Rad/MC &Pelv/Tib upper limbs missing	<3-4 months
L	Hum/Rad/Uln (also right pelv)	<12-15 months
R	Upper halves only Uln PF	>42-48 months
L&R	Missing toes and left jaw	adult
L&R	P2 absent	
		>20-24 months
R	Rad/Uln/Carp/MC/P1&2 & Tib/Ast/NQ/MT/P1	>42-48 months
R	Lower half Tib only	>24-30 months
R	Rad PF	>12-15 months
R	Cal PF	<36 months
	P1/P2	
L&R	2 R & L Pelvis	all fused
L	Rad/Uln	all fused
L	Fem/Fib/Tib/Ast/Cal/MT	all fused
R	Fib/Tib/Ast/Cal/MT	all fused
R	Tib/Ast/Cal/MT	>24 months
R	Ast/Cal/MT(upper)	<36 months
R	Fused	>42 months
	P1/P2	>2 years
	Very fragmented mostly unfused L and R	
L&R	Limbs, no Scap/Pelv	3-4 months
L&R	L & R	foetal
L&R	Max/mand LandR lower fore and complete hindlimb	<15-20 months
		foetal
L&R	2 indivs? Skull, neck, part of fore and hind limbs	
L	L Scap/Rad/Fem/Tib/MP and Pelvis	<9-10 months
	L & R	
	Skull/Hyoid/ L Scap/Hum/Rad/Uln/Pel & R Scap/Pel/Fem/Tib/VC	adult
	Not sure if artic as L/R fragmentary	
L&R		
R	12 Fem 2 PF, 10 PUF all DUF+ 2 Tib UF	<36-42 & >36-42 months
L&R	Anterior half	
	4 VT/7 Rib	
	P1/P2	>2 years
L&R		
		fused
R	R Scap/Hum/Rad/Uln & LScap 3VC/12VT	<12 months
R		
L&R	Complete missing LMC/Ast/Cal all spine/ribs/limbs	<5 months

left dog radius and ulna and the lower leg bone of a horse, from tibia to tarsal. Another lower horse leg was recovered from pit 8195. Both sets of horse limbs were fully fused indicating that these were adult animals.

Nine further groups of articulated cattle bones were noted in this period, but these can all be interpreted as associations likely to persist within normal rubbish practises. For example, pit 7173 only contained an articulating radius/ulna and a calcaneum/astragalus – these small associations are those likely to survive butchery processes, such as carcass division, and suggest only routine domestic waste.

Middle Iron Age

The middle Iron Age has fewer recorded ABGs. Pit 273 contained a partial sheep skeleton aged below 15-20 months. This consisted of bones of the head, torso and limb bones, excluding the scapula and humerus. Nothing below the proximal half of the metacarpal or tibia was present and few of the bones were complete.

The only evidence for foals at Yarnton came from pit 511 (510). Both fore and hind left hand side limbs were recovered, but no bones from the torso or the head. The unfused state of all the bone indicates an animal of less than 9-12 months. A cattle torso was also recovered from pit 511, represented by a group of cervical and thoracic vertebra.

A partial dog burial was recovered from pit 1744. The skull, mandibles, atlas, cervical vertebrae, pelvis and sacrum were present along with the opposing front and hind limbs; the left scapula, humerus and radius were present with the right femur and tibia and a few metacarpals. There was also a second pair of mandibles present.

A concentration of cattle femora was found in ditch 7789 (7791); the 28 femoral fragments are derived from a minimum of two left femurs and five right femurs. Elements of all other species in this context only occur singly, with four sheep/goat bones, two pig bones and two dog bones present. These cattle femurs were from sub-adult animals; the unfused proximal and distal epiphyses were present, suggesting a primary deposit. As the femur fuses distally at around three to three and a half years, and proximally at three and a half to four years, it is only possible to say that some were below the age of three and others below the age of four.

Pit 8149 contained two groups of very young sheep bone. A partial skeleton of a 3-4 month old animal was present, consisting of the limb bones minus the scapula or pelvis. The second group of bones was a pair of foetal tibia. This information can be used to consider the time at which the pit was infilled. Sheep are likely to have birthed in the spring (eg Hamilton 2000a), so the presence of foetal remains suggests a spring infilling for some of the pit, but the slightly older animal of 3-4 months suggests a later summer date. As both are found in the same context either the pit filled up over a period of a couple of months or some of the bone was a secondary deposit. The latter is unlikely because of the presence of the articulating and paired bones.

Foetal bones were also recovered from pit 8467. The lower part of a sheep left hind limb was present, again suggesting a spring infilling.

Late Iron Age and late Iron Age/early Roman

The number of special deposits in the late Iron Age/LIR phase is relatively small. A pair of sheep mandibles and a broken up horse mandible were found in ditches 1000 and 1634 (enclosure 175) respectively, and a dog skeleton and a partial horse forelimb were found in pits 1608 and 594.

The dog, like that in pit 1744, had opposing front and hind limbs missing. The skull, mandibles, left scapula, entire right front limb, right pelvis and entire left hind limb were present along with sixteen ribs and a single neck vertebra. No metapodials or phalanges were recovered, nor the remaining vertebra. This was a fully fused adult animal.

The horse bone also came from an adult animal, with parts of the scapula, humerus, radius and metacarpal recorded along with two first phalanges in section 594/C. Another first phalange was recovered in section 594/A. These bones formed a composite limb, as the humerus was from the left side and the other limb bones from the right.

Early Roman

As for the middle Iron Age an unusual quantity of cattle femurs, all from the right hand side, was noted in a single pit, (1060). There were at least 12 right femurs, most of which were complete, unfused shafts from animals less than three and a half years old. The epiphyses were missing, which suggests the bone had degenerated sufficiently for the unfused ends to be lost before being placed in the pit as a secondary deposit. This could indicate a period of time between death and placement in the pit, although the process of cooking (particularly boiling) could swiftly loosen the unfused ends. The femurs were accompanied by a couple of right cattle tibiae and a single right humerus. Other material in the context included a right pig mandible, a left horse tibia and a few loose sheep teeth. Such a bias towards a single element and side is highly unusual, although this is the second pit at Yarnton that shows a bias towards the femur (see above).

The enclosure ditches contained a cattle torso (enclosure 138), a pair of cattle mandibles (enclosure 187) and articulating toes (enclosure 279). A pair of sheep mandibles was found in a pit, 171, together with a partial pig burial. The latter is a young animal (less than 12 months old) represented by the right limb, scapula to ulna, the left scapula and part of the torso (cervical and thoracic vertebra). Also present in pit 171 were numerous elements of a second, similarly aged pig. These were not noted as in articulation on recording, but do make up an almost entire second skeleton – the presence of a second right radius and ulna indicates there is more than one individual present.

Late Roman

The late Roman period only has two groupings of what is probably waste cattle bone in two ditch contexts (toes and hock bones), and a sheep skeleton in pit 1084. The latter was about five months old indicating an autumn/late summer infilling of the pit. The majority of bone from the head to the toes was present. The missing elements are the left astragalus, calcaneum and metacarpal and the right ulna.

Summary

In the early Iron Age there are two instances of cattle hind and/or fore limbs being deposited in pits, and a single torso. A sheep skeleton and a deposit of the fore and hind limbs of another individual were recorded. There were two dog skeletons, two other incidences of dog bones and two of horse hind limbs. All other material was classified as 'waste'. In the middle Iron Age a group of cattle femora and a torso, two sheep skeletons and a pair of neonatal tibiae, as well as the partial skeletons of a horse and a dog were recorded. 'Waste' articulations were also noted. In the late Iron Age there is a dog skeleton, a horse forelimb, and paired mandibles of a horse and a sheep. The early Roman had few records not identified as possible waste; a second deposit of cattle femora, a cattle torso, cattle and sheep mandible pairs, and a pig forelimb were present. The waste articulations included both cattle and horse bones. The skeleton of a sheep and two incidents of articulating cattle waste bone were recorded for the late Roman period.

Yarnton shows an overall decline in the number of ABGs over time (Table 17.19). If the waste associations are excluded then eleven incidents of burials, articulated limbs/torso and skulls were recorded in the early Iron Age, seven in the middle Iron Age and two in the LIR. The ABGs continue through into the Roman phases with small numbers in the early Roman (3) and the late Roman periods (1). It must, however, be remembered that quantifying these groups is difficult as the number of ABGs is a function of the size of the assemblage

Elsewhere Wait (1985) identified a decrease in the numbers of ABGs from the early Iron Age to middle Iron Age. Hill (1995, 120) found no evidence of this, or of a decrease in the frequency of cattle and pig deposits in the Hampshire sites over this time, but he did identify a decline in ABGs during the late Iron Age. He suggested (ibid., 121) that this reflected a change in the way meat was used, with food employed in strategies for building social obligations amongst the living instead of being reserved for offerings.

In addition to changes in the number of burials over time variation in the proportions of species in ABGs can be considered. In the Thames Valley at Yarnton dog ABGs are most common in the early Iron Age, sheep in the middle Iron Age and cattle in the Roman phases. This is the reverse of that predicted on the basis of bone counts within which cattle predominate during the middle Iron Age, with their numbers falling in the Roman period. In general the rarer species, horse and dog, appear in ABGs in greater frequencies than they do in the whole assemblage (both make up less than 4% of the major domestic species, Table 17.2). This phenomenon has already been noted by Grant (1984), Wait (1985) and is re-stated by Morris (2010), and implies that these species were treated differently. The evidence suggests that dogs and horses were less commonly consumed. This may have been a reflection of their special status as working or (for dogs) companion animals, and this difference in status appears to persist in their deposition. Wait suggested that there was an increase in the amount of dog ABG deposits over the entire Iron Age but, as noted above, this is not the case at Yarnton or at Gravelly Guy (Mulville and Levitan 2004), nor was this identified in Wessex by Morris (2008). As Hill (1995, 120) points out, dog ABGs are absent from Danebury and Winklebury.

At Gravelly Guy both the early and middle Iron Age is dominated by dog ABGs, and by sheep in the Roman period, again this does not reflect the general animal abundance, for example cattle predominate in the middle Iron Age. In other periods the pattern is less clear and the numbers of cattle and sheep ABGs are generally too small to allow firm conclusions to be drawn (cf Lambrick and Allen 2004, 223, table 6.1). Pig deposits are rare in all periods at both Yarnton and Gravelly Guy.

Other sites in the area also have some evidence of Iron Age ABGs, although few have as many as Gravelly Guy and Yarnton. They are recorded from Ashville, for example, where cattle, sheep, horse and dog articulations and cattle skulls were recovered (Wilson *et al.* 1978). At Watkins Farm there were five dog skeletons, two sets of articulated cattle vertebrae and articulated horse limb bones, while two piglet burials and fragmentary associated remains of a puppy, but no other articulated limbs, were described at Mingies Ditch. The concise report at Ditches mentions that much of the canine material was articulated (Reilly 1988), suggesting that dog burials were again common at that site. It is interesting to note that no ABGs are recorded from Thornhill Farm (Levine 2004).

Morris' (2010) recent work on Wessex, reviewing 64 sites and 845 Iron Age ABGs, has identified some overarching trends for this region, with an emphasis on sheep/goat, followed by dog, horse and cattle, but this appears to be in contrast to the dog/cattle dominated Thames Valley sites. Hill (1995, 120) has previously commented on the high degree of variability of practice between Iron Age sites and considers intra-site variation to be more important than chronological changes.

As noted above ABGs are still present in Roman contexts at Yarnton although the number falls over time. They also occurs in significantly smaller numbers at Gravelly Guy, and for both sites the range of species represented is similar to that from the Iron Age. At Gravelly Guy the Roman burials are a cattle skull in a ditch (2527), two adult and three neonatal/foetal sheep in a pit (1553), two infant pig burials from another ditch (1506), an adult horse tightly packed into a pit (617) and the burial of two complete dogs (one a very large male) and parts of a third dog.

The type of material contained within each ABG can be considered and trends identified for the different species. In Iron Age Wessex the majority were partial rather than complete skeletons (Morris 2010). Cattle and horses were generally deposited as partial ABGs, whilst for sheep/goat the proportion of complete skeletons increased during the late Iron Age. Pigs showed a reverse trend with more complete skeletons present in the early Iron Age. Dogs were often deposited as skeletons in the early and late Iron Age, but more commonly deposited as partial ABGs, particularly heads and neck, in the middle Iron Age.

The small group of animal burials at Yarnton partially agrees with this model, in that horses and cattle are only present as partial burials, but the changing emphasis on complete sheep skeletons is not identifiable, nor is an emphasis on dog heads in the Middle Iron Age. The single pig burial, made up of the right hand side of the forequarter, is in a late Roman context. Looking in detail at the composition of the ABGs, Morris (2010) concluded that for Wessex the axial skeleton, mainly the vertebral column, was the most common ABG for cattle, horse and sheep. At Yarnton there is a similar emphasis on cattle torsos (vertebrae and ribs), but horses are most commonly represented by limbs and sheep by partial skeletons. The dog ABGs at Yarnton are complete/partial skeletons or articulating hindlimbs.

The two large groups of Roman cattle femurs at Yarnton are without parallel. The middle Iron Age example with fragmented bones of both sides could represent food debris, although the selection and re-deposition of a large group of single elements is still of interest. The early Roman example, featuring complete bones and a distinct side bias, has parallels only with classical votive deposits (Davis 1987a; 1987b; Stallibrass pers. comm.) where the right hand side of limbs were deposited.

Whilst Roman studies have accepted diversity in expressions of ritual behaviour it is only recently that the range of ritual activity of structured deposition that is not associated with cult buildings, formal or informal burials or particular kinds of natural or man-made contexts has been considered (Fulford 2001). As Fulford notes, this behaviour is strongly reminiscent of evidence from the British Iron Age; so the fills found in pits at Newstead, for example, have been compared with those from Danebury (Clarke 1997). Fulford's (2001) review of Roman evidence from non-rural sites identifies ABGs and repeating elements at Silchester, London, Neatham, Baldock, Verulamium and Portchester. Other notable examples include Cambridge (Alexander and Pullinger 1999, 51-6) and Springhead (Andrews *et al.* forthcoming), which demonstrate the link between pits and features which may more specifically be described as 'ritual shafts'. The majority of these types of deposits are found in pits and wells and they range in date from the later 1st century BC to the 5th century AD. Fulford (2001) sees these deposits as forming a strong link to the pre-Roman past in lowland Britain; however the connection is in the structured or special natures of the deposits, rather than the substance of the deposits themselves. The common Roman themes for some sites are complete or near complete skeletons of dogs, whereas for other animals only selected body parts, such as the skull, were selected. At other sites the deposits contain a wider range of species; whilst a further group has a link between infants and animal remains (birds, dogs or young animals).

As noted above, at Yarnton and Gravelly Guy the proportion of dogs in ABGs falls in the Roman period, contra Morris (2010, 7). Apart from a slight emphasis on younger animals at Gravelly Guy, there is no noticeable change to a Romano-British pattern of ABGs on these Thames Valley sites. If anything there would appear to be continuity in practice, particularly in the unusual femora deposits, which suggests that Romanisation of these sites has not affected the practices associated with special deposits. A good local example is a shallow pit of late 2nd century date from Alchester, the fills of which included bird bone and articulated horse limbs as well as a notable ceramic assemblage (Booth *et al.* 2001, 101, 103-4).

The contextual analysis necessary for understanding ABGs is a complex process (Morris 2008; Maltby 2010) and extremely detailed analysis lies outside the scope of this report. In addition to considering the overall proportion of animals, the significance of different type of deposit, the links between different types of ABGs, different species and the relationship between the bone and other material found within pits require further investigation.

Floodplain causeway deposits

The middle Iron Age deposits found lying over the limestone causeway (Fig. 17.10) can be separated out and compared to the main assemblage. It was initially thought that this material formed some sort of 'hard-core' for the construction of the limestone causeway, but stratigraphic analysis identifies the

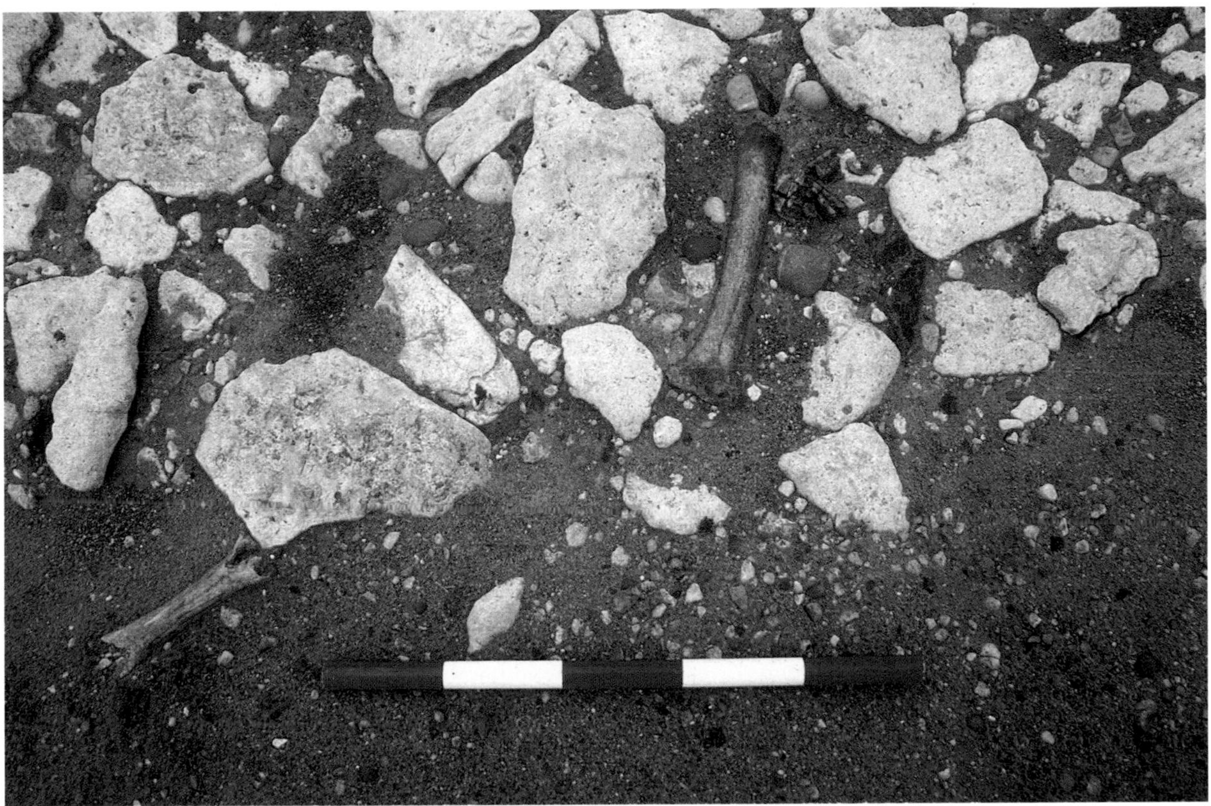

Fig. 17.10 Animal bone on limestone causeway. Scale 0.5 m

majority of bone as having been recovered from both within and on the surface of the causeway.

The proportions of the animals present within the 402 fragments identified to species are very different from those in the settlement contexts. For the major domestic species there is more cattle and horse bone present in the causeway and less of the smaller species (Table 17.20). There is also a larger percentage of wild species present, with the small amount of red and roe deer making up 3% of the total assemblage, a much higher figure than is found in any other part or phase of the site. If we examine the cattle assemblage in more detail, we can identify a minimum of thirty cattle deposited within the causeway, with smaller amounts of horse (5), sheep (3), red deer (2), and a single pig, dog and roe deer represented.

The cattle MNI is based upon right humeri, and a brief examination of the other cattle material indicates a distinct bias towards right cattle limbs in the causeway deposits. Whilst such a bias may

Table 17.20 Comparison of the relative abundance of species in causeway and settlement contexts.

	% NISP						
	Cattle	*Sheep/goat*	*Pig*	*Horse*	*Dog*	*Red deer*	*Roe deer*
Settlement	57	33	4	3	2	3	-
Causeway	81	6	2	10	2	7	2

Table 17.21 Ratio of left to right sides found in channel deposits.

Cattle Element	Ratio *NISP*	*MNI*
Jaw	1:0.6	1:0.8
Scapula	1:1.7	1:2
Humerus	**1:3.4**	**1:3.8**
Radius	**1:2.9**	**1:2.6**
Ulna	1:0.5	1:0.3
Metacarpal	**1:2.6**	**1:2.5**
Pelvis	1:0.5	1:0.8
Femur	**1:6**	**1:5.7**
Tibia	1:0.8	1:0.9
Astragalus	1:1.7	1:1.7
Calcaneum	All Right	All Right
Metatarsal	**1:3**	**1:3.2**
All elements	**1:2.19**	**1:2.7**
Total Cattle NISP	223	
Other species - all elements	*Ratio NISP*	*NISP*
Sheep	1:1.43	17
Pig	**1:2**	3
Horse	1:0.86	27
Dog	1:1	4
Red deer	**1:2**	6
Roe deer	1:1	2

Bold identifies those with more than twice as many rights as lefts

occur easily in small samples, the large collection of bone from the causeway does suggest that such a bias is not just a slight unevenness in the material. Table 17.21 show the ratio of right to left limb bones for cattle, using both the NISP (based on fragments) and the MNI (based on zones). If there were parity in the sides of limbs deposited the ratios would be 1:1. For some of the smaller limbs with only a few fragments present there is a bias towards the left limbs, but for the larger samples there are anything up to six times as many right as left bones present (femur). This pattern is particularly interesting in the light of the bias towards right limb bones recovered in the early Roman pit 1060 and the less pronounced bias towards right femora in the middle Iron Age pit 7791, as described above.

A brief comparison of the maximum number of left and right-hand zones for all elements from the largest groups was undertaken to see if the side bias occurs in contexts within or overlying the causeway. This reveals that both have a bias towards right-hand elements; although it is more pronounced in material within or beneath the causeway.

Wilson (1996) has identified the preferential deposition of larger species in larger features away from the core of settlements, and this could account for the higher proportions of cattle, horse and red deer in the palaeochannel. Additionally, bone, particularly the long bones of large animals, could provide a structural component of the causeway, the movement of water perhaps washing away smaller bone. However, the remarkable bias towards the right side of cattle both within and overlying the causeway suggests that more than simple utility was a factor. There is plentiful evidence that water courses were used for deposition of human and animal bones in the Bronze Age and Iron Age. Examples include the human burials at Eton Rowing Lake (Allen *et al.* 2000), the human and animal remains in the Trent at Langford (Garton *et al.* 1997), the deposits of animal bone around the causeway at Fiskerton, Lincolnshire (Field and Parker Pearson 2003) and the many human skulls recovered from the Thames (Bradley and Gordon 1988; Knüsel and Carr 1995). Whilst the present deposit is extremely unusual it does suggest that for Yarnton in the middle Iron Age the watercourse on the floodplain became a focus for the deposit of cattle remains. As with the contents of pit 1060 the evidence suggests that the right side, in particular, of cattle had a special significance.

Metrical Data

The measurements are presented as supplementary digital data on the Oxford Archaeology website

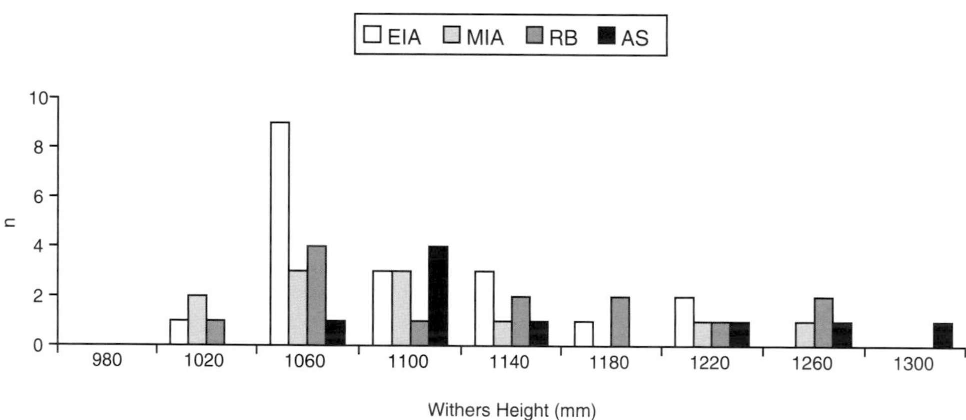

Fig. 17.11 Cattle withers height

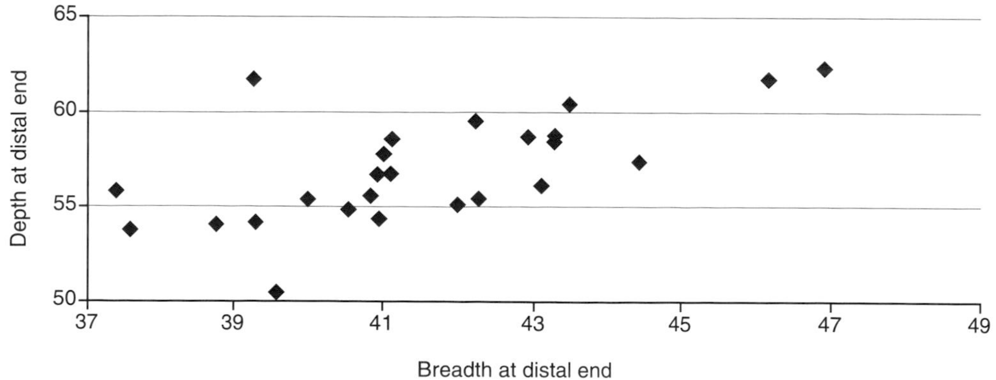

Fig. 17.12 Cattle tibia measurements

(http://library.thehumanjourney.net). Despite the relatively large assemblage, much of the metrical data is not sufficient for a detailed chronological analysis. For many measurements there are only Iron Age examples whilst for most (including metapodials) there were too few examples to allow bivariate statistics to be calculated. Data for each of the species are compared to Anglo-Saxon measurements from Yarnton (Mulville and Ayres 2004) and to those for other Iron Age and Roman sites.

Cattle

The most abundant measurements come from the small robust bones, such as the astragalus and phalanges. The former demonstrates an increase in length between Iron Age and Roman periods, whilst the latter decreases. Cattle withers heights were calculated and are compared with the results from Anglo-Saxon Yarnton in Figure 17.11. The average height of cattle increases from the early Iron Age to the middle Iron Age to the Roman period, although Anglo-Saxon cattle on average are not taller than those in the Roman period. The range of sizes remains wide, although there are no taller cattle in the early Iron Age and no small cattle in the Anglo-Saxon period.

The larger samples of measurements from the tibia are used to compare distal breadth and distal depth in a scatter plot. There are some more robust specimens present (Fig. 17.12). The larger individuals are not the few Roman specimens, which cluster in the centre of the scatter plot. There could be a small number of larger males and/or castrate males present. This could suggest that surplus males were culled earlier than females (before the distal tibia fuses at 24-30 months, so cannot be measured), and that only a few survived into adulthood as working/breeding animals.

If we compare the measurements with those from other Iron Age and Roman sites (Table 17.22) the Yarnton cattle astragali are a similar size to those from other sites. The smaller samples of metacarpals have a wide range with a few larger specimens present, whilst the metatarsals fall within the range found at other sites. Iron Age withers heights are both smaller and larger than in the comparative sites, but the Roman measurements fall within the expected range.

Sheep

There are few Roman measurements for sheep, making an intra-site chronological comparison difficult for individual measurements. The withers height calculation demonstrates a reduction in the average height of sheep between the Iron Age and the Roman with taller Anglo-Saxon sheep present (Fig. 17.13). The Roman metacarpals and metatarsals are on average smaller than those on other sites, although the range of measurements is similar. Other measurements, such as the distal humerus

Table 17.22 Comparative cattle measurements after Wilson et al. (1978).

Withers height (m)		*no.*	*range*	*mean*	*s.d.*
IA	Yarnton	20	0.93-1.21	1.08	
	Ashville	10	1.0-1.11		
	Appleford	1		1.03	
	Farmoor	6	1.01-1.18		
RB	Yarnton	2	1.12-1.18	1.15	
	Appleford	2	1.21-1.25	1.23	
	Farmoor	1	1.13-1.18	1.15	
Astragalus length (mm)					
IA	Yarnton	31	63	58.3	3.1
	Ashville	18	53-64	58.5	3.4
	Appleford	8	55-60	58	
	Farmoor	1	57	57	
	Barton Court Farm	13	54-62	58.5	2.4
	Catcote	14	51-63	57	
	Croft Ambrey	20	55-63	57.7	1.3
	Grimthorpe	8	56-61	59.5	
RB	Yarnton	30	55-67	60.2	3.08
	Appleford	4	58-70	64.3	
	Farmoor	5	59-75	65.2	
	Corbridge	9	53-63	58	
	Shakenoak	11	56-66	62.8	3.5
Metacarpal length (mm)					
IA	Yarnton	12	164-203	180.5	11.4
	Ashville	5	167-183	175.4	
	Appleford	1	171	171	
	Farmoor	4	174-182	177.8	
	All Cannings Cross	14	167-185		
	Catcote	6	155-184	176	
	Croft Ambrey	10	162-178	171.8	1.8
	Glastonbury	12	158-181	169.5	
RB	Yarnton	5	171-202	181.3	
	Ashville	2	189-192	187	
	Farmoor	2	189-192	187.5	
	Corbridge	96	182	182	
	Shakenoak	8	174-190	184.1	
Metatarsal length (mm)					
IA	Yarnton	9	192-208	198	
	Ashville	5	197-213	204.9	
	Farmoor	4	188-216	203.3	
	Tripontium	24	182-208		
	Catcote	8	179-226	198.4	
	Croft Ambrey	3	193-204	197.7	
	Glastonbury	16+	185-206	194	
	Grimthorpe	5	200-216	208.7	
RB	Yarnton	2	192-203	186.6	
	Appleford	2	226-233	229.5	
	Portchester	##	183-240		
	Shakenoak	2	208-210	209	
	Tripontium	6	205-217	210.7	

Table 17.23 Comparative sheep measurements after Wilson et al. (1978).

Withers height (m)		*no.*	*range*	*mean*	*s.d.*
IA	Yarnton	19	0.54-0.62	0.59	
	Ashville	14	0.53-0.64	0.59	
	Appleford	2	0.60-0.63	0.61	
	Ashville	1		0.63	
RB	Yarnton	11	0.53-0.61	0.57	
	Appleford	1		0.61	
	Farmoor	1		0.67	
Metacarpal length (mm)					
IA	Yarnton	3	116-127	122.4	
	Ashville	3	109-120	115.3	
	Appleford	2	123-128	125	
	Croft Ambrey	2	108-125	116.5	
	All Cannings Cross	2+	112-128		
	Glastonbury	10+	104-134		
RB	Yarnton	3	110-112	110.3	
	Gad	3	126-134	130.6	
	Tripontium	3	122-123	122.3	
Metatarsal length (mm)					
IA	Yarnton	2	118-137	125.5	
	Ashville	7	122-140	133	
	All Cannings Cross	2+	122-141		
	Glastonbury	110	109-136		
RB	Yarnton	3	125-135	130.4	
	Ashville	1	139	139	
	Appleford	1	134	134	
	Farmoor	1	147	147	
	Gad	6	128-144	135	
	Tripontium	6	125-137	131.2	
Width of distal humerus (mm)					
IA	Yarnton	18	23-30	26.2	2.04
	Ashville	30	23-32	26.3	1.4
	Appleford	3	25-28	27	
	Barton Court Farm	26	23-28	25.4	1.5
	Croft Ambrey	18	24-30	26.8	1.2
	Grimthorpe	3	27-30	28.7	
RB	Ashville	2	23-28	25	
	Farmoor	3	30-31	30.3	
	Gadebridge	5	25-28		
Width of distal metatarsal (mm)					
IA	Yarnton	3	21-22	21.6	
	Ashville	7	21-24	22.3	
	Appleford	2	22-23	22.5	
	Farmoor	1	24	24	
	Barton Court Farm	18	18-20	19.3	1
	Grimthorpe	3	20-22	21.2	
RB	Yarnton	4	21-26	22.7	
	Gad	4	21-23	22	
	Tripontium	6	20-24	21.8	

and metatarsal do not show this reduction in size, and as all the Roman samples are very small no firm conclusions can be drawn. If we compare the withers height to other sites the Iron Age sheep (Table 17.23) are of similar height to those at Ashville, and the Roman sheep are smaller than those at the two other Roman sites.

As for cattle the distal tibia measurements have been plotted (Fig. 17.14). Again a few individuals belonging to the Iron Age group are larger (a single Roman animal is in the centre of the chart). It is possible that, as for cattle, these larger specimens are males, with only a few surviving beyond the age of distal tibia fusion (15-20 months) as breeding males or castrates.

Pig

There is only a small amount of pig data; for withers height there is a wide range of pig sizes, and the few Anglo-Saxon animals are smaller (Fig. 17.15). Other comparative measurements demonstrate that the

Table 17.24 Comparative pig measurements after Wilson et al. (1978).

3rd molar length (mm)		*no.*	*range*	*mean*	*s. d.*
IA	Yarnton	4	28-32	30.5	
	Ashville	8	30-35	32	
	Farmoor	1	31		
	Glastonbury	3	29-33	30.3	
	Balksbury Camp	3	30-41	34.3	
	Durrington	25	31-38		
RB	Farmoor	1	30	30	
	Fishbourne	53	28-44	*c* 33	*c* 2.8

Table 17.25 Comparative horse measurements after Wilson et al. (1978).

Withers height (m)		*no.*	*range*	*mean*
IA	Yarnton	3	1.29-1.4	1.35
	Ashville	6	1.20-1.42	
	Farmoor	1		1.28
RB	Yarnton	4	1.13-1.49	1.33
	Ashville	2		1.41
	Farmoor	3	1.22-1.41	
	Appleford	1		1.28
Metacarpal length (mm)				
IA	Ashville	3	204-231	214.3
	Farmoor	1	208	208
	All Cannings Cross	7+	191-212	
	Glastonbury	8+	183-204	
RB	Yarnton	1	221	221
	Ashville	1	227	227
	Appleford	1	206	206
	Tripontium	8	206-217	210.9

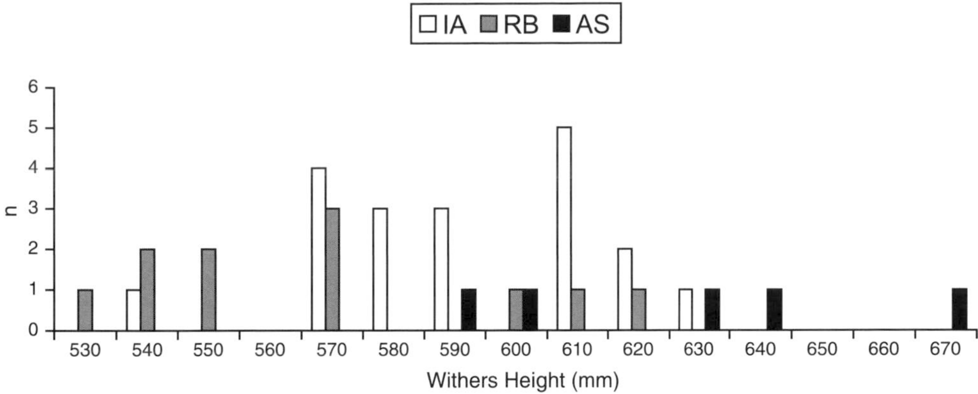

Fig. 17.13 Sheep withers height

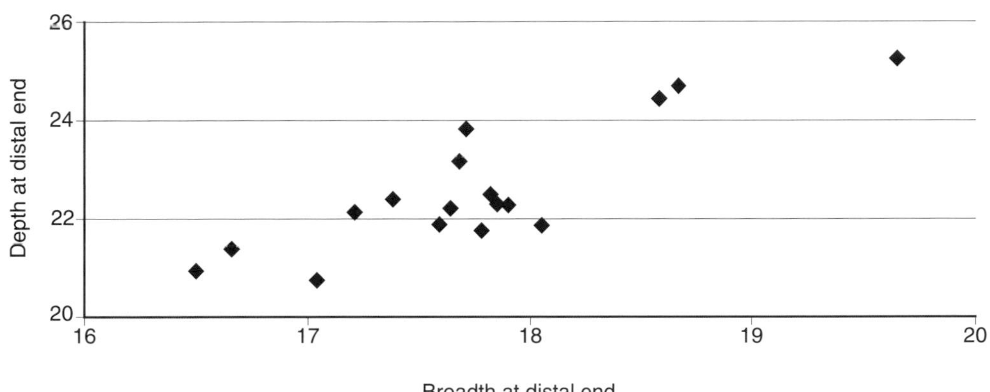

Fig. 17.14 Sheep tibia measurements

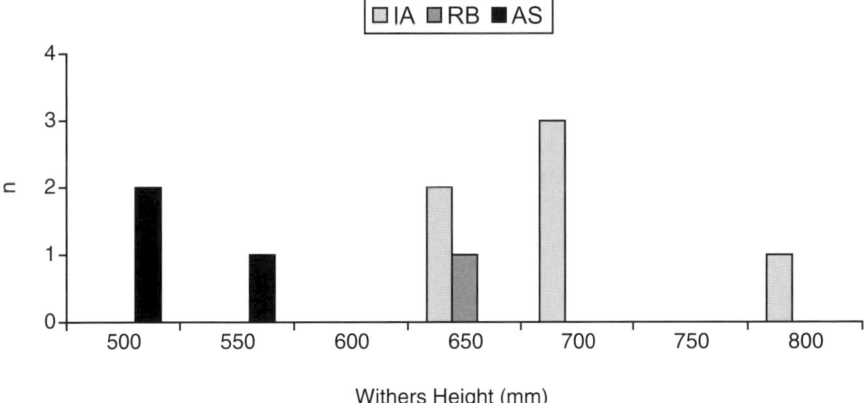

Fig. 17.15 Pig withers height

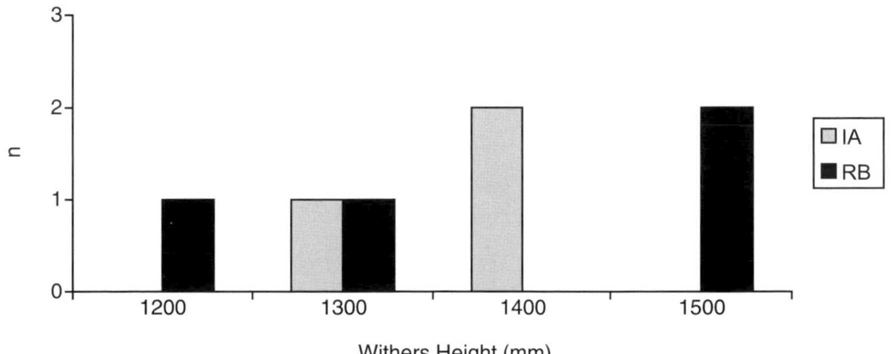

Fig. 17.16 Horse withers height

Yarnton animals are similar to those from other sites in terms of tooth size (Table 17.24).

Horse

The few horse measurements show a large range in withers heights (Fig.17.16) with a possible increase in the range of withers heights in the Roman period with individuals both larger and smaller than in the Iron Age (Table 17.25). The only comparative measurement shown is for the metacarpal, which falls within the size range of other sites.

In general, the Yarnton measurements fall within the range seen at other sites. There is some evidence that cattle are increasing in height over time and sheep are decreasing. The pig sample is too small for conclusions to be drawn. There is slight evidence for increasing variation in the size-range of horses from the Iron Age to the Roman period as noted by King (1991), although for cattle withers heights the reverse is true. There is no evidence of dual size ranges for any of the species, indicating Romano-British improvement of stock, although this lack is likely to be a product of the small sample size.

DISCUSSION

The role that animals play at Yarnton (here used in the sense of both YWRF and Cresswell Field parts of the site) can be summarised as follows; for the Iron Age and Roman phases domestic animals were the mainstay of the food economy. Yarnton has a higher proportion of cattle than is seen at many other Thames Valley sites. The numbers of cattle increased from the early to the middle Iron Age and then steadily declined, whilst those of sheep and to a lesser extent pig increased.

The age of death information identifies a farming regime that focused on meat production for all species, with only a small number of adult animals retained as breeding stock, although there is the potential for some use of cattle for secondary products (milk, traction). Whilst sheep fleeces were probably utilised and the few goats may have been milked; there is little evidence of a specialised focus on ovi-caprid secondary products. This regime suggests reasonably large herd and flock sizes capable of sustaining high levels of sub-adult mortality. The environment of the Thames Valley would have encouraged the development of larger cattle herds than, for example, those found in Wessex. The river valleys and gravel terraces have a permanent water supply, an essential requirement for cattle as they need to drink at least twice daily. Sheep are less well suited to damp ground.

There was little evidence for calves or lambs on site. The absence of small, young, fragile bone could be ascribed to preservation and recovery factors, but could also be a demonstration of an extensive farming system with animals breeding away from the settlement and only food animals returned to the site.

Although all parts of the main food animals are recovered from the site, Yarnton does not show the same skeletal element abundance as other Iron Age sites. Yarnton has less waste bone than found at other sites (for example the smaller than expected number of mandibles in some periods), which could be indicating the importation of meat. Whether these are coming from another settlement or from outlying areas, where the community's stock is grazed, cannot be ascertained.

The other two domestic mammals, horse and dog, are present in small amounts and there was little evidence for the young of either of these animals. The carcasses of both animals were utilised, although the sparse evidence for dogs suggests that they were merely skinned, whilst horses were more comprehensively butchered. Dogs were mostly recovered as complete burials, which could indicate that they were not consumed. Domestic fowl is found in the early Iron Age but with only a single bone recovered it is likely they contributed little to the site economy.

Wild animals play only a very minor role in terms of food production, with little evidence for them on site. As in other Thames Valley sites, red deer antler is present, but Yarnton (like Gravelly Guy) differs in that a small amount of deer bone is also deposited on the settlement in the Iron Age. What is perplexing is that these elements do not represent joints of venison, returned from hunting expeditions or traded with other communities, but are the limb extremities and skull fragments (although the latter could be associated with unshed antler). These low-utility remains could be the remnants of animals traded in from farther afield or, as the evidence from the causeway deposits suggests, the hunting of these animals was followed by the disposal of the prime meat elements outside settlements. In either scenario, whether a local population with a proscription against the return of bones or the trade in 'waste' red deer bone, these animals were treated very differently from domestic food animals. The differential treatment of wild and domestic species is not unexpected; the farmers at Yarnton would have a very different relationship with deer as hunted animals. The process of hunting itself would have had its own rituals, social grouping and tools, whilst the food obtained through a different type of skill, from an untamed animal, was probably imbued with significance.

In addition to red deer, there is some indication that roe deer were also hunted in the Iron Age, although their bones are even rarer on sites and again it is mostly waste bones that are deposited with the settlements. Other wild species are mostly present as occasional bones, with few wild mammals or birds recovered. The exception to this is the hare which increases in abundance in the Roman periods. As discussed above, its absence in the Iron Age probably results from a proscription against its consumption, which then disappears with the Romanisation of the settlement. As at other sites of this period there were no fish bones recovered from Yarnton.

Yarnton differs from many of the Thames Valley sites in the higher quantities of cattle present but has similarities with Gravelly Guy, Thornhill Farm and Appleford in this respect. Grant considered the Upper Thames Valley and Wessex as one region and found differences relating to topography; the chalk downland sites above *c* 76 m OD exhibit a greater emphasis on sheep while the lowland sites, below *c* 76 m OD are biased towards cattle. At only about 60 m above OD, Yarnton is consistent with this model in its abundance of cattle.

Lambrick (1992b) suggested that there was an increase in production from the early Iron Age, and that in the middle Iron Age there is an increased intensification of pastoral and arable farming which continues into the late Iron Age. This middle Iron Age intensification resulted in intra-regional variation in animal husbandry regimes, and Lambrick considered there to be evidence for the development of specialised pastoralism with a strategy of seasonal transhumance exploiting the summer pastures of the flood plain. Hambleton (1999) considered there to be too few data to allow Lambrick's models to be tested, although she conceded that the intra-regional variation in cattle mortality profiles may be indicative of variation in animal husbandry strategy, whilst the reasonably high percentage of cattle may indicate a specialised pastoral economy. At Yarnton there is no evidence for a change in the relative abundance of stock between the early and middle Iron Age, but there is a change in the age at which cattle are dying. The intensity of the cull of prime cattle is greatest in the middle Iron Age with more animals dying during age stage D, at 18-30 months, than at any other time. There is no such change in sheep management over this time.

In general, the farming strategy at Yarnton utilised extensive farming methods with sheep and cattle grazing away from the settlement, at least during the spring. Hambleton interprets low sheep mortality at stage C (6-12 months), as seen at Yarnton, to indicate a more permanent occupation here than at some other Thames Valley sites. Thus the site remains occupied all year round and the stock are moved in a form of seasonal transhumance. It is unlikely that sheep were permanently returned to this low-lying ground for the winter as they do not thrive on damp ground, although it is possible that they and the cattle were used to manure the agricultural land as necessary.

The age at death information indicates that sheep are managed in a similar manner to that of other Iron Age sites, but the cattle found at Yarnton are being kept until a slightly older age and culled at two specific times, at 8-18 months and as adults. This slight increase in age is consistent with culling animals at the age of prime meat production. This could demonstrate the presence of a consumer site to which meat is imported, or one with abundant pasture allowing animals to be kept to an older age. The lack of very young or old pigs is again consistent with prime meat production.

At Yarnton there seems to be a focus on meat throughout time, although there is greater emphasis on prime animals in the Roman period compared to the Iron Age. This change is in line with the conclusions drawn by King (1991) that more animals are killed when adult or sub-adult in the Roman period than in the Iron Age, and he sees this as implying a husbandry system that emphasised meat and wool production. King also concluded that Romano-British farming communities in general must have been richer; since more live animals were occupying the land at the same time, consuming valuable pasture and fodder.

The presence of many ABGs within the numerous Iron Age pits at Yarnton, and continuity of this type of deposition, though in admittedly smaller quantities, through to the Roman period give an impression of a community for whom animals provide both food and social meaning through time. The changing nature of British society and the inevitable Romanisation of the settlement changed the emphasis of animal husbandry strategies but did not entirely exclude the role of 'special deposits'. The careful composition of many skeletons and limbs, including the few composite skeletons made of more than one individual, suggest that on some occasions it was the completeness of a deposited animal that was important. On the other hand, the large collections of right cattle limbs in the causeway deposits and right femora in an early Roman pit suggest that at other times it was important to place the appropriate portion of many different animals within special deposits. The proscriptions against fish, and other wild species, the changing relationship with hares and the returning of only some parts of deer to the sites provide further evidence of people for whom animals had symbolic significance. A detailed examination of the role of wild animal and special deposits within the Thames Valley lies outside the scope of this report. Nevertheless the differences between sites in terms of the presence or absence of wild species and special deposits suggest that there are characteristics of communities that cannot be defined by examining farming strategies alone.

Chapter 18: Environmental Evidence

The charred plant remains from Yarnton and Cresswell Field were reported upon at widely different stages in the project. The work by Chris Stevens on Yarnton was undertaken initially as part of the research for his Ph.D. (Stevens 1996). The Cresswell Field assemblage was examined rather later by Ruth Pelling. Their separate texts have been retained but the tabulated data are presented in a similar way. The texts have not, however, been updated otherwise. Nomenclature for the plant remains follows Stace (1997) for indigenous species and Zohary and Hopf (2000) for cultivated species. The traditional binomial system for the cereals is maintained here, following Zohary and Hopf (2000, 28, table 3, 65, table 5). The Cresswell Field report is placed first because of the earlier chronological emphasis of the material.

CHARRED PLANT REMAINS FROM CRESSWELL FIELD *by Ruth Pelling*

Introduction

A number of recent excavations of Iron Age settlements in the Upper Thames Valley have involved systematic sampling for carbonised plant remains. The available assemblages have enabled detailed studies of the nature of the arable economy of the sites and the role of the settlements within the landscape. Most significantly, the relationship between the nature of the assemblages, and hence the role of agriculture, has been linked with the topographical location of the settlements. Settlements associated with arable agriculture appear to occupy sites on the Second Gravel Terrace, while sites with a greater reliance on pasture tend to be situated on the lower ground closer to the river. The excavation of the component sites of the Yarnton project has allowed a landscape study to be made within one fairly limited geographical area, which covers both the floodplain and the Second Gravel Terrace. The project also allows the examination of developments through time.

During the excavation of the multi-period Second Gravel Terrace site of Cresswell Field, 61 samples were extracted for the analysis of carbonised plant remains and wood charcoal. A variety of contexts were sampled, representing the full range of feature date and type, although preservation and quantities of remains were such that the analysis concentrated on the Iron Age and Anglo-Saxon samples. The latter samples from Cresswell Field have been discussed previously (Pelling 2004).

Method

Sampling strategy

The abundance and density of features across the site meant that it was only possible to excavate a percentage of the discrete features. The site was therefore divided into approximately 50 m square blocks and 40% of the pits in each square were sectioned and sampled. The selected pits covered a range of sizes and types. Pits which produced important pottery assemblages or other significant deposits from the initial half were excavated totally and soil samples were taken from across the range of date and feature type. In addition, an initial sample of 20% of the postholes was treated in the same manner as the pits. If any groups of postholes appeared to form a structure a further representative sample was examined. Samples for charred plant remains were taken from selected features examined in this way. In total, 61 samples of 10-20 litres in size were taken. The samples were floated onto a 0.5 mm mesh and slowly air dried.

Analytical methods

All flots were scanned under a binocular microscope at up to x50 magnification. Any charred seeds and chaff observed were provisionally identified and their abundance estimated. In addition, charcoal fragments were broken transversely and examined at up to x50 magnification, and thus identified as either ring-porous taxa, such as *Fraxinus* (ash) and *Quercus* (oak), or diffuse-porous.

On the basis of the scanning results, a total of 24 samples from Iron Age features and one late Bronze Age deposit were identified as containing sufficient material to warrant detailed analysis of seeds and chaff. The samples came from pits, possible cremation burials, ring gullies and a hearth. Eight samples were examined for charcoal, one sample (sample 7047/8) from a late Bronze Age 'burnt mound' feature 7108 (7107), six from early Iron Age deposits and one from a middle Iron Age feature.

Samples for detailed analysis were sorted under a binocular microscope at magnifications of x10 to x50 for the retrieval of charred plant remains. Identifications were made by morphological characteristics and by comparison with modern reference material held by the Environmental Archaeology Department, University Museum, Oxford. Random fragments of charcoal were extracted from a 2 mm mesh for identification. Individual fragments of charcoal were fractured and examined in transverse section at magnifications of x20 and x40, and in tangential and radial sections at x100 and x400. Identifications were based on reference to the key for European Hardwoods in Schweingruber (1978) and by comparison with modern reference material held in the University Museum, Oxford.

Results

The results of the analysis (Tables 18.1-18.3) are first discussed in terms of species present, including the ecological implications of the weed/wild component. Secondly, the samples are discussed in terms of their composition.

Triticum (wheat)

Triticum species are represented by grains, glume bases and rachis internodes. Grains showing visible signs of distortion, such as blistering or bursting, were simply identified as *Triticum* sp. Of the remaining grains, both hulled and free-threshing varieties were identified. *Triticum spelta* (spelt) is the most commonly represented species in both the grain and the chaff components. Preservation and the inherent difficulties in distinguishing between *T. spelta* and *T. dicoccum* (emmer) meant that some grains could not be assigned to a species. Given that no grain or glume bases of *Triticum dicoccum* could be positively identified it is plausible that it is not a major component and that the majority of the indeterminate hulled wheat grains are in fact of spelt. Spelt appears to be the principal crop of the Iron Age, replacing emmer in the first half of the first millennium BC, and is commonly encountered in Iron Age cereal assemblages of the Upper Thames valley (eg Jones 1978; 1986b; Moffett 2004). It is a very hardy wheat which has good milling and baking properties. The decline of spelt as an arable crop is probably largely due to the difficulties of threshing.

Grains of free-threshing *Triticum* sp. form a minor component of the cereal assemblage. Both compact and more elongated free-threshing wheat grains were present. Free-threshing wheats are present in botanical assemblages from the Neolithic onwards, but only sporadically and in small quantities, although the species may be under-represented in the charred record in relation to hulled wheats. They have many advantages, such as being winter hardy, high yielding and free-threshing, but the loose glumes also mean that they are prone to attack from birds and fungi, are poor competitors with weeds and need greater soil fertility than other forms of wheat (Jones 1981). It has been suggested that free-threshing wheat only became an important crop when greater amounts of fertiliser were available and the man-hours necessary for cultivation and weeding could be invested (ibid.).

Several wheat grains were very short and compact in the manner of compact free-threshing grain, but displayed surface detail consistent with grain that had been charred while restricted by a tightly fitting glume, indicating that they were in fact hulled. Jones (1978) demonstrated that the shape of some well-preserved wheat grains from the Ashville site, Abingdon, suggests a continuous cline between bread/club wheat and spelt, thus highlighting the difficulties in the identification of wheat grains (but see also Campbell and Straker 2003).

Hordeum (barley)

Barley is represented by grains and by a single rachis internode. The presence of *Hordeum vulgare*, the hulled 6-row variety, is attested by two asymmetrical lateral grains. Further grains could be identified as hulled on the basis of two parallel ridges on their dorsal surfaces or by the presence of fragments of palea and lemma. No grains of naked barley were identified. The one rachis internode was too poorly preserved to be identified as either the dense or the lax-eared form. *H. vulgare* occurs continuously in the Upper Thames Valley from the Neolithic onwards. Nationally the naked varieties seem to have disappeared by the early Iron Age (Helbaek 1952; Hillman 1981), which has been interpreted as a result of barley ceasing to be a crop for human consumption and becoming a crop principally for fodder, for which hulled varieties are sufficient (van der Veen 1992; Gill and Vear 1980).

Other edible plants

Nut shell fragments of *Corylus avellana* (hazel nut) occur in small numbers in a few samples. Hazel nut is a major component of early prehistoric assemblages in Southern Britain (Moffett 2004, 423), and continues to occur, although in smaller quantities, throughout the Iron Age (eg Moffett 1988; 2004, 428).

Weed/wild component

The weed/wild component represented in the assemblage is a mixture of common weeds of arable/cultivated ground and some species of damp ground and grassland (Table 18.2). Two species of damp ground represented are *Eleocharis palustris* (spike rush), a rhizomatous perennial herb commonly associated with grazed damp meadows (Walters 1949) and *Montia fontana* subsp. *chondrosperma* (blinks) which prefers light, usually sandy or gravelly, acid soils, (Clapham *et al.* 1987). Both species require marsh conditions at least in the spring but can tolerate drier summer conditions. Seeds of *Carex* spp. (sedge) occur in several of the samples. These are again rhizomatous perennials, many of which, although not all, grow on wet or damp ground. *Ranunculus* spp. (buttercup) is also commonly associated with damp grassland.

These damp ground species, notably *Eleocharis*

Table 18.1 Cresswell Field charred plant remains.

Context Number	*7180*	*7202*	*7058*	*7077*	*7061*	*7171*	*8356*	*7915*	*7915*
Sample Number	*7041/2*	*7004*	*7009*	*7056*	*7059*	*7060/1*	*7063*	*7032*	*7033*
Context Type	*Burnt Mound*	*Pit*	*Pit*	*Pit*	*Pit*	*Pit*	*Pit*	*Pit*	*Pit*
Phase	*LBA*	*EIA*	*EIA*	*EIA*	*EIA*	*EIA*	*EIA*	*EIA*	*EIA*
Sample Volume (L)	*20*	*10*	*10*	*20*	*10*	*20*	*10*	*10*	*10*
Seeds/litre of sediment	*4.8*	*26.9*	*3.3*	*0.6*	*7.1*	*0.7*	*4.3*	*4.6*	*7.3*
CEREAL GRAIN									
Hordeum vulgare L. (hulled, lateral/twisted)	-	-	-	-	-	-	-	-	-
Hordeum spp. (hulled)	2	1	2	-	1	1	1	-	-
Hordeum spp.	7	3	4	-	8	1	2	1	2
Triticum dicoccum Schübl./spelta L.	-	3	-	-	-	-	-	-	-
Triticum spelta L.	-	7	-	1	-	-	-	-	-
Triticum spp. free-threshing (small-grained)	1	-	1	-	-	-	-	-	-
Triticum spp. - free-threshing indeterminate		-	-	-	-	-	-	-	-
Triticum spp. - indeterminate	5	13	3	1	4	1	-	-	1
Cereal - indeterminate	35	38	9	3	30	7	9	7	6
Cereal - indeterminate large-sized detached embryo	-	-	-	-	-	-	-	-	2
CEREAL CHAFF									
Hordeum spp. (rachis fragments)	-	-	-	-	-	-	-	-	-
Triticum dicoccum Schübl./*spelta* L. (glume bases)	13	104	5	4	11	-	7	9	23
Triticum spelta L. (glume bases)	11	40	4	3	2	1	5	5	7
Triticum spp. (rachis internodes)	-	-	-	-	-	-	-	-	-
Cereal (indeterminate basal rachis nodes)	1	16	-	-	-	-	-	-	-
Cereal/POACEAE (large-sized culm node)	-	1	-	-	-	-	-	-	-
OTHER FOOD PLANTS									
Corylus avellana L. - nutshell frags	2	2	-	-	-	-	-	1	2
WEED/WILD PLANTS									
Ranunculus acris L./*repens* L./*bulbosus* L.	-	1	-	-	-	-	-	-	-
Chenopodium album L.	-	1	-	-	-	-	-	-	-
Chenopodium cf. *album* L.	1	-	1	-	-	1	-	-	-
Chenopodium spp.	-	-	-	-	-	-	-	-	1
Atriplex spp.	-	1	-	-	-	-	-	-	-
CHENOPODIACEAE (indeterminate)	-	5	-	-	-	-	1	-	-
Montia fontana ssp. *chondrosperma* (Fenzl.) Walters	-	-	-	-	-	-	-	-	-
cf. *Montia fontana* subsp. *chondrosperma* (Fenzl.) Walters	-	-	-	-	-	-	-	-	-
Stellaria media (L.) Vill.									
Stellaria cf. *media* (L.) Vill.	-	2	-	-	-	-	-	-	-
Stellaria palustris Retz./*graminea* L.									
Stellaria spp.	-	-	-	-	-	-	1	-	-
Silene sp.	-	-	-	-	-	-	-	-	-
CARYOPHYLLACEAE indeterminate.	-	1	-	-	1	-	-	-	-
Polygonum aviculare L. agg.	-	-	-	-	-	-	2	1	-
Polygonum spp.	-	-	-	-	-	-	-	-	1
cf. *Fallopia convolvulus* (L.) Á. Löve	-	-	-	-	-	-	-	-	-
Rumex spp. (indeterminate)	1	1	-	-	-	-	-	1	-
POLYGONACEAE (indeterminate)	1	-	-	-	2	-	2	-	-
Malva sp.	-	-	-	-	-	-	-	-	-
Brassica rapa subsp. *campestris* (L.) A. R. Clapham	-	1	-	-	-	-	-	-	-
Prunus sp./*Crataegus* sp. (thorn)	-	-	-	-	-	-	-	1	-
Crataegus cf. *monogyna* Jacq. (fruit stone)	-	-	-	-	-	-	-	-	-
Vicia sp.	-	-	-	-	-	-	-	-	-
Vicia spp./Lathyrus spp.	-	-	-	-	-	-	-	-	-
Lathyrus cf. *nissolia* L. (type)	-	-	-	-	-	-	-	-	-
Lathyrus sp.	-	-	-	-	-	-	-	-	-
cf. *Trifolium* sp.	-	1	-	-	-	-	-	-	-
FABACEAE (small) indeterminate	1	1	-	-	2	-	-	-	-

Table 18.1 Cresswell Field charred plant remains (continued).

Context Number	*7180*	*7202*	*7058*	*7077*	*7061*	*7171*	*8356*	*7915*	*7915*
Sample Number	*7041/2*	*7004*	*7009*	*7056*	*7059*	*7060/1*	*7063*	*7032*	*7033*
cf. *Ballota nigra* L.	-	-	-	-	-	-	-	1	-
cf. *Nepeta cataria* L.	-	-	-	-	-	-	-	-	-
LAMIACEAE indeterminate	-	-	-	-	-	-	-	-	-
Plantago cf. *media* L./*lanceolata* L.	1	-	-	-	-	-	-	-	-
Odontites vernus (Bellardi) Dumort.	1	1	-	-	-	-	1	-	-
Sherardia arvensis L.	-	-	-	-	-	-	-	-	-
Galium aparine L.	2	2	-	-	-	-	-	-	-
Galium spp.	-	-	-	-	-	-	-	-	1
Anthemis cotula L.	-	-	-	-	-	-	-	-	-
Eleocharis palustris (L.) Roem. & Schult./*uniglumis* (Link.) Schult.	-	-	-	-	1	-	2	-	-
Carex spp. (indeterminate - trigonous)	-	-	-	-	-	-	-	3	2
cf. *Carex* spp.	-	-	-	-	-	-	-	-	2
CYPERACEAE indeterminate	-	-	-	-	-	-	-	-	-
Avena fatua L. (floret base)	-	-	-	-	-	-	-	-	-
Avena spp. (caryopses)	-	1	-	-	-	-	-	-	1
Bromus hordeaceus L./*secalinus* L. (type)	1	6	-	-	-	-	2	5	4
Anisantha sterilis (L.) Nevski (type)	-	2	-	-	-	-	1	-	-
POACEAE >4 mm undifferentiated	4	6	-	-	-	-	-	6	-
POACEAE indeterminate (tuber)	1	-	-	-	-	-	-	-	-
INDETERMINATE	4	8	4	-	9	2	7	5	10
MINERALISED SEEDS									
Montia fontana ssp. *chondrosperma* (Fenzl.) Walters	-	-	-	-	-	-	-	-	1
cf. *Potentilla* spp.	-	-	-	-	-	-	-	-	3
LAMIACEAE (indeterminate)	-	-	-	-	-	-	-	-	1
Carex spp.	-	-	-	-	-	-	-	-	2
Bromus hordeaceus L./*secalinus* L. (type)	-	-	-	-	-	-	-	-	1
TOTALS									
Cereal Grain	50	65	19	5	43	10	12	8	11
Cereal Chaff	25	161	9	7	13	1	12	14	30
Other Crops	2	2	0	0	0	0	0	1	2
Weed/Wild	14	33	1	0	6	1	12	18	12
Unidentified/Indeterminate	4	8	4	0	9	2	7	5	10
Mineralised seeds	0	0	0	0	0	0	0	0	8
TOTAL IDENTIFICATIONS	95	269	33	12	71	14	43	46	73
PROPORTIONS									
Cereal Grain	52.6%	24.2%	57.6%	41.7%	60.6%	71.4%	27.9%	17.4%	15.1%
Cereal Chaff	26.3%	59.9%	27.3%	58.3%	18.3%	7.1%	27.9%	30.4%	41.1%
Other Crops	2.1%	0.7%	0.0%	0.0%	0.0%	0.0%	0.0%	2.2%	2.7%
Weed/Wild	14.7%	12.3%	3.0%	0.0%	8.5%	7.1%	27.9%	39.1%	16.4%
Unidentified/Indeterminate	4.2%	3.0%	12.1%	0.0%	12.7%	14.3%	16.3%	10.9%	13.7%
Mineralised Seeds	0.0%	0.0%	0.0%	0.0%	0.0%	0.0%	0.0%	0.0%	11.0%

palustris and various species of *Carex*, are not regarded as arable weeds in modern phytosociological classifications. However, they are commonly associated with charred Iron Age and Romano-British cereal assemblages in Upper Thames valley sites such as Ashville and Barton Court Farm, Abingdon (Jones 1978; 1986b), Gravelly Guy (Moffett 2004) and Mingies Ditch (Jones and Robinson 1993). Examples of *Eleocharis* sp. have also been found in the granary deposits at South Shields, Tyne and Wear (van der Veen 1992) associated with stored grain, and from grain stores and the stomach contents of Iron Age corpses in Denmark. The regular occurrence of *Eleocharis palustris* and *Carex* spp. in charred seed assemblages does suggest that they were weeds of arable fields in the past, but have disappeared in more recent times, presumably due to improved drainage (Jones 1984a; 1988a; 1988b). Their appearance in the Cresswell Field assemblages therefore suggests the utilisation of damper ground, possibly extending onto the floodplain itself.

Table 18.1: Charred plant remains from Cresswell Field (continued).

Context Number	*8252*	*7242*	*8067*	*8428*	*7335*	*7348*	*7294*	*7003*
Sample Number	*7066*	*7070*	*7039/40*	*7073*	*7010/15*	*7014/17/18*	*7005/8*	*7003*
Context Type	*Pit*	*Hearth*	*Pit*	*Pit*	*Pit*	*Pit*	*Crem pit*	*Pit*
Phase	*EIA*	*EIA*	*EIA*	*EIA*	*EIA*	*EIA*	*EIA*	*EIA*
Sample Volume (L)	*10*	*10*	*20*	*10*	*20*	*30*	*20*	*10*
Seeds/litre of sediment	*1.8*	*0.8*	*4.2*	*0.5*	*0.5*	*1.4*	*0.6*	*5.8*
CEREAL GRAIN								
Hordeum vulgare L. (hulled, lateral/twisted)	1	-	-	-	-	-	-	-
Hordeum spp. (hulled)	1	-	-	-	1	3	1	-
Hordeum spp.	-	-	3	-	1	1	-	2
Triticum dicoccum Schübl./spelta L.	-	1	5	-	-	-	-	-
Triticum spelta L.	-	-	1	-	-	-	-	-
Triticum spp. free-threshing (small-grained)	1	-	-	-	-	-	-	-
Triticum spp. - free-threshing indeterminate	-	-	-	-	-	-	-	-
Triticum spp. - indeterminate	-	-	-	-	-	1	1	2
Cereal - indeterminate	-	-	3	-	3	26	7	16
Cereal - indeterminate large-sized detached embryo	3	3	31	-	-	1	-	-
CEREAL CHAFF								
Hordeum spp. (rachis fragments)	-	-	-	-	-	-	-	-
Triticum dicoccum Schübl./*spelta* L. (glume bases)	7	-	12	2	1	4	-	18
Triticum spelta L. (glume bases)	1	-	7	1	-	1	1	11
Triticum spp. (rachis internodes)	-	-	-	-	-	-	-	-
Cereal (indeterminate basal rachis nodes)	-	-	1	-	-	1	-	-
Cereal/POACEAE (large-sized culm node)	-	-	-	-	-	-	-	-
OTHER FOOD PLANTS								
Corylus avellana L. - nutshell frags	-	-	2	-	-	-		-
WEED/WILD PLANTS								
Ranunculus acris L./*repens* L./*bulbosus* L.	-	-	-	-	-		-	-
Chenopodium album L.	-	-	-	-	-	-	-	-
Chenopodium cf. *album* L.	-	-	-	-	1	-	-	-
Chenopodium spp.	-	-	-	-	-	-	-	-
Atriplex spp.	-	-	-	-	-	-	-	-
CHENOPODIACEAE (indeterminate)	-	-	2	-	-	-	-	-
Montia fontana ssp. *chondrosperma* (Fenzl.) Walters	-	-	-	-	-	-	-	-
cf. *Montia fontana* subsp. *chondrosperma* (Fenzl.) Walters	-	-	-	-	-	-	-	-
Stellaria media (L.) Vill.								
Stellaria cf. *media* (L.) Vill.	-	-	-	-	-	-	-	-
Stellaria palustris Retz./*graminea* L.								
Stellaria spp.	-	-	-	-	-	-	-	1
Silene sp.	-	-	1	-	-	-	-	-
CARYOPHYLLACEAE indeterminate	-	-	-	-	-	-	-	-
Polygonum aviculare L. agg.	-	-	-	-	-	-	-	-
Polygonum spp.	-	-	-	-	-	-	-	-
cf. *Fallopia convolvulus* (L.) Á. Löve	-	-	-	-	-	-	-	-
Rumex spp. (indeterminate)	-	-	-	-	1	-	-	1
POLYGONACEAE (indeterminate)	-	-	-	-	-	-	-	-
Malva sp.	-	-	-	-	-	-	1	-
Brassica rapa subsp. *campestris* (L.) A. R. Clapham	-	-	-	-	-	-	-	1
Prunus sp./*Crataegus* sp. (thorn)	-	-	-	-	-	-	-	-
Crataegus cf. *monogyna* Jacq. (fruit stone)	-	-	-	-	-	-	-	-
Vicia sp.	-	-	-	-	-	-	-	-
Vicia spp./*Lathyrus* spp.	-	-	-	-	-	-	-	-
Lathyrus cf. *nissolia* L. (type)	-	-	-	-	-	-	-	-
Lathyrus sp.	-	-	-	-	-	-	-	-
cf. Trifolium sp.	-	-	-	-	-	-	-	-
FABACEAE (small) indet	1	1	2	-	1	1	1	-

Table 18.1: Charred plant remains from Cresswell Field (continued).

Context Number *Sample Number*	*8252* *7066*	*7242* *7070*	*8067* *7039/40*	*8428* *7073*	*7335* *7010/15*	*7348* *7014/17/18*	*7294* *7005/8*	*7003* *7003*
cf. *Ballota nigra* L.	-	-	-	-	-	-	-	-
cf. *Nepeta cataria* L.	-	-	-	-	-	-	-	1
LAMIACEAE indet	-	-	-	-	-	-	-	-
Plantago cf. *media* L./*lanceolata* L.	-	1	-	-	-	-	-	-
Odontites vernus (Bellardi) Dumort.	-	-	-	-	-	-	-	-
Sherardia arvensis L.	-	-	-	-	-	1	-	-
Galium aparine L.	-	-	-	-	-	-	-	-
Galium spp.	-	-	1	-	-	-	-	-
Anthemis cotula L.	-	-	-	-	-	-	-	1
Eleocharis palustris (L.) Roem. & Schult./*uniglumis* (Link.) Schult.	-	-	-	-	-	-	-	-
Carex spp. (indeterminate - trigonous)	-	-	-	-	-	-	-	1
cf. *Carex* spp.	-	-	-	-	-	-	-	-
CYPERACEAE indeterminate	-	-	-	-	-	-	-	-
Avena fatua L. (floret base)	-	-	-	-	-	-	-	-
Avena spp. (caryopses)	-	-	-	-	-	-	-	-
Bromus hordeaceus L./*secalinus* L. (type)	-	-	2	-	-	-	-	-
Anisantha sterilis (L.) Nevski (type)	-	-	-	-	-	-	-	-
POACEAE >4 mm undifferentiated	1	-	6	-	-	-	-	-
POACEAE indeterminate (tuber)	-	-	-	-	-	1	-	-
INDETERMINATE	2	2	5	2	1	1	-	2
MINERALISED SEEDS								
Montia fontana ssp. *chondrosperma* (Fenzl.) Walters	-	-	-	-	-	-	-	-
cf. *Potentilla* spp.	-	-	-	-	-	-	-	-
LAMIACEAE (indeterminate)	-	-	-	-	-	-	-	-
Carex spp.	-	-	-	-	-	-	-	1
Bromus hordeaceus L./*secalinus* L. (type)	-	-	-	-	-	-	-	-
TOTALS								
Cereal Grain	6	4	43	0	5	32	9	20
Cereal Chaff	8	0	20	3	1	6	1	29
Other Crops	0	0	2	0	0	0	0	0
Weed/Wild	2	2	14	0	3	3	2	6
Unidentified/Indeterminate	2	2	5	2	1	1	0	2
Mineralised seeds	0	0	0	0	0	0	0	1
TOTAL IDENTIFICATIONS	18	8	84	5	10	42	12	58
PROPORTIONS								
Cereal Grain	33.3%	50.0%	51.2%	0.0%	50.0%	76.2%	75.0%	34.5%
Cereal Chaff	44.4%	0.0%	23.8%	60.0%	10.0%	14.3%	8.3%	50.0%
Other Crops	0.0%	0.0%	2.4%	0.0%	0.0%	0.0%	0.0%	0.0%
Weed/Wild	11.1%	25.0%	16.7%	0.0%	30.0%	7.1%	16.7%	10.3%
Unidentified/Indeterminate	11.1%	25.0%	6.0%	40.0%	10.0%	2.4%	0.0%	3.4%
Mineralised Seeds	0.0%	0.0%	0.0%	0.0%	0.0%	0.0%	0.0%	1.7%

Grassland species represented include cf. *Trifolium* sp. (clovers) and cf. *Potentilla* sp. (cinquefoil). Species of grassland which can also occur as arable weeds include *Lathyrus nissolia* (grass vetchling) and other leguminous species, and *Odontites verna* (red bartsia). Grassland species may have entered the assemblage via a number of routes. If former grassland had been brought into cultivation some plants may have continued to survive as arable weeds for a few seasons. Grassland species may also have entered the site as animal fodder or amongst vegetation cut for litter.

The majority of the weeds are arable species which are common to charred cereal assemblages and have no specific ecological requirements other than their adaptation to disturbed ground. A few species are of further interest, however. Single seeds of *Anthemis cotula* (stinking mayweed) appear in one early Iron Age sample (7003) from pit 7057 and two middle Iron Age samples; sample 7081 from gully 7886 and sample 7076 from pit 8467. The species occurs in a number of Romano-British charred plant assemblages in the area but only as occasional individual finds in Iron Age assemblages, such as at

Table 18.1: Charred plant remains from Cresswell Field (continued).

Context Number	*8466*	*8466*	*7986*	*8493*	*7657*	*8229*	*7887*	*7863*
Sample Number	*7076*	*7077*	*7034/5*	*7087*	*7045/6*	*7108*	*7081*	*7082*
Context Type	*Pit*	*Pit*	*Pit*	*Pit*	*Pit*	*Ditch*	*Gully*	*Gully*
Phase	*MIA*	*MIA*	*MIA*	*MIA*	*MIA*	*MIA*	*MIA*	*MIA*
Sample Volume (L)	*10*	*10*	*20*	*10*	*20*	*10*	*10*	*10*
Seeds/litre of sediment	*8.2*	*3.5*	*6.6*	*6.3*	*3.8*	*2.0*	*5.2*	*10.5*
CEREAL GRAIN								
Hordeum vulgare L. (hulled, lateral/twisted)	-	-	-	-	-	-	-	1
Hordeum spp. (hulled)	1	-	1	-	-	-	1	7
Hordeum spp.	2	6	4	1	2	-	3	8
Triticum dicoccum Schübl./*spelta* L.	1	-	-	-	-	-	-	1
Triticum spelta L.	-	-	-	1	-	-	-	-
Triticum spp. free-threshing (small-grained)	1	1	-	-	-	-	-	-
Triticum spp. - free-threshing indeterminate		1	-	-	-	-	-	-
Triticum spp. - indeterminate	-	-	1	-	-	-	2	3
Cereal - indeterminate	28	18	16	12	17	4	15	22
Cereal - indeterminate. large-sized detached embryo	-	-	-	-	-	-	1	-
CEREAL CHAFF								
Hordeum spp. (rachis fragments)	-	-	-	1	-	-	-	-
Triticum dicoccum Schübl./*spelta* L. (glume bases)	18	2	35	21	12	3	10	23
Triticum spelta L. (glume bases)	12	3	9	4	8	-	5	16
Triticum spp. (rachis internodes)	-	-	-	-	-	-	-	-
Cereal (indeterminate basal rachis nodes)	1	-	1	-	-	-	-	2
Cereal/POACEAE (large-sized culm node)	-	-	-	-	-	-	-	-
OTHER FOOD PLANTS								
Corylus avellana L. - nutshell frags	1	-	1	-	1	-	3	
WEED/WILD PLANTS								
Ranunculus acris L./*repens* L./*bulbosus* L.	-	-	-	-	-	-	-	-
Chenopodium album L.	1	-	-	-	-	-	-	-
Chenopodium cf. *album* L.	-	-	1	-	-	-	-	-
Chenopodium spp.	2	-	-	-	-	-	-	5
Atriplex spp.	-	-	2	-	-	-	-	-
CHENOPODIACEAE (indeterminate)	-	-	2	2	2	-	2	-
Montia fontana subsp. *chondrosperma* (Fenzl.) Walters	-	-	1	-	-	1	-	-
cf. *Montia fontana* subsp. *chondrosperma* (Fenzl.) Walters	-	-	-	-	-	-	-	-
Stellaria media (L.) Vill.								
Stellaria cf. *media* (L.) Vill.	-	-	-	-	-	-	-	-
Stellaria palustris Retz./*graminea* L.								
Stellaria spp.	-	-	-	-	-	-	-	-
Silene sp.	-	-	-	-	-	-	-	-
CARYOPHYLLACEAE indeterminate	-	-	-	-	-	-	-	-
Polygonum aviculare L. agg.	-	-	-	1	-	-	-	-
Polygonum spp.	-	-	1	-	-	-	-	-
cf. *Fallopia convolvulus* (L.) Á. Löve	-	-	-	-	1	-	-	-
Rumex spp. (indeterminate)	-	1	1	-	-	1	1	1
POLYGONACEAE (indeterminate)	1	-	-	1	-	-	1	-
Malva sp.	-	-	-	-	-	-	-	-
Brassica rapa subsp. *campestris* (L.) A. R. Clapham	-	-	-	-	-	-	-	-
Prunus sp./*Crataegus* sp. (thorn)	-	-	-	-	-	-	-	-
Crataegus cf. *monogyna* Jacq. (fruit stone)	-	1	-	-	-	-	-	-
Vicia sp.	-	-	-	1	-	-	-	-
Vicia spp./*Lathyrus* spp.	-	-	1	1	-	-	-	-
Lathyrus cf. *nissolia* L. (type)	-	-	2	-	-	-	-	-
Lathyrus sp.	-	-	-	1	-	-	-	-
cf. *Trifolium* sp.	-	-	-	-	-	-	-	-
FABACEAE (small) indet	1	-	6	5	4	-	2	5

Table 18.1: Charred plant remains from Cresswell Field (continued).

Context Number	*8466*	*8466*	*7986*	*8493*	*7657*	*8229*	*7887*	*7863*
Sample Number	*7076*	*7077*	*7034/5*	*7087*	*7045/6*	*7108*	*7081*	*7082*
cf. *Ballota nigra* L.	-	-	-	-	-	-	-	-
cf. *Nepeta cataria* L.	-	-	-	-	-	-	-	-
LAMIACEAE indet	-	-	-	-	-	-	-	-
Plantago cf. *media* L./lanceolata L.	-	-	1	2	-	-	-	1
Odontites vernus (Bellardi) Dumort.	-	-	2	-	1	-	-	-
Sherardia arvensis L.	-	-	-	-	-	-	-	-
Galium aparine L.	-	-	3	1	-	-	-	1
Galium spp.	-	-	1	-	2	1	-	-
Anthemis cotula L.	1	-	-	-	-	-	1	-
Eleocharis palustris (L.) Roem. & Schult./*uniglumis* (Link.) Schult.	-	-	2	-	2	-	1	1
Carex spp. (indeterminate - trigonous)	-	-	-	-	-	-	-	-
cf. *Carex* spp.	-	-	-	-	-	-	-	-
CYPERACEAE indet	-	-	-	-	-	-	-	-
Avena fatua L. (floret base)	-	-	1	-	-	-	-	-
Avena spp. (caryopses)	-	-	-	-	-	-	-	-
Bromus hordeaceus L./*secalinus* L. (type)	-	-	5	-	2	3	-	3
Anisantha sterilis (L.) Nevski (type)	-	-	-	-	-	-	-	-
POACEAE >4 mm undifferentiated	4	-	3	-	8	-	-	5
POACEAE indeterminate (tuber)	-	-	-	-	-	-	-	-
INDETERMINATE	7	2	28	8	14	7	4	-
MINERALISED SEEDS								
Montia fontana ssp. *chondrosperma* (Fenzl.) Walters	-	-	-	-	-	-	-	-
cf. *Potentilla* spp.	-	-	-	-	-	-	-	-
LAMIACEAE (indeterminate)	-	-	-	-	-	-	-	-
Carex spp.	-	-	-	-	-	-	-	-
Bromus hordeaceus L./*secalinus* L. (type)	-	-	-	-	-	-	-	-
TOTALS								
Cereal Grain	33	26	22	14	19	4	22	42
Cereal Chaff	31	5	45	26	20	3	15	41
Other Crops	1	0	1	0	1	0	3	0
Weed/Wild	10	2	35	15	22	6	8	22
Unidentified/Indeterminate	7	2	28	8	14	7	4	0
Mineralised seeds	0	0	0	0	0	0	0	0
TOTAL IDENTIFICATIONS	82	35	131	63	76	20	52	105
PROPORTIONS								
Cereal Grain	40.2%	74.3%	16.8%	22.2%	25.0%	20.0%	42.3%	40.0%
Cereal Chaff	37.8%	14.3%	34.4%	41.3%	26.3%	15.0%	28.8%	39.0%
Other Crops	1.2%	0.0%	0.8%	0.0%	1.3%	0.0%	5.8%	0.0%
Weed/Wild	12.2%	5.7%	26.7%	23.8%	28.9%	30.0%	15.4%	21.0%
Unidentified/Indeterminate	8.5%	5.7%	21.4%	12.7%	18.4%	35.0%	7.7%	0.0%
Mineralised Seeds	0.0%	0.0%	0.0%	0.0%	0.0%	0.0%	0.0%	0.0%

Ashville (Jones 1978). This pattern is also reflected in waterlogged assemblages in the region. If the species is a Roman introduction then the occasional Iron Age find must be due to later contamination, although if it was present during the Iron Age its rarity in the assemblages may be due to other factors, such as behavioural changes due to hybridisation. *Galium aparine* (goose grass) occurs in small numbers in some of the samples along with seeds of unidentifiable *Galium* species. *Galium aparine* normally germinates in the autumn, so when occurring as an arable weed is often associated with autumn sown crops (Fryer and Evans 1963, 15). It occurs in small numbers in assemblages from other Iron Age sites in the region such as Barton Court Farm (Jones 1986b) and Gravelly Guy (Moffett 2004), and occurred in large numbers at Ashville (Jones 1978), which was interpreted as indicating that much of the cereal crop was autumn sown.

Leguminous plants are present in the majority of samples, being slightly better represented in the middle Iron Age weed floras than in earlier

Table 18.2 Cresswell Field weed/wild species list with ecological requirements.

LATIN BINOMIAL	ENGLISH COMMON NAME	HABITAT TYPE
Ranunculus acris L. / *repens* L./ *bulbous* L.	meadow / creeping / bulbous buttercup	Gw
Chenopodium album L.	fat hen	An
Chenopodium spp.	fat hen / goosefoot	A
Atriplex spp.	orache	A
Montia fontana L. subsp. *chondrosperma* (Fen.) Walt	blink	M+Gw
Stellaria media (L.) Vill.	common chickweed	An
Silene spp.	campion	A
Polygonum aviculare L. agg.	knotgrass	A
Fallopia convolvolous (L.) Á. Löve	black bindweed	A
Rumex spp.	dock	A+G
Malva sp.	mallow	D+G
Brassica rapa subsp. *campestris* (L.) A. R. Clapham	wild turnip	A
Potentilla sp.	cinquefoil	G
Crataegus cf. *monogyna* Jacq.	hawthorn	H
Vicia spp. / *Lathyrus* spp.	vetch / vetchling	A+G
Lathyrus cf. *nissolia* L. (type)	grass vetchling type	A+G
Trifolium spp.	clover	G
cf. *Ballota nigra* L.	possible black horehound	D
cf. *Nepeta cataria* L.	possible cat mint	G+D
Plantago cf. *media* L. / *lanceolata* L.	possible hoary / ribwort plantain	(A)+G
Odontites vernus (Bellardi) Dumort.	red bartsia	G+A
Sherardia arvensis L.	field madder	Ad
Galium aparine L.	cleaver (goosegrass)	An
Anthemis cotula L.	stinking chamomile	Awbh
Eleocharis palustris (L.) Roem. & Schult. / uniglumis (Link.) Schult.	common / slender spike rush	M+Gwb
Carex spp.	sedges	M+aw
Avena fatua L.	wild oat	A
Bromus hordeaceus L. / *secalinus* L. (type)	soft / rye brome	D+A
Anisantha sterilis (L.) Nevski (type)	barren brome	Ad

Key			
A	Arable / disturbed	a	preference for acid soils
D	Disturbed ground on field margins / waysides	b	preference for basic soils
G	Grassland	d	preference for dry ground
M	Marshy / very damp ground	h	preference for heavy soils
H	Woods / hedgerows	w	preference for wet soils
		n	nitrophilous plants

deposits. Legumes generally compete well on nitrogen-poor soils because they are host to bacteria in root nodules which convert nitrogen from the atmosphere to a form the plant can absorb. An increase in such species, particularly where nitrophilous species such as the Chenopodiaceae decrease, might therefore be associated with a depletion in soil fertility and implied agricultural intensification. The Cresswell Field samples actually demonstrate an increase in plant species requiring nitrogen-rich soil. Any identification of soil depletion is therefore tentative.

Minor components of the weed flora are seeds of two weed species which prefer dry or well drained soils, *Sheradia arvensis* and (to a lesser extent) *Bromus sterilis*. Hedgerow or scrub species are represented by two fruit stones of *Crataegus* sp. (hawthorn) and a rosaceous thorn. The latter items could have entered the assemblages as introductions with fire wood.

Some low growing weed seeds are present in the samples, such as *Odontites verna*, *Trifolium* sp., *Stellaria media* and *Sheradia arvensis*. Such seeds cannot have entered the assemblages with the harvested crop products unless the crop had been reaped low on the straw. This appears to have been a common practice in the Iron Age of the Upper Thames Valley as low growing weed species are frequent components of the carbonised assemblages, such as at Gravelly Guy and Ashville (Moffett 2004; Jones 1978). It is therefore of interest that culm nodes are not frequently recovered in the assemblages. Charred remains of straw in any quantity generally tend to be exceptional, as for example a charred mass of straw from the medieval site at The Hamel, Oxford (Jones 1980), which was also waterlogged and may have been the remains of an entire burnt sheaf of straw. It is also likely that straw was not reaching the settlement fires, possibly because it was a valuable resource in its own right, for example, as thatch or bedding.

Larger non-cereal grass seeds, including *Bromus* subsect *Eubromus*, are a fairly common component of the weed assemblages. Seeds of *Bromus* sp. were deliberately collected in Denmark in the early 20th century to bulk up poor rye harvests (Hjelmqvist 1955). The seeds are smaller and more difficult to thresh, but can be processed and used in the same way as rye. The high concentration of *Bromus* seeds in some prehistoric assemblages has been suggested to be a result of deliberate harvesting (eg Hubbard 1975; Jones 1978; 1986b; Knörzer 1967), or at least to reflect a tolerable impurity.

The Cresswell Field weed assemblage is typical of the mature weed floras encountered in assemblages from Iron Age sites in the Upper Thames Valley such as Ashville (Jones 1978), Barton Court Farm (Jones 1986b), Mingies Ditch (Jones and Robinson 1993) and Gravelly Guy (Moffett 2004). By the early Iron Age the weed flora had increased in diversity throughout Southern Britain. As discussed, several of the species not considered to be arable weeds in modern phytosociological classifications could have been included in this list. Jones (1988b) suggests that the isolation of various crop/weed communities from one another had become progressively diminished by their closer proximity to one another as a result of more intensive agriculture, and by the increasing movement between ecosystems. The presence of species not normally associated with cereal crops suggests the utilisation of agriculturally marginal land.

Sample composition

The composition of carbonised seed assemblages tends to represent the harvested grain crops and their assorted impurities in varying ratios. The assemblages generally represent secondary refuse, however, relating to the final function of the features from which they are recovered rather than the original function. Hillman (1981; 1984a) and G Jones (1983; 1984; 1987) have demonstrated that ethnographic models based on modern agricultural practices can provide a method of analysing the internal composition of assemblages, thus giving an indication of the processing stages from which the material has been derived, independent of the archaeological contexts. This is because the actual stages involved in processing a cereal crop are in the greater part dependent on the nature of the crop, irrespective of the tools and methods applied. The crop processing stages are discussed in detail by Hillman (1984a).

Following the approach applied to other sites within the Upper Thames Valley (Jones 1978; Jones and Robinson 1993), as well as in landscape studies elsewhere (eg van der Veen 1992), the Cresswell Field assemblages are examined in terms of relative percentages of grain, chaff and weeds. For ease of summarising the results the sample composition is displayed in graph form in Figure 18.1 by period, although the composition of individual samples is also considered.

Late Bronze Age

This phase is represented by one sample only (sample 7041 context 7180). Grain dominates the assemblage with weeds and chaff each forming *c* 20%. Such proportions are characteristic of a cereal product with some contaminants, or an unprocessed crop in which some chaff has been destroyed during charring.

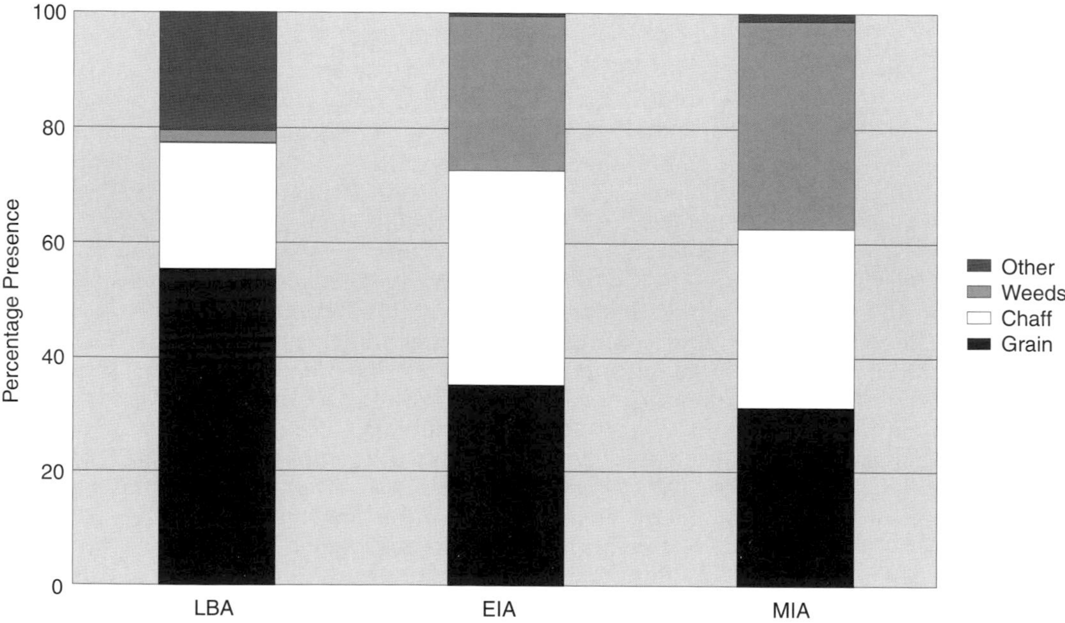

Fig. 18.1 Cresswell Field: composition of samples of charred plant remains by period

Early Iron Age

This phase is represented by 16 samples. The overall proportion of grain to chaff to weeds suggests roughly equal proportions of chaff and grain (equivalent to an unprocessed crop) with slightly fewer weed seeds. This pattern is generally represented in the individual samples, with weeds more numerous in some samples than others. One sample (7004, context 7202) can be regarded as chaff rich, while the numbers of grains to chaff and weeds are slightly higher in samples 7039/40, 7010, 7014/17/18, 7003 and 7001, although the actual numbers of items are small in all these samples. Generally, therefore, the samples can be regarded as mixed, with grain, chaff and weeds in more or less equal proportions. While these proportions might be regarded as representing an unprocessed crop, it should be considered that the surviving sample sizes are small; they are not characteristic of the large scale destruction of stored material, for example. As chaff survives burning less readily than grain it is likely to be underrepresented, therefore the assemblages might still represent cereal processing waste in which the loss of some grain is inevitable.

Middle Iron Age

The overall ratio of chaff to weeds to grain in the middle Iron Age samples indicates that chaff and weeds outnumber grain and that the remains are therefore most characteristic of cereal processing waste (particularly if it is assumed that chaff is likely to be underrepresented). Generally the difference in the proportions of these components in the individual samples is slight, and as with the early Iron Age deposits they can on the whole be regarded as mixed. Sample 7034 is dominated by weed seeds, but the actual numerical difference is not particularly significant.

Discussion

The mixed composition of grain, chaff and weeds in similar proportions in the samples is characteristic of unprocessed spikelets. As such it does not fit Martin Jones' (1985) model for 'producer' sites, as might be expected from its situation on the Second Gravel Terrace and by the associated evidence for arable activity. The problems of the simplistic division of 'producer' and 'consumer' sites as proposed by Jones (1985) have been discussed recently by Stevens (2003a) and van der Veen (1992). Such models do not take into account differences in storage methods (eg sheafs versus spikelets), the trade of chaff as a commodity, small scale routine year round processing of crops for individual use, or preservation differences.

The chaff represented in the samples consists predominantly of glume bases, with very rare rachis or culm nodes. The weeds are mostly small, light seeded or grain sized. The absence of culm nodes (ie straw) in any number, and of heavy large weed seeds or seed heads, indicates that the early stages of processing the harvest (ie threshing and early sieving) are not represented. This is typical of most settlement sites where the early stages of processing are conducted in the fields or perhaps in a threshing barn away from the domestic structures. The overall proportions therefore suggest that whole spikelets had been brought into the site. However, glume bases are likely to be under-represented because of preservation biases. Chaff survives charring less well than grain (Boardman and Jones 1990) and the longer waste material is left exposed to the elements or the more it is redeposited the more the chance of survival of chaff is reduced. It is therefore more realistic to regard the assemblages as consisting of the waste product of the late stages of cereal processing (fine sieving waste) in which the grain is separated from the glumes and weeds prior to milling or cooking, with grain present as occasional spoilt or lost grain. Such assemblages are typical of small scale processing where grain is stored as spikelets and is then processed on a day a day basis (Stevens 2003a). Such a scenario is independent of site status in terms of 'producer' or 'consumer', but is more characteristic of the day to day activities which took place within the settlement. The assemblage composition is not related to feature type at the site, which perhaps further indicates the secondary nature of the deposits.

Charcoal

Charcoal identification

Charcoal was identified in samples from both the Yarnton and Cresswell Field sites. In the case of Yarnton the samples generally did not contain sufficient wood charcoal to merit a detailed study. Analysis was therefore restricted to an examination of sufficient detail to gain an impression of the character of the samples and the range of wood species represented

The results of the charcoal analysis are shown in Table 18.3. Three taxa have been identified to generic or species level, *Quercus* sp. (oak), *Prunus* sp. (blackthorn, plum etc.) and *Rhamnus cartharticus* (buckthorn), while a possible fragment of *Fraxinus excelsior* (ash) was also present. The Pomoideae group consists of the pomaceous trees including hawthorn, apple and pear. Their charcoal is not easily distinguishable to generic level, so they are recorded as a single group.

Those fragments of charcoal prefixed with 'cf.' were most reminiscent of the genus recorded, but distortion or mineral encrustation prevented definite identification. The indeterminate fragments in sample 7041 (late Bronze Age burnt mound 7180) showed signs of the large vessels characteristic of *Quercus*, but which had exploded during carbonisation. The remaining indeterminate fragments were too poorly preserved or too encrusted with minerals to allow identification.

Fragments of heartwood of both *Quercus* sp. and Pomoideae were identified on the basis of the presence of tyloses or gum in the pores. The presence of heartwood suggests the use of mature wood as timbers.

A combination of environmental evidence, including charcoal, plant macrofossils, pollen and Coleoptera, indicates that during the early Iron Age there were still remnants of tree and scrub cover surviving in the floodplains of the Thames tributaries (Robinson and Wilson 1987). There is also an indication of mature oak woodland surviving on higher ground, for example from pollen taken from the small hillfort of Eynsham Hall Camp in the Wychwood area (Robinson and Wilson 1987). The Cresswell Field wood charcoal demonstrates the utilisation of both scrub/hedgerow species and oak wood throughout the Iron Age, suggesting their availability within the vicinity of the site.

Conclusions

The carbonised seed assemblage from Cresswell Field is consistent with those from other Second Gravel Terrace Iron Age sites in the Upper Thames Valley. Spelt wheat and hulled barley are the principal cereal crops, with free-threshing wheat and collected wild plants forming a minor component.

The individual assemblages represent mixtures of processing by-products including weed impurities reflecting the range of habitats utilised for cereal cultivation. Samples tend to be mixed with grain and chaff in similar proportions. They are not comparable to the grain-rich samples recovered from some Second Gravel Terrace sites within the Upper Thames Valley such as Ashville, although this is not necessarily related to an absence of arable production, but rather reflects the specific nature of the material present. The Cresswell Field assemblages are characteristic of routine year round processing of cereals on a small scale, the waste from which is likely to be redeposited and mixed before its final deposition. The weed/wild component suggests a mature arable weed flora reflecting the utilisation of agriculturally marginal land as well as the relatively fertile and well drained soils of the Second Gravel Terrace.

CROP-HUSBANDRY AS SEEN FROM THE CHARRED BOTANICAL SAMPLES FROM YARNTON *by Chris Stevens*

During the course of the excavations of the Iron Age and Roman settlement at Yarnton (YWRF) numerous features; pits, ditches, gullies, layers and kilns, were sampled for the retrieval of archaeobotanical material. In total 18 early Iron Age, 25 middle Iron Age, 24 early Roman and 17 late Roman samples were taken. The samples were processed by the Oxford Archaeological Unit. The flots were then examined in the George Pitt-Rivers Laboratory at the McDonald Institute Cambridge. The flots were sorted for archaeobotanical material, which was then extracted, identified and listed by sample and phase in Tables 18.4-18.8. The nomenclature used follows that of Stace (1997).

Results

The crops

The main crops represented in the sample were barley (*Hordeum vulgare (sensu lato)*) and hulled wheats (*Triticum* sp.) with smaller amounts of free-threshing type wheat grains (*Triticum aestivum sl*). On the basis of the identification of rachis fragments and grains, the barley was predominantly of the 6-row hulled variety. Only spelt wheat (*Triticum spelta*)

Table 18.3 Cresswell Field results of charcoal identification.

Sample	*7004*	*7009*	*7014*	*7032*	*7041*	*7047*	*7070*	*7082*
Context	*7202*	*7058*	*7348*	*7915*	*7180*	*7107*	*7242*	*7863*
Quercus sp.	5	7	4	2	9	4	7	6
Quercus sp. heartwood	-	-	-	-	-	2	3	-
cf *Quercus* sp.	-	-	-	-	-	4	-	-
Prunus sp.	1	2	-	-	-	6	-	1
MALOIDEAE*	3	-	2	8	-	13	-	3
MALOIDEAE heartwood	-	-	1	-	-	-	-	-
Cf. MALOIDEAE	-	-	-	-	-	2	-	-
Rhamnus catharticus L.	-	-	-	-	1	-	-	-
cf *Rhamnus catharticus* L.	-	1	1	-	-	2	-	-
cf *Fraxinus excelsior* L.	1	-	-	-	-	-	-	-
Indeterminate	-	-	2	-	-	2	-	-
Total	10	10	10	10	10	35	10	10

*MALOIDEAE is the new name applied by Stace to POMOIDEAE, the taxa included remain unchanged.

Table 18.4 Yarnton charred plant remains: early Iron Age.

Context Number	26/A	276/A	371/A	389	438	544/A/2	1163/A	1415/A	1528/A	1529/A/2	1692	1695	1716	1729	2647/A/1	2649/A/1	2650/A/1
Sample Number	103	123	120	128	164	160	114	127	159	156	170	171	173	174	89	85	88
Context Type	ditch	pit	pit	pit	pit	pit	pit	pit	pit	pit	pit	pit	pit	pit	pit	pit	pit
Sample Vol (L)	n/a	n/a	n/a	n/a	10	10	n/a	n/a	10	10	10	10	10	10	20	20	20
Seeds/litre of sediment	-	-	-	-	1.1	1.6	-	-	0.6	6.0	20.0	3.3	24.9	1.7	7.5	9.3	6.4
CEREAL GRAIN																	
Hordeum cf. *vulgare* L (lateral/twisted)	-	-	-	-	-	-	-	-	-	2	-	-	-	-	-	-	-
Hordeum spp. (hulled)	-	4	13	1	1	-	-	2	1	7	7	8	6	2	14	2	3
Hordeum spp.	-	-	-	-	-	1	-	-	-	-	4	3	-	1	1	2	5
Secale cereale L.	-	-	-	3	-	-	-	-	-	-	-	-	-	-	-	-	-
Triticum cf. *diccocum* Schübl.	1	-	-	-	-	-	-	-	-	-	-	-	-	-	-	-	-
Triticum dicoccum Schübl./spelta L.	-	-	10	-	1	-	-	-	1	12	4	2	-	-	-	2	2
Triticum cf. *dicoccum* Schübl./spelta L.	-	-	7	3	-	-	1	-	-	-	-	-	-	-	4	2	1
Triticum spp. free-threshing (small-grained)	2	-	-	1	-	-	-	-	-	-	-	-	-	-	-	-	-
Triticum spp. - indeterminate	1	1	18	5	-	3	-	4	-	16	7	-	4	3	4	2	9
cf. *Triticum* spp. free-threshing (small-grained)	-	-	-	-	-	-	-	-	-	-	-	-	-	-	-	-	-
Cereal - indeterminate	1	4	4	-	2	5	4	2	2	3	5	4	-	-	2	6	6
CEREAL CHAFF																	
Hordeum spp. (rachis fragments)	-	-	1	-	-	-	-	-	-	-	1	-	-	-	2	-	-
Triticum cf. *diccocum* Schübl. (glume bases)	-	-	-	-	-	-	-	-	-	-	-	-	-	-	-	-	-
Triticum diccocum Schübl./*spelta* L. (spikelet forks = 2 glume bases)	-	-	5	-	-	-	-	-	-	-	2	-	-	1	1	-	-
Triticum dicoccum Schübl./*spelta* L. (glume bases)	-	43	279	4	3	1	17	3	-	3	40	7	80	2	57	42	42
Triticum dicoccum Schübl./*spelta* L. (unquant. minute glume base frags)	-	+	++++	+	-	-	-	+	-	-	++	-	+++	-	+	+	-
Triticum dicoccum Schübl./*spelta* L. (rachis internodes)	-	-	-	-	-	-	-	-	-	-	-	-	-	-	-	-	-
Triticum spelta L. (spikelet forks = 2 glume bases)	-	-	1	-	-	-	-	-	-	1	-	-	-	-	-	-	-
Triticum spelta L. (glume bases)	-	1	9	-	-	-	-	-	-	1	-	-	-	-	12	6	13
Triticum spp. (free-threshing type rachis node)	-	-	-	-	-	-	-	-	-	-	-	-	-	-	-	-	-
Cereal (indeterminate basal rachis nodes)	-	-	2	-	-	-	-	-	-	-	-	-	-	-	2	-	-
Cereal (indeterminate unquantified straw frags)	-	-	++	+	-	+	+	-	-	+	+	++	-	+	++	-	+
Cereal (indeterminate culm nodes)	2	2	3	-	1	-	-	-	-	-	7	-	-	1	-	2	-
Cereal (indeterminate basal culm node)	-	-	-	-	-	-	-	-	-	-	-	-	-	-	1	-	2
OTHER FOOD PLANTS																	
Linum cf. *usitatissimum* L.	-	-	-	-	-	-	-	1	-	-	-	-	-	-	-	-	-
WEED/WILD PLANTS																	
Ranunculus cf. *repens* L.	-	-	3	-	-	-	-	-	-	-	-	-	-	-	-	-	-
Adonis annua L.	-	-	-	-	-	-	-	-	-	-	-	-	-	-	-	-	-

Table 18.4 Yarnton charred plant remains: early Iron Age (continued).

Context Number	26/A	276/A	371/A	389	438	544/A/2	1163/A	1415/A	1528/A	1529/A/2	1692	1695	1716	1729	2647/A/1	2649/A/1	2650/A/1
Sample Number	103	123	120	128	164	160	114	127	159	156	170	171	173	174	89	85	88
WEED/WILD PLANTS continued…																	
Papaver cf. *rhoeas* L./*dubium* L.	-	-	-	-	-	-	-	-	-	-	-	-	-	-	-	3	-
Papaver spp.	-	-	1	-	-	-	-	-	-	-	-	-	-	-	-	-	-
Urtica urens L.	-	-	-	20	-	-	-	-	-	-	-	-	-	-	-	-	-
Chenopodium cf. *polyspermum* L.	-	-	-	2	-	-	-	-	-	-	-	-	-	-	-	-	-
Chenopodium album L.	2	1	25	-	1	-	-	-	-	2	13	-	26	-	8	5	5
Chenopodium spp.	-	-	-	1	-	-	-	-	-	-	-	-	-	-	-	-	-
Atriplex prostrata Boucher ex DC./*patula* L.	-	1	-	1	-	-	-	2	-	1	20	-	6	-	2	-	1
CHENOPODIACEAE (indeterminate)	-	-	1	-	-	1	-	-	-	1	-	-	-	-	-	-	-
Montia fontana ssp. *chondrosperma* (Fenzl.) Walters	-	-	-	-	-	-	-	-	-	-	1	-	-	-	-	-	-
Stellaria media (L.) Vill.	-	-	1	-	-	-	-	-	-	-	1	-	4	-	2	3	-
Stellaria spp.	1	-	1	2	-	-	-	-	-	-	-	-	-	-	-	-	-
Stellaria sp./*Cerastium* sp.	-	-	1	-	-	-	-	-	-	-	-	-	-	-	-	-	-
Cerastium cf. *fontanum* Baumg.	-	-	-	-	-	-	1	-	-	-	-	-	-	-	-	-	-
Spergula arvensis L.	-	-	-	-	-	-	-	-	-	-	1	-	-	-	-	1	-
Lychnis flos-cuculi L.	-	-	-	-	-	-	-	-	-	-	-	-	1	-	-	-	-
Agrostemma githago L.	-	-	-	-	-	-	-	-	-	-	-	-	-	-	-	1	-
Silene cf. *nutans* L.	-	1	-	-	-	-	-	-	-	-	-	-	-	-	-	-	-
Silene cf. *latifolia* Poir.	-	-	-	-	-	-	-	-	-	-	-	-	-	-	1	-	1
CARYOPHYLLACEAE indeterminate	-	-	-	-	-	-	-	2	-	-	-	-	1	-	-	-	-
Persicaria maculosa Gray	-	-	-	-	-	-	-	-	-	-	-	1	-	-	-	-	-
Persicaria cf. *hydropiper* (L.) Spach	-	-	-	-	-	-	-	-	-	-	1	-	-	-	-	-	-
Polygonum aviculare L. agg.	-	-	-	2	-	-	-	-	-	-	-	-	1	-	1	2	-
Polygonum spp./*Fallopia* spp. (indeterminate)	-	-	4	-	-	-	-	-	-	-	1	-	-	-	-	-	-
Fallopia convolvulus (L.) Á. Löve	-	-	-	-	-	-	-	-	-	-	-	-	-	-	-	-	2
Rumex acetosella L.	-	-	-	-	-	-	-	-	-	-	-	-	-	-	-	-	1
Rumex cf. *crispus* L.	-	-	1	-	-	-	-	-	-	-	3	-	1	1	-	5	3
Rumex cf. *conglomeratus* Murray/*sanguineus* L./*obtusifolius* L.	-	-	-	-	-	-	-	-	-	-	-	-	2	-	-	-	1
Rumex spp. (indeterminate)	-	-	1	-	-	-	-	-	-	-	3	-	4	-	-	-	-
POLYGONACEAE (indeterminate)	-	-	-	1	-	-	1	1	-	-	-	-	1	-	-	-	-
Malva sylvestris L.	-	-	-	-	-	-	-	-	-	-	-	-	-	-	1	1	-
Viola cf. *tricolor* L./*arvensis* Murray	-	-	-	-	-	-	-	-	-	-	-	-	1	-	-	-	-
Brassica spp.	-	-	-	-	-	-	1	1	-	-	-	-	-	-	-	-	-
Sinapis arvensis L./*alba* L.	-	1	-	-	-	-	-	-	-	-	-	-	-	-	-	-	-
Potentilla cf. *neumanniana* Rchb./*erecta* (L.) Raeusch./*anglica* Laichard	-	-	-	-	-	-	-	-	-	-	-	-	2	-	-	-	-
Potentilla cf. *reptans* L.	-	-	3	-	-	-	-	-	-	-	-	-	-	-	-	1	-
Potentilla spp.	-	-	1	-	-	-	1	-	-	-	-	-	-	-	-	-	-

Table 18.4 *Yarnton charred plant remains: early Iron Age (continued).*

Context Number	*26/A*	*276/A*	*371/A*	*389*	*438*	*544/A/2*	*1163/A*	*1415/A*	*1528/A*	*1529/A/2*	*1692*	*1695*	*1716*	*1729*	*2647/A/1*	*2649/A/1*	*2650/A/1*
Sample Number	*103*	*123*	*120*	*128*	*164*	*160*	*114*	*127*	*159*	*156*	*170*	*171*	*173*	*174*	*89*	*85*	*88*
WEED/WILD PLANTS continued...																	
Vicia spp./*Lathyrus* spp.	1	2	3	-	-	1	2	1	1	2	19	1	-	-	2	3	1
Medicago lupilina L.	-	-	6	2	-	-	-	1	-	-	-	-	13	-	-	1	-
Medicago spp./*Trifolium* spp.	-	-	-	-	-	-	-	-	-	-	-	-	-	-	3	-	-
Trifolium repens L./*campestre* Schreb./*dubium* Sibth./*arvense* L. (type)	-	3	9	-	-	-	2	-	-	-	10	-	12	-	4	1	1
Trifolium repens L./*pratense* L.	-	-	3	2	-	1	-	-	-	-	2	-	-	-	5	-	1
Trifolium cf. *pratense* L.	-	1	1	1	-	-	-	-	-	-	-	-	3	-	-	-	-
Trifolium spp.	1	-	-	-	-	1	-	1	-	-	-	-	-	-	-	1	1
FABACEAE indeterminate	-	-	-	-	-	-	-	1	-	-	-	-	-	-	-	-	2
Myosotis cf. *arvensis* (L.) Hill	1	-	-	-	-	-	-	-	-	-	-	-	-	-	-	1	-
Plantago lanceolata L.	-	-	1	-	-	-	-	-	-	-	-	-	-	-	-	-	-
Veronica cf. *arvensis* L.	-	-	-	-	-	-	-	-	-	-	-	-	-	1	-	-	-
cf. *Odontites vernus* (Bellardi) Dumort.	-	-	1	-	-	-	-	-	-	1	1	-	7	-	-	2	-
Galium aparine L.	-	-	-	-	-	1	-	-	-	-	2	-	-	-	1	2	2
Valerianella locusta (L.) Laterr.	-	-	-	-	-	-	-	-	-	-	-	-	-	-	-	-	1
Centaurea spp.	-	-	1	-	-	-	-	-	-	-	-	-	-	-	-	-	-
Lapsana communis L.	-	-	-	-	-	-	-	-	-	-	-	-	-	-	-	5	-
Achillea spp./*Artemisia* spp./*Anthemis* spp./*Tripleurospermum* spp.	-	-	-	-	-	-	-	-	-	-	-	-	-	-	1	1	-
Anthemis cotula L.	1	-	-	-	-	-	1	-	-	-	-	-	-	1	1	-	-
cf. *Leucantheum vulgare* L.	-	-	-	-	-	-	-	-	-	-	-	-	-	-	-	-	-
Tripleurospermum inodorum (L.) Sch. Bip.	-	1	-	-	-	-	1	-	-	-	-	-	18	-	-	2	1
ASTERACEAE (indeterminate)	-	-	1	-	-	-	1	1	-	-	1	-	1	-	-	-	-
Juncus spp. (seed capsules)	-	-	1	-	-	-	-	-	-	-	-	-	-	-	-	-	-
Eleocharis palustris (L.) Roem. & Schult./*uniglumis* (Link.) Schult.	-	-	23	1	-	-	-	-	-	-	5	1	3	-	6	-	6
Carex spp. (indeterminate - flat/2-sided)	-	-	6	-	-	-	-	-	-	-	1	-	1	-	-	-	-
Carex spp. (indeterminate - trigonous)	-	-	3	2	-	-	-	-	-	-	2	-	-	-	2	-	1
cf. *Festuca* spp./*Lolium* spp.	-	-	5	-	-	-	1	-	-	-	-	-	-	-	-	1	-
Lolium cf. *perenne* L.	-	-	3	-	-	-	-	-	-	-	-	1	3	-	1	-	-
Briza media L./*Glyceria maxima* (Hartm.) Holmb./*Milium effusum* L.	-	-	-	-	-	-	-	-	-	-	10	-	-	-	-	-	-
Poa cf. *annua* L.	-	-	2	2	-	1	-	2	-	4	-	1	4	1	-	-	1
Poa cf. *trivialis* L./*pratensis* L.	-	-	-	-	-	-	-	-	-	-	4	-	-	-	-	-	-
Phleum sp./*Poa* sp.	-	3	-	-	1	-	-	-	-	2	3	3	13	-	2	2	-
Avena spp. (caryopses)	1	-	7	2	-	-	-	-	-	-	6	-	1	-	1	1	1
Avena spp. (awns)	-	2	1	-	-	-	-	-	-	-	1	-	1	-	-	2	1
Avena spp./*Bromus* spp.	1	-	10	3	-	-	2	-	-	1	4	-	5	1	1	6	2
cf. *Deschampsia* spp.	-	-	1	-	-	-	-	-	-	-	-	-	-	-	-	-	-
cf. *Alopecurus* sp.	-	-	-	1	-	-	-	-	-	-	-	-	-	-	-	-	-

Table 18.4 Yarnton charred plant remains: early Iron Age (continued).

Context Number	*26/A*	*276/A*	*371/A*	*389*	*438*	*544/A/2*	*1163/A*	*1415/A*	*1528/A*	*1529/A/2*	*1692*	*1695*	*1716*	*1729*	*2647/A/1*	*2649/A/1*	*2650/A/1*
Sample Number	*103*	*123*	*120*	*128*	*164*	*160*	*114*	*127*	*159*	*156*	*170*	*171*	*173*	*174*	*89*	*85*	*88*
WEED/WILD PLANTS continued…																	
Phleum sp.	-	-	12	-	-	-	-	-	-	-	-	-	8	-	1	55	-
Bromus hordeaceus L./*secalinus* L. (type)	-	-	6	-	-	-	-	-	-	-	-	-	-	-	1	-	-
Bromus spp.	-	1	5	-	-	-	1	-	-	-	1	-	5	-	-	2	2
POACEAE >4 mm undifferentiated	-	-	1	-	-	-	-	-	-	-	-	-	3	-	-	-	-
POACEAE <3.5 mm undifferentiated	-	-	1	-	-	-	-	-	-	-	-	-	-	-	2	1	-
POACEAE (indeterminate)	-	-	1	-	-	-	-	1	-	-	-	-	4	1	-	-	1
Unidentified - seeds (undifferentiated)	2	-	9	8	1	-	4	1	1	-	5	1	3	-	-	7	6
Unidentified - tree/shrub buds	-	-	5	-	-	-	-	-	-	-	-	-	-	-	-	1	-
TOTALS																	
Cereal Grain	5	9	52	13	4	9	5	8	4	40	27	17	10	6	25	16	26
Cereal Chaff	2	46	306	4	4	1	18	3	0	6	52	7	80	5	76	50	57
Other Crops	0	0	0	0	0	0	0	1	0	0	0	0	0	0	0	0	0
Weed/Wild	9	17	157	45	2	6	15	14	1	14	116	8	156	6	49	111	39
Unidentified/Indeterminate	2	0	14	8	1	0	4	1	1	0	5	1	3	0	0	8	6
TOTAL IDENTIFICATIONS	18	72	529	70	11	16	42	27	6	60	200	33	249	17	150	185	128
PROPORTIONS																	
Cereal Grain	27.8%	12.5%	9.8%	18.6%	36.4%	56.3%	11.9%	29.6%	66.7%	66.7%	13.5%	51.5%	4.0%	35.3%	16.7%	8.6%	0.3%
Cereal Chaff	11.1%	63.9%	57.8%	5.7%	36.4%	6.3%	42.9%	11.1%	0.0%	10.0%	26.0%	21.2%	32.1%	29.4%	50.7%	27.0%	4.5%
Other Crops	0.0%	0.0%	0.0%	0.0%	0.0%	0.0%	0.0%	3.7%	0.0%	0.0%	0.0%	0.0%	0.0%	0.0%	0.0%	0.0%	0.0%
Weed/Wild	50.0%	23.6%	29.7%	64.3%	18.2%	37.5%	35.7%	51.9%	16.7%	23.3%	58.0%	24.2%	62.7%	35.3%	32.7%	60.0%	0.5%
Unidentified/Indeterminate	11.1%	0.0%	2.6%	11.4%	9.1%	0.0%	9.5%	3.7%	16.7%	0.0%	2.5%	3.0%	1.2%	0.0%	0.0%	4.3%	4.7%

Key: + = <5 items, ++ = 5 – 25 items, +++ = 26 – 100 items, ++++ = >100 items
N.B. Sample 87 from context 2658/A/1 was unproductive.
Some samples did not have a volume recorded, however, it is likely that the samples were either 10 L or 20 L in volume based on the other volumes recorded.

Table 18.5 Yarnton charred plant remains: middle Iron Age.

Context Number	*241/C/2*	*259/A*	*261/A*	*268/A*	*270/A*	*273/A*	*301/D*	*327*	*369/A*	*415/A*
Sample Number	*154*	*39*	*132*	*40*	*45*	*41*	*43*	*131*	*130*	*44*
Context Type	*gully*	*ditch/enc*	*ditch*	*pit*	*gully*	*pit*	*gully*	*gully*	*gully*	*ditch*
Sample Volume (L)	*10*	*10*	*20*	*10*	*10*	*10*	*10*	*n/a*	*n/a*	*10*
Seeds per litre of sediment	*2.1*	*6.1*	*6.0*	*4.4*	*2.7*	*6.5*	*2.0*	-	-	*2.1*
CEREAL GRAIN										
Hordeum cf. *vulgare* L (lateral/twisted)	-	-	-	-	-	-	-	-	-	-
Hordeum spp. (hulled)	4	4	6	1	-	4	1	6	-	2
Hordeum spp.	4	6	8	2	-	11	2	-	1	1
cf. *Secale cereale* L. (grains)	-	-	-	-	-	-	-	-	-	-
Triticum dicoccum Schübl./*spelta* L.	-	-	2	-	3	-	-	-	-	-
Triticum cf. *dicoccum* Schübl./*spelta* L.	-	3	1	-	-	-	1	-	-	1
Triticum spp. free-threshing (small-grained)	-	-	-	-	3	1	2	-	1	1
Triticum spp. - indeterminate	2	2	4	-	-	-	-	5	1	1
cf. *Triticum* spp. free-threshing (small-grained)	-	-	-	-	4	-	1	-	-	-
Cereal - indeterminate	3	3	8	1	-	4	2	2	1	1
CEREAL CHAFF										
Hordeum spp. (rachis fragments)	-	-	2	-	-	-	-	-	-	-
Triticum diccocum Schübl./*spelta* L. (spikelet forks)	-	-	4	-	1	-	-	4	-	-
Triticum cf. *diccocum* Schübl. (glume bases)	-	-	-	-	-	-	-	-	-	-
Triticum dicoccum Schübl./*spelta* L. (glume bases)	-	12	34	18	-	4	-	5	1	3
Triticum dicoccum Schübl./*spelta* L. (unquant. minute glume base frags)	-	-	++	-	-	-	-	+	-	-
Triticum spelta L. (spikelet forks = 2 glume bases)	-	-	-	-	1	-	-	-	-	-
Triticum spelta L. (glume bases)	-	-	1	-	1	-	1	-	-	-
Cereal (indeterminate rachis nodes)	-	-	-	-	-	-	-	-	-	-
Cereal (indeterminate unquantified straw frags)	-	-	-	+	+	+	-	-	+	-
Cereal (indeterminate culm nodes)	-	1	-	1	-	-	-	-	-	-
Cereal (indeterminate basal culm node)	-	-	-	-	-	-	-	-	-	-
OTHER FOOD PLANTS										
Corylus avellana L. - nutshell frags	-	-	-	-	-	-	-	-	-	-
WEED/WILD PLANTS										
Urtica dioica L.	-	-	-	-	-	1	-	-	-	-
Urtica urens L.	-	-	-	-	-	-	-	-	-	-
Chenopodium cf. *polyspermum* L.	-	1	1	-	-	-	-	-	-	-
Chenopodium album L.	-	1	7	1	-	1	1	1	-	-
Atriplex prostrata Boucher ex DC./*patula* L.	-	-	-	4	2	6	1	1	-	-
CHENOPODIACEAE (indeterminate)	-	-	-	-	-	2	-	-	-	-
Montia fontana ssp. *chondrosperma* (Fenzl.) Walters	-	-	-	1	-	-	-	-	-	-
Stellaria media (L.) Vill.	-	-	-	-	-	1	-	-	-	-
Agrostemma githago L.	-	1	-	-	-	-	-	-	-	-
Silene cf. *latifolia* Poir.	-	-	-	-	-	-	-	-	-	-
Dianthus deltoides L./*armeria* L.	-	-	-	-	-	-	-	-	-	-
CARYOPHYLLACEAE indeterminate	-	-	-	-	-	7	-	-	-	-
Persicaria maculosa Gray	1	-	-	-	-	-	-	-	-	-
Polygonum aviculare L. agg.	-	-	-	-	-	-	-	1	-	3
Polygonum spp./*Fallopia* spp. (indeterminate)	-	-	-	-	-	-	1	-	-	3
Fallopia convolvulus (L.) Á. Löve	-	-	-	-	-	-	-	-	-	-
Rumex acetosella L.	-	-	1	-	-	-	-	-	-	-
Rumex cf. *crispus* L.	-	-	1	-	-	-	1	2	-	-
Rumex cf. *conglomeratus* Murray/*sanguineus* L./*obtusifolius* L.	-	-	3	-	-	-	-	-	-	-
Rumex spp. (indeterminate)	-	-	-	-	-	-	-	-	-	-
POLYGONACEAE (indeterminate)	-	-	-	-	-	-	-	-	-	-
Malva sylvestris L.	-	-	-	-	-	-	-	-	-	-
Brassica spp.	-	-	-	-	-	-	-	-	-	-
Brassica sp./*Sinapsis* sp.	-	-	-	-	-	-	-	-	-	-
Raphanus raphanistum L. (seed capsule)	-	-	-	-	-	-	-	-	-	-
Potentilla spp.	-	-	-	-	-	-	-	-	-	-
Vicia spp./*Lathyrus* spp.	-	5	4	1	3	1	1	2	-	3

Table 18.5 Yarnton charred plant remains: middle Iron Age (continued).

Context Number	*241/C/2*	*259/A*	*261/A*	*268/A*	*270/A*	*273/A*	*301/D*	*327*	*369/A*	*415/A*
Sample Number	*154*	*39*	*132*	*40*	*45*	*41*	*43*	*131*	*130*	*44*
Medicago lupilina L.	-	-	-	1	-	-	-	-	-	-
Medicago spp./*Trifolium* spp.	-	-	-	-	-	-	-	-	-	-
Trifolium repens L./*campestre* Schreb./*dubium* Sibth./ *arvense* L. (type)	-	5	2	3	3	6	-	2	-	-
Trifolium repens L./*pratense* L.	1	-	5	-	-	-	-	-	-	-
Trifolium cf. *pratense* L.	-	-	-	-	-	-	-	-	-	1
Trifolium spp.	-	-	-	-	-	2	-	-	-	-
Torilis japonica (Houtt.) DC./*arvensis* (Huds.) Link	-	-	-	-	-	-	-	-	-	-
Lithospermum arvense L.	-	-	-	-	-	-	-	-	-	-
Myosotis cf. *arvensis* (L.) Hill	-	-	1	-	-	-	-	-	-	-
Lamium cf. *album* L./*purpurum* L./*hybridum* Vill./*amplexicaule* L.	1	-	-	-	-	-	-	-	-	-
Mentha cf. *arvensis* L./*aquatica* L.	-	-	-	-	-	-	-	-	-	-
Plantago lanceolata L.	-	-	-	-	-	1	-	-	-	-
Veronica cf. *arvensis* L.	-	-	-	-	-	-	-	-	-	-
cf. *Odontites vernus* (Bellardi) Dumort.	-	1	1	1	1	-	-	-	1	-
Galium palustre L./*verum* L./*mollugo* L./*saxatile* L./*spurium* L.	-	-	-	-	-	-	-	-	-	-
Galium aparine L.	-	1	1	2	-	-	1	2	-	-
Valerianella dentata (L.) Pollich.	-	-	-	-	-	-	-	-	-	-
VALERIANACEAE (indeterminate)	-	1	-	-	-	-	-	-	-	-
Carduus spp./*Cirsium* spp.	-	-	-	-	-	-	-	-	-	-
Achillea spp./*Artemisia* spp./*Anthemis* spp./*Tripleurospermum* spp.	-	2	-	-	-	1	-	-	-	-
Anthemis cotula L.	2	-	-	-	-	-	-	1	-	-
Tripleurospermum inodorum (L.) Sch. Bip.	-	1	-	-	-	-	-	-	-	-
Eleocharis palustris (L.) Roem. & Schult./*uniglumis* (Link.) Schult.	-	-	-	-	-	-	-	2	1	-
Carex spp. (indeterminate - flat/2-sided)	-	-	-	-	-	-	-	-	-	-
Carex spp. (indeterminate - trigonous)	-	-	1	-	-	2	-	-	-	-
CYPERACEAE indet	1	-	-	-	-	-	-	-	-	-
cf. *Festuca* spp./*Lolium* spp.	-	-	-	-	-	-	-	-	-	-
Lolium cf. *perenne* L.	-	-	-	-	-	-	-	-	-	-
Poa cf. *annua* L.	-	3	4	-	2	-	-	2	-	-
Phleum sp./*Poa* sp.	-	-	-	2	-	1	-	2	2	-
cf. *Dactylis glomerata* L.	-	-	-	-	-	-	-	-	-	-
cf. *Arrhenatherum* spp. *Avena* spp.	-	-	1	-	-	-	-	1	-	-
Avena spp. (caryopses)	-	1	1	2	1	4	-	1	-	-
Avena spp. (awns)	-	1	2	-	-	-	-	1	-	-
Avena spp./*Bromus* spp.	-	-	1	3	-	-	-	-	-	-
cf. *Alopecurus* sp.	-	-	-	-	-	1	-	-	-	-
Phleum sp.	-	1	-	-	-	-	-	-	-	-
Bromus hordeaceus L./*secalinus* L. (type)	-	1	-	-	-	-	-	-	-	1
Bromus sp.	-	1	3	-	-	-	-	-	-	-
POACEAE >4 mm undifferentiated	1	-	-	-	-	-	-	-	-	-
POACEAE <3.5 mm undifferentiated	-	-	-	-	-	-	1	-	-	-
POACEAE (indeterminate)	-	-	2	-	-	-	-	-	1	-
POACEAE indeterminate (rachis)	-	-	-	-	-	-	-	-	-	-
Unidentified	1	2	4	-	-	4	3	1	-	-
TOTALS										
Cereal Grain	13	18	29	4	10	20	9	13	4	7
Cereal Chaff	0	13	41	19	3	4	1	9	1	3
Other Crops	0	0	0	0	0	0	0	0	0	0
Weed/Wild	7	27	42	21	12	37	7	21	5	11
Unidentified/Indeterminate	1	2	4	0	0	4	3	1	0	0
TOTAL IDENTIFICATIONS	21	60	116	44	25	65	20	44	10	21
PROPORTIONS										
Cereal Grain	61.9%	30.0%	25.0%	9.1%	40.0%	30.8%	45.0%	29.5%	40.0%	33.3%
Cereal Chaff	0.0%	21.7%	35.3%	43.2%	12.0%	6.2%	5.0%	20.5%	10.0%	14.3%
Other Crops	0.0%	0.0%	0.0%	0.0%	0.0%	0.0%	0.0%	0.0%	0.0%	0.0%
Weed/Wild	33.3%	45.0%	36.2%	47.7%	48.0%	56.9%	35.0%	47.7%	50.0%	52.4%
Unidentified/Indeterminate	4.8%	3.3%	3.4%	0.0%	0.0%	6.2%	15.0%	2.3%	0.0%	0.0%

Table 18.5 Yarnton charred plant remains: middle Iron Age (continued).

Context Number	*584/B/2*	*715/A*	*731/A*	*746/A*	*944/A*	*1189*	*1277/A*	*1357/A*	*1530/A*
Sample Number	*37*	*161*	*121*	*122*	*125*	*162*	*124*	*126*	*133*
Context Type	*pit*	*pit*	*pit*	*pit*	*pit*	*pit*	*pit*	*pit*	*pit*
Sample Volume (L)	*10*	*10*	*10*	*n/a*	*n/a*	*n/a*	*10*	*n/a*	*n/a*
Seeds per litre of sediment	*9.0*	*3.4*	-	-	-	*7.7*	-	-	*1.7*
CEREAL GRAIN									
Hordeum cf. *vulgare* L (lateral/twisted)	-	-	-	-	-	-	-	-	-
Hordeum spp. (hulled)	1	-	-	2	2	-	3	3	-
Hordeum spp.	3	4	-	-	-	2	-	-	3
cf. *Secale cereale* L. (grains)	-	-	-	1	-	-	-	-	-
Triticum dicoccum Schübl./*spelta* L.	-	-	-	-	3	3	-	2	4
Triticum cf. *dicoccum* Schübl./*spelta* L.	1	-	-	-	-	-	2	-	-
Triticum spp. free-threshing (small-grained)	-	-	-	-	-	-	-	-	-
Triticum spp. - indeterminate	1	-	2	2	8	4	-	7	-
cf. *Triticum* spp. free-threshing (small-grained)	1	-	-	-	-	-	-	-	-
Cereal - indeterminate	2	3	2	2	3	1	2	-	2
CEREAL CHAFF									
Hordeum spp. (rachis fragments)	2	4	-	-	-	1	-	2	-
Triticum diccocum Schübl./*spelta* L. (spikelet forks)	4	-	-	-	3	-	-	4	-
Triticum cf. *diccocum* Schübl. (glume bases)	-	1	-	-	-	-	-	-	-
Triticum dicoccum Schübl./*spelta* L. (glume bases)	20	11	5	12	88	28	51	256	1
Triticum dicoccum Schübl./*spelta* L. (unquant. minute glume base frags)	++	-	+	++	++	-	++	+++	-
Triticum spelta L. (spikelet forks = 2 glume bases)	-	-	-	-	-	-	-	-	-
Triticum spelta L. (glume bases)	2	-	-	-	5	-	4	13	1
Cereal (indeterminate rachis nodes)	-	-	-	-	5	-	-	-	-
Cereal (indeterminate unquantified straw frags)	-	+	-	-	-	-	+	+	-
Cereal (indeterminate culm nodes)	-	2	1	-	-	3	1	2	-
Cereal (indeterminate basal culm node)	-	-	-	1	-	2	-	-	-
OTHER FOOD PLANTS									
Corylus avellana L. - nutshell frags	-	-	-	-	-	-	-	-	-
WEED/WILD PLANTS									
Urtica dioica L.	2	-	-	-	-	-	-	-	-
Urtica urens L.	-	-	-	-	-	-	-	-	-
Chenopodium cf. *polyspermum* L.	-	-	-	-	-	-	-	-	-
Chenopodium album L.	-	5	7	1	4	4	5	6	2
Atriplex prostrata Boucher ex DC./*patula* L.	1	-	-	-	4	-	3	3	-
CHENOPODIACEAE (indeterminate)	1	-	-	-	-	-	-	-	-
Montia fontana ssp. *chondrosperma* (Fenzl.) Walters	-	-	-	-	-	-	-	-	-
Stellaria media (L.) Vill.	1	-	-	-	1	2	-	-	-
Agrostemma githago L.	-	-	-	-	-	-	-	-	-
Silene cf. *latifolia* Poir.	-	-	-	-	-	1	-	-	-
Dianthus deltoides L./*armeria* L.	-	-	-	-	-	-	-	-	-
CARYOPHYLLACEAE indeterminate	-	-	-	-	-	-	-	-	-
Persicaria maculosa Gray	-	-	-	-	-	-	-	-	-
Polygonum aviculare L. agg.	1	-	-	-	-	2	-	1	-
Polygonum spp./*Fallopia* spp. (indeterminate)	-	-	-	-	-	-	-	-	-
Fallopia convolvulus (L.) Á. Löve	-	-	-	-	-	1	-	-	-
Rumex acetosella L.	-	-	-	-	-	-	1	1	-
Rumex cf. *crispus* L.	2	-	3	-	-	3	1	5	-
Rumex cf. *conglomeratus* Murray/*sanguineus* L./*obtusifolius* L.	-	-	-	-	-	-	-	-	-
Rumex spp. (indeterminate)	1	-	2	1	-	1	-	-	1
POLYGONACEAE (indeterminate)	-	-	-	-	-	-	2	-	-
Malva sylvestris L.	1	-	-	-	-	-	-	-	-
Brassica spp.	-	-	-	-	-	-	-	-	-
Brassica sp./*Sinapsis* sp.	-	-	-	-	-	-	-	1	-
Raphanus raphanistum L. (seed capsule)	-	-	-	2	-	-	-	-	-
Potentilla spp.	-	-	-	-	-	-	-	-	-
Vicia spp./*Lathyrus* spp.	5	-	-	2	1	4	7	1	-

Table 18.5 Yarnton charred plant remains: middle Iron Age (continued).

Context Number	*584/B/2*	*715/A*	*731/A*	*746/A*	*944/A*	*1189*	*1277/A*	*1357/A*	*1530/A*
Sample Number	*37*	*161*	*121*	*122*	*125*	*162*	*124*	*126*	*133*
Medicago lupilina L.	-	-	1	-	-	-	-	3	-
Medicago spp./*Trifolium* spp.	-	-	-	-	-	-	-	3	-
Trifolium repens L./*campestre* Schreb./*dubium* Sibth./*arvense* L. (type)	2	-	2	-	-	2	-	5	1
Trifolium repens L./*pratense* L.	-	1	-	-	-	1	-	-	-
Trifolium cf. *pratense* L.	-	-	-	-	4	-	-	-	-
Trifolium spp.	3	-	-	3	-	-	-	-	-
Torilis japonica (Houtt.) DC./*arvensis* (Huds.) Link	-	-	-	-	-	-	-	-	-
Lithospermum arvense L.	-	-	-	-	-	-	-	-	-
Myosotis cf. *arvensis* (L.) Hill	-	-	-	-	-	-	-	-	-
Lamium cf. *album* L./*purpurum* L./*hybridum* Vill./*amplexicaule* L.	-	-	-	-	-	-	-	-	-
Mentha cf. *arvensis* L./*aquatica* L.	-	-	-	-	-	-	-	-	-
Plantago lanceolata L.	-	-	-	-	-	-	-	-	-
Veronica cf. *arvensis* L.	-	-	-	-	-	-	-	-	-
cf. *Odontites vernus* (Bellardi) Dumort.	-	1	-	-	-	-	-	-	-
Galium palustre L./*verum* L./*mollugo* L./*saxatile* L./*spurium* L.	-	-	-	-	-	-	-	-	-
Galium aparine L.	-	-	-	-	-	-	-	1	-
Valerianella dentata (L.) Pollich.	-	-	-	-	-	-	-	-	-
VALERIANACEAE (indeterminate)	-	-	-	-	-	-	-	-	-
Carduus spp./*Cirsium* spp.	-	-	-	-	-	-	-	-	-
Achillea spp./*Artemisia* spp./*Anthemis spp./Tripleurospermum* spp.	-	-	-	-	-	-	-	-	-
Anthemis cotula L.	-	-	-	-	-	-	-	-	-
Tripleurospermum inodorum (L.) Sch. Bip.	3	-	-	-	1	-	1	2	-
Eleocharis palustris (L.) Roem. & Schult./*uniglumis* (Link.) Schult.	2	-	-	1	4	4	1	2	-
Carex spp. (indeterminate - flat/2-sided)	-	-	-	-	-	-	-	1	-
Carex spp. (indeterminate - trigonous)	-	-	-	-	2	-	2	-	-
CYPERACEAE indeterminate	-	-	-	-	-	-	-	-	-
cf. *Festuca* spp./*Lolium* spp.	-	-	-	-	1	-	-	4	-
Lolium cf. *perenne* L.	1	-	-	-	1	-	-	-	-
Poa cf. *annua* L.	9	-	-	-	-	3	2	-	1
Phleum sp./*Poa* sp.	-	-	-	1	-	-	2	7	-
cf. *Dactylis glomerata* L.	-	-	-	-	-	-	-	-	-
cf. *Arrhenatherum* spp./*Avena* spp.	-	-	-	-	-	-	-	-	-
Avena spp. (caryopses)	6	2	1	1	3	3	2	3	-
Avena spp. (awns)	2	-	-	-	3	1	4	1	-
Avena spp./*Bromus* spp.	-	-	-	2	4	-	7	3	-
cf. *Alopecurus* sp.	-	-	-	-	-	-	-	-	-
Phleum sp.	-	-	-	-	3	-	1	-	-
Bromus hordeaceus L./*secalinus* L. (type)	1	-	1	-	-	-	-	2	-
Bromus sp.	-	-	-	2	1	-	1	4	-
POACEAE >4 mm undifferentiated	2	-	-	-	1	-	-	1	-
POACEAE <3.5 mm undifferentiated	-	-	-	-	-	-	-	-	-
POACEAE (indeterminate)	-	-	-	3	3	-	-	6	-
POACEAE indeterminate (rachis)	-	-	-	-	-	-	-	-	-
Unidentified	3	-	-	2	4	-	2	2	1
TOTALS									
Cereal Grain	9	7	4	7	16	10	7	12	9
Cereal Chaff	28	18	6	13	101	34	56	277	2
Other Crops	0	0	0	0	0	0	0	0	0
Weed/Wild	46	9	17	19	41	32	42	66	5
Unidentified/Indeterminate	3	0	0	2	4	0	2	2	1
TOTAL IDENTIFICATIONS	86	34	27	41	162	76	107	357	17
PROPORTIONS									
Cereal Grain	10.5%	20.6%	14.8%	17.1%	9.9%	13.2%	6.5%	3.4%	52.9%
Cereal Chaff	32.6%	52.9%	22.2%	31.7%	62.3%	44.7%	52.3%	77.6%	11.8%
Other Crops	0.0%	0.0%	0.0%	0.0%	0.0%	0.0%	0.0%	0.0%	0.0%
Weed/Wild	53.5%	26.5%	63.0%	46.3%	25.3%	42.1%	39.3%	18.5%	29.4%
Unidentified/Indeterminate	3.5%	0.0%	0.0%	4.9%	2.5%	0.0%	1.9%	0.6%	5.9%

Table 18.5 Yarnton charred plant remains: middle Iron Age (continued).

Context Number	*1603/A*	*1696/A/2*	*1696/A/9*	*1730*	*1733*
Sample Number	*151*	*172*	*172*	*175*	*177*
Context Type	*ditch*	*pit*	*pit*	*pit*	*pit*
Sample Volume (L)	*10*	*10*	*10*	*10*	*10*
Seeds per litre of sediment	*1.8*	*36.3*	*18.8*	*10.8*	*7.1*
CEREAL GRAIN					
Hordeum cf. *vulgare* L (lateral/twisted)	-	-	-	2	-
Hordeum spp. (hulled)	4	20	-	6	3
Hordeum spp.	-	15	9	1	3
cf. *Secale cereale* L. (grains)	-	-	-	-	-
Triticum dicoccum Schübl./*spelta* L.	-	35	30	1	-
Triticum cf. *dicoccum* Schübl./*spelta* L.	2	10	-	-	-
Triticum spp. free-threshing (small-grained)	-	-	-	-	-
Triticum spp. - indeterminate	1	10	6	1	2
cf. *Triticum* spp. free-threshing (small-grained)	1	-	-	-	-
Cereal - indeterminate	4	14	6	-	5
CEREAL CHAFF					
Hordeum spp. (rachis fragments)	-	1	-	2	-
Triticum diccocum Schübl./*spelta* L. (spikelet forks)				3	2
Triticum cf. *diccocum* Schübl. (glume bases)	-	-	-	-	-
Triticum dicoccum Schübl./*spelta* L. (glume bases)	1	36	27	39	5
Triticum dicoccum Schübl./*spelta* L. (unquant. minute glume base frags)	-	++	-	-	-
Triticum spelta L. (spikelet forks = 2 glume bases)	-	7	2	-	-
Triticum spelta L. (glume bases)	-	3	-	-	-
Cereal (indeterminate rachis nodes)	-	-	-	-	-
Cereal (indeterminate unquantified straw frags)	-	-	+	-	-
Cereal (indeterminate culm nodes)	-	5	1	1	-
Cereal (indeterminate basal culm node)	-	2	2	-	-
OTHER FOOD PLANTS					
Corylus avellana L. - nutshell frags	-	-	-	2	1
WEED/WILD PLANTS					
Urtica dioica L.	-	-	-	-	-
Urtica urens L.	-	-	-	-	1
Chenopodium cf. *polyspermum* L.	-	-	-	-	-
Chenopodium album L.	-	2	3	5	9
Atriplex prostrata Boucher ex DC./*patula* L.	-	16	6	3	1
CHENOPODIACEAE (indeterminate)	-	-	-	-	-
Montia fontana ssp. *chondrosperma* (Fenzl.) Walters	-	2	1	2	2
Stellaria media (L.) Vill.	-	1	-	-	1
Agrostemma githago L.	-	1	-	-	-
Silene cf. *latifolia* Poir.	-	-	-	1	-
Dianthus deltoides L./*armeria* L.	-	1	-	-	-
CARYOPHYLLACEAE indeterminate	-	-	-	-	-
Persicaria maculosa Gray	-	1	1	-	-
Polygonum aviculare L. agg.	-	4	6	-	1
Polygonum spp./*Fallopia* spp. (indeterminate)	-	-	-	-	-
Fallopia convolvulus (L.) Á. Löve	-	1	-	1	-
Rumex acetosella L.	-	-	-	-	-
Rumex cf. *crispus* L.	-	9	13	2	1
Rumex cf. *conglomeratus* Murray/*sanguineus* L./*obtusifolius* L.	-	1	1	3	1
Rumex spp. (indeterminate)	-	1	-	5	3
POLYGONACEAE (indeterminate)	-	-	-	-	-
Malva sylvestris L.	-	-	-	-	1
Brassica spp.	-	13	6	-	-
Brassica sp./*Sinapsis* sp.	-	-	-	-	-
Raphanus raphanistum L. (seed capsule)	-	-	-	-	-
Potentilla spp.	-	-	-	-	1
Vicia spp./*Lathyrus* spp.	4	32	14	2	3
Medicago lupilina L.	-	-	3	-	-

Table 18.5 Yarnton charred plant remains: middle Iron Age (continued).

Context Number *Sample Number*	*1603/A* *151*	*1696/A/2* *172*	*1696/A/9* *172*	*1730* *175*	*1733* *177*
Medicago spp./*Trifolium* spp.	-	-	-	2	1
Trifolium repens L./*campestre* Schreb./*dubium* Sibth./*arvense* L. (type)	-	7	4	-	2
Trifolium repens L./*pratense* L.	-	3	1	2	-
Trifolium cf. *pratense* L.	-	-	-	-	-
Trifolium spp.	-	-	-	-	-
Torilis japonica (Houtt.) DC./*arvensis* (Huds.) Link	-	-	2	-	-
Lithospermum arvense L.	-	2	-	-	-
Myosotis cf. *arvensis* (L.) Hill	-	-	-	-	-
Lamium cf. *album* L./*purpurum* L./*hybridum* Vill./*amplexicaule* L.	-	-	-	-	-
Mentha cf. *arvensis* L./*aquatica* L.	-	1	-	-	-
Plantago lanceolata L.	-	-	-	-	-
Veronica cf. *arvensis* L.	-	1	-	-	-
cf. *Odontites vernus* (Bellardi) Dumort.	-	3	-	1	2
Galium palustre L./*verum* L./*mollugo* L./*saxatile* L./*spurium* L.	-	2	-	-	-
Galium aparine L.	-	11	7	3	-
Valerianella dentata (L.) Pollich.	-	1	1	-	-
VALERIANACEAE (indeterminate)	-	-	-	-	-
Carduus spp./*Cirsium* spp.	-	2	-	1	1
Achillea spp./*Artemisia* spp./*Anthemis* spp./*Tripleurospermum* spp.	-	-	-	-	-
Anthemis cotula L.	1	-	-	-	6
Tripleurospermum inodorum (L.) Sch. Bip.	-	8	3	-	1
Eleocharis palustris (L.) Roem. & Schult./*uniglumis* (Link.) Schult.	-	4	3	-	-
Carex spp. (indeterminate - flat/2-sided)	-	-	-	-	1
Carex spp. (indeterminate - trigonous)	-	-	1	-	-
CYPERACEAE indet	-	-	-	3	-
cf. *Festuca* spp./*Lolium* spp.	-	-	-	-	-
Lolium cf. *perenne* L.	-	-	-	-	-
Poa cf. *annua* L.	-	4	3	5	1
Phleum sp./*Poa* sp.	-	1	2	-	1
cf. *Dactylis glomerata* L.	-	-	1	-	-
cf. *Arrhenatherum* spp./*Avena* spp.	-	2	-	-	-
Avena spp. (caryopses)	-	9	5	2	-
Avena spp. (awns)	-	1	-	2	-
Avena spp./*Bromus* spp.	-	26	13	-	7
cf. *Alopecurus* sp.	-	-	-	-	-
Phleum sp.	-	3	1	-	-
Bromus hordeaceus L./*secalinus* L. (type)	-	-	-	-	-
Bromus sp.	-	12	2	1	-
POACEAE >4 mm undifferentiated	-	-	-	-	-
POACEAE <3.5 mm undifferentiated	-	1	-	-	-
POACEAE (indeterminate)	-	-	-	1	-
POACEAE indeterminate (rachis)	-	3	-	-	-
Unidentified	-	6	-	-	-
TOTALS					
Cereal Grain	12	104	51	11	13
Cereal Chaff	1	54	32	45	7
Other Crops	0	0	0	2	1
Weed/Wild	5	192	103	47	48
Unidentified Indeterminate	0	6	0	0	0
TOTAL IDENTIFICATIONS	18	356	186	105	69
PROPORTIONS					
Cereal Grain	66.7%	29.2%	27.4%	10.5%	18.8%
Cereal Chaff	5.6%	15.2%	17.2%	42.9%	10.1%
Other Crops	0.0%	0.0%	0.0%	1.9%	1.4%
Weed/Wild	27.8%	53.9%	55.4%	44.8%	69.6%
Unidentified/Indeterminate	0.0%	1.7%	0.0%	0.0%	0.0%

Some samples did not have a volume recorded, however, it is likely that the samples were either 10 L or 20 L in volume based on the other volumes recorded. Key: + = <5 items, ++ = 5 – 25 items, +++ = 26 – 100 items, ++++ = >100 items

Table 18.6 Yarnton charred plant remains: late Iron Age.

Context Number	*592/A/2*	*120/A*	*121/B*	*236/F/3*	*246*	*300/A*	*347/B/2*	*370*
Sample Number	*73*	*113*	*107*	*142*	*165*	*42*	*58*	*30*
Context Type	*pot*	*ditch*	*ditch*	*ditch*	*pit*	*pit*	*ditch*	*layer*
Sample Volume (L)	*6*	*n/a*	*n/a*	*10*	*10*	*10*	*10*	*30*
Seeds per litre of sediment	*0.2*	-	-	*3.2*	*0.8*	*3.7*	*43.9*	*14.4*
CEREAL GRAIN								
Hordeum cf. *vulgare* L (lateral/twisted)	-	-	-	-	-	-	-	1
Hordeum spp. (hulled)	-	-	-	8	-	-	93	3
Hordeum spp.	1	-	-	1	-	4	30	-
Triticum dicoccum Schübl./*spelta* L.	-	-	-	6	-	-	-	-
Triticum cf. *dicoccum* Schübl./*spelta* L.	-	-	3	-	1	-	-	-
Triticum spp. - indeterminate	-	-	4	-	-	1	-	-
cf. Triticum spp. free-threshing (small-grained)	-	-	-	2	-	-	-	-
Cereal - indeterminate	-	2	5	-	2	1	-	1
CEREAL CHAFF								
Hordeum spp. (rachis fragments)	-	-	-	-	-	-	-	-
Triticum dicoccum Schübl./*spelta* L. (spikelet forks)	-	-	-	-	-	-	1	-
Triticum dicoccum Schübl./*spelta* L. (glume bases)	-	-	4	2	1	8	5	3
Triticum dicoccum Schübl./*spelta* L. (unquant. minute glume base frags)	-	-	-	-	-	-	-	++
Triticum spelta L. (spikelet forks = 2 glume bases)	-	-	-	-	-	-	-	-
Triticum spelta L. (glume bases)	-	-	1	-	-	1	3	-
Cereal (indeterminate basal rachis nodes)	-	-	-	-	-	-	-	-
Cereal (indeterminate unquantified straw frags)	-	+	+	-	-	-	++	++
Cereal (indeterminate culm nodes)	-	-	1	4	-	-	12	5
Cereal (indeterminate basal culm node)	-	-	-	-	-	-	-	-
WEED/WILD PLANTS								
Ranunculus cf. *repens* L.	-	-	-	-	-	-	5	-
Ranunculus parviflorus L.	-	-	-	-	-	-	2	-
Adonis annua L.	-	-	-	-	-	-	-	-
Papaver cf. *rhoeas* L./*dubium* L.	-	-	-	-	-	-	-	-
Papaver cf. *argemone* L.	-	-	-	-	-	-	1	-
Urtica dioica L.	-	-	-	-	-	-	7	37
Urtica urens L.	-	-	-	-	-	-	-	-
Chenopodium cf. *urbicum* L.	-	-	-	-	-	-	-	-
Chenopodium album L.	-	-	-	-	-	1	20	-
Chenopodium spp.	-	-	-	-	-	-	-	-
Atriplex prostrata Boucher ex DC./*patula* L.	-	-	-	1	-	-	12	3
Atriplex spp.	-	-	-	-	-	-	2	-
CHENOPODIACEAE (indeterminate)	-	-	-	-	-	-	-	2
Montia fontana ssp. *chondrosperma* (Fenzl.) Walters	-	1	-	-	-	-	1	1
Stellaria media (L.) Vill.	-	-	-	-	-	-	53	46
Stellaria spp.	-	-	1	-	-	-	-	-
Stellaria sp./*Cerastium* sp.	-	-	-	-	-	-	5	1
Cerastium cf. *fontanum* Baumg.	-	1	-	-	-	-	-	-
Silene cf. *latifolia* Poir.	-	-	-	-	-	-	-	-
CARYOPHYLLACEAE indeterminate	-	1	-	-	-	-	37	8
Persicaria maculosa Gray	-	-	-	-	-	-	1	-
Polygonum aviculare L. agg.	-	-	-	-	-	-	10	1
Polygonum spp./*Fallopia* spp. (indeterminate)	-	-	-	-	-	-	5	3
Fallopia convolvulus (L.) Á. Löve	-	-	-	-	-	-	3	-
Rumex acetosella L.	-	-	-	-	-	-	-	1
Rumex cf. *longifolius* DC./*crispus* L.	-	-	-	-	-	-	-	-
Rumex cf. *crispus* L.	-	-	-	-	-	2	-	-
Rumex cf. *conglomeratus* Murray/*sanguineus* L./*obtusifolius* L.	-	-	-	-	-	-	3	6
Rumex spp. (indeterminate)	-	-	-	-	-	-	-	4
POLYGONACEAE (indeterminate)	-	-	-	-	-	-	-	-
cf. *Lepidum* spp.	-	-	-	-	-	-	-	-
Brassica spp.	-	-	1	-	-	-	-	-
Potentilla cf. *neumanniana* Rchb./*erecta* (L.) Raeusch./*anglica* Laichard	-	-	-	-	-	-	-	1
Potentilla cf. *reptans* L.	-	-	-	-	-	-	1	-
Potentilla spp.	-	-	-	-	-	-	1	-
Aphanes arvensis L.	-	-	-	-	-	-	-	1
Vicia spp./*Lathyrus* spp.	-	4	-	1	1	3	9	11
Medicago lupilina L.	-	-	-	-	-	-	1	1

Table 18.6 Yarnton charred plant remains: late Iron Age (continued).

Context Number	*592/A/2*	*120/A*	*121/B*	*236/F/3*	*246*	*300/A*	*347/B/2*	*370*
Sample Number	73	113	107	142	165	42	58	30
WEED/WILD PLANTS continued...								
Medicago spp./*Trifolium* spp.	-	-	-	-	-	-	-	-
Trifolium repens L./*campestre* Schreb./*dubium* Sibth./*arvense* L. (type)	-	1	-	1	-	4	3	40
Trifolium repens L./*pratense* L.	-	-	6	-	-	-	22	4
Trifolium cf. *pratense* L.	-	-	-	-	-	-	-	2
Trifolium spp.	-	-	-	-	-	1	3	5
FABACEAE indeterminate	-	-	-	-	-	-	-	2
Torilis japonica (Houtt.) DC./*arvensis* (Huds.) Link	-	-	-	-	-	-	-	1
APIACEAE indeterminate <4 mm	-	-	-	-	-	-	-	-
Myosotis cf. *arvensis* (L.) Hill	-	-	-	1	-	-	-	-
Lamium cf. *album* L./*purpurum* L./*hybridum* Vill./*amplexicaule* L.	-	-	1	1	-	-	-	-
Mentha cf. *arvensis* L./*aquatica* L.	-	-	-	-	-	-	-	-
Mentha spp.	-	-	-	-	-	-	1	-
Plantago major L.	-	-	-	-	-	-	-	2
Plantago cf. *media* L.	-	-	-	-	-	-	1	-
Plantago lanceolata L.	-	-	-	-	-	-	3	1
cf. *Euphrasia*/*Odontites* spp.	-	-	-	-	-	-	-	1
cf. *Odontites vernus* (Bellardi) Dumort.	-	-	-	-	-	-	1	-
Rhinanthus augustifolius C. C. Gmel./*minor* L.	-	-	-	-	-	-	-	1
Galium palustre L./*verum* L./*mollugo* L./*saxatile* L./*spurium* L.	-	-	-	-	-	-	-	-
Galium aparine L.	-	-	-	-	-	-	-	-
Valerianella dentata (L.) Pollich.	-	-	-	-	-	-	-	-
Lapsana communis L.	-	-	-	-	-	-	2	-
Anthemis cotula L.	-	-	2	-	-	-	1	-
Tripleurospermum inodorum (L.) Sch. Bip.	-	-	-	-	-	-	1	-
ASTERACEAE (indeterminate)	-	-	-	-	-	-	-	-
Potamogeton sp.	-	-	-	-	-	-	1	-
Eleocharis palustris (L.) Roem. & Schult./*uniglumis* (Link.) Schult.	-	-	1	1	1	4	32	141
Carex cf. *sylvatica* Huds./*laevigata* Sm./*distans* L.	-	-	-	-	-	-	1	-
Carex spp. (indeterminate - flat/2-sided)	-	-	-	-	-	-	2	7
Carex spp. (indeterminate - trigonous)	-	-	-	-	-	-	-	30
CYPERACEAE indet	-	-	-	-	-	-	-	17
cf. *Festuca* spp./*Lolium* spp.	-	-	2	-	-	-	-	-
Lolium cf. *perenne* L.	-	-	-	-	-	-	-	4
Poa cf. *annua* L.	-	-	-	-	-	-	-	21
Poa spp./*Alopecurus* spp.	-	-	-	-	-	-	1	2
Phleum sp./Poa sp.	-	-	2	-	-	1	-	-
Avena spp. (caryopses)	-	-	-	3	2	-	11	-
Avena spp. (awns)	-	1	-	-	-	2	8	-
Avena spp./*Bromus* spp.	-	-	2	-	-	2	2	2
cf. *Deschampsia* spp.	-	-	-	-	-	-	2	-
cf. *Agrostis capillaris* L.	-	-	-	-	-	-	-	1
Phleum sp.	-	-	-	-	-	-	1	1
Bromus hordeaceus L./*secalinus* L. (type)	-	-	-	-	-	-	-	-
Bromus sp.	-	-	-	-	-	-	-	-
POACEAE <4 mm undifferentiated	-	-	-	-	-	-	3	-
POACEAE >3.5 mm undifferentiated	-	1	-	-	-	-	1	-
POACEAE (indeterminate)	-	1	-	-	-	-	3	1
Unidentified - plant stem	-	-	-	-	-	-	-	2
Unidentified - seeds (undiff.)	-	3	4	-	-	1	9	5
Unidentified - tree/shrub buds	-	-	-	-	-	-	-	-
TOTALS								
Cereal Grain	1	2	12	17	3	6	123	5
Cereal Chaff	0	0	6	6	1	9	21	8
Weed/Wild	0	11	18	9	4	20	285	413
Unidentified/Indeterminate	0	3	4	0	0	1	9	7
TOTAL IDENTIFICATIONS	1	16	40	32	8	36	438	433
PROPORTIONS								
Cereal Grain	100.0%	12.5%	30.0%	53.1%	37.5%	16.7%	28.1%	1.2%
Cereal Chaff	0.0%	0.0%	15.0%	18.8%	12.5%	25.0%	4.8%	1.8%
Weed/Wild	0.0%	68.8%	45.0%	28.1%	50.0%	55.6%	65.1%	95.4%
Unidentified/Indeterminate	0.0%	18.8%	10.0%	0.0%	0.0%	2.8%	2.1%	1.6%

Table 18.6 Yarnton charred plant remains: late Iron Age (continued).

Context Number	*372/A/1*	*406/A/1*	*479/A/1*	*671/A/1*	*683/C/3*	*852/A*	*913/B*	*1000/A/2*
Sample Number	*146*	*27*	*166*	*145*	*141*	*110*	*53*	*96*
Context Type	*ditch*	*posthole*	*ditch*	*ditch*	*ditch*	*hearth*	*pit*	*ditch*
Sample Volume (L)	*10*	*6*	*10*	*10*	*10*	*n/a*	*10*	*20*
Seeds per litre of sediment	*0.4*	*73.3*	*2.0*	*1.9*	*1.4*	*-*	*5.2*	*5.9*
CEREAL GRAIN								
Hordeum cf. *vulgare* L (lateral/twisted)	-	-	-	-	-	-	-	-
Hordeum spp. (hulled)	-	1	2	2	2	-	-	2
Hordeum spp.	-	13	2	1	-	4	5	3
Triticum dicoccum Schübl./*spelta* L.	-	2	-	-	1	-	-	1
Triticum cf. *dicoccum* Schübl./*spelta* L.	-	8	-	-	-	-	-	-
Triticum spp. - indeterminate	-	13	-	-	-	4	6	4
cf. Triticum spp. free-threshing (small-grained)	-	-	-	-	-	-	3	2
Cereal - indeterminate	1	15	4	2	-	2	3	4
CEREAL CHAFF								
Hordeum spp. (rachis fragments)	-	1	-	-	-	1	-	1
Triticum dicoccum Schübl./*spelta* L. (spikelet forks)	-	4	-	-	-	-	1	1
Triticum dicoccum Schübl./*spelta* L. (glume bases)	-	43	2	7	5	4	6	10
Triticum dicoccum Schübl./*spelta* L. (unquant. minute glume base frags)	-	+++	-	-	-	++	-	+
Triticum spelta L. (spikelet forks = 2 glume bases)	-	-	1	-	-	-	-	-
Triticum spelta L. (glume bases)	-	21	-	-	-	-	1	-
Cereal (indeterminate basal rachis nodes)	-	1	-	-	-	1	-	-
Cereal (indeterminate unquantified straw frags)	-	+	-	-	-	++	++	++
Cereal (indeterminate culm nodes)	-	5	-	-	-	3	-	3
Cereal (indeterminate basal culm node)	-	1	1	-	-	-	-	-
WEED/WILD PLANTS								
Ranunculus cf. *repens* L.	-	-	-	-	-	-	-	-
Ranunculus parviflorus L.	-	-	-	-	-	-	-	-
Adonis annua L.	-	1	-	-	-	-	-	-
Papaver cf. *rhoeas* L./*dubium* L.	-	2	-	-	-	-	-	-
Papaver cf. *argemone* L.	-	-	-	-	-	-	-	-
Urtica dioica L.	-	-	-	-	-	-	-	-
Urtica urens L.	-	4	-	-	-	-	-	-
Chenopodium cf. *urbicum* L.	-	1	-	-	-	-	-	-
Chenopodium album L.	-	37	-	1	-	20	1	3
Chenopodium spp.	-	1	-	-	-	-	-	-
Atriplex prostrata Boucher ex DC./*patula* L.	1	41	-	-	-	-	2	3
Atriplex spp.	-	-	-	-	-	-	-	-
CHENOPODIACEAE (indeterminate)	-	-	1	-	-	-	-	-
Montia fontana ssp. *chondrosperma* (Fenzl.) Walters	-	-	-	-	-	-	1	-
Stellaria media (L.) Vill.	-	-	-	-	-	-	-	3
Stellaria spp.	-	-	-	-	-	-	-	-
Stellaria sp./*Cerastium* sp.	-	-	-	-	-	2	-	-
Cerastium cf. *fontanum* Baumg.	-	-	-	-	-	-	-	-
Silene cf. *latifolia* Poir.	-	-	-	-	-	-	3	-
CARYOPHYLLACEAE indeterminate	-	-	-	-	-	-	-	-
Persicaria maculosa Gray	-	-	-	-	-	1	-	-
Polygonum aviculare L. agg.	-	2	-	-	-	1	-	1
Polygonum spp./*Fallopia* spp. (indeterminate)	-	2	-	-	-	-	-	2
Fallopia convolvulus (L.) Á. Löve	-	4	-	-	-	-	-	-
Rumex acetosella L.	-	4	-	-	-	-	2	-
Rumex cf. *longifolius* DC./*crispus* L.	-	1	-	-	-	-	-	-
Rumex cf. *crispus* L.	-	-	-	1	-	-	1	-
Rumex cf. *conglomeratus* Murray/*sanguineus* L./*obtusifolius* L.	-	12	-	1	-	-	3	-
Rumex spp. (indeterminate)	-	3	-	-	-	-	-	2
POLYGONACEAE (indeterminate)	1	-	-	-	-	-	-	-
cf. *Lepidum* spp.	-	3	-	-	-	-	-	-
Brassica spp.	-	-	-	-	-	-	-	1
Potentilla cf. *neumanniana* Rchb./*erecta* (L.) Raeusch./*anglica* Laichard	-	-	-	-	-	-	-	-
Potentilla cf. *reptans* L.	-	3	-	-	-	-	-	-
Potentilla spp.	-	1	-	-	-	-	-	-
Aphanes arvensis L.	-	-	-	-	-	-	-	-
Vicia spp./*Lathyrus* spp.	1	1	-	1	1	11	3	21
Medicago lupilina L.	-	3	-	-	-	-	-	-

Table 18.6 Yarnton charred plant remains: late Iron Age (continued).

Context Number / *Sample Number*	372/A/1 146	406/A/1 27	479/A/1 166	671/A/1 145	683/C/3 141	852/A 110	913/B 53	1000/A/2 96
WEED/WILD PLANTS (continued)								
Medicago spp./*Trifolium* spp.	-	-	-	-	-	1	1	-
Trifolium repens L./*campestre* Schreb./*dubium* Sibth./*arvense* L. (type)	-	17	-	-	-	-	-	6
Trifolium repens L./*pratense* L.	-	-	-	-	-	4	-	-
Trifolium cf. *pratense* L.	-	3	-	-	-	-	-	2
Trifolium spp.	-	-	-	-	-	-	-	-
FABACEAE indeterminate	-	4	-	-	-	-	-	-
Torilis japonica (Houtt.) DC./*arvensis* (Huds.) Link	-	-	-	-	-	-	-	-
APIACEAE indeterminate <4 mm	-	2	-	-	-	-	-	-
Myosotis cf. *arvensis* (L.) Hill	-	-	-	-	-	1	-	-
Lamium cf. *album* L./*purpurum* L./*hybridum* Vill./*amplexicaule* L.	-	-	-	-	-	-	-	-
Mentha cf. *arvensis* L./*aquatica* L.	-	-	-	-	-	-	1	-
Mentha spp.	-	-	-	-	-	-	-	-
Plantago major L.	-	-	-	-	-	-	-	-
Plantago cf. *media* L.	-	-	-	-	-	-	-	-
Plantago lanceolata L.	-	4	-	-	-	1	2	1
cf. *Euphrasia* /*Odontites* spp.	-	1	-	-	-	-	-	-
cf. *Odontites vernus* (Bellardi) Dumort.	-	-	-	-	-	-	-	-
Rhinanthus augustifolius C. C. Gmel./*minor* L.	-	-	-	-	-	-	-	-
Galium palustre L./*verum* L./*mollugo* L./*saxatile* L./*spurium* L.	-	2	-	-	-	-	-	-
Galium aparine L.	-	-	-	1	1	-	-	2
Valerianella dentata (L.) Pollich.	-	-	-	-	-	-	-	1
Lapsana communis L.	-	2	-	-	-	-	-	-
Anthemis cotula L.	-	-	1	-	-	-	-	-
Tripleurospermum inodorum (L.) Sch. Bip.	-	2	1	-	-	3	-	1
ASTERACEAE (indeterminate)	-	1	-	-	-	-	-	-
Potamogeton sp.	-	-	-	-	-	-	-	-
Eleocharis palustris (L.) Roem. & Schult./*uniglumis* (Link.) Schult.	-	74	2	-	-	1	2	1
Carex cf. *sylvatica* Huds./*laevigata* Sm./*distans* L.	-	-	-	-	-	-	-	-
Carex spp. (indeterminate - flat/2-sided)	-	4	-	-	-	-	-	-
Carex spp. (indeterminate - trigonous)	-	5	-	-	1	-	-	1
CYPERACEAE indet	-	-	-	-	-	-	-	-
cf. *Festuca* spp./*Lolium* spp.	-	-	-	-	-	2	1	-
Lolium cf. *perenne* L.	-	-	-	-	-	2	-	-
Poa cf. *annua* L.	-	6	-	-	-	-	1	3
Poa spp./*Alopecurus* spp.	-	-	-	-	-	-	-	-
Phleum sp./Poa sp.	-	-	-	-	-	-	-	2
Avena spp. (caryopses)	-	34	-	1	1	-	1	4
Avena spp. (awns)	-	2	-	-	-	4	1	8
Avena spp./*Bromus* spp.	-	13	-	-	1	2	-	2
cf. *Deschampsia* spp.	-	-	-	-	-	-	-	-
cf. *Agrostis capillaris* L.	-	-	-	-	-	-	-	-
Phleum sp.	-	-	-	1	-	2	-	1
Bromus hordeaceus L./*secalinus* L. (type)	-	2	-	-	-	-	-	2
Bromus sp.	-	3	-	-	-	-	-	-
POACEAE <4 mm undifferentiated	-	1	1	-	-	-	-	1
POACEAE >3.5 mm undifferentiated	-	-	-	-	-	1	-	2
POACEAE (indeterminate)	-	-	-	-	-	-	-	1
Unidentified - plant stem	-	-	-	-	-	-	-	-
Unidentified - seeds (undiff.)	-	-	1	-	1	5	-	8
Unidentified - tree/shrub buds	-	-	-	-	-	1	-	-
TOTALS								
Cereal Grain	1	52	8	5	3	10	17	16
Cereal Chaff	0	76	4	7	5	9	8	15
Weed/Wild	3	308	6	7	5	59	26	77
Unidentified/Indeterminate	0	0	1	0	1	6	0	8
TOTAL IDENTIFICATIONS	4	436	19	19	14	84	51	116
PROPORTIONS								
Cereal Grain	25.0%	11.9%	42.1%	26.3%	21.4%	11.9%	33.3%	13.8%
Cereal Chaff	0.0%	17.4%	21.1%	36.8%	35.7%	10.7%	15.7%	12.9%
Weed/Wild	75.0%	70.6%	31.6%	36.8%	35.7%	70.2%	51.0%	66.4%
Unidentified/Indeterminate	0.0%	0.0%	5.3%	0.0%	7.1%	7.1%	0.0%	6.9%

Table 18.6 Yarnton charred plant remains: late Iron Age (continued).

Context Number	*1016/A/6*	*1490*	*1593/A/3*	*1606/C/1*	*1685*
Sample Number	*101*	*147*	*134*	*144*	*169*
Context Type	*pit*	*gully*	*ditch*	*ditch*	*pit*
Sample Volume (L)	*n/a*	*10*	*10*	*10*	*10*
Seeds per litre of sediment	-	*0.8*	*0.9*	*3.2*	*4.3*
CEREAL GRAIN					
Hordeum cf. *vulgare* L (lateral/twisted)	-	-	-	-	2
Hordeum spp. (hulled)	1	-	4	3	2
Hordeum spp.	-	1	-	1	-
Triticum dicoccum Schübl./*spelta* L.	-	1	-	2	-
Triticum cf. *dicoccum* Schübl./*spelta* L.	-	-	-	-	-
Triticum spp. - indeterminate	-	-	-	-	3
cf. Triticum spp. free-threshing (small-grained)	-	-	-	-	-
Cereal - indeterminate	1	1	2	3	-
CEREAL CHAFF					
Hordeum spp. (rachis fragments)	-	-	-	-	-
Triticum diccocum Schübl./*spelta* L. (spikelet forks)	-	-	-	-	4
Triticum dicoccum Schübl./*spelta* L. (glume bases)	-	1	2	2	20
Triticum dicoccum Schübl./*spelta* L. (unquant. minute glume base frags)	-	-	-	-	++
Triticum spelta L. (spikelet forks = 2 glume bases)	-	-	-	-	-
Triticum spelta L. (glume bases)	-	-	-	-	3
Cereal (indeterminate basal rachis nodes)	-	-	-	-	-
Cereal (indeterminate unquantified straw frags)	-	-	-	-	-
Cereal (indeterminate culm nodes)	-	-	-	-	-
Cereal (indeterminate basal culm node)	-	-	-	-	-
WEED/WILD PLANTS					
Ranunculus cf. *repens* L.	-	-	-	-	-
Ranunculus parviflorus L.	-	-	-	-	-
Adonis annua L.	-	-	-	-	-
Papaver cf. *rhoeas* L./*dubium* L.	-	-	-	-	-
Papaver cf. *argemone* L.	-	-	-	-	-
Urtica dioica L.	-	-	-	-	-
Urtica urens L.	-	-	-	-	-
Chenopodium cf. *urbicum* L.	-	-	-	-	-
Chenopodium album L.	1	1	-	1	-
Chenopodium spp.	-	-	-	-	-
Atriplex prostrata Boucher ex DC./*patula* L.	-	1	-	-	2
Atriplex spp.	-	-	-	-	-
CHENOPODIACEAE (indeterminate)	-	-	-	-	-
Montia fontana ssp. *chondrosperma* (Fenzl.) Walters	-	-	-	-	-
Stellaria media (L.) Vill.	-	-	-	-	-
Stellaria spp.	-	-	-	-	-
Stellaria sp./*Cerastium* sp.	-	-	-	-	-
Cerastium cf. *fontanum* Baumg.	-	-	-	-	-
Silene cf. *latifolia* Poir.	-	-	-	-	-
CARYOPHYLLACEAE indeterminate	-	-	-	-	-
Persicaria maculosa Gray	-	-	-	-	-
Polygonum aviculare L. agg.	-	-	-	-	-
Polygonum spp. /*Fallopia* spp. (indeterminate)	-	-	-	-	1
Fallopia convolvulus (L.) Á. Löve	-	-	-	-	-
Rumex acetosella L.	-	-	-	-	-
Rumex cf. *longifolius* DC./*crispus* L.	-	-	-	-	-
Rumex cf. *crispus* L.	-	-	1	1	-
Rumex cf. *conglomeratus* Murray/*sanguineus* L./*obtusifolius* L.	-	-	-	-	-
Rumex spp. (indeterminate)	-	-	-	2	-
POLYGONACEAE (indeterminate)	-	-	-	-	-
cf. *Lepidum* spp.	-	-	-	-	-
Brassica spp.	-	-	-	-	-
Potentilla cf. *neumanniana* Rchb./*erecta* (L.) Raeusch./*anglica* Laichard	-	-	-	-	-
Potentilla cf. *reptans* L.	-	-	-	-	-
Potentilla spp.	-	-	-	-	-
Aphanes arvensis L.	-	-	-	-	-
Vicia spp./*Lathyrus* spp.	-	1	-	2	1
Medicago lupilina L.	-	-	-	-	-
Medicago spp./*Trifolium* spp.	-	-	-	2	-

Table 18.6 Yarnton charred plant remains: late Iron Age (continued).

Context Number	*1016/A/6*	*1490*	*1593/A/3*	*1606/C/1*	*1685*
Sample Number	*101*	*147*	*134*	*144*	*169*
Trifolium repens L./*campestre* Schreb./*dubium* Sibth./*arvense* L. (type)	-	-	-	-	-
Trifolium repens L./*pratense* L.	-	-	-	-	-
Trifolium cf. *pratense* L.	-	-	-	-	-
Trifolium spp.	-	-	-	-	-
FABACEAE indeterminate	-	-	-	-	-
Torilis japonica (Houtt.) DC./*arvensis* (Huds.) Link	-	-	-	-	-
APIACEAE indeterminate <4mm	-	-	-	-	-
Myosotis cf. *arvensis* (L.) Hill	-	-	-	-	-
Lamium cf. *album* L./*purpurum* L./*hybridum* Vill./*amplexicaule* L.	-	-	-	-	-
Mentha cf. *arvensis* L./*aquatica* L.	-	-	-	-	-
Mentha spp.	-	-	-	-	-
Plantago major L.	-	-	-	-	-
Plantago cf. *media* L.	-	-	-	-	-
Plantago lanceolata L.	-	-	-	-	-
cf. *Euphrasia* / *Odontites* spp.	-	-	-	-	-
cf. *Odontites vernus* (Bellardi) Dumort.	-	-	-	-	-
Rhinanthus augustifolius C. C. Gmel./*minor* L.	-	-	-	-	-
Galium palustre L./*verum* L./*mollugo* L./*saxatile* L./*spurium* L.	-	-	-	-	-
Galium aparine L.	-	-	-	1	-
Valerianella dentata (L.) Pollich.	-	-	-	-	-
Lapsana communis L.	-	-	-	-	-
Anthemis cotula L.	-	-	-	-	-
Tripleurospermum inodorum (L.) Sch. Bip.	-	-	-	-	-
ASTERACEAE (indeterminate)	-	-	-	-	-
Potamogeton sp.	-	-	-	-	-
Eleocharis palustris (L.) Roem. & Schult./*uniglumis* (Link.) Schult.	-	-	-	1	-
Carex cf. *sylvatica* Huds./*laevigata* Sm./*distans* L.	-	-	-	-	-
Carex spp. (indeterminate - flat/2-sided)	-	-	-	-	-
Carex spp. (indeterminate - trigonous)	-	-	-	1	-
CYPERACEAE indet	-	-	-	1	-
cf. *Festuca* spp./*Lolium* spp.	-	-	-	1	-
Lolium cf. *perenne* L.	-	-	-	-	-
Poa cf. *annua* L.	-	-	-	-	1
Poa spp./*Alopecurus* spp.	-	-	-	-	-
Phleum sp./Poa sp.	1	-	-	3	-
Avena spp. (caryopses)	-	1	-	4	-
Avena spp. (awns)	-	-	-	-	-
Avena spp./*Bromus* spp.	-	-	-	-	-
cf. *Deschampsia* spp.	-	-	-	-	-
cf. *Agrostis capillaris* L.	-	-	-	-	-
Phleum sp.	-	-	-	-	-
Bromus hordeaceus L./*secalinus* L. (type)	-	-	-	-	-
Bromus sp.	-	-	-	-	-
POACEAE <4 mm undifferentiated	-	-	-	-	-
POACEAE >3.5 mm undifferentiated	-	-	-	-	-
POACEAE (indeterminate)	-	-	-	-	-
Unidentified - plant stem	-	-	-	-	-
Unidentified - seeds (undiff.)	-	-	-	1	-
Unidentified - tree/shrub buds	-	-	-	-	-
TOTALS					
Cereal Grain	2	3	6	9	7
Cereal Chaff	0	1	2	2	27
Weed/Wild	2	4	1	20	5
Unidentified/Indeterminate	0	0	0	1	0
TOTAL IDENTIFICATIONS	4	8	9	32	39
PROPORTIONS					
Cereal Grain	50.0%	37.5%	66.7%	28.1%	17.9%
Cereal Chaff	0.0%	12.5%	22.2%	6.3%	69.2%
Weed/Wild	50.0%	50.0%	11.1%	62.5%	12.8%
Unidentified/Indeterminate	0.0%	0.0%	0.0%	3.1%	0.0%

Key: + = >5 items, ++ = 5 – 25 items, +++ = 26 – 100 items, ++++ = <100 items

Table 18.7 Yarnton charred plant remains: early Roman.

Context Number	*71/A/1*	*172/A*	*256/A/1*	*295/A/1*	*310/A*	*313/A/1*	*343/B*	*348/A*	
Sample Number	20	22	140	139	25	168	94	71	
Context Type	*pit*	*ditch*	*ditch*	*gully*	*layer*	*ditch*	*gully*	*ditch*	
Sample Volume (L)	10	10	10	10	10	10	20	20	
Seeds per litre of sediment	6.5	1.6	1.4	1.9	6.5	2.8	2.7	2.7	
CEREAL GRAIN									
Hordeum cf. *vulgare* L (lateral/twisted)	1	-	-	-	-	-	-	1	
Hordeum spp. (hulled)	2	-	-	2	2	5	-	1	
Hordeum spp.	6	-	3	1	1	-	2	1	
Secale cereale L.	-	-	-	-	-	-	-	-	
Secale cereale L./*Triticum* spp. - indeterminate	-	-	-	-	-	-	-	-	
Triticum dicoccum Schübl./*spelta* L.	1	-	-	-	-	3	-	1	
Triticum cf. *dicoccum* Schübl./spelta L.	-	-	-	-	1	-	1	-	
Triticum spp. free-threshing (small-grained)	-	-	-	-	1	-	-	2	
Triticum spp. - indeterminate	3	-	1	-	2	-	-	1	
cf. Triticum spp. free-threshing (small-grained)	1	-	-	-	-	-	1	-	
Cereal - indeterminate	3	-	1	1	1	-	2	3	
CEREAL CHAFF									
Hordeum spp. (rachis fragments)	-	-	-	-	-	-	-	1	
Triticum diccocum Schübl./*spelta* L. (spikelet forks)	-	-	-	-	5	-	-	-	
Triticum cf. *diccocum* Schübl. (glume bases)	-	-	-	-	-	-	-	-	
Triticum dicoccum Schübl./*spelta* L. (glume bases)	1	-	2	3	3	2	10	3	
Triticum dicoccum Schübl./*spelta* L. (unquant. minute glume base frags)		-	-	-	-	+	+	-	-
Triticum dicoccum Schübl./spelta L. (rachis internodes)	-	-	-	-	-	-	-	-	
Triticum spelta L. (spikelet forks = 2 glume bases)	-	-	-	-	-	-	-	-	
Triticum spelta L. (glume bases)	-	-	-	-	-	-	-	-	
Cereal (indeterminate basal rachis nodes)	-	-	-	-	-	-	-	-	
Cereal (indeterminate unquantified straw frags)	+	+++	-	-	++	-	-	-	
Cereal (indeterminate culm nodes)	-	5	2	2	6	-	-	-	
Cereal (indeterminate basal culm node)	-	-	-	-	-	-	-	-	
WEED/WILD PLANTS									
Ranunculus acris L./*repens* L./*bulbosus* L.	-	-	-	-	-	-	-	-	
Ranunculus spp.	-	-	-	-	-	-	-	-	
Papaver cf. *rhoeas* L./*dubium* L.	-	-	-	-	-	-	-	-	
Papaver spp.	-	-	-	-	-	-	-	-	
Urtica urens L.	-	3	-	-	-	-	-	1	
Chenopodium album L.	2	-	-	2	2	2	-	-	
Atriplex prostrata Boucher ex DC./*patula* L.	3	-	-	1	1	1	-	-	
CHENOPODIACEAE (indeterminate)	1	-	-	-	-	-	-	-	
Montia fontana ssp. *chondrosperma* (Fenzl.) Walters	-	-	-	-	-	-	-	-	
Stellaria media (L.) Vill.	-	-	-	-	-	-	1	-	
Stellaria palustris Retz./*graminea* L.	-	-	-	-	-	-	-	-	
Stellaria sp./*Cerastium* sp.	-	-	-	-	-	-	-	-	
Cerastium spp.	-	-	-	-	-	-	-	-	
Agrostemma githago L.	-	-	-	-	-	-	-	-	
CARYOPHYLLACEAE indeterminate	-	-	-	-	-	-	-	-	
Persicaria maculosa Gray	4	-	-	-	-	-	-	-	
Polygonum aviculare L. agg.	-	-	-	-	2	1	-	1	
Polygonum spp./*Fallopia* spp. (indeterminate)	1	-	-	-	-	1	1	-	
Fallopia convolvulus (L.) Á. Löve	-	-	-	-	-	-	-	-	
Rumex acetosella L.	-	-	-	-	-	-	-	-	
Rumex cf. *crispus* L.	1	-	-	-	-	-	-	-	
Rumex cf. *conglomeratus* Murray/*sanguineus* L./*obtusifolius* L.	1	-	-	-	-	-	2	-	
Rumex spp. (indeterminate)	-	-	1	-	1	-	1	-	
POLYGONACEAE (indeterminate)	-	-	-	-	-	-	-	-	
Malva sylvestris L.	-	-	-	1	-	-	-	-	
Sinapis arvensis L./*alba* L.	-	-	-	-	-	-	-	1	
Raphanus raphanistum L. (seed capsule)	-	-	-	-	-	-	-	-	
Aphanes arvensis L.	-	-	-	-	-	-	-	-	
Vicia spp./*Lathyrus* spp.	5	-	-	1	9	7	7	6	
Medicago lupilina L.	-	-	-	-	-	-	-	-	
Medicago spp./*Trifolium* spp.	5	-	-	-	-	-	-	-	
Trifolium repens L./*campestre* Schreb./*dubium* Sibth./*arvense* L. (type)		4	-	-	-	1	1	1	3
Trifolium repens L./*pratense* L.	-	-	-	-	-	-	-	4	
Trifolium cf. *pratense* L.	-	-	-	-	-	-	-	-	

Table 18.7 Yarnton charred plant remains: early Roman (continued).

Context Number *Sample Number*	*71/A/1* *20*	*172/A* *22*	*256/A/1* *140*	*295/A/1* *139*	*310/A* *25*	*313/A/1* *168*	*343/B* *94*	*348/A* *71*
Trifolium spp.	-	-	-	-	-	-	-	-
FABACEAE indeterminate	1	-	-	-	-	-	-	2
Geranium sp.	-	-	-	-	-	-	-	-
Apium spp.	-	-	-	-	-	-	-	-
Torilis japonica (Houtt.) DC./*arvensis* (Huds.) Link	-	-	-	-	-	-	-	-
Lithospermum arvense L.	-	-	-	-	-	-	-	-
Myosotis cf. *arvensis* (L.) Hill	-	-	-	-	-	-	-	-
Lamium cf. *album* L./*purpurum* L./*hybridum* Vill./*amplexicaule* L.	-	-	-	-	-	-	-	1
Prunella vulgaris L.	-	-	-	-	-	-	-	-
Mentha cf. *arvensis* L./*aquatica* L.	-	-	-	-	-	-	-	-
Mentha spp.	-	-	-	-	1	-	-	-
Plantago lanceolata L.	1	-	-	-	-	-	-	1
Veronica cf. *arvensis* L.	-	-	-	-	-	-	-	-
cf. *Euphrasia*/*Odontites* spp.	-	-	-	-	2	-	-	-
cf. *Odontites vernus* (Bellardi) Dumort.	1	-	-	-	1	-	1	2
Galium palustre L./*verum* L./*mollugo* L./*saxatile* L./*spurium* L.	-	-	-	-	-	-	-	-
Galium aparine L.	-	-	-	-	-	1	1	-
Valerianella locusta (L.) Laterr.	-	-	-	-	-	-	-	1
Valerianella dentata (L.) Pollich.	-	-	-	-	-	-	-	-
Centaurea spp.	-	-	-	-	-	-	-	1
Achillea spp./*Artemisia* spp./*Anthemis* spp./*Tripleurospermum* spp.	-	-	-	-	-	-	-	2
Anthemis cotula L.	1	-	-	1	6	-	2	-
cf. *Leucantheum vulgare* L.	-	-	-	-	-	-	-	1
Tripleurospermum inodorum (L.) Sch. Bip.	1	-	-	-	-	-	-	-
cf. *Senecio* sp.	-	-	-	-	1	-	-	-
ASTERACEAE (indeterminate)	-	-	-	-	1	-	1	-
Juncus cf. *bufonius* (seed capsules)	-	-	-	-	-	-	-	1
Juncus spp. (seed capsules)	-	-	-	-	-	-	-	-
Eleocharis palustris (L.) Roem. & Schult./*uniglumis* (Link.) Schult.	11	-	-	-	1	-	-	2
Carex spp. (indeterminate - flat/2-sided)	1	7	-	-	-	-	-	-
Carex spp. (indeterminate - trigonous)	-	-	-	-	-	1	1	-
CYPERACEAE indet	-	-	-	-	-	-	-	-
cf. *Festuca* spp./*Lolium* spp.	-	-	-	-	-	-	-	2
Lolium cf. *perenne* L.	-	-	-	-	-	-	2	-
Briza media L./*Glyceria maxima* (Hartm.) Holmb./*Milium effusum* L.	-	-	-	-	-	-	-	- -
Poa cf. *annua* L.	-	1	-	-	-	1	2	1
Phleum sp./Poa sp.	-	-	-	1	-	-	-	-
cf. *Dactylis glomerata* L.	-	-	-	-	-	-	-	-
Avena spp. (caryopses)	-	-	1	-	1	1	2	1
Avena spp. (awns)	1	-	-	-	4	-	3	1
Avena spp./*Bromus* spp.	-	-	2	-	-	1	2	-
Phleum sp.	-	-	-	-	-	-	-	-
Bromus hordeaceus L./*secalinus* L. (type)	-	-	-	-	1	-	-	-
Bromus sp.	-	-	-	-	-	-	-	-
POACEAE >4 mm undifferentiated	-	-	-	-	-	-	-	1
POACEAE <3.5 mm undifferentiated	-	-	-	1	-	-	-	-
POACEAE (indeterminate)	-	-	-	2	1	-	2	1
Unidentified - plant stem	-	-	-	-	-	-	-	-
Unidentified	2	-	1	-	1	-	5	3
TOTALS								
Cereal Grain	17	0	5	4	8	8	6	10
Cereal Chaff	1	5	4	5	14	2	10	4
Weed/Wild	45	11	4	10	36	18	32	37
Unidentified/Indeterminate	2	0	1	0	1	0	5	3
TOTAL IDENTIFICATIONS	65	16	14	19	59	28	53	54
PROPORTIONS								
Cereal Grain	26.2%	0.0%	35.7%	21.1%	13.6%	28.6%	11.3%	18.5%
Cereal Chaff	1.5%	31.3%	28.6%	26.3%	23.7%	7.1%	18.9%	7.4%
Weed/Wild	69.2%	68.8%	28.6%	52.6%	61.0%	64.3%	60.4%	68.5%
Unidentified/Indeterminate	3.1%	0.0%	7.1%	0.0%	1.7%	0.0%	9.4%	5.6%

Table 18.7 Yarnton charred plant remains: early Roman (continued).

Context Number	*395/A*	*442/A*	*480/C/1*	*624/B/1*	*821/E*	*836*	*837*	*846/C*
Sample Number	*91*	*92*	*167*	*56*	*93*	*111*	*50*	*105*
Context Type	*ditch*	*ditch*	*ditch*	*gully*	*ditch*	*pit*	*pit*	*ditch*
Sample Volume (L)	*10*	*10*	*10*	*10*	*10*	*n/a*	*10*	*n/a*
Seeds per litre of sediment	*5.3*	*0.6*	*2.3*	*1.5*	*7.8*	*-*	*0.6*	*-*
CEREAL GRAIN	2	-	-	-	-	-	-	-
Hordeum cf. *vulgare* L (lateral/twisted)	1	-	1	-	2	2	-	-
Hordeum spp. (hulled)	3	2	1	-	1	4	-	2
Hordeum spp.	-	-	-	-	-	-	-	-
Secale cereale L.	-	-	-	-	-	-	-	-
Secale cereale L./*Triticum* spp. - indeterminate	2	-	1	-	-	-	-	-
Triticum dicoccum Schübl./*spelta* L.	-	-	-	-	-	5	-	4
Triticum cf. *dicoccum* Schübl./*spelta* L.	-	-	1	-	1	2	-	1
Triticum spp. free-threshing (small-grained)	-	-	3	3	-	8	2	-
Triticum spp. - indeterminate	-	-	-	-	-	-	-	-
cf. Triticum spp. free-threshing (small-grained)	3	-	3	-	5	4	2	2
Cereal - indeterminate								
CEREAL CHAFF	-	-	-	-	-	-	-	-
Hordeum spp. (rachis fragments)	-	-	-	1	-	-	-	-
Triticum diccocum Schübl./*spelta* L. (spikelet forks)	-	-	-	-	-	-	-	-
Triticum cf. *diccocum* Schübl. (glume bases)	11	-	4	4	14	4	1	3
Triticum dicoccum Schübl./*spelta* L. (glume bases)	-	-	-	-	-	++	-	-
Triticum dicoccum Schübl./*spelta* L. (unquant. minute glume base frags)		-	-	-	-	-	-	- -
Triticum dicoccum Schübl./spelta L. (rachis internodes)	-	-	-	-	-	-	-	-
Triticum spelta L. (spikelet forks = 2 glume bases)	-	-	-	1	1	1	-	1
Triticum spelta L. (glume bases)	-	-	-	-	-	-	-	-
Cereal (indeterminate basal rachis nodes)	+	+	-	-	-	++	+	-
Cereal (indeterminate unquantified straw frags)	2	2	1	-	2	-	-	-
Cereal (indeterminate culm nodes)	-	-	1	-	-	-	-	-
Cereal (indeterminate basal culm node)								
WEED/WILD PLANTS	-	-	-	-	-	1	-	-
Ranunculus acris L./*repens* L./*bulbosus* L.	-	-	-	-	-	-	-	-
Ranunculus spp.	-	-	-	-	-	-	-	-
Papaver cf. *rhoeas* L./*dubium* L.	-	-	-	-	-	-	-	-
Papaver spp.	-	-	-	-	1	-	-	-
Urtica urens L.	-	-	-	-	-	6	-	-
Chenopodium album L.	2	-	-	-	2	3	-	-
Atriplex prostrata Boucher ex DC./*patula* L.	-	-	-	-	1	-	-	-
CHENOPODIACEAE (indeterminate)	-	-	-	-	-	1	-	-
Montia fontana ssp. *chondrosperma* (Fenzl.) Walters	-	-	-	-	2	-	-	-
Stellaria media (L.) Vill.	-	-	-	-	1	-	-	-
Stellaria palustris Retz./*graminea* L.	2	-	-	-	-	-	-	-
Stellaria sp./*Cerastium* sp.	-	-	-	-	-	6	-	-
Cerastium spp.	-	-	-	-	1	-	-	-
Agrostemma githago L.	-	-	-	-	1	1	-	-
CARYOPHYLLACEAE indeterminate	-	-	-	-	-	-	-	-
Persicaria maculosa Gray	-	-	-	-	-	1	-	-
Polygonum aviculare L. agg.	1	-	-	-	-	-	-	-
Polygonum spp./*Fallopia* spp. (indeterminate)	-	-	-	-	-	-	-	1
Fallopia convolvulus (L.) Á. Löve	-	-	-	-	-	-	-	-
Rumex acetosella L.	1	1	-	-	2	1	-	-
Rumex cf. *crispus* L.	-	-	-	-	-	-	-	-
Rumex cf. *conglomeratus* Murray/*sanguineus* L./*obtusifolius* L.	2	-	-	1	1	1	-	-
Rumex spp. (indeterminate)	-	-	-	-	-	-	-	-
POLYGONACEAE (indeterminate)	-	-	-	-	-	-	-	-
Malva sylvestris L.	-	-	-	-	-	-	-	-
Sinapis arvensis L./*alba* L.	-	-	-	-	-	-	-	-
Raphanus raphanistum L. (seed capsule)	-	-	-	-	-	-	-	-
Aphanes arvensis L.	8	-	3	3	5	11	-	-
Vicia spp./*Lathyrus* spp.	-	-	-	-	-	1	-	-
Medicago lupilina L.	4	-	-	-	-	-	-	-
Medicago spp./*Trifolium* spp.	-	-	-	-	11	5	-	2
Trifolium repens L./*campestre* Schreb./*dubium* Sibth./*arvense* L. (type)								
Trifolium repens L./*pratense* L.	-	-	1	-	-	-	-	-

Table 18.7 Yarnton charred plant remains: early Roman (continued).

Context Number	*395/A*	*442/A*	*480/C/1*	*624/B/1*	*821/E*	*836*	*837*	*846/C*
Sample Number	*91*	*92*	*167*	*56*	*93*	*111*	*50*	*105*
Trifolium cf. *pratense* L.	-	-	-	-	2	-	-	3
Trifolium spp.	-	-	-	-	-	-	-	-
FABACEAE indeterminate	-	-	-	-	2	1	-	-
Geranium sp.	-	-	-	-	-	-	-	-
Apium spp.	-	-	-	-	-	-	-	-
Torilis japonica (Houtt.) DC./*arvensis* (Huds.) Link	-	-	-	-	-	-	-	-
Lithospermum arvense L.	-	-	-	-	-	-	-	-
Myosotis cf. *arvensis* (L.) Hill	-	-	-	-	-	1	-	-
Lamium cf. *album* L./*purpurum* L./*hybridum* Vill./*amplexicaule* L.	-	-	-	-	-	-	-	-
Prunella vulgaris L.	-	-	-	-	-	1	-	-
Mentha cf. *arvensis* L./*aquatica* L.	-	-	-	-	-	-	-	-
Mentha spp.	-	-	-	-	-	-	-	-
Plantago lanceolata L.	-	-	-	-	-	2	-	-
Veronica cf. *arvensis* L.	-	-	-	-	-	1	-	-
cf. *Euphrasia*/*Odontites* spp.	-	-	-	-	-	-	-	-
cf. *Odontites vernus* (Bellardi) Dumort.	-	1	-	-	-	4	-	-
Galium palustre L./*verum* L./*mollugo* L./*saxatile* L./*spurium* L.	-	-	-	-	-	-	-	-
Galium aparine L.	-	-	-	-	-	2	-	-
Valerianella locusta (L.) Laterr.	-	-	-	-	-	-	-	-
Valerianella dentata (L.) Pollich.	-	-	-	-	-	1	-	-
Centaurea spp.	-	-	-	-	-	-	-	-
Achillea spp./*Artemisia* spp./*Anthemis* spp./*Tripleurospermum* spp.	-	-	-	-	-	-	-	-
Anthemis cotula L.	-	-	-	-	-	1	-	-
cf. *Leucantheum vulgare* L.	-	-	-	-	-	-	-	-
Tripleurospermum inodorum (L.) Sch. Bip.	1	-	-	-	1	13	-	-
cf. *Senecio* sp.	-	-	-	-	-	-	-	-
ASTERACEAE (indeterminate)	-	-	-	-	-	-	-	-
Juncus cf. *bufonius* (seed capsules)	-	-	-	-	-	-	-	-
Juncus spp. (seed capsules)	-	-	-	-	-	-	1	-
Eleocharis palustris (L.) Roem. & Schult./*uniglumis* (Link.) Schult.	2	-	-	1	5	5	-	-
Carex spp. (indeterminate - flat/2-sided)	1	-	-	-	-	-	-	-
Carex spp. (indeterminate - trigonous)	-	-	-	-	-	-	-	-
CYPERACEAE indet	-	-	-	-	-	-	-	-
cf. *Festuca* spp./*Lolium* spp.	1	-	-	-	1	-	-	1
Lolium cf. *perenne* L.	-	-	-	-	3	9	-	-
Briza media L./*Glyceria maxima* (Hartm.) Holmb./*Milium effusum* L.	-	-	-	-	-	-	-	- -
Poa cf. *annua* L.	-	-	1	-	2	5	-	-
Phleum sp./*Poa* sp.	-	-	-	-	-	1	-	-
cf. *Dactylis glomerata* L.	-	-	-	-	-	-	-	-
Avena spp. (caryopses)	1	-	-	-	1	3	-	1
Avena spp. (awns)	-	-	-	-	-	4	-	1
Avena spp./*Bromus* spp.	-	-	1	-	-	6	-	-
Phleum sp.	-	-	-	-	-	-	-	-
Bromus hordeaceus L./*secalinus* L. (type)	-	-	-	-	-	-	-	-
Bromus sp.	-	-	1	-	-	-	-	-
POACEAE >4 mm undifferentiated	1	-	-	-	-	1	-	-
POACEAE <3.5 mm undifferentiated	-	-	-	-	-	-	-	-
POACEAE (indeterminate)	-	-	-	-	1	-	-	-
Unidentified - plant stem	-	-	-	-	-	-	-	-
Unidentified	2	-	-	-	3	5	-	-
TOTALS								
Cereal Grain	11	2	10	3	9	25	4	9
Cereal Chaff	13	2	6	6	17	5	1	4
Weed/Wild	27	2	7	5	46	99	1	9
Unidentified/Indeterminate	2	0	0	0	3	5	0	0
TOTAL IDENTIFICATIONS	53	6	23	14	75	134	6	22
PROPORTIONS								
Cereal Grain	20.8%	33.3%	43.5%	21.4%	12.0%	18.7%	66.7%	40.9%
Cereal Chaff	24.5%	33.3%	26.1%	42.9%	22.7%	3.7%	16.7%	18.2%
Weed/Wild	50.9%	33.3%	30.4%	35.7%	61.3%	73.9%	16.7%	40.9%
Unidentified/Indeterminate	3.8%	0.0%	0.0%	0.0%	4.0%	3.7%	0.0%	0.0%

Table 18.7 Yarnton charred plant remains: early Roman (continued).

Context Number	*1088/A*	*1151/A*	*1157/A*	*1633/A/1*	*2525/A/10*	*2537*	*2656*
Sample Number	*115*	*108*	*84*	*137*	*76*	*83*	*69*
Context Type	*pit*	*ditch*	*ditch*	*gully*	*kiln*	*kiln fill*	*layer*
Sample Volume (L)	*n/a*	*n/a*	*10*	*10*	*10*	*10*	*10*
Seeds per litre of sediment	*-*	*-*	*0.6*	*4.9*	*2.3*	*19.6*	*53.5*
CEREAL GRAIN							
Hordeum cf. *vulgare* L (lateral/twisted)	1	-	-	-	-	-	-
Hordeum spp. (hulled)	1	-	-	13	1	9	3
Hordeum spp.	-	-	-	-	1	-	7
Secale cereale L.	-	-	-	-	1	-	1
Secale cereale L./*Triticum* spp. - indeterminate	-	-	-	-	-	1	-
Triticum dicoccum Schübl./*spelta* L.	15	-	-	-	-	-	-
Triticum cf. *dicoccum* Schübl./*spelta* L.	-	1	-	-	-	-	2
Triticum spp. free-threshing (small-grained)	-	-	-	-	-	-	-
Triticum spp. - indeterminate	8	1	1	2	1	2	9
cf. Triticum spp. free-threshing (small-grained)	-	-	-	-	-	-	5
Cereal - indeterminate	7	-	1	5	1	2	13
CEREAL CHAFF							
Hordeum spp. (rachis fragments)	6	-	-	-	-	1	2
Triticum diccocum Schübl./*spelta* L. (spikelet forks)	3	-	-	-	-	-	1
Triticum cf. *diccocum* Schübl. (glume bases)	-	-	-	-	-	-	-
Triticum dicoccum Schübl./*spelta* L. (glume bases)	239	4	-	10	4	53	83
Triticum dicoccum Schübl./*spelta* L. (unquant. minute glume base frags)	++++	-	+	-	-	-	++
Triticum dicoccum Schübl./*spelta* L. (rachis internodes)	1	-	-	-	-	-	-
Triticum spelta L. (spikelet forks = 2 glume bases)	2	-	-	-	-	-	-
Triticum spelta L. (glume bases)	15	-	-	-	1	2	11
Cereal (indeterminate basal rachis nodes)	-	-	-	-	-	2	-
Cereal (indeterminate unquantified straw frags)	+	+	-	+	+	++	++
Cereal (indeterminate culm nodes)	2	-	-	7	-	-	1
Cereal (indeterminate basal culm node)	-	-	-	-	-	-	-
WEED/WILD PLANTS							
Ranunculus acris L./*repens* L./*bulbosus* L.	-	-	-	-	-	-	-
Ranunculus spp.	-	-	-	-	-	-	1
Papaver cf. *rhoeas* L./*dubium* L.	-	-	-	-	-	2	-
Papaver spp.	-	-	-	-	-	-	5
Urtica urens L.	-	-	-	-	-	-	-
Chenopodium album L.	2	-	-	1	-	2	4
Atriplex prostrata Boucher ex DC./*patula* L.	4	-	-	-	-	2	-
CHENOPODIACEAE (indeterminate)	-	-	-	1	-	-	2
Montia fontana ssp. *chondrosperma* (Fenzl.) Walters	1	-	-	-	-	-	-
Stellaria media (L.) Vill.	-	1	-	-	-	2	9
Stellaria palustris Retz./*graminea* L.	-	-	-	-	-	-	-
Stellaria sp./*Cerastium* sp.	-	-	-	-	-	-	-
Cerastium spp.	-	-	-	-	-	-	-
Agrostemma githago L.	1	-	-	-	-	-	-
CARYOPHYLLACEAE indeterminate	-	-	-	-	-	1	1
Persicaria maculosa Gray	-	-	-	-	-	-	-
Polygonum aviculare L. agg.	1	-	-	-	-	-	-
Polygonum spp./*Fallopia* spp. (indeterminate)	1	1	-	-	-	1	2
Fallopia convolvulus (L.) Á. Löve	2	-	-	-	-	2	4
Rumex acetosella L.	-	-	-	-	-	-	2
Rumex cf. *crispus* L.	2	1	-	1	-	8	-
Rumex cf. *conglomeratus* Murray/*sanguineus* L./*obtusifolius* L.	-	5	-	-	-	-	2
Rumex spp. (indeterminate)	3	-	-	1	-	-	3
POLYGONACEAE (indeterminate)	-	2	-	-	-	-	-
Malva sylvestris L.	-	-	-	-	-	-	-
Sinapis arvensis L./*alba* L.	-	-	-	-	-	-	-
Raphanus raphanistum L. (seed capsule)	1	-	-	-	-	-	-
Aphanes arvensis L.	-	-	-	-	-	1	-
Vicia spp./*Lathyrus* spp.	22	4	1	-	3	33	125
Medicago lupilina L.	2	-	-	-	-	-	28
Medicago spp./*Trifolium* spp.	-	1	-	-	-	5	-
Trifolium repens L./*campestre* Schreb./*dubium* Sibth./*arvense* L. (type)	4	-	-	-	1	6	6
Trifolium repens L./*pratense* L.	3	-	-	-	-	-	-
Trifolium cf. *pratense* L.	-	-	-	-	-	1	-

Table 18.7 Yarnton charred plant remains: early Roman (continued).

Context Number	*1088/A*	*1151/A*	*1157/A*	*1633/A/1*	*2525/A/10*	*2537*	*2656*
Sample Number	*115*	*108*	*84*	*137*	*76*	*83*	*69*
Trifolium spp.	-	-	-	-	1	-	-
FABACEAE indeterminate	-	-	-	-	-	-	-
Geranium sp.	-	-	1	-	-	-	-
Apium spp.	-	-	-	-	-	-	2
Torilis japonica (Houtt.) DC./*arvensis* (Huds.) Link	-	-	-	-	-	-	2
Lithospermum arvense L.	-	-	-	-	-	-	2
Myosotis cf. *arvensis* (L.) Hill	-	-	-	-	-	-	-
Lamium cf. *album* L./*purpurum* L./*hybridum* Vill./*amplexicaule* L.	-	-	-	-	-	-	-
Prunella vulgaris L.	-	-	-	-	-	-	-
Mentha cf. *arvensis* L./*aquatica* L.	-	-	-	-	1	-	-
Mentha spp.	-	-	-	-	-	-	-
Plantago lanceolata L.	3	-	-	-	-	2	-
Veronica cf. *arvensis* L.	-	-	-	-	-	-	-
cf. *Euphrasia* / *Odontites* spp.	-	1	-	-	-	-	-
cf. *Odontites vernus* (Bellardi) Dumort.	2	-	-	1	-	5	16
Galium palustre L./*verum* L./*mollugo* L./*saxatile* L./*spurium* L.	-	-	-	-	-	1	-
Galium aparine L.	-	-	-	-	-	-	-
Valerianella locusta (L.) Laterr.	-	-	-	-	-	-	1
Valerianella dentata (L.) Pollich.	-	-	-	-	-	-	-
Centaurea spp.	2	-	-	-	-	-	-
Achillea spp./*Artemisia* spp./*Anthemis* spp./*Tripleurospermum* spp.	-	-	-	-	-	-	7
Anthemis cotula L.	-	-	-	-	-	1	3
cf. *Leucantheum vulgare* L.	-	-	-	-	-	-	-
Tripleurospermum inodorum (L.) Sch. Bip.	2	-	-	-	-	-	15
cf. *Senecio* sp.	-	-	-	-	-	-	-
ASTERACEAE (indeterminate)	-	-	-	-	-	1	-
Juncus cf. *bufonius* (seed capsules)	-	-	-	-	-	-	-
Juncus spp. (seed capsules)	-	-	-	-	-	-	-
Eleocharis palustris (L.) Roem. & Schult./*uniglumis* (Link.) Schult.	2	2	-	-	-	-	1
Carex spp. (indeterminate - flat/2-sided)	-	-	-	-	-	-	-
Carex spp. (indeterminate - trigonous)	-	-	-	1	-	2	-
CYPERACEAE indet	-	-	-	-	-	1	-
cf. *Festuca* spp./*Lolium* spp.	3	-	-	-	-	3	66
Lolium cf. *perenne* L.	13	-	-	1	2	3	-
Briza media L./*Glyceria maxima* (Hartm.) Holmb./*Milium effusum* L.	-	-	-	-	-	-	-
Poa cf. *annua* L.	1	3	-	1	-	-	-
Phleum sp./*Poa* sp.	-	-	-	-	-	-	3
cf. *Dactylis glomerata* L.	2	-	-	-	-	-	-
Avena spp. (caryopses)	5	-	-	2	-	7	9
Avena spp. (awns)	-	1	-	-	-	20	7
Avena spp./*Bromus* spp.	10	-	1	2	2	3	9
Phleum sp.	3	-	-	-	-	-	5
Bromus hordeaceus L./*secalinus* L. (type)	-	-	-	-	-	2	5
Bromus sp.	7	-	-	-	-	-	-
POACEAE >4 mm undifferentiated	25	4	-	-	2	4	41
POACEAE <3.5 mm undifferentiated	-	-	-	-	-	-	2
POACEAE (indeterminate)	-	-	-	-	-	-	-
Unidentified - plant stem	-	1	-	-	-	-	-
Unidentified	8	2	1	-	1	3	6
TOTALS							
Cereal Grain	32	2	2	20	5	14	40
Cereal Chaff	268	4	0	17	5	58	98
Weed/Wild	129	26	3	12	12	121	390
Unidentified/Indeterminate	8	3	1	0	1	3	6
TOTAL IDENTIFICATIONS	437	35	6	49	23	196	534
PROPORTIONS							
Cereal Grain	7.3%	5.7%	33.3%	40.8%	21.7%	7.1%	7.5%
Cereal Chaff	61.3%	11.4%	0.0%	34.7%	21.7%	29.6%	18.4%
Weed/Wild	29.5%	74.3%	50.0%	24.5%	52.2%	61.7%	73.0%
Unidentified/Indeterminate	1.8%	8.6%	16.7%	0.0%	4.3%	1.5%	1.1%

Key: + = <5 items, ++ = 5 – 25 items, +++ = 26 – 100 items, ++++ = >100 items. Some samples did not have a volume recorded, however, it is likely that the samples were either 10 L or 20 L in volume based on the other volumes recorded.

Table 18.8 Yarnton charred plant remains: late Roman.

Context Number	*134/A/2*	*151A/1*	*216/C/2*	*258/B/1*	*304/B*	*354*	*379/A/1*	*494/F/1*	*522/A/2*	*522/A*	*522*	*1031/D*	*1041/D*	*1049/B*	*1061/A*	*1651/A*
Sample Number	102	49	153	143	117	70	176	149	35	33	36	104	106	112	109	179
Context Type	*pit*	*pit*	*gully*	*gully*	*ditch*	*layer*	*ditch*	*feature*	*c.dryer*	*c.dryer*	*c.dryer*	*ditch*	*ditch*	*ditch*	*ditch*	*ditch*
Sample Volume (L)	*n/a*	*10*	*10*	*10*	*n/a*	*20*	*10*	*10*	*10*	*20*	*10*	*n/a*	*n/a*	*n/a*	*n/a*	*10*
Seeds per litre of sediment	-	*1.9*	*1.4*	*3.4*	-	*1.6*	*2.7*	*2.4*	*1.8*	*1.7*	*21.8*	-	-	-	-	*1.7*
CEREAL GRAIN																
Hordeum cf. *vulgare* L (lateral/twisted)	-	-	-	-	1	-	-	-	-	-	-	-	-	-	-	-
Hordeum spp. (hulled)	19	-	3	-	1	1	2	2	2	1	4	-	1	1	-	-
Hordeum spp.	5	-	-	2	1	-	-	1	-	1	2	3	1	-	5	-
Secale cereale L.	2	-	-	-	-	-	-	-	-	-	-	-	-	-	-	-
cf. *Secale cereale* L. (grains)	8	-	-	-	-	-	-	-	-	-	-	-	-	-	-	-
Secale cereale L./*Triticum* spp. - indeterminate	8	-	-	-	-	-	-	-	-	-	-	-	-	-	-	-
Triticum dicoccum Schübl./*spelta* L.	2	1	-	-	1	1	-	-	-	-	-	-	-	-	-	-
Triticum cf. *dicoccum* Schübl./*spelta* L.	-	-	-	-	-	-	-	-	-	-	1	-	-	-	8	1
Triticum spp. free-threshing (small-grained)	3	-	-	-	-	1	-	-	2	1	4	-	2	-	-	-
Triticum spp. - indeterminate	30	1	4	1	1	-	14	4	-	2	2	-	1	-	3	-
cf. Triticum spp. free-threshing (small-grained)	-	-	-	-	-	-	-	-	2	1	5	-	5	3	1	-
Cereal - indeterminate	9	-	4	8	3	1	2	2	3	2	9	1	4	12	14	4
CEREAL CHAFF																
Hordeum spp. (rachis fragments)	-	-	-	1	-	1	-	-	-	1	1	-	-	-	-	2
Triticum diccocum Schübl./*spelta* L. (spikelet forks)	-	-	-	-	-	-	-	-	-	1	19	1	-	-	3	-
Triticum cf. *diccocum* Schübl. (glume bases)	-	-	-	-	-	-	-	-	-	-	-	-	-	-	-	-
Triticum dicoccum Schübl./*spelta* L. (glume bases)	5	-	1	6	10	5	2	4	4	7	62	2	24	-	67	3
Triticum dicoccum Schübl./*spelta* L. (unquant. minute glume base frags)	++	+	-	-	-	-	-	-	-	-	++	+	-	-	-	-
Triticum spelta L. (glume bases)	0	0	0	0	1	2	0	0	0	3	6	0	1	0	2	0
Triticum spp. (free-threshing type rachis node)	0	0	0	0	0	0	0	0	1	0	1	0	0	0	0	0
Cereal (indeterminate unquantified straw frags)	+	-	-	-	+	+	-	-	+	-	++	+	++	+	-	-
Cereal (indeterminate culm nodes)	3	-	-	-	-	2	-	-	1	-	2	1	1	3	-	1
Cereal (indeterminate basal culm node)	-	-	-	-	-	-	-	-	-	-	-	-	-	-	-	1
OTHER FOOD PLANTS																
Linum cf. *usitatissimum* L.	-	-	-	-	-	-	-	-	-	-	1	-	-	-	-	-
WEED/WILD PLANTS																
Ranunculus acris L./*repens* L./*bulbosus* L.	-	-	-	-	-	-	-	-	-	-	1	-	-	-	-	-
Ranunculus cf. *repens* L.	1	-	-	-	-	-	-	-	-	-	-	-	-	-	-	-
Papaver cf. *rhoeas* L./*dubium* L.	-	-	-	-	-	-	-	-	-	1	1	-	-	-	-	-
Urtica urens L.	4	-	-	-	-	1	-	-	-	-	-	-	-	-	-	-
Chenopodium album L.	3	4	-	3	-	2	-	-	-	1	1	-	-	-	4	-
Atriplex prostrata Boucher ex DC./*patula* L.	3	-	-	-	1	-	-	-	-	-	2	-	2	-	2	-

Table 18.8 Yarnton charred plant remains: late Roman.

Context Number	134/A/2	151A/1	216/C/2	258/B/1	304/B	354	379/A/1	494/F/1	522/A/2	522/A	522	1031/D	1041/D	1049/B	1061/A	1651/A
Sample Number	*102*	*49*	*153*	*143*	*117*	*70*	*176*	*149*	*35*	*33*	*36*	*104*	*106*	*112*	*109*	*179*
Atriplex spp.	-	-	-	-	-	1	-	-	-	-	-	-	-	-	-	-
CHENOPODIACEAE (indeterminate)	2	-	-	-	-	-	-	-	-	-	-	1	-	-	-	-
Montia fontana ssp. *chondrosperma* (Fenzl.) Walters	-	-	-	-	-	-	-	-	-	-	-	-	-	-	1	-
Stellaria media (L.) Vill.	-	-	-	-	-	1	-	-	-	-	-	-	3	-	4	-
Stellaria spp.	-	-	-	-	-	-	-	-	-	-	-	-	-	3	-	-
Cerastium cf. *fontanum* Baumg.	1	-	-	-	-	-	-	-	-	-	-	-	-	-	-	-
Silene cf. *latifolia* Poir.	-	1	-	-	-	-	-	-	-	-	-	-	-	-	-	-
Persicaria maculosa Gray	-	-	-	-	-	-	-	-	-	-	-	-	-	-	2	-
Polygonum aviculare L. agg.	1	-	-	1	-	-	-	-	-	-	-	-	1	-	-	1
Fallopia convolvulus (L.) Á. Löve	1	-	-	-	-	-	-	-	-	-	-	-	4	-	-	-
Rumex acetosella L.	2	-	-	-	-	-	-	-	-	-	-	-	-	-	-	-
Rumex cf. *crispus* L.	2	-	-	-	-	-	1	1	-	-	2	-	-	-	-	-
Rumex cf. *conglomeratus* Murray / *sanguineus* L. / . *obtusifolius* L	-	1	-	-	-	-	-	-	-	-	-	-	-	-	-	-
Rumex spp. (indeterminate)	7	-	-	-	-	-	1	-	-	-	-	-	1	-	3	1
POLYGONACEAE (indeterminate)	-	-	-	-	-	-	-	-	-	-	-	-	3	-	-	-
Hypericum perforatum L.	-	-	-	-	-	-	-	-	-	-	-	-	-	-	1	-
Malva sylvestris L.	5	-	-	-	-	-	-	-	-	-	-	-	-	-	-	-
Viola cf. *tricolor* L. / *arvensis* Murray	-	-	-	-	-	-	-	-	-	-	1	-	-	-	-	-
Brassica sp. / *Sinapsis* sp.	1	-	-	-	-	-	-	-	-	-	-	-	-	-	-	-
Raphanus raphanistum L. (seed capsule)	-	-	-	-	-	-	-	-	-	-	-	-	-	-	1	-
Vicia spp. / *Lathyrus* spp.	2	-	-	2	5	2	2	-	-	2	6	4	7	7	25	1
Medicago lupilina L.	-	-	-	-	-	-	-	-	-	-	-	-	-	2	-	-
Medicago spp. / *Trifolium* spp.	1	-	-	-	-	-	-	1	-	-	3	-	-	-	6	-
Trifolium repens L. / *campestre* Schreb. / *dubium* Sibth. / *arvense* L. (type)	1	2	-	4	2	-	2	2	-	-	1	2	7	7	33	-
Trifolium repens L. / *pratense* L.	9	-	-	-	-	2	-	2	-	-	2	-	3	-	-	-
Trifolium cf. *pratense* L.	-	1	-	-	-	-	-	-	-	-	-	-	-	-	-	-
Trifolium spp.	-	-	-	-	-	-	-	-	-	-	1	-	-	-	-	-
Torilis japonica (Houtt.) DC. / *arvensis* (Huds.) Link	-	-	-	-	-	-	-	-	-	-	-	-	-	-	1	-
Myosotis cf. *arvensis* (L.) Hill	-	-	-	-	-	-	-	-	-	-	-	-	-	1	-	-
Prunella vulgaris L.	1	-	-	-	-	-	-	-	-	-	-	-	-	-	1	-
Plantago cf. *media* L. / *lanceolata* L.	1	-	-	-	-	-	-	-	-	-	-	-	-	-	-	-
cf. *Euphrasia* / *Odontites* spp.	-	-	-	-	-	-	-	-	-	-	1	-	-	-	-	-
cf. *Odontites vernus* (Bellardi) Dumort.	-	-	-	-	1	-	-	-	-	-	-	-	1	-	1	-
Galium aparine L.	-	-	-	-	1	-	-	-	-	-	-	-	-	-	-	-
Valerianella dentata (L.) Pollich.	-	-	-	-	-	-	-	-	-	-	-	-	-	-	-	1
Carduus spp. / *Cirsium* spp.	1	-	-	-	-	-	-	-	-	-	1	-	-	-	-	-
Centaurea spp.	1	-	-	-	1	-	-	-	-	-	-	-	-	-	-	-

Achillea spp./*Artemisia* spp./*Anthemis* spp./ *Tripleurospermum* spp.	-	-	-	-	-	-	-	1	-	-	-	-	-	-	-	-
Anthemis cotula L.	20	-	-	2	1	-	-	2	-	1	2	2	6	4	1	-
cf. *Leucantheum vulgare* L.	-	-	-	-	-	-	-	-	-	-	-	-	-	-	-	-
Tripleurospermum inodorum (L.) Sch. Bip.	-	-	-	-	1	-	-	1	-	1	2	-	-	-	4	-
ASTERACEAE (indeterminate)	-	-	-	-	-	1	-	-	-	-	-	-	-	-	-	-
Eleocharis palustris (L.) Roem. & Schult./ *uniglumis* (Link.) Schult.	8	2	1	1	-	2	-	-	-	-	-	1	4	1	2	-
Carex spp. (indeterminate - trigonous)	-	-	1	-	1	-	-	-	-	-	1	-	-	-	-	-
cf. *Festuca* spp./*Lolium* spp.	-	-	-	-	-	1	-	-	-	-	1	-	2	-	-	-
Lolium cf. *perenne* L.	-	-	-	-	-	-	-	-	1	-	3	-	1	-	2	-
Poa cf. *annua* L.	2	1	-	1	-	-	-	-	-	-	9	-	-	-	8	-
Phleum sp./*Poa* sp.	-	-	-	-	2	-	-	1	-	-	-	1	2	1	-	-
cf. *Dactylis glomerata* L.	-	-	-	-	-	-	-	-	-	-	2	-	-	-	-	-
cf. *Dactylis* spp./*Holcus* spp.	-	3	-	-	-	-	-	-	-	-	-	-	-	-	-	-
Avena spp. (caryopses)	6	-	-	1	-	-	-	-	1	4	21	1	-	-	2	-
Avena spp. (awns)	-	2	-	1	-	-	-	-	-	-	2	-	2	1	4	-
Avena spp./*Bromus* spp.	3	-	-	-	-	-	-	-	-	-	1	1	-	-	2	1
cf. *Alopecurus* sp.	1	-	-	-	-	-	-	-	-	-	-	-	-	-	-	-
Phleum sp.	1	-	-	-	-	-	-	-	-	-	-	-	-	-	-	-
Bromus hordeaceus L./*secalinus* L. (type)	-	-	-	-	-	-	-	-	1	-	3	-	1	-	-	-
Bromus sp.	1	-	-	-	-	-	-	-	-	2	3	-	1	-	-	-
POACEAE <4 mm undifferentiated	-	-	-	-	-	1	-	-	-	-	2	-	-	-	-	-
POACEAE >3.5 mm undifferentiated	-	-	-	-	1	-	-	-	-	-	-	-	-	-	-	-
POACEAE (indeterminate)	1	-	-	-	-	-	-	-	-	-	-	-	-	-	2	-
POACEAE indeterminate (rachis)	-	-	-	-	-	-	-	-	-	-	-	-	-	1	-	-
Unidentified - seeds (undiff.)	5	-	-	-	-	3	1	-	-	-	4	2	3	5	8	-
Unidentified - tree/shrub buds	-	-	-	-	-	-	-	-	-	-	1	-	-	-	-	-
TOTALS																
Cereal Grain	86	2	11	11	8	4	18	9	9	8	27	4	14	16	31	5
Cereal Chaff	8	0	1	7	11	10	2	4	6	12	91	4	26	3	72	7
Other Crops	0	0	0	0	0	0	0	0	0	0	1	0	0	0	0	0
Weed/Wild	93	17	2	16	17	14	6	11	3	12	75	13	51	28	112	5
Unidentified/Indeterminate	5	0	0	0	0	3	1	0	0	0	5	2	3	5	8	0
TOTAL IDENTIFICATIONS	192	19	14	34	36	31	27	24	18	32	199	23	94	52	223	17
PROPORTIONS																
Cereal Grain	44.8%	10.5%	78.6%	32.4%	22.2%	12.9%	66.7%	37.5%	50.0%	25.0%	13.6%	17.4%	14.9%	30.8%	13.9%	29.4%
Cereal Chaff	4.2%	0.0%	7.1%	20.6%	30.6%	32.3%	7.4%	16.7%	33.3%	37.5%	45.7%	17.4%	27.7%	5.8%	32.3%	41.2%
Other Crops	0.0%	0.0%	0.0%	0.0%	0.0%	0.0%	0.0%	0.0%	0.0%	0.0%	0.5%	0.0%	0.0%	0.0%	0.0%	0.0%
Weed/Wild	48.4%	89.5%	14.3%	47.1%	47.2%	45.2%	22.2%	45.8%	16.7%	37.5%	37.7%	56.5%	54.3%	53.8%	50.2%	29.4%
Unidentified/Indeterminate	2.6%	0.0%	0.0%	0.0%	0.0%	9.7%	3.7%	0.0%	0.0%	0.0%	2.5%	8.7%	3.2%	9.6%	3.6%	0.0%

could be identified from glume remains. Although oat grains, *Avena* sp., were present there was no reason to suspect, in the absence of identifiable floret fragments, that they were of the cultivated variety *Avena sativa*. Most were assumed to be more likely representative of the non-cultivated varieties, most probably *Avena fatua*

Arable husbandry techniques and practice

The charred assemblages were investigated in terms of the transformations, both natural and cultural, that contributed to their composition. These include circumstances surrounding the charring of the material, as well as human interactions with the crop itself that led to the formation of the weed flora within the assemblage. Such transformations can be traced back in time to provide a 'history' of the assemblages' formation. So we may use each sample's internal composition to assess post-depositional changes and the nature of its deposition. We may examine the circumstances surrounding the charring of each sample, including the processing of cereals taken from storage in readiness for their preparation as food. We may also examine the processing of the crop following harvest in preparation for its storage. From the seeds of wild species believed to represent weeds growing within the crop when it was harvested we may examine the nature of the harvest itself, the conditions under which the crop was sown and grew. Observations gleaned from such an examination then allow for the comparison of crop husbandry techniques with those of a number of sites in the region for which archaeobotanical assemblages are also available.

Post-depositional changes

Preservation varied from highly degraded to very good. One of the main observations on post-depositional effects concerned the appearance of a group of taxa in Iron Age samples that are more commonly recovered in Roman and Saxon contexts. These taxa included stinking mayweed (*Anthemis cotula*), corncockle (*Agrostemma githago*) and rye (*Secale cereale*). Stinking mayweed has been recovered from late 3rd-4th century Roman contexts from Barton Court Farm (Jones 1986b) and Alchester (Pelling 2001). It is generally absent from British sites before this date (cf Tomlinson and Hall 1996). Corncockle is also rare and thought to be a Roman introduction (Greig 1991). Rye too is relatively unknown before the Saxon period (Greig 1991) yet a few grains do appear in Iron Age contexts at Yarnton. All of these species were common from Saxon Yarnton (Stevens 2004).

Post-harvest – pre-storage crop-processing and daily post-storage processing

The association of wild species seeds with chaff and crop remains has led many authors to view them as weeds growing in past fields (Knörzer 1971) and to associate the charred assemblages themselves with crop processing (Hillman 1981). The examination of the assemblage then allows us to see how crops were stored and processed (Stevens 2003a; Hillman 1981; 1984a).

Hillman suggested, on the basis of comparison with the wet areas of Turkey where hulled wheats are still grown, that emmer and spelt wheat in prehistoric Britain would be most likely to have been stored in the spikelet. In part this would be because of the limited time following harvest, in which the number of consecutive dry days would rarely be enough to allow the full processing of crop. Further, storage in the glumes in wet areas would help protect the crop against insect and fungal attack. The finding of spikelets from storage pit contexts at Danebury (Jones 1984b), Fifield Down (Biffen 1924) and Twywell, Northamptonshire (Arthur in Jackson 1975) further suggests that the storage of hulled cereals as spikelets was commonplace in prehistoric Britain.

Van der Veen (1992) argued that the higher ratio of glume bases to estimated glume wheats demonstrated that many samples from Iron Age sites in north-east England represent the waste from fine-sieving after pounding. If glume wheats are stored as spikelets, and if most samples are higher in glume bases than glume wheat grains, then it follows that most charred remains are the result of the burning of waste from the 'daily processing' of cereals taken from storage as and when needed (Stevens 2003a). Such waste would be produced throughout the year, as opposed to waste from post-harvest processing which would be produced only for a limited period following harvest in mid to late summer. The time at which cereals ripen depends on prevailing climatic and soil conditions. Although ripening may vary from year to year and geographically according to soil type, when it occurs the crop must be quickly harvested and processed to facilitate its successful storage in a dry condition.

Processing following harvest has therefore to be carried out over a relatively short period in order to store the crop safely before the autumn rains set in. If labour and/or time are limited then relatively little processing may be carried out. If both are freely available then more processing can be conducted. It is probable that such patterns will be embedded within any single community. Such variations in processing and their relationship to the wider community between wet and dry regions were seen in Hillman's (1973; 1981) studies in Turkey.

The samples from Yarnton have the potential to reveal the processing stages conducted every day as grain was prepared for food. In turn they can reveal the state in which crops were stored; as semi-spikelets or almost clean grain with only grain-sized contaminants, or at the other extreme as sheaves. Lastly, from the absence of material associated with earlier stages – for example, straw nodes, small weed seeds and free-threshing rachis fragments – the amount of processing carried out after harvest may be demonstrated.

In order to investigate such patterns for Yarnton, the number of glume bases (spikelet forks were counted as two) and the estimated number of hulled wheat grains were calculated for each sample. This latter figure was arrived at through dividing the number of unidentified cereal grains proportionally, according to the fraction of identified barley, free-threshing and/or hulled wheat grains in the sample. Unidentified wheat grains were similarly apportioned. The resultant values were then added to the number of identified hulled wheat grains. In cases where no cereals had been identified to species level, all cereal grains were assumed to come from hulled wheats. The ratio of glumes to hulled wheat grains is around 1 to 1 in the living plant (van der Veen 1992). If glumes are more numerous than grain then the sample must be derived, at least in part, from the separation of glumes after pounding.

This first analysis was conducted to ascertain whether most of the samples could be assumed to derive from processing waste of grain taken from storage (glume rich) rather than from other operations such as the burning of harvest processing waste, storage, or parching waste, all of which would involve the burning of whole unpounded spikelets and result in grain-rich assemblages. Studies of the differential effects of preservation by charring on glumes and grains have shown that glumes tend to be destroyed much more readily than grains (Boardman and Jones 1990; Robinson and Straker 1991; Hillman 1981). Even at Danebury and Wandlebury (Jones 1984b; author's own observation) where spikelets were preserved *in situ* with conditions more suited for exceptional preservation (a slow burning, reduced atmosphere), grains outnumbered glume bases by at least two to one. On the basis of this observation it is probable that samples representative of the burning of whole spikelets would be extremely grain rich, whilst even those representative of the burning of processing waste, if under less suitable preservation conditions, might still be slightly grain rich

The second analysis was to ascertain the amount of processing prior to storage. Glynis Jones (1987) noted differences between the representation of small, large, headed and light weed seeds according to the stage of processing. In van der Veen's analysis of sites from Northern England most weed seeds were placed in one or two categories, small heavy-seeded, or large (grain-sized) weed seeds. These two categories correspond to two of the later processing stages of Hillman (1981, stages 6b/13 and 14), in which weed seeds are removed. These are fine sieving to remove small weed seeds (stage 6b and stage 13), while spikelets are retained in the sieve, and hand sorting (stage 14) which removes large grain-sized weed seeds.

Evidence for earlier stages of processing, threshing, raking, winnowing, and coarse sieving, (Hillman stages 3 to 6a) is more difficult to ascertain. Headed weed seeds are often difficult to classify, as some are removed by coarse sieving (stage 6a), prior to fine sieving, while others will be released from the head during threshing (stage 3) and only removed later during fine sieving. Similarly, species whose seeds are small and light may be removed via first winnowing (stage 5) and by fine sieving; many very light seeds, removed by winnowing, will not survive charring. Alternative indicators may be the relative quantities of stems and culm nodes, all of which are more likely to be removed in earlier stages, such as coarse sieving, raking and threshing.

Weed seeds from the archaeologically recorded species were classified on the basis of the normal size category of modern seeds (Grime *et al.* 1981; 1988). They were classified as large, if greater than 2.5 mm, or small, <2.5 mm. Charring tends to reduce seed size, but the classification of unidentified seeds (especially grass seeds) as large or small may help in such an analysis. For species whose seeds are generally longer than 2.5 mm, but less than 2.5 mm wide, the average measurement was used. For example, *Polygonum aviculare* has seeds approximately 3.75 mm in length, but only 2.1 mm in width, the average is therefore 2.9 mm and the seeds of this species were classified as large. Some seeds, such as those of *Lolium perenne*, proved more difficult to classify. They are on average 4 to 6 mm long, but only 1.8 mm wide. For this reason an intermediate group was also created in which *Lolium perenne* and *Medicago lupulina*, amongst other species, were placed. The intermediate group created little variation within trial calculations in which they were classified as large or small.

The last analysis concerns the ratio of weed seeds to grain. Van der Veen notes that this ratio will enable the distinction of the crop product from crop waste, where grain will be better-represented within the product and weed seeds in the waste. As each stage of processing removes weed seeds the proportion of weed seeds within the crop product will decline. As cereal grains are also inevitably lost during processing the proportion of weed seeds to cereal grains will also diminish in the waste from any single stage as processing progresses. This will be especially true where hulled wheat crops are stored as semi-clean spikelets. The removal of the glumes inevitably leads to a fair amount of wastage of grain, while relatively few seeds are removed (mainly those of a similar size to the grain) through hand sorting. If crops are stored unclean, then 'daily processing' will remove vast amounts of weed seeds compared to the amount of grain lost, so conversely samples derived from the waste generated through processing of these crops will be richer in weed seeds.

Results of processing

The results from Yarnton are shown in Figures 18.2 and 18.4. Figure 18.2 shows the negative logged values of grains divided by spikelets forks against the percentage of large, grain sized weed seeds (from a total of all classified weed seeds). The samples are plotted by period. Only samples with over 20 crop and 15 weed seeds were plotted. Figure 18.3 shows possible interpretations of scatters. Whilst individual samples may contain mixtures of material derived from various activities, the diagram indicates at least the predominant sources of material.

The first thing noticeable from the results is that glume bases are more numerous than estimated glume wheat grains in almost every sample. This indicates that most samples come from the 'daily' post-storage processing of grain stored as spikelets. The high incidence of smaller weed seeds compared to larger ones seems to indicate that the crops were probably stored prior to at least fine-sieving. Hillman comments that for wet climates crops were sometimes stored before coarse sieving, as threshed or partially threshed ears (Hillman 1981, 132-3).

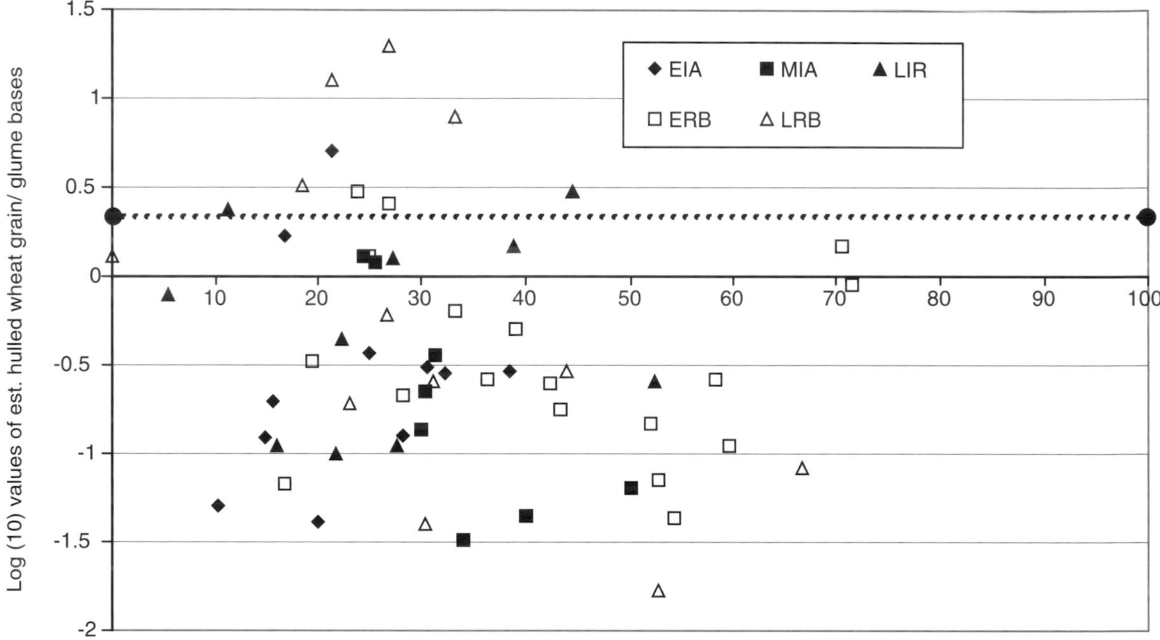

Fig. 18.2 The logged values of estimated glume wheat grains divided by glume bases plotted against the percentage of grain sized (>2.5 mm) weed seeds, for samples from Iron Age and Roman Yarnton. The dotted line indicates the optimal 2:1 grain to glume base ratio that might be expected for the burning of spikelets.

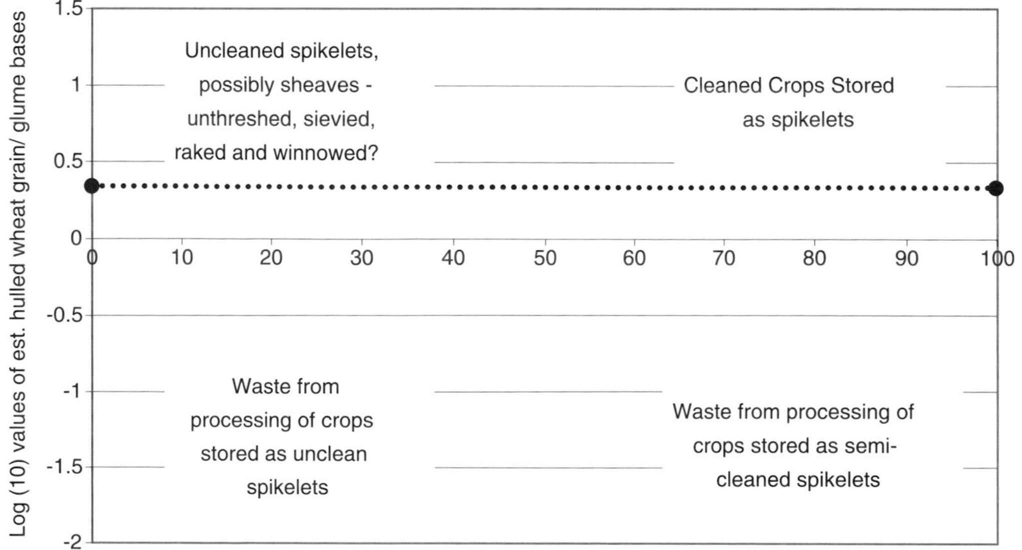

Fig. 18.3 Diagram showing possible interpretations for the distribution of samples according to the logged number of estimated grains divided by glume bases plotted against the percentage of large weed seeds within samples.

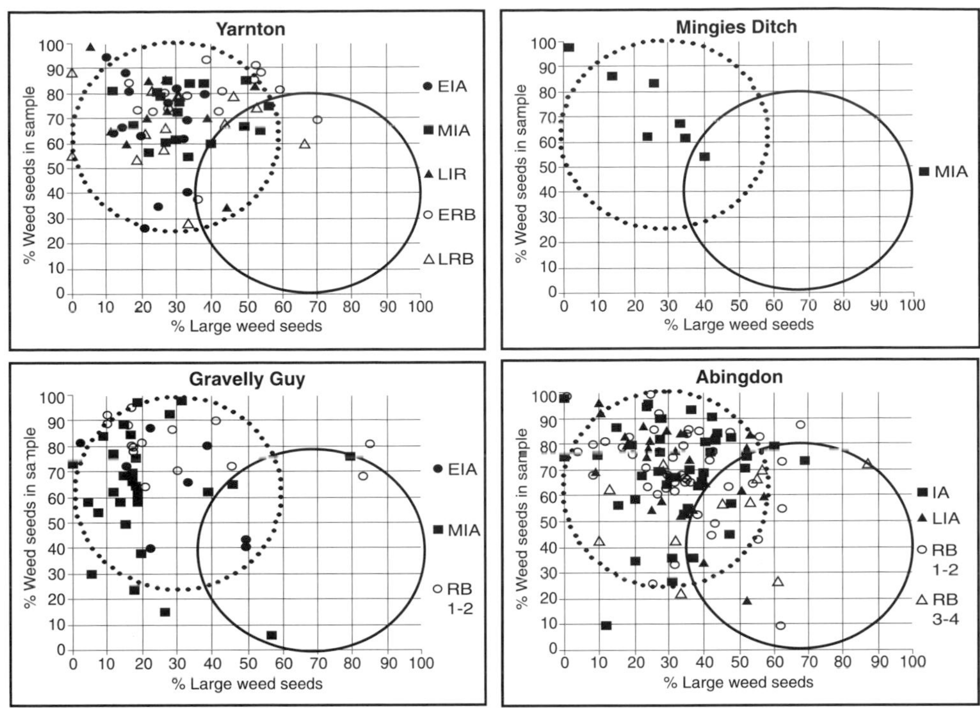

Fig. 18.4 The percentage of large (>2 mm) 'grain size' weeds (from a total of all size classified weed seeds) against the percentage of weed seeds (from a total of all weed seeds and cereal grain) plotted for individual samples. The samples are plotted by period for Yarnton, Mingies Ditch, Gravelly Guy and Abingdon

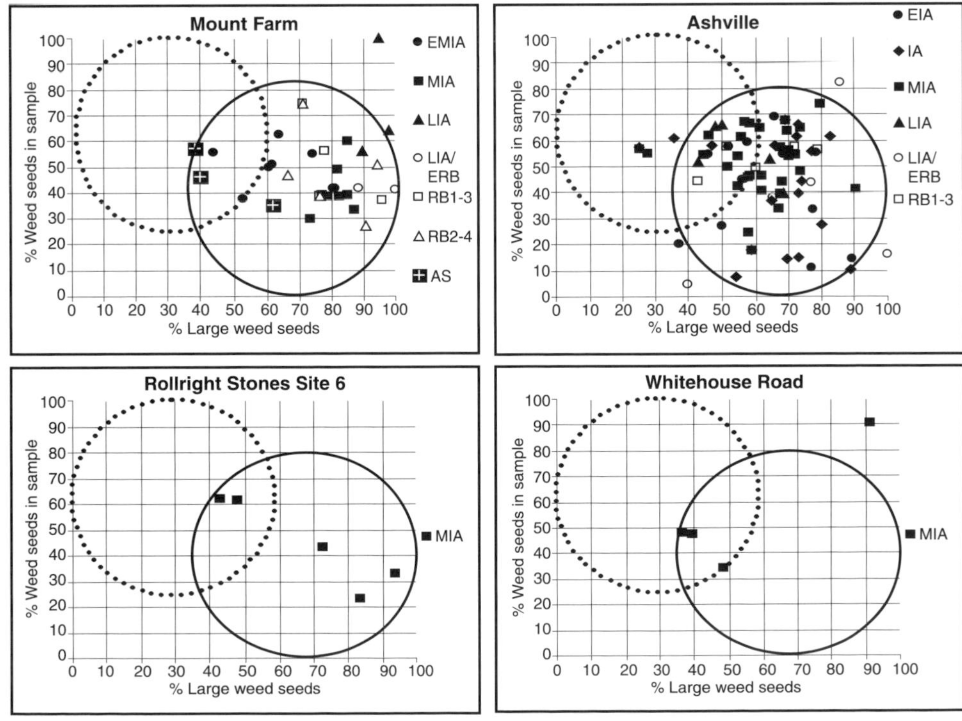

Fig. 18.5 The percentage of large (>2 mm) 'grain size' weeds (from a total of all size classified weed seeds) against the percentage of weed seeds (from a total of all weed seeds and cereal grain) plotted for individual samples. The samples are plotted by period for Mount Farm, Ashville, Rollright Site 6 and Whitehouse Road, Oxford

The results from Yarnton are then compared to those from other sites in the region (Figs 18.4 and 18.5. These are Mount Farm and Ashville (Jones M 1984a; 1978), Mingies Ditch (Jones and Robinson 1993), Abingdon (Stevens 1996), Rollright Stones Site Six and Gravelly Guy, (Moffett 1988; 2004) and Whitehouse Road (Letts 1993). The comparisons, especially with Ashville, provide some interesting observations. The samples from Ashville, like those from Yarnton, were glume rich (Stevens 2003a, cf. Jones 1978; 1984a). However, unlike Yarnton, Ashville contained mainly large weed seeds, indicative of cleanings, mainly through hand sorting. Ashville also contained only one culm node in eighty-nine samples with over 8000 grains, compared to Yarnton that had some 123 culm nodes and 295 cereal/grass internodes. As straw and culm nodes are mainly separated prior to fine sieving, by coarse sieving, threshing and raking, this might suggest that at Yarnton grain was stored as partially threshed ears or in the sheaf. Such patterns were noted for Mingies Ditch (cf Jones and Robinson 1993), and are probably similar for many other sites in the region, eg Sherborne House, Lechlade and Abingdon (Stevens 1996; 2003a; 2003b).

These differences in storage and hence in processing mean that cross-comparisons between some sites may be problematic. Seed size is also often linked to other attributes such as life cycle (annuals or perennials), germination time, and other ecological aspects (Stevens 1996; Jones 1992; van der Veen 1992).

Daily activities

The indication for Yarnton is that after harvest the crop was gathered in, perhaps threshed with the straw raked off and then stored relatively unclean. The settlement at Yarnton may have been only relatively small at any one period, comprising no more than one to two households. This would imply that arable production was probably carried out on a household level. With only a small amount of labour available for harvesting, crops were then stored as sheaves or partially threshed ears. The opposite may be seen to be true of Ashville, where the settlement would always appear to have been relatively large (Parrington 1978; Muir and Roberts 1999) and the pattern would seem to indicate farming beyond the household unit.

At regular periods, perhaps every day, at Yarnton crops were taken from storage, perhaps further threshed, winnowed to remove light, fine chaff, coarse-sieved to remove remaining straw fragments and seed heads and then fine-sieved to remove small weed seeds. They would then be pounded with a pestle and mortar, with further sieving and winnowing to remove the glumes and unpounded spikelets. Lastly they would be hand sorted to pick out grain-sized weed seeds. Some grass seeds, such as oats or brome grass, may have been left in with the crop and eaten according to personal taste or in cases of bad harvests/grain shortage (Jones 1978, 101). The grain would then have been ground or crushed on saddle querns (see Roe, Chapter 15) for flour. This may have then been cooked and consumed as dough balls, porridge, bread and gruel. Some may also have been malted and brewed, but as such processing/preparation activities would have been carried out less frequently or involved similar initial processing, evidence of them is less likely to be seen from charred remains alone.

Harvesting height and method

Hillman (1984a) suggested that the presence of twining and/or low growing weeds can be used to distinguish the method and height of harvesting. At Yarnton the commonest lowest growing seeds of probable weed species were those of clover (*Trifolium* sp.) growing at 20-30 cm and annual meadow grass (*Poa annua*) at 30 cm (Stace 1997). The high presence of these species from the Iron Age to the Roman period in the majority of samples would then indicate harvesting, probably with a sickle, low at the culm. Such harvesting methods were probably widespread, as seen from the ubiquity of these species upon other sites in the region (Stevens 1996).

Sowing, manuring and weeding

Two methods of sowing are possible; either broadcast sowing that is most commonly known in historical Britain prior to the invention of Jethro Tull's seed drill, and depicted in countless medieval manuscripts, or the planting of individual grains in rows that allows weeding between the rows.

The approaches available for detecting the method of sowing are numerous. One is through identification of the presence of large seeded species, which often have short seed banks and germinate on contact with the soil (Stevens 1996; cf Grime *et al.* 1988). Many of these species, as noted by Salisbury (1961, 31) became extinct from corn fields with the change in practise from broadcast sowing to individual seed planting (dibbling), and with the advent of improved seed cleaning which prevented them getting back into the arable field. A second approach is to identify evidence of improved weeding through the absence of species that are particularly susceptible to such weeding.

In terms of the first method, several species present in the samples are indicative of broadcast sowing. These are *Agrostemma githago*, *Adonis annua*, *Centaurea cyanus* and most species of *Bromus*. All these produce short-term seed banks (Grime *et al.* 1988) and are removed by hand-sorting. *Galium aparine* has a short-lived seed bank that allows it to germinate best in spring (ibid.). It is destroyed by spring ploughing (Reynolds 1981a; Jones 1978; 1981; 1988b), but would be less susceptible to elimination by spring tillage if it was resown with the crop in the seed corn. The practise of autumn sowing, without its having been resown in the seed corn, would also have gradually diminished it, as most of the seed would be harvested with the crop and removed from the field.

Seeds of *Agrostemma githago*, as stated earlier, are likely to be Roman or Saxon in date, while those of *Adonis annua* and *Centaurea* sp. were uncommon. Both *Galium aparine* and *Bromus* were, however, common enough in many samples to suggest that fields were more probably broadcast rather than row planted. The common occurrence of perennials and annual species with short seed banks that would otherwise be reasonably easily weeded out by hoeing, such as *Bromus* sp., *Trifolium* sp., *Lolium perenne*, *Phleum pratense* and *Eleocharis* sp., also indicates that it is unlikely that fields were planted and weeded in rows.

Determining the time of sowing is more problematic than resolving the questions asked previously. The presence of *Galium aparine* has been taken as an indicator of autumn sowing from experiments at Butser Ancient Farm (Jones 1981; 1988a; 1988b; Reynolds 1981a). However, as noted, *Galium aparine* may be introduced via seed corn, something the experiments at Butser did not account for (see Reynolds 1981a, 108).

It is difficult to accurately assess from the archaeobotanical information whether crops were spring or autumn sown, as few species are specific indicators of just one time of sowing. On the continent two groups of species are traditionally noted. The Chenopodietea, with species of the Chenopodiaceae being most prominent, are associated with spring crops and the Secalietea are associated with winter sown crops, especially rye (Behre 1975; van Zeist 1988; van Zeist *et al* 1987; Jones 1992; van der Veen 1992, 102). The differences between these two groups have been attributed partly to climate, with species of the Chenopodietea being susceptible to frost (Ellenberg 1950). Nevertheless, the differences still survive in Britain to some extent in spite of its milder climate and for this reason Silverside (1977) attributed these differences to nitrogen levels rather than to climatic differences.

Nitrogen cycles in the soil follow seasonal patterns according to the activity of soil fauna. These are mainly responsible for the breaking down of organic matter and its conversion into organic nitrogen that can then be taken up by plants. The nitrogen cycle follows a pattern in which during autumn to winter nitrogen levels are low, rising in spring into summer, when soil organisms are most active (Runge 1983). Species of the Chenopodiaceae are particularly adapted to germination in spring, especially in terms of using nitrogen as a dormancy breaker in the seeds (Henson 1970; Harper 1977, 67; Grime *et al.* 1981; 1988; Karssen and Hilhorst 1992). While some seeds do germinate in autumn the seedlings do not go on to flower (Williams 1963).

Leguminosae are noted for being well adapted for nitrogen-poor, but not nutrient-poor soils, where the association with *Rhizobium* spp. within their roots allows them to uptake nitrogen in situations where overall soil nitrogen is low. This then gives them a competitive advantage in such soils (Black 1957; Hanf 1983; Sprent 1981). Differences between the proportion of seeds from legumes (especially *Vicia* sp. and *Lathyrus* sp.) to those of the Chenopodiaceae in samples have been noted to alter through time for prehistoric Britain (Green 1981; Jones 1981). Martin Jones (1981; 1984a; 1984c; 1988a; 1988b) has argued that this is due to removal of soil nitrogen and other nutrients by over-cropping. Over-cropping has been demonstrated to quickly reduce nitrogen levels to a base level within a year, at which point it stabilises, but this only appeared to occur in the absence of manuring (Catt 1994; Hall 1905, 40). Rather it is probably declining phosphorus levels that are the major detrimental consequence of over-cropping (Jeffry 1987; Piggot

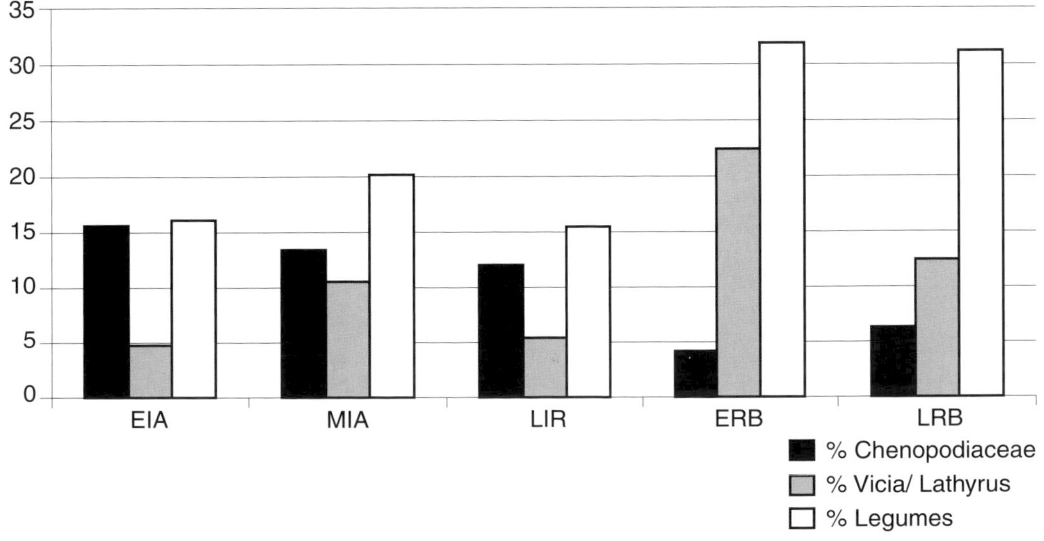

Fig. 18.6 The percentage of legumes (including Vicia and Lathyrus), Vicia spp. and Lathyrus spp. and Chenopodiaceae, as a total of all identified seeds from all samples from Yarnton for each period.

and Taylor 1964). At Yarnton there is evidence that manuring certainly continued from the Iron Age into the Roman period (Hey *et al.* 1993; see Chapter 11 above). This might suggest that nitrogen levels are unlikely to have become so limited. Increased manuring during the Iron Age to Roman period is also seen at other sites in the region (Lambrick 1992b). From this point of view the reduction in the number of species of the Chenopodiaceae might indicate a gradual switch to increased amounts of autumn sowing. The high presence of seeds of the Chenopodiaceae has not been taken as an indicator of spring sowing by van der Veen (1992) for her sites in north-east England. Rather she dismisses this possibility, on the basis of evidence from modern studies in the Netherlands that showed that the time of sowing was less influential than the presence of manuring, soil disturbance and weeding. There are, however, several problems with the use of such observations. As already noted it is highly likely that most crops in the past were broadcast rather than planted in rows. With modern crops planting in rows allows for the potential use of the hoe or harrow. This creates spaces within the crop that allow spring-sown weeds to germinate. With broadcast sowing it is unlikely that the crops could have been weeded. Legumes only compete well in the absence of nitrogen, but not with overall low nutrient availability (Warrington 1924), as would occur with over-cropping (Catt 1994, Hall 1905, 40).

It is therefore suggested that the changes seen at Yarnton (Fig. 18.6), as well as at Ashville, Gravelly Guy, and Abingdon (Jones 1978; Moffett 2004; Stevens 1996), continuing from the early Iron Age to the Roman period, are reflective of a change in the time of sowing, from spring to autumn. It is suggested that both spring and autumn sowing were practised in all periods, but it is further suggested that the Iron Age period sees a predominance of spring sowing, which is replaced in the Roman period by an increase in autumn sowing.

Tillage, crop rotations, length of arable

Van der Veen (1992) has linked the ratio of annuals and perennials, seen on prehistoric and Roman sites in north-east Britain, to corresponding levels of soil disturbance. The scenario is that annuals are better adapted to a disturbed environment than perennial species are. Van der Veen (ibid.) attributes the ratio of annuals to perennials to the level of soil disturbance between hoed and arded crops. However, other factors may affect this ratio. Perennials tend to be better-represented for example where arable fields replace those previously used for grassland (Chancellor 1985; 1986). Some will also survive better where grazing is less frequent or heavy, as will be the case for many of the species seen, such as *Lolium perenne*, *Eleocharis palustris* and *Phleum* sp. In general most of these species will be diminished by arable cultivation, as is seen in the experiments of Chancellor (1986), although a plough rather than an ard was used, and over a fourteen year period most had diminished. The second cause of higher rates of perennials may be a change from spring to autumn sowing. The longer growing season allows perennials much more growing time and the chance of maintaining a population in the arable field (Haas and Streibig 1982).

There is generally little variation within the ratio of seeds of perennials to annuals through time (Fig. 18.7). The samples dated to the later Iron Age/early Roman period seem to contain more perennials and fewer seeds of annuals. If it is assumed that ards were used for all these periods (as seen at Ashville; Fowler 1978), and that in the absence of any evidence for planting in rows the inhabitants sowed their seed by broadcasting, then it may be postulated that the suggested change in the time of sowing does not occur until the earlier Roman period rather than in the transitional period. An explanation might then be found in the possibility that the fields from which these samples came had either not been under cultivation for a long period,

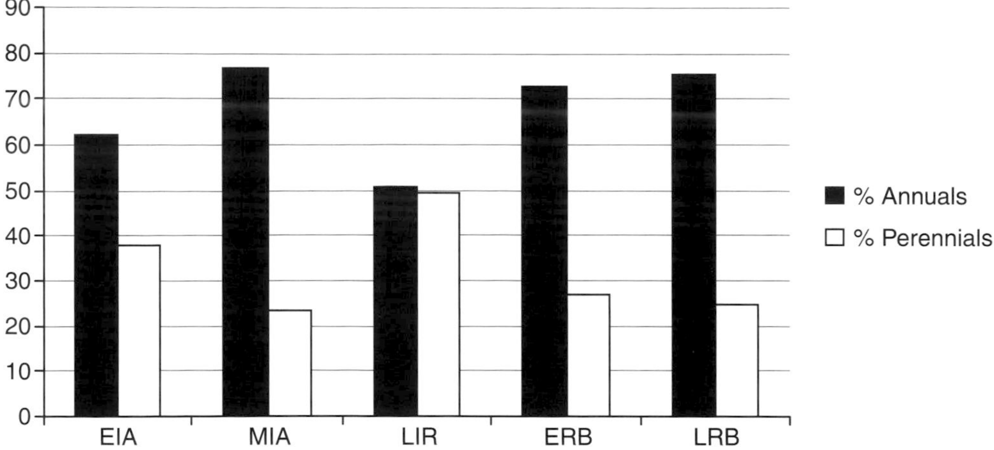

Fig. 18.7 The ratio of annuals to perennials for the total of all annuals and perennials as a total of all classifiable weed seeds by period for Yarnton.

or were more regularly rotated with periods of ley. That the later Iron Age sees a reorganisation of existing field systems as well as settlement patterns (Lambrick 1992b) might provide at least one explanation for these differences.

The location of the fields and changes within the location

The site, like many in the Thames valley, contains several elements. For example, spikerush, *Eleocharis palustris*, a species of wetlands, requires the water-table to be within its rooting zone during its main season of growth in spring (Walters 1949). The other wetland species, which is relatively common within the samples, is blinks, *Montia fontana* subsp. *chondrosperma*. Both species would have been frequent components of the partially flooded soils on the lower parts of the gravel terrace around the site, as they are in similar conditions today (Rodwell 1995). Many fields would then appear to have been located on or at least encroached onto these wet, gravelly, silt circum-neutral soils (cf Jones 1978). The Iron Age to Roman period sees increased flooding and alluviation in the region (Robinson 1992a; 1992b). Such flooding and alluviation continued until the palaeochannels that run around the site silted (see Chapter 2), and so may have limited the area suited for settlement and forced the shifting of fields onto wetter areas. Species more commonly associated with drier soils were also present, for example, *Valerianella locusta*, *V. dentata*, *Ranunculus parviflorus*, *Silene* sp. and *Adonis annua*, although none was common in the samples. These, as well as seeds of *Medicago lupulina*, also associated with drier soils, do, however, either point to at least some exploitation of such areas or the existence of drier patches within wet and damp fields.

Seeds of *Anthemis cotula* within earlier samples, as noted, may be contaminants. However, they appear to increase in number in the late Roman period (Fig. 18.8). This may signify the movement of fields onto clay soils. The increase may be more closely related to the colonisation of this species in Britain during this period, or alternatively it may be indicative of the increased alluviation of clayey material onto already existing fields within the area of the floodplain (cf Lambrick 1992b; Robinson 1992b). *Anthemis cotula* has been noted by Jones (1981) to increase during the late Roman period at other sites, for example at Barton Court Farm (Jones 1986b), and a slight increase is seen at other sites in the region, for instance Abingdon Vineyard (Stevens 1996). Jones associated this rise with a movement of arable onto clay soils.

Comparisons with other sites

The differences between Yarnton and Gravelly Guy in terms of species composition were relatively small. Comparisons of the frequency of species, based on the percentage of samples in which species were present, also generated similar results. The samples from Gravelly Guy were generally richer so that the increased frequency of some species such as *Galium aparine*, *Eleocharis* sp., *Stellaria* sp., *Chenopodium album*, *Lithospermum arvense*, *Valerianella dentata*, *Fallopia convovulus* and *Polygonum aviculare*, and the presence of *Fumaria* sp. there may be largely attributed to this.

Summary

The charred plant remains have been largely attributed to the waste from 'daily crop-processing'. The general indication is one suited to the patterns observed by Hingley (1984) of small, relatively independent farmsteads, the occupants of which were probably solely responsible for the farming and tillage of fields allotted to or 'owned' by them around the farmstead. The fields appear to have been lying close to former small channels and from this perspective were almost certainly relatively wet and damp, and probably subjected to some flooding. Fields appear to have been only minimally disturbed prior to sowing, probably by ard, though possibly with mattocks and spades. Crops appear to have been sown in both spring and autumn, probably using the broadcast method in which spikelets for hulled wheats and grain in the case of barley are scattered

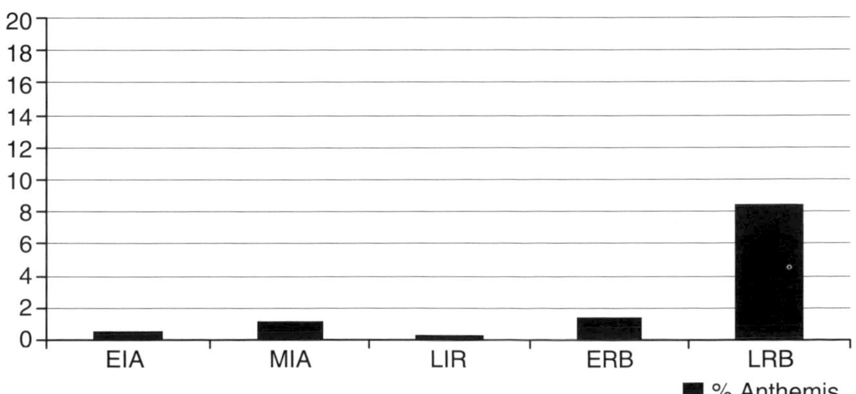

Fig. 18.8 The percentage of Anthemis cotula (from a total of all identifiable seeds) in all the samples by period.

evenly by hand across the field. Such a method of sowing does not allow for weeding once the crops become relatively well-established.

The crops would have been harvested in late summer. Some were certainly cut low on the culm. A point noted by Reynolds (1981a) is that the ears of hulled wheats grew at a variety of heights. Some would therefore inevitably have been harvested low to the ground. A scythe blade was recovered from Roman Farmoor, but it is believed that at this period scythes were more probably used for harvesting hay rather than cereals (Rees 1979). It is probable that the crops were harvested by sickle low on the culm. They would then appear to have been stored as sheaves, possibly in house roofs or in four-post structures. It is interesting to note the comments of the Roman writers Diodorus Siculus (*Hist* 5.21.5) and Strabo (*Geog* 4.5.5) who not only record the Britons cutting off the ears of grain and storing them in roofed houses, but also note that ears rather than grain were stored. While this does not appear true for all sites it might possibly apply for sites such as Yarnton.

Most of the samples appear to relate to the processing of crops taken from these stores and the discard of the waste into the hearth. There is little suggestion that any of the samples resulted from other activities. Those from the pottery kilns (2525 and 2537), or the corn-drying oven (522) showed the burning of similar material. They were more glume-rich than the others, but this is most likely a reflection of the reduced environment of charring and the fact they were probably burnt and recovered *in situ*, leading to the increased preservation of the more fragile glumes.

IRON AGE AND ROMAN POLLEN RESULTS FROM YARNTON FLOODPLAIN, YARNTON CRESSWELL FIELD AND OXEY MEAD

by James Greig

Summary

Two profiles of peat and alluvium from former river channels at Yarnton and from Oxey Mead were analysed for pollen, in connection with extensive archaeological investigations on the gravel terraces and floodplain around Yarnton and Cassington. An Iron Age ditch fill from the Cresswell Field part of the site has also been investigated. The parts of the sequences which correspond to the Iron Age and Roman periods indicate an open landscape already cleared of most of its original woodland cover, and with grasslands and cornfields.

Introduction

The Yarnton profile discussed here was sampled in part of a palaeochannel, at grid reference SP 472 112. Another profile in an old river channel was sampled in Oxey Mead at SP 482 109. In addition, some pollen spectra from another part of the excavation area, Cresswell Field, are discussed. This report discusses the pollen results from these sedimentary sequences, which correspond to the Iron Age and Roman periods.

Methods

The Yarnton channel profile, sampled in November 1992, is a 125 cm section of sediment which was also sampled for insects and plant macrofossils (Chapter 2 above, see also Robinson below). The pollen samples were collected in 25 x 10 x 10 cm aluminium boxes which were hammered into the clean section, and then dug away. Radiocarbon dating material was obtained from the macrofossil samples. Alluvium samples were collected from the profile to test optical dating techniques.

The stratigraphy of the Yarnton profile is as follows:-

depth cm	*material*	*period*
c 33 cm	topsoil and alluvium (not sampled)	
0-30	alluvium (sampled)	medieval
10-20	alluvium	medieval
20-30	alluvium	late Saxon
30-50	organic alluvial material	
40-50	organic	Saxon
50-70	alluvium	
50-65	organic	Saxon
65-75	organic alluvium	Roman
75-90		Roman
90-105	organic	?Iron Age
70-115	more organic material	
105-115	organic	Bronze Age
115-125	merging into clay	?Devensian
125-	gravel (not sampled)	

The Oxey Mead core was collected by Petra Day and Mark Robinson; the writer did not see the site. The profile consists of a single monolith of 100 cm in plastic guttering. The top 50 cm of the material is alluvial material, becoming more organic and peaty with increasing depth, and becoming stony from 95-100 cm.

Laboratory work

Pollen preparation and counting

The Yarnton core pollen subsamples for analysis were taken from the boxed material at a 5 cm interval and stored in a fridge. At first, samples at a 10 cm interval were prepared for pollen analysis by traditional methods using hydrofluoric acid and counted (30, 40, 50, 60 70, 80, 100 cm). In the Oxey Mead core, samples were prepared at an interval of 5 cm (except 85 cm), all measured from the top of the plastic guttering, although at 10, 15 and 25 cm there was insufficient pollen to count.

Pollen preparation was done on the first few of the Oxey Mead samples (20, 40, 60, 80 and 100 cm) using the traditional preparation process; phosphate pre-treatment to disperse clay, hydrofluoric acid treatment to remove siliceous material, followed by acetolysis and staining. The other samples from both cores were prepared using a newer technique. The material was dispersed in dilute alkali, sieved through a 75 μm mesh and the organic fraction of the material separated from the inorganic fractions by swirl separation on a 15 cm watchglass. Microfiltration on a 10 μm mesh was used to remove fine material such as clay, and acetolysis was carried out to remove cellulose-related material. The new preparation method has been tested to see whether much pollen is lost during swirling or filtration. It is difficult to say whether there are statistically significant differences between the counts made on samples prepared in the two different ways.

The samples were stained and mounted in glycerol jelly, and the pollen was counted with a Leitz Dialux microscope, using phase-contrast lighting. Identification was done using the writer's pollen reference collection, and also the standard literature (Andrew 1984; Fægri and Iversen 1989). Names of pollen types follow Bennett (1994).

In the Yarnton core, pollen is preserved from 0 cm down to 110 cm. In some of the samples, especially in the middle of the core, the pollen was quite well preserved, but in the top and bottom parts preservation and concentration were rather poor, and it took a long time to count a minimum number of pollen grains. Pollen concentration was also rather low in some Oxey Mead samples, particularly towards the top of the core, and two slides were needed for a high enough count in some cases. The pollen counts were of 200 grains or more, although with the pollen sum of dry land taxa, the percentage base was rather low in some cases. Pollen slides were scanned after counting to record some extra pollen types on a presence or absence basis. The samples above 20 cm did not produce a significant pollen count.

Pollen diagrams

The pollen diagrams have been drawn up using the TILIA programme (Grimm 1990). The Yarnton diagram is shown in Figure 18.9A-B, the Oxey Mead diagram in Figure 18.10A-B. The pollen sum is that of land plants, and these records are drawn as black saw-edge curves, with a x10 exaggeration in stipple. The wetland herbs, aquatics and spores have been excluded from the pollen sum, since the first two are likely to have been mainly local, and might obscure the more regional record. For example, Apiaceae pollen may be largely from *Oenanthe* (water dropwort) which is present in the macrofossil record, and *Ranunculus*-tp is mainly of the aquatic type (*R.* subg. *Batrachium*) so these pollen records are therefore considered as (mainly) aquatic and wetland. The pollen taxa used for the pollen sum are drawn in solid black, while the others are in outline (white) only. The pollen types in the sum have x10 exaggeration curves to make the smaller records more visible; much of the interpretation depends on small changes in a number of slight pollen records.

The pollen types are arranged in the following ecological groups: trees and shrubs, dry land herbs, wetland herbs, aquatics. Spores are listed at the end. Within these groups, the trees have been subgrouped to keep the main wildwood components, *Quercus*, *Tilia* and *Ulmus* together. The dry land herbs are also subdivided into mainly grassland taxa (*Potentilla* tp. to Poaceae), weeds and crops (Chenopodiaceae to Cerealia tp.), and various (*Urtica* to *Aster* tp.). The nomenclature and order of the taxa within the groups and sub-groups follows Bennett (1994) and Kent (1992). The diagrams have not been zoned in the conventional sense because the rather small changes of pollen assemblage do not lend themselves to division in this way.

Dating

The Iron Age and Roman part of the Yarnton profile seems to be from 65-105 cm, based on a series of three accelerator radiocarbon dates on plant macrofossils, and two optical dates from the alluvium. However, the radiocarbon dates have variations of 1-2 centuries, so the dating is not very exact.

The Iron Age and Roman part of the Oxey Mead profile may be at 85-100 cm, on the basis of one radiocarbon accelerator date (OxA-7360) from 85-95 cm giving a calibrated date range which seems to be Roman (cal AD 240-540), and another (Oxa-3643) at 75-85 cm giving a Saxon or Norman date range of cal AD 660-1010 (Hey 2004, 258).

Results

Pollen preservation was generally adequate in the parts of the diagrams thought to correspond to the Iron Age and Roman periods. As the sites are channels, they should act mainly as small catchments which collected pollen more from local vegetation within several hundred metres of the sites, than from the whole Thames floodplain region. The discussion is ordered according to vegetation types.

Trees and woodland

Tree and shrub pollen is fairly low throughout in this part of both the Yarnton and Oxey Mead pollen diagrams, around 5-10%, consisting mainly of *Quercus* (oak), Coryloid (hazel type) and *Alnus* (alder) with some *Pinus* (pine) pollen, and other taxa such as *Fraxinus* (ash), *Betula* (birch), and *Ulmus* (elm) occasionally present. There is slightly more tree pollen, notably *Quercus* and Coryloid, in the Oxey Mead diagram than in the Yarnton one. The pollen evidence at Yarnton agrees with the general lack of evidence for trees or woodland in the seed and beetle records (Chapter 2, see also Robinson

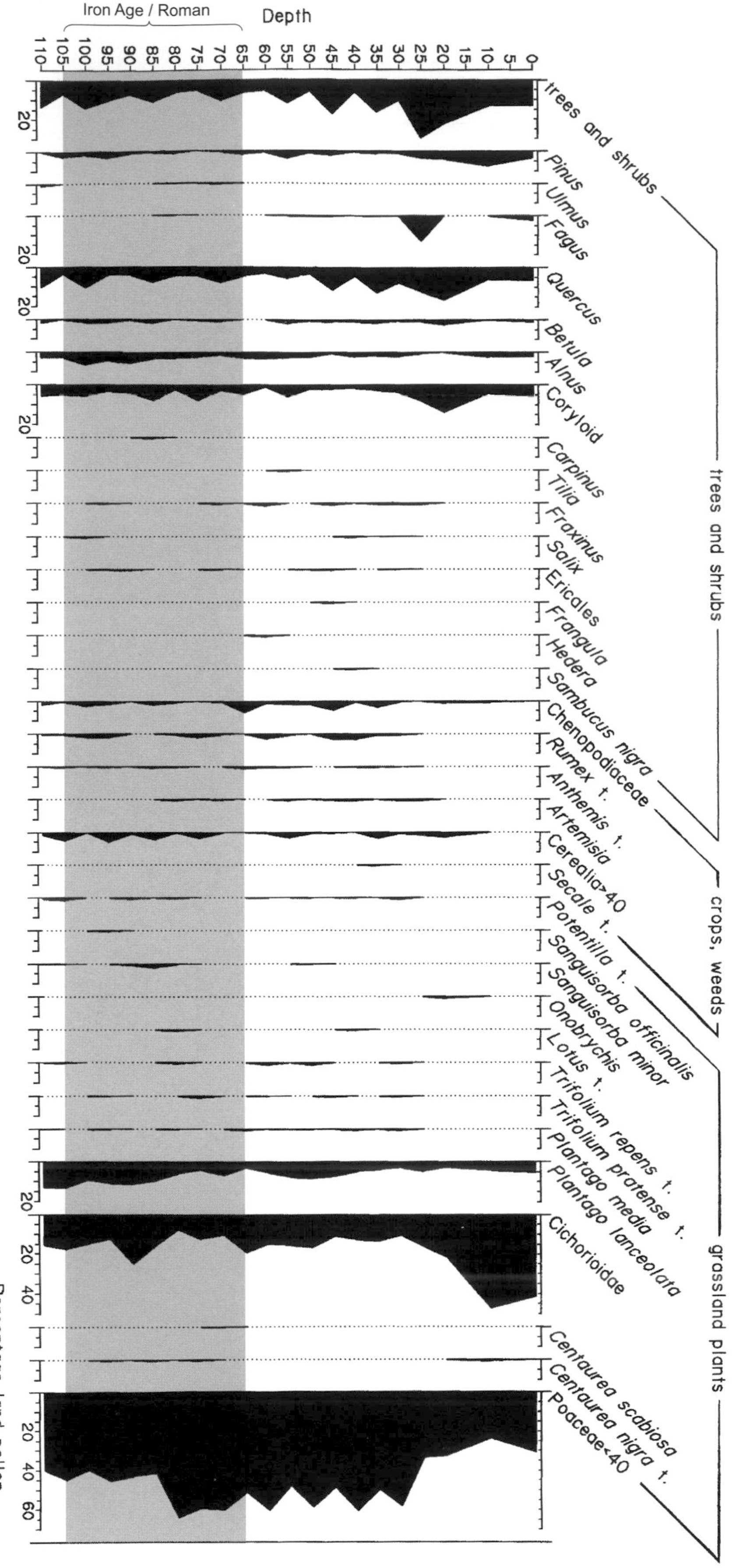

Fig. 18.9A Yarnton YFPB 92 pollen diagram with: trees and shrubs; dry land herbs from grassland; dry land herbs, crops and their weeds. The percentage curves are based on the sum of dry land pollen (black curves), and 10x exaggeration (stippled curves).

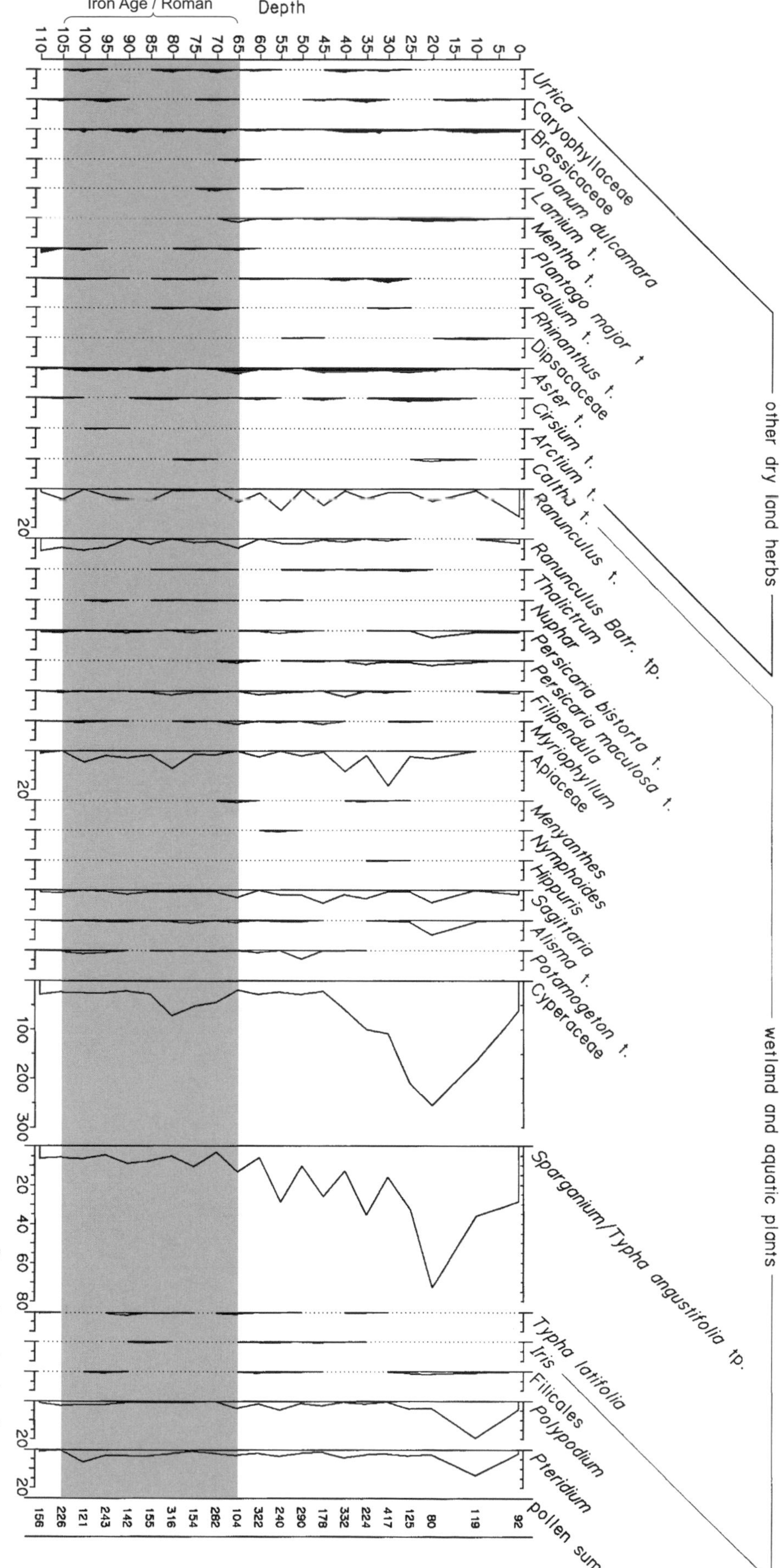

Fig. 18.9B Yarnton YFPB 92 pollen diagram (continued): wetland herbs; aquatic herbs; spores. The white curves are those taxa not in the pollen sum (based on the sum of dry land pollen).

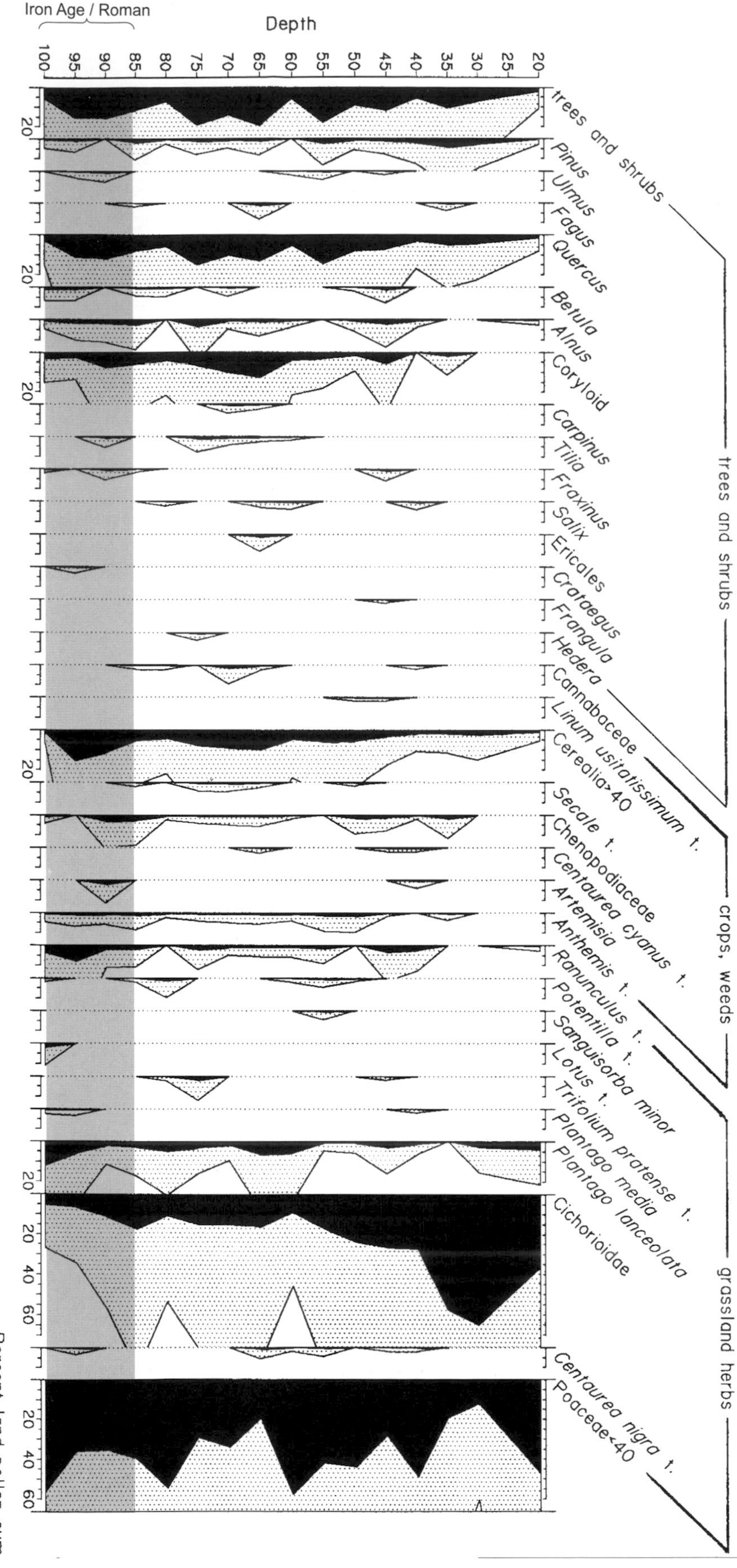

Fig. 18.10A Oxey Mead pollen diagram with: trees and shrubs; dry land herbs from grassland; dry land herbs, crops and their weeds. The percentage curves are based on the sum of dry land pollen (black curves)

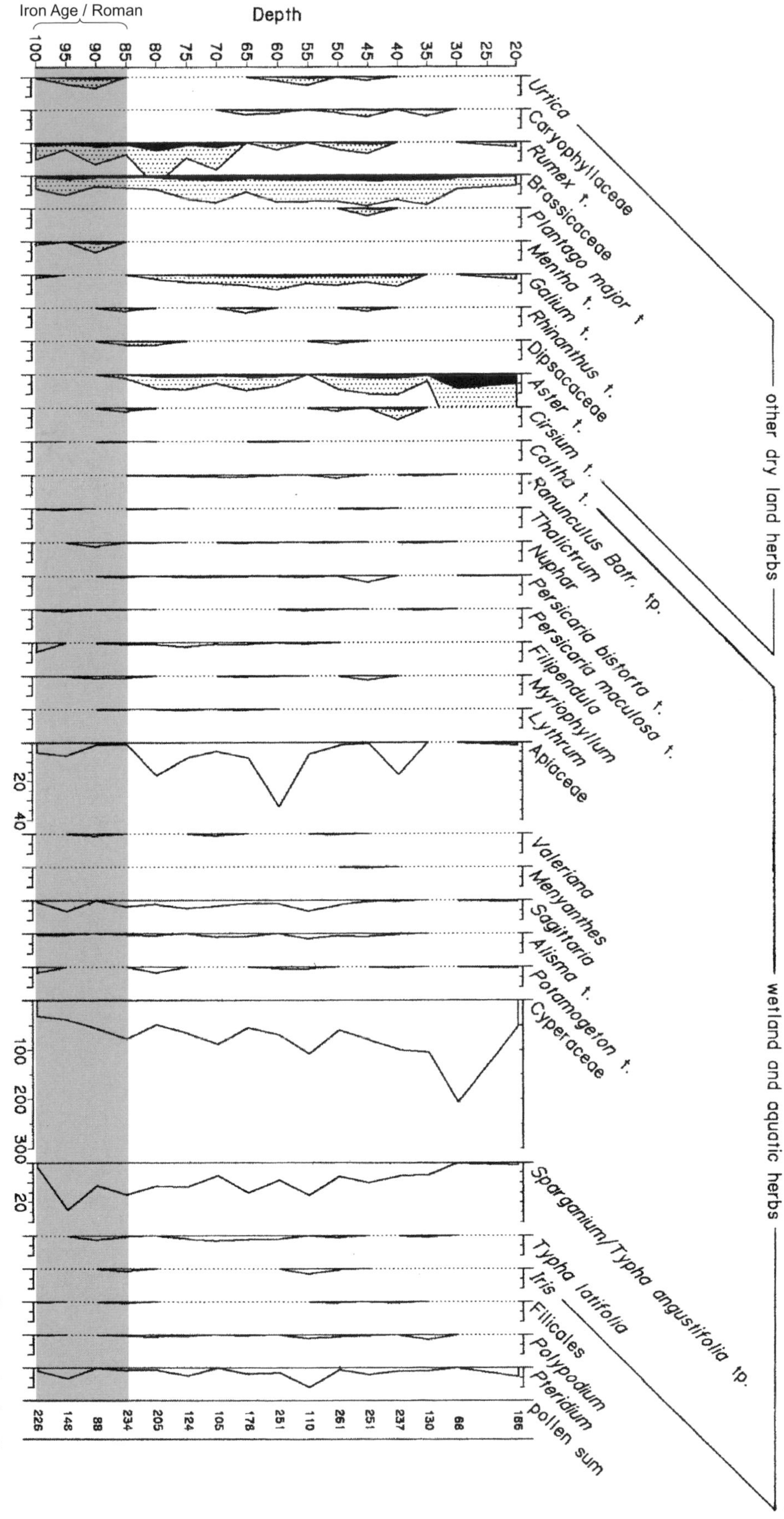

Fig. 18.10B Oxey Mead pollen diagram (continued): dry land herbs of various habitats; wetland herbs; aquatic herbs; spores. The percentage curves are based on the sum of dry land pollen (black curves). White curves are those taxa not in the pollen sum, as percentages of pollen sum.

below). Trees generally leave rather a poor macrofossil record, so pollen usually provides most evidence. Some charcoal was mainly of *Quercus* (oak), *Corylus/Alnus* (hazel or alder) and Rosaceae (Pelling, above). The first two correspond to the most abundant tree and shrub pollen types. Pollen is more easily transported and tends to reflect the whole region as well as the locality, so what woodland or scrub there was probably grew some distance away from the site.

The low tree and shrub pollen counts suggests that this landscape, which had already been substantially cleared of woodland by the early prehistoric, remained an open occupied landscape during the Iron Age and Roman period. An interesting question is whether there is any sign of change at the end of the Roman period. The Yarnton diagram has a possible increase in *Fagus* (beech) and possibly of *Fraxinus* (ash) following the Roman part of the sequence. Both of these are trees which spread in secondary woodland.

Grassland

The best evidence of grassland comes from the pollen of a range of rather characteristic grassland herbs in the Yarnton diagram. These include *Sanguisorba officinalis* (greater burnet), *Lotus* tp. (birds foot trefoil), *Trifolium repens* and *T. pratense* (white and red clovers), *Plantago media* and *P. lanceolata* (hoary and ribwort plantains), *Centaurea scabiosa* and *C. nigra* (greater knapweed and knapweed). Although the pollen records of Poaceae <40 μm (grasses) and Cichorioidae (Compositae Liguliflorae) (composites including dandelions, hawkbits, etc) probably mainly represent grassland, taxa within these groups do grow in a range of other habitats too. A similar although smaller range is seen in the Oxey Mead pollen diagram.

Signs of damper fen grassland come from taxa such as *Ranunculus* tp. (buttercups, spearworts), *Thalictrum* (meadow rue), *Persicaria bistorta* tp. (bistort) and *Filipendula* (meadowsweet), probably with some of the large Cyperaceae (sedge) pollen record, in both the Yarnton and Oxey Mead diagrams.

There are a few corresponding indications of grassland from some of the fauna and macrofossil flora from Yarnton. Seed records of *Ranunculus acris* (meadow buttercup) and *Prunella vulgaris* (self-heal) have no corresponding pollen records, although the *Plantago media* (hoary plantain) seed corresponds with the pollen record. Dung beetles were present, an indication of the presence of grazing animals and therefore that some of the grassland may have been pasture. This lack of macrofossil evidence for grassland may reflect the filtering effect of dense waterside vegetation hindering the transfer of seeds and beetles from grasslands that were probably fairly close to the forming deposit. At Oxey Mead, the pollen also gives far more sign of a grassland flora than does the macrofossil record. Here *Centaurea* cf. *nigra* (knapweed) is present, corresponding to the pollen record, and the presence of *Leontodon* sp. (hawkbit) suggests what may be represented by the large Cichorioidae pollen record. The beetle records from Oxey Mead also provide evidence of grassland, beetles such as *Apion* and *Sitona* corresponding to pollen records of the weevils' food plants *Trifolium* (clover) and *Lotus* (birdsfoot trefoil), while *Gymnetron* species correspond to pollen records of its food plant *Plantago lanceolata*.

The predominance of pollen evidence of grassland suggests that the local drier landscape may have been mainly grassy, ranging from fen grassland typified by *Thalictrum* (rue) through to dry calcareous meadow with *Centaurea scabiosa* (greater knapweed). The large records of Poaceae (grasses) are probably the least good indicator of grassland, because grasses are found in almost every habitat type. Such grassland may have had some similarity to that still surviving in the flood meadow at Pixey Mead.

Arable land and crops – identification

A small amount of Cerealia-type pollen is present in this part of the Yarnton diagram, and rather more in the Oxey Mead diagram, and in both cases the records are greatest in the Iron Age and Roman parts of the diagrams (Figs 18.9A and 18.10A).These records do probably represent cereals, which were found charred in deposits on site (see Pelling and Stevens above), although there is still the possibility that some could have come from wild grasses with large pollen, such as *Glyceria*, which was also present (M Robinson pers. comm.).

The cereal pollen raises the question of how close to the excavated site the cornfields were. Crop storage, and especially processing, releases much cereal pollen. A third possible cereal pollen source is from straw used as fodder and bedding and reappearing as the dung of animal stock, so the cereal-type pollen records do not necessarily represent cornfields located close to the find site.

Possible crop weeds

Both pollen diagrams have records of Chenopodiaceae at the bottom, which could either indicate open cultivated soil, or wet mud. There are pollen records of *Anthemis* tp. (mayweed type) but there are no equivalent waterlogged macrofossils (*Anthemis cotula*, however, is a regular component of the charred plant remains at Yarnton). Crop weed communities were fairly undifferentiated in the early prehistoric period, and seem to have contained a number of plants associated with other types of vegetation today, such as plantains. Therefore it is not easy to identify the likely weeds in this part of the pollen diagrams. However, the cover of Roman alluvium and then medieval alluvium over the site must have come from open ground, such as ploughsoil, in the vicinity.

Wetland and aquatic plants

Aquatic and swamp vegetation is very well-represented in both pollen diagrams (Figs 18.9B and 18.10B), which include large amounts of Cyperaceae (sedges) and *Sparganium* tp. (bur-reed), together with Apiaceae (probably including *Oenanthe*, water dropwort), indicating vegetation typical of a channel edge and growing in the channel itself, as can be seen on Pixey Mead today. Further taxa which would grow in such habitats are *Sagittaria* (arrowhead), *Iris pseudacorus* (yellow flag) and *Typha latifolia* type (bulrush). This flora can be seen now with wetland plants growing on the banks of the river channels.

There is a large seed flora of wetland and aquatic plants (see Chapter 2, and Robinson below) which includes all the pollen types listed as aquatics in the Yarnton profile. The macrofossils provide some extra information on wetland herbs, so *Ranunculus* type can be seen to include both dry land (*R. parviflorus*) and marshland (*R. flammula*) taxa. The Brassicaceae record listed under dry land plants should have been moved to wetland, since all three macrofossil records belong here. The Apiaceae record mainly comes from *Oenanthe aquatica* (water dropwort) and other wetland and aquatic taxa. Pollen records of Cyperaceae probably correspond to macrofossils of *Schoenoplectus* (bulrush) and *Eleocharis* species (spike-rush) as well as species of *Carex* (sedge). There are pollen records of a number of additional taxa such as *Caltha* (kingcup), *Thalictrum* (meadow rue) and *Persicaria bistorta* (bistort), adding to the picture of damp fen grassland, The correspondence of pollen and seed flora is similar in the case of the Oxey Mead profile, except that *Filipendula* (meadowsweet) and *Sparganium* (bur-reed) are represented among the macrofossils here.

Comparison with other results (Fig. 18.11)

The results from Yarnton and Oxey Mead can be compared with pollen spectra from a number of sites, such as the Iron Age ditch samples at Farmoor analysed by Dimbleby (Lambrick and Robinson 1979, 81-3). They are dominated by Poaceae (grasses), Lactuceae (composites) and *Plantago lanceolata* (ribwort plantain), with small amounts of tree and herb pollen. Likewise, similar spectra were obtained from Port Meadow, Oxford (quoted in Lambrick and Robinson 1988, 66, 68) and Mingies Ditch (Allen and Robinson 1993, 164). These are typical spectra of an occupied landscape.

More natural sites such as Sidlings Copse (Day 1991; 1993; Preece and Day 1994) seem to show what was happening in the less intensively

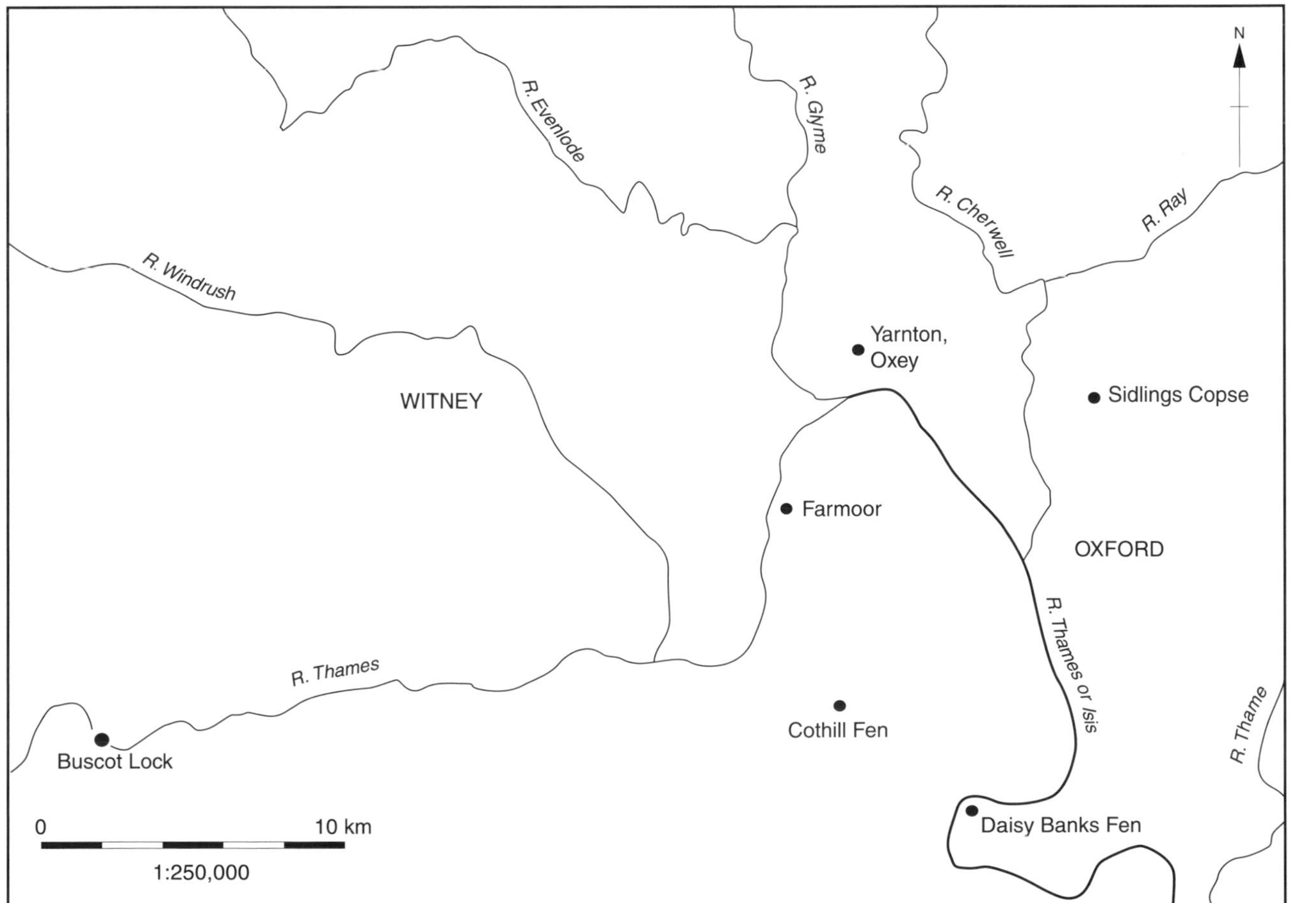

Fig. 18.11 Map showing location of pollen sites in the Upper Thames Valley

occupied parts of the landscape, although this site was not far from a Roman villa. There, much of the wildwood must have been cleared during prehistoric times, particularly during the Bronze Age, leaving some remaining woodland on the wet ground around the site, which was probably less suitable for clearing and settling, until *c* 1700 BP when it too was cleared. It is uncertain whether this reflects local activity around Sidlings Copse in the Roman period, or a more general phase of woodland clearance. Other sites such as Daisy Banks Fen and Spartum Fen and work still in progress are adding detail to the evidence for the formation of this landscape (Parker 1995a).

Conclusion

The Iron Age and Roman period was a time of broad continuity of occupation. The pattern of cultivated fields and meadows, together with remaining woodlands, which had been established in the prehistoric period, was to remain more or less the same through the succeeding ages (Dark and Dark 1998).

IRON AGE AND ROMAN PALAEOCHANNEL AND PALAEOENVIRONMENTAL SEQUENCES ON THE FLOODPLAIN *by Mark Robinson*

The palaeochannel sequence at Yarnton Floodplain A (Sites 1 and 2)

Introduction

The area under consideration as Yarnton Floodplain A comprised a block of Thames floodplain about 500 m x 500 m bounded by the Second Gravel Terrace to the north and the A40 to the south. The area was surrounded by a continuation of the floodplain on all sides except the north, Oxey Mead (see below) lying to the east. The main extant channel of the River Thames runs west-east a further 500 m south of the A40. A parallel minor palaeochannel of the Thames enters the area at the south-west corner and leaves through the eastern side. A second minor palaeochannel of the Thames enters the area at the north-west corner, runs along the edge of the gravel terrace and then joins the southern channel. Both channels left the main channel of the Thames further upstream and, below their junction, formed the channel which bounded the northern and eastern sides of Oxey Mead. This channel flowed into what is now the Wolvercote Mill Stream of the Thames. Above Floodplain A, the northern channel was joined by two minor valleys from the north. These valleys, which dissected the Second Gravel Terrace, were of Devensian origin but there were probably episodes of spring activity from water draining out of the gravels during the Flandrian (see also Chapter 2 above).

The floodplain to the south of the southern channel (Site 2) is low-lying and had a depth of up to 1.5 m of fine alluvial sediment over the floodplain gravel, but the area between the channels (Sites 1 and 3-4) comprised a 'gravel island' with only a thin covering of alluvium. In places, the alluvium on Sites 1 and 3-4 had been entirely mixed with the underlying deposits by modern ploughing. Excavation showed that there had been much human activity on Sites 1-4 prior to alluviation. Between the northern channel and the Second Gravel Terrace lies the Long Pond, which is probably a medieval fish pond.

As part of the excavation programme, a complete section was cut southwards from Site 1 (the gravel island) across the southern palaeochannel (for location see Fig. 11.39). Trenches were also extended into the channel from Sites 2 and 4. They showed evidence for a surprising degree of human activity associated with the channel, including a late Bronze Age timber and brushwood platform at Site 1. There were also at least four late prehistoric gravel causeways which ran across the channel from Sites 1 and 4 and a line of stakes along the channel edge in Site 1. The northern channel was trenched to the west of Floodplain A as part of the Floodplain B Project (see below), further causeways across it being discovered, while the combined palaeochannel was trenched downstream at Oxey Mead (see below).

Sequences of samples were analysed for macroscopic plant and invertebrate remains from the Bronze Age platform in Site 1, the palaeochannel sequence at Site 1 (sample Column 1; Tables 18.9-18.11) and the palaeochannel sequence in Section B of Site 2 (for location see Fig. 1.6). The locations of the Site 2 Section B samples are shown in Figure 11.12. Well-preserved organic remains were found in the Bronze Age platform and in the samples from the lower part of the palaeochannel sequences. Mollusc shells were present throughout the deposits. Full details of analyses, sample descriptions and techniques are given in the project archive. The species identifications relating to Section B are presented in Tables 18.12 to 18.17. A Coleopteran histogram is shown in Figure 18.12. Pollen analysis was also undertaken alongside the analysis of macroscopic remains from Section B of Site 2 and has been reported on by James Greig (above). Radiocarbon determinations were made on wood from the Bronze Age platform and seeds from the organic part of the sequence of Section B (see Chapter 13). Optically stimulated luminescence (OSL) dating was undertaken of the sediments of the palaeochannel in Site 1 and Section B (see Chapter 13). Dates have been given calibrated at 95% confidence.

The consideration of the evidence from the palaeochannel has been divided into two parts. The first is concerned with the processes of channel development and the palaeohydrology of the channel. The second deals with the evidence from the biological remains for the wider environment and for human activities.

The southern palaeochannel

Pre-Iron Age

The bed of the palaeochannel was possibly dry in the mid Holocene but the water table rose during the middle Bronze Age. By the late Bronze Age there was sufficient water in the channel to result in the preservation of the timber and brushwood platform on Site 1. An upright oak stake, which gave a radiocarbon date of 900-410 BC (OxA-3644), survived to a height of 57.40 m OD, suggesting that the channel held 0.80 m of water for much of the year. This would give a width to the water-filled channel of perhaps 20 m. The occurrence of shells of flowing water molluscs including *Bithynia tentaculata* and *Pisidium amnicum* in the sediments trapped by the platform suggested that there was at least a seasonal flow of water from the main river along the channel. The macroscopic plant remains showed that a full aquatic flora had developed, with seeds from submerged water plants such as *Zannichellia palustris* (horned pondweed) and reedswamp vegetation such as *Sagittaria sagittifolia* (arrow-head) and *Schoenoplectus lacustris* (bulrush).

Little sedimentation occurred in the channel during the late Bronze Age other than around the obstruction of the platform. However, an OSL date (866c) of 1440-860 BC was obtained on black organic shelly loam towards what would have been the southern edge of the channel in Site 1. The channel would have been very shallow at this point and the bed almost flat. Emergent vegetation probably impeded the flow of water and the initial sedimentation resulted in the narrowing of the channel.

Early to middle Iron Age

At least four gravel causeways believed to be of early or middle Iron Age date were constructed across the southern palaeochannel in the area under consideration. They rested directly on the gravel in the centre of the channel bed, pre-dating any accumulation of fine sediment. The sandy gravel of all the causeways contained numerous shells of aquatic molluscs such as *Bithynia tentaculata* and *Pisidium amnicum*, suggesting that the material for their construction had been derived from the channel bed rather than the terrace gravels. The causeways did not, however, block the channel and they seem to have served more as ford surfaces rather than dry crossings. Indeed, the biological evidence suggested that the southern channel was part of a permanent stable channel system carrying flowing water.

At some stage after the middle Bronze Age but before the end of the middle Iron Age, clean water flooding occurred over the low-lying area of floodplain of Site 2, depositing shells of aquatic molluscs but little sediment in archaeological features. This gave way to alluviation in the middle Iron Age, organic alluvial sediment filling the top of an archaeological feature on Site 2 giving a radiocarbon date of 400-160 BC (OxA-6616), while a date of 50 BC-AD 130 (OxA-6618) was obtained from the earliest alluvial sediment on the gravel surface of the floodplain itself (see Chapter 13). Relatively little fine sediment of this date seems to have accumulated in the channel.

Late Iron Age to Roman

Extensive alluviation occurred on the lower part of the floodplain (Site 2) from the late Iron Age onwards. Initially, flood levels did not reach the higher ground of the 'gravel island' to the north (Sites 1, 3 and 4) but during the later Roman period these areas also experienced alluviation. Substantial sedimentation occurred in the palaeochannel.

Initially, very organic sediments accumulated at Section B and an OSL date of 130 BC-AD 230 (957a) was obtained for 0.28-0.42 m. This gave way to sedimentation with a higher clay content in which organic remains were still preserved, an OSL date of 160 BC-AD 140 (957b) being obtained from 0.43-0.50 m and radiocarbon dates of AD 130-430 (OxA-7362) and AD 250-540 (OxA-7361) being given by waterlogged seeds from 0.50-0.62 m.

More organic sediments at sample Column 1 were also followed by sediments with a higher clay content, an OSL date of AD 40-360 (866b) being obtained for the latter deposit at 0.53-0.63 m. In this sequence, however, sedimentation continued above the level of permanent waterlogging in the Roman period, an OSL date of AD 140-440 (866a) being obtained for inorganic grey clay at 0.71-0.83 m.

The Roman alluviation would have had a substantial influence on the drainage pattern of the floodplain, with the low-lying parts tending to be levelled up to a height more similar to that of the remainder. Although much sediment was deposited in the southern channel, this did not occur evenly, possibly as a result of the gravel causeways crossing the channel bed. The channel certainly performed a drainage function at times of flood. The plant and invertebrate remains from throughout the Roman part of the sequence in Section B suggested a channel with a well-developed reedswamp but at least a seasonal flow of water. In Column 1, sample 0.71-0.83 m contained shells of riverine molluscs such as *Bithynia tentaculata* but the absence of waterlogged organic remains suggested that there could have been episodes when the bed of the channel there was dry. It is possible that the channel was reduced in dry summers during the late Roman period to little more than a series of discontinuous pools.

After the end of the Roman period, the organic content of the sediments accumulating at Section B rose. This would suggest a reduction in the sediment load carried in suspension by the water and thus a decrease in alluviation. A radiocarbon date of AD 560-690 (OxA-7363) and an OSL date of AD 680-920 (957c) were given by sample 0.62-0.75 m from Section B (Hey 2004, 258-9).

Table 18.9 Waterlogged seeds from Yarnton Floodplain A Site 1 palaeochannel.

	Sample		*Palaeochannel Column 1*		
	Height (m.)	*0.33-0.43*	*0.43-0.53*	*0.53-0.63*	*0.63-0.71*
	Sample weight (kg.)	*0.5*	*0.5*	*0.5*	*0.5*
RANUNCULACEAE					
Ranunculus cf. *repens* L.	creeping buttercup	3	-	2	1
R. S. *Batrachium* sp.	water crowfoot	69	57	34	26
CRUCIFERAE					
Barbarea vulgaris R. Br.	yellow rocket	2	1	-	-
Nasturtium officinale R. Br.	water-cress	-	-	1	-
VIOLACEAE					
Viola S. *Viola* sp.	violet	-	-	-	1
CARYOPHYLLACEAE					
Cerastium cf. *fontanum* Baum.	mouse-ear chickweed	-	1	-	-
Myosoton aquaticum (L.) Moen.	water chickweed	-	1	-	-
Stellaria cf. *palustris* Retz.	marsh stitchwort	-	-	1	-
PORTULACACEAE					
Montia fontana L. ssp. *chondrosperma* (Fen.) Walt.	blinks	-	1	-	-
CHENOPODIACEAE					
Atriplex sp.	orache	-	-	1	-
LINACEAE					
Linum catharticum L.	fairy flax	1	-	-	-
ROSACEAE					
Potentilla anserina L.	silverweed	1	1	-	1
P. reptans L.	creeping cinquefoil	1	-	-	-
Aphanes arvensis L.	parsley-piert	1	-	-	-
LYTHRACEAE					
Lythrum salicaria L.	purple loosestrife	-	-	1	-
HIPPURIDACEAE					
Hippuris vulgaris L.	mare's tail	-	1	1	-
CALLITRICHACEAE					
Callitriche sp.	starwort	-	3	-	-
UMBELLIFERAE					
Sium latifolium L.	water parsnip	-	-	-	2
Oenanthe aquatica gp.	water-dropwort	26	17	6	5
Aethusa cynapium L.	fool's parsley	-	-	-	-
POLYGONACEAE					
Polygonum persicaria L.	red shank	1	1	2	1
Rumex conglomeratus Mur.	sharp dock	1	-	3	1
R. maritimus L.	golden dock	11	7	8	4
Rumex spp. (not *maritimus*)	dock	1	2	2	-
URTICACEAE					
Urtica dioica L.	stinging nettle	6	2	2	1
MENYANTHACEAE					
Nymphoides peltata (Gml.) Kz.	fringed water-lily	-	-	2	3
BORAGINACEAE					
Myosotis sp.	forget-me-not	-	6	-	2
SOLANACEAE					
Solanum dulcamara L.	woody nightshade	-	-	1	-
SCROPHULARIACEAE					
Veronica Sect. *Beccabunga* sp.	water speedwell	60	1	20	-
LABIATAE					
Mentha cf. *aquatica* L.	water mint	54	37	48	34
Lycopus europaeus L.	gipsywort	1	-	1	-
Prunella vulgaris L.	selfheal	-	-	1	-
PLANTAGINACEAE					
Plantago major L.	great plantain	-	1	-	-
RUBIACEAE					
Galium sp. (not *aparine*)	bedstraw	1	-	1	-
COMPOSITAE					

Table 18.9 Waterlogged seeds from Yarnton Floodplain A Site 1 palaeochannel (continued).

	Sample	*Palaeochannel Column 1*			
	Height (m.)	*0.33-0.43*	*0.43-0.53*	*0.53-0.63*	*0.63-0.71*
	Sample weight (kg.)	*0.5*	*0.5*	*0.5*	*0.5*
cf. *Cirsium* sp.	thistle	-	1	-	-
Onopordum acanthium L.	cotton thistle	-	-	1	-
Sonchus asper (L.) Hill	sow-thistle	-	1	-	-
ALISMATACEAE					
Alisma sp.	water-plantain	90	87	49	45
Sagittaria sagittifolia L.	arrow-head	22	22	45	57
POTAMOGETONACEAE					
Potamogeton sp.	pondweed	2	4	17	16
ZANNICHELLIACEAE					
Zannichellia palustris L.	horned pondweed	42	61	50	54
JUNCACEAE					
Juncus effusus gp.	tussock rush	-	-	10	40
J. bufonius gp.	toad rush	160	60	30	40
J. articulatus gp.	rush	30	10	40	20
Juncus spp.	rush	30	10	-	10
IRIDACEAE					
Iris pseudacorus L.	yellow flag	-	2	-	1
SPARGANIACEAE					
Spargunium sp.	bur-reed	1	-	1	-
CYPERACEAE					
Eleocharis palustris (L.) R. & S. ssp. *palustris*	spike rush	-	-	-	-
Eleocharis cf. *palustris* (L.) R. & S. ssp. *vulgaris* Walt.	spike rush	6	9	3	1
Scirpus sylvaticus L.	wood club-rush	-	-	-	-
Schoenoplectus lacustris (L.) Pal.	bulrush	12	21	6	4
Carex spp.	sedge	8	4	3	1
GRAMINEAE					
Glyceria sp.	reed-grass	1	1	6	14
Gramineae indeterminate	grass	3	3	-	1
Total		647	436	399	386

Table 8.10 Other waterlogged plant remains from Yarnton Floodplain A Site 1 palaeochannel.

	Palaeochannel Column 1					
	Sample					
	Height (m.)		*0.33-0.43*	*0.43-0.53*	*0.53-0.63*	*0.63-0.71*
	Sample weight (kg.)		*0.5*	*0.5*	*0.5*	*0.5*
Bryophyta indeterminate	- stem with leaves	moss	+	-	-	-
Chara sp.	- oospores	stonewort	1193	539	1392	441

+ present

Summary of the Iron Age and Roman palaeohydrological and alluvial sequence

During the late Bronze Age, the southern channel held water throughout the year and there was at least a seasonal flow of water from the main channel of the Thames. However, there was little sedimentation. At some stage clean-water flooding was occurring over low-lying areas of floodplain; this gave way during the middle Iron Age to alluviation. More general organic sedimentation occurred in the channel, which was fully active. Extensive clay alluviation took place in the Roman period and eventually reached even the highest areas of the floodplain. This sedimentation began to fill the palaeochannel, which was perhaps reduced to a series of pools by the end of this period. In the early to middle Saxon period, the river carried a reduced sediment load, with organic accumulation in the palaeochannel and the development of a palaeosol on the alluvium at Oxey Mead (see below). The sequence entirely fits into the pattern which has already been established for the Upper Thames Valley (Robinson 1992b, 200-2).

Table 18.11 Mollusca from Yarnton Floodplain A Site 1 palaeochannel.

Palaeochannel Column 1				
Sample				
Height (m.)	*0.33-0.43*	*0.43-0.53*	*0.53-0.63*	*0.63-0.71*
Sample weight (kg.)	*0.5*	*0.5*	*0.5*	*0.5*
GASTROPODA				
Valvata cristata Müll.	12	5	11	23
V. piscinalis (Müll.)	-	2	9	15
Bithynia tentaculata (L.)	1	1	6	10
Bithynia spp.	34	47	125	136
Carychium sp.	1	-	-	-
Lymnaea truncatula (Müll.)	4	1	2	5
L. stagnalis (L.)	-	-	1	-
L. peregra (Müll.)	1	-	-	3
Lymnaea sp.	-	-	1	-
Planorbis planorbis (L.)	-	1	1	2
P. carinatus (Mill.)	-	-	1	-
Anisus leucostoma (Mill.)	1	-	-	-
A. vortex (L.)	-	-	-	1
Bathyomphalus contortus (L.)	4	-	-	2
Gyraulus albus (Müll.)	2	2	8	7
Armiger crista L.	8	1	4	8
Acroloxus lacustris (L.)	1	-	-	-
Succinea or *Oxyloma* sp.	-	1	1	-
BIVALVIA				
Sphaerium corneum (L.)	1	-	2	1
Sphaerium sp.	-	1	2	1
Pisidium amnicum (Müll.)	-	-	-	-
Pisidium spp.	4	3	12	9
Total	74	65	186	223

The Iron Age to Roman environmental sequence

The organic sequence provided by the sections through the palaeochannel on Site 1 at the timber platform and on Site 2 at Section B extended from the late Bronze Age to the Saxon period. Although there were changes in channel activity and sedimentation over this time span, while the floodplain became much wetter, the fauna and flora remained essentially characteristic of a river flowing through a landscape with much grassland. Therefore changes will be highlighted rather than the environment described in full for each period.

Early to middle Iron Age

The organic sediments at the bottom of Section B on Site 2 which filled a hollow in the channel bed (samples -0.10-0, 0-0.12) were of uncertain date, other than that they pre-dated an Iron Age deposit. They gave similar results to those from the lowest organic sediments of Column 1, which were late Bronze Age in date.

The organic sediments from column 1 between the Bronze Age and Roman optical dates (samples 0.33-0.43, 0.43-0.53) probably spanned the Iron Age and perhaps continued into the Roman period. The lowest general organic sediment in Section B (sample 0.12-0.28) was also possibly of Iron Age date.

The occurrence of shells of flowing water molluscs such as *Bithynia tentaculata* in the platform sediments has already been noted. However, the insects were mostly species of stagnant or slowly moving water such as *Helophorus* cf. *brevipalpis* and *Ochthebius minimus*. Beetles of well-oxygenated flowing water from the family Elmidae were absent.

Seeds of submerged-leaved aquatic plants, particularly *Ranunculus* S. *Batrachium* sp. (water crowfoot) and *Zannichellia palustris* (horned pondweed) were abundant. There was also evidence for a well-developed reedswamp, with many seeds of *Oenanthe aquatica* gp. (water-dropwort), *Sagittaria sagittifolia* (arrow-head), *Schoenoplectus lacustris* (bulrush) and *Glyceria* sp. (reed-grass) (Table 18.12).

The phytophagous Coleoptera likewise gave strong evidence for reedswamp vegetation with the following Chrysomelidae (leaf beetles) being dependant on the following plants:

Donacia dentata on *Sagittaria sagittifolia* (arrow-head) and *Alisma* sp. (water plantain)

D. impressa on *Schoenoplectus lacustris* (bulrush)

Prasocuris phellandrii on aquatic Umbelliferae esp. *Oenanthe aquatica* (water-dropwort)

Aphthona nonstriata on *Iris pseudacorus* (yellow flag)

In places, probably as a result of grazing pressure, the reedswamp had been replaced by shorter shallow water and marsh vegetation, including *Mentha* cf. *aquatica* (water mint), *Alisma* sp. (water plantain), *Juncus articulatus* (rush) and *Eleocharis palustris* (spike rush). There were also a few seeds from annual plants which possibly grew on waterside mud, such as *Myosoton aquaticum* (water chickweed), *Chenopodium album* (fat hen) and *Polygonum persicaria* (red shank). The insect fauna included species of wet bankside habitats. The staphylinid *Micropeplus caelatus*, which no longer occurs in England, was also identified.

The floodplain seems largely to have been cleared of trees before the end of the Bronze Age. Wood and tree-dependent Coleoptera (Fig. 18.12, Species Group 4) were absent and there was little evidence for scrub. Grassland probably predominated on the floodplain. Chafer and elaterid beetles with larvae that feed on the roots of grassland herbs, such as *Phyllopertha horticola* (Species Group 11), made up around 3% of the terrestrial Coleoptera. Scarabaeoid dung beetles which occur in the droppings of domestic animals on grassland (Species Group 2) comprised around 6% of the terrestrial Coleoptera. They were almost all from the genus *Aphodius*. Their abundance was sufficient to show the presence of domestic animals, although it suggests only a low intensity of grazing. The majority of the seeds were from aquatic and waterside plants, but there was also a small grassland element of species such as *Ranunculus* cf. *repens*

Table 18.12 Waterlogged seeds from Yarnton Floodplain A Site 2 section B.

		Section B					
Sample		*1*	*2*	*3*	*4*	*5*	*6*
Height (m.)		*-0.10 - 0*	*0 - 0.12*	*0.12 - 0.28*	*0.28 - 0.42*	*0.43 - 0.50*	*0.50 - 0.62*
Sample weight (kg.)		*1.0*	*1.0*	*0.5*	*0.5*	*0.5*	*0.5*
RANUNCULACEAE							
Ranunculus cf. *acris* L.	meadow buttercup	-	1	-	3	2	-
R. cf. *repens* L.	creeping buttercup	1	12	2	7	2	2
R. parviflorus L.	small-flowered buttercup	-	-	-	1	-	-
R. flammula L.	lesser spearwort	-	-	1	-	-	-
R. S. *Batrachium* sp.	water crowfoot	38	139	98	74	77	26
NYMPHAEACEAE							
Nuphar lutea (L.) Sm.	yellow water-lily	-	-		1	1	- -
PAPAVERACEAE							
Papaver rhoeas tp.	poppy	-	1	-	-	-	-
FUMARIACEAE							
Fumaria sp.	fumitory	-	1	-		-	- -
CRUCIFERAE							
Brassica rapa L. ssp. *sylvestris* (L.) Jan.	wild turnip	-	1	-	-	-	-
Rorippa cf. *palustris* (L.) Bes.	marsh yellow cress	-	1	-	-	1	-
Nasturtium officinale R. Br.	water-cress	-	1	3	1	9	3
N. microphyllum (Boenn.) Reich.	water-cress	-	-	-	-	-	-
VIOLACEAE							
Viola S. *Viola* sp.	violet	-	-	1	-	-	-
CARYOPHYLLACEAE							
Lychnis flos-cuculi L.	ragged robin	-	-	-	-	1	-
Cerastium cf. *fontanum* Baum.	mouse-ear chickweed	1	1	-	-	4	-
Myosoton aquaticum (L.) Moen.	water chickweed	-	1	-	1	-	-
Stellaria media gp.	chickweed	1	2	-	-	-	-
Arenaria sp.	pearlwort	-	-	10	-	-	-
PORTULACACEAE							
Montia fontana L. ssp. *chondrosperma* (Fen.) Walt.	blinks	-	2	-	1	1	-
CHENOPODIACEAE							
Chenopodium album L.	fat-hen	11	11	1	2	1	-
C. ficifolium Sm.	fig-leaved goosefoot	2	1	-	-	-	-
C. rubrum gp.	red goosefoot	-	-	1	-	-	-
Atriplex sp.	orache	-	1	1	-	-	-
ROSACEAE							
Potentilla anserina L.	silverweed	-	2	3	5	2	1
P. erecta (L.) Räu.	tormentil	-	-	-	-	1	-
P. reptans L.	creeping cinquefoil	-	1	-	1	1	-
Aphanes arvensis L.	parsley-piert	-	3	3	-	1	-
A. microcarpa (B.& R.) Roth.	slender parsley-piert	-	1	1	1	-	-
HIPPURIDACEAE							
Hippuris vulgaris L.	mare's tail	-	-	1	1	2	2
CALLITRICHACEAE							
Callitriche sp.	starwort	-	2	2	-	-	-
UMBELLIFERAE							
Hydrocotyle vulgaris L.	marsh pennywort	-	-	1	-	-	-
Sium latifolium L.	water parsnip	-	-	-	-	1	-
Berula erecta (Huds.) Cov.	narrow-leaved parsnip	-	-	2	2	1	-
Oenanthe aquatica gp.	water-dropwort	10	37	46	54	10	5
Apium nodiflorum (L.) Lag.	fool's watercress	2	-	2	2	5	-
POLYGONACEAE							
Polygonum aviculare agg.	knotgrass	-	1	-	-	-	-
P. persicaria L.	red shank	-	2	-	1	3	1
P. lapathifolium L.	pale persicaria	-	2	2	-	-	-
Rumex conglomeratus Mur.	sharp dock	-	1	2	2	3	2
R. maritimus L.	golden dock	1	-	3	8	3	2
Rumex spp. (not *maritimus*)	dock	1	3	3	1	1	-

Table 18.12 Waterlogged seeds from Yarnton Floodplain A Site 2 section B (continued).

URTICACEAE							
Urtica urens L.	small nettle	-	-	-	1	1	-
U. dioica L.	stinging nettle	-	1	3	4	11	5
MENYANTHACEAE							
Menyanthes trifoliata L.	bogbean	-	-	-	-	-	-
Nymphoides peltata (Gml.) Kz.	fringed water-lily	-	-	-	-	1	2
BORAGINACEAE							
Myosotis sp.	forget-me-not	-	1	3	2	1	-
SOLANACEAE							
Solanum dulcamara L.	woody nightshade	-	-	-	1	1	-
SCROPHULARIACEAE							
Veronica Sect. *Beccabunga* sp.	water speedwell	20	10	40	52	1	-
LABIATAE							
Mentha cf. *aquatica* L.	water mint	4	25	36	54	66	38
Lycopus europaeus L.	gipsywort	-	1	2	2	-	-
Prunella vulgaris L.	selfheal	1	1	1	1	-	-
Ballota nigra L.	black horehound	-	-	-	1	-	-
PLANTAGINACEAE							
Plantago major L.	great plantain	-	3	2	-	1	-
RUBIACEAE							
Galium sp. (not *aparine*)	bedstraw	-	-	1	1	-	-
CAPRIFOLIACEAE							
Sambucus nigra L.	elder	-	2	-	-	-	-
VALERIANACEAE							
Valerianella dentata (L.) Pol.	corn salad	1	-	-	-	1	-
COMPOSITAE							
Senecio cf. *aquaticus* Hill	marsh ragwort	-	1	1	1	-	-
Carduus sp.	thistle	-	1	-	2	-	-
cf. *Cirsium* sp.	thistle	1	1	1	-	-	-
Leontodon sp.	hawkbit	-	1	-	-	-	-
Sonchus asper (L.) Hill	sow-thistle	-	-	-	3	-	-
ALISMATACEAE							
Alisma sp.	water-plantain	6	10	62	106	29	17
Sagittaria sagittifolia L.	arrow-head	3	9	19	38	81	20
POTAMOGETONACEAE							
Potamogeton sp.	pondweed	2	26	17	6	49	11
ZANNICHELLIACEAE							
Zannichellia palustris L.	horned pondweed	10	79	37	27	94	49
JUNCACEAE							
Juncus effusus gp.	tussock rush	40	10	10	10	20	20
J. bufonius gp.	toad rush	20	173	124	263	11	61
J. articulatus gp.	rush	30	110	30	111	-	30
Juncus sp.	rush	30	60	30	30	10	20
Luzula sp.	woodrush	-	-	-	-	1	-
IRIDACEAE							
Iris pseudacorus L.	yellow flag	-	-	-	-	1	-
CYPERACEAE							
Eleocharis palustris (L.) R. & S. ssp. *palustris*	spike rush	1	3	-	-	-	-
Eleocharis cf. *palustris* (L.) R. & S. ssp. *vulgaris* Walt.	spike rush	2	11	7	7	13	3
Schoenoplectus lacustris (L.) Pal.	bulrush	6	37	28	47	48	6
Isolepis setacea (L.) R.Br.	bristle club-rush	-	-	-	-	1	-
Carex spp.	sedge	2	9	2	8	3	1
GRAMINEAE							
Glyceria sp.	reed-grass	3	8	6	4	3	1
Gramineae indeterminate	grass	-	1	-	-	-	-
Total		250	825	652	951	580	328

+ present

(creeping buttercup), *Potentilla anserina* (silverweed) and *Rumex conglomeratus* (sharp dock), all of which would readily have grown in pasture on the floodplain. Many of the beetles can occur in grassland habitats.

Late Iron Age to Roman

The top two organic samples in Column 1 (samples 0.53-0.63, 0.63-0.71) had a higher clay content. OSL dates suggested that they spanned the Roman period. They showed a general decline in seed concentration but *Nymphoides peltata* (fringed water-lily) appeared for the first time. *Glyceria* sp. (reed-grass) seems to have expanded amongst the reedswamp vegetation at the expense of *Schoenoplectus lacustris* (bulrush).

An Iron Age to Roman OSL date was obtained on the top part of the first general organic deposit (sample 0.28-0.42) at Section B. The layer of slightly organic alluvial clay which overlay it (samples 0.43-0.50 and 0.50-0.62) was dated by OSL and radiocarbon determinations to the Roman period. There were few differences between sample 0.28-0.42 and the underlying sample, although a substantial rise in numbers of the snail *Lymnaea truncatula* was perhaps a reflection of increasingly muddy conditions alongside the channel. The samples from the organic clay (samples 0.43-0.50, 0.50-0.62) showed greater differences, although mostly to their aquatic flora and fauna. There was a major decline in seed numbers of *Oenanthe aquatica* gp. (water dropwort), *Veronica* Sect. *Beccabunga* sp. (water speedwell) and *Juncus* spp. (rushes) whereas seed numbers of *Sagittaria sagittifolia* (arrow-head), *Potamogeton* sp. (pondweed) and *Zannichellia palustris* (horned pondweed) rose. Some similarity can be seen with Section 1 with the appearance of *N. peltata* (fringed water-lily) and, in sample 0.50-0.62, a decline in *S. lacustris* (bulrush). No obvious explanation can be found for these changes in the aquatic and marginal flora (Table 18.12).

Aquatic Coleoptera declined by 50% from sample 0.28-0.42 to the overlying organic clay layer (samples 0.43-0.50, 0.50-0.62) (Fig. 18.12, Species Group 1; Table 18.15). The decline was particularly evident amongst two small water beetles characteristic of stagnant water, *Helophorus* cf. *brevipalpis* and *Ochthebius minimus*. It is possible that the increased flow of water and major flood episodes in winter resulted in conditions that were unfavourable for these species to build up high population levels. However, despite the increased sediment load carried by the water, there was still a slight presence of beetles from the family Elmidae, with single individuals of *Normandia nitens* and *Oulimnius* sp. These species require clean, well-oxygenated flowing water.

The Coleoptera from the late Iron Age and Roman samples from Section B (Table 18.15) suggested that the landscape remained open and there was still much grassland. Scarabaeoid dung beetles of Species Group 2 comprised 11% of the terrestrial Coleoptera (Fig. 18.12). There was a single example of the dung beetle *Aphodius varians*, a species which is now extinct in Britain (Jessop 1986, 25), from sample 0.43-0.50. Otherwise the

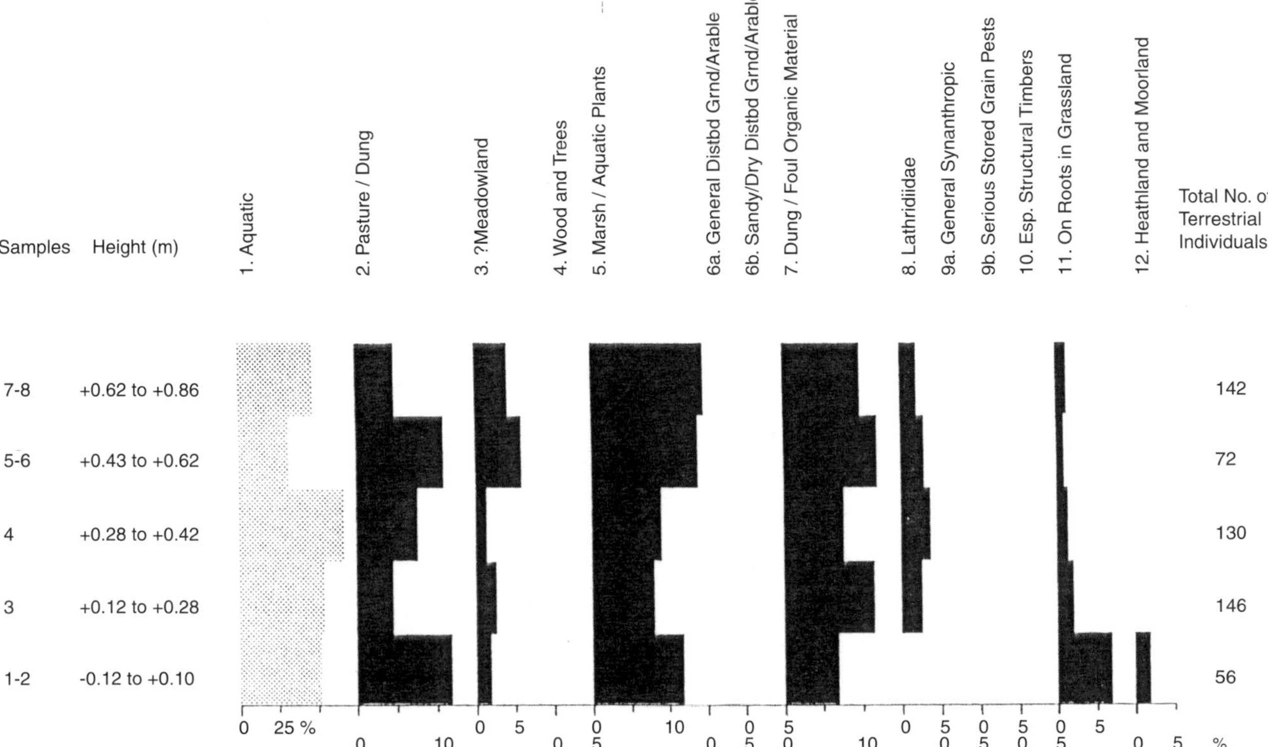

Fig. 18.12 Percentages of species groups of Coleoptera by habitat type: Yarnton Floodplain A Site 2 Section B

Table 18.13 Other waterlogged plant remains from Yarnton Floodplain A Site 2 section B.

			Section B					
Sample			1	2	3	4	5	6
Height (m.)			-0.10 - 0	0 - 0.12	0.12 - 0.28	0.28 - 0.42	0.43 - 0.50	0.50 - 0.62
Sample weight (kg.)			1.0	1.0	0.5	0.5	0.5	0.5
Alnus glutinosa (L.) Gaert.	- female catkin	alder	1	-	-	-	-	-
Bryophyta indeterminate	- stem with leaves	moss	-	+	+	-	+	+
Bud scale			-	3	-	-	-	-
Chara sp.	- oospores	stonewort	1101	261	425	234	592	575
Triticum spelta L.	- glume	spelt wheat	-	-	-	-	1	-

Table 18.14 Wood from Yarnton Floodplain A Site 2 section B.

Section B							
Sample		1	2	3	4	5	6
Height (m.)		-0.10 - 0	0 - 0.12	0.12 - 0.28	0.28 - 0.42	0.43 - 0.50	0.50 - 0.62
Sample weight (kg.)		1.0	1.0	0.5	0.5	0.5	0.5
Pomoideae indeterminate	hawthorn, apple etc.	-	1	-	-	-	-
Quercus sp.	oak	3	-	-	-	1	-

dung beetles from the Roman samples, indeed from all the samples from Section B, were species which are still common in the area, including *Colobopterus erraticus*, *Aphodius contaminatus* and *A.* cf. *sphacelatus*. Members of the genus *Onthophagus* were absent. Although the percentage of weevils which are favoured by hay meadow conditions (Species Group 3) rose from 1.5% of the terrestrial Coleoptera in sample 0.28-0.42 to 6% in the samples from the organic clay layer above, they did not even approach the number of scarabaeoid dung beetles. The assemblages from the organic clay layer were also rather small. Therefore, in the absence of supporting evidence it cannot be taken as showing a transition to hay meadow.

Unfortunately only small proportions of seeds from Column 1 and Section B were from plants likely to have been growing much beyond the margin of the channel. The seeds of *Potentilla anserina* (silverweed) and *Rumex conglomeratus* (sharp dock) would be appropriate to marshy pasture. *Mentha* cf. *aquatica* (water mint) and *Eleocharis* S. *Palustris* sp. (spike rush) could also have been members of this community, although they could also have been growing along the edge of the channel. There were insufficient seeds of *Juncus inflexus* gp. (tussock rush) to suggest rush pasture.

The excavation showed that there was an early Roman arable field a little to the north of the palaeochannel, on the higher area of floodplain (see Chapter 11). In the late Roman period the field bank was overwhelmed by alluvial clay, which formed a thin covering over the field. This clay was continuous with the organic clay layer of Roman date in the palaeochannel at Section B. There were very few seeds of annual weeds of drier ground from either of the sequences. The assemblages were too small to give any reliable evidence for the field falling out of cultivation. Carabidae (ground beetles) which flourish under arable conditions (Species Group 6) were absent. The only crop remain was a glume of *Triticum spelta* (spelt wheat) from Section B, sample 0.43-0.50. The Coleoptera gave no indication of the proximity of any settlement.

The palaeoenvironmental sequence of Yarnton Floodplain A Site 2

Introduction

Site 2 of Yarnton Floodplain A comprised an excavation of a low-lying block of floodplain 60 m wide and running 100 m south-east from the Bronze Age margin of the southern palaeochannel. The surface of the floodplain gravel sloped gently towards the palaeochannel and was covered by up to 1.5 m of alluvial clay. The gravel surface beneath a palaeosol sealed by the clay had resulted from the northerly migration of the palaeochannel eroding into a higher area of floodplain during the Late Devensian. Indeed much of the floodplain surface represented the bed of this very broad and shallow channel when it ceased to be active towards the end of the Late Devensian. Between 0.2 m and 0.4 m of alluvial sandy silt to clay loam was deposited over the gravel at the close of the Late Devensian. This weathered to form a circum-neutral brown earth soil.

The excavation showed that there had been a long sequence of prehistoric activity on Site 2 before the substantial alluviation of the Roman period. There was a scatter of Neolithic flints along the palaeochannel edge and a late Neolithic penannular

Table 18.15 Coleoptera from Yarnton Floodplain A Site 2 section B.

	Section B						
Sample	1	2	3	4	5	6	
Height (m.)	-0.10 - 0	0 - 0.12	0.12 - 0.28	0.28 - 0.42	0.43 - 0.50	0.50 -0.62	*Species Group*
Sample weight (kg.)	1.0	1.0	4.0	4.0	0.5	0.5	
CARABIDAE							
Carabus monilis F.	-	-	1	-	-	-	
Nebria brevicollis (F.)	-	1	-	-	-	-	
Notiophilus sp.	-	1	-	-	-	-	
Elaphrus riparius (L.)	-	-	-	1	-	-	
Loricera pilicornis (F.)	-	1	1	1	-	-	
Dyschirius globosuss (Hbst.)	-	1	2	3	2	-	
Clivina collaris (Hbst.) or *fossor* (L.)	1	-	-	-	-	-	
Trechus obtusus Er. or *quadristriatus* (Schr.)	-	-	2	1	-	1	
Bembidion dentellum (Thun.)	-	-	-	1	-	-	
B. semipunctatum Don.	-	-	1	-	-	-	
B. gilvipes Sturm	-	1	-	-	2	-	
B. assimile Gyl.	-	-	1	-	-	-	
B. doris (Pz.)	-	-	1	1	-	-	
B. biguttatum (F.)	-	-	2	4	-	1	
B. guttula (F.)	-	1	1	1	1	-	
Pterostichus cupreus (L.)	-	-	-	1	-	-	
P. gracilis (Dej.)	-	-	-	1	1	-	
P. vernalis (Pz.)	-	-	-	1	-	-	
P. cupreus (L.) or *versicolor* (Sturm)	-	1	2	-	-	-	
Agonum marginatum (L.)	-	1	1	1	-	-	
A. muelleri (Hbst.)	-	-	1	1	-	-	
Agonum sp.	-	-		1	-	-	
Amara sp.	-	-	-	-	-	1	
Harpalus S. *Harpalus* sp.	-	-	1	-	-	-	
Acupalpus dorsalis (F.)	-	-	-	-	1	-	
A. exiguus Dej.	-	-	-	1	-	-	
Odacantha melanura (L.)	-	-	-	1	-	-	
HALIPLIDAE							
Haliplus sp.	1	-	1	3	-	-	1
NOTERIDAE							
Noterus clavicornis (Deg.)	-	-	1	-	-	-	1
DYTISCIDAE							
Hygrotus inaequalis (F.)	-	-	2	1	-	-	1
H. versicolor (Schal.)	-	2	4	4	-	-	1
Coelambus impressopunctatus (Schal.)	-	-	-	-	-	-	1
Hydroporus sp.	-	1	1	5	-	-	1
Graptodytes pictus (F.)	-	1	-	-	-	-	1
Porhydrus lineatus (F.)	-	-	2	1	-	-	1
Agabus bipustulatus (L.)	-	-	2	1	-	-	1
Agabus sp. (not *bipustulatus*)	-	1	3	3	1	-	1
Rhantus sp.	-	-	1	1	-	-	1
Colymbetes fuscus (L.)	-	-	1	1	-	-	1
Dytiscus sp.	-	-	-	1	-	-	1
GYRINIDAE							
Gyrinus sp.	-	-	1	1	1	-	1
HYDROPHILIDAE							
Georissus crenulatus (Ros.)	-	1	-	-	-	-	1
Helophorus aquaticus (L.)	-	-	4	1	1	-	1
H. grandis Ill.	-	-	1	-	-	-	1
H. aquaticus (L.) or *grandis* Ill.	1	1	-	2	1	-	1
Helophorus sp. (*brevipalpis* size)	1	4	13	19	3	3	1
Sphaeridium bipustulatum F.	-	-	-	-	1	-	
S. lunatum F. or *scarabaeoides* (L.)	-	1	-	-	-	-	

Table 18.15 Coleoptera from Yarnton Floodplain A Site 2 section B (continued).

	Section B						
Sample	*1*	*2*	*3*	*4*	*5*	*6*	
Height (m.)	*-0.10 - 0*	*0 - 0.12*	*0.12 - 0.28*	*0.28 - 0.42*	*0.43 - 0.50*	*0.50 -0.62*	*Species Group*
Sample weight (kg.)	*1.0*	*1.0*	*4.0*	*4.0*	*0.5*	*0.5*	
Cercyon analis (Pk.)	-	-	1	-	-	1	7
C. haemorrhoidalis (F.)	-	-	2	1	-	-	7
C. cf. *sternalis* Sharp	-	-	3	3	-	-	7
C. cf. *tristis* (Ill.)	-	2	3	3	4	1	7
C. ustulatus (Preys.)	-	-	1	-	-	-	7
Cercyon sp.	-	1	1	-	-	1	7
Megasternum obscurum (Marsh.)	-	1	3	2	-	-	7
Hydrobius fuscipes (L.)	-	3	3	2	2	-	1
Anacaena bipustulata (Marsh.) or *limbata* (F.)	-	-	1	1	-	-	1
Laccobius sp.	-	-	1	1	-	-	1
Enochrus sp.	-	-	1	1	-	-	1
HISTERIDAE							
Hister bissexstriatus F.	-	1	-	1	1	-	
HYDRAENIDAE							
Ochthebius cf. *bicolon* Germ.	-	-	-	1	-	-	1
O. minimus (F.)	-	-	12	6	2	-	1
O. cf. *minimus* (F.)	2	7	17	22	2	3	1
Hydraena riparia Kug.	-	-	1	1	-	-	1
Limnebius papposus Muls.	-	1	1	2	-	-	1
LEIODIDAE							
Choleva or *Catops* sp.	-	-	1	-	-	-	
STAPHYLINIDAE							
Micropeplus caelatus Er.	-	-	1	-	-	-	
Lesteva sp.	-	-	-	2	-	-	
Carpelimus bilineatus Step.	-	-	3	2	-	-	
C. cf. *corticinus* (Grav.)	-	1	3	2	1	1	
C. cf. *rivularis* (Mots.)	-	-	1	-	-	-	
Platystethus cornutus gp.	-	1	2	-	1	-	
P. nitens (Sahl.)	-	1	-	-	-	-	
P. nodifrons (Man.)	-	-	15	18	6	1	
Anotylus rugosus (F.)	-	-	3	1	1	1	7
A. sculpturatus gp.	-	-	-	-	-	1	7
Stenus spp.	-	3	7	5	3	1	
Paederus riparius (L.)	-	-	1	1	-	-	
Xantholinus longiventris Heer	-	-	-	3	1	-	
X. linearis (Ol.) or *longiventris* Heer	-	-	3	-	-	-	
Philonthus spp.	-	1	3	2	1	2	
Gabrius sp.	-	1	1	1	-	-	
Mycetoporus sp.	-	-	2	-	-	-	
Tachyporus sp.	-	1	2	-	-	-	
Tachinus sp.	-	-	1	-	1	-	
Aleocharinae indeterminate	-	1	8	8	1	1	
PSELAPHIDAE							
Pselaphidae indeterminate	-	-	1	1	-	-	
GEOTRUPIDAE							
Geotrupes sp.	-	-	-	1	1	-	2
SCARABAEIDAE							
Colobopterus erraticus (L.)	1	-	1	1	1	-	2
Aphodius ater (Deg.)	-	-	-	1	-	-	2
A. contaminatus (Hbst.)	-	-	3	3	-	-	2
A. cf. *foetens* (F.)	-	-	-	-	1	-	2
A. granarius (L.)	-	-	-	-	1	-	2
A. luridus (F.)	-	-	-	-	1	-	2
A. pusillus (Hbst.)	1	-	-	-	-	-	2
A. cf. *sphacelatus* (Pz.)	1	-	2	3	1	-	2

Table 18.15 Coleoptera from Yarnton Floodplain A Site 2 section B (continued).

	Section B						
Sample	*1*	*2*	*3*	*4*	*5*	*6*	
Height (m.)	*-0.10 - 0*	*0 - 0.12*	*0.12 - 0.28*	*0.28 - 0.42*	*0.43 - 0.50*	*0.50 -0.62*	*Species Group*
Sample weight (kg.)	*1.0*	*1.0*	*4.0*	*4.0*	*0.5*	*0.5*	
A. varians Duft.	-	-	-	-	1	-	2
Aphodius sp.	-	4	1	1	-	1	2
Hoplia philanthus (Fues.)	-	1	-	-	-	-	11
Phyllopertha horticola (L.)	-	1	2	2	-	-	11
SCIRTIDAE							
cf. *Cyphon* sp.	-	-	-	1	-	-	
HETEROCERIDAE							
Heterocerus sp.	-	-	2	3	1	-	
DRYOPIDAE							
Dryops sp.	-	2	2	6	1	1	1
ELMIDAE							
Normandia nitens (Müll.)	-	-	-	-	1	-	1
Oulimnius sp.	-	-	3	-	1	-	1
ELATERIDAE							
Agrypnus murinus (L.)	-	1	-	-	-	-	11
Agriotes lineatus (L.)	-	-	1	-	-	-	11
Agriotes sp.	-	1	-	-	1	-	11
CANTHARIDAE							
Cantharis sp.	-	1	1	-	-	-	
Silis ruficollis (F.)	-	-	1	-	-	-	
CRYPTOPHAGIDAE							
Atomaria sp.	-	-	1	2	-	-	
PHALACRIDAE							
Phalacrus cf. *corruscus* (Pz.)	-	1	-	-	-	-	
Olibrus sp.	-	-	-	1	-	-	
CORYLOPHIDAE							
Corylophus cassidoides (Marsh.)	-	-	1	-	-	-	
COCCINELLIDAE							
Scymnus frontalis (F.)	1	-	-	-	-	-	
Coccinella septempunctata Marsh.	1	-	-	1	-	-	
LATHRIDIIDAE							
Enicmus transversus (Ol.)	-	-	-	1	-	-	8
Corticaria punctata Marsh.	-	-	1	-	-	-	8
Corticariinae indeterminate	-	-	3	4	2	-	8
CHRYSOMELIDAE							
Donacia cinerea Hbst.	-	-	1	-	-	-	5
D. clavipes F.	-	-	-	-	1	-	5
D. dentata Hoppe	1	1	-	1	-	-	5
D. impressa Pk.	2	1	1	2	1	1	5
D. marginata Hoppe	-	-	-	-	-	1	5
D. simplex F.	-	-	1	3	1	-	5
D. versicolorea (Brahm)	-	-	1	1	-	-	5
Donacia or *Plateumaris* sp.	-	-	1	-	-	-	5
Chrysolina polita (L.)	-	-	-	1	1	-	
Prasocuris phellandrii (L.)	-	-	2	1	-	-	5
Phaedon sp. (not *tumidulus*)	-	-	1	1	-	-	
Phyllotreta atra (F.)	-	-	2	1	-	-	
P. nigripes (F.)	-	1	-	1	-	-	
P. vittula Redt.			1	1	-	-	
Aphthona nonstriata (Gz.)	-	-	2	-	1	-	5
Longitarsus spp.	1	2	3	4	1	-	
Epitrix pubescens (Koch.)	-	-	-	1	-	-	
Chaetocnema concinna (Marsh.)	1	1	3	1	-	-	
Chaetocnema sp. (not *concinna*)	-	-	1	-	-	-	

Table 18.15 Coleoptera from Yarnton Floodplain A Site 2 section B (continued).

	Section B						
Sample	*1*	*2*	*3*	*4*	*5*	*6*	
Height (m.)	*-0.10 - 0*	*0 - 0.12*	*0.12 - 0.28*	*0.28 - 0.42*	*0.43 - 0.50*	*0.50 -0.62*	*Species Group*
Sample weight (kg.)	*1.0*	*1.0*	*4.0*	*4.0*	*0.5*	*0.5*	
APIONIDAE							
Apion malvae (F.)	-	-	1	-	-	-	
Apion spp.	-	-	1	2	2	1	3
CURCULIONIDAE							
Strophosomus faber (Hbst.)	-	-	1	-	-	-	
Sitona lepidus Gyl.	-	-	1	-	-	-	3
S. cf. *sulcifrons* (Thun.)	-	-	1	-	-	-	3
S. suturalis Step.	-	-	1	-	-	-	3
Sitona sp.	-	1	-	-	1	-	3
Hypera punctata (F.)	-	-	1	-	-	-	
Bagous sp.	-	-	-	-	1	-	5
Grypus equiseti (F.)	-	-	1	-	-	-	
Orthochaetes setiger (Beck)	-	-	1	-	-	-	
Notaris acridulus (L.)	-	2	2	2	1	1	5
Thryogenes cf. *festucae* (Hbst.)	-	-	1	1	-	-	5
Micrelus ericae (Gyl.)	-	1	-	-	-	-	12
Ceutorhynchus floralis (Pk.)	-	-	1	-	-	-	
Ceuthorhynchinae indeterminate	-	-	1	2	1	-	
Anthonomus cf. *rubi* (Hbst.)	-	-	-	1	-	-	
Tychius sp.	-	-	1	-	-	-	
Miccotrogus picirostris (F.)	-	1	1	-	-	-	
Gymnetron labile (Hbst.)	-	-	1	-	-	-	
G. villosulum Gyl.	-	-	-	1	1	-	5
Total	16	69	225	217	69	26	

enclosure on the bankside. A pair of middle Bronze Age ditches created an avenue running down to the palaeochannel, enclosing the penannular ditch. Subsequently, a gravel causeway was laid within the avenue, also running to the edge of the palaeochannel. Series of alignments of small pits and slots of probable Iron Age date ran towards the channel. Finally, dendritic ditches were dug flanking the causeway in the Iron Age (see Chapter 11 above).

Samples were analysed for macroscopic plant and invertebrate remains from a wide range of contexts on Site 2. The species identifications are presented in Tables 18.18 to 18.22 except for the charred plant remains, which are the subject of a separate report (Robinson in Hey *et al.* forthcoming). Radiocarbon determinations were made on organic remains from the earliest alluvial sediments. The consideration of the evidence from Site 2 begins with features of late Bronze Age or Iron Age date.

The gravel causeway

The soil sealed beneath the causeway was the brown earth soil of the floodplain which occurs beneath the alluvium. Although the soil was circumneutral, the calcareous gravel of the causeway had a buffering effect and a few mollusc shells were found in sample 0-0.02 m from the soil surface beneath the northern end of the causeway. Although this was the closest point of the causeway to the palaeochannel, shells of marsh and aquatic species were absent. The shells identified included *Trichia hispida* gp., which occurs in a wide range of terrestrial habitats, and *Vallonia costata*, a species of dry open habitats. This suggests that the causeway was constructed when this part of the floodplain was at least seasonally dry. The sandy gravel of the causeway (Table 18.22) contained numerous shells of flowing-water molluscs, suggesting that it had been dug from the bed of one of the channels.

The later eastern ditch

At some stage during the late Bronze Age or Iron Age, a shallow ditch was dug along the eastern side of the avenue on a somewhat different alignment from the middle Bronze Age ditch and its recuts. The lower layer in the ditch where it was sampled (context 2710) was brown sandy loam which appeared to have been derived from the weathering of the soil through which the ditch had been cut. The two mollusc samples from this deposit (sample -0.30 to -0.40 m and sample -0.13 to -0.19 m) contained many shells of aquatic molluscs. The most abundant were from *Lymnaea truncatula*, a stagnant water to amphibious species which was

Table 18.16 Other insects from Yarnton Floodplain A Site 2 section B.

		Section B					
	Sample	*1*	*2*	*3*	*4*	*5*	*6*
	Height (m.)	*-0.10 - 0*	*0 - 0.12*	*0.12 - 0.28*	*0.28 - 0.42*	*0.43 - 0.50*	*0.50 - 0.62*
	Sample weight (kg.)	*1.0*	*1.0*	*4.0*	*4.0*	*0.5*	*0.5*
ODONATA							
Odonata indeterminate	- adult	-	1	1	-	-	-
HEMIPTERA- HETEROPTERA							
Drymus sylvaticus (F.)		1	-	1	-	-	-
Saldula S. *Saldula* sp.	-	1	2	-	-	-	-
HOMOPTERA							
Aphrodes flavostriatus (Don.)	-	-	-	1	-	-	
Aphidoidea indeterminate	-	-	1	-	2	-	
Homoptera indeterminate	-	-	1	-	-	-	
TRICHOPTERA							
Orthotrichia sp	- case	-	1	1	-	-	-
Trichoptera indeterminate	- larva	3	21	9	8	43	5
Trichoptera indeterminate	- case	8	31	16	13	72	10
HYMENOPTERA							
Lasius flavus gp.	- worker	-	-	2	-	-	-
Hymenoptera indeterminate	- adult head	-	1	15	6	1	-
DIPTERA							
Chironomidae indeterminate	- larva	-	+	+	+	+	+
Dilophus febrilis (L.) or *femoratus* (Meig.)		-	1	5	-	1	1
Bibionidae indeterminate		1	-	-	-	-	-
Diptera indeterminate	- puparium	-	-	1	2	2	-
Diptera indeterminate	- adult	-	5	1	2	1	1

\+ present

probably living in the ditch. However, there were also shells of the flowing-water aquatic species *Valvata cristata* and *Bithynia tentaculata* which would have been unable to live in the ditch. Their occurrence implies flooding from the river but with little alluvial sediment being deposited. There were some badly-preserved seeds of aquatic plants from sample -0.13 to -0.19 m) including *Ranunculus* S. *Batrachium* sp. (water crowfoot), *Mentha* cf. *aquatica* (water mint) and *Zannichellia palustris* (horned pondweed). This suggested that the water table continued to rise.

The small pits and slots

The small pits and slots presented particular problems of interpretation. They were features within the floodplain soil which had not been cut into the underlying gravel. They could be discerned easily on the excavated surface of the soil because they were still hollow at the onset of alluviation in the middle Iron Age. However, they were extremely difficult to detect as features below the alluvial interface with the soil because their pre-alluvial fills were so similar to the floodplain soil. There were only a few example where it proved possible to excavate convincingly a pre-alluvial fill to any of them. In most instances the pre-alluvial fill was entirely devoid of biological remains. However, a slot which joined the later eastern ditch had a lower fill (context 2709) that appeared continuous with context 2710. This was sampled in the same section as samples -0.30 to -0.40 m and -0.13 to -0.19 m. It contained a similar range of shells to those from samples -0.30 to -0.40 m and -0.13 to -0.19 m, although in lower concentration. *Lymnaea truncatula* predominated but the flowing-water species *Valvata costata* and *Bithynia* sp. were again present. A single, badly preserved waterlogged seed of *Mentha* sp. was also found.

The results showed that at least some of these curious features were open to receive clean floodwaters before the onset of alluviation. They also possibly had the snail *Lymnaea truncatula* living in temporary puddles of water in the bottom of them. The slots were certainly not cultivation trenches that were immediately filled in. If they held timbers, they must have remained open after the timbers decayed or were removed, but it seems unlikely that the pits and slots held timbers that were allowed to decay *in situ*. The survival of badly preserved organic remains in the samples from the later eastern ditch and the slot which related to it, which were from a relatively high area of Site 2, would suggest that some trace of decayed wood might have been expected from the features on the lowest part of the site if they had held timbers. There was not even the mineral staining which sometimes results from the decay of organic material. Some of

Table 18.17 Mollusca from Yarnton Floodplain A Site 2 section B.

	Section B					
Sample	*1*	*2*	*3*	*4*	*5*	*6*
Height (m.)	*-0.10 - 0*	*0 - 0.12*	*0.12 - 0.28*	*0.28 - 0.42*	*0.43 - 0.50*	*0.50 - 0.62*
Sample weight (kg.)	*0.5*	*0.5*	*0.5*	*0.5*	*0.5*	*0.5*
GASTROPODA						
V. cristata Müll.	43	74	72	39	27	10
V. piscinalis (Müll.)	22	24	23	3	32	6
Bithynia tentaculata (L.)	4	4	3	4	13	-
Bithynia spp.	51	124	124	82	177	44
Carychium sp.	-	-	-	1	2	-
Physa fontinalis (L.)	1	-	-	1	1	-
Lymnaea truncatula (Müll.)	9	18	12	2	33	4
L. palustris (Müll.)	1	5	2	2	2	-
L. stagnalis (L.)	-	1	-	-	-	-
L. peregra (Müll.)	9	4	6	2	5	-
Lymnaea sp.	-	3	2	3	-	-
Planorbis planorbis (L.)	-	2	2	3	1	2
P. carinatus (Mill.)	-	-	1	-	-	-
Anisus leucostoma (Mill.)	-	1	2	2	1	1
A. vortex (L.)	-	-	-	-	2	-
Bathyomphalus contortus (L.)	-	-	1	2	1	-
Gyraulus albus (Müll.)	29	37	14	3	11	1
Armiger crista L.	6	8	11	2	6	3
Hippeutis complanatus (L.)	4	2	5	-	-	-
Acroloxus lacustris (L.)	-	-	-	1	-	-
Succinea or *Oxyloma* sp.	2	-	1	3	-	-
Vallonia sp.	-	1	2	-	1	-
Limax or *Deroceras* sp.	-	-	-	1	1	-
Arianta arbustorum (L.) or *Cepaea* sp.	-	-	1	-	-	-
BIVALVIA						
Sphaerium corneum (L.)	1	5	2	2	2	-
Sphaerium sp.	5	4	3	2	2	1
Pisidium amnicum (Müll.)	-	-	-	-	1	-
Pisidium spp.	37	59	53	10	24	5
Total	224	376	342	170	345	77

the pits and slots were, however, sufficiently shallow that they need not even have been cut features. They could have resulted from earthworm action undermining timbers which had been placed on the ground.

The most simple explanation for these features is that they were cut and left open for ceremonial purposes at a time of increasing wetness on the site shortly before the onset of alluviation.

The earliest overbank alluviation

During the middle Iron Age, alluviation began to occur on the lowest areas of Site 2. It filled the top 0.12 m of the northern end of the western middle Bronze Age ditch, filled some of the slots which cut the ditch and sealed the scatter of Neolithic flints alongside the palaeochannel. The water table of the site rose sufficiently that organic remains were preserved in the sediment so it was possible for radiocarbon determinations to be made on seeds extracted from them. A date of 440-160 BC (OxA-6616) was obtained on sample 0 to 0.12 m and 50 BC-AD 130 (OxA-6618) on a sample from the alluvium over the Neolithic flints (calibrated, 95% confidence).

The macroscopic plant and invertebrate remains from these sediments very much reflected their riverine origin. Shells of flowing-water molluscs were well-represented, including *Valvata cristata, V. piscinalis, Bithynia tentaculata* and *Pisidium amnicum* (Table 18.22). Seeds of aquatic plants were numerous and included *Ranunculus* S. *Batrachium* sp. (water crowfoot), *Nymphoides peltata* (fringed water-lily), *Sagittaria sagittifolia* (arrow-head), *Potamogeton* sp. (pondweed), *Zannichellia palustris* (horned pondweed) and *Schoenoplectus lacustris* (bulrush) (Table 18.18).

The water beetles were mostly species of slowly moving to stagnant water such as *Agabus bipustulatus, Colymbetes fuscus* and *Hydrobius fuscipes*. However, larval cases of the flowing-water caddis *Ithytrichia* sp. were present. Phytophagous

Table 18.18 Waterlogged seeds from Yarnton Floodplain A Site 2.

		Alluvium over OGS	Causeway	Late east ditch & slot ditch 2710	alluvium in top	Dendritic feature
Depth (m.)				-0.13 to -0.19		
Sample weight (kg.)		1.0	0.5	1.0	1.0	1.0
RANUNCULACEAE						
Ranunculus cf. *acris* L.	meadow buttercup	-	1	-	-	-
R. cf. *repens* L.	creeping buttercup	4	-	-	-	-
R. parviflorus L.	small-flowered buttercup	1	-	-	-	-
R. flammula L.	lesser spearwort	-	-	1	-	-
R. S. *Batrachium* sp.	water crowfoot	51	2	2	-	-
CRUCIFERAE						
Brassica rapa L. ssp. *sylvestris* (L.) Jan.	wild turnip	1	-	-	-	-
Rorippa cf. *palustris* (L.) Bes.	marsh yellow cress	1	-	-	-	-
Nasturtium officinale R. Br.	water cress	1	-	-	-	-
Cruciferae indeterminate		-	-	-	-	-
CARYOPHYLLACEAE						
Stellaria media gp.	chickweed	1	-	-	-	-
CHENOPODIACEAE						
Chenopodium album L.	fat hen	-	1	-	-	-
HIPPURIDACEAE						
Hippuris vulgaris L.	mare's tail	2	-	-	-	-
CALLITRICHACEAE						
Callitriche sp.	starwort	3	2	-	-	-
UMBELLIFERAE						
Berula erecta (Huds.) Cov.	narrow-leaved water-parsnip	1	-	-	-	-
Oenanthe aquatica gp.	water-dropwort	5		-	-	-
POLYGONACEAE						
Polygonum persicaria L.	red shank	1	1	-	-	-
P. lapathifolium L.	pale persicaria	-	1	-	-	-
Rumex acetosella agg.		1	-	-	-	-
R. hydrolapathum Huds.	water dock	1	-	-	-	-
R. maritimus L.	golden dock	2	-	-	-	-
Rumex spp. (not *maritimus*)	dock	5	-	-	-	-
URTICACEAE						
Urtica dioica L.	stinging nettle	3	-	1	-	-
BORAGINACEAE						
Myosotis sp.	forget-me-not	1	-	-	-	-
LABIATAE						
Mentha cf. *aquatica* L.	water mint	41	-	8	1	3
Glechoma hederacea L.	ground-ivy	1	-	-	-	-
COMPOSITAE						
cf. *Cirsium* sp.	thistle	2	-	-	-	-
Sonchus palustris L.	marsh sow-thistle	1	-	-	-	-
S. asper (L.) Hill	sow-thistle	1	-	-	-	-
ALISMATACEAE						
Alisma sp.	water-plantain	13	1	2	-	2
Sagittaria sagittifolia L.	arrow-head	28	1	-	-	-
POTAMOGETONACEAE						
Potamogeton sp.	pondweed	46	8	1	-	-
ZANNICHELLIACEAE						
Zannichellia palustris L.	horned pondweed	44	5	3	-	3
JUNCACEAE						
Juncus effusus gp.	tussock rush	20	-	-	-	98
J. bufonius gp.	toad rush	41	-	-	-	10
J. articulatus gp.	rush	1	-	-	-	8
Juncus spp.	rush	-	-	-	-	58
IRIDACEAE						
Iris pseudacorus L.	yellow flag	1	-	-	-	-
CYPERACEAE						
Eleocharis cf. *palustris* (L.) R. & S. ssp. *vulgaris* Walt.	spike rush	6	1	-	-	1
Schoenoplectus lacustris (L.) Pal.	bulrush	17	4	1	-	-
Carex spp.	sedge	4	4	6	-	-
GRAMINEAE						
Glyceria sp.	reed-grass	2	9	-	-	1
Gramineae indeterminate	grass	-	-	1	-	-
Total		354	41	26	1	184

OGS = old ground surface

Table 18.19 Other waterlogged plant material from Yarnton Floodplain A Site 2.

			Alluvium	Causeway ditch 2710	Late east ditch & slot alluvium in top		Dendritic feature
Depth (m.)				-0.13 to -0.19			
Sample weight (kg.)		1.0	0.5	1.0	1.0	1.0	
Bryophyta indeterminate	- stem with leaves	moss	-	-	+	-	-
Bud scales			1	-	-	-	-
Chara sp.	- oospores	stonewort	2756	213	12	10	54
Leaf abscission pad			1	-	-	-	-

Table 18.20 Coleoptera from Yarnton Floodplain A Site 2.

	Late east ditch & slot ditch 2710	 alluvium in top	
Depth (m.)			
Sample weight (kg.)	1.0	1.0	*Species Group*
CARABIDAE			
Dyschirius globosus (Hbst.)	-	1	
Bembidion biguttatum (F.)	-	1	
B. lunulatum (Fouc.)	-	1	
Pterostichus nigrita (Pk.)	-	1	
P. cupreus (L.) or *versicolor* (Sturm)	-	1	
Agonum muelleri (Hbst.)	-	1	
DYTISCIDAE			
Dytiscus sp.	-	1	1
HYDROPHILIDAE			
Helophorus cf. *obscurus* Muls.	-	1	1
Helophorus sp. (*brevipalpis* size)	-	-	1
Cercyon cf. *tristis* (Ill.)	-	1	7
Megasternum obscurum (Marsh.)	1	1	7
Hydrobius fuscipes (L.)	-	1	1
HYDRAENIDAE			
Ochthebius cf. *minimus* (F.)	-	2	1
STAPHYLINIDAE			
Anotylus rugosus (F.)	1	-	7
Xantholinus angularis Gang.	1	-	
Philonthus spp.	-	2	
Gabrius sp.	-	3	
Tachyporus sp.	-	1	
Aleocharinae indeterminate	-	1	
SCARABAEIDAE			
Aphodius sp.	-	1	2
Phyllopertha horticola (L.)	1	-	11
DRYOPIDAE			
Dryops sp.	1	1	1
ELATERIDAE			
Agrypnus murinus (L.)	1	-	11
CHRYSOMELIDAE			
Donacia impressa Pk.	-	1	5
APIONIDAE			
Apion spp.	1	-	3
CURCULIONIDAE			
Sitona cf. *lineatus* (L.)	1	-	3
Bagous sp.	-	1	5
Total	8	24	

Table 18.21 Other Insects from Yarnton Floodplain A Site 2.

		East Bronze Age ditch	Alluvium over old ground surface
Depth (m.)			
Sample weight (kg.)		1.0	1.0
HYMENOPTERA			
Hymenoptera indeterminate	- adult head	-	2
DIPTERA			
Diptera indeterminate	- adult	-	1

Coleoptera which feed on marsh and aquatic plants (Species Group 5) comprised over 13% of the terrestrial Coleoptera (Table 18.20). Many of them feed on the larger plants of reedswamp communities, including:

Donacia clavipes on *Phragmites australis* (common reed)

D. dentata on *Alisma* sp. (water plantain) and *Sagittaria sagittifolia* (arrow-head)

D. impressa on *Schoenoplectus lacustris* (bulrush)

Prasocuris phellandrii on *Oenanthe aquatica* (water dropwort) and other aquatic Umbelliferae

Aphthona nonstriata on *Iris pseudacorus* (yellow flag)

All these plants were represented by their seeds. The aquatic mollusc, plant and insect remains from the early overbank alluvium were also identified from the two columns of samples through the palaeochannel.

As the water table rose, so the water-filled area of the channel would have become wider and it is possible that the reedswamp extended over some of the lowest-lying archaeological features. However, the grazing of domestic animals could have confined the taller aquatic plants to deeper water. There were also seeds from smaller plants of shallow water and marsh habitats such as *Mentha* cf. *aquatica* (water mint) and *Alisma* sp. (water plantain) which were perhaps growing along the edge of the channel. The amphibious to stagnant water snail *Lymnaea truncatula*, which flourishes in such habitats, was well-represented in both samples.

Table 18.22 Mollusca from Yarnton Floodplain A Site 2.

	Alluvium over OGS	*Causeway*		*Late east ditch & slot*			*Dendritic feature*	
		OGS below	*causeway*	*ditch 2710*	*ditch 2710*	*slot 2709*	*alluvium*	*in top*
Depth (m.)				*-0.30 to -0.40*	*-0.13 to -0.19*			
Sample weight (kg.)	*1.0*	*0.5*	*0.5*	*1.0*	*1.0*	*1.0*	*1.0*	*1.0*
GASTROPODA								
V. cristata Müll.	15	-	22	30	22	5	58	-
V. piscinalis (Müll.)	15	-	-	-	-	-	-	-
Bithynia tentaculata (L.)	9	-	9	4	3	-	16	3
Bithynia spp.	58	-	42	20	22	1	28	3
Carychium sp.	-	-	-	-	-	-	1	-
Lymnaea truncatula (Müll.)	34	-	32	113	36	14	17	1
L. stagnalis (L.)	1	-	-	-	-	-	-	-
L. palustris (Müll.)	-	-	3	1	3	-	4	-
L. peregra (Müll.)	8	-	6	5		1	28	2
Lymnaea sp.	12	-	8	16	3	1	15	1
Planorbis planorbis (L.)	1	-	1	6	3	-	30	-
P. carinatus (Mill.)	3	-	-	-	-	-	1	-
Anisus leucostoma (Mill.)	1	-	-	2	-	-	10	-
A. vortex (L.)	-	-	-	-	-	-	1	-
Bathyomphalus contortus (L.)	1	-	2	1	2	-	2	-
Gyraulus albus (Müll.)	7	-	6	4	2	-	22	-
Armiger crista L.	9	-	3	13	14	5	64	-
Hippeutis complanatus (L.)	-	-	1	-	1	-	-	-
Succinea or *Oxyloma* sp.	2	-	3	10	-	2	-	-
Vallonia costata (Müll.)	-	1	-	-	-	-	-	-
Vallonia sp.	2	2	-	-	-	-	-	-
Limax or *Deroceras* sp.	1	1	1	-	-	-	-	-
Trichia hispida (L.) or *plebeia* (Drap.)	-	1	-	-	-	-	-	-
BIVALVIA								
Sphaerium corneum (L.)	1	-	-	-	-	-	-	-
Sphaerium sp.	3	-	6	-	1	-	2	-
Pisidium amnicum (Müll.)	1	-	-	-	-	-	-	-
Pisidium spp.	32	-	11	18	6	2	21	2
Total	216	5	156	243	118	31	320	12

OGS = old ground surface

The seeds of plants of drier grassland which grew on the site in the middle Bronze Age were largely absent. Grazing, however, continued and scarabaeoid dung beetles (Species Group 2) comprised 5% of the terrestrial Coleoptera. The Coleoptera, which were probably derived from a wider catchment than the seeds, ranged from species of marshy or waterside habitats such as *Blethisa multipunctata* and *Notaris acridulus* to beetles of grassland such as the weevils *Ceuthorhynchidius troglodytes* and *Gymnetron labile* which both feed on *Plantago lanceolata* (ribwort plantain).

The dendritic ditches

Flanking the gravel causeway was a pattern of irregular dendritic ditches which cut some of the enigmatic slots. Conditions on Site 2 were certainly becoming increasingly wet and it seems likely that the ditches were dug in response to problems with standing surface water after floods. They were filled with gleyed alluvial clay but with a lower organic content than the early overbank alluvium described above. There were inwash bands of sand from the causeway in the parts of the ditch system alongside the causeway itself. A sample of alluvium from the bottom of one of the deeper dendritic features (Tables 18.18 and 18.22) contained a few shells of flowing-water aquatic molluscs which had presumably been deposited from the river, and some badly preserved seeds, mostly of *Juncus* spp. (rushes). There were also many calcareous oospores of *Chara* sp. (stonewort), an aquatic algae. (Table 18.19).

The oak tree surrounded by a penannular ditch

When the alluvial clay was removed from Site 2 by mechanical excavator, tree roots were exposed *in situ* in the underlying soil within the penannular enclosure. They had been preserved by waterlogging. They were identified as *Quercus* sp. (oak). No other tree roots were found immediately beneath the alluvium on Site 2 (although roots of *Alnus gluti-*

nosa from the mid Flandrian woodland of the floodplain do survive at depth in the gravel). Oak trees will not grow roots into permanently waterlogged anaerobic sediments, so the remains were from a tree growing when waterlogging reached the surface of the soil in the Iron Age. The absence of roots in the soil elsewhere on Site 2 implies that trees had already been cleared from the site before the rise in water table that would have resulted in the preservation of their roots. The upper fill of the penannular enclosure ditch was alluvial sediment, so the monument would still have been a visible feature in the Iron Age. It is suggested that an isolated oak tree grew within the enclosure at some stage during the middle Iron Age.

General alluviation

Alluviation with clay sediment with a low organic content occurred over all of Site 2 from the later Iron Age and throughout the Roman period. The southern part of the later eastern ditch (sample 0 to -0.08 m) and the dendritic ditches became filled with this sediment and the whole site was levelled up, obscuring all traces of the prehistoric features. Details of subsequent alluviation were obtained from Section B (see above).

Summary of the Iron Age and Roman environmental sequence of Site 2

The low area of floodplain gravel represented by Site 2 was created by the migration of a channel northwards in the late Devensian. During the early Flandrian a soil developed from the Devensian sediments and the palaeochannel was dry. The channel had, however, become re-activated by the late Bronze Age, carrying a parallel stream of the Thames. The floodplain supported grassland. A gravel causeway was constructed along the avenue created by a pair of middle Bronze Age ditches which ran towards the palaeochannel, possibly in response to the increasing wetness of a rising water table, but there was no direct evidence of flooding. In the late Bronze Age or Iron Age a ditch was dug along the eastern side of the avenue. Alignments of slots and small pits also ran down to the edge of the channel. Their earliest sediments gave evidence of clean-water flooding. Subsequently, dendritic drainage ditches were dug alongside the causeway. All these features pointed at ceremonial activity directed towards the edge of the channel occurring on a site experiencing increasing flooding. The character of the flooding changed and alluvium began to be deposited over the lowest parts of the floodplain in the middle Iron Age. This was accompanied by a rise in water table such that these sediments remained waterlogged and the bed of the channel extended over the lowest-lying archaeological features. Finally, extensive clay alluviation from the later Iron Age onwards covered the entire site, obliterating the remaining archaeological features and beginning to fill the palaeochannel.

The palaeoenvironmental sequence of Yarnton Floodplain A Sites 1 and 3 and Floodplain B Sites 4, 4A, 4B and 5

Introduction

Sites 1 and 3 of Yarnton Floodplain A and Sites 4, 4a, 4b and 5 comprised a series of excavations of a relatively elevated block of floodplain up to 250 m wide, running 500 m along the north-west bank of a palaeochannel (the southern palaeochannel of earlier Floodplain A reports). The surface of the floodplain gravel sloped steeply down to the palaeochannel, which had a distinct edge. The palaeochannel had ceased to be active towards the end of the Late Devensian and the bed remained dry until the Bronze Age (see above). The gravel surface of the floodplain was covered by up to 0.2 m of yellow brown silt loam to silty clay loam of a truncated circumneutral brown earth soil similar to the Sutton Series, although not as deep as the typical examples described by Jarvis (1973). In places ancient cultivation had incorporated sand and gravel from the underlying Pleistocene gravel into the soil. Towards the edge of the palaeochannel, this soil survived to its full thickness and was sealed by up to 0.3 m of grey alluvial clay. However, alluvial sediment was not evident over most of the area excavated and the palaeosol was truncated by the modern ploughsoil. Nevertheless, it is likely that much of the site had been sealed beneath a layer of alluvium of late Roman or medieval date, but this covering had largely been mixed by modern cultivation.

The archaeological remains on Sites 1, 3, 4a and 4b mostly related to Neolithic and Bronze Age domestic activities. The main feature on Site 4 was a late Neolithic to early Bronze Age segmented ring ditch. Discoveries on Site 5 included part of an early Neolithic rectangular ditched enclosure (Hey *et al.* forthcoming). A rectilinear system of Roman enclosure ditches and a ditched trackway crossed the sites. One of these ditches ran through Sites 3 and 4 parallel to the edge of the palaeochannel. There was an entrance through it on Site 4 and it cut the Neolithic segmented ring ditch on Site 4. Consideration is given here to the evidence from these sites which relates to the Iron Age and Roman environment.

The pre-Iron Age soils and palaeohydrology

The majority of the Neolithic and Bronze Age archaeological features were filled with what had originally been non-calcareous brown earth soil mixed with varying quantities of limestone gravel. Where the proportion of limestone gravel was high, conditions eventually became calcareous and bone survived. However, in many of the other archaeological features, the soil fill developed a blocky clay layer suggestive of the illuvial B horizon of an argillic brown earth soil. Conditions were sufficiently acidic in such deposits to result in the almost complete loss of bone. Although it is possible that there was pre-Iron Age cultivation on these parts of the floodplain, no evidence for cultivation was found either in the surviving soils or in the fills of the archaeological features. The water table seems to have remained low and there was no evidence for any episodes of flooding on Sites 1, 3, 4, 4a, 4b or 5.

The late Neolithic to early Bronze Age ring ditch (Site 4)

Molluscs were absent from three samples from the lower fills of the ring ditch. However, one sample from the lower fill on the north-west contained some large eroded shells, including the open-country species *Helicella itala*, as well as *Cepaea* sp. The upper fill of the ditch on the north-west contained a gravelly ploughsoil of Roman date from which shells were absent, but to the south of the east-west Roman ditch cut through the ring ditch (context group 107), the upper fill of the ring ditch was an alluvial clay in which shells were well-preserved. They included flowing water aquatic species such as *Bithynia tentaculata* and other species characteristic of the Thames, such as *Gyraulus albus* (Table 18.23).

These results suggested that the ring ditch was constructed in open grassland. Conditions remained stable throughout the Bronze Age and Iron Age. However, in the earlier Roman period, an east-west field boundary ditch cut through the ring ditch and cultivation occurred to the north of the boundary. The ring ditch rapidly became filled with ploughsoil to the north of the boundary. To the south of the boundary, in the absence of cultivation, the ring ditch remained open until later Roman alluviation extended onto this part of the floodplain and filled it with sediment.

The Roman field boundary ditch (Site 3, context group 27, feature 5013)

Samples were analysed from the primary sediment and the alluvial sediment in ditch 5013 at the eastern end of Site 3. This feature comprised a Roman field boundary ditch, which ran along the edge of Site 3 and through Site 4, parallel to the palaeochannel. Both samples contained mollusc shells but the sample from the bottom of the ditch additionally contained poorly-preserved water-logged macroscopic plant remains.

Table 18.23 Mollusca from Yarnton Floodplain Sites 4 and 3.

	Site 4		*Site 3*	
Context Group			*27*	
Context	*7108*	*7113*	*5014*	*6003*
Sample	*7081*	*7076*		
Feature	*ring ditch lower fill*	*alluvium in top of ring ditch*	*ditch bottom*	*alluvium in top*
Sample weight (kg.)	*0.5*	*0.5*	*0.5*	*0.5*
GASTROPODA				
Valvata cristata Müll.	-	-	-	12
V. macrostoma Mörch.	-	-	-	8
V. piscinalis (Müll.)	-	-	-	10
Bithynia tentaculata (L.)	-	2	1	7
Bithynia spp.	-	4	5	92
Lymnaea truncatula (Müll.)	-	11	2	10
L. palustris (Müll.)	-	-	-	4
L. stagnalis (L.)	-	-	1	1
L. peregra (Müll.)	-	4	1	-
Planorbis planorbis (L.)	-	6	1	4
Anisus leucostoma (Mill.)	-	-	-	2
A. vortex (L.)	-	-	-	1
Bathyomphalus contortus (L.)	-	2	-	-
Gyraulus albus (Müll.)	-	15	-	4
Armiger crista L.	-	6	-	8
Planorbarius corneus (L.)	-	-	-	1
Succinea or *Oxyloma* sp.	-	1	-	4
Vallonia sp.	-	-	1	1
Limax or *Deroceras* sp.	-	-	1	1
Helicella itala L.	1	-	-	-
Trichia hispida (L.) or *plebeia* (Drap.)	-	-	1	-
Cepaea sp.	2	-	-	-
Arianta or *Cepaea* sp.	1	-	-	-
BIVALVIA				
Sphaerium sp.	-	-	-	1
Total	4	51	14	171

Both the shells (Table 18.23) and the seeds from the bottom of the ditch suggested that the ditch either had water flowing along it or experienced episodes of flooding from the river. The snails included the flowing water species *Bithynia tentaculata*, while there were seeds of *Sagittaria sagittifolia* (arrow-head), which is characteristic of slowly-flowing ditches and channels of the Thames. There were also seeds of *Ranunculus* S. *Batrachium* sp. (water crowfoot). The seeds included weeds of disturbed ground which could have grown in the field. There were no certain remains of crops but a pod of *Brassica* sp. (cabbage, wild turnip, mustard etc) could have been from a cultivated plant or a weed.

The sediment in the bottom of the ditch was mixed, with a high proportion of sand and gravel likely to have eroded from the ditch sides. In contrast, the upper fill of the ditch was an alluvial clay. It contained numerous shells of aquatic molluscs, particularly flowing water species from the genera *Valvata* and *Bithynia*.

Iron Age to modern soils and palaeohydrology

Whereas Site 2, which was on a low-lying area of floodplain, experienced a gradual rise on the water table from the middle Bronze Age onwards and the onset of flooding during the Iron Age (see above), Sites 1, 3, 4, 4a, 4b and 5 showed no evidence for a rise in water table or flooding during the Iron Age. Hydrological change did, however, have an impact on these sites in the Roman period. The preservation of organic remains in the bottom of ditch 5022 was a reflection of the continuing rise in water table on the floodplain at Yarnton. The ditch and its associated bank were perhaps constructed to protect the field to the north from flooding. Certainly the ditch carried flowing water or experienced flooding early in its life. Initially, it was probably successful in its purpose, for the north-east corner of the ring ditch became filled with ploughsoil without any evidence for an alluvial component.

It is difficult to ascertain when extensive cultivation began on these sites. The evidence from the ring ditch on Site 4, where ploughsoil extended southwards up to, but not beyond, the line of ditch 5022, suggested either that the onset of cultivation was associated with the digging of the ditch or that the ditch exactly corresponded with an earlier field boundary. However, a small Roman ditch on Site 3, on a different alignment from the entrance to the field, could represent an earlier boundary to cultivation to the north of the ring ditch. Roman cultivation resulted in sand and gravel becoming incorporated into the overlying soil, creating a calcareous brown earth soil. Traces of a possible Roman ploughsoil were quite widespread on Sites 1, 3, 4, 4a, 4b and 5 beneath alluvium or the modern topsoil.

Roman period flooding eventually extended onto Site 3 and presumably the other sites considered here. There was a spread of alluvial clay which extended through the entrance to the field and onto the soil surface. Cultivation ceased. The Roman field boundary ditch became entirely filled with alluvium. As noted above, it is likely that much of the area of these sites was sealed beneath a thin layer of alluvium of late Roman or early medieval date, but this covering had largely been mixed by modern cultivation.

The palaeoenvironmental sequence of Yarnton Floodplain B Sites 9, 10 and 21

Introduction

Yarnton Floodplain Sites 9, 10 and 21 were situated on, or extended from, a pair of gravel 'islands', areas of floodplain at an intermediate height. The islands were defined by a major palaeochannel to the south, which divided them from a high area of floodplain, and a minor palaeochannel to the north. The islands were separated by another minor palaeochannel. The palaeochannels appeared to be of Late Devensian origin and had no indications of Flandrian migration or even very active flow. All the channels showed evidence of pre-Bronze Age trees growing on the beds, with iron-pan root pseudomorphs and, at depth, preserved woody roots. A rising water table, however, was beginning to re-activate the channels in the late Bronze Age.

A thin circumneutral brown-earth soil had developed over the floodplain gravels. There was evidence from the higher areas of the floodplain that ancient cultivation had incorporated gravel into this soil. Alluvial layers of Roman or medieval date could be traced from the upper fills of the palaeochannels onto the lower areas of floodplain. Only a thin band of alluvium sealed the palaeosol where the floodplain was of intermediate height, and on the highest area of floodplain, for example to the south of the islands on Site 4d, modern cultivation had entirely incorporated the alluvium into the ploughsoil.

There was Bronze Age activity on the two islands which included the digging of several waterholes (Chapter 11 above). Site 21 spanned the minor palaeochannel which separated the two islands. A narrow gravel causeway, presumed to be of Iron Age date, ran obliquely over the bottom of the channel. A ditch system appeared to be related to the causeway, a segmented ditch running alongside the causeway, cutting into the bed of the palaeochannel. On Site 9, a substantial limestone causeway of middle Iron Age date was discovered sealing the earliest channel sediments. A narrower gravel causeway of middle to late Iron Age date had been constructed along the top of the limestone causeway. There was also a double row of small alluvium-filled pits running down to the edge of the channel. They were similar to the enigmatic rows of Iron Age pits and slots on Floodplain A Site 2. Site 10 was situated further upstream on the major palaeochannel and a second causeway was found crossing the channel, likewise sealing sediments beneath it.

Consideration is given here to the evidence from these sites which related to the Iron Age and Roman environments (Tables 18.24-18.26).

The presumed Iron Age ditch alongside the causeway between the islands (Site 21, context group 51)

That it was possible to dig the ditch along the bed of the channel suggested that the bed was at least seasonally dry, and the poor preservation of organic remains in the ditch confirms this observation. The limited range of seeds from sample 15008 from context 15032, the lower fill of the ditch, included *Ranunculus* S. *Batrachium* sp. (water crowfoot) and *Glyceria* sp. (reed-grass) which were probably from vegetation growing in the ditch bottom. By far the most numerous seeds, however, were of *Juncus bufonius* gp. (toad rush), a low-growing annual of disturbed marshy habitats and exposed mud. This plant probably reflects conditions on the channel bed. Other seeds included *Potentilla anserina* (silverweed), *Plantago major* (great plantain) and *Eleocharis palustris* (spike rush), suggesting trampled marshy pasture.

When the causeway was constructed, the sediments beneath it were not sufficiently waterlogged for the preservation of organic remains. This evidence, plus the results from the ditch, suggested that the causeway was constructed in relatively dry conditions. Unfortunately, the sediments both below and above the causeway were decalcified, so no mollusc evidence was available. The causeway was sealed beneath alluvial clay of presumed Roman date which extended onto the floodplain (context group 52).

The limestone and gravel causeways (Site 9, context groups 2, 5, 6, 9 and 12)

Sample 13106 from context 13289, alluvial clay under the limestone causeway in the major palaeochannel (context group 2), was decalcified and the preservation of organic remains was very poor. However, many seeds of *Juncus* spp. (rushes) survived, particularly from the *J. articulatus* group. These are creeping rushes of marshy places and wet grassland. A Bronze Age spearhead which had been placed in context 13266, directly beneath the causeway (context group 5), was dated to 410-200 cal BC at 95% confidence (OxA-9377) on a seed cluster of *Juncus effusus* gp. (tussock rush) from its socket. Three individuals of the beetle *Ptinus fur* were also found in the socket of the spear. The other evidence suggested that the limestone causeway was constructed across a marshy hollow, on which rushes grew and which was perhaps flooded in winter. This is a very unlikely habitat for *P. fur*, which is naturally a beetle of birds' nests, where it eats rather dry food waste left by the nest occupants. However, it also flourishes inside buildings, where it is omnivorous on rather dry decaying animal and vegetable material, including hay waste, old straw and kitchen debris (Horion 1961, 265). The most likely explanation for the occurrence of the beetles in the socket of the spear was that the spear had been kept inside a house, giving them the opportunity to crawl in. Given that the spear was several hundred years old when it was deposited, it is possible that it was a treasured item which had long been hidden, for example in thatch or at the base of a house wall where the beetles flourished.

Some poorly-preserved waterlogged seeds and leached mollusc shells were found associated with the gravel causeway which had been laid along the top of the limestone causeway (context group 9). The most numerous seeds were of aquatic plants including *Ranunculus* S. *Batrachium* sp. (water crowfoot), *Callitriche* (starwort) and *Zannichellia palustris* (horned pondweed). Shells of stagnant water aquatic molluscs, such as *Lymnaea truncatula* and *Planorbis planorbis*, were present, although no flowing-water species were noted amongst the fragmentary remains. It is possible that when the causeway was raised, the channel held pools of stagnant water for much of the year and only had an active flow in winter. There were also a few seeds of plants of marshy pasture, such as *Potentilla anserina* (silverweed) and *Eleocharis palustris* (spike rush), and weeds of disturbed ground, such as *Thlaspi arvense* (field pennycress) and *Polygonum persicaria* (red shank).

Decalcified alluvial clay (context group 12) sealed the top of the gravel causeway. Waterlogged remains and shells were absent. The upper part of the alluvial sequence over the causeway contained shells of flowing-water molluscs, such as *Bithynia tentaculata*. Up to one metre of alluvial clay (context group 23) accumulated in the deepest part of the palaeochannel during the Roman period.

The pit rows (Site 9, context group 19)

The double row of enigmatic small pits was entirely filled with shell-rich alluvial clay. No pre-alluvial fill could be detected in these fills and there was no evidence of decayed timber. Samples were analysed in detail from two of the pits, sample 13000 from context 13030 and sample 13001 from context 13032. Flowing-water aquatic molluscs in both samples, including *Valvata cristata*, *V. piscinalis* and *Bithynia tentaculata*, showed that the alluvial sediment had been derived from the bed of the Thames (Table 18.26). Shells of fully terrestrial species were absent but numerous shells of the amphibious snail *Lymnaea truncatula* probably reflected muddy conditions on the floodplain, with seasonal pools of stagnant water. While the results suggested that the pits were open features, dug around or shortly after the onset of alluviation, the investigations shed no light on their purpose.

The Iron Age and Roman floodplain surface (Site 9, context groups 22 and 23; Site 10, context groups 37, 38 and 39)

There was no evidence for cultivation of the lower parts of the floodplain, where in most areas there

Table 18.24 Waterlogged seeds from Yarnton Floodplain Sites 9, 10 and 21.

		Site 21	*Site 9*	*Site 10*
Context Group		*51*	*2*	*28*
Context		*15032*	*13289*	*14014*
Sample		*15008*	*13106*	*14001*
Sample weight (kg.)		*1.0*	*1.0*	*1.0*
Ranunculus cf. *repens* L.	creeping buttercup	2	-	2
R. sardous Crantz.	hairy buttercup	-	-	2
R. S. *Batrachium* sp.	water crowfoot	72	-	118
Papaver rhoeas tp.	poppy	-	-	1
Cerastium cf. *fontanum* Baum.	mouse ear chickweed	-	-	2
Myosoton aquaticum (L.) Moen.	water chickweed	-	-	2
Chenopodium album L.	fat hen	-	-	8
Atriplex sp.	orache	-	-	1
Potentilla anserina L.	silverweed	5	-	1
P. reptans L.	creeping cinquefoil	-	-	1
Epilobium sp.	willow-herb	2	-	-
Callitriche sp.	starwort	-	-	3
Oenanthe aquatica gp.	water-dropwort	-	-	9
Polygonum persicaria L.	red-shank	-	-	1
Rumex acetosella agg.	sheep's sorrel	-	-	1
R, maritimus L.	golden dock	-	-	1
Rumex sp.	dock	-	-	1
Urtica dioica L.	stinging nettle	-	-	21
Corylus avellana L.	hazel	-	-	1
cf. *Anagallis* sp.	pimpernel	-	-	1
Mentha cf. *aquatica* L.	water mint	1	-	11
Prunella vulgaris L.	selfheal	-	-	2
Plantago major L.	great plantain	18	-	4
Anthemis cotula L.	stinking mayweed	-	-	3
Alisma sp.	water plantain	1	-	16
Sagittaria sagittifolia L.	arrow-head	-	-	7
Potamogeton sp.	pondweed	-	-	9
Zannichellia palustris L.	horned pondweed	1	-	143
Juncus effusus gp.	tussock rush	-	-	10
J. bufonius gp.	toad rush	6370	30	40
J. articulatus gp.	rush	40	730	30
Juncus sp.	rush	1220	-	50
Eleocharis palustris (L.) R. & S. ssp. *palustris* L.	spike rush	15	-	4
E. palustris (L.) R. & S. ssp. *vulgaris* Walt.	spike rush	7	-	5
Schoenoplectus lacustris (L.) Pal.	bulrush	-	-	21
Carex spp.	sedge	7	-	11
Glyceria sp.	reed-grass	16	-	3
Gramineae indeterminate	grass	4	-	-
Total		7,781	760	546

Table 18.25 Other waterlogged macroscopic plant remains from Yarnton Floodplain Sites 10 and 21.

			Site 21	*Site10*
Context Group			*51*	*28*
Context			*15032*	*14014*
Sample			*15008*	*14001*
Sample weight (kg.)			*1.0*	*1.0*
Chara sp.	stonewort	oospore	30	7840
Linum usitatissimum L.	flax	capsule frag	-	1

was yellow-brown circumneutral sandy silt to clay loam above the Pleistocene gravel. However, this palaeosol appeared to have been removed from the northern end of Site 10, where undisturbed alluvial clay (context group 38) lay directly on the gravel. This implies that at some stage, probably in the Iron Age or Roman period, the soil had been stripped from the site and bare gravel exposed. The palaeosol was intact alongside the channel, so it is unlikely that the soil was removed by river action.

Some of the higher areas of the floodplain had, however, experienced cultivation. A cultivation soil of brown loam with some gravel was found on both sides of the palaeochannel on Site 9 (context group 22) and on a small area of Site 10 to the south of the palaeochannel (context group 39). While the final date of cultivation was probably Roman and Roman artefacts were found in the ploughsoil, the possibility of earlier cultivation cannot be excluded.

Alluvial clay sealed both the non-cultivated soil on the lower areas and the Roman ploughsoil on Sites 9 (context group 23) and 10 (context group 38). It is difficult to date the onset of the alluviation, but shelly alluvial clay entirely filled a short length of Iron Age-Roman gully on Site 10 (context group 37). Sample 14002 from context 14010, the fill of the gully, contained shells of the riverine molluscs *Valvata piscinalis* and *Bithynia* sp. This suggested that alluviation had begun no later than in the late Roman period.

The upstream gravel causeway (Site 10, context groups 28 and 29)

Waterlogged calcareous alluvial clay (context 14014) was found sealed beneath the gravel causeway. Sample 14001 from this deposit contained shells of flowing-water molluscs, including *Valvata piscinalis* and *Bithynia tentaculata*, in company with numerous seeds of submerged to floating-leaved aquatic plants, such as *Ranunculus* S. *Batrachium* sp. (water crowfoot), *Zannichellia palustris* (horned pondweed) and *Potamogeton* sp. (pondweed). Seeds were also present from vegetation of tall reedswamp, including *Oenanthe aquatica* gp. (water dropwort), *Sagittaria sagittifolia* (arrow-head), *Schoenoplectus lacustris* (bulrush) and *Glyceria* sp. (reed-grass) (Table 18.24). These results suggested a causeway crossing a channel that was certainly actively flowing in winter (in which case the causeway would have served as a ford) but in summer was a well-vegetated pool with perhaps only intermittent flow over the causeway. Seeds from terrestrial plants included those typical of herbaceous bankside vegetation, such as *Urtica dioica* (stinging nettle) and various species which can occur in damp grassland, for example *Prunella vulgaris* (self heal). However, there were also seeds of annual weeds such as *Papaver rhoeas* tp. (poppy) and *Anthemis cotula* (stinking mayweed). These plants readily grow as arable weeds and it is possible they had been derived from cultivated fields on the higher ground alongside the channel. Interestingly, *A. cotula* appears to have been a Roman introduction to Britain, so its occurrence dated the causeway as Roman or later.

Table 18.26 Mollusca from Yarnton Floodplain Sites 9 and 10.

	Site 9		*Site 10*	
Context Group	*19*	*19*	*37*	*28*
Context	*13030*	*13032*	*14010*	*14014*
Sample	*13000*	*13001*	*14002*	*14001*
Sample weight (kg.)	*1.0*	*1.0*	*1.0*	*1.0*
GASTROPODA				
Valvata cristata Müll.	39	10	2	1
V. piscinalis (Müll.)	57	31	2	6
Bithynia tentaculata (L.)	4	2	1	1
Bithynia sp.	9	8	3	8
Lymnaea truncatula (Müll.)	84	44	2	1
L. palustris (Müll.)	11	3	-	-
L. peregra (Müll.)	9	4	1	-
Planorbis planorbis (L.)	12	3	-	-
P. carinatus (Müll.)	-	-	-	1
Anisus leucostoma (Mill.)	3	3	1	-
A. vortex (L.)	4	1	-	1
Bathyomphalus contortus (L.)	1	-	-	-
Gyraulus albus (Müll.)	21	10	-	5
Armiger crista L.	43	15	4	4
Succinea or *Oxyloma* sp.	-	1	-	-
Trichia plebeia (Drap.) or *hispida* (L.)	-	-	1	-
BIVALVIA				
Sphaeridium sp.	-	-	-	1
Pisidium spp.	13	11	1	6
Total	310	146	18	35

Summary of the Iron Age and Roman environmental sequence of Sites 9, 10 and 21

The environmental sequences from all three sites gave evidence for a rising water table followed by alluviation. The bed of the minor palaeochannel between the two islands at Site 21 was sufficiently dry for a ditch to be dug along its bottom during the late Bronze Age or Iron Age. When the limestone causeway was constructed across the major palaeochannel at Site 9 in the Iron Age, it was laid over damp ground with rushy vegetation. The causeway was subsequently raised, suggesting a continuing rise in water level. The causeway across the major palaeochannel on Site 10 was possibly Roman in date and crossed a reedswamp which experienced at least a seasonal flow of water. Roman clay alluviation eventually covered the causeways on the three sites. There was no evidence for cultivation on the lower areas of the floodplain. On Site 9, an alignment of small pits of presumed Iron Age date which ran down to the palaeochannel was filled with alluvium of probable Iron Age date. Some higher areas of the floodplain were cultivated at least in the early Roman period but during the late Roman period extensive clay alluviation was covering the floodplain and filling the palaeochannel over all three sites.

The palaeoenvironmental sequence of Yarnton Floodplain B Site 25

Introduction

Site 25 of Yarnton Floodplain comprised a relatively high area of floodplain to the north of a palaeochannel. It was crossed by a middle Iron Age ditch with two re-cuts which ran towards the palaeochannel (see Figs 11.15 and 11.16). Waterlogged sediments were present towards the southern end of the ditch. The ditch was covered by a ploughsoil which extended over the entire site, which in turn was sealed beneath a layer of alluvial clay.

Biological remains from the middle Iron Age ditch (context group 26)

A sequence of three samples from the waterlogged sediments of the ditch was analysed, the earliest being sample 14 from context 37/8, followed by sample 13 from the lower part of context 37/7 and sample 12 from the upper part of context 37/7 (Tables 18.27-18.31). In addition, sample 20 was taken from context 40/7, less well-preserved organic sediments nearer the junction with the palaeochannel (Table 18.27). The non-waterlogged sediments further to the north in the ditch were sampled for molluscs at two sections: sample 9 from context 17/9 and sample 11 from context 16/6 (Table 18.31).

Samples 14, 13 and 12 all contained numerous seeds of aquatic and emergent plants which suggested that the ditch held shallow stagnant water. The submerged vegetation included *Ranunculus* S. *Batrachium* sp. (water crowfoot) and *Callitriche* sp. (starwort) while the emergent vegetation included *Apium nodiflorum* (fool's watercress), *Veronica* S. *Beccabunga* sp. (water speedwell) and *Alisma* sp. (water plantain). The stagnant water conditions were confirmed by the occurrence of water beetles, such as *Agabus bipustulatus*, *Helophorus* cf. *brevipalpis* and *Ochthebius minimus*. However, flowing-water species were absent. Likewise, the molluscs from sample 14 were species of stagnant water such as *Lymnaea peregra* and *Bathyomphalus contortus*. Sample 20 suggested somewhat different aquatic vegetation, with *Potamogeton* sp. (pondweed) and *Zannichellia palustris* (horned pondweed) amongst the submerged to floating-leaved aquatic plants and tall emergent vegetation including *Schoenoplectus lacustris* (bulrush). A diverse aquatic molluscan fauna included flowing-water species such as *Bithynia tentaculata* which had presumably entered the ditch from the palaeochannel.

The seeds from samples 12-14 included various plants which could have been growing on the ditch sides, such as *Filipendula ulmaria* (meadowsweet), *Epilobium* sp. (willow-herb), *Pulicaria* sp. (fleabane) and *Carex* sp. (sedge). There were also a few seeds of annual weeds which could have grown on exposed gravel on the ditch sides, for example *Atriplex* sp. (orache). There was no evidence from the macroscopic plant remains or the insect remains for the presence of a hedge or even scattered scrubs alongside the ditch. Indeed, the Coleoptera of Species Group 4, which are

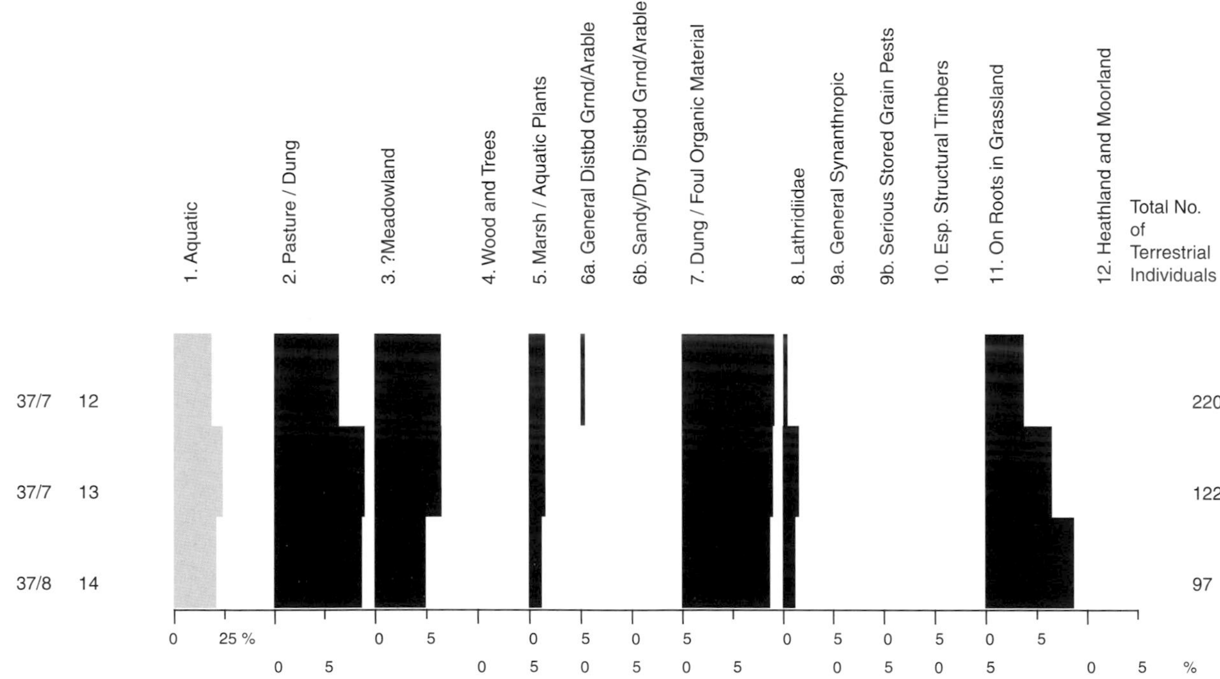

Fig. 18.13 Percentages of species groups of Coleoptera by habitat type: Yarnton Floodplain B Site 25 Iron Age ditch (context group 26)

Table 18.27 Waterlogged seeds from Yarnton Floodplain Site 25 Iron Age ditch (context group 26).

Context		37/8	37/7	37/7	40/7
Sample		14	13	12	20
Sample weight (kg.)		1.0	1.0	1.0	0.5
RANUNCULACEAE					
Ranunculus cf. *acris* L.	meadow buttercup	2	-	3	-
R. cf. *repens* L.	creeping buttercup	15	8	8	2
R. cf. *bulbosus* L.	bulbous buttercup	-	2	-	-
R. S. *Batrachium* sp.	water crowfoot	46	21	54	22
CRUCIFERAE					
Brassica rapa L. ssp. *sylvestris* (L.) Jan.	wild turnip	1	-	-	-
Rorippa cf. *palustris* (L.) Bes.	marsh yellow cress	1	-	1	1
Nasturtium officinale R. Br.	water cress	2	1	-	-
HYPERICACEAE					
Hypericum sp.	St John's wort	-	-	1	
CARYOPHYLLACEAE					
Cerastium cf. *fontanum* Baum.	mouse-ear chickweed	45	2	15	-
Stellaria media gp.	chickweed	7	-	2	-
S. graminea L.	stitchwort	3	-	1	-
Arenaria serpyllifolia L.	sandwort	10	12	13	-
CHENOPODIACEAE					
Chenopodium polyspermum L.	all-seed	-	-	2	-
C. ficifolium Sm.	fig-leaved goosefoot	1	-	-	-
Atriplex sp.	orache	3	15	18	1
LINACEAE					
Linum catharticum L.	fairy flax	5	2	4	-
ROSACEAE					
Filipendula ulmaria (L.) Max.	meadowsweet	6	-	2	-
Potentilla anserina L.	silverweed	12	6	8	2
Aphanes arvensis L.	parsley piert	-	3	2	-
ONAGRACEAE					
Epilobium sp.	willow-herb	-	116	126	-
CALLITRICHACEAE					
Callitriche sp.	starwort	73	159	711	2
UMBELLIFERAE					
Oenanthe pimpinelloides gp.	water-dropwort	-	-	-	1
Apium nodiflorum (L.) Lag.	fool's watercress	1	74	5	-
POLYGONACEAE					
Polygonum aviculare agg.	knotgrass	2	1	-	-
P. persicaria L.	red shank	9	1	-	1
P. lapathifolium L.	pale persicaria	-	-	-	1
P. hydropiper L.	water-pepper	1	-	-	-
Rumex hydrolapathum Huds.	water dock	-	-	-	1
R. cf. *crispus* L.	curled dock	1	-	-	-
R. conglomeratus Mur.	sharp dock	41	22	43	-
R. maritimus L.	golden dock	2	2	-	1
Rumex spp. (not *maritimus*)	dock	12	12	6	-
URTICACEAE					
Urtica dioica L.	stinging nettle	-	-	-	5
BORAGINACEAE					
Myosotis sp.	forget-me-not	3	53	24	-
SCROPHULARIACEAE					
Veronica S. *Beccabunga* sp.	water speedwell	30	620	802	30
Odontites verna (Bell.) Dum.	red bartsia	-	-	2	-
LABIATAE					
Mentha cf. *aquatica* L.	water mint	2	687	52	8
Lycopus europaeus L.	gipsywort	-	2	-	-
Prunella vulgaris L.	selfheal	8	7	15	-
PLANTAGINACEAE					
Plantago major L.	great plantain	25	19	41	-

Table 18.27 Waterlogged seeds from Yarnton Floodplain Site 25 Iron Age ditch (context group 26) (continued).

Context		*37/8*	*37/7*	*37/7*	*40/7*
Sample		*14*	*13*	*12*	*20*
Sample weight (kg.)		*1.0*	*1.0*	*1.0*	*0.5*
RUBIACEAE					
Galium sp. (not *aparine*)	bedstraw	1	1	1	-
VALERIANACEAE					
Valerianella mimosa Bast	cornsalad	-	1	1	-
Valeriana sp.	valerian	1	-	-	-
COMPOSITAE					
Senecio sp.	ragwort	-	1	-	-
Pulicaria sp.	fleabane	-	13	14	-
Achillea sp.	yarrow	4	-	2	-
Leucanthemum vulgare Lam.	ox-eye daisy	2	-	-	-
Carduus sp.	thistle	-	3	3	-
cf. *Cirsium* sp.	thistle	13	8	6	-
Lapsana communis L.	nipplewort	-	-	-	1
Leontodon sp.	hawkbit	16	13	19	-
Sonchus asper (L.) Hill	sow-thistle	2	29	5	-
Taraxacum sp.	dandelion	-	-	1	-
ALISMATACEAE					
Alisma sp.	water plantain	57	41	51	7
Sagittaria sagittifolia L.	arrow-head	-	-	-	1
POTAMOGETONACEAE					
Potamogeton sp.	pondweed	-	-	-	12
ZANNICHELLIACEAE					
Zannichellia palustris L.	horned pondweed	-	-	-	71
JUNCACEAE					
Juncus effusus gp.	tussock rush	10	10	-	10
Juncus bufonius gp.	toad rush	120	80	150	30
J. articulatus gp.	rush	30	40	30	20
Juncus spp.	rush	60	20	40	30
IRIDACEAE					
Iris pseudacorus L.	yellow flag	-	1	-	1
CYPERACEAE					
Eleocharis palustris (L.) R. & S. ssp. *vulgaris* L.	spike rush	1	-	-	9
E. palustris (L.) R. & S. ssp. *vulgaris* Walt.	spike rush	1	-	-	2
Schoenoplectus lacustris (L.) Pal.	bulrush	-	-	-	2
Carex spp.	sedge	4	62	59	1
GRAMINEAE					
Glyceria sp.	reed-grass	14	12	19	4
Gramineae indeterminate	grass	26	23	15	-
Total		731	2,205	2,377	279

Table 18.28 Other waterlogged plant material from Yarnton Floodplain Site 25 Iron Age ditch (context group 26).

Context			*37/8*	*37/7*	*37/7*	*40/7*
Sample			*14*	*13*	*12*	*20*
Sample weight (kg.)			*1.0*	*1.0*	*1.0*	*0.5*
Bryophyta indeterminate	- stem with leaves	moss	+	-	+	-
Chara sp.	- oospores	stonewort	20	1	30	3161
Rumex sp.	- stem	dock	-	-	3	-
cf. *Trifolium* sp.	- flower	clover	3	3	5	-
Triticum dicoccum Schübl. or *spelta* L.	- charred glume	emmer or spelt	-	-	1	-

Table 18.29 Coleoptera from Yarnton Floodplain Site 25 Iron Age ditch (context group 26).

Context	37/8	37/7	37/7	
Sample	*14*	*13*	*12*	
Sample weight (kg.)	*5.0*	*5.0*	*5.0*	*Species Group*
CARABIDAE				
Carabus granulatus L.	-	1	1	
Carabus sp.	1	-	-	
Dyschirius globosus (Hbst.)	3	2	4	
Clivina collaris (Hbst.) or *fossor* (L.)	1	1	2	
Trechus obtusus Er. 1 or *quadristriatus* (Schr.)	-	3		
T. secalis (Pk.)	-	1	-	
Bembidion lampros (Hbst.)	-	-	2	
B. lampros (Hbst.) or *properans* (Step.)	-	1	-	
B. gilvipes Sturm.	1	1	-	
B. assimile Gyl.	-	2	1	
B. obtusum Serv.	-	-	3	
B. biguttatum (F.)	-	1	2	
B. guttula (F.)	2	2	5	
Pterostichus cf. *anthracinus* (Pz.)	1	-	-	
P. cupreus (L.)	-	1	2	
P. gracilis (Dej.)	-	1	-	
P. melanarius (Ill.)	-	1	1	
P. nigrita (Pk.)	-	1	1	
P. vernalis (Pz.)	-	1	1	
P. cupreus (L.) or *versicolor* (Sturm.)	1	-	-	
Calathus fuscipes (Gz.)	1	2	-	
C. melanocephalus (L.)	2	1	2	
Olisthopus rotundatus (Pk.)	-	-	1	
Agonum dorsale (Pont.)	-	-	1	6a
Agonum sp.	-	1	-	
Amara spp.	-	1	5	
Harpalus S. *Ophonus* sp.	-	1	-	
H. affinis (Schr.)	-	-	1	
Panagaeus bipustulatus (F.)	-	-	1	
Chlaenius nigricornis (F.)	-	-	2	
Lebia chlorocephala (Hoff.)	-	-	1	
Dromius linearis (Ol.)	1	-	-	
Metabletus sp.	-	-	1	
Brachinus crepitans (L.)	-	-	1	
HALIPLIDAE				
Haliplus sp.	1	1	1	1
DYTISCIDAE				
Hydroporus sp.	-	1	1	1
Agabus bipustulatus (L.)	1	1	4	1
Agabus sp. (not *bipustulatus*)	-	1	1	1
Colymbetes fuscus (L.)	-	1	1	1
HYDROPHILIDAE				
Helophorus aquaticus (L.)	1	-	1	1
H. grandis Ill.	-	2	3	1
H. aquaticus (L.) or *grandis* Ill.	2	-	-	1
H. rufipes (B. d'A.)	-	-	1	
Helophorus sp. (*brevipalpis* size)	5	5	8	1
Cercyon analis (Pk.)	-	-	1	7
C. haemorrhoidalis (F.)	-	1	2	7
C. lugubris (Ol.)	-	1	-	7
C. sternalis Sharp	-	-	1	7

Table 18.29 Coleoptera from Yarnton Floodplain Site 25 Iron Age ditch (context group 26) (continued).

Context	37/8	37/7	37/7	
Sample	*14*	*13*	*12*	
Sample weight (kg.)	*5.0*	*5.0*	*5.0*	*Species Group*
C. terminatus (Marsh.)	1	-	-	7
C. tristis (Ill.)	1	1	-	7
Cercyon sp.	-	-	2	7
Megasternum obscurum (Marsh.)	3	5	7	7
Hydrobius fuscipes (L.)	-	1	1	1
Anacaena bipustulata (Marsh.) or *limbata* (F.)	1	-	1	1
Laccobius sp.	-	1	-	1
HISTERIDAE				
Hister bissexstriatus F.	-	-	1	
Paralister purpurascens (Schr.)	-	-	1	
Atholus duodecimstriatus (Schr.)	1	-	-	
HYDRAENIDAE				
Ochthebius cf. *bicolon* Germ.	1	3	2	1
O. minimus (F.)	1	2	1	1
O. cf. *minimus* (F.)	4	9	5	1
Limnebius papposus Muls.	-	-	3	1
PTILIIDAE				
Ptenidium sp.	-	-	1	
LEIODIDAE				
Choleva or *Catops* sp.	-	1	-	
SILPHIDAE				
Nicrophorus sp. (not *humator*)	-	1	-	
SCYDMAENIDAE				
Scydmaenidae indeterminate	-	-	1	
STAPHYLINIDAE				
Metopsia retusa (Step.)	-	1	-	
Lesteva longoelytrata (Gz.)	1	-	1	
Omalium sp.	-	1	-	
C. cf. *corticinus* (Grav.)	1	-	-	
Platystethus cornutus gp.	-	1	-	
P. nitens (Sahl.)	1	-	-	
P. nodifrons (Man.)	1	-	1	
Anotylus nitidulus (Grav.)	1	-	-	
A. rugosus (F.)	1	3	4	7
A. sculpturatus gp.	1	-	-	7
Stenus spp.	2	4	5	
Lathrobium longulum Grav.	-	1	-	
Lathrobium sp.	-	1	1	
Astenus sp.	-	-	1	
Rugilus orbiculatus (Pk.)	-	1	-	
Gyrohypnus fracticornis (Müll.) or *punctulatus* (Pk.)	-	-	1	
Xantholinus longiventris Heer	2	1	4	
X. linearis (Ol.) or *longiventris* Heer	-	3	2	
Philonthus spp.	1	2	4	
Gabrius sp.	-	1	-	
Staphylinus aeneocephalus Deg. or *fortunatarum* (Wol.)	1	-	-	
S. olens Müll.	-	-	1	
Mycetoporus sp.	-	1	-	
Tachyporus sp.	1	1	5	
Tachinus sp.	-	2	2	

Table 18.29 Coleoptera from Yarnton Floodplain Site 25 Iron Age ditch (context group 26) (continued).

Context	37/8	37/7	37/7	
Sample	*14*	*13*	*12*	
Sample weight (kg.)	*5.0*	*5.0*	*5.0*	*Species Group*
Aleocharinae indeterminate	3	5	7	
GEOTRUPIDAE				
Geotrupes sp.	-	-	1	2
SCARABAEIDAE				
Aphodius ater Deg.	1	-	-	2
A. contaminatus (Hbst.)	-	1	-	2
A. cf. *fimetarius* L.	-	-	1	2
Aphodius granarius (L.)	2	4	3	2
A. luridus (F.)	-	-	1	2
A. cf. *sphacelatus* (Pz.)	2	4	4	2
A. sus (Hbst.)	-	-	2	2
Aphodius spp.	1	1	-	2
Onthophagus ovatus (L.)	1	-	1	2
Onthophagus sp. (not *ovatus*)	-	1	-	2
Serica brunnea (L.)	1	1	-	11
Phyllopertha horticola (L.)	2	3	3	11
DASCILLIDAE				
Dascillus cervinus (L.)	-	1	-	
SCIRTIDAE				
Cyphon sp.	-	-	1	
BYRRHIDAE				
Byrrhus sp.	1	-	1	
DRYOPIDAE				
Dryops sp.	-	2	2	1
ELATERIDAE				
Agrypnus murinus (L.)	1	2	2	11
Athous hirtus (Hbst.)	1	-	-	11
Agriotes lineatus (L.)	1	-	1	11
A. sputator (L.)	1	2	-	11
Agriotes sp.	-	-	1	11
CANTHARIDAE				
Cantharis sp.	-	1	1	
Rhagonycha sp.	1	1	-	
MELYRIDAE				
Malachius sp. (not *aeneus*)	-	1	-	
CRYPTOPHAGIDAE				
Atomaria spp.	-	1	2	
PHALACRIDAE				
Olibrus sp.	-	-	1	
CORYLOPHIDAE				
Corylophus cassidoides (Marsh.)	-	1	1	
Orthoperus sp.	-	1	-	
COCCINELLIDAE				
Coccidula rufa (Hbst.)	-	1	-	
Coccinella septempunctata (L.)	-	-	1	

Table 18.29 Coleoptera from Yarnton Floodplain Site 25 Iron Age ditch (context group 26) (continued).

Context	37/8	37/7	37/7	
Sample	*14*	*13*	*12*	
Sample weight (kg.)	*5.0*	*5.0*	*5.0*	*Species Group*
LATHRIDIIDAE				
Enicmus transversus (Ol.)	1	-	-	8
Corticariinae indeterminate	-	2	1	8
CHRYSOMELIDAE				
Donacia impressa (L.)	1	-	-	5
Chrysolina hyperici (Forst.)	-	-	1	
C. polita (L.)	-	1	2	
Hydrothassa glabra (Hbst.)	1	-	1	
Prasocuris phellandrii (L.)	-	1	1	5
Phyllotreta nigripes (F.)	-	-	2	
P. vittula Redt.	-	-	1	
Longitarsus spp.	5	5	9	
Altica sp.	-	-	1	
Crepidodera ferruginea (Scop.)	1	2	3	
Chaetocnema concinna (Marsh.)	3	1	4	
Chaetocnema sp. (not *concinna*)	-	1	2	
APIONIDAE				
Apion spp.	2	4	7	3
CURCULIONIDAE				
Trachyphloeus bifoveolatus (Beck)	-	-	1	
Phyllobius roboretanus Gred. or *viridiaeris* (Laich.)	2	-	1	
Phyllobius sp.	1	-	-	
Sitona hispidulus (F.)	-	2	-	3
S. lepidus Gyll.	-	-	1	3
S. cf. *lineatus* (L.)	1	-	1	3
S. sulcifrons (Thun.)	-	2	3	3
Sitona sp.	1	-	-	3
Hypera punctata (F.)	-	2	1	
Hypera sp. (not *punctata*)	-	1	-	
Alophus triguttatus (F.)	1	-	3	
Liparus coronatus (Gz.)	-	1	-	
Notaris acridulus (L.)	-	1	2	5
Orthochaetes setiger (Beck)	1	-	-	
Cidnorhinus quadrimaculatus (L.)	-	1	1	
Ceuthorhynchidius troglodytes (F.)	-	-	1	
Ceuthorhynchinae indeterminate	-	1	3	
Baris lepidii Germ	1	-	-	
Tychius sp.	1	2	-	
Mecinus pyraster (Hbst.)	2	1	2	
Gymnetron pascuorum (Gyl.)	1	-	1	
SCOLYTIDAE				
Hylastinus obscurus (Marsh.)	-	2	-	
Total	97	152	220	

dependent on trees and shrubs, were entirely absent.

The macroscopic plant, insect and mollusc evidence suggested that the ditch was set amidst open grassland. The insects could have been derived from the widest catchment and the elaterid and chafer beetles of Species Group 11, such as *Phyllopertha horticola*, whose larvae feed on the roots of grassland plants, averaged over 5.5% of the terrestrial Coleoptera from samples 12-14 (Fig. 18.13). The more host-specific phytophagous Coleoptera included *Hydrothassa glabra*, which feeds on *Ranunculus* spp. (buttercups) and three species of weevil which feed on plantains, probably *Plantago*

Table 18.30 Other insects from Yarnton Floodplain Site 25 Iron Age ditch (context group 26).

Context		*37/8*	*37/7*	*37/7*
Sample		*14*	*13*	*12*
Sample weight (kg.)		*5.0*	*5.0*	*5.0*
Tingidae indeterminate		-	1	-
Gerris sp.		1	-	-
Philaenus or *Neophilaenus* sp.		-	1	1
Megophthalmus sp.		-	1	-
Aphrodes cf. *albifrons* (L.)		1	-	2
A. bicinctus (Schr.)		3	1	3
Aphrodes sp.		2	1	2
Aphidoidea indeterminate		1	2	2
Trichoptera indeterminate	- larva	-	-	2
Trichoptera indeterminate	- larval case	-	2	11
Lasius flavus gp.	- worker	2	-	3
L. niger gp.	- worker	2	1	1
Hymenoptera indeterminate		3	3	2
Chironomidae indeterminate		+	+	+
Dilophus febrilis (L.) or *femoratus* (Meig.)	-	1	1	
Diptera indeterminate	- puparium	-	1	1
Diptera indeterminate	- adult	5	2	-

+ present

Table 18.31 Mollusca from Yarnton Floodplain Site 25 Iron Age ditch (context group 26).

Context	*17/19*	*16/6*	*37/8*	*40/7*
Sample	*9*	*11*	*14*	*20*
Sample weight (kg.)	*1.0*	*1.0*	*1.0*	*0.5*
GASTROPODA				
Valvata cristata Müll.	-	-	5	11
Bithynia tentaculata (L.)	-	-	-	4
Bithynia sp.	-	-	-	15
Lymnaea truncatula (Müll.)	-	2	11	10
L. palustris (Müll.)	-	-	1	2
L. peregra (Müll.)	-	-	28	2
Planorbis planorbis (L.)	-	-	1	1
Anisus leucostoma (Mill.)	-	1	3	2
A. vortex (L.)	-	-	-	1
Bathyomphalus contortus (L.)	-	-	13	-
Gyraulus albus (Müll.)	-	-	-	3
Armiger crista L.	-	-	-	6
Hippeutis complanatus (L.)	-	-	-	1
Succinea or *Oxyloma* sp.	-	-	-	1
Pupilla muscorum (L.)	-	2	-	-
Vallonia excentrica Sterki	1	1	-	-
Vallonia sp.	-	5	2	-
Limax or *Deroceras* sp.	3	-	-	-
Trichia hispida (L.) or *plebeia* (Drap.)	3	7	1	-
BIVALVIA				
Sphaerium sp.	-	-	-	1
Pisidium sp.	-	-	4	3
Total	7	18	69	63

+ present

lanceolata (ribwort plantain): *Ceuthorhynchidius troglodytes*, *Mecinus pyraster* and *Gymnetron pascuorum*. Grass-feeding insects included the leaf beetle *Crepidodera ferruginea* and the bug *Aphrodes bicinctus*. The mound-building ant of grassland, *Lasius flavus*, was also present.

The seeds from samples 12-14 would have had a much more local origin than the insects, mostly being derived from a strip, one or two metres wide, alongside the ditch. They too gave evidence for grassland and included *Ranunculus* cf. *acris* (meadow buttercup), *R.* cf. *repens* (creeping buttercup), *R.* cf. *bulbosus* (bulbous buttercup), *Cerastium* cf. *fontanum* (mouse-ear chickweed), *Rumex acetosella* (sharp dock), *Prunella vulgaris* (selfheal), cf. *Cirsium* sp. (thistle) and *Leontodon* sp. (hawkbit).

Scarabaeoid dung beetles, such as *Aphodius granarius* and *A.* cf. *sphacelatus*, suggested that there was grazing by domestic animals occurring on the grassland. However, the scarabaeoid dung beetles of Species Group 2 only averaged 7.8% of the terrestrial Coleoptera (Fig. 18.13), suggesting that grazing pressure on the grassland was relatively light. There was certainly no evidence that there was a high concentration of domestic animals, as sometimes occurs in small enclosures adjacent to settlements. Weevils of the genera *Apion* and *Sitona*, which feed on clovers and vetches (Species Group 3) and are favoured by hay meadow conditions, were quite well-represented, at 6.2% of the terrestrial Coleoptera (Fig. 18.13). They included four species of *Sitona*: *S. hispidulus*, *S. lepidus*, *S.* cf. *lineatus* and *S. sulcifrons*. Their abundance likewise suggested that the grassland was not closely grazed.

Many of the Carabidae (ground beetles) occur in grassland habitats and some, for example

Pterostichus vernalis, favour wet conditions, but there were also species of dry grassland on light soil, such as *Panagaeus bipustulatus* and *Lebia chlorocephala*. As is often the case for non-alluvial sediments in archaeological features on the Thames gravels, the concentrations of shells in the two non-waterlogged samples from further north along the ditch were low. The few terrestrial snails were species of dry open habitats, for example the species of *Vallonia* that was present was *V. excentrica* rather than *V. pulchella*, a species of moist pastures and meadows. *Pupilla muscorum* was also present. These results suggested dry, well-drained grassland on the higher areas of the floodplain during the Iron Age.

It has already been suggested that some annual weeds were growing on the ditch sides but there was no evidence from the seeds for cultivation on the floodplain alongside the ditch. There was only a single beetle, *Agonum dorsale*, from Species Group 6a, Coleoptera of general disturbed ground and arable.

The beetles gave no evidence for the proximity of human habitation. The woodworm beetles of Species Group 10, which infest structural timbers, were absent, as were the synanthropic beetles of Species Group 9 which tend to occur in indoor habitats. The beetles of general accumulations of decaying organic material, including Species Group 7, were no more abundant than might be expected given that there would have been some plant debris on the ditch sides and that there were droppings of domestic animals on the grassland.

The biological remains from the ditch probably gave a very good picture of conditions on the higher areas of floodplain which were above any flood levels during the Iron Age, with vegetation of herb-rich grassland. The grassland was used as pasture for domestic animals but does not seem to have been grazed closely. It is possible that summer grazing was not intensive because areas of pasture above the levels of seasonal waterlogging were important for the overwintering of stock.

Roman ploughsoil and alluvium (context groups 25 and 23)

The gravel surface of the floodplain at Site 25 was covered by a red-brown layer of slightly gravelly sandy to clay loam which represented a Roman ploughsoil (context group 25). This was sealed by grey alluvial clay (context group 23), at least the lower part of which was probably later Roman in date.

Palaeoenvironmental investigations of Iron Age and Roman deposits at Oxey Mead

Introduction

Oxey Mead was one of three alluvial flood-meadows alongside the Thames above Oxford. Their modern hay-meadow flora has attracted considerable interest (Baker 1937; Tansley 1939, 568-70; McDonald 1984) and there has been speculation amongst botanists as to its origin. This study covers the Iron Age to Roman part of the palaeoenvironmental sequence, which predated the establishment of such vegetation.

Trial trenching established that a palaeochannel ran along the northern and eastern sides of Oxey Mead. The channel was a minor parallel channel of the Thames which had its origin in the late Devensian but was dry in the Flandrian until it was re-activated in the middle or late Bronze Age. Full details of the channel system at Yarnton are given elsewhere (Robinson in Hey *et al*. forthcoming). The terrace gravels of the floodplain were close to the surface over most of Oxey Mead and mollusc shells were absent from the thin covering of alluvial clay. However, fine overbank alluvial sediments shelved down gently into the palaeochannel and areas had remained sufficiently calcareous for the survival of at least some shells. Organic sediments were sparse in most of the palaeochannel trenches, probably because the trenches did not extend to the deepest part of the Flandrian channel, but one had 0.55 m of organic silt at the bottom in which was discovered a beet (bundle) of flax stems (see Hey 2004, 214 and 215, plate 11.3).

It was decided to analyse sequences of samples from the deepest exposure of overbank alluvium on the edge of the palaeochannel (Section 2, see Fig. 11.10) and the organic sediments from which the flax beet was recovered (Section 3, see Figs 11.10 and 11.12). Full details of analyses, sample descriptions and techniques are given in the project archive. The species identifications are presented in Tables 18.32-18.36, and a coleopteran histogram for Trench 3 is shown in Fig. 18.14. Pollen analysis was also undertaken alongside the analysis of macroscopic remains from Trench 3 and is the subject of a separate report (see Greig above).

Interpretation of the floodplain alluvial sequence

The base of the sequence comprised somewhat leached limestone gravel of the floodplain terrace (layer 2/2). The ground was of Late Devensian date and was overlain by non-calcareous sandy loams and silty clays (layers 2/14-2/13). By analogy with similar deposits elsewhere in the channel system, they probably represented fine sedimentation at the end of the Devensian. The greenish coloration shown by layer 2/13 is characteristic of non-gleyed sediments on the site that have subsequently become waterlogged. This would be consistent with evidence both from Yarnton and throughout the remainder of the Upper Thames Valley (Robinson 1992b) for a rising water table in the middle to late Bronze Age.

Above layer 2/13 was a dark brown humic clay containing rootlets which represented the prehistoric soil which had developed from the early sediment. Mollusc shells were absent but the upper part of this horizon (sample 7) contained some seeds which were probably derived from the vegetation growing on it and preserved by the continuing rise in water table. They suggested marshy pasture, with many seeds of *Juncus effusus* gp. (tussock rush). Other species represented by seeds included *Potentilla anserina* (silverweed), *Mentha* cf. *aquatica* (water mint), *Eleocharis* S. *Palustris* sp. (spike rush) and *Carex* sp. (sedge). Alluviation began on other low-lying areas on the site related to this palaeochannel in the middle Iron Age and it is probable that the seeds indicated the floodplain vegetation just prior to this alluviation.

Sealing the soil was 0.33 m of grey alluvial clay which graded upwards into grey/buff, alluvial clay (layers 2/7 and 2/5). The lower part was non-calcareous but the upper part was calcareous. It probably corresponded with the later Iron Age and Roman overbank alluvium which has been recorded elsewhere in the Upper Thames Valley (Robinson and Lambrick 1984). The clay sediment above, layer 2/4, was dark grey, possibly as a result of manganese staining. This layer had a distinct organic component where it continued into the palaeochannel. It is assumed that this horizon represented an episode of soil development which occurred as a result of a reduction in the rate of sedimentation in the early Saxon period. (Radiocarbon and OSL dates have confirmed a corresponding organic layer in a palaeochannel on Yarnton Floodplain A Site 2 to be Saxon in date, Chapter 13 above). Above this soil horizon was further alluvial sediment.

Mollusc shells were preserved in the top of layer 2/5 (samples 10-11), which contained shells of aquatic and amphibious species. The aquatic species, particularly *Bithynia* sp., *Valvata cristata* and *Armiger crista*, had probably been derived from the well-vegetated moving water of the channel. The amphibious to stagnant water species, of which *Lymnaea truncatula* was the most abundant followed by *Anisus leucostoma*, probably lived on mud and in pools of stagnant water left by the retreating floodwaters, retreating into cracks if the ground surface became dry (Robinson 1988b).

Comparative studies on the floodplain of the Upper Thames Valley have shown that under overbank conditions, the amphibious molluscs occur in both pastures and hay meadows but the terrestrial species only occur in hay meadows (ibid.). The results, therefore, would suggest that Oxey Mead was pasture until the end of the Roman period.

Interpretation of the organic deposits from the palaeochannel

The organic sequence from the bottom of Trench 3 was divided into four samples, sample 3/8 (bottom)-3/5 (top). A calibrated radiocarbon date (at 95% confidence) of AD 240-540 (OxA-7360) was obtained for sample 3/7, while the beet of flax, which was from sample 3/6, gave a date of AD 660-1010 (OxA-3643). Samples 3/8 and 3/7 were probably of Roman date so have been considered here.

The majority of the macroscopic plant and mollusc remains from the palaeochannel samples were aquatic species which had been living in the channel. The insects had been derived from a larger catchment, but even so the majority of them were probably from the channel and bankside habitats.

The mollusc shells had apparently experienced differential preservation because the calcite opercula of *Bithynia* sp. greatly outnumbered the aragonite shells of this genus. Even so, the range of flowing water species included *Valvata piscinalis*, *Bithynia tentaculata* and *Pisidium amnicum* which showed that there were at least episodes of flow along the channel. There was a slight presence of beetles from the family Elmidae (which require clean, well oxygenated flowing water) with the occurrence of *Elmis aenea* and *Oulimnius* sp. The majority of the water beetles, however, were species most usually found in stagnant or slowly moving water, for example *Helophorus* cf. *brevipalpis* and *Ochthebius minimus*.

The seeds suggested a richly vegetated slowly flowing channel. The submerged-leaved community included *Ranunculus* S. *Batrachium* sp. (water crowfoot) and *Zannichellia palustris* (horned pondweed). The most abundant seeds of floating-leaved aquatic plants were from *Potamogeton* sp., but *Nuphar lutea* (yellow water-lily), *Nymphoides peltata* (fringed water-lily) and *Lemna* sp. (duckweed) were all present. A tall dense reedswamp evidently fringed much of the channel, the major plants including *Oenanthe aquatica* gp. (water dropwort), *Sagittaria sagittifolia* (arrow head), *Schoenoplectus lacustris* (bulrush) and *Glyceria* sp. (reed-grass).

Where the reedswamp was not so tall, plants such as *Mentha* cf. *aquatica* (water mint), *Alisma* sp. (water-plantain) and *Eleocharis* cf. *palustris* (spike rush) grew at the water's edge. The phytophagous insects supported and amplified the evidence from the seeds. The two most numerous donaciine chrysomelids were *Donacia semicuprea*, which feeds on *Glyceria maxima* (reed-grass), followed by *D. dentata*, which feeds on *Alisma* sp. and *Sagittaria sagittifolia*. *Prasocuris phellandrii*, which feeds on aquatic Umbelliferae, especially *Oenanthe* spp., was identified from all the samples, while *Tanysphyrus lemnae* confirmed the evidence from the seeds for *Lemna* sp. carpeting the surface of the water at the height of the summer. One aquatic plant added to the species list by the insects was *Butomus umbellatus* (flowering rush), the host of *Bagous nodulosus*.

The vegetation suggested by the plant and insect remains is still to be found on the quieter reaches and lushly vegetated back streams of the Thames,. A similar flora was described by Tansley in the vicinity of Yarnton at Medley Weir (Tansley 1939, 627-8). The sequence of waterlogged deposits described here perhaps spanned the Roman period but sedimentation continued into the Saxon period.

The seeds provided limited information on the bankside vegetation. Areas of exposed mud were suggested by *Myosoton aquaticum* (water chickweed), *Chenopodium rubrum* gp. (red goosefoot), *Rumex maritimus* (golden dock), *Polygonum persicaria* (red shank) and *P. lapathifolium* (pale persicaria). There was, however, little evidence for tall bankside vegetation beyond the reedswamp other than relatively low numbers of seeds of *Urtica dioica* (stinging nettle).

The Coleoptera included many species of marshy waterside habitats, for example the Carabidae *Blethisa multipunctata, Bembidion assimile, B. doris, Pterostichus nigrita, Agonum marginatum* and *A. viduum*. Staphylinidae from the genus *Stenus*, many of which occur in marshy habitats, were numerous. Coleoptera of Species Group 7 (Fig. 18.14) which occur in a range of types of foul organic material were well-represented, rising to 14% of the terrestrial Coleoptera in sample 3/7. The most abundant of these was *Cercyon* cf. *tristis*, a species which tends to be associated with accumulations of decaying plant debris in marshes and on river banks. *Anotylus rugosus*, another member of the group, was also abundant. Other small Staphylinidae of foul vegetable material such as fallen reeds included *Platystethus nodifrons*.

Unfortunately, the macroscopic plant remains did not give much evidence of the terrestrial landscape. There were few remains of trees or shrubs apart from several seeds of *Sambucus nigra* (elder). The insects suggested very open conditions. There were relatively few seeds of grassland plants. The most numerous were from *Ranunculus* cf. *repens* (creeping buttercup) but others included *Ranunculus acris* (meadow buttercup), *Filipendula ulmaria* (meadow sweet), *Potentilla anserina* (silverweed) and *Prunella vulgaris* (selfheal). These seeds do suggest grassland on the floodplain and give some indication of the range of species present. Seeds of species which are resilient to grazing, for example *R. repens* and *P. anserina*, were present, but there were insufficient seeds to allow characterisation of the grassland.

The Coleoptera gave clearer evidence for the occurrence of the grassland even though the percentages of all the grassland-related species groups were reduced by the high proportion of beetles from reedswamp and marginal habitats. (Fig. 18.14). Chafers and elaterids, with larvae that feed on the roots of grassland herbs (Species Group 11) including *Phyllopertha horticola*, species of *Athous* and species of *Agriotes* ranged from 2.2-3.1% of the terrestrial Coleoptera. Some of the Carabidae and Staphylinidae readily occur in grassland, for example *Pterostichus cupreus* and *Xantholinus linearis* or *longiventris*.

Scarabaeoid dung beetles which feed on the droppings of the larger herbivores, particularly domestic animals, on pastures (Species Group 2) (Robinson 1983, 30-4; 1991, 278-80), such as *Aphodius paykulli* and *A.* cf. *sphacelatus*, comprised around 4.6% of the terrestrial Coleoptera from samples 3/8 and 3/7. Weevils of the genera *Apion* and *Sitona*, which feed on clovers and vetches and are favoured by hay meadow conditions (Species Group 3) were not so well represented, comprising 2.2% of the terrestrial Coleoptera from these samples. Such results suggested the floodplain grassland to have been pasture.

The macroscopic plant and insect remains gave little evidence of the nearby settlement on the

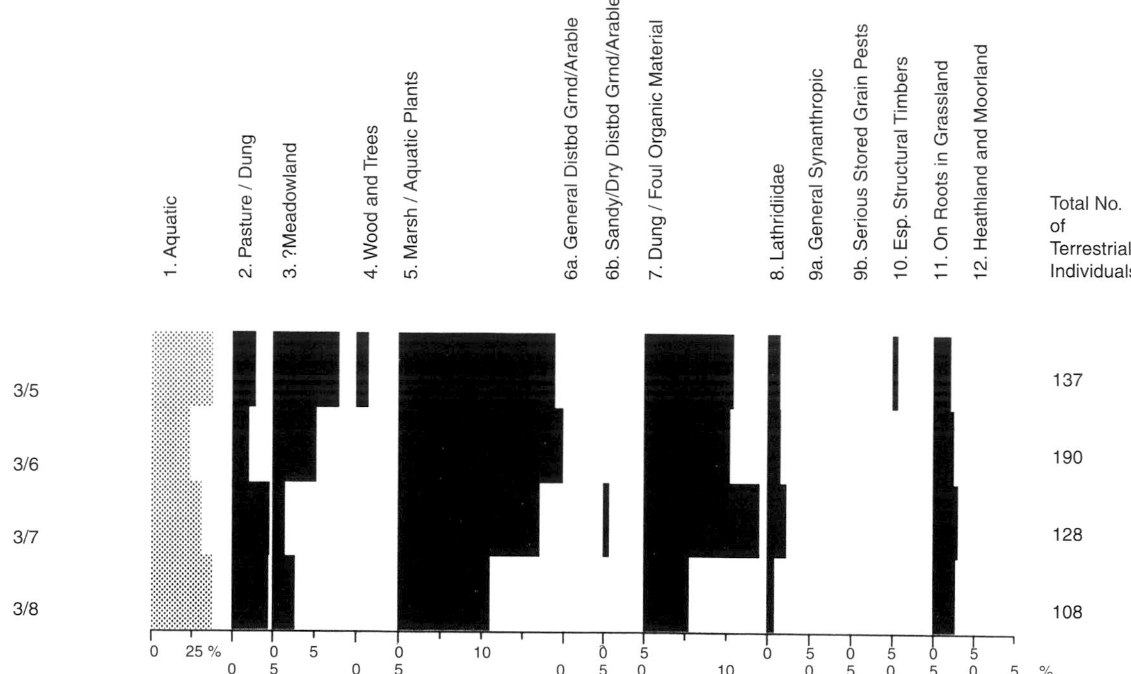

Fig. 18.14 Percentages of species groups of Coleoptera by habitat type: Yarnton Oxey Mead

Table 18.32 Waterlogged seeds from Yarnton Oxey Mead.

		Old ground surface	Oxey Mead palaeochannel	
Context		*2/10*	*3/8*	*3/7*
Sample		*7*		
Sample weight (kg.)		*0.5*	*0.5*	*0.5*
RANUNCULACEAE				
Ranunculus cf. *acris* L.	meadow buttercup	-	1	1
R. cf. *repens* L.	creeping buttercup	-	17	10
R. cf. *bulbosus* L.	bulbous buttercup	-	-	1
R. sceleratus L.	celery-leaved crowfoot	-	1	2
R. S. *Batrachium* sp.	water crowfoot	-	106	89
NYMPHAEACEAE				
Nuphar lutea (L.) Sm.	yellow water-lily	-	-	2
FUMARIACEAE				
Fumaria sp.	fumitory	-	1	-
CRUCIFERAE				
Rorippa cf. *palustris* (L.) Bes.	marsh yellow cress	-	1	-
Nasturtium microphyllum (Boenn.) Reich.	water-cress	-	-	3
CARYOPHYLLACEAE				
Cerastium cf. *fontanum* Baum.	mouse-ear chickweed	-	1	-
Myosoton aquaticum (L.) Moen.	water chickweed	-	-	9
Stellaria media gp.	chickweed	-	2	2
Sagina sp.	pearlwort	-	20	10
CHENOPODIACEAE				
Chenopodium album L.	fat hen	-	7	1
C. rubrum gp.	red goosefoot	-	5	4
Atriplex sp.	orache	1	-	-
ROSACEAE				
Filipendula ulmaria (L.) Max.	meadowsweet	-	-	1
Potentilla anserina L.	silverweed	4	2	5
P. reptans L.	creeping cinquefoil	1	-	-
HALORAGIDACEAE				
Myriophyllum sp.	water-milfoil	-	10	1
HIPPURIDACEAE				
Hippuris vulgaris L.	mare's tail	-	31	5
CALLITRICHACEAE				
Callitriche sp.	starwort	-	-	1
UMBELLIFERAE				
Hydrocotyle vulgaris L.	marsh pennywort	3	-	-
Sium latifolium L.	water parsnip	-	-	1
Oenanthe aquatica gp.	water-dropwort	-	38	75
Apium nodiflorum (L.) Lag.	fool's watercress	-	-	3
POLYGONACEAE				
Polygonum aviculare agg.	knotgrass	-	1	1
P. persicaria L.	red shank	-	2	13
P. lapathifolium L.	pale persicaria	-	-	3
Rumex acetosella agg.	sheep's sorrel	-	-	1
R. hydrolapathum Huds.	water dock	-	-	1
R. conglomeratus Mur.	sharp dock	-	-	-
R. maritimus L.	golden dock	-	11	11
Rumex spp. (not *maritimus*)	dock	-	2	2
URTICACEAE				
Urtica urens L.	small nettle	-	1	-
U. dioica L.	stinging nettle	-	38	12
PRIMULACEAE				
cf. *Anagallis arvensis* L.	pimpernel	-	-	1
MENYANTHACEAE				
Nymphoides peltata (Gml.) Kz.	fringed water-lily	-	4	4
BORAGINACEAE				
Myosotis sp.	forget-me-not	-	-	3

Table 18.32 Waterlogged seeds from Yarnton Oxey Mead (continued).

		Old ground surface	*Oxey Mead palaeochannel*	
Context		*2/10*	*3/8*	*3/7*
Sample		*7*		
Sample weight (kg.)		*0.5*	*0.5*	*0.5*
SOLANACEAE				
Hyoscyamus niger L.	henbane	-	-	1
Solanum dulcamara L.	woody nightshade	-	-	1
SCROPHULARIACEAE				
Veronica Sect. *Beccabunga* sp.	water speedwell	-	40	-
LABIATAE				
Mentha cf. *aquatica* L.	water mint	15	17	32
Lycopus europaeus L.	gipsywort	-	2	-
Prunella vulgaris L.	selfheal	-	1	-
PLANTAGINACEAE				
Plantago major L.	great plantain	-	1	-
RUBIACEAE				
Galium sp. (not *aparine*)	bedstraw	-	-	1
CAPRIFOLIACEAE				
Sambucus nigra L.	elder	-	-	2
COMPOSITAE				
Sonchus asper (L.) Hill	sow-thistle	-	-	1
ALISMATACEAE				
Alisma sp.	water-plantain	-	30	18
Sagittaria sagittifolia L.	arrow-head	-	31	64
POTAMOGETONACEAE				
Potamogeton sp.	pondweed	-	14	20
ZANNICHELLIACEAE				
Zannichellia palustris L.	horned pondweed	-	52	24
JUNCACEAE				
Juncus effusus gp.	tussock rush	130	30	-
J. bufonius gp.	toad rush	-	32	10
J. articulatus gp.	rush	20	30	10
Juncus sp.	rush	80	20	-
IRIDACEAE				
Iris pseudacorus L.	yellow flag	-	1	-
LEMNACEAE				
Lemna sp.	duckweed	-	2	-
SPARGANIACEAE				
Sparganium sp.	bur-reed	-	-	1
CYPERACEAE				
Eleocharis cf. *palustris* (L.) R. & S. ssp. *vulgaris* Walt.	spike rush	25	14	2
Schoenoplectus lacustris (L.) Pal.	bulrush	-	14	21
Isolepis setacea (L.) R. Br.	bristle club-rush	-	1	-
Carex spp.	sedge	18	2	2
GRAMINEAE				
Glyceria sp.	reed-grass	-	2	3
Gramineae indeterminate	grass	-	-	2
Total		297	638	493

Table 18.33 Other waterlogged plant remains from Yarnton Oxey Mead.

			Oxey Mead palaeochannel	
Context			*3/8*	*3/7*
Sample weight (kg.)			*0.5*	*0.5*
Bryophyta indeterminate	- stem with leaves	moss	+	+
Chara sp.	- oospores	stonewort	396	568

+ present

Table 18.34 Coleoptera from Yarnton Oxey Mead.

Context	Oxey Mead palaeochannel 3/8	3/7	Species Group
Sample weight (kg.)	4.0	4.0	
CARABIDAE			
Blethisa multipunctata (L.)	1	-	
Elaphrus riparius (L.)	1	-	
Dyschirius globosus (Hbst.)	1	1	
Bembidion gilvipes Sturm	-	2	
B assimile Gyl.	1	1	
B. doris (Pz.)	1	1	
B. biguttatum (F.)	1	3	
B. guttula (F.)	1	1	
Bembidion sp.	1	2	
Pterostichus cupreus (L.)	-	1	
P. cf. *gracilis* (Dej.)	-	1	
P. nigrita (Pk.)	2	1	
Agonum marginatum (L.)	1	-	
A. piceum (L.)	1	1	
A. cf. *versutum* Sturm	1	1	
Amara bifrons (Gyl.)	-	1	
Amara sp.	1	-	
Harpalus azureus (F.)	1	-	
Acupalpus exiguus Dej.	1	-	
Badister bipustulatus (F.)	-	1	
HALIPLIDAE			
Haliplus sp.	2	1	1
NOTERIDAE			
Noterus clavicornis (Deg.)	1	2	1
DYTISCIDAE			
Hygrotus inaequalis (F.)	1	-	1
H. versicolor (Schal.)	-	1	1
Hydroporus sp.	1	-	1
Porhydrus lineatus (F.)	-	2	1
Platambus maculatus (L.)	1	1	1
Agabus bipustulatus (L.)	1	1	1
Agabus sp. (not *bipustulatus*)	1	1	1
Colymbetes fuscus (L.)	1	1	1
Dytiscus sp.	1	-	1
GYRINIDAE			
Gyrinus sp.	-	1	1
HYDROPHILIDAE			
Helophorus aquaticus (L.)	3	2	1
Helophorus sp. (*brevipalpis* size)	9	5	1
Coelostoma orbiculare (F.)	-	1	1
Cercyon haemorrhoidalis (F.)	1	1	7
C. melanocephalus (L.)	-	1	7
C. cf. *sternalis* Sharp	2	1	7
C. cf. *tristis* (Ill.)	2	8	7
Megasternum obscurum (Marsh.)	-	3	7
Hydrobius fuscipes (L.)	2	2	1
Laccobius sp.	1	1	1
HISTERIDAE			
Histerinae indeterminate	1	-	
HYDRAENIDAE			
Ochthebius bicolon Germ.	1	-	1
O. minimus (F.)	5	5	1
O. cf. *minimus* (F.)	8	5	1
Hydraena cf. *riparia* Kug.	-	2	1
Limnebius papposus Muls.	1	1	1

Table 18.34 Coleoptera from Yarnton Oxey Mead (cont'd).

Context	Oxey Mead palaeochannel 3/8	3/7	Species Group
Sample weight (kg.)	4.0	4.0	
PTILIIDAE			
Ptiliidae indeterminate (not *Ptenidium*)	2	-	
LEIODIDAE			
Choleva or *Catops* sp.	1	-	
STAPHYLINIDAE			
Carpelimus bilineatus Step.	1	1	
C. cf. *corticinus* (Grav.)	2	3	
Platystethus cornutus gp.	-	1	
P. nodifrons (Man.)	5	3	
Anotylus nitidulus (Grav.)	1	3	
A. rugosus (F.)	1	3	7
A. sculpturatus gp.	-	1	7
Stenus spp.	3	4	
Paederus littoralis (Grav.)	2	2	
Lathrobium sp.	2	-	
Rugilus orbiculatus (Pk.)	1	-	
Xantholinus linearis (Ol.) or *longiventris* Heer	1	2	
Philonthus spp.	6	4	
Gabrius sp.	4	-	
Mycetoporus sp.	-	1	
Tachyporus sp.	-	1	
Tachinus sp.	1	1	
Aleocharinae indeterminate	9	6	
GEOTRUPIDAE			
Geotrupes sp.	1	-	2
SCARABAEIDAE			
Aphodius granarius (L.)	-	1	2
A. cf. *niger* (Pz.)	1	-	
A. paykulli Bed.	-	1	2
A. rufipes (L.)	-	1	2
A. cf. *sphacelatus* (Pz.)	3	2	2
Aphodius sp.	1	-	2
Onthophagus ovatus (L.)	1	-	2
Onthophagus sp. (not *ovatus*)	-	1	2
Phyllopertha horticola (L.)	1	2	11
CLAMBIDAE			
Clambus sp.	-	1	
HETEROCERIDAE			
Heterocerus sp.	1	2	
DRYOPIDAE			
Dryops sp.	1	3	1
ELMIDAE			
Elmis aenea (Müll.)	-	1	1
Oulimnius sp.	-	1	1
ELATERIDAE			
Agrypnus murinus (L.)	-	1	11
Agriotes obscurus (L.)	1	-	11
Agriotes sp.	1	1	11
CANTHARIDAE			
Cantharis sp.	1	1	
NITIDULIDAE			
Brachypterus urticae (F.)	1	-	
Meligethes sp.	1	1	
CRYPTOPHAGIDAE			

Table 18.34 Coleoptera from Yarnton Oxey Mead (cont'd).

Context	*Oxey Mead palaeochannel* 3/8	3/7	
Sample weight (kg.)	*4.0*	*4.0*	*Species Group*
Atomaria sp.	2	-	
PHALACRIDAE			
Stilbus sp.	1	-	
CORYLOPHIDAE			
Corylophus cassidoides (Marsh.)	-	2	
COCCINELLIDAE			
Scymnus frontalis (F.)	-	1	
LATHRIDIIDAE			
Enicmus transversus (Ol.)	-	2	8
Corticariinae indeterminate	1	1	8
OEDEMERIDAE			
Oedemera lurida (Marsh.)	1	-	
BRUCHIDAE			
Bruchus or *Bruchidius* sp.	-	1	
CHRYSOMELIDAE			
Donacia aquatica (L.)	-	1	5
D. dentata Hoppe	3	2	5
D. impressa Pk.	1	1	5
D. semicuprea Pz.	-	3	5
Donacia sp.	-	1	5
Plateumaris sp.	1	-	5
Chrysolina hyperici (Forst.)	-	1	
Gastrophysa viridula (Deg.)	-	1	
Phaedon sp. (not *tumidulus*)	1	1	
Prasocuris phellandrii (L.)	1	2	5
Phyllotreta atra (F.)	2	-	

Table 18.34 Coleoptera from Yarnton Oxey Mead (cont'd).

Context	*Oxey Mead palaeochannel* 3/8	3/7	
Sample weight (kg.)	*4.0*	*4.0*	*Species Group*
P. vittula Redt.	-	1	
Aphthona nonstriata (Gz.)	1	1	5
Longitarsus spp.	-	1	
Chaetocnema concinna (Marsh.)	3	2	
Chaetocnema sp. (not *concinna*)	-	3	
APIONIDAE			
Apion spp. (not above)	2	2	3
CURCULIONIDAE			
Phyllobius sp.	-	1	
Sitona sp.	1	-	3
Lixus paraplecticus (L.)	-	-	5
Tanysphyrus lemnae (Pk.)	-	2	5
Bagous nodulosus Gyl.	-	1	5
Bagous sp.	1	1	5
Notaris acridulus (L.)	2	3	5
Thryogenes cf. *nereis* (Pk.)	-	2	5
Eubrychius velutus (Beck)	1	-	5
Litodactylus leucogaster (Marsh.)	-	1	5
Ceuthorhynchinae indeterminate	3	1	
Limnobaris pilistriata (Step.)	1	-	5
Anthonomus cf. *rubi* (Hbst.)	-	1	
Tychius sp.	1	1	
Gymnetron villosulum Gyl.	-	1	5
Total	149	168	

Table 18.35 Other insects from Yarnton Oxey Mead.

Context		*Oxey Mead palaeochannel* 3/8	3/7	3/6	3/5
Sample weight (kg.)		*4.0*	*4.0*	*4.0*	*4.0*
HEMIPTERA - HETEROPTERA					
Saldula S. *Saldula* sp.		1	-	1	
- HOMOPTERA					
Aphrodes bicinctus (Schr.)		1	-	2	2
Aphrodes sp.		-	1	1	-
TRICHOPTERA					
Trichoptera indeterminate	- larva	11	14	21	17
Trichoptera indeterminate	- case	8	51	126	102
HYMENOPTERA					
Lasius sp. (not *fuliginosus*)	- female	1	-	-	-
Apis mellifera L.	- worker	-	1	-	-
Hymenoptera indeterminate	- adult head	4	6	7	3
DIPTERA					
Chironomidae indeterminate	- larva	+	+	+	+
Dilophus febrilis (L.) or *femoratus* (Meig.)		1	1	2	-
Diptera indeterminate	- puparium	-	2	-	-
Diptera indeterminate	- adult	4	3	2	5

\+ present

Table 18.36 Mollusca from Yarnton Oxey Mead.

	Oxey Mead floodplain alluvium		*Oxey Mead palaeochannel*	
Context	2/4	2/4	3/8	3/7
Sample	10	11		
Sample weight (kg.)	0.5	0.5	0.5	0.5
GASTROPODA				
Valvata cristata Müll.	4	65	2	27
V. piscinalis (Müll.)	-	-	-	59
Bithynia tentaculata (L.)	-	6	1	12
Bithynia spp.	18	103	55	459
Lymnaea truncatula (Müll.)	27	61	-	2
L. palustris (Müll.)	2	2	1	2
L. peregra (Müll.)	2	2	2	3
Lymnaea sp.	-	1	-	-
Planorbis planorbis (L.)	-	1	3	6
Anisus leucostoma (Mill.)	-	15	-	1
A. vortex (L.)	-	-	3	2
Bathyomphalus contortus (L.)	-	1	1	1
Gyraulus albus (Müll.)	1	1	2	3
Armiger crista L.	9	52	-	5
Planorbarius corneus (L.)	-	-	-	2
Succinea or *Oxyloma* sp.	1	6	1	2
Limax or *Deroceras* sp.	-	2	-	1
BIVALVIA				
Sphaerium corneum (L.)	-	-	-	1
Pisidium amnicum (Müll.)	-	-	-	1
Pisidium spp.	1	4	6	14
Total	65	322	77	603

Second Gravel Terrace. The various Coleoptera which tend to be associated with human habitation (Species Groups 8-10) were either absent or gave very low percentage values. A single seed of *Hyoscyamus niger* (henbane) from sample 3/7 perhaps reflected midden vegetation. One record of interest was the head of a worker of *Apis mellifera* (honey bee) from sample 3/7.

The results for the Coleoptera from samples 3/8 and 3/7 from the palaeochannel suggested that Oxey Mead was grazed grassland during the Roman period. The contrast shown by the results from these samples with the results from samples 3/6 and 3/5 presented in Figure 18.14 were consistent with a post-Roman origin for the hay meadow of Oxey Mead.

YARNTON FLOODPLAIN GEOARCHAEOLOGICAL ANALYSIS *by Matt Canti*

Floodplain profile development

A typical soil profile on the floodplain site shows gravel at a depth of 60 cm over which is a fairly coarse layer which has been referred to as a Roman ploughsoil. Over this, alluvium is found from about 40 cm upwards going into a modern ploughed layer at the top. It is currently believed that the Roman ploughsoil became increasingly unworkable due to flooding and alluvial deposition. If this is correct, then there should be some alluvial material in the ploughsoil itself. Two scenarios present themselves as possibilities:-

Either (a) the 'ploughsoil' is derived from the gravels (by decalcification and fine earthworm sorting along with perhaps some loess deposition) and the later alluvium is significantly different; if this is the case, there may be a particle size or heavy mineral variation which can be used as a signature to separate them.

Alternatively (b) since the 'ploughsoil' and the alluvium are both derived from the same source area (mainly Cotswold limestones) they are texturally and mineralogically similar despite significantly different modes of formation.

Methods

To test these ideas, two profiles 1 metre apart were selected in the road cutting at SP 47208 10862. They were sampled as follows:-

Floodplain Profile 1		
0-25 cm	Topsoil and spoil from gravel workings	(Sample 1A from 25-30 cm)
25-40 cm	Grey-orange alluvium	(Sample 1B from 30-35 cm)
40-55 cm	Orange 'ploughsoil'	(Sample 1C from 45-50 cm)
55 cm -	Gravel	(Sample 1D from 55-60 cm)
Floodplain Profile 2		
0-25 cm	Topsoil and spoil from gravel workings	(Sample 2A from 25-30 cm)
25-35 cm	Grey alluvium	(Sample 2B from 30-35 cm)
35-60 cm	Orange 'ploughsoil'	(Sample 2C from 45-50 cm)
60 cm -	Gravel	(Sample 2D from 60-65 cm)

The eight samples were tested for particle size using a mixture of sieves and Sedigraph (Canti 1991) and for the heavy mineral percentages in the 125-63 μm fraction, using 1,1,2,2, tetrabromoethane extraction.

Results

The profiles (Figs 18.15 and 18.16) both show fine materials (A, B and C samples) overlying very coarse gravels (D samples). In both cases, the C samples are not quite parallel with the other two from the upper part of the profile. Both cross the A and B lines and become flatter, due to lower silt contents. However, it is not practicable to try and relate this to the fine content of the gravel. There is simply too little silt in the gravel (around 7% at most) to make a meaningful assessment of its particle size characteristics.

The heavy mineral counts did not support the view that there was any fundamental variation between the gravelly basal materials, the ploughsoil and the alluvial layers. There are some differences

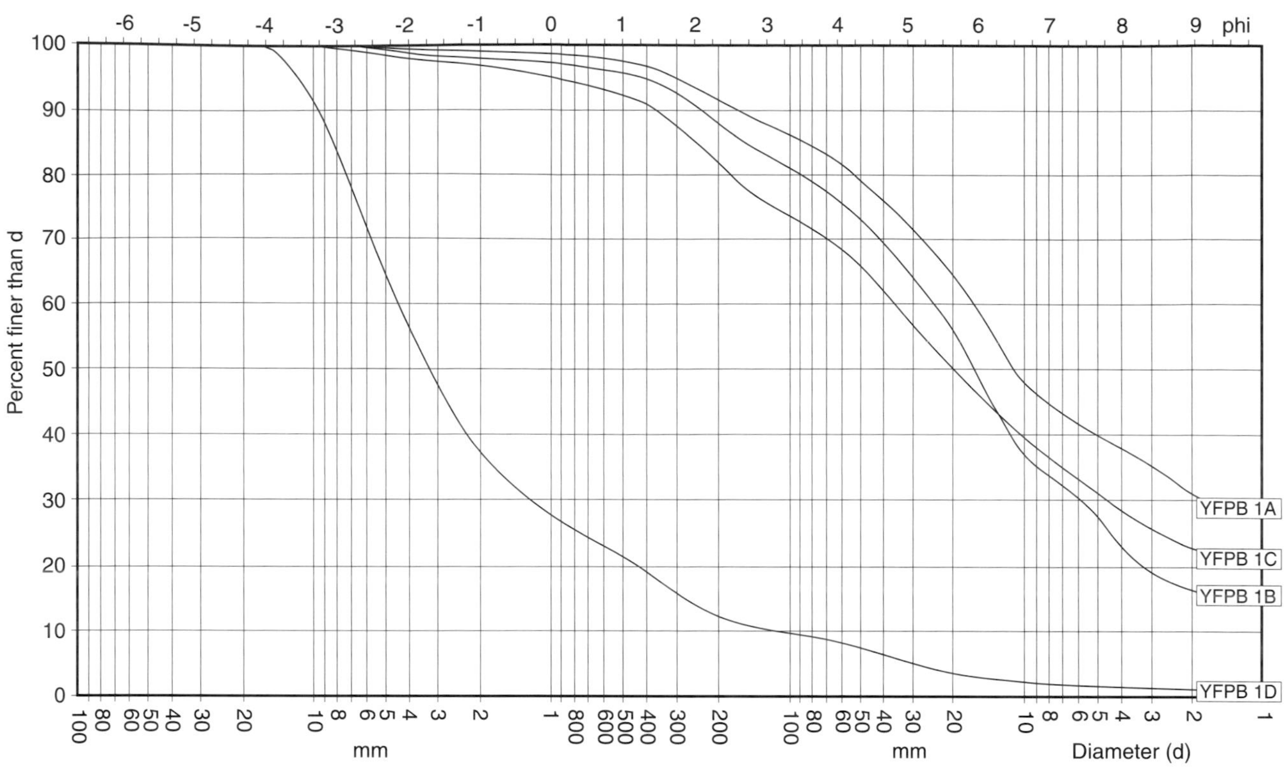

Fig. 18.15 Particle-size distributions of samples from Flooplain Profile 1

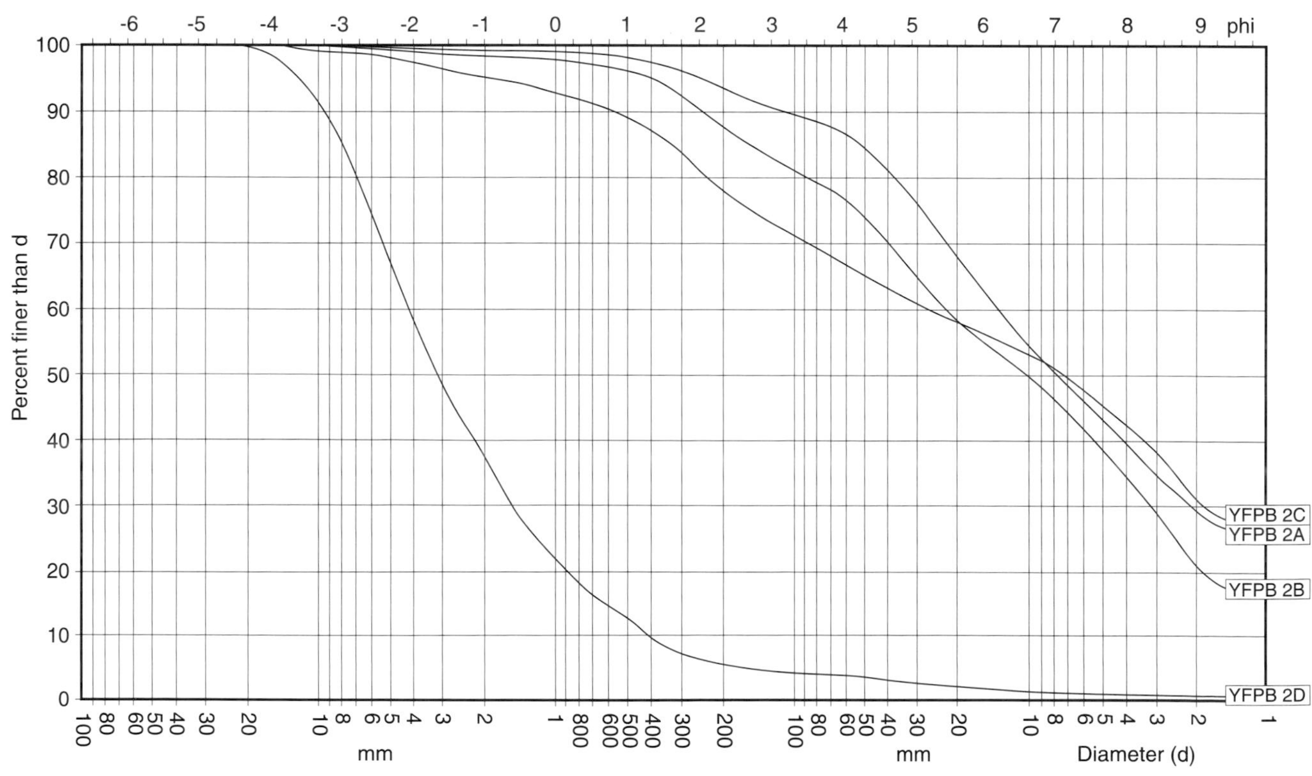

Fig. 18.16 Particle-size distributions of samples from Flooplain Profile 2

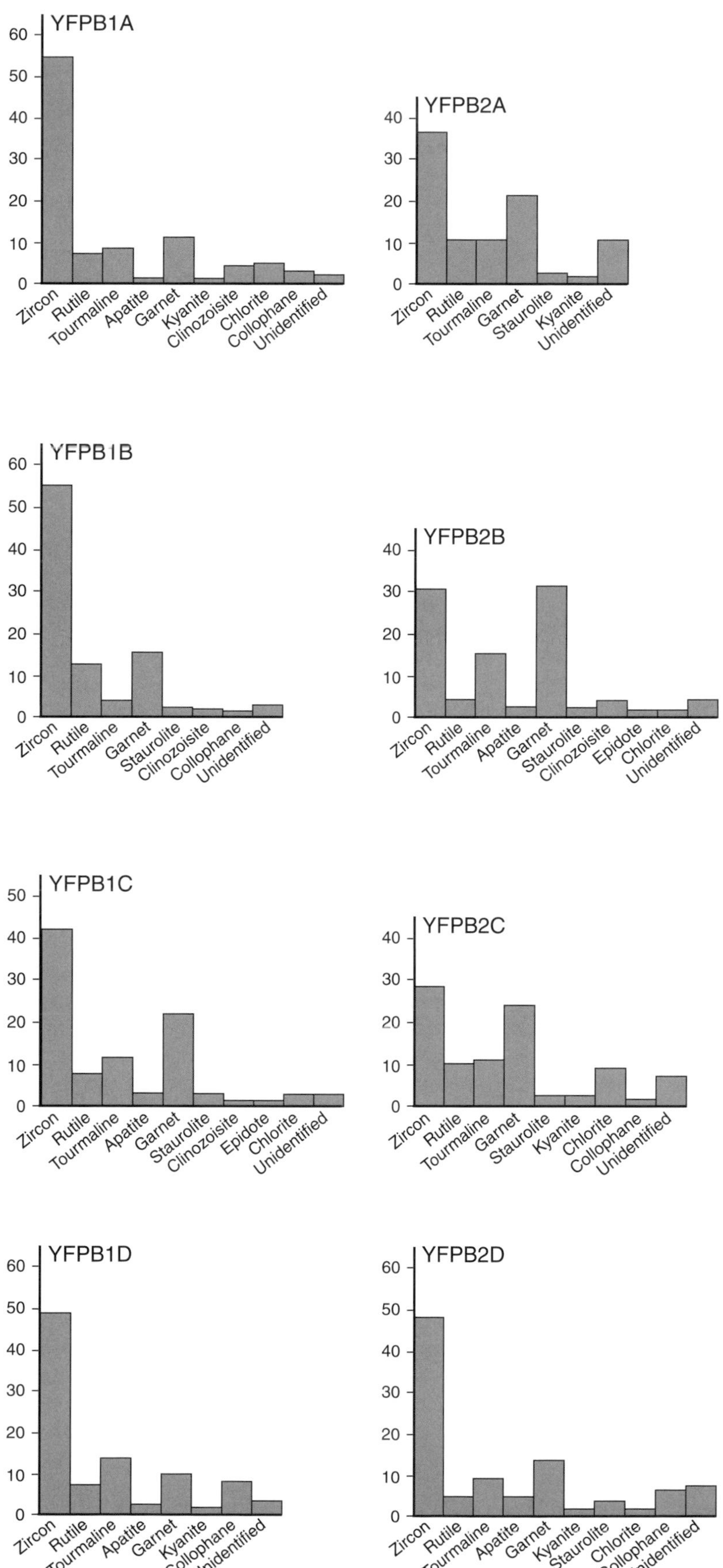

Fig. 18.17 Heavy minerals (>1%) in the samples from the two floodplain profiles

in the details of both the zircon and garnet levels, but they are as variable between similar deposits (eg the C samples) as they are between top and bottom of the profiles (Fig. 18.17).

It has therefore not been possible to show conclusively that an alluvial component has been added to the upper parts of the ploughsoil, due to the very low silt content of the underlying gravel and the mineralogical similarity (see option (b), above) of the alluvial and ploughsoil layers.

Chapter 19: Waterlogged wood

by Maisie Taylor

INTRODUCTION

Nearly 200 pieces of wood relating to the middle Iron Age causeway in Yarnton Floodplain Site 9 were submitted for analysis. The wood was examined in three groups:

- Wood which was part of a pre-stone phase of the causeway.
- Wood (vertical and horizontal) on the edge of the structure
- Wood used as patching or repair

There were also rows of uprights running parallel with the causeway but at a distance; the phasing of these is uncertain.

The condition of the wood was very variable, and often not good, depending on whether it overlay the limestone or not, but some data were retrieved and the assemblage represents a reasonable selection of Iron Age wood working practices. The assemblage was examined for evidence of woodworking as well as the type of wood and evidence for woodland management. A great deal of information was recorded in the field and samples were taken for identification of species. Much of this later work had been completed in the Post-excavation Room at Flag Fen in Peterborough when there was a serious fire which totally destroyed the building. Most of the notes and paperwork had gone to another building for adding to the computer record and filing when the fire happened, but everything that was left in the post-excavation room was destroyed. Wood which was stored in tanks adjacent to the building was also destroyed as the heat melted plastic (including labels) and evaporated water etc. This means that there are fewer species identifications than would be ideal and the amount of material for radiocarbon dating was limited.

RESULTS

Causeway phase 1

Uprights associated with earliest surviving causeway (contexts 18128 and 18193)

There are 25 pieces of wood from these contexts, most of which (19) are roundwood with four showing signs of coppicing. The diameters range from 12-52 mm (Table 19.1). The split wood is worked in various ways: a half split, two quarter splits, two radial splits and one hewn square. All the split wood is generally smaller than the roundwood with sizes varying from 20 mm square to 32 x 37 mm.

Timber 18193 is a vertical, possibly from the earliest surviving causeway. It has a flat top, possibly cut off to accommodate later phases of the trackway.

Horizontals of earliest surviving causeway (context 18192)

There was a group of small diameter roundwood timbers beneath the limestone causeway. This was in very poor condition. It was noted, however, that there were a number of coppiced heels. The material identified to species for radiocarbon dating was willow or poplar (*Salix/Populus* sp.). There is no apparent pattern in the deposition of the material, which suggest that it was probably a simple brushwood structure. The diameters of the roundwood ranged between 10 mm and 19 mm.

Causeway phase 2

Verticals to the east (contexts 18000, 18001, 18095, 18133 and 18139-18146)

The vertical wood from these contexts is mainly radial splits (9) but there is also some roundwood (6) and a few other modified pieces: four quarter splits, two half splits, one squared piece and one cross-grained. There is a large variation in the dimensions of the verticals (see Table 19.2). The typical dimensions of a smaller piece might be 33 x 11 mm, with larger pieces up to 142 x 36 mm.

Verticals to the west (18002, 18134 and 18050)

The verticals to the west of the causeway are also mainly radial splits (26) with small numbers of other modified pieces: four half splits, two quarter splits and two squared timbers. There are also two pieces of roundwood. The dimensions of the verticals to the west suggest a slightly lighter weight structure with a range of 20 x 15 mm to 100 x 33 mm (Table 19.2).

Horizontals to the east (18000, 18001, 18080, 18106 and Misc. 18092, 18093 and 18096)

The character of the horizontal wood is very similar to that of the verticals with radially split planks

Table 19.1: Measurements (in mm) of verticals Phase 1

No.	Species	Length	Width	Thickness	Diameter	Comment
18128						**context group**
18124	Q	225			50	coppice curve, trimmed one end
18125	Q	625			39	coppice curve, trimmed one end
18126	nr	530			44	coppice curve, trimmed one end
18127	Q	450			47	coppice curve, trimmed one end
18131	nr	c 220	32	13		half split
18132	nr	?			40	
18135	nr	?	12	12		quarter split, original dia 25 mm
18136	nr	?			28	
18137	nr	?			42	
18138	nr	?			32	
18178	nr	?			40	
18179	nr	?			46	
18180	nr	?			41	
18181	Q	?			44	
18182	Q	?			34	
18183	Q	?			28	
18184	Q	?			24	
18185	Q	?			30	
18186	Q	?			36	
18187	Q	?			26	
18188	Q	?	20	20		quarter split, original dia 40 mm
18189	Q	?			52	radial
18190	nr	?			24	radial
18191	Q	?	32	37		squared roundwood
Misc						
18193						
	nr	?			50	possible upright of earliest surviving causeway

Q = *Quercus* (sp.); nr = species not recorded

predominating (17). Additionally there are five quarter split pieces, two of which are worked across the grain, one which is half split, and one piece which is roundwood. The two tangentially split timbers, however, are a type not represented among the verticals. Typical measurements suggest that much of the material is also similar in size to the verticals with dimensions between 30 x 18 mm and 114 x 25 mm (Table 19.3).

Horizontal to the west (18003, 18097, 18106, 18134 and 18050)

Once again the horizontal element appears to be closely similar technologically to the vertical element with most of the pieces being radially split (27). There are also four quarter split pieces and one which is cross-grained. There are a further four tangentially split timbers on this side of the causeway. The dimensions follow the same pattern as before with the horizontals to the west being slightly lighter in weight than the verticals, with dimensions ranging from 25 x 12 mm to 100 x 33 mm (Table 19.3).

Causeway phase 3

Possible repairs (18077)

There are nine pieces of wood in this group. It was suggested in the field notes that this may be the remains of some kind of 'chestnut paling' fencing or repairs, but this suggestion is problematic. Most of the strength of modern chestnut paling comes from the wire that binds it together and there is no ancient equivalent. Wood bound together with twine or rope might be quite strong when first constructed but would not retain its strength for very long, deteriorating quickly with the water and weather. The individual pieces are generally longer and finer than those from phase 2.

Uncertain phasing (18075, 18076, 18094, 18109 and 18110)

The material which makes up the rows of verticals is quite variable: 18075 and 18076 are both small diameter roundwood, while 18094 is radially split oak. The two groups 18109 and 18110 are both double rows aligned north-south. None of this material is very heavy.

Table 19.2: Measurements (in mm) of verticals Phase 2

No.	Species	Length	Width	Thickness	Diameter	Comment
18000						**context group E side**
18008	Q	>160	55	55		roundwood, rotted, estimated original dia c 90
18018	Q	>100	62	35		radial post
18081	Q	>50	75	16		radial split
18091	Q	760	60	32		radial split
18001						**context group E side**
18062	Q	825	114	20		radial post, fallen
18106						**context group E side**
18070	Q	605	100	33		radial, long point
18071	Q	>85			45/70	roundwood?
18072	Q	330	98	69		roughly quarter split
18073	Q	530	58	46		quarter split, long point, possible joint
18074	Q	?	58	24		radial
18078	Q	380	55	54		radial
18979	Q	250	56	18		tangential
18133						**context group E side**
18130	Q	330	142	36		split cross-grain
18139	Q	?			40/50	
18140	nr	?			50	
18141	nr	?	35	17		half split, original dia 35
18142	Q	?	60	31		squared roundwood
18143	nr	?			31	
18144	nr	?	70	46		quarter split
18145	nr	85			30	
18146	Q	270	40	32		radial
18002						**context group W side**
18052	Q	280	54	31		half split
18050						**context group W side**
18037	Q	>90	90	32		radial post
18134						**context group W side**
18129	Q	496	95	44		squared roundwood
18147	Q	?	25	20		radial
18148	Q	?	30	20		radial
18149	Q	?	34	20		radial
18150	Q	?	50	20		radial
18151	Q	?	35	32		radial
18152	Q	?	40	15		radial
18153	Q	?	48	27		radial
18154	Q	?	25	20		radial
18155	Q	?	55	28		radial
18156	Q	?	30	15		radial
18157	Q	?	38	20		radial
18158	Q	?	28	25		radial
18159	nr	?	38	25		half split
18160	Q	?	40	20		radial
18161	Q	?	20	15		radial
18162	Q	?	32	32		half split
18163	Q	?	40	30		radial
18164	Q	?			20	
18165	nr	?	40	24		half split
18166	Q	?	42	30		radial
18167	Q	?	42	30		radial
18168	nr	?	47	30		half split
18169	nr	?	36	32		radial
18170	Q	?			38	
18171	Q	?	34	34		quarter split
18172	Q	?	86	42		radial
18173	Q	?			37	
18174	Q	?	71	15		radial
18175	Q	?	35	26		quarter split
18176	Q	?	60	16		radial
Misc						**W side**
18095	Q	>35	32	11		radial
18102	Q	?	60	25		hewn or split square
18103	Q	?	32	10		radial
18104	Q	70	40	15		radial
18105	Q	180	60	30		radial, trimmed one end

Q = *Quercus* (sp.); nr = species not recorded

Table 19.3: Measurements (in mm) of horizontals Phase 2

No.	Species	Length	Width	Thickness	Comment
18000					**context group E side**
18004	Q	532	110	46	radial plank
18005	Q	670	80	43	radial plank
18006	Q	535	70	27	radial plank
18007	Q	1027	55	30	quarter split plank
18009	Q	150	40	18	radial
18010	Q	480	82	20	quarter split
18011	Q	240	35	20	half split
18012	Q	320	32	28	quarter split
18013	Q	295	30	25	quarter split
18014	Q	520	60	22	radial split
18015	Q	110	35	22	radial split
18016	Q	150		12	roundwood, poor condition , one trimmed end,
18017	Q		32	20	split across grain
18001					**context group E side**
18058	Q	230	70	16	radial
18059	Q	545	45	14	radial
18060	Q	530	60	35	quarter split
18061	Q	510	40	37	radial, possible trimmed end
18063	Q	448	54	25	radial, possibly notched
18064	Q	620	92	18	radial
18065	Q	340	80	14	radial
18066	Q	380	73	11	radial
18067	Q	305	70	17	radial
18068	Q	370	48	26	radial
18069	Q	470	75	52	cross grained
Misc					**E side**
18092	Q	350	50	15	radial
18093	Q	106	45	33	tangential
18101	Q	820	35	10	radial
18002					**context group W side**
18019	Q	690	52	30	radial split
18020	Q	900	32	18	radial and tapering
18021	Q	320	32	13	quarter split
18022	Q	190	36	9	tangential split
18023	Q	360	42	14	radial
18024	Q	190	45	37	radial
18025	Q	450	36	30	radial
18026	Q	570	37	26	radial
18027	Q	555	74	20	radial
18028	Q	680	75	21	radial
18029	Q	190	41	30	radial, one end trimmed
18030	Q	290	50	35	tangential, one end trimmed
18032	Q	84	22	14	cross-grained
18003					**context group W side**
18045	Q	250	31	13	radial
18046	Q	642	61	35	quarter split
18047	Q	515	52	34	radial
18048	Q	1160	45	26	radial, smooth flat rounded end
18049	Q	530	60	20	radial
18054	Q	480	40	17	radial
18055	Q	410	54	28	quarter split
18056	Q	610	40	30	radial

Table 19.3: Measurements (in mm) of horizontals Phase 2 (continued).

No.	Species	Length	Width	Thickness	Comment
18057	Q	330	26	17	radial
18050					**context group W side**
18033	Q	560	50	25	radial
18034	Q	150	30	10	tangential
18035	Q	1170	25	23	radial
18036	Q	220	35	9	radial
18038	Q	250	33	6	radial
18039	Q	615	38	9	radial
18040	Q	350	63	7	radial
18041	Q	>160	72	14	radial
18042	Q	>350	30	12	radial, ?attached to 18043 & 18044
Misc					**W side**
18096	Q	520	90	13	radial
18097	Q	630	38	23	tangential
18098	Q	680	30	30	quarter split
18099	Q	215	59	21	radial
18100	Q	415	50	22	radial

Q = *Quercus* (sp.); nr = species not recorded

Rope (18053)

The rope appears to have been quite extensive but was not in very good condition and was difficult to excavate, with the longest piece exposed only 190 mm long. It was not clear during excavation whether there was any pattern which would help with interpreting the use of the rope. It seemed most likely that the rope had been used to bind together several of the timbers (probably 18042 to 18043 and 18044) lining the causeway. Unfortunately it was not well enough preserved to allow detailed understanding of how it was manufactured, but photographs of the material *in situ* suggest that it was made of a simple twisted stem. Long woody stems of plants such as honeysuckle can be made quite pliable by soaking and twisting.

Joints (18031 and 18071)

Two possible joints were identified in the field but at the time neither was thought to be very convincing. 18031 is a split vertical with a horizontal (18032) possibly resting on it or possibly articulated in a joint. 18071 is a roundwood vertical in a similar arrangement, but the top is better preserved. The open faced joint is carved into the end grain of the roundwood with two 'ears' or 'fingers' to hold the horizontal. This is a common type of joint, usually used in prehistoric contexts to join two roundwood timbers (see Taylor 2001, figs 7.33 1, 2 and 6 for example, where similar joints are referred to as 'eared housing joints').

DISCUSSION

Woodland management

A number of pieces (eg 18125-7) show classic evidence for coppicing such as heels or curved stems, but there were also some strangely shaped pieces and some which were very knotty. Further evidence for coppicing lies in the small radial planks which are typical of those split out of trunks derived from overgrown coppice. Work ongoing on Iron Age woodworking from other sites (Fiskerton, Lincolnshire and Eton Rowing Lakes for example) is beginning to indicate that material from overgrown coppice is a feature of the period. Coppice cut on a short rotation will produce thin, flexible rods for wattle work, hurdling and so on, but if the coppice is either neglected, or cut on a much longer rotation then a completely different kind of material is produced. Oak which is coppiced and then left for twenty years or more will produce fewer stems but the trunks will be largely straight grained and of a useful size for radial splitting into planks. Feather edge planks from these stems will be of uniform quality and excellent for buildings. The presence of so much knotty and misshapen material suggests that these coppices might have been neglected rather than worked on an extended cycle, or that the wood simply represents regrowth from felling.

Thin, radially split planks are easily manufactured from long, straight poles and would show a distinctive pattern in the growth rings if the poles were derived from coppices. Almost all these planks seem to have growth rings which are 2 or 3 mm wide or narrower, which seems rather slow grown for coppices. After cutting back, coppice stems usually grow strongly for several years producing wide growth rings, but this does not appear to be the case here. If the oak was growing on low lying ground close by then its re-growth may have been slower because of the stress caused by growing in an over-wet environment.

Causeway construction

There are a number of problems with the interpretation of the causeway construction. There is, for example, no obvious pairing of the uprights which might suggest that there could have been some kind of superstructure. The verticals could have fulfilled various non-structural functions such as indicating the edge of the causeway or preventing the causeway from spreading.

The phase 1 causeway could have been a simple drovers' crossing with verticals required to hold brushwood in place. Willow or poplar for coppicing would very likely be growing nearby and plenty of material could have been generated to replace the surface annually. The fact that there are coppice heels present in the material supports the idea that the causeway was of brushwood rather than wattle. The heels would have been trimmed off rods if they were being prepared for weaving wattle. A structure of wattle would have entailed a great deal of work which would only have been worthwhile if the causeway was permanent.

In the phase 2 causeway there is no pairing of the verticals, which would be necessary if they were part of a structure. The verticals are more dense on the west side and sparser on the east. There does not appear to be a strong pattern in the distribution. The timbers are reasonably large and chunky (roundwood, half split or quarter), but are not regularly spaced and never particularly close together. There is no pairing across the rows and no repetition in the pattern. Horizontals on both sides of the causeway are predominantly radial oak planks with one or two other pieces which are split differently; quartered or split across the grain.

One function of the verticals may have been to indicate the position of the causeway when it was under water. It was noted in the field that the flat sides of the timbers were aligned with the line of the causeway. It was also suggested that they may have been intended for retaining or to act as a revetment (eg 18097). This is unlikely because they seem too far apart and it is not clear how the revetment would work, although the key might lie in the notches. Post revetments are not particularly common in watery environments because wattle is easier to use, more flexible and very strong. The notches suggest horizontal planking, but such revetments would be rather weak and difficult to maintain. This also does not entirely fit with the evidence of the rounded ends of some planks (eg 18067, 18027) which suggest that they were probably set vertically. 18062 (on the east side) has a rounded end as has 18063. 18063 also has a distinct notch but is quite frail if required to support any horizontal structure. There is also a problem with the spacing as the interval between the timbers seems rather far apart for a revetment but too close together for hurdles.

Timber 18062, which has a very distinctive shape, was identified in the field as a fallen vertical. 18063 is similar but the shaping is sharper. There is a clear step or notch which has not formed naturally as it is cut across the grain. One possibility is that the planks were set in the ground with a revetment resting on the step. This method of construction, however, would not produce a very high fence, or a very strong one. Other pieces (eg 18020) show a similar shape, but not so clearly. Some of the shaping could be due to the wood having weathered, or possibly having been water-worn, before it became waterlogged.

The quality of the raw material is quite characteristic of Iron Age structures in that much of it is quite knotty (eg 18028, 18037, 18098 etc). Straight grained wood is unusual enough that a piece that is not knotty is invariably mentioned in the field notes.

18062 is the only timber which was excavated lying horizontally but interpreted as a definite fallen vertical. It is a plank with a width of 114 mm and a thickness of 14-25 mm ,which would make it fairly frail if used as a vertical. Posts too, such as 18018 on the east side which has a section of 62 x 35 mm, or 18031 (60 x 47 mm) and 18052 (54 x 31 mm) on the west side, are not large enough to take much weight or strain. If the length of 18062 is complete (825 mm) this would suggest that there would have been a little over half a metre above ground when it was set vertically, which would be too short to work as a fence; it is more likely to have been used as part of a retaining structure. 18062 and 18063 are both notched. The notches do not appear to be related to the grain or knots in the wood, but rather seem to be something to do with weathering. It was suggested in the field that if the decayed end had been in the ground the notch would have made a 'ledge' to carry horizontal planking. This would have to have been tied into place as there does not appear to be any evidence for joints which would have fulfilled this function.

There is evidence for a rope or twine used to hold some pieces together. When excavated it was thought possible that 18042 was attached to 18043 and 18044 (which was below it) with rope. This arrangement runs perpendicular to 18039-41 which may have originally extended into the same structure. Rope and twine rarely survive in prehistoric contexts and it is not possible to judge how frequently they may have been used, or how effectively. The early Bronze Age find of honeysuckle rope *in situ* on the central tree of the timber circle at Holme-next-the-Sea was surprising in the sophistication of the rope and the knot (Brennand and Taylor 2003). This rope, which dates to 2049 BC, is made from three stems of honeysuckle which have been individually twisted and flexed to soften the fibres and then plied back together for maximum strength. Rope and twine were certainly more important, and their manufacture more sophisticated, than their rare presence on later prehistoric sites might suggest. The rope associated with the central tree at Holme is twisted and plied, while that from Yarnton appears to have been simply twisted until virtually reduced to fibres. The rope from Yarnton was not well enough preserved for it to be possible to be entirely sure how it was manufactured, but photographs of the material *in situ* suggest that it may have been more like that from Baston Fen. Work in progress on material excavated from a deep pit at Baston Fen (which is probably middle Bronze Age in date) indicates a simple kind of rope with fibres twisted together rather than plied.

A structure made of relatively lightweight wood and rope such as this would not act as a 'fence' in the sense that animals might be contained, or as a hand rail that might be used for support. A structure made from planks and rope would be effective in defining the route of the causeway and also in providing protection from flotsam without impeding water movement. The need to protect from flotsam would be necessary because in a flood there would be a tendency for the water to drop any load onto the causeway. Once weed and detritus was dumped on the surface, the causeway could soon become quite treacherous.

The small amount of material from phase 3 appears to represent repair or renewal.

Species

Approximately 90% of the wood is oak, which, given the availability of other species in the area suggests selection for function. Much of the oak is deried from coppiced or re-grown stems after felling larger trunks. Almost without exception the worked wood is oak, the species favoured throughout prehistory and later for almost all structures, large or small and for indoors or outside. The remaining material, where identified, was willow or poplar. This would be the kind of material which would be expected to be growing in a damp, low-lying environment and which would respond well to coppicing.

Woodworking

Although the picture is far from complete, it seems that there is less use of large forest trees in Iron Age woodworking than earlier. Even in the Bronze Age, at sites such as Flag Fen, most of the domestic woodworking appears to have used roundwood and poles, with large forest trees reserved for monumental structures, such as the post alignment. Domestic woodworking techniques were adapted to working smaller and, sometimes, poorer quality wood. This is not to suggest that overall there was necessarily a shortage of the larger material, but rather that there was plenty of regenerated material which was more useful for working on a domestic scale. Roundwood with a diameter of 40 mm, for example, as found in phases 1 and 2, could be split to produce posts of varying sizes and radially split planks between 15 and 20 mm wide.

Timber 18071 has a classic load-bearing joint of a type which appears to be quite common by the Bronze Age. It is used to join two pieces of roundwood. 18031 and 19032 may also be joined by a similar joint but they are too decayed for this to be certain. The joint in 18071 appeared during excavation to be distorted, but it does seem to be quite a convincing example.

General

The wooden structures associated with the causeway are not sufficiently heavy-duty to have had a long-term function. A hand-rail, for example, must be sturdy enough to take a person's weight if they should slip in treacherous conditions. Any structure set where conditions can get very wet, however, will be very short-lived as the bottom ends of all the timbers will rot quite quickly when subjected to repeated wetting and drying. A renewable structure would be much more serviceable. Much of the wood appeared water-worn or decayed at one end, suggesting that it did not penetrate the ground, but either rested upon the surface or dangled in water.

Although the quantity of material from the site is quite large there is an insurmountable problem in the poor quality of preservation. This is not only true of the individual pieces which, because of weathering, produce very little clear or 'sharp' data, but also of the structure as a whole. Much of the material was spread out across the causeway and little was *in situ*, while virtually nothing remains articulated. All this, together with the unusual nature of the structure, makes the task of trying to reconstruct its original appearance and function very difficult.

Bibliography

Ainslie, R, 1988 Bladon Round Castle, *South Midlands Archaeol* **18**, 94

Ainslie, R, 1992 Excavations at Thrupp near Radley, Oxon, *South Midlands Archaeol* **22**, 63-6

Aitken, M J, 1985 *Thermoluminescence dating*, Academic Press, London

Alexander, J and Pullinger, J, 1999 *Roman Cambridge: Excavations at Castle Hill 1956-1988*, Proc Cambridge Antiquarian Soc **88**

Allason-Jones, L, 1996 *Roman jet in the Yorkshire Museum*, Yorkshire Museum, York

Allen, L, 1995 Bone small finds, in Hey 1995, 146

Allen, S, Allen, J R L and Fulford, M G, 1993 A late Iron Age – early Roman site at Streatley, *Berks Archaeol J* **74**, 145-6

Allen, T G, 1981 Hardwick with Yelford: Smith's Field, *CBA Group 9 Newsletter* **11**, 124-7

Allen, T G, 1990a *An Iron Age and Romano-British enclosed settlement at Watkins Farm, Northmoor, Oxon*, Oxford Archaeol Thames Valley Landscapes: The Windrush Valley **1**, Oxford

Allen, T G, 1990b The Iron Age pottery, in Allen 1990a, 32-46

Allen, T G, 1990c Briquetage, in Allen 1990a, 52-3

Allen, T G, 1990d Fired clay, in Allen 1990a, 53

Allen, T G, 1990e Abingdon Vineyard redevelopment, *South Midlands Archaeol* **20**, 73-4

Allen, T G, 1993 Clay objects, in Allen and Robinson 1993, 78

Allen, T G, 2000 The Iron Age Background, in Henig and Booth 2000, 1-33

Allen, T G and Kamash, Z, 2008 *Saved from the grave: Neolithic to Saxon discoveries at Spring Road Municipal Cemetery, Abingdon, Oxfordshire*, Oxford Archaeol Thames Valley Landscapes Monograph No. **28**, Oxford

Allen, T G and Moore, J, 1987 Standlake: Eagle Farm, *South Midlands Archaeol* **17**, 96-7

Allen, T G and Robinson, M A, 1993 *Mingies Ditch, Hardwick-with-Yelford, Oxon.*, Oxford Archaeol Unit Thames Valley Landscapes: the Windrush Valley **2**, Oxford

Allen, T, Miles, D and Palmer, S, 1984 Iron Age buildings in the Upper Thames Region, in Cunliffe and Miles 1984, 89-102

Allen, T, Darvill, T, Green, S and Jones, M, 1993 *Excavations at Roughground Farm, Lechlade, Gloucestershire: a prehistoric and Roman Landscape*, Oxford Archaeol Thames Valley Landscapes: the Cotswold Water Park **1**, Oxford

Allen, T, Hey, G and Miles, D, 1997 A line of time: approaches to archaeology in the upper and middle Thames valley, England, *World Archaeol* **29(1)**, 114-29

Allen, T, Hacking P and Boyle A, 2000 Eton Rowing Course at Dorney Lake. The burial traditions, *Tarmac Papers* **IV**, 65-106

Allen, T G, Cramp, K, Lamdin-Whymark, H and Webley, L, 2010 *Castle Hill and its landscape; Archaeological investigations at the Wittenhams, Oxfordshire*, Oxford Archaeol Monograph No. **9**, Oxford

Allen, T G, Anderson, L, Barclay, A, Petts, D and Robinson, M, in prep *Bridging the river, dividing the land. The archaeology of a Middle Thames Landscape: the Eton College Rowing Lake Project and the Maidenhead, Windsor and Eton Flood Alleviation Scheme. Volume 2: Middle Bronze Age to Roman*, Oxford Archaeol Monograph

Amorosi, T, 1989 *A postcranial guide to domestic neo-natal and juvenile mammals: the identification and ageing of old world species*, BAR Int Ser **533**, Oxford

Anderson, A S, 1979 *The Roman pottery industry in North Wiltshire*, Swindon Archaeol Soc Rep **2**

Anderson, T, 1995 The human skeletons, in K Parfitt, *Iron Age burials from Mill Hill, Deal*, British Museum Press, London, 114-44

Andrew, R, 1984 *A practical pollen guide to the British flora*. Quaternary Research Association, Technical Guide 1, QRA, Cambridge

Andrews, C W, 1917 Report on the remains of birds found at the Glastonbury Lake Village, in A Bulleid and H St G Gray, *The Glastonbury lake village*, Glastonbury, 631-7

Andrews, P, Biddulph, E, Hardy, A and Smith, A, forthcoming *Settling the Ebbsfleet Valley: CTRL excavations at Springhead and Northfleet, Kent. The late Iron Age, Roman, Saxon and medieval landscape*, Oxford Wessex Archaeology

Annable, F K, 1962 A Romano-British pottery in Savernake Forest, kilns 1-2, *Wiltshire Archaeol and Nat Hist Mag* **58**, 142-55

Annable, F K and Simpson, D D A, 1964 *Guide catalogue of the Neolithic and Bronze Age collections in Devizes Museum*, Devizes

Anon, 1936 Notes and news, *Oxoniensia* **1**, 196-203

Anon, 1937 Notes and news, *Oxoniensia* **2**, 201-9

Anon, 1938 Notes and news, *Oxoniensia* **3**, 162-78

Arkell, W K, 1947 *The Geology of Oxford,* Oxford

Armstrong, L, 1979 Standlake, Oxfordshire, *CBA Group 9 Newsletter* **9**, 31-7

Arthur, B V and Jope, E M, 1962-3 Early Saxon pottery kilns at Purwell Farm, Cassington, Oxfordshire, *Medieval Archaeol* **6-7**, 1-14

Ashbee, P, 1978 Amesbury barrow 51: excavations 1960, *Wiltshire Archaeol Mag* **70-1**, 1-60

Ashmolean Museum 1942 *University of Oxford, Ashmolean Museum, Report of the Visitors for 1942*

Atkinson, R J C, 1941 A Romano-British Potter's Field at Cowley, Oxon, *Oxoniensia* **6**, 9-21

Atkinson, R J C, 1942 Archaeological sites in Port Meadow, Oxford, *Oxoniensia* **7**, 24-35

Atkinson, R J C, 1952-3 Excavations in Barrow Hills Field, Radley, Berks, 1944-45, *Oxoniensia* **17-18**, 14-35

Atkinson, R J C, Piggott, C M and Sandars, N K, 1951 *Excavations at Dorchester, Oxon*, Oxford

Aufderheide, A C and Rodríguez-Martín, C, 1998 *The Cambridge encyclopedia of human paleopathology*, Cambridge University Press

Avery, M, Sutton, J E and Banks, J W, 1967 Rainsborough, Northants, England: excavations 1961-5, *Proc Prehist Soc* **33**, 207-95

Bagnall-Smith, J, 1998 More votive finds from Woodeaton, Oxfordshire, *Oxoniensia* **63**, 147-85

Bakels, C C, 1982 Zum wirtschaftlichen Nutzungsraum einer bandkeramischen Siedlung, in J Pavúk (ed.), *Siedlungen der Kultur mit Linearkeramik in Europa*, Archäologisches Institut der Slowakischen Akademie der Wissenschaften, Nitra, 9-16

Baker, H, 1937 Alluvial meadows; a comparative study of grazed and mown meadows, *J of Ecology* **205**, 408-20

Baker, S, 2002 Prehistoric and Romano-British landscapes at Little Wittenham and Long Wittenham, Oxfordshire, *Oxoniensia* **67**, 1-28

Bakkeorg, S, 1980 Phosphate analysis in archaeology: problems and recent progress, *Norwegian Archaeological Review* **13** (2), 1

Barber, A and Holbrook, N, 2001 A Romano-British settlement to the rear of Denchworth Road, Wantage, Oxfordshire: evaluation and excavation in 1996 and 1998, *Oxoniensia* **66**, 289-335

Barber, K E, 1976 History of vegetation, in S B Chapman (ed.) *Methods in plant ecology*, Oxford, 5-83

Barclay, A, 1999 The fired clay, in Muir and Roberts 1999, 42-4

Barclay, A and Halpin, C, 1999 *Excavations at Barrow Hills, Radley, Oxfordshire 1, The Neolithic and Bronze Age monument complex*, Oxford Archaeol Unit Thames Valley Landscapes **11**, Oxford

Barclay, A J and Wait, G A, 2004 Fired Clay, in Lambrick and Allen 2004, 376-86

Barclay, A, Glass, H and Hey, G, 1995 Fired clay, in Hey 1995, 136-8

Barclay, A, Gray, M and Lambrick, G, 1995 *Excavations at the Devil's Quoits, Stanton Harcourt, Oxfordshire 1972-3 and 1988*, Thames Valley Landscapes: the Windrush Valley **3**, Oxford

Barclay, A, Serjeantson, D and Wallis, J M, 1999 Worked bone and antler, in Barclay and Halpin 1999, 235-6

Barclay, A, Boyle, A and Keevill, G D, 2001 A Prehistoric enclosure at Eynsham Abbey, Oxfordshire, *Oxoniensia* **66**, 105-62

Barclay, A, Lambrick, G, Moore, J and Robinson, M, 2003 *Lines in the landscape. Cursus monuments in the Upper Thames Valley: excavations at the Drayton and Lechlade cursuses*, Oxford Archaeol Thames Valley Landscapes Monograph No **15**, Oxford

Barfield, L, 1991 Wessex with and without Mycenae: new evidence from Switzerland, *Antiquity* **65**, 102-7

Barford, P M, 1985 Objects of stone, in K Blockley, *Marshfield Ironmongers Piece: excavations 1982-3*, BAR Brit Ser **141**, Oxford, 217-51

Barnes, I, 1985 The non-ferrous metalwork from Hunsbury hillfort, Northamptonshire, dissertation for Diploma in Post-Excavation Studies, Univ. Leicester

Barnes I, Butterworth C A, Hawkes J W and Smith L 1997 *Excavations at Thames Valley Park, Reading, Berkshire, 1986-88*, Wessex Archaeol Report No. **14**, Salisbury

Barrett, J C, 1980 The pottery of the later Bronze Age in lowland England, *Proc Prehist Soc* **46**, 297-319

Barrett, J C, Bradley, R and Green, M, 1991 *Landscape, monuments and society: the prehistory of Cranborne Chase*, Cambridge

Bartlett, A, 1999 Geophysical survey, in Barclay and Halpin 1999, 11-14

Bass, W M, 1987 *Human osteology: A field guide*, Special publication of the Missouri Archaeological Society, Columbia

Bayley, J, 1986 Metallurgical analysis: the brooches, in I M Stead and V Rigby, *Baldock: The excavation of a Roman and pre-Roman settlement 1968-72 (Herts.)*, Britannia Monograph Ser No **7**, London, 381-4

Bayne, N, 1957 Excavations at Lyneham Camp, Lyneham, Oxon, *Oxoniensia* **22**, 1-10

Becker, H, 1995 From nanoTesla to picoTesla – a new window for magnetic prospecting in archaeology, *Archaeological Prospection* **2**, 217-28

Behre, K E, 1975 Wikingerzeitlicher Ackerbau in der Seemarsh bei Elisenhof, Schleswig-Holstein, Deutsche Nordseeküste, *Folia Quaternaria*, **46**, 49-62

Bell, C, 1997 Yarnton Worton Rectory Farm recycling plant, *South Midlands Archaeol* **27**, 64

Bell, C, 1998 Yarnton Worton Rectory Farm recycling plant, *South Midlands Archaeol* **28**, 92

Bell, M, 1989 Environmental archaeology as an index of continuity and change in the medieval landscape, in M Aston, D Austin and C Dyer (eds), *The rural settlements of medieval England*, Oxford, 269-86

Bennett, K A 1965 The aetiology and genetics of wormian bones, *Amer J of Physical Anthrop* **23**, 255-60

Bennett, K D, 1994 Annotated catalogue of pollen and pteridophyte spore types in the British Isles. Unpublished document

Benson, D and Miles, D, 1974 *The Upper Thames Valley: an archaeological survey of the river gravels*, Oxford Archaeological Unit Survey **2**, Oxford

Bersu, G, 1940 Excavations at Little Woodbury: part 1, *Proc Prehist Soc* **6**, 30-111

Biddle, M, 1976 Hampshire and the origins of Wessex, in G de G Sieveking, I H Longworth and K E Wilson (eds), *Problems in economic and social archaeology*, London, 323-42

Biddulph, E, 2005 Roman pottery, in P Bradley, B Charles, A Hardy and D Poore, Prehistoric and Roman activity and a Civil War ditch: excavations at the Chemistry Research Laboratory, 2-4 South Parks Road, Oxford, *Oxoniensia* **70**, 155-67

Biffen, R H, 1924 Report on the cereals, in R C C Clay, An early Iron Age site on Fifield Bavant Down, *Wiltshire Archaeological Magazine,* **42**, 493-4

Binford, L R, 1978 *Nunamiut Ethnoarchaeology*, New York

Black, C A, 1957 *Soil-Plant Relationships*, London

Black, S and Scheuer, L, 1996 Age changes in the clavicle: from the early neonatal period to skeletal maturity, *Internat J Osteoarchaeology* **6**, 452-534

Blair, J, 1994 *Anglo-Saxon Oxfordshire*, Stroud

Blinkhorn, P, 2007 Anglo-Saxon pottery, in R A Chambers and E Macadam, *Excavations at Barrow Hills, Radley, Oxfordshire. Volume II: the Romano-British cemetery and Anglo-Saxon settlement*, Oxford Archaeol Thames Valley Landscapes Monograph **25**, Oxford, 229-47

Boardman, S and Jones, G, 1990 Experiments on the effects of charring on cereal plant components, *J Archaeol Science* **17**, 1-11

Boessneck, J A, 1969 Osteological differences between sheep (*Ovis aries* Linné) and goat (*Capra hircus* Linné), in D R Brothwell and E S Higgs (eds), *Science in Archaeology*, London, 331-358

Böhme, H W, 1986 Das Ende der Römerherrschaft in Britannien und die angelsächsische Besiedlung Englands im 5. Jahrhundert, *Jahrbuch des Römisch-Germanischen Zentralmuseums Mainz* **33**, 469-574

Booth, P, 1991a Gill Mill, *South Midlands Archaeol* **21**, 95-6

Booth, P M, 1991b Inter-site comparisons between pottery assemblages in Roman Warwickshire: ceramic indicators of social status, *J Roman Pottery Stud* **4**, 1-10

Booth, P M, 1993 Archaeological evaluation at Appleford Sidings, nr Didcot, Oxfordshire, 1993, Oxford Archaeol Unit internal report

Booth, P, 1996 Pottery and other ceramic finds, in C Mould, An archaeological excavation at Oxford Road, Bicester, Oxfordshire, *Oxoniensia* **61,** 75-89

Booth, P M, 1997a *Asthall, Oxfordshire, excavations in a Roman 'small town', 1992*, Oxford Archaeol Unit Thames Valley Landscapes Monograph No. **9**, Oxford

Booth, P, 1997b A prehistoric-early Roman site near Lock Crescent, Kidlington, *Oxoniensia* **62**, 21-49

Booth, P, 1997c The Iron Age pottery, in C Cropper and A Hardy, The excavation of Iron Age and medieval features at Glympton Park, Oxfordshire, *Oxoniensia* **62**, 104-7

Booth, P, 1999a Ralegh Radford and the Roman villa at Ditchley: a review, *Oxoniensia* **64**, 39-49

Booth, P, 1999b Pink grogged ware again, *Study Group for Roman Pottery Newsletter* **27**, 2-3

Booth, P M, 2000 The Iron Age and Roman pottery, in Iron Age and early Romano-British settlement at Manor House Farm, Hatford, in R J Zeepvat (ed.) *Three Iron Age and Romano-British Rural Settlements on English Gravels*, BAR Brit Ser **312**, Oxford, 25-45

Booth, P, 2001 Late Roman cemeteries in Oxfordshire: a review, *Oxoniensia* **66**, 13-42

Booth, P, 2004a Quantifying status: some pottery data from the Upper Thames Valley, *J Roman Pottery Stud* **11**, 39-52

Booth, P, 2004b Iron Age and Roman pottery from Saxon features, in Hey 2004, 274-6

Booth, P, 2007 Cotswold Water Park Roman ceramic assemblages in their regional context, in Miles *et al.* 2007, 319-335

Booth, P, 2009 Fired clay and ceramic building material, in Booth and Simmonds 2009, 85-88

Booth, P, 2010 Roman and post-Roman fired clay and ceramic building material [from Castle Hill], in Allen *et al.* 2010, 67-68

Booth, P and Edgeley-Long, G, 2003 Prehistoric settlement and Roman pottery production at Blackbird Leys, Oxford, *Oxoniensia* **68**, 201-262

Booth, P and Green, S, 1989 The nature and distribution of certain pink, grog tempered vessels, *J Roman Pottery Stud* **2**, 77-84

Booth, P and Hayden, C, 2000 A Roman settlement at Mansfield College, Oxford, *Oxoniensia* **65**, 291-331

Booth, P and Simmonds, A, 2009 *Appleford's earliest farmers: archaeological work at Appleford Sidings, Oxfordshire, 1993-2000*, Oxford Archaeol Occ Paper No **17**, Oxford

Booth, P, Boyle, A and Keevill, G D, 1993 A Romano-British kiln site at Lower Farm, Nuneham Courtenay, and other sites on the Didcot to Oxford and Wootton to Abingdon water mains, Oxfordshire, *Oxoniensia* **58**, 87-217

Booth, P M, Evans, J and Hiller, J, 2001 *Excavations in the extramural settlement of Roman Alchester, Oxfordshire, 1991*, Oxford Archaeol Monograph No. **1,** Oxford

Booth, P, Dodd, A, Robinson, M, and Smith, A, 2007 *The Thames through time; the archaeology of the gravel terraces of the Upper and Middle Thames. The early historical period: AD 1-1000*, Oxford Archaeol Thames Valley Landscapes Monograph **27**, Oxford

Bowen, H J M, 1968 *Flora of Berkshire*, Oxford

Boyle, A, nd. The human bone, in A Boyle and R Early, *Excavations at Springhead Roman Town, Southfleet, Kent,* Oxford Archaeol Unit Occasional Paper No. **1**, 33-4

Boyle, A, 1997 The human skeletal assemblage, in Booth 1997a, 135-7

Boyle, A, 1999 The human remains, in A Barclay

and C Halpin, *Excavations at Barrow Hills, Oxfordshire. Volume 1: The Neolithic and Bronze Age Monument Complex*, Oxford Archaeological Unit Thames Valley Landscapes Volume **11**, Oxford, 171-83

Boyle, A, 2000 Human skeletal assemblage, in A Mudd and P Booth, Site of the former Hockley Chemical Works, Stratford Road, Alcester: excavations 1994, *Trans Birmingham Warwickshire Archaeol Soc* **104**, 45-9

Boyle, A, 2001a The human skeletal assemblage, in Booth *et al*. 2001, 385-94

Boyle, A 2001b The human skeletal assemblage in E Biddulph, G D Keevill and I R Scott, Redlands Farm, Stanwick, Northamptonshire: The Roman evidence, Oxford Archaeol unpublished report

Boyle, A, 2002 The Romano-British Cemetery, in A Mudd, *Excavations at Melford Meadows, Brettenham, 1994*, East Anglian Archaeol Rep No. **99**, 35-51

Boyle, A, 2004 The human burials, in Hey 2004, 317-23

Boyle, A, unpublished manuscript The human remains from a Romano-British cemetery at Crowmarsh, Wallingford

Boyle, A and Wait, G A, 2004 Shale, in Lambrick and Allen 2004, 368

Boyle, A, Jennings, D, Miles, D and Palmer, S, 1998 *The Anglo-Saxon cemetery at Butler's Field, Lechlade, Gloucestershire* **1**, *prehistoric and Roman activity and Anglo-Saxon grave catalogue*, Oxford Archaeol Thames Valley Landscapes **10**, Oxford

Bradford, J S P, 1942a An Early Iron Age settlement at Standlake, Oxon., *Antiq J* **22**, 202-14

Bradford, J S P, 1942b An Early Iron Age site at Allen's Pit, Dorchester, *Oxoniensia* **7**, 36-60

Bradford, J S P and Goodchild, R G, 1939 Excavations at Frilford, Berks., 1937-8, *Oxoniensia* **4**, 1-70

Bradley, P, Charles, B, Hardy A and Poore, D, 2005 Prehistoric and Roman activity and a Civil War ditch: excavations at the Chemistry Research Laboratory, 2-4 South Parks Road, Oxford, *Oxoniensia* **70**, 141-202

Bradley, R, 1985 Exchange and social distances: the structure of bronze artefact distributions, *Man* **20**, 692-704

Bradley, R, 1990 *The passage of arms: an archaeological analysis of prehistoric hoards and votive deposits*, Cambridge

Bradley, R and Ellison, A, 1975 *Rams Hill: a Bronze Age defended enclosure and its landscape*, BAR Brit Ser **19**, Oxford

Bradley, R and Gordon, K, 1988 Human skulls from the River Thames, their dating and significance, *Antiquity* **62**, 503-9

Bradley, R and Yates, D, 2007 After 'Celtic' fields: the social organisation of Iron Age agriculture, in C Haselgrove and R Pope (eds), *The earlier Iron Age in Britain and the Near Continent*, Oxbow Books, Oxford, 94-102

Bradley, R, Lobb, S, Richards, J and Robinson, M, 1980 Two late Bronze Age settlements on the Kennet gravels: excavations at Aldermaston Wharf and Knight's Farm, Burghfield, Berkshire, *Proc Prehist Soc* **46**, 217-95

Brailsford, J W 1962 *Hod Hill. Vol I. Antiquities from Hod Hill in the Durden Collection*, British Museum, London

Brain, C K, 1981 *The Hunters or the Hunted? An introduction to African Cave Taphonomy*, University of Chicago Press, Chicago and London

Brennand, M and Taylor, M, 2003 The survey and excavation of a Bronze Age timber circle at Holme-next-the-Sea, Norfolk, 1998-9, *Proc Prehist Soc* **69**, 1-84

Bridgland, D, 1994 *The Quaternary of the Thames*, London

Briggs, D J, Coope, G R and Gilbertson, D D, 1985 *The chronology and environmental framework of early man in the Upper Thames valley: a new model*, BAR Brit Ser **137**, Oxford

Britnell, W J, 1976 Antler cheekpieces of the British Late Bronze Age, *Antiq J* **56**, 24-34

Brodribb, A C C, Hands, A R, and Walker, D R, 1968 *Excavations at Shakenoak Farm, near Wilcote, Oxfordshire, Part I: Sites A & D*, Oxford

Brodribb, A C C, Hands, A R, and Walker, D R, 1971 *Excavations at Shakenoak Farm, near Wilcote, Oxfordshire, Part II: Sites B and H*, Oxford

Brodribb, A C C, Hands, A R, and Walker, D R, 1972 *Excavations at Shakenoak Farm, near Wilcote, Oxfordshire, Part III: Site F*, Oxford

Brodribb, A C C, Hands, A R, and Walker, D R, 1973 *Excavations at Shakenoak Farm, near Wilcote, Oxfordshire, Part IV: Site C*, Oxford

Bronk Ramsey, C, 1995 Radiocarbon calibration and analysis of stratigraphy, *Radiocarbon* **36**, 425–30

Bronk Ramsey, C, 1998 Probability and dating, *Radiocarbon* **40**, 461–74

Bronk Ramsey, C, 2001 Development of the radiocarbon calibration program, *Radiocarbon* **43**, 355-63

Bronk Ramsey, C and Hedges, R E M, 1997 Hybrid ion sources: radiocarbon measurements from microgram to milligram, *Nuclear Instruments and Methods in Physics Research* **B 123**, 539–45

Bronk Ramsey, C, Pettitt, P B, Hedges, R E M, Hodgins, G W L, and Owen, D C, 2000 Radiocarbon dates from the Oxford AMS system: *Archaeometry* datelist 29, *Archaeometry* **42**, 243-54

Brooks, H, 1988 Stansted Airport project, *Essex Archaeol Hist* **19**, 269

Brooks, S and Suchey, J M, 1990 Skeletal age determination based on the os pubis: a comparison of the Acsádi-Nemeskéri and Suchey-Brooks methods, *Human Evolution* **5**, 227-238

Brossler, A, Gocher, M, Laws, G and Roberts, M, 2002 Shorncote Quarry: excavation of a late prehistoric landscape in the Upper Thames Valley, *Trans Bristol Gloucestershire Archaeol Soc* **120**, 37-87

Brothwell, D R, 1981 *Digging up bones* 3rd edn, London and Oxford

Brown, A, 1991 Structured deposition and technological change among the flaked stone artefacts from Cranborne Chase, in J Barrett, R Bradley and M Hall (eds), *Papers on the prehistoric archaeology of Cranborne Chase*, Oxbow Monograph **11**, Oxford, 101-33

Brown, A, 1994 A Romano-British shell-gritted pottery and tile manufacturing site at Harrold, Beds, *Bedfordshire Archaeol* **21**, 19-107

Brown, K, 1999 The pottery, in Cromarty *et al.* 1999, 182-95

Brown, P D C, 1972 Excavations at Shakenoak III – Site F [Review], *Britannia* **3**, 376-7

Bruce, M, 1986 Skeletal report, in M R Pointing, Two Iron Age cists from Galson, Isle of Lewis, *Proc Soc Antiqs of Scotland* **119**, fiche 3: F1-G14

Brück, J, 1995 A place for the dead: the role of human remains in Late Bronze Age Britain, *Proc Prehist Soc* **61**, 245-77

Buck, C E, Kenworthy, J B, Litton, C D and Smith, A F M, 1991 Combining archaeological and radiocarbon information: a Bayesian approach to calibration, *Antiquity* **65**, 808–21

Buck, C E, Litton, C D and Smith, A F M, 1992 Calibration of radiocarbon results pertaining to related archaeological events, *J Archaeol Science*, **19**, 497–512

Buck, C E, Christen, J A, Kenworthy, J B and Litton, C D, 1994 Estimating the duration of archaeological activity using 14C determinations, *Oxford J Archaeol* **13,** 229–40

Buckley, D G, 1979 The stone, in G J Wainwright, *Gussage All Saints: an Iron Age settlement in Dorset*, Dept Environment Archaeol Rep **10**, London, 89-97

Budd, P, Gale, D, Ixer, R A and Thomas, R G, 1995 Tin sources for prehistoric bronze production in Ireland, *Antiquity* **68** (260), 518-24

Budd, P, Gale, D and Thomas, R G, 1997 Cornish copper and the origins of extractive metallurgy in the British Isles: some scientific considerations, in P Budd and D Gale (eds), *Prehistoric extractive metallurgy in Cornwall*, Truro, 15-17

Bulleid, A and Gray, H St G, 1917 *The Glastonbury Lake Village: A Full Description of the Excavations and the Relics Discovered, 1892–1907*, Vol 2. Glastonbury Antiquarian Society, Taunton

Burgess, C B, 1979 The background of early metalworking in Ireland and Britain, in M Ryan (ed.), *The origins of metallurgy in Atlantic Europe: proceedings of the fifth Atlantic Colloquium*, Dublin, 207-14

Burnham, B C and Wacher, J S, 1990 *The 'small towns' of Roman Britain*, London

Butler, R F, 1992 *Paleomagnetism: magnetic domains to geological terranes*, Boston

Calkin, J B, 1953 'Kimmeridge coal-money': the Romano-British shale armlet industry, *Proc Dorset Nat Hist Archaeol Soc* **75**, 45-71

Campbell, G and Straker, V, 2003 Prehistoric crop husbandry and plant use in Southern England: development and regionality, in K Robson Brown (ed.), *Archaeological Sciences 99*, BAR Int Ser **1111**, Oxford, 14-30

Canti, M G, 1991 Soil particle size analysis: a revised interpretative guide for excavators, *English Heritage Ancient Monuments Lab Rep* 1/91

Canti, M, 1996 Geoarchaeological work, in Hey 1996, 21-5

Carr, G and Knüsel, C, 1997 The ritual framework of excarnation by exposure as the mortuary practice of the early and middle Iron Ages of central southern Britain, in Gwilt and Haselgrove 1997, 167-173

Case, H, 1956 Beaker pottery from the Oxford region: 1939-1955, *Oxoniensia* **21**, 1-21

Case, H, 1958 A late Belgic burial at Watlington, Oxon, *Oxoniensia* **23**, 139-41

Case, H J, 1963 Notes on the finds and on ring ditches in the Oxford region, *Oxoniensia* **28**, 19-52

Case, H J, 1982a Cassington, 1950-2: late Neolithic pits and the big enclosure, in Case and Whittle 1982, 118-51

Case, H J, 1982b The Vicarage Field, Stanton Harcourt, in Case and Whittle 1982, 103-117

Case, H J, 1982c Introduction, in Case and Whittle 1982, 1-9

Case, H J and Whittle, A W R, 1982 *Settlement patterns in the Oxford region: excavations at the Abingdon causewayed enclosure and other sites*, CBA Res Rep **44**, London

Case, H, Bayne, N, Steele, S, Avery, G and Sutermeister, H, 1964-5 Excavations at City Farm, Hanborough, Oxon, *Oxoniensia* **29-30**, 1-98

Catling, H W, 1982 Six ring-ditches at Standlake, in Case and Whittle 1982, 88-102

Catt, J A, 1994 Long-term consequences of using artificial and organic fertilisers: the Rothampstead Experiments, in S Foster and T C Smout (eds), *The History of Soils and Field Systems*, Scottish Cultural Press, Aberdeen, 119-34

Challands, A, 1995 Report on the magnetic suspeceptibility survey at the ARC quarry, Yarnton, Oxfordshire, June 1995, unpub geophysical report commissioned by English Heritage, London

Challands A, 1998 Report on the magnetic suspeceptibility survey at the ARC quarry, Yarnton, Oxfordshire, May 1998, unpub geophysical report commissioned by English Heritage, London

Chambers, R A, 1976 Late Iron Age material from Ducklington, *Oxoniensia* **41**, 36-7

Chambers, R A 1977 A crouched pit burial at Cassington Mill, Oxon., 1976, *Oxoniensia* **42,** 256-7

Chambers, R A, 1987 The late- and sub-Roman cemetery at Queensford Farm, Dorchester-on-Thames, Oxon., *Oxoniensia* **52**, 35-69

Chambers, R, 1988 Bampton: Calais Farm Redevelopment, *South Midlands Archaeol* **18**, 73

Chambers, R and Boyle, A, 2007 The Romano-British cemetery, in R Chambers and E Macadam, *Excavations at Barrow Hills, Radley, Oxfordshire. Volume II: the Romano-British cemetery and Anglo-Saxon settlement*, Oxford Archaeol Thames Valley Landscapes Monograph **25**, Oxford, 13-64

Chambers, R A and Williams, G, 1976 A Late Iron Age and Romano-British settlement at Hardwick, *Oxoniensia* **41**, 21-35

Chancellor, R.J, 1985 Changes in the weed flora of an arable field cultivated for 20 years, *J Applied Ecology* **22**, 491-501

Chancellor, R J, 1986 Decline of arable weed seeds during 20 years in soil under grass and periodicity of seedling emergence after cultivation, *J Applied Ecology* **23**, 631-7

Charles, B M, Parkinson, A and Foreman, S, 2000 A Bronze Age ditch and Iron Age settlement at Elms Farm, Humberstone, Leicester, *Trans Leicestershire Archaeol Hist Soc* **74**, 113-220

Charlesworth D, 1973 The Aesica hoard, *Archaeol Aeliana 5th ser.* **1**, 225-34

Charlton, O P, Gehweiler, J A, Martinez, S, Morgan, C L and Daffner, R H, 1978 Spondylolosis and spondylolisthesis of the cervical spine, *Skeletal Radiology* **3**, 79-85

Charters, S, Evershed, R P, Goad, L J, Heron, C and Blinkhorn, P, 1993 Quantification and distribution of lipid in archaeological ceramics: implications for sampling potsherds for organic residue analysis, *Archaeometry* **35**, 211-23

Charters, S, Evershed, R P, Blinkhorn, P W and Denham, V, 1995 Evidence for the mixing of fats and waxes in archaeological ceramics, *Archaeometry* **37**, 113-27

Charters, S, Evershed, R P, Quye, A, Blinkhorn, P and Reeves, V, 1997 Simulation experiments for determing the use of ancient pottey vessels: the behaviour of epicuticular leaf wax during boiling of a leafy vegetable, *J Archaeol Science* **24** (1), 1-7

Christie, W W, 1981 *Lipid Metabolism in Ruminant Animals*, Oxford

Clapham, A R, Tutin, T G and Moore, D M, 1987 *Flora of the British Isles* (3rd edn), Cambridge

Clark, A J, 1992 Archaeogeophysical prospecting on alluvium, in Needham and Macklin 1992, 43-9

Clarke, G, 1979 *The Roman cemetery at Lankhills*, Winchester studies **3**, Pre-Roman and Roman Winchester, Part II, Oxford

Clarke, S, 1997 Abandonment, rubbish disposal and 'special' deposits at Newstead, in K Meadows, C Lemke and J Heron (eds), *TRAC 96. Proceedings of the Sixth Annual Theoretical Roman Archaeology Conference, Sheffield 1996*, Oxford, 73-81

Clay, R C C, 1924 An early Iron Age site on the Fifield Bavant Down, *Wiltshire Archaeol Mag* **42**, 457-96

Cleal, R M J, 1984 The later Neolithic in eastern England, in R Bradley and J Gardiner (eds), *Neolithic studies: a review of some current research*, BAR Brit Ser **133**, Oxford, 135-58

Cleal, R M J, 1991 Cranborne Chase: the earlier prehistoric pottery, in J Barrett, R Bradley and M Hall, *Papers on the prehistoric archaeology of Cranborne Chase*, Oxbow Monograph **11**, Oxford, 134-200

Cleere, H, 1978 The slag and crucible fragments, in Parrington 1978, 88-90

Coe, D, Jenkins, V and Richards, J, 1991 Cleveland Farm, Ashton Keynes: Second Interim Report: Investigations May-August 1989, *Wiltshire Archaeol Nat Hist Mag* **84**, 40-50

Cole, M A, 1995 Hoe Hills, Dowsby, Lincolnshire. Report on the geophysical surveys October 1994 and March 1995, Report **17/95**, Ancient Monuments Laboratory, London

Cole, M A, Linford, N T, Payne, A P and Linford, P K, 1993 Soil Magnetic Susceptibility Measurements and their Application to Archaeological Site Investigation, in J Beavis and K Barker (eds), *Science and site: archaeological sciences conference 1993*, Bournemouth University, 144-162

Cole, M, David, A, Fassbinder J, Linford N, Linford, P and Payne, W, 1999 Comparative high resolution caesium vapour and fluxgate gradiometer survey at a range of archaeological sites in England, in J W E Fassbinder and W E Irlinger (eds), *Archaeological Prospection 1999*, Arbeitshefte des Bayerischen Landesamtes Für Denkmalpflege, Munich, 22-3

Coles, J M, 1987 *Meare Village East: the excavations of A Bulleid and H St George Gray 1932-1956*, Somerset Levels Papers **13**

Collingwood, R G and Richmond I, 1969 *The Archaeology of Roman Britain*, revised edn, London

Collins, A E P, 1947 Excavations on Blewburton Hill, 1947, *Berkshire Archaeol J* **50**, 4-29

Collins, A E P, 1953 Excavations on Blewburton Hill, 1948 and 1949, *Berkshire Archaeol J* **53**, 21-64

Collis, J R (ed.), 1977 *The Iron Age in Britain – a review*, Sheffield

Collis, J, 1994 An Iron Age and Roman cemetery at Owlesbury, Hampshire, in Fitzpatrick and Morris 1994, 106-08

Cook, J, Guttman, E B A and Mudd, A, 2004 Excavations of an Iron Age site at Coxwell Road, Faringdon, *Oxoniensia* **69**, 181-285

Cook, S and Hayden, C, 2000 Prehistoric and Roman settlement near Heyford Road, Steeple Aston, Oxfordshire, *Oxoniensia* **65**, 161-210

Cool, H E M, 1998 A general overview of the finds assemblage from Kingscote, in J R Timby, *Excavations at Kingscote and Wycomb, Gloucestershire*, Cotswold Archaeol Trust, Cirencester, 220-7

Coombs, D G, 2001 Metalwork, in Pryor 2001, 255-98

Copeland, T, 1988 The North Oxfordshire Grim's Ditch: a fieldwork survey, *Oxoniensia* **53**, 277-292.

Copley, M S, Berstan, R, Dudd, S N, Docherty, G, Mukherjee, A J, Straker, V, Payne, S and Evershed, R P, 2003 Direct chemical evidence for widespread dairying in prehistoric Britain. *Proc National Academy Sciences* **100** (4), 1524-9

Corney, M, 2000 The brooches, in M Fulford and J Timby, *Late Iron Age and Roman Silchester. Excavations on the site of the forum-basilica 1977, 1980-86*, Britannia Monograph Ser **15**, London, 322-38

Cotton, M and Frere, S, 1968 Ivinghoe Beacon excavations 1963-65, *Recs Buckinghamshire* **18**, 187-260

Cowell, M R, 1990 Scientific report, in R Jackson, *Camerton: the late Iron Age and early Roman metalwork*, London, 69-90

Craddock, P T, 1978 The composition of the alloys used by the Greek, Etruscan and Roman civilisations 3: the origins and early use of brass, *J Archaeol Sci* **5**, 1-16

Cromarty, A M, Foreman, S and Murray, P, 1999 The excavation of a late Iron Age enclosed settlement at Bicester Fields Farm, Bicester, Oxon, *Oxoniensia* **64**, 154-233

Cromarty, A M, Barclay, A, Lambrick, G and Robinson, M, 2006 *Late Bronze Age ritual and habitation on a Thames eyot at Whitecross Farm, Wallingford: The archaeology of the Wallingford Bypass, 1986-92*, Oxford Archaeol Thames Valley Landscapes Monograph No **22**, Oxford

Cropper, C, and Hardy, A, 1997 The excavation of Iron Age and medieval features at Glympton Park, Oxfordshire, *Oxoniensia* **62**, 101-7

Crowfoot, G M, 1945 The bone 'gouges' from Maiden Castle and other sites, *Antiquity* **19**, 157-8

Crummy, N, 1983 *The Roman small finds from excavations in Colchester 1971-9* Colchester Archaeol Rep **2**

Cunliffe, B W, 1968 Excavations at Eldon's Seat, Dorset, *Proc Prehist Soc* **34,** 191-237

Cunliffe, B, 1983 *Danebury: the anatomy of an Iron Age hillfort*, London

Cunliffe, B, 1984a *Danebury: an Iron Age hillfort in Hampshire* **2**, *the excavations 1969-78: the finds*, CBA Res Rep **52**, London

Cunliffe, B, 1984b The Iron Age pottery, in Cunliffe 1984a, 232-331

Cunliffe, B, 1984c Objects of Kimmeridge shale, in Cunliffe 1984a, 396

Cunliffe, B, 1984d Iron Age Wessex: continuity and change, in Cunliffe and Miles 1984, 12-45

Cunliffe, B, 1991 *Iron Age communities in Britain* (3rd edn), London

Cunliffe, B, 1992 Pits, preconceptions and propitiation in the British Iron Age, *Oxford J Archaeol* **11**, 69-83

Cunliffe, B, 2000 *The Danebury Environs Programme; the prehistory of a Wessex Landscape. Volume 1: introduction,* English Heritage and OUCA Monograph No. **48**, Institute of Archaeol, Oxford

Cunliffe, B, 2005 *Iron Age communities in Britain* (4th edn), London

Cunliffe, B and Miles, D (eds), 1984 *Aspects of the Iron Age in Central Southern Britain,* Univ of Oxford: Comm for Archaeol Monograph **2**, Oxford

Cunliffe, B and Poole, C, 1991a *Danebury: an Iron Age hillfort in Hampshire* **4**, *the excavations, 1979-1988: the site*, CBA Res Rep **73**, London

Cunliffe, B and Poole, C, 1991b *Danebury: an Iron Age hillfort in Hampshire* **5**, *the excavations, 1979-1988: the finds*, CBA Res Rep **73**, London

Cunliffe, B and Poole, C, 2000 *Suddern Farm, Middle Wallop, Hants, 1991 and 1996. The Danebury Environs Programme. The prehistory of a Wessex Landscape*, English Heritage and OUCA Monograph No. **49**, Institute of Archaeol, Oxford

Cunnington, M E, 1923 *The Early Iron Age inhabited site at All Cannings Cross Farm, Wiltshire*, Devizes

Cunnington, M E and Goddard, E H, 1911 *Catalogue of Antiquities in the Museum of the Wiltshire Archaeological and Natural History Society, at Devizes*, part II, Devizes

Curwen, E C, 1937 Querns, *Antiquity* **11**, 133-51

Curwen, E, and Curwen, E C, 1925 Earthworks and Celtic Roads, Binderton, *Sussex Archaeol Coll* **66**, 131-71

Dalwood, H and Edwards, R, 2004 *Excavations at Deansway, Worcester, 1988-89 Romano-British small town to late medieval city*, CBA Res Rep **139**, York

Dannell, G B, 1977 The samian from Bagendon, in J Dore and K Greene (eds), *Roman pottery in Britain and beyond*, BAR Int Ser **30**, Oxford, 229-34

Dark, K and Dark P, 1998 *The landscape of Roman Britain*. Sutton, Stroud

David, A, 1995 Geophysical survey in Archaeological Field Evaluation, *Research and Professional Services Guideline,* **1,** English Heritage, London

David, A E U and Payne, A W, 1993 Croughton, Northamptonshire, interim report on geophysical survey on geophysical surveys 1992-93, report series, **15/93,** Ancient Monuments Laboratory, London

Davies, B, Richardson, B and Tomber, R, 1994 *A dated corpus of early Roman pottery from the City of London,* CBA Res Rep **98**, London

Davis, S J M, 1987a The faunal remains from Tell Qiri, in A Ben-Tor and Y Portugali, *Tell Qiri: a village in the Jezreel valley*, Qedem **24**, Jerusalem, 249-251

Davis, S J M, 1987b Animal sacrifices, in O D Buitron (ed.), *The sanctuary of Apollo Hylates at Kourion: Excavations in the Archaic Precinct*, Jonsered, Sweden, Paul Åströms förlag, 181-2

Davis, S J M, 1992 *Rapid Method for Recording Information about Mammal Bones from*

Archaeological Sites, Ancient Monuments Laboratory Res Rep **19/92**
Dawes, J, nd Wetwang Slack human bone report, unpublished manuscript
Dawkins, 1862 Traces of the early Britons, *The Gentleman's Magazine and Scientific Review*, London, August 1862, 144-9
Dawkins, W B, 1862 On the traces of the early Britons in the neighbourhood of Oxford, *Proc Oxford Archit Hist Soc* NS Vol **1**
Dawson, G J, 1961-2 Excavations at Purwell Farm, Cassington, *Oxoniensia* **26**, 1-6
Day, C J, 1990 Yarnton, in A Crossley (ed.), *A history of the county of Oxford, Volume XII Wootton Hundred (south) including Woodstock*, Victoria County History, Oxford, 470-90
Day, P, 1989 Reconstructing the environment of Shotover Forest, Oxfordshire, *Medieval Settlement Reaserch Group Ann Rep* **4**, 6
Day S P, 1991 Post-glacial vegetational history of the Oxford region, *New Phytologist* **119**, 445-70.
Day, S P, 1993 Woodland origin and 'ancient woodland indicators': a case-study from Sidlings Copse, Oxfordshire, UK, *The Holocene* **3(1)** 45-53
De Roche, C D, 1978 The Iron Age pottery, in Parrington 1978, 40-74
Dent, J S, 1982 Cemeteries and settlement patterns of the Iron Age on the Yorkshire Wolds, *Proc Prehist Soc* **48**, 120-8
Dent, J S 1985 Three cart burials from Wetwang, Yorkshire, *Antiquity* **59,** 85-92
Dickinson, B, 2001 Samian ware, in Booth *et al*. 2001, 277-85
Dickinson, T M, 1976 The Anglo-Saxon burial sites of the Upper Thames Region and their bearing on the history of Wessex, circa AD 400-700, unpubl DPhil thesis, Univ of Oxford
Druce, G C, 1886 *Flora of Oxfordshire*, Oxford and London
Druce, G C, 1897 *Flora of Berkshire*, Oxford
Dudd, S N, Regert, M and Evershed, R P, 1998 Assessing microbial lipid contributions during laboratory degradations of fats and oils and pure triacylglycerols absorbed in ceramic potsherds, *Organic Geochemistry* **29** (5-7), 1345-54
Duncan, D, Lambrick, G and Barclay, A, 2004 Final Bronze Age to Middle Iron Age pottery, in Lambrick and Allen 2004, 259-303
Dungworth, D B, 1995 Iron Age and Roman copper alloys from northern Britain, unpubl PhD thesis, Univ of Durham
Dungworth, D B, 1996 The production of copper alloys in Iron Age Britain, *Proc Prehist Soc* **62**, 399-422
Dunning, G C, 1976 Salmonsbury, Bourton-on-the-Water, Gloucestershire, in Harding 1976, 75-118

Eames, B W, 1998 *The archaeology of Swalcliffe Lea*, OUDCE Diploma in Applied Archaeology dissertation unpub
Edwards, E, 1978 The human remains, in Parrington 1978, 90-2
Edwards, R and Hurst, D, 2000 Iron Age settlement and a medieval and later farmstead: excavation at 93-97 High Street, Evesham, *Trans Worcestershire Archaeol Soc* 3s **17**, 73-124
Ehrenreich, R E, 1985 *Trade, technology and the ironworking community in the Iron Age of Southern Britain*, BAR Brit Ser **144**, Oxford
El-Najjar, M Y and Dawson, G L, 1977 The effect of artificial cranial deformation on the incidence of wormian bones in the lambdoid suture, *Amer J Physical Anthropology* **46**, 155-60
Ellenberg, H, 1950 *Landwirtschaftliche Pflanzensoziologie I: Unkrautgemeinschaften als Zeiger für Klima und Boden*, Stuttgart
Ellenberg, H, 1974 Zeigerwerte der Gefäßpflanzen Mitteleuropas, *Scripta Geobotanica* **9**, 1-97
Ellis, C and Brown, A G, 1998 Archaeomagnetic dating and palaeochannels sediments: data from the mediaeval channel fills at Hemington, Leicester, *J Archaeol Science* **25**, 149-63
Ellis, P, Hughes, G and Jones, L, 2001 An Iron Age boundary and settlement features at Slade Farm, Bicester, Oxfordshire: a report on the excavations, 1996, *Oxoniensia* **65**, 211-65
English Heritage, 1991 *Management of archaeological projects* (2nd edn), London
Esmonde Cleary, A S, 1995 Changing constraints on the landscape AD 400-600, in D Hooke and S Burnell (eds), *Landscape and settlement in Britain AD 400-1066*, Exeter, 11-26
Evans, J, 2001a Iron Age, Roman and Anglo-Saxon pottery, in Booth *et al*. 2001, 263-383
Evans, J, 2001b Material approaches to the identification of different Romano-British site types, in S James and M Millett (eds), *Britons and Romans: advancing an archaeological agenda*, CBA Res Rep **125**, York, 26-35
Evans, J G, 1972 *Land snails in archaeology*, London
Evans, M, 1995 The mollusca from the henge ditch, in A Barclay, M Gray and G Lambrick, *Excavations at the Devil's Quoits, Stanton Harcourt, Oxfordshire, 1972-3 and 1988*, Oxford Archaeol Thames Valley Landscapes: The Windrush Valley **3**, Oxford, 62-7
Everett, R N and Eeles, B M G, 1999 Investigations at Thrupp House Farm, Radley, near Abingdon, *Oxoniensia* **64**, 118-52
Evershed, R P, 1993 Biomolecular archaeology and lipids, *World Archaeol* **25**(1), 74-93
Evershed, R P, Heron, C and Goad, L J, 1990 Analysis of organic residues of archaeological origin by high-temperature gas-chromatography and gas-chromatography mass-spectrometry. *Analyst* **115**(10), 1339-42
Evershed, R P, Heron, C, Charters, S and Goad, L J, 1992 The survival of food residues: new methods of analysis, interpretation and application, in A M Pollard (ed.), *New Developments in Archaeological Science*, Oxford University Press, Oxford, 187-208
Evershed, R P, Arnot, K I, Collister, J, Eglinton, G

and Charters, S, 1994 Application of isotope ratio monitoring gas-chromatography mass-spectrometry to the analysis of organic residues of archaeological origin, *Analyst* **119**(5), 909-14

Evershed, R P, Stott, A W, Raven, A, Dudd, S N, Charters, S and Leyden, A, 1995 Formation of long-chain ketones in ancient pottery vessels by pyrolysis of acyl lipids, *Tetrahedron Letters* **36**(48), 8875-8

Evershed, R P, Dudd, S N, Charters, S, Mottram, H, Stott, A W, Raven, A, van Bergen, P F and Bland, H A, 1999 Lipids as carriers of anthropogenic signals from prehistory, *Philosophical Trans Royal Soc London Series B-Biological Sciences* **354**(1379), 19-31

Evershed, R P, Dudd, S N, Copley, M S, Berstan, R, Stott, A W, Mottram, H, Buckley, S A and Crossman, Z, 2002 Chemistry of archaeological animal fats, *Accounts of Chemical Research* **35**(8), 660-8

Fasham, P J, 1985 *The prehistoric settlement at Winnall Down, Winchester*, Hampshire Field Club and Archaeol Soc Monograph **2**, M3 Archaeol Rescue Committee Rep **8**, Winchester

Fægri, K and Iversen, J, 1989 *Textbook of pollen analysis* (4th edn, by K Fægri, P E Kaland and K Krzywinski), Wiley, Chichester

Fazekas, I G and Kosa, F, 1966 Neuere Beiträge und vergleichende Untersuchungen von Feten zur Bestimmung der Korperlange auf Grund der Diaphysenmasse der Extremitatenknochen, *Deutsche Zeitschrift für gerichtliche Medizin* **58**, 142-60

Featherstone, R and Bewley, R, 2000 Recent aerial reconnaissance in North Oxfordshire, *Oxoniensia* **65**, 13-27

Featherstone, R and Dyer, C, 1994 RCHME cropmark plot, in Hey 1994a

Fell, C I, 1936 The Hunsbury hill-fort, Northants: a new survey of the material, *Archaeol J* **93**, 57-100

Fell, C I, 1961 The coarse pottery of Bagendon, in E M Clifford, *Bagendon: a Belgic oppidum*, Cambridge, 212-67

Fell, V and Salter, C, 1998 Metallographic examination of seven Iron Age ferrous axeheads from England, *J Historical Metallurgy Soc* **32(1)**, 1–6

Fenton, A J, 1978 *The Northern Isles, Orkney and Shetland*, Edinburgh

Ferembach, D, Skloukal, M and Schwidetzky, I, 1980 Recommendations for age and sex diagnoses of skeletons, *Proc Royal Soc Medicine* **55**, 517-49

Field, N and Parker Pearson, M, 2003 *Fiskerton: An Iron Age Timber Causeway with Iron Age and Roman Votive Offerings, the 1981 excavations*, Oxbow, Oxford

Fitter, A, 1978 *An atlas of the wild flowers of Britain and northern Europe*, London

Fitzpatrick, A P, 1997 Everyday life in Iron Age Wessex, in Gwilt and Haselgrove 1997, 73-86

Fitzpatrick, A P and Morris, E L, 1994 *The Iron Age in Wessex: Recent work*, Association Française D'Etude de L'Age du Fer, Trust for Wessex Archaeol Ltd, Salisbury

Ford, S, 1990 The archaeology of the Cleeve-Didcot pipeline in South Oxfordshire 1989, *Oxoniensia* **55**, 1-40

Ford, S and Hazell, A, 1989 Prehistoric, Roman and Anglo-Saxon settlement patterns at North Stoke, Oxfordshire, *Oxoniensia* **54**, 7-23

Forenbaher, S, 1993 Radiocarbon dates and absolute chronology of the central European early Bronze Age, *Antiquity* **67**, 218-56

Foster, J, 1980 *The Iron Age moulds from Gussage All Saints*, British Museum Occ Paper **12**, London

Foster, J 1995 Metalworking in the British Iron Age: the evidence from Weelsby Avenue, Grimsby, in B Raftery (ed.), *Sites and sights of the Iron Age: essays on fieldwork and museum research presented to Ian Matthiesen Stead*, Oxbow Monograph **56**, Oxford, 49-61

Fowler, P J, 1978 The Abingdon ard-share, in Parrington 1978, 83-8

Frederickson, B E, Baker, D, McHolick, W J, Yuan, H A and Lubicky, J P, 1984 The natural history of spondylolysis and spondylolisthesis, *J Bone and Joint Surgery* **66**, 699-705

Freestone, I, 1991 Petrography of the stone materials, in S Needham, *Excavation and salvage at Runnymede Bridge, 1978: the Late Bronze Age waterfront site*, London, 138-9

Frere, S S, 1962 Excavations at Dorchester on Thames, 1962, *Archaeol J* **119**, 114-49

Frere, S S, 1984 Excavations at Dorchester on Thames, 1963, *Archaeol J* **141**, 91-174

Freundlich, J C, Schröter, P and Velicky, P, 1979 C-14 Datierung hominider Knochenfunde aus Süddeutschland, *Kölner Jahrbuch für Ur- und Frühgeschichte* **16**, 165-72

Fryer, J D and Evans, S A, 1963 *Weed Control Handbook*, Oxford

Fulford, M, 1975 *New Forest Roman pottery*, BAR Brit Ser **17**, Oxford

Fulford, M, 1992 Iron Age to Roman: a period of radical change on the gravels, in Fulford and Nichols (eds) 1992, 23-38

Fulford, M, 2001 Links with the past: Pervasive 'ritual' behaviour in Roman Britain, *Britannia* **32**, 199-218

Fulford, M and Nichols, E, 1992 (eds) *Developing Landscapes of Lowland Britain, The Archaeology of the British Gravels, A Review*, Occasional Papers from the Society of Antiquaries of London, Vol **14**

Fulford, M G and Rippon, S J, 1994 Lowbury Hill, Oxon: a re-assessment of the probable Romano-Celtic temple and the Anglo-Saxon barrow, *Archaeol J* **151**, 158-211

Gale, J, 1983 Iron Age spears and sling missiles in southern Britain, unpublished M Phil thesis, Univ of Oxford

Garton, D, Howard, A and Pearce, M, 1997

Archaeological investigations at Langford Quarry, Nottinghamshire, 1995-6, *Tarmac Papers* **1**, 29-40

Gelfand, A E and Smith, A F M, 1990 Sampling approaches to calculating marginal densities, *J Amer Stat Assoc* **85**, 398–409

Gelling, P S and Peacock, D P S, 1970 The pottery from Caynham Camp, near Ludlow, *Trans Shropshire Archaeol Soc* **58** (for 1965-1968), 96-100

Gent, H, 1983 Centralized storage in late prehistoric Britain, *Proc Prehist Soc* **49**, 243-68

Gentry Steele, D and Bramblett, C A 1988 *The anatomy and biology of the human skeleton*, Texas A&M University Press, College Station

Gerloff, S, 1975 *The early Bronze Age daggers in Great Britain and a reconsideration of the Wessex culture*, Prähistorische Bronzefunde **6** (2), Munich

Gerloff, S, 1993 Zu Fragen der mittelmeerländischen Kontakte und absoluten Chronologie der Frühbronzezeit in Mittel- und Westeuropa, *Prähistorische Zeitschrift* **68** (1), 58-102

Getty, R, 1975 *Sisson and Grossman's The Anatomy of Domestic Animals*. 5th edition. W B Saunders Company, Philadephia

Gilks, W R, Richardson, S and Spiegelhalther, D J, 1996 *Markov Chain Monte Carlo in Practice*, London

Gill, N T and Vear, K C, 1980 *Agricultural Botany, vol 2. Monocotyledonous Crops*, London

Gingell, C, 1982 Excavation of an Iron Age enclosure at Groundwell Farm, Blunsdon St Andrew, 1976-7, *Wiltshire Archaeol Mag* **76**, 33-75

Girling, M A, 1988 The bark beetle *Scolytus scolytus* (Fabricius) and the possible role of elm disease in the early Neolithic, in M Jones (ed.), *Archaeology and flora of the British Isles*, Oxford Univ Comm for Archaeol Monograph **14**, Oxford, 34-8

Godelier, M, 1977 `Salt money' and the circulation of commodities among the Baruya of New Guinea, in M Godelier (ed.), *Perspectives in Marxist anthropology*, Cambridge, 127-51

Godwin, H, 1956 *The history of the British flora*, Cambridge

Godwin, H, 1975 *The history of the British flora* (2nd edn), Cambridge

Goodman, A H, Armelagos, G J and Rose, J C,1980 Enamel hypoplasias as indicators of stress in three prehistoric populations from Illinois, *Human Biology* **52**, 515-28

Goodman, A H and Rose, J C, 1990 Assessment of systemic physiological perturbations from dental enamel hypoplasias and associated histological structures, *Yearbook of Physical Anthropology* **33**, 59-110

Goodman, C N and Morant, G M, 1940 The human remains of the Iron Age and other periods from Maiden Castle, Dorset, *Biometrika* **31**, 295-312

Gosden, C and Lock, G, 2003 Becoming Roman on the Berkshire Downs; the evidence from Alfred's Castle, *Britannia* **34**, 65-80

Grant, A, 1982 The use of tooth wear as a guide to the age of domestic ungulates, in B Wilson, C Grigson and S Payne (eds), *Ageing and sexing animal bones from archaeological sites*, BAR Int Ser **109**, Oxford, 91-108

Grant, A, 1984 Animal Husbandry in Wessex and the Thames Valley, in Cunliffe and Miles 1984, 102-19

Grant, M, 1996 (translated and edited by) *Anthimus 'De obseruatione ciborum': On the observance of foods*, Blackawton, Totnes

Gray, H St G, 1909 Excavations at the 'amphitheatre', Charterhouse-on-Mendip, *Somerset Archaeol Natur Hist* **55**, 118-37

Gray, M, 1970 Excavations at Northfield Farm, Long Wittenham, Berkshire, *Oxoniensia* **35**, 107-9

Gray, M, 1973 A Romano-British site at Camp Corner, Milton Common, *Oxoniensia* **38**, 6-22

Green, C and Rollo-Smith, S, 1984 The excavation of eighteen round barrows near Shrewton, Wiltshire, *Proc Prehist Soc* **50**, 255-318

Green, F J, 1981 The plant remains, in S M Davies, Excavations at Old Down Farm, Andover Part II, *Proc Hampshire Field Club Archaeol Soc* **37**, 96-161 passim

Green, S and Booth, P 1993 The Roman pottery, in Allen *et al*. 1993, 113-142

Green, S, Booth, P and Allen, T, 2004 Late Iron Age and Roman pottery, in Lambrick and Allen 2004, 303-334

Gregory, C, 1982 *Gifts and commodities*, London

Greig, J R A, 1982 Past and present lime woods of Europe, in M Bell and S Limbrey (eds), *Archaeological aspects of woodland ecology*, BAR Int Ser **146**, Oxford, 23-55

Greig, J, 1991 The British Isles, in W van Zeist, K Wasylikowa and K Behre (eds), *Progress in Old World Palaeoethnobotany*, Blakema, Rotterdam, 299-334

Greig, J, 2004 Pollen from Yarnton floodplain, in Hey 2004, 369-79

Grieve, M, 1980 *A modern herbal*, Harmondsworth

Grime, J P, Mason, G, Curtis, A V, Rodman, J, Bard, S R, Mowforth, M A G, Neal, A M and Shaw, S, 1981 A comparative study of germination characteristics in a local flora, *J of Ecology* **69**, 1017-59

Grime, J P, Hodgson, J G and Hunt, R, 1988 *Comparative Plant Ecology: A functional approach to common British Species*, Unwin Hyman, London

Grimes, W F, 1943 Excavations at Stanton Harcourt, Oxon, 1940, *Oxoniensia* **8-9**, 19-63

Grimes, W F and Close-Brooks. J, 1993 The excavation of Caesar's Camp, Heathrow, Harmondsworth, Middlesex, 1944, *Proc Prehist Soc* **59**, 303-60

Grimm, E C, 1990 TILIA and TILIA.GRAPH. PC spreadsheet and graphics software for pollen data, *INQUA Working Group for Data-handling Methods Newsletter* **4**, 5-7

Gwilt, A, and Haselgrove, C (eds), 1997 *Reconstructing Iron Age Societies*, Oxbow Monograph **71**, Oxford

Haas, H and Streibig, J C, 1982 Changing patterns of weed distribution as a result of herbicide use and other agronomic factors, in H M Le Baron and J Gressel (eds), *Herbicide Resistance in Plants*, Wiley, New York, 57-79

Haigh, J G B, 1989 Rectification of aerial photographs by means of desk-top systems, in S Rahtz and J Richards (eds), *Computer applications and quantitative methods in archaeology*, BAR Int Ser **548**, Oxford, 111-8

Halden, R with Mellor, M, 1977 Late Saxon and medieval pottery, in B Durham, Archaeological investigations in St Aldates, Oxford, *Oxoniensia* **42**, 111-39

Hall, A D, 1905 *An account of the Rothampstead Experiments,* John Murray, London

Hall, D, 1988 The late Saxon countryside: villages and their fields, in D Hooke (ed.), *Anglo Saxon settlements*, Oxford, 99-122

Hall, M, 1998 The archaeology of the Ashbury to Bishopstone pipeline, South Oxfordshire/Wiltshire, 1993, *Oxoniensia* **63,** 199-220

Halpin, C, 1983 Abingdon: ex-MG car factory site, *South Midlands Archaeol* **13**, 113-4

Halpin, C, 1985 Blewbury London Road, *South Midlands Archaeol* **15**, 93-4

Halstead, P, 1985 A study of mandibular teeth from Romano-British contexts at Maxey, in F Pryor *et al.* (eds), *The Fenland project*, **1**: *archaeology and environment in the Lower Welland Valley*, East Anglian Archaeol Rep **27**, 219-24

Hambleton, E, 1999 *Animal Husbandry Regimes in Iron Age Britain. A comparative study of faunal assemblages from British Iron Age sites*, BAR Brit Ser **282**, Oxford

Hamilton, J, 2000a Animal husbandry: the evidence from the animal bones, in B Cunliffe *The Danebury Environs Programme: the prehistory of a Wessex landscape. Vol 1 Introduction*, Oxford University Comm for Archaeol Monograph No. **48**, Oxford, 59-76

Hamilton, J, 2000b Animal bones, in B Cunliffe and C Poole, *Bury Hill, Upper Clatford, Hants, 1990*, The Danebury Environs Programme: the prehistory of a Wessex landscape Vol 2 – Part 2, Oxford University Comm for Archaeol Monograph No. **49**, Oxford, 67-72

Hamilton-Dyer, S, 1993 Animal bone, in A Mudd, Excavations at Whitehouse Road, Oxford, 1992 *Oxoniensia* **58**, 68-71

Hamlin, A, 1963 Excavations of ring ditches and other sites at Stanton Harcourt, *Oxonienia* **28**, 1-19

Hamlin, A, 1966 Early Iron Age sites at Stanton Harcourt, *Oxoniensia* **31**, 1-27

Hands, A R, 1993 *The Romano-British roadside settlement at Wilcote, Oxfordshire I. Excavations 1990-92*, BAR Brit Ser **232**, Oxford

Hands, A R, 1998 *The Romano-British Roadside Settlement at Wilcote, Oxfordshire II. Excavations 1993-96*, BAR Brit Ser **265**, Oxford

Hanf, M, 1983 *The arable weeds of Europe with their seedlings and seeds*, BASF, Ipswich

Harbison, P, 1969 *The daggers and halberds of the early Bronze Age in Ireland*, Prähistorische Bronzefunde **6** (1), Munich

Harcourt, R, 1979 The animal bones, in G J Wainwright, *Gussage All Saints: an Iron Age settlement in Dorset,* Dept of Environment Archaeol Rep No **10**, London, 150-60

Harden, D B and Taylor, M V, 1939 Romano-British remains, in *VCH Oxfordshire I*, 267-345

Harden, D B and Treweeks, R C, 1945 Excavations at Stanton Harcourt, Oxon, 1940, *Oxoniensia* **10**, 16-42

Harding, D W, 1966 The pottery from Kirtlington, and its implications for the chronology of the earliest Iron Age in the Upper Thames region, *Oxoniensia* **31,** 158-61

Harding, D W, 1972 *The Iron Age in the Upper Thames Basin*, Clarendon Press, Oxford

Harding, D W, 1974 *The Iron Age in Lowland Britain*, London

Harding, D W (ed.), 1976 *Hillforts: Later Prehistoric Earthworks in Britain and Ireland,* Academic Press, London

Harding, D W, 1987 *Excavations in Oxfordshire, 1964-66*, University of Edinburgh Department of Archaeol Occ Paper **15**, Edinburgh

Hardy, A, Dodd, A and Keevill, G, 2003 *Ælfric's Abbey Excavations at Eynsham Abbey, Oxfordshire, 1989-92*, Oxford Archaeol Thames Valley Landscapes Vol **16**, Oxford

Harley, J L and Harley, E L, 1987 A checklist of mycorrhiza in the British Flora, *New Phytologist* **105** (supplement), 1-102

Harman, M, 1990 The human bones, in Allen 1990a, 57

Harman, M, 2004 The human remains, in Lambrick and Allen 2004, 457-463

Harman, M, Lambrick, G, Miles, D and Rowley, T, 1978 Roman burials around Dorchester-on-Thames, *Oxoniensia* **43**, 1-16

Harman, M, Molleson, T I and Price, J L, 1981 Burials, bodies and beheadings in Romano-British and Anglo-Saxon cemeteries, *Bull Brit Mus Nat Hist (Geol)* **35 (3)**, 145-88

Harper, J L, 1977 *Population Biology of Plants*, London

Harris, E and Young, C J, 1974 The 'Overdale' kiln site at Boar's Hill, near Oxford, *Oxoniensia* **39**, 12-25

Hasdorf, C A and DeNiro, M J, 1985 New isotope method used to reconstruct prehistoric plant production and cooking practices, *Nature* **315**, 489-91

Haselgrove, C, 1985 Inferences from ploughsoil artefact samples, in C Haselgrove, M Millett and I Smith (eds), *Archaeology from the ploughsoil*, Dept of Archaeol and Prehist, University of Sheffield, 7-29

Hassall, T G, 1972 Roman finds from the Radcliffe Science Library extension, *Oxoniensia* **37**, 38-50

Hattatt, R, 1985 *Iron Age and Roman Brooches. A second selection from the author's collection*, Oxford

Hattatt, R, 1987 *Brooches of Antiquity. A third selection of brooches from the author's collection*, Oxford

Hattatt, R, 1989 *Ancient Brooches and other artefacts. A fourth selection of brooches together with some other antiquities from the author's collection*, Oxford

Havinga, A J, 1964 Investigation into the differential corrosion susceptibility of pollen and spores, *Pollen et Spores* **6**, 621-35

Havinga, A J, 1974 Problems in the interpretation of pollen diagrams of mineral soils, *Geologie en Mijnbouw* **53**, 449-53

Hawkes, C F C and Hull, M R, 1947 *Camulodunum: First Report on the excavations at Colchester 1930-1939*, Rep Res Comm Soc Antiqs London **14**, London

Hawkes, S, 1986 The early Saxon period, in G Briggs, J Cook and T Rowley (eds), *The archaeology of the Oxford region*, Oxford, 64-108

Hawkes, S and Dunning, G C, 1961 Soldiers and settlers in Britain, fourth to fifth century, *Med Archaeol* 5, 1-70

Hawkes, S C and Gray, M, 1969 Preliminary note on the early Anglo-Saxon settlement at New Wintles Farm, Eynsham, *Oxoniensia* **34**, 1-4

Hayden, C, Hey, G and Laws, G, forthcoming Excavations on Cassington Floodplain, in Hey *et al.* forthcoming

Healy, F, 1984 The Neolithic in Norfolk, in C Barringer (ed.), *Aspects of East Anglian prehistory*, Geo Books, Norwich, 77-140

Healy, F, Cleal, R M J and Kinnes, I, 1993 Excavations on Redgate Hill, Hunstanton, 1970 and 1971, in R Bradley, P Chowne, R M J Cleal, F Healy and I Kinnes, *Excavations at Redgate Hill, Hunstanton, Norfolk and at Tattershall Thorpe, Lincolnshire*, East Anglian Archaeol Rep **57**, 1-77

Hearne, C M and Adam, N, 1999 Excavation of an extensive Late Bronze Age settlement at Shorncote Quarry, near Cirencester, 1995-6, *Trans Bristol Gloucestershire Archaeol Soc* **117**, 35–73

Hearne, C M and Heaton, M J, 1994 Excavations at a Late Bronze Age settlement in the Upper Thames Valley at Shorncote Qarry near Cirencester, 1992, *Trans Bristol Gloucestershire Archaeol Soc* **112**, 17–57

Hedges, J D and Buckley, D G, 1981 *Springfield cursus and the cursus problem*, Essex County Council Occas Pap **1**, Chelmsford

Hedges, R E M, Bronk, C R and Housley, R A, 1989 The Oxford Accelerator Mass Spectrometry facility: technical developments in routine dating, *Archaeometry* **31**, 99-113

Hedges, R E M, Housley, R A, Ramsay, C B and van Keinken, G J, 1995 Radiocarbon dates from the Oxford AMS system: *Archaeometry* datelist 20, *Archaeometry* **37(2)**, 417-30

Helbaek, H, 1952 Early crops in Southern Britain, *Proc Prehistoric Soc* **18**, 194-233

Helbæk, H, 1964 The Isca grain, a Roman plant introduction in Britain, *New Phytologist* **63**, 158-64

Henig, M, 1995 *The Art of Roman Britain*, London

Henig, M and Booth, P, 2000 *Roman Oxfordshire*, Sutton, Stroud

Hensinger, R N, 1989 Spondylolysis and spondylolisthesis in children and adolescents, *J Bone and Joint Surgery* (71A), 1098-1107

Henson, I E, 1970 The effects of light, potassium nitrate and temperature on the germination of *Chenopodium album*, *Weed Research* **10**, 27-39

Heron, C and Evershed, R P, 1993 The analysis of organic residues and the study of pottery use, in M Schiffer (ed.), *Archaeological method and theory* **5**, University of Arizona Press, Arizona, 242

Hey, G, 1991a Yarnton Worton Rectory Farm, *South Midlands Archaeol* **21**, 86-92

Hey, G, 1991b Mead Farm, Yarnton archaeological assessment, internal OAU and client report, January 1991

Hey, G, 1991c Yarnton & Cassington Worton Rectory Farm; 1990/91 assessments, internal OAU and English Heritage report, July 1991

Hey, G, 1992 Yarnton Floodplain: 1991 field evaluation, internal OAU and English Heritage report, January 1992

Hey, G, 1993a Witney-Eynsham-Cassington A40 dualling, *South Midlands Archaeol* **23**, 60-3

Hey, G, 1993b Yarnton Floodplain 1992: post-excavation assessment, internal OAU and English Heritage report, November 1993

Hey, G, 1994a Yarnton-Cassington evaluation 1993, internal OAU and English Heritage report, March 1994

Hey, G, 1994b Yarnton-Cassington Project: A Neolithic to Medieval landscape, internal OAU and English Heritage report, November 1994

Hey G, 1994c Yarnton-Cassington evaluation, *South Midlands Archaeol* **24**, 49-52

Hey, G, 1995 Iron Age and Roman settlement at Old Shifford Farm, *Oxoniensia* **60**, 93-176

Hey, G, 1996 Yarnton-Cassington Project: Yarnton Floodplain B 1995 post-excavation assessment, internal OAU and English Heritage report, February 1996

Hey, G, 1998 The Yarnton-Cassington project: evaluating a floodplain landscape, *Lithics* **19**, 47-60

Hey, G, 2001 Danebury's Landscape, *Antiquity* **75**, 630-2

Hey, G, 2004 *Yarnton Saxon and medieval settlement and landscape*, Oxford Archaeol Thames Valley Landscapes Monograph **20**, Oxford

Hey, G, 2007 Unravelling the Iron Age landscape of the Upper Thames Valley, in C Haselgrove and T Moore (eds), *The Later Iron Age in Britain and Beyond*, Oxbow, Oxford, 156-172

Hey G and Miles, D, 1989 Archaeological investigation in the Upper Thames Valley: a proposal for research in the Cassington/Eynsham/Yarnton area (Evenlode confluence), unpublished OAU report

Hey, G, Bell, C and Parsons, M, 1993 Yarnton Floodplain, *South Midlands Archaeol* **23**, 82-5

Hey, G, Bayliss, A and Boyle, A, 1999 Iron Age inhumation burials at Yarnton, Oxfordshire,

Antiquity **73**, 551-62

Hey, G, Dennis, C and Bell, C, forthcoming *Yarnton: Neolithic and Bronze Age settlement and landscape*, Oxford Archaeol Thames Valley Landscapes Monograph

Higham, N, 1992 *Rome, Britain and the Anglo-Saxons*, Seaby, London

Hill, J D, 1995 *Ritual and rubbish in the Iron Age of Wessex: A study on the formation of a specific archaeological record*, BAR Brit Ser **242**, Oxford

Hillman, G, 1973 Crop husbandry and food production: modern models for the interpretation of plant remains, *Anatolian Studies* **23**, 241-44

Hillman, G C, 1981 Reconstructing crop husbandry practices from charred remains of crops, in R Mercer (ed.), *Farming practice in British prehistory*, Edinburgh, 123-62

Hillman, G C, 1984a Interpretation of archaeological plant remains: the application of ethnographic models from Turkey, in van Zeist and Casparie 1984, 1-41

Hillman, G C, 1984b Traditional husbandry and processing of archaic cereals in recent times: the operations, products and equipment which might feature in Sumerian texts, part 1, the glume wheats, *Bulletin on Sumerian Agriculture* **1**, 114-52

Hillson, S 1996 *Dental anthropology*, Cambridge University Press

Hinchliffe, J and Thomas, R, 1980 Archaeological investigations at Appleford, *Oxoniensia* **45**, 9-111

Hingley, R, 1980 Excavations by R A Rutland on an Iron Age site at Wittenham Clumps, *Berkshire Archaeol J* **70**, 21-55

Hingley, R, 1984 Towards social analysis in archaeology: Celtic society in the Iron Age of the Upper Thames Valley (400-0 B.C.), in Cunliffe and Miles 1984, 72-88

Hingley, R and Miles, D, 1984 Aspects of Iron Age settlement in the Upper Thames Valley, in Cunliffe and Miles 1984, 52-71

Hirst, S and Rahtz, P, 1996 Liddington Castle and the Battle of Badon: excavations and research 1976, *Archaeol J* **153**, 1-59

Hjelmqvist, H, 1955 Die älteste Geschichte der Kulturpflanzen in Schweden, *Opera Botanica (a societate botanica lundensi)* **I.3**, 1-186

Hodder, I, 1974 The distribution of Savernake ware, *Wiltshire Archaeol Mag* **69**, 67-84

Hodder, I and Hedges, J W, 1977 Weaving combs – their typology and distribution with some introductory remarks on date and function, in Collis 1977, 17-28

Hodder, M and Barfield, L H (eds), 1991 *Burnt mounds and hot stone technology, Papers from the Second International Burnt Mound Conference*, Sandwell

Hodgson, G, 1968 A comparative account of the animal remains from Corstopitum and the iron age site of Catcote near Hartlepool, County Durham, *Archaeol Aeliana* (4th series) **46**, 127-62

Holbrook, N and Thomas, A, 1996 The Roman and early Saxon settlement at Wantage, Oxfordshire: excavations at Mill Street, 1993-4, *Oxoniensia* **61**, 109-79

Holgate, R, 1988 *Neolithic settlement of the Thames basin*, BAR Brit Ser **194**, Oxford

Hooper, B, 1984 Anatomical considerations, in Cunliffe 1984a, 463-74

Hooper, B, 1991 Anatomical considerations, in Cunliffe and Poole 1991b, 425-31

Hooper, B, 2000 The cemetery population, in Cunliffe and Poole 2000, 168-70

Horion, A D, 1961 *Faunistik der Mitteleuropäischen Käfer* 8, Feyel, Überlingen-Bodensee

Howard, H, 1983 The bronze casting industry in later prehistoric southern Britain, unpubl PhD thesis, Univ of Southampton

Hubbard, R N L B, 1975 Assessing the botanical component of human palaeo-economies, *Bull Inst Archaeol Univ London* **12**, 197-205

Hubbard, R N L B, 1976 On the strength of the evidence for prehistoric crop processing activities, *J Archaeol Science* **3**, 257-65

Hull, M R and Hawkes, C F C, 1987 *Corpus of ancient brooches in Britain. Pre-Roman bow brooches*, BAR Brit Ser **168**, Oxford

Huntley, D J, Godfrey-Smith, D I and Thewalt, M L W, 1985 Optical dating of sediments, *Nature* **313**, 105–7

Hurst, D and Rees, H, 1992 Pottery fabrics; a multi-period series for the county of Hereford and Worcester, in S Woodiwiss (ed.), *Iron Age and Roman salt production and the medieval town of Droitwich*, CBA Res Rep **81**, London, 200-9

Ingle, C, 2004 Greensand querns, in Lambrick and Allen 2004, 357

Institute of Geological Sciences, 1972 *Geological Survey of Great Britain, Sheet 236, Witney, Solid and Drift*, 1:50,000, London

Iscan, M and Loth, S, 1986 Estimation of age and determination of sex from the sternal rib, in K J Reichs (ed.), *Forensic archaeology: advances in the identification of human remains*, Thomas, Springfield, Illinois, 68-89

Jackson, D A, 1975 An Iron Age site at Twywell, Northamptonshire, *Northamptonshire Archaeol* **10**, 31-93

Jacobi, R M, 1973 Aspects of the `Mesolithic Age' in Great Britain, in S Kozlowski (ed.), *The Mesolithic in Europe*, Warsaw, 237-65

Janssen, C R, 1959 *Alnus* as a disturbing factor in pollen diagrams, *Acta Botanica Neerlandica* **8**, 55-8

Jarman, M and Fagg, A, 1968 Animal Remains, in I M Stead, An Iron Age hill-fort at Grimthorpe, Yorkshire, England, *Proc Prehist Soc* **34**, 182-9

Jarvis, M G, 1973 *Soils of the Wantage and Abingdon district*, Memoir of the Soil Survey of Great Britain: England and Wales, Harpenden

Jecock, H M, 1985 The querns: some observations, in P J Fasham, *The prehistoric settlement at Winnall*

Down, Winchester, Hampshire Field Club and Archaeol Soc Monograph **2**, M3 Archaeol Rescue Comm Rep **8**, Winchester 77-80

Jeffry, D W, 1987 *Soil-plant relationships: an ecological approach*, London

Jennings, D, 1998 Prehistoric and Roman activity, in Boyle *et al*. 1998, 9-34

Jennings, D, Muir, J Palmer, S and Smith, A, 2004 *Thornhill Farm, Fairford, Gloucestershire. An Iron Age and Roman pastoral site in the Upper Thames Valley*, Oxford Archaeol Thames Valley Landscapes Monograph **23**, Oxford

Jessop, L, 1986 *Dung beetles and chafers*, Royal Entomological Society Handbook for the Identification of British Insects **5**, pt 11, London

Jessup, R F, 1932 Bigberry Camp, Harbledown, Kent, *Archaeol J* **89**, 87–115

Johnstone, J and Bowden, M, 1985 Excavations at Pingewood, *Berkshire Archaeol J* **72**, 17-52

Jones, G E M, 1983 The ethnoarchaeology of crop processing: seeds of a middle range methodology, *Archaeol Rev from Cambridge* **2**, Part 2, 17-26

Jones, G E M, 1984 Interpretation of archaeological plant remains: ethnographic models from Greece, in van Zeist and Casparie 1984, 43-61

Jones, G E M, 1987 A statistical approach to the archaeological identification of crop processing, *J Archaeol Science* **14**, 311-23

Jones, G E M, 1992 Weed phytosociology and crop husbandry: identifying a contrast between ancient and modern practice, in J P Pals, J Buurman, and M van der Veen (eds), *Review of Palaeobotany and Palynology* **73**, Festschrift for Professor van Zeist, Amsterdam, 133-43

Jones, M, 1975 Seed report, in M Parrington, Excavations at the Old Gaol, Abingdon, *Oxoniensia* **40**, 77-8

Jones, M K, 1978 The plant remains, in Parrington 1978, 93-110

Jones, M, 1980 Carbonised plant remains, in Palmer 1980 fiche G07

Jones, M K, 1981 The development of crop husbandry, in M K Jones and G Dimbleby (eds), *The Environment of Man, the Iron Age to the Anglo-Saxon Period*, BAR Brit Ser **87**, Oxford, 95-127

Jones, M K, 1984a The Ecological and Cultural Implications of Carbonised Seed Assemblages from Selected Archaeological Contexts in Southern Britain, unpublished D Phil thesis, Univ of Oxford

Jones, M K, 1984b The plant remains, in Cunliffe 1984a, 483-95

Jones, M K, 1984c Regional patterns in crop production, in Cunliffe and Miles 1984, 120-5

Jones, M K, 1985 Archaeobotany beyond subsistence reconstruction, in G Barker and C Gamble (eds), *Beyond Domestication in Prehistoric Europe. Investigations on subsistence archaeology and social complexity*, London, 107-28

Jones, M, 1986a, Towards a model of the villa estate, in D Miles (ed) *Archaeology at Barton Court Farm, Abingdon, Oxon*, CBA Res Rep **50**, 38-42

Jones, M K, 1986b The carbonised plant remains, in Miles 1986, Fiche 9:A1-9:B5

Jones, M, 1987 Carbonised grain, in D Mynard (ed.), *Roman Milton Keynes: Excavations and fieldwork 1971-82*, Buckinghamshire Archaeol Soc Monograph **1**, 192-3

Jones, M K, 1988a The phytosociology of early arable weed communities with special reference to southern England, in H Küster (ed.), *Der Prähistoriche Mensch und Seine Umwelt*, Forschungen und Berichte zur Vor- und Frühgeschichte in Baden-Württemberg, Band **31**, Stuggart, Theiss, 43-51

Jones, M K, 1988b The arable field: a botanical battleground, in M Jones (ed.), *Archaeology and the Flora of the British Isles*, Oxford Univ Comm Archaeol, Oxford, 86-91

Jones, M, 1991 Food production and consumption – plants, in R F J Jones (ed.), *Britain in the Roman period, recent trends*, Department of Archaeol and Prehist, University of Sheffield, 21-7

Jones, M with Robinson, M, 1993 The carbonised plant remains, in Allen and Robinson 1993, 120-3

Karssen, C M and Hilhorst, H W M, 1992 Effect of chemical environment on seed germination, in M Fenner (ed.), *Seeds: The Ecology of Regeneration in Plant Communities*, C.A.B. International, Oxford, 327-48

Katz, D and Suchey, J M, 1986 Age determination of the male *os pubis*, *Amer J Physical Anthropology* **69**, 427-35

Kay, Q O N, 1971 Anthemis cotula L., *J of Ecology* **59**, 623-36

Keely, J, 1986 The coarse pottery, in A McWhirr, *Cirencester Excavations III; houses in Roman Cirencester*, Cirencester, 158-89

Keepax, C A, 1979 The human bones, in Wainright 1979, 161-71

Keevill, G D and Durden, T, 1997 Archaeological work at the Rover Plant Site, Cowley, Oxford, *Oxoniensia* **62**, 87-99

Kent, D H, 1992 *A list of vascular plants of the British Isles*, Botanical Soc of the British Isles, London

Kenward, H K and Williams, D, 1979 Biological evidence from the Roman warehouses in Coney Street, in P V Addyman (ed.), *The archaeology of York* **14** (2), CBA, London, 45-100

King, A C, 1978 A comparative survey of bone assemblages from Roman sites in Britain. *Bull Institute of Archaeol University of London* **15**, 207-32

King, A C, 1991 Food production and consumption – meat, in R F J Jones (ed.), *Roman Britain: Recent Trends*, Department of Archaeol and Prehist, University of Sheffield, 15-8

King R, 1998 Excavations at Gassons Road, Lechlade 1993, in Boyle *et al.* 1998, 269-81

Kinnes, I, 1977 Finds, in P Donaldson, The excavation of a multiple round barrow at Barnack,

Cambridgeshire, 1974-1976, *Antiq J* **57**, 197-231
Kirk, J and Case, H, 1950 Notes and news, *Oxoniensia* **15**, 104-9
Kirk, J R and Leeds, E T, 1952/53 Three early Saxon graves from Dorchester, Oxon., *Oxoniensia* **17/18**, 63-76
Kitchener, A C and O'Connor, T P, 2010 Wild, domestic and feral cats, in T P O'Connor, and N Sykes (eds), *Extinctions and Invasions. A social history of British fauna*, Windgather Press, Oxford, 83-94
Kloet, G S and Hincks, W D, 1977 *A checklist of British insects: Coleoptera and Strepsiptera*, (2nd edn), Royal Entomological Society Handbook for the Identification of British Insects **11**, pt. 3, London
Knight, D, 1984 *Late Bronze Age and Iron Age settlement in the Nene and Great Ouse basins*, BAR Brit Ser **130**, Oxford
Knörzer, K-H, 1967 Die Roggentrespe (*Bromus secalinus* L.) als prahistorische Nutzpflanze, *Archaeo-Physika* **2**, 3-29
Knörzer, K-H, 1971 Urgeschichtliche Unkräuter im Rheinland, ein Beitrag zur Entstehung der Segetalgesellschaften, *Vegetatio* **23**, 89-111
Knüsel, C J and Carr, G C, 1995 On the significance of the crania from the River Thames and its tributaries, *Antiquity* **69**, 162-9
Kosnick, E J, Johnson, J C, Scoles, P V and Rossel, C W, 1979 Cervical spondylolisthesis, *Spine* **4**, 203-9

Lambrick, G, 1979a Mount Farm, Berinsfield, *CBA Group 9 Newsletter* **9**, 113-5
Lambrick, G, 1979b Finds: the Iron Age pottery, in Lambrick and Robinson 1979, 35-46
Lambrick, G, 1984 Pitfalls and possibilities in Iron Age pottery studies: experiences in the Upper Thames Valley, in Cunliffe and Miles 1984, 162-77
Lambrick, G (ed.), 1985 *Archaeology and nature conservation*, Oxford
Lambrick, G, 1988 *The Rollright Stones: megaliths, monuments and settlement in the prehistoric landscape*, Historic Buildings and Monuments Commission for England Archaeol Rep **6**, London
Lambrick, G, 1992a Alluvial archaeology of the Holocene in the Upper Thames Basin 1971-1991: a review, in Needham and Macklin (eds) 1992, 209-26
Lambrick, G, 1992b The development of late prehistoric and Roman farming on the Thames gravels, in Fulford and Nichols (eds) 1992, 78-105
Lambrick, G, 1996 Gill Mill, *South Midlands Archaeol* **26**, 56
Lambrick, G, 1999 Community and change in the Iron Age of the Upper Thames, unpublished paper presented to the Prehistoric Society Conference, May 1999
Lambrick, G, 2009 *The Thames through time; the archaeology of the gravel terraces of the Upper and Middle Thames. Volume 2: The foundation of modern society in the Thames Valley 1500 BC-AD 50*, Oxford Archaeol Thames Valley Landscapes Monograph No. **29**, Oxford
Lambrick, G, 2010 *Neolithic to Saxon social and environmental change at Mount Farm, Berinsfield, Dorchester on Thames*, Oxford Archaeol Occ Paper No. **19**, Oxford
Lambrick, G and Allen, T, 2004 *Gravelly Guy, Stanton Harcourt: the development of a prehistoric and Romano-British community*, Oxford Archaeol Thames Valley Landscapes Monograph No. **21**, Oxford
Lambrick, G and De Roche, C D, 1980 The Iron Age pottery, in Hinchliffe and Thomas 1980, 45-59
Lambrick, G and McDonald, A, 1985 The archaeology and ecology of Port Meadow and Wolvercote Common, Oxford, in Lambrick 1985, 95-109
Lambrick, G and Roaf, M, 1992 Gravelly Guy, Stanton Harcourt: revised research design and post-excavation reassessment, document prepared by OAU for English Heritage
Lambrick, G and Robinson, M, 1979 *Iron Age and Roman riverside settlements at Farmoor, Oxfordshire*, CBA Res Rep **32**, Oxford Archaeol Unit Rep **2**, London
Lambrick, G and Robinson, M, 1988 The development of floodplain grassland in the upper Thames valley, in M Jones (ed.), *Archaeology and the flora of the British Isles*, Oxford University Comm for Archaeol Monograph **14**, 55-75
Lambrick, G and Wallis, J, 1989 Ducklington, Gill Mill, *South Midlands Archaeol* **19**, 49-50
Lamdin-Whymark, H, Brady, K and Smith, A, forthcoming Excavation of a Neolithic to Roman landscape at Horcott Pit, near Fairford, Gloucestershire, 2002-3, *Trans Bristol Gloucestershire Archaeol Soc* **128**
La Niece, S, 1983 Niello: an historical and technical survey, *Antiq J* **63**, 279-97
La Niece, S, 1993 Silvering, in S La Niece and P T Craddock (eds), *Metal plating and patination: cultural, technical and historical developments*, London, 201-10
Law, I A and Hedges, R E M, 1989 A semi-automated pre-treatment system and the pre-treatment of older and contaminated samples, *Radiocarbon* **31**, 247–53
Laws, K, 1991a The copper alloy objects, in Sharples 1991, 153-6
Laws, K, 1991b The copper alloy objects, in Sharples 1991, 162-5
Laws, K, 1991c The shale, in Sharples 1991, 233-4
Laws, K, 1991d The worked bone objects, in Sharples 1991, 236-8
Laws, K, Brown, L and Roe, F, 1991 Objects of stone, in Cunliffe and Poole 1991, 382-404
Lawson, A J, 1976 Shale and jet objects from Silchester, *Archaeologia* **105**, 241-75

Lawson, J D, 1955 The Geology of the May Hill Inlier, *Quarterly J Geological Soc* **111**, 85-116

Leech, R, 1977 *The Upper Thames Valley in Gloucestershire and Wiltshire: an archaeological survey of the river gravels,* Comm for Rescue Archaeol in Avon, Gloucestershire and Somerset, Survey No **4**

Leeds, E T, 1931 An Iron-Age site near Radley, Berks, *Antiq J* **11**, 399-404

Leeds, E T, 1935 Recent Iron Age discoveries in Oxfordshire and north Berkshire, *Antiq J* **15**, 30-41

Leeds, E T and Atkinson R J C, 1943-4 Notes and News, *Oxoniensia* **8-9**, 200-1

Letts, J, 1993 The charred plant remains, in Mudd 1993, 71-8

Levine, M, 1982 The use of crown height measurements and eruption-wear sequences to age horse teeth, in B Wilson, C Grigson and S Payne (eds), *Ageing and sexing animal bones from archaeological sites,* BAR Int Ser **109**, Oxford, 223-50

Levine, M A, 1999 The origins of horse husbandry on the Eurasian Steppe, in M A Levine, Y Y Rassamakin, A M Kislenko and N S Tatarintseva (eds), *Late prehistoric exploitation of the Eurasian steppe,* McDonald Institute, Cambridge, 5-58

Levine, M A, 2004 The faunal remains, in Jennings *et al.* 2004, 109-33

Lightfoot, E, 2003 An Investigation into Iron Age Diet at Yarnton, using Stable Carbon and Nitrogen Isotopes, unpublished Univ of Oxford BA dissertation (Candidate Number 21101)

Limbrey, S, 1995 The sediments and soils in the henge ditch, in Barclay *et al.* 1995, 68-9

Lindroth, C H, 1974 *Coleoptera: Carabidae,* Royal Entomological Society Handbook for the Identification of British Insects **4**, pt. 2, London

Linford, N, 1994 Mineral magnetic profiling of archaeological sediments, *Archaeol Prospection* **1**, 37-52

Linford, N, 1995 Yarnton Cassington Project, Oxfordshire. Cresswell Field. Report on geophysical survey, March 1995, *Ancient Monuments Laboratory Report Series,* **16/95**, English Heritage, London

Linford, N, 2004 Geophysical Survey, in Hey 2004, 229-51

Linford, N, Linford, P and Platzman, E, 2005 Dating environmental change using magnetic bacteria in archaeological soils from the upper Thames Valley, *J Archaeol Science* **32 (7)**, 1037-43

Lloyd-Morgan, G, 1997 Copper alloy and bone objects, in Booth 1997a, 77-82

Lock, G, Gosden, C and Daly, P, 2005 *Segsbury Camp: Excavations in 1996 and 1997 at an Iron Age Hillfort on the Oxfordshire Ridgeway,* Oxford Univ School of Archaeol Monograph **61**, Oxford

Locker, A, 2007 *In piscibus diversis*: the bone evidence for fish consumption in Roman Britain, *Britannia* **38**, 141-80

Longin, R, 1971 New method of collagen extraction for radiocarbon dating, *Nature* **230**, 241–2

Lovejoy, C O, Meindl, R S, Pryzbeck, T R and Mensforth, R, 1985 Chronological metamorphosis of the auricular surface of the ilium: a new method for the determination of adult skeletal age at death, *American J Physical Anthropology* **68**, 15-28

LRBCI = Hill, P V, and Kent, J P C, 1976 *Late Roman Bronze Coinage Part I,* London

LRBCII = Carson, R A G, and Kent, J P C, 1976 *Late Roman Bronze Coinage Part II,* London

Lynch, F, 1991 *Prehistoric Anglesey,* 2nd edn, Anglesey Antiquarian Soc, Llangefni

MacGregor, A, 1985 *Bone, antler, ivory and horn: The technology of skeletal materials since the Roman period,* London

Mackreth, D F, 1973 The brooches, in Brodribb *et al.* 1973, 112-6

Mackreth, D F, 1982 The brooches, in Wacher and McWhirr 1982, 88-92

Mackreth, D F, 1993 The brooches, in Hands 1993, 27-37

Mackreth, D F, 1996 *Orton Hall Farm: a Roman and early Anglo-Saxon farmstead,* East Anglian Archaeol Rep No. **76**

Maier, A, 1972 Ein frühbronzeitlicher Grabdolch mit Griffknauf, *Germania* **50**, 235-7

Maltby, M, 2010 Pits and wells, in J Morris and M Maltby (eds), *Integrating social and environmental archaeologies: Reconsidering deposition,* BAR Int Ser **2077**, Oxford, 24-32

Manning, W H, 1985 *Catalogue of the Romano-British iron tools, fittings and weapons in the British Museum,* London

Manning, W H and Scott, I R, 1989 *Report on the excavations at Usk 1965-1976: the fortress excavations 1972-1974 and minor excavations on the fortress and Flavian fort,* Cardiff

Manning, W H, Price J and Webster, J, 1995 *Report on excavations at Usk 1965-1976. The Roman small finds,* University of Wales, Cardiff

Marchant, T, 1989 The evidence for textile production in the Iron Age, *Scottish Archaeol Rev* **6**, 5-12

Mays, S 1993 Infanticide in Roman Britain, *Antiquity* **67**, 883-8

McCormac, F G, 1992 Liquid scintillation counter characterization, optimization, and benzene purity correction, *Radiocarbon* **34**, 37-45

McDonald, A W, 1984 The historical ecology of some unimproved alluvial grasslands in the Upper Thames Valley, unpubl D. Phil. thesis, Univ of Oxford

McDonald, P, Edwards, R A and Greenhalgh, J F D, 1988 (eds) *Animal nutrition,* Harlow (4th edn)

McGavin, N, 1980 A Roman cemetery and trackway at Stanton Harcourt, *Oxoniensia* **45**, 112-22

McKinley, J I, 1993 Bone fragment size and weights of bone from modern British cremations and its implications for the interpretation of archaeological cremations, *Internat J Osteoarchaeology* **3**, 283-7

Meadows, K, 1999 The appetites of households in early Roman Britain, in P M Allison (ed.), *The archaeology of household activities*, London, 101-20

Meindl, R S and Lovejoy, C O, 1985 Ectocranial suture closure: A revised method for the determination of skeletal age at death based on the lateral-anterior sutures, *American J Physical Anthropology* **68**, 29-45

Meyer-Arendt, H (ed.), 1993 *Bronzezeit in Ungarn: Forschungen in Tell-Siedlungen an Donau und Theiss*, Ausstellungskatalog des Museums für Vor- und Frühgeschichte Frankfurt am Main

Middleton, A, 1987 Technological investigations of the coatings on some 'haematite-coated' pottery from southern England, *Archaeometry* **29**(2), 250-61

Miles, A E W, 1962 Assessment of the ages of a population of Anglo-Saxons from their dentitions, *Proc Royal Soc Medicine* **55**, 881-6

Miles, D, 1975 Excavations at West St. Helens St, 1972, *Oxoniensia* **40**, 79-101

Miles, D, 1982 Confusion in the countryside: some comments from the Upper Thames region, in D Miles (ed.), *The Romano-British countryside: studies in rural settlement and economy*, BAR Brit Ser **103**, Oxford, 53-79

Miles, D (ed.), 1986 *Archaeology at Barton Court Farm, Abingdon, Oxon*, Oxford Archaeol Unit Rep **3**, CBA Res Rep **50**, Oxford and London

Miles, D, 1997 Conflict and complexity: the later prehistory of the Oxford region, *Oxoniensia* **62**, 1-19

Miles, D and Palmer, S, 1984 Fairford/Lechlade: Claydon Pike, *South Midlands Archaeol* **14**, 93-8

Miles, D, Hofdahl, D and Moore, J, 1986 The pottery, in Miles 1986, microfiche 7

Miles, D, Palmer, S, Lock, G, Gosden, C and Cromarty, A M, 2003 *Uffington White Horse and its landscape: investigations at White Horse Hill, Uffington, 1989-95, and Tower Hill, Ashbury, 1993-4*, Oxford Archaeol Thames Valley Landscapes Monograph No. **18**, Oxford

Miles, D, Palmer, S, Smith, A and Jones, G P, 2007 *Iron Age and Roman settlement in the Upper Thames Valley: Excavations at Claydon Pike and other sites within the Cotswold Water Park*, Oxford Archaeol Thames Valley Landscapes Monograph No. **26**, Oxford

Millett, M, 1990 *The Romanization of Britain*, Cambridge

Moffett, L, 1986 Crops and crop processing in a Romano-British village at Tiddington: the evidence from the charred plant remains, *Ancient Monuments Lab Rep* **15/86**

Moffett, L, 1988 Charred seeds and crop remains from the Iron Age enclosure, in G Lambrick, *The Rollright Stones: megaliths, monuments and settlement in the prehistoric landscape*, English Heritage Archaeol Rep **6**, London, 103-5

Moffett, L, 1999 The prehistoric use of plant resources, in Barclay and Halpin 1999, 243-7

Moffett, L, 2004 The evidence for crop-processing products from the Iron Age and Romano-British periods and some earlier prehistoric plant remains, in Lambrick and Allen 2004, 421-45

Moffett, L, Robinson, M A and Straker, V, 1989 Cereals, fruit and nuts: charred plant remains from Neolithic sites in England and Wales and the Neolithic economy, in A Milles, D Williams and N Gardner (eds), *The beginnings of agriculture*, BAR Int Ser **496**, Oxford, 243-61

Molleson, T, 1992 The anthropological evidence for change through Romanisation of the Poundbury population, *Anthropologische Anzeiger* **50**, 178-89

Mook, W G, 1986 Business meeting: Recommendations/Resolutions adopted by the Twelfth International Radiocarbon Conference, *Radiocarbon* **28**, 799

Moore, P D and Webb, J A, 1978 *An illustrated guide to pollen analysis*, London

Morris, E L, 1981 Ceramic exchange in western Britain: a preliminary view, in H Howard and E L Morris (eds), *Production and distribution: a ceramic viewpoint*, BAR Int Ser **120**, Oxford, 67-81

Morris, E L, 1985 Prehistoric salt distributions: two case studies from western Britain, *Bull Board Celtic Stud* **32**, 336-79

Morris, E L, 2004 Briquetage, in Lambrick and Allen 2004, 357-60

Morris, J, 2008 Associated bone groups; one archaeologist's rubbish is another's ritual deposition, in O Davis, K Waddington and N, Sharples (eds), *Changing perspectives on the first millennium BC*, Oxbow, Oxford, 83-98

Morris, J, 2010 Associated bone groups: beyond the Iron Age, in J Morris and M Maltby (eds), *Integrating social and environmental archaeologies: reconsidering deposition*, BAR Int Ser **2077**, Oxford, 12-23

Mottram, H R, Dudd, S N, Lawrence, G J, Stott, A W and Evershed, R P, 1999 New chromatographic, mass spectrometric and stable isotope approaches to the classification of degraded animal fats preserved in archaeological pottery, *J Chromatography* A **833**(2), 209-21

Mudd, A, 1993 Excavations at Whitehouse Road, Oxford, 1992, *Oxoniensia* **58**, 33-85

Mudd, A, 1995 The excavation of a late Bronze Age/early Iron Age site at Eight Acre Field, Radley, *Oxonienisa* **60**, 21-65

Muir, J and Roberts, M K, 1999 *Excavations at Wyndyke Furlong, Abingdon, Oxfordshire, 1994*, Oxford Archaeol Unit Thames Valley Landscapes Monograph No **12**, Oxford

Mullin, D, Laws, G and Smith, A, 2009 Horcott Quarry (Churchberry Manor), Fairford, Gloucestershire, Post-excavation assessment and project design, Oxford Archaeol unpublished client report

Mulville, J and Ayres, K, 2004 Animal bone, in Hey 2004, 325-50

Mulville, J and Levitan, B, 2004 The animal bone, in Lambrick and Allen 2004, 463-78

Murphy, P, 1994 The Anglo-Saxon landscape and rural economy: some results from sites in East Anglia and Essex, in J Rackham (ed.), *Environment and Economy in Anglo-Saxon England*, CBA Res Rep **89**, London, 23-39

Musson, C R, Britnell, W J, Northover, J P and Salter, C J, 1992 Excavations and metalworking at Llwyn-Bryn Dinas hillfort, Llangedwyn, Clwyd, *Proc Prehist Soc* **58**, 265-83

Myres, J N L, 1937 A prehistoric and Roman site on Mount Farm, Dorchester, *Oxoniensia* **2**, 12-40

Mytum, H, 1986 An early Iron Age site at Wytham Hill, near Cumnor, Oxford, *Oxoniensia* **51**, 15-24

Mytum, H and Taylor, J W, 1981 Stanton Harcourt: Linch Hill Corner, *CBA Group 9 Newsletter* **11**, 139-41

Needham, S and Evans, J, 1987 Honey and dripping: Neolithic food residues from Runnymede Bridge, *Oxford J Archaeol* **6**, 21-8

Needham, S and Macklin, M G (eds), 1992 *Alluvial archaeology in Britain*, Oxbow Monograph **27**, Oxford

Noakes, J E, Kim, S M and Stipp, J J, 1965 Chemical and counting advances in Liquid Scintillation Age dating, in E A Olsson and R M Chatters (eds), *Proc Sixth International Conference on Radiocarbon and Tritium Dating*, Washington, 68–92

Northover, J P, 1989 Non-ferrous metallurgy, in J Henderson (ed.), *Scientific analysis in archaeology and its interpretation*, Oxford Univ Comm Archaeol Monograph **19**, 213-34

Northover, J P, 1991a Non-ferrous metalwork and metallurgy, in Sharples 1991, 159-65 and microfiche

Northover, J P, 1991b Non-ferrous metalwork and metallurgy, in Cunliffe and Poole 1991b, 407-12

Northover, J P, 1997 The metalwork, in N Nayling and A Caseldine, *Excavations at Caldicot, Gwent: Bronze Age palaeochannels in the lower Nedern valley*, CBA Res Rep **108**, York, 249-53

Northover, J P, 2000 Copper alloy analysis, in J C Barrett, P W M Freeman and A Woodward, *Cadbury Castle, Somerset: the later prehistoric and early historic archaeology*, English Heritage Archaeol Rep **20**, 271-5

Northover, J P, forthcoming Analysis of Bronze Age metalwork, in Hey *et al*. forthcoming

Northover, J P and Salter, C J, 1990 Decorative metallurgy of the Celts, *Materials Characterisation* **25**(1), 47-62

OAU 1991 Yarnton and Cassington, Worton Rectory Farm: 1990/91 Assessments, July 1991, unpublished report

OAU 1992a Yarnton Cassington Project. Project design specification: recording in Stage 4, April 1992, unpublished report

OAU 1992b A40 Witney-Cassington Dualling. An archaeological evaluation 1991/92, unpublished report

OAU 1993a Yarnton Worton Rectory Farm. Post-excavation assessment and revised research design, February 1993, unpublished report

OAU 1993b Yarnton Cassington project. Project design specification. Evaluation of the study area, 2nd edn. May 1993, unpublished report

OAU 1993c Yarnton Floodplain 1992. Post-excavation assessment, November 1993, unpublished report

OAU 1994 Yarnton Cassington evaluation 1993, March 1994, unpublished report

O'Connor, B J and Foster, J, 2000 Composite rings, in J C Barrett, P W M Freeman and A Woodward, *Cadbury Castle, Somerset: the later prehistoric and early historic archaeology*, English Heritage Archaeol Rep **20**, 194-6

O'Connor, T P, 1988 Bones from the General Accident Site, Tanner Row, in V E Black (ed.), *Archaeology of York* **15(2)**, CBA, London, 61-136

Ortner, D J and Putschar, W G J, 1985 *Identification of pathological conditions in human skeletal remains*, Smithsonian Institution Press, Contributions to Anthropology **28**, Washington

Orton, C, 2000 *Sampling in Archaeology*, Cambridge manuals in archaeology, Cambridge Univ Press

Oswald, A, 1997 A doorway on the past: practical and mystical concerns in the orientation of roundhouse doorways, in Gwilt and Haselgrove 1997, 87-95

Palmer, N, 1980 A Beaker burial and medieval tenements in the Hamel, Oxford, *Oxoniensia* **45**, 124-225

Parfitt, K, 1995 *Iron Age burials from Mill Hill, Deal*, British Museum Press, London

Parker, A J, 1988 The birds of Roman Britain, *Oxford J Archaeol* **7**(2), 197-226

Parker, A, 1995a Quaternary environmental change in the upper Thames basin, central southern England, unpubl D Phil thesis, Univ of Oxford

Parker, A G, 1995b Pollen analysis, in A Mudd, The excavation of a late Bronze Age/early Iron Age site at Eight Acre Field, Radley, *Oxoniensia* **60**, 50-3

Parrington, M, 1978 *The excavation of an Iron Age settlement, Bronze Age ring ditches and Roman features at Ashville Trading Estate, Abingdon (Oxfordshire) 1974-76*, Oxford Archaeological Unit Report **1**, CBA Res Rep **28**, London and Oxford

Parrington, M, 1979 Excavations at Stert Street, Abingdon, Oxon, *Oxoniensia* **44**, 1-25

Parry, C, 1999 Iron Age, Romano-British and medieval occupation at Bishops Cleeve, *Trans Bristol Gloucestershire Archaeol Soc* **117**, 89-118

Parry, S, 2006 *Raunds Area Survey: An archaeological study of the landscape of Raunds, Northamptonshire 1985-94*, Oxbow, Oxford

Payne, S, 1969 A metrical distinction between sheep and goat metacarpals, in P J Ucko and G W Dimbleby (eds), *The domestication and exploitation of plants and animals*, London, 295-306

Payne, S, 1973 Kill off patterns in sheep and goats:

the mandibles from Asvan Kale, *Anatolian Studies* **23**, 281-303

Payne, S and Bull, G, 1986 Components of variation in measurements of pig bones and teeth and the use of measurements to distinguish wild from domestic pig remains, *Archaeozoologia* **II 1.2**, 27-65

PCRG, 1991 *The study of later prehistoric pottery: general policies*, Prehistoric Ceramics Research Group, Occas Pap **1**, Oxford

PCRG, 1992 *The study of later prehistoric pottery: guidelines for analysis and publication*, Prehistoric Ceramics Research Group, Occas Pap **2**, Oxford

Peacock, D P S, 1967 Romano-British pottery production in the Malvern district of Worcestershire, *Trans Worcestershire Archaeol Soc* **1**, 15-28

Peacock, D P S, 1968 A petrological study of certain Iron Age pottery from western England, *Proc Prehist Soc* **34**, 414-27

Peacock, D P S, 1987 Iron Age and Roman quern production at Lodsworth, West Sussex, *Antiq J* **67**, 61-85

Pearson, G W, 1984 The development of high-precision 14C measurements and its application to archaeological timescale problems, unpubl PhD thesis, Queen's Univ, Belfast

Pearson, G W, Pilcher, J R, Baillie, M G L, Corbett, D M and Qua, F, 1986 High-precision 14C measurements of Irish oaks to show the natural 14C variations from AD 1840-5210 BC, *Radiocarbon* **28(2B)**, 911-34

Pearson, G W and Stuiver, M, 1986 High-precision calibration of the radiocarbon time scale, 500-2500 BC, *Radiocarbon* **28(2B)**, 839-62

Peck, R W, 1986 Applying Contemporary Analogy to the Understanding of Animal Processing Behaviour on Roman Villa Sites, unpubl PhD thesis, Univ of Southampton

Pelling, R, 2001 Charred plant remains, in Booth *et al*. 2001, 418-22

Pelling, R, 2004 Cresswell Field: charred plant remains and charcoal, in Hey 2004, 367-8

Percival, J, 1921 *The wheat plant*, Duckworth, London

Phillips, F C, 1964 Metamorphism in south-west England, in K F G Hosking and G J Shrimpton (eds), *Some aspects of the geology of Cornwall and Devon*, Truro, 185-200

Philpott, R, 1991 *Burial practices in Roman Britain: a survey of grave treatment and furnishing AD 43-410*, BAR Brit Series **219**, Oxford

Piggott, C D and Taylor, K, 1964 The distribution of some woodland herbs in relation to the supply of nitrogen and phosphorous in the soil, *J of Ecology* **52**, 175-85

Pine, J and Preston, S, 2004 *Iron Age and Roman settlement and landscape at Totterdown Lane, Horcott near Fairford, Gloucestershire*, Thames Valley Archaeol Services Monograph **6**, Reading

Pitt-Rivers, A H L F, 1887 *Excavations in Cranborne Chase* **1**, London

Poole, C, 1984 Objects of fired clay, in Cunliffe 1984a, 398-407

Poole, C, 1991 Briquetage containers, in Cunliffe and Poole 1991b, 404-7

Poole, C, 1995 Pits and propitiation, in B Cunliffe, *Danebury Vol. 6. A hillfort community in perspective*, CBA Res Rep **102**, York, 80-6

Pope, R, 2007 Ritual and the roundhouse: a critique of recent ideas on the use of domestic space in later British prehistory, in C Haselgrove and R Pope (eds), *The earlier Iron Age in Britain and the Near Continent*, Oxbow Books, Oxford, 204-28

Powell, A and Clark, K M, 1996 Exploitation of domestic animals in the Iron Age at Rooksdown, unpublished report, Centre for Human Economy and Ecology, Univ. Southampton

Powell, A, Clark, K and Serjeantson, D, 1997 The animal bones, in Booth 1997a, 141-7

Powell, K, Laws G and Brown, L, 2009 A Late Neolithic/Early Bronze Age enclosure and Iron Age and Romano-British settlement at Latton Lands, Wiltshire, *Wiltshire Archaeol and Nat Hist Mag* **102**, 22-113

Powell, K, Smith, A and Laws, G, 2010 *Evolution of a farming community in the Upper Thames Valley. Excavation of a prehistoric, Roman and post-Roman landscape at Cotswold Community, Gloucestershire and Wiltshire Volume 1: narrative and overview*, Oxford Archaeol Thames Valley Landscapes Monograph No. **31**, Oxford

Powlesland, D, 1986 Excavations at Heslerton, North Yorkshire 1978-82, *Archaeol J* **143**, 53-175

Preece, R C and Day, S P, 1994 Comparison of Post-glacial molluscan and vegetational successions from a radiocarbon-dated tufa sequence in Oxfordshire, *J Biogeography* **21**, 463-78

Pryor, F, 2001 *The Flag Fen Basin: archaeology and environment of a Fenland landscape*, English Heritage Archaeol Rep, Swindon

Raftery, B, 1984 *La Tène in Ireland*, Veröffentlichung des Vorgeschichtlichen Seminars Marburg, Sonderband **2**, Marburg

Raftery, B, 1988 *Hollow two-piece metal rings in La Tène Europe*, Marburger Studien zur Vor- und Frühgeschichte **11**, Marburg

Rahtz, S and Rowley, T, 1984 *Middleton Stoney, excavation and survey in a North Oxfordshire parish 1970-1982*, Oxford

Randsborg, K, 1992 Historical implications. Chronological studies in European archaeology *c.* 2000-500 BC, *Acta Archaeologia* **62**, 89-108

Raven, A M, van Bergen, P F, Stott, A W, Dudd, S N and Evershed, R P, 1997 Formation of long-chain ketones in archaeological pottery vessels by pyrolysis of acyl lipids, *J Analytical and Applied Pyrolysis* **40-1**, 267-85

Raven, S, 1990 The Romano-British pottery, in Allen 1990a, 46-51

Rawes, B, 1982 Gloucester Severn Valley Ware, *Trans Bristol Gloucestershire Archaeol Soc* **100**, 33-46

Raymond, F, 1997 The investigation of Roman and medieval settlements found during the construction of the Theale to Bradfield Pipeline, *Berkshire Archaeol J* **75**, 41-73

RCHME, 1995 *Thames valley aerial photographic transcriptions*, Royal Commission on the Historical Monuments of England

Reece, R, 1972 A short survey of the Roman coins found on fourteen sites in the British Isles, *Britannia* **3**, 269-76

Rees, A I, 1961 The effect of water currents on the magnetic remanence and anisotropy of susceptibility of some sediments, *Geophysical J Royal Astronomical Soc* **5**, 235–51

Rees, H, 1986 Ceramic salt working debris from Droitwich, *Trans Worcestershire Archaeol Soc* **10**, 47-54

Rees, H, 1992 Briquetage, in S Woodiwiss (ed.), *Iron Age and Roman salt production and the medieval town of Droitwich*, CBA Res Rep **81**, London, 52

Rees, S, 1979 The Roman scythe blade, in Lambrick and Robinson 1979, 61-4

Rees-Jones, J, 1995 Optical dating of selected archaeological sediments, unpubl DPhil thesis, Univ of Oxford

Rees-Jones, J and Tite, M S, 1994 Recuperation of IRSL after bleaching and consequences for dating young sediment, *Radiation Measurements* **23**, 569-74

Reid-Henry, D and Harrison, C, 1988 *The history of the birds of Britain*, London

Rielly, K, 1988 The animal bone, in S D Trow, Excavations at Ditches Hillfort, North Cerney, Gloucestershire 1982-3, *Trans Bristol Gloucesterhire Archaeol Soc* **106**, 77-9, fiche 71/B13 – 72/C77

Resnick, D and Niwayama, G, 1981 *Diagnosis of bone and joint disorders*, Philadelphia

Reynolds, P J, 1974 Experimental Iron Age storage pits: an interim report, *Proc Prehist Soc* **40**, 118-31

Reynolds, P J, 1979 *Iron-Age farm: the Butser experiment*, London

Reynolds, P J, 1981a Deadstock and livestock, in R Mercer (ed.), *Farming Practice in British Prehistory*, Edinburgh University Press, 97-122

Reynolds, P J 1981b New approaches to familiar problems, in M Jones and G Dimbleby (eds), *The environment of man: the Iron Age to the Anglo-Saxon period*, BAR Brit Ser **87**, Oxford, 19-49

Reynolds, P J, 1987 *Butser Ancient Farm Yearbook 1986*

Reynolds, P J, 1988 *Butser Ancient Farm Yearbook 1987*

Reynolds, P J, 1989 *Butser Ancient Farm Yearbook 1988*

Reynolds, P J, 1995 The life and death of a posthole, *Interpreting stratigraphy* **5**, 21-5

Reynolds, P J and Langley, J K, 1979 Romano-British corn-drying oven: an experiment, *Archaeol J* **136**, 27-42

RIC VII = Bruun, P M, 1966 *The Roman Imperial Coinage Volume VII*, London

Richards, J, 1990 *The Stonehenge environs project*, Historic Buildings and Monuments Commission for England Archaeol Rep **16**, London

Richardson, L, Arkell, W J and Dines, H G, 1946 *Geology of the Country around Witney*, Memoir for Sheet 236, Geological Survey of Great Britain, HMSO, London

Richardson, K M and Young, A, 1951 An Iron Age A site on the Chilterns, *Antiq J* **31**, 132-48

Richmond, I, 1968 *Hod Hill: excavations carried out between 1951 and 1955 for the Trustees of the British Museum* **2**, London

Roberts, M R, 1995 Excavations at Park Farm, Binfield, 1990: an Iron Age and Romano-British settlement and Mesolithic flint scatters, in I Barnes, W A Boismier, R M J Cleal, A P Fitzpatrick and M R Roberts, *Early settlement in Berkshire: Mesolithic-Roman occupation sites in the Thames and Kennet valleys*,Wessex Archaeol Rep **6**, Salisbury, 93-132

Roberts, C and Cox, M, 2003 *Health and disease in Britain from prehistory to the present day*, Sutton Publishing, Stroud

Roberts, C and Manchester, K, 1995 *The archaeology of disease*, 2nd edn, Alan Sutton Publishing Limited, New York

Robinson, M, 1980 Roman waterlogged plant and invertebrate evidence, in Hinchliffe and Thomas 1980, 90-106

Robinson, M A, 1981 The Iron Age to early Saxon environment of the Upper Thames Terraces, in M Jones and G Dimbleby (eds), *The environment of man: the Iron Age to the Anglo-Saxon period*, BAR Brit Ser **87**, Oxford, 251-86

Robinson, M A, 1983 Arable/pastoral ratios from insects? in M Jones (ed.), *Integrating the subsistence economy*, BAR Int Ser **181**, Oxford, 19-55

Robinson, M A, 1984 Landscape and environment of Central Southern England in the Iron Age, in Cunliffe and Miles 1984, 1-11

Robinson, M A, 1985 Plant and invertebrate remains from the priory drains, in G H Lambrick, Further excavations on the second site of the Dominican Priory, Oxford, *Oxoniensia* **50**, 196-201 and fiche E10-F1

Robinson, M, 1986 Waterlogged plant and invertebrate evidence, in Miles 1986, microfiche 8; 9:C1-9, E9 and 11

Robinson, M, 1988a The significance of *Arrhenatherum elatius* (L) Beauv. from site 4, cremation 15/11, in G Lambrick, *The Rollright Stones: megaliths, monuments and settlement in the prehistoric landscape*, Historic Buildings and Monuments Commission for England, Archaeol Rep **6**, London, 102

Robinson, M A, 1988b Molluscan evidence for pasture and meadowland on the floodplain of the Upper Thames basin, in P Murphy and C French (eds), *The exploitation of wetlands*, BAR Brit Ser **186**, Oxford, 101-12

Robinson, M A, 1990 The waterlogged seeds, insects, molluscs and other biological evidence, in Allen 1990a, 64-72

Robinson, M A, 1991 Neolithic and late Bronze Age insect assemblages, in S Needham, *Excavation and salvage at Runnymede Bridge, 1978: the late Bronze Age waterfront site*, London, 277-326

Robinson, M, 1992a Environmental archaeology of the river gravels: past achievements and future directions, in Fulford and Nichols 1992, 47-62

Robinson, M, 1992b Environment, archaeology and alluvium on the river gravels of the South Midlands, in Needham and Macklin 1992, 197-208

Robinson, M A, 1993a The Iron Age environmental evidence, in Allen and Robinson 1993, 101-23

Robinson, M A, 1993b The radiocarbon dates in Allen and Robinson 1993, 139-40

Robinson, M A, 1995 Plant and invertebrate remains, in A Mudd, The excavation of a late Bronze Age / early Iron Age site at Eight Acre Field, Radley, *Oxoniensia* **60**, 41-50

Robinson, M A, 1999 The prehistoric environmental sequence of the Barrow Hills area, in Barclay and Halpin 1999, 269-74

Robinson, M A, 2002 Waterlogged macroscopic plant and insect remains, in A Brossler, M Gocher, G Laws and M Roberts, Shorncote Quarry: excavations of a late prehistoric landscape in the upper Thames Valley, 1997 and 1998, *Trans Bristol Gloucestershire Archaeol Soc* **120**, 74-8

Robinson, M, 2003 Palaeoenvironmental studies, in A Barclay, G Lambrick, J Moore and M Robinson, *Lines in the landscape. Cursus monuments in the Upper Thames Valley: excavations at the Drayton and Lechlade cursuses*, Oxford Archaeol Thames Valley Landscapes Monograph No **15**, Oxford, 163-78

Robinson, M, 2004 Waterlogged plant and invertebrate remains and mollusca, in Hey 2004, 379-409

Robinson, M, 2007 Waterlogged plant and invertebrate remains [from the 2nd to 3rd century AD Roman complex], in Miles *et al.* 2007, 158-9

Robinson, M A and Lambrick, G H, 1984 Holocene alluviation and hydrology in the Upper Thames basin, *Nature* **308**, 809-14

Robinson, M A and Straker, V, 1991 Silica skeletons of macroscopic plant remains from ash, in J M Renfrew (ed.), *New light on early farming*, Proceedings of the 7th Symposium of the International Work Group of Palaeoethnobotanists, Edinburgh, 3-13

Robinson, M and Wilson, B, 1987 A survey of environmental archaeology in the South Midlands, in H C M Keeley (ed.), *Environmental archaeology, a regional review* 2, English Heritage Occasional Paper **1**, London, 16-99

Rodwell, J S (ed.), 1992 *British plant communities, vol. 3. Grasslands and montane communities*, Cambridge University Press

Rodwell, J S (ed.), 1995 *British plant communities, vol. 4. Aquatic communities, swamps and tall-herb fens*, Cambridge University Press

Rodwell, W, 1978 Buildings and settlements in south-east Britain in the late Iron Age, in B Cunliffe and T Rowley (eds), *Lowland Iron Age communities in Europe*, BAR Int Ser **48**, Oxford, 25-41

Roe, F, 2001 Worked stone, in Booth *et al.* 2001, 248-53

Roe, F E S, forthcoming a The worked stone, in Hey *et al.* forthcoming

Roe, F E S, forthcoming b Worked stone, in J Wills, *Excavations at Beckford 1975-79*

Rohl, B M, 1995 Application of lead isotope analysis to Bronze Age metalwork from England and Wales, unpubl DPhil thesis, Univ of Oxford

Rolleston, G, 1884 *Scientific Papers and Addresses, vol 2*, Oxford

Rottländer, R C A, 1990 Die Resultate der modernen Fettanalytik und ihre Anwendung auf praehistorische Forschung, *Archaeo-Physika* **12**, 1-354

Rowley, T, 1973 An Iron Age settlement site at Heath Farm, Milton Common, *Oxoniensia* **38**, 23-40

Rozanski, K, Stichler, W, Gonfiantini, R, Scott, E M, Beukens, R P, Kromer, B and van der Plicht, J, 1992 The IAEA 14C intercomparison exercise 1990, *Radiocarbon* 34, 506-19

Ruckdeschel, W, 1978 *Die frühbronzezeitlichen Gräber Südbayerns: ein Beitrag zur Kenntnis der Straubinger Kültur*, Antiquitas **2**,**11**, Bonn

Runge, M, 1983 Physiology and ecology of nitrogen nutrition, in O L Lange, P S Nobel, C B Osmond and H Zieger (eds), *Physiological Plant Ecology III, Encyclopedia of Plant Physiology*, New Series, Vol **12c**, Berlin, Springer-Verlag, 163-200

Sahlins, M, 1976 *Culture and practical reason*, Chicago

St. Joseph, J K, 1961 Air reconnaissance in Britain, 1958-1960, *J Roman Stud* **51**, 119-35

Salisbury, S, 1961 *Weeds and aliens*, London

Salter, C J, 1984 Metallurgical aspects of the ironwork, in Cunliffe 1984a, 433–36

Salter, C, 1993 Metalworking, in Allen and Robinson 1993, 77

Salter, C and Ehrenreich, R, 1984 Iron Age iron metallurgy in central southern Britain, in Cunliffe and Miles 1984, 146-61

Salter, C and Wait, G A, 2004 Slag, in Lambrick and Allen 2004, 366-368

Salzman, L F, 1952 *Building in England down to 1540; a documentary history*, Oxford

Sandford, K S, 1924 The River Gravels of the Oxford District, Quaternary, *J Geol Soc* **80**, 113

Sangmeister, E, 1964 Die schmalen `Armschutzplatten', in K J Naur (ed.), *Studien aus Alteuropa* **1**, *Festschrift für Kurt Tackenburg*, Köln, 93-122

Sauer, E, 1999 The military origins of the Roman town of Alchester, Oxfordshire, *Britannia* **30**, 289-97

Sauer, E, 2000 Alchester, a Claudian 'Vexillation Fortress' near the western boundary of the Catuvellauni: new light on the Roman invasion of Britain, *Archaeol J* **157**, 1-78

Sauer, E, 2001 Wendlebury (Alchester), a vexillation fortress of the year AD 44 (SP 570 203), *South Midlands Archaeol* **31**, 72-6

Sauer, E, 2002 Wendlebury (Alchester), an annexe of AD 44 and the earlier(?) main fortress, *South Midlands Archaeol* **32**, 84-94

Sauer, E W, 2005 Inscriptions from Alchester: Vespasian's base of the Second Augustan Legion(?), *Britannia* **36**, 101-33

Savory, H N, 1937 An early Iron Age site at Long Wittenham, Berks, *Oxoniensia* **2**, 1-11

Savory, H N, 1976 *Guide catalogue to the Iron Age collections*, Cardiff, National Museum of Wales

Scaife, R G, 1988 The elm decline in the pollen record of south-east England and its relationship to early agriculture, in M Jones (ed.), *Archaeology and flora of the British Isles*, Oxford Univ Comm for Archaeol Monograph **14**, Oxford, 21-33

Scheuer, L and MacLaughlin-Black, S, 1994 Age estimation from the pars basilaris of the fetal and juvenile occipital bone, *Int J Osteoarchaeology* **4**, 377-80

Scheuer, L, Musgrave, J H and Evans, S P, 1980 The estimation of late fetal and perinatal age from limb bone length by linear and logarithmic regression, *Annals of Human Biology* **7**(3), 257-65

Schiffer, M, 1972 Archaeological context and systematic context, *American Antiquity* **48**, 156-65

Schultz, P D and McHenry, H M, 1975 Age distributions of enamel hypoplasia in prehistoric California Indians, *J Dental Research* **54**, 913

Schweingruber, F H, 1978 *Microscopic wood anatomy*, Zurich

Scott, E, 1991 Animal and infant burials in Romano-British villas: a revitalisation movement, in P Garwood, D Jennings, R Skeates and J Toms (eds), *Sacred and profane: proceedings of a conference on archaeology, ritual and religion, Oxford 1989*, Oxford Univ Comm for Archaeol Monograph **32**, Oxford, 115-21

Scott, E M, Harkness, D D and Cook, G T, 1998 Inter-laboratory comparisons: lessons learned, *Radiocarbon* **40**, 331-40

Sellwood, L, 1984a Tribal boundaries viewed from the perspective of numismatic evidence in Cunliffe and Miles 1984, 191-204

Sellwood, L, 1984b Objects of iron, in Cunliffe 1984a, 346-71

Sellwood, L, 1984c Objects of bone and antler, in Cunliffe 1984a, 371-95

Sellwood, L, 1984d Textile manufacture, in Cunliffe 1984a, 438-9

Sellwood, L, 1991 Objects of bone and antler in Cunliffe and Poole 1991b, 354-68

Serjeantson, D, 1991 Rid Grasse of Bones: a taphonomic study of the bones from midden deposits at the Neolithic and Bronze Age site of Runneymede, Surrey, *International J Osteoarchaeology* **1**, 73-89

Serjeantson, D, Wales, S, *et al*. 1994 Fish in later prehistoric Britain, in D Heinrich (ed.), *Archaeo-ichthyological studies: papers presented at the 6th Meeting of the I.C.A.Z. Fish Remains Working Group, Offa*, Neumunster, Wachholz, 332-9

Shahriaree, H, Sajadi, K and Rooholamini, S A, 1979 A family with spondylolisthesis, *J Bone and Joint Surgery* **61**, 1256-61

Sharples, N M, 1991 *Maiden Castle: excavations and field survey 1985-6*, English Heritage Archaeol Rep **19**, London

Shennan, S J, 1981 Settlement history in East Hampshire, in S J Shennan and R T Schadla-Hall (eds), *The archaeology of Hampshire from the Palaeolithic to the Industrial Revolution*, Hampshire Field Club Archaeol Soc Monograph **1**, 106-21

Sherriff, L, Tisdale, M A, Sayer, BG, Schwarcz, H P and Knyf, M, 1995 Nuclear magnetic resonance spectroscopic and isotopc analysis of carbonized residues from subarctic Canadian prehistoric pottery, *Archaeometry* **37**, 95-111

Siculus, Diodorus, 1992 *Les fragments de l'histoire des Grecques dans la 'Bibliothèque' de Diodore de Sicile*, par Paula Botteri, Librairie Droz, Genèvre

Sieveking, G de G (ed.), 1971 *Prehistoric and Roman Studies*, British Museum, London

Silverside, A J, 1977 *A phytosociological survey of British arable weed and related communities*, unpubl PhD thesis, Univ of Durham

Smith, A and Muir, J, 2004 Discussion and synthesis, in Jennings *et al*. 2004, 147-159

Smith, P and Kahila, G, 1992 Identification of infanticide in archaeological sites: a case study from the late Roman-early Byzantine periods at Ashkelon, Israel, *J Archaeol Science* **19**, 667-75

Smith, R J C, 1986 Winson, *Trans Bristol Gloucestershire Archaeol Soc* **104**, 246

Soil Survey of England and Wales, 1983 *Soils of England and Wales, Sheet 6, South East England*, 1:250000

Spooner, N A, Aitken, M J, Smith, B W, Franks, M and McElroy, C, 1990 Archaeological dating by infrared-stimulated luminescence using a diode array, *Radiation Protection Dosimetry* **34**, 83–6

Sprent, J I, 1981 Adaptive variation in legume nodule physiology resulting from host-rhizobial interactions, in J A Lee, S McNeill and I H Rorison (eds), *Nitrogen as an ecological factor*, British Ecological Symposium **22**, Oxford, 29-42

Stace, C, 1997 *New Flora of the British Isles*, 2nd edn, Cambridge University Press

Stead, I M, 1971 The reconstruction of Iron Age buckets from Aylesford and Baldock, in Sieveking 1971, 250-82

Stead, I M, 1991 *Iron Age cemeteries in East Yorkshire*, English Heritage Archaeol Rep **22**, London

Steinbock, R T, 1976 *Palaeopathological diagnosis and interpretation*, Charles C Thomas, Springfield, Illinois

Stenhouse, M J and Baxter, M S, 1983 14C dating

reproducibility: evidence from routine dating of archaeological samples, *PACT* **8**, 147-61

Stevens, C J, 1996 Iron Age and Roman Agriculture in the Upper Thames Valley: Archaeobotanical and Social Perspectives, unpubl PhD thesis, Univ of Cambridge

Stevens, C, 2003a An investigation of agricultural consumption and production models for Prehistoric and Roman Britain, *Environmental Archaeology* **8.1**, 61-76

Stevens, C J, 2003b The arable economy, in C Bateman, D Enright and N Oakey, Prehistoric and Anglo-Saxon settlements of the rear of Sherbourne House Lechlade: excavations in 1997, *Trans Bristol Gloucestershire Archaeol Soc* **121**, 76-81

Stevens, C, 2004 Yarnton charred plant remains, in Hey 2004, 351-64

Stevens, C and Wilkinson, K, 2001 Economy and environment, in Walker *et al.* 2001, 33-42

Strabo, 1960 *Geographica*, edited by H L Jones, Loeb, London-Cambridge

Stone, E C, 1987 Aspects of later Iron Age metal-craft in southern Britain, unpublished dissertation for Part II of BA degree in Metallurgy and the Science of Materials, University of Oxford

Stone, S, 1857 Account of certain (supposed) British and Saxon remains, *Proc Soc Antiq Lond* 1st ser. **4**, 92-100

Straker, V, Jones, M and Perry, A, 2007 Charred plant macrofossils, in Miles *et al.* 2007, CD Section 4.5

Stuart-Macadam, P S, 1989 Nutritional deficiency disease: a survey of scurvy, rickets and iron deficiency anaemia, in M Y Iscan and K A R Kennedy (eds), *Reconstruction of life from the skeleton*, New York, 211-22

Stuart-Macadam, P, 1991 Anaemia in Roman Britain: Poundbury Camp, in H Bush and M Zvelebil (eds), *Health in past societies – biocultural interpretations of human skeletal remains in archaeological contexts*, BAR Int Ser **567**, Oxford, 101-14

Stuiver, M, and Kra, R S, 1986 Editorial comment, *Radiocarbon* **28(2B)**, ii

Stuiver, M, and Polach, H A, 1977 Reporting of 14C data, *Radiocarbon* **19**, 355–63

Stuiver, M and Reimer, P J, 1986 A computer program for radiocarbon age calculation, *Radiocarbon* **28**, 1022-30

Stuiver, M and Reimer, P J, 1987 *User's guide to the programs CALIB and DISPLAY, Rev 2.1*, Quarternary Isotope Laboratory, University of Washington

Stuiver, M and Reimer, P J, 1993 Extended 14C data base and revised CALIB 3.0 14C age calibration program, *Radiocarbon* **35**, 215–30

Stuiver, M, Reimer, P J, Bard, E, Beck, J W, Burr, G S, Hughen, K A, Kromer, B, McCormac, F G, van der Plicht, J and Spurk, M, 1998 INTCAL98 radiocarbon age calibration, 24,000–0 cal BP, *Radiocarbon* **40**, 1041–84

Sturdy, D and Case, H, 1963 Begbroke, Oxon, in Notes and News, *Oxoniensia* **28**, 87

Sturdy, D and Young, C J, 1976 Two early Roman kilns at Tuckwell's Pit, Hanborough, Oxon, *Oxoniensia* **41**, 56-64

Sunter, N and Woodward, P J, 1987 *Romano-British industries in Purbeck: Excavations at Norden by Nigel Sunter Excavations at Ower and Rope Lake Hole by Peter J Woodward*, Dorset Nat Hist and Archaeol Soc Monograph Ser No **6**, Dorchester

Swan, V G, 1975 Oare reconsidered and the origins of Savernake Ware in Wiltshire, *Britannia* **6**, 36-61

Swan, V G, 1984 *The pottery kilns of Roman Britain*, Royal Commission on Historical Monuments Supplementary Series **5**, London

Tansley, A G, 1939 *The British Islands and their vegetation*, Cambridge University Press

Taylor, M, 2001 The wood, in Pryor 2001, 167-228

Teichert, M, 1975 Osteometrische Untersuchungen zur Berechnung der Wideristhohe bei Schafen, in A Clason (ed.), *Archaeozoological Studies*, Amsterdam, 51-69

Thomas, N, 1955 Excavations at Vicarage Field, Stanton Harcourt, 1951, *Oxoniensia* **20**, 1-28

Thomas, R, Robinson, M, Barrett, J and Wilson, B, 1986 A late Bronze Age riverside settlement at Wallingford, Oxfordshire, *Archaeol J* **143**, 174-200

Thompson, I, 1982 *Grog-tempered `Belgic' pottery of south-eastern England*, BAR Brit Ser **108**, Oxford

Thompson, R and Oldfield, F, 1986 *Environmental Magnetism*, Allen and Unwin, London

Timby, J, 1990 Severn Valley wares: a reassessment, *Britannia* **21**, 243-51

Timby, J R, 1993 Pottery, in Mudd 1993, 56-63

Timby, J R, 1995a Pottery, in Hey 1995, 124-36

Timby, J R, 1995b The Pottery, in Walker 1995, 78-82

Timby, J, 1996 The pottery, in Holbrook and Thomas 1996, 131-47

Timby, J R, 1998 *Excavations at Kingscote and Wycomb, Gloucestershire*, Cotswold Archaeol Trust, Cirencester

Timby, J, 1999 The pottery, in Muir and Roberts 1999, 31-40

Timby, J, 2001a A reappraisal of Savernake ware, in P Ellis (ed.), *Roman Wiltshire and after: Papers in honour of Ken Annable*, Wiltshire Archaeol Nat Hist Soc, Devizes, 73-84

Timby, J, 2001b The pottery, in Walker *et al.* 2001, 19-26

Timby, J, 2004a The pottery, in Jennings *et al.* 2004, 90-108

Timby J, 2004b Fired clay, in Jennings *et al.* 2004, 88-9

Timby, J R, forthcoming The pottery, in Lamdin-Whymark *et al.* forthcoming

Timby, J, Booth, P and Allen, T G, 1997 A new early Roman fineware industry in the Upper Thames Valley, unpublished report, Oxford Archaeol Unit

Tomlinson, P and Hall, A R, 1996 A review of the archaeological evidence for food plants from the

British Isles: an example of the use of the Archaeobotanical Computer Database (ABCD), *Internet Archaeology* **1,** intarch.ac.uk/journal/issue1/tomlinson_index.html

Toynbee, J M C, 1971 *Death and burial in the Roman world*, Thames and Hudson, London

Trotter, M and Gleser, G C 1952 Estimation of stature from long bones of American Whites and Negroes, *Amer J Physical Anthrop* (ns) **10**, 463-514

Trotter, M and Gleser, G C 1958 A re-evaluation of estimation of stature based on measurements of stature taken during life and long bones after death, *Amer J Physical Anthropology* **16**, 79-123

Trow, S D, 1988 Excavations at Ditches hillfort, North Cerney, Gloucestershire, 1982-3 *Trans Bristol Gloucestershire Archaeol Soc* **106**, 19-85

Trust for Wessex Archaeology, 1996 Clarendon to Cockey Down Water Main, Salisbury, Wiltshire, internal report prepared for Wessex Water

Tuohy, C, 1992 Long-handled "weaving combs" in the Netherlands, *Proc Prehist Soc* **58**, 385-7

Tylecote, R F and Gilmour, B, 1986 *The metallography of early ferrous edge tools and edged weapons*, BAR Brit Ser **155**, Oxford

Underwood-Keevill C, 1993 Bone objects *and* Fired clay, in Mudd 1993, 64

van Beek, G, 1983 *Dental morphology. An illustrated guide*, 2nd edn, Bristol

van der Veen, M, 1989 Charred grain assemblages from Roman-period corn driers in Britain, *Archaeol J* **146**, 302-19

van der Veen, M, 1992 *Crop husbandry regimes; an archaeobotanical study of farming in northern England 1000 B.C.–A.D. 500*, Sheffield Archaeol Monograph **3**, J R Collis Publications, Dept of Archaeol and Prehist, University of Sheffield

van Zeist, W, 1988 Botanical evidence of relations between the sand and clay districts of the north of The Netherlands in medieval times, in H Küster (ed.), *Der Prähistorische Mensch und Seine Umwelt*, Forschungen und Berichte zur Vor- und Frühgeschite in Baden-Württemberg, Band **31**, Stuttgart, Theiss, 381-7

van Zeist, W and Casparie, W A (eds), 1984 *Plants and Ancient man: studies in the palaeoethnobotany*, Proc 6th symposium of the international work group for Palaeobotanists, A A Balkema, Rotterdam

van Zeist, W, van Cappers, R, Neef, R and During, H, 1987 A palaeobotanical investigation of medieval occupation deposits in Leeuwarden, The Netherlands, *Proc Koninklijke Nederlandse Akademie van Wetenschappen*, Series B, **90**(4), 371-426

Viner, L, 1996 Worked bone, in R King, A Barber and J Timby, Excavations at West Lane, Kemble: An Iron Age, Roman and Saxon burial site and Medieval building, *Trans Bristol Gloucestershire Archaeol Soc* **114**, 21-2

von den Driesch, A, 1976 *A guide to the measurement of animal bones from archaeological sites*, Peabody Museum Bulletin **1**

von den Driesch, A and Boessneck, J, 1974 Kritische Anmerkungen zur Widerristhohenberechnung aus Längenmassen vor- und frühgeschichtlicher Tierknochen, *Säugetierkundliche Mitteilungen* **40**(4), 325-48

Wacher, J and McWhirr A, 1982 *Early Roman Occupation at Cirencester*, Cirencester Excavations I, Cirencester Excavation Comm, Cirencester

Wainwright, G J, 1968 The Excavation of a Durotrigian farmstead near Tollard Royal in Cranborne Chase, Southern England, *Proc Prehist Soc* **34**, 102-47

Wainwright, G J, 1979 *Gussage All Saints: an Iron Age settlement in Dorset*, Department of the Environment Archaeol Rep **10**, London

Wainwright, G J, 1990 *Archaeology review 1989-90*, London

Wainwright, G J and Longworth, I H, 1971 *Durrington Walls: excavations 1966-1968* Rep Res Comm Soc Antiq London **29**

Wait, G A, 1985 *Ritual and religion in Iron Age Britain*, BAR Brit Ser **149**, Oxford

Waldén, H W, 1976 A nomenclatural list of the land mollusca of the British Isles, *J Conchology London* **29**, 21-5

Waldron, T, 1991 Spondylolysis in early populations, *Int J Osteoarchaeology* **1**, 64-7

Walker, G, 1995 A middle Iron Age settlement at Deer Park Road, Witney. Excavations in 1992, *Oxoniensia* **60**, 67-92

Walker, G, Langton, B and Oakey, N, 2001 *An Iron Age site at Groundwell West, Wiltshire: excavations in 1996*, Cotswold Archaeol Trust, Cirencester

Walker, L, 1984 The deposition of human remains, in Cunliffe 1984a, 442-63

Wallis, J, 1981 Radley, Thrupp Farm, *CBA Group 9 Newsletter* **11**, 134-7

Wallis, J and Lambrick, G, 1989 Ducklington: Gill Mill Farm, *South Midlands Archaeol* **19**, 49-50

Walter, H, 1923 Some recent finds on Ham Hill, Somerset, *Antiq J* **3**, 149

Walters, S M, 1949 Biological Flora of the British Isles: *Eleocharis palustris* (L) R. Br. em R and S, *J Ecology* **37**, 194-202

Ward, G K and Wilson, S R, 1978 Procedures for comparing and combining radiocarbon age determinations: a critique, *Archaeometry* **20**, 19-31

Warrington, K, 1924 The influence of manuring on the weed flora of arable land, *J Ecology* **12**, 111-26

Watson, J, 1995 Mineral preserved organic material associated with metalwork from Gravelly Guy, Stanton Harcourt, Oxon, *Ancient Monuments Laboratory Report Series*

Watt, R J, 1979 The evidence for decapitation, in Clarke 1979, 342-4

Watts, D, 1991 *Christians and pagans in Roman Britain*, Routledge, London

Weaver, S D G and Ford, S, 2004 An early Iron Age occupation site, a Roman shrine and other prehistoric activity at Coxwell Road, Faringdon, *Oxoniensia* **69**, 119-80

Webster, J 1995 Brooches, in Manning *et al.* 1995, 60-96

Welch, F B A and Trotter, F M, 1961 *Geology of the Country around Monmouth and Chepstow*, Memoir for Sheets 233 & 250, Geological Survey of Great Britain. HMSO, London

Wheeler, R E M and Wheeler, T V, 1932 *Report on the excavations of the Prehistoric, Roman and post Roman site in Lydney Park, Gloucestershire*, Rep Res Comm Soc Antiqs London No **9**

Whimster, R, 1981 *Burial practices in Iron Age Britain*, BAR Brit Ser **90**, Oxford

Wild, J P, 1970 *Textile manufacture in the northern Roman provinces*, Cambridge

Williams, A, 1946-7 Excavations at Langford Downs, Oxon (near Lechlade) in 1943, *Oxoniensia* **11-12**, 44-64

Williams, A, 1948 Excavations in Barrow Hills Field, Radley, Berkshire, 1944, *Oxoniensia* **13**, 1-17

Williams, A, 1951 Excavations at Beard Mill, Stanton Harcourt, Oxon, 1944, *Oxoniensia* **16**, 5-22

Williams, D F, 1977 The Romano-British black-burnished industry: an essay in characterization by heavy mineral analysis, in D P S Peacock (ed.), *Pottery and early commerce: characterization and trade in Roman and later ceramics*, London, 163-220

Williams, J T, 1963 Chenopodium album L., *J Ecology* **51**, 711-25

Wilson, B, 1979 The vertebrates, in Lambrick and Robinson 1979, 128-33

Wilson, B, 1980 Bone and shell report, in Hinchliffe and Thomas 1980, 84-9

Wilson, B, 1986 Faunal remains: animals and marine shells, in Miles 1986, microfiche 8: A1-G10

Wilson, B, 1992 Considerations for the identification of ritual deposits of animal bones in Iron Age pits, *Int J Osteoarchaeol* **2**, 341-9

Wilson, B, 1993a Reports on the bones and oyster shell, in Allen and Robinson 1993, 123-34

Wilson, B, 1993b Bone and shell evidence [Technical Appendix], in Allen and Robinson 1993, 168-91

Wilson, B, 1996 *Spatial patterning among animal bones in settlement archaeology*, BAR Brit Ser **251**, Oxford

Wilson, B and Allison, E, 1990 The animal and fish bones, in Allen 1990, 57-61

Wilson, B, Hamilton, J, Bramwell, D and Armitage, P, 1978 The animal bones, in Parrington 1978, 110-38

Wilson, C E, 1981 Burials within settlements in southern Britain during the pre-Roman Iron Age, *Bull Inst Archaeol Univ London* **18**, 127-70

Wilson, D, 1993 Iron Age pottery, in Allen and Robinson 1993, 70-5

Wilson, G, 1979 Horse dung from Roman Lancaster: a botanical report, *Archaeo-Physica* **8** (Festschrift for Maria Hopf), 331-49

Wilson, G, 1984 The carbonization of weed seeds and their representation in macrofossil assemblages, in van Zeist and Casparie 1984, 201-6

Winton, H, 2001 A possible Roman small town at Sansom's Platt, Tackley, Oxon., *Britannia* **32**, 304-9

Wood, P 1954 The early Iron Age camp on Bozedown, Whitchurch, Oxon, *Oxoniensia* **19,** 8-14

Woodbury S E, Evershed, R P, Rossell, J B, Griffiths, R E and Farnell, P, 1995 Detection of vegetable oil adulteration using gas chromatography combustion/isotope ratio mass spectrometry, *Anaytical Chemistry* **67**, 2685-90

Woodward, A and Leach, P, 1993 *The Uley shrines, excavation of a ritual complex on West Hill, Uley, Gloucestershire: 1977-9*, English Heritage Archaeol Rep **17**, London

Workshop of European Anthropologists 1980 Recommendations for age and sex diagnoses of skeletons, *J Human Evolution* **9**, 517-49

Yates, D T, 1999 Bronze Age field systems in the Thames Valley, *Oxford J Archaeol* **18**, 157-70

Young, C J, 1975 The defences of Roman Alchester, *Oxoniensia* **60**, 136-70

Young, C J, 1977 *The Roman pottery industry of the Oxford region*, BAR Brit Ser **43**, Oxford

Young, C J, 1980 The late Roman finewares, in B Rawes, The Romano-British site at Wycomb, Andoversford; excavations 1969-70, *Trans Bristol Gloucestershire Archaeol Soc* **98**, 41-6

Young, C J, 1982 Late Iron Age and Roman pottery, in Case 1982a, 139-47

Young, C, 1986 The Upper Thames Valley in the Roman period, in G Briggs, J Cook and T Rowley (eds), *The Archaeology of the Oxford Region*, Oxford, 58-63

Zohary, D and Hopf, M, 2000 *Domestication of plants in the Old World: The origin and spread of cultivated plants in West Asia, Europe, and the Nile Valley*, Oxford (3rd edn)

Index